Mastering Borland® C++

Mastering Borland® C++

Tom Swan

SAMS

A Division of Prentice Hall Computer Publishing
11711 North College, Carmel, Indiana 46032 USA

International Standard Book Number: 0-672-30274-8

Library of Congress Catalog Card Number: 92-81456

95 94 93   4   3

Interpretations of the printing code: the rightmost double-digit number is the year of the book's printing; the rightmost single-digit number, the number of the book's printing. For example, a printing code of 92-1 shows that the first printing of the book occurred in 1992.

Trademarks

Composed in Carmel, Indiana by Prentice Hall Computer Publishing

Printed in the United States of America

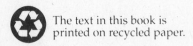

The text in this book is printed on recycled paper.

Publisher
Richard K. Swadley

Managing Editor
Neweleen A. Trebnik

Acquisitions Editor
Greg Croy

Production Editor
Erik Dafforn

Editors
Fran Hatton
Gayle Johnson
Hugh Vandivier
Colleen Flanagan
Grant Fairchild
Kathy Ewing
Tad Ringo
Lori Cates

Editorial Coordinators
Becky Freeman
Bill Whitmer

Technical Editors
Brad Jones
Greg Guntle

Editorial Assistants
Rosemarie Graham
San Dee Phillips
Lori Kelley
Mary Croy

Cover Designer
Dan Armstrong

Director of Production and Manufacturing
Jeff Valler

Production Manager
Corinne Walls

Book Design
Michele Laseau

Production Analyst
Mary Beth Wakefield

Page Layout Coordinator
Matthew Morrill

Proofreading/Indexing Coordinator
Joelynn Gifford

Graphic Image Specialist
Dennis Sheehan

Book Shepherd
Carla Hall-Batton

Production
Jeff Baker
Claudia Bell
Keith Davenport
Brook Farling
Tim Groeling
Denny Hager
John Kane
Carrie Keesling
Bob LaRoche
Laurie Lee
Juli Pavey
Linda Quigley
Joe Ramon
Angie Trzepacz
Julie Walker

Index
Jeanne Clark
Sharon Hilgenberg
Loren Malloy
John Sleeva

Dedication

To Anne, my best friend and partner,
on our 20th wedding anniversary.

Overview

Contents

Part 4 DOS and Windows Development Tools

Borland C++ 3.0—and now 3.1—are taking the programming world by storm. What is it about C++, and particularly about Borland C++, that is capturing so much attention? Why are programmers migrating to C++ in record numbers—and should you join them? If you have already adopted C++, how can you learn more about this remarkable language?

These are questions I've tried to answer in *Mastering Borland C++*. The exploding popularity of C++ is more than a fad; it's evidence of a revolution in computer science. If you are a professional developer, if you are aiming for a career in programming, or if you are serious about computers and want to write your own code, you simply can't ignore C++. I'm convinced that C++ soon will be the language of choice for software publishers and professional developers—worldwide.

In writing *Mastering Borland C++,* I've attempted to convey my 15 years of experience with programming in the context of a specific compiler (Borland C++ 3.1), operating on a specific computer (the IBM PC and compatibles), for specific operating environments (DOS and Windows). This is a practical nuts-and-bolts book for programmers who write code in the real world. It's short on theory; long on actual programming techniques.

Parts 2 and 3 present complete ANSI C and C++ tutorials. Other chapters concentrate on features unique to Borland C++, such as BGI graphics, Borland's class library in class and template forms, Turbo Vision, inline and external assembly language, memory models, overlays, optimizations, and Windows. Reading this book, you'll find C and C++ language tutorials that cover most every facet of ANSI C and C++ programming, including object-oriented techniques, classes, constructors, destructors, and advanced topics such as templates, operator overloading, and polymorphism.

You'll also find reams of source code—over 800 complete programming examples in C and C++. The accompanying disk includes every listing ready to compile and run, along with answers to exercises and several shareware and public domain programs graciously donated by EMS Professional Shareware Libraries. I've always believed that there's no better way to learn programming than to dig into lots of code and see what makes real programs tick, so I've tried to pack this book and disk with as many complete listings as possible.

By the way, feel free to use any and all of the programming printed in this book. *You have my permission to incorporate my listings into your own programs in any way you choose.* Determining the suitability and proper use of my listings is, of course, your responsibility. But I hope you *will* use them. I'd consider it a high honor if you do. After all, if I wanted to keep my listings secret, I wouldn't publish them in a book! (Please respect the copyrights, however, of contributing authors for the extra shareware and public domain programs provided on disk.)

Concerning authorship, that brings up a subject of some importance to me— and, I hope, to you. Some computer book authors hire ghost writers to write their books for them. That's not my way. I personally wrote every listing and every word in this book. (Okay, I confess to having help with the index.) I am fortunate to enjoy the assistance of many talented editors at Sams Publishing, and also to benefit from the keen eyes of my wife Anne, who read the manuscript and found many mistakes. But these are my words as I typed them. Someday I may *become* a ghost, but I'll not hire one to write my words.

I owe a note also to my Turbo Pascal readers and friends. Is this goodbye to Turbo Pascal? Never! I see no reason why programmers shouldn't learn many languages, and use them all whenever it makes sense to do so. In fact, by knowing both Borland C++ and Turbo Pascal, you'll gain many insights into programming that you might miss if you stick to only one language. When it comes to programming, part of the fun is playing the field. May reading this book be as much fun and be as rewarding to you as it was for me to write.

Tom Swan

CompuServe ID: 73627,3241

Acknowledgments

In writing this book, I've been fortunate to have the assistance—and more importantly, the friendship—of many individuals. Thanks to all in Sams' Editorial, Production, and Sales departments, especially Erik Dafforn, Richard Swadley, Joe Wikert, Greg Croy, Fran Hatton, Gayle Johnson, Hugh Vandivier, Colleen Flanagan, Becky Freeman, Bill Whitmer, San Dee Phillips, Mary Croy, Brad Jones, and Greg Guntle; and at Borland, Ghopin Yen, Nan Borreson, Paul Gross, David Intersimone, and Eugene Wang. Thanks also to Jeff and Carol Duntemann for a place to work, but most of all for good company. And I truly lack the words to thank my friends, family, and CompuServe buddies for all of your contributions. It's been fun. Let's do it again sometime.

Part 1

Environments

PART 1

Introducing Borland C++

Borland C++ 3.1 is a highly sophisticated programming system for DOS and Windows developers. The box alone weighs almost 20 pounds and comes with nearly 4,000 pages of documentation and dozens of software tools. How can you learn to use this tremendously capable package? Where do you begin?

Experienced developers probably welcome the complexity of Borland C++—PC programming isn't getting any easier, and as developers, we need all of the help, tools, and utilities that we can cram onto our disks. The days are gone when compilers took only a few thousand bytes of disk space.

Treat this book as a guide and tutorial to the C and C++ languages and to the critical components of Borland C++. C and C++ gurus probably can read the chapters in any order. Ancient veterans might turn directly to Part 3, "Programming with C++," and Part 4, "DOS and Windows Development Tools."

Beginners in the audience need only their wits and a computer, although some knowledge of programming is helpful. If you're just getting started, read this book from front to back. The ANSI C and C++ tutorials assume no prior programming experience, but for smooth sailing, you should be somewhat familiar with bits, bytes,

DOS commands, and so on. If you have written a couple of programs in Turbo Pascal or BASIC, you're already ahead of the pack. You don't need to be a programming wizard. Beginners and experts are equally welcome.

Read this chapter for an overview of the book's parts and chapters. Continue with the next several chapters to configure your development system for DOS or Windows. Dig into the tutorials to learn about ANSI C and C++ programming. Use the reference in Chapter 22, "Functions and Examples," to look up unfamiliar functions. Go slowly, install the accompanying diskette, send complimentary letters to the author, and take time out occasionally to look out your window (better still, when frustration mounts, take a stroll in the park). Programming is a tough business, but also an extremely rewarding one. If this book has a goal, it's to help you discover *on your own* what programming has to offer *you*.

Requirements

You can use this book's programs with a wide variety of software, hardware, and memory capacities. No single configuration is right for all. If you can install Borland C++ or Turbo C++, you're ready to begin.

Some requirements need no mention, but I'll mention them anyway: To use the Windows examples, you of course need to have Microsoft Windows 3.0 or 3.1. To run the Turbo Vision demonstrations, you need Borland's Application Frameworks, which includes the Turbo Vision and ObjectWindows class libraries. Printer-output programs usually work best if you have a printer. (Don't you just love software manuals that list a color monitor as required to show colors on-screen? I will try not to insult your intelligence in a similar manner.)

Hardware

For most programs, depending on which compiler version you have, you need to acquire some or all of the following hardware components:

- A 100-percent compatible IBM PS/2 or AT-class computer, the fastest one you can beg, borrow, steal, or preferably, purchase legally. Your PC must have an 80286, 80386, 80486, or a compatible processor. SX processors (such as 80386SX) also are fine. I wrote much of this book using a Toshiba T3100SX system with 5 megabytes (often abbreviated *M*) of RAM. I also used my main development system, an Everex Step 386/25 with 16M of RAM.

- As much RAM as possible, at least 640K of real-mode memory and one megabyte of extended RAM. On 80386 and 80486 speed demons, if you are running Windows, you need at least two megabytes of extended RAM, you'll be happier with four, and the sky's the limit if you have eight. *You cannot have too much memory.*

- A hard disk drive. Borland C++ does not run on floppy disks. This is no great loss, because compiling on floppies takes so long, you might fall asleep midway through Chapter 5 waiting for the compiler to finish.

- A 1.2M floppy disk drive to install the compiler and to copy the files on this book's accompanying diskette. See the last page for installation instructions and for how to obtain a 3 1/2-inch floppy disk. *Every code listing plus extra goodies are included on the diskette included with this book. There's nothing else to buy.*

- One of the Turbo Vision programs in Chapter 18, "Turbo Vision," and some of the Windows examples in Chapter 21, "Windows Tools and Techniques," require a mouse. Except for these few exceptions, you don't need a mouse. Assuming you intend to distribute your programs to others, however, you'll need a mouse if only to test your program's mouse capabilities.

Software

Now for the best part—the software. You can mix and match software configurations in many different ways. To compile and run most of this book's example programs, you'll need some or all of the following:

- Borland C++ 3.0 or 3.1; *or* Turbo C++ for DOS; *or* Turbo C++ for Windows 3.0; *or* Borland C++ for Windows 3.1. Chapters 2 through 4 discuss configurations and give hints for using different environments, IDEs, and the command-line compiler. Regardless of which C++ compiler you have or prefer to use, you should be able to compile and run most of this book's example programs using your favorite working environment. You can run DOS or Windows or both as you please.

- Borland's Application Frameworks are optional (but recommended). You need the Turbo Vision class library for the examples in Chapter 18, "Turbo Vision." You need the ObjectWindows library (OWL) for the listings in Chapter 21, "Windows Tools and Techniques."

- DOS 5.0 or any version of DOS from Version 3.31 up. For best results, use DOS 5.0 to take advantage of improved memory management and utilities.

- Windows 3.1 or 3.0. (Version 3.1 is *far* more stable than 3.0. Upgrade from 3.0 to 3.1 as soon as possible if you haven't already.) I used Windows 3.1 exclusively to write this book and all of its programs. You can compile and run most example programs in a DOS prompt window, or you can use Turbo C++ for Windows or Borland C++ for Windows to run programs in a *Windows* window (see the discussion of Borland's EasyWin interface in Chapter 4, "Borland C++ for Windows").

Installing Borland C++

Run Borland's automated installation program to install the compiler. Just insert the first master diskette into A: and type **a:install**. Following are a few tips that might settle questions during installation and thereafter:

- This book assumes that you install to the default C:\BORLANDC directories. If you specify a different base directory, you'll have to modify some examples. (Turbo C++ for DOS users who install to C:\TC might have to make a few changes here and there.)

- Add C:\BORLANDC\BIN or equivalent to your system path. For example, in AUTOEXEC.BAT, add a one-line command such as PATH C:\DOS;C:\WINDOWS;C:\BORLANDC\BIN. *BIN* stands for *binaries*—the location where you store Borland C++ binary code files. Reboot after installing and modifying AUTOEXEC.BAT.

- If you have enough disk space, install *everything*. You can always delete (or copy to floppy disks) files that you don't need. It's much easier to install every component now than it is to install only some files and then reinstall other files later.

- If you receive errors when compiling, check whether you have defined an INCLUDE environment variable. (Type **set** at a DOS prompt.) Utilities such as MAKE and Resource Workshop, but not the compiler, recognize INCLUDE, which may cause mysterious conflicts, especially if you have other compilers that also depend on INCLUDE.

- It's probably best, however, not to configure your system to use Borland C++ and other C++ compilers (or other languages) at the same time. Create separate

AUTOEXEC.BAT and CONFIG.SYS files for each development environment. On the other hand, you can configure your system for Turbo Pascal, Turbo Pascal for Windows, and Borland C++. In case of conflicts, use the most recent files—use Borland C++'s Turbo Debugger to debug Turbo Pascal programs, for instance. *Perform thorough tests before deleting old utilities.* (I usually copy old files to a temporary directory, which I clean out once a week or so. That way, if conflicts arise, I can recover earlier file versions without having to reinstall from scratch.)

- If you have Windows installed (it doesn't have to be running), the automated installation program permits you to create a Program Manager folder with icons for various Borland C++ compilers and utilities. Allow the installer to create this folder. You can always edit or delete it later from the Program Manager. (The installer might prepare files to create the folder the *next* time you run Windows.)

Protected Mode and DPMI

The DOS Protected Mode Interface (DPMI) is a memory access protocol by which programs can use a PC's extended memory—RAM above the one-megabyte high water mark available in 80x86 real-mode operation. (In this book, the x in 80x86 represents the family of Intel 8088, 8086, 80186, 80286, 80386, 80486, and compatible processors and emulation modes. 80386 processors, for example, can emulate 8086 real mode operation.)

Borland C++ is a memory-based compiler— during compilation, the compiler writes *only* object-code instructions to disk files. It never writes any intermediate symbols or other data to disk. This means that, if you run out of memory when compiling large programs, your only option is to add more memory (or, perhaps, to reorganize your program into smaller modules).

For most users, Borland C++ and Turbo C++ use DPMI automatically with no help on your part. If you receive a message that your machine is "not in the database," change to the C:\BORLANDC\BIN or C:\TC\BIN directory and run the DPMIINST utility to configure the compiler for your system. If you experience trouble, contact Borland directly for assistance. If the compiler can't support your system, you can't go any further until you fix what's wrong. This kind of trouble should be extremely rare. The *best* solution is to purchase a supported, name-brand, 100-percent compatible development system.

To limit the compiler's extended memory use, include the following environment variable command in your AUTOEXEC.BAT file:

```
DPMIMEM=MAXMEM 1000
```

That tells the compiler to use no more than one megabyte (1000K) of extended RAM. Normally, the compiler uses all available extended memory, and you might need to use this command if other programs also need memory from the DPMI kernel. 1000 is the smallest possible value.

Unless you are using Windows 3.0 or 3.1, you might need to install Borland's DPMI server by running DPMIRES. This program installs a resident DPMI memory manager and executes a DOS command shell.

Do *not* use DPMIRES with Microsoft Windows running in enhanced mode, which provides its own DPMI services. You can use DPMIRES to run Windows in standard (/s) mode, however, which you might do on an 80286-based system.

WARNING: The Windows EMM386.EXE memory manager is not compatible with Borland C++ when running in DOS (in other words, when Windows is *not* running). If you have trouble using Borland C++ from DOS—typically the computer hangs on using the compiler a second or third time—do not install EMM386.EXE. You might also specify EMM386.EXE /NOEMS in CONFIG.SYS. If you run Windows, you may install EMM386.EXE, or not, as you please.

Part and Chapter Summaries

This book's chapters build on each other. Simpler subjects come before advanced topics. Consult this section for summaries of each part and chapter.

The Parts

Five parts divide the book into natural boundaries:

- *Part 1, "Environments,"* describes Borland and Turbo C++ compilers, provides configuration tips, explains how to compile example programs, and helps you set up for DOS and Windows programming.

- *Part 2, "Programming with ANSI C,"* is a complete tutorial to ANSI C programming. Borland C++ is actually two compilers in one—an ANSI C compiler and a C++ compiler. Read the chapters in this part if you plan to program in ANSI C, and also to prepare for the C++ tutorial in Part 3. Exercises at the end of each chapter help you test your progress. Every answer is included near the end of the book. Any listings also are included on disk.

- *Part 3, "Programming with C++,"* builds on the material in Part 2 with a complete guide to C++ programming, classes, and object-oriented programming. Borland C++ (and this book) complies with AT&T's C++ specification version 2.1, but also recognizes templates as proposed by AT&T for C++ 3.0. The material in this part's chapters should also be applicable to other C++ 2.1-compatible compilers (possibly excluding templates). As in Part 2, exercises at the ends of each chapter in this part help you to test your progress.

- *Part 4, "DOS and Windows Development Tools,"* tours various Borland C++-specific tools and programming techniques for DOS and Windows developers. Read the chapters in this part to learn about BGI graphics, Borland's class library (including the new template-based containers), Turbo Vision, assembly language (external and inline modes), memory models, optimizations, and ObjectWindows techniques.

- *Part 5, "Function Encyclopedia,"* follows in the tradition of *Mastering Turbo Pascal* and *Mastering Turbo Assembler,* providing an alphabetic reference to the Borland C++ standard function library. Individual parameter lists, a new key feature, help you quickly identify function argument types.

> **NOTE:** Parts 2 and 3 include exercises at the end of each chapter. You'll find answers to all exercises near the end of this book. The accompanying disk also includes listings for exercises that ask you to write programs (most do).

The Chapters

In its five parts, the book's 22 chapters cover DOS and Windows programming using ANSI C and C++. The following notes briefly describe each chapter's contents.

- *Chapter 1. Introducing Borland C++ 3.1*, as you are discovering, introduces the compiler and suggests how to make the most of this book.

- *Chapter 2. The Integrated Environment* describes how to use Borland's text-based integrated development environment (IDE) to compile and run this book's example programs.

- *Chapter 3. The Command-Line Environment* describes how to use the command-line compiler and linker to compile this book's examples. Introduces Turbo Debugger and Turbo Profiler.

- *Chapter 4. Borland C++ for Windows* describes how to use Borland C++ for Windows 3.1 or Turbo C++ for Windows 3.0 to compile and run most of this book's examples. You can run most DOS programs directly in BCW and TCW; you don't have to use a DOS prompt window unless you want to.

- *Chapter 5. Data: What a Program Knows* begins the ANSI C tutorial. You examine the parts of a C program and learn about data types and variables.

- *Chapter 6. Action: What a Program Does* shows how to create `while` loops, use `if` statements, and use other C elements to perform actions.

- *Chapter 7. Functions: Divide and Conquer* explains structured, top-down programming techniques, using functions to divide large programs into manageable pieces.

- *Chapter 8. Data Structures* covers structs, unions, arrays, and other higher-level data structures.

- *Chapter 9. Pointers* eases you into one of programming's trickier subjects: using pointers to address data in memory. The chapter also covers dynamic heap allocation techniques.

- *Chapter 10. Strings* is devoted to ASCII character strings—how to create them, and how to use them. This chapter also covers standard string functions.

- *Chapter 11. Input and Output* details file I/O, showing how to read and write disk files.

- *Chapter 12. Introducing C++* is the first of several chapters on C++ programming. Read this chapter for an overview of C++ and to learn how C++ differs from C.

- *Chapter 13. Programming with Classes* introduces the class—C++'s object-oriented tool for creating new data types. Covers encapsulation, constructors, and destructors.

- *Chapter 14. Inheritance and Polymorphism* builds on chapter 13's introduction to object-oriented programming, showing how to use inheritance to derive new classes and how to put virtual member functions (polymorphism) to work.

- *Chapter 15. Advanced Topics in C++* covers other C++ object-oriented topics such as friends, operator overloading, copy constructors, and templates.

- *Chapter 16. The Borland Graphics Interface* is one of many chapters about programming techniques specific to Borland C++. In this chapter, you learn how to write BGI graphics programs for DOS.

- *Chapter 17. Borland's Class Library* is one of the most poorly documented components in Borland C++. This chapter explains how to use "container classes" in standard class form *and* as templates.

- *Chapter 18. Turbo Vision* introduces the Turbo Vision class library, which you can use to write DOS text-based interfaces with pull-down menus, overlapping windows, and dialog boxes. Chapter 18 also covers event-driven programming techniques.

- *Chapter 19. Assembly Language Optimizations* tours the ins and outs of using BASM, Borland's inline assembler, to write statements and functions in assembly langauge. This chapter also covers external assembly language programming using Turbo Assembler.

- *Chapter 20. DOS Tools and Techniques* offers guidance for selecting memory models, using overlays, and for choosing from the compiler's many optimizations.

- *Chapter 21. Windows Tools and Techniques* introduces ObjectWindows, showing how to write Windows applications. This chapter covers graphics, message handling, dialog boxes, and custom controls using DLLs. It also discusses Windows 3.1 programming techniques (which require Borland C++ 3.1).

- *Chapter 22. Functions and Examples* ends the book with an alphabetic reference to the standard function library. Every Borland C++ 3.0 and 3.1 function is here, and most include complete examples (also supplied on disk). Parameters are separately listed.

  In addition to its chapters, the book includes five appendixes. These are

- *Appendix A—Extended ASCII Characters.* IBM PC standard and extended ASCII characters.

- *Appendix B—Compiler (BCC) Options.* Command-line compiler options.

- *Appendix C—Linker (TLINK) Options.* Turbo Linker options.

- *Appendix D—Operator Precedence and Associativity.* Table of C and C++ operators and their left-to-right or right-to-left associativity.

- *Appendix E—C and C++ Keywords.* Complete list of ANSI C, C++, and Borland C++ keywords (also called reserved words).

  Last but hardly least is the book's bibliography. As big as this book is, it can't possibly cover every topic in PC and Borland C++ programming. Consult the bibliography for references in which you can find additional information on DOS and Windows programming techniques.

Summary

- Borland C++ is a sophisticated software development system for DOS and Windows programming. Experienced developers can probably read this book's chapters in any order. Beginners should read the book from front to back.

- Borland C++ requires an 80286 or later-model processor, 640K of real-mode RAM, and at least one megabyte of extended memory, or at least two megabytes to run Windows. Under DOS, you might need to run the DPMIRES utility to provide a DOS Protected Mode Interface memory manager. Don't do this, however, if you run Windows 3.0 or 3.1 in enhanced mode.

- This chapter lists hardware and software requirements, and it summarizes the book's parts and chapters.

- Now that you have a rough idea of the book's contents, turn to the next three chapters for tips on using the Borland C++ integrated development environment (IDE), the command-line compiler, and Borland C++ for Windows 3.1 (or Turbo C++ for Windows 3.0). You can run most example listings in this book using whatever configuration of DOS and Windows you like.

The Integrated Environment

Borland popularized the concept of an integrated development environment, or IDE, with the company's first Turbo Pascal compiler. In the past, other compilers such as UCSD Pascal offered IDEs, but none worked as well or as *fast* as Turbo Pascal 1.0.

Turbo C provided the first Borland IDE with overlapping windows, pull-down menus, and other user interface features that are virtual standards in DOS software. Today, the Borland C++ 3.1 IDE gives you a state-of-the-art IDE complete with text editor, compiler, debugger, and file manager rolled into one easy-to-use package. For many programmers, their Borland C++ or Turbo C++ IDE is the only program they run from dawn to dusk (or, for nighttimers, from dusk to dawn).

The Borland C++ IDE

Figure 2.1 shows the Borland C++ 3.1 IDE in operation. The 3.0 IDE in Verison 3.0 looks similar but lacks the syntax-highlighting capabilities contained in Version 3.1 and also Turbo C++ for DOS 3.0. Refer to this figure as you read the following descriptions.

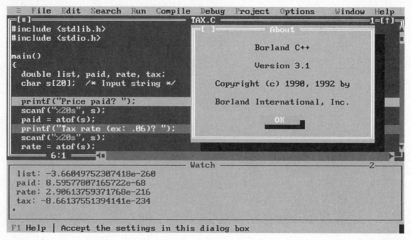

Figure 2.1. The Borland C++ 3.1 IDE.

Run the IDE by typing **bc** at a DOS prompt. (Turbo C++ for DOS users type **tc**.) If you are using Windows, run the IDE from a DOS prompt window or select the Borland C++ icon from the Program Manager. It's probably best to select the icon, which is programmed to configure the DOS session using BC.PIF—a Windows program information file that specifies memory and other runtime options.

Naturally, Borland's references cover every aspect of the editor, debugger, and compiler. The following general notes are meant to help you get started using the IDE's commands to compile and run this book's sample listings.

- To select menus, press Alt+*x* where *x* is a boldface letter. To select commands, type the letter alone. For example, to select the File|Open command, press Alt+F, release Alt, and press O.

- Generally, pressing Esc cancels a prompt, a command, an open menu, or a dialog box (a window for selecting program options, often called a dialog for short). Press Enter to select highlighted items. Use the mouse and the tab and arrow keys to move from command to command or from field to field in a dialog.

- Menu commands ending with an ellipsis (...) open dialog boxes. Commands that end with a triangle lead to another nested menu of additional commands. Commands with no suffix execute immediate actions.

- Some commands have associated hot keys. For example, rather than select File|Open, you can simply press F3. The best way to learn hot-key assignments is to use the menus and pay attention to hot-key labels. Eventually, you'll wean yourself from the menu system as you gain experience.

- Hot keys and various messages appear on the status line at the bottom of the display. Be sure to refer to this line often.

- Press F1 at just about any time for online help. Use Borland's online help along with this book. If you see an unfamiliar function name in a listing, load the file into the IDE, highlight a menu command or select a window, and press F1. You can also move the cursor to a programming term and press Crtl+F1 for context-sensitive help. Choose the Help on help option from the Help menu for detailed instructions.

Setting Options

Use the Options menu to select an application type—a DOS program, an overlay module, a Windows program, or a Windows dynamic link library (DLL). (We'll get to each of these types of programs in later chapters.) You also can select individual compiler options such as memory models and optimizations—descriptions of which appear throughout this book. Following are some Option menu commands you might want to change now.

- Use the Transfer command to edit the programs listed in the system menu, represented by a three-bar symbol at upper left. Select the Edit and Help commands for instructions.

- Select Directories and enter directory paths for the Include and Library input boxes. Separate multiple directories with semicolons. For example, you might enter C:\BORLANDC\CLASSLIB\INCLUDE;C:\BORLANDC\INCLUDE (on a single line). If you receive compiler errors for the examples in this book, check the text for notes about include and library paths that you might need to enter using this command.

- On disk, you'll find project .PRJ files for some multifile programs. Load these projects using the Project menu's Open project command. Directories in these projects assume you've installed your compiler in C:\BORLANDC. If you use a different root path, use the Options|Directories command to edit include and library paths.

- Spend some time becoming familiar with the Environment options. Most options have obvious purposes, but you might want to use the Colors command to customize the syntax highlighter in Borland C++ 3.1 or Turbo C++ for DOS. After selecting Colors, highlight Edit Window in the Group panel at left, then press Tab and select an Item to change. Some of these items affect window items such as scroll bar colors. Others affect identifiers, strings, numbers, and other program elements. (Hint: The syntax highlighter in Borland C++ for Windows 3.1 is *much* easier to use than the text-based IDE command. You might want to adjust syntax highlighting in Windows and then copy your settings manually to the DOS IDE.)

> **NOTE:** If you find syntax highlighting to be too much of a good (if colorful) thing, you can use Options|Environment|Editor to turn off syntax highlighting, or you can do as I do: reconfigure all program elements to use the same colors (white on blue by default), then recolor only one or two elements. I color comments yellow—they pop out like Post-it Notes on-screen. I also color strings green. These changes aren't merely for show. If I forget to type a closing comment bracket or a closing quote, the editor instantly colors subsequent text down to the end of the window, graphically highlighting my mistake.

- After selecting the options you will use most of the time, close any open files or projects and select Options|Save. The command's three options—Environment, Desktop, and Project—update three files in C:\BORLANDC\BIN: TCCONFIG.TC (IDE configurations), TCDEF.DPR (default project), and TCDEF.DSK (current desktop settings and filenames). The next time you start the IDE, it loads these settings so you can continue working where you stopped.

Files and Directories

The File menu (as you might suppose) has commands for working with disk files. By convention, this menu also has directory and system commands. Here are some of the key File commands you need for this book:

- Use the **O**pen command to select a text filename from the current directory. Files ending in .C are ANSI C programs. Those ending in .CPP are C++ programs. You might have to enter ***.c** or ***.cpp** into the "Open a File" dialog's **N**ame field before you'll see any filenames.

- To change directories temporarily, choose **O**pen and select a pathname ending with a backslash (\). Select the double dot (..) to move up one directory level.

- To change the *current* directory, use the **C**hange dir command and select a path. Or you can type a new path into the **D**irectory Name input box.

- You can open just about any number of files simultaneously. Use the **W**indow menu's commands to arrange windows, tiling them like bricks or cascading them like a fanned-out deck of cards. Use this menu's List all command to select windows by name in case they become buried under other windows. This command also reopens recently closed files.

Editing Text Files

After loading a text file, or after creating a new window with File|New, a flashing cursor (usually an underline) tells you where you can begin typing. Here are some tips about editing text files:

- Use the **O**ptions|**E**nvironment|**E**ditor command to select editor options. You can choose to have the editor insert tab control codes when you press Tab, or to insert spaces. You can also select a Tab Size, which affects the number of spaces by which the editor indents lines. (The text files on disk are indented in two-space increments and do not include tabs.)

- Select **A**utoindent Mode to have the editor position the cursor at the same depth as the preceding line when you press Enter to begin a new line. Because C and C++ programs use indenting for better clarity, autoindenting simplifies typing.

- The **O**ptimal fill option tells the editor to adjust tabs in lines when you move the cursor to a new line. I leave this one off because I don't insert tab control codes into my text files.

- **O**verwrite blocks affects whether typing replaces a highlighted block. I enable this feature, but some people find it disconcerting, so try this one both ways.

- If you accidentally delete something, don't be concerned. When editing, press Alt+Backspace to use the editor's multilevel undo feature, which can recover lost text and can reverse other operations.

- After changing text in a window, an asterisk appears on the bottom border at left. Pay attention to this mark—it means you haven't saved the current window. Every so often, you might want to use File|Save all to save all changes in all windows.

- Use the Search menu to search for text and to perform global search and replace operations. In the top panel, enter the text to find. When replacing text, enter new text below. Hint: For speed, toggle Prompt off, and press Alt+A to replace all instances without prompting. You can use multilevel undo to reverse changes. For safety, however, *always save your work before giving a nonprompted global search-and-replace command.*

- The Edit menu has Cut (delete highlighted text to clipboard), Copy (copy to clipboard but don't delete), Paste (insert text from clipboard), and Clear (delete but don't copy to clipboard) commands. Memorize the hot keys for these commands—you'll use them often to shuffle text from here to there and from one window to another.

Compiling and Running Programs

After entering or loading a program file, press F9 to compile or Crtl+F9 to compile and run. To run most examples in this book, these are the only two commands you need. Here are some other ideas, however, that might help in various situations.

- To compile a program but not create an executable .EXE code file, press Alt+F9 or select Compile|Compile. This command creates an object code .OBJ file.

- Use the Build all command to compile all modules in a multifile program. (Most of the examples in this book are stored in single files, so you won't use this command often. Developers use it to rebuild a complex program from scratch.)

- Use the Information command to check on the IDE's memory use and for a report about the most recent compilation.

Using Turbo C++ for DOS

If you are using Turbo C++ for DOS, your IDE looks much the same as in Figure 2.1. You can use TC with most of the programs in this book. Be aware, however, that TC lacks the following items available in Borland C++:

- The stand-alone Turbo Debugger. Use the built-in debugger described in this chapter.

- The stand-alone Turbo Profiler.

- The stand-alone Turbo Assembler. Turbo C++ has a built-in assembler described in Chapter 19, "Assembly Language Optimizations."

- Sophisticated code-generation optimizations (see Chapter 20, "DOS Tools and Techniques").

- Turbo Vision (supplied with Borland's Application Frameworks).

- Windows code generation. You must use Borland C++ 3.0 or 3.1 (IDE or command-line compilers), Turbo C++ for Windows 3.0, or Borland C++ for Windows 3.1 to compile Windows programs.

- The ObjectWindows class library, Borland's object-oriented framework for Windows programming (supplied with Application Frameworks).

NOTE: After a program ends, the IDE immediately returns. Short example programs in this book might therefore appear to have no visual effect. If you run a program and the screen just flashes briefly, press Alt+F5 to view the program's output. Press any key to return to the IDE. You can also use the File menu's DOS shell command to return temporarily to a DOS prompt, where you can run a compiled example. Type **exit** to return to the IDE.

Introducing Projects

Projects are configuration files that specify the parts and pieces of multifile programs. You don't need to create projects for simple programs—you can just load their files, press F9 to compile, or press Ctrl+F9 to compile and run.

To create a new project, select Project|Open project and enter a nonexisting file name. The IDE automatically supplies the extension .PRJ. The Project menu strangely lacks a Save command. Closing a project *always* saves it, a feature of some questionable value. (If you delete a file from a project, for example, there appears to be no recovery short of again adding that same file to the project window.)

If you start the IDE in a directory with a single .PRJ file, the IDE opens that project automatically. To take advantage of this feature, store your projects in separate directories, then from a DOS prompt change to a directory and type **bc**.

Examples in this book that require projects include instructions in the text about which files to add. For most programs, you simply add their .C and .CPP files, plus any auxiliary files such as Windows .DEF definitions and .RES resources. The compiler compiles and links all files in the correct order to create a finished .EXE executable code file on disk.

> **NOTE:** If you find a .PRJ file in a directory (for example, after installing this book's diskette), load that project to compile and run the example program. If you load only one file of a multifile project into the IDE, you might not be able to compile the program successfully.

The IDE Debugger

Debugging is a chore that all programmers need to perform but few enjoy. Nobody likes bugs. That's why we need good debuggers like the stand-alone and built-in IDE Turbo Debuggers. This section describes the built-in model. See Chapter 3, "The Command-Line Environment," for information about the stand-alone debugger.

Turbo Debugger might just as well be named Turbo Investigator. Use the debugger not only to locate problems in programs, but also as a kind of software microscope through which you can peer into your code's inner secrets. Use TD to examine variables, to single-step programs one statement at a time, and to test sections of programs while you observe results. Load any program into the IDE, then follow these suggestions:

- Move the cursor to any program statement and press Ctrl+F8 to set a breakpoint at that location. When and if the program reaches the breakpoint, it halts *before* executing the marked statement. Use breakpoints to stop programs at strategic places so you can examine variables and perform other operations.

- After executing one or more statements, select Debug|Inspect, and enter a variable name. The debugger shows you the variable's value in a small window, which you can close by selecting the window's close button on its upper-left border, or by pressing Alt+F3.

- Use the Watches command to open a window for one or more variables that you want to examine while the program operates.

- Instead of running a program at full speed by pressing Ctrl+F9, press F7 and F8 to single-step, or *trace,* statements one at a time. F7 traces into function calls, showing you their statements (see Chapter 7, "Functions: Divide and Conquer"). F8 executes function calls at full speed, then stops at the next statement.

- Select Evaluate/modify and enter an expression to evaluate. You can use this command also as a handy hex-to-decimal converter. For example, enter `0xff` to see that hexadecimal value's decimal equivalent, 255.

- Use Call stack to see a list of the currently active functions. This command is useful in larger programs, but has little value in this book's many short examples.

HINT: Use the built-in debugger extensively to investigate the sample listings in this book. Slow programs down to your speed by using the IDE's debugger so you can see how each statement works.

Using Precompiled Headers

Borland C++ and Turbo C++ for DOS can make use of precompiled headers to reduce compilation times. Use the Options|Compiler|Code generation command and select Precompiled headers to enable this feature.

With precompiled headers on, compiling a program creates an associated .SYM file that contains declarations in a precompiled form that the compiler can load quickly the *next* time you compile that same module. If you make any changes that would affect the accuracy of the precompiled information (adding a new "include" directive, for example, as described in Chapter 5, "Data: What a Program Knows"), the compiler simply recompiles from scratch, again creating an updated .SYM file.

Precompiled .SYM files take acres of disk space, so be careful when using this command to delete .SYM files that you no longer need. You can delete a .SYM file at any time. Another way to reduce .SYM file size is to insert an instruction that tells the compiler not to add any more information to a precompiled header file. Insert the line

```
#pragma hdrstop
```

where you want the compiler to stop collecting precompiled data. Insert the line

```
#pragma hdrfile
```

to resume precompiled header information. If you add new include directives after the #pragma hdrstop command, the compiler uses old precompiled information without starting over from scratch. This can save lots of time when compiling large programs.

NOTE: If you don't know what include directives are, don't be concerned. We'll get to those and other program elements in Part 2, "Programming with ANSI C." For compiling this book's examples, it's probably best not to use precompiled headers. The benefits are nil for short programs that you compile only one time.

Summary

- The Borland C++ and Turbo C++ for DOS integrated development environments, or IDEs, provide a text editor, compiler, debugger, and file manager rolled into one easy-to-use package.

- IDEs are popular, but they are not the only way to compile, link, and run programs. In the next chapter, "The Command-Line Environment," you'll learn how to use the Borland C++ command-line compiler and linker to construct program code files from the DOS prompt.

The Command-Line Environment

Simply stated, the Borland C++ command-line compiler and this chapter are for programmers who want a no-frills development environment. No menus, no windows, no dialog boxes—just you and the DOS prompt. We'll also briefly examine the stand-alone Turbo Debugger and Turbo Profiler programming tools.

The Command-Line Compiler

To start the command-line compiler, run BCC.EXE from DOS. For example, to compile and link a program WELCOME.C, enter **bcc welcome.c**. You must supply a filename and extension for .C programs. For .CPP (C++) program files, just enter the filename. The command **bcc welcome** compiles and links WELCOME.CPP. Type **bcc** alone for an abbreviated options list.

The command-line compiler offers several advantages over the IDEs described in Chapter 2, "The Integrated Environment." These advantages include

- *Memory savings.* IDEs take memory, which the command-line compiler can use to compile large programs.

- *Editing.* You can use a programmer's editor such as Brief to enter and edit text files (see instructions later in this chapter).

- *Making multifile programs.* You can use the MAKE utility with the command-line compiler to compile only the minimum number of modules required to keep complex multifile programs up to date. See Chapter 20, "DOS Tools and Techniques," for instructions on using MAKE and converting IDE project files to MAKE files.

- *Background compilation.* Under Windows you can run the command-line compiler in a DOS window. Use the system menu Settings command to select Background operation, or select that option in the task's .PIF file. You then can start a lengthy compilation and switch to another window while the command-line compiler runs. (You can also perform background compilation using an IDE, but that only wastes memory for features you aren't using.)

NOTE: The following sections explain some of the ways to use the Borland C++ command-line compiler BCC.EXE. You can use these same techniques with the Turbo C++ for DOS command-line compiler TCC.EXE. See also Appendixes B and C for command-line compiler and linker options.

If you plan to use a command-line environment regularly, run the THELP utility to install a resident online help system. Press the 5 key on your keyboard's numeric pad to activate a help screen. (The NumLock key must be off.) Unfortunately, unlike the IDE's similar online help windows, the resident THELP does not respond to mouse commands.

Compiling with Batch Files

One way to use BCC is to insert DOS commands into batch files. For example, suppose you have a program composed of three modules, MAIN.CPP, SUB1.CPP, and SUB2.CPP. You can create a batch file named C.BAT (you might as well use a short filename) with the lines

```
bcc -c main
bcc -c sub1
bcc -c sub2
bcc main.obj sub1.obj sub2.obj
```

From DOS simply type **c** to compile and link your program. The first three lines compile each separate module using the -c option to "compile only"—that is, to create an object-code .OBJ file. The final line executes Turbo Linker (TLINK) to combine the .OBJ modules into an executable code (.EXE) file.

BCC can do all of that in a single command. This line is equivalent to the four above:

```
bcc main sub1 sub2
```

The command-line compiler recognizes typical filename extensions. It compiles files ending in .C and .CPP, links files ending in .OBJ (by running the TLINK.EXE linker), and assembles files ending in .ASM (by running the TASM.EXE assembler). You can mix and match extensions in one command. The command

```
bcc main.c sub1 sub2.obj
```

compiles MAIN.C to MAIN.OBJ, compiles SUB1.CPP (the default extension) to SUB1.OBJ, and calls TLINK to link the resulting two .OBJ files plus SUB2.OBJ to create MAIN.EXE.

> **NOTE:** As mentioned earlier, you can also use the MAKE utility described in Chapter 20, "DOS Tools and Techniques," to run the command-line compiler. Rather than insert BCC commands in batch files, you might use this more sophisticated technique, especially for complex multifile projects.

Selecting Options

Select command-line options by typing a hyphen, a letter, and a minus sign (in other words, another hyphen) to turn off an option or a plus sign to turn it on. The plus sign is understood. For example, the command

```
bcc -v main
```

compiles MAIN.CPP to MAIN.OBJ, then links that file to create MAIN.EXE. The -v option (equivalent to -v+) tells the compiler to add debugging information to the resulting code for use with Turbo Debugger. The command

```
bcc -f- main
```

disables floating point emulation when compiling MAIN.CPP.

Option letters are case-sensitive. The option -c is *not* the same as -C. This command:

```
bcc -c main
```

compiles MAIN.CPP to MAIN.OBJ and does not run the linker. This command:

```
bcc -C main
```

enables nested comments for MAIN.CPP, compiles that file to MAIN.OBJ, and links to create MAIN.EXE.

Combine multiple options by separating them with spaces. You can write commands such as

```
bcc -c -C -v main
```

In almost all cases, options precede any filenames. See Chapter 20, "DOS Tools and Techniques," for an exception when compiling overlays.

Some options require strings, filenames, and so on. To define a symbol (which the compiler can detect via instructions in the program text), use the -D option like this:

```
bcc -DTEST main
```

That defines a symbol TEST for MAIN.CPP. (In later chapters you'll see the -D option again.) There is no space between the option letter and its argument. The same is true of filenames and pathnames. To specify an include directory (containing .h header files of declarations needed during compilation), use the -I directive. The command

```
bcc -Ic:\borlandc\include main
```

tells the compiler to look for .h header files in the specified directory. You can type path strings in upper- or lowercase, and you can separate multiple paths with semicolons, as in

```
bcc -Ic:\borlandc\classlib\include;c:\borlandc\include main
```

Typing long commands like these is extremely tedious. Fortunately, as explained next, there's an easier way to issue complex command-line options.

Creating a Configuration File

The C:\BORLANDC\BIN directory contains two default configuration files, TURBOC.CFG and TLINK.CFG. Insert options into these text files to select them as defaults for the command-line compiler and linker. To compile the programs in this book, edit TURBOC.CFG to contain these lines:

```
-Ic:\borlandc\owl\include
-Ic:\borlandc\classlib\include
-Ic:\borlandc\include
-Lc:\borlandc\owl\lib
-Lc:\borlandc\classlib\lib
-Lc:\borlandc\lib
```

For Turbo Vision examples, replace owl with tvision, and unless instructed otherwise, delete the two lines that reference classlib. (Turbo Vision does not use Borland's class library, but the ObjectWindows library, or OWL, does.)

You can insert *any* options listed in Appendix B into a .CFG file. Just insert them on separate lines. You might, for example, include the -v option to compile with debugging information. The TLINK.CFG file specifies default linker options, listed in Appendix C.

Rather than edit the default TURBOC.CFG and TLINK.CFG files for different configurations, you can store files of those names in the current directory. The command-line compiler then uses those files instead of the ones in C:\BORLANDC\BIN.

Using the Brief Programming Editor

The Brief programmer's editor is one of the most highly regarded programming tools among professional developers. When not using the IDE, I used Brief to write many of this book's sample programs.

Configure Brief by running its SETUP program. Select File Extensions and enter or select the .C and .CPP entries to prepare for automatic compilation using the Borland C++ or Turbo C++ command-line compilers. For each extension, if you want to use my settings, enter these options:

- Set tab stops to 3 5 7.

- Set Language type to C++.

- Select Regular Automatic indenting.

- Disable Word processing (that is, word wrap).

- Set "Compile inside Brief using:" to Borland.

- Insert the compiler command `bcc -c example.cpp`. Change this to `tcc -c example.cpp` for Turbo C++. Specify `.c` for .C files, and `.cpp` for .CPP files.

- Select Yes for "Show warning messages even if compile succeeds."

- Reserve at least 320 bytes for swapping.

Enter these options also for .h header files, but don't select an automatic compilation method. Optionally also set Miscellaneous options to swap DOS commands to "EMS or disk." Other options depend on your personal tastes.

To use Brief with THELP, you might have to specify the -p option or turn off multipage display swapping by using SETUP's Video Page Test command. (Set both options in this command to "No.") Brief's page swapping conflicts with THELP's pop-up windows and the only reported solution is to disable Brief's use of multiple text pages.

Press Alt+F10 to compile programs from within Brief. Brief recognizes Borland C++ compilation errors and shows you their associated lines. Press Ctrl+N to step to the next error message, and Ctrl+P for a list of all errors. Hint: Brief seems to be confused by errors that begin with punctuation characters. If an error message at the bottom of the display appears senseless, press Ctrl+P to read the full message.

I typically run Brief, enter or load selected files, press Alt+F10 to compile, then exit temporarily to a DOS prompt (Alt+Z). I can then type a command such as **bcc myfile.obj** to link, and if no errors occur, I run the program by typing its name. I type **exit** to return to Brief. I also sometimes open two DOS prompt windows under Microsoft Windows, one to run Brief and one to link and execute programs. Another possibility is to write a Brief macro that runs MAKE. You can probably perform similar commands with other popular third-party editors such as Epsilon and the capable Multi-Edit from American Cybernetics.

NOTE: Beginners are probably best advised to use the supplied IDE rather than Brief or another editor. You might not realize the value of an external programmer's editor unless you regularly switch between many different environments and languages. The main reason that I use Brief is to provide a single environment that works with all of my languages, compilers, and other tools.

Using Turbo Debugger for DOS

Figure 3.1 shows Turbo Debugger's display. There isn't room here for an exhaustive treatment of TD's extensive commands. These notes will help you to load the book's examples into the debugger to investigate how they operate.

The stand-alone and IDE debuggers recognize similar commands (see Chapter 2, "The Integrated Environment"). With TD, however, you can press F2 or Ctrl+F8 to set breakpoints. In the IDE, F2 saves the current file. Most other hot keys and commands are the same in the built-in and stand-alone models. The stand-alone debugger also offers numerous features such as hardware debugging (run TD286.EXE or TD386.EXE) and remote debugging via TDREMOTE.

To prepare a program for debugging, compile it using the -v option. For example, you might compile the TAX.C program in Chapter 5, "Data: What a Program Knows," with the command

```
bcc -v tax.c
```

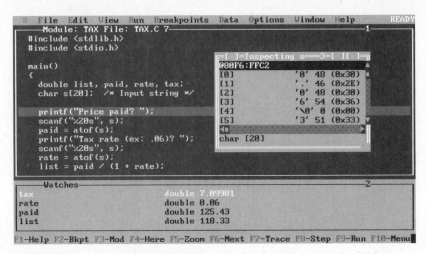

Figure 3.1. Turbo Debugger.

Use a similar command to compile all modules for which you want to view source code in the debugger. Load the resulting TAX.EXE file into TD with the command

```
td tax
```

In a moment, the debugger's display appears. Press F7 and F8 to single-step statements as explained in Chapter 2, "The Integrated Environment." Press Ctrl+I to inspect variables, or Ctrl+W to add them to the Watches window. Press Alt+X to exit the debugger and return to DOS.

> **NOTE:** My book, *Mastering Turbo Debugger*, gives detailed descriptions of TD's options and commands. See Bibliography.

Using Turbo Profiler for DOS

Beginners can postpone using Turbo Profiler for the time being (see Figure 3.2). You don't need this utility until you are ready to optimize your code to improve performance—usually one of the last jobs to perform when developing new software. (Fix the bugs first. Then worry about efficiency.)

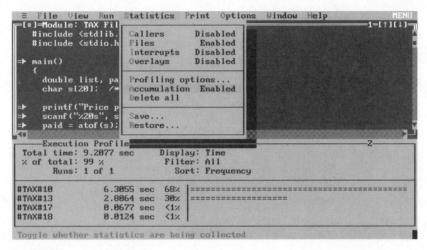

Figure 3.2. Turbo Profiler.

Use TPROF to test your program's runtime activity, collecting data that can help you to identify critical code—those sections where your program spends most of its time. After profiling, you can rewrite critical code in assembly language, and according to the theory, gain the best possible speed advantages for the least amount of effort. (Chapter 19, "Assembly Language Optimizations," covers assembly language. Chapter 20, "DOS Tools and Techniques," lists other optimization techniques for boosting performance.)

To prepare a program for profiling, use the same techniques as for debugging. For example, to compile, link, and profile the TAX.C program, enter the commands

```
bcc -v tax.c
tprof tax
```

Press F9 to run the program and use the profiler's default settings. At the bottom of the display, you see a report of the program's activities. Press Alt+X to return to DOS.

Summary

- Programmers who want a no-frills environment, or those who use a programmer's editor such as Brief, can run the Borland C++ command-line compiler and linker from a DOS prompt.

- The command-line compiler uses less memory, and can therefore compile larger programs than the IDE. You can also use command-line compilation with the MAKE utility described in Chapter 20, "DOS Tools and Techniques."

- This completes Part 1's introduction to DOS programming environments. In the next chapter, you'll investigate two graphical IDEs: Borland C++ for Windows and Turbo C++ for Windows.

Borland C++ for Windows

Windows fans will be pleased to learn that they can use Borland C++ for Windows 3.1 to compile and run not only Windows programs, but also DOS programs using EasyWin. Turbo C++ for Windows 3.0 can be used the same way. This chapter explains how to use these graphical integrated development environments (IDEs) along with EasyWin to compile and run many of this book's listings. Chapter 21, "Windows Tools and Techniques," covers fully fledged Windows programming techniques.

The Windows IDE

Figure 4.1 shows Borland C++ for Windows 3.1 (BCW), which includes similar options and features found in the text-based IDE.

Figure 4.1. Borland C++ for Windows.

Like its text-mode partner, the BCW IDE supports projects. All .PRJ files are transferrable between DOS and Windows, and the Project menu commands in the two IDEs are exactly the same. BCW's editor also works like the text-based IDE BC's, and most other commands and options are the same or similar.

BCW's predecessor, Turbo C++ for Windows 3.0 (TCW), lacked the sophisticated optimizations available in the text IDE and command-line compilers. BCW 3.1 includes the identical optimizations found in the text IDE and command-line compilers, but still lacks one significant text-mode feature: a built-in debugger. To debug programs under Windows, you must use the stand-alone Turbo Debugger for Windows (TDW), introduced later in this chapter.

One unique feature in BCW is a class browser (Borland calls it ObjectBrowser), activated with the **B**rowse menu (see Figure 4.2).

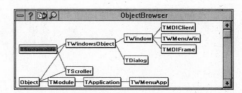

Figure 4.2. Borland's Class Browser.

Use the browser's commands to investigate class library hierarchies and to inspect variables, symbols, and functions. Also use BCW's extensive online help (press F1 or use the Help menu) for more information about the class browser, other BCW commands, and library functions including the Windows API (application programming interface).

BCW's editor provides the same syntax highlighting feature described in Chapter 2, "The Integrated Environment." Turbo C++ for Windows does not implement syntax highlighting.

There is one other significant new feature: BCW 3.1 can generate only 80286 and 80386 instructions; it no longer creates 8088/8086 code. (See the Options|Compiler|Advanced code generation command.) This means that programs compiled with BCW must run on systems with 80286 or later processors. You may, however, target programs to run under Windows 3.0 and 3.1, or for Windows 3.1 use exclusively. (See Options|Resources.)

NOTE: Windows 3.1 itself also runs only on model 80286, 80386, and 80486 systems, so the new restriction on output isn't too severe. BCW 3.1 can generate Windows 3.0-compatible programs, but those programs, as well, can't run on 8088/8086-powered computers. These restrictions apply only to BCW, not to the text-based IDE or command-line compilers.

Using EasyWin

You can use BCW to compile many of this book's sample listings. Figure 4.1, for example, shows BCW running the TAX.C program from Chapter 5, "Data: What a Program Knows." TAX.C is not a Windows application. It's a DOS program that BCW has compiled to run in a window that resembles a PC's text-mode display.

BCW automatically compiles DOS-style programs using the EasyWin library, a tool that allows programs to call standard input and output functions but still run under Windows. EasyWin simply redirects I/O to a graphical window. You might have trouble using EasyWin for running some of this book's more complex programs, such as the examples in Chapter 18, "Turbo Vision." You should, however, be able to run most listings in the ANSI C and C++ tutorials in Parts 2 and 3.

The best part about EasyWin is its simplicity. There are no commands to issue or options to select. You don't have to modify the listings. Just load any .C or .CPP program into BCW, press F9 to compile, or press Ctrl+F9 to compile and run. After the program finishes, close the inactive output window by using standard Windows commands (press Alt+F4, for example).

NOTE: EasyWin supports only standard I/O. It doesn't support BGI graphics or other unique Borland C++ features intended for DOS programming. Also, you can't compile programs with BCW and then run the results from DOS. BCW, TCW, and EasyWin can generate only Windows .EXE code files. To create DOS .EXE files you must use the text based IDE or command-line compilers.

Turbo Debugger for Windows

Select Run|Debugger to load the current program into Turbo Debugger for Windows (TDW). If necessary, this command recompiles the program to add debugging information that TDW needs. You can use TDW to debug EasyWin and also full Windows applications.

TDW runs in text mode, hiding Windows' graphics display, which remains active in the background. TDW takes control of your development system, which is necessary to debug applications on the processor instruction level. Windows and your application are still there—you just can't see them. Press Alt+F5 to switch between the text and Windows displays.

TDW's commands are similar to those in the text-mode stand-alone debugger (see Chapter 3, "The Comand-Line Environment"). You can single-step statements (press F7 or F8), inspect variables (Ctrl+I), add variables to the Watches window (Ctrl+W), and set breakpoints (F2 or Ctrl+F8). If you know how to use TD, you should have little trouble getting around in TDW.

> **NOTE:** You can install a monochrome card and tell TDW to use it for output, leaving the graphics screen untouched. Because monochrome cards are designed for 8-bit operation, however, this can drastically slow a fast 16-bit graphics card's performance. For a list of TDW command-line options, including those to enable dual screen debugging, from the Windows Program Manager (or File Manager), select File|Run and enter `tdw -h`. You must have C:\BORLANDC\BIN or another installation directory on the current path for this trick to work.

When debugging EasyWin and Windows programs, TDW switches from its text display to the Windows graphics screen so you can see your code in operation. The debugger's display returns when the program reaches a breakpoint or when it ends. For EasyWin programs, this means you must close the program's inactive window to return to TDW, which you can then exit (Alt+X) to get back to Windows. *Don't accidentally leave TDW running in the background.*

> **NOTE:** In TDW it's usually best to run a program to completion. Aborting a Windows program midstream might leave DOS, Windows, or both in an unstable condition. If any errors cause a program to end prematurely, for safety, exit Windows and reboot as soon as possible.

Chapter 21, "Windows Tools and Techniques," explains how to create and compile full Windows applications, complete with pull down menus, overlapping windows, dialog boxes, and controls. The chapter also includes additional instructions for using TDW to debug Windows programs.

Turbo Profiler for Windows

Like TDW, Turbo Profiler for Windows (TPROFW) runs in a text display while Windows remains active but hidden. Run the profiler from the Windows Program

Manager, and then use its File|Open command to load a compiled Windows application.

You can't profile DOS programs using TPROFW. Use Turbo Profiler for DOS as explained in Chapter 3, "The Command-Line Environment." TPROFW is intended to profile only Windows applications. The commands in the DOS and Windows programs are similar.

Summary

- You can use BCW's EasyWin capability to run many of this book's sample programs—at least those that call standard input and output functions. EasyWin directs I/O to a graphical window that resembles the DOS text-mode display.

- You can use BCW also to write complete Windows applications. That's a topic we'll have to postpone, however, until Chapter 21, "Windows Tools and Techniques."

- This completes Part 1's introduction to Borland C++ environments. Select a programming environment suitable for your tastes and computer, and turn to Part 2 to begin learning how to program using ANSI C.

Part 2

Programming
with ANSI C

PART 2

5

Data: What a Program Knows

Data are facts that a computer program knows. By storing data in programs, you teach facts—your bank balance, or the name and address of your stock broker, for example—to a computer.

As you'll discover in this chapter, a C program's data may take various forms such as integers, floating-point values, and character strings. Before exploring these and other data types, however, let's take a close look at the parts and pieces of a typical C program.

Anatomy of a C Program

The best way to learn a programming language is to enter, compile, and run small- to medium-size listings on your own computer. Using Borland C++, Turbo C++ for DOS, Borland C++ for Windows, or your favorite text editor, enter Listing 5.1 (excluding the reference numbers and colons at the left), save as WELCOME.C, then compile and run the program.

Listing 5.1. WELCOME.C (A sample program in C).

```
1:  #include <stdio.h>
2:
3:  main()
4:  {
5:    printf("Welcome to Borland C Programming!\n");
6:    return 0;
7:  }
```

INSTRUCTIONS: Press Ctrl+F9 to compile and run listings from an integrated development environment (IDE). From DOS, enter **bcc welcome.c** (BCC.EXE must be in the system PATH, and you must type the .c extension to compile C programs). In the DOS IDE, press Alt+F5 to view the output screen, then press any key to return to the editor. You also can use the Window|Output command. From Windows, press Alt+F4 to close an inactive output window. To run compiled programs from the DOS command line, enter the program's name (**welcome** in this case). Refer to Part 1, "Environments," for additional help compiling and running listings.

Line 1 of Listing 5.1 is an include directive. The directive's name (#include) tells the compiler to read the text from the specified file. Bracketing the filename as <stdio.h> tells the compiler to look for stdio.h in a preset directory, usually C:\BORLANDC\INCLUDE. Enclosing a filename with quotes—"anyfile.h", for example—tells the compiler to look for anyfile.h in the current directory. In Listing 5.1, the included file stdio.h is called a header file, which typically ends with the extension .h. The stdio.h file contains various standard input and output declarations needed by the program. Other header files contain different kinds of declarations, most of which you'll see by the time you finish this book.

Line 2 is blank—don't laugh, blank lines are important in programming, and they help separate key sections. The compiler ignores blank lines.

The opening and closing braces in lines 4 and 7 form a block—a group of items that you want the compiler to treat as a unit. A block is also called a compound statement. The block in Listing 5.1 encloses two statements at lines 5 and 6. In general, statements are actions that you want a program to perform. The first statement in

Listing 5.1 calls C's formatted-output function `printf()` to display a line of quoted text that ends with a two-character symbol \n, which starts a new line on the output window or terminal. In this book, empty parentheses remind you that a symbol such as `printf()` is a function. (By the way, most people pronounce `printf()` as "print F.")

Line 6 is a `return` statement. It ends the program and returns a value to DOS. Usually, nonzero values indicate errors; 0 means success.

That leaves one line unexplained. At line 3 is one of the most important elements in every C program—the `main()` function. It deserves closer inspection.

The *main()* Function

C programs run in a linear fashion. They start at one instruction, execute others, and unless lightning strikes and the power fizzes away, they usually end at a planned time and location.

All C programs start at the same spot: the first statement inside a function called `main()`. (You'll learn more about functions, and how to write your own, in Chapter 7, "Functions: Divide and Conquer.") When you run a compiled C program, no matter how large or how small, it always begins at `main()`.

Listing 5.2, SMALLEST.C, is the smallest possible complete C program (however, see Exercise 5.1). Despite its Lilliputian appearance, the program still has a `main()` function.

Listing 5.2. SMALLEST.C (Smallest possible C program).

```
1:  main()
2:  {
3:    return 0;
4:  }
```

Functions begin with a name (`main` at line 1), followed by a pair of parentheses. Later in this book, you'll learn how to declare function parameters to which you can pass argument values. Functions that have no parameters are written with empty parentheses.

The function's block follows its name (lines 2–4). Everything inside the block belongs to the function. In this case, there's only one statement: a single `return` (line

3). In other programs, main() may have many statements, each terminated with a semicolon so the compiler can easily find their ends.

Running this extremely simple program under a debugger's watchful eye reveals how C programs start, run, and stop (see Figure 5.1).

Figure 5.1. A typical C program runs in three stages.

From the DOS IDE (don't use Turbo C++ for Windows for this experiment), enter Listing 5.2, but instead of compiling in the usual way, follow these steps:

1. Press F8 to compile and run the program one statement at a time. The first time you press F8, main() is highlighted. The program is poised at its beginning like a drag racer waiting for the light to turn green.

2. Press F8 again. Now the return statement is highlighted. You have just executed an invisible section called the startup code. A C program's startup code performs various initializations that are usually of little concern except in advanced programming.

3. Press F8 once more to execute the return statement. Now the final brace is highlighted, showing you that the program is ready to execute another invisible section called the exit code. Like the startup code, the exit code performs miscellaneous chores that you can ignore for now.

4. Press F8 a final time to end the program.

You can perform a similar experiment from the DOS command line using the stand-alone Turbo Debugger. Save Listing 5.2 in a file named SMALLEST.C. Then, from DOS, enter **bcc -v smallest.c** to compile. The compiler switch -v adds debugging information to the finished code file. After compiling, load the specially prepared code file into Turbo Debugger with the command **td smallest**. Then, skipping step 1 (automatically executed when you start the debugger), follow steps 2–4.

When the program ends, unlike the IDE, the stand-alone debugger displays the return value. Try an experiment: Change Listing 5.2's return value to 1, compile from DOS (remember to specify -v), load into Turbo Debugger, and repeat steps 2–4. The debugger again shows you the program's return value, which, in a more sophisticated program, might represent an error code.

> **NOTE:** To exit Turbo Debugger, press Esc or Enter to clear any open dialog boxes, then press Alt+X. See Chapter 3, "The Command-Line Environment," for more information about using the stand-alone Turbo Debugger.

Error Messages

Don't be surprised if, when typing and writing programs, you make more than your fair share of mistakes. Programming demands perfection. Misplace just one itsy-bitsy symbol and the compiler will squawk in discontent.

There are two categories of compiler complaints.

- *Errors.* Errors indicate relatively serious mistakes that prevent the compiler from finishing its job. You must correct all errors before you can run a program.

- *Warnings.* Warnings direct your attention to problems that may or may not cause the program to fail. You may run programs for which the compiler generates warnings, but the results are unpredictable. When you receive a warning, proceed with caution and repair the trouble as soon as possible.

Because you will undoubtedly make countless errors over the course of your programming career, it's helpful to make a few mistakes on purpose now so that you know how to deal with your own problems later. Enter and compile Listing 5.3, BAD.C, which contains several nasty typos.

Listing 5.3. BAD.C (A good program with many bad errors).

```
1:  include <stdio.h)
2:
3:  main{}
4:  (
5:    printf("Problems, problems\n");
6:    printf("Problems all day long!\n");
7:    printf("  -- The Everly Brothers\n")
8:  )
```

When you compile the listing, the compiler informs you that BAD.C has a few errors. Compiling from the DOS command line displays the lines:

```
Error bad.c 1: Declaration syntax error
Error bad.c 6: ) expected
Error bad.c 6: Unterminated string or character constant
*** 3 errors in Compile ***
```

Each error message gives you the filename (more important in multifile programs), the line number, and a brief explanation. Obviously, there are problems with lines 1 and 6. Reload the program (or switch back to the appropriate editor window) and fix the mistakes in those lines. Change line 1 to

```
#include <stdio.h>
```

Line 6 appears to have two errors. The first says a closing parenthesis is missing. The text seems okay, however, so skip this error and go to the next, "Unterminated string...". The string of characters in the printf() statement is missing its closing quotation. Change line 6 to

```
printf("Problems all day long!\n");
```

Compile the modified program. Again, the compiler complains with a list of problems:

```
Error bad.c 3: Declaration syntax error
Error bad.c 6: ) expected
Error bad.c 7: ) expected
*** 3 errors in Compile ***
```

Now line 3 has developed a problem. This is typical—you fix some errors and others appear. Although the compiler tries to find all mistakes, some types of errors may hide others, so after fixing one set of problems, it's common to receive others.

Try to fix the rest of the errors on your own. (Hint: use Listing 5.1 as a guide.) Listing 5.4, GOOD.C, shows the corrected program.

Listing 5.4. GOOD.C (Repaired version of BAD.C).

```
1:  #include <stdio.h>
2:
3:  main()
4:  {
5:    printf("Problems, problems\n");
```

```
6:    printf("Problems all day long!\n");
7:    printf("  -- The Everly Brothers\n");
8:    return 0;
9:  }
```

Header Files

Directives such as `#include <stdio.h>` tell the compiler to read file stdio.h as though its lines were written at the directive's location. Examine stdio.h with a text editor (the file is probably stored in C:\BORLANDC\INCLUDE), and search for `printf`. Near the middle of the file is the line

```
int    _Cdecl printf(const char _FAR *_format, ...);
```

This is called a prototype. It informs the compiler about function `printf()`'s form and requirements—in other words, its syntax. Don't be concerned with understanding every detail in this sample prototype—just be aware that including header files such as stdio.h is how you import various predeclared items into your programs.

> **NOTE:** Specifying header files isn't always required by ANSI C. For example, you can remove line 1 from Listing 5.1 and still compile the program. This practice is dangerous, however, because it forces the compiler to make assumptions about functions such as `printf()` in the absence of a formal prototype. For best results, always include header files for every function and other library items used in a program.

Listings 5.5 and 5.6 demonstrate two ways to use `#include` directives. Enter Listing 5.5 and save as MYSTUFF.INC. Also enter Listing 5.6 and save as INCLUDES.C in the same directory. Then, compile and run INCLUDES.C.

Listing 5.5. MYSTUFF.INC.

```
1:  printf("Inside MYSTUFF.INC\n");
```

Listing 5.6. INCLUDES.C.

```
1:  #include <stdio.h>
2:
3:  main()
4:  {
5:  #include "mystuff.inc"
6:    printf("Inside INCLUDES.C\n");
7:    return 0;
8:  }
```

Line 1 includes the standard STDIO.H header file in the usual way. Line 5 includes MYSTUFF.INC, causing the compiler to read the single `printf()` statement from Listing 5.5 into `main()`. When you run the program, you see the two lines:

```
Inside MYSTUFF.INC
Inside INCLUDES.C
```

proving that both `printf()` statements were compiled. The program also demonstrates a useful debugging technique. Inserting `printf()` statements at strategic locations gives you a handy way to trace a program's execution.

When the compiler processes an `#include` directive, it looks for specified files according to these rules:

- If the filename is bracketed (`#include <stdio.h>`), the compiler looks for the file in the Include Directories, as specified by the IDE's Options|Directories command, or the command-line compiler's `-I` switch.

- If the filename is quoted (`#include "anyfile.ext"`), the compiler looks for the file in the current directory.

- If the compiler can't find a quoted file, it treats the name as though it were surrounded by angle brackets (in other words, if "anyfile.ext" isn't in the current directory, the compiler looks for the file in the Include Directories).

- Case is not significant for `#include` filenames. MyFile.H, MYFILE.H, and myfile.h all refer to the same file. The `#include` directive itself must be typed in lowercase.

- Filenames may include drive letters and paths as in the directive `#include "c:\mydir\myfile.inc"`. Single backslashes separate directory pathnames.

Comments

Comments are a kind of private data for your eyes only. The compiler completely ignores comments. Like a footnote in a book, a comment adds a clarifying note about the program.

Bracket comments with the double-character symbols /* and */. Here's a sample:

```
/* My first C program */
```

The compiler completely ignores all characters in this comment, including the two brackets. Comments may come at the end of a statement:

```
printf("Print this text");  /* Display text on-screen */
```

They may not, however, come between quoted text or identifiers:

```
printf("Not /*a comment*/");   /* ??? */
int bad/*comment*/Identifier;  /* ??? */
```

In this text, I'll attach the comment /* ??? */, borrowed from traditional chess commentary, to a faulty construction or a questionable practice. The two lines above are bad moves for a programmer.

You can write single or multiline comments with a single pair of brackets. The following three lines of text are one comment:

```
/* My second C program
   Written 11/10/1998
   By: Your Name */
```

As with single-line comments, the compiler ignores all text between and including the opening and closing brackets. Taking advantage of this fact, programmers often write fancy comments like:

```
/*
** Program: My third C program
** Date: 12/10/1998
** Author: Your name
*/
```

The compiler ignores all text between and including the comment brackets on the top and bottom lines. The extra asterisks are just for show.

Nested Comments

Normally, comments may not nest inside of each other. This is not a legal comment:

```
/* Outer /* inner comment */ comment */
```

If you want to use nested comments, turn on Nested comments with the IDE's Options|Compiler|Source command, or use the -C command-line switch. Don't do this, however, if you want your code to work with other compilers, which may not support nested comments.

Debugging with Comments

Nested comments are often useful for debugging an ornery piece of code. Sometimes, removing a statement or two and running the program minus some of its parts can reveal the cause of a problem. This technique is similar to a doctor being able to remove someone's heart, and, upon observing that the patient remains sick, determining there's probably nothing wrong with the subject's ticker. (Don't try this at home.)

Suppose you want to find out what happens if Listing 5.1 neglects to execute a return statement. Rather than delete the line, disable it by surrounding the statement with comment brackets:

```
main()
{
  printf("Welcome to Borland C Programming!\n");
/*
  return 0;
*/
}
```

The compiler now ignores the statement, which you can easily restore by removing the brackets.

Suppose next, however, that the program already had a comment at that same position:

```
main()
{
  printf("Welcome to Borland C Programming!\n");
  return 0;  /* return 0*/
}
```

To *comment-out* the return statement, you could switch on nested comments, and write

```
main()
{
  printf("Welcome to Borland C Programming!\n");
/*
  return 0;  /* return 0*/
*/
}
```

This technique is especially useful when commenting out large sections of programming containing numerous comments. With nested comments off, however, the modified program will not compile.

NOTE: Use comments sparingly. Good programs should be readable on their own, and you should get in the habit of reading code, not only comments. To encourage you to develop this skill, many of the listings in this book have few or no comments. Don't hesitate to add comments to your own listings, however, to clarify the purpose of a section, or to document (at the beginning of a file) a program's purpose, parameters, author, and other miscellaneous information.

Variables and Data Types

You store facts in a program by assigning values to variables. A variable is a name that is associated with memory set aside for storing a variable's value. The reserved memory region is called an *object*, but don't confuse this use of the word "object" with object-oriented programming introduced in Chapter 13, "Programming with Classes." An object is just a place in memory to store a value.

Programs must declare variables before using them. This rule helps the compiler complete its job quickly and forces programmers to plan their work carefully. Listing 5.7, INTEGER.C, demonstrates how to declare, initialize, and use a simple integer variable. Integers are whole numbers. In C, an integer is abbreviated as int.

Listing 5.7. INTEGER.C (Displays an integer variable).

```
 1:  #include <stdio.h>
 2:
 3:  main()
 4:  {
 5:    int value;
 6:
 7:    value = 1234;
 8:    printf("Value = %d\n", value);
 9:    return 0;
10:  }
```

Line 5 declares an int variable named value. The declaration ends with a semicolon. The symbol int is called a data type and is built into the C language. The symbol value is an identifier, a name that you invent. By convention, a blank line (line 6) separates a program's variable declarations from its statements.

Line 7 assigns the value 1234 to the variable named value. When this assignment statement is executed, the program stores a binary representation of 1234 in the memory that belongs to value. (See Figure 5.2.)

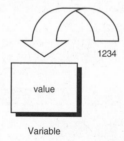

Figure 5.2. An assignment statement stores a value in a variable.

Line 8 displays value with the statement

```
printf("Value = %d\n", value);
```

Examine this line's printf() statement closely. Buried inside the string is the argument %d, a special command that tells printf() where and in what form a value should appear. The printf() function replaces %d with the value of a variable listed after the string. When line 8 executes, printf() converts value's binary value to text, inserts that text in place of the %d argument, and sends the result to the terminal. The \n characters at the end of the string start a new line on the terminal.

Listing 5.8, VARIABLE.C, declares and displays a few more variables of many different types.

Listing 5.8. VARIABLE.C (Displays variables of various types).

```
 1:  #include <stdio.h>
 2:
 3:  main()
 4:  {
 5:    char slash = '/';
 6:    short month = 4;
 7:    int year = 2001;
 8:    long population = 308700000L;
 9:    float pi = 3.14159;
10:    double velocity = 186281.7;
11:    long double lightYear = 5.88e12;
12:
13:    printf("Date = %02d%c%d\n", month, slash, year);
14:    printf("Population of the U.S.A. = %ld\n", population);
15:    printf("Pi = %f\n", pi);
16:    printf("Velocity of light =%12.2f miles/sec\n", velocity);
17:    printf("One light year = %.0Lf miles\n", lightYear);
18:    return 0;
19:  }
```

You'll investigate all of Listing 5.8's data types (lines 5–11) in this chapter. To display the program's values, printf() uses a variety of arguments (%d, %c, %f, and so on), each of which inserts a value of a particular type and form into the displayed strings. As you meet various data types, you'll learn how to format their values in printf() statements. (For a full description of this powerful function, look up printf() in Chapter 22, "Functions and Examples.")

Line 7 shows a handy way to declare and initialize a variable in one easy step. You could also write this line in two parts:

```
int year;
...
year = 2001;
```

The end result is the same, but before 2001 is assigned to year, that variable's value is uninitialized. Using an uninitialized variable can lead to all sorts of problems, because variables such as year and velocity would then have values equal to the bit patterns left in their memory locations from previous operations. Always initialize your variables before using them. (The compiler warns you about this mistake if you forget.)

Global Variables

As Listing 5.8 shows, you may declare variables inside of the main() function's block. You can also declare variables outside of main(). These are called global variables.

Unlike local variables declared inside main(), global variables are preinitialized to all zero bytes. Listing 5.9, GLOBAL.C, is identical to 5.7, but declares value as a global variable.

Listing 5.9. GLOBAL.C (Declares a global variable).

```
 1:  #include <stdio.h>
 2:
 3:  int value;
 4:
 5:  main()
 6:  {
 7:    value = 1234;
 8:    printf("Value = %d\n", value);
 9:    return 0;
10:  }
```

Because int value; appears at line 3, outside of main(), the compiler stores the variable in the program's data segment. At runtime, the program's startup code sets every byte in this memory area to 0, thus also initializing value to 0. If you remove line 7, the program will display value as 0. If you remove the similar assignment from Listing 5.7, however, the local value would not be zeroed. Only global variables are guaranteed to equal 0 when the program begins.

Compile and run Listing 5.10, DEFAULT.C, for a demonstration of the differences between initialized and uninitialized global and local variables.

> **NOTE:** The compiler may warn you about the use of `localDefault` before it is initialized. You can ignore this warning for the test program, but you should not ignore a similar message in your own programs. If you don't receive a warning for Listing 5.10, edit the TURBOC.CFG file usually stored in C:\BORLANDC\BIN, and add the command -w on a separate line. This will enable all warnings for the command-line compiler. To do the same for the IDE, select Compiler from the Options menu, choose Messages and Display, and set Display warnings to All. Use Options|Save to save this setting for future sessions.

Listing 5.10. DEFAULT.C (Global vs. local default values).

```
 1:  #include <stdio.h>
 2:
 3:  int global = 100;
 4:  int globalDefault;
 5:
 6:  main()
 7:  {
 8:    int local = 200;
 9:    int localDefault;
10:
11:    printf("global = %d\n", global);
12:    printf("local  = %d\n", local);
13:
14:    printf("globalDefault = %d\n", globalDefault);
15:    printf("localDefault  = %d\n", localDefault);
16:    return 0;
17:  }
```

The variables `global` and `local` (lines 3 and 8) are assigned initial values. Variables `globalDefault` and `localDefault` are not. When you run the code, only `globalDefault` is guaranteed to equal zero. In one test, the program displayed:

```
global = 100
local  = 200
globalDefault = 0
localDefault  = 262
```

On your terminal, the value for `localDefault`, which is not preinitialized, may be *any* value, including 0.

Keywords

Keywords such as `int` in Listing 5.9 are built-in symbols. You may never use keywords for your own purposes; they are reserved for specific purposes. Keywords must be typed in lowercase. Table 5.1 lists ANSI C keywords reserved by Borland C++.

Table 5.1. ANSI C keywords.

asm	default	for	short	union
auto	do	goto	signed	unsigned
break	double	if	sizeof	void
case	else	int	static	volatile
char	enum	long	struct	while
const	extern	register	switch	
continue	float	return	typedef	

Borland C++ extends the standard ANSI keyword list with several more reserved words, listed in Table 5.2. Some of these words begin with underscores—a convention that indicates a special word belonging to the compiler or to a component of a standard library. You may not use any of these words for your own purposes.

Table 5.2. Extended ANSI C keywords.

_cdecl	_es	_fastcall	_near	_saveregs
cdecl	_export	huge	near	_seg
_cs	_far	interrupt	_pascal	_ss
_ds	far	_loadds	pascal	

Use the command-line switch -A to restrict the compiler to recognize only standard ANSI C keywords. You could also use the Option|Compiler|Source command and select ANSI. You need to do this only if you plan to port (transfer) your programs to another ANSI-compatible compiler.

NOTE: The C++ language and Borland C++ add additional keywords to those listed in Tables 5.1 and 5.2. See Appendix E for a complete keyword list.

Identifiers

The word value in Listing 5.9 is called an identifier. Identifiers are words that you invent, usually to identify variables or functions of your own design. (Chapter 7, "Functions: Divide and Conquer," covers functions in depth.)

Identifiers must begin with a letter, and they may contain only letters, digits, or underscores. Identifiers may be any practical length. However, they must differ in their first 32 characters, or by the number specified using the IDE's Options|Compiler|Source command or the -i*n* command-line switch where *n* is the maximum length. The switch -i8, for example, specifies eight significant characters. Some ANSI compilers may use as few as six significant characters to distinguish among identifiers; Borland C++ guarantees 32.

NOTE: Identifiers may begin with one or more underscores as in _myIdentifier or __myWord. However, this form is best reserved for system-level identifiers used by Borland C++. If you never begin identifiers with underscores, you will never cause a conflict with a predeclared system identifier.

The C and C++ languages are case-sensitive, meaning that upper- and lowercase letters are significant. MyVar, myvar, and MYVAR are three distinctly unique identifiers. Traditionally, C programmers begin variable identifiers and standard library functions with lowercase letters. In this book, most new functions are capitalized so you can tell them apart from library functions, although this plan is imperfect because Borland's Turbo Vision, ObjectWindows, and other libraries use a mix of capitalized and uncapitalized function names. Keywords are always in lowercase. For example, a program might have several variables named

```
value          balance          result          name
```

and the program might call functions named

```
printf      MyFunc          getchar          GetUp
```

Remember, these are conventions, not rules. You may use upper- and lowercase letters in your own identifiers such as MyFunc and GetUp in any way you wish. You must capitalize existing names like printf and getchar exactly as declared. Conventions like these help you to organize your programs and to understand code written by others.

Badly formed identifiers cause the compiler to complain, often by issuing the error "Declaration terminated incorrectly." The error refers to the fact that a preceding item such as a data type name is followed by an incorrect identifier. Here are a few samples of incorrect identifiers:

```
3rdValue      $balance          my-Var          bigMistake!           /* ??? */
```

Identifiers may never begin with digits, and they may not contain punctuation characters other than underscores.

For extra clarity, some programmers separate multiword identifiers with underscores. The meanings of these identifiers are obvious, and their forms are easy to read:

```
balance_of_power                          speed_of_light
```

Underscores are significant characters. To the compiler, balance_of_power is a *single* word, not three.

Another popular convention, which you might refer to as *camel caps*, uses a lowercase letter to begin the first word and initial capitals for subsequent words, resembling a camel's humps. Using camel caps, you could write the previous two identifiers like this:

```
balanceOfPower                speedOfLight
```

NOTE: I prefer the camel cap style because underscores are sometimes hard to see in print and on computer terminals. Underscores, however, are more traditional.

Integer Types

Integer data types such as `int` occupy a fixed amount of memory, thus limiting the range of values they can represent. In Borland C++, an `int` variable takes two bytes and can hold values ranging from −32,768 to +32,767 (including 0). For clarity in this text, large values are segmented with commas. Never add commas to numeric values in programs. In a program, type `32767`.

If you need a wider integer range, you can declare variables of type `long int` like this:

```
long int bigValue;
```

Declared that way, `bigValue` can store values from −2,147,483,648 to +2,147,483,647, including 0. You can abbreviate `long int` as `long`:

```
long bigValue;
```

You can also declare `short int` values such as

```
short int smallValue;
```

which you can abbreviate as

```
short smallValue;
```

In Borland C++, a `short int` is identical to an `int`, and can represent the same range of values.

> **NOTE:** Exact ranges and memory sizes of data types may differ from compiler to compiler, especially for compilers running under different operating systems. ANSI C guarantees only that an `int` value takes no less space than a `short int`, and that a `long int` takes no less space than an `int`. Another compiler could store all three types in the same amount of space, having them all represent the same value ranges, and the compiler would still conform to ANSI C's rules. Don't assume that specific types have a certain size and range—your code may not work properly on different systems.

Use a `char` for very small values. Although `char` variables may of course represent characters, they may also hold integers ranging from −128 to +127 (including 0). Here's a sample:

```
char oneByte;
```

Variable `oneByte` may store signed values that can be stored in one 8-bit byte. As with other integer types, however, another ANSI C compiler could store `char` variables in more than one byte, and still be consistent with ANSI's rules and regulations.

Signed and Unsigned Values

All integer types—`char`, `short`, `int`, and `long`—are signed by default. In other words, variables of those types can hold negative and positive values. You may use the `signed` keyword to designate signed values, such as

```
signed int plusOrMinus;
```

Just plain `int` means the same, so it's unnecessary to preface `int` with the `signed` keyword.

If you don't need to store negative values, you can preface any integer type with the keyword `unsigned`. Here are a few samples of unsigned variables:

```
unsigned char oneChar;
unsigned short oneShort;
unsigned int oneInt;
unsigned long oneLong;
```

Unsigned values take the same amount of space as their signed compatriots, but can represent only positive values. Because unsigned variables don't need to store negative values, they can represent twice as many positive values (including 0) as their signed equivalents. Table 5.3 summarizes the Borland C++ signed and unsigned integer data types, listing their memory sizes and value ranges.

Table 5.3. Integer data types.

Data type	Size in bytes	Size in bits	Minimum value	Maximum value
signed char	1	8	−128	127
unsigned char	1	8	0	255
signed short	2	16	−32,768	32,767
unsigned short	2	16	0	65,535
signed int	2	16	−32,768	32,767

Data type	Size in bytes	Size in bits	Minimum value	Maximum value
unsigned int	2	16	0	65,535
signed long	4	32	−2,147,483,648	2,147,483,647
unsigned long	4	32	0	4,294,967,295

NOTE: See the standard library header file limits.h for exact ranges of Borland C++ integer data types. A similar file should be supplied with all ANSI C compilers.

When used in expressions, because integers occupy fixed amounts of memory, integer values can wrap around like an automobile speedometer going back to zero after many long journeys. If an unsigned int variable i equals 15,000, the expression

```
j = i + 60000;
```

assigns to unsigned int j the value 9464, not 75,000, which is beyond the capacity of a Borland C++ unsigned int value. The result wraps around to fit into the smaller space. This is not an error—it's an intentional effect that avoids time-wasting checks for integer overflow. Be aware, however, that if you rely on the wrap-around effect, your programs might not operate on systems that use a different int size.

char Values

Borland C++ treats char values specially. By default, char and signed char are synonymous. Use unsigned char to represent single-byte positive values from 0 to 255.

To use unsigned char as the default for char declarations, use the Options|Compiler|Code generation command and select Unsigned characters. You can also use the -K switch for the command-line compiler. Do this only if you plan to transfer your code to another compiler, or to compile foreign code with Borland C++.

Multiple Variable Declaration

When declaring multiple variables of the same type, you can write them one after the other this way:

```
int v1; int v2; int v3; int v4;
```

or you can stack them on separate lines:

```
int v1;
int v2;
int v3;
int v4;
```

Rather than type int over and over, you can also use the shorthand notation

```
int v1, v2, v3, v4;
```

In all three cases, variables v1, v2, v3, and v4 are variables of type int. You can replace int with another type name to declare multiple variables of any type. Some programmers object to the shorthand style, arguing that declarations are clearer when written on separate lines. It's your choice; these are all legal ways to declare variables.

True and False Values

Integers can represent true and false values, which make it possible for programs to make decisions. In C, 0 means false; nonzero values mean true.

We'll get back to true and false values in Chapter 6, "Action: What a Program Does." For now, just be aware that C uses integers to represent true and false conditions.

Literal Integer Values

Literal values are those you type directly in a program's text. Because you can't change their values after compiling a program, literal values are also called constants. To process constants such as 1234 and -96, the compiler uses the smallest possible data types that can represent the values.

Sometimes, it's necessary to force the compiler to store constants as specific data types. For example, to store 1234 internally as a long rather than an int, add L after the last digit:

```
long bigValue = 1234L;
```

The value 1234 is an int. With a trailing L, it's a long. To specify an unsigned value, add U. The constant 1234U is stored as type unsigned int. The constant 1234UL is stored as an unsigned long integer.

You can also specify literal values in hex and octal. Constants that start with a leading 0 are octal values. Decimal constants may *not* begin with 0. Constants that start with 0x are hexadecimal. Listing 5.11, HEXOCT.C, demonstrates sample values in hexadecimal, octal, and decimal, and shows how to display their unformatted and formatted values.

Listing 5.11. HEXOCT.C (Hexadecimal and octal constants).

```
 1:  #include <stdio.h>
 2:
 3:  main()
 4:  {
 5:     int hexValue = 0xf9ac;
 6:     int octalValue = 0724;
 7:     int decimalValue = 255;
 8:
 9:     printf("As decimal integers:\n");
10:     printf(" hexValue = %d\n", hexValue);
11:     printf(" octalValue = %d\n", octalValue);
12:     printf(" decimalValue = %d\n", decimalValue);
13:
14:     printf("\nAs formatted integers:\n");
15:     printf(" hexValue = %x\n", hexValue);
16:     printf(" octalValue = %o\n", octalValue);
17:     printf(" decimalValue = %#x\n", decimalValue);
18:     return 0;
19:  }
```

Running Listing 5.11 displays the following lines:

```
As decimal integers:
 hexValue = -1620
 octalValue = 468
 decimalValue = 255

As formatted integers:
 hexValue = f9ac
 octalValue = 724
 decimalValue = 0xff
```

Formatting the hexadecimal values with `%d` commands in the `printf()` statements at lines 10–12 displays their equivalent values in decimal. To display hex values, use the command `%x` (or `%X` for capital hex letters A through F). Preface X or x with # to select an alternate format. For example, line 15 uses `%#x` to display the decimal value 255 as hexadecimal `0xff`. Specify `%o` for octal format.

> **NOTE:** The octal number base, or radix, is popular in mainframe circles, but most PC programmers prefer decimal and hexadecimal formats for integer values. You don't need to understand the octal radix to use this book.

The *const* Keyword

As you know, you can store values in integer variables with statements such as

```
intValue = 1234;
```

where `intValue` is type `int` (or another integer type that can hold the literal value 1234).

Of course, any other statement is free to change `intValue` by assigning it another value. The statement

```
intValue = 4321;
```

assigns 4321 to `intValue`, replacing the variable's current value. If `newValue` is another `int` variable, the statement

```
intValue = newValue;
```

makes `intValue` equal to `newValue`.

To restrict statements from changing variables, preface their declarations with the keyword `const`. For example, if you modify line 5 of Listing 5.11 to

```
const int hexValue = 0xf9ac;
```

and then add the statement

```
hexValue = 0xa9bc;
```

the compiler will issue the error message "Cannot modify a const object in function main." Variables declared as `const` may be assigned initial values, but other statements can't change them—a safety measure for ensuring that values remain constant throughout the runtime life of a program.

> **NOTE:** Variables declared with const may be placed in read-only memory (ROM). Chapter 9, "Pointers," discusses how to address values stored anywhere in memory.

Floating Types

A floating-point value (sometimes referred to as a "real number") is written with a decimal point. The value of pi, 3.14159, is a floating-point constant.

You can also represent floating-point values using scientific notation. The value 3.755E+02 is equivalent to the decimal value 375.5. (Mathematicians would write that same value as 3.755×10^2.) To form the decimal equivalent of a scientific value, move the decimal point right for positive exponents, left for negative ones. Thus, 5.123E+03 equals 5123.0; 6.5E–03 equals 0.0065, and so on.

There are three floating-point data types, float, double, and long double. (A long float is not allowed, except in a parade.) Table 5.4 lists the memory sizes and value ranges for the Borland C++ floating-point types.

Table 5.4. Floating-point data types.

Data type	Size in bits	Size in bytes	Minimum value	Maximum value
float	4	32	3.4E–38	3.4E+38
double	8	64	1.7E–308	1.7E+308
long double	10	80	3.4E–4932	1.1E+4932

> **NOTE:** See the standard library header file float.h for exact ranges and other details about Borland C++ floating-point values. A similar file should be supplied with all ANSI C compilers.

Create floating-point variables the same way you do integer variables. For example, to declare a variable named `balance`, you can write

```
float balance;
```

You can also use the `double` data type:

```
double balance;
```

Initialize floating-point values by assigning literal constants, either in the declaration like this:

```
double balance = 525.49;
```

or by using a separate assignment statement:

```
balance = 99.99;
```

Floating-point constants such as `525.49` and `99.99` are of the `double` type unless followed by f or F. The value 3.14159F is type `float`. Use l or L for a `long double` as in 3.14159L.

Listing 5.12, TAX.C, shows a typical use for floating-point values. The program solves a simple mathematical problem: how to calculate the amount of tax paid and the retail price of an item given its total purchase price and the local tax rate.

Listing 5.12. TAX.C (Calculates tax paid given amount and rate).

```
 1:  #include <stdlib.h>
 2:  #include <stdio.h>
 3:
 4:  main()
 5:  {
 6:    double list, paid, rate, tax;
 7:    char s[20];   /* Input string */
 8:
 9:    printf("Price paid? ");
10:    scanf("%20s", s);
11:    paid = atof(s);
12:    printf("Tax rate (ex: .06)? ");
13:    scanf("%20s", s);
14:    rate = atof(s);
15:    list = paid / (1 + rate);
```

```
16:     tax = paid - list;
17:     printf("List price = $%8.2f\n", list);
18:     printf("Tax paid   = $%8.2f\n", tax);
19:     return 0;
20:  }
```

Line 6 declares four `double` floating-point variables. Line 7 declares a string for inputting new data. (More about strings later.) Line 9 prompts you to enter the total purchase price, which line 10 reads into the string s. The statement

```
scanf("%20s", s);
```

pauses for you to enter up to 20 characters, copied into the string s. Function `scanf()` is declared in the stdio.h header file, and is similar in form, but opposite in purpose, to `printf()`. Function `printf()` sends output to the standard output file, usually the display. Function `scanf()` reads input from the standard input file, usually the keyboard.

A `scanf()` statement includes one or more format specifiers, such as `"%20s"`. After that comes the name of a variable to hold the input, in this case, a character string. The declaration

```
char s[20];
```

reserves space for 19 characters plus one byte to hold a terminating zero (called a null character) that marks the end of the string.

Line 11 in Listing 5.12 calls another function, `atof()`, declared in stdlib.h, to convert a string to a floating-point value. The statement

```
paid = atof(s);
```

assigns to `paid` a binary floating-point value converted from the characters stored in string s.

Listing 5.12 contains another new element: an expression. This statement at line 15:

```
list = paid / (1 + rate);
```

divides the value of `paid` by 1 plus the tax rate, and assigns the result to `list`.

Precision

Like markings on a ruler, floating-point values are approximates. A common error is to expect floating-point values to behave as integers, which can represent exact counts. Unlike integers, the accuracy of floating-point values depends on their precision, a function of their storage size.

A float value can have about 6 or 7 significant digits; double values can have 15 or 16; long double values can have 19. Significant digits denote relative error. Beyond the stated number of significant digits, round-off errors in expression results may cause a loss of information. You can represent any value within a floating-point data type's allowed range, but you can't represent every value with perfect accuracy.

Conceptually, there are an infinite number of values between any two real numbers. Between 1.0 and 2.0 there's a value 1.5; between 1.0 and 1.5 there's 1.25, and so on. However, because floating-point values are stored in fixed numbers of bits, some values cannot be represented precisely in memory. Floating-point values in a computer only approximate true real numbers in mathematics.

Listing 5.13, PRECISE.C, demonstrates three key concepts of floating-point expressions.

Listing 5.13. PRECISE.C (Demonstrates floating-point precision).

```
 1:  #include <stdio.h>
 2:
 3:  main()
 4:  {
 5:    double d1 = 4.0 / 2.0;
 6:    double d2 = 1.0 / 3.0;
 7:    double d3 = 2.0E40 * 2.0E30 + 1;
 8:
 9:    printf("d1 = %G\n", d1);
10:    printf("d2 = %G\n", d2);
11:    printf("d3 = %G\n", d3);
12:    return 0;
13:  }
```

Lines 5–7 assign the results of three expressions to double variables d1, d2, and d3. Dividing 4.0 by 2.0 creates an exact result, 2.0, fully within the range of values a `double` variable can accurately represent. Dividing 1.0 by 3.0, however, results in something like 0.333333—close but no cigar. The repeating decimal continues infinitely, and any finite representation of that value is therefore less than totally precise. The third expression adds one to the product of two very large values expressed in scientific notation. Because the result requires more than 64 bits to represent it, `d3`'s reported value is 4E+70, one less than the correct answer.

Don't let such oddities wreck your day. A few simple guidelines will help you to use floating-point values correctly, despite their limitations.

- Declare variables of 64-bit `double`, not 32-bit `float`, whenever possible. The `double` data type can safely represent more significant digits than `float`, and gives more accurate results in most cases.

- Don't use `long double` unless you really need the extra precision provided by this 80-bit floating-point value, which takes more memory and more time to process. Plain `double` values offer the ideal balance between size and precision for most applications.

- Use the command-line compiler option `-ff-` (in the IDE use Options| Compiler|Advanced code generation) to disable fast floating point, which might affect the results of some computations that involve `float` and `double` values. The fast floating point option is on by default to prevent compiled expressions from demoting `double` precision values to `float` when those values are then immediately promoted back to `double`, a situation that effectively reduces a `double` value to a `float`'s precision.

- Don't use floating-point types to store important financial figures. Round-off errors are not acceptable when counting cold cash. Instead, you might use the `bcd` class (see Chapter 17, "Borland's Class Library").

IEEE Formats and Math Coprocessors

Many PCs have 80x87 math coprocessor chips, also called numeric data processors (NDP). This family of coprocessors, including the 8087, 80287, and 80387, store and process floating-point values in the standard format of the IEEE, the Institute of Electrical and Electronics Engineers.

Borland C++ `float`, `double`, and `long double` data types are stored in this same format. As a result, calculations and values are NDP-compatible whether or not a computer has a coprocessor. The `float` data type is equivalent to the 32-bit IEEE real format. The `double` data type is equivalent to the 64-bit IEEE real. The `long double` data type is equivalent to the 80-bit IEEE extended real.

On systems without a coprocessor, compiled programs automatically use a software emulator that mimics most of the real chip's capabilities. When you run a compiled program, it detects and uses a coprocessor if present.

When you know for certain that a coprocessor is installed, you may delete the emulator from a compiled .EXE code file, thus saving about 10K of disk space and memory. To do this, use the IDE's Options|Compiler command, select Advanced code generation, and set Floating Point to None. You can also specify the -f87 switch with the command-line compiler. Either way, the resulting code requires a math coprocessor, and the program will hang or run wild if an NDP is not installed.

In some situations, the autodetection logic can fail, either due to a faulty NDP chip, or a nonstandard PC. To force a program to use the emulator (even if a coprocessor is present), enter the following DOS command at the DOS command line:

```
set 87=N
```

Typing this command (or inserting it into a batch file such as AUTOEXEC.BAT) sets an environment variable named 87 to N. If a compiled program senses this value, it uses the coprocessor emulator whether or not an NDP is present. To return to automatic NDP detection, enter

```
set 87=Y
```

You can delete the environment variable by typing

```
set 87=
```

Character Types

Borland C++ stores characters as 8-bit bytes formatted according to the extended ASCII character set, a standard feature on all PCs. (See Appendix A for a complete list of extended ASCII characters.) Strictly speaking, ANSI C compilers are free to store characters in different formats, or even use multibyte characters. On PCs (at least those running English-language DOS operating systems) it's safe to assume that char values take exactly one byte and represent ASCII symbols.

Using Single Characters

You learned earlier how to store small signed byte values from –128 to +127 (including 0) in char variables. You can also store unsigned byte values from 0 to 255 in unsigned char variables.

Of course, char variables can store single characters. For example, the declaration

```
char c = 'A';
```

declares a char variable c and assigns it the ASCII value of the symbol A. The compiler converts the literal character constant 'A' to an int value, equal to the character's ASCII code, which is then stored in the byte reserved for c. Single character constants are delimited by single quote marks.

Listing 5.14, ASCII.C, takes advantage of a char value's internal representation to display characters in ASCII, decimal, octal, and hexadecimal.

Listing 5.14. ASCII.C (Displays ASCII characters in decimal and hex).

```
 1:  #include <stdio.h>
 2:
 3:  main()
 4:  {
 5:    char c;
 6:
 7:    printf("Enter character: ");
 8:    c = getchar();
 9:    printf(" Character   = %c\n", c);
10:    printf(" ASCII (dec) = %d\n", c);
11:    printf(" ASCII (hex) = %#x\n", c);
12:    return 0;
13:  }
```

Line 5 declares a single char variable c. Line 8 calls the stdio.h library function getchar() to read a character from the keyboard. The function waits until you type a character and press Enter, then returns the character's value, assigned here to c. Three printf() statements then display c in character format (%c), as a decimal ASCII value (%d), and in hexadecimal (%#x).

Because literal characters are stored internally as int values, and not char types as you might reasonably suppose, you can change line 5 to

```
int c;
```

and the program continues to work perfectly well. In fact, many library functions (and many programs) are designed to store single characters as int values—a throwback to C's early days, but also a convenient size for 16-bit computers.

Using Literal String Constants

You've seen many samples of character string constants in this chapter. Character strings consist of zero or more characters delimited by double quotes. The string `"Oh, what a beautiful morning"` is stored in memory as a series of single-byte ASCII `char` values, terminated with a zero byte, called a null character. The null character allows string functions to detect the ends of strings. (More on this subject and other string goodies in Chapter 10, "Strings.")

Most often, you should type literal string constants on single lines. For example, a typical `printf()` statement such as

```
printf("Oh what a beautiful day");
```

displays the quoted text. (Actually, output is directed to the standard output device, which is probably attached to a display terminal, but might be redirected elsewhere. Such topics are covered in Chapter 11, "Input and Output.")

Borland C++ also allows long strings to be entered on separate lines:

```
"This looks like "
"three strings,"
"but it's really just one."
```

When two or more quoted strings are logically adjacent (meaning they can be physically next to each other or on separate lines as long as only whitespace comes between them), Borland C++ concatenates the strings into one long string, ending with a single null character.

Whether long or short, however, string constants are just that—as constants they can't be modified. Clever programmers may be able to break this rule by finding the string constants in memory and poking new characters into them, but this is a nonstandard practice that might fail if strings are placed in read-only memory, or in a multitasking computer's protected RAM.

In addition to the characters you can type, string constants may also contain escape codes—special symbols that represent control codes and other ASCII values, which can't be typed into text editors. Table 5.5 lists the Borland C++ escape codes.

Table 5.5. String escape codes.

Code	Meaning	ASCII value(s) Decimal	Hexadecimal	Symbol(s)
'\a'	Bell ("alert!")	7	0x07	BEL
'\b'	Backspace	8	0x08	BS
'\f'	Formfeed	12	0x0C	FF
'\n'	New line	10	0x0a	LF
'\r'	Return	13	0x0d	CR
'\t'	Horizontal tab	9	0x09	HT
'\v'	Vertical tab	11	0x0b	VT
'\\'	Backslash	92	0x5c	\
'\''	Single quote	39	0x27	'
'\"'	Double quote	34	0x22	"
'\?'	Question mark	63	0x3f	?
'\000'	ASCII octal 000	all	all	all
'\x00	ASCII hex 00	all	all	all

Each of the escape codes in Table 5.5 is a single character, stored internally as an int value, and composed of a backslash followed by a letter, punctuation symbol, or octal digits. The octal and hex code make it possible to enter any ASCII code into a string or character constant. For example, the declaration

```
char c = '\x27';
```

assigns the ASCII value 0x27 (a single quote) to c. You can do the same for int values:

```
int c = '\x27';
```

Escape codes can appear anywhere a visible character can. For example, to end a string with the code for a new line, you can write

```
"This string ends with a new line code\n"
```

The compiler replaces the \n newline symbol with a line-feed control code having the value 10 (0x0a in hexadecimal). On PCs when \n is sent to a character output device, or when \n is written to a text file, the newline symbol is translated to a carriage return and a line feed.

Because a backslash begins an escape code, a special trick is needed to enter a backslash character—just type two of them. For example, to enter a DOS path as a string, you can type something like this:

```
"c:\\borlandc\\test\\funny.c";
```

If you forget to double up on the backslashes, a string such as

```
"c:\borlandc\test\funny.c";   /* ??? */
```

may cause all sorts of strange events when displayed. For this sample string, the compiler interprets the \b in c:\borlandc as a backspace, \t as a horizontal tab, and \f as a form feed character. If your pathname strings aren't working, check whether you typed single backslashes by mistake.

NOTE: There's one exception to this rule. You must use single backslashes to separate directory names in #include directives such as

```
#include "c:\anydir\anyfile.h"
```

Creating and Reading Character Strings

The simplest way to create character string variables is to add square brackets and a maximum string length to a char declaration. For example, the line

```
char string[80];
```

declares a variable named string that can hold from 0 to 80 characters including a null terminator. (In future chapters, you'll learn that this format is a special case of an array, which can store many different kinds of values. You'll also learn how to use pointers to address strings. For now, however, it's best to postpone these advanced topics.)

To read a string of characters from the keyboard, execute a statement such as

```
scanf("%80s", string);
```

You can then display the result with printf():

```
printf("You entered %s", string);
```

If you try this string input technique, however, you will discover a problem. Function scanf() terminates input upon the first space (or other whitespace characters such as a tab) or when you press Enter. If you enter This is a string, only This is stored in string.

To read strings along with any spaces entered, use the library function gets() like this:

```
printf("Enter a string: ");
gets(string);
```

Unfortunately, the stdio.h function gets() does not prevent users from typing more characters than allotted to the string. If string is declared as

```
char string[10];
```

then gets() will merrily store the 11th and any subsequent characters beyond the end of the string, thus overwriting whatever other data happens to be stored at those locations. To prevent such errors, you can declare 128-character strings like this:

```
char string[128];
```

Because the standard DOS internal input buffer is limited to 128 characters, users cannot enter more than that many characters into string.

NOTE: This technique works only on MS-DOS systems with 128-character input buffers, the typical case for PCs. The same trick might not work for other ANSI C compilers or on systems that modify the default input buffer length.

Converting Strings to Values

Character strings are especially useful for holding input entered at the keyboard. When that data is numerical, programs need a way to convert strings to integers and floating-point values.

Three standard functions make fast work of string-to-value conversions. Use atof() to convert ASCII strings to floating-point double values. (Despite the function name atof, or "ASCII to float," the result is a double value.) Use atoi() to convert strings to integers. Use atol to convert strings to long int values.

A couple of sample programs demonstrate how to use these functions. Listing 5.15, CONVERT.C, converts integer values to hexadecimal. Compile and run the program, then enter an integer when prompted.

Listing 5.15. CONVERT.C (Converts integers to hexadecimal and octal).

```
 1:  #include <stdio.h>
 2:  #include <stdlib.h>
 3:
 4:  main()
 5:  {
 6:    int value;
 7:    char string[128];
 8:
 9:    printf("Enter value: ");
10:    gets(string);
11:    value = atoi(string);
12:    printf("Value in decimal = %d\n", value);
13:    printf("Value in hex     = %#x\n", value);
14:    printf("Value in octal   = %o\n", value);
15:    return 0;
16:  }
```

The program operates by calling gets() to read keyboard input into a character string. The function atoi() converts that string to an integer value, assigned to value. Three printf() statements then display value in decimal (%d), hexadecimal (%#x), and octal (%o).

To convert strings to long int values, use atol(). For example, you could change line 6 to long value; and then execute value = atol(string); in line 11.

A similar program shows how to convert strings to floating-point values. Listing 5.16, KILO.C, prompts for a value in miles and displays the equivalent distance in kilometers.

Listing 5.16. KILO.C (Converts miles to kilometers).

```
 1:  #include <stdio.h>
 2:  #include <stdlib.h>
 3:
```

```
 4:  main()
 5:  {
 6:    double miles;
 7:    char string[128];
 8:
 9:    printf("Convert miles to kilometers\n");
10:    printf("How many miles? ");
11:    gets(string);
12:    miles = atof(string);
13:    printf("Kilometers = %f\n", miles * 1.609344);
14:    return 0;
15:  }
```

As in the preceding listing, gets() reads a string of characters from the keyboard (line 11). Function atof() converts that string to a floating-point double value, assigned to miles (line 12). Then, a printf() statement (line 13) displays miles times 1.609344, the approximate number of kilometers in one mile. The format %f displays the result of the multiplication as a floating-point value.

Sizes of Variables

ANSI C compilers may differ in how they store values of various integer and floating-point types. Rather than assume that a certain variable occupies a particular number of bytes, you can use the sizeof operator to calculate a variable's storage requirements.

Listing 5.17, SIZEOF.C, demonstrates one way to use sizeof, and also makes a handy test program for displaying the sizes of any ANSI C compiler's fundamental data types.

Listing 5.17. SIZEOF.C (Demonstrates sizeof() function).

```
1:  #include <stdio.h>
2:
3:  main()
4:  {
5:    char c;
6:    short s;
7:    int i;
8:    long l;
```

continues

Listing 5.17. continued

```
 9:    float f;
10:    double d;
11:    long double ld;
12:
13:    printf("Size of char ...... = %2d byte(s)\n", sizeof(c));
14:    printf("Size of short ..... = %2d byte(s)\n", sizeof(s));
15:    printf("Size of int ....... = %2d byte(s)\n", sizeof(i));
16:    printf("Size of long ...... = %2d byte(s)\n", sizeof(l));
17:    printf("Size of float ..... = %2d byte(s)\n", sizeof(f));
18:    printf("Size of double .... = %2d byte(s)\n", sizeof(d));
19:    printf("Size of long double = %2d byte(s)\n", sizeof(ld));
20:    return 0;
21:  }
```

> **NOTE:** With all warnings enabled (-w), compiling SIZEOF.C generates numerous warnings about variables that are "declared but never used." The warning can help you get rid of variables left over from past versions. For this simple test program, you can just ignore the messages (you might not even see them).

The program declares variables of seven types (lines 5–11), then displays the size in bytes of each type (lines 13–19). For example, the statement

```
printf(..., sizeof(c));
```

displays the size in bytes of the char variable c. It's important to realize that sizeof is a unary operator, similar to a unary minus sign in the value −59 or the unary plus in +68. The compiler converts the expression sizeof(item) to an integer value equal to the size of an item. This item can be a data type name such as int or float, or the name of any variable, not just those in the sample listing.

Technically, sizeof returns a value of type size_t, a symbol defined in the header file stddef.h. (Pre-ANSI C compilers define sizeof as type int, causing the operator to return negative values for the sizes of large structures, causing more than a little confusion.) In Borland C++, size_t is defined more sensibly as unsigned int. Another ANSI C compiler might define size_t as some other kind of value, however, thus also affecting the type of sizeof (and other declarations of type size_t).

> **NOTE:** You can also use `sizeof` without parentheses. The compiler evaluates the expression `sizeof item` without also evaluating `item`, a fact that may seem meaningless now, but is important in cases where evaluating `item` causes an unwanted action to occur.

Symbolic Constants

Some C programs read like cryptograms. Others seem easy to follow and understand. The difference may have nothing to do with a program's complexity, but more with the programmer's choice of identifiers, comments, and symbolic constants.

A symbolic constant is an identifier that stands for something else. For example, in a slot machine (most of which today are just computers in sly disguise) the identifier JACKPOT might represent the maximum amount the machine pays for a win. The identifier is usually declared in a header file or at the beginning of the program, using a `#define` directive like

```
#define JACKPOT 45000
```

The directive (`#define`) is a command to the compiler—it doesn't generate any code or instructions in the compiled program. A `#define` directive associates a symbol (such as JACKPOT) with some text (such as 45000). By convention, symbolic constants are typed in uppercase, making them easy to spot in a complex program.

It's important to understand that 45000 may look like an integer value, but to the compiler, it's just a collection of ASCII digit characters. Symbolic constants such as these

```
#define NAME "Jack Pot"
#define FALSE 0
#define TRUE 1
```

are not variable declarations. They merely create temporary symbols NAME, FALSE, and TRUE associated with whatever text follows, including the double quote marks on the first line. You can use the symbolic names at any place (except inside a string) where their associated literal constants make sense. For instance, the compiler interprets

```
printf(NAME);
```

as though you had written

```
printf("Jack Pot");
```

A common mistake is to end a symbolic constant definition with a semicolon. The following does not work:

```
#define JACKPOT 45000;  /* ??? */
```

When you try to use this faulty JACKPOT symbol (which includes the digits 45000 *and* the trailing semicolon), perhaps in a statement such as

```
printf("Jackpot = $%d\n", JACKPOT);  /* ??? */
```

the compiler attempts to compile that line as

```
printf("Jackpot = $%d\n", 45000;);  /* ??? */
```

causing an error at the misplaced semicolon after 45000.

On the other hand, you may follow a symbolic constant with a comment. For example, the line

```
#define JACKPOT 45000  /* Maximum payoff */
```

associates the text 45000 with the symbol JACKPOT. The compiler does not include the comment as part of JACKPOT's value.

Defining Your Own Symbolic Constants

Defining symbolic constants at the beginning of the program or in a header file creates a set of easily modified symbols. Listing 5.18, DEFINE.C, demonstrates typical ways to use #define.

Listing 5.18. DEFINE.C (Displays symbolic constants).

```
1:  #include <stdio.h>
2:
3:  #define CHARACTER       '@'
4:  #define STRING          "Mastering Borland C++\n"
5:  #define OCTAL           0233
6:  #define HEXADECIMAL     0x9b
7:  #define DECIMAL         155
```

```
 8:  #define FLOATING_POINT  3.14159
 9:
10:  main()
11:  {
12:    printf("CHARACTER = %c\n", CHARACTER);
13:    printf("STRING = " STRING);
14:    printf("OCTAL = %o\n", OCTAL);
15:    printf("HEXADECIMAL = %#x\n", HEXADECIMAL);
16:    printf("DECIMAL = %d\n", DECIMAL);
17:    printf("FLOATING_POINT = %f\n", FLOATING_POINT);
18:    return 0;
19:  }
```

In a large program, storing numerous symbolic constants in one place makes it easy to change those values and various statements that make use of those values.

Examine the printf() statements in lines 12–17. Line 13 is not a mistake. When the compiler processes the line

```
printf("STRING = " STRING);
```

the compiler replaces STRING with the symbol's associated text value, in effect compiling that line as

```
printf("STRING = " "Mastering Borland C++\n");
```

As you recall from earlier in this chapter, Borland C++ concatenates adjacent strings. Therefore, this statement displays the single string

```
STRING = Mastering Borland C++
```

For a useful exercise, rewrite each of the printf() statements in lines 12–17, manually replacing the symbolic constants with the associated values. This will help you to understand how the statements operate.

> **NOTE:** Symbolic constants are translated during compilation by the compiler's preprocessor, which also replaces #include directives with included text. For better speed, Borland C++ emulates a classic preprocessor, but the results are the same as if they were from a compiler with a preprocessing stage. It's often useful to examine a preprocessor's output to see exactly how the compiler translates defined symbols. Although Borland C++ doesn't

have a preprocessor, you can use the CPP.EXE utility to generate preprocessed output. For example, from DOS, use the command `cpp define.c` to expand DEFINE.C's lines to a new file DEFINE.I, which you can examine with a text editor.

Using Predefined Symbolic Constants

In addition to defining your own symbolic constants, you can use those predefined in various header files. For instance, in the math.h header file are several useful symbols including

```
#define M_E          2.71828182845904523536
#define M_LOG2E      1.44269504088896340736
#define M_PI         3.14159265358979323846
#define M_PI_2       1.57079632679489661923
#define M_PI_4       0.78539816339744830961
#define M_SQRT2      1.41421356237309504880
```

Inserting the line `#include <math.h>` makes these and other mathematical symbolic constants available to your program. If you need the value of pi in an expression, you can write

```
result = M_PI * value;
```

which is clear and neatly avoids the possibility of introducing an error by mistyping pi as a literal value.

Borland C++ also defines a few symbols that don't require reading a header file. (Look these up under "predefined macros" in the *Borland C++ Programmer's Guide*.) Two of the most useful of these symbols are `_ _DATE_ _` and `_ _TIME_ _`. The symbols are preceded and followed by double underscore characters—an attempt to guard against any possible conflict with your own identifiers, or those that might be added to future compiler versions.

To display the date and time, you can write

```
printf("The time is " _ _TIME_ _ "\n");
printf("The date is " _ _DATE_ _ "\n");
```

Because these two symbols represent character strings, they can be concatenated with other strings and used directly in `printf()` statements as shown here. Be aware that the date and time represent the moment when the program was compiled, not the current date and time when you run the code (see `getdate()` and `gettime()` in Chapter 22, "Functions and Examples").

Another useful symbol, `_ _BORLANDC_ _`, represents the compiler version. The statement

```
printf("Compiler version is %#x\n", _ _BORLANDC_ _);
```

displays the current version number. A similar constant, `_ _BCPLUSPLUS_ _`, represents the compiler version when compiling a C++ program. These constants are associated with literal hexadecimal values such as 0x0300 for Version 3.0.

NOTE: The `#define` directive is also capable of creating text macros, a kind of minilanguage built into all ANSI C compilers. Some low-level library functions are defined as text macros to avoid numerous subroutine calls for simple operations such as reading single characters from keyboards. In time, you may want to study how to build your own macros; however, you are wise to postpone this task until you first become expert in C. Plenty of experienced C programmers have never written a macro in their lives, and you won't miss anything by joining their ranks.

Enumerated Types

Suppose you want to represent the colors of the rainbow. You could define light's visible hues as symbolic constants like this:

```
#define RED 0
#define ORANGE 1
#define YELLOW 2
#define GREEN 3
#define BLUE 4
#define INDIGO 5
#define VIOLET 6
```

The values are meaningless—they just give programs a convenient way to represent color names as unique integer values. Given these symbols, a program can declare an int variable like this:

```
int color;
```

and then assign to `color` any of the color symbols:

```
color = GREEN;
```

The compiler replaces GREEN with that symbol's associated text, in this case the single digit 3. In effect, the statement is compiled as

```
color = 3;
```

Obviously, the symbol GREEN is more meaningful to humans than the literal value 3. Typing a long series of color names and other relatively fixed symbols (the months of the year, for instance) is drudge work. Also, there's nothing in the program to indicate that the individual color symbols go together.

To make creating such lists easier, ANSI C provides a helpful device, called an enumerated type. Using the keyword enum, you can create the preceding seven color constants like this:

```
enum {RED, ORANGE, YELLOW, GREEN, BLUE, INDIGO, VIOLET};
```

This has the identical effect as the #define directives listed earlier. The enum keyword is followed by a list of identifiers (typically in uppercase) separated by commas, delimited by curly braces, and ending with a semicolon. Each symbol is assigned a sequential integer value, beginning with 0. RED equals 0, ORANGE is 1, YELLOW is 2, and so on, up to VIOLET, which equals 6.

Given the enum declaration above, to declare an int variable named color and assign it the color value for BLUE, you can write

```
int color = BLUE;
```

Enumerated data types are stored internally as integer values in the smallest possible space—either signed or unsigned char or int types—and therefore, can always be assigned to int variables.

With the help of another keyword, typedef (for "type definition"), you can create a new data type for enumerated symbolic constants. Using typedef, a more formal enumeration for the colors of the rainbow might be written like this:

```
typedef enum
{
  RED, ORANGE, YELLOW, GREEN, BLUE, INDIGO, VIOLET
} Colors;
```

The `typedef` keyword creates a new data type name. In this case, the name (`Colors`) is associated with the enumerated list of color names. Now that `Colors` is defined as a new data type, a program can declare variables of that type in the usual way:

```
Colors oneColor;
```

Declared like that, `oneColor` is a variable of type `Colors`. You can assign color symbolic constants to `oneColor` with statements such as

```
oneColor = INDIGO;
```

and, because `Colors` is an enumerated type, you can also assign integer values to variables of that type:

```
oneColor = 5;
```

The compiler automatically enumerates the elements in an `enum` declaration. Sometimes, however, it's necessary to take over that job and assign explicit values to one or more symbols. For example, consider the problem of creating an enumerated type for the months of the year. You might begin by typing

```
enum {JAN, FEB, MAR, APR, MAY, JUN, JUL, AUG, SEP, OCT, NOV, DEC};
```

There's nothing wrong with this `enum` declaration. However, because the first symbol in the enumerated list is assigned the value 0, JAN equals 0, not 1—the normal value associated with the first month of the year.

You can fix this problem by assigning an explicit value to any member of an enumerated list. For example, to set JAN to 1, you can change the preceding declaration to

```
enum {JAN = 1, FEB, MAR, APR, MAY, JUN, JUL, AUG, SEP, OCT, NOV, DEC};
```

The expression JAN = 1 assigns 1 to the symbol JAN. Subsequent symbols continue the sequence from that point, making FEB equal to 2, MAR to 3, APR to 4, and so on.

You can use a similar trick anywhere in an enumerated list. If you wanted to number the months by tens, you could write

```
enum {JAN = 10, FEB = 20, ..., DEC = 120};
```

Forcing values on enumerated elements this way is rarely necessary (but sometimes useful), and it's probably best to let the compiler assign the values. The symbolic names are what matter—they lend clarity to the code by replacing numbers with easy-to-recognize names.

Type Conversions

Although int and long values are both integers, they are not exactly petals of the same flower. To close this chapter, it's time to consider what happens when programs mix values of different data types in expressions.

Remember always that variables are stored in fixed numbers of bytes—a fact that, if ignored, can shoot holes through your code. Consider these declarations:

```
long getalong = 12345678;
int intbyint;
```

Now consider what happens if a statement assigns getalong to intbyint:

```
intbyint = getalong;  /* ??? */
```

Because intbyint can store values ranging from −32,768 to +32,767 (see Table 5.3), it can't hold getalong's large positive value. Despite the obvious error, the compiler allows the assignment, in this case setting intbyint to 24,910—not at all what you might have expected.

The number 24,910 happens to be the remainder of 12345678 divided by 65,536, the largest unsigned value that two bytes can represent. This is no accident! The long value stored in getalong is truncated to fit into the shorter int variable intbyint.

In general, assigning values from larger variables to smaller ones may cause a similar loss of information, and may or may not also produce a warning from the compiler. Assigning smaller values to larger ones usually does not cause any trouble. For example, if intbyint equals 4321, the assignment

```
getalong = intbyint;
```

sets getalong to the same value 4321, which is well within a long int's range.

To carry out the assignment of an int to a long, the compiler generates code to perform a promotion. In this case, intbyint is promoted from a two-byte int to a four-byte long. Promotions also occur in expressions involving integers or floating-point values of different types. If fp is a float variable and db is of type double, the statement

```
db = fp;
```

promotes fp to db, with no loss of information. However, the reverse assignment,

```
fp = db;
```

may cause trouble, because a float value can't represent the same range as a double.

Another kind of promotion occurs when assigning floating-point values to integers. The assignment is allowed, but of course, any fractional value is lost. The reverse case—assigning integers to floating-point variables—is also permitted.

Mixing integer and floating-point values also causes a type conversion, but the results are not always easy to predict. To see why, consider these declarations:

```
int i = 4;
float f = 2.8;
```

Then, execute the statement

```
i = f * i;
```

What does i equal? Generally, in mixed-type expressions, "narrow" values are promoted to "wider" ones, and to process the expression f * i, the compiler first converts the int variable i (equal to 4) to a float, multiplies that value by f (giving 4 * 2.8, or 11.2), and assigns the result back to i. At that stage, the floating-point value 11.2 is demoted to an int, thus giving i the final value 11.

Using Typecasts

It's possible to defeat, or at least to control more closely, the compiler's default promotion rules. Using the declarations from the preceding section,

```
int i = 4;
float f = 2.8;
```

if you want to multiply the unrounded integer equivalent of f by i, thus giving 8, not 11, use a typecast in the expression like this:

```
i = (int)f * i;
```

The typecast expression (int) f tells the compiler to force f to an int value before using that value in the expression. Consequently, the compiler converts f's value of 2.8 to an int value 2 (truncating the fractional part), and then multiplies 2 by i's value to give 8.

Mixing Signed and Unsigned Values

When mixing signed and unsigned values, another headache may pound its way into your code. If u is an unsigned int and i is a signed int, then

```
i = u;
```

may or may not work as expected. If u equals hexadecimal 0xff, for example, i is assigned the equivalent value 255 in decimal. If u equals 0xffff, equal to the unsigned decimal value 65,535, i is assigned the value −1, which, as a signed quantity, also equals 0xffff in hexadecimal.

Mixing signed values is usually safe, as long as the recipient of an assignment is as large or larger than the source. Borland C++ extends the value's sign from source to target, so that int values may safely be assigned to long variables.

Mixing Signed and Unsigned Characters

Because char values may or may not be represented by signed integers (as they are in Borland C++), the following code may not give identical results for all ANSI C compilers:

```
char c = '\xf0';
int i = c;
printf("i = %d", i);
```

Character c is assigned the ASCII value 0xf0, equivalent as a signed integer to −16. However, if the char type were stored as an unsigned value, i would equal 240. Such oddities usually cause problems only for code that must be ported between different ANSI C compilers. In that case, use a declaration such as

```
unsigned char c;
```

or change `unsigned` to `signed` to force the compiler to use the format you need. Another trick that's useful is to declare character variables as type `int` like this:

```
int c = 'A';
```

Because characters are stored internally as integer values, you can declare character variables as type `int`. Therefore, you can be assured that an unsigned representation is used.

NOTE: ANSI C defines a series of promotion rules for all data types, which you may want to study later. (See the Bibliography section of this book.) Memorizing these rules, especially if you are just getting started with programming, isn't too important. What matters most is to understand that, when mixing data types in expressions, utmost care is needed to produce correct results.

Summary

- All C programs begin at the first statement inside function `main()`. All C programs must have a `main()` function.

- Error messages indicate serious mistakes and prevent the compiler from finishing its job. Warnings are less serious and may allow programs to run, but should be fixed as soon as possible.

- Header files declare function prototypes and other items. Read header files with `#include` directives.

- Comments are bracketed by the symbols `/*` and `*/`. The compiler ignores the brackets and all text between them.

- Global variables are declared outside of `main()` and are preinitialized to zero. Local variables declared inside of `main()` are not preinitialized.

- Keywords are reserved. Identifiers are words that you make up. Identifiers must begin with a letter or underscore, and they may include only letters, digits, and underscores.

- C is case-sensitive. Identifiers `myVar` and `MyVAR` are unique words.

- Integer data types are `char`, `int`, and `long`, which are signed by default. These types may be prefaced with `signed` or `unsigned` keywords. The word `unsigned` alone is a synonym for `unsigned int`.

- Floating-point types are `float`, `double`, and `long double`. These types conform to IEEE standards, and are compatible with a math coprocessor.

- Literal characters are written like this: `'a'`. Literal strings are written like this: `"abcdefg"`.

- Use the `sizeof` operator to determine the storage sizes of data types and variables.

- Use `#define` to define symbolic constants.

- Use `enum` to define enumerated symbolic constants.

- Beware of expressions that mix data types.

Exercises

5.1 Write the smallest possible C program (see Listing 5.2).

5.2 Shorten Listing 5.7 to declare and initialize variable `value` in one easy step.

5.3 If `k` is an `int` variable, what does `k` equal after executing the expression `k = 1000 * 2000`? If `k` is declared as type `long`, what does `k` equal? (Try to guess the answers, then write programs to test your assumptions.)

5.4 Explain why the following program halts with a "Divide error."

```
/* diverr.c */

#include <stdio.h>

int value;

main()
{
  int k = 100 / value;
  printf("k = %d\n", k);
  return 0;
}
```

5.5 Write a program that prompts for a name, then displays "Hello *x*" where *x* is replaced by the entered text.

5.6 Fix the following program, which contains several errors. (Hint: Enter and compile the program, then use the resulting error messages to track down the bugs.)

```
(* badcode.c *)

include "stdio.h"

main
{
  int ivalue
  double fvalue

  ivalue = 32767;
  fvalue = 3.14159;
  printf("ivalue = %d", ivalue);
  printf("fvalue = %f", fvalue);
}
```

5.7 Write a program to convert kilometers to miles.

5.8 Write a program that prompts for a signed integer value, then displays the value's unsigned equivalent in decimal and hexadecimal.

5.9 Create an enumerated data type for the days of the week.

5.10 The circumference of a circle equals its diameter times pi. Write a program that prompts for the diameter of a circle and displays its circumference.

Action: What a Program Does

Computer programs written in C can sort databases, evaluate formulas, print tables, and do all kinds of other action-packed jobs. Without action, a program would be as stiff and boring as a movie with motionless actors who say nothing. A film's action gives a picture its life. A program's action performs work on data by evaluating expressions and executing statements.

Expressions

Expressions are operations that programs perform. If valueA, valueB, and valueC are int variables, the expression

```
valueB + valueC
```

computes the sum of valueB plus valueC. The result of an expression is usually assigned to a variable with a statement such as

```
valueA = valueB + valueC;
```

After this statement executes, `valueA` equals the sum of `valueB` plus `valueC`. The plus sign (+) is one of C's many operators. It tells the compiler what kind of operation to perform on adjacent operands.

There are seven kinds of operators in C, and it's the rare program that doesn't use a healthy mix of them. In the following sections, you'll meet C's arithmetic, relational, logical, negation, increment, decrement, and bitwise operators.

Arithmetic Operators

In your early school days, you undoubtedly learned how to use the arithmetic operators +, -, *, and / (see Table 6.1). In C, these operators work as expected. The modulus operator % might be less familiar. Use % to calculate the remainder of an integer division. For example, the expression 24 % 11 ("24 modulo 11") equals 2—the remainder of the integer division 24 / 11. The expression 8 % 2 equals 0 because 2 divides evenly into 8.

Table 6.1. Arithmetic operators.

Operator	Description	Example
*	Multiplication	(a * b)
/	Division	(a / b)
+	Addition	(a + b)
–	Subtraction	(a - b)
%	Modulus	(a % b)

As an example of numeric expressions using arithmetic operators, Listing 6.1, CELSIUS.C, converts degrees Fahrenheit to Celsius, the system named for the Swedish astronomer Anders Celsius (1701–1744), who invented the temperature scale with 0° at the freezing point of water and 100° at the boiling point.

Listing 6.1. CELSIUS.C (Converts degrees Fahrenheit to degrees Celsius).

```
 1:  #include <stdio.h>
 2:  #include <stdlib.h>
 3:
 4:  main()
 5:  {
 6:     double fdegrees, cdegrees;
 7:     char answer[128];
 8:
 9:     printf("Fahrenheit to Celsius conversion\n\n");
10:     printf("Degrees Fahrenheit? ");
11:     gets(answer);
12:     fdegrees = atof(answer);
13:     cdegrees = ((fdegrees - 32.0) * 5.0) / 9.0;
14:     printf("Degrees Celsius = %f\n", cdegrees);
15:     return 0;
16:  }
```

The program uses two `double` floating-point values, `fdegrees` and `cdegrees`. After the program prompts for input, function `atof()` converts string `answer` to floating-point, assigning the result to `fdegrees`. The expression

```
((fdegrees - 32.0) * 5.0) / 9.0
```

calculates the equivalent temperature in Celsius. In the expression, parentheses force a planned evaluation order by performing innermost operations before others. The expression in this example is evaluated in this sequence:

1. 32.0 is subtracted from `fdegrees`.

2. The result from step 1 is multiplied by 5.0.

3. The result from step 2 is divided by 9.0.

> **NOTE:** Always use as many parentheses as necessary to clarify an expression's parts. Parentheses cost you nothing in execution speed; they merely force expressions to be evaluated in the order you want.

In the absence of parentheses, multipart expressions are evaluated according to a fixed precedence level, a property of every operator. Because the operators * and / have a higher precedence than + and -, the expression

```
(A + B * C)
```

is logically identical to the expression

```
(A + (B * C))
```

Because multiplication is performed before addition, the inner pair of parentheses aren't needed. However, to force the addition to occur before the multiplication, you must write

```
((A + B) * C)
```

We'll get back to precedence levels later, after covering all the operators in C.

> **NOTE:** Children are taught the phrase "My Dear Aunt Sally" to help them remember the arithmetic precedence order: multiply, divide, add, and subtract. In C programming, however, / and * have the same precedence, thus A / B * C is evaluated in left-to-right order as (A / B) * C, not as A / (B * C).

Relational Operators

Relational operators evaluate their operands to produce a true (nonzero) or false (zero) result. The expression

```
(A < B)
```

is true only if A is less than B. Both A and B must be types that can be compared, usually integer or floating-point values, or pointers, a subject for Chapter 9, "Pointers." (You may not use relational operators to compare strings. Chapter 10, "Strings," explains how to compare strings alphabetically.)

Table 6.2 lists all of C's relational operators. Later in this chapter, you'll use some of these operators in statements that can make decisions and perform operations based on true and false expressions.

Table 6.2. Relational operators.

Operator	Description	Example
<	Less than	(a < b)
<=	Less than or equal	(a <= b)
>	Greater than	(a > b)
>=	Greater than or equal	(a >= b)
==	Equal	(a == b)
!=	Not equal	(a != b)

> **NOTE:** The equality operator is represented by a double equal-to sign, thus the expression (A == B) is true (nonzero) only if A is equal to B. Don't mistake such expressions for statements like A = B;, which assigns the value of B to A. Confusing the two forms is a common source of bugs. Always use a single equal-to sign (=) for assignments; a double equal-to sign (==) to compare two values.

Logical Operators

Two logical operators, && and ||, combine relational expressions according to the rules for logical AND and logical OR. Use the logical AND operator && in multipart relational expressions such as

```
(A < B) && (B < C)
```

which is true (nonzero) only if A is less than B *and* B is less than C.

Use the logical OR operator || similarly. The expression

```
(A < B) || (B < C)
```

is true if A is less than B *or* B is less than C.

Multipart logical expressions are evaluated efficiently. Given the expression

```
(A <= B) && (B <= C)
```

if A is greater than B, the expression result is known to be false upon evaluating (A <= B); therefore, (B <= C) is not evaluated. This short-circuiting of complex logical expressions helps keep programs running quickly. For any relational expression, only the minimum number of operations are performed to produce an accurate result.

Negation Operator *(!)*

Invert the result of any logical expression by using the unary NOT operator !. The expression

```
!(A < B)
```

literally "not A is less than B" is equivalent to

```
(A >= B)
```

The not-equal operator != is related to !. The expression

```
!(A == B)
```

or "not A equals B" is equivalent to

```
(A != B)
```

This expression is true only if A is not equal to B.

Increment and Decrement Operators

Two of C's most intriguing operators are ++ (increment) and -- (decrement). The ++ operator (pronounced "plus plus") adds one to an operand. The -- operator ("minus minus") subtracts one.

A few examples clarify how these important operators work. The following two statements give identical results:

```
i = i + 1;    /* Add one to i */
i++;          /* Same as above */
```

The expression i++ in the second line is shorthand for the longer addition and assignment in the first. The expression i++ adds one to the current value of integer i. The following two expressions also have identical effects:

```
i = i - 1;    /* Subtract one from integer i */
i--;          /* Same as above */
```

The expression i-- subtracts one from i.

In addition to incrementing and decrementing their operands, expressions such as i++ and i-- also have values, as do all expressions. However, the value of increment and decrement expressions depends on the position of the ++ and -- operators.

When ++ or -- follow their operands, the values of the expressions i++ and i-- equal the premodified values of i. In other words, the statement

```
j = i++;
```

assigns to j the premodified value of i. If i equals 7, after executing j = i++; j equals 7 and i equals 8.

A different result occurs when increment and decrement operators preface their operands. In that case, the expressions equal the postmodified operand values. The statement

```
j = ++i;
```

assigns the incremented value of i to j and also increments the current value of i. If i equals 7, after executing j = ++i; both j and i equal 8.

Another way to visualize these effects is to write increment and decrement expressions in long form. The statement

```
j = i++;
```

operates as though it were two statements:

```
j = i;
i++;
```

And the statement

```
j = ++i;
```

operates as though it were written

```
++i;
j = i;
```

Listing 6.2, INCDEC.C, demonstrates the effects of the ++ and -- operators. Compile and run the program, then enter an integer value for a report on the effects of applying the increment and decrement operators to that value.

Listing 6.2. INCDEC.C (Demonstrates ++ and -- operators).

```
 1:  #include <stdio.h>
 2:
 3:  main()
 4:  {
 5:    int a, b, c, v, k;
 6:
 7:    printf("Enter an integer value: ");
 8:    scanf("%d", &v);
 9:    k = v;
10:    printf("\n    Before  During  After\n");
11:    v = k; a = v; b = v++; c = v; printf("v++%8d%8d%8d\n", a, b, c);
12:    v = k; a = v; b = v--; c = v; printf("v--%8d%8d%8d\n", a, b, c);
13:    v = k; a = v; b = ++v; c = v; printf("++v%8d%8d%8d\n", a, b, c);
14:    v = k; a = v; b = --v; c = v; printf("--v%8d%8d%8d\n", a, b, c);
15:    return 0;
16:  }
```

Executing the program and entering the integer 8 displays a table of values showing the effect of C's increment and decrement operators:

	Before	During	After
v++	8	8	9
v--	8	8	7
++v	8	9	9
--v	8	7	7

Study these results closely. The Before column shows the value of v before the expression is evaluated. The During column shows the value of the expression (what k would equal, for example, if you were to execute the statement k = v++;). The After column shows the final value of v after the expression is evaluated.

The use of scanf() in line 8 is a little different from that function's uses in Chapter 5, "Data: What a Program Knows." The statement

```
scanf("%d", &v);
```

reads a decimal integer value ("%d") and stores the result in v. The expression &v passes the address of v to scanf(). Except for string variables (as demonstrated in Chapter 5), arguments to scanf() must be passed by address.

Bitwise Operators

Like all binary computers, PCs crunch numbers represented in the number base 2. Binary digits, or bits, in values such as 1011 correspond perfectly to on-off switches inside the computer's memory. As switches, bit 0 is off; bit 1 is on.

To keep computers running fast, the computer's processor reads, writes, and transfers multiple bits grouped as 8-bit bytes and 16-bit words rather than one bit at a time. C programs can manipulate such values directly in binary.

C's six bitwise operators perform Boolean logic operations, named after the English mathematician George Boole (1815–1864). Table 6.3 summarizes C's bitwise operators.

Table 6.3. Bitwise operators.

Operator	Description	Example
&	Bitwise AND	C = A & B;
¦	Bitwise inclusive OR	C = A ¦ B;
^	Bitwise exclusive OR	C = A ^ B;
<<	Shift bits left	C = A << B;
>>	Shift bits right	C = A >> B;
~	One's complement	C = ~A;

In expressions, the first three bitwise operators in Table 6.3 combine two operands according to the rules for logical AND (&), inclusive OR (¦), and exclusive OR (^). The next two operators, << and >>, shift bits in values left and right. The final operator, ~, flops bits in its operand value, changing all 0s to 1s and 1s to 0s, creating a result called the one's complement.

To help you learn how to twiddle bits in C (the popular phrase for bitwise operations), the following sections demonstrate each of the operators in Table 6.3.

Displaying Values in Binary

The Borland C++ printf() can display values in many formats, but unfortunately, binary isn't one of the supplied configurations. Before examining C's bitwise operators, you need a way to display values in binary.

Listing 6.3, PBIN.INC, adds this missing capability. However, PBIN.INC contains programming not yet introduced, and therefore, it is not explained here. Enter the listing and save as PBIN.INC. Listings 6.4–6.9 include the file to display values in binary form.

Listing 6.3. PBIN.INC (Include file for displaying binary values).

```
 1:  void pbinc(unsigned char n)
 2:  {
 3:    int i;
 4:    for (i = 0; i < 8; i++) {
 5:      if (n & 0x80)
 6:        putc('1', stdout);
 7:      else
 8:        putc('0', stdout);
 9:      n = n << 1;
10:    }
11:  }
12:
13:  void pbin(unsigned int n)
14:  {
15:    pbinc(n / 256);
16:    pbinc(n % 256);
17:    putc('\n', stdout);
18:  }
```

> **NOTE:** Any program that includes PBIN.INC must also include the standard header stdio.h.

Bitwise AND

Listing 6.4, TAND.C, demonstrates the bitwise AND operator &. (The *T* in the program's name stands for *test*.) Compile and run the program. When prompted, enter two values such as 1234 15 (two numbers separated with a single blank). Press Enter for a report of the values ANDed together in decimal, hexadecimal, and binary.

Listing 6.4. TAND.C (Demonstrates bitwise AND).

```
 1:  #include <stdio.h>
 2:  #include "pbin.inc"
 3:
 4:  main()
 5:  {
 6:    unsigned v1, v2, v3;
 7:
 8:    printf("Enter values to AND: (ex: 1234 15) ");
 9:    scanf("%u %u", &v1, &v2);
10:    v3 = v1 & v2;
11:    printf("      %5u  %#06x  ", v1, v1); pbin(v1);
12:    printf("AND   %5u  %#06x  ", v2, v2); pbin(v2);
13:    printf("====================================\n");
14:    printf("      %5u  %#06x  ", v3, v3); pbin(v3);
15:    return 0;
16:  }
```

Line 10 assigns to the unsigned variable v3 the result of the expression v1 & v2. Lines 11–14 display the original values and the final result. (Statements in these lines call the pbin() function in file PBIN.INC, included at line 2, to display binary digits.)

Table 6.4 lists the rules for a bitwise AND operation. The table shows the result (c) of applying the bitwise AND operator (&) to two single-bit operands (A and B). According to the rules for bitwise AND, the result equals 1 only if both operands are 1; otherwise, the result is 0.

A typical use for the bitwise AND operator is to mask a portion of a value, allowing only part of that value to pass through to the result. For example, run TAND, and enter the two values 1021 15 (separated with a single space). The program reports

```
      1021    0x03fd    0000001111111101
AND     15    0x000f    0000000000001111
====================================
        13    0x000d    0000000000001101
```

Table 6.4. Rules for bitwise AND.

A	&	B	==	C
0	&	0	==	0
0	&	1	==	0
1	&	0	==	0
1	&	1	==	1

The second input value, 15, in binary equals 1111 (not including the leading zeros). When ANDed with another value, 15 is called a mask. Bits corresponding to 1 in the mask pass through to the result. Bits corresponding to 0 in the mask are stripped from the result (set to 0), regardless of their original value.

Figure 6.1 illustrates the effect of a logical AND operation. Bits equal to 1 in the mask allow operand bits to pass through unchanged to the result. Bits equal to 0 in the mask block corresponding operand bits, forcing them to 0 in the result.

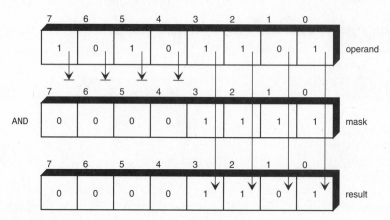

Figure 6.1. Result of logically ANDing an operand and mask.

NOTE: In Figure 6.1 and in other binary illustrations in this book, bits are numbered from right to left. By convention, the least significant bit (LSB) at far right in a binary value is numbered 0. Bits that are more significant increase in number moving left. Bit number 7 is therefore the most significant bit (MSB) in an 8-bit binary value. Bit number 15 is the MSB in a 16-bit value, and so on.

Bitwise Inclusive OR

Listing 6.5, TOR.C, demonstrates C's bitwise inclusive OR operator (¦). Compile and run the program as you did with TAND.C. When prompted, enter two values separated by a single space.

Listing 6.5. TOR.C (Demonstrates bitwise inclusive OR).

```
 1:  #include <stdio.h>
 2:  #include "pbin.inc"
 3:
 4:  main()
 5:  {
 6:    unsigned v1, v2, v3;
 7:
 8:    printf("Enter values to OR inclusively: (ex: 1234 15) ");
 9:    scanf("%u %u", &v1, &v2);
10:    v3 = v1 ¦ v2;
11:    printf("     %5u  %#06x  ", v1, v1); pbin(v1);
12:    printf("OR   %5u  %#06x  ", v2, v2); pbin(v2);
13:    printf("====================================\n");
14:    printf("     %5u  %#06x  ", v3, v3); pbin(v3);
15:    return 0;
16:  }
```

The rules for a bitwise inclusive OR complement those for a bitwise AND. Table 6.5 lists the bitwise inclusive OR results on every combination of two single-bit operands. The result equals 0 only if both operands are 0; otherwise, if either or both operands equal 1, the result is 1.

Table 6.5. Rules for bitwise inclusive OR.

A	I	B	==	C
0	¦	0	==	0
0	¦	1	==	1
1	¦	0	==	1
1	¦	1	==	1

The bitwise inclusive OR operator is often used to insert (or include) bits into values. Test this by running TOR and entering 153 and 5. The program reports

```
     153    0x0099   0000000010011001
OR   5      0x0005   0000000000000101
=====================================
     157    0x009d   0000000010011101
```

The result (157) in binary contains all of the bits from the original (153) plus new 1 bits where 1s appear in the mask (5). This is true regardless of the operand's value: 1s in the mask insert 1s into the result; 0s in the mask allow the operands original bits to pass through. Compare this with the results of the bitwise AND, which allows bits to pass through to the result only for 1 bits in the mask.

Figure 6.2 illustrates the effect of inclusive ORing an operand value with a mask. Bits equal to 1 in the mask insert 1s into the result, regardless of the operand's corresponding bit values. Bits equal to 0 in the mask allow corresponding operand bits to pass through unchanged to the result.

Bitwise Exclusive OR

The bitwise exclusive OR operator (^) seems to have magical properties. Listing 6.6, TXOR.C, demonstrates how the operator works. As you did with the preceding two programs, compile and run the listing. When prompted, enter two values separated by a space.

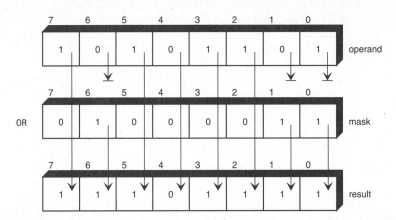

Figure 6.2. Result of logically ORing an operand and mask.

Listing 6.6. TXOR.C (Demonstrates bitwise exclusive OR).

```
 1:  #include <stdio.h>
 2:  #include "pbin.inc"
 3:
 4:  main()
 5:  {
 6:    unsigned v1, v2, v3;
 7:
 8:    printf("Enter values to OR exclusively: (ex: 1234 15) ");
 9:    scanf("%u %u", &v1, &v2);
10:    v3 = v1 ^ v2;
11:    printf("      %5u  %#06x  ", v1, v1); pbin(v1);
12:    printf("XOR   %5u  %#06x  ", v2, v2); pbin(v2);
13:    printf("=================================\n");
14:    printf("      %5u  %#06x  ", v3, v3); pbin(v3);
15:    return 0;
16:  }
```

Table 6.6 shows the results of applying a bitwise exclusive OR operator to every possible combination of two single-bit values. The result is 0 if both operands are equal. The result is 1 if both operands differ. Another way to view the result of an exclusive OR operation is to observe that a 1 in an operand toggles the other operand's value from 1 to 0 or 0 to 1.

Table 6.6. Rules for bitwise exclusive OR.

A	^	B	==	C
0	^	0	==	0
0	^	1	==	1
1	^	0	==	1
1	^	1	==	0

A simple experiment demonstrates an important benefit of the bitwise exclusive OR operator. Run TXOR and enter 45000 and −1 (two values separated by one space). The program reports

```
      45000    0xafc8    1010111111001000
XOR   65535    0xffff    1111111111111111
=====================================
      20535    0x5037    0101000000110111
```

The value −1 in hexadecimal is 0xffff—a 16-bit unsigned value with all bits equal to 1. The result of exclusive ORing that value as a mask with 45000 equals 20535. In binary, 1s replace the original value's 0s. Because every bit in the second operand equals 1, applying the bitwise exclusive OR operator effectively toggles the original bits on and off. Even more interesting is the effect of repeating the same experiment, this time entering the result from the previous test *along with the same mask*. Run TXOR again, enter 20535 and −1 (two values separated by a single space), and the program displays

```
      20535    0x5037    0101000000110111
XOR   65535    0xffff    1111111111111111
=====================================
      45000    0xafc8    1010111111001000
```

Applying the mask −1 to the result from the first experiment recovers the original operand, 45000. In general, this fact is true for the 1 bits in any mask, not only −1. Executing the statements

```
C = A ^ B;
D = C ^ B;
```

sets D equal to A's original value.

This property is often put to good use in animated graphics, where shapes are represented by bit patterns (called bitmaps) in memory. Displaying an image by exclusive ORing its bits with a background bitmap and using the identical operation to exclusive OR those same bits again restores the original image. This gives the visual appearance of one shape moving independently on top of another. (We'll investigate this property again in Chapter 17, "Borland's Class Library.")

Figure 6.3 illustrates the effect of applying a mask to an operand value using an exclusive OR operator. Bits equal to 1 in the mask toggle the bit values in the operand. Bits equal to 0 in the mask allow operand bits to pass through unchanged to the result.

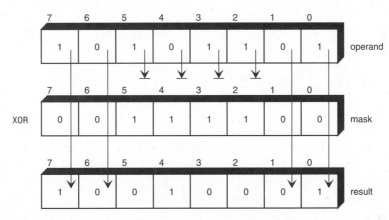

Figure 6.3. Result of exclusive ORing an operand and mask.

Shift Bits Left

Use the shift-left operator (<<) to shift bits by zero or more positions to the left. The statement

```
C = A << 3;
```

assigns to C the value of A shifted three bits left.

Listing 6.7, TLEFT.C, displays the result of the bitwise shift-left operator applied to two 16-bit unsigned values. Compile and run the program, then enter two values such as 89 3 (separated by a space) to see the effect of shifting 89 three bits to the left.

Listing 6.7. TLEFT.C (Demonstrates bitwise shift left).

```
 1:  #include <stdio.h>
 2:  #include "pbin.inc"
 3:
 4:  main()
 5:  {
 6:    unsigned v1, v2, v3;
 7:
 8:    printf("Enter values to SHIFT LEFT: (ex: 1234 3) ");
 9:    scanf("%u %u", &v1, &v2);
10:    v3 = v1 << v2;
11:    printf("     %5u  %#06x  ", v1, v1); pbin(v1);
12:    printf("<<   %5u  %#06x  ", v2, v2); pbin(v2);
13:    printf("===================================\n");
14:    printf("     %5u  %#06x  ", v3, v3); pbin(v3);
15:    return 0;
16:  }
```

In binary, shifting bits one position to the left effectively multiplies the original value by 2, a binary value's radix or number base. Actually, the same is true for values in any number base. Shifting the digits in the decimal value 1234 one position to the left, and bringing a zero digit in at right, gives 12340, or ten times the original base-ten value. In C, however, all shifts are performed in binary.

Because binary computers can shift bits left very rapidly, left shift operations are fast ways to multiply values by powers of two. Try this using TLEFT. Run the program, enter 4 1, and you see this report:

```
     4    0x0004    0000000000000100
<<   1    0x0001    0000000000000001
===================================
     8    0x0008    0000000000001000
```

Shifting the value 4 left one bit position gives 8, which of course equals 4 times 2.

Figure 6.4 illustrates the effect of the statement C = A << B; where A equals the binary value 01011001 and B equals 3. As the result (C) shows, the shift-left operator shifts zero bits in from the right while shifting high-order bits out at left, illustrated here by an electrical grounding symbol, as the bits disappear like electrons to ground.

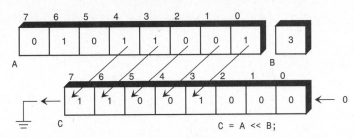

Figure 6.4. The effect of the bitwise shift-left operator.

Shift Bits Right

As you might suppose, C's bitwise shift-right operator (>>) works like the shift-left model, but shifts bits in the other direction. The statement

```
C = A >> 3;
```

assigns to C the value of A shifted three bits to the right.

Listing 6.8, TRIGHT.C, displays the result of the bitwise shift-right operator applied to two 16-bit unsigned values. Compile and run the program, then enter two values such as 89 3 to see the effect of shifting 89 three bits to the right.

Listing 6.8. TRIGHT.C (Demonstrate bitwise shift right).

```
 1:  #include <stdio.h>
 2:  #include "pbin.inc"
 3:
 4:  main()
 5:  {
 6:    unsigned v1, v2, v3;
 7:
 8:    printf("Enter values to SHIFT RIGHT: (ex: 1234 3) ");
 9:    scanf("%u %u", &v1, &v2);
10:    v3 = v1 >> v2;
11:    printf("    %5u  %#06x  ", v1, v1); pbin(v1);
12:    printf(">>  %5u  %#06x  ", v2, v2); pbin(v2);
13:    printf("==================================\n");
14:    printf("    %5u  %#06x  ", v3, v3); pbin(v3);
15:    return 0;
16:  }
```

As shift-left operations multiply values by powers of two, shift-right operations divide values. The same is true for any number base. Shifting the value 12340 right one digit and discarding the 0 gives 1234, the original value divided by 10. In C, all shifts are performed in binary.

To see how shifting binary values right divides by powers of 2, run TRIGHT, enter 89 3, and study this report:

```
       89   0x0059   0000000001011001
>>      3   0x0003   0000000000000011
======================================
       11   0x000b   0000000000001011
```

Using integer arithmetic, dividing 89 by 2^3 (8 decimal) equals 11.

Figure 6.5 illustrates the effect of the statement `C = A >> B;` for the same values in Figure 6.4.

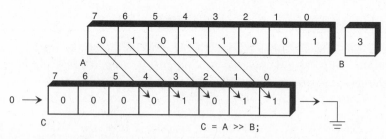

Figure 6.5. The effect of the bitwise shift-right operator.

One's Complement

The bitwise one's complement operator in C, represented by a tilde, ~ (in mathematics, the difference symbol), toggles the bits in a value from 1 to 0 and 0 to 1. The one's complement is a unary operator—it prefaces its operand the way unary plus and minus do in expressions such as -34 and +value.

Use unary one's complement operations to negate binary values. For example, the expression

```
A = ~B;
```

assigns to A the complement, or negated value, of B.

Listing 6.9, TCOMP.C, demonstrates the bitwise one's complement operator. Enter and run the program, then enter a single value for a report of its complement.

Listing 6.9. TCOMP.C (Demonstrates bitwise one's complement).

```
 1:  #include <stdio.h>
 2:  #include "pbin.inc"
 3:
 4:  main()
 5:  {
 6:    unsigned int v1, v2;
 7:
 8:    printf("Enter value to complement: ");
 9:    scanf("%u", &v1);
10:    v2 = ~v1;
11:    printf("     %5d  %#06x  ", v1, v1); pbin(v1);
12:    printf("====================================\n");
13:    printf("COMP %5d  %#06x  ", v2, v2); pbin(v2);
14:    return 0;
15:  }
```

The one's complement is a common low-level operation that most computer processors can perform in the blink of an eye. As a binary logic operation, one's complement has two main purposes: to reverse true and false values, and to convert between negative and positive quantities.

If 0 represents false, ~0 is true, because zero negated equals –1 (65535 unsigned) and any nonzero value means true. (Run TCOMP and enter 0 to see these values.) The reverse is also true: ~–1 equals 0. However, not every nonzero value negated is 0.

The one's complement operator also plays a part in converting between negative and positive integers. Adding one to the result of a one's complement expression forms another quantity called the two's complement. Try this: Run TCOMP and enter –45. You see this report:

```
     -45   0xffd3   1111111111010011
====================================
COMP  44   0x002c   0000000000101100
```

Obviously, 44 + 1 equals 45—the absolute (unsigned equivalent) value of –45. Next, enter 45 for another report:

```
      45   0x002d   0000000000101101
====================================
COMP -46   0xffd2   1111111111010010
```

117

Adding 1 to –46 gives the original value –45. One plus the one's complement of any signed integer v equals that same value with the opposite sign.

Figure 6.6 illustrates the effect of the one's complement operator applied to the binary value 00101100. Compare bits 2 to 5 in this figure with the exclusive OR example in Figure 6.3. Exclusive ORing a bit with 1 toggles the bit's value, as does the one's complement operator—an important relationship to memorize. For instance, the value 00101100 exclusive ORed with 11111111 gives the same result as the expression ~00101100.

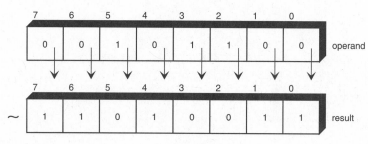

Figure 6.6. The effect of the one's complement operator.

Assignment Operators

You've already been introduced to C's assignment operator, and now that you're such good friends, it's time to take a closer look at this important symbol, represented by the single equal-to sign =. Consider the following simple statement:

```
A = B;   /* Assign B to A */
```

which assigns B's value to A. Following this statement, B's value is unchanged, but A's former value disappears like fog in sunshine.

Technically speaking, A is called an lvalue (pronounced "L Value"); B is called an rvalue ("R Value"). Generally, an lvalue is any expression that might appear to the left of an assignment operator =. An rvalue is any expression that might appear to the right of =. An lvalue such as A must refer to an object that can receive values—usually a reference to a memory location. An rvalue is any expression that has a value (all do) but can't necessarily store one—it may be a reference or it could be a literal constant. The statement

```
A = 1234;
```

is perfectly reasonable, provided A can hold numeric values. The expression

```
1234 = A;   /* ??? */
```

doesn't make sense because a literal constant such as 1234 is not an lvalue.

Expressions of Value

Expressions can range from modestly plain to mind-searingly complex. The simplest expression is a value. For example, written by itself, an int variable A is an expression that represents the value of A. In fact, all expressions have values. The expression (A + B) equals the value of A plus B.

Although the concept may seem odd at first, assignments are expressions, and like all expressions, they have values. As you know, the expression (A = B) assigns B to A. As an expression, however, (A = B) also has a value equal to the assigned result. The statement

```
C = (A = B);
```

is therefore perfectly acceptable. First, the parenthetical subexpression (A = B) assigns B to A. The value of that subexpression (equal to A) is then assigned to C. Consequently, both C and A now equal B. You don't even need the parentheses. The statement

```
C = A = B;
```

assigns B to A and C.

With these facts in mind, here's a hot tip for initializing multiple variables. The statement

```
A = B = C = 451;
```

assigns 451 to A, B, and C.

Assignment Operators

Assignment statements sometimes do more work than necessary. In the statement

```
A = A + 45;
```

the compiler generates code to evaluate the expression A + 45, which is then assigned back to A. The two references to A require the compiled code to compute A's memory location twice—once to find A's original value, and again to determine where to store the result. You can write the same expression more simply as

```
A += 45;
```

This helps the compiler generate more efficient code. The double symbol += is called an assignment operator, a kind of shorthand that tells the compiler to add 45 to A's value and stuff the result back in A. The full set of assignment operators is *=, /=, +=, -=, %=, <<=, >>=, &=, ^=, and ¦=. Each reduces the pseudocode expression

```
i = i op j;
```

to the shorter form

```
i op= j;
```

> **NOTE:** *Pseudocode* is an informal way to show the form of statements without using actual C (or another language's) elements. The *op* in the above pseudocode statements is just a conceptual placeholder, not an actual operator.

A few samples of assignment operators in action for an int variable named count, with the equivalent longhand expressions written as comments, demonstrate how this shorthand notation works:

```
count += 10;   /* count = count + 10 */
count *= 2;    /* count = count * 2 */
count /= 3;    /* count = count / 3 */
count %= 16;   /* count = count % 16 */
```

Optimizing compilers such as Borland C++ may be able to generate efficient code for the equivalent longhand expressions, but in complex settings where count is not a simple variable as it is here, the multiple references to count may reduce a program's performance. Use assignment operators whenever possible. They can add extra zip to code.

Operator Precedence

In complex expressions, subexpressions with operators of higher precedence are evaluated before subexpressions with operators of lower precedence. Operators of different kinds are applied in left-to-right or right-to-left order, a property known as *associativity*.

In most expressions, common sense and a good helping of parentheses are your best guides to accurate results. You don't need to memorize lots of precedence and associativity rules to understand the evaluation order of expressions such as this:

```
y = ((a * x) + b) / (x + C);
```

Even though the purpose of this formula isn't obvious (it describes a hyperbolic curve, in case you're interested), the parentheses make perfectly clear which subexpressions belong together.

Relying on operator precedence to produce a correct answer, the above statement could also be written as

```
y = (a * x + b) / (x + C);
```

Because multiplication and division associate from left-to-right, one set of parentheses in the first expression can be removed. Even so, the first expression is unambiguous. The second is correct, but less clear.

By all means, study the precedence and associativity rules in Table 6.7, but don't rely solely on precedence levels to obtain correct expression results. A few extra parentheses cost nothing in performance, and they lend more than their weight in clarity.

The *if* Statement

C's if statement operates just as you might expect. If an expression is true, the statement performs an action; otherwise, execution continues directly to the following statement.

In this section and in those that follow, pseudocode provides a handy way to explain various statement forms. C's if statement in pseudocode is

```
if (expression)
  statement;
```

The expression can be any expression that evaluates to a true-false value. If expression is true (nonzero), then the statement is executed. If expression is false (zero), then the statement is skipped. You can write if statements on one line:

```
if (expression) statement;
```

You also can divide them into multiple lines, typically indenting statements for emphasis. The statement may be compound:

```
if (expression) {
  statement1;
  statement2;
}
```

Table 6.7. Operator precedence and evaluation order (associativity).

Level	Operators	Evaluation Order
1.	`() . [] ->`	left-to-right
2.	`* & ! ~ ++ -- + - (typecast) sizeof`	right-to-left
3.	`* / %`	left-to-right
4.	`+ -`	left-to-right
5.	`<< >>`	left-to-right
6.	`< <= > >=`	left-to-right
7.	`== !=`	left-to-right
8.	`&`	left-to-right
9.	`^`	left-to-right
10.	`¦`	left-to-right
11.	`&&`	left-to-right
12.	`¦¦`	left-to-right
13.	`?:`	right-to-left
14.	`= *= /= += -= %= <<= >>= &= ^= ¦=`	right-to-left
15.	`,`	left-to-right

*NOTE: Unary plus (+) and unary minus (-) are at level 2, and have precedence over arithmetic plus and minus at level 4. The & symbol at level 2 is the address-of operator; the & symbol at level 8 is the bitwise AND operator. The * symbol at level 2 is the pointer-dereference operator; the * symbol at level 3 is the multiplication operator. In the absence of clarifying parentheses, operators on the same level are evaluated according to their evaluation order. You'll meet some of these symbols in future chapters. Also, see Appendix D for a complete C and C++ operator-precedence table.*

The location of the braces in a compound `if` statement is optional. Some programmers align them like this:

```
if (expression)
{
  statement1;
  statement2;
}
```

You might also use a relational operator to write comparative expressions such as

```
if (expression == value)
  statement;
```

Only if `expression` is equal to `value` does the `statement` execute. Never write such expressions as

```
if (expression = value)  /* ??? */
  statement;
```

or you'll receive a warning from the compiler about a possibly faulty assignment. The compiler senses that in `if` statement expressions, you probably do not want to assign `value` to `expression`. More likely, you accidentally typed a single equal sign rather than two—one of the most common errors C programmers make.

Expert C programmers (who may not be so expert in typing skills) frequently shorten `if` statement expressions to the extreme. The statement

```
if (expression != 0)
  statement;
```

when stripped to the bone, is functionally identical to

```
if (expression)
  statement;
```

Be sure to understand this common trick. As relational true-false expressions, `(expression != 0)` and `(expression)` are equivalent, because any nonzero value represents true. Substitute the literal value 5 for `expression`, and you can see the reason this trick works. Obviously, 5 is not equal to 0. Because any nonzero value represents true, the value 5 alone represents true as well.

> **NOTE:** This kind of shorthand pops up all the time in `if` statements. There is no functional difference between `if (expression)`... and `if (expression != 0)`... By using the longer form, however, which is certainly the clearer of the two, you lose no style points, and you give up no runtime performance.

Listing 6.10, CHOICE.C, shows how to use `if`. Compile and run the program, then enter a number from 1 to 10. If you enter a value outside of that range, the program displays an error message.

Listing 6.10. CHOICE.C (Demonstrates the `if` statement).

```
1:  #include <stdio.h>
2:
3:  main()
4:  {
5:    int number;
6:    int okay;
7:
8:    printf("Enter a number from 1 to 10: ");
9:    scanf("%d", &number);
10:   okay = (1 <= number) && (number <= 10);
11:   if (!okay)
12:     printf("Incorrect answer!\n");
13:   return okay;
14: }
```

Line 10 assigns to `int okay` the true or false result of the relational expression

`(1 <= number) && (number <= 10)`

The expression result is an integer value—0 when the evaluation is false, nonzero when true. That value is assigned to `okay`, after which line 11 examines the expression `!okay`, literally *not okay*. If `okay` is false (indicating an error has occurred), then `!okay` evaluates as true, and line 12 displays an error message.

> **HINT:** For storing and using relational expressions in `if` statements, choose identifiers such as `okay`, `isPeachy`, and `makesGoodSense` to avoid painful mental gymnastics figuring out whether a complex logical expression is true or false. A few carefully chosen identifiers can add a lot of clarity to a program's text.

Just for effect, line 13 returns the value of `okay`—passing the true or false result back to DOS. Though not used here, a similar return value in a more complex program might indicate whether a critical error occurred.

You can also write complex logical expressions directly in `if` statements. For example, you can combine lines 10–12 into one statement:

```
if ((1 <= number) && (number <= 10))
  printf("Incorrect answer!\n");
```

Notice the additional parentheses around the logical expression. The expression that `if` evaluates must always be enclosed in parentheses.

The *else* Statement

The `else` statement is the `if` statement's sidekick. Following any `if` statement, you can insert an `else` statement to perform an alternative action. Use `else` like this:

```
if (expression)
  statement1;
else
  statement2;
```

If expression is true (nonzero), `statement1` executes; otherwise, `statement2` runs. The statements may be simple or compound. You can write

```
if (expression) {
  statement1;
  statement2;
} else
  statement3;
```

Or both parts can be compound, surrounded by braces:

```
if (expression) {
  statement1;
  statement2;
} else {
  statement3;
  statement4;
}
```

In this construction, statements 1 and 2 execute when `expression` is true; otherwise, statements 3 and 4 run.

Compound statements can nest to any depth, so `statement1` might be another `if` statement, which could execute still more `if` statements. The logic of deeply nested `if` statements may be obscure, but the compiler imposes no limit on how many statements can nest inside of others. For best results, limit nesting to a couple of levels or so.

As with plain `if` statements, brace placement in complex `if-else` constructions is a personal choice of style. Some programmers align the braces in the preceding example as shown in the following:

```
if (expression)
{
  statement1;
  statement2;
}
else
{
  statement3;
  statement4;
}
```

You may nest multiple `if-else` statements together, creating a multiway decision maker:

```
if (expression1)
  statement1;
else if (expression2)
  statement2;
else
  statement3;
```

Take that a line at a time, and be sure to understand how this works. If `expression1` is true, then `statement1` is executed; if `expression2` is true, `statement2` runs. When both `expression1` and `expression2` are false, `statement3` executes. You can carry this idea to extremes, writing

```
if (expression1)
  statement1;
else if (expression2)
  statement2;
else if (expression3)
  statement3;
else if (expressionN)
  statementN;
else                 /* Optional */
  defaultStatement;  /* Optional */
```

Nested `if-else` statements are useful for selecting one of several possible actions, and are guaranteed to execute only the statement (or statements) associated with the first true expression. If no expressions are true, the final (and optional) `defaultStatement` executes.

As a practical example of nested `if-else` statements, Listing 6.11, LEAP.C, detects leap years. Compile and run the program, then enter a year such as 2000. A new century is a leap year when evenly divisible by 400. (Actually, because there was no year 0, 2001 will be the first year of the 21st century, but who's counting?) Noncentury dates such as 1996 are leap years if evenly divisible by 4.

Listing 6.11. LEAP.C (Uses `if-else` to detect leap years).

```
 1: #include <stdio.h>
 2:
 3: main()
 4: {
 5:   int leapYear;
 6:   int year;
 7:
 8:   printf("Leap Year Calculator\n");
 9:   printf("Year? ");
10:   scanf("%d", &year);
11:   if (year > 0) {
12:     if ((year % 100) == 0)
13:       leapYear = ((year % 400) == 0);
14:     else
```

continues

Listing 6.11. continued

```
15:          leapYear = ((year %    4) == 0);
16:      if (leapYear)
17:        printf("%d is a leap year\n", year);
18:      else
19:        printf("%d is not a leap year\n", year);
20:    }
21:    return 0;
22:  }
```

Like a movie villain, a badly written if-else statement may fail due to bad character—a badly placed brace character, that is. Listing 6.12, BADIF.C, demonstrates the damage that a broken nested if-else statement can do.

Listing 6.12. BADIF.C (The wrong way to nest if-else statements).

```
 1:  #include <stdio.h>
 2:
 3:  main()
 4:  {
 5:    int value;
 6:
 7:    printf("Value (1 ... 10)? ");
 8:    scanf("%d", &value);
 9:    if (value >= 1)
10:      if (value > 10)
11:        printf("Error: value > 10\n");
12:    else
13:      printf("Error: value < 1\n");
14:    return 0;
15:  }
```

Run BADIF and enter a value from 1 to 10. Although programmed to reject values outside of that range, the program reports errors for good values and reports the wrong errors for some bad ones. The if statement at line 9 checks whether value is greater than or equal to 1. If so, an inner `if` statement tests whether `value` is greater than 10, displaying an error message. Trouble is, the code doesn't work as expected.

The `else` at line 12 is the culprit. Although physically aligned with the `if` at line 9, the `else` statement logically connects to the nearest `if` above—in this case, the `if` statement at line 10. This is wrong. Somehow, you must change the program so the `else` goes with the correct `if`.

Remember this rule: *Never rely on indentation to control a program's logic.* The compiler doesn't care about indentations—they are for your benefit. Use braces around statements to keep nested `if-else` statements working smoothly. Listing 6.13, GOODIF.C, shows the corrected code.

Listing 6.13. GOODIF.C (The right way to nest `if-else` statements).

```
 1:  #include <stdio.h>
 2:
 3:  main()
 4:  {
 5:    int value;
 6:
 7:    printf("Value (1 ... 10)? ");
 8:    scanf("%d", &value);
 9:    if (value >= 1) {
10:      if (value > 10)
11:        printf("Error: value > 10\n");
12:    } else
13:      printf("Error: value < 1\n");
14:    return 0;
15:  }
```

Compare Listings 6.12 and 6.13. The extra braces at lines 9 and 12 in GOODIF force the `else` statement to go with the `if` at line 9. The inner `if`, at lines 10–11, now operates correctly.

The Conditional Expression

A shorthand `if-else` statement called a *conditional expression* is sometimes useful. In pseudocode, a conditional expression looks like this:

```
expression1 ? expression2 : expression3;
```

The program evaluates `expression1`. If `expression1` is true, the result of the entire expression equals `expression2`. If `expression1` is false, the result equals `expression3`. The conditional expression is exactly equivalent to the `if-else` statement

```
if (expression1)
  expression2;
else
  expression3;
```

The purpose of an `if-else` statement is usually clearer than the equivalent conditional expression. Consider this fact when choosing between the two forms.

Usually, you'll assign a conditional expression's result to a variable. Suppose, for example, you are writing a menu-driven program. If an `int` variable `menuChoice` equals `'Y'`, you want to set a `testValue` to 100; otherwise, you want to set `testValue` to zero. The straightforward solution uses an `if-else` statement:

```
if (menuChoice == 'Y')
  value = 100;
else
  value = 0;
```

That's certainly clear enough, but the statement requires two references to `value`. To refer to `value` only once and perform the identical job, you can write

```
value = (menuChoice == 'Y') ? 100 : 0;
```

If the expression (`menuChoice == 'Y'`) is true, the statement assigns 100 to `value`. If the expression is false, the statement assigns 0 to `value`.

Don't use conditional expressions just because they take up only one line instead of four. In most cases, the compiler generates similar code for the longer `if-else` statement as it does for an equivalent conditional expression. On the other hand, to avoid two references to the same expression such as `value` (possibly critical if `value` is a complex expression), the conditional expression may be a wise choice.

The *switch* Statement

A nested collection of if-else statements can look as twisted as the plumbing in an old building. The system works, but you're not sure which pipe goes where.

Consider the following series of if-else statements, each of which compares an expression with a value:

```
if (expression == value1)
  statement1;
else if (expression == value2)
  statement2;
else if (expression == value3)
  statement3;
else                 /* Optional */
  defaultStatement;  /* Optional */
```

You can use a simpler switch statement to reduce such expressions to

```
switch (expression) {
  case value1:
    statement1;    /* Executes if expression == value1 */
    break;         /* Exit the switch statement */
  case value2:
    statement2;    /* Executes if expression == value2 */
    break;         /* Exit the switch statement */
  case value3:
    statement3;    /* Executes if expression == value3 */
    break;         /* Exit the switch statement */
  default:
    defaultStatement;  /* Executes if no values match expression */
}
```

At first glance this may seem longer, but in practice, a switch statement is easier to manage than the equivalent if-else construction. Following the switch keyword is the expression to be compared to a set of values. Inside the switch's block, case selectors compare the expression to specified values. The line

```
case value1:
```

compares value1 with the result of the switch statement's expression. If that comparison is true, the statement (or statement block) following this case is executed. If the comparison is false, the next case is evaluated. The default: selector at the end specifies an optional action if no values match the expression.

The `break` statements in each `case` immediately exit from the `switch`. Because of the way `switch` statements are designed, if you write them without using `break`:

```
switch (expression) {
  case value1:
    statement1;  /* ??? */
  case value2:
    statement2;  /* ??? */
  case value3:
    statement3;
}
```

and `expression` equals `value1`, `statement1` executes. `statement2` and `statement3` also execute, however—probably not what you intended. Likewise, if `expression` equals `value2`, `statement2` and `statement3` execute. In `switch` statements, the first true `case` falls through to the subsequent statements until reaching a `break` statement or the end of the `switch`.

> **NOTE:** Clever programmers (perhaps *too* clever) sometimes purposely omit `break`s from `switch` statements to allow one case to select multiple actions, including those listed for other cases. Although this is technically allowed, the results can be difficult to follow and even more difficult to modify. For best results, end every `case` with `break`.

Listing 6.14, MENU.C, demonstrates how to write a selection menu using a `switch` statement. Compile and run the program, then enter a letter A, D, S, or Q to select a command. (The commands don't do anything useful, so feel free to experiment.) Enter an unlisted letter to see how the `switch` statement detects input errors.

Listing 6.14. MENU.C (Demonstrates `switch` statement).

```
1:  #include <stdio.h>
2:  #include <ctype.h>
3:
4:  main()
5:  {
6:    int choice;
7:
8:    printf("Menu: A(dd D(elete S(ort Q(uit: ");
```

```
 9:    choice = toupper(getchar());
10:    switch (choice) {
11:      case 'A':
12:        printf("You selected Add\n");
13:        break;
14:      case 'D':
15:        printf("You selected Delete\n");
16:        break;
17:      case 'S':
18:        printf("You selected Sort\n");
19:        break;
20:      case 'Q':
21:        printf("You selected Quit\n");
22:        break;
23:      default:
24:        printf("\nIllegal choice!!!\n");
25:    }
26:    return choice;
27:  }
```

Line 9 calls a standard library function getchar() to read a character typed at the keyboard. Function toupper() converts that character to uppercase, thus simplifying the job of finding a match for a keypress.

The switch statement begins at line 10, listing the chosen character as the statement's expression. Subsequent case sections compare choice with literal characters, printing a confirmation message for the first match. If no matches are found, the default section at lines 23–24 displays an error message.

At line 26, the program returns the chosen character. Although not important here, a similar statement might pass the menu's result from one function to another to select commands. (We'll get to functions in Chapter 7, "Functions: Divide and Conquer.")

The *while* Statement

The while statement is one of three loops that repeat actions. Programs use while to execute statements repeatedly as long as a specified condition holds true. In pseudocode, while looks like this:

```
while (expression)
  statement;
```

In English, you can read that as "while expression is true, execute statement." As usual, the statement can be simple or compound:

```
while (expression) {
  statement1;
  statement2;
  ...
}
```

In such constructions, each statement executes one after the other while the expression is true.

A while statement—also called a while loop—typically executes at least one statement that affects the specified expression. Obviously, this must be so, or once begun, the statement would loop forever—at least, that is, until you pull the computer's plug or halt the code by some other means.

Listing 6.15, WCOUNT.C, uses a while statement to count from 1 to 10.

Listing 6.15. WCOUNT.C (Counts from 1 to 10 with a while loop).

```
1:  #include <stdio.h>
2:
3:  main()
4:  {
5:    int counter;
6:
7:    printf("while count\n");
8:    counter = 1;
9:    while (counter <= 10) {
10:     printf("%d\n", counter);
11:     counter++;
12:   }
13:   return 0;
14: }
```

Line 8 initializes an int counter, called a control variable. The while statement in lines 9–12 uses the relational operator <= to compare counter with 10. While counter is less than or equal to 10, the statements at lines 10–11 execute. Line 11 advances counter by one each time through the loop, thus guaranteeing that the statement eventually ends.

What is the final value of counter after the end of the while statement? Prove your guess by inserting this statement between lines 12 and 13:

```
printf("counter == %d\n", counter);
```

Does counter's final value (11) make sense? What would counter equal if you changed the expression in line 9 to (counter < 10)? Try also changing counter's starting value at line 8. What happens if you initialize counter to 11? Does the loop still execute?

This test demonstrates an important property of while loops: They do not execute any of their statements if the controlling expression is initially false.

You may use other kinds of control variables in while statements. For example, Listing 6.16, WALPHA.C, displays the alphabet, using a character as the loop's control value.

Listing 6.16. WALPHA.C (Display the alphabet with a while loop).

```
1:  #include <stdio.h>
2:
3:  main()
4:  {
5:    int c;
6:
7:    printf("while alphabet\n");
8:    c = 'A';
9:    while (c <= 'Z') {
10:     printf("%c", c);
11:     c++;
12:   }
13:   return 0;
14: }
```

The expression in line 9 (c <= 'Z') is true if character c's ASCII value is less than or equal to Z's.

135

The *do-while* Statement

The do-while (which sounds like a '60s pop-group vocal embellishment), is a sort of upside down while loop. Expressed in pseudocode, C's do-while (diddy dum diddy do) looks like this:

```
do {
  statement;
} while (expression);
```

The statement executes while expression is true. Compare this with a plain while, which evaluates its expression before executing any statements. A while may never execute its statements if the controlling expression is initially false. But a do-while always executes its statements at least once because it doesn't get around to evaluating its expression until the end of the loop. This leads to a general rule for choosing between while and do-while:

- Ask yourself: "Is there at least one condition when the statements in the loop should not execute, not even once?" If the answer is yes, a while loop probably is the correct choice.

- If the answer to the preceding question is no, a do-while may be appropriate. If the statements in a loop must execute at least once, regardless of the controlling expression's value, use do-while.

The do-while's statement may be single or compound. You can write single-statement do-while loops on one line:

```
do statement; while (expression);
```

Or, you can write them on separate lines, indenting the statement for clarity:

```
do
  statement;
while (expression);
```

However, braces typically are added to make clear that this is one statement and not several:

```
do {
  statement;
} while (expression);
```

Write multistatement do-whiles like this:

```
do {
  statement1;
  statement2;
  ...
} while (expression);
```

Listing 6.17, DWCOUNT.C, is similar to the earlier WCOUNT program which counts from 1 to 10, but uses do-while.

Listing 6.17. DWCOUNT.C (Count from 1 to 10 with a do-while loop).

```
 1:  #include <stdio.h>
 2:
 3:  main()
 4:  {
 5:    int counter;
 6:
 7:    printf("do-while count\n");
 8:    counter = 0;
 9:    do {
10:      counter++;
11:      printf("%d\n", counter);
12:    } while (counter < 10);
13:    return 0;
14:  }
```

In addition to running DWCOUNT, execute the code by hand, writing the values of counter on paper. Aim for a clear understanding of why the expression (counter < 10) properly ends the loop after displaying the 10th value. Why would the expression (counter <= 10) not work (as it did in WCOUNT)? Test your assumptions by inserting printf() statements that display counter's value at strategic locations (a good debugging trick to remember).

You can use any sort of controlling true-false expression for a do-while loop. To demonstrate do-while's versatility, Listing 6.18, DWALPHA.C, uses do-while to display the alphabet.

Listing 6.18. DWALPHA.C (Display the alphabet with a do-while loop).

```
1:  #include <stdio.h>
2:
3:  main()
4:  {
5:    int c;
6:
7:    printf("do-while alphabet\n");
8:    c = 'A' - 1;
9:    do {
10:     c++;
11:     printf("%c", c);
12:   } while (c < 'Z');
13:   return 0;
14: }
```

The *for* Statement

When you know, or when a program can calculate in advance, the number of times a statement block should execute, a for statement is usually the best choice of loops. In pseudocode, a for statement looks like this:

```
for (expression1; expression2; expression3) {
  statement;
}
```

This for statement may look complicated on a first glance, but is easier to understand when expressed as an equivalent while statement. The following pseudocode has the identical effect as the preceding for:

```
expression1;
while (expression2) {
  statement;
  expression3;
}
```

Technically, you may use any expressions in a for loop, but some types of expressions are more appropriate for expression1, expression2, and expression3 than others. For example, to count from 1 to 10 using a for loop, assuming variable i is type int, you can write

```
for (i = 1; i <= 10; i++)   /* expressions 1, 2, and 3 */
  printf("i == %d\n", i);   /* statement */
```

The first expression in this sample for loop initializes i to 1—an action that occurs only once, just before the loop begins. The second expression is typically relational, in this case evaluating to true if i is less than or equal to 10. The third and final expression increments i, thus moving the loop along to its conclusion.

The preceding for may be easier to visualize as the equivalent while loop:

```
i = 1;                        /* expression1 */
while (i <= 10) {             /* expression2 */
  printf("i == %d\n", i);    /* statement */
  i++;                        /* expression3 */
}
```

Compare the for and while versions, and note the location of each expression and statement. They are functionally identical, and at least in this simple example, the compiler generates identical code for each.

Listing 6.19, ASCII.C, uses a for loop to display the visible ASCII character set (characters with values from 32 to 127).

Listing 6.19. ASCII.C (Display ASCII characters with a for loop).

```
 1:  #include <stdio.h>
 2:
 3:  main()
 4:  {
 5:    unsigned char c;
 6:
 7:    for (c = 32; (c < 128); c++) {
 8:      if ((c % 32) == 0) printf("\n");
 9:      printf("%c", c);
10:    }
11:    printf("\n");
12:    return 0;
13:  }
```

139

When you run ASCII, the program displays the following 96-character report:

```
!"#$%&'()*+,-./0123456789:;<=>?
@ABCDEFGHIJKLMNOPQRSTUVWXYZ[\]^_
'abcdefghijklmnopqrstuvwxyz{|}~△
```

The program's for loop at lines 7–10 initializes the unsigned char control variable c to the ASCII value for a blank character (32). The controlling expression, (C < 128), ends the loop after displaying the final character—when c equals 128, that is. The expression c++ advances the control variable by one for each pass through the loop.

Inside the for statement, an if statement tests whether (c % 32)—equal to the remainder of c divided by 32—is zero. If so, a printf() statement starts a new display line. Change 32 to 16 for a 16 character-per-line report. Line 9 displays each character.

A for statement's expressions may also be blank, an advanced technique that requires forethought to be used correctly. One handy trick is the "do-forever" loop:

```
for (;;) ;  /* Loop forever */
```

This for loop initializes no control variable, has no controlling expression, and performs no action to end the loop. It also has no statements. When executed, the statement "hangs" the program until an external event occurs—the power fails, for example, or an interrupt signal causes the processor to begin executing some other code. In the absence of any such external activity, the program remains stuck inside this loop until the cows come home (whenever that is).

By the way, the blank space between the closing parenthesis and terminating semicolon is intentional. Without the blank, some C compilers (but, unfortunately, not Borland C++) display a warning, helping to guard against a common mistake, shown here in pseudocode:

```
for (i = 1; i < 100; i++);  /* ??? */
  statement;
```

Because a for loop's statement part may be blank, the compiler processes this faulty construction as two syntactically correct statements—a for loop with three expressions, and a *separate* statement that executes after the for loop finishes. The for loop runs correctly, but performs no useful action. When you intend to construct for loops this way (usually not recommended), insert an extra blank before the semicolon like this:

```
for (i = 1; i < 100; i++) ;  /* Semicolon is intentional! */
```

By convention, the blank indicates that the unusual construction is intentional and is not a typing error. Adding a comment can't hurt, either.

> **NOTE:** Because a `for` statement's expressions may be any expressions, it's possible to create `for` loops that do nothing or that perform various actions as the results of evaluating expressional parts. Such code is difficult to write, even harder to maintain, and is more likely than not to develop serious bugs. For best results, use `for` loops as intended. Just because the C language allows you to write obscure statements doesn't mean you have to do so.

The *break* Statement

It's sometimes useful to interrupt a `while`, `do-while`, or `for` loop in progress. Listing 6.20, BREAKER.C, demonstrates how a `break` statement can interrupt a program like a news break on TV.

Listing 6.20. BREAKER.C (Demonstrates `break` statement).

```
 1:  #include <stdio.h>
 2:
 3:  main()
 4:  {
 5:    int count;
 6:
 7:    printf("\n\nfor loop:\n");
 8:    for (count = 1; count <= 10; count++) {
 9:      if (count > 5) break;
10:      printf("%d\n", count);
11:    }
12:
13:    printf("\n\nwhile loop:\n");
14:    count = 1;
15:    while (count <= 10) {
16:      if (count > 5) break;
```

continues

141

```
17:        printf("%d\n", count);
18:        count++;
19:      }
20:
21:      printf("\n\ndo/while loop:\n");
22:      count = 1;
23:      do {
24:        if (count > 5) break;
25:        printf("%d\n", count);
26:        count++;
27:      } while (count <= 10);
28:
29:      return 0;
30:    }
```

BREAKER executes for (lines 8–11), while (lines 15–19), and do-while (lines 23–27) statements. Each statement counts from 1 to 10 using an int variable count. Each loop also executes a break statement before count reaches its final value (see lines 9, 16, and 24). Due to the breaks in their armor, the loops end prematurely. The technique is useful for getting out of a loop in a hurry—to respond to an error condition, for example.

You can use break statements at other times. (You saw them earlier inside switch statements.) For example, a so-called do-forever loop can use a break to shorten "forever" to a more reasonable length of time:

```
for (;;) {           /* Do figuratively "forever" */
  ...                /* Various statements */
  if (expression)    /* If expression is true, */
    break;           /*   break out of loop */
}
```

Lacking any controlling expressions, the for statement executes forever—until, that is, expression becomes true, causing the inner if statement to execute break, and halting the do-forever loop long before its time. Such code has all the appeal of a Rube Goldberg invention, which is about all you can say in favor of the technique.

The *continue* Statement

Similar to break, a continue statement forces a loop to start its next iteration from the top. Listing 6.21, CONTINUE.C, demonstrates the difference between break and continue.

Listing 6.21. CONTINUE.C (Demonstrates continue statement).

```
 1:  #include <stdio.h>
 2:
 3:  main()
 4:  {
 5:    int count;
 6:
 7:    printf("\nStarting for loop with continue...\n");
 8:    for (count = 1; count <= 10; count++) {
 9:      if (count > 5) continue;
10:      printf("%d\n", count);
11:    }
12:    printf("After for loop, count = %d\n", count);
13:
14:    printf("\n\nStarting for loop with break...\n");
15:    for (count = 1; count <= 10; count++) {
16:      if (count > 5) break;
17:      printf("%d\n", count);
18:    }
19:    printf("After for loop, count = %d\n", count);
20:    return 0;
21:  }
```

The CONTINUE program uses two for loops (lines 8–11 and 15–18) to count from 1 to 10. Line 9, inside the first for loop, executes a continue statement if count is greater than 5. Line 16 executes a break statement for the same condition. Except for this difference, the loops are identical.

The program displays count's value inside and out of the loops. After the first loop, count equals 11. After the second, it equals 6. The continue statement starts the first loop over from the top, skipping the printf() statement at line 10, but allowing count to reach its final value. The break statement exits the second loop immediately, also skipping printf() at line 17, but not continuing to advance count.

The *goto* Statement

A goto statement directs a program to execute any other statement and to continue executing subsequent statements starting from that location. Because a goto can "jump" to any place in a program, using goto is like leaving a highway through a field rather than at a marked exit. Be prepared for a bumpy ride.

At first glance, goto seems tremendously useful. In practice, however, the statement gives programmers too much freedom to jump from here to there and over yonder. At best, it's difficult to fathom the results of a program that has several goto statements. At worst, the code won't work well at all.

If you must use goto, insert a label (an unused identifier and colon) above any statement. Execute goto LABEL to direct the program to that location. Listing 6.22, GCOUNT.C, demonstrates how to use goto to count from 1 to 10.

Listing 6.22. GCOUNT.C (Counts from 1 to 10 with a goto statement).

```
 1:  #include <stdio.h>
 2:
 3:  main()
 4:  {
 5:    int count = 1;
 6:
 7:  TOP:
 8:    printf("%d\n", count);
 9:    count++;
10:    if (count <= 10) goto TOP;
11:    return 0;
12:  }
```

The label, TOP:, at line 7 marks a target location for a goto statement. The if statement at line 10 examines an integer variable count. If count is less than or equal to 10, goto transfers control to TOP:, executing the printf() and count++ statements again until count becomes larger than 10. When that happens, the if statement does not execute the goto, and the program continues to line 11 and ends.

The program works, but it lacks the intuitive clarity of the while, do-while, and for demonstrations in this chapter. Understanding the goto version requires tracing each statement by hand. In a complex program, debugging gotos that way is painstaking work. Worse yet, the compiler can do nothing to optimize a goto's performance. To the compiler, the loop at lines 7–10 (if you can bear to call it a "loop") is merely a series of unrelated statements.

By all means, learn how to use goto. You might stumble over one in somebody else's code. Avoid using goto in your own programs. This is one statement you can do without.

Halting a Program with *exit*

Left to their own devices, programs stop after executing the final statement in main(). To avoid a compiler warning, main() should end with the statement

```
return value;
```

where value is any integer expression. The value returned from main() is available to the program that executed the code—usually DOS's COMMAND.COM, but it might be another "shell," a batch file, or a program designed to execute others.

Another way to halt a program is to call exit(), a function defined in stdlib.h. Executing the statement

```
exit(0);
```

terminates the program immediately, closes all open files, and performs other miscellaneous shutdown chores. The value in parentheses is passed back to DOS (or to the program that executed this one).

Listing 6.23, YESNO.C, shows how to use `exit()` to alter the normal top-to-bottom flow of a program. YESNO is also a practical utility you can use to add Yes-No prompts to DOS batch files. Enter and compile the listing, but don't run it just yet. The next listing shows how to use YESNO.

Listing 6.23. YESNO.C (Ends a program with `exit()`).

```
 1:  #include <stdio.h>
 2:  #include <stdlib.h>
 3:  #include <ctype.h>
 4:
 5:  main()
 6:  {
 7:    char answer;
 8:
 9:    printf("\nType Y for yes, N for no: ");
10:    answer = toupper(getchar());
11:    if (answer == 'Y')
12:      exit(1);
13:    else
14:      exit(0);
15:    printf("This statement never executes!\n");
16:    return 99;  /* This statement doesn't execute either! */
17:  }
```

Lines 12 and 14 call `exit()`, passing either 1 or 0 as an argument in parentheses. The exit value 1 indicates that the Y key was pressed; 0 indicates any other key. Lines 15–16 never execute.

Listing 6.24, TESTYN.BAT, is a DOS batch file that runs YESNO. Enter the listing. From a DOS prompt, type **testyn** to run the batch file. Type Y to repeat the prompt; N to quit.

Listing 6.24. TESTYN.BAT (Batch file for running YESNO.C).

```
echo off
rem
rem - Test YESNO.C
rem
```

```
goto START
:YES
echo You answered yes!
:START
echo.
echo Continue program?
yesno
if errorlevel == 1 goto YES
echo You answered no!
```

The batch file tests the value of a system variable named `errorlevel`, using an `if` command, which doesn't work exactly the same as C's `if` statement. In batch files, `if expression == value` is true when `expression` is greater than or equal to `value`. (For unknown reasons, the `==` symbol in DOS batch files is equivalent to C's `>=` operator.) The batch file uses a `goto` command to jump to the label `:YES` for positive responses. Negative responses continue at the final `echo`.

You might want to store the compiled YESNO.EXE program with your other system-level utilities. Use the program as demonstrated here in any batch file that needs a yes-no response from users.

Summary

- A program performs actions by evaluating expressions and executing statements.

- Expressions are operations that programs perform.

- C's operators `*`, `/`, `+`, `-` and `%` perform arithmetic operations on operands. Relational operators `<`, `<=`, `>`, `>=`, `==`, and `!=` compare two operands. Logical operators `&&` and `¦¦` compare true-false expressions. The negation operator `!` inverts a logical expression's value.

- The increment operator `++` adds one to its operand. The decrement operator `--` subtracts one. The operators may come before or after their operand. The expressions `value++` and `++value` have the same effect on `value`.

- In addition to performing operations, all expressions have values. The value of the expression `(A = B)`, for example, equals the value assigned to `A`. The value

147

of value++ equals value's preincremented value. The value of ++value equals value's postincremented value.

- Bitwise operators &, ¦, ^, <<, >>, and ~ perform Boolean logic operations on the bits in their operands.

- Assignment operators can reduce statements like value = value + 10 to value += 10. C's assignment operators are *=, /=, +=, -=, %=, <<=, >>=, &=, ^=, and ¦=.

- All operators have fixed precedence levels. In expressions with mixed operators, subexpressions that use operators with higher precedence are evaluated before subexpressions that use operators with lower precedence.

- Expressions are evaluated in the associativity order defined for their operators. Most operators associate from left to right, but some associate in the other direction.

- Parentheses may always be used in expressions to control expression evaluation order, and therefore, to override the default precedence and associativity properties of any operator.

- Use if and if-else statements to make decisions by selecting one statement or another based on an expression's result.

- Use switch statements to simplify lengthy nested if-else constructions. Be sure to end every case in a switch with a break.

- Use while statements to create loops that execute while a condition holds true. A while loop evaluates its condition at the top, and therefore its statements may never execute if the controlling expression is initially false.

- Use do-while to create loops that execute until a condition is no longer true. A do-while loop evaluates its condition at the bottom, and therefore always executes its statements at least once.

- The for statement is probably the most popular of all statements in C. Use a for statement when you know or can calculate in advance the number of times a loop should execute.

- A break statement ends a while, do-while, or for loop immediately.

- A continue statement forces a loop to start its next iteration immediately.

- A goto statement jumps to any labeled statement. Because programs with many gotos tend to be difficult to understand and debug, the goto statement is one that's best never used.

- Programs typically end with a return statement in function main(). However, programs may also end at any time by executing exit().

Exercises

6.1 Write a program that determines whether an integer value is even or odd.

6.2 The unsigned complement of 88 decimal is 65447 (0xffa7 in hexadecimal). What value exclusive ORed with 88 gives this same answer?

6.3 Replace the for loop in Listing 6.19, ASCII.C, with an equivalent while loop.

6.4 Modify Listing 6.23, YESNO.C, to reject all responses other than Y or N.

6.5 Write a program using a loop that prompts for a value between 1 and 100. If someone types a value outside of that range, the program should display an error message and redisplay the prompt.

6.6 Using bitwise operators, write a program with an expression that limits the range of an int variable's value to 0 through 31.

6.7 Write a program that confirms whether one integer value divides evenly into another.

6.8 Modify Listing 6.15, WCOUNT.C, to count down from 10 to 1.

6.9 To convert more than one temperature, you have to rerun Listing 6.1, CELSIUS.C. Add a loop to the program, making it repeat until you want to stop.

6.10 In mathematics, a factorial *n!* of a nonnegative integer is defined by the equation

```
n! = 1 * 2 * ... * n;
```

In other words, *n!* equals the product of the integer values from 1 up to and including *n*. Write a program to calculate *n!* for any positive integer. (Note: The factorial of 0 is 1, not 0. Your program should handle this special condition.)

7

Functions: Divide and Conquer

Writing computer programs is like building bridges. You can't start pouring concrete in midair; you've got to anchor the foundations on land before you can span the water.

Functions are to C what girders, cable, and stone are to bridge builders. Similar to, but more powerful than BASIC's subroutines, functions divide a large program into manageable pieces. They can also save space by storing repeatable operations.

Top-Down Programming

To write a complex program in C, few experts merely would sit down at the terminal and start typing. Experienced programmers carve big problems into small pieces, and then, as they might assemble a jigsaw puzzle, work on a section at a time until the entire job is done.

The divide-and-conquer method is at the heart of top-down programming. Start at the top with the main goal, divide the goal into tasks, and further divide the tasks into subtasks until you have a set of relatively simple problems to solve. You then write functions for each of those problems, finishing a complex program while never working on more than a few lines of code at a time.

Programmers aren't the only ones to take advantage of top-down problem solving. A musician begins with a melody before adding the trills and completing the score. House builders start with a blueprint then dig the foundation before framing the walls. This book started with an idea, then progressed from an outline into chapters, paragraphs, and sentences. The top-down method is a natural way to tackle seemingly overwhelming problems.

In the next sections, you learn how to write functions. Then you learn how to apply functions to writing programs in a top-down fashion.

Functions that Return Void

Every C program has at least one function, main(). Most have many more functions, each with a specific task to perform. Generally, it's best to assign functions jobs that are narrowly defined. When writing functions, simplicity is the golden rule.

Listing 7.1, FNCOUNT.C, shows the correct way to write and use functions. The program counts from 1 to 10, then counts down from 10 to 1.

HINT: Although simplistic, programs such as FNCOUNT.C help demonstrate new concepts. When you encounter a programming term that you don't understand, write a similar test program. Learn to be your own teacher, using the compiler as a guide.

Listing 7.1. FNCOUNT.C (Demonstrates functions).

```
1:  #include <stdio.h>
2:
3:  void CountUp(void);
4:  void CountDown(void);
5:
```

```
 6:  main()
 7:  {
 8:    CountUp();
 9:    CountDown();
10:    return 0;
11:  }
12:
13:  void CountUp(void)
14:  {
15:    int i;
16:
17:    printf("\n\nCounting up to 10\n");
18:    for (i = 1; i <= 10; i++)
19:      printf("%4d", i);
20:  }
21:
22:  void CountDown(void)
23:  {
24:    int i;
25:
26:    printf("\n\nCounting down from 10\n");
27:    for (i = 10; i >= 1; i--)
28:      printf("%4d", i);
29:  }
```

Lines 3–4 declare function prototypes—schematics that tell the compiler the name and form of each function in a program. Study line 3 closely:

```
void CountUp(void);
```

CountUp is the function's name, which can be any unused identifier. Try to choose meaningful names for functions. That way, you can tell at a glance what the functions do. Because CountUp() performs an action, but does not return a value, the keyword void prefaces the function name. A second void inside parentheses (called the parameter list, or sometimes, the declarator list) tells the compiler that CountUp() requires no input arguments. CountUp() is the simplest kind of function: It returns nothing and requires no input.

Void functions operate like simple BASIC subroutines or Pascal procedures. They serve as commands that other program statements can give. To use a void function, simply write its name in a statement as lines 8–9 demonstrate. The statement

```
CountUp();
```

executes function CountUp(), temporarily pausing at this location in the program while the function's statements run. The empty parentheses are required to match the prototype's (void) parameter list. When the function is done (programmers say "when the function returns"), the program continues where it paused. In this case, the program executes the statement at line 9, which calls another function, CountDown(). When that function returns, line 10 executes, and the program ends.

Somewhere in the program, after the function's prototype declaration but not inside another function, every declared function must be defined. To define a function, fill it with statements to perform. CountUp()'s definition:

```
void CountUp(void)
{
  int i;

  printf("\n\nCounting up to 10\n");
  for (i = 1; i <= 10; i++)
    printf("%4d", i);
}
```

resembles main(). First comes the function's header—identical to the function prototype declared earlier, but lacking a terminating semicolon. Like the covers of a book, braces delimit the function's body, which may declare variables such as int i and execute statements such as printf() and for.

Any variables declared inside a function have temporary life spans, existing in memory only while the function is active. These are called local variables. Integer i, for example, is local to CountUp. The variable i at line 15 is distinct from the variable i at line 24.

> **NOTE:** Inside a function, you may declare one or more variables, call other functions, and execute statements. You cannot declare a function inside another function, however. This rule has no negative consequences—except, perhaps, to require a little extra work when translating programs from another language such as Pascal, which allows nested procedures and functions.

A function's prototype and header (see lines 3 and 13, 4 and 22) must match exactly, or the compiler issues an error. In large programs, this rule forces you to plan your function designs carefully and to implement your designs as planned. Any deviations between a function's declaration and its definition might cause hard-to-find bugs—errors that are easily avoided by using function prototypes.

Figure 7.1 illustrates the sequence of events that occurs when you run Listing 7.1. Calling the CountUp and CountDown functions temporarily transfers control to the statements in those functions.

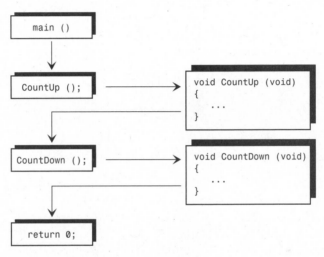

Figure 7.1. The function calls of Listing 7.1.

At each function call (see lines 8–9 in Listing 7.1), the compiled code pushes the program's current address onto the stack, an area of memory that operates like a spring-loaded bin of dishes in a restaurant. The last dish in is the first to come out—a concept often abbreviated as the acronym LIFO, for *last in, first out*. The stacked return addresses provide functions with the means to return to where they were called. Due to the stack's LIFO organization, the most recent function to be called uses (pops) the first return address from the stack. Local variables such as int i (see lines 15 and 24) are also stored on the stack. (You'll examine stacks again in Chapter 9, "Pointers.")

Any statement may call a function, including statements inside other functions. For example, insert the statement

```
CountDown();
```

between lines 19 and 20 in Listing 7.1, calling CountDown() from inside CountUp(). When you run the modified program, line 8 calls CountUp(), which calls CountDown() before returning.

To exit a function at any time, execute a `return` statement. For example, using pseudocode, the function

```
void AnyFn(void)
{
  if (condition)
    return;
  statement;
}
```

exits immediately if `condition` is true. The `statement` executes only if `condition` is false.

Functions that Return Values

A symbolic constant such as

```
#define LAST_CRT_ROW 25
```

puts a face on the arbitrary value 25. Out of context, 25 is meaningless. As a symbol, `LAST_CRT_ROW` clarifies the value's significance.

Function names also lend meaning to programs. Unlike constants, functions typically perform actions to compute their results. Operating like specialized calculators, functions can be inserted into programs to solve equations, perform mathematical operations, and return judgments.

Integer Functions

Listing 7.2, QUITEX.C, demonstrates how to use a function that returns an integer value representing true or false. The program also shows how functions can lend clarity to a program's meaning.

Listing 7.2. QUITEX.C (Demonstrates a true-false `int` function).

```
1:  #include <stdio.h>
2:  #include <ctype.h>
3:
4:  #define FALSE 0
5:  #define TRUE 1
6:  int UserQuits(void);
```

```
 7:
 8:  main()
 9:  {
10:    int i = 0;
11:    int quitting = FALSE;
12:
13:    printf("Quit example\n");
14:    while (!quitting) {
15:      i++;
16:      printf("i == %d\n", i);
17:      quitting = UserQuits();
18:    }
19:    return 0;
20:  }
21:
22:  int UserQuits(void)
23:  {
24:    int c;
25:
26:    printf("Another value? (y/n) ");
27:    do {
28:      c = toupper(getchar());
29:    } while ((c != 'Y') && (c != 'N'));
30:    return (c == 'N');
31:  }
```

If you have trouble remembering that zero means false and any nonzero value means true, define TRUE and FALSE symbols as QUITEX does at lines 4–5. The symbols can greatly simplify logical expressions.

For example, skip to line 11 in function main(). An int variable named quitting is declared and assigned the value FALSE. The symbolic constant makes the line perfectly clear, and also reminds you that quitting is to be used as a true-false flag.

HINT: When reading any program with functions, it's often easiest to start at main(), and then branch out, following the program's logic rather than reading the text line by line.

When you run QUITEX, you are asked whether you want to see another value. If you type Y for yes, the program displays the previous value plus one. If you type N, the program ends. QUITEX demonstrates a common task: prompting for yes or no responses to questions.

Study the program's while loop at lines 14–18. The loop executes while *not* quitting (in other words, while quitting's value is not true). Inside the loop, after incrementing a variable and displaying its value (actions that in another example could be replaced by any task), line 17 assigns to quitting the result of a function named UserQuits().

The prototype for the function appears at line 6. The declaration

```
int UserQuits(void);
```

specifies UserQuits() as a function that returns an int value and requires no arguments. As an int function, UserQuits() may be called at any place where an integer constant might appear. The quitting variable is also of type int (see line 11), and the statement

```
quitting = UserQuits();
```

directly assigns to quitting the value returned by function UserQuits().

Function UserQuits() is defined at lines 22–31. As always, the function's header (line 22) duplicates its declared prototype, minus a trailing semicolon. The function's body (lines 23–31), delimited with braces, contains a local variable declaration (line 24) and a few statements (lines 26–30). The statements display a prompt and pause for you to type a response. Line 28,

```
c = toupper(getchar());
```

demonstrates how expressions can call multiple functions. As in all expressions, inner parenthetical parts have priority. First, getchar() returns a character typed at the keyboard. Then, function toupper() converts that character to uppercase, leaving nonalphabetic symbols unchanged. The result is assigned to int variable c and examined at line 29. Only if c equals Y or N does the while loop relinquish control, ensuring that only those responses are permitted.

> **NOTE:** In Borland C++, getchar() is implemented as a macro, a topic discussed later in this chapter. Nevertheless, getchar() and other similar library macros are used as functions, and are therefore typically referred to as functions.

Line 30 in function `UserQuits()` returns the function's result. The statement

```
return (c == 'N');
```

evaluates the expression in parentheses, giving a true or false value depending on whether c equals N. If c does not equal N, zero is returned (meaning false); otherwise, a nonzero value is returned (meaning true).

> **NOTE:** All functions that return values must execute at least one `return` statement, or the compiler issues the warning: "Function should return a value...." Do not ignore this warning! Functions that end without explicitly returning a value actually return a value selected at random, and there's no telling what damage such a fickle function might cause.

Executing a `return` statement inside a function ends that function immediately. Consider the pseudocode

```
int Anyfunction(void)
{
  if (condition)
    return 0;
  statement;
  return 1;
}
```

If condition is true, the first `return` statement passes 0 back as the function's value, and the subsequent `statement` and second `return` do not execute. If condition is false, `statement` executes and the second `return` passes 1 back as the function's result.

Floating-Point Functions

One of the most common program interfaces is a menu of commands. Although many programs today sport fancy pull-down menus and graphical user interfaces (subjects to be covered later in this book), there's still room for a simple, but effective, menu-driven design.

As Listings 7.3, metrics.h, and 7.4, METRICS.C, demonstrate, functions and the top-down method are tailored for writing menu-driven programs. The program also demonstrates how to write and use floating-point functions. METRICS is unfinished—a good example of top-down programming in progress. The program is syntactically complete, and you can compile and run the code, but only its first command works. Let's examine the header file, metrics.h, first.

Listing 7.3. metrics.h (Header file for METRICS.C).

```
1:  #include <conio.h>
2:
3:  #define FALSE 0
4:  #define TRUE 1
5:  #define CENT_PER_INCH 2.54;
6:
7:  /* Function prototypes */
8:
9:  void DisplayMenu(void);
10: int MenuSelection(void);
11: double GetValue(void);
12: void InchesToCentimeters(void);
```

Modularize your programs by storing #include and #define directives in header files such as metrics.h. This is also a good place to declare function prototypes, such as those at lines 9–12. All these lines can be inserted into a program module, but then those declarations are available only to that module. With header files, two or more modules can use the directive

```
#include "metrics.h"
```

to gain access to the module's declarations.

> **NOTE:** It's best never to declare variables or define functions in header files. Think of header files as information folders that provide symbolic constants and describe functions that are implemented elsewhere.

The header file metrics.h declares four function prototypes. The first, DisplayMenu(), and the last, InchesToCentimeters(), are void functions. The second, MenuSelection(), returns an int value representing a selected command. GetValue() returns a double floating-point value. METRICS calls GetValue() to prompt you to enter a value to convert from one measurement to another. No function requires any arguments. The main listing follows.

Listing 7.4. METRICS.C (Menu-driven program demonstration).

```
 1:  #include <stdio.h>
 2:  #include "metrics.h"
 3:
 4:  main()
 5:  {
 6:    int quitting = FALSE;
 7:
 8:    printf("Welcome to Metrics\n");
 9:    while (!quitting) {
10:      DisplayMenu();
11:      switch(MenuSelection()) {
12:        case 1:
13:          InchesToCentimeters();
14:          break;
15:        case 9:
16:          quitting = TRUE;
17:          break;
18:        default:
19:          printf("\nSelection error!\a\n");
20:      }
21:    }
22:    return 0;
23:  }
24:
25:  /* Function implementations */
26:
27:  void DisplayMenu(void)
28:  {
29:    printf("\nMenu\n");
30:    printf("----\n");
31:    printf("1 -- Inches to centimeters\n");
32:    printf("2 -- Centimeters to inches\n");
33:    printf("3 -- Feet to meters\n");
34:    printf("4 -- Meters to feet\n");
35:    printf("5 -- Miles to kilometers\n");
36:    printf("6 -- Kilometers to miles\n");
37:    printf("9 -- Quit\n");
38:  }
```

continues

Listing 7.4. continued

```
39:
40:   int MenuSelection(void)
41:   {
42:     printf("\nSelection? (Don't press ENTER!): ");
43:     return (getche() - '0');
44:   }
45:
46:   double GetValue(void)
47:   {
48:     double value;  /* Temporary place to store value */
49:
50:     printf("\nValue to convert? ");
51:     scanf("%lf", &value);
52:     return value;
53:   }
54:
55:   void InchesToCentimeters(void)
56:   {
57:     double value;  /* Holds value passed back from GetValue */
58:     double result; /* Holds computed result */
59:
60:     printf("\nInches to Centimeters\n");
61:     value = GetValue();
62:     result = value * CENT_PER_INCH;
63:     printf("%.3f inches == %.3f centimeters\n", value, result);
64:   }
```

Line 1 includes the usual stdio.h header. Line 2 includes metrics.h, the header file from listing 7.3. metrics.h includes another header file, conio.h, which declares various console I/O functions, available only with Borland C++.

> **NOTE:** Use the CONIO functions sparingly if you plan to port your code to other compilers. These functions are not listed in standard ANSI C.

To understand how METRICS works, start by examining the statements in main(). At line 9, a while statement examines a true-false flag, quitting, looping while the flag is not true. Line 10 calls `DisplayMenu()`, a function that (as you might guess) displays a menu of commands. You have examined only a couple of statements so far, but the descriptive function names give plenty of useful clues about the program's operation.

Lines 11–20 execute a `switch` statement that selects among the program's operations. The statement's expression calls function `MenuSelection()` to obtain the user's choice. It then examines that choice in a series of `case` selectors, calling `InchesToCentimeters()` at line 13 for choice 1, setting the `quitting` flag to `TRUE` at line 16 for choice 9, and displaying a noisy error message at line 19 for any other selection. (The `\a` escape code in the `printf()` statement beeps your computer's speaker.)

Cases 2 through 8 are missing from the `switch` statement, a good illustration of top-down programming. Even though METRICS is still in development, the parts that are finished are available for testing. Later, you may want to complete the program, adding new commands one at a time until the entire job is done (see Exercise 7.6).

> **NOTE:** Top-down design can help locate errors in programs before the errors become serious. Don't postpone debugging until you're done writing a large program. Test as you go, verifying that each completed part works as expected before you move on to the next.

The program's functions are implemented at lines 27–64. Each function performs a specific job. Each begins with a header that exactly matches the prototype in metrics.h. The following notes explain a few points that might not be clear in the listing:

- `DisplayMenu()` (lines 27–38) executes a series of `printf()` statements to display the program's menu. The double `\n` escape codes in line 29 ensure that the menu begins on a new line.

- `MenuSelection()` (lines 40–44) prompts users to choose a menu command. The expression `(getche() - '0');` calls CONIO's `getche()` function to get a key press without requiring users to press Enter. Subtracting the ASCII value of the digit character `'0'` (literal characters are stored internally as ASCII values) converts the character to a decimal value from 0 to 9. Subtracting ASCII character values in the expression `'0' - '0'` gives 0. Because ASCII digits progress sequentially, `'1' - '0'` equals 1, `'2' - '0'` equals 2, and so on.

- GetValue() (lines 46–53) prompts for a value to convert, calling scanf() to read a floating-point value directly into a local variable, value. Line 52 returns this value as the function's result.

- InchesToCentimeters() (lines 55–64) displays a message and calls GetValue() (line 61), assigning the result to a local variable value. Another local variable is assigned the result of value converted from inches to centimeters, displayed by printf() at line 63. If you want to try your hand at completing METRICS, use InchesToCentimeters() as a guide to supplying the missing commands.

Other Function Types

Functions may return values of types other than integer and floating point. Any function may return any of the data types covered in Chapter 5. For example, you can declare a long int function as

```
long AnyLongFn(void);  /* long and long int are synonymous */
```

Or, you can have a function return an unsigned long value by declaring it like this:

```
unsigned long AnyUnsignedLongFn(void);
```

Most floating-point functions should probably return double, which is more accurate than float, but takes less space than long double. You can certainly declare functions of these types:

```
float AnyFloatFn(void);
double AnyDoubleFn(void);
long double AnyLongDoubleFn(void);
```

Functions may also return strings and pointers, subjects for chapters 9 and 10.

Common Function Errors

If your functions don't work correctly, the cause might be one of the following common errors:

- *No return*—The compiler warns about all nonvoid functions that lack a return statement. If a typed function ends without executing return, it returns an unpredictable value, which might cause serious bugs.

- *Skipped return*—The compiler also warns about functions that fail to execute a return statement for all possible conditions. Pay special attention to functions that have `if` statements, and be sure that a `return` statement is executed for every possible exit path.

- *No prototype*—Functions that lack prototypes are considered to return `int`, even if they are defined to return a value of another type. Don't rely on this rule. For best results, declare prototypes for all functions.

- *Side effect*—This problem is usually caused by a function that changes the value of one or more global variables. Because functions may be called by expressions, and because other statements may rely on the same variables, changes to global variables may cause hard-to-find bugs.

The first two common mistakes, forgetting or skipping a `return` statement, are easily prevented by paying attention to compiler warnings. The error is most common in code such as

```
int AnyIntFn(void)
{
  if (condition) {
    statement1;
    return 0;
  } else
    statement2;  /* ??? */
}
```

This function executes a `return` statement only if `condition` is true. If `condition` is false, `statement2` is executed normally, but the program ends without executing `return`.

The third common error, not supplying a prototype for a function, frequently shows up in older C programs. Watch for this problem, especially when updating older programs to modern ANSI C. Functions without prototypes are considered to return `int`. You may therefore remove prototypes such as the one at line 6 in Listing 7.2 without harmful effects. This practice is not recommended, however. (C++, but not C, requires prototypes for all functions.)

NOTE: Although typically written without an explicit data type, `main()` actually returns an `int` value, and could be declared as `int main()`. This fact explains why `main()` must execute a `return` statement to avoid a compiler warning. Lacking a prototype, `main()` is considered to return `int` by default. As with all typed functions, the compiler expects `main()` to execute `return` for all exit paths.

Of all the errors you might make in functions, a side effect is the most subtle, and often the most exasperating to find and correct. Listing 7.5, SIDE.C, demonstrates how side effects can get programmers in hot water. The program is supposed to display the values 1 through 19, identifying values that are even. Unfortunately, a bug causes the program to display only odd values—a quirk that needs immediate attention.

Listing 7.5. SIDE.C (Demonstrates function side effects).

```
 1:  #include <stdio.h>
 2:
 3:  int Even(void);
 4:  int Odd(void);
 5:
 6:  int i = 1;              /* ??? */
 7:
 8:  main()
 9:  {
10:    while (i < 20) {
11:      printf("%2d", i);
12:      if (Even())
13:        printf(" : is even");
14:      printf("\n");
15:      i++;                /* ??? */
16:    }
17:    return 0;
18:  }
19:
20:  int Even(void)
21:  {
22:    i++;                  /* ??? */
23:    return Odd();
24:  }
25:
26:  int Odd(void)
27:  {
28:    return (i % 2);
29:  }
```

The SIDE program displays the values (on separate lines) 1, 3, 5, 7, 9, 11, 13, 15, 17, and 19, failing to identify any even values despite the statement at lines 12–13.

The main() function attempts to count from 1 to 19, using a global variable i initialized to 1 (line 6). Because the variable is global, any statement anywhere may use i, including the statements at lines 15 and 22.

The function Even() is supposed to return true if variable i is even. The function performs its job in a most unusual fashion, incrementing i and then returning the result of another function, Odd(). Even() should therefore be true if Odd() is false, a logical if roundabout way to determine a value's evenness.

Trouble is, incrementing the global variable at line 22 affects the program's use of that same variable in the while loop (lines 10–16). By changing the global variable, function Even() causes a side effect on another part of the program. When similar problems occur in large programs, the bug can be difficult to find because its symptom (an improperly executing while loop in this case) might be far removed from the cause (the function that changes the global value.)

There are much better ways to construct functions like Even() and Odd(). As a rule, it's best never to change the values of global variables from inside functions. If you must break that rule, do so with great care and lots of documenting comments.

Local Variables

Variables declared inside functions are local to those functions. Variables declared outside functions, including main(), are global. In code such as

```
int global;   /* Global--outside of main() */
main()
{
  int local;  /* Local--inside main() (or another function) */
  ...
}
```

statements anywhere in the program may refer to global, but only statements inside of main() have access to local. If this same program defines a function such as

```
void AnyFn(void)
{
  global = 5;  /* Okay */
  local = 6;   /* ??? */
  ...
}
```

the assignment to `local` does not compile. That variable is local to `main()`, and it does not exist anywhere else.

Learning to use local variables correctly is crucial to your success with C. Let's take a closer look at some important characteristics of local variables.

Scope and Variables

Variables and other items have a property called *scope*. A variable's scope defines its range of view. Statements within the variable's scope can "see" the variable's value. Statements outside the variable's scope have no access to that variable, and therefore can't use its value. Outside of its scope, the variable might not even exist.

Figure 7.2 illustrates the concept of a local variable's scope in relation to the variable's declaring function. Function `AnyFn()` declares a local `int` variable named `i`. Because `i` is local to `AnyFn()`, only that function has access to `i`. Function `OtherFn()` is outside of the scope of `i`; thus the assignment to `i` in that function is not allowed.

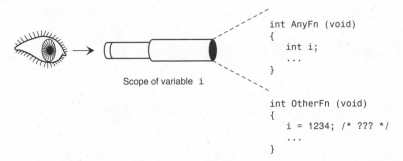

```
int AnyFn (void)
{
    int i;
    ...
}
```

```
int OtherFn (void)
{
    i = 1234; /* ??? */
    ...
}
```

Scope of variable `i`

Figure 7.2. The scope of local variable `i` extends to its declaring function.

Local Variables

Local variables are stored on the stack along with function return addresses. Conceptually, the stack grows and shrinks dynamically as statements call functions and as those functions return.

Local variables also are called *automatic variables*—a term that generally refers to an object created and destroyed automatically by the program's code. You may declare local variables by prefacing them with the storage class specifier `auto` like this:

```
void AnyFn(void)
{
  auto int i;
  i = 1;
  ...
}
```

There's little reason to use this form, however, because local variables are auto by default.

You can also declare local variables to be constant. For example, in this function:

```
void AnyFn(void)
{
  const myAge = 39;
  ...
  myAge++; /* ??? */
}
```

the initial assignment is acceptable, but increasing myAge is not allowed (I wish!).

When a function begins, it allocates space on the stack to hold its local variables. As Figure 7.3 illustrates, this space exists only while the function is active. After the function returns, it deletes the allocated stack space, thus discarding any values stored there.

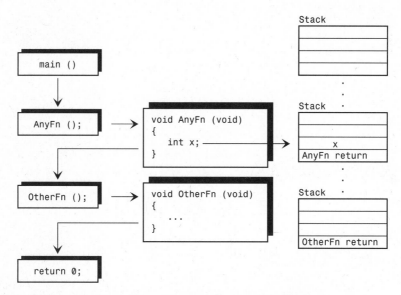

Figure 7.3. A local variable is temporarily stored on the stack.

Local variables are stored temporarily on the stack, helping functions to make efficient use of memory. If two independent functions (A and B) declare a local variable, as long as one function does not call the other (or a function that eventually calls the other), their local variables can potentially share the same stack space—not at the same time, of course. In some programs with many functions, the total space occupied by all local variables may be larger than the amount of memory available! Global variables, which take up room as long as the program remains active, make less efficient use of RAM.

Because the scope of a local variable is limited to its declaring function, two functions may declare identically named local variables without conflict. You don't have to choose different identifiers for your local variables in different functions. Forty functions may each declare a local for-loop control variable named i with no conflict. Listing 7.6, LOCAL.C, demonstrates this important concept.

Listing 7.6. LOCAL.C (Demonstrates nonconflicting local variables).

```
 1:  #include <stdio.h>
 2:  #include <conio.h>
 3:
 4:  void Pause(void);
 5:  void Function1(void);
 6:  void Function2(void);
 7:
 8:  main()
 9:  {
10:    Function1();
11:    return 0;
12:  }
13:
14:  void Pause(void)
15:  {
16:    printf("Press <Spacebar> to continue...");
17:    while (getch() != ' ') ;
18:  }
19:
20:  void Function1(void)
21:  {
22:    char s[15] = "Philadelphia\n";
23:
```

```
24:    printf("\nBegin function #1.   s = %s", s);
25:    Pause();
26:    Function2();   /* Call function2 from function1 */
27:    printf("\nBack in function #1. s = %s", s);
28: }
29:
30: void Function2(void)
31: {
32:   char s[15] = "San Francisco\n";
33:
34:    printf("\nBegin function #2.   s = %s", s);
35:    Pause();
36: }
```

Compile and run LOCAL. When prompted, press the Spacebar. The program displays

```
Begin function #1.   s = Philadelphia
Press <Spacebar> to continue...
Begin function #2.   s = San Francisco
Press <Spacebar> to continue...
Back in function #1. s = Philadelphia
```

Function1() and Function2() each declare and display a string variable s (lines 22 and 32). Function1() calls Function2() at line 26. If there was a conflict between the two local variables, Function2() would change the other function's string value, thus causing line 27 to display "San Francisco" rather than "Philadelphia."

This does not happen because, even though the two variables have the same name, their scopes extend only to their declaring functions. Each is a distinct variable with a distinct value.

The program also has a function, Pause() (lines 14–18), that you can extract for your own projects. Pause() prints the message "Press <Spacebar> to continue..." and executes the while loop

```
while (getch() != ' ') ;
```

The statement loops while the CONIO function getch() does not return a blank character. The loop performs no other action—conventionally indicated by a blank in front of the semicolon. Function getch() does not echo (display) its returned character; use the similar getche() to get a key press and echo the character on-screen.

Local variables do not retain their values between calls to their declaring functions. In this fragment:

```
void AnyFn(void)
{
  int anyInt;
  ...
}
```

variable anyInt is newly created each time AnyFn() is called. Any assignments to anyInt are not preserved between such calls. When the function returns, the value of anyInt and other local variables are thrown out with the bath water.

A less typical way to declare local variables is to insert the declaration directly in a statement block. For instance, you can declare a local variable in an if statement such as

```
if (condition) {
  int i = 1;
  ...
}
```

The integer variable i is allocated memory only if condition is true. If i is created, its scope extends to the if statement's closing brace.

Global Variables

Global variables exist for the duration of a program. They are stored in the program's data segment, and occupy space whether needed or not. As a rule, you should use global variables sparingly. They are the data equivalents of goto statements—perhaps too powerful for their own good (or ours).

You may declare global variables anywhere outside main(). The typical location is just before main(). This pseudocode

```
#include <stdio.h>
int globalint;
double globaldouble;
main()
{
  statements;
}
```

declares two global variables globalint and globaldouble. Any statement in any function can read and write these two values.

Global variables cause trouble mostly because they are so readily accessible. In a complex program, it may be difficult to avoid conflicts between functions that modify the same globals, a problem that local variables neatly avoid.

On the other hand, global variables are useful for storing large arrays and structures—topics for the next chapter. In some cases, it may be wiser to store large variables globally rather than locally, where they consume precious stack space.

Register Variables

A register variable is stored directly in a processor register. Because a register might not be available, however, you can only suggest, not demand, which of your variables should be stored in registers.

To declare a register variable, preface it with the storage class specifier `register`. The declaration must be local to a function; register variables may never be global. For example, to declare an integer variable `countDracula` and place it in a register, you can write

```
register int countDracula;
```

Values in processor registers are directly processed by machine code instructions, and their use can boost a program's performance. Use register variables for loop controllers and other small values that have a critical impact on your code's operation.

NOTE: Borland C++ can store a variable in a register whether or not it's declared with `register`. Use the `-r-` command-line switch to disable register variables—useful for debugging so that you can inspect values in memory. You can also use the IDE's **O**ptions|**C**ompiler|**O**ptimizations command. Under Register Variables, choose **N**one for no register variables, Register keyword to restrict register variables to those explicitly labeled `register`, or **A**utomatic to let the compiler choose when to put variables in registers (but still recognize the `register` specifier).

Volatile Variables

A volatile variable is a register variable's counterpart. To explicitly state that a local variable in a function is *not* to be considered for register storage, preface its declaration with the keyword `volatile` like this:

```
volatile int memoryCounter;
```

As a volatile variable, `memoryCounter` is guaranteed storage space in memory. Using `volatile` also tells the compiler to disable any optimizations it may perform for this value.

Typically, volatile variables are needed only for values that might be altered by an interrupt routine that operates independently of the program. If the compiler stores a variable temporarily in a register—one of the optimizations performed by Borland C++ to keep code running quickly—an interrupt routine can store a value in the variable's assigned memory location while the main program is using a copy of the previous value stored in a register. (Chapter 19, "Assembly Language Optimizations," covers interrupts.) Listing 7.7, REG.C, demonstrates register and volatile variables.

Listing 7.7. REG.C (Demonstrates register and volatile variables).

```
 1:  #include <stdio.h>
 2:
 3:  void UseRegister(void);
 4:  void UseVolatile(void);
 5:
 6:  main()
 7:  {
 8:    UseRegister();
 9:    UseVolatile();
10:    return 0;
11:  }
12:
13:  void UseRegister(void)
14:  {
15:    register int k;
16:
17:    printf("\nCounting with a register variable\n");
18:    for (k = 1; k <= 100; k++)
19:      printf("%8d", k);
20:  }
21:
22:  void UseVolatile(void)
23:  {
24:    volatile int k;
```

```
25:
26:    printf("\nCounting with a volatile variable\n");
27:    for (k = 1; k <= 100; k++)
28:      printf("%8d", k);
29:  }
```

To see the difference between register and volatile variables, compile the program from the DOS prompt with the command **bcc -v reg.c**. Load the program into Turbo Debugger (type **td reg**). Move the cursor to the first printf() statement inside each function and press F2 to set a breakpoint on each of the two lines. Press F9 to run. When the program pauses at the breakpoint locations, move the cursor to k and press Ctrl+I to inspect the variable's value. Press F9 to run the code up to the next breakpoint and repeat the inspection. Notice that only one variable is marked "register." The other is given an address in memory. If you have some assembly language experience, to see how the compiler treats register and volatile variables, you might also want to view the compiled code in the CPU window (Alt+VC). Press Alt+X to quit.

External Variables

Declaring a variable describes its data type. Defining a variable reserves storage space for the variable's value. A program may declare a variable any number of times (provided all such declarations agree), but may define a variable only once.

In multifile programs, functions in one module may need to refer to variables defined in another module. Variables defined outside of a module in which they are used are called external variables. There's nothing special about an external variable—it's just a global variable like any other. Consider a variable defined in module A like this:

```
int outsider;
```

If a function in another module (module B) wants to use that variable, module B's function must tell the compiler the variable is defined externally. It does so by prefacing the declaration with the storage class specifier extern:

```
extern int outsider;
```

B's function doesn't have to specify where the definition occurs, only that it takes place somewhere else in the program.

A two-file program demonstrates how to use external variables. Although simple, the program shows how functions in multiple files can refer to the same variables—an important technique in complex programs composed of many modules.

Listing 7.8, EXTERN1.C, is the main program. Type it (or locate the file on the included disk), but don't compile the code just yet.

Listing 7.8. EXTERN1.C (External variables, Part 1 of 2).

```
 1:  #include <stdio.h>
 2:
 3:  void GetFloat(void);
 4:
 5:  float f;
 6:
 7:  main()
 8:  {
 9:    GetFloat();
10:    printf("Value of float = %f\n", f);
11:    return 0;
12:  }
```

Listing 7.9, EXTERN2.C, is the program's submodule, which, in a larger project, might contain common functions shared by the main program and other modules. Type in this file or locate it on disk. To compile and link both listings from a DOS prompt, enter **bcc extern1.c extern2.c**. From the IDE, select Project|Open and enter **extern1**, creating a project file named EXTERN1.PRJ. Use Project|Add item to add EXTERN1.C and EXTERN2.C to the project. Press Ctrl+F9 to compile and run. Select Project|Close to close and save the project file.

Listing 7.9. EXTERN2.C (External variables, Part 2 of 2).

```
 1:  #include <stdio.h>
 2:
 3:  void GetFloat(void)
 4:  {
 5:    extern float f;
 6:
```

```
7:    printf("Enter floating point value: ");
8:    scanf("%f", &f);
9:  }
```

When you run EXTERN1.EXE, the program prompts you to enter a floating-point value. Enter the value, and you see it confirmed. Line 7 in Listing 7.9 displays the prompt. Line 8 reads the value you enter. The value is displayed in the main program, Listing 7.8, line 10.

Examine EXTERN1.C. Line 5 declares a global `float` variable `f`. Now look at EXTERN2.C. Line 5 declares the identical variable marked `extern` inside function `GetFloat()` (prototyped in EXTERN1.C so `main()` can call it). Even though `f` is declared inside `GetFloat()`, because the variable is tagged with `extern`, the compiler knows that `f` is defined elsewhere.

NOTE: In EXTERN2.C, `f`'s scope is local to its declaring function. Other functions in EXTERN2.C may not access `f`—unless, that is, they also declare it as `extern`. The external `f` is not automatic—its storage space is defined in EXTERN1.C, and its value is retained between function calls. Unlike automatic local variables, external variables are not created and destroyed automatically by functions.

The `extern` declaration in EXTERN2.C tells the compiler that storage space for `f` is allocated elsewhere in the program. The compiler doesn't care where that is—that's the job of the linker when it joins the separately compiled modules.

Static Variables

As mentioned earlier, local variables do not retain their values between function calls. In the function:

```
void AnyFn(void)
{
  int finalCount = 1;
  ...
}
```

variable finalCount is created on the stack and initialized to one each time the function is called. Between function calls, finalCount does not exist, and its value is not retained.

At times, functions need to define variables that keep their values between calls to the functions. One way to accomplish this goal is to declare the variables as extern in the functions, and then define them as global variables elsewhere. Declaring variables in this way, however, opens the door for any program statement to declare the same variables extern and gain access to them.

To restrict access to critical variables while allowing them to retain their values between function calls, declare them as static. Like other storage class specifiers, static prefaces a declaration:

```
void AnyFn(void)
{
  static int finalCount = 1;
  ...
}
```

Unlike common local variables, the static finalCount is not automatically created and destroyed when the function is called. The compiler allocates permanent storage for finalCount and initializes its value to one. However, the program does not repeat that initialization every time the function is called. At the first call to AnyFn(), variable finalCount equals one; thereafter, it equals whatever value it has when the function ends.

> **NOTE:** The scope of a static variable is limited to its declaring function. Functions do not have access to static variables declared in other functions.

Listing 7.10, STATIC.C, demonstrates how static variables retain their values between function calls.

Listing 7.10. STATIC.C (Demonstrates static variables).

```
1:  #include <stdio.h>
2:
3:  int Next1(void);
4:  int Next2(void);
```

```
 5:
 6:  main()
 7:  {
 8:    int i;
 9:
10:    printf("\nCalling Next1():\n");
11:    for (i = 1; i <= 10; i++)
12:      printf(" %d", Next1());
13:    printf("\nCalling Next2():\n");
14:    for (i = 1; i <= 10; i++)
15:      printf(" %d", Next2());
16:    return 0;
17:  }
18:
19:  int Next1(void)
20:  {
21:    static int value = 1;      /* Static variable */
22:
23:    return value++;
24:  }
25:
26:  int Next2(void)
27:  {
28:    int value = 1;             /* Normal local variable */
29:
30:    return value++;
31:  }
```

The program declares two int functions (lines 3–4). Two for loops (lines 11–12 and 14–15) call the functions ten times each, displaying their returned values. Running STATIC displays

```
Calling Next1():
 1 2 3 4 5 6 7 8 9 10
Calling Next2():
 1 1 1 1 1 1 1 1 1 1
```

Function Next1() declares a local static variable value (line 21), initialized to one. The value of value is returned and incremented at line 23. As the sample printout shows, value retains its value between calls to Next1(), thus causing the program to display 1 through 10.

Function Next2() declares an automatic local variable also named value. Because value is created and initialized at each function call, the return statement at line 30 always returns the same value.

Function Parameters and Arguments

Functions may receive input values from their callers. Suppose you need the cube of a value r, declared as type double. To compute the result, you can use an expression such as this:

```
r = r * r * r;
```

Suppose, however, you need the cubes of many different variables. All those expressions take space in the code, and, if strewn throughout a large program, may complicate maintenance.

Functions make ideal packages for common operations that you need to perform repeatedly. They also can collect various statements in one handy location, where you can easily modify them. Rather than write each expression individually, you can write a function that returns the cube of an argument. You might declare the function as

```
double cube(double r);
```

Function cube() returns a double value. The declaration in parentheses specifies a double value named r. This is called a parameter. If x and y are double variables, a statement can assign to x the cube of y with the assignment

```
x = cube(y);   /* x = cube of y */
```

The variable y is called an argument. Its value is passed to the cube() function's r parameter. In the function's definition:

```
double cube(double r)
{
  return r * r * r;
}
```

parameter r equals whatever argument value that a statement passes to the function. In the Cube() function, parameter r is cubed and returned as the function's result. Figure 7.4 illustrates how an argument is passed by value to a function's parameter.

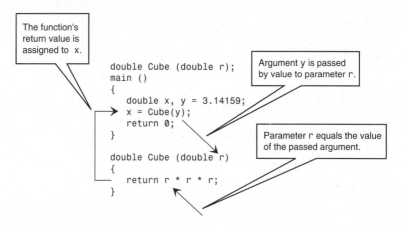

The function's return value is assigned to `x`.

Argument `y` is passed by value to parameter `r`.

Parameter `r` equals the value of the passed argument.

```
double Cube (double r);
main ()
{
    double x, y = 3.14159;
    x = Cube(y);
    return 0;
}

double Cube (double r)
{
    return r * r * r;
}
```

Figure 7.4. An argument passed to a function parameter.

> **NOTE:** Some authors use the terms "formal parameters" for a function's declared parameters, and "actual values" for arguments passed to functions. These older terms are not in vogue, but you may encounter them in articles and other books.

Functions may declare multiple parameters, in which case statements may pass them multiple arguments. Consider the problem of calculating the cost of running an appliance for a number of hours at a certain number of watts. On your electric bill, you find the cost per kilowatt hour (kwh), perhaps 0.0687. Given the kwh rate, a length of time in hours, and the appliance's power consumption in watts, the cost in dollars of running the appliance is equal to

```
cost = rate * (power * 0.001 * time);
```

To package this formula as a function, you might declare a `double` function named `Cost()` like this:

```
double Cost(double time, double power, double rate);
```

`Cost()` returns a `double` value. It declares three parameters—`time`, `power`, and `rate`—each of type `double`. Commas separate multiple parameters. The function's definition:

```
double Cost(double time, double power, double rate)
{
   return rate * (power * 0.001 * time);
}
```

applies the cost formula to the parameters, returning the result. Elsewhere in the program, statements can pass arguments to the function for processing. If `result` is type `double`, a simple statement computes the cost of running a 100-watt appliance for 10 hours at a kwh rate of 0.0687:

```
result = Cost(10.0, 100.0, 0.0687);
```

When this statement executes, inside the `Cost()` function, parameter `time` equals 10.0, power equals 100.0, and `rate` equals 0.0687. The parameters receive copies of the passed argument values—internally using the identical mechanism as assignment statements. In other words, the function begins as though it first executes

```
time = 10.0;
power = 100.0;
rate = 0.0687;
```

When passing arguments to function parameters of different types, C promotes (or demotes) the passed values in the same way it does for assignments. For example, if `i` is type `int` and `r` is type `double`, the assignment

```
r = i;
```

converts `i`'s value to `double` and assigns the result to `r`. The identical process takes place when passing argument values to function parameters of different, but compatible, types. Given the declarations

```
int intTime = 10;
int intPower = 100;
double rate = 0.0687;
double result;
```

you can pass the values of these variables to the `Cost()` function by writing

```
result = Cost(intTime, intPower, rate);
```

Variable `intTime` is promoted to a `double` value, and passed (assigned) to the function's `time` parameter. Variable `intPower` is also promoted to `double` and passed to the function's `power` parameter. Variable `rate` is already type `double`, and its value is therefore passed directly to the function's `rate` parameter.

> **NOTE:** For best results, arguments should match the function's declared parameter types. If a function declares a `long` parameter, you should pass it a `long` value. Values of compatible types (for example, passing an `int` argument to a `float` parameter) are promoted automatically, but might cause a loss of information due to roundoff errors. Incompatible types (such as a string argument passed to an `int` parameter) cause a "Type mismatch..." compiler error.

Like local variables, in the `Cost()` function, parameters `time`, `power`, and `rate` are stored on the stack. Function parameters operate identically to local variables except for one difference—they are initialized to the values passed as arguments to the function.

This is a vital concept. In a function, parameters receive copies of the values passed as arguments. If the `Cost()` function were written like this:

```
double Cost(double time, double power, double rate)
{
  power = 4.51;  /* ??? */
  return rate * (power * 0.001 * time);
}
```

the assignment to `power` is made only to that local variable. The value 4.51 is not passed back to the caller's argument. In other words, if q, x, y, and z are `doubles`, the statement

```
q = Cost(x, y, z);
```

is guaranteed not to alter the values of x, y, and z. Those variables are passed by value to the function's parameters. The function cannot reach back to the originating statement and change x, y, and z's values.

Listing 7.11, ELECTRIC.C, puts the `Cost()` function into action. The program also demonstrates how to display a row-and-column table, similar to a spreadsheet's output.

Listing 7.11. ELECTRIC.C (Displays table of electric costs per kwh).

```
1:  #include <stdio.h>
2:  #include <ctype.h>
3:  #include <conio.h>
```

continues

Listing 7.11. continued

```
 4:
 5:  #define MAXROW 12       /* Number of rows in table */
 6:  #define MAXCOL 8        /* Number of columns in table */
 7:
 8:  /* Function prototypes */
 9:
10:  void Initialize(void);
11:  double Cost(double time, double power, double rate);
12:  void PrintTable(void);
13:  int Finished(void);
14:
15:  /* Global variables */
16:
17:  double startHours;
18:  double hourlyIncrement;
19:  double startWatts;
20:  double wattsIncrement;
21:  double costPerKwh;
22:
23:  main()
24:  {
25:    do {
26:      Initialize();
27:      PrintTable();
28:    } while (!Finished());
29:    return 0;
30:  }
31:
32:  void Initialize(void)
33:  {
34:    puts("Cost of electricity\n");
35:    printf("Starting number of hours .. ? ");
36:      scanf("%lf", &startHours);
37:    printf("Hourly increment .......... ? ");
38:      scanf("%lf", &hourlyIncrement);
39:    printf("Starting number of Watts .. ? ");
40:      scanf("%lf", &startWatts);
41:    printf("Watts increment ........... ? ");
42:      scanf("%lf", &wattsIncrement);
43:    printf("Cost per kilowatt hour (KWH)? ");
44:      scanf("%lf", &costPerKwh);
45:  }
```

```
46:
47: double Cost(double time, double power, double rate)
48: {
49:   return rate * (power * 0.001 * time);
50: }
51:
52: void PrintTable(void)
53: {
54:   int row, col;
55:   double hours, watts;
56:
57:   /* Print top line of table */
58:   printf("\nHrs/Watts");
59:   watts = startWatts;
60:   for (col = 1; col <= MAXCOL; col++) {
61:     printf("%8.0f", watts);
62:     watts += wattsIncrement;
63:   }
64:   /* Print table rows */
65:   hours = startHours;
66:   for (row = 1; row <= MAXROW; row++) {
67:     printf("\n%6.1f - ", hours);
68:     watts = startWatts;
69:     for (col = 1; col <= MAXCOL; col++) {
70:       printf("%8.2f", Cost(hours, watts, costPerKwh));
71:       watts += wattsIncrement;
72:     }
73:     hours += hourlyIncrement;
74:   }
75:   printf("\n\nCost of electricity @ $%.4f per KWH\n", costPerKwh);
76: }
77:
78: int Finished(void)
79: {
80:   int answer;
81:
82:   printf("\nAnother table (y/n) ? ");
83:   answer = getch();
84:   putchar(answer);
85:   putchar('\n');
86:   return (toupper(answer) != 'Y');
87: }
```

Compile and run the program. When prompted, enter a starting number of hours (100 is good), an hourly increment (10, for example), a starting number of watts (try 4), a watts increment (2), and the cost per kwh (0.0687).

Hrs/Watts	4	6	8	10	12	14	16	18
100.0 -	0.03	0.04	0.05	0.07	0.08	0.10	0.11	0.12
110.0 -	0.03	0.05	0.06	0.08	0.09	0.11	0.12	0.14
120.0 -	0.03	0.05	0.07	0.08	0.10	0.12	0.13	0.15
130.0 -	0.04	0.05	0.07	0.09	0.11	0.13	0.14	0.16
140.0 -	0.04	0.06	0.08	0.10	0.12	0.13	0.15	0.17
150.0 -	0.04	0.06	0.08	0.10	0.12	0.14	0.16	0.19
160.0 -	0.04	0.07	0.09	0.11	0.13	0.15	0.18	0.20
170.0 -	0.05	0.07	0.09	0.12	0.14	0.16	0.19	0.21
180.0 -	0.05	0.07	0.10	0.12	0.15	0.17	0.20	0.22
190.0 -	0.05	0.08	0.10	0.13	0.16	0.18	0.21	0.23
200.0 -	0.05	0.08	0.11	0.14	0.16	0.19	0.22	0.25
210.0 -	0.06	0.09	0.12	0.14	0.17	0.20	0.23	0.26

Cost of electricity @ $0.0687 per KWH

Figure 7.5. Sample output from Listing 7.11, ELECTRIC.C.

ELECTRIC.C is the most complex program listing you've examined so far. Although more involved, the program follows the general layout of earlier examples. Lines 1–3 include header files that declare function prototypes and other items the program uses. Lines 5–6 declare two symbolic constants. To change the table's format, just alter the constants—there's no need to hunt through the program's statements to make such changes.

Lines 10–13 declare four function prototypes. Well-chosen function names make their purposes clear. Function Initialize() performs miscellaneous chores at the start of each table. You've already seen function Cost(). PrintTable() displays the program's output. Finished() returns true if the user does not request another chart.

The declarations at lines 17–21 break the rule about avoiding global variables. The values, however, aren't critical to the program's correct operation. Changing a global value in this case merely produces a different table.

> **NOTE:** It's often difficult to decide whether to make a variable global or local. Parameters such as those in ELECTRIC.C at lines 17–21 are global by nature—they affect the program's output. Variables of more narrowly defined purpose, such as while and for loop controls, should never be global.

The program's main() function is short and sweet—a good example of how functions can simplify complex programs. Lines 25–28 execute a do-while loop until Finished() returns true. Literally, the loop is designed to "do statements while not finished."

Those statements call functions Initialize() and PrintTable() (lines 26–27). Function Initialize() (lines 32–45) displays the program's name and prompts users to enter values, stored in the program's global variables.

Function PrintTable() uses for statements to display the row and column table. The statement at line 67:

```
printf("\n%6.1f - ", hours);
```

displays the value of hours as a floating-point value in six columns with one decimal place (%6.1f). The statement at line 70:

```
printf("%8.2f", Cost(hours, watts, costPerKwh));
```

calls the Cost() function, passing local variables hours, watts, and the global costPerKwh as arguments. The printf() statement displays Cost()'s return value in eight columns with two decimal places (%8.2f).

The final function in the program, Finished() at lines 78–87, prompts for a yes or no response to the question, "Another table (y/n)?" Line 83 calls CONIO's getch() function for a character, displayed by the statements

```
putchar(answer);
putchar('\n');
```

Function putchar(), prototyped in stdio.h, is useful for displaying single characters. The second line produces a newline character, causing the terminal to start a new display line.

Nameless Parameters

The Cost() function from the preceding section could be prototyped using nameless parameters like this:

```
double Cost(double, double, double);
```

Compare this declaration with the actual prototype used at line 11 in Listing 7.11:

```
double Cost(double time, double power, double rate);
```

The two forms are equivalent because the compiler ignores the parameter names time, power, and rate. In order to generate code for statements that call Cost(), the compiler needs to know only the parameter data types. The names are for your benefit and for the benefit of others who have to read your code.

Unlike the prototype, however, the function's definition must name its parameters, as shown here:

```
double Cost(double time, double power, double rate)
{
  return rate * (power * 0.001 * time);
}
```

Ascribing names time, power, and rate to the parameter types identifies the parameters so statements can use them.

You may occasionally run into a related method for ascribing parameter names, a dying relic from C's stone-age days. Using archaic C style, you could implement the Cost() function as

```
double Cost(double, double, double)      /* Header */
double time;                             /* Name 1st parameter */
double power;                            /* Name 2nd parameter */
double rate;                             /* Name 3rd parameter */
{
  return rate * (power * 0.001 * time);
}
```

Unlike ANSI C, the function header does not specify parameter names. Rather, the three lines that follow (before the function's opening brace) assign identifiers to the declared parameters. Statements in the function can then refer to the parameters by those names.

The archaic and modern styles generate identical code, but the old way is disappearing like a dinosaur sinking into a tar pit. Borland C++ supports the older form solely for the purpose of maintaining existing C programs. Don't use this format in your own code.

Pointer Parameters

This chapter would not be complete without at least mentioning pointer parameters. Pointers are the addresses of other variables. If you see a parameter written with an asterisk (int *value, for example), value is a pointer to an integer variable stored somewhere in RAM.

Chapter 9, "Pointers," covers pointers, so it's pointless to discuss pointer parameters here, except to confirm their existence. Never fear; I clear up this mystery soon.

Parameter Modifiers

Keep in mind that parameters are treated internally as preinitialized local variables. In the function

```
void AnyFn(int x)
{
   int y;
   ...
}
```

integers x and y are both stored on the stack, and are limited in scope to statements in AnyFn(). Integer x receives an initial value from the statement that calls AnyFn(); integer y must be initialized in the function itself.

Because parameters are local variables, they may be declared using the register, volatile, and const modifiers you examined earlier. If you declare a function like this:

```
void AnyFn(const int x, const int y, register int value);
```

statements may pass argument values to parameters x and y, but the const modifiers prevent function statements from changing those values. Integer value is placed in a register if one is available.

> **NOTE:** Arguments to register parameters are passed on the stack. Inside the function, the argument values are copied to registers if any are free; otherwise, they are treated as normal parameters. Register parameters are passed in registers to functions only when using the -pr command-line option, the equivalent IDE command (Options|Compiler|Entry/Exit Code, **R**egister Calling Convention), or the _fastcall modifier as explained in Chapter 20, "DOS Tools and Techniques."

Although rarely necessary, you can also declare volatile parameters. For example, in the function prototype

```
void AnyFn(volatile int value);
```

the value parameter is guaranteed never to be optimized or placed in a register. This is important when an external event such as an interrupt modifies value, which must therefore be stored in memory, not in a register unknown to the interrupt routine.

Recursion: What Goes In Must Come Out

Recursion may seem like a difficult scientific term, something straight out of nuclear physics or brain surgery. Recursion is actually a common everyday event. Literally, a recursion is a "return." When you peer into a mirror with another mirror behind, you see an endless series of images returning themselves to infinity. Each image is a recursion of light from the one before.

In programming, recursion occurs when a function calls itself one or more times. The return addresses of such calls are stacked in memory like reflections in facing mirrors, until some event causes the recursions to stop. Some algorithms are naturally recursive. For example, the factorial of a value equals the product of its preceding sequential values. The factorial of 5 equals 1 * 2 * 3 * 4 * 5, or 120. You can write a recursive factorial function like this:

```
double Factorial(int number)
{
  if (number > 1)
    return number * Factorial(number - 1);
  return 1;
}
```

When you understand this small function, you'll understand all there is to know about recursion. First, consider the essential fact: The factorial of *n* equals *n* times the factorial of *n – 1*. (The factorial of 4 equals 4 * 3 * 2 * 1. The factorial of 3 equals 3 * 2 * 1. So, the factorial of 4 must equal 4 times the factorial of 3.)

The Factorial() function uses recursion to implement this self-defining algorithm. The statement:

```
d = Factorial(8);
```

sets d equal to 40,320 (8 * 7 * ... * 1). As you can see, factorials grow big quickly.

Factorial() returns a double value and declares a single int parameter, number. The function begins with an if statement that examines the value of number. If number is greater than one, the function returns the value of number multiplied by the factorial of that number *minus* one. The statement expresses in programming terms the factorial algorithm.

Figure 7.6 illustrates the successive levels for the expression factorial(5).

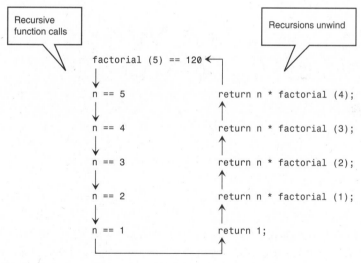

Figure 7.6. Recursive function calls for the expression factorial(5).

Inclusively Recursive Functions

Because they call themselves directly, functions such as Factorial() are inclusively recursive. A simple program demonstrates the key properties of an inclusively recursive function. Enter Listing 7.12, RECOUNT.C. Compile and run it. On-screen, you see a count of values from 1 to 10. Before reading on, try to figure out how RECOUNT uses recursion to perform this simple job.

Listing 7.12. RECOUNT.C (Counts from 1 to 10 using recursion).

```
 1:  #include <stdio.h>
 2:
 3:  void Recount(int top);
 4:
 5:  main()
 6:  {
 7:    Recount(10);
 8:    return 0;
 9:  }
10:
11:  void Recount(int top)
12:  {
13:    if (top > 1)
14:      Recount(top - 1);
15:    printf("%4d", top);
16:  }
```

Line 7 calls function Recount(), which uses recursion to count from 1 to 10 (admittedly, the hard way of solving a simple problem).

Line 13 examines parameter top. If greater than one, the function calls itself recursively at line 14, passing top - 1 as the new argument. When top reduces to 0 (as it evidently must), line 15 displays the value of top.

Notice that ten values are displayed; therefore, the printf() statement at line 15 *must* have executed ten times. This demonstrates that each recursive call returns in kind, thus executing printf() once for each time Recount() is called.

> **NOTE:** If a recursive function declares any local variables, those variables are newly created on each level of recursion. If function `A()` declares a local variable `i`, when `A()` calls itself recursively, a brand new `i` is created on the stack.

Mutually Recursive Functions

A less common form of recursion occurs when one function calls another, which eventually ends up calling the first function again. If you position three mirrors so that mirror 1 reflects mirror 2, which reflects mirror 3, which again reflects mirror 1, you'd have a graphic illustration of mutual recursion. Kids call them kaleidoscopes. In fact, you might call mutual recursion "the house-of-mirrors effect."

Mutual recursion is useful for writing co-routines—functions that depend on each other, but don't necessarily require one function to be called before the other. Listing 7.13, ONFIRST.C, demonstrates mutual recursion in a somewhat frivolous way. Named for Abbott and Costello's famous and comically recursive "Who's on First?" routine, ONFIRST displays the alphabet. Before continuing, can you figure out how?

Listing 7.13. ONFIRST.C (Displays alphabet using mutual recursion).

```
 1:  #include <stdio.h>
 2:
 3:  void A(int c);
 4:  void B(int c);
 5:
 6:  main()
 7:  {
 8:    A('Z');
 9:    puts("");   /* Starts a new line */
10:    return 0;
11:  }
12:
```

continues

Listing 7.13. continued

```
13:  void A(int c)
14:  {
15:    if (c > 'A')
16:      B(c);
17:    putchar(c);
18:  }
19:
20:  void B(int c)
21:  {
22:    A(--c);
23:  }
```

The main program starts the recursive ball rolling at line 8, calling function A() with the argument 'Z'. Function A() examines its parameter c. If c is alphabetically greater than 'A', the function calls B(), which immediately calls A(), passing the predecessor of c. That causes A() to again examine c, and again call B(), until c equals 'A'. At this point, the recursion unwinds, executing putchar() 26 times at line 17, and displaying the alphabet, one character at a time.

This effect demonstrates an important characteristic of recursion. Parameter values are stored on the stack for each recursive entry in the function. This observation also implies that recursion is potentially costly in stack space. In fact, unless the recursion ends decisively, too many recursive function calls can exhaust the stack, causing an overflow error, and usually halting the program.

> **NOTE:** All recursive functions may be written without using recursion, although not always as simply. Also, function calls take time, and nonrecursive functions may run faster than their recursive equivalents. See Exercise 7.10.

Function Modifiers

An external function is available outside of the module in which it is defined. Functions are external by default. Any statement in one module may call the functions defined in any other.

To restrict a function's use to the module defining that function, precede its header with the keyword static. A static function's scope is limited to the module that defines the function.

For an example of static functions, modify the EXTERN1.C program (Listing 7.8), changing line 3 to

```
static void GetFloat(void)
```

After saving the modified file, compile the program from the DOS prompt with the command **bcc extern1.c extern2.c**. Rather than success, you receive the error "Undefined symbol 'GetFloat'...." Function GetFloat() is now static, and is not available externally. Even though file EXTERN1.C supplies a prototype, it cannot call the restricted function.

You may also declare functions as extern. For example, GetFloat()'s header could be written

```
extern void GetFloat(void)
```

Because functions are external by default, an explicit extern modifier is unnecessary.

You may also preface function declarations with a few other modifiers, briefly explained here. You'll meet some of these again in later chapters:

pascal	When a statement calls a function, the statement pushes argument values on to the stack. With the pascal calling convention in effect, before returning, functions are responsible for removing from the stack any such argument values.
cdecl	The direct opposite of the pascal calling convention, a cdecl function (the default) makes the calling statement responsible for removing from the stack any arguments passed to functions.
_fastcall	Passes function arguments in registers rather than on the stack (see Chapter 20, "DOS Tools and Techniques).
interrupt	Declares a function as an interrupt service routine. Cannot be used with near, far, or huge. See Chapter 19, "Assembly Language Optimizations."
near	Declares a function that can be called only from within the same memory segment. The default for tiny, small, and compact memory models (see Chapter 20, "DOS Tools and Techniques").

far   Declares a function that can be called from any memory
             segment. The default for medium and large memory models.

huge   Same as a far function. The default for the huge memory
             model.

Macros

Earlier, you learned how to create symbolic constants using #define. The line

```
#define GOODYEAR 1950
```

associates the symbol GOODYEAR with the text 1950. GOODYEAR is a macro—a symbol that, when compiled, expands into something else.

Macros can be far more complex than simple one-for-one symbolic constants. In fact, some library functions are written entirely as macros. For example, the statement

```
c = getchar();
```

appears to call function getchar(), prototyped in stdio.h. In Borland C++ (but not necessarily all ANSI C compilers) getchar() is declared as the macro

```
#define getchar()  getc(stdin)
```

The compiler's preprocessor replaces every occurrence of the macro getchar() with getc(stdin), which gets a character from the standard input file, stdin. Function getchar() is just a stand-in. In reality, there is no such function! You also may be surprised to learn that, although getc() looks like a function, it too is actually a macro, declared in stdio.h as

```
#define getc(f) \
  ((--((f)->level) >= 0) ? (unsigned char)(*(f)->curp++) : \
   _fgetc (f))
```

As you can see, this is a mouthful and a half. Fortunately, there's no need to learn the built-in cryptic macro language of C. Just be aware that some functions are actually macros, expanded at compile time into something else.

One of the most useful supplied macros is assert(), declared in assert.h. It performs a simple task—halting a program with an error message.

To use assert(), add #include <assert.h> to your program module. It's handy for debugging. For example, suppose that you suspect an error is caused by an int variable waterLevel falling below a defined high mark. To test for that condition, insert a statement such as

```
assert(waterLevel < 10000);
```

If the program executes this statement, and if waterLevel is greater than or equal to 10000, the program halts with an error message similar to

```
Assertion failed: waterLevel < 10000, file name.c, line 13
Abnormal program termination
```

The assert() macro expands into an if statement. If the test condition in assert()'s parentheses is false (0), the program is halted by calling stdlib.h's abort(). If the test condition is true (nonzero), then the program continues normally.

After debugging your code, you do not have to delete the assert() statements. Leave them in, and begin the module with the lines

```
#define NDEBUG
#include <assert.h>
```

The first line defines a symbol NDEBUG, which causes the assert.h header to declare assert() as a do-nothing macro. Because the macro now expands into nothing, the compiler effectively removes all assert() statements, thus disabling debugging statements from the code. If problems develop later, simply remove #define NDEBUG and recompile to reenable all assertions.

is...() Macros

Use the is...() character classification macros to determine the nature of ASCII character values. For example, this statement:

```
if (isalpha(c))
  statement;
```

executes statement only if int c contains an alphabetic ASCII value. Other similar macros, most of which have obvious meanings, include isdigit(), islower(), and ispunct(). See Chapter 22, "Functions and Examples," for complete descriptions of all is...() macros.

Variable-Argument Macros

You can use the variable-argument macros, va_arg(), va_end(), and va_start(), to write functions that can accept a variable number of arguments. The standard printf() is a good example of such a function—statements can pass to printf() one, two, or more argument values.

Many C programmers rely heavily on variable-argument macros, but I suggest avoiding them if possible. The macros are difficult to use correctly, and if you are just getting started with programming, writing functions with variable numbers of arguments is a technique best postponed until later. Chapter 22, "Functions and Examples," explains how to use the macros and includes a sample program listing (look up va_arg() in that chapter).

Debugging Macros

Macros are difficult to debug because they expand into other instructions, which are immediately compiled. Borland C++ lacks a separate preprocessor that, in some C compilers, expands macros and creates an intermediate text file, giving you the opportunity to investigate the expansions and track down errors.

To see how macros expand, use the separate CPP.EXE utility. This utility is supplied with Borland C++ but is not used during normal compilation. The utility, introduced in Chapter 5, "Data: What a Program Knows," performs the job of a more traditional C preprocessor.

CPP.EXE is easy to use. For example, to preprocess Listing 7.11, ELECTRIC.C, from a DOS prompt, enter the command **cpp electric.c**. The result is a file ELECTRIC.I with all include files included, all macros expanded, leading white space stripped, line numbers and include file pathnames added, and various other preliminary operations performed just as they will be when using the real compiler.

If you are following along, examine the end of ELECTRIC.I at function Finished(). As you can see, the supposed calls to function putchar() are actually expanded into other commands. This happens because, even though putchar() looks like and is used as a function, it's implemented in Borland C++ as a macro.

> **HINT:** From a DOS prompt, enter **cpp** for a list of available options that you can use with the utility.

Conditional Compilation

The #define NDEBUG directive in the preceding section defines a symbol NDEBUG that has no associated text. The symbol, however, is still defined in the sense that the compiler now recognizes NDEBUG's existence, a fact that other directives may determine.

This fact leads to another useful macro technique called conditional compilation. Use the #ifdef directive to test whether a symbolic constant exists. For example, suppose you define a symbol named DEBUGGING:

```
#define DEBUGGING
```

You can then insert directives such as

```
#ifdef DEBUGGING
   statement;
#endif
```

If a symbol named DEBUGGING is defined, the compiler compiles statement. Otherwise, statement is ignored. An #endif directive ends the preceding #ifdef and tells the compiler to continue compiling normally.

To select between two sections, use #else like this:

```
#ifdef DEBUGGING
   statement1;
#else
   statement2;
#endif
```

Always remember to terminate conditional compilation directives with #endif. Remember, these are instructions to the compiler; they are not program statements and do not generate code. They merely affect which sections of a program the compiler processes.

For multiway #if directives, use #elif, the rough equivalent of an if-else statement:

```
#ifdef DEBUGGING
   statement1;
#elif BETATESTING
   statement2;
#else
   statement3;
#endif
```

Simply defining or not defining symbols DEBUGGING and BETATESTING affect which statements are compiled. Clever selection of symbols and conditional directives can be used to create modules that can be drastically altered simply by defining or not defining certain symbols. You can even nest directives, defining symbols if they are not already defined:

```
#ifndef BUFFER
  #define BUFFER 255
#endif
```

This defines a symbol BUFFER as 255 only if that symbol is not already defined elsewhere. The directive #ifndef stands for "if not defined." To undefine a symbol, you can write

```
#undef BUFFER
```

which might be useful in modules that need to redefine BUFFER to be something else.

Preventing Multiple Includes

Conditional compilation macros are often useful in large programs to prevent including the same header file more than once. If the header file is named calc.h, start with the following two lines:

```
#ifndef __CALC_H
#define __CALC_H  /* Prevent multiple #includes */
```

and end on the last line with

```
#endif   /* __CALC_H */
```

The first line states that, if a symbol named __CALC_H is *not* defined, compile all lines up to #endif. If there is no such symbol, the file is compiled normally. If __CALC_H is defined, however, *all text is ignored between the top and bottom lines.* Because the second line defines __CALC_H, if the same file is included again, its declarations are ignored. The double leading underscores in __CALC_H are optional, but they are recommended to help prevent potential conflicts with other identifiers. You could use any symbol name, but the filename (with the period replaced by an underscore) is convenient.

This trick can speed compilation by preventing several modules in a large program from recompiling function prototypes and other declarations that are already known due to another module's including the header file.

Summary

- The top-down technique is a natural way to tackle big problems by dividing them into smaller problems, which are more easily solved. In programming, apply the top-down method by dividing goals into subgoals, then writing functions that carry out narrowly defined tasks until the entire program is done.

- Void functions operate like BASIC subroutines. Statements can call void functions as commands.

- Functions may also return values of any type. A `double` function, for example, returns a value of type `double`.

- Variables declared inside functions have local scope, and may be accessed only by statements inside the same functions.

- Local variables are stored on the stack and are allocated space each time the function is called. Local variables do not retain their values between calls to their declaring functions. Static variables do retain their values and are allocated space only the first time a function is called.

- Global variables exist for the duration of a program, and occupy fixed storage space for that time.

- Register variables are placed in fast processor registers, if available. Volatile variables are never placed in registers.

- Declaring variables as `extern` allows modules to access variables defined globally in other modules.

- Functions may declare parameters. Statements pass values as arguments to function parameters, providing input data to the function.

- Recursion is what happens when a function calls itself. Mutual recursion occurs when a function calls another function, which calls the original function again. Some event must eventually stop the successive recursions; otherwise, a stack overflow error is certain to halt the program. Self-referential algorithms (such as the steps to compute a value's factorial) are naturally programmed recursively. Recursive functions may operate more slowly and consume more stack space than their nonrecursive equivalents.

- Some functions may actually be written as macros, symbols created by #define that are expanded at compile time into something else. C has a full macro language, which is cryptic, and best learned only after mastering the C language. You don't have to learn how to write macros to use supplied ones such as assert(), which is useful for debugging.

- Related to macros are several conditional compilation directives such as #ifdef and #elif. Use these along with #defined symbols to select between sections of a program at compile time. Conditional directives are useful also for preventing multiple modules from wastefully including the same header files.

Exercises

7.1   Add parameters to the functions in Listing 7.1, FNCOUNT.C. In your program, the statement CountUp(10) should display 1 through 10; the statement CountDown(100) should display 100 down to 1, and so on.

7.2   Write and test a function to compute the volume of a sphere, using the formula

$$V_{sphere} = \frac{4\pi r^3}{3}$$

7.3   A harmonic series is defined by the expression 1 + 1/2 + 1/3 + ... + 1/n. Write a function that returns the number of terms required to satisfy the expression [harmonic series] > limit.

7.4   Write and test a function that prompts for a value and limits a user's response to within a stated minimum and maximum range.

7.5   Fuses and circuit breakers are rated by how many amperes it takes to break the connection. Ohm's law says that current measured in amperes equals voltage divided by resistance. Write a program that uses a function named Amps() to compute the amount of current for a given voltage and resistance.

7.6   Finish Listing 7.4, METRICS.C. Use the top-down method to write the final program one stage at a time. (Hints: There are 0.3937 inches in one centimeter, 0.3048 meters in one foot, 3.28084 feet in one meter, 1.609 kilometers in one mile, and 0.621 miles in one kilometer.)

7.7 Write a function named InRange() that accepts three arguments: a minimum integer value, a maximum integer value, and a test value. The function should return true if the test value is within the stated range; otherwise, the function should return false. Also write a program that tests your function.

7.8 Write a function named Error() that displays a message based on an integer error code argument.

7.9 Modify your Error() function from Exercise 7.8 to keep track of how many times the function is called. The function should halt the program after reaching a certain maximum number of errors. You may not use any global variables in your solution.

7.10 Write a nonrecursive version of the factorial function described in the section that discussed recursion.

Data Structures

Imagine a database program that stores its information piecemeal in variables. What a mess that would be! Variables like brendasName and robertsZipCode would clutter the code while complicating general purpose operations such as sorting and printing.

Fortunately, C doesn't require programmers to work so hard. The language provides two data types, arrays and structures, that can help you to organize data.

Arrays

Arrays collect variables of the same type. You can have an array of integers, an array of floating-point values, or an array of characters. Arrays can store as few as one element, or as many as memory allows.

To declare an array, begin with a variable declaration, and end with an integer value in square brackets. The value represents the number of elements in the array. For example, this declaration:

```
int scores[100];
```

declares an array named scores capable of holding 100 int values. If scores is a global variable, its elements are zeroed. If the array is local to a function, its values are uninitialized.

Alone, the array name, scores, represents the *entire* data structure. After the array name, add brackets and a subscript to form an expression that refers to an individual element. The subscript can be any integer expression. For instance, this statement:

```
scores[5] = 89;
```

assigns the value 89 to the sixth element in scores. Why the sixth? Because the first element of an array is indexed with the subscript 0. This statement:

```
scores[0] = 100;
```

gives the array's first element a perfect score.

NOTE: Because the first subscript of an array is 0, for any declaration of the form T name[N]; where T is a type, the allowable subscript values range from 0 to N – 1. Using a subscript outside of that range—name[-2] for example—refers to a memory location that does not belong to the array, a dangerous practice that can cause serious bugs.

Array elements are stored sequentially in memory. Each element holds one value of the array's declared type. As Figure 8.1 shows, an array is like a stack of boxes. The expression scores[0] represents the first box—that is, the element at the array's lowest memory address. The next value at scores[1] immediately follows the first. Then come scores[2], scores[3], scores[4], and so on. The last element in this 100-integer array is at scores[99].

Subscripts can be any integer expressions—constants, variables, function results, and others. Given an int variable index, you might use the following statements to display the sixth value in scores:

```
index = 5;
printf("Score = %d\n", scores[index]);
```

An expression such as scores[index] is treated as a variable of the array's declared data type. The expression scores[index] can therefore be used anywhere an int variable can.

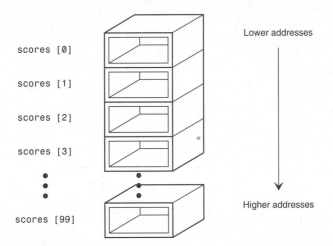

Figure 8.1. An array is like a stack of boxes. Subscript expressions in brackets refer to individual elements in the array.

Sorting Arrays

Programs can perform all sorts of operations on values stored in arrays. Typically, a `for` loop uses a control variable as an index to zip through an array's elements. Here is one way to display each element in `scores`:

```
for (index = 0; index < 100; index++)
  printf("scores[%d] == %d\n", index, scores[index]);
```

Sorting array elements into an orderly sequence is another common operation. There are dozens of ways to sort arrays—too many to explain here. Listing 8.1, SORTER.C, demonstrates one of the best and most famous sorting algorithms, called the Quicksort. Invented by C. A. R. Hoare, the technique is generally regarded as the fastest available for putting an array's ducks in a row.

Listing 8.1. SORTER.C (Sorts an array using the Quicksort algorithm).

```
1:  #include <stdio.h>
2:  #include <stdlib.h>
3:  #include <time.h>
```

continues

Listing 8.1. continued

```
 4:
 5:  #define ARRAYSIZE 100
 6:
 7:  void FillArray(void);
 8:  void DisplayArray(void);
 9:  void Quicksort(int left, int right);
10:  void SortArray(int n);
11:
12:  int array[ARRAYSIZE];   /* Array of integers */
13:
14:  main()
15:  {
16:    FillArray();
17:    DisplayArray();
18:    SortArray(ARRAYSIZE);
19:    DisplayArray();
20:    return 0;
21:  }
22:
23:  /* Fill global array with values taken at random */
24:  void FillArray(void)
25:  {
26:    int i;
27:
28:    srand((unsigned)time(NULL));        /* Randomize */
29:    for (i = 0; i < ARRAYSIZE; i++)     /* Fill array */
30:      array[i] = rand();
31:  }
32:
33:  /* Display contents of array before and after sorting */
34:  void DisplayArray(void)
35:  {
36:    int i;
37:
38:    puts("");  /* Start new display line */
39:    for (i = 0; i < ARRAYSIZE; i++)
40:      printf("%8d", array[i]);
41:  }
42:
```

```
43:  /* Quicksort algorithm by C. A. R. Hoare */
44:  void Quicksort(int left, int right)
45:  {
46:    int i = left;
47:    int j = right;
48:    register int test = array[(left + right) / 2];
49:    int swap;
50:
51:    do {
52:      while (array[i] < test) i++;
53:      while (test < array[j]) j--;
54:      if (i <= j) {
55:        swap = array[i];
56:        array[i] = array[j];
57:        array[j] = swap;
58:        i++;
59:        j--;
60:      }
61:    } while (i <= j);
62:    if (left < j) Quicksort(left, j);
63:    if (i < right) Quicksort(i, right);
64:  }
65:
66:  /* Sort n elements in global array */
67:  void SortArray(int n)
68:  {
69:    if (n > 1) Quicksort(0, n - 1);
70:  }
```

The array declaration at line 12 specifies a global array of 100 int values. The array is named array, but it could be named something else. Using the symbolic constant ARRAYSIZE for the array declaration and other program statements makes future modifications easier. If the number of elements changes, a quick adjustment to line 5 is all that's needed to update the program.

Function FillArray() (lines 24–31) uses a for loop to fill the sample array with values selected at random. In another setting, this function might read values from disk or prompt for users to enter values to sort. Line 28 calls the srand() function, prototyped in stdlib.h to seed a random number generator. Using the current time as the seed ensures a different sequence of values for each run.

Line 30 indexes `array` using the subscript `i`. Similarly, line 40 indexes `array` to display its values. Loops such as these are common methods for processing all the elements of an array.

The `Quicksort()` function at lines 44–64 implements the Quicksort algorithm. The technique partitions the target array into left and right subarrays, and then compares selected elements against a test value, which is best kept in a register to boost performance (see line 48). Elements found to be in the wrong partitions are exchanged (see lines 55–57), thus moving them closer to their final destinations. The array is repeatedly partitioned by the recursive function calls in lines 62–63 until the elements are sorted. For large, unordered sets of data, this partition-exchange method tends to minimize the number of elements moved, while using simple and fast array subscripting to scan the array.

> **NOTE:** For a detailed description of the Quicksort algorithm, see Donald E. Knuth's *Sorting and Searching*, Vol. 3 of *The Art of Computer Programming* (Addison-Wesley, 1973). See also Chapter 9, "Pointers," and Chapter 22, "Functions and Examples," for discussions of the `qsort()` library function prototyped in stdlib.h. The library function employs a number of refinements, and it probably runs faster (and may take less memory) than the textbook model listed here.

Initializing Arrays

It's often useful to preinitialize arrays with values rather than use program statements to assign values to array elements. To preinitialize an array, declare it as usual, but follow the declaration with a list of constant values in braces. For example, this declaration:

```
int digits[10] = {0, 1, 2, 3, 4, 5, 6, 7, 8, 9};
```

creates a 10-integer array named `digits` and assigns the values 0 to 9 to each successive array element from `digits[0]` to `digits[9]`. Commas separate multiple elements listed in braces. The declaration has the same effect as

```
int i, digits[10];  /* index i and array of ten ints */
for (i = 0; i < 10; i++)
  digits[i] = i;
```

Notice how the first line declares an index i and an array of ten integers.

You can also have the compiler automatically calculate the size of an array. The declaration

```
int digits[] = {0, 1, 2, 3, 4, 5, 6, 7, 8, 9};
```

creates an array of ten integers as before. In this case, however, the empty brackets instruct the compiler to allocate the exact amount of space needed to hold the listed elements.

When specifying an explicit array count, you do not have to supply values for every array position. For example, the declaration

```
int digits[10] = {0, 1, 2, 3, 4};
```

creates an array of ten integers, but initializes only the first five. The remaining elements at subscripts 5 through 9 are zeroed if the array is global or set to unpredictable values if the array is local to a function.

Specifying too many elements is an error. The compiler coughs out "Too many initializers" if you feed it

```
int digits[5] = {0, 1, 2, 3, 4, 5, 6};
```

Preinitialized arrays are commonly used for holding values that are known when you write the program. Uninitialized arrays are useful for storing test results or other data elements that can be indexed by subscripts.

Listing 8.2, DICE.C, uses initialized and uninitialized arrays. The program simulates the roll of a pair of dice and saves the results in an array. The program then applies a standard statistical technique, known as the chi-square test, as a benchmark for the random number generator in Borland C++. Compile and run the program. When prompted, specify how many rolls to simulate—between 10,000 and 50,000 for best results.

Listing 8.2. DICE.C (Uses a random number benchmark).

```
1:  #include <stdio.h>
2:  #include <stdlib.h>
3:  #include <time.h>
4:
5:  void Initialize(void);
6:  long GetNumThrows(void);
```

continues

Listing 8.2. continued

```
 7:  void ThrowDice(long numThrows);
 8:  double sqr(double r);
 9:  double ChiSquare(long numThrows);
10:  void DisplayResults(long numThrows);
11:
12:  #define MAX 13   /* Indexes 0 to 12; 0 & 1 wasted */
13:
14:  double count[MAX];
15:  double prob[MAX] = {
16:    0.0, 0.0, 1.0 / 36, 1.0 / 18, 1.0 / 12, 1.0 / 9, 5.0 / 36,
17:    1.0 / 6, 5.0 / 36, 1.0 / 9, 1.0 / 12, 1.0 / 18, 1.0 / 36
18:  };
19:
20:  main()
21:  {
22:    long numThrows;
23:
24:    printf("\nDice -- A random number benchmark\n\n");
25:    numThrows = GetNumThrows();
26:    if (numThrows > 0) {
27:      ThrowDice(numThrows);
28:      DisplayResults(numThrows);
29:    }
30:    return 0;
31:  }
32:
33:  long GetNumThrows(void)
34:  {
35:    char answer[128];
36:
37:    printf("How many throws? ");
38:    gets(answer);
39:    return atol(answer);
40:  }
41:
42:  void ThrowDice(long numThrows)
43:  {
44:    long i;
45:    int k;
46:
```

```
47:    randomize();
48:    for (i = 1; i <= numThrows; i++) {
49:      k = (1 + random(6)) + (1 + random(6));
50:      count[k]++;
51:    }
52:  }
53:
54:  double sqr(double r)
55:  {
56:    return r * r;
57:  }
58:
59:  double ChiSquare(long numThrows)
60:  {
61:    double v = 0.0;
62:    int i;
63:
64:    for (i = 2; i < MAX; i++)
65:      v += ((sqr(count[i])) / prob[i]);
66:    return ((1.0 / numThrows) * v) - numThrows;
67:  }
68:
69:  void DisplayResults(long numThrows)
70:  {
71:    int i;
72:
73:    printf("\nDice    Proba-    Expected    Actual  \n");
74:    printf("Value    bility    Count      Count   \n");
75:    printf("=====================================\n");
76:    for (i = 2; i < MAX; i++) {
77:      printf("%5d%10.3f%12.0f%10.0f\n",
78:        i, prob[i], prob[i] * numThrows, count[i]);
79:    }
80:    printf("\nChi square == %f\n", ChiSquare(numThrows));
81:  }
```

Lines 14 and 15–18 declare two arrays, count and prob, each capable of holding 13 double values. A symbolic constant, MAX, is defined at line 12 so other statements can easily limit subscripts to the range 0 to MAX - 1. (Because dice values range from 2 to 12, array positions 0 and 1 are not used.)

Lines 15–18 declare and preinitialize the prob array with the probabilities for each possible combination of the dice. Assuming the dice are on the up and up, there are three ways that 4 can be made—3+1, 2+2, and 1+3. Because there are 36 (6*6) different pairings of two six-sided dice, the probability of rolling 4 is 3/36 (three ways out of thirty-six combinations), or 1/12. The expressions at lines 16–17 compute these probabilities, which are assigned to the prob array. The subscripts indicate the dice values, thus prob[4] equals the probability of rolling a 4.

Function ThrowDice() (lines 42–52) runs the simulation. To produce different results on each new run, a call to randomize() seeds the random number generator—similar to calling srand() as SORTER.C demonstrated earlier. Remove the call to randomize() to reproduce the same random sequence for each run—a useful technique that stabilizes the program's output and can help you debug code that uses random numbers. When using the randomize() function, include the time.h header as shown at line 3.

The for loop at lines 48–51 cycles once for each simulated shake, rattle, and roll. Line 49 assigns to local integer k the expression

```
(1 + random(6)) + (1 + random(6))
```

The expression random(N) returns a value limited to a positive integer modulo N; therefore, random(6) returns a value from 0 to 5 selected at random. Adding one gives a value in the range 1 to 6—the possible values from a single die. In this program, it's vital to call random() twice to give values at random from 2 to 12. The expression 2 + random(11) would also generate values in that range, but would equalize the probabilities of each value, destroying the test (to say nothing of the house percentage). To see this effect, change line 48 to

```
k = 2 + random(11);  /* ??? */
```

The actual reported counts for all dice combinations are now more or less equal. Be sure to change the statement back before continuing.

Line 50 executes count[k]++, which increments the arrayed value at subscript k, equal to the value of the current dice roll. After the for loop runs its course, count holds the number of rolls for each possible value.

Running the program displays these values, the probabilities, the expected number of rolls, and the actual counts stored in the count array. Figure 8.2 shows a sample run of 50,000 dice throws—the equivalent of one solid week of crap shooting at Vegas. (Two weeks if you take time to sleep.)

```
Dice -- A random number benchmark
How many throws? 50000
  Dice       Proba-    Expected     Actual
  Value      bility    Count        Count
===============================================
    2        0.028      1389         1365
    3        0.056      2778         2798
    4        0.083      4167         4156
    5        0.111      5556         5509
    6        0.139      6944         7074
    7        0.167      8333         8494
    8        0.139      6944         6942
    9        0.111      5556         5413
   10        0.083      4167         4105
   11        0.056      2778         2772
   12        0.028      1389         1372

Chi square == 11.279080
```

Figure 8.2. Sample output from Listing 8.2, DICE.C.

As you can see from Figure 8.2, and from your own trials, the actual counts differ slightly from the expected values. This should come as no surprise—after all, if dice were perfectly predictable, there'd be few profitable casinos in the world.

To analyze the program's output, and thus determine whether the output from the random number generator falls within expected tolerances, a statistician might apply a chi-square test using the actual counts compared with the expected probabilities. Written X^2, the chi-square formula is

$$V = \frac{1}{n} \sum_{1 \le i \le K} \left(\frac{o_i^2}{P_i}\right) - n$$

Even if you don't have a background in statistics, you should be able to convert such formulas into functions. In English, the formula defines the chi-square as 1 divided by the number of independently obtained samples *(n)* times the summation for *i* equals 1 to *K* of the observed data squared (o_i^2) over the expected probability (p_i) minus the number of samples.

Substituting the number of throws for *n*, the range of dice values for *i*, the actual counts for *o*, and the probabilities for *p*, function ChiSquare() (lines 58–66) returns 11.279080 for the data in Figure 8.2. Compare the function statements with the chi-square formula to see how the formula is converted to C.

To use the function, look up the result in a chi-square distribution table, found in most elementary statistics books. (Table 8.1 shows a portion of a typical table.) Table rows *(v)* represent degrees of freedom, equal to one less than the number of categories in the original data. For your dice throws, there are 11 categories in the range of possible values 2 to 12. One less than that is 10—the row to examine.

Table 8.1. Chi-square distribution (sample).

v	99%	95%	75%	50%	25%	5%	1%
9	2.088	3.325	5.899	8.343	11.39	16.92	21.67
10	2.558	3.940	6.737	9.342	12.55	18.31	23.21
11	3.053	4.575	7.584	10.34	13.70	19.68	24.73

From Table 8.1, DICE should report a chi-square value between 6.737 and 12.55 about 50% of the time. A value greater than 23.21 should occur no more often than about 1% of the time (that is, once out of every 100 program runs). A value less than 3.940 would indicate nonrandomness. (Substituting the expected dice counts for the actual counts gives a chi-square value of 0.000, indicating that the data is unbelievably good.) The program's reported value of 11.279080 falls within the table's midrange, suggesting that the random number generator probably is working—at least the results compare favorably with real-world statistical observations.

> **NOTE:** For best results, run the DICE program at least three times. A bad chi-square value has a low statistical probability, but does not necessarily indicate a faulty random number generator.

The DICE program uses array indexing to display its output in a nicely formatted table. Lines 76–79 execute a for loop with a complex printf() statement to align
output into columns. The string

```
"%5d%10.3f%12.0f%10.0f\n"
```

formats four variables—one decimal integer and three floating-point values. The
integer is aligned in five columns; the floating-point values are aligned in 10, 12, and
10 columns respectively, with the first value given three decimal places and the others
none.

Complex printf() formatting strings such as this one are easier to write and
debug as separate statements. For example, when developing the program, instead of
the printf() statement at lines 77–78, you might use these lines:

```
printf("%5d", i);
printf("%10.3f", prob[i]);
printf("%12.0f", prob[i] * numThrows);
printf("%10.0f", count[i]);
printf("\n");
```

After debugging the individual output statements, combine them into one as
shown in the listing.

Using *sizeof* with Arrays

If anyArray is the name of an array, the expression sizeof(anyArray) equals the
number of bytes the array occupies in memory. The expression sizeof(anyArray[0])
equals the size of a single element.

When preinitializing arrays, you can use sizeof() to find the number of elements, a technique that can help eliminate a common mistake—assigning a value to
a nonexistent array element. Instead of writing

```
#define MAX 5
int anyArray[MAX] = {0, 1, 2, 3, 4};
```

you can write

```
int anyArray[] = {0, 1, 2, 3, 4};
#define MAX (sizeof(anyArray) / sizeof(anyArray[0]))
```

The first line declares an array of unspecified size and assigns initial element
values. Because the array size is not given in brackets, the compiler allocates exactly as

much space as needed to store the listed values. The second line defines a symbolic constant MAX equal to the size of the array in bytes divided by the size of one element. Because array elements are stored sequentially in memory, MAX must equal the number of elements in the array. Although resembling a function call, sizeof() expressions reduce to constants. Because only constants are involved, the compiler folds (reduces) the division to a single constant value—there is no performance penalty for using this safe method for computing array sizes.

Using this technique can help prevent a common error caused by assigning too few elements to an array. For example, the compiler does not complain about declarations such as

```
#define MAX 5
int anyArray[MAX] = {0, 1, 2, 3};
```

The value anyArray[4] is not assigned an explicit value (this fact is easy to miss) and could cause a serious bug.

Aligning Array Elements

With word alignment enabled (use the -a command-line option or the IDE Options|Compiler|Code Generation command and switch on Word alignment), the first array element is aligned at an even address. Except for early PCs with 8088 processors, word alignment results in better performance because the processor can read aligned 16-bit words faster than it can read values divided into two bytes starting at odd-numbered addresses.

Subsequent array elements butt up against preceding ones. If you want to have all array values aligned, the entire array must be aligned and each element must have an even number of bytes.

Using Constant Arrays

To prevent changes to array elements, preface the array declaration with const. This technique can be especially useful when programs are maintained by different people who may be tempted to subvert a module's design rules. The declaration

```
const int anyArray[] = {0, 1, 2, 3, 4};
```

creates a five-element array named `anyArray`. Because of the `const` modifier, any statement, such as the following, that attempts to change an array value does not compile:

```
anyArray[4]++;   /* ??? */
```

Character Arrays

Strings are arrays of `char` values. You've already seen several examples of strings, although thinking of them as arrays may seem new. The declaration

```
char name[128];
```

declares a character array `name` with room for 128 `char` elements. As you can with all arrays, you can use subscript expressions to refer to individual elements—in this case, elements of type `char`. If `c` is a variable of type `char`, the statement

```
c = name[3];
```

assigns the fourth character in `name` to `c`. The first character in a string is at `name[0]`, thus `name[3]` refers to the fourth, not the third, element.

To preinitialize a string, assign a literal string in quotes:

```
char composer[] = "Paul McCartney";
```

As with all array declarations, the empty brackets instruct the compiler to calculate the amount of room needed to store the initialized value. However, strings are terminated by an invisible null byte (ASCII 0), and therefore, the `composer` string in this sample is 15 bytes long (not 14).

You may also initialize strings using the conventional array-initialization techniques described earlier. If you follow this course, however, you are responsible for adding the terminating null byte. This declaration:

```
char myABCs[] = "ABC";
```

is exactly equivalent to

```
char myABCs[] = {'A', 'B', 'C', 0};
```

You can use the `sizeof()` trick explained earlier to define a constant equal to the length of a preinitialized string variable. For example, these lines:

```
char author[] = "Robertson Davies";
#define AUTHORSIZE (sizeof(author))
```

declare a string author initialized to "Robertson Davies" and also declare a symbolic constant AUTHORSIZE equal to the array's size. Because characters occupy single bytes, there's no need to divide sizeof(author) by the size of an individual element as in the preceding examples. When using this technique with strings, be aware that AUTHORSIZE equals the size of the array in bytes, including the null terminator. The AUTHORSIZE symbolic constant does not represent the length of the string.

You may specify an array size in a declaration along with an initial value. The declaration

```
char cook[128] = "Julia Child";
```

declares a string named cook with room for 128 characters, and assigns to the array the string "Julia Child" plus a terminating null character. As with all arrays where the initializer is smaller than the declared size, the remaining array bytes are zeroed if the array is global, or set to unpredictable values if the array is local to a function.

To display a string, pass it to the printf() function. For example, these two lines create, initialize, and display a string named company:

```
char company[] = "Borland International";
printf(company);
```

Generally, however, printf() is best reserved for solving complex formatting problems. To display a string and start a new line, it's usually easier to call puts() from stdio.h like this:

```
char processor[] = "80486";
puts(processor);
```

To display a string and not start a new line, use the conio.h cputs() instead:

```
cputs("I wish my PC had an ");
cputs(processor);
puts(" CPU");
```

These three lines display the string "I wish my PC had an 80486 CPU." (Be sure to add #include <conio.h> before using cputs().) Of course, you can use printf() to do the same:

```
printf("I wish my PC had an %s CPU\n", processor);
```

You may pass character arrays to function parameters, and functions may pass character arrays back to statements. You can write a DisplayString() function like this:

```
void DisplayString(char string[])
{
  printf(string);
}
```

Then, elsewhere in the program, you can declare a string variable and pass it to the function:

```
char title[] = "Alice in Wonderland";
DisplayString(title);
```

Despite appearances, however, the `title` string's characters are not passed to `DisplayString()` directly on the stack. In a large program with many functions and string parameters, passing large amounts of data on the stack (typically limited to a single 64K segment) may lead to a stack overflow error. Borland C++ therefore passes the *addresses* of strings and other arrays to functions, not the actual characters or other array elements.

NOTE: See Chapter 10, "Strings," for more information about strings and string functions.

Multidimensional Arrays

Arrays such as `int count[100]` are one-dimensional—their values are stacked in one column. A single subscript is all that's needed to reference any arrayed element.

Arrays can also have two or more dimensions. The most common multidimensional arrays store values in row-and-column format, conceptually resembling a spreadsheet's layout or a checkerboard's squares. Another good example of a two-dimensional array, or matrix, is a PC row-and-column display. In a program, you could represent the character positions of the display as

```
char display[25][80];
```

Conceptually, `display` is a 25-by-80 character matrix. It is an array of arrays—specifically, a 25-element array of 80-byte strings. The statement

```
puts(display[4]);
```

displays the fifth 80-character row. The expression `display[0]` references the first row. The statement

```
putc(display[4][2]);
```

displays the third character in the fifth row.

Using Two-Dimensional Arrays

Two-dimensional arrays are stored in memory in row-and-column order. To access array elements, use double sets of brackets. If `c` is a variable of type `char`, the statement

```
c = display[4,2];   /* ??? */
```

does not compile, as it might in some other programming languages that support multidimensional arrays. However, the statement

```
c = display[4][2];
```

although a little more difficult to type, does the job. Here's another sample declaration:

```
int multi[7][8];
```

This declares array `multi` as an array of seven eight-integer arrays, although it's convenient to view the structure as a seven-by-eight matrix, illustrated in Figure 8.3.

Using Three-Dimensional Arrays

Despite the conceptual view of multidimensional arrays as matrixes, in memory array elements are physically stacked one after the other. This fact is true no matter how many dimensions an array has. For example, the three-dimensional array

```
int cubic[10][20][4];
```

declares `cubic` as an array of integers. The array has a height of 10, a width of 20, and a depth of 4. Literally, `cubic` is an array of arrays of arrays. Conceptually, it's a three-dimensional structure.

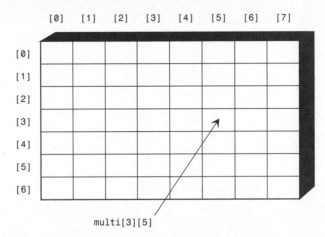

Figure 8.3. A two-dimensional array is stored as an array of arrays, but it is conveniently treated as a row-and-column matrix.

In all such multidimensional arrays, if you scan the arrayed elements in memory order, the leftmost subscript varies slowest and the rightmost varies fastest. In other words, to display the values of cubic in memory-storage order, you can use the nested for loop

```
for (i = 0; i < 10; i++)
  for (j = 0; j < 20; j++)
    for (k = 0; k < 4; k++)
      printf("%d\n", cubic[i][j][k]);
```

> **NOTE:** Multidimensional arrays grow very large very quickly. A ten-by-ten-by-eight array of two-byte integers occupies 1600 bytes. Adding a fourth dimension of ten values takes that total up to 16,000 bytes.

Initializing Multidimensional Arrays

It's often useful to preinitialize multidimensional arrays. As an example, consider an array of strings that appears to have only one dimension, but actually has two.

Listing 8.3, MONTHS.C, shows a typical use for a preinitialized multidimensional array—storing the names of the months.

Listing 8.3. MONTHS.C (Stores month names in an array).

```
1:  #include <stdio.h>
2:
3:  #define NUMMONTHS 12
4:
5:  char months[NUMMONTHS][4] = {
6:    "Jan", "Feb", "Mar", "Apr",
7:    "May", "Jun", "Jul", "Aug",
8:    "Sep", "Oct", "Nov", "Dec"
9:  };
10:
11: main()
12: {
13:   int month;
14:
15:   for (month = 0; month < NUMMONTHS; month++)
16:     puts(months[month]);
17:   return 0;
18: }
```

The months array declared at line 5 stores 12 three-character strings, each terminated with a null byte. The expression months[0] references *Jan;* months[1] equals *Feb;* and so on. Such expressions make months appear to have only one dimension, but it actually has two. The expression months[1][2], for example, references the character *b* in the char array *Feb.*

> **NOTE:** The string techniques described here require all strings in arrays to have the same lengths. In Chapter 9, "Pointers," you learn how to use pointers to create arrays of strings with different lengths.

Listing 8.4, CHESS.C, uses multidimensional arrays to display a sample chessboard. (Unfortunately, the program knows only a single move, and it doesn't actually play chess.) CHESS also demonstrates how the typedef keyword can help make programs more readable.

Listing 8.4. CHESS.C (Displays a sample chessboard as a multidimensional array).

```
 1:  #include <stdio.h>
 2:
 3:  /* Chess-piece symbols. Stored in board array */
 4:  #define NUMPIECES 13
 5:  typedef enum piece {
 6:    EMPTY, WPAWN, WROOK, WKNIGHT, WBISHOP, WQUEEN, WKING,
 7:    BPAWN, BROOK, BKNIGHT, BBISHOP, BQUEEN, BKING
 8:  } Piece;
 9:
10:  /* New name for an int */
11:  #define NUMRANKS 8
12:  typedef int Ranks;
13:
14:  /* Names of files */
15:  #define NUMFILES 8
16:  typedef enum files {
17:    A, B, C, D, E, F, G, H
18:  } Files;
19:
20:  /* The 8-by-8 playing surface with initial pieces */
21:  Piece board[NUMRANKS][NUMFILES] =
22:  {
23:    {WROOK, WKNIGHT, WBISHOP, WQUEEN, WKING, WBISHOP, WKNIGHT, WROOK},
24:    {WPAWN, WPAWN,   WPAWN,   WPAWN,  WPAWN, WPAWN,   WPAWN,   WPAWN},
25:    {EMPTY, EMPTY,   EMPTY,   EMPTY,  EMPTY, EMPTY,   EMPTY,   EMPTY},
26:    {EMPTY, EMPTY,   EMPTY,   EMPTY,  EMPTY, EMPTY,   EMPTY,   EMPTY},
27:    {EMPTY, EMPTY,   EMPTY,   EMPTY,  EMPTY, EMPTY,   EMPTY,   EMPTY},
28:    {EMPTY, EMPTY,   EMPTY,   EMPTY,  EMPTY, EMPTY,   EMPTY,   EMPTY},
29:    {BPAWN, BPAWN,   BPAWN,   BPAWN,  BPAWN, BPAWN,   BPAWN,   BPAWN},
30:    {BROOK, BKNIGHT, BBISHOP, BQUEEN, BKING, BBISHOP, BKNIGHT, BROOK},
31:  };
32:
33:  /* String array of abbreviated piece names */
34:  char pieceNames[NUMPIECES][3] =
```

continues

Listing 8.4. continued

```
35:  {
36:      "..", "wP", "wR", "wN", "wB", "wQ", "wK",
37:             "bP", "bR", "bN", "bB", "bQ", "bK"
38:  };
39:
40:  /* Function prototypes */
41:  void MovePiece(Ranks r1, Files f1, Ranks r2, Files f2);
42:  void DisplayBoard(void);
43:
44:  main()
45:  {
46:    DisplayBoard();  /* Before move */
47:    MovePiece(2, D, 4, D);
48:    printf("\nPawn to Q4 (d2-d4)\n");
49:    DisplayBoard();  /* After move */
50:    return 0;
51:  }
52:
53:  void MovePiece(Ranks r1, Files f1, Ranks r2, Files f2)
54:  {
55:    board[r2 - 1][f2] = board[r1 - 1][f1];
56:    board[r1 - 1][f1] = EMPTY;
57:  }
58:
59:  void DisplayBoard(void)
60:  {
61:    Ranks r;
62:    Files f;
63:
64:    for (r = NUMRANKS; r > 0; r--) {
65:      printf("\n%d: ", r);
66:      for (f = A; f <= H; f++)
67:        printf(" %s", pieceNames[board[r - 1][f]]);
68:    }
69:    printf("\n    a  b  c  d  e  f  g  h\n");
70:  }
```

Even without studying CHESS closely, you can easily spot the two-dimensional chessboard array. Rather than use cryptic literal numbers, lines 21–31 are written entirely with meaningful symbols. Strive for this same degree of readability in your own code. Months or years later when you have to update your programs, you will appreciate the care you took to make your programs readable.

The `typedef` keyword can help clarify programs by introducing new symbols that stand for data type declarations. Similar in use to storage class specifiers such as `extern` and `static`, `typedef` creates a data type alias. Contrary to popular myth (and the keyword's misleading name), `typedef` does *not* define a new data type. Similar in purpose to `#define`, `typedef` merely associates a data type declaration—usually a complex one with many parts—with a simpler name.

Use `typedef` like this:

```
typedef declaration Alias;
```

This creates a symbol `Alias` that can be used in place of `declaration`. The `Alias` is typically capitalized, although this is not a hard-and-fast rule. Line 12 in CHESS uses `typedef` to provide a new name for `int`:

```
typedef int Ranks;
```

There's only one reason for taking this step: clarity. Because the symbol `Ranks` is now equivalent to `int`, `Ranks` can be used in place of `int`, thus making various other declarations crystal clear. For example, in the function prototype in line 41:

```
void MovePiece(Ranks r1, Files f1, Ranks r2, Files f2);
```

parameters `r1` and `r2` are obviously chessboard rank numbers. In reality, they are just `int`s, but their new `typedef` data type name clarifies their purpose.

NOTE: Various system-dependent declarations use `typedef` to ensure portability as well as clarity. A good example is `size_t`, declared in stddef.h as `typedef unsigned size_t;`. The `size_t` symbol, in other words, is simply an alias for `unsigned`. Another ANSI C installation could declare `size_t` differently—as `int` or `long`, for instance—and all uses of that symbol would automatically adjust to the new meaning.

You can also use `typedef` with more complex data types. Lines 5–8 show a typical case, declaring alias `Piece` for the enumerated symbols used to identify empty chessboard squares and playing pieces. The declaration takes advantage of the case-sensitive nature of C. Writing

```
typedef enum piece {
  ...
} Piece;
```

declares an alias `Piece` for `enum piece {...}`. The capitalized name is the alias; the lowercase version of that same name is part of the original data type declaration. Because C is case-sensitive, the two symbols are distinct. Given this `typedef`, you can declare a variable named `anyPiece` of the alias type `Piece`:

```
Piece anyPiece;
```

which has the same meaning as

```
enum piece anyPiece;
```

Lines 16–18 use a similar upper- and lowercase naming trick to declare an alias `Files` for the enumerated chessboard files A through H. In the program, the letters A through H are not characters; they are single-character enumerated symbols. Internally, A equals 0, B equals 1, and so on.

Armed with these symbols, lines 21–31 declare the two-dimensional chessboard, using symbolic constants `NUMRANKS` and `NUMFILES` in the declaration to clarify the meanings of the rows and columns. The declaration also demonstrates how to preinitialize a two-dimensional array, using nested braces.

One other multidimensional array appears at lines 34–38, which declare a string array of piece names. The string `".."` represents an empty square. The order of elements in the `pieceNames` array matches the enumerated piece names. Thus, `pieceNames[WROOK]` is the name of a white rook; `pieceNames[BQUEEN]` is the name of a black queen.

These easy-to-understand relationships between array elements and subscripts make the code easy to write and maintain. Function `MovePiece()` (lines 53–57), for instance, clearly assigns a piece from one square to another.

Function `DisplayBoard()` is equally clear. Two `for` loops at lines 64 and 66 display the playing surface. There are almost no literal values here; except for 0 and 1, everything is symbolic, making explanatory comments unnecessary.

Line 67 shows an example of a nested array subscript. The expression `pieceNames[board[r - 1][f]]` refers to the string name for the piece at the board position with rank `r - 1` and file `f`.

> **HINT:** Many expert programmers suggest never typing any literal numeric values other than 1 and 0 in program statements. All other literal values should have associated symbolic constants.

Passing Arrays to Functions

You can pass arrays to functions. Suppose, for example, you need to sum the values stored in an array. Given the declarations

```
#define MAX 100
double data[MAX];
```

you can declare a function that accepts an array of `double` values as a parameter. You might prototype the function as

```
double SumOfData(double data[MAX]);
```

Even better, you can leave the brackets blank and add a second parameter that indicates the size of the array:

```
double SumOfData(double data[], int n);
```

To `SumOfData()`, you can then pass array arguments along with an integer `n` that informs the function how many values the array contains. For example, this statement displays the sum of the values in the array `data`:

```
printf("Sum == %lf\n", SumOfData(data, MAX));
```

The `SumOfData()` function is not difficult to write. A simple `for` loop sums the array's elements, and a `return` statement passes the result back to the caller:

```
double SumOfData(double data[], int n)
{
  double sum = 0;

  while (n > 0)
    sum += data[--n];
  return sum;
}
```

Passing Strings to Functions

A similar array-parameter technique is useful for passing character strings to functions. Consider these declarations of a symbolic constant and a function that accepts a string parameter and a length value:

```
#define MAXLEN 128
void AnyFn(char s[], int len);
```

Parameter s is a character array of unspecified length. Parameter len tells the function how many bytes s occupies (which might be different from the number of characters stored in s). Given these declarations, you can write

```
char president[MAXLEN] = "George Washington";
AnyFn(president, MAXLEN);
```

The first line declares and initializes a char array named president, capable of storing up to MAXLEN - 1 characters plus a null terminating byte. The second line passes the string to the function.

As mentioned earlier, to conserve stack space, C passes the addresses of arrays to functions, not to the actual arrayed contents. The array's elements stay in their original locations. This rule holds true for character arrays as well. As Figure 8.4 illustrates, passing array arguments by address conserves stack space, but it means that changing elements in the function also affects the original data. The same is not true for parameters of other types, such as int and double. Because copies of these simpler values are passed to function parameters, changing values inside the function does not affect the original arguments.

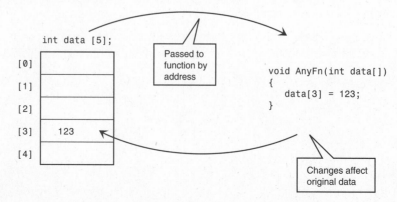

Figure 8.4. Array arguments are passed by address to function parameters.

Listing 8.5, GETSTR.C, demonstrates a common technique for passing character arrays to functions, and also shows that modifying array elements in functions affects the original argument values. Compile and run the program. When prompted, enter your name or another string. The program includes a function that limits your response to nine characters—a handy technique for designing data-entry screens and similar programs where responses from users must be limited to a maximum length.

Listing 8.5. GETSTR.C (Limits string input to a specified length).

```
 1:  #include <stdio.h>
 2:
 3:  void GetString(char s[], unsigned maxlen);
 4:
 5:  main()
 6:  {
 7:    char name[10];
 8:
 9:     printf("Enter your name (9 character limit): ");
10:     GetString(name, 10);
11:     printf("Result == %s\n", name);
12:     return 0;
13:  }
14:
15:  void GetString(char s[], unsigned maxlen)
16:  {
17:    char buffer[128];  /* Place to hold raw input */
18:    int i;             /* Array index */
19:
20:     gets(buffer);                       /* Get raw input */
21:     if (maxlen != 0)                    /* If maxlen > 0 */
22:       --maxlen;                         /*   reduce maxlen by 1 */
23:     i = buffer[maxlen] = 0;             /* Init i; put null in buffer */
24:     while ((s[i] = buffer[i]) != 0)     /* Loop till null found */
25:       i++;                              /*   incrementing index */
26:  }
```

Line 3 prototypes a GetString() function, which declares a char array s of unspecified length. A second parameter, maxlen, tells the function the size of the array in bytes.

The function uses these parameters at lines 15–26. A 128-byte local `buffer` (line 17) holds raw keyboard input. Line 20 calls the library function `gets()` to read characters into `buffer`. Lines 21–22 subtract one from `maxlen` (if it's not zero), and assign a null byte (0) to `buffer[maxlen]`, thus truncating any input that is longer than requested. A `while` loop at lines 24–25 copies characters from `buffer` to parameter `s`, stopping at the first null found. This may be the null inserted by `gets()`, or the one inserted at line 23, whichever comes first.

The `while` loop at lines 24–25 may seem odd at first. Remember, expressions have values; therefore, the expression `(s[i] = buffer[i])` copies one character from `buffer[i]` to `s[i]`. As evaluated, however, the expression also has the value of the copied character. The `while` loop tests this value, continuing until the expression equals zero.

This observation leads some programmers to use a popular (but potentially dangerous) trick. In various C programs, you might see similar loops abbreviated as

```
while (s[i] = buffer[i])  /* ??? */
  i++;
```

If the value of the loop's controlling expression is not zero, the loop continues. (Nonzero values are true, remember.) The explicit comparison operator `!=` that appears in line 24 is redundant. However, the only advantage gained from using this trick is a few less characters to type. The two expression forms produce identical code. For clarity, use the complete form shown at line 24 in Listing 8.5.

> **NOTE:** A `while` loop expression such as `(s[i] = buffer[i])` causes the compiler to warn about a "Possibly incorrect assignment...." After all, the compiler seems to reason, you might have meant to type `(s[i] == buffer[i])`, comparing two characters rather than assigning one to the other. No warning is given for the equivalent long form `((s[i] = buffer[i]) != 0)`, which is perfectly clear—to programmers and to the compiler.

Passing Multidimensional Arrays to Functions

When passing multidimensional arrays as arguments to function parameters, you must specify the minimum information that the compiler needs to translate subscript expressions into memory addresses. In a two-dimensional array, the compiler needs to know how many columns there are in order to calculate the address of the elements at the beginning of each row.

This fact has important consequences when declaring multidimensional arrays as function parameters. Given the symbolic constants ROWS and COLS, equal to the number of rows and columns in a two-dimensional array, you can declare a function with an array parameter like this:

```
void AnyFn(int data[ROWS][COLS]);
```

or, you can specify only the number of columns:

```
void AnyFn(int data[][COLS]);
```

Given either declaration, the compiler can translate the expression data[n][m] into an address. If the number of columns were unknown, however, subscript n would be ambiguous. (In other words, the meaning of a row is undefined unless you specify how many columns a row has.) The following line does not compile:

```
void AnyFn(int data[][]);  /* ??? */
```

Ideally, there would be a way to pass the array's dimensions to AnyFn, but C has no such feature. When passing two-dimensional arrays to functions, you must specify at least the number of columns. Usually, you should also pass another parameter that specifies the number of rows in a specific array argument:

```
void AnyFn(int data[][COLS], int numRows);
```

The numRows parameter tells the function how many rows are in the array data, a technique that allows arrays with different numbers of rows to be passed to the same function. The global COLS constant informs the compiler and the function of how many columns are in one row. Because the number of columns is fixed, a parameter for this value is not needed.

Listing 8.6, MULTIPAR.C, demonstrates how to design and use multidimensional array function parameters. When you run the program, you see two tables, with different numbers of rows, proving that the program's functions can handle arrays of different sizes.

Listing 8.6. MULTIPAR.C (Passes multidimensional arrays to functions).

```
 1:  #include <stdio.h>
 2:  #include <stdlib.h>
 3:  #include <time.h>
 4:
 5:  #define COLS 8
 6:
 7:  void FillArray(int data[][COLS], int numRows);
 8:  void DisplayTable(int data[][COLS], int numRows);
 9:
10:  main()
11:  {
12:    int data1[7][COLS];
13:    int data2[4][COLS];
14:
15:    randomize();
16:    FillArray(data1, 7);
17:    DisplayTable(data1, 7);
18:    FillArray(data2, 4);
19:    DisplayTable(data2, 4);
20:    return 0;
21:  }
22:
23:  void FillArray(int data[][COLS], int numRows)
24:  {
25:    int r, c;
26:
27:    for (r = 0; r < numRows; r++)
28:      for (c = 0; c < COLS; c++)
29:        data[r][c] = rand();
30:  }
31:
32:  void DisplayTable(int data[][COLS], int numRows)
33:  {
34:    int r, c;
35:
36:    for (r = 0; r < numRows; r++) {
37:      printf("\n");
38:      for (c = 0; c < COLS; c++)
```

```
39:         printf("%8d", data[r][c]);
40:     }
41:     printf("\n");
42: }
```

Functions `FillArray()` and `DisplayTable()` specify only the number of columns in their `data` array parameters. The actual number of rows is passed as a separate `int` parameter, `numRows`. This device gives both functions the advantage of being able to accept variable-size arrays, as long as the number of columns remains fixed.

Lines 15–19 insert random values into two sample arrays, one with seven rows and the other with four. The functions use the global `COLS` constant in `for` loops along with the `numRows` parameters to subscript the `data` arrays.

Structures

A structure forms a shell around one or more values of the same or different types. To declare a structure, start with the `struct` keyword, and follow with an identifier and a list of variables (called members) in braces. End the structure and each member declaration with a semicolon.

Structures can be complex data types with many members, or they can be simple, such as this two-member model:

```
struct coordinate {
  int x;
  int y;
};
```

This `coordinate` structure has two integer members, named `x` and `y`, which might represent data points for a chart or graph.

A structure declaration is merely a schematic that describes the structure's components. To use a structure, you first have to declare a variable of the structure's type:

```
struct coordinate point;
```

The variable `point` is a single entity that contains two integers. Use dot notation to refer to the structure's members. For example, to assign values to the two integer components of `point`, you can write:

235

```
point.x = 5;
point.y = 6;
```

Technically, the dot in dot notation is called the structure-member operator. It informs the compiler of how and where to find a structure's member. The expression `point.x` refers to the `int` member in the structure `point`, and can therefore be used wherever an `int` variable is allowed.

Member names must be unique within the same structure, but they do not conflict with names used in other contexts. It would not be an error, for instance, if a program declared the `coordinate` structure and also declared other variables named `x` and `y`.

A structure could have just one member, although in that case, there would be little justification for the structure's existence. The simplest practical structure, therefore, has two members.

There are different ways to declare structures and structure variables. You can use the forms just described, or you can follow the structure declaration's closing brace with a variable identifier:

```
struct coordinate {
  int x;
  int y;
} point;
```

This declares the `coordinate` structure and allocates space for a structure variable `point`, all in one easy motion.

You must precede structure variable declarations with the `struct` keyword, even though you declared the structure data type earlier. This does not compile:

```
coordinate p;  /* ??? */
```

You might think that, having declared `coordinate`, the compiler should recognize the name. It does, but only if you include the `struct` keyword:

```
struct coordinate p;
```

> **NOTE:** This is one of the rare C rules that C++ relaxes. As you'll discover in Part 3, "Programming with C++," in C++ you do not have to use the `struct` keyword to declare variables of a structure data type.

Declare multiple structure variables as you do variables of other types, separating identifiers with commas:

```
struct coordinate var1, var2, var3;
```

To avoid having to type `struct` over and over, you might want to use `typedef` in the structure declaration:

```
typedef struct coordinate {
  int x;
  int y;
} Coordinate;
```

As explained earlier, `typedef` does not create a new data type—it just associates a type with a simpler alias, which is usually capitalized. When declaring structures with `typedef`, you may omit the structure tag, and just write

```
typedef struct {
  int x;
  int y;
} Coordinate;
```

Either way, alias `Coordinate` represents a structure data type with two integer members. You can use the alias to declare a variable:

```
Coordinate point;
```

and then use dot notation to access the structure's members. For example, the statement

```
point.x = 5;
```

assigns 5 to the x member in the `Coordinate` structure named `point`.

Structures can store variables of any and all types, including arrays and even other structures. Here's a sample of a complex structure:

```
typedef struct complexStruct {
  float aFloat;
  int anInt;
  char aString[8];
  char aChar;
  long aLong;
} ComplexStruct;
```

`ComplexStruct` is a structure of five members: a floating-point value, an integer, an eight-element `char` array, a single character, and a long integer. A variable named `data` declared as

```
ComplexStruct data;
```

can store member values of these five types in one handy package. As with all structures, you can store values in `data`'s members using dot notation:

```
data.aFloat = 3.14159;
data.aChar = 'X';
```

As Figure 8.5 illustrates, `ComplexStruct`'s members are stored together in memory.

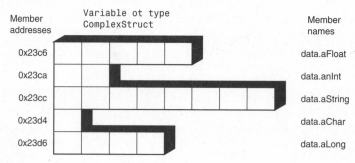

Figure 8.5. A structure's members are stored together in memory.

Normally, a structure's members butt up against each other with no wasted space between. However, when using the -a command-line alignment option, or the IDE Options|Compiler|Code generation command to enable Word alignment, the structure and all members except for `char` or `char[]` arrays are forced to begin at even memory addresses. To enforce this rule, the compiler inserts extra bytes, called *padding,* as needed between structure members. In addition, when word-alignment is in effect, the compiler adds a byte to the end of structures if necessary so that all structure objects have an even number of bytes.

Comparing and Assigning Structures

You may assign one structure variable to another of the same type. Given the declaration

```
Coordinate var1, var2;
```

this statement assigns var2 to var1:

```
var1 = var2;
```

In the compiled program, fast 80x86 instructions copy the bytes for var2 directly to the memory reserved for var1. Any padding in a structure is also copied.

Two structures cannot be compared directly. Statements like this one do not compile:

```
if (var1 == var2)  /* ??? */
  statement;
```

Structure members may be padded with extra bytes, char array members may contain leftover characters, and the exact storage details for structure members are left to individual compilers; therefore, a byte-by-byte comparison of two structures isn't possible to do in a general way.

Even though you cannot compare two structures, you can compare their members. Here's the correct way to execute a statement if the two structures var1 and var2 are equal:

```
if ((var1.x == var2.x) && (var1.y == var2.y))
  statement;
```

> **NOTE:** Lengthy expressions that compare structures member-by-member may seem grossly inefficient. However, due to the short-circuiting of logical expressions in C, only the minimum number of comparisons is made. In the preceding example, if the two x members are not equal, the entire expression must be false, and the second part of the logical AND (&&) expression is not considered.

Initializing Structures

A date is a good example of the kind of data-storage problem that structures neatly solve. The three components of a date—the day, the month, and the year—are conveniently represented by integer values, and even more convenient to use when housed in a structure. You might declare a date structure like this:

```
typedef struct dateStruct {
  char month;  /* 0 == no date */
  char day;
  unsigned year;
} DateStruct;
```

Structure DateStruct represents a structure with three members: a char named month, another char named day, and an unsigned integer named year. The two char members can represent values from 0 to 255—plenty of room for month values from 1 to 12 and days from 1 to 31. To provide a way to determine whether a date is initialized, the structure stipulates that, if month is zero, the member values are invalid.

The DateStruct declaration also demonstrates how structures can pack information tightly in memory. On PCs, DateStruct variables occupy only four bytes. Even with alignment enabled, there's no wasted space between this structure's members. Listing 8.7, DATETEST.C, demonstrates how to use DateStruct in a program.

Listing 8.7. DATETEST.C (Stores the date in a structure).

```
 1:  #include <stdio.h>
 2:
 3:  typedef struct dateStruct {
 4:    char month;  /* 0 == no date */
 5:    char day;
 6:    unsigned year;
 7:  } DateStruct;
 8:
 9:  main()
10:  {
11:    DateStruct date;
12:
13:    printf("Date test\n");
14:    date.month = 5;
15:    date.day = 16;
16:    date.year = 1972;
17:    printf("The date is: %02d/%02d/%04d\n",
18:      date.month, date.day, date.year);
19:    return 0;
20:  }
```

Lines 14–16 use dot notation to assign values to a variable `date` of the structure `DateStruct`. Lines 17–18 also use dot notation to display `date`'s member values. The `printf()` statement adds slashes and leading zeros, displaying

```
Date test
The date is: 05/16/1972
```

Rather than use dot-notation expressions to assign values to structure members, you can also initialize structures directly in a declaration. Use the form:

```
struct tag v = {elements};
```

where `struct tag` is the structure name or a `typedef` alias, `v` is the variable of that structure type, and `elements` are constant expressions to assign to members. Separate multiple constants with commas. For example, this assigns 7/15/2012 to `date`:

```
DateStruct date = {7, 15, 2012};
```

The order of the initializers in braces corresponds to the order of the structure's declared members. Thus 7 is assigned to the `date.month` member, 15 is assigned to `date.day`, and 2012 is assigned to `date.year`.

Using Nested Structures

If a structure's member is another structure, the result is a nested structure—one structure inside another. Suppose you declare a structure to store the time:

```
typedef struct timeStruct {
  char hour;      /* 0 to 23 */
  char minute;    /* 0 to 59 */
  char second;    /* 0 to 59 */
} TimeStruct;
```

Using `DateStruct` from the preceding section, you can create a nested `DateTime` structure like this:

```
typedef struct dateTime {
  DateStruct theDate;
  TimeStruct theTime;
} DateTime;
```

`DateTime` declares two members, `theDate` and `theTime`, each another structure. Member `theDate` is a structure of type `DateStruct`. Member `theTime` is a structure of type `TimeStruct`. Given a variable declared as

```
DateTime dt;
```

the expression `dt.theDate` refers to the `DateStruct` member `theDate` in `dt`. The expression `dt.theTime` refers to the `TimeStruct` member `theTime`.

> **NOTE:** A structure may not declare a member of the structure's own type. In other words, a structure cannot declare itself as a member. Chapter 9, "Pointers," explains how to get around this limitation, using pointers to address structures that are members of their own structure data types.

Use multiple dot-notation expressions to reference nested members. For example, the expression `dt.theDate.month` refers to the `month` member in `theDate` member belonging to `dt`. Expressions such as `dt.theDate.year` and `dt.theTime.minute` form pathways to a specified structure member—much in the way a DOS path such as C:\BORLANDC\BIN locates a subdirectory BIN nested inside another directory BORLANDC on the root drive and directory C:\.

Listing 8.8, DATETIME.C, expands the DATETEST program, using `TimeStruct` and the nested `DateTime` structures to store and display date and time values.

Listing 8.8. DATETIME.C (Stores date and time in a nested structure).

```
 1: #include <stdio.h>
 2:
 3: typedef struct dateStruct {
 4:    char month;  /* 0 == no date */
 5:    char day;
 6:    unsigned year;
 7: } DateStruct;
 8:
 9: typedef struct timeStruct {
10:    char hour;
11:    char minute;
12:    char second;
13: } TimeStruct;
14:
15: typedef struct dateTime {
```

```
16:    DateStruct theDate;
17:    TimeStruct theTime;
18:  } DateTime;
19:
20:  main()
21:  {
22:    DateTime dt;
23:
24:    printf("Date and time test\n");
25:    dt.theDate.month = 5;
26:    dt.theDate.day = 16;
27:    dt.theDate.year = 1972;
28:    dt.theTime.hour = 6;
29:    dt.theTime.minute = 15;
30:    dt.theTime.second = 0;
31:    printf("The date is: %02d/%02d/%04d\n",
32:       dt.theDate.month, dt.theDate.day, dt.theDate.year);
33:    printf("The time is: %02d:%02d:%02d\n",
34:       dt.theTime.hour, dt.theTime.minute, dt.theTime.second);
35:    return 0;
36:  }
```

Lines 25–30 assign values to the members of the nested structures in `DateTime` structure dt. Two `printf()` statements at lines 31–34 display those values, formatted with leading zeros, and punctuated with slashes and colons. On-screen, the program displays

```
Date and time test
The date is: 05/16/1972
The time is: 06:15:00
```

Using Structures and Functions

A structure's members can be any data types, but they cannot be functions. (C++ allows a structure to have member functions—a topic for Part 3, "Programming with C++.") Despite this limitation, there's a lot you can do with structures and functions. Structures may be passed to function parameters, and functions can return structures as their results.

For designing good-looking displays, a useful structure defines a rectangle, with coordinates representing the CRT character positions. Coordinate (0,0) is at the top-left corner, and on standard PC text screens, (24,79) represents the bottom-right corner. Here's one possible design:

```
typedef struct rectangle {
  int left;
  int top;
  int right;
  int bottom;
} Rectangle;
```

The Rectangle structure has four integer members, representing the left, top, right, and bottom coordinates of a display's characters. (You could use a similar structure to define coordinates for graphics displays.)

Programs that use many Rectangle structure variables would probably need various support functions. For example, rather than declare a variable r of type Rectangle and assign it four coordinate values like this:

```
Rectangle r;
r.left = 5;
r.top = 8;
r.right = 60;
r.bottom = 18;
```

you could write a function that returns an initialized Rectangle. Then, you could simply write

```
Rectangle r;
r = RectAssign(5, 8, 60, 18);
```

Function RectAssign() returns a Rectangle structure with its members initialized to the specified arguments. Here's one way to write RectAssign():

```
Rectangle RectAssign(int l, int t, int r, int b)
{
  Rectangle rtemp;

  rtemp.left = l;
  rtemp.top = t;
  rtemp.right = r;
  rtemp.bottom = b;
  return rtemp;
}
```

Even though `rtemp` is local to the function, and therefore, the variable doesn't exist outside of the function's scope, it's okay to return `rtemp` as the function's result. The statement `return rtemp;` copies `rtemp`'s bytes to temporary stack space, which is then copied to the variable to which the function's result is assigned. The temporary bytes on the stack are then removed.

You can also pass structures to function parameters. For example, if you need to compare two rectangles for equality, you could write a rectangle comparison function like this:

```
int RectsEqual(Rectangle r1, Rectangle r2)
{
  return ((r1.left   == r2.left  ) &&
          (r1.top    == r2.top   ) &&
          (r1.right  == r2.right ) &&
          (r1.bottom == r2.bottom));
}
```

> **HINT:** In complex expressions such as the one in function `RectsEqual()`, align the parentheses and operators to make typing and debugging easier.

You can then call `RectsEqual()` wherever a logical true-false expression is allowed. An `if` statement, for instance, can execute `statement` if two `Rectangle` structures `var1` and `var2` are equal:

```
if (RectsEqual(var1, var2))
  statement;
```

One caution about passing structures to and from functions: Like arrays, structures can consume gobs of memory, and because the stack is limited in size, passing too many large structures around on the stack may cause a stack overflow error. (Chapter 9, "Pointers," explains how to pass structures efficiently to and from functions.)

Unions

Unions are nearly identical to structures, and in fact, if you're not careful, you can easily confuse them with disastrous results. Although structures and unions have near mirror-image forms, they are related more like cousins than identical twins.

As you have learned in this chapter, structures collect members into a convenient package. Unions, declared with the union keyword where struct normally goes, also house multiple members. Unlike a structure, where each member follows the other, in a union, all members overlap each other at the same address.

This fact may seem odd, but there are many times when a union comes in handy. A common case is a union that permits statements to access variables as more than one data type. Listing 8.9, UNION.C, demonstrates.

Listing 8.9. UNION.C (Permits a union to access bytes, words, and double words).

```
 1:  #include <stdio.h>
 2:
 3:  /* WARNING: Implementation dependent code! */
 4:
 5:  typedef char Byte;
 6:
 7:  union word {
 8:    unsigned w;
 9:    struct {
10:      Byte lobyte;
11:      Byte hibyte;
12:    } bytes;
13:  };
14:
15:  union dword {
16:    long dw;
17:    struct {
18:      union word loword;
19:      union word hiword;
20:    } words;
21:  };
22:
23:  main()
24:  {
25:    union dword d;
26:
27:    d.dw = 0x12345678L;
28:    printf("d.dw == %#lx\n", d.dw);
29:    printf("d.words.loword.w == %#x\n",
```

```
30:       d.words.loword.w);
31:     printf("d.words.hiword.w == %#x\n",
32:       d.words.hiword.w);
33:     printf("d.words.loword.bytes.lobyte == %#x\n",
34:       d.words.loword.bytes.lobyte);
35:     printf("d.words.loword.bytes.hibyte == %#x\n",
36:       d.words.loword.bytes.hibyte);
37:     printf("d.words.hiword.bytes.lobyte == %#x\n",
38:       d.words.hiword.bytes.lobyte);
39:     printf("d.words.hiword.bytes.hibyte == %#x\n",
40:       d.words.hiword.bytes.hibyte);
41:     return 0;
42: }
```

The program might be easier to understand after examining its output. Enter the listing, compile, and run. On-screen, you see

```
d.dw == 0x12345678
d.words.loword.w == 0x5678
d.words.hiword.w == 0x1234
d.words.loword.bytes.lobyte == 0x78
d.words.loword.bytes.hibyte == 0x56
d.words.hiword.bytes.lobyte == 0x34
d.words.hiword.bytes.hibyte == 0x12
```

Although many values are listed, each is a portion of the same long integer assigned to d.dw. Look closely at each value. The expression d.words.loword.w equals hexadecimal 0x5678, the low-order word of the initial value, 0x12345678L. The trailing capital *L* tells the compiler that the constant is a long integer. The expression d.words.hiword.bytes.lobyte equals 0x34, the low-order byte of the high-order word in the initial value.

Figure 8.6 shows how 0x12345678L is stored in memory. In 80x86-based PCs, words and double words are stored in *little-endian* fashion—that is, with the least significant (low-order) values at lower (littler) addresses than more significant (high-order) values. A big-endian computer, such as the Macintosh, stores multibyte values the other way around. From a traditional mathematics point of view, little-endian storage is all mixed up. As shown in Figure 8.6, the value 0x12345678L is actually stored as the series of byte values 0x78, 0x56, 0x34, and 0x12, in that order.

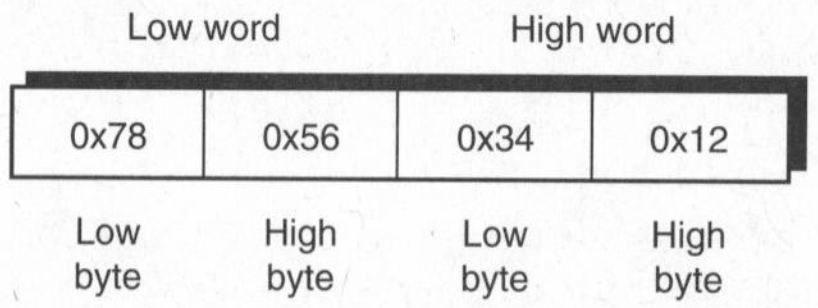

Figure 8.6. Hexadecimal 0x12345678 stored in little-endian fashion.

Storage details like these complicate a programmer's life. Many times, you can ignore a computer's internal peculiarities, but when writing system software—programs targeted for a specific computer system—it's often necessary to pick apart long integers and examine bytes and words as stored in memory.

Getting back to UNION.C, the two unions at lines 7–13 and 15–21 provide handy structures for accessing bytes and words in long integers. Be aware, however, that the same program may not operate correctly on other computers. Examine the first union:

```
union word {
  unsigned w;        /* Overlays lobyte and hibyte */
  struct {
    Byte lobyte;     /* Overlays first byte of w   */
    Byte hibyte;     /* Overlays second byte of w  */
  } bytes;
};
```

A union's members are stored at the same address; therefore, member `unsigned w` overlays the `bytes` structure, which declares two of its own members, `lobyte` and `hibyte`. In memory, `lobyte` begins at the same location as `w`, and `hibyte` begins one byte beyond. Because in Borland C++ an `unsigned int` occupies two bytes, the inner `bytes` structure provides access to those bytes as separate values; the outer `unsigned w` accesses the same bytes as a single word.

A similar trick dissects a long integer in the union `dword`:

```
union dword {
  long dw;                  /* Overlays loword and hiword */
  struct {
    union word loword;  /* Overlays first word of dw */
    union word hiword;  /* Overlays second word of dw */
  } words;
};
```

For a variable d of type `union dword`, the expression `d.loword` represents the low-order word of the long integer value `dw`. The expression `d.hiword` represents the high-order word of that *same* value.

Keeping these facts in mind, examine the UNION.C `printf()` statements at lines 28–40. In each case, a different portion of the same value is printed in hexadecimal simply by referring to different overlaid members of the `dword union d`.

Initializing Unions

Like structures, unions may be initialized in a declaration, but you may specify a value for only the first of a union's members. For example, given the `dword` union from the preceding section, the declaration

```
union dword d = {0x12345678L};
```

assigns hexadecimal 0x12345678L to member `dw` in the `dword union d`.

The restriction on initializing union members is not so much a limitation as it is an understandable consequence of a union's nature. Because all union members begin at the same address, assigning a value to the first member effectively assigns values to all others overlaid by that value.

This fact is true, however, only for unions with members of the same size. In a union such as

```
union tricky {
  int i;
  char c[8];
};
```

the int member `i` overlays only the first two bytes of the eight-character array c (a fact that might not be true for all ANSI C compilers). You can initialize a `tricky` union's i member like this:

```
union tricky t = {1234};
```

You can't assign an initial value to both members as you could if `tricky` were a structure. Given the comparable structure declaration:

```
struct notTricky {
  int i;
  char c[8];
};
```

you can initialize members i and c by writing

```
struct notTricky n = {1234, 'A', 'B', 'C', 'D', 'E', 'F', 'G'};
```

This assigns 1234 to n.i, and the seven characters A through G to n.c. The same technique does not work for unions. If you try to write

```
union tricky t = {1234, 'A', 'B', 'C', 'D', 'E', 'F', 'G'}; /* ??? */
```

you receive a compiler error, because only t.i can be initialized this way.

Using Tagged Unions

Using unions is like playing the children's game "Button, button," in which a child guesses which of several other children holds a button in a clenched fist. Any one of a union's members could contain valid data, but which one holds the prize?

Because union members overlay each other, only one member at a time can have valid information. In the tricky union from the preceding section:

```
union tricky {
  int i;
  char c[8];
};
```

a variable v of type tricky may contain an integer value or a string, but not both. Only a structure can store two such values simultaneously.

One way to distinguish between a union's members is to use multiple structures, each beginning with a tag member that tells you which other member currently holds valid data. For clarity, it's best to define a few symbols to use as tag values:

```
typedef enum tags = {U_INT, U_CHAR} Tags;
```

The Tags alias is associated with the type enum tags, an enumeration of two symbols U_INT (equal to 0) and U_CHAR (equal to 1). Next, declare tricky with multiple structure members, each topped with a Tags member:

```
union tricky {
  Tags tag;        /* Overlays t1 and t2 */
  struct {
    Tags t1;       /* Overlays tag */
    int i;         /* Overlays beginning of c[] */
  } intStruct;     /* Overlays charStruct */
  struct {
```

```
    Tags t2;       /* Overlays tag */
    char c[8];     /* Overlays i */
  } charStruct;    /* Overlays intStruct */
};
```

The first member, tag of type Tags, is the tag field. It should equal one of the enumerated symbols U_INT or U_CHAR. A statement can inspect tag to determine what kind of data the union holds.

The two inner structure members intStruct and charStruct overlay tag and each other. The tag and the two structure members t1 and t2 therefore reside at the *same* location. The other members, i and c, also overlay each other, but because they are declared inside the inner structs, they follow tag.

Given this design, a program could declare a variable t of type union tricky, and then assign data to the integer member like this:

```
t.tag = U_INT;
t.intStruct.i = 1234;
```

Elsewhere in the program, another statement can inspect t.tag. If t.tag equals U_INT, the program can use the union's integer member; otherwise, the character array is assumed to hold valid information. For example, to display the data in the union, you can write

```
if (t.tag == U_INT)
  printf("%d", t.intStruct.i);
else
  printf(t.charStruct.c);
```

As these samples demonstrate, using unions requires a lot of picky work. You must be very careful to determine exactly what data you are accessing in one member or another, and you must be wary of introducing any system dependencies that tie your program to a specific memory architecture. Don't use unions unless there's an excellent reason for going to all this trouble.

Other Union Facts

Here are some other facts to keep in mind when using unions:

- The size of a union equals the size of its largest member.

- Structures may be members of unions, and unions may be members of structures (or other unions).

- Because union members overlay each other at the same address, padding is never added between union members, even when word alignment is in effect. However, the entire union may be aligned to an even address.

Bit-Field Structures

It often happens that one or more structure members never exceed a certain small value. For example, in a personnel database, a member that holds the number of an employee's children is unlikely to be higher than 15. Likewise, a member that represents a person's sex needs only a single bit if 0 is taken to mean male and 1 female. You might design the structure like this:

```
struct person {
  unsigned age;          /* 0 ... 99 */
  unsigned sex;          /* 0=male, 1=female */
  unsigned children;     /* 0 ... 15 */
};
```

Unfortunately, on PCs, the person structure takes six bytes, two per int field, leaving lots of wasted space. For example, sex requires only a single bit to hold its value—the other 15 bits in sex are unused. If the structure could pack information into a smaller space that takes only as many bits as needed to represent each member, it could squeeze out most of those wasted bits.

That's exactly what bit-field structures are designed to do. A bit-field structure resembles a common structure: It uses the same struct keyword and layout, but it specifies the number of bits that each member occupies. Here's how the previous structure looks when converted to a bit-field structure:

```
struct person {
  unsigned age : 7;      /* 0 ... 127 */
  unsigned sex : 1;      /* 0=male, 1=female */
  unsigned children : 4; /* 0 ... 15 */
  unsigned : 4;          /* Not used */
};
```

Members are declared as usual, but are followed by a colon and an unsigned literal value that specifies the size of the member in bits. The age member is stored in seven bits—room enough to hold values from 0 to 127. The sex bit field takes only one bit, and can therefore specify values of 0 or 1. Because adjacent bit-field members are packed together in the structure, person occupies exactly 16 bits—the total number of bits occupied by all members.

You may declare bit fields in structs or unions. (You may also declare bit fields in C++ classes, a subject for Part 3, "Programming with C++.") You cannot calculate the address of a bit-field member by applying the & operator because a bit field might be *inside* of a byte, and only whole bytes in memory have addresses.

Although not shown here, bit-field members may be signed or unsigned char or int values. Most C programming experts suggest specifying signed or unsigned keywords for better portability. However, by their very nature, bit-field structures tend to be nonportable. You might not even be able to use the same bit-field structures for two compilers on the same computer and operating system.

Using Bit-Field Placeholders

The last unnamed bit field in person from the preceding section is a placeholder, which keeps the total number of bits in the structure equal to 16. A placeholder is optional, but it is recommended because it accounts for every bit in a bit-field structure. You may also use more than one placeholder to force fields to begin at certain bits. For example, this fictitious bit-field structure has three placeholders labeled with comments as "Not used":

```
struct hardware {
  unsigned reset : 1;     /* 0 ... 1  */
  unsigned level : 4;     /* 0 ... 15 */
  unsigned : 1;           /* Not used */
  char selector : 2;      /* 0 ... 3  */
  unsigned : 3;           /* Not used */
  unsigned active : 1;    /* 0 ... 1  */
  unsigned : 4;           /* Not used */
};
```

Multiple placeholders can help you to create bit-field structures that match the positions of bits stored in hardware registers. For example, an input port might define certain bits to mean various things—whether a byte is available from an external source, the port's status, and so on. Other bits might be undefined or reserved. You could use a bit-field structure to match the port's documented bits, and insert placeholders for other undocumented bit values.

Using Bit-Field Structures

Use bit-field structures as you do common structs. For example, to display the age and number of children in a person bit-field structure, you could write:

```
struct person p;
...
printf("\nAge      = %d", p.age);
printf("\nChildren = %d", p.children);
```

The expressions p.age and p.children generate the necessary code to extract bit-field values from the structure and convert the values to their designated types. In this case, the age and children members are converted to unsigned integer values.

Listing 8.10, EQUIP.C, uses a bit-field structure to extract information packed inside PCs. The program also demonstrates one of the best reasons for using bit-field structures—to avoid having to write bitwise logical expressions to extract values packed into bytes and words.

Listing 8.10. EQUIP.C (Uses bit fields to extract system information).

```
 1:  #include <stdio.h>
 2:  #include <bios.h>
 3:
 4:  struct equipment {
 5:    unsigned hasdiskette : 1;
 6:    unsigned hascoprocessor: 1;
 7:    unsigned planar : 2;
 8:    unsigned videomode : 2;
 9:    unsigned numfloppy : 2;
10:    unsigned hasdma: 1;
11:    unsigned numserial : 3;
12:    unsigned gameadaptor : 1;
13:    unsigned serialprinter: 1;
14:    unsigned numprinters : 2;
15:  };
16:
17:  union twotypes {
18:    struct equipment eq;   /* The bit-field structure */
19:    int k;                 /* Same bytes as an integer */
20:  };
```

```
21:
22:   main()
23:   {
24:     union twotypes t;
25:
26:     t.k = biosequip();    /* Get list as integer */
27:     printf("\nNumber of printers         %d", t.eq.numprinters);
28:     printf("\nGame adaptor installed (1) %d", t.eq.gameadaptor);
29:     printf("\nNumber of serial ports     %d", t.eq.numserial);
30:     printf("\nNumber of diskette drives  ");
31:     if (t.eq.hasdiskette)
32:       printf("%d", t.eq.numfloppy + 1);
33:     else
34:       printf("0");
35:     printf("\nInitial video mode (2)     %d", t.eq.videomode);
36:     printf("\nPlanar RAM size (3)        %d", t.eq.planar);
37:     printf("\n\n(1): 0=FALSE, 1=TRUE");
38:     printf("\n(2): 1=40x25 color, 2=80x25 color, 3=monochrome");
39:     printf("\n(3): 3=64K on XTs\n");
40:     return 0;
41:   }
```

The program uses a bit-field structure to interpret the information returned by function biosequip(), prototyped in header file bios.h. EQUIP displays the number of diskette drives, serial ports, and printers installed on a PC. It also indicates the startup video mode and tells whether a game adaptor is available. (The program limits output to values that exist on XTs and later PC-compatible systems; it does not use every bit-field member declared at lines 4–15.)

Use dot notation as you do for other structures to extract individual bit-field member values. For example, the expression t.eq.numserial equals the number of serial ports. (See line 29.)

EQUIP also makes good use of a union (lines 17–20). The twotypes union contains two members, eq of type struct equipment and k of type int. Remember, all members in a union overlay each other at the same address. Because the equipment member occupies 16 bits, as does k, the two members in twotypes overlay each other in memory.

Line 26 calls the biosequip() function, which returns an integer value. Assigning that value to the k member in twotypes t also initializes the bit-field structure t.equipment.

> **NOTE:** Bit-field structures that access system hardware are unlikely to work on other computers. Running EQUIP on anything but a true-blue PC, XT, AT, PS/2, or clone will almost certainly fail.

Other Bit-Field Facts

Here are a few other facts to keep in mind when using bit-field structures:

- Bit-field members are not arrays, and you cannot access individual bits using array subscripting.

- The compiled code that extracts bit-field values may not be as efficient as a bitwise logical expression, or a fine-tuned assembly language routine. Using bit-field structures may cause a loss of performance.

- You may declare bit-field members only in structures—never in unions.

- In Borland C++, bit-field members may cross word boundaries in memory, but any individual member may not be larger than two bytes.

- Borland C++ allocates storage to bit-field members beginning with the low-order bits for the first member, and progressing to higher-order bits for subsequent members. Member order may differ on other computers and compilers.

Arrays and Structures

Combining arrays and structures creates powerful data structures that can help you to organize information in nearly limitless ways. There are two fundamental combinations:

- Arrays of structures

- Structures with array members

    Let's take a look at each of these multipart data types.

Arrays of Structures

Two or more arrays of related information can often be translated to a single array of structures, usually with improved efficiency. Consider, for example, how you might store a 100-element set of three-dimensional coordinates. You could declare three arrays:

```
double X[100];
double Y[100];
double Z[100];
```

To access one data point, however, requires three array index operations. Using a hypothetical function `PlotPoint()`, to plot the value at an index 9, you would have to write something like this:

```
PlotPoint(X[9], Y[9], Z[9]);
```

A much better plan is to declare a structure with three `double` members:

```
struct point3D {
  double X;
  double Y;
  double Z;
};
```

Now the program has a convenient way to represent three-dimensional coordinates. Even better, only a single array is needed to store the 100-value data collection:

```
struct point3D points[100];
```

Expressions such as `points[9]` and `points[50]` refer to the three-member `point3D` structures stored at those subscripted locations. It's now possible to design a `PlotPoint()` function to accept a single `point3D` parameter:

```
void PlotPoint(struct point3D p);
```

You can then pass arrayed structures to `PlotPoint()` using a statement such as

```
PlotPoint(points[9]);
```

The three indexing operations are reduced to one. Inside the `PlotPoint` function, the structure members are accessible as `p.X`, `p.Y`, and `p.Z`.

Structures with Array Members

Structures may also have array members. A typical case is a structure with one or more arrays of char:

```
struct person {
  char name[20];
  char address[20];
  char city[15];
  ...
};
```

Other arrays of various types can also be structure members. You can even declare members as arrays of other structures. Be aware, however, that such arrays occupy fixed amounts of storage. Any unused array positions are wasted—a disconcerting fact considering the minimal memory capacities of typical desktop computers. In the next chapter, you'll investigate pointers along with techniques that can help use memory more efficiently by creating data structures that expand and contract to take only as much RAM as necessary.

Summary

- Arrays collect variables of the same type. Declare an array with brackets. For example, int scores[100]; declares an array named scores with room to store 100 int values.

- To refer to individual array elements, use subscript expressions such as scores[9], which references the tenth int in scores. The first array subscript is zero, thus scores[0] is the first value in the array, scores[1] is the second, and so on.

- In memory, array elements are stored one after the other. The entire array may be aligned to an even address using the -a option or the equivalent IDE word-alignment setting.

- Strings are arrays of char values. You can use subscript expressions to operate on individual characters stored in strings.

- Two-dimensional arrays are typically viewed as row-and-column matrixes; however, they are literally arrays of arrays, and their values are stored sequentially in memory. Use double bracket expressions such as point[row][col] to reference individual elements in two-dimensional arrays.

- Multidimensional arrays may have any number of subscripts. It's rare, however, to use more than three. A cubic array could be declared as
  `int cubic[10][20][4];`

- To conserve memory, C passes arrays to function parameters by address. In functions that declare array parameters, any statements in the functions that modify array elements also change the original array data passed to the function.

- When passing multidimensional arrays to functions, you must specify (at a minimum) enough information to enable the compiler to evaluate subscript expressions. For example, in the case of a two-dimensional array parameter, you must specify the number of columns in the array parameter, but you do not have to specify the number of rows.

- A structure can store one or more members of the same or of different data types. Use the struct keyword to declare a structure.

- Use dot notation in expressions such as point.x and person.name to refer to individual members of a structure.

- Structures may be assigned but not compared. They may be passed as arguments to functions, and functions may return structures. Structure arguments and function return values are passed onto the stack.

- Unions resemble structures in form, but use the union keyword in place of struct. All members of a union overlay one another at the same location in memory. The size of a union equals the size of its largest member.

- A bit-field structure specifies the number of bits each member occupies. Use bit-field structures to pack members into as small a space as possible, and also to access bit-packed system data that might be stored in hardware registers.

- You may declare arrays of structures, and you may declare arrays as structure members.

Exercises

8.1 Write a function that calculates the length of an argument string.

8.2 Write a function that rotates a series of values in an array one position to the right. In other words, given the arrayed values 1,2,3,4,5, calling the function would change the array to 5,1,2,3,4. Calling it again would modify the values to 4,5,1,2,3, and so on.

8.3 Write a function that returns the average of a series of `double` floating-point values stored in an array.

8.4 Design an array that simulates a deck of cards. Also design a function to shuffle the deck.

8.5 Write a function `spos()` that returns the index position of a specific character in a string. The statement `spos("abcd", 'c');` should return 2, the subscript of the character 'c' in "abcd".

8.6 Declare a telephone-number structure. The structure should have members named `areaCode`, `exchange`, and `number`. Use the structure in a test program. Also declare a nested structure with two telephone numbers, one for voice communication and the other for a fax.

8.7 Write a function that compares two telephone-number structures from Exercise 8.6, returning true if the structures are equal or false if they are not.

8.8 Define an array of 100 telephone-number structures from Exercise 8.6. Insert the array into a program that lists member values.

8.9 Create a bit-field structure for setting and resetting specific bits in word values.

8.10 Write a program that initializes a two-dimensional unit matrix `matrix[s][s]` (where s is the size of the array) defined by the rules

```
matrix[n][m] == 1 if n == m
matrix[n][m] == 0 if n != m
```

Pointers

Programs use pointers to locate data the way post offices use mailing addresses to locate people and places. A mailing address represents a postal destination. In a C program, a pointer represents the address of information stored in memory. In fact, that's all a pointer is—a memory address that points to another value.

Despite the apparent simplicity, however, pointers are among C's most versatile tools. By chaining pointers together, programs can link multiple instances of data, forming complex structures such as stacks, lists, and trees. You can also use pointers to read and write hardware registers, poke text into video buffers, and access normally hidden system values.

Learning to use pointers correctly takes practice. With pointers, programs can read and write information at any location in memory—a powerful capability that, if misused, can wreck data and code in unprotected memory locations faster than you can lick a postage stamp. Don't let that potential danger turn you off from using pointers, however. After you master the twists and turns of pointers, you might wonder how anyone ever wrote programs without them.

Introducing Pointers

To declare a pointer, add a space and an asterisk after any data type identifier. For example, `int` is an integer; `int *` is a pointer *to* an integer. The declaration `int p` declares p as an integer variable; `int *p` declares p as a pointer to an integer stored elsewhere. (The placement of the asterisk is not critical, and you can write `int* p` or `int * p`, but the most common style is `int *p`.)

Memorize the following facts about pointers:

- A pointer is a variable similar to `int` or `float` variables.

- A pointer variable contains an address that points to another location in memory.

- Stored at this location is the data the pointer addresses.

Remember: A pointer points to a value stored in memory. If you declare `ptr` like this:

```
int *ptr;
```

you are telling the compiler `ptr` is a pointer to an integer value stored somewhere else in RAM. (See Figure 9.1.) The pointer (left) addresses the value 100 (right) stored in memory.

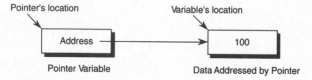

Figure 9.1. A pointer is a variable that contains an address.

Like all variables, `ptr` requires initializing before use. Until you initialize a pointer, it holds an unpredictable value, possibly left in memory from another operation. When you initialize a pointer, you give it an address you know points to a valid location. Never use uninitialized pointers. They are like arrows spilled from a quiver—a bunch of dangerous pick-up sticks that point every which way, often causing hard-to-find bugs.

This chapter covers several techniques for initializing pointers. Study these methods and use them religiously to prevent bugs before they happen.

Declaring and Dereferencing Pointers

Using a pointer to get to its addressed data is called *dereferencing the pointer.* Given the pointer and int declarations

```
int i;   /* An integer variable i */
int *p;  /* A pointer p to an integer value */
```

you can assign to p the address of the integer variable i:

```
p = &i;
```

The unary address-of operator & returns the address of an object in memory. The expression &i represents the address of i. (You may use & to calculate the addresses of variables and functions, but not expressions, symbolic constants, or register variables—none of which have addresses.) After assigning i's address to p, the pointer p points to the location where i's value is stored. To display i's value directly, you can write

```
printf("%d", i);
```

To perform the same job using the pointer p, you can instead write

```
printf("%d", *p);
```

The expression *p dereferences the pointer p, instructing the compiler to use p's addressed integer value.

C knows from the pointer's declaration what kind of value the pointer addresses. Because p was declared as int *p, the compiler understands *p refers to an int value stored at the address in p. For all practical purposes, *p *is* an int, and can be used anywhere a plain integer variable is allowed.

Pointers as Aliases

Listing 9.1, ALIAS.C, demonstrates the concepts of declaring, initializing, and dereferencing a pointer variable. These are vital facts to learn, and you should run the sample program several times until the statements and their effects are perfectly clear.

Listing 9.1. ALIAS.C (Declares, initializes, and dereferences a pointer).

```
 1:  #include <stdio.h>
 2:
 3:  char c;              /* A character variable */
 4:
 5:  main()
 6:  {
 7:    char *pc;          /* A pointer to a character variable */
 8:
 9:    pc = &c;
10:    for (c = 'A'; c <= 'Z'; c++)
11:      printf("%c", *pc);
12:    return 0;
13:  }
```

Are you surprised at ALIAS's output? Running the program displays the alphabet—nothing to shake the earth, but consider for a moment how the program accomplishes this simple task. The only output statement is at line 11, which does not refer directly to the global character variable c to which the for loop at line 10 assigns the characters 'A' through 'Z'. If the output statement does not use the character variable directly, how can it display the letters assigned to c?

To solve this riddle, first examine line 7. The declaration char *pc informs the compiler that pc is a pointer to a char value. Line 9 assigns to pc the address of c. After that assignment, pc addresses c's value in memory. (See Figure 9.2.) In the line 11 printf() statement, the expression *pc dereferences the pointer, passing to the function the addressed data—in this case, the character stored in c.

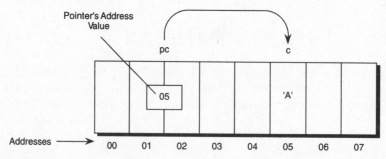

Figure 9.2. Variable c and pointer pc refer to the same value.

When a pointer addresses the location where another variable's value is stored, that pointer is called an alias. Like a gangster's alias, a pointer alias conceals an object's true identity.

To prove pc addresses the same data as c, load ALIAS.C into your editor and change the output statement to printf("%c", c);. In other words, change the dereferenced pointer expression *pc to c. Compile and run the modified program. Despite the change you made, the program operates no differently, proving that pc is an alias for c.

> **NOTE:** All pointers are not aliases, only those that point to the location where another program variable is stored.

When you dereference other pointers using expressions such as *pc, think of the expressions as variables of the pointers' declared data types. Consider these sample pointer declarations:

```
double *dp;
char *s;
long *lp;
```

Pointer dp addresses a double value. Pointer s addresses a character—which might be the first character of a string. Pointer lp addresses a long integer. To dereference these and other pointers, preface their names with asterisks. The expression *dp refers to the double value addressed by dp; *s refers to the char addressed by s; and *lp refers to the long integer addressed by lp. The pointer-dereference expressions *dp, *s, and *lp may be used in exactly the same ways as variables of type double, char, and long. The nondereferenced expressions dp, s, and lp may be used only where pointers are allowed.

Pointers and Type Checking

Because pointers are bound to specific data types, the compiler can verify that you don't accidentally assign the address of one sort of data to the wrong kind of pointer. You receive a "Suspicious pointer conversion" message for programming such as

```
float *fp;
char c;
fp = &c;    /* ??? */
```

Because c is type char and fp is type float *, the compiler warns against assigning c's address to fp—in effect, a suspicious attempt to convert one type of pointer into another. If fp addresses a char variable, storing a floating-point value in that location would be a serious error. Because char values in Borland C++ don't take as much space as float, using the pointer to store a value might overwrite other data stored next to c.

NOTE: C++ does an excellent job of guarding against assigning the address of one type of variable to a pointer bound to a different type. Where ANSI C issues a warning about the suspicious pointer conversion, C++ gives an error and refuses to compile the code.

Null Pointers

A null pointer points nowhere in particular. It's like an arrow without a tip, or a sign that's fallen to the ground. A null pointer is C's way of saying that, at least for the moment, "this pointer does not address any valid data in memory."

As you learned at the beginning of this chapter, pointers hold numeric values that represent memory addresses. A null pointer's value equals zero—the only address a pointer cannot reach. (This is no great loss, because low memory addresses are reserved for the system's use and can't be used for data storage.) Rather than use the literal 0 digit for null, however, you can define a symbol NULL somewhere in a header file:

```
#define NULL 0
```

Even better, include a header file such as stddef.h, stdio.h, stdlib.h, or string.h. These and several other headers test whether NULL is already defined, and if not, include _null.h, located in C:\BORLANDC\INCLUDE. This defines NULL as one of three possible values:

- If this is an OS/2 program, NULL is defined as ((void *)0). (You learn about void pointers in the next section.) This form of NULL isn't needed for MS-DOS or Windows programming.

- If the current memory model is tiny, small, or medium (see Chapter 21, "Windows Tools and Techniques"), NULL is defined as a macro that represents the integer value 0.

- Some memory models define NULL as 0L, in other words, a long integer constant equal to zero.

Because pointers are numeric, you can assign integer values to them. Given the pointer declaration double *fp;, the following statements compile without error:

```
fp = NULL;
fp = 0;
fp = 12345;   /* ??? */
```

The first two lines have the same effect—assigning NULL to fp. The first line, however, is safest and is guaranteed to work correctly in all memory models. The last line compiles, but causes the compiler to issue the warning "Nonportable pointer conversion." Never assign integer values to pointers this way. See the section entitled "Advanced Pointer Techniques" later in this chapter for the correct way to assign specific memory addresses to pointer variables.

Having assigned NULL to a pointer, the program can check whether the pointer is valid:

```
if (fp != NULL)
  statement;
```

Use similar programming to execute one or more statements if a pointer such as fp addresses valid data. If the pointer equals NULL, you should assume the pointer does not address actual data—a simple but useful device that goes a long way in preventing bugs caused by using uninitialized pointers. If all uninitialized pointers are set to NULL, such bugs are squashed before they can do any damage.

Because NULL equals zero, and because zero means false, many programmers use the shorthand expression

```
if (fp)
  statement;
```

This has the identical effect as the preceding longer form because, if fp is not null, it is assumed to address a valid memory location, and its nonzero value is evaluated as true by the if statement.

NOTE: The expressions (fp) and (fp != NULL) compile to the same code. There's no technical advantage to using one form or the other. The shorthand is popular and clear if you keep in mind that nonzero means true and non-null pointers are assumed to be valid. Hint: Silently, read if (fp) as "if fp is valid."

Like all global variables, global pointers are initialized to zero. If you declare pointer `fp` as a global variable:

```
float *fp;      /* fp == NULL */
main()
{
  ...
}
```

`fp` is guaranteed to equal NULL when the program begins. If, however, you declare `fp` or any other pointer as a local variable in a function, like all local variables, the pointer has an unpredictable value when the function runs. To guard against using uninitialized pointers, you can assign NULL to a local pointer:

```
void f(void)
{
  float *fp = NULL;  /* fp == NULL */
  ...
}
```

Void Pointers

Like a void function that does not return any value, a void pointer points to an unspecified type of data. Declare a void pointer like this:

```
void *nowhereLand;
```

The void pointer `nowhereLand` may address any location in memory, and is not bound to a specific data type. A void pointer might address a `double` variable, a `char`, or an arbitrary location, perhaps one that belongs to DOS or to the ROM BIOS. A void pointer is a generic pointer for addressing data without having to specify the type of that data in advance.

> **NOTE:** Don't confuse null and void pointers. A null pointer does not address valid data. A void pointer addresses data of an unspecified type. A void pointer may also be null. Warning: Early C programs used `char *` as a generic pointer type. Don't use this form. Use `void *` to declare pointers to data of unknown type.

One of the most common uses for void pointers is to address buffers that hold raw data traveling on its way to and from memory. Other uses include filling memory blocks with values and reading hardware registers.

Casting Roles for Pointers to Play

When using void pointers to address buffers, you may need to use a type cast to view raw data in its true form. For example, a database program might quickly read records directly from disk sectors, and then process that data as an array of double floating-point values. A type cast instructs the compiler to consider an item of one type (a void pointer in this case) to be an item of another type (a double pointer, for example).

One way (not necessarily the best) to create data buffers is to define some memory and then create one or more pointers to address the buffer's location:

```
char buffer[1024];    /* A 1,024-byte buffer */
void *bp;             /* A pointer to nothing in particular */
bp = &buffer;         /* Assign buffer's address to bp */
```

This fragment defines buffer as an array of 1024 char values. A void pointer bp is then declared and assigned the address of buffer. The pointer bp points to buffer's first byte.

Though hypothetical, this fragment poses a common question: How does a program use data that a void pointer such as bp addresses? One way is to use a type cast, prefacing a pointer or other identifier with a data type declaration in parentheses. For example, if c is a variable of type char, to assign to c the first character in the char buffer addressed by void pointer bp, you can write

```
c = *(char *)bp;
```

The expression (char *)bp instructs the compiler to treat bp temporarily as a pointer to type char. Dereferencing that expression as *(char *)bp refers to bp's addressed data as a char value.

If the buffer contains int values, and if i is a variable of type int, a similar type cast expression assigns an integer value from the buffer to i:

```
i = *(int *)bp;
```

The type cast expression (int *)bp treats bp as a pointer to int. Dereferencing that expression refers to an int value stored at bp's addressed location. It's up to you to ensure an integer value is actually stored there.

269

Listing 9.2, VOID.C, demonstrates pointer type casts. The program also has a useful function that uses a void pointer to display the address value stored in any pointer—useful for debugging broken pointers.

Listing 9.2. VOID.C (Uses a void pointer to address a buffer).

```
 1:  #include <stdio.h>
 2:  #include <dos.h>
 3:
 4:  void DispPointer(void *p);
 5:
 6:  main()
 7:  {
 8:    char buffer[1024];
 9:    void *bp;
10:
11:    bp = &buffer;          /* Assign buffer address to bp */
12:    *(char *)bp = 'A';     /* Store character via pointer */
13:    buffer[1] = 'B';       /* Store character directly */
14:    buffer[2] = 0;         /* Insert null after "AB" */
15:
16:    printf("Address of buffer == ");
17:    DispPointer(&buffer);
18:    printf("Data in buffer == %s", (char *)bp);
19:    return 0;
20:  }
21:
22:  void DispPointer(void *p)
23:  {
24:    printf("%04x:%04x\n", FP_SEG(p), FP_OFF(p));
25:  }
```

Line 4 declares a void function DispPointer with a void *p parameter. The declaration states that pointer p addresses a value of an unspecified type. Because p is typeless, statements can pass it the address of any variable. For example, the statement at line 17:

```
DispPointer(&buffer);
```

passes the address of `buffer` to `DispPointer`. Line 11 performs a similar job, assigning the address of `buffer` to a void pointer `bp`. Void pointers are generic—they can hold any addresses.

Line 12 uses a type cast expression to assign data to the location addressed by `bp`. This statement has the identical effect as the simpler

```
buffer[0] = 'A';
```

but is used here to demonstrate how void pointers may address raw data.

Lines 16–18 display the buffer's address and its data. The assignments at lines 12–14 store in `buffer` two characters, A and B, plus a zero byte, creating a small string. Line 18 displays this string by using a type cast expression `(char *)bp`, which passes to `printf()` `bp`'s address value recast as a pointer to `char`. Actually, `printf()` doesn't care about `bp`'s type, and the statement at line 18 could be shortened to

```
printf("Data in buffer == %s", bp);
```

The full expression `(char *)bp` makes it perfectly clear, however, that `bp` addresses character data.

The `DispPointer()` function (lines 22–25) displays a pointer's address value. The program uses the function to display buffer's location:

```
Address of buffer == 194c:fbf6
```

If you prefer uppercase hexadecimal digits, change the two *x* characters in line 24 to *X*, or you can use this alternate statement:

```
printf("%p\n", p);
```

Option `%p` in a format string tells `printf()` to display a pointer's address. You can also use `%Fp` to display a far pointer with segment and offset components. Conceptually, pointers are integer values, but actually, their internal forms depend on the computer's memory architecture. On 80x86-based PCs, memory addresses are represented by 16-bit offsets from a base location, called a segment. These 16-bit *near* pointers can address data that's relatively close—from 0 to 65535 bytes above (at a higher address than) an assumed segment boundary. *Far* pointers contain complete segment and offset values, and therefore can reach any location.

To extract a pointer's segment and offset values, `DispPointer()` uses two macros, `FP_SEG` and `FP_OFF`, defined in dos.h. For any pointer p, the expression `FP_SEG(p)` equals that pointer's 16-bit segment value; the expression `FP_OFF(p)` equals the pointer's 16-bit offset. You can use these expressions anywhere unsigned integers are allowed. `DispPointer()` employs them in the `printf()` statement:

```
printf("%04x:%04x\n", FP_SEG(p), FP_OFF(p));
```

The formatting string specifies two hexadecimal values padded with leading zeros and right justified in four places.

A simple experiment demonstrates the versatility of void pointers. Add the following statements to VOID.C, immediately after line 9:

```
double f = 3.14159;
double *fp = &f;
printf("*fp == %f\n", *fp);
printf(" fp == ");
DispPointer(fp);
```

The first line declares and initializes a `double` variable `f` to 3.14159. The second line declares a `double` pointer `fp`, and assigns it the address of `f`. The `fp` pointer now points to the location where `f`'s value is stored. In other words, `fp` is an alias for `f`. Next, a `printf()` statement displays `f`'s dereferenced value `*fp`. Running the modified program displays 3.14159, proving `fp` addresses `f`'s value. The last two lines display `fp`'s address by passing the pointer to `DispPointer()`.

NOTE: Writing programs that rely on the 80x86's segmented memory makes those programs highly system-dependent. Other computers may or may not use segmented addresses, and programs written as described in the preceding section probably won't run on systems that are not 80x86-based.

Pointers and Dynamic Variables

Sample programs up to this point stored values in global and local variables. Global variables reside at fixed locations in the program's data segment. Local variables are stuffed on the stack and exist only while their declaring functions are active.

Both kinds of variables share one characteristic—you declare them directly in the program's text. When the compiled code runs, declarations such as `int x;` or `float *fp;` define storage space for values of the declared data types.

Another technique allocates space for variables at runtime. Such variables are dynamic—they are created on demand and stored in a variable-size block of memory known as the heap. Dynamic variables are also called pointer-addressable variables because they are always addressed by pointers. (See Figure 9.3.)

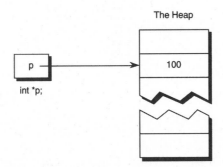

Figure 9.3. Pointers can address dynamic variables on the heap.

The heap's exact size and location depend on how much memory is available and other factors, such as which memory model the program uses (see Chapter 20, "DOS Tools and Techniques"). Some memory models provide two heaps—a near one with limited capacity, and a far one that is usually much larger. It's best to postpone studying these details until you are comfortable with the general concepts of allocating heap space and using pointers to address that space. For now, think of the heap as a capacious memory space that tends to provide more room than is typically available for global and local variables, and is therefore a good place to store large buffers and data structures that grow and shrink as needed to accommodate varying amounts of information.

Reserving Heap Space

There are several ways to reserve space on the heap for dynamic variables. The most common technique uses a library function named `malloc()`, an abbreviation for *memory allocation* or *memory allocator*. Calling `malloc()` reserves a specified number of bytes on the heap for the program's use. The function returns the reserved block's address, which is usually assigned to a pointer.

To use `malloc()`, include the header file alloc.h, and declare a pointer:

```
#include <alloc.h>
...
char *sp;          /* sp is a pointer to char */
```

Then, call `malloc()`, specifying in the parentheses the number of bytes to reserve, and assigning the function's returned value to the pointer:

```
sp = malloc(129);  /* Reserve 129 bytes */
```

Because `malloc()` returns type `void *`, not `char *`, some programmers prefer to use a type cast, making the purpose of the assignment perfectly clear:

```
sp = (char *)malloc(129);  /* Reserve 129 bytes */
```

This form is required in C++ to assign a `void *` address to a typed pointer. The type cast is optional in ANSI C. (This form, however, is rarely used in C++; as discussed in later chapters, there are better ways to allocate heap memory for C++ programs.)

Either way, pointer `sp` now addresses a block of 129 bytes reserved for the exclusive use of `sp`. The statement might fail if the heap is already full or isn't big enough to accommodate the requested number of bytes. In that case, `malloc()` returns null. For best results, after calling `malloc()`, check whether `sp` is null:

```
sp = malloc(129);  /* Reserve 129 bytes */
if (sp == NULL)    /* If malloc fails, */
  error();         /*  call error function */
```

To execute a statement if a memory allocation is successful, you can write

```
sp = malloc(129);  /* Allocate 129 bytes of memory */
if (sp)            /* If sp is non-null... */
  statement;       /* ... execute statement */
```

Because expressions such as `sp = malloc(129)` have values, you can also write

```
if ((sp = malloc(129)) != NULL)
  statement;
```

Either technique allocates 129 bytes of memory, assigns the returned address to `sp`, and executes `statement` if `sp` is non-null.

After reserving a memory block and assigning its address to a pointer, you can dereference that pointer and use the memory as though it belonged to a local or global variable. For example, to copy characters from a string to the memory addressed by `sp`, you can write

```
#include <string.h>
...
char *sp;
sp = malloc(129);
if (sp)
  strcpy(sp, "Throw me onto the heap!");
```

You cannot use the assignment operator (=) to copy character strings. You must instead call a string function such as strcpy(), which transfers characters from one string (the literal "Throw me...") to another (the reserved block of bytes addressed by sp). In Chapter 10, "Strings," you'll examine strcpy() and other string functions prototyped in string.h.

Pointers can address dynamic variables of any types. For instance, if you declare a pointer v to a double value:

```
double *v;
```

you can allocate space on the heap for a double value, and assign the address of that space to v. You now have a riddle to solve, however: How many bytes should you allocate? You could look up the size of double in a reference and use the statement

```
v = malloc(n);
```

where n equals a double value's size in bytes. For better portability, however, use sizeof to pass double's size to malloc():

```
v = malloc(sizeof(double));
```

After this statement, if pointer v is not null, it addresses a reserved space on the heap exactly large enough to hold a double value—a space that might be a different size on another ANSI C installation.

After allocating space for a double value, and assigning the reserved block's address to v, you can dereference v and use it as a double variable. This assigns the value of pi to the reserved memory:

```
*v = 3.14159;
```

This displays the value stored on the heap:

```
printf("Value == %lf\n", *v);
```

In each case, the expression *v dereferences the pointer, instructing the compiler to use the reserved memory as a variable of the pointer's declared type.

Rather than call `malloc()` to reserve memory, you can call the similar function `calloc()`, prototyped in alloc.h. The function works like `malloc()`, but requires two arguments—the number of objects you want to allocate and the size of one object. Use `calloc()` like this:

```
long *p;
p = calloc(1, sizeof(long));
```

This reserves space for one `long` value, and assigns the address of that space to `p`. To reserve 10 objects, you could write

```
p = calloc(10, sizeof(long));
```

This reserves a block of 10 `long` values, and assigns the address of the first value to `p`. Interestingly, `calloc()`'s parameters can be specified in either order. The expression `calloc(num, size)` reserves `num*size` bytes; therefore, the statement

```
p = calloc(4, sizeof(long));
```

has the same effect as

```
p = calloc(sizeof(long), 4);
```

Technically speaking, if n equals `sizeof(long)`, the former statement allocates four objects of n bytes each; the latter allocates n four-byte blocks. In practice, however, the two statements are functionally identical, although statements such as

```
buffer = calloc(n, 1);
```

are typically used to reserve buffers of n bytes.

In addition to allocating memory, `calloc()` sets every reserved byte to zero. Use this feature to initialize memory blocks and as a debugging aid. Load the program into Turbo Debugger and, after executing various statements, inspect memory blocks allocated by `calloc()`. Any bytes equal to zero might not have been used. (Of course, another operation could have zeroed those bytes, but this is still a handy, if informal, method for investigating memory use.)

Deleting Heap Space

When finished with a reserved memory block, you should free it so `malloc()`, `calloc()`, and other memory-allocation functions can reuse that memory. If you don't free reserved heap space that you no longer need, it remains unusable until the program ends.

To free a reserved memory block, call `free()`. If you allocate space for a 255-character string (which takes 256 bytes including the null terminator):

```
char *s;
s = malloc(256);
```

after using the memory addressed by `char` pointer `s`, release that space by executing this statement:

```
free(s);
```

You do not have to specify how much space to free—the block's size is saved in a few miscellaneous bytes attached to every reserved block. As you might suppose, it's vital to free only as much space as originally reserved for a pointer's use. Fortunately, C takes care of that requirement for you.

> **WARNING:** After calling `free(p)` to release the space addressed by `p`, *never* under any circumstances use `p` to read or write values in that now-unprotected memory. You may call `malloc()` or a similar function to reserve another memory block and assign its address to `p`, but a freed pointer's address value is invalid and must not be used. Some programmers assign `NULL` to freed pointers, which helps prevent accidental use of unprotected memory blocks.

Declaring Near and Far Pointers

The terms *near pointer* and *far pointer* are not part of the ANSI C specification, but are needed by Borland C++ to accommodate the 80x86 segmented memory architecture. When data resides in a memory location that is not reachable as an offset from a segment boundary, it's necessary to address that data with a far pointer. A 16-bit near pointer can reach memory addresses within 64K (exactly 65,536) bytes from any segment, which may begin at any 16-byte boundary address, typically kept in a processor segment register. A far pointer's 32 bits include a segment address value, and can therefore reach any memory location (see Figure 9.4).

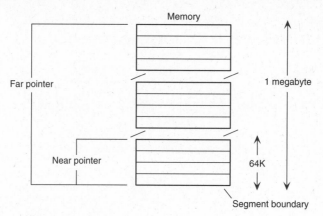

Figure 9.4. Far pointers can address all memory locations; near pointers can reach only locations within 64K of a segment boundary.

One myth about 80x86-based memory is that a segment is 64K bytes long. It isn't. A segment isn't a fixed chunk of memory. It's one of 65,536 possible segment starting locations (called paragraphs) in a typical PC's first megabyte of RAM. (65,536*16 equals 1,048,576.) Segments can range from 16 to 65,536 bytes. Two or more segments may begin at the same boundaries and multiple segments may overlap. Segments are simply divisions of memory—a convenient scheme for managing large amounts of RAM in relatively small chunks.

A simple example demonstrates near and far pointers. Listing 9.3, NEARFAR.C, shows how to declare each pointer type and displays their internal sizes in bytes.

Listing 9.3. NEARFAR.C (Demonstrates near and far pointers).

```
 1:  #include <stdio.h>
 2:
 3:  /* Disable warning "xxx is declared but never used" */
 4:  #pragma warn -use
 5:
 6:  main()
 7:  {
 8:    float *fp1;        /* A "near" pointer */
 9:    float far *fp2;    /* A "far" pointer */
10:
```

```
11:    printf("Size of fp1 == %d bytes\n", sizeof(fp1));
12:    printf("Size of fp2 == %d bytes\n", sizeof(fp2));
13:    return 0;
14:  }
```

Line 4 is a #pragma command that disables the compiler warning "[identifier] is declared but never used." The sample program simply displays the sizes of two pointers. Because the code doesn't otherwise use the pointers, the compiler issues the warning.

Running NEARFAR displays the small report:

```
Size of fp1 == 2 bytes
Size of fp2 == 4 bytes
```

The plain float pointer fp1 at line 8 takes two bytes of memory—exactly enough room for a 16-bit offset address value. The far pointer fp2 takes four bytes—two for a segment value and two for an offset. You can also designate fp1 to be near by changing line 8 to

```
float near *fp1;
```

Usually, however, it's best to declare pointers without near and far qualifiers. In the absence of these words, the compiler can adjust a pointer's storage format and size to accommodate different memory models. Use near and far only when you must declare a pointer to have a specific format.

Out of Memory

The main disadvantage of using dynamic variables occurs after creating and disposing many of them. Freeing a few unused dynamic variables while leaving others reserved may create holes in memory equal to the sizes of the freed items. As Figure 9.5 illustrates, the holes fragment the heap, dividing it into small spaces, which might not be large enough to accommodate new memory requests from malloc() and calloc().

A fragmented heap is a serious condition. If the heap becomes significantly fragmented, for a given memory allocation request, the total amount of unused (but separated) memory areas may be far more than needed. If, however, all indivisible spaces are smaller than the requested amount, malloc() and calloc() return zero. Due to fragmentation, it's possible to receive an out-of-memory error when, in fact, there's plenty of memory available. It's just not all in one place.

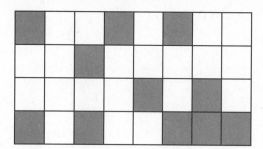

Figure 9.5. After disposing numerous variables, available memory (shaded boxes) may be divided, or fragmented, into unconnected regions.

Unfortunately, Borland C++ doesn't provide the means to collect unused heap fragments into one large space for new variables. Adjacent disposed blocks are combined, but nonadjacent blocks remain separated. Some languages, such as Lisp, include a garbage collector that can compact the heap's unused areas. However, garbage collection tends to reduce performance considerably, and the Borland C++ memory manager therefore trades efficient heap use for speed—a good bargain in most cases.

NOTE: Windows 3.0 and 3.1 in 386-Enhanced mode can move memory blocks to reduce heap fragmentation without requiring programs to perform any special actions. Better memory management is one reason developers are gravitating toward Windows. See Chapter 21, "Windows Tools and Techniques," in Part 4.

One answer to the heap fragmentation dilemma is to reserve only large structures, preferably of the same sizes, or of sizes that are multiples of each other. For example, you might request memory in fixed-block sizes of 32, 64, 128, and 256 bytes. When those spaces are freed, they tend to create unused areas of the sizes that are more likely to satisfy other memory allocation requests.

Another possible solution is to allocate arrays of variables. With this strategy, you are assured of having at least a minimum number of dynamic variables available. Also, disposing relatively large arrays tends to produce less fragmentation than disposing multiple lone-wolf variables.

Heap Granularity

The Borland C++ memory manager tacks on four extra bytes to every heap allocation request. Two of these extra bytes hold the segment address of the preceding block, and the other two equal the size of the block in 16-byte paragraphs (see Figure 9.6). In other words, if the block's size is 4, it has room for 64 (16*4) bytes of data.

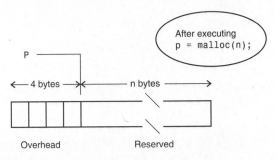

Figure 9.6. Reserved heap blocks have four bytes of overhead each.

Like sand in a dune, a program's memory heap is composed of grains, each having a minimum number of bits. In Borland C++, the smallest possible non-null reserved area on the heap (often called the heap's granularity) is 20 bytes—four bytes of overhead plus one 16-byte paragraph. Because actual data begins four bytes beyond the physical beginning of every reserved memory block, a dynamic variable's far pointer has an offset equal to 4.

Although these facts suggest that heap memory is full of wasted bytes, Borland C++'s 16-byte granularity tends to reduce heap fragmentation—a trade-off worth much more than a small amount of waste. However, it's best not to store individual small variables on the heap. A single dynamic int value, for example, occupies 20 bytes of heap space! An array of several int variables uses the heap much more efficiently.

Determining Free Space

Calculating the amount of free space on the heap requires a good understanding of how the heap is organized. At any one time, the heap contains three kinds of items:

- Reserved areas allocated by malloc(), calloc(), or a similar heap allocation function.

• Previously used areas released by free() or a similar heap deallocation function.

• Virgin memory areas.

The total heap space available to a program equals the sum of the sizes of all previously used areas plus the size of the heap's virgin territory. Listing 9.4, HEAPNEAR.C, calculates the amount of free space available in the near heap.

Listing 9.4. HEAPNEAR.C (Calculates near heap's free space).

```
 1:  #include <stdio.h>
 2:  #include <alloc.h>
 3:
 4:  #define MSIZE 1024      /* Size as an integer */
 5:  #define SSIZE "1024"    /* Same size as a string */
 6:
 7:  void Report(char *s);
 8:  long NearHeapSize(void);
 9:
10:  main()
11:  {
12:    void *p1;
13:    void *p2;
14:
15:    Report("Before calling malloc()");
16:    p1 = malloc(MSIZE);
17:    Report("After allocating "SSIZE" bytes");
18:    p2 = malloc(MSIZE);
19:    Report("After allocating another "SSIZE" bytes");
20:    free(p1);
21:    Report("After freeing "SSIZE" bytes");
22:    free(p2);
23:    Report("After freeing another "SSIZE" bytes");
24:    return 0;
25:  }
26:
27:  void Report(char *s)
28:  {
29:    long result;
30:
```

```
31:    puts(s);
32:    result = NearHeapSize();
33:    if (result < 0)
34:      puts("- No near heap or error!");
35:    else
36:      printf("- Near heap size = %lu\n", result);
37:  }
38:
39:  /* Return size of near heap free space or -1 for error */
40:  long NearHeapSize(void)
41:  {
42:    unsigned long count;
43:    struct heapinfo info;
44:
45:    info.ptr = NULL;
46:    if (heapcheck() != _HEAPOK)
47:      return -1L;
48:    count = coreleft();
49:    while (heapwalk(&info) == _HEAPOK)
50:      if (info.in_use == 0)
51:        count += info.size;
52:    return count;
53:  }
```

You might want to extract function `NearHeapSize()` for your own programs. The function is prototyped at line 8 and implemented at lines 40–53. Call it to find out how many free bytes are available on the near heap.

Just to make things interesting, the test program allocates two memory blocks of 1024 bytes (see lines 16 and 18). It frees those blocks at lines 20 and 22, thus temporarily fragmenting the heap, but not seriously. At each stage, the program reports the amount of heap space available:

```
Before calling malloc()
- Near heap size = 63344
After allocating 1024 bytes
- Near heap size = 62320
After allocating another 1024 bytes
- Near heap size = 61296
After freeing 1024 bytes
- Near heap size = 62324
After freeing another 1024 bytes
- Near heap size = 63344
```

Two local variables inside `NearHeapSize()` help the function compute the amount of available heap space. The `unsigned long count` declared at line 42 holds the function result, returned at line 52. A second variable, `info` of type `struct heapinfo`, stores information about used and freed memory blocks. The structure is declared in the alloc.h header file, which the program includes at line 2.

To calculate free heap space, `info.ptr` is initialized to `NULL`, a requirement before "walking the heap"—in other words, examining the heap's structure by walking through its blocks. Before starting the program's walking tour of the heap, lines 46–47 call function `heapcheck()`, which might return one of three values: `_HEAPEMPTY` if there is no heap for the current memory model, `_HEAPOK` if the heap passes internal tests, or `_HEAPCORRUPT` if an error is detected in the heap's structure. Only if `heapcheck()` returns `_HEAPOK` is it safe to walk the heap.

After these preliminary steps, line 48 initializes `count` to the value returned by another function, `coreleft()`. This value equals the amount of virgin territory. Next, a `while` loop calls `heapwalk()`, passing the `info` structure as an argument. If `heapwalk()` returns `_HEAPOK`, then an inner `if` statement examines the structure's `in_use` member, which is zero (false) for blocks previously freed. Upon finding a freed block, the statement at line 51 adds the block's size to `count`.

> **NOTE:** *Core* is another word for memory. The term is a holdover from the early days of computing when some memory systems consisted of tiny donut-shaped ferrite magnets, strung up inside a matrix of wires through which the computer could read bit values.

Listing 9.5, HEAPFAR.C, determines the amount of free space available on the far heap.

Listing 9.5. HEAPFAR.C (Calculates far heap's free space).

```
1:  #include <stdio.h>
2:  #include <alloc.h>
3:
4:  #define MSIZE 1024      /* Size as an integer */
5:  #define SSIZE "1024"    /* Same size as a string */
6:
```

```
 7:   void Report(char *s);
 8:   long FarHeapSize(void);
 9:
10:   main()
11:   {
12:     void far *p1;
13:     void far *p2;
14:
15:     Report("Before calling farmalloc()");
16:     p1 = farmalloc(MSIZE);
17:     Report("After allocating "SSIZE" bytes");
18:     p2 = farmalloc(MSIZE);
19:     Report("After allocating another "SSIZE" bytes");
20:     farfree(p2);
21:     Report("After freeing "SSIZE" bytes");
22:     farfree(p1);
23:     Report("After freeing another "SSIZE" bytes");
24:     return 0;
25:   }
26:
27:   void Report(char *s)
28:   {
29:     long result;
30:
31:     puts(s);
32:     result = FarHeapSize();
33:     if (result < 0)
34:       puts("- No far heap or error!");
35:     else
36:       printf("- Far heap size = %lu\n", result);
37:   }
38:
39:   /* Return size of far heap free space or -1 for error */
40:   long FarHeapSize(void)
41:   {
42:     unsigned long count;
43:     struct farheapinfo info;
44:
45:     info.ptr = NULL;
46:     if (farheapcheck() != _HEAPOK)
47:       return -1L;
```

continues

Listing 9.5. continued

```
48:     count = farcoreleft();
49:     while (farheapwalk(&info) == _HEAPOK)
50:       if (info.in_use == 0)
51:         count += info.size;
52:     return count;
53:   }
```

HEAPFAR calls `farmalloc()` to allocate space on the far heap (see lines 16 and 18). The function works the same as `malloc()`, but reserves far heap space, which typically has more room for dynamic variables than the near heap. You must use far pointers when addressing objects on the far heap, so be sure to use the proper memory model (see Chapter 20, "DOS Tools and Techniques") or declare your pointers `far` as done here at lines 12–13.

Function `FarHeapSize()` at lines 40–53 is similar to `NearHeapSize()` in HEAPNEAR. The new function uses an `info` variable of type `farheapinfo` and calls `farheapcheck()`, `farcoreleft()`, and `farheapwalk()` to calculate available far heap space. (Look up other `far...` functions in Chapter 22, "Functions and Examples," and in your Borland C++ Library Reference.)

Try compiling and running HEAPNEAR and HEAPFAR using different memory models. Either select a model using the IDE Options|Compiler|Code Generation command, or from a DOS prompt, specify -m*x* where *x* is t for tiny, s for small, m for medium, c for compact, 1 for large, or h for huge memory models. Not all memory models support near and far heaps, and the programs correctly issue errors for any illegal commands.

NOTE: To compile tiny (that is, .COM style) programs, use the DOS command **bcc -mt file.c**. Ignore the "No stack" warning from the linker, and *don't run the resulting .EXE code file!* Instead, give the command **exe2bin file.exe**, creating FILE.BIN, which you can rename to FILE.COM and run.

Setting the Heap and Stack Sizes

For better control over a program's memory resources, you can specify minimum stack and heap sizes. There's no guarantee the space you request will be available on a particular computer system, but it doesn't hurt to ask.

The smallest possible stack is 256 bytes. The default size for small memory-model programs is 4096 bytes. That should be plenty of room for small- to medium-size programs, but if you need more space, add this line to your program:

```
extern unsigned _stklen = 8192U;
```

The _stklen identifier refers to a global variable, one of several that are available to Borland C++ programs. Redeclaring _stklen and assigning it an unsigned integer sets the program's stack to the requested length. If enough space is not available, however, the program displays "Abnormal program termination" and refuses to run.

Listing 9.6, SETSTACK.C, demonstrates how to redeclare _stklen. It also makes a handy benchmark for verifying the Borland C++ default stack size. From the DOS prompt, compile the program with the command **bcc setstack.c** and run it to display the size of the default stack. Recompile with the command **bcc -DDEBUG setstack.c** to double the stack length to 8192 bytes.

Listing 9.6. SETSTACK.C (Sets the minimum stack size).

```
 1:  #include <stdio.h>
 2:
 3:  #ifdef DEBUG
 4:  extern unsigned _stklen = 8192U;
 5:  #else
 6:  extern unsigned _stklen;
 7:  #endif
 8:
 9:  main()
10:  {
11:    printf("Stack length == %u\n", _stklen);
12:    return 0;
13:  }
```

The program uses #ifdef, #else, and #endif to detect whether the symbol DEBUG is defined, selecting either line 4 or 6 for compilation.

Listing 9.7, SETHEAP.C, is similar to SETSTACK, but modifies the default near heap size. The default near heap size varies for different memory models, and for some models, is affected by the size of the stack and the number of global variables the program uses. (The far heap typically equals all the space left in memory after a program's data, code, stack, and near heap are accounted for, so there's no need to specify the far heap's size. When a program begins, there *is* no far heap until space is requested.)

Listing 9.7. SETHEAP.C (Sets the minimum heap size).

```
 1:  #include <stdio.h>
 2:  #include <alloc.h>
 3:
 4:  #ifdef DEBUG
 5:  extern unsigned _heaplen = 16000U;
 6:  #else
 7:  extern unsigned _heaplen;
 8:  #endif
 9:
10:  main()
11:  {
12:    printf("_heaplen == %u\n", _heaplen);
13:    printf("coreleft() == %u\n", coreleft());
14:    return 0;
15:  }
```

The global _heaplen variable works differently than _stklen. Normally, _heaplen equals zero, which specifies the maximum possible size. Potentially, the near heap can have up to about 64K of memory, but is usually smaller because, in the small and medium memory models, its space is shared with the stack and global variables. In the tiny model's .COM code files, the heap, stack, code, and data must all fit in one 64K segment—a tight squeeze that is unsuitable for most applications.

Because the default _heaplen variable is set to zero, you can't use this value to determine how much near heap space is available. Instead, call coreleft() as demonstrated at line 13. As explained before, coreleft() returns the size of virgin near heap territory. At the start of the program, this value equals the size of the heap. After allocating and freeing various dynamic variables on the heap, however, `coreleft()` does not give an accurate picture of the amount of free space available. For that, you must walk the heap as explained earlier.

Pointers and Data Structures

Pointers may address variables of all kinds—including simple variables of types such as int and double, but also arrays and structures. When using pointers to address these relatively complex data structures, several new rules come into play.

Pointers and Arrays

Most beginning C programmers are surprised to discover arrays and pointers are one and the same. All array identifiers are actually pointers, and all pointers can address arrays.

Sound strange? If so, consider the nature of an array. As you learned earlier, an array collects a series of one or more variables of the same data type. If collection is an array, the expression collection[0] refers to the first element of the array. In a sense, a subscript expression such as collection[0], points to the array's first variable, and is internally the same as a dereferenced pointer.

A simple example, Listing 9.8, ARRAYPTR.C, demonstrates this important relationship between pointers and arrays.

Listing 9.8. ARRAYPTR.C (Demonstrates arrays and pointers).

```
1:  #include <stdio.h>
2:
3:  #define MAX 10        /* Size of array */
4:
5:  void showFirst(void);
6:
7:  int array[MAX];       /* Global array of MAX integers */
8:
```

continues

Listing 9.8. continued

```
 9:  main()
10:  {
11:    array[0] = 123;     /* Assign value using indexing */
12:    showFirst();        /* Display value both ways */
13:    *array = 321;       /* Assign value using pointer */
14:    showFirst();        /* Display value both ways */
15:    return 0;
16:  }
17:
18:  void showFirst(void)
19:  {
20:    printf("array[0] = %d\n", array[0]);
21:    printf("*array   = %d\n", *array);
22:  }
```

Line 7 declares a global array of int values. Line 11 assigns 123 to array[0], using common array subscripting. Function showFirst() displays the array's first element, using a subscript expression (line 20) and then using the same array identifier as a pointer (line 21). Because arrays are pointers in disguise, C allows programs to dereference array names with expressions such as *array. Line 13 assigns another value to the array's first position, but also uses the dereferenced pointer expression *array.

The relationship between arrays and pointers may be easier to visualize if you consider what the compiler must do in order to evaluate a subscripted expression such as array[4]. In order to find the fifth element in the array, the program's compiled code has to

- Locate the starting address of the array.

- Calculate the distance from the starting address to the indexed element. If the array contains two-byte integers, the fifth element is 4*2, or eight bytes, beyond the first.

- To the starting address, add the distance calculated from the preceding step, forming a pointer to the subscripted element.

The result of these steps is a pointer the program uses when it executes an expression such as i = array[4]. To find the array's fifth element, the compiled code converts the expression array[4] into a pointer to the subscripted element (let's call the pointer p). The program then executes the equivalent of i = *p to assign the array's element value to i.

Although it's usually best to let the compiler handle array addressing details, it's sometimes useful to take over that job and use explicit pointers rather than subscripts to address array elements. For an example of this trick, compile and run Listing 9.9, PTRARRAY.C.

Listing 9.9. PTRARRAY.C (Addresses array elements with pointers).

```
 1:  #include <stdio.h>
 2:
 3:  #define MAX 10       /* Size of array */
 4:
 5:  void showFirst(void);
 6:
 7:  int array[MAX];       /* Global array of MAX integers */
 8:
 9:  main()
10:  {
11:    int *p = array;    /* p is an int pointer to array */
12:    int i;            /* i is a plain int variable */
13:
14:    for (i = 0; i < MAX; i++)
15:      array[i] = i;
16:    for (i = 0; i < MAX; i++)
17:      printf("%d\n", *p++);
18:    p = &array[5];
19:    printf("array[5] = %d\n", array[5]);
20:    printf("*p ..... = %d\n", *p);
21:    return 0;
22:  }
```

PTRARRAY is similar to the preceding ARRAYPTR demonstration, but shows how to use pointers to access any array element. Line 11 declares a pointer variable p as a pointer to type int, the same type as the array's elements (see line 7). Line 11 also assigns the address of array to p. Using the address-of operator in an expression such as &array to compute array's address is an error, and would cause the compiler to issue the warning "Suspicious pointer conversion." Remember, array *is* a pointer; you can assign its value directly to another pointer of an appropriate type.

Lines 14–15 use common indexing to fill array with values from 0 to MAX - 1. A second for loop at lines 16–17 then displays array's contents. This time, however, the program uses the pointer p instead of subscripting to refer to each array value.

Carefully study the expression *p++ in line 17. Two actions take place. Dereferencing *p gives the value addressed by p. The increment operator ++ then advances p to the next int in array, causing the loop to display all array elements.

Pointer Arithmetic

From the preceding section, you might wonder how it's possible for an expression such as *p++ to advance p to the address of the array's next integer. Because p is declared as int *p, the compiler knows p addresses variables of type int. The compiler also knows the size of an int variable (two bytes in Borland C++). To evaluate the expression p++, the compiler simply adds two to p's address value (see Figure 9.7).

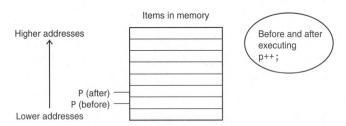

Figure 9.7. The expression p++ advances pointer p to the next item.

You can use pointer arithmetic expressions such as p += 10 to advance p 10 units from its present position, or p -= 2 to move p back two units. In arithmetic expressions involving pointers, only plus and minus operations are allowed. You can also compare pointers with expressions such as (p1 < p2) and (p1 >= p2). Although the compiler accepts such statements, they may not work correctly with far pointers. You may compare pointers reliably only if they are not far.

The reason for this restriction is that, in segmented memory such as found on all 80x86-based computers, it's possible for two or more different address values to refer to the same physical location. For example, the hexadecimal address 0000:0010 is equivalent to 0001:0000. The first value represents a location 16 bytes beyond 0000:0000. The second represents the start of a segment boundary at that exact same spot.

Far pointers contain both segment and offset values, and they may therefore differ in value while pointing to the same memory location. For two pointers p1 and p2, the expression (p1 == p2) may be false even though both pointers address the identical data.

One way out of this dilemma is to use huge pointers, which are physically the same as far pointers but have normalized offset values in the range of 0 to 15 decimal. Every location in memory has a unique normalized far address. In other words, for every address, there is only one pair of segment and offset values with an offset in the range of 0 to 15.

To declare huge pointers, use the huge keyword similar to the way you use far. For example, this line:

```
char huge *fp;
```

declares pointer fp as a huge pointer, which may be used as a far pointer with one difference: In any expressions involving huge pointers, the pointer values are normalized to ensure a correct result. Huge pointers are Borland C++ specialties—they may not be available in other ANSI C compilers.

Listing 9.10, FARHUGE.C, demonstrates how huge pointers can be used to compare two pointers for equality.

Listing 9.10. FARHUGE.C (Compares far and huge pointers).

```
 1:  #include <stdio.h>
 2:  #include <dos.h>
 3:
 4:  main()
 5:  {
 6:    char far *fp1;    /* Far char pointer #1 */
 7:    char far *fp2;    /* Far char pointer #2 */
 8:    char huge *hp1;   /* Huge char pointer #1 */
 9:    char huge *hp2;   /* Huge char pointer #2 */
10:
11:    fp1 = MK_FP(0, 0x0010);
12:    fp2 = MK_FP(0x0001, 0);
13:    if (fp1 == fp2)
14:      printf("Far pointers are equal\n");
15:    else
```

continues

Listing 9.10. continued

```
16:     printf("Far pointers are NOT equal\n");
17:   hp1 = MK_FP(0, 0x0010);
18:   hp2 = MK_FP(0x0001, 0);
19:   if (hp1 == hp2)
20:     printf("Huge pointers are equal\n");
21:   else
22:     printf("Huge pointers are NOT equal\n");
23:   return 0;
24: }
```

Lines 6–7 declare two far pointers, fp1 and fp2. To the first pointer, the program assigns the hexadecimal address 0000:0010. To the second, it assigns 0001:0000. Though different in value, the two addresses point to the same location in memory. Despite that fact, however, the comparison at line 13 is false. The expression (fp1 == fp2) compares only the far pointer values—it doesn't take the segmented memory architecture of the PC into account.

Lines 8–9 declare two more pointers, this time using the huge keyword to inform the compiler that these pointers should be normalized in expressions. Lines 17–18 assign the same address values as before, but this time the expression (hp1 == hp2) at line 19 evaluates to true. In making that comparison, the compiler generates code that normalizes the pointer values, thus making it possible to compare them.

> **NOTE:** Normalization takes time, and for that reason, huge pointers should be used only when absolutely necessary. Programs with many huge pointers may operate more slowly than programs that use far pointers.

Dynamic Arrays

Fixed-size arrays can waste space. For instance, if you declare a 100-element array of double values like this:

```
double myArray[100];
```

but use only 70 elements, 30 double values are wasted. At eight bytes each, that's 240 bytes that are unusable for other operations. In a large program with many such arrays, the amount of waste in fixed-size arrays can reach staggering levels.

When you don't need to determine in advance how big to declare arrays, use the following technique to create a dynamic array that can change size at runtime. First, declare a pointer of the data type for variables to be stored in the array:

```
double *myArrayP;
```

Then, elsewhere in the program, call malloc() to allocate heap space for the array. For example, if the program needs 70 elements, use the statement

```
myArrayP = malloc(70 * sizeof(double));
```

You might also call calloc() or, to create an array on the far heap, farmalloc() or farcalloc(). To allocate a 70-element array of double values, and clear those values to zero, you could write

```
myArrayP = calloc(70, sizeof(double));
```

After allocating space for the array, if myArrayP is non-null, it addresses a block of memory capable of holding 70 double values. Because arrays and pointers are directly related, you can use the pointer identifier as though it had been declared as an array. This stores 3.14159 in the array's 12th element:

```
myArrayP[11] = 3.14159;
```

After using the array, release its memory by calling free():

```
free(myArrayP);
```

You can then call malloc() again to reserve a different amount of space for another array, and assign the new address to myArrayP.

Arrays of Pointers

A useful construction is an array of pointers. Each element in such an array points to the *real* data located elsewhere. This is a good way to keep track of related dynamic variables, for example, a series of strings loaded from a text file. If those strings were stored in fixed-character arrays declared as char c[128], each 80-character string would waste 48 bytes.

Listing 9.11, READSTR.C, shows a good way to avoid such waste. The program uses an array of char pointers, each of which addresses a string that takes only as much space as necessary.

Listing 9.11. READSTR.C (Uses an array of pointers to address dynamic strings).

```
 1:  #include <stdio.h>
 2:  #include <string.h>
 3:  #include <alloc.h>
 4:
 5:  #define MAX 3     /* Maximum number of strings */
 6:
 7:  char *ReadString(void);
 8:
 9:  main()
10:  {
11:    int i;               /* Array index */
12:    char *array[MAX]; /* Array of MAX char pointers */
13:
14:    printf("Enter %d strings:\n", MAX);
15:    for (i = 0; i < MAX; i++)
16:      array[i] = ReadString();
17:    puts("\n\nYour strings are:\n");
18:    for (i = 0; i < MAX; i++)
19:      puts(array[i]);
20:    return 0;
21:  }
22:
23:  char *ReadString(void)
24:  {
25:    char *p;          /* p is a pointer to a char array */
26:    char buffer[128]; /* buffer for reading each string */
27:
28:    gets(buffer);
29:    p = (char *)malloc(1 + strlen(buffer));
30:    strcpy(p, buffer);
31:    return p;
32:  }
```

The key feature in READSTR is the char *array[MAX]; declaration at line 12. Declared like this, array is an array of char pointers. Assigning to these pointers the addresses of variable-length strings (themselves char arrays) creates an efficient data structure, illustrated in Figure 9.8.

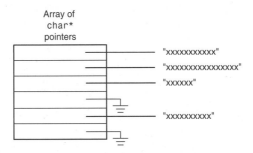

Figure 9.8. An array of char pointers addresses variable-length strings.

Line 16 calls function ReadString(), which returns a pointer to a char array. The pointer is saved in the array. Line 19 then displays those strings, passing their addresses to puts().

Function ReadString() (lines 23–32) declares a local buffer. Because local variables exist only while their functions are active, any waste from this fixed-size string is recovered automatically when the function ends.

After line 28 reads a string from the keyboard (or from the operating system's standard input file), the function executes the statement

```
p = (char *)malloc(1 + strlen(buffer));
```

As in earlier examples, malloc() reserves space on the heap, in this case equal to one plus the length of the string in the local buffer. Function strlen() returns the length of a string—that is, the number of characters it holds. Reserving that much space plus one byte for the string's null terminator allocates the smallest amount of space possible to store the string. Function malloc()'s result is recast to a char *, avoiding a warning from the compiler.

After allocating space for the string and assigning its address to p, the program calls strcpy() at line 30 to copy the characters from the temporary buffer to the newly reserved heap space. Finally, the function returns p, passing back the address of the reserved space.

> **NOTE:** For simplicity, READSTR.C assumes that enough space is available on the heap for storing a few short strings. In a larger program, such assumptions may be dangerous, and except for short tests and examples, you should always verify that pointers are valid before using them. (See Exercise 9.5)

Pointers and Strings

The declaration char *c is exactly equivalent to char c[]. Each creates a pointer to an array of char, which typically addresses a null-terminated string.

The preceding section explained how to create and use an array of char pointers to address a collection of variable-size strings. A pointer *to* such an array is literally a pointer to an array of pointers, which could be declared as

```
char **array;
```

The double pointer symbols ** declare a pointer to a pointer. Because pointers and arrays are equivalent, this declaration is exactly equivalent to

```
char *array[];
```

This form is clearer than the latter, and usually preferred. Either way, array is a pointer that addresses an array of char pointers. Probably the most typical use for this two-way pointer is to access command-line parameters from DOS, passed to main() as demonstrated by Listing 9.12, CMDLINE.C.

Listing 9.12. CMDLINE.C (Displays command-line parameters).

```
1:  #include <stdio.h>
2:
3:  main(int argc, char *argv[])
4:  {
5:    if (argc <= 1) {
6:      puts("");
7:      puts("CMDLINE by Tom Swan");
8:      puts("Enter CMDLINE [x[y][z]] to test");
9:      puts("command-line arguments.");
```

```
10:    } else
11:    while (--argc > 0)
12:      puts(*++argv);
13:    return 0;
14:  }
```

Line 3 declares `main()` differently than in previous listings. Parameter `argc` equals the number of parameters entered after the program's name, plus one additional argument for the program's path. Parameter `argv` is a pointer to an array of `char` pointers, each of which addresses a command-line string.

Compile and run CMDLINE, then from a DOS prompt, enter a command such as **`cmdline arg1 arg2 arg3`**. CMDLINE displays each of the arguments, extracted from DOS and passed to `main()` by the program's startup code. The `while` statement at line 11 decrements `argc`, and ends after the count reaches zero. Line 12 passes one string to `puts()`, using the expression `*++argv` to dereference the pointer and increment it to the next `char *` in the array.

Lines 11 and 12 might be unclear until you are familiar with C's shorthand tricks. To understand these lines, rewrite them the long way using separate statements. First, declare a `char` pointer between lines 4 and 5:

```
char *p;
```

Then, modify the `while` loop at lines 11–12 to

```
while (argc > 0) {
  argc--;
  p = *argv;
  puts(p);
  argv++;
}
```

Carefully study this loop. It reveals several pointer tricks you can use in many other situations. The loop cycles while the count of arguments in `argc` is greater than zero. On each pass through the loop, `argc` is decremented by `argc--;`. Next, the dereferenced `*argv` is assigned to the `char` pointer `p`. Because `argv` is a pointer to an array of `char` pointers, dereferencing the pointer as `*argv` locates the first of those pointers. After function `puts()` displays the string addressed by `p`, the statement `argv++` increments the array pointer to the next `char *` in line.

Figure 9.9 illustrates parameters `argc` and `argv` as organized in memory when CMDLINE is executed with the command **`cmdline filename.c -x a.out`**, which

299

simulates the kinds of arguments that might be passed to a more sophisticated program such as a C compiler. Compare CMDLINE's output with the figure while you examine the code, and be sure to understand that argv addresses an array of other pointers that address the program's command-line argument strings. (Hint: Use Turbo Debugger to inspect CMDLINE's argc and argv parameters.)

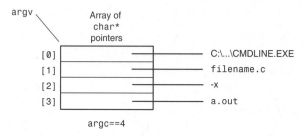

Figure 9.9. Parameters argc and argv as they appear in memory.

Character pointers are useful enough to deserve their own type name. For example, you might want to include this line in a header file or at the top of your program:

```
typedef char *Pchar;
```

You can then use Pchar ("pointer to char") in place of char *, reducing the number of hard-to-read asterisks in C programs.

> **NOTE:** See Chapter 10, "Strings," for more information about char pointers, strings, and string functions.

Pointers to the Environment

Function main() can also have a third parameter that resembles argv but addresses a series of strings in the operating system's environment. From DOS, you can create new environment strings by using the SET command. For example, typing **SET MYVAR=TRUE** creates an environment variable named MYVAR equal to the string TRUE. Type **SET** alone for a list of the current environment's strings. The system PATH is also stored as an environment string.

Every program receives a copy of the system's environment strings. To access those strings, declare main() like this:

```
main(int argc, char *argv[], char *env[])
```

Use env as you do argv. The expression env[0] addresses the first string in the environment; env[1] addresses the second string, and so on.

HINT: Declaring env in main() isn't the only way to access environment strings. To read the environment, you can also call function getenv(). To write new environment strings, call putenv(). For more information about these functions, look them up in Chapter 22, "Functions and Examples."

Pointers and Structures

When a pointer addresses a structure, a special syntax is used to refer to the structure's members. Given this structure:

```
struct xyrec {
  int x;
  int y;
};
```

which might be used to store x,y coordinates, you can declare a variable v of type struct xyrec by writing

```
struct xyrec v;   /* v is an xyrec structure */
```

Then, to assign values to v's x and y integer members, you can use statements such as

```
v.x = 123;
v.y = 321;
```

To make better use of the computer's memory, it might be best to allocate heap space for large structures rather than storing them in global or local variables. First, declare a pointer to the struct type:

```
struct xyrec *p;   /* p is a pointer to an xyrec structure */
```

Then, call `malloc()` to allocate some heap memory and assign its address to p:

```
p = (struct xyrec *)malloc(sizeof(struct xyrec));
```

Pointer p now addresses a block of memory exactly big enough to hold one `xyrec` structure. Unlike global and local structure variables, however, you can't use dot notation to access the structure's members. These statements do *not* work:

```
p.x = 123;   /* ??? */
p.y = 321;   /* ??? */
```

Pointer p is not a structure variable. It is a pointer *to* a structure, and to access the structure's members, you must use a different symbol, ->, which resembles an arrow:

```
p->x = 123;
p->y = 321;
```

The structure member access operator -> (which Borland C++ calls the "indirect (or pointer) member selector"), when applied between a structure pointer and a member name, points to that member's location, relative to the beginning of the structure. You can also dereference a structure pointer in the usual way. The expression *p refers to the structure addressed by p. The expression (*p).x is equivalent to p->x. Listing 9.13, DSTRUCT.C, demonstrates how to use structures addressed by pointers.

Listing 9.13. DSTRUCT.C (Addresses structure members with a pointer).

```
 1:  #include <stdio.h>
 2:  #include <stdlib.h>
 3:
 4:  typedef struct xyrec {
 5:    int x;
 6:    int y;
 7:  } Xyrec;
 8:
 9:  typedef Xyrec *PXyrec;
10:
11:  main()
12:  {
13:    PXyrec xyp;    /* Declare pointer to struct xyrec */
14:
15:    xyp = (PXyrec)malloc(sizeof(Xyrec));
16:    if (xyp == NULL) {
17:      puts("Out of memory!");
```

```
18:     exit(1);
19:   }
20:   xyp->x = 10;   /* Assign 10 to x member */
21:   xyp->y = 11;   /* Assign 11 to y member */
22:   printf("x == %d\n", xyp->x);
23:   printf("y == %d\n", xyp->y);
24:   return 0;
25: }
```

Lines 4–7 declare a structure with two int members, x and y. To simplify the programming, typedef associates the name Xyrec with struct xyrec. A second typedef at line 9 specifies PXyrec as an Xyrec structure pointer. Line 13 can then declare xyp as a pointer variable. Without the typedefs, the declaration:

```
PXyrec xyp;
```

would have to be written using the more confusing line:

```
struct xyrec *xyp;
```

The typedefs also simplify line 15's call to malloc(), which allocates memory for a dynamic Xyrec structure. Without typedefs, this statement becomes almost terrifyingly complex:

```
xyp = (struct xyrec *)malloc(sizeof(struct xyrec));
```

Either form works equally well, but the typedefs make the listing easier to read, and may help to prevent bugs caused by typing errors.

After allocating memory for the structure, the program assigns values to the variable's members, using the -> operator (lines 20–21). Two printf() statements at lines 22–23 display those values. The expression:

```
xyp->x;
```

points to the x member in the structure addressed by pointer xyp. Because that member is type int, the expression can be used wherever an int variable is normally allowed.

Pointers and Functions

Functions can return pointers, and you can pass pointer arguments to function parameters. It's also possible for a pointer to address a function—in other words, the pointer points to code rather than data.

This section explores these "functional" pointer techniques. First, you need to take a detour through a potentially confusing but related topic: double indirection.

Understanding Double Indirection

Remember command-line parameters, introduced a bit earlier? To use command-line parameters, you can declare main() like this:

```
main(int argc, char *argv[])
{
    ...
}
```

Pointer argv, a pointer to an array of char pointers, is an example of a double indirection—literally a pointer to a pointer. As explained earlier, you could also declare argv like this:

```
char **argv;
```

Listing 9.14, INDIRECT.C, demonstrates how to declare and use double indirection pointers.

Listing 9.14. INDIRECT.C (Demonstrates double indirection).

```
 1:  #include <stdio.h>
 2:
 3:  main()
 4:  {
 5:    double d;       /* A double variable */
 6:    double *dp;     /* Pointer to a double */
 7:    double **dpp;   /* Indirect pointer to a double */
 8:
 9:    d = 3.14159;
10:    dp = &d;
11:    dpp = &dp;
12:    printf("Value of d     == %f\n", d);
13:    printf("Value of *dp   == %f\n", *dp);
14:    printf("Value of **dpp == %f\n", **dpp);
15:    return 0;
16:  }
```

Line 5 declares a double variable d. Line 6 declares a pointer to a double variable. Line 7 declares a pointer to a pointer to a double variable. You could carry this scheme further, creating pointers to pointers to pointers to some kind of data type, but there's rarely much use for more than two levels of indirection.

Carefully examine the statements at lines 9–11. First, the value of pi is assigned to the double variable d. Next, d's address is assigned to the double pointer, dp. *That* pointer's address is then assigned to dpp. At this point, dpp points to a pointer dp which points to d, which holds a double value.

Any one of these pointers and variables can be used to refer to that same value. Line 12 simply uses the variable's name in a printf() statement. Line 13 dereferences pointer dp to refer to d's value. Line 14 double dereferences dpp—again, reaching the same value. Consequently, running the program displays the value of pi three times:

```
Value of d     == 3.141590
Value of *dp   == 3.141590
Value of **dpp == 3.141590
```

The expression **dpp dereferences dpp twice, and actually performs two distinct operations. The simpler expression *dpp dereferences dpp, forming a double pointer. The result from that operation is again dereferenced, locating the addressed value.

You may be thinking double indirection is an interesting oddity of little practical use, but it is much more than that—in fact, the technique is vital for passing information efficiently to and from functions. Keep double indirection in mind as you continue with the next topic: passing pointers to function parameters.

Pointers as Function Parameters

Functions may declare pointer parameters, and then use the pointers to address information stored somewhere in memory. Suppose you declare a structure to represent the date:

```
struct date {
  int day;
  int month;
  unsigned year;
};
```

You could then design a function `DisplayDate()` to receive a `struct date` pointer passed as an argument. The function's prototype might be

```
void DisplayDate(struct date *pd);
```

Inside the function, parameter `pd` is assumed to address a `date` structure. As with all structures addressed by pointers, you can use the `->` operator to access the structure's members:

```
void DisplayDate(struct date *pd)
{
  printf("%02d/%02d/%04d", pd->month, pd->day, pd->year);
}
```

To display a date, the program could declare and initialize a `date` structure variable, then pass its address to `DisplayDate()`'s pointer parameter:

```
struct date theDate = {31, 12, 1999};
DisplayDate(&theDate);
```

C evaluates the expression `&theDate` as the address of `theDate`, which is passed to `DisplayDate()`'s `pd` parameter. The function uses that pointer to refer to `theDate`'s members.

Passing pointers to functions this way usually saves time and memory over passing information directly. For example, if `DisplayDate()` had been declared as

```
void DisplayDate(struct date d);
```

then the program could pass `date` structure variables without using the address-of operator:

```
DisplayDate(theDate);
```

However, `theDate`'s bytes are now copied onto the stack, wasting time and memory. In this example, the waste is minuscule, but for larger structures, it's probably best to pass structure pointers to functions rather than pass the structures themselves.

Many library functions also declare pointer parameters. One of the most common functions is `scanf()`, which reads information into variables. To read a `double` value, for instance, pass it by address to `scanf()`:

```
float value;
printf("Enter a float value: ");
scanf("%f", &value);
printf("You entered %f\n", value);
```

The argument &value passes the address of value to scanf(), which reads input from the keyboard (or other standard input source), and converts ASCII text to the form specified by the format string—in this case "%f", signifying a floating-point value. That value is deposited directly in value, which scanf() can do because it knows value's address. To display that same value, however, the variable is passed by value (without the & operator). Function printf() does not modify value; therefore, it needs only the variable's value, not its address.

Double-Indirect Pointer Parameters

Getting back to double indirection, as explained earlier, a double-indirect pointer is literally a pointer to a pointer to a value. Passing such pointers to function parameters requires careful planning—at all times, it must be perfectly clear whether a statement is addressing a pointer, a pointer to a pointer, or another value.

The following program helps clear the foggy atmosphere that surrounds the topic of double-indirect pointer parameters. Listing 9.15, PTRPARAM.C, shows the basic requirements for passing a pointer to a pointer parameter. (Later listings in this chapter demonstrate a more practical side of the technique.)

Listing 9.15. PTRPARAM.C (Uses double-indirect pointers and functions).

```
 1:  #include <stdio.h>
 2:
 3:  void Assign(double **dpp);
 4:
 5:  main()
 6:  {
 7:    double d;        /* A double variable */
 8:    double *dp;      /* Pointer to a double */
 9:
10:    d = 0;
11:    dp = &d;
12:    Assign(&dp);
13:    printf("Value of d   == %f\n", d);
14:    printf("Value of *dp == %f\n", *dp);
```

continues

Listing 9.15. continued

```
15:     return 0;
16:  }
17:
18:  void Assign(double **dpp)
19:  {
20:     **dpp = 3.14159;
21:  }
```

Assign()'s prototype at line 3 declares a double-indirect pointer dpp—literally a pointer to a pointer to a double value. To the function, the program passes the address of a pointer, which points to the actual value to modify (see line 12).

For the demonstration, line 7 declares a double variable d (initialized at line 10), the value to be changed by the Assign() function. Line 8 declares a pointer, assigned the address of d at line 11. Line 12 passes the address of the pointer dp to Assign().

In the function, line 20 doubly dereferences dpp to get to the actual addressed value. The expression **dpp locates the double value stored in d. Lines 13–14 prove Assign() was able to modify d by doubly dereferencing dpp. The first printf() statement displays d directly; the second dereferences the pointer dp. Despite this difference, both statements display the same value.

A simple experiment demonstrates a related and powerful technique. Add the following global declaration to PTRPARAM.C:

```
double q = 1.234;
```

then modify the Assign() function's statement at line 20 to

```
*dpp = &q;
```

You have reprogrammed Assign() to modify the pointer passed to the function, rather than the actual addressed double value. When line 12 calls Assign(), the function modifies dp's value, causing that pointer to address the new global q. After this statement, *dp refers to the new global value.

When combined with structures, double-indirect pointer parameters require even more care. Pointers to structures—and pointers to structure *pointers*—are commonplace in C programs, and these techniques are important ones to stick under your belt. Listing 9.16, INSTRUCT.C, demonstrates a few tricks with structures and pointers.

Listing 9.16. INSTRUCT.C (Demonstrates structures and double-indirect pointers).

```
 1:  #include <stdio.h>
 2:
 3:  typedef struct item {
 4:    int a;
 5:    int b;
 6:  } Item;
 7:
 8:  typedef Item *Itemptr;
 9:  typedef Itemptr *Itemref;
10:
11:  main()
12:  {
13:    Item i;
14:    Itemptr ip;
15:    Itemref ir;
16:
17:    i.a = 1;
18:    i.b = 2;
19:    ip = &i;
20:    ir = &ip;
21:    printf("Value of i.a == %d\n", (*ir)->a);
22:    printf("Value of i.b == %d\n", (*ir)->b);
23:    return 0;
24:  }
```

INSTRUCT puts typedef to good use, reducing the number of confusing pointer operators in the program. Item is associated with the data type struct item, which has two integer members, a and b. Itemptr is associated with an Item pointer—in other words, Itemptr is an alias for Item *. Likewise, Itemref is associated with the type Itemptr *—a pointer to a pointer to a struct Item.

> **NOTE:** A pointer to a pointer is sometimes called a reference. If you name your pointer variables ending with Ptr and your pointer-pointer references ending with Ref, a quick glance at your code tells you which is the pointer and which is the pointer to a pointer.

Lines 17–18 assign values to an Item structure, i. Line 19 assigns i's address to ip, an Itemptr. Line 20 assigns the address of the pointer to ir, an Itemref.

At this point, ir is a pointer to a pointer to an Item. Lines 21–22 show how to address the structure's members using this doubly indirected reference. The expression (*ir)->a addresses member a in the structure addressed by a pointer that is in turn addressed by ir. The parentheses are required. If you wrote the expression as

```
*ir->a   /* ??? */
```

the compiler would complain because -> has a higher precedence than *. To force the compiler to dereference the pointer-pointer ir and then use the result as a pointer to a structure, you must instead write

```
(*ir)->a
```

Listing 9.17, PTRSTRUC.C, takes these concepts to the next logical step— passing a structure reference (a pointer to a pointer to a structure) to a function parameter.

Listing 9.17. PTRSTRUC.C (Passes a structure reference to a function).

```
 1:  #include <stdio.h>
 2:
 3:  typedef struct item {
 4:    int a;
 5:    int b;
 6:  } Item;
 7:
 8:  typedef Item *Itemptr;
 9:  typedef Itemptr *Itemref;
10:
11:  void Assign(Itemref ir);
12:
13:  main()
14:  {
15:    Item i;          /* An item struct */
16:    Itemptr ip;      /* Pointer to an item struct */
17:
18:    i.a = 1;
19:    i.b = 2;
20:    ip = &i;
```

```
21:    Assign(&ip);
22:    printf("Value of i.a == %d\n", ip->a);
23:    printf("Value of i.b == %d\n", ip->b);
24:    return 0;
25: }
26:
27: void Assign(Itemref ir)
28: {
29:    (*ir)->a = 4;
30:    (*ir)->b = 5;
31: }
```

As in the INSTRUCT demonstration, typedef is used to declare various symbols that help clarify the code (lines 3–9). Function Assign() at line 11 is prototyped with a single parameter ir of type Itemref. Literally, ir is a pointer to a pointer to an Item structure.

Line 21 passes the address of an Item pointer ip to Assign(), which executes the statements

```
(*ir)->a = 4;
(*ir)->b = 5;
```

to assign values to the structure's members. The expression forms are the same as demonstrated a moment ago. The expression (*ir)->a dereferences the pointer-pointer ir, forming an Item pointer to which the -> operator is applied, locating member a in the structure.

As you did earlier in PTRPARAM.C (Listing 9.15), you can change PTRSTRUC's Assign() function to modify the pointer passed as an argument. Add the following global declaration to PTRSTRUC:

```
Item q = {100, 200};
```

Then, replace the Assign() function's two statements at lines 29–30 with

```
*ir = &q;
```

When you run the modified code, Assign() assigns the address of q to *ir, thus modifying the pointer ip passed to the function at line 21. As a result, the two printf() statements now display the values of the global structure's members.

Pointers as Function Results

Functions that return pointers typically fall into one of two categories:

- Functions that modify an argument passed by address to the function, and return a pointer to that same argument.

- Functions that allocate heap space for a new dynamic variable, returning the address of that space or null if the heap is full or damaged.

Listing 9.18, UPPER.C, demonstrates a typical case—a function that returns a pointer to char.

Listing 9.18. UPPER.C (Returns a pointer from a function).

```
 1:  #include <stdio.h>
 2:  #include <ctype.h>
 3:  #include <string.h>
 4:
 5:  char *Uppercase(char *s);
 6:
 7:  main()
 8:  {
 9:    char title[] = "The case of the capital letter";
10:    char *cp;
11:
12:    cp = Uppercase(title);
13:    puts(cp);
14:    return 0;
15:  }
16:
17:  char *Uppercase(char *s)
18:  {
19:    int i;
20:
21:    for (i = 0; i < strlen(s); i++)
22:      s[i] = toupper(s[i]);
23:    return s;  /* return address of argument */
24:  }
```

Line 5 prototypes function Uppercase to return a char * (pointer to char). The function's single parameter is also a char pointer—a common design that you'll see more of in Chapter 10, "Strings."

As you might guess, function Uppercase capitalizes lowercase characters in a string. Line 12 executes the statement

```
cp = Uppercase(title);
```

which passes title to Uppercase, and assigns the returned pointer to cp, a char pointer declared in main(). Line 13 displays the string addressed by cp, thus proving the function returned the correct address value. As a result of the function call, cp becomes an alias for title.

Inside the function, a for loop calls function toupper() (implemented as a macro in ctype.h) to convert each character in string s to uppercase. Line 22 assigns that character back to the string, thus changing the argument passed to the function. Line 23 returns the function's parameter. Because the function returns a char * value, it can be used wherever a char pointer is allowed. For example, rather than assign the function's result to a temporary variable as done at line 11, you could replace lines 12 and 13 with the single statement

```
puts(Uppercase(title));
```

Function puts() requires a char * argument. Because function Uppercase() returns a value of that type, it can be passed directly to puts(). Functions that return pointers are most commonly used this way.

The next program, Listing 9.19, MAKEBLOK.C, demonstrates another common use for functions that return pointers—allocating new dynamic variables on the heap.

> **NOTE:** MAKEBLOK.C displays no output, so postpone compiling and running the program until later.

Listing 9.19. MAKEBLOK.C (Calls a function to allocate memory).

```
 1:  #include <stdio.h>
 2:  #include <alloc.h>
 3:  #define SIZE 64
 4:
 5:  void *MakeBlok(unsigned size, char init);
 6:
 7:  main()
 8:  {
 9:    void *p = NULL;
10:
11:    p = MakeBlok(SIZE, 0xff);  /* Block of SIZE 0xFF bytes */
12:    free(p);
13:    return 0;
14:  }
15:
16:  void *MakeBlok(unsigned size, char init)
17:  {
18:    void *p;
19:    int i;
20:
21:    p = (void *)malloc(size);
22:    if (p) {
23:      for (i = 0; i < size; i++)
24:        ((char *)p)[i] = init;
25:    }
26:    return p;
27:  }
```

The program's MakeBlok() function is prototyped to return a general-purpose void pointer that might address data of any kind, or perhaps, a buffer to serve as a holding tank for information on its way in and out of memory (see line 5).

To allocate heap space, the function calls malloc() at line 21, assigning the function result to a local void pointer p. Typecasting malloc()'s return value as (void *) avoids a warning from the compiler. If malloc() does not return null (indicating a full or damaged heap), a for loop fills the newly allocated memory with the value of char init, passed as an argument to the function. The statement at line 24:

```
((char *)p)[i] = init;
```

takes some effort to understand. Pointer p is a void pointer—it doesn't address data of any specified type and must therefore be recast before use. The expression (char *)p instructs the compiler to treat p temporarily as a pointer to char. However, p actually addresses not one char variable, but a memory block of many chars (provided size is greater than one, that is). An array subscript [i] is used to refer to individual chars in this block. The extra parentheses are required because the expression

```
(char *)p[i]   /* ??? */
```

is ambiguous. Variable p is a pointer, not an array, and it can't be subscripted. However, ((char *)p) is a pointer to a char, and because pointers and arrays are equivalent, the expression may be subscripted to refer to one char in the block of memory p addresses.

Filling memory blocks with known values this way is useful for debugging. From a DOS prompt, compile MAKEBLOK.C with the command **bcc -v makeblok.c**. The -v switch generates debugging information, making it possible to load the program into Turbo Debugger with the command **td makeblok**. Do that, and when the debugger's display appears, follow these steps:

1. Press F8 twice to execute the program's startup code and initialize p to NULL.

2. Cursor to p and press Ctrl+I to inspect the pointer's value, which should equal ds:0000.

3. Press F8 to call MakeBlok(). Watch p change as the program assigns the function's pointer return value. The pointer now addresses a newly allocated block of memory at the reported address.

4. Press Alt+VD to open a memory-dump view window.

5. Press Ctrl+G and enter p to view the block of data addressed by the pointer. All bytes equal FF hexadecimal, the value passed to the function (see line 11 in Listing 9.19).

> **NOTE:** If the value of a pointer or another variable mystifies you, load the code into the debugger, and use various commands to peer into variables and examine values. Beginning programmers often forget they have at their fingertips one of the best teachers available—Turbo Debugger. Use the debugger not only to fix broken code, but also as a guide to reveal how programs operate.

Pointers to Functions

So far in this chapter, you've spent a lot of time examining pointers to data. It's also possible to create pointers to functions—literally, pointers that address executable code.

To understand how to use pointers to functions, it's helpful to review a couple of basics. To declare a pointer to a variable, preface the variable's name with an asterisk. For example, this declares myptr as a pointer to a float value:

```
float *myptr;
```

You can also declare a function that returns a float pointer value:

```
float *myfn(void);
```

Declared this way, function myfn returns a pointer to a float value. Suppose, however, you don't want a pointer to a value; you instead want a pointer to the function's executable code. A special rule of C syntax accomplishes this goal:

```
float (* myfnptr)(void);
```

The parentheses around (* myfnptr) inform the compiler that the pointer operator (*) binds to the function name, not to its float data type. This creates a pointer to a function that returns a float value, rather than a function that returns a float pointer.

If the function requires parameters, add them as usual inside parentheses in the function's parameter list:

```
float (* myfnptr)(int x, int y);
```

This declares myfnptr as a pointer to a function that returns a float value and requires two integer arguments. To call the function, assign to myfnptr the address of a conforming function. In other words, if you declare a pointer to a function that declares two parameters and returns a double value, the actual function *must* declare the two expected parameters and return the expected type of value. Suppose the function you want to call is named TheFunction. Assign the function's address to myfnptr with the statement

```
myfnptr = TheFunction;
```

This is no different from the way you assign addresses of other variables to pointers, but you do not need to preface TheFunction with the address-of operator &. Function names such as TheFunction are assumed to be pointers to code. TheFunction could be written in the usual way:

```
float TheFunction(int x, int y)
{
  ...
}
```

You can, of course, call TheFunction directly, perhaps assigning its result to a float variable answer:

```
answer = TheFunction(5, 6);
```

Because myfnptr addresses TheFunction's executable code, however, you can also call it by dereferencing the pointer:

```
answer = (* myfnptr)(5, 6);
```

or, if the function requires no arguments, just leave the parentheses blank:

```
answer = (* myfnptr)();
```

In each case, the parentheses around (* myfnptr) instruct the compiler to generate a function call to the code addressed by the function pointer.

NOTE: When using function pointers, be sure they actually address functions in the correct form. The compiler doesn't check whether function pointers address executable code. If you accidentally "call" data instead of code, the results are likely to be disastrous to your program's health.

Now that you've investigated the basic forms of function pointers, examine a program that puts the technique to good use. Listing 9.20, PLOT.C, plots a simple graph of a mathematical function, using text commands (see Figure 9.10). Using a function pointer makes it easy to replace the function to plot a different graph without requiring modifications to other parts of the program.

Listing 9.20. PLOT.C (Plots a mathematical function with a function pointer).

```
1:  #include <stdio.h>
2:  #include <math.h>
3:  #include <dos.h>
4:  #include <conio.h>
```

continues

Listing 9.20. continued

```
 5:
 6:  #define XSCALE 20
 7:  #define YSCALE 10
 8:  #define XMIN 1
 9:  #define XMAX 79
10:  #define YMIN 1
11:  #define YMAX 25
12:
13:  typedef double (* Pfptr)(int x);
14:
15:  void Yplot(int x, double f);
16:  double Afunction(int x);
17:
18:  main()
19:  {
20:    int x;
21:    Pfptr pf = Afunction;
22:
23:    clrscr();
24:    for (x = XMIN; x <= XMAX; x++)
25:      Yplot(x, (* pf)(x * XSCALE));
26:    gotoxy(XMIN, YMAX - 2);
27:    return 0;
28:  }
29:
30:  void Yplot(int x, double f)
31:  {
32:    gotoxy(x, YMIN + (YSCALE + (f * YSCALE)));
33:    delay(50);    /* Optional. Remove to plot at full speed */
34:    putch('*');
35:  }
36:
37:  double Afunction(int x)
38:  {
39:    return sin((x * M_PI) / 180.0);
40:  }
```

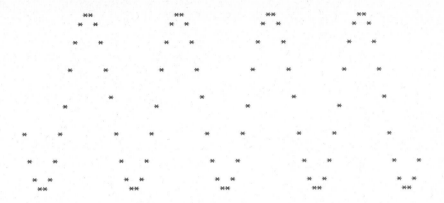

D:\TSWAN\MBC\SOURCE\C09>

Figure 9.10. Sample output from PLOT.C.

Line 13 uses `typedef` to create a symbol for the mathematical function to be plotted. The line

```
typedef double (* Pfptr)(int x);
```

specifies `Pfptr` as a function pointer type that returns a `double` value and expects to receive an `int` argument `x`.

Line 16 prototypes the mathematical function to be plotted. The declaration

```
double Afunction(int x);
```

conforms to `Pfptr`'s design; therefore, a pointer of type `Pfptr` may be used to address `Afunction`.

At line 21, the program makes use of this fact by declaring a `Pfptr` pointer variable `pf` and assigning to it the address of `AFunction`. To obtain Y coordinate values for the plot, line 25 executes

```
Yplot(x, (* pf)(x * XSCALE));
```

which might seem as cryptic as hieroglyphics on a first reading. The expression `(* pf)(x * XSCALE)` calls the function addressed by `pf`, passing as an argument the value of `(x * XSCALE)`. (The two constants XSCALE and YSCALE help keep the plot on-screen.) Dereferencing `pf` as `* pf` instructs the compiler to call the code `pf` addresses.

That code, of course, is the mathematical function to be plotted (see lines 37–40).In this small example, you could just call `Afunction` directly, replacing line 25 with

```
Yplot(x, Afunction(x * XSCALE));
```

This statement has the identical effect as the one in the listing. In a large program, however, where the plotting code might be in one module and the mathematical function in another, passing a function pointer to the plotter might be more convenient than modifying the call to Yplot(). Also, this change could be made *without having access to the plotter's source code.*

NOTE: PLOT.C uses Borland C++'s direct-video console I/O library, including file conio.h at line 4. Several functions in this library are tailor made for writing fast text-screen display code. For example, line 23 calls clrscr() to clear the screen. Line 26 calls gotoxy() to position the cursor—coordinate (1,1) is at upper left. Line 34 displays a single character via putch(), the fastest way to display text. Examine conio.h in your C:\BORLANDC\INCLUDE or equivalent directory for other direct-video functions, also described in Chapter 22, "Functions and Examples."

Function Pointers as Hooks

Some library functions use function pointers as hooks on which you can hang your own code. One of the most useful of these functions is qsort(), which is similar but faster and more efficient than the QuickSort function demonstrated in SORTER.C from Chapter 8, "Data Structures." Listing 9.21, QSORTER.C, shows how to use qsort(). The program is nearly identical to SORTER.C, but calls the library function to sort an array of integer values.

Listing 9.21. QSORTER.C (Uses function pointers and the qsort() function).

```
1:  #include <stdio.h>
2:  #include <stdlib.h>
3:  #include <time.h>
4:
5:  #define ARRAYSIZE 100
6:
7:  int compare(const void *a, const void *b);
8:  void FillArray(void);
```

```
 9:  void DisplayArray(void);
10:  void SortArray(int n);
11:
12:  int array[ARRAYSIZE];   /* Array of integers */
13:
14:  main()
15:  {
16:    FillArray();
17:    DisplayArray();
18:    SortArray(ARRAYSIZE);
19:    DisplayArray();
20:    return 0;
21:  }
22:
23:  int compare(const void *a, const void *b)
24:  {
25:    int aint = *(int *)a;
26:    int bint = *(int *)b;
27:    if (aint < bint)
28:      return -1;
29:    else if (aint > bint)
30:      return +1;
31:    else
32:      return 0;
33:  }
34:
35:  /* Fill global array with values taken at random */
36:  void FillArray(void)
37:  {
38:    int i;
39:
40:    srand((unsigned)time(NULL));      /* Randomize */
41:    for (i = 0; i < ARRAYSIZE; i++)   /* Fill array */
42:      array[i] = rand();
43:  }
44:
45:  void DisplayArray(void)
46:  {
47:    int i;
48:
49:    puts("");  /* Start new display line */
```

continues

Listing 9.21. continued

```
50:    for (i = 0; i < ARRAYSIZE; i++)
51:      printf("%8d", array[i]);
52:  }
53:
54:  void SortArray(int n)
55:  {
56:    if (n > 1)
57:      qsort((void *)array, n, sizeof(array[0]), compare);
58:  }
```

The qsort() library function, prototyped in stdlib.h, can sort arrays of any kind of data. That powerful capability has a price, however, in the form of a comparison function that you must supply. Line 7 in QSORTER demonstrates how to meet this requirement. The function—named compare(), though it could be another name—is prototyped as

```
int compare(const void *a, const void *b);
```

The two parameters are declared as const void pointers, and are assumed to address two instances of the data to be sorted. Using const prevents accidental changes to the pointer address values, which would cause sorting to fail.

A qsort() comparison function returns an int value that indicates the result of comparing two argument values. While sorting, qsort() calls the supplied comparison function, which returns one of three values:

- −1 if argument a is less than argument b
- 0 if arguments a and b match exactly
- +1 if argument a is greater than argument b

In place of −1, any negative integer will do. Similarly, any positive integer may be returned in place of +1. The function must return zero if the two arguments are equal.

By supplying a comparison function and returning an appropriate value, you effectively teach qsort() how to sort arrays of any types. It's up to you to figure out how to compare two values, which could be simple integers or complex structures.

In this case, compare() is written inefficiently, just to demonstrate how qsort() works (see lines 23–33). To make the comparison easy to program, two local int variables `aint` and `bint` are assigned the values addressed by pointers `a` and `b`. These local variables are then compared by an `if` and two `else` statements, returning an appropriate value that represents the comparison's result.

Supplying a different comparison function affects `qsort()`'s outcome. For example, to sort the array of values from high to low rather than from low to high, swap lines 28 and 30. That is, return +1 if `aint` is less than `bint`, and −1 if the first value is greater than the second.

Dynamic Data Structures

Dynamic data structures grow and shrink as needed to accommodate whatever you need to store in them. They are often called self-referential structures, because they typically use pointers to refer to like images of themselves. The three most common dynamic data structures are lists, stacks, and trees.

Lists

A structure may have a pointer member that points to an instance of its own data type. You might declare this structure as

```
struct item {
  int data;            /* Any data members */
  struct item *next;  /* Pointer to another item */
};
```

This `struct item` has two members: an integer `data`, which represents the information to be stored in the structure, and a `struct item` pointer `next`. In any structure declaration, C allows a member to be declared as a pointer to that same kind of structure, forming a data type that can refer to instances of itself.

What a powerful capability this is! As Figure 9.11 illustrates, two or more `item` variables can form a list simply by linking their `next` pointers together.

Lists are useful for storing all sorts of information. For example, a word processor might keep text as a list strings. A database might link its records in sorted order, and so on.

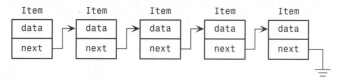

Figure 9.11. Member pointers link structures into a list.

To create a list, first declare a structure such as item, in which you may store any kind of data members. Use typedef to simplify the programming:

```
typedef struct item {
  int data;
  struct item *next;
} Item;
typedef Item *Itemptr;
typedef Itemptr *Itemref;
```

Item with a capital *I* is an alias for struct item. Itemptr stands for struct Item *, a pointer to an Item instance. Itemref is a pointer to a pointer to an Item. These typedef symbols are optional, but keep the code clear and understandable.

Next, declare a pointer to an Item, which serves as the list head (the item at the top of the list):

```
Itemptr head = NULL;
```

When the pointer head equals null, the list is empty, so it's a good idea to initialize the pointer in its declaration as shown here. To start the list, examine head, and if it's null, allocate space for a new Item:

```
if (head == NULL) {
  head = (Itemptr)malloc(sizeof(Item));
  head->data = 1;
  head->next = NULL;
}
```

The new Item's data member is set to 1 (you could assign other data at this point), and its next member is set to the NULL macro. At this stage, the list appears as illustrated in Figure 9.12. There's only one element in the list, addressed by the head pointer. The electrical grounding symbol represents null, showing that the element's next member pointer is at the end of the line.

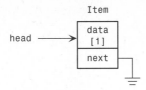

Figure 9.12. A list of one element.

It's the rare list that has only one element. Sooner or later, the program adds new information to the list. If p addresses an Item structure, the following statements insert a new structure into the list addressed by head:

```
Itemptr p;
...
p = (Itemptr)malloc(sizeof(Item));
p->data = 2;
p->next = head->next;
head->next = p;
```

Study these statements carefully. After the program allocates memory for an item addressed by p, it assigns 2 to the structure's data member. The list head's next value (currently null) is assigned to p->next. Then, head->next is made to address the new structure at p. The list now appears as illustrated by Figure 9.13. The temporary pointer p is no longer needed; however, it should not be freed as the new item now belongs to the list.

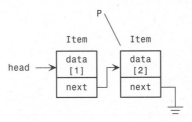

Figure 9.13. After inserting a new element into the list.

After inserting several more structures, the list appears as shown in Figure 9.14. Each Item structure is linked to the next by next pointers.

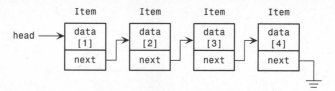

Figure 9.14. A list of several items chained by next member pointers.

By dereferencing the list head pointer, it's possible to access any element of a list. The expression head->data refers to the data member in the list's first element. To refer to the other members, you could use statements such as these, each of which assigns the value of a different item's data member to an int variable i:

```
i = head->data;                     /* i == 1 */
i = head->next->data;               /* i == 2 */
i = head->next->next->data;         /* i == 3 */
i = head->next->next->next->data;   /* i == 4 */
```

Corresponding data values from Figure 9.14 are shown in comments. Using the next members as successive pointers to structures locates each data field, much in the way you use successive pathnames to locate files in subdirectories on your computer's disk drive.

Such multipath expressions are unwieldy, and are rarely used as shown here. Instead, to walk through a list's elements, most programmers use a loop. For example, this fragment displays the values of the list addressed by head:

```
Itemptr p;
...
p = head;
while (p != NULL) {
  printf("%d\n", p->data);
  p = p->next;
}
```

> **NOTE:** The statement while (p != NULL) {...} can be shortened to while (p) {...}. The longer form is used here for clarity.

Using a temporary `Itemptr` p, initialized to the same value as `head`, while p is not null, the `while` loop's `printf()` statement displays the `data` member in the structure addressed by p. Then, p is assigned the value of the addressed structure's `next` member, thus causing p to point to the next structure in the list until reaching the end. For this to work, the last structure *must* have a `next` member equal to null.

Deleting items is another common list operation. Given the list illustrated in Figure 9.14, these statements delete the item addressed by `head`:

```
Itemptr p;
...
p = head;
head = head->next;
free(p);
```

A temporary `Itemptr` p is assigned the value of `head`, after which `head` is assigned the value of the addressed structure's `next` member. This step unlinks the structure, causing `head` to address the next item. (See Figure 9.15.) The final statement passes p to `free()`, deleting the unused list element from the heap and making its memory available for other uses.

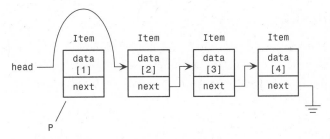

Figure 9.15. After deleting one element from the list.

Incomplete *struct* Declarations

An ambiguous situation occurs when two or more structures refer to each other with pointer members. You must declare the `struct`s before you can use them, but you can't declare them all ahead of one another!

To resolve the dilemma, use an incomplete `struct` declaration, which begins like a normal `struct` but has no body. For example, here's how to declare two `struct`s,

AStruct and BStruct, each with a pointer member to an object of the other struct's type:

```
struct BStruct;  /* Incomplete struct declaration */

struct AStruct {
  struct BStruct *bp;  /* Pointer to BStruct object */
};

struct BStruct {
  struct AStruct *ap;  /* Pointer to AStruct object */
};
```

The first line declares the bodyless BStruct so that AStruct may declare a pointer to a BStruct object. At some point, you have to finish the incomplete declaration, giving BStruct its missing body. You can use this technique only to declare struct pointer members. You could not, for example, declare a BStruct member directly in AStruct, because until BStruct grows a body, the compiler can't determine how large BStruct is.

Stacks

Programmers ordinarily think of the stack as a gray area of memory that holds function return addresses and local variables. Stacks, however, are useful data structures in their own right. With the help of a few lists, a program can have any number of stacks for saving various kinds of information.

By nature, a stack is a last-in-first-out (LIFO) data structure. They are like stacks of books. The item on top is easily accessible, but to reach those below, you must remove others above. (Of course, you can cheat and slide a book out of the middle, but then you are on your own. When programming stacks, it pays to play by the rules.)

Listing 9.22 demonstrates how to use a list to create stacks of Item structures. The program keeps two lists—an Item list of active structures, and an Avail list of deleted items. Compile and run the program, then press A a few times to add new items to the stack. Notice their numbers. Press D that same number of times to delete items and add them to the Avail list. If you delete more items than you add, the program creates dummy structures equal to −1, adding these to the Avail list. Next, press A to add items. Rather than create new structures, the program takes any from the Avail list and attaches them again to the active Items. You can use the program's design in any situation where you have a varying number of items to maintain.

> **NOTE:** For simplicity, STACK assumes you won't add or delete too many items. If you do, the display may appear jumbled. No harm done—just press **Q** to quit.

Listing 9.22. STACK.C (Uses a list to create a stack).

```
1:  #include <stdio.h>
2:  #include <stdlib.h>
3:  #include <ctype.h>
4:  #include <conio.h>
5:
6:  #define FALSE 0
7:  #define TRUE 1
8:
9:  typedef struct item {
10:    int data;                /* Data to store in stack */
11:    struct item *next;       /* Pointer to next item */
12:  } Item;
13:
14:  typedef Item *Itemptr;     /* Pointer to struct item */
15:  typedef Itemptr *Itemref;  /* Reference to struct item */
16:
17:  void Push(Itemptr newitem, Itemref list);
18:  void Pop(Itemref newitem, Itemref list);
19:  void AddItem(void);
20:  void DelItem(void);
21:  void ShowList(Itemptr p);
22:  void Display(void);
23:
24:  Itemptr avail;             /* The "avail" stack pointer */
25:  Itemptr itemlist;          /* The "item" stack pointer */
26:
27:  main()
28:  {
29:    int done = FALSE;        /* When TRUE, program ends */
30:    int c;                   /* User command character */
31:
```

continues

Listing 9.22. continued

```
32:    while (!done) {
33:      Display();
34:      gotoxy(1, 25);
35:      cprintf("A-dd, D-elete, Q-uit");
36:      c = getch();
37:      switch (toupper(c)) {
38:        case 'A':
39:          AddItem();
40:          break;
41:        case 'D':
42:          DelItem();
43:          break;
44:        case 'Q':
45:          done = TRUE;
46:          break;
47:      }
48:    }
49:    return 0;
50: }
51:
52: /* Push newitem onto list. Modifies list pointer. */
53: void Push(Itemptr newitem, Itemref list)
54: {
55:    newitem->next = *list;  /* Item's next now points to list */
56:    *list = newitem;          /* List now points to new item */
57: }
58:
59: /* Pop newitem from list, or create new item if list is empty */
60: void Pop(Itemref newitem, Itemref list)
61: {
62:    if (*list == NULL) {      /* If list is empty... */
63:      *newitem = malloc(sizeof(struct item));  /* Create item */
64:      (*newitem)->data = -1;  /*  Initialize data to -1 */
65:    } else {                  /* Else... */
66:      *newitem = *list;       /*  Pass back item at top of list */
67:      *list = (*list)->next;  /*  Adjust list to next item */
68:    }
69: }
70:
71: /* Add item with random data to item stack */
```

```
72:  void AddItem(void)
73:  {
74:    Itemptr newitem;
75:
76:    Pop(&newitem, &avail);       /* Get or create new item */
77:    if (newitem->data < 0)       /* If this is a new item */
78:      newitem->data = rand();    /* Assign random data to it */
79:    Push(newitem, &itemlist);    /* Put new item onto item stack */
80:  }
81:
82:  /* Delete item from item stack. Save same item on avail stack */
83:  void DelItem(void)
84:  {
85:    Itemptr newitem;
86:
87:    Pop(&newitem, &itemlist);    /* Get new item from item stack */
88:    Push(newitem, &avail);       /* Save item on avail stack */
89:  }
90:
91:  /* Display contents of list addressed by p */
92:  void ShowList(Itemptr p)
93:  {
94:    while (p != NULL) {
95:      gotoxy(1, wherey() + 1);
96:      cprintf("%d", p->data);
97:      clreol();
98:      p = p->next;           /* Address next item in the list */
99:    }
100: }
101:
102: /* Display the avail and item stacks */
103: void Display(void)
104: {
105:   clrscr();
106:   gotoxy(1, wherey() + 1);
107:   cprintf("Avail list:");
108:   ShowList(avail);
109:   gotoxy(1, wherey() + 2);
110:   cprintf("Item list:");
111:   ShowList(itemlist);
112: }
```

Except for demonstrating how stacks operate, the program contains no new techniques, and you should be able to understand most of the statements. Two functions, Push() and Pop(), demonstrate practical uses for double indirect pointers of type Itemref.

Function Push() (lines 53–57) assigns to a new item's next member the address of a list, passed as a pointer to a pointer in the function's list parameter. After this step, that list's pointer is updated to address the new item—similar to the way the preceding section inserted a new item into a list.

Function Pop() (lines 60–69) performs the reverse operation, removing one item from the stack and adjusting the pointer to address the next item in line. However, if the list is empty, Pop() allocates space for a new item. (In other programs, it may be more appropriate to call an underflow-error function rather than allocate a new item, in which case the statements at lines 63–64 aren't needed.)

Examine the calls to Push() and Pop() throughout the listing. Notice how the address-of operator (&) is used to pass the list pointers to the functions, giving the functions the capability of modifying those pointers to add and subtract items from the stacks.

Trees

By adding a second pointer member to the Item structure from the preceding sections, a structure can point to two instances of its own type. The result is usually viewed as a kind of tree, with pointers for branches and variables for leaves. You might declare the new Item structure like this:

```
typedef struct item {
  char *data;
  struct item *left;
  struct item *right;
} Item;
typedef Item *Itemptr;
typedef Itemptr *Itemref;
```

This time, item's data member is declared as a char * pointer, but it could be any type. Two struct item * pointers, named left and right, address other item structures. The names don't matter, and the pointers are sometimes called next and previous.

Linking various `item` structures together creates a binary tree-like structure. It's a *binary* tree because every leaf (also called a node) can address up to two other nodes. The left branches point to nodes on the left side of the tree; the right branches point to nodes on the right. Compared to trees in nature, a tree of data leaves is upside down and has its root in the clouds. Never mind, though: The structure still bears plenty of fruit for programmers, as Figure 9.16 illustrates.

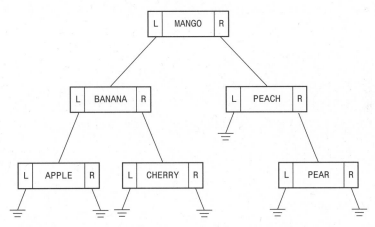

Figure 9.16. A binary "fruit tree" as it might appear in memory.

By tracing node pointers, a program can visit (examine) each item in the tree. Simple, but powerful, algorithms provide easy ways to locate every node, and also dictate the order in which multiple nodes are visited. The three main tree-traversal algorithms are pre-order, in-order, and post-order (see Table 9.1).

Table 9.1. Binary tree-traversal algorithms.

Pre-order	In-order	Post-order
Process node	Go left	Go left
Go left	Process node	Go right
Go right	Go right	Process node

In Table 9.1, *Process node* means to perform some operation on a node's data and go to the next step; *Go left* means to shift the program's focus to the node addressed by the current node's left pointer *and then start over;* and *Go right* means to shift the focus to the node addressed by the right pointer *and then start over.* If a left or right pointer is null, the algorithm moves to the next step.

Reading each traversal method's steps from top to bottom reveals the meaning of their names. The pre-order method processes the current node in advance of moving to other nodes. The in-order method processes nodes in between moving left then right. The post-order method moves through the tree before processing nodes.

Because of the tree's self-referential nature, the traversal algorithms are easiest to program using recursion. (Remember, recursion is what happens when a function calls itself.) Listing 9.23, TREE.C, includes functions that implement each of the tree-traversal algorithms from Table 9.1.

Listing 9.23. TREE.C (Traverses a binary tree in three ways).

```
 1:  #include <stdio.h>
 2:  #include <string.h>
 3:  #include <alloc.h>
 4:
 5:  typedef struct item {
 6:    char *data;            /* Addresses character data */
 7:    struct item *left;     /* Pointer to left tree branch */
 8:    struct item *right;    /* Pointer to right tree branch */
 9:  } Item;
10:  typedef Item *Itemptr;
11:  typedef Itemptr *Itemref;
12:
13:  Itemptr root;  /* Global root tree pointer */
14:
15:  void Search(Itemref tree, const char *s);
16:  void Process(Itemptr node);
17:  void PreOrder(Itemptr node);
18:  void InOrder(Itemptr node);
19:  void PostOrder(Itemptr node);
20:
21:  main()
22:  {
23:    int done = 0;
24:    char s[128];
```

```
25:
26:    puts("Tree demonstration");
27:    while (!done) {
28:      printf("Data (Enter to quit): ");
29:      gets(s);
30:      done = (strlen(s) == 0);
31:      if (!done)
32:        Search(&root, s);
33:    }
34:    puts("\nPREORDER:\n");
35:    PreOrder(root);
36:    puts("\n\nINORDER:\n");
37:    InOrder(root);
38:    puts("\n\nPOSTORDER:\n");
39:    PostOrder(root);
40:    puts("");
41:    return 0;
42: }
43:
44: /* Search for existing item or create new one */
45: void Search(Itemref tree, const char *s)
46: {
47:    Itemptr p;
48:    int cmpresult;
49:
50:    if (*tree == NULL) {
51:      p = (Itemptr)malloc(sizeof(Item));
52:      p->data = strdup(s);
53:      p->left = NULL;
54:      p->right = NULL;
55:      *tree = p;
56:    } else {
57:      p = *tree;
58:      cmpresult = strcmp(s, p->data);
59:      if (cmpresult < 0)
60:        Search(&p->left, s);
61:      else if (cmpresult > 0)
62:        Search(&p->right, s);
63:      else {
64:        puts("Duplicate data!");
65:        Process(p);
```

continues

Listing 9.23. continued

```
 66:         puts("");
 67:       }
 68:     }
 69:   }
 70:
 71:   void Process(Itemptr node)
 72:   {
 73:     printf("%s  ", node->data);
 74:   }
 75:
 76:   void PreOrder(Itemptr node)
 77:   {
 78:     if (node != NULL) {
 79:       Process(node);
 80:       PreOrder(node->left);
 81:       PreOrder(node->right);
 82:     }
 83:   }
 84:
 85:   void InOrder(Itemptr node)
 86:   {
 87:     if (node != NULL) {
 88:       InOrder(node->left);
 89:       Process(node);
 90:       InOrder(node->right);
 91:     }
 92:   }
 93:
 94:   void PostOrder(Itemptr node)
 95:   {
 96:     if (node != NULL) {
 97:       PostOrder(node->left);
 98:       PostOrder(node->right);
 99:       Process(node);
100:     }
101:   }
```

Compile and run TREE, and when prompted, type the fruit names mango, banana, apple, cherry, peach, and pear. You may enter any other short strings. Press Enter after the last name, and the program displays the tree's data using the three traversal algorithms:

```
PREORDER:
mango         banana        apple         cherry        peach         pear
INORDER:
apple         banana        cherry        mango         peach         pear
POSTORDER:
apple         cherry        banana        pear          peach         mango
```

Notice that the in-order algorithm displays your entries sorted alphabetically. One advantage of binary trees is their ability to keep data in sorted order without requiring the use of a sort function such as qsort().

Skip to the end of the listing, where you'll find three functions: PreOrder(), InOrder(), and PostOrder(), corresponding to the three traversal algorithms. The functions are mirror images of the algorithms. Function Process() displays the data addressed by parameter Itemptr node. To go left—in other words, to move to the node to the left of the current one—the functions call themselves with the argument node->left, passing as an argument the value of the current node's left member pointer. To go right, the functions execute similar recursive function calls but pass the current item's right pointer.

Inserting new items into the tree takes a bit more effort. Function Search() at lines 45–69 performs that duty while also hunting for existing items. As an example of how to use Search(), see line 32, which passes the address of the tree's root pointer plus the new information to insert—in this case, a character string.

Search() initializes an empty tree branch (lines 50–55), or it seaches for specified data (lines 56–68). Two if-else statements at lines 59–67 examine the result of a comparison between the data at the current node and the specified data (line 58). If the new data is less than the data stored at a node, Search() calls itself recursively for the node to its left (line 60). If the new data is greater than the current node's information, the search proceeds to the right (line 62). If the new data is found, an else statement at lines 63–67 displays it and the search ends.

NOTE: The first time you inspect the Search() function in TREE, it may not be clear how new nodes are inserted into the tree. By calling itself recursively at lines 60 and 62, the function eventually reaches a node with a null left or right member. Passing this null pointer to Search() causes it to allocate a new node at line 51. For example, if p->left at line 60 equals null, passing that pointer member's address to Search()'s Itemref tree parameter causes line 51 to allocate a new node and assign its address to p. At this point, p addresses the left member pointer from the call to Search() back at line 60—therefore, the assignment at line 51 attaches the new node to the node for which Search() was called recursively. To see these ideas in action, load TREE into Turbo Debugger and execute the code in slow motion while examining the tree's pointers.

Advanced Pointer Techniques

This chapter would not be complete if I did not at least mention the darker side of pointers: accessing system locations. Be warned: Poking around inside your computer can cause all sorts of strange occurrences. If you aim just one pointer at the wrong location, you can accidentally wipe out a hard drive, destroy files, and even physically damage certain kinds of display monitors.

WARNING: The programs in this section probably won't harm 100% compatible IBM PC computers, but even so, you should proceed with caution. Using pointers to access system locations is always risky and should *never* be attempted without first backing up all important data.

Pointers to System Locations

Listing 9.24, CRTSTAT.C, demonstrates how to use pointers to gain access to some of a PC's system information stored in the lower reaches of memory. Run the program for a small report about your system's startup video mode and the number of columns supported by your display—information that might be useful to know in planning a program's output.

Listing 9.24. CRTSTAT.C (Accesses system information using a pointer).

```
 1:  #include <stdio.h>
 2:  #include <dos.h>
 3:
 4:  main()
 5:  {
 6:    char far *mode = (char far *)MK_FP(0x0040, 0x0049);
 7:    int far *cols = (int far *)MK_FP(0x0040, 0x004a);
 8:
 9:    printf("CRT startup mode = %d\n", *mode);
10:    printf("CRT columns      = %d\n", *cols);
11:    return 0;
12:  }
```

Lines 6 and 7 define and initialize two far pointers, mode and cols. Pointer mode addresses a value of type char, equivalent in Borland C++ to a single byte. Pointer cols addresses an int value. Each pointer is initialized using macro MK_FP (*make far pointer*) defined in dos.h.

The result of MK_FP is a far pointer containing a 16-bit segment value and a 16-bit offset. Both mode and cols use the same segment value—0x0040, the base address in hexadecimal where DOS and the PC's ROM BIOS routines store various system variables. The other values (0x0049 and 0x004a) represent the offset addresses that locate values specifying the system's startup video mode and the number of columns available for text displays.

After these setup chores, mode and cols address system values inside the segment at 0x0040. You can use similar techniques to assign other addresses to pointers in order to read and even change various system-dependent values.

Far Pointers and the Keyboard

Another example shows how to use far pointers to detect whether a program's user is pressing the Alt, Ctrl, Shift Left, or Shift Right keys. The program also detects the current on or off state of the Insert, Caps Lock, Num Lock, and Scroll Lock keys. Without pointers, this highly system-dependent program would be next to impossible to write.

Compile and run Listing 9.25, KEYSTAT.C. Press one of the keys displayed by name on-screen. Notice that some keys turn on (1) and off (0) as soon as you press and release them, and that the program distinguishes between Shift Left and Shift Right. Other keys such as Caps Lock and Num Lock serve as toggles, and may be on or off when you start the program. When you're done experimenting with KEYSTAT, press and hold the three keys Ctrl+Alt+Shift Left simultaneously to quit.

Listing 9.25. KEYSTAT.C (Detects states of special keys).

```
 1:  #include <stdio.h>
 2:  #include <dos.h>
 3:  #include <string.h>
 4:  #include <conio.h>
 5:
 6:  typedef struct keyboard {
 7:    unsigned shiftRight  : 1;      /* Keyboard flags */
 8:    unsigned shiftLeft   : 1;
 9:    unsigned ctrl        : 1;
10:    unsigned alt         : 1;
11:    unsigned scrollLock  : 1;
12:    unsigned numLock     : 1;
13:    unsigned capsLock    : 1;
14:    unsigned insert      : 1;
15:    unsigned             : 8;     /* Not used */
16:  } Keyboard;
17:
18:  int CmpKeys(void far* p1, void far* p2);
19:  void ShowString(int *y, char *s);
20:  void ShowValue(int *y, char *s, unsigned v);
21:
22:  main()
23:  {
24:    Keyboard far *keys;  /* Pointer to keyboard struct */
```

```
25:    Keyboard oldkeys;     /* Holds copy of last known key state */
26:    int done = 0;         /* True when user quits program */
27:    int y;                /* Display y coordinate */
28:
29:    clrscr();
30:    keys = (Keyboard far *)MK_FP(0x0040, 0x0017);
31:    while (!done) {
32:      y = 1;
33:      ShowString(&y, "Keyboard State");
34:      y++;
35:      ShowString(&y, "State bits (press and release):");
36:      ShowValue(&y, " <Insert> ....... ", keys->insert);
37:      ShowValue(&y, " <Caps lock> .... ", keys->capsLock);
38:      ShowValue(&y, " <Num lock> ..... ", keys->numLock);
39:      ShowValue(&y, " <Scroll lock> .. ", keys->scrollLock);
40:      y++;
41:      ShowString(&y, "Shift bits. (press, hold, and release):");
42:      ShowValue(&y, " <Alt> .......... ", keys->alt);
43:      ShowValue(&y, " <Ctrl> ......... ", keys->ctrl);
44:      ShowValue(&y, " <Shift left> ... ", keys->shiftLeft);
45:      ShowValue(&y, " <Shift right> .. ", keys->shiftRight);
46:      y++;
47:      ShowString(&y, "Press above keys to change state");
48:      ShowString(&y, "Press <Ctrl>-<Alt>-<shiftLeft> to quit");
49:      done = (   keys->alt
50:              && keys->ctrl
51:              && keys->shiftLeft);
52:      oldkeys = *keys;  /* Save key state */
53:      while (CmpKeys(&oldkeys, keys)) ;  /* Pause for change */
54:    }
55:    gotoxy(1, 25);
56:    return 0;
57: }
58:
59: /* Return true (1) if bytes at p1 and p2 are the same */
60: int CmpKeys(void far* p1, void far* p2)
61: {
62:    return *(char far *)p1 == *(char far *)p2;
63: }
64:
65: /* Display string s at (1,y) and increment y */
```

continues

Listing 9.25. continued

```
66:  void ShowString(int *y, char *s)
67:  {
68:    gotoxy(1, *y);
69:    cputs(s);
70:    (*y)++;
71:  }
72:
73:  /* Display string s and value v at (1,y) */
74:  void ShowValue(int *y, char *s, unsigned v)
75:  {
76:    ShowString(y, s);
77:    cprintf("%u", v);
78:  }
```

In addition to showing a good use for far pointers, KEYSTAT also demonstrates how to address bit-field structures. Lines 6–16 declare a bit-field structure named Keyboard. Each member in the structure corresponds to a bit stored in memory by the ROM BIOS when certain keys are pressed. Inspecting this value, called the keyboard flag byte, and extracting its various bits gives programs a way to detect the states of these special keys, which normally can't be read in the same way common ASCII keys can.

Line 18 declares a prototype for a function CmpKeys(), which returns true if the bytes addressed by the void far pointers p1 and p2 are equal. If those bytes differ, CmpKeys() returns false. Comparing the before and after values of the keyboard flag byte gives the program a way to detect a change in a key's status.

To address the keyboard flag byte, line 30 uses MK_FP to create a far pointer keys. The address assigned to keys, 0x0040:0x0017, is the location of the keyboard flag byte. (A good PC reference lists the addresses of this and other system variables.)

Most of KEYSTAT's action occurs inside a while loop (lines 31–54). To display each key value, the program calls ShowValue(), passing the address of a variable y, which is incremented to display text on successive lines.

While running KEYSTAT, you may wonder how the program somehow manages to detect changes in the keyboard's status. Line 53 reveals the answer—surprisingly simple when you understand the trick. Structure oldkeys holds a copy of the keyboard flag values. The while statement at line 53 compares that information with the current flag, addressed by keys, pausing at this location until a keypress changes a flag value, causing the "do-forever" while loop to end.

Summary

- Pointers are addresses that "point" to values stored somewhere in memory.

- Declare a pointer with the * operator. The declaration int p declares p as an int variable; int *p declares p as a pointer to an int value stored elsewhere.

- Dereference pointers to get to their values. The expression *p instructs the compiler to use the value addressed by p.

- Use the address-of operator to find the address of a variable or function. The expression &x represents the address of x.

- When a pointer addresses another variable, the pointer is called an alias. It hides the variable's true identity.

- A null pointer, represented by the macro NULL (which equals 0 or 0L), does not address valid data. Null pointers must never be used to read or write information in memory.

- A void pointer, declared as void *p, is a generic pointer, capable of addressing values of any type at any location. Don't confuse null and void pointers. Null pointers do not address valid data. Void pointers address data of unspecified types.

- Use type casting to inform the compiler about the type of data a void pointer addresses. If p is a void pointer, the type cast expression (int *)p instructs the compiler to treat p temporarily as a pointer to an int value.

- Borland C++ programs can store dynamic variables on the near or far heap, or both, depending on which memory model is in effect. Use malloc() or calloc() to allocate near heap space. Use farmalloc() or farcalloc() to allocate space from the far heap. Assign the results from these functions to pointers. Far pointers must be used to address items on the far heap.

- When finished using a dynamic variable, delete its memory by calling free(), or for items on the far heap, farfree(). Freeing unused dynamic variables places their memory back into the heap's free space, making the memory available for new variables. Never use a freed pointer except in another call to malloc() or a similar function.

- Freeing many small dynamic variables can fragment the heap by dividing it into relatively tiny used and unused chunks. Avoid fragmentation by using dynamic variables of sizes that are powers of two or another value. You might also allocate arrays rather than single variables.

- Borland C++ uses near and far pointers to accommodate the 80x86's segmented memory architecture, which uses segment and offset 16-bit address values to locate bytes in memory. A near pointer takes two bytes and represents the offset from a fixed segment boundary. A far pointer is four bytes long, and includes segment and offset values. Because far pointers may differ in value but refer to the identical locations, Borland C++ also defines huge pointers, which are normalized to force a pointer's offset portion to range from 0 to 15, thus creating a unique far address.

- Determining the amount of free heap space available requires "walking the heap." It's also possible to request heaps of specific sizes, although the requests are not guaranteed to be filled.

- Pointers and arrays are equivalent. An array is actually a pointer to the first of several items stored consecutively in memory. A pointer may also be subscripted like an array.

- C allows arithmetic operations on pointers. If p addresses an array, the expression p++ advances pointer p to the next item stored at a higher address.

- To obtain arguments entered after the program's name on the DOS command line, declare int argc and char *argv[] parameters in function main().

- Pointers may address structures. Use the structure member access operator -> to refer to an addressed structure's member. If p is a pointer to a struct, the expression p->x refers to a member x declared in the struct.

- Pointers may also address functions. One use for this device is to provide hooks, onto which modules can attach code to be called by a precompiled routine.

- Double-indirect pointers are literally pointers to pointers, and have many uses in C. A double-indirect pointer might be declared as char **argv or char *argv[]. Dereference double-indirect pointers twice, as in the expression **argv, to refer to the addressed information.

- Pointer parameters make it possible for functions to modify actual variables passed as arguments to functions. Pointers may also be returned as function results.

- Dynamic data structures declare pointer members in structs that address instances of themselves. Typical uses for these kinds of structures are lists, stacks, and trees.

- Pointers may be used to address locations that belong to the system. Use the MK_FP macro prototyped in dos.h to assign a specific address to a pointer. The technique makes it possible to address any location in memory at will—a powerful and potentially dangerous capability that requires great care to use successfully.

Exercises

9.1 Write a function that declares a char * argument and returns the length of a string passed to the function as an argument.

9.2 Given the declaration char str[10], use only pointer techniques to set the string addressed by str to a null string.

9.3 Write a memory check program that uses pointers to fill and verify memory blocks of test values.

9.4 Write a function that deletes an array of pointers to objects passed to the function as an argument. The function should work correctly regardless of the type of objects addressed. (Assume all objects are allocated by malloc().)

9.5 Modify Listing 9.11 READSTR.C to include appropriate checks for out of memory conditions.

9.6 Given the declaration int *p, write a statement that uses the ++ operator to increment the value addressed by p.

9.7 Write a function that uses pointers to swap any two variables of any type. (Assume the two variables are the same size.)

9.8 Write a function that computes the largest possible free space available on the near heap.

9.9 Modify Listing 9.21 (QSORTER.C) to accept command line arguments -u to sort up (that is, in ascending order) or -d to sort down (in descending order). The program should display an error message for incorrect or missing arguments.

9.10 Write a program that resets the NumLock, CapsLock, and ScrollLock keys.

Strings

Strings give computer programs the gift of speech. With strings, programs can display error messages, prompt for input, and report facts about internal events. Strings can also store character data, such as filenames and database search keys.

Almost all programs use one or more strings, which are so important in C programming, they deserve their own chapter. You've already seen many examples of strings. Now it's time to dig more deeply into the topic. In the following sections, you learn how strings of different kinds are stored in memory, and you investigate several string functions that can take strings apart, put them back together, search for patterns, and perform a variety of other operations. This chapter also covers related low-level functions for moving and filling blocks of memory.

The Nature of a String

As introduced in Chapter 8, "Data Structures," a string is an array of char values terminated with a null byte equal to zero. Each character in a string is actually an integer ASCII byte value associated with a visible symbol or an operation such as a carriage return or a line feed. As Figure 10.1 shows, in memory, a string's characters are stored one after the other, with leftmost characters at lower addresses. A null character (represented by /0 in the figure) follows the final significant character. If the string doesn't fill its allotted space exactly, bytes after the null terminator are wasted.

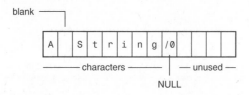

Figure 10.1. A typical character string as stored in memory.

On a PC, char values in strings represent ASCII characters. The standard ASCII character set specifies symbols for values in the range of 0 to 127, with 0 to 30 reserved for control codes. An extended ASCII character set adds more symbols for values from 128 to 255. You can store any of these standard and extended characters in Borland C++ strings. (See Appendix A for a complete ASCII character chart.)

> **NOTE:** Single-byte characters are of type char, which is unsigned by default in Borland C++. Multibyte characters are of type int. For representing ASCII characters, you may use either int or char.

Strings are typically stored in one of three forms:

- As literal strings entered directly into the program's text.

- As fixed-size variables stored along with other variables such as integers and floating-point numbers.

- As pointers that address strings, typically stored on the heap.

Understanding the nature of these forms is important to your understanding of strings, and later in this chapter, your understanding of how to use string functions. Begin by taking a close look at these common string formats.

String Literals

A literal string is typed directly in a program's text. Quotes surround the string's characters as in this symbolic constant declaration:

```
#define TITLE "My Program"
```

The constant TITLE is associated with the literal string "My Program", which is stored in the program's global data segment. Unseen is a null terminator byte added after the character 'm', causing this literal string to occupy 11 bytes including the space between the two words. Spaces are significant but invisible characters, as are other white-space characters such as tabs.

In expressions, literal strings such as "My Program" are treated as the address of the string's first character. Because the compiler sees literal strings as addresses, this is a legal statement:

```
char *stringPtr = "My Program";
```

Variable stringPtr is declared as a char pointer. The assignment initializes stringPtr to the address of 'M', the first character of the literal string "My Program". Despite appearances, the statement does not copy characters from one location to another. Instead, the characters are stored at a fixed address, which is assigned to stringPtr. Figure 10.2 shows the relationship of stringPtr and the literal string "My Program".

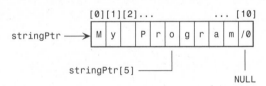

Figure 10.2. A string pointer addressing a literal character string.

To enter long literal strings, type a single backslash at the end of a line to tell the compiler the string continues on the *next* line. For example, to assign a long string to a char pointer p, you can write

```
  char *p = "This is a long string that \
I have typed on multiple lines \
ending with backslashes.";
```

The result is one string consisting of the characters between the quotes, but not the backslashes. The second and third lines in this example are purposely not indented. If they were, the indented spaces would also be inserted into the string.

Because arrays and pointers are equivalent—an array being represented internally as the address of the array's first element—the following declaration is also acceptable to the compiler:

```
char stringVar[] = "My Program";
```

This declares stringVar as an array of char values, and is exactly equivalent to the previous char pointer declaration of stringPtr. Internally, stringVar is a char * that addresses a string. In this case, however, the literal characters from "My Program" are copied to another location reserved for the stringVar array. You can use this declaration form if program statements modify the string. Use the declaration

```
char *stringPtr = "My Program";
```

to address a literal string directly, and avoid copying any characters. To prevent statements from changing the literal string, add const to the declaration:

```
const char *stringPtr = "My Program";
```

> **NOTE:** Modifying literal strings is unwise, though it still may be possible by using an alias pointer even when strings are declared with const. Attempting to modify literal strings, however, might not work under all conditions. If the string's characters are burned into a ROM chip or stored in protected memory, for example, changing the string's characters is impossible.

You can use either form (char s[] or char *s) to declare string pointers. To declare a string as a specific size, you must use array brackets. For example, this line:

```
char bigString[80] = "My Program";
```

reserves an 80-character array into which the literal string "My Program" is copied. Because the string's length is specified, a later statement may store up to 79 characters into the space addressed by bigString. Always remember to reserve one character for a string's null terminator (represented in programs by the macro NULL). The declaration char myString[80]; reserves memory for up to 79 characters plus null. To store an 80-character string in myString, declare it as char myString[81];

Be careful when using the assignment operator with strings. The results may be unexpected. Given the declaration

```
char *stringPtr = "A literal string";
```

a statement may later reassign `stringPtr` to address a different literal string:

```
stringPtr = "A new literal string";
```

Despite the equivalence of arrays and pointers, however, the same is not possible with string arrays. If you declare a string like this:

```
char stringVar[] = "A literal string";
```

you cannot assign a different string later with the statement

```
stringVar = "A new literal string";  /* ??? */
```

That does not compile because the assignment operator is not defined for string variables. Although `stringVar` is represented internally as a pointer, it addresses space reserved for the string's characters, and an assignment statement cannot copy new characters into that space. Such an assignment is allowed only in a `char` array's declaration. Later in this chapter, you learn how to copy strings using a function such as `strcpy()`.

String Variables

A string variable occupies a fixed amount of space determined when you write the program. Like all variables, strings may be global or local to a function. Because strings are arrays, you declare them using brackets enclosing a positive integer equal to the size of the string in bytes:

```
char stringVar[128];
```

Declared like this, `stringVar` can hold from 0 to 127 characters plus a null terminator. If the declaration is outside of any function, it's global, and may be used by any statement. All bytes in global strings (and other global variables) are stored in the program's data segment and are set to zero when the program runs. Other modules linked to a program can access the global `stringVar` by including the declaration

```
extern char stringVar[128];
```

which might be included from a header file, thus making `stringVar` and other global variables available to modules other than the one that declares them.

If `stringVar` is declared inside a function, then only statements in the function may use it. Local strings (and other local variables) are stored temporarily on the stack and are not zeroed. They contain initial values equal to whatever bytes existed on the stack when the function begins; therefore, you must initialize local strings before their use.

Using string variables generally involves calling various functions to copy characters, compare one string with another, join two strings, and so on. This chapter covers many such functions. You can find others in Chapter 22, "Functions and Examples," and in your Borland C++ Library Reference.

String Pointers

String pointers are *not* strings. They are pointers—that is, addresses—that locate the first character of a string stored elsewhere. String pointers are declared as type `char *` or, if you don't want statements to be able to modify their addressed data, as `const char *`. Here are a few samples:

```
char *stringPtr;          /* String pointer */
const char *fixedString;  /* Pointer to a fixed string */
char far *stringFPtr;     /* String far pointer */
```

There's nothing special about string pointers—they are just pointers to arrays of `char` values, and they behave exactly like other pointers (see Chapter 9, "Pointers"). There are many functions that operate on strings addressed by string pointers, and `char *` declarations are commonplace in C.

To allocate heap space for a string pointer, call `malloc()`, and specify a size value that includes one extra byte for the string's terminating null. This statement:

```
stringPtr = (char *)malloc(81);
```

reserves 81 bytes of heap space and assigns to `stringPtr` the address of the first byte. The string can hold up to 80 characters plus a null terminator. When finished with the string, call `free()` to place the reserved heap space back into the available pool of memory for future `malloc()` statements:

```
free(stringPtr);
```

Remember that arrays and pointers are equivalent. To refer to individual characters in a string, you may use subscript expressions. For example, to display the third character in the string addressed by pointer `stringPtr`, you can write

```
printf("%c", stringPtr[2]);
```

When indexing strings like this, it's your responsibility to ensure that a valid character exists at `stringPtr[2]`. If the addressed string has fewer than three significant characters, this expression probably displays incorrect information.

Null Strings and Null Characters

Null has many meanings in C programming, and it's important to understand the different uses of null:

- A null character has the ASCII value zero and is typically represented in programs by the `NULL` macro, defined in stdio.h and other header files. `NULL` may be type `int` or `long` depending on the current memory model.

- A null-terminated string is any array of `char` with an ASCII null character after the last significant character in the string. All strings must have one extra `char` position to hold a terminating null character.

- A null string is one that begins with a null character. A null string's length is zero because it has no significant characters, but its size in memory may occupy from one to several bytes. Null strings typically represent blank lines in text editors and blank fields in database entry screens. A literal null string is written `""`.

- A null string pointer addresses no character data—it is *not* equivalent to a null (zero-length) string. To create a null string pointer, assign the macro `NULL` to the pointer. To create a null string, assign `NULL` to the string's first byte.

Figure 10.3 illustrates an important concept: that a string's contents may take up less space than the total amount of memory allocated to a string. A string might have from 0 to *n*–1 characters where *n* is the declared length. The top string in the figure is null—it contains no significant characters, only a null terminator in its first byte. All other bytes in the string are unused. The middle string in the figure fills the character array completely. There's no waste in this string. The bottom string in the figure represents the most typical case—a character array partially occupied by characters, leaving a few wasted bytes after the terminating null.

During its existence, a string occupies a fixed amount of memory, but its character content may vary in length. String variables do *not* grow and shrink as needed to hold their characters, and unless the entire string is filled, some of its space may at times be wasted. In the next sections, you'll learn ways to minimize this waste.

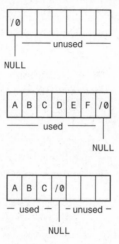

Figure 10.3. Typical strings in memory.

Using String Functions

Borland C++ has a rich library of string functions, all of which begin with str, making them easy to find in your Borland C++ Library Reference and in Chapter 22, "Functions and Examples." To use one or more of these functions, include the string.h header by inserting this line near the top of your module:

```
#include <string.h>
```

Do the same for all modules that call one or more of the string functions described in this chapter.

Displaying Strings

Libraries other than string.h also have functions that use strings. For example, you've already seen many samples of printf() and puts(), both of which accept char * arguments to display strings. To use these functions, include the header file stdio.h like this:

```
#include <stdio.h>
```

Generally, printf() is best reserved for displaying multiple variables formatted in columns or with fixed numbers of decimal places, and other formats. To simply display a string variable, puts() is faster and more efficient than printf(). The statement

```
puts(string);
```

displays string, which may be a string variable declared as char string[n] or a string pointer declared as char *string. Function puts() starts a new display line, making the function convenient for displaying multiple strings, perhaps stored in an array:

```
for (i = 0; i < MAX; i++)
  puts(stringArray[i]);
```

If you are not concerned with writing strictly ANSI C-compatible programs, include the conio.h header file and use cputs() rather than puts(). The cputs() function writes directly to the PC video display buffer, or if that's impossible (due to hardware limitations on some types of PC compatibles), cputs() calls video BIOS routines to display text. Either way, cputs() is probably faster than puts(). However, the statement

```
cputs(string);
```

does not start a new line. Instead, it's up to you to position the cursor. For example, to display a string at coordinate (1,5), you can write

```
gotoxy(1, 5);
cputs(string);
```

Function gotoxy() is also prototyped in conio.h. The function considers coordinate (1,1) to be the upper-left corner of the display. To start a new display line after cputs(), use programming such as

```
cputs(string);
gotoxy(1, wherey() + 1);
```

Function wherey() returns the cursor's current Y coordinate value. That value plus one sends the cursor to the next line—however, unlike puts(), the display does not scroll when writing to the bottom line. A similar function, wherex(), returns the cursor's current X coordinate value. See file conio.h in C:\BORLANDC\INCLUDE or the equivalent directory for other direct-video console functions you can use. For information about the functions, look them up in Chapter 22, "Functions and Examples."

Reading Strings

In addition to displaying strings, most programs also need to read characters from the keyboard, disk files, and other sources. (See Chapter 11, "Input and Output," for general-purpose file-handling techniques.) The easiest way to read a string from the standard input is to call gets(). As explained in Chapter 5, "Data: What a Program Knows," because there's no way to tell gets() how many characters to read, the best course is to give it a string variable at least as big as DOS's type-ahead input buffer, typically 128 bytes:

```
char buffer[128];
gets(buffer);
```

To read input into shorter strings, use gets() as shown here, then call a string function to copy some or all characters from buffer to another variable.

If you don't need to port your programs to other ANSI C compilers, include conio.h and call cgets() for string input. The cgets() function requires a specially prepared string argument. Declare the string as usual, but add three to its size. For example, declare a 40-character string as

```
char string[43];
```

The cgets() function expects a string's first byte to equal the string's maximum length. Before calling cgets(), assign that length with a statement such as

```
string[0] = 41;
```

This length value includes one byte for the null terminator added by cgets() to the returned result. You can now call the function like this:

```
cgets(string);
```

After the program's user presses Enter, cgets() stores in byte string[1] the actual number of characters typed. The first significant character (if any) starts at string[2]. As Figure 10.4 shows, a cgets() string variable has 3 bytes of overhead, including the terminating null. To read 40-character strings with cgets() therefore requires a string variable 43 bytes long. Because bytes are used to represent the string's maximum and actual lengths, the largest string you can read with cgets() is 256 bytes long and can hold from 0 to 253 characters.

Listing 10.1, GETSTR.C, shows how to use cgets() to read character strings. Enter the program and type up to 15 characters, with or without spaces. GETSTR echoes your typing in three ways, including a breakdown of each character in the result.

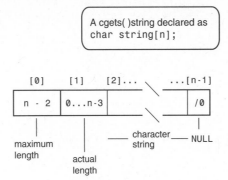

Figure 10.4. Function `cgets()` requires a specially prepared string.

Listing 10.1. GETSTR.C (Reads strings using `cgets()` function).

```
 1:  #include <stdio.h>
 2:  #include <conio.h>
 3:
 4:  #define MAXLEN 18   /* Room for 15 characters */
 5:
 6:  void ShowChars(char *s);
 7:
 8:  main()
 9:  {
10:    char buffer[MAXLEN];
11:    char *result;
12:
13:    clrscr();
14:    gotoxy(1, 12);
15:    cputs("Enter a string: ");
16:    buffer[0] = MAXLEN - 2;
17:    result = cgets(buffer);
18:    gotoxy(1, 14);
19:    cputs("result == ");
20:    cputs(result);
21:    gotoxy(1, 16);
22:    cputs("&buffer[2] == ");
23:    cputs(&buffer[2]);
```

continues

Listing 10.1. continued

```
24:    gotoxy(1, 18);
25:    ShowChars(buffer);
26:    gotoxy(1, 24);
27:    return 0;
28:  }
29:
30:  void ShowChars(char *s)
31:  {
32:    int i;
33:
34:    cprintf("[%d] [%d]", s[0], s[1]);
35:    for (i = 2; s[i] != NULL; i++)
36:      cprintf(" [%c]", s[i]);
37:    cputs(" [NULL]");
38:  }
```

If you run GETSTR and enter Borland C++, the program displays

```
Enter a string: Borland C++
result == Borland C++
&buffer[2] == Borland C++
[16] [11] [B] [o] [r] [l] [a] [n] [d] [ ] [C] [+] [+] [NULL]
```

The last line shows the resulting buffer's contents. The first character equals the maximum length of the string, including the terminating null. This value has to be assigned *before* calling cgets(). After the function returns, the second value equals the number of characters entered, in this case 11, which does not include the terminating null. Entered characters begin at subscript [2], and the final character is, as always, NULL.

Line 16 in the listing shows the proper way to prepare a string for cgets(). Line 17 shows the proper way to call the function, saving the function result in a char pointer:

```
result = cgets(buffer);
```

Pointer result now addresses the location of buffer[2], where the first character of the new string begins. (If the program's user presses Enter without entering any text, buffer[2] equals null.) Line 20 displays the resulting string. Line 23 does the same, but uses the expression &buffer[2] to locate the new string's beginning.

Function ShowChars() at lines 30–38 displays the character-by-character view of the buffer after calling cgets(). Lines 34 and 36 call cprintf(), which is similar to printf() but is available only in Borland C++ programs that include conio.h. The cprintf() function displays text quickly by writing directly to the PC video buffers or by calling BIOS routines. It is not portable, however, and does not recognize escape characters such as '\n' to start a new display line.

Determining a String's Length

Finding the length of a string is simple. Just pass a string pointer to strlen(), which returns the string's length in characters. Given the declarations

```
char *c = "Any old string";
int len;
```

this sets len equal to the length of the string addressed by c:

```
len = strlen(c);
```

Listing 10.2, LENGTH.C, demonstrates how to use strlen() along with the specially prepared string buffer required by cgets().

Listing 10.2. LENGTH.C (Uses the strlen() function).

```
 1:  #include <stdio.h>
 2:  #include <conio.h>
 3:  #include <string.h>
 4:
 5:  #define MAXLEN 256
 6:
 7:  main()
 8:  {
 9:    char string[MAXLEN];  /* Room for 253 characters */
10:    char *result;         /* Points to result from cgets() */
11:
12:    printf("\nEnter a string: ");
13:    string[0] = MAXLEN - 2;
14:    result = cgets(string);
15:    puts("");
16:    puts(result);
```

continues

Listing 10.2. continued

```
17:    printf("Length == %d characters\n", strlen(result));
18:    return 0;
19:  }
```

Lines 13–14 prepare a char array string for cgets(), which returns the address of a string entered at the keyboard. As explained before, this address is equal to &string[2]. When line 17 calls strlen() to display the string's length, it must use the pointer returned by cgets()—it can't use string directly.

When not using specially prepared buffers for cgets(), you may pass char arrays directly to strlen(). For a string declared as

```
char buffer[128] = "Copied to buffer";
```

the following statement sets an int variable len equal to 16, the length of the assigned literal string:

```
len = strlen(buffer);
```

Copying Strings

The assignment operator is not defined for strings. If c1 and c2 are char arrays, you may not copy one to the other like this:

```
c1 = c2;  /* ??? */
```

This statement does not compile. If c1 and c2 are declared as type char *, however, the compiler accepts the statement, but does not produce the results that you might expect. Instead of copying the characters from one string to another, the statement c1 = c2 copies the *pointer* c2 to c1, thus overwriting the address in c1, potentially losing that pointer's addressed information.

To copy one string to another, rather than use an assignment statement, call a string-copy function such as strcpy(). For two char * pointers c1 and c2, this statement:

```
strcpy(c1, c2);
```

copies the characters addressed by c2 to the memory addressed by c1, including the string's null terminator. It's your responsibility to ensure that the destination string has enough room to hold the copy.

A similar function, strncpy(), limits how many characters are copied. If source and destination are pointers of type char * or char arrays, the statement

```
strncpy(destination, source, 10);
```

copies up to 10 characters from the string addressed by source to the location addressed by destination. If the source string has more than 10 characters, the result is truncated. If the source has fewer than 10 characters, the result's unused bytes are set to nulls.

> **NOTE:** Generally, string functions with an extra n in their names declare a numeric parameter that limits the function's action in some way. These functions tend to be safer or more restrictive, but slower, than their n-less counterparts. Examples include strcpy() and strncpy(), strcat() and strncat(), and strcmp() and strncmp().

Duplicating Strings

Having to prepare special buffers for cgets() is tedious in large programs with many string variables. What's needed is a function that prompts for and returns a string entered at the keyboard. The string should be stored on the heap, and it should occupy only as much space as needed. Down with wasted bytes!

Listings 10.3, gets.h, and 10.4, GETS.C, form a small module with a single function, GetStringAt(), that fits the bill, using another string function, strdup(), to make a duplicate copy of an input string. Other programs in this chapter use the GETS module—a good example of how storing common routines separately can save time, effort, and disk space. Enter both listings now and compile with the command **bcc -c gets.c**. The -c command instructs the compiler to "compile only" and not to call the linker to produce an executable code file. At this stage, you want to create the object-code file GETS.OBJ for other programs to use, not as a finished application.

Listing 10.3. gets.h (Header file for GETS.C).

```
1:  /* gets.h -- Header for gets.c */
2:
3:  #define MAXLEN 256  /* Maximum string size (+3) */
4:
5:  char *GetStringAt(int x, int y, int maxlen);
```

Listing 10.4. GETS.C (Uses get-string module).

```
 1:  #include <string.h>
 2:  #include <conio.h>
 3:  #include "gets.h"
 4:
 5:  char *GetStringAt(int x, int y, int maxlen)
 6:  {
 7:    static char buffer[MAXLEN];
 8:
 9:    buffer[0] = maxlen - 2;
10:    gotoxy(x, y);
11:    return strdup(cgets(buffer));
12:  }
```

The module in Listing 10.4 includes its own header file (line 3), which defines a MAXLEN constant and lists a prototype for the GetStringAt() function (see Listing 10.3). Back in Listing 10.4, the function declares a static string buffer at line 7. Using the static keyword as shown here creates a variable that is stored permanently in the data segment, but is available only inside of GetStringAt().

The static buffer holds raw keyboard input, which is copied to a new string returned by the function. The reason for using a static buffer is to guarantee that the function has room to store input. One disadvantage of this technique, however, is that buffer is overwritten on every call to the function, which therefore must not be called recursively. A static buffer as shown here is a common device, but the technique is optional, and you could write GetStringAt() to use a local variable or a string stored on the heap (see Exercise 10.4).

The static buffer is prepared for cgets() (line 9). Then, after positioning the cursor by calling gotoxy(), the function executes the statement

```
return strdup(cgets(buffer));
```

The char * address value returned by cgets() is passed directly to another string function, strdup(). Cascading multiple string-function calls this way avoids having to save string pointers in temporary variables. As its name implies, strdup() returns the address of a duplicate of a string addressed by its argument. The string is created by calling malloc(), and it occupies only as much space as needed. If c is type char *, the statement

```
c = strdup("Double trouble");
```

allocates exactly 15 bytes of heap space, copies the 14-character string `"Double trouble"` plus a terminating null to that space, and returns the reserved memory's address. When done with the string, free it in the usual way:

```
free(c);
```

> **WARNING:** You may modify strings created by `strdup()`, but you must never cause such strings to grow beyond their allotted lengths. If a string must grow larger, copy it to a new, larger buffer allocated by `malloc()`, then free the original string.

Listing 10.5, DUPED.C, demonstrates how to use the `GetStringAt()` function in gets.h and GETS.C. Because the program uses the GETS module, compile it with the command **bcc duped.c gets.obj**. This two-part command compiles DUPED.C and links it to GETS.OBJ, which you compiled earlier, creating the finished application.

Listing 10.5. DUPED.C (Demonstrates `GetStringAt()` function).

```
 1:  #include <stdio.h>
 2:  #include <conio.h>
 3:  #include <string.h>
 4:  #include <alloc.h>
 5:  #include "gets.h"
 6:
 7:  #define X_ENTRY 12        /* Entry X coordinate */
 8:  #define Y_ENTRY 10        /* Entry Y coordinate */
 9:  #define PROMPT "String: "  /* Entry prompt */
10:
11:  main()
12:  {
13:    char *s;  /* Pointer to result from GetStringAt() */
14:
15:    clrscr();
16:    gotoxy(X_ENTRY - strlen(PROMPT), Y_ENTRY);
17:    printf("String: ");
```

continues

Listing 10.5. continued

```
18:      s = GetStringAt(X_ENTRY, Y_ENTRY, MAXLEN);
19:      gotoxy(1, 24);
20:      if (s) {
21:        puts("Your entry is:");
22:        puts(s);
23:        printf("Length == %d characters\n", strlen(s));
24:        free(s);
25:      } else
26:        puts("Error duplicating string!");
27:      return 0;
28:    }
```

Line 18 calls `GetStringAt()`, passing three arguments: an X coordinate, a Y coordinate, and the result's maximum length. The function positions the cursor at the specified location (useful for designing data-entry screens), and restricts input to the requested number of characters.

At line 20, the program examines `GetStringAt()`'s result. If the function returns null, then `strdup()` was unable to create a copy of the input—probably due to a shortage of heap space. Notice also how line 24 frees the string's space after that space is no longer needed.

Comparing Strings

By using `GetStringAt()` from the GETS module, and with the help of a little trickery, you can write a program that prompts for a secret password. To determine whether you typed the correct password, Listing 10.6, PASSWORD.C, calls `strcmp()`, which compares two strings. Compile with the command **bcc password.c gets.obj**, and then run PASSWORD. To end the program, enter **Borland C++** exactly, using upper- and lowercase letters. If you don't enter the correct password, the program displays an error message and makes you start over. As in all good password-entry routines, PASSWORD blanks your typing to prevent someone from looking over your shoulder and stealing your secret code.

Listing 10.6. PASSWORD.C (Prompts for a secret password).

```
 1:  #include <stdio.h>
 2:  #include <stdlib.h>
 3:  #include <conio.h>
 4:  #include <string.h>
 5:  #include <alloc.h>
 6:  #include "gets.h"
 7:
 8:  #define FALSE 0
 9:  #define TRUE 1
10:  #define X_ENTRY 20
11:  #define Y_ENTRY 10
12:  #define PASSWORD "Borland C++"
13:  #define PROMPT "Enter password: "
14:
15:  main()
16:  {
17:    char *s;
18:    int done = FALSE;
19:
20:    clrscr();
21:    while (!done) {
22:      gotoxy(X_ENTRY - strlen(PROMPT), Y_ENTRY);
23:      cputs(PROMPT);
24:      clreol();
25:      textbackground(BLACK);
26:      textcolor(BLACK);
27:      s = GetStringAt(X_ENTRY, Y_ENTRY, MAXLEN);
28:      if (!s) {
29:        cputs("Error: Out of memory");
30:        clreol();
31:        exit(1);
32:      } else {
33:        normvideo();
34:        done = (strcmp(s, PASSWORD) == 0);
35:        gotoxy(1, Y_ENTRY + 2);
36:        if (!done) {
37:          cputs("ERROR in password! Type "PASSWORD" to quit");
38:          clreol();
```

continues

365

Listing 10.6. continued

```
39:        }
40:        free(s);   /* Delete memory allocated by GetStringAt() */
41:      }
42:    }
43:    cputs("Correct password given");
44:    clreol();
45:    gotoxy(1, 24);
46:    return 0;
47: }
```

To hide your typing, lines 25–26 set the foreground and background to black—a simple trick that makes all conio.h output routines invisible. Use functions textbackground() and textcolor() to select from 16 possible colors. For example, for yellow letters on a blue background, you can write

```
textbackground(BLUE);
textcolor(YELLOW);
```

These functions affect only conio.h output routines, not those defined in stdio.h. On systems without color monitors, text is shaded various levels of gray. On systems with monochrome adapters, text is given bold, underline, and blinking attributes. See file conio.h in C:\BORLANDC\INCLUDE or the equivalent directory for a full list of color constants.

You can also call functions normvideo(), highvideo(), and lowvideo() to select different output effects. PASSWORD calls normvideo() at line 33 to reset output to normal.

Line 34 shows how to compare two strings, in this case, to determine whether the correct password was given. The statement

```
done = (strcmp(s, PASSWORD) == 0);
```

sets int variable done to true (nonzero) if the strings addressed by s and PASSWORD (a macro that expands to a literal string) are equal. If i is an int variable, and if a and b are pointers of type char * or char arrays, this statement:

```
i = strcmp(a, b);
```

sets i to –1 or another negative value if the string addressed by a is alphabetically less than the string addressed by b. The function returns zero if the two strings are exactly equal. It returns +1 or another positive value if the string at a is alphabetically greater than the string at b.

Function strcmp() is case-sensitive—it considers lowercase letters to be alphabetically greater than their uppercase equivalents (because lowercase letters have higher ASCII values than uppercase letters). For a caseless (but not tasteless) comparison between two strings, call stricmp(). The extra "i" stands for "ignore case." This function works identically to strcmp(), but converts all characters to uppercase before comparing. When compared using strcmp(), "Apple" is alphabetically less than "apple". When compared using stricmp(), "Apple" and "apple" are considered identical.

> **NOTE:** For compatibility with other C compilers, Borland C++ defines function strcmpi() as a macro that expands to stricmp(). Both these functions produce identical compiled code, but the macro strcmpi() takes a tiny bit longer to compile. Use stricmp() in new programs. Use strcmpi() only to compile programs that use this alternate spelling. Generally, string functions with i at the end of their names are macros; those with i in the middle are native functions.

To compare only a portion of two strings, use strncmp(). For example, this statement:

```
i = strncmp(s1, s2, 2);
```

sets int variable i to zero only if the first two characters of the strings addressed by s1 and s2 match exactly. For a caseless comparison, call function strnicmp(). (Macro strncmpi() expands to strnicmp(), and like strcmpi(), is provided for compatibility reasons only.)

Concatenating Strings

Concatenating two strings joins them, creating a new, longer string. Given an existing string declared as

```
char original[128] = "Testing ";
```

the statement

```
strcat(original, "one, two, three!");
```

sets the original string to "Testing one, two, three!".

When calling strcat(), be sure that the first char * argument is initialized, and that there is enough room in that string to hold the result. If c1 addresses a string that is already full, and c2 addresses a non-null string, the statement

```
strcat(c1, c2);  /* ??? */
```

overwrites the end of the string at c1, causing a serious bug.

Function strcat() returns the address of the final string (the same as its first parameter), and may be cascaded in multiple function calls:

```
strcat(strcat(c1, c2), c3);
```

This appends the string at c2 and the string at c3 to the string addressed by c1, and is equivalent to the separate statements

```
strcat(c1, c2);
strcat(c1, c3);
```

Listing 10.7, CONCAT.C, demonstrates how to use strcat() to solve a typical problem: joining a full name out of a person's first, middle, and last names, stored separately as strings might be in a name-and-address database. Compile the program with the DOS command **bcc concat.c gets.obj** (assuming you have compiled module GETS as explained earlier). Run CONCAT, and enter your first, middle, and last names. The program concatenates your entries, displaying your name as a single string.

Listing 10.7. CONCAT.C (Demonstrates string concatenation).

```
1:  #include <conio.h>
2:  #include <stdlib.h>
3:  #include <string.h>
4:  #include <alloc.h>
5:  #include "gets.h"
6:
7:  char *PromptFor(char *prompt);
8:
```

```
 9:  main()
10:  {
11:    char *firstName;
12:    char *middleName;
13:    char *lastName;
14:    char fullName[128];
15:
16:    clrscr();
17:    firstName = PromptFor("first name");
18:    middleName = PromptFor("middle name");
19:    lastName = PromptFor("last name");
20:    strcpy(fullName, firstName);
21:    strcat(fullName, " ");
22:    strcat(fullName, middleName);
23:    strcat(fullName, " ");
24:    strcat(fullName, lastName);
25:    gotoxy(1, 20);
26:    cprintf("Your name is: %s", fullName);
27:    free(firstName);   /* Delete allocated string memory */
28:    free(middleName);  /*     "      "     "     "      "      "       */
29:    free(lastName);    /*     "      "     "     "      "      "       */
30:    gotoxy(1, 24);
31:    return 0;
32:  }
33:
34:  char *PromptFor(char *prompt)
35:  {
36:    char *temp;   /* Temporary string pointer */
37:
38:    gotoxy(1, wherey() + 1);
39:    cprintf("Enter your %s: ", prompt);
40:    temp = GetStringAt(wherex(), wherey(), 40);
41:    if (!temp) {
42:      gotoxy(1, wherey());
43:      clreol();
44:      cputs("Error: Out of memory");
45:      exit(1);
46:    }
47:    return temp;
48:  }
```

Lines 20–24 illustrate an important principle of string concatenation: *Always initialize the initial string argument.* In this case, char array fullName is initialized by calling strcpy(), inserting firstName into fullName. After this step, the program appends blanks and two other strings, middleName and lastName. Never call strcat() for an uninitialized first argument. For example, if line 20 had been written

```
strcat(fullName, firstName);   /* ??? */
```

the program would append firstName to the unpredictable contents of the uninitialized fullName. This is a serious and common error, easily avoided by always initializing strcat()'s destination argument.

When you can't be sure that a string has enough room to hold concatenated substrings, call strncat(), which is similar to strcat() but requires a numeric argument that specifies the maximum number of characters to copy. For two strings, s1 and s2, which can be char * pointers or char arrays, the statement

```
strncat(s1, s2, 4);
```

appends, at most, four characters from s2 to the end of s1. The result is null terminated.

One way to use strncat() to ensure a safe string concatenation is to pass the destination's free space to strncat()'s third argument. Consider these declarations:

```
#define MAXLEN 128
char s1[MAXLEN] = "The Cat ";
char s2[] = "in the Hat";
```

You can append s2 to s1, forming the string "The Cat in the Hat", with strcat():

```
strcat(s1, s2);
```

If you can't be certain that s1 has enough room to hold the result, use the alternate statement

```
strncat(s1, s2, (MAXLEN - 1) - strlen(s1));
```

This technique guarantees that s1 does not overflow, even if s2 must be truncated to fit. It also works correctly if s1 is a null string.

Searching Strings for Patterns

Often, a program needs to search strings for characters and substrings. One of the most common uses for the technique is to examine filenames for a certain extension. For example, after prompting users to enter a filename, you might want to check if they entered the extension .TXT, and if so, take a different action than for the extension .EXE. You may also want to reject all but a specific extension, thus helping to prevent bugs caused by loading the wrong type of data file.

Searching for Characters

Listing 10.8, EXT1.C, demonstrates how to use function strchr() to hunt for single characters in strings.

Listing 10.8. EXT1.C (Checks filename extensions, demonstration #1).

```
 1:  #include <stdio.h>
 2:  #include <string.h>
 3:
 4:  main()
 5:  {
 6:    char fileName[128];
 7:
 8:    printf("Enter file name: ");
 9:    gets(fileName);
10:    printf("As entered: %s\n", fileName);
11:    if (strchr(fileName, '.'))
12:      printf("File name is probably complete\n");
13:    else
14:      strcat(fileName, ".TXT");
15:    printf("Final file name: %s\n", fileName);
16:    return 0;
17:  }
```

Compile and run EXT1, then enter a filename with an extension. For example, if you type **test.txt**, the program displays

```
Enter file name: test.txt
As entered: test.txt
File name is probably complete
Final file name: test.txt
```

If you enter **test** with no extension, however, the program appends .TXT, displaying

```
Enter file name: test
As entered: test
Final file name: test.TXT
```

EXT1 detects the presence of a filename extension by searching the input string for a period. (There can be only one period in a DOS filename, and the period must precede the extension, if there is one.) The key to this program is the if-else statement at lines 11–14:

```
if (strchr(fileName, '.'))
  printf("File name is probably complete\n");
else
  strcat(fileName, ".TXT");
```

The expression strchr(fileName, '.') returns a pointer to the period character in the string addressed by fileName. If no such character is found, strchr() returns null. Because non-null values mean true, you can use strchr() as though it returned a true/false value. You can also use strchr() to assign a pointer to a substring, located at a specific character. For instance, if p is a pointer declared as char *, and if fileName from EXT1 addresses the string "TEST.TXT", Figure 10.5 illustrates the effect of the statement

```
p = strchr(fileName, '.');
```

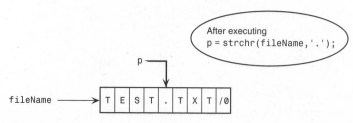

Figure 10.5. Function strchr() finds a character in a string.

Figure 10.5 also points out a subtle, and important, consideration when using pointers to address substrings—a variation of pointer aliases that takes great care to use correctly. In the figure, there is only one string, `"TEST.TXT"`, terminated with a null. There are *two* string pointers, however—`fileName` and `p`. The `fileName` pointer addresses the entire string. The `p` pointer addresses a substring inside that same set of characters. String functions don't care about any bytes that precede a string's designated first character; therefore, the statement

```
puts(p);
```

displays `".TXT"` as though this substring were a complete string variable, and not part of another string.

In C programming, it's common to have many pointers addressing substrings this way, and there is nothing wrong with using the technique. If Figure 10.5's string is stored on the heap, however, the statement

```
free(fileName);
```

correctly frees the string's occupied space. The program, however, must *never* execute a statement such as

```
free(p);   /* ??? */
```

as this would attempt to free the substring addressed by `p`, an action that would undoubtedly corrupt the heap, causing a hard-to-find bug.

Function `strchr()` locates the first occurrence of a character in a string. These declarations and statements:

```
char *p;
char s[] = "Abracadabra";
p = strchr(s, 'a');
```

set `p` to the address of the first lowercase `'a'` in the string `"Abracadabra"`.

The `strchr()` function considers a string's null terminator to be a significant character. Given this fact, a useful trick locates the end of a string. Using the preceding declarations, the statement

```
p = strchr(s, 0);
```

sets `p` equal to the address of the null character in `s`. Use this technique to find the end of a string.

To locate the last occurrence of a character in a string, call `strrchr()`. Using the preceding declarations, the statement

```
p = strrchr(s, 'b');
```

sets p to the address of the substring "bra" at the end of "Abracadabra".

Searching for Substrings

In addition to searching for characters in strings, you can also hunt for substrings. Listing 10.9, EXT2.C, demonstrates the technique. The program is similar to EXT1, but forces a filename's extension to .TXT.

Listing 10.9. EXT2.C (Checks filename extensions, demonstration #2).

```
 1:  #include <stdio.h>
 2:  #include <string.h>
 3:
 4:  main()
 5:  {
 6:    char fileName[128];
 7:    char *p;
 8:
 9:    printf("Enter file name: ");
10:    gets(fileName);
11:    printf("As entered: %s\n", fileName);
12:    strupr(fileName);
13:    p = strstr(fileName, ".TXT");
14:    if (p)
15:      printf("File name is complete\n");
16:    else {
17:      p = strchr(fileName, '.');
18:      if (p)
19:        *p = NULL;  /* Delete any other extension */
20:      strcat(fileName, ".TXT");
21:    }
22:    printf("Final file name: %s\n", fileName);
23:    return 0;
24:  }
```

The new program creates a filename that's guaranteed to end in .TXT. Run EXT2 and enter **test** or **test.txt**, which produce similar results as from EXT1. If you enter **test.c**, however, EXT2 displays

```
Enter file name: test.c
As entered: test.c
Final file name: TEST.TXT
```

To determine whether a filename has the extension .TXT, the program executes this statement at line 13:

```
p = strstr(fileName, ".TXT");
```

Like strchr(), strstr() returns the address of a substring or null if the target string is not found. If the target is found, p is set to its address—in the example, to the period in .TXT. Because that extension might not be in uppercase, the program also executes

```
strupr(fileName);
```

to convert the original string to all uppercase letters before calling strstr().

EXT2 also demonstrates a useful trick for truncating a string at a specified character or substring. Line 17 calls strchr() to set pointer p to the address of the first period in fileName. If the result of this search is non-null (see line 18), line 19 executes

```
*p = NULL;
```

which overwrites the period with a null byte. This affixes the new end of the string at the location of its former extension in preparation for adding a new extension with a call to strcat() at line 20.

Tokenizing a String

Programs frequently need to extract substrings from char buffers or other large strings. For example, a database indexer might need to locate all the words in a text file. (See Chapter 11, "Input and Output," for the file-handling techniques required to solve this problem.)

Finding a string's components, or tokens—a process called parsing—often requires custom programming. If a string's parts are delimited with commas, spaces, or other unique characters, however, you can use function strtok() to tokenize a string into multiple substrings.

It might take some effort to understand how to use strtok() properly, but the time is well spent, and you are likely to find dozens of uses for this powerful string function. Examine these declarations:

```
char s[] = "Now I know my ABCs";
char *p1, *p2, *p3, *p4, *p5;
```

String s is an array of char, initialized to a line from a child's alphabet jingle. The five char pointers are not yet initialized—in a moment, you will see how strtok() uses these pointers to parse the string addressed by s. First, call strtok(), passing the string pointer as the first argument and the delimiter character (represented in this case as a string equal to a single blank character) as the second:

```
p1 = strtok(s, " ");
```

The strtok() function returns the address of the first component separated from the next by the specified delimiter—a blank in this example. The delimiter must be a string containing a single character. For example, to parse strings with items separated by commas, use the string "," as strtok()'s second argument, not the character ','. Figure 10.6 illustrates the state of the program's variables at this stage.

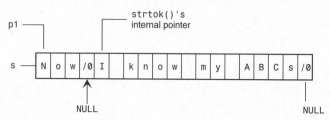

Figure 10.6. After calling strtok() the first time to parse a string.

As Figure 10.6 shows, strtok() inserts a null byte (represented in the figure as /0) at the location of the first specified delimiter. This creates a small substring, the address of which is passed back by strtok(), and in this example, assigned to p1. If no more delimiters are found, strtok() returns null. The function also keeps an internal pointer to the character that follows the end of the last-formed substring, so that subsequent calls to strtok() can parse more of the string. To continue parsing, pass the NULL macro as the first argument—a signal that strtok() interprets as a command to use its internal pointer as the starting address for another delimiter search. Parsing the other components of the string is therefore a simple matter of calling strtok() multiple times, in each case passing NULL as the initial argument:

```
p2 = strtok(NULL, " ");
p3 = strtok(NULL, " ");
p4 = strtok(NULL, " ");
p5 = strtok(NULL, " ");
```

Figure 10.7 illustrates the tokenized string and its pointers p1 through p5. Each pointer addresses a null-terminated substring inside the original string. Each of the substrings is a distinct string variable, and the five pointers can be passed to other string functions such as strlen(), strcpy(), strdup(), and others.

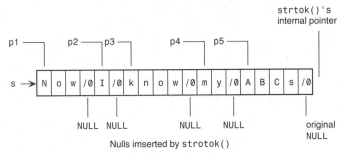

Figure 10.7. After tokenizing a string with strtok().

NOTE: Function strtok() directly modifies the destination string, so before tokenizing a string, be sure to copy it for safekeeping if necessary.

The preceding samples assume that it's possible to know in advance how many components a string has. Most of the time, of course, that isn't possible, and addressing a string's components with individual pointers is impractical.

A more sensible solution uses a loop to extract a string's tokens, passing the results of multiple strtok() function calls to other string functions. This loop can usually be written something like this:

```
p = strtok(buffer, ";");
while (p) {
  /* Process substring addressed by p */
  p = strtok(NULL, ";");
}
```

First, set a `char *` pointer p to the result of `strtok()`, passing a pointer to the original string such as `buffer` and a delimiter such as `";"`. Examine p in a `while` loop, ending if p equals null. If p is non-null, it addresses the next substring in `buffer`, and you can pass p to another string function. Find other substrings by calling `strtok()` again inside the loop, but pass the `NULL` macro as the initial argument.

Listing 10.10, TOKENS.C, demonstrates how to use `strtok()` this way to extract words from any string. Compile and run the program. When prompted, enter a string of words separated by blanks. The statements at lines 14–18 tokenize your entry, and display its individual words.

Listing 10.10. TOKENS.C (Tokenizes a string of words).

```
 1:  #include <stdio.h>
 2:  #include <string.h>
 3:
 4:  main()
 5:  {
 6:    char buffer[128];
 7:    char *p;
 8:
 9:    printf("Enter a string of words separated by blanks.\n");
10:    printf(": ");
11:    gets(buffer);
12:    printf("As entered: %s\n", buffer);
13:    printf("As words (tokens):\n");
14:    p = strtok(buffer, " ");
15:    while (p) {
16:      puts(p);
17:      p = strtok(NULL, " ");
18:    }
19:    return 0;
20:  }
```

Related Memory Functions

When writing programs that use strings, you may run into situations that require general-purpose memory functions such as those described in this section. Although you can use these functions to fill, move, and compare memory blocks containing any type of data, the functions are frequently used with character strings, so it's appropriate to discuss them in this chapter.

Filling Memory

Borland C++ provides two functions for filling a number of bytes with values: memset() and setmem(), prototyped in mem.h. Because memset() works with DOS, UNIX, and Windows (and is part of the ANSI C standard library), this function is preferred over setmem(), which works only with DOS and Windows. (Chapter 22, "Functions and Examples," describes setmem().)

Use memset() as demonstrated in Listing 10.11, MEMFILL.C. The program fills all available heap memory, less a few overhead bytes, with zeros. Use MEMFILL as a debugging utility to help find bugs caused by leftover values in RAM. If a bug tends to disappear *after* running MEMFILL, the program might be suffering from the illicit use of an uninitialized pointer.

Listing 10.11. MEMFILL.C (Stores zero in available memory).

```
 1:  #include <stdio.h>
 2:  #include <alloc.h>
 3:  #include <mem.h>
 4:
 5:  #define BLOCK_SIZE 4092
 6:
 7:  main()
 8:  {
 9:    unsigned long len;
10:    unsigned char far *p;
11:
```

continues

Listing 10.11. continued

```
12:    puts("Memory Filler");
13:    printf("Filling %lu bytes...", farcoreleft());
14:    do {
15:      len = farcoreleft();
16:      if (len > BLOCK_SIZE)
17:        len = BLOCK_SIZE;
18:      p = (unsigned char far *)farmalloc(len);
19:      if (p)
20:        _fmemset(p, 0, (size_t)len);
21:    } while (p);
22:    printf("\nDone");
23:    return 0;
24:  }
```

Line 20 calls `_fmemset()`, the far counterpart of the near function `memset()`. Given a buffer addressed by a pointer p, this sets the buffer's first 10 bytes to 1:

```
memset(p, 1, 10);
```

If p is a far pointer, as it is in MEMFILL, replace `memset()` with `_fmemset()`.

Moving Memory

Another useful low-level memory operation moves a block of bytes from one location to another. The mem.h header file prototypes two functions for this purpose—`memmove()` and `memcpy()`, both of which are demonstrated by Listing 10.12, MEMMOVE.C. The program uses memory-move operations to insert a substring into another string.

Listing 10.12. MEMMOVE.C (Inserts a substring in a string).

```
1:  #include <stdio.h>
2:  #include <string.h>
3:  #include <mem.h>
4:
5:  main()
6:  {
```

```
 7:    char original[128] = "How now cow?";
 8:    char insert[] = " brown";
 9:    char *p;
10:    int len;
11:
12:    printf("Original string == %s\n", original);
13:    printf("Insert string == %s\n", insert);
14:    len = strlen(insert);
15:    p = strrchr(original, ' ');   /* Find last blank */
16:    memmove(p + len, p, len);    /* Cut "hole" in string */
17:    memcpy(p, insert, len);       /* Drop insert into hole */
18:    printf("Final string == %s\n", original);
19:    return 0;
20:  }
```

Line 7 declares the original string, a rhyme that is obviously missing something. The missing word is assigned to char array insert at line 8. To insert the word into the string, line 16 calls memmove(). The first argument to the function is the destination address to which you want to move some bytes. The second argument is the address of the source of the bytes to be moved. The third and final argument represents the number of bytes to move. The statement at line 16 punches a hole in the original string just large enough to hold the missing word.

The next line calls memcpy() to drop the missing word into the punched-out hole in the original string. This function's arguments are the same as memmove()'s. In this case, p addresses the destination (the beginning of the hole punched by line 16). Argument insert is the source address—the string to be inserted. The number of bytes to move is represented by len.

The two functions, memmove() and memcpy(), perform similar jobs, but differ in one important characteristic:

- memmove() can copy a block of memory to another location, even when one or more bytes in both blocks overlap.

- memcpy() can also copy a block of memory to another location; however, the two blocks must not overlap. In other words, if any of the addresses in the destination block fall within the source block's location, the result of calling memcpy() is undefined.

> **NOTE:** If you can't determine in advance whether two blocks have any overlapping bytes, use the safer `memmove()` to copy one block to another.

Comparing Memory

At times, you might also need to compare two blocks of data with no regard for the information those blocks contain. For this purpose, call `memcmp()`, prototyped in mem.h, and demonstrated by Listing 10.13, MEMCMP.C. The program fills and compares two `char` buffers, an operation that might be part of a file compare program, or any other application that needs to compare bytes quickly.

Listing 10.13. MEMCMP.C (Compares memory blocks).

```
 1:  #include <stdio.h>
 2:  #include <mem.h>
 3:
 4:  void Report(const char *message);
 5:
 6:  char buffer1[1024];
 7:  char buffer2[1024];
 8:
 9:  main()
10:  {
11:    memset(buffer1, 1, sizeof(buffer1));
12:    memset(buffer2, 2, sizeof(buffer2));
13:    Report("Before memcpy()");
14:    memcpy(buffer2, buffer1, sizeof(buffer2));
15:    Report("After memcpy()");
16:    return 0;
17:  }
18:
19:  void Report(const char *message)
20:  {
21:    puts("");
22:    puts("Comparing buffer1 and buffer2");
23:    puts(message);
```

```
24:    if (memcmp(buffer1, buffer2, sizeof(buffer1)) == 0)
25:      puts("Buffers are equal");
26:    else
27:      puts("Buffers are NOT equal");
28: }
```

Lines 11–12 fill the program's two buffers with different values, 1 and 2. As you can see when you run the program, line 13 reports

```
Comparing buffer1 and buffer2
Before memcpy()
Buffers are NOT equal
```

Line 24 calls memcmp() to compare buffer1 and buffer2, also passing as a third argument the number of bytes to compare. If memcmp() returns 0, the buffers are equal; otherwise, they differ in at least one byte.

Line 14 copies buffer1 to buffer2, thus making the two buffers equal. After this step, line 15 reports

```
Comparing buffer1 and buffer2
After memcpy()
Buffers are equal
```

Internally, memcmp() compares bytes as unsigned chars, and the function therefore works almost the same as strcmp(). The memcmp() function returns −1 (or another negative value) if its first argument's characters are alphabetically less than those in its second argument, or +1 (or another positive value) if the first buffer is alphabetically greater than the second. You can use memcmp() to compare noncharacter data only for equality.

When comparing character buffers, you may also use memicmp(), which performs a caseless unsigned comparison on the characters in two buffers. The function's parameters and result are the same as for memcmp().

Summary

- A string is an array of char values terminated with a null byte equal to zero and represented in programs by the NULL macro. If a string doesn't fill its allotted space exactly, bytes after the null terminator are wasted.

- Strings usually have one of three forms: literal strings entered directly in the program's text, fixed-size char arrays, or pointers of type char *, which typically address strings stored on the heap.

- A null string has no significant characters, only a null character stored in its first byte.

- Borland C++ has a rich library of string functions such as strcpy() and strcmp(). Use string functions to copy, search, compare, concatenate, tokenize, and perform other operations on strings.

- For PC-only programs, include the header file conio.h and, to display strings, use this library's fast direct-video output routines such as cputs(). Call textbackground() and textcolor() to select background and foreground text-screen colors or other attributes. Call gotoxy() to position the cursor, and wherex() and wherey() to find the cursor's location. To read strings from the keyboard, call cgets(), which requires a specially-prepared string buffer.

- Many string functions return char * pointers, and can be cascaded by passing the result of one function to another.

- mem.h prototypes several functions that are typically applied to character strings, but can also be used for general low-level memory operations. Function memset() fills memory blocks with any value, memmove() and memcpy() copy one block to another, and memcmp() compares the bytes in two blocks.

Exercises

10.1 Write a program with a function that returns a copy of a string with its lowercase letters converted to uppercase. The original string passed to the function should not be modified.

10.2 Design a function that compares the string data in two arrays of char * pointers. The function should indicate whether the two string arrays are equal.

10.3 Sort into alphabetic order an array of char * pointers that address strings.

10.4 Revise GetStringAt() (Listings 10.3, 10.4) so it can be called recursively.

10.5 Revise EXT2.C (Listing 10.9) so it doesn't use strstr() to search for a filename extension. In other words, your program should force the filename extension to .TXT without having to search for that extension.

10.6 Write a program that prompts for a string and then displays the string's individual words sorted into reverse alphabetic order regardless of case.

10.7 Write a function that searches for and deletes a substring in a string. Hint: Use a combination of string and memory-move functions.

Input and Output

You've probably heard the expression "garbage in, garbage out." That may be so, but even good data can be turned to mush by a single bad input or output statement.

To help you write robust I/O routines, C provides a wealth of functions and declarations for reading and writing files, and for performing related operations. In this chapter, you'll learn about standard files, direct-video techniques, disk-file functions, database methods, directory structures, and advanced file-handling tools. You may not be able to prevent users from feeding your programs bad data, but there's a lot you can do to prevent your code from adding any more scrap to the world's garbage dump.

Standard File I/O

It's hard to imagine a computer program that doesn't have any I/O statements. For simple I/O, C defines standard files, listed in Table 11.1.

The filenames in Table 11.1 are called streams because of the way data is read and written, or streamed, one byte at a time to and from these files. Associated with a stream is a current position—an internal pointer that designates the location where data is read from next, or where new data is to be deposited. As you read and write data, a file's internal pointer moves like a boat moving up and down a stream.

Table 11.1. Standard I/O files.

Standard filename	Description
stdaux	Serial I/O (low speed only)
stderr	Error output
stdin	Standard input
stdout	Standard output
stdprn	Printer output

You may pass any of the filenames in Table 11.1 to any function that requires a file stream of type FILE *. For example, to display a string on the standard error output (in computer jargon, you write data *on*, not *in*, a standard file), use the statement

```
fputs("ERROR: Something's amiss!", stderr);
```

Function fputs() works like puts(), but requires you to specify the file stream to which you want to write text. The reason for using stderr to display an error message is because stdout—the default output file for functions such as puts()—may have been redirected by a DOS command to write data to a text file. File stderr is normally not redirectable, and writing text to this predefined file is therefore guaranteed to display an important message on-screen.

Use other standard files to direct text to associated devices. To print text, for instance, specify stdprn in an fputs() statement:

```
fputs("All the text that's fit to print!", stdprn);
```

> **NOTE:** The symbol FILE is a typedef alias for a structure declared in stdio.h. This structure contains various details about an active file. You may examine a FILE's members, but should never change those values directly. Always use file functions to manipulate FILE variables.

File Functions

Many of C's most popular file function names begin with a lowercase f. Look these up in Chapter 22, "Functions and Examples," and also in the Borland C++ Library Reference. Other functions are scattered throughout the library—functions such as open() and close(). DOS functions begin with _dos, and provide access to various internal DOS subroutines. Many of these functions have overlapping purposes, and it can be difficult to determine which sets of functions you should use. This chapter helps cut through this tangled jungle by detailing the functions that are suitable for solving most I/O problems. Also keep these general facts in mind:

- Some file functions require integer handles—values that DOS associates with internal details about active files. The value of a handle is meaningless to a program. It's simply a means to distinguish between multiple files. The actual details about the files are stored internally, and are not normally accessible to programs.

- File functions that declare or return objects of type FILE * use file streams rather than handles. In most cases, these functions (which mostly begin with lowercase f) are preferred by expert C programmers. The functions are part of the ANSI C standard library, and are therefore portable to other environments. To use a file stream with a function that requires a file handle, you can use function fdopen() to obtain a handle for the stream.

- Borland C++ also provides a slew of DOS functions, the names of which begin with _dos and are prototyped in dos.h. Use these functions only if you absolutely must have direct access to DOS file-handling subroutines. Programs that use DOS functions might not be portable to other C compilers. They are almost certainly not portable to other operating systems (however, DOS functions are available to Windows programs). See Chapter 22, "Functions and Examples," for information on specific _dos functions.

- Except for standard files (see Table 11.1), you must open a file before you can use it. With disk files, you also must specify a file-access mode—for example, whether you intend to read or write data to the file, and whether the file contains text or binary information.

- After opening a file, you can read and write data to it. In the case of a disk file, you can also position the file's current pointer to read and write data at any position.

• When done using a file, always remember to close it. DOS permits only a limited number of files to be open simultaneously, and if you don't close your files, your program may lose the capability of opening additional files.

• I/O may be buffered, either by DOS or by various file library functions. For example, when reading from a disk file, data is typically brought into memory one sector (512 bytes usually) or more at a time, thus limiting the number of disk accesses in hopes of improving runtime performance. Similarly, data written to disk may be buffered until a full sector or more is collected, which is then transferred all at once to the output file. Closing a file flushes any data buffered in memory—another good reason always to close a file, especially one to which you've written new information.

• All open files are closed automatically when the program ends. This does no harm, but it is generally considered to be a wise practice to close files explicitly.

Writing a Filter Program

With a few simple I/O statements, you can write text file filters—programs that operate like valves through which every byte from an input source flows (see Figure 11.1).

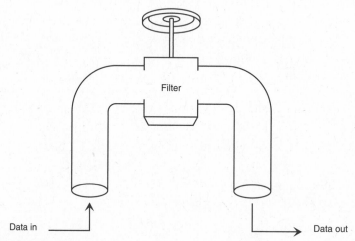

Figure 11.1. A filter acts like an information valve.

The simplest of filters, demonstrated by Listing 11.1, FILTER.C, merely copies bytes from stdin to stdout. Though simplistic, the program demonstrates several key concepts about using file streams.

Listing 11.1. FILTER.C (Demonstrates a standard input and output filter).

```
 1:  #include <stdio.h>
 2:
 3:  main()
 4:  {
 5:    int c;
 6:
 7:    while ((c = getchar()) != EOF)
 8:      putchar(c);
 9:    return 0;
10:  }
```

A while statement at line 7 calls getchar(), which reads and returns a byte from stdin. The program assigns this byte to int variable c, and also compares its value with a predefined symbolic constant, EOF, meaning *end of file*. This value is guaranteed to be different from any valid data that getchar() might return. When EOF is received, the program has reached the end of the input data. Until then, line 8 sends every byte on its way by calling putchar().

At first glance, FILTER may seem to be a silly piece of code, but it's actually a useful utility in disguise. To use FILTER, compile the program, and then from DOS, enter a command such as

filter <filter.c >newfile.txt

The input redirection symbol (<) instructs DOS to redirect stdin to obtain its characters from FILTER.C rather than from the keyboard. The output redirection symbol (>) prompts DOS to redirect stdout to NEWFILE.TXT. Given these redirections, FILTER copies FILTER.C to NEWFILE.C—a simple but effective text file copier.

That's not all FILTER can do. Turn on your printer, and enter the DOS command

filter >prn

which redirects stdout to the printer. (DOS maintains certain device names like PRN, CON, and AUX, which correspond with the standard filenames in Table 11.1). Type one or more lines of text, and press the DOS end-of-file key, Ctrl+Z, when done. As this experiment proves, FILTER can convert your computer to a quick-and-dirty typewriter—useful for addressing the odd envelope or printing out a quick memo.

> **NOTE:** Because a filter expects to receive input from stdin, running a filter program may appear to hang your system. Don't reboot! To end a filter program, just type Ctrl+Z, the DOS end-of-file control code.

By adding some programming to FILTER.C, you can also create utilities that modify text as it passes through the program's plumbing. For example, add #include <ctype.h> to FILTER.C and change the while loop to

```
while ((c = getchar()) != EOF)
  putchar(toupper(c));
```

The new program passes each character from stdin to toupper(), which returns uppercase equivalents for lowercase letters, leaving other characters unchanged. Running FILTER with the command

```
filter <anyfile.txt >newfile.txt
```

copies a text file named ANYFILE.TXT to NEWFILE.TXT, converting every character to uppercase.

> **WARNING:** In typical unfriendly fashion, DOS erases without warning an existing file to which you redirect output. Filters are an interesting class of I/O programs—the DOS MORE and SORT commands are written as filters—but there are other more versatile techniques to read and write file data, as you will soon see.

Direct Console I/O

The trouble with standard I/O is its lack of speed. Contributing to this sluggishness are levels upon levels of function calls, DOS subroutines, and internal programming that has to accommodate a wide variety of input and output devices.

Your programs might not require such demanding versatility. Few, if any, commercial programs use standard I/O, except perhaps to display a brief startup message or error. Programs written for PCs can take advantage of memory-mapped video—a term that refers to memory buffers that are dedicated to the PC display. In general, when operating in text mode, video buffer bytes are interpreted as ASCII characters and attributes such as colors or, on monochrome displays, as underlines or bold face. Simply poking a few bytes into the appropriate buffer is the hands-down fastest way to display text on PC screens.

In earlier chapters, you've already met some of the Borland C++ direct-video routines prototyped in conio.h. Use this console-I/O library to write superfast display output routines, but be aware that Borland's conio.h functions are unlikely to be available on another compiler or operating system.

Using Direct-Video I/O

Because conio.h functions are available only with Borland C++, it makes good sense to hide them inside a separate module containing new functions of your own designs. That way, if it should become necessary to port the program to another environment, you can rewrite the one module rather than track down individual conio.h function calls strewn throughout a large project.

To get you started on this track, Listing 11.2, crt.h, and Listing 11.3, CRT.C, provide sample text-screen functions that encapsulate many conio.h routines, and also provide some new ones. CRT can display overlapping, pop-up windows—a basic requirement for modern text-based PC software. Enter both listings now and compile with the DOS command **bcc -c crt.c**, or use the IDE Compile|Compile (Alt+F9) command. Other programs in this chapter are linked to the resulting CRT.OBJ file, giving them direct-video capabilities.

Listing 11.2. crt.h (Creates header file for CRT.C direct-video module).

```
 1:  /* crt.h -- Header file for crt.c */
 2:
 3:  #ifndef __CRT_H
 4:  #define __CRT_H  1      /* Prevent multiple #includes */
 5:
 6:  #include <conio.h>
 7:
 8:  #define CRT_REVERSEVIDEO 0x70
 9:  #define CRT_NORMAL 0x07
10:
11:  void CrtGotoxy(int x, int y);
12:  void CrtEeop(void);
13:  void CrtBox(int type, int attr, unsigned trow, unsigned lcol,
14:     unsigned brow, unsigned rcol);
15:  void CrtPokew(int row, int col, unsigned attrchar);
16:  void CrtPeekBox(void *save, unsigned trow, unsigned lcol,
17:     unsigned brow, unsigned rcol);
18:  void CrtFillBox(unsigned attrchar, unsigned trow, unsigned lcol,
19:     unsigned brow, unsigned rcol);
20:  void CrtPokeBox(void *save, unsigned trow, unsigned lcol,
21:     unsigned brow, unsigned rcol);
22:  void CrtHideCursor(void);
23:  void CrtShowCursor(void);
24:  void CrtScroll(int lines, unsigned ulrow, unsigned ulcol,
25:     unsigned lrrow, unsigned lrcol, unsigned attr);
26:  int CrtGetMode(void);
27:
28:  #endif   /* __CRT_H */
```

The header file, crt.h, begins with conditional compilation directives that prevent the file's text from being included more than once, even if many modules in the same project #include "crt.h". The header file crt.h includes conio.h (line 6), thus every program that makes use of CRT's functions can also use functions prototyped in conio.h.

Table 11.2 describes the functions prototyped in crt.h and implemented in Listing 11.3, CRT.C. After the listing are a few sample programs that demonstrate how to use the module for fast, direct-video output.

Table 11.2. CRT direct-video display functions.

Function	Description
CrtBox	Draws outlined box (see the sample listing, BOX.C, later in this chapter). Set type to 0-4 to select the type of box, set attr to a display-attribute or color byte value, and trow, lcol, brow, and rcol to the top row, left column, bottom row, and right column coordinates of the box's upper-left and lower-right corners.
CrtEeop	Erases text screen from current cursor position to the end of the page.
CrtFillBox	Fills a rectangle with character values equal to attrchar. Other parameters are the same as for CrtBox().
CrtGetMode	Returns current video display mode. If equal to macro MONOCHROME, the display is a monochrome display adapter; otherwise, it's a color display.
CrtGotoxy	Positions cursor to an (X,Y) coordinate. Unlike the conio.h gotoxy() function, CrtGotoxy() considers coordinate (0,0) to be the upper-left corner of the display.
CrtHideCursor	Turns off text-screen cursor.
CrtPeekBox	Copies characters and attributes from the system's video display buffer (color or monochrome) to a block of RAM addressed by void *save. The other parameters mark the upper-left and lower-right corners of a rectangle as with CrtBox(). POPUP.C, later in this chapter, is an example of how to use CrtPeekBox().
CrtPokeBox	Copies information saved by CrtPeekBox() back to the video display buffer. Parameters are the same as for CrtPeekBox(). See POPUP.C later in this chapter for an example of how to use CrtPokeBox().
CrtPokew	Displays at coordinate (row,col) a 16-bit word composed of a character in the low-order byte and an attribute value in the high-order byte. See ASC.C later in this chapter for an example of how to use CrtPokew.

continues

Table 11.2. continued

Function	Description
CrtScroll	Scrolls a portion or the entire display up or down. Parameter lines equals the number of lines to scroll—positive values scroll up, negative values scroll down. Parameters ulrow, ulcol, lrrow, and lrcol represent the upper-left row, upper-left column, lower-right row, and lower-right column coordinates of the rectangle to be scrolled. Parameter attr is the attribute value to display on blank lines inserted from the bottom when scrolling up, or from the top when scrolling down.
CrtShowCursor	Displays text-mode cursor after hiding with CrtHideCursor().

Listing 11.3, CRT.C, implements the CRT module's functions. The module includes the dos.h header (line 1) for CrtScroll(), which calls a system BIOS scroll-text routine. The code for this and other functions is highly system-dependent—one good reason for isolating the functions inside a single module. Highlights of potentially unfamiliar statements follow the listing.

Listing 11.3. CRT.C (Implements the CRT direct-video function module).

```
 1:  #include <dos.h>
 2:  #include "crt.h"
 3:
 4:  #define VIDEO 0x010   /* BIOS video interrupt number */
 5:
 6:  /* Character sets for CrtBox function */
 7:  const char *scul = "\xc9\xda\xdb\xd5\xd6"; /* "╔┌█╒╓";  */
 8:  const char *scur = "\xbb\xbf\xdb\xb8\xb7"; /* "╗┐█╕╖";  */
 9:  const char *scbl = "\xc8\xc0\xdb\xd4\xd3"; /* "╚└█╘╙";  */
10:  const char *scbr = "\xbc\xd9\xdb\xbe\xbd"; /* "╝┘█╛╜";  */
11:  const char *schz = "\xcd\xc4\xdb\xcd\xc4"; /* "═─█═─";  */
12:  const char *scvt = "\xba\xb3\xdb\xb3\xba"; /* "║│█│║";  */
13:
14:  /* Position cursor with 0,0 in upper-left corner (home) */
```

```
15:   void CrtGotoxy(int x, int y)
16:   {
17:     gotoxy(x + 1, y + 1);
18:   }
19:
20:   /* Erase from cursor to end of page */
21:   void CrtEeop(void)
22:   {
23:     int xx, yy, y;
24:     struct text_info info;
25:
26:     gettextinfo(&info);
27:     clreol();
28:     yy = wherey();
29:     xx = wherex();
30:     for (y = yy + 1; y <= info.screenheight; y++) {
31:       gotoxy(1, y);
32:       clreol();
33:     }
34:     gotoxy(xx, yy);
35:   }
36:
37:   /* Draw a box outline */
38:   void CrtBox(int type, int attr, unsigned trow, unsigned lcol,
39:     unsigned brow, unsigned rcol)
40:   {
41:     unsigned cul, cur, cbl, cbr, chz, cvt;   /* Drawing characters */
42:     unsigned uattr = attr * 256;             /* Attr in high byte */
43:     int x, y;                                /* for-loop controls */
44:
45:   /* Create drawing characters based on type and attribute */
46:     if (type < 0 || type > 4) type = 0;
47:     cul = uattr + (unsigned char)scul[type];
48:     cur = uattr + (unsigned char)scur[type];
49:     cbl = uattr + (unsigned char)scbl[type];
50:     cbr = uattr + (unsigned char)scbr[type];
51:     chz = uattr + (unsigned char)schz[type];
52:     cvt = uattr + (unsigned char)scvt[type];
53:
54:   /* Display four corners of box */
55:     CrtPokew(trow, lcol, cul);
```

continues

Listing 11.3. continued

```
56:     CrtPokew(trow, rcol, cur);
57:     CrtPokew(brow, lcol, cbl);
58:     CrtPokew(brow, rcol, cbr);
59:
60:   /* Display box outline */
61:     for (x = lcol + 1; x < rcol; x++) {
62:       CrtPokew(trow, x, chz);
63:       CrtPokew(brow, x, chz);
64:     }
65:     for (y = trow + 1; y < brow; y++) {
66:       CrtPokew(y, lcol, cvt);
67:       CrtPokew(y, rcol, cvt);
68:     }
69:   }
70:
71:   /* Poke unsigned character and attribute into display */
72:   void CrtPokew(int row, int col, unsigned attrchar)
73:   {
74:     col++;
75:     row++;
76:     puttext(col, row, col, row, &attrchar);
77:   }
78:
79:   /* Copy display buffer bytes to buffer at save pointer */
80:   void CrtPeekBox(void *save, unsigned trow, unsigned lcol,
81:     unsigned brow, unsigned rcol)
82:   {
83:     gettext(lcol + 1, trow + 1, rcol + 1, brow + 1, save);
84:   }
85:
86:   /* Paint a box on-screen with an attribute and character */
87:   void CrtFillBox(unsigned attrchar, unsigned trow, unsigned lcol,
88:     unsigned brow, unsigned rcol)
89:   {
90:     int i;
91:
92:     while (trow <= brow) {
93:       for (i = lcol; i <= rcol; i++)
94:         CrtPokew(trow, i, attrchar);
95:       trow++;
```

```
 96:    }
 97:  }
 98:
 99:  /* Copy data saved by CrtPeekBox back to display */
100:  void CrtPokeBox(void *save, unsigned trow, unsigned lcol,
101:    unsigned brow, unsigned rcol)
102:  {
103:    puttext(lcol + 1, trow + 1, rcol + 1, brow + 1, save);
104:  }
105:
106:  /* Remove cursor from display */
107:  void CrtHideCursor(void)
108:  {
109:    _setcursortype(_NOCURSOR);
110:  }
111:
112:  /* Redisplay hidden cursor */
113:  void CrtShowCursor(void)
114:  {
115:    _setcursortype(_NORMALCURSOR);
116:  }
117:
118:  /* Scroll the defined area up or down */
119:  void CrtScroll(int lines, unsigned ulrow, unsigned ulcol,
120:    unsigned lrrow, unsigned lrcol, unsigned attr)
121:  {
122:    union REGS regs;
123:
124:    if (lines < 0){
125:      regs.h.ah = 7;        /* Scroll down */
126:      lines = -lines;
127:    }
128:    else
129:      regs.h.ah = 6;        /* Scroll up */
130:    regs.h.ch = ulrow;
131:    regs.h.cl = ulcol;
132:    regs.h.dh = lrrow;
133:    regs.h.dl = lrcol;
134:    regs.h.bh = attr;
135:    if (ulrow >= lrrow)
136:      regs.h.al = 0;        /* Clear window if top >= bottom row */
```

continues

Listing 11.3. continued

```
137:    else
138:      regs.h.al = lines;   /* Else scroll the specified number of lines */
139:    int86(VIDEO, &regs, &regs);
140:  }
141:
142:  /* Return current display mode */
143:  int CrtGetMode(void)
144:  {
145:    struct text_info info;
146:
147:    gettextinfo(&info);
148:    return info.currmode;
149:  }
```

You should be able to read and understand most of CRT.C and its header file crt.h. The following are a few highlights that explain some of the less obvious sections:

- Lines 7–12 declare six constant character strings. The hexadecimal escape values such as \xc9 and \xda represent extended ASCII PC line-drawing symbols, which are used by CrtBox() to display corners and line segments. The strings shown as comments at the end of each line could be substituted for the escape values—if, that is, your editor lets you type these characters.

- Some functions, such as CrtGotoxy() at lines 15–18, merely call a conio.h routine, possibly adjusting a value here and there. These functions are often called wrappers because of the way they envelope a library function. Calling an original function is, of course, faster than calling a wrapper. The wrapper, however, offers the advantage of hiding system-dependent code in a single place where it's more easily ported to another environment.

- Function CrtBox() (lines 38–69) displays one of five box styles, selected by setting attr to a value from 0 to 4. Try these in a test program to see the different box styles (see Figure 11.2). At lines 47–52, the function sets six unsigned integers to the attribute and line-drawing characters to use for displaying the box. Lines 55–58 poke the box's four corners into the display. Two for loops at lines 61–68 fill in the box's borders.

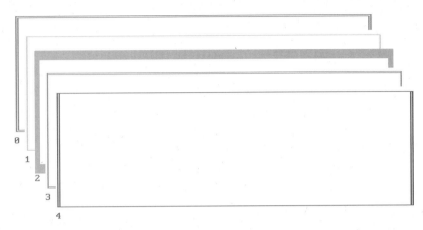

Figure 11.2. The CRT module's CrtBox() styles.

- CrtPokew() is another wrapper function that calls the conio.h puttext routine, which inserts a 16-bit word value into the system's video buffer. The function's col and row parameters are incremented to make them conform to function gotoxy()'s home coordinate of (1,1).

- CrtPeekBox() (lines 80–84) calls CONIO's gettext() function to copy a rectangle from the display to a program buffer. The contents of this buffer are not directly usable, except for CrtPokeBox(), which transfers a saved buffer of text and attributes back to the screen. CrtPeekBox() and CrtPokeBox() (lines 100–104) are typically used to create pop-up windows, as demonstrated by POPUP.C later in this chapter. When calling CrtPeekBox(), pointer save must address a buffer large enough to hold the requested display area. The size of this buffer is calculated by the statement

```
bufsize =
   ((brow - trow + 1) * (rcol - lcol + 1)) * sizeof(unsigned);
```

- Function CrtScroll() (lines 119–140) uses a few techniques that you haven't seen before. Line 122 declares a REGS union, declared in dos.h. This structure's members are designed to hold processor register values for simulated calls to DOS and BIOS subroutines. For example, line 125 sets the union's pseudo ah register to 7, selecting the BIOS scroll-down function. (Consult a PC reference for other BIOS routines and requirements.) Other assignments to pseudo registers are at lines 130–134, which prepare coordinate and attribute values for the scroll.

- The actual scrolling action takes place at line 139, which calls function int86(). This function simulates calling the interrupt service routine specified in the first argument—here, constant VIDEO—set to interrupt number 0x010 at line 4. The two &reg arguments passed to int86() give the function pseudo register values, and also pass back values from the BIOS routine to the program. (In this case, no usable values are returned, however.)

Direct-video output functions such as those provided by the CRT module are crucial components of modern, PC software. Listing 11.4, BOX.C, demonstrates how to use CRT to display boxes—useful for organizing a busy display into visually pleasing compartments. Compile the program from DOS with the command **bcc box.c crt.obj** (or specify **crt.c** if you did not compile the CRT module previously), and when prompted, enter two pairs of values separated by a space, such as **3 7** and **20 64**. The program displays a box with those values as the upper-left and lower-right corner coordinates.

Listing 11.4. BOX.C (Draws a box using CRT module).

```
 1:  #include <stdio.h>
 2:  #include "crt.h"
 3:
 4:  void GetCoords(int *topRow, int *topCol, int *botRow, int *botCol);
 5:  void DrawBox(int topRow, int topCol, int botRow, int botCol);
 6:
 7:  main()
 8:  {
 9:    int topRow, topCol, botRow, botCol;
10:
11:    GetCoords(&topRow, &topCol, &botRow, &botCol);
12:    CrtGotoxy(0, 0);
13:    CrtEeop();
14:    DrawBox(topRow, topCol, botRow, botCol);
15:    CrtGotoxy(0, 23);
16:    return 0;
17:  }
18:
19:  void GetCoords(int *topRow, int *topCol, int *botRow, int *botCol)
```

```
20:  {
21:    printf("\nEnter top row and column (ex: 3 7): ");
22:    scanf("%d %d", topRow, topCol);
23:    printf("Enter bottom row and column (ex: 20 64): ");
24:    scanf("%d %d", botRow, botCol);
25:  }
26:
27:  void DrawBox(int topRow, int topCol, int botRow, int botCol)
28:  {
29:    CrtBox(0, CRT_NORMAL, topRow, topCol, botRow, botCol);
30:  }
```

Function DrawBox at lines 27–30 calls CRT's CrtBox() function to draw the box. Change the first argument to a value from zero to four to display boxes in the five available styles. The second argument, CRT_NORMAL, selects attributes to use for the box border.

Creating Pop-Up Text Windows

Pop-up text windows have become all the rage in PC software. Because a CRT's display is a two-dimensional surface, however, overlapping windows are illusions—tricks done with mirrors in the form of functions that copy and restore selected portions of the screen. The eye tends to see windows on top of other windows, when in fact, there is only one smooth display surface.

Listing 11.5, POPUP.C, demonstrates how to use CRT's direct-video routines to create simple pop-up windows. Compile the program from DOS with the command **bcc popup.c crt.obj** (assuming you previously compiled the CRT module as instructed). Run the program, which displays several overlapping windows at random locations and colors (see Figure 11.3). Press the spacebar repeatedly to remove the windows one by one. The program ends automatically when you remove the final window.

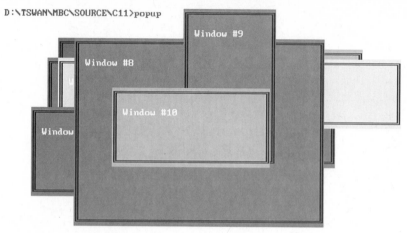

Figure 11.3. Sample output from POPUP.C.

Listing 11.5. POPUP.C (Uses CRT module to display pop-up windows).

```
 1:  #include <stdio.h>
 2:  #include <stdlib.h>
 3:  #include <dos.h>
 4:  #include <time.h>
 5:  #include "crt.h"
 6:
 7:  #define MAXWINDOW 10      /* Maximum number of windows */
 8:  #define MAXCOLOR 7        /* Maximum background color (min = 0) */
 9:  #define MAXROW 22         /* Maximum row number (min = 0) */
10:  #define MAXCOL 79         /* Maximum column number (min = 0) */
11:  #define WHITE 15          /* Color number for whiter than white */
12:  #define MONOCHROME 7      /* Monochrome display mode number */
13:
14:  typedef struct winrec {   /* Window record */
15:     void *bufptr;          /* Saved text. NULL if window closed */
16:     unsigned trow;         /* Top row number */
17:     unsigned lcol;         /* Left column number */
18:     unsigned brow;         /* Bottom row number */
19:     unsigned rcol;         /* Right column number */
20:     int attribute;         /* Background & foreground color */
```

```
21:  } Winrec;
22:
23:  typedef Winrec *Winrecptr;
24:
25:  void Pause(void);
26:  int RandRange(int low, int high);
27:  void OpenWindow(Winrecptr wrp, int backcolor, unsigned trow,
28:    unsigned lcol, unsigned brow, unsigned rcol);
29:  void DisplayText(Winrecptr wrp, char *message);
30:  void CloseTopWindow(Winrecptr wrp);
31:
32:  main()
33:  {
34:    int wnum;
35:    unsigned trow, lcol, brow, rcol;   /* Window coordinates */
36:    Winrec buffer[MAXWINDOW];          /* Array of winrecs */
37:    char string[20];
38:
39:  /* Display windows at randomly selected positions */
40:
41:    randomize();
42:    for (wnum = 0; wnum < MAXWINDOW; wnum++) {
43:      trow = RandRange(0, MAXROW / 2);       /* Set top row */
44:      lcol = RandRange(0, MAXCOL / 2);       /* Set left column */
45:      brow = RandRange(trow + 4, MAXROW);    /* Set bottom row */
46:      rcol = RandRange(lcol + 12, MAXCOL);   /* Set right column */
47:      OpenWindow(
48:        &buffer[wnum],             /* Pass winrec pointer */
49:        RandRange(1, MAXCOLOR),    /* Background color */
50:        trow, lcol, brow, rcol);   /* Location */
51:      sprintf(string, "Window #%d", wnum + 1);
52:      DisplayText(&buffer[wnum], string);
53:    }
54:
55:  /* Close windows one by one */
56:
57:    CrtGotoxy(0, 24);
58:    cprintf("Press <Space> to erase top window...");
59:    for (wnum = MAXWINDOW - 1; wnum >= 0; wnum--)
60:      CloseTopWindow(&buffer[wnum]);
61:    CrtGotoxy(0, 24);    /* Move cursor to last row */
```

continues

Listing 11.5. continued

```
 62:    return 0;
 63:  }
 64:
 65:  /* -- Pause for a keypress */
 66:  void Pause(void)
 67:  {
 68:    getch();
 69:  }
 70:
 71:  /* -- Return random number from low ... high */
 72:  int RandRange(int low, int high)
 73:  {
 74:    return low + (rand() % ((high - low) + 1));
 75:  }
 76:
 77:  /* -- Open new window */
 78:  void OpenWindow(Winrecptr wrp, int backcolor, unsigned trow,
 79:    unsigned lcol, unsigned brow, unsigned rcol)
 80:  {
 81:    int bcolor, tcolor;  /* Border color, text color */
 82:    unsigned bufsize;     /* Saved-text buffer size */
 83:
 84:  /* -- Determine color to use for background and foreground */
 85:
 86:    if (CrtGetMode() == MONOCHROME) {
 87:      bcolor = CRT_REVERSEVIDEO;           /* Monochrome display */
 88:      tcolor = bcolor;
 89:    } else {
 90:      bcolor = (backcolor << 4) + WHITE;   /* Color display */
 91:      tcolor = bcolor - WHITE;
 92:    }
 93:
 94:  /* -- Calculate bytes needed to save text behind window */
 95:
 96:    bufsize =
 97:    ((brow - trow + 1) * (rcol - lcol + 1)) * sizeof(unsigned);
 98:
 99:    wrp->bufptr = malloc(bufsize);  /* Reserve space for buffer */
100:    if (wrp->bufptr == NULL)         /* If that fails, return */
101:      return;                        /*  leaving bufptr == NULL */
```

```
102:
103:   /* -- Save text behind window in buffer just created */
104:
105:     CrtPeekBox(wrp->bufptr, trow, lcol, brow, rcol);
106:     wrp->trow = trow;    /* Save coordinates and color, too */
107:     wrp->lcol = lcol;
108:     wrp->brow = brow;
109:     wrp->rcol = rcol;
110:     wrp->attribute = tcolor;    /* Text color */
111:
112:   /* -- Pause and then display the window */
113:
114:     delay(250);    /* Pause for 1/4 second */
115:     CrtFillBox(((bcolor * 256) + ' '), trow, lcol, brow, rcol);
116:     CrtBox(0, bcolor, trow, lcol, brow, rcol);
117:   }
118:
119:   /* -- Display text inside this window */
120:   void DisplayText(Winrecptr wrp, char *message)
121:   {
122:     if (wrp->bufptr == NULL)
123:       return;   /* Exit if window not open */
124:     CrtGotoxy(wrp->lcol + 2, wrp->trow + 2);
125:     textattr(wrp->attribute);
126:     cprintf(message);
127:     textattr(CRT_NORMAL);
128:   }
129:
130:   /* -- Close window using winrec struct addressed by wrp. */
131:   void CloseTopWindow(Winrecptr wrp)
132:   {
133:     if (wrp->bufptr == NULL)
134:       return;   /* Exit if window not open */
135:     Pause();
136:     CrtPokeBox(
137:       wrp->bufptr, wrp->trow, wrp->lcol, wrp->brow, wrp->rcol);
138:     free(wrp->bufptr);    /* Dispose buffer */
139:     wrp->bufptr = NULL;   /* Prevent further use of buffer */
140:   }
```

Function OpenWindow() (lines 78–117) creates a new window, using the values assigned to struct Winrec, declared at lines 14–21. When designing functions that require multiple parameters, it's often a good idea to store those values in a structure rather than pass too many individual values as arguments. This technique keeps the program text clear and simple. It also helps the compiler generate more efficient function calls by copying entire structures to the stack, instead of pushing multiple values onto the stack one at a time.

Lines 96–97 calculate the size of the buffer required to hold the text now on display where the new window will appear. Line 99 calls malloc() to reserve heap space for storing this area's characters and attributes. Line 105 then calls CrtPeekBox() to transfer the display information to the buffer for safekeeping, after which the window is displayed by CrtFillBox() and CrtBox() at lines 115–116. Text is displayed inside the window by function DisplayText().

To close the window, and restore the text and attributes saved in the heap buffer, function CloseTopWindow() calls CrtPokeBox(). The function also frees the buffer space at line 138, and for safety, sets the buffer pointer to NULL.

> **NOTE:** CRT's simple pop-up window capability is useful for quick-and-dirty programs. For more sophisticated text-based windowing, see Chapter 18, "Turbo Vision," for a discussion of the Turbo Vision library supplied with Borland C++.

Displaying Extended ASCII Characters

As a final example of CTR's capabilities, Listing 11.6, ASC.C, offers a handy ASCII-character utility. Compile the program with the DOS command **bcc asc.c crt.obj** (assuming that you have previously compiled CRT as instructed). Run ASC and use the cursor keys to select a character, which is displayed as a symbol, in decimal, and in hex above and to the right of the program's window (see Figure 11.4). Notice how a simple text box contributes to the program's good-looking display. Press Esc to quit.

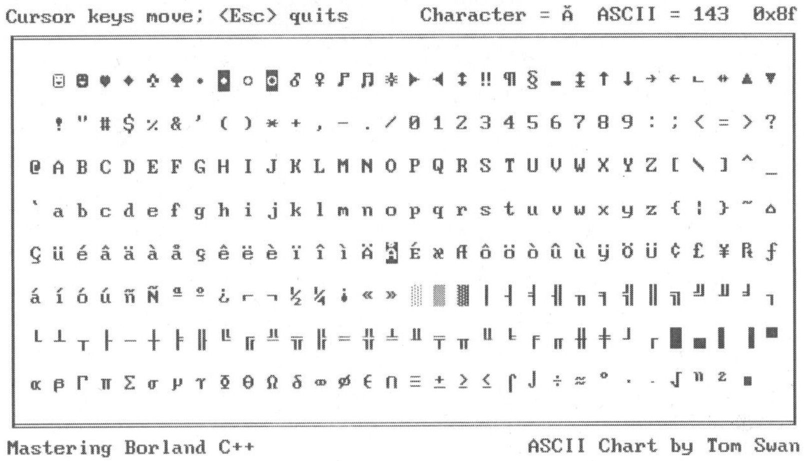

```
Cursor keys move; <Esc> quits      Character = Å   ASCII = 143   0x8f
```

```
Mastering Borland C++                    ASCII Chart by Tom Swan
```

Figure 11.4. Screen shot of program ASC.C.

Listing 11.6. ASC.C (Displays interactive ASCII chart using CRT module).

```
 1:  #include <stdio.h>
 2:  #include "crt.h"
 3:
 4:  #define ESC 27
 5:  #define TOPROW  3
 6:  #define TOPCOL  7
 7:  #define BOTROW 21
 8:  #define BOTCOL 73
 9:
10:  void ShowChart(void);
11:  void ShowASCII(unsigned c, int attrib);
12:  void MoveCursor(unsigned c);
13:  void ShowValues(unsigned c);
14:  int RowChar(unsigned c);
15:  int ColChar(unsigned c);
16:
17:  int oldc;       /* Previously displayed character */
18:
19:  main()
20:  {
```

continues

Listing 11.6. continued

```
21:    unsigned c = 1;      /* Currently highlighted character */
22:    unsigned key;        /* Command from keyboard */
23:
24:    CrtHideCursor();                      /* Make cursor invisible */
25:    ShowChart();                          /* Display ASCII chart */
26:    MoveCursor(c);                        /* Init cursor position */
27:    while ((key = getch()) != ESC) {  /* Get user command */
28:      switch (key) {
29:        case 'H': c -= 32; break;     /* Move up */
30:        case 'P': c += 32; break;     /* Move down */
31:        case 'K': c--; break;         /* Move left */
32:        case 'M': c++; break;         /* Move right */
33:      }
34:      c %= 256;          /* Make sure c is in range 0 ... 255 */
35:      MoveCursor(c);     /* Highlight and report on character c */
36:    }
37:    CrtShowCursor();     /* Make system cursor visible */
38:    CrtGotoxy(0, 24);    /* Move cursor to last line before ending */
39:    return 0;
40:  }
41:
42:  void ShowChart(void)
43:  {
44:    unsigned c = 0;         /* for-loop control variable */
45:
46:  /* Clear display */
47:    CrtGotoxy(0, 0);
48:    CrtEeop();
49:
50:  /* Display box and ASCII characters inside */
51:    CrtBox(3, CRT_NORMAL, TOPROW, TOPCOL, BOTROW, BOTCOL);
52:    for (c = 0; c <= 255; c++)
53:      ShowASCII(c, CRT_NORMAL);
54:
55:  /* Display other text on-screen */
56:    CrtGotoxy(TOPCOL, TOPROW - 1);
57:    cprintf("Cursor keys move; <Esc> quits");
58:    CrtGotoxy(TOPCOL, BOTROW + 1);
59:    cprintf("Mastering Borland C++");
60:    CrtGotoxy(BOTCOL - 22, BOTROW + 1);
```

```
61:     cprintf("ASCII Chart by Tom Swan");
62:  }
63:
64:  /* Display one ASCII character using a display attribute */
65:  void ShowASCII(unsigned c, int attrib)
66:  {
67:     CrtPokew(RowChar(c), ColChar(c), (attrib * 256) + c);
68:  }
69:
70:  /* Return row number for character c */
71:  int RowChar(unsigned c)
72:  {
73:     return(2 + TOPROW + ((c / 32) * 2));
74:  }
75:
76:  /* Return column number for character c */
77:  int ColChar(unsigned c)
78:  {
79:     return(2 + TOPCOL + ((c % 32) * 2));
80:  }
81:
82:  /* Unhighlight old character and highlight a new one */
83:  void MoveCursor(unsigned c)
84:  {
85:    ShowASCII(oldc, CRT_NORMAL);
86:    ShowASCII(c, CRT_REVERSEVIDEO);
87:    oldc = c;
88:    ShowValues(c);
89:  }
90:
91:  /* Display character and its ASCII value in decimal and hex */
92:  void ShowValues(unsigned c)
93:  {
94:    CrtGotoxy(TOPCOL + 35, TOPROW - 1);
95:    cprintf("Character =    ASCII = %d  %#x", c, c);
96:    clreol();
97:    CrtPokew(TOPROW - 1, TOPCOL + 47, (CRT_NORMAL * 256) + c);
98:  }
```

The ASC program contains numerous comments that help explain the code. At this stage in your quest to learn C programming—a turning point of sorts—you should be able to read and understand ASC.C on your own. The listing contains no new techniques. If you get stuck, recompile with the command **bcc -v asc.c crt.c**, then enter **td asc** to run the program in Turbo Debugger. Observe the display as you scan the listing, set breakpoints, and investigate the values of various variables.

If you still don't understand a section, write your own test program and use the debugger to investigate the results of expressions. The experience you gain from digging into a foreign piece of code is invaluable, and will help you to understand complex listings in later chapters.

Reading and Writing Text Files

A program's display routines are only part of the I/O story. Many programs also need ways to read and write data stored on relatively permanent devices such as disks, hard drives, and other media. C's rich library of file-handling routines make the language an ideal choice for these tasks. In this section, you investigate text file techniques. Then, you explore similar, but more generally useful, binary file I/O methods.

Basic Text File Techniques

You saw one kind of text file program in Listing 11.1, FILTER.C. The standard I/O files listed in Table 11.1 are text file streams designed expressly for reading and writing character data.

Filters, however, are not the only kinds of text file programs. You can also write programs that create, read, and write named text files stored (usually) on disks. The same general file-handling tips presented earlier apply to text files. Before using a file, you must open it, and when done with it, you must close the file, which flushes any modified in-memory buffers to disk.

There are two fundamental ways to read and write text files: a character at a time, or a line at a time. The choice of techniques, which the following sections help you to make, depends on how the text is stored and the needs of the program.

Reading Text Files

Reading a text file is an easy way to get lots of information quickly into a program. The next two sections show how to read text files one character at a time and one line at a time.

One Character at a Time

Reading text files one character at a time gives you the opportunity to examine a file's individual characters. Listing 11.7, RCHAR.C, demonstrates the method. Compile the program, and run it with a command such as **rchar name.ext** where name.ext is the name of a text file. For example, enter **rchar rchar.c** to display the program's own source code.

Listing 11.7. RCHAR.C (Reads a text file one character at a time).

```
 1:  #include <stdio.h>
 2:  #include <stdlib.h>
 3:
 4:  void Error(const char *message);
 5:  void Instruct(void);
 6:
 7:  main(int argc, char *argv[])
 8:  {
 9:    FILE *fp;
10:    char c;
11:
12:    if (argc <= 1)
13:      Instruct();
14:    fp = fopen(argv[1], "r");
15:    if (!fp)
16:      Error("Opening file");
17:    while ((c = fgetc(fp)) != EOF)
18:      putchar(c);
19:    fclose(fp);
20:    return 0;
21:  }
22:
23:  void Error(const char *message)
```

continues

Listing 11.7. continued

```
24:  {
25:    printf("\n\nError: %s\n\n", message);
26:    exit(1);
27:  }
28:
29:  void Instruct(void)
30:  {
31:    puts("\nSyntax: RCHAR filename");
32:    puts("Enter the name of a text file. Or, you can");
33:    puts("enter `rchar filename ¦ more' to display");
34:    puts("lengthy files (requires DOS's MORE.COM to be");
35:    puts("in the current path).");
36:    exit(0);
37:  }
```

Line 9 declares the program's text file stream variable, fp, of type FILE *. Line 14 calls function fopen() to open the file specified on the command line. For instance, if you run RCHAR with the command **rchar rchar.c**, argv[1] equals the string "rchar.c". In addition to a filename, function fopen()'s second parameter is one of the string options listed in Table 11.3. These options select a variety of access modes, which specify the actions you intend to take on a file. For instance, opening a file in read-only mode (as done at line 14 in the sample listing) prevents the program from accidentally writing new information to a file that should not be changed.

Table 11.3. File access mode strings for function fopen().

Mode string	Description
"r"	Opens a file for reading only. Modifications to file data are not allowed.
"w"	Creates a new file for writing only. Overwrites any existing file of the same name. Reading information from the file is not allowed.
"a"	Opens file in write-only mode for appending new information to its end. A file is created if it does not exist, and any existing file of the same name is overwritten. Reading information from the file is not allowed.

Mode string	Description
"r+"	Opens an existing file for reading and writing.
"w+"	Creates a new file for reading and writing. Overwrites any existing file of the same name.
"a+"	Opens a file in read-and-write mode for appending new information to its end. A file is created if it does not exist, and any existing file of the same name is overwritten.

Function fopen() returns a FILE * stream pointer, which you should save in a variable as demonstrated at line 14. If the value returned is NULL, the file could not be opened for some reason—a situation that you must detect, as shown at lines 15–16. If fopen() returns a non-null value, the file is open and ready for use.

Lines 17–18 demonstrate the bare-minimum requirements for processing text files one character at a time. The while loop calls fgetc(), passing the file pointer fp as an argument, and assigning the function result to char variable c. The fgetc() function is similar to fgetchar(), which you saw earlier in FILTER.C. Unlike fgetchar(), however, fgetc() requires a FILE * argument, and can therefore read text from any file opened by fopen().

Line 18 displays every character returned by fgetc(). In your own programs, replace this statement with whatever action you want to perform on a text file's contents.

The while loop ends when fgetc() returns EOF after having read the last character in the file. Line 19 then closes the file by calling fclose()—not strictly required because ending the program also closes any open files.

One Line at a Time

Many, if not most, text files are organized into lines—series of characters terminated with carriage return and line feed control codes. You can process these files one line at a time, which improves the program's speed by cutting down on the number of loops and function calls. Reading text a line at a time has one serious disadvantage, however: You must be able to determine in advance how long the maximum line is, and to provide a buffer for storing lines up to that length.

Listing 11.8, RLINE.C, demonstrates how to read a text file a line at a time. Run the program as you did RCHAR, but supply the name of a text file that contains lines no longer than 255 characters each.

> **NOTE:** Some word processors, such as Microsoft Word, are capable of storing text files with carriage return and line feed control codes marking the ends of paragraphs. These files resemble text files divided into potentially long lines, which RLINE.C might not be able to read properly. It's probably best to process these kinds of text files using the one-character-at-a-time technique demonstrated by RCHAR.C.

Listing 11.8. RLINE.C (Reads a text file one line at a time).

```
 1:  #include <stdio.h>
 2:  #include <stdlib.h>
 3:
 4:  void Error(const char *message);
 5:  void Instruct(void);
 6:
 7:  main(int argc, char *argv[])
 8:  {
 9:    FILE *fp;
10:    char buffer[256];
11:
12:    if (argc <= 1)
13:      Instruct();
14:    fp = fopen(argv[1], "r");
15:    if (!fp)
16:      Error("Opening file");
17:    while (fgets(buffer, 255, fp) != NULL)
18:      fputs(buffer, stdout);
19:    fclose(fp);
20:    return 0;
21:  }
22:
23:  void Error(const char *message)
```

```
24:  {
25:    printf("\n\nError: %s\n\n", message);
26:    exit(1);
27:  }
28:
29:  void Instruct(void)
30:  {
31:    puts("\nSyntax: RLINE filename");
32:    puts("Enter the name of a text file. Or, you can");
33:    puts("enter `rline filename ¦ more' to display");
34:    puts("lengthy files (requires DOS's MORE.COM to be");
35:    puts("in the current path).");
36:    exit(0);
37:  }
```

RLINE differs from RCHAR in only one significant way. Its `while` loop at lines 17–18 calls `fgets()` to read a line's worth of characters into a `buffer`, declared at line 10. Function `fgets()` requires three arguments: the address of a variable to hold a line of text, the maximum number of characters to read, and a `FILE *` variable previously opened with `fopen()` for any reading mode. When `fgets()` reads a line from an open file, it appends a terminating null. The function also places a newline character, `'\n'`, into the destination buffer if that character is read from the file. Be sure to supply a large enough buffer for `fgets()`. Any lines longer than the specified size of the buffer are truncated.

Writing Text Files

Writing text files is similar to reading them. The main differences are: You must open an existing file or create a new one using one of the "write" modes in Table 11.3, and you must use functions such as `fputc()` and `fputs()` to write characters and lines (represented as strings) to text files.

Another significant difference between reading and writing text files occurs when calling `fclose()`. For any file opened with a write mode, closing that file updates its date and time in the DOS directory, and also flushes any buffered data in memory that has not been written to disk.

One Character at a Time

To create a new text file, declare a `FILE *` variable named `fp` (or another name), and open it like this:

```
fp = fopen("NEWFILE.TXT", "w");
```

Mode `"w"` creates a new file, overwriting an existing file of the same name. Be sure that's what you want to do! To open an existing file for reading and writing, use mode `"r+"`. This does not overwrite an existing file. After calling `fopen()`, if `fp` is not null, the new file is open and ready to receive characters. For example, to write the characters A, B, and C to the file, you can write

```
fputc('A', fp);
fputc('B', fp);
fputc('C', fp);
```

Because output is buffered, a disk write may not occur at this time. To force data to be written to disk, you can flush the file by calling `fflush()` like this:

```
fflush(fp);
```

To flush all open files, call `flushall()`:

```
flushall();
```

which requires no arguments. Notice that `fflush()` begins with two fs, but that `flushall` begins with one—a minor inconsistency that makes the function names somewhat hard to remember.

Closing the file also flushes any buffered data to disk. Use the same technique to close files, regardless of the mode in which they were opened:

```
fclose(fp);
```

One Line at a Time

Writing lines of text to files requires using the identical opening, flushing, and closing techniques outlined in the preceding section. Assuming `fp` is the valid `FILE *` variable, write a line of text by calling `fputs()`:

```
fputs("Write me to disk please!", fp);
```

Unlike `puts()`, `fputs()` does *not* append a carriage return and line feed to the output. For this reason, you should follow `fputs()` with a call to `fputc()` and a single newline character as an argument:

```
fputc('\n', fp);
```

Together, `fputs()` and `fputc()` write a line of text terminated with carriage return and line feed control codes. It's far preferable, however, to use the symbol `'\n'` rather than write explicit carriage return and line feed control characters. On a different system, the `'\n'` escape code might be translated internally into that system's line-ending symbol, which is not always a carriage return.

printf and Family

Throughout the example listings of this book, you've seen many uses of the versatile `printf()` function. Actually, this function is one of several that can output all sorts of values formatted in countless ways. Function `printf()` directs its output to `stdout`, and is therefore suitable for formatting output directly to the display (or to another file or device if `stdout` is redirected by a DOS command).

To format direct-video output, include conio.h and call `cprintf()` exactly as you do `printf()`. The main difference is that `cprintf()` does not recognize escape codes such as `'\n'`. Before calling the function, position the cursor by calling `gotoxy()`. (You can also call the CRT module's `CrtGotoxy()` function. See Listing 11.3, lines 15–18.)

You can also write formatted text to disk files. Open a file by calling `fopen()`, using one of the write modes from Table 11.3. Then call `fprintf()` exactly as you do `printf()`, but supply a `FILE *` variable as the initial argument. For example, this writes a `double` value `d` formatted in eight columns and two decimal places:

```
fprintf(fp, "%8.2f", d);
```

> **NOTE:** See the discussion of `printf()` in Chapter 22, "Functions and Examples," for more information about the formatting capabilities of function `fprintf()` and others in the `printf()` family.

Particularly useful is `sprintf()`—a string version of `printf()`. Declare a buffer to hold `sprintf()`'s result, then call it like this:

```
char buffer[256];  /* Buffer to hold result */
sprintf(buffer, "%8.2f", d);
```

Assuming d is a `double` variable, this deposits in `buffer` a null-terminated string representation of d's value. You might call other string functions to massage the result further, and then use file output functions to write the string to disk:

```
strcat(buffer, " == balance paid");
fputs(buffer, fp);
fputc('\n', fp);
```

Listing 11.9, NUMBER.C, demonstrates a practical use for `fprintf()`—adding line numbers to text files like in the listings printed in this book. After compiling the program, enter a DOS command such as **number myfile.txt** to add line numbers to MYFILE.TXT's lines, saving a copy of the original file as MYFILE.BAK (and erasing any old backup of that same name).

> **CAUTION:** NUMBER modifies the original copy of the specified file. If you add line numbers to a program listing, it no longer compiles. For best results, even though NUMBER creates a backup file, *never run NUMBER on your only copy of an important file.*

Listing 11.9. NUMBER.C (Adds line numbers to text files).

```
 1:  #include <stdio.h>
 2:  #include <stdlib.h>
 3:  #include <string.h>
 4:
 5:  void Error(const char *message);
 6:  void Instruct(void);
 7:  char *NewExt(const char *fname, const char *ext);
 8:
 9:  main(int argc, char *argv[])
10:  {
11:    char *inpfname, *bakfname, *outfname;
12:    FILE *inpf, *outf;
13:    char buffer[256];
14:    int lineNumber = 0;
15:
16:    if (argc <= 1)
17:      Instruct();
```

```
18:
19:   /* Make filenames and open files */
20:
21:     inpfname = strdup(argv[1]);
22:     bakfname = NewExt(inpfname, ".BAK");
23:     if (!bakfname)
24:       Error(bakfname);
25:     outfname = tempnam(".", "~");
26:     remove(bakfname);
27:     outf = fopen(outfname, "w+");
28:     if (!outf)
29:       Error(outfname);
30:     inpf = fopen(inpfname, "r+");
31:     if (!inpf)
32:       Error(inpfname);
33:
34:   /* Add line numbers to input file */
35:
36:     printf("Numbering %s\n", inpfname);
37:     while (fgets(buffer, 255, inpf) != NULL) {
38:       fprintf(outf, "%4d: %s", ++lineNumber, buffer);
39:       putchar('.');   /* Display feedback on-screen */
40:     }
41:     puts("");
42:
43:   /* Close files and backup original */
44:
45:     fclose(inpf);
46:     fclose(outf);
47:     rename(inpfname, bakfname);
48:     rename(outfname, inpfname);
49:     printf("Line numbers added to %s\n", inpfname);
50:     printf("Backup copy saved as %s\n", bakfname);
51:     return 0;
52:   }
53:
54:   /* Return copy of filename with new extension */
55:   char *NewExt(const char *fname, const char *ext)
56:   {
57:     char *p;     /* Pointer to string result */
58:     int fnlen;   /* Filename length minus any extension */
```

continues

Listing 11.9. continued

```
59:
60:    if (fname == NULL)
61:      return NULL;
62:    fnlen = strcspn(fname, ".");   /* Where is "."? */
63:    if (fnlen == 0)
64:      fnlen = strlen(fname);
65:    p = (char *)calloc(1, fnlen + strlen(ext) + 1);
66:    if (p) {
67:      strncpy(p, fname, fnlen);   /* Copy fname minus extension */
68:      strcat(p, ext);             /* Concatenate new extension */
69:    }
70:    return p;   /* Return pointer to new filename (or NULL) */
71: }
72:
73: void Error(const char *message)
74: {
75:    if (errno == 0)
76:      printf("Internal error: %s", message);
77:    else
78:      perror(message);  /* Print system error */
79:    exit(1);
80: }
81:
82: void Instruct(void)
83: {
84:    puts("\nSyntax: NUMBER infile");
85:    puts("Enter the name of an input text file. The program ");
86:    puts("appends line numbers to every line, and saves a ");
87:    puts("copy of the original file with its extension ");
88:    puts("changed to .BAK.");
89:    exit(0);
90: }
```

NUMBER makes good use of the file-handling principles outlined earlier. The program also demonstrates a few new techniques. Lines 21–32 prepare three char * variables: inpfname (input filename), bakfname (backup filename), and outfname (output filename). The input filename is assigned the address of the command-line argument argv[1] (see line 21). A local function, NewExt(), returns any filename with its extension changed to something else—".BAK" in this case (see line 22). If this filename is null, line 24 calls function `Error()` to halt the program. Line 25 calls a function you haven't seen before:

```
outfname = tempnam(".", "~");
```

Function `tempnam()`, prototyped in stdio.h, returns a temporary filename guaranteed not to exist in one of four paths, in this order:

- The path specified by a TMP environment variable.

- The path specified as `tempnam()`'s first argument.

- The path indicated by `P_tmpdir`, declared in stdio.h.

- The current directory.

The sample statement uses the pathname `"."` to indicate the current directory if a TMP environment variable is not defined. The second argument, `"~"` in the sample, is the initial character used for the temporary name. This string may be from zero to five characters and it cannot contain a period. Function `tempnam()` does not open a file. It merely returns a unique filename, which should be used as soon as possible after calling the function.

Another new function, `remove()` (line 26), deletes a specified file. The statement

```
remove("OLDFILE.XXX");
```

deletes OLDFILE.XXX from the current directory. The argument may also have drive and path information as in this string:

```
remove("C:\\MYDIR\\MYOLD.TXT");
```

The double backslashes are necessary because string escape codes such as `'\n'` begin with backslashes. Two backslashes together translate to a single backslash character, used by DOS as a separator in a pathname string.

For best results, the file specified to `remove()` should not be open. Try never to delete an open file. That's like shutting a door with your foot in the doorway—a painful experience best avoided.

After creating the program's filenames, and opening input and output files (see lines 27 and 30), NUMBER executes a `while` loop at lines 37–40. The loop calls `fgets()` to read lines from the input file, and calls `fprintf()` to write those lines, reformatted with line numbers attached. Line 39 displays a period on-screen for each line processed—a useful feedback technique that provides assurance of some activity while a program performs a lengthy task. There are few things more disconcerting than to run a program and not know whether it has decided to take a trip to the moon or is moving faithfully along, though traveling in total silence. Always try to provide constant feedback of a program's activity, or your program's users, fearing disaster, may be tempted to reboot their systems needlessly.

One other new function demonstrated by NUMBER is rename() at lines 47–48. Call rename() to change the name of a file. The first argument is the existing filename. The second is the new name. NUMBER uses rename() to backup the original file, and to change the temporary output filename to the original's name.

Finally in NUMBER, function perror() (see line 78) demonstrates a handy way to display error messages for a variety of I/O functions. Most functions set an internal errno variable to a value that represents one or many possible error conditions. Calling perror() with any string argument (a message or a filename, for example) displays that string plus a description of the faulty condition.

> **NOTE:** Any detected I/O errors prevent further I/O until the error is cleared. Call function clearerr() to reset the internally stored error code for an open file stream. Call function rewind() to reset a file to its beginning, which also clears any detected error. After clearing an error condition, you may perform additional I/O on the file. It is your responsibility, however, to repair the conditions that led to the error in the first place.

scanf and Family

Function scanf() and its associates cscanf(), fscanf(), sscanf(), and a few others (consult scanf()'s "See also" references in Chapter 22, "Functions and Examples") input binary values from text sources. When data is stored in text files, but you want to read those values as binary representations, use one of these functions. For example, a text file of floating-point numbers—perhaps created by a spreadsheet—could be loaded into an array of double variables by fscanf().

Listing 11.10, RARRAY.C, demonstrates how to use fscanf() to read several floating-point values stored in a text file. Before compiling and running the program, create a sample data file using your favorite ASCII text editor. Save the file as TEST.DAT in the same directory as RARRAY.C. The data file's first line is an integer equal to the number of entries that follow, one entry per line. Use these sample lines or make up your own values:

```
10
3.14159
79.86
100
85.3
24.329
7.0
66.32
89.99
12.31
9.99
```

> **NOTE:** Rather then enter the preceding lines with a text editor, you can also use the FILTER program from Listing 11.1 as a simple data entry utility. At a DOS prompt, enter **filter >test.dat**, then type the numbers as printed here. End with Ctrl+C and press Enter.

Next, enter RARRAY.C, and compile. Run the program to load TEST.DAT into an array of double variables, displayed on-screen for confirmation.

Listing 11.10. RARRAY.C (Reads array of double values from a text file).

```
 1:  #include <stdio.h>
 2:  #include <stdlib.h>
 3:
 4:  main()
 5:  {
 6:    FILE *inpf;
 7:    int i, count;
 8:    double *array;
 9:
10:  /* Open file */
11:
12:    inpf = fopen("TEST.DAT", "r");
13:    if (!inpf) {
14:      puts("Can't open TEST.DAT");
```

continues

425

Listing 11.10. continued

```
15:      exit(1);
16:    }
17:
18:  /* Read count of values */
19:
20:    fscanf(inpf, "%d", &count);
21:    if (count <= 0) {
22:      printf("Bad count value of %d\n", count);
23:      exit(2);
24:    }
25:
26:  /* Create array and read values from file */
27:
28:    printf("\nCreating array of %d values\n", count);
29:    array = (double *)malloc(count * sizeof(float));
30:    for (i = 0; i < count; i++)
31:      fscanf(inpf, "%lf", &array[i]);
32:    fclose(inpf);
33:
34:  /* Display array of values */
35:
36:    for (i = 0; i < count; i++)
37:      printf("array[%2d] == %lf\n", i, array[i]);
38:    free(array);  /* Free memory allocated to array */
39:    return 0;
40:  }
```

Function fscanf() requires an input file stream, opened in the usual way by calling fopen() (see line 12). Line 20 demonstrates how to call fscanf(). Pass the opened file variable as the initial argument (inpf in the listing), then pass a formatting string ("%d") as the second argument, which tells the function what kind of value to expect. The third argument is the address of a variable suitable for holding the value loaded from the file. In this case, &count is the address of an int variable. The statement at line 20 sets count to the first entry in the data file, representing the number of entries that follow.

Those entries are loaded into an array of double values allocated by malloc() at line 29. Rather than declare an explicit array, the program creates the array at runtime just big enough to hold the specified number of entries. A for loop at lines 30–31 again calls `fscanf()`, this time specifying the format string `"%lf"` (a "long float," equivalent to a `double`). The destination address, `&array[i]`, informs `fscanf()` where to deposit the result.

You can also use `fscanf()` and other similar functions to read multiple values. See Chapter 22, "Functions and Examples," for more information.

Reading and Writing Binary Files

Text files are certainly common, but they are only one of many kinds of files that can be stored on computer disks. Rather than store values in text form, for instance, you can write `double`, `int`, and other binary values directly to files, and read those and other data types from disk into memory.

One advantage to storing binary data directly in files is speed. Converting text to and from binary representations takes time. Another advantage is space. A `double` value takes 8 bytes of storage in Borland C++. That same value in text form may take many more bytes, including carriage return and line feed control codes if values are stored on separate lines. Binary files tend to be smaller, and in most cases, programs can process binary files faster than they can read and write text.

Basic Binary File Techniques

C makes working with binary files easy. The techniques are nearly the same as those explained for text files. Instead of dealing with characters and lines, however, programs read and write binary data as collections of bytes, from one to many thousands.

When opening files for binary processing, call `fopen()` as before, but add a lowercase b to any of the access modes in Table 11.3. For example, if `fp` is a variable of type `FILE *`, the statement

```
fp = fopen("MYFILE.DAT", "r+b");
```

opens MYFILE.DAT for reading and writing in binary mode. You don't have to type the plus sign. Other binary access-mode strings include `"rb"` (read-only), `"wb"` (create new file), `"ab"` (append), and so on. After calling `fopen()`, if `fp` is not null, it can be used in subsequent calls to binary file functions such as `fread()` and `fwrite()`.

> **NOTE:** Don't attempt to mix text file functions with binary file I/O techniques. Process files in text or binary mode exclusively.

There are two basic ways to read and write binary files—sequentially or randomly. Take a close look at these two methods, and then investigate how, with binary file techniques, you can use C as a database programming language.

Sequential-Access Files

Sequential processing is useful for storing values quickly in files, and for manipulating file data as a stream of bytes—as though those bytes were stored on computer tape rather than a disk drive. When performing an operation on all data in a file, it makes good sense (and saves time) to read and write that data sequentially.

A simple example demonstrates the principles of sequential binary file processing. Listing 11.11, WINT.C, writes an array of integers to a binary file. Compile and run the program to create file INT.DAT in the current directory.

Listing 11.11. WINT.C (Writes an array of integers to a binary file).

```
 1:  #include <stdio.h>
 2:  #include <stdlib.h>
 3:
 4:  main()
 5:  {
 6:    FILE *outf;
 7:    int i;
 8:
 9:    outf = fopen("INT.DAT", "wb");
10:    if (!outf) {
11:      puts("Can't create INT.DAT");
12:      exit(1);
13:    }
14:    puts("Writing 100 integer values to INT.DAT");
15:    for (i = 0; i < 100; i++)
16:      fwrite(&i, sizeof(int), 1, outf);
```

```
17:     fclose(outf);
18:     return 0;
19: }
```

Line 9 shows how to create a new binary file, using option "wb" with function fopen(). If the function returns a valid file stream, the for loop at lines 15–16 calls fwrite() to write 100 integer values to file INT.DAT. Because in Borland C++ an int takes two bytes, the resulting file is exactly 200 bytes long. Function fwrite() requires four parameters:

- The address of a variable or array of variables from which bytes are copied to disk.

- The number of bytes in one variable.

- The number of items to write—1 for a single value, or another positive integer to write an array of items.

- A FILE * stream variable opened in binary mode for writing (see Table 11.3).

You can also use fwrite() to write arrays of values to disk. For example, given the array

```
int array[100];
```

a single call to fwrite() writes the entire array to a file:

```
fwrite(&array, sizeof(int), 100, outf);
```

Reading binary values sequentially from disk files uses similar programming, demonstrated by Listing 11.12, RINT.C. Compile and run this program to read and display the values in the INT.DAT file created by WINT.C.

Listing 11.12. RINT.C (Reads binary values from INT.DAT).

```
1: #include <stdio.h>
2: #include <stdlib.h>
3:
4: main()
5: {
6:     FILE *inpf;
```

continues

Listing 11.12. continued

```
 7:    int i, value;
 8:
 9:    inpf = fopen("INT.DAT", "rb");
10:    if (!inpf) {
11:      puts("Can't open INT.DAT");
12:      exit(1);
13:    }
14:    for (i = 0; i < 100; i++) {
15:      fread(&value, sizeof(int), 1, inpf);
16:      printf("%8d", value);
17:    }
18:    return 0;
19:  }
```

Line 9 opens INT.DAT using option `"rb"`, literally "read-only binary mode." To load values one-by-one from disk, a `for` loop at lines 14–17 calls `fread()`, which requires the same arguments as `fwrite()`. The `fread()` function's initial argument is the destination address to which the function should copy bytes from disk. Be sure this variable is at least as large as the number of bytes you request!

Function `fread()` can load more than one value from disk at a time. In fact, if you add an array of 100 integers to RINT.C:

```
int array[100];
```

you can replace RINT's `for` loop with a single function call to `fread()`:

```
fread(&array, sizeof(int), 100, inpf);
```

This code loads 100 `int` values from file `inpf` into `array`, and is the fastest way to read multiple values from disk into memory.

Random-Access Files

When disk drives first appeared on the computer scene, they vastly improved the state of the art of data storage. At that time, the most common storage medium was tape, which reads and writes data in sequential fashion only. Disk drives give computers the added luxury of being able to store information at *random* locations—a capability that makes it possible to pluck records from the middle of a file, and to insert new information at any location.

Random-access files have one basic requirement: All records in them must be exactly the same size. Except for that fact, there's no physical difference between a random and a sequential file, and you can mix random and sequential file techniques on the same data files.

To demonstrate the concept of random-access techniques, Listing 11.13, RINTR.C, reads the eleventh integer value stored in INT.DAT by WINT.C. Each value in a random-access file has an associated record number, similar to the index values that arrays use as subscripts. Beginning with zero for the first value in a file, the eleventh value is numbered 10, and in INT.DAT, has the value 10. When you compile and run RINTR, this is the value the program displays on-screen.

Listing 11.13. RINTR.C (Reads value at random from INT.DAT).

```
1:  #include <stdio.h>
2:  #include <stdlib.h>
3:
4:  main()
5:  {
6:    FILE *inpf;
7:    int value;
8:
9:    inpf = fopen("INT.DAT", "rb");
10:   if (!inpf) {
11:     puts("Can't open INT.DAT");
12:     exit(1);
13:   }
14:   fseek(inpf, 10 * sizeof(int), SEEK_SET);
15:   fread(&value, sizeof(int), 1, inpf);
16:   printf("Record #10 == %d\n", value);
17:   fclose(inpf);
18:   return 0;
19: }
```

Use fopen() as before to open a file for random-access processing. Be sure to include a lowercase "b" in the option string passed to fopen()'s second parameter. To read a record at a randomly selected position, first call fseek(), as shown at line 14, to move the file's internal pointer to the desired record's first byte. After seeking the record's position, call fread() to load bytes starting from that location. Function fseek() requires three arguments:

- A FILE * stream variable opened for binary access.

- An offset value.

- One of three constants: SEEK_SET, SEEK_CUR, or SEEK_END.

The purpose of the offset value passed to fseek()'s second parameter depends on the value of the third argument. If that argument is SEEK_SET, the offset equals the number of bytes to move the internal file pointer forward from the beginning of the file. If the argument is SEEK_CUR, the offset is a signed value that represents the number of bytes to move the pointer forward or back from its present position. If the argument is SEEK_END, the offset represents the number of bytes to move the pointer from the end of the file back toward the beginning.

In RINTR, line 14 calls fseek() like this:

```
fseek(inpf, 10 * sizeof(int), SEEK_SET);
```

The first argument is the opened FILE * variable. The second is the product of the size in bytes of an int variable times the record number (10) of the sought-after value. Because the third argument is SEEK_SET, the second represents the offset in bytes from the beginning of the file. Function fseek() returns zero if successful; due to DOS limitations, however, seeking to a nonexistent location might not generate an error. Always keep track of the maximum number of records in a file, and include programming to prevent seeking beyond a file's known boundaries.

Some other examples demonstrate fseek()'s versatility. Given a FILE * variable f opened to a file of records of type t, the statement

```
fseek(f, sizeof(t), SEEK_CUR);
```

moves the current file pointer from the current record to the next. The statement

```
fseek(f, -sizeof(t), SEEK_CUR);
```

moves the current file pointer back one record. Calling fread() also moves the file pointer forward, so after reading one record with fread(), you can use the preceding statement to reposition the file pointer, perhaps in preparation for rewriting new information to that same location.

Another handy statement seeks to the end of the file:

```
fseek(f, 0, SEEK_END);
```

which you might use before calling fwrite() to append new records to a file not opened in an append mode.

Listing 11.14, WINTR.C, demonstrates how to position the file pointer and call fwrite() to write a value at random in file INT.DAT, without disturbing other values that come before and after. Run the program, and then rerun RINT and RINTR. As you can see, lines 15–16 seek the eleventh record, and change its value from 10 to 99. Other values are unaffected.

Listing 11.14. WINTR.C (Writes value at random to IND.DAT).

```
 1:  #include <stdio.h>
 2:  #include <stdlib.h>
 3:
 4:  main()
 5:  {
 6:    FILE *outf;
 7:    int value = 99;  /* New value to write */
 8:
 9:    outf = fopen("INT.DAT", "r+b");
10:    if (!outf) {
11:      puts("Can't open INT.DAT");
12:      exit(1);
13:    }
14:    printf("Writing %d to record #10\n", value);
15:    fseek(outf, 10 * sizeof(int), SEEK_SET);
16:    fwrite(&value, sizeof(int), 1, outf);
17:    fclose(outf);
18:    return 0;
19:  }
```

Notice that line 9 opens INT.DAT for reading and writing in binary mode—probably the most common way to open existing files for random-access processing. Line 15 calls fseek() to position the file's internal pointer to the eleventh integer (record number 10). Line 16 calls fwrite() to modify the value stored at that location.

> **NOTE:** Be aware that writing a value at random to a file is preceded by an internal read operation that loads the target value—and possibly others—into a buffer somewhere in memory. Calling `fwrite()` transfers a new value into that buffer, but an actual disk write might not occur until later when another read operation requires the same buffer. Closing or flushing the file also writes to disk any modified buffers. Never assume that calling `fwrite()` ensures data security. If the computer happens to be turned off before a disk write occurs, data stored temporarily in memory buffers is permanently lost.

Database Programming

You've now seen all the basic ways to read and write text and binary data in sequential and random-access files. Armed with this knowledge, you are ready to begin writing database programs that can store, search, sort, and retrieve records in disk files. There isn't room in this chapter (possibly not even in this entire book) to present a complete database system. The following few programs, however, give you a running start toward completing your own database projects.

A database is conveniently written in C as a file of structures. Each record is a `struct` data type, with members representing fixed-size fields of strings, integers, floating-point, and other values. Anything you can store in a `struct`, you can read and write at random to a binary file.

Designing the Database

The first step in writing a database program is to design your record `struct`. You also need a few functions to create a new file, to read and write records, and to input data fields. Listing 11.15, db.h, declares these items for use by other programs in this section.

Lines 8–11 declare symbolic constants for string-field lengths. The constants are used at lines 18–21 to declare char arrays for the database record's text information. Don't use char * fields in record structures—they simply complicate the works and require you to call `malloc()` to allocate fields individually. You can still allocate space for an entire structure on the heap and store character fields there.

Line 22 shows that record structures can have noncharacter data, in this case, a `double` value named `balance`. Structures are stored in binary fashion in the database file, and they may have members of any data types.

Listing 11.15. db.h (Creates a sample database header file).

```
 1:  /* db.h -- Sample data base header file */
 2:
 3:  #include <stdio.h>
 4:  #include <limits.h>
 5:
 6:  #define FALSE 0
 7:  #define TRUE 1
 8:  #define NAMELEN 30
 9:  #define ADDRLEN 30
10:  #define CSZLEN 30
11:  #define PHONELEN 13
12:
13:  typedef struct record {
14:     union {
15:       long numrecs;          /* Header == number of records */
16:       long custnum;          /* Record == customer number */
17:     } info;
18:     char name[NAMELEN];      /* Customer name */
19:     char addr[ADDRLEN];      /* Customer address */
20:     char csz[CSZLEN];        /* Customer city, state, zip */
21:     char phone[PHONELEN];    /* Customer telephone */
22:     double balance;          /* Current account balance */
23:  } Record;
24:
25:  #define MAXREC (LONG_MAX / sizeof(Record))
26:
27:  /* Create new database named path. 0==success; -1==failure */
28:  int CreateDB(const char *path);
29:
30:  /* Open database named path. Return FILE* or NULL and header */
31:  FILE *OpenDB(const char *path, Record *header);
32:
33:  /* Read record number recnum into rec. Return TRUE/FALSE */
34:  int ReadRecord(FILE *f, long recnum, Record *recp);
35:
36:  /* Write record number recnum from rec. Return TRUE/FALSE */
37:  int WriteRecord(FILE *f, long recnum, Record *recp);
38:
```

continues

Listing 11.15. continued

```
39:  /* Append record onto end of file. Return recnum, TRUE/FALSE */
40:  int AppendRecord(FILE *f, long *recnum, Record *recp);
41:
42:  /* Display label and input long integer */
43:  void InputLong(const char *label, long *lp);
44:
45:  /* Display label and input character string */
46:  void InputChar(const char *label, char *cp, int len);
47:
48:  /* Display label and input double */
49:  void InputDouble(const char *label, double *dp);
```

Lines 14–17 use a union to help organize the database. A union's fields are stored on top of one another. Though two long values (numrecs and custnum) are declared, only one of those values is in use at one time. The union might have other members as well, of the same or different types.

The purpose of the union is to record the number of records in the database file. In the file, record number zero stores this information, using field numrecs (but no others) in the structure. Records numbered 1 and higher contain valid information—in this example, a customer number, name, address, and other data. Figure 11.5 shows how the file is organized.

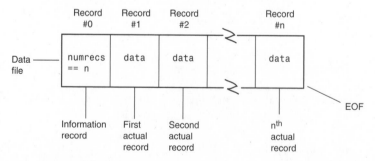

Figure 11.5. The sample database and information header record.

Listing 11.16, DB.C, implements the functions prototyped in db.h. Enter db.h and DB.C, and compile with the DOS command **bcc -c db.c**. The -c option creates

DB.OBJ, which is linked to other programs in this section in order to provide common database functions.

Listing 11.16. DB.C (Implements common database functions).

```
 1:  #include <stdlib.h>
 2:  #include <string.h>
 3:  #include "db.h"
 4:
 5:  int CreateDB(const char *path)
 6:  {
 7:    FILE *f;
 8:    Record rec;
 9:    int result;
10:
11:    f = fopen(path, "wb");
12:    if (!f)
13:      return FALSE;
14:    memset(&rec, 0, sizeof(Record));
15:    rec.info.numrecs = 0;
16:    result = WriteRecord(f, 0, &rec);
17:    fclose(f);
18:    return result;
19:  }
20:
21:  FILE *OpenDB(const char *path, Record *header)
22:  {
23:    FILE *f = fopen(path, "r+b");
24:    if (f)
25:      ReadRecord(f, 0, header);
26:    return f;
27:  }
28:
29:  int ReadRecord(FILE *f, long recnum, Record *recp)
30:  {
31:    if (recnum > MAXREC)
32:      return FALSE;
33:    if (fseek(f, recnum * sizeof(Record), SEEK_SET) != 0)
34:      return FALSE;
```

continues

Listing 11.16. continued

```
35:    return (fread(recp, sizeof(Record), 1, f) == 1);
36:  }
37:
38:  int WriteRecord(FILE *f, long recnum, Record *recp)
39:  {
40:    if (recnum > MAXREC)
41:      return FALSE;
42:    if (fseek(f, recnum * sizeof(Record), SEEK_SET) != 0)
43:      return FALSE;
44:    return (fwrite(recp, sizeof(Record), 1, f) == 1);
45:  }
46:
47:  int AppendRecord(FILE *f, long *recnum, Record *recp)
48:  {
49:    if (fseek(f, 0, SEEK_END) != 0)
50:      return FALSE;
51:    *recnum = ftell(f) / sizeof(Record);
52:    return WriteRecord(f, *recnum, recp);
53:  }
54:
55: void InputLong(const char *label, long *lp)
56: {
57:    char buffer[128];
58:
59:    printf(label);
60:    gets(buffer);
61:    *lp = atol(buffer);
62: }
63:
64: void InputChar(const char *label, char *cp, int len)
65: {
66:    char buffer[128];
67:
68:    printf(label);
69:    gets(buffer);
70:    strncpy(cp, buffer, len - 1);
71: }
72:
73: void InputDouble(const char *label, double *dp)
74: {
```

```
75:     char buffer[128];
76:
77:     printf(label);
78:     gets(buffer);
79:     *dp = atof(buffer);
80:   }
```

You should recognize most of the programming in DB.C. Function CreateDB() (lines 5–19) calls fopen() with the option "wb" to create a new database file. The function sets the initial information record's numrecs field to zero because, at this stage, the database has no customer records.

Function OpenDB() (lines 21–27), which returns a FILE * value, calls fopen() to open an existing file for reading and writing. The function also reads the file's information record, giving the program the means to detect how many records the file contains.

Function ReadRecord() (lines 29–36) reads record number recnum from file f into the record structure addressed by pointer recp. Notice how fseek() is used to move the file's internal pointer to the location of the record, after which fread() loads the record's bytes from disk.

Function WriteRecord() (lines 38–45) has the same parameters as ReadRecord(), but transfers to disk the record structure addressed by recp. Again, fseek() positions the file's internal pointer. Then, fwrite() writes the record to that location.

Function AppendRecord() (lines 47–53) calls fseek() using the SEEK_END option to position the file's internal pointer to just beyond the file's end. Line 51 calls function ftell(), which returns the file's internal pointer. Divided by the size of one record, this value equals the number of the record to be appended. Line 52 calls WriteRecord to attach this new record to the end of the file.

Functions InputLong(), InputChar(), and InputDouble() (lines 55–80) are simple editing routines for obtaining new data from the keyboard. These functions are oversimplified to keep the listings in this section reasonably short. A more sophisticated database program would need more extensive editing capabilities (much of which you can accomplish easily with Turbo Vision—see Chapter 18, "Turbo Vision").

Creating the Database File

After designing the database's structure and support functions, it's usually a good idea to create an empty database file as a separate operation. Listing 11.17, MAKEDB.C, illustrates one way to accomplish this goal. Compile the program from DOS with the command **bcc makedb.c db.obj**, and run the result. (This assumes you previously compiled DB.C.) When prompted, enter a filename such as DB.DAT to create that file in the current directory.

Listing 11.17. MAKEDB.C (Creates empty database file).

```
 1:  #include <stdlib.h>
 2:  #include <string.h>
 3:  #include "db.h"
 4:
 5:  int FileExists(const char *path);
 6:
 7:  main()
 8:  {
 9:    char path[128];
10:
11:    puts("Create new database file");
12:    printf("File name? ");
13:    gets(path);
14:    if (strlen(path) == 0)
15:      exit(0);
16:    if (FileExists(path)) {
17:      printf("%s already exists.\n", path);
18:      puts("Delete file and try again.");
19:      exit(1);
20:    }
21:    if (!CreateDB(path))
22:      perror(path);
23:    else
24:      printf("%s created.\n", path);
25:    return 0;
26:  }
27:
28:  int FileExists(const char *path)
29:  {
30:    FILE *f = fopen(path, "r");
31:
```

```
32:    if (!f)
33:      return FALSE;
34:    else {
35:      fclose(f);
36:      return TRUE;
37:    }
38: }
```

Line 21 calls module DB's `CreateDB()` function to create the empty database file using the name you specify. If this file exists, the program refuses to overwrite it. In that case, use DOS's DEL command to delete the old file, or rerun the program and specify a different name.

Lines 28–38 list a handy function, `FileExists()`, which returns true if the specified file identified by `char` pointer `path` exists. You might want to copy the function to your own library of C routines, and use it whenever you need to detect the existence of named files.

Adding Database Records

Your database system needs a program to add new records. Listing 11.18, ADDREC.C, shows one solution. Compile with the DOS command **bcc addrec.c db.obj**. Run the program, and enter information as prompted to append one new record to the end of the specified file.

Listing 11.18. ADDREC.C (Adds a record to a database file).

```
1:  #include <stdlib.h>
2:  #include <string.h>
3:  #include <mem.h>
4:  #include "db.h"
5:
6:  void GetNewRecord(Record *recp);
7:
8:  main()
9:  {
10:    char path[128];
11:    FILE *dbf;
```

continues

441

Listing 11.18. continued

```
12:     Record rec;
13:     long numrecs;
14:
15:     printf("Database file name? ");
16:     gets(path);
17:     dbf = OpenDB(path, &rec);
18:     if (!dbf) {
19:       printf("Can't open %s\n", path);
20:       exit(1);
21:     }
22:     numrecs = rec.info.numrecs;
23:     printf("Number of records == %lu\n", numrecs);
24:     GetNewRecord(&rec);
25:     if (AppendRecord(dbf, &numrecs, &rec))
26:         printf("Record #%lu added to database\n", numrecs);
27:     memset(&rec, 0, sizeof(Record));   /* Zero header record */
28:     rec.info.numrecs = numrecs;        /* Update record count */
29:     WriteRecord(dbf, 0, &rec);         /* Write header */
30:     fclose(dbf);
31:     return 0;
32: }
33:
34: void GetNewRecord(Record *recp)
35: {
36:     memset(recp, 0, sizeof(Record));
37:     InputLong("Customer #       : ", &recp->info.custnum);
38:     InputChar("Name             : ", recp->name, NAMELEN);
39:     InputChar("Address          : ", recp->addr, ADDRLEN);
40:     InputChar("City, State, Zip : ", recp->csz, CSZLEN);
41:     InputChar("Telephone        : ", recp->phone, PHONELEN);
42:     InputDouble("Account balance  : ", &recp->balance);
43: }
```

ADDREC.C, clearly, would be a lot more useful if it could add more than one record at a time. You might want to consider adding a loop to the program, and after each record, ask users whether they want to continue adding new ones.

Editing Database Records

Most databases require frequent maintenance. In addition to entering records, you probably need to edit existing information without disturbing other records. Using the random-access techniques described earlier, Listing 11.19, EDITREC.C, requests a record number, and lets you retype that record's information. Compile the program with the DOS command **bcc editrec.c db.obj**.

Listing 11.19. EDITREC.C (Edits a record in a database file).

```
 1:  #include <stdlib.h>
 2:  #include "db.h"
 3:
 4:  void EditRecord(FILE *f, long recnum, Record *recp);
 5:
 6:  main()
 7:  {
 8:    char path[128];
 9:    FILE *dbf;
10:    Record rec;
11:    long numrecs, recnum;
12:
13:    printf("Database file name? ");
14:    gets(path);
15:    dbf = OpenDB(path, &rec);
16:    if (!dbf) {
17:      printf("Can't open %s\n", path);
18:      exit(1);
19:    }
20:    numrecs = rec.info.numrecs;
21:    printf("Number of records == %lu\n", numrecs);
22:    InputLong("Record number? ", &recnum);
23:    if ((recnum <= 0) || (recnum > numrecs)) {
24:      puts("Record number out of range");
25:      fclose(dbf);
26:      exit(1);
27:    }
28:    EditRecord(dbf, recnum, &rec);
```

continues

443

Listing 11.19. continued

```
29:    if (WriteRecord(dbf, recnum, &rec))
30:      printf("Record #%lu written to %s\n", recnum, path);
31:    else
32:      perror("Write record");
33:    fclose(dbf);
34:    return 0;
35:  }
36:
37:  void EditRecord(FILE *f, long recnum, Record *recp)
38:  {
39:    if (!ReadRecord(f, recnum, recp)) {
40:      perror("Reading record");
41:      exit(1);
42:    }
43:    printf(    "Customer #        : %lu\n", recp->info.custnum);
44:    InputLong("Customer #        : ", &recp->info.custnum);
45:    printf(    "Name              : %s\n", recp->name);
46:    InputChar("Name              : ", recp->name, NAMELEN);
47:    printf(    "Address           : %s\n", recp->addr);
48:    InputChar("Address           : ", recp->addr, ADDRLEN);
49:    printf(    "City, State, Zip : %s\n", recp->csz);
50:    InputChar("City, State, Zip : ", recp->csz, CSZLEN);
51:    printf(    "Telephone         : %s\n", recp->phone);
52:    InputChar("Telephone         : ", recp->phone, PHONELEN);
53:    printf(       "Account balance  : %8.2f\n", recp->balance);
54:    InputDouble("Account balance  : ", &recp->balance);
55:  }
```

EDITREC.C suffers from a touch of unfriendliness. As written, the program requires you to reenter every field of a selected record—hardly an ideal editing technique. As mentioned earlier, the Turbo Vision library described in Chapter 18, "Turbo Vision," has features that you can use to design vastly superior editing functions. Also, if you are writing a Windows application, you can take advantage of built-in editors in Windows.

Writing a Database Report

As a final demonstration of the kinds of programs a typical database system needs, Listing 11.20, REPORT.C, displays a report of the information entered in a database file. Compile with the DOS command **bcc report.c db.obj**, run the program, and supply a filename when prompted. REPORT displays selected fields from the file's current records.

Listing 11.20. REPORT.C (Displays a report for a database file).

```
 1:  #include <stdlib.h>
 2:  #include "db.h"
 3:
 4:  main()
 5:  {
 6:    char path[128];
 7:    FILE *dbf;
 8:    Record rec;
 9:    long numrecs, recnum;
10:
11:    printf("Database file name? ");
12:    gets(path);
13:    dbf = OpenDB(path, &rec);
14:    if (!dbf) {
15:      printf("Can't open %s\n", path);
16:      exit(1);
17:    }
18:    numrecs = rec.info.numrecs;
19:    printf("\nNumber of records == %lu\n\n", numrecs);
20:    for (recnum = 1; recnum <= numrecs; recnum++)
21:      if (ReadRecord(dbf, recnum, &rec))
22:        printf("%4lu: #%4lu; %s; Phone:%s; Balance: $%.2f\n",
23:           recnum, rec.info.custnum, rec.name, rec.phone,
24:           rec.balance);
25:    fclose(dbf);
26:    return 0;
27:  }
```

Directories and Drives

In addition to reading and writing files, programs often also need to scan directories, make new subdirectories, update file dates and times, and perform other related

445

operations. The following sections explain some of the more common Borland C++ directory functions.

Changing Directories and Drives

As you probably know, from DOS you can use the CHDIR (often abbreviated to CD) command to change the current directory. To do the same in a program, call function chdir(), prototyped in dir.h. Listing 11.21, CDIR.C, demonstrates. Compile and run the program with no arguments to display the current directory. You can also enter a DOS command such as **cdir c:\borlandc\include** to change to a different directory.

Listing 11.21. CDIR.C (Changes or displays current directory).

```
 1:  #include <stdio.h>
 2:  #include <dir.h>
 3:
 4:  main(int argc, char *argv[])
 5:  {
 6:    char *buffer;
 7:
 8:    if (argc == 1) {
 9:      if ((buffer = getcwd(NULL, MAXPATH)) != NULL)
10:        puts(buffer);
11:    } else {
12:      if (chdir(argv[1]) != 0)
13:        printf("Can't change to %s\n", argv[1]);
14:    }
15:    return 0;
16:  }
```

To obtain the current directory, line 9 calls function getcwd() (get current working directory). The function requires two arguments:

- A char * pointer to a buffer large enough to hold the current directory's pathname. You can also pass NULL to have getcwd() create a new string on the heap (by calling malloc()) of the length specified by the second parameter.

- A value equal to the size in bytes of the char buffer passed to the function. If the first argument is NULL, getcwd() returns the address of a newly allocated string containing the current directory as a null-terminated string.

To change the current directory, line 12 calls chdir(), passing a pathname—in this case equal to the string entered in the DOS command line. If the directory is found, chdir() returns 0. The function returns −1 if it detects an error.

It may also be necessary to change the current drive. In that case, call _chdrive(). (The leading underscore indicates this function's system-dependent nature. It works only on MS-DOS systems.) Pass to _chdrive() an integer representing the new drive; 1 for drive A, 2 for drive B, 3 for drive C, and so on. The function returns 0 if successful, −1 if an error is detected. For example, to make drive A current, use programming such as

```
if (_chdrive(1) == 0)
  ...;  /* success */
else
  ...;  /* error */
```

Creating and Deleting Directories

Subdirectories help to organize massive numbers of files on large disk drives. To create a subdirectory from within a program, include the dir.h header file and call mkdir() like this:

```
result = mkdir("c:\\temp\\myfiles");
```

The function returns 0 for success, −1 if an error occurs. To remove an existing directory, which is possible only if that directory is empty of all files and other directories, call rmdir(), also prototyped in dir.h:

```
result = rmdir("c:\\temp\\myfiles");
```

Displaying Directories

A directory's entries are normally locked away on disk, accessible only to the DOS DIR command. With the help of a couple of library functions, findfirst() and findnext(), a C program can easily have DOS cough up directory information for any drive or path.

Listing 11.22, LF.C, shows how to use these two functions, which operate in tandem to scan a directory's contents one file and directory name at a time. Enter and compile the program. Then, from DOS, run it to display a list of filenames in the current directory. You can specify wildcards such as *.C, as you can with DIR. The program's output is redirectable. To save a list of files in a text file, enter a command such as **lf *.c >newfile.txt**.

Listing 11.22. LF.C (Lists files in a directory).

```
 1:  #include <stdio.h>
 2:  #include <string.h>
 3:  #include <dos.h>
 4:  #include <dir.h>
 5:
 6:  main(int argc, char *argv[])
 7:  {
 8:    struct ffblk fb;
 9:    char wildCard[13] = "*.*";
10:    int done;
11:
12:    if (argc > 1)
13:      strncpy(wildCard, argv[1], 12);
14:    done = findfirst(wildCard, &fb, FA_DIREC);
15:    while (!done) {
16:      puts(fb.ff_name);
17:      done = findnext(&fb);
18:    }
19:    return 0;
20:  }
```

Lines 14–18 show the correct way to call findfirst() and findnext(). Call findfirst() to initiate a directory search, and then using the same ffblk structure, call findnext() to continue searching until no more files are found. The two functions return zero if successful, or –1 if an error is detected or there are no more directory entries to read. Line 14 starts the directory scan, calling findfirst() with three arguments:

- A pointer to a wildcard string such as "*.*" or "*.C".

- The address of a struct ffblk structure. Information about each located file is deposited in this structure.

• One or more file attributes indicating the types of files desired.

If findfirst() returns zero, to continue searching for more files, pass the same ffblk structure to findnext() (see line 17). The struct ffblk is declared in dir.h as

```
struct ffblk {
  char      ff_reserved[21];   /* Don't use */
  char      ff_attrib;         /* File attributes */
  unsigned  ff_ftime;          /* File time */
  unsigned  ff_fdate;          /* File date */
  long      ff_fsize;          /* File size in bytes */
  char      ff_name[13];       /* File or directory name */
};
```

After calling findfirst() or findnext(), you can use the fields in this structure to find the file's attributes, size, date, time, and name. Attributes passed to findfirst() may be any logical-OR combination of the dir.h constants listed in Table 11.4. Unfortunately, however, DOS returns files and directories even when you ask only for directories—a fact that LF.C proves (see line 14). Even though FA_DIREC is specified to findfirst(), the program lists all directory and filenames in the specified path.

Table 11.4. File and directory attributes.

Constant	Meaning
FA_ARCH	Archive bit
FA_DIREC	Directory
FA_HIDDEN	Hidden file
FA_LABEL	Volume label
FA_RDONLY	Read-only file
FA_SYSTEM	System file

Scanning Directory Paths

To locate only the subdirectories in a path requires programming similar to that demonstrated by LF.C. Because DOS doesn't return only directory names, however, an additional check is needed to weed out the files from the subdirectories. Listing

11.23, LP.C, demonstrates the technique, which might be useful in a program that lists directories, perhaps to give users the means to change the current path without having to return to DOS. You can specify a wildcard. The command **lp xyz*.*** lists all subdirectories that begin with xyz. Enter **lp** alone for a list of the current directory's subdirectories, including current and previous ones (represented by one and two dots).

Listing 11.23. LP.C (Lists subdirectory paths in current directory).

```
 1:  #include <stdio.h>
 2:  #include <string.h>
 3:  #include <dos.h>
 4:  #include <dir.h>
 5:
 6:  main(int argc, char *argv[])
 7:  {
 8:    struct ffblk fb;
 9:    char wildCard[13] = "*.*";
10:    int done;
11:
12:    if (argc > 1)
13:      strncpy(wildCard, argv[1], 12);
14:    done = findfirst(wildCard, &fb, FA_DIREC);
15:    while (!done) {
16:      if ((fb.ff_attrib & FA_DIREC) == FA_DIREC)
17:        puts(fb.ff_name);
18:      done = findnext(&fb);
19:    }
20:    return 0;
21:  }
```

LP is almost the same as LF. In the directory scan at lines 14–19, however, an if statement uses a logical AND expression to detect whether each file's FA_DIREC attribute bit is set. Only if it is set does the program display the directory's name at line 17.

Advanced File Techniques

It's difficult to know where to begin discussing all the possible advanced file and disk operations that you can perform with C programs. This section by no means covers the entire field, but it does present three useful techniques, which show how to modify a file's attributes, how to determine how much space is available on a drive, and how to access a drive's sectors in their raw, untamed state.

File Attributes

Listing 11.24, TOUCH.C, "touches" one or more files in a specified directory to update the file dates and times. The program's traditional name probably refers to the fact that only the file directory entries are modified. The files themselves are opened briefly, but their contents remain undisturbed—a mere touch on the file rather than a push or a shove.

> **NOTE:** A similar TOUCH utility is provided with Borland C++. Both programs perform the same operation.

Listing 11.24. TOUCH.C (Updates file dates and times).

```
 1:  #include <stdio.h>
 2:  #include <stdlib.h>
 3:  #include <string.h>
 4:  #include <errno.h>
 5:  #include <dos.h>
 6:  #include <dir.h>
 7:  #include <io.h>
 8:
 9:  int UpdateTime(const char *fname, struct ftime ft);
10:
11:  main(int argc, char *argv[])
```

continues

451

Listing 11.24. continued

```
12:  {
13:    struct ffblk fb;              /* Directory info */
14:    struct ftime ft;              /* File date and time */
15:    struct time t;                /* System time structure */
16:    struct date d;                /* System date structure */
17:    char wildCard[129] = "*.*";   /* Default wildcard string */
18:    int done;                     /* For findfirst, findnext */
19:
20:    gettime(&t);                  /* Get system date and time */
21:    getdate(&d);
22:    ft.ft_tsec  = t.ti_sec;       /* Assign time to file struct */
23:    ft.ft_min   = t.ti_min;
24:    ft.ft_hour  = t.ti_hour;
25:    ft.ft_day   = d.da_day;       /* Assign date to file struct */
26:    ft.ft_month = d.da_mon;
27:    ft.ft_year  = d.da_year - 1980;
28:    if (argc > 1)
29:      strcpy(wildCard, argv[1]);
30:    printf("\nUpdating %s", wildCard);
31:    done = findfirst(wildCard, &fb, 0);
32:    while (!done) {
33:      printf("\n%s", fb.ff_name);
34:      if (UpdateTime(fb.ff_name, ft) == -1) {
35:        printf("\nError setting time for file %s", fb.ff_name);
36:        printf("\nERROR #%d: %s\n", errno, strerror(errno));
37:        exit(errno);
38:      }
39:      printf(" updated");
40:      done = findnext(&fb);
41:    }
42:    return 0;
43:  }
44:
45:  /* Update time and date of specified file */
46:  int UpdateTime(const char *fname, struct ftime ft)
47:  {
48:    FILE *fp;
49:    int result;
50:
51:    if ((fp = fopen(fname, "r")) == NULL)
```

```
52:        return -1; /* Error opening file */
53:     result = setftime(fileno(fp), &ft);
54:     fclose(fp);
55:     return result;
56:  }
```

Lines 20–21 obtain the current time and date, which are assigned to a struct ftime variable declared at line 14. Executing a directory scan of all files (lines 31–41) locates candidate names to be updated by UpdateTime() at line 34.

The UpdateTime() function (lines 46–56) opens the file in read-only mode by calling fopen(). Line 53 calls setftime(), also calling fileno() to convert the FILE * pointer fp to a handle, which setftime() requires. Use this method to pass file streams to any file-handle function. Closing the file at line 54 updates the file's directory entry, making its date and time current.

Determining Disk Free Space

When you can calculate in advance how much storage space a file needs, do your users a favor: Make sure at least that much room is available before starting a lengthy file operation. Almost nothing is more annoying than a disk-file program that spins its wheels for minutes on end, only to report an out-of-room error when nearly finished. Time is money. Don't waste either for your program's users.

Determining a disk's free space is simple, so there's no excuse not to perform this important task. Listing 11.25, FREE.C, shows how to write the code, and also makes a handy utility for quick checks on a disk's free space. Compile FREE.C and then from DOS, run the program for a report on the current drive's free space. You can also enter a command such as **free a:** to determine the amount of available room on another drive.

Listing 11.25. FREE.C (Reports free space on current or specified drive).

```
1:  #include <stdio.h>
2:  #include <dos.h>
3:  #include <ctype.h>
4:
```

continues

Listing 11.25. continued

```
 5:  main(int argc, char *argv[])
 6:  {
 7:    int drive = 0;
 8:    unsigned long freeSpace;
 9:    struct dfree free;
10:
11:    if (argc > 1)
12:      drive = toupper(*argv[1]) - ('A' - 1);
13:    getdfree(drive, &free);
14:    if (free.df_sclus == 0xFFFF)
15:      freeSpace = -1;
16:    else
17:      freeSpace = (long)free.df_avail * (long)free.df_bsec
18:        * (long)free.df_sclus;
19:    if (freeSpace == -1)
20:      puts("Error reading drive");
21:    else
22:      printf("Free space on drive = %lu bytes", freeSpace);
23:    return 0;
24:  }
```

Function getdfree() (line 13) takes two arguments: an integer representing the drive number and the address of a struct dfree variable. Set the drive number to 0 for the current drive, 1 for drive A, 2 for drive B, 3 for drive C, and so on. Structure dfree is declared in dos.h as

```
struct dfree {
  unsigned df_avail;  /* Number of available clusters */
  unsigned df_total;  /* Total clusters on drive */
  unsigned df_bsec;   /* Bytes per sector */
  unsigned df_sclus;  /* Sectors per cluster */
};
```

After calling getdfree(), if member df_sclus equals 0xffff, an error occurred; otherwise, the values have the meanings shown as comments here. The total amount of free space in bytes equals df_avail * df_bsec * df_sclus, calculated at lines 17–18 using typecasts to ensure a long integer result. The total amount of space available on a large hard drive might easily be greater than the largest possible unsigned value, so the calculation should be done using the longest possible integer size available.

Using BIOS Disk Functions

The final program in this chapter introduces a subject that, like a wild animal, might best be kept under lock and key and never allowed to roam freely through your code. By using a special function, `biosdisk()`, it's possible to read and write disk data without regard to its content or whether it belongs to a file, a directory, DOS, or is unused. It's also possible to wipe out entire disks with this function, so please be careful with it.

WARNING: Just in case that message didn't sink in, here it is again: *The* `biosdisk()` *function can wipe out hard drives in a flash. Be extremely careful when using it!*

To demonstrate `biosdisk()` using relatively safe code (but be sure to backup your disk before running the program), Listing 11.26, RSECT.C, reads four 512-byte sectors from a floppy disk inserted into drive A. Insert the disk before running RSECT, as some disk drive's signal a disk change, which causes `biosdisk()` to return an error. If that happens, leave the disk in place and rerun the program.

Listing 11.26. RSECT.C (Reads absolute disk sector from drive A).

```
 1:  #include <stdio.h>
 2:  #include <bios.h>
 3:  #include <conio.h>
 4:
 5:  #define DRIVE 0   /* 0==A:, 1==B:, 2==C:, etc. */
 6:  #define HEAD 0
 7:  #define TRACK 1
 8:  #define SECTOR 1
 9:  #define SECTORSIZE 512
10:  #define NUMSECTORS 4
11:  #define SIZE (SECTORSIZE * NUMSECTORS)
12:  #define DISKREAD 2
13:
14:  main()
```

continues

Listing 11.26. continued

```
15:  {
16:    char buffer[SIZE];
17:    int result;
18:
19:    puts("Insert scratch floppy in drive A:");
20:    puts("Press Enter to read from disk");
21:    getch();
22:    result = biosdisk(DISKREAD, DRIVE, HEAD, TRACK,
23:      SECTOR, NUMSECTORS, buffer);
24:    if (result == 0)
25:      puts("Disk read successful");
26:    else
27:      puts("Error detected");
28:    return 0;
29:  }
```

Lines 22–23 call `biosdisk()`, passing a command, drive, head, track, sector, number of sectors, and the address of a buffer for saving or providing data. The command listed here, `DISKREAD` (equal to 2), reads data from disk and is therefore relatively safe. Table 11.5 lists other commands, but again, please do not try these without careful study and *never* on a drive containing your only copies of valuable information.

Table 11.5. Commands for function `biosdisk()`.

Command	Description
0	Reset disk
1	Return status of previous function call
2	Read one or more sectors
3	Write one or more sectors
4	Verify one or more sectors
5	Format a track
6	Format track and set bad sector flags

Command	Description
7	Format drive starting at specified track
8	Return drive parameters
9	Initialize drive-pair characteristics
10	Perform long read, equal to 512 + 4 bytes overhead per sector
11	Perform long write, equal to 512 + 4 bytes overhead per sector
12	Seek to specified location
13	Alternate disk reset
14	Read sector buffer
15	Write sector buffer
16	Test if drive is ready
17	Recalibrate drive
18	Perform RAM diagnostic on disk controller
19	Perform drive diagnostic
20	Perform internal drive controller diagnostic

The biosdisk() function returns zero if successful, or an error code if not. More information about biosdisk() can be found in your Borland C++ Library Reference and in a PC reference that discusses BIOS interrupt 0x13.

Summary

- Most text I/O is handled by five, predefined standard file streams: stdaux, stderr, stdin, stdout, and stdprn. These files can be passed to any function that requires a FILE * argument. Many functions such as puts() and gets() use standard I/O files by default.

- Some file functions use integer handles to identify active files. Other functions, most of which begin with lowercase f, use and return FILE * streams. Borland C++ also provides many pure DOS functions, all of which are named beginning with _dos.

- Except for standard I/O files, you must open a file before you can use it. Open files should be closed when no longer needed. Closing a file flushes to disk any modified data held in memory buffers. When a program ends, all open files are automatically closed, but it's still a good idea to close files explicitly.

- A filter program reads input from a source, and writes possibly modified data to a destination. The simplest filter program merely copies stdin to stdout.

- Modern PC software typically uses direct-video techniques to display text in a variety of colors and attributes. Use the Borland C++ conio.h functions for ultra-fast, direct-video I/O. Because these routines are unlikely to be available on other compilers and operating systems, however, you might want to provide CONIO wrapper functions, such as those used in this chapter's CRT module. The CRT module also shows one way to create pop-up, overlapping windows on text screens.

- Use printf() and the related fprintf() functions to write values of many types as formatted text. Use scanf() and fscanf() to read text input into binary variables.

- You can read and write text files either one character at a time, or one line at a time. The choice depends on how the text is stored and the needs of your program.

- You can also read and write files in binary mode, loading bytes into memory and writing bytes back to disk. Any data of any type can be stored in a binary file.

- Binary files may be read and written in sequential-access or in random-access modes. A random-access file's records must all be exactly the same size. Internally, a pointer marks the file's current position. By seeking to new positions, it's possible to read and write data at any location in a file without disturbing other information in the file.

- With its binary-file and random-access functions, C makes an ideal database programming language. Records in binary files correspond to structures. Any data that can be stored in a struct member can be stored in a random-access database file.

- Borland C++ provides various directory functions, which by nature are dependent on MS-DOS services. You can change directories, create new ones, and delete empty subdirectories. You can also scan a directory's files, using the functions `findfirst()` and `findnext()`.

- Various advanced file-handling functions are also available. File attributes, including file dates and times, may be modified by programs. You can determine a disk drive's free space—a good feature to include in programs that create large files.

- One relatively dangerous function, `biosdisk()`, provides low-level disk drive services. The function can read and write disk sectors in their raw, untamed state. It can also format disk tracks, however, and perform other operations that can easily wipe out an entire hard drive. *Use `biosdisk()` with extreme care.*

> **NOTE:** This chapter completes Part 2's tour of ANSI C programming with Borland C++. In the next part, you'll investigate features of C++ that enhance C's basic capabilities. You've learned C. Now it's time to extend your knowledge to the world of object-oriented programming and C++.

Exercises

11.1 Write a filter program SKIP.C that prints a text file and skips printout paper folds.

11.2 Write a program that reads and sorts a text file's lines in alphabetic order.

11.3 Write a program that joins two text files into one larger file.

11.4 Write a program that splits a large text file into multiple smaller files.

11.5 Write a filter that converts a text file's characters to lowercase.

11.6 Given the database file structure as listed in db.h (Listing 11.15), write a program that totals all customer balances.

11.7 Write a program that displays a disk drive's subdirectory tree, using indentation to show directory levels.

11.8 Write a program that searches for and displays all files with their archive bit set, indicating the file has not been backed up. Compute the total sizes of all such files—useful for checking how many disks a backup operation requires. Due to the fact that files are stored in multiples of a disk's cluster size, simply adding the byte sizes of all unarchived files does not give an accurate tally. Your program should deal with this problem.

Part 3

Programming
with C++

Introducing C++

Many programmers think of C++ as an object-oriented version of C. That's not an entirely accurate description, although the major contribution of C++ is the class—a special kind of structure that can have data and function members. In Chapter 13, "Programming with Classes," you explore classes and learn how they are used for object-oriented programming. In this chapter, you tour other less profound, but no less important, features that make C++ special.

The language's name, C++ (pronounced "C plus plus") is something of a pun—a play on C's ++ increment operator. The language C++ is literally "one step beyond C." Early on, C++ was known as "C with Classes," but the modern name C++ quickly won popularity, and is in fact the perfect title for this enhanced flavor of C.

The inventor of C++, Bjarne Stroustrup, calls the language "a better C." In addition to the class, C++ adds to ANSI C several new keywords and operators, inline and overloaded functions, overloaded operators, new memory management techniques, and a few other odds and ends. In every instance, these C++ features were designed to correct an oversight or inconsistency in C, or to add new tools for building solid code. If C is an ice cream cone, C++ is a fudge sundae.

Since the humble beginnings of C++ in the early 1980s at AT&T Bell Laboratories, some of the language's unique features have spilled back into ANSI C, thus muddying the waters that divide C++ from its direct ancestor, Classic C. Today,

ANSI C and C++ are as close as kissing cousins, and most ANSI C programs are compatible with C++. Many of C++'s more advanced features, however, such as classes, are not found in ANSI C.

Anatomy of a C++ Program

Most of what you have learned about ANSI C programming applies to C++. ANSI C and C++ programs look pretty much the same. They use nearly identical syntax, as well as the same kinds of loops, data types, pointers, and other elements.

Because the Borland C++ compiler can tackle ANSI C and C++ programs, you must tell the compiler which of these languages you intend to use. The easiest way to fulfill this requirement for C++ programs is to name your source code files with the extension .CPP rather than .C. From DOS, the command **bcc file.c** compiles FILE.C as an ANSI C program. The command **bcc file.cpp** compiles FILE.CPP as a C++ program. Because .CPP is the Borland C++ default file extension, the commands **bcc file** and **bcc file.cpp** give the same results. From the IDE, to compile C++ programs, save them with the extension .CPP and compile normally.

> **NOTE:** You can also use the -P option or the equivalent IDE setting (Options|Compiler|C++ options...|C++ always) to force Borland C++ to compile in C++ mode. Naming your source files with .CPP is simpler, however, and helps to distinguish ANSI C program files from those that use C++ features. Some programmers also name C++ header files ending with .hpp rather than .h. The compiler makes no distinction between .hpp and .h, so in this book, all header files end with .h.

Back in Chapter 5, "Data: What a Program Knows," you compiled and ran a simple program, WELCOME.C. Listing 12.1, WELCOME.CPP, is a C++ version of that same code. Compile and run the program using the command **bcc welcome** and then enter **welcome**. To compile and run from the IDE, press Ctrl+F9 and then Alt+F5 to see the program's output.

Listing 12.1. WELCOME.CPP (A sample C++ program).

```
1:   #include <iostream.h>
2:
3:   main()
4:   {
5:     cout << "Welcome to Borland C++ programming!\n";
6:     return 0;
7:   }
```

There are two main differences between Listing 12.1 and Listing 5.1. First, line 1 includes iostream.h rather than the usual stdio.h. (You can include both of these headers if necessary.) Second, line 5 displays a line of text using the iostream library's cout ("character out") standard output stream. To send information to a destination (in this case, to the display), iostream uses the C++ "put to" operator <<. Think of << as an arrow that tosses some data, such as the literal string in WELCOME, to an I/O stream, such as cout.

You can also write multipart iostream statements. If firstName and lastName are char * pointers to strings, the statement

```
cout << lastName << ", " << firstName << '\n';
```

writes the two names, last name first, separating the two strings with a comma and ending with a new line. You can write the string "\n" or the character '\n' to start a new line. Some programmers prefer to write each section of a multipart iostream on a separate line. Despite appearances, this is one statement, not four:

```
cout << lastName
  << ", "
  << firstName
  << '\n';
```

An iostream has the attractive property of being able to output a wide variety of data types, including all built-in types such as int, long, and double, and also types of your own making. If count is type long, the statement

```
cout << "Count == " << count << '\n';
```

displays a string followed by count's value and a new line.

You'll dig deeper into iostreams later in this chapter. Meanwhile, keep your eye out for different kinds of iostream statements in most of the listings in Part 3.

> **NOTE:** You may mix stdio and iostream techniques, and you may still use `printf()` and similar functions in C++ programs. However, as you'll learn in Chapter 15, "Advanced Topics in C++," iostreams can be extended to accommodate new data types. Function `printf()` can handle only built-in types, and its output formats, while extensive, are not programmable.

Comparing C and C++

Before beginning to learn about the features of C++, you need to memorize a few rules that alter some of the facts you learned earlier in this book. Following are critical notes and differences between ANSI C and C++:

- ANSI C and C++ generally use the same syntax, operators, expressions, built-in data types, structures, arrays, unions, loops, functions, and pointers. These fundamental elements are used identically in both languages.

- C++ has several new reserved keywords, listed along with words specific to C++ (denoted with an asterisk) in Table 12.1. (See Appendix E for a complete list of ANSI C and C++ reserved words, plus others reserved specifically by Borland C++.) C++ also has a few new operators, introduced later. (Appendix D lists all ANSI C and C++ operators.)

Table 12.1. ANSI C and C++(*) keywords.

asm	default	for	operator*	sizeof	unsigned
auto	delete*	friend*	private*	static	virtual*
break	do	goto	protected*	struct	void
case	double	if	public*	switch	volatile*
char	else	inline*	register	template*	while
class*	enum	int	return	this*	
const	extern	long	short	typedef	
continue	float	new	signed	union	

- C++ requires all functions to have formal prototypes before being called. ANSI C encourages, but does not require, function prototypes.

- Type checking in expressions is more strictly performed by C++. In general, values in expressions must be of the same types, or they must be readily convertible to appropriate types. Where ANSI C gives an incompatible type warning, C++ tends to generate a compiler error. However, ANSI C and C++ are much closer in their type-checking rules than are Classic C and C++.

- The need for `typedef` declarations is greatly reduced in C++. You can declare a `struct` like this:

```
struct mystruct {
...
};
```

  and then declare variables as `mystruct x;`. To do the same in ANSI C, you need to write `struct mystruct x;`, or you need to use a `typedef` alias for `struct mystruct`.

- In C++, a `char` is an 8-bit byte. In ANSI C, a `char`'s size is not defined, although in Borland C++, `char`s are *always* 8 bits long.

- In ANSI C, character constants are type `int`, and the expression `sizeof('X')` equals `sizeof(int)`. In C++, character constants are type `char`, and the expression `sizeof('X')` equals `sizeof(char)`.

NOTE: The preceding list of rules is not a complete comparison of ANSI C and C++. Other new C++ features are introduced at the appropriate times.

C++ Comments

C++ supplements ANSI C comments with a new comment style, resurrected from the Classic C predecessor language, BCPL. In a C++ program, a double slash `//` begins a comment. The compiler ignores every character from `//` to the end of the line. In ANSI C, the comment

```
/* This is a comment */
```

can also be written in C++ as

```
// This is a comment
```

The ANSI C comment, which you can use in C++ programs, requires two symbols: `/*` to begin the comment and `*/` to end it. The C++ comment requires only one `//` symbol; it ends at the end of the line. ANSI C comments may continue for two or more lines; C++ comments occupy single lines only. Either kind of comment may come at the end of a line. In ANSI C, you can add a comment to a statement like this:

```
count++;   /* Increment count */
```

In C++, that line might also be written

```
count++;   // Increment count
```

Only ANSI C comments may be embedded in a statement. The following is a valid (though confusing) statement in ANSI C and C++:

```
result = count /* Embedded comment */ + 100;
```

However, the statement

```
result = count // Embedded comment??? + 100;
```

causes a syntax error because C++ comments extend to the end of the line, and they cannot be embedded inside statements.

Mixing Comment Styles

ANSI C and C++ comments may be mixed in the same program. Listing 12.2, COMMENTS.CPP, shows several examples of ANSI C and C++ comments.

Listing 12.2. COMMENTS.CPP (Compares ANSI C and C++ comment styles).

```
1:  #include <iostream.h>
2:
3:  // ----------------------------------------
4:  // Author   : Tom Swan
5:  // Revision : v1.0
6:  // Purpose  : Demonstrates C++ comment styles
7:  // ----------------------------------------
8:
9:  main()
```

```
10:  {
11:    cout << "A Brief C++ Commentary\n";  // Display title
12:    cout << "\n";  // Display blank line under title
13:
14:  /* This paragraph demonstrates that C-style
15:  comments can occupy more than one line.
16:  C++ comments are restricted to single lines. */
17:
18:    cout << "// This is not a comment.\n\n";  // This is a comment
19:    cout << "/* This also is not a comment.*/ \n\n";
20:    cout /* This is a comment. */ << "This text is displayed.\n";
21:    return 0;
22:  }
```

Lines 3–7 use C++ comments for a small information header that describes the program. Many programmers like to "sign" their source listings with a uniquely styled header, which might list facts about the program, bug repairs, modification dates, and so on.

Lines 11–12 show the classic way to end C++ statements with explanatory comments. Lines 14–16 show a multiline ANSI C comment. To write similar C++ styled comments, each line would have to begin with //.

Lines 18–19 illustrate an important principle: Comments of any style may not occur in the middle of character strings. Line 20 shows that only ANSI C style comments may be embedded inside statements—a commenting style that's more confusing than helpful, and is best avoided.

Debugging with Comments

You can nest C++ comments inside ANSI C comments, a fact that leads to a useful debugging trick. Consider this fragment:

```
char buffer[128];          // Input buffer
gets(buffer);              // Get string into buffer
cout << '\n';              // Start new display line
cout << buffer << '\n';    // Display buffer and start new line
```

Suppose these statements do not produce the expected display, and you decide to test what happens if you delete the cout << '\n'; statement, which begins a new line before displaying `buffer`. Rather than delete the line, you can remove its effect by turning it into a comment:

```
char buffer[128];        // Input buffer
gets(buffer);            // Get string into buffer
/*
cout << '\n';            // Start new display line
*/
cout << buffer << '\n';  // Display buffer and start new line
```

The `/*` and `*/` brackets "comment out" the surrounded statement. The compiler ignores all characters between the brackets, including the C++ comment `// Start new display line`. You can now recompile and run the temporarily modified program. If you decide to restore the original statement, simply delete the ANSI C comment brackets.

Introducing Input/ Output Streams

A few sample programs demonstrate the power of the C++ iostream library. (See Chapter 15, "Advanced Topics in C++.") As in ANSI C, I/O in C++ is not part of the language but is provided as an external library module. This means programmers writing code for embedded systems or special-purpose computers are free to devise their own I/O functions and techniques—one of the reasons C and C++ are popular for low-level programming tasks. Most programmers, however, may as well take advantage of the standard libraries. These libraries have been tweaked to the hilt by superb software specialists, and it would be difficult to outdo their efforts.

An iostream behaves much like the standard input and output file streams introduced in Part 2 and covered in Chapter 11, "Input and Output." The `cout` (character out) and `cin` (character in) streams have many capabilities. To display a character `c`, you can write

```
cout << c;
```

or you can write

```
cout.put(c);
```

Function `put()` is a member of `cout`—a new concept that you'll be seeing frequently in the coming chapters. To call a member function, separate it from `cout` with a period—similar to the dot notation used to access structure members. The cout stream is an instance of a *class,* which can have associated functions such as put(). (The next chapter, "Programming in Classes," covers this in greater depth.) You must call member functions in reference to an object such as cout. Alone, the statement

```
put(c);  // ???
```

attempts to call a separate put() function (if there is one). The statement

```
cout.put(c);
```

calls the put() function that *belongs* to cout.

To read a character from the standard input, use the input stream cin along with the >> (get from) operator. The statement

```
cin >> c;
```

reads one character from the standard input and assigns that character to c. You also can call cin's get() member function to do the same:

```
cin.get(c);
```

As with standard I/O, a C++ iostream uses the system's standard input and output files, and can be used to write filter programs. Listing 12.3, FILTER.CPP, demonstrates the basic technique.

Listing 12.3. FILTER.CPP (A basic C++ filter program).

```
 1:  #include <iostream.h>
 2:
 3:  main()
 4:  {
 5:    char c;
 6:
 7:    while (cin.get(c))
 8:      cout.put(c);
 9:    return 0;
10:  }
```

Run FILTER as you do other filters, redirecting I/O with DOS commands. For example, to use FILTER to display its own source code file, enter the DOS command **filter <filter.cpp**. To send console input to a printer, enter **filter >prn**. To print a file, enter **filter <filename.ext >prn**.

Line 7 in FILTER.CPP calls `cin.get(c)` to obtain a character. The expression `cin.get(c)` returns an `int` value, or null upon reaching the end of the input source. Line 8 passes every character from the source to the standard output.

Reading Built-in Types

Reading and writing multiple data types are main attractions under the big tent of the C++ iostream library. Listing 12.4, GETVAL.CPP, tames a few iostream statements into reading integer and floating-point values. Compile and run the program, then enter values as prompted. Try entering mistakes (XXX rather than a floating-point value, for example) to see how the program handles errors.

Listing 12.4. GETVAL.CPP (Uses iostreams to read built-in types).

```
 1:  #include <iostream.h>
 2:  #include <stdlib.h>
 3:
 4:  void test(void);
 5:
 6:  main()
 7:  {
 8:    double fp;   // A floating-point value
 9:    long k;      // A long int value
10:
11:    cout << "Enter a floating-point value: ";
12:    cin >> fp;
13:    test();
14:    cout << "Value entered is: " << fp << '\n';
15:    cout << "Enter an integer value: ";
16:    cin >> k;
17:    test();
18:    cout << "Value entered is: " << k << '\n';
19:    return 0;
20:  }
21:
22:  void test(void)
23:  {
24:    if (!cin.good()) {
25:      cout << "Error detected";
```

```
26:      exit(1);
27:    }
28:  }
```

Line 11 prompts for a floating-point value, read by an iostream input statement into a `double` variable `fp` at line 12. A similar input statement at line 16 reads an integer. Unlike standard I/O, which requires you to specify data types in `scanf()` statements or to call functions that can read and convert specific types, iostreams automatically detect the types of variables used in I/O statements. Because you don't have to specify the data type in advance, you can't make a data-type selection mistake as you can with standard I/O. It's very hard in C++ to input data into the wrong kind of variable!

Lines 13 and 17 demonstrate another important quality of iostreams. These lines call a local function, `test()`, implemented at lines 22–28. The function examines `cin.good()`, a member function that returns TRUE if no unresolved errors exist for the specified stream. Use `cout.good()` to do the same for output streams. In the sample program, if `cin.good()` is FALSE, lines 25–26 display a message and halt the program.

You don't have to halt a program upon detecting an error. To clear a pending error, use a statement such as

```
cin.clear();
```

See Chapter 15, "Advanced Topics in C++," for other member functions available to iostreams.

Reading Character Strings

You already saw how iostreams can output character strings. For example, given the declaration

```
char *s = "Gently down the iostream";
```

the statement

```
cout << s;
```

sends the string `"Gently down the iostream"` on its way to the system's standard output, usually the display. To read a string, reverse the process using the `cin` input stream identifier and the `>>` ("put to") operator:

```
char buffer[128];  // Declare string buffer
cin >> buffer;     // ???
```

This works, but poses a hidden danger: If the user enters more than 127 characters, the input statement overwrites the end of the buffer, possibly destroying code or data after the array. Statements like this might crash your system!

Fortunately, there is a safer way to enter strings, as demonstrated by Listing 12.5, GETSTR.CPP. Compile and run the program, then enter a 24-character or smaller string at the first prompt. (You must enter at least one character before pressing Enter.) At the second prompt, enter a string longer than 24 characters, which is safely truncated to fit in the program's string buffer declared at line 5.

> **WARNING:** An intentional bug in GETSTR.CPP can crash your system if you enter more than 24 characters at the first prompt. The purpose of the listing is to show how to avoid this bug in your own code.

Listing 12.5. GETSTR.CPP (Uses iostreams to read character strings).

```
 1:  #include <iostream.h>
 2:
 3:  main()
 4:  {
 5:    char s[25];
 6:    char c;
 7:
 8:  // Bad string input technique
 9:    cout << "Enter a 24-char string unsafely: \n";
10:    cin >> s;     // Dangerous!
11:    cout << "You entered: " << s << '\n';
12:    cin.get(c);  // Throw out pending new-line char
13:
14:  // Good string input technique
15:    cout << "Enter a 24-char string safely: \n";
16:    cin.get(s, 25, '\n');
17:    cout << "You entered: " << s << '\n';
18:    if (cin.get(c) && c != '\n')
19:      cout << "Maximum line length reached\n";
20:    return 0;
21:  }
```

Line 10 shows the simplest, but a potentially dangerous, way to read strings with iostream statements. Line 16 shows a safer solution—call member function `cin.get()` with three arguments:

- The destination address of a `char` array. The resulting string read into this array is null-terminated.

- The size of the array in bytes.

- The character that, when typed, should end input. If not supplied, this character defaults to `'\n'`;

Reading input as shown at line 10 is safe as long as you correctly specify the size of the destination buffer. One problem, however, remains. The newline or other character that ends input is left in the stream and must be read by another `cin.get()` statement as shown at lines 12 and 18. Line 12 simply throws this character away. Line 18 uses it as a check of the input. If `cin.get()` does not read a newline character, input has been truncated—a fact that may be important for some programs to determine.

The problem of a leftover newline character can be solved by calling a different member function, `cin.getline`. To read a 24-character string into a 25-byte buffer (leaving one byte for the null terminator), you can write

```
char buffer[25];
cin.getline(buffer, 25);
```

Writing Values

In general, you can write any kind of variable in an output stream statement. For a variable v, regardless of type, the statement

```
cout << v;
```

should write something reasonable to the system's standard output. The exact form of some kinds of data may not be as you expect, and this advice does not apply to structures or arrays. However, you can display the values of pointers. Given a pointer declared as `int *p` (or as another pointer type), the statement

```
cout << p;
```

displays p's value as a long integer. This may be useful for debugging, but it's probably not a good idea to expect similar results with all C++ compilers and operating systems.

Formatting iostream Output

An iostream understands a variety of output formatting commands, some of which are discussed in Chapter 15, "Advanced Topics in C++." Listing 12.6, CONVERT.CPP, shows how to use three output stream identifiers—dec, hex, and oct—to write integer values in decimal, hexadecimal, and octal formats.

Listing 12.6. CONVERT.CPP (Uses iostreams to display formatted output).

```
 1:  #include <iostream.h>
 2:  #include <stdlib.h>
 3:
 4:  #define SIZE 35
 5:
 6:  main()
 7:  {
 8:    int value;
 9:    char s[SIZE];
10:
11:    cout << "Value? ";
12:    cin.get(s, SIZE, '\n');
13:    value = atoi(s);
14:    cout << "Decimal=" << dec << value
15:      << "  Hexadecimal=0x" << hex << value
16:      << "  Octal=0" << oct << value << '\n';
17:    return 0;
18:  }
```

Lines 14–16 form a single output stream statement with many parts. Some of those parts are literal strings. Others write an int variable value. Just before writing value, the identifiers dec, hex, and oct modify the output stream's current format, changing the result.

You can also specify output width by calling cout.width(n), where n is the number of columns you want. For example, to have your output right-justified in 15 columns, use programming such as

```
int value = 1234;   // Value to be formatted
cout.width(15);     // Specify 15-character column
cout << value;      // Output value in 15 columns
```

It may not always be convenient to use iostream formatting. Complex iostream statements (see lines 14–16 in Listing 12.6) might be difficult to read. Judging from published listings, expert C++ programmers prefer a mix of standard ANSI C and C++ formatting methods. Listing 12.7, CONVERT2.CPP, shows a typical case, and produces the same output as CONVERT.CPP.

Listing 12.7. CONVERT2.CPP (Displays formatted output in an alternative way).

```
1:  #include <iostream.h>
2:  #include <stdio.h>
3:  #include <stdlib.h>
4:
5:  #define SIZE 35
6:
7:  main()
8:  {
9:    int value;
10:   char s[SIZE];
11:   char buffer[80];
12:
13:   cout << "Value? ";
14:   cin.get(s, SIZE, '\n');
15:   value = atoi(s);
16:   sprintf(buffer, "Decimal=%d  Hexadecimal=%#x  Octal=%#o\n",
17:     value, value, value);
18:   cout << buffer;
19:   return 0;
20: }
```

The complex output stream statement from CONVERT.CPP is replaced by a call to sprintf() at lines 16–17. The sprintf() function, prototyped in stdlib.h, prepares a character string with values formatted according to the same rules for printf() and related functions. Line 16 specifies %d (decimal) %#x (hexadecimal) and $#o (octal) formats to be inserted at these locations in the final string, which is deposited into buffer. A single output stream statement at line 18 writes the completed buffer to the system's standard output.

Scope and Variable Definitions

Scope ambiguities can easily arise in ANSI C and C++ programs. For example, given a global variable int count, a function can declare a local variable of that same name without producing an error:

```
int count;    // Global variable
void AnyFunction()
{
  int count;  // Local variable
  ...
}
```

The local count's scope extends to its declaring function. In that function, local count effectively hides the global variable of the same name. In C++, you can use the scope resolution operator, ::, to unhide the global name. Writing the above function as

```
int count;    // Global variable
void AnyFunction()
{
  int count;        // Local variable
  count = 1234;     // Assign value to local count
  ::count = 4321;   // Assign value to global count
}
```

assigns 1234 to the local count and 4321 to the global count. The expression ::count instructs C++ to refer to the count in the outer scope rather than the count in the local scope (see Figure 12.1).

Listing 12.8, SCOPE.CPP, shows how to use the C++ scope resolution operator. This listing also illustrates a related concept: C++ declarations may appear anywhere inside a statement block, not only globally or at the beginning of a function as in ANSI C. As in ANSI C, however, you must declare variables before you can use them.

Line 3 declares a global variable k, initialized to 100; Line 7 declares a variable i, local to main(). Lines 9–10 display the values of k and i. There's no need to use the C++ scope resolution operator at line 9 because there is only one k.

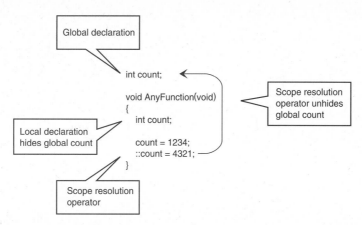

Figure 12.1. The scope resolution operator unhides a global variable.

Listing 12.8. SCOPE.CPP (Demonstrates scope resolution operator).

```
1:  #include <iostream.h>
2:
3:  int k = 100;     // Global variable
4:
5:  main()
6:  {
7:    int i = 200;  // Local variable
8:
9:    cout << "Global k == " << k << '\n';
10:   cout << "Local i  == " << i << '\n';
11:   {
12:     int k = 300;
13:     cout << "Local k  == " << k << '\n';
14:     cout << "Global k == " << ::k << '\n';
15:   }
16:   return 0;
17: }
```

Lines 11–15 form a new statement block, nested inside `main()`. Although this programming technique is unusual, blocks can be declared this way inside other blocks (see lines 11 and 15). However, in practice, such a nested block typically belongs to an `if`, `while`, or other compound statement. Inside the nested block, line 12 declares a new local variable named `k`, initialized to 300. Unlike ANSI C, C++ allows variables to be declared and initialized anywhere in a statement block. Now there are two `k`s: the global one declared at line 3 and the local one at line 12. Because the new local `k` hides the global variable of the same name, line 13 displays the local variable's value. To refer to the global variable, use the scope resolution operator as demonstrated at line 14.

Variables declared inside a statement block (in line 12, for example) exist only within that block. In other words, their scope is limited to the place of their declaration. The compiler rejects code such as

```
if (expression) {
  int count = 0;   // Declare variable within if's scope
  ...
}
cout << "count == " << count << '\n';  // ???
```

The last line does not compile because `int count` is declared within the scope of the `if` statement, and the variable does not exist outside of that scope.

A useful related trick is to declare and initialize a `for` loop's control variable at the same time. ANSI C `for` loops are typically written like this:

```
void f()
{
  int i;
  for (i = 0; i < MAX; i++)
    ...
}
```

In C++, you can declare the loop index directly inside the `for` loop, shortening the code to

```
void f()
{
  for (int i = 0; i < MAX; i++)
    ...
}
```

However, this does not declare `int i` within the `for` loop's exclusive scope. A `for` loop's initializer (`int i = 0;` in this case) is executed *before* the `for` loop begins, thus i in this example falls within the scope of f(), and the control variable is available to any statements that follow for.

Constants

The const identifier is a C++ innovation, adopted by ANSI C. Declaring variables with const throws a force field around them, preventing changes to their values at runtime. If you declare an integer count like this:

```
const int count = 1234;
```

The compiler rejects the statement:

```
count++;  // ???
```

Some C++ programmers recommend using const declarations rather than symbolic constants created with #define. The symbolic constant

```
#define MAX 100
```

declares a macro named MAX associated with the text 100 (*not* an integer value 100). If MAX appears in an expression such as

```
for (int i = 0; i < MAX; i++)
  ...
```

the compiler replaces MAX with the text digits 100 and compiles the statement as though you had typed those digits at this location.

Some C++ experts argue that symbolic constants such as MAX are too easily misused. Proponents of const would have you declare MAX like this:

```
const int MAX = 100;
```

The for loop remains the same, but with MAX declared as a true constant rather than a macro symbol, you gain two supposed advantages:

- The compiler can perform stricter type checking on MAX. C++ knows that the constant MAX is an int value; the compiler doesn't know any such type information about the text macro MAX.

- Turbo Debugger recognizes the true constant MAX. The debugger does not recognize symbolic macro constants created with #define.

These are important considerations. Unfortunately, however, the true constant MAX requires permanent storage in the program's data segment. Numerous constants in a program can take up hundreds or thousands of bytes, wasting disk space. Worse, using those values may require time-wasting memory references. Using #defined symbolic constants typically generates efficient instructions that load values directly into registers.

True const constants are useful for declaring values that behave like variables, but must not change at runtime. However, the advantages are not so great to warrant giving up #define.

Inline Functions

One of the sad truths of programming languages such as C and C++ is that function calls waste time. Although a function call takes place in the barest flutter of an eyelash, numerous function calls can shave points off a program's performance. Avoiding functions is not an acceptable solution to this problem! Functions make programs modular and easier to maintain. Without functions, it's extremely difficult, perhaps impossible, to write even medium-size programs that run correctly.

On the other hand, unrolling loops and removing multiple function calls are time-honored techniques for improving a program's runtime performance. Consider this hypothetical for loop:

```
for (int i = 0; i < MAX; i++) {
  AnyFunction();
  ...
}
```

If MAX is very large, the numerous calls to AnyFunction() might steal precious time from the program's overall performance. Suppose that AnyFunction() is written like this:

```
void AnyFunction(void)
{
  cout << AnyValue << '\n';
  AnyValue++;
}
```

All of this is hypothetical, but one fact is apparent: Inserting AnyFunction()'s statements directly into the for loop ought to speed up the program:

```
for (int i = 0; i < MAX; i++) {
  cout << AnyValue << '\n';
```

```
AnyValue++;
    ...
}
```

The amount of time saved should equal the value of MAX times the amount of time it takes to execute one function call. An even better solution is to unroll the loop completely, doing away with the for statement's overhead altogether:

```
cout << AnyValue << '\n';
AnyValue++;
cout << AnyValue << '\n';
AnyValue++;
    ...
cout << AnyValue << '\n';
AnyValue++;
```

Never mind that you have to type MAX * 2 statements, and if MAX is large, the compiled code will probably grow to elephantine proportions. No matter—*you have improved the program's performance by at least a millisecond or two!*

Ridiculous? Yes, but even though saving time is important, giving up functions and loops is too high a price to pay for a small improvement. Luckily, C++ offers an alternative. Rather than do away with function calls, you can declare functions *inline,* injecting their statements directly into the code stream. Listing 12.9, INLINE.CPP, shows how.

Listing 12.9. INLINE.CPP (Demonstrates inline functions).

```
 1:  #include <iostream.h>
 2:
 3:  inline int max(int a, int b)
 4:  {
 5:    if (a >= b)
 6:      return a;
 7:    else
 8:      return b;
 9:  }
10:
11:  main()
12:  {
13:    int x, y, z;
```

continues

Listing 12.9. continued

```
14:
15:    cout << "X? ";
16:    cin >> x;
17:    cout << "Y? ";
18:    cin >> y;
19:    z = max(x, y);
20:    cout << "max(a, b) == " << z << '\n';
21:    return 0;
22: }
```

To declare an inline function, precede it with the C++ inline keyword as shown at line 3. Implement the function normally (see lines 4–9). There is nothing special about an inline function's contents—anything that can go in a normal function can also go in one declared inline. Usually, inline functions such as the one at lines 3–9 are declared in header files and included in each module that needs to use the function. The inline function must appear, in full, before that function may be used, and storing the text in a header is a simple way to fulfill this requirement.

Use inline functions the same way you use normal functions. Line 19, for instance, calls max() to determine which of two integers is greater, assigning that value to z. In the compiled code, however, Borland C++ does not call a max() function at line 19. Instead, the compiler inserts the function's statements directly into the program, effectively compiling this statement as though it had been written

```
if (x >= y)
  z = x;
else
  z = y;
```

The amount of time saved in this small example is miniscule. If max() were called thousands of times in a loop, however, the program's performance might gain a significant boost from the inline code.

> **NOTE:** Inline functions are akin to register variables. When you declare an inline function, you are telling the compiler that, *if possible,* the function's statements should be inserted directly where the function is called. The compiler is not an obedient genie, however, and there is no guarantee that it

will carry out your every command. If the inline code is very large, for example, the compiler might refuse to inject it into the code stream, and instead, the compiler generates a common function call. Also, when compiling programs for Turbo Debugger, all inline functions are converted to common ones so they may be traced. Good C++ programs work correctly whether or not their inline functions are actually compiled inline.

Managing Memory with *new* and *delete*

You may use the same heap-memory routines in ANSI C and C++ programs. Functions `malloc()`, `farmalloc()`, `calloc()`, `farcalloc()`, `free()`, `farfree()`, and others are available to all Borland C++ programs. C++, however, offers alternate memory allocation *operators* new and `delete`, which can do everything standard heap-memory functions can do—and more.

Use new to allocate space for new dynamic variables. Use delete to free space allocated by new, returning allocated memory to the heap for use in subsequent new expressions. Keep in mind that new and delete are unary operators, not functions. This fact is significant because, as you'll discover in a later chapter, C++ makes it possible to reprogram most operators, including new and delete. Using these operators rather than the standard heap-memory routines makes it possible to take over memory-management details if that should be necessary. The operators also play important roles in object-oriented programming, a topic for Chapter 13, "Programming with Classes."

To allocate space in memory for a double variable and assign its address to a pointer, you can write

```
double *dp = new double;
```

You might often see similar declarations written as

```
double *dp = new(double);
```

which makes new appear to be a function. It's not, and the extra parentheses are ignored. Use dp as you do any pointer allocated by `malloc()` or a similar function. To assign a value to the memory addressed by dp, write

```
*dp = 3.14159;
```

When you are done using a dynamic variable, delete it like this:

```
delete dp;
```

Deleting the pointer returns the memory addressed by dp to the heap, making that memory available for other uses. Always use delete to free memory allocated by new. Dynamic variables allocated by malloc() or other memory-allocation functions should be freed by free() (or perhaps farfree()). You may use malloc() and new in the same program, but you must not mix standard ANSI C and C++ heap-memory techniques.

Using Simple Dynamic Variables

If successful, a new expression returns a pointer to a new dynamic object. If enough space is not available, new returns null. Always test whether new succeeded in allocating space for an object, as demonstrated by Listing 12.10, NEWVAR.CPP.

Listing 12.10. NEWVAR.CPP (Declares simple variables with new).

```
 1:  #include <iostream.h>
 2:  #include <math.h>
 3:
 4:  main()
 5:  {
 6:    double *dp;
 7:
 8:    dp = new double;
 9:    if (dp) {
10:      *dp = M_PI;
11:      cout << "Pi == " << *dp << '\n';
12:    }
13:    delete dp;
14:    return 0;
15:  }
```

Line 6 declares a pointer dp to type double. Line 8 uses new to allocate space for a dynamic double variable, and assigns the address of that variable to dp. Lines 10–11 use dp the same as pointers allocated space by malloc() and other functions. Line 13 uses delete to dispose dp's addressed space—unnecessary in this small example because the program soon ends. In most cases, however, variables created by new should be disposed by delete when those variables are no longer needed.

Unlike malloc(), new automatically calculates an allocated variable's size. You never have to specify the size in bytes of an object created with new, a fact that helps eliminate errors caused by miscalculating memory allocation sizes with malloc() and calloc().

Dynamic variables such as the double value allocated at line 8 have global scope. If you allocate space to a global pointer from inside a function:

```
void f()
{
  globalPtr = new double;
  ...
}
```

unlike local variables, the memory addressed by globalPtr is not automatically freed when the function ends. If you allocate a dynamic variable and assign its address to a *local* pointer, you should delete that space before the end of the function:

```
void f()
{
  double *localPtr = new double;
  ...
  delete localPtr;
}
```

If this function did not delete the dynamic variable allocated by new, the variable's address would be permanently lost when the function ends because, at that time, localPtr would cease to exist.

Using Dynamic Strings

You can use new to allocate dynamic character strings of any practical size. Listing 12.11, NEWSTR.CPP, demonstrates the technique.

Listing 12.11. NEWSTR.CPP (Declares strings with new).

```
 1:  #include <iostream.h>
 2:
 3:  #define SIZE 80
 4:
 5:  main()
 6:  {
 7:    char *sp;
 8:
 9:    sp = new char[SIZE];
10:    if (sp) {
11:      cout << "String? ";
12:      cin.getline(sp, SIZE);
13:      cout << "You entered: " << sp << '\n';
14:    }
15:    delete[] sp;
16:    return 0;
17:  }
```

Line 9 allocates a char array of SIZE bytes, and assigns the address of the array's first byte to sp. Lines 10–14 demonstrate how to use the dynamic string, prompting you to enter a line of text, which line 13 displays.

Line 15 deletes the dynamic char array. Borland C++ permits this statement to be written without brackets as

```
delete sp;  // ???, but okay in Borland C++
```

To stay in tune with strict C++ protocol, the empty brackets should be used in the expression delete[], which tells the compiler that an array, rather than just a simple variable, is being deleted. (In Borland C++, the brackets are required only when deleting arrays of class objects, but more on that later.)

> **NOTE:** Early versions of C++ required specifying the number of elements when deleting an array. In C++ Version 2.0, for example, line 15 would be written delete[SIZE] sp;. Borland C++ ignores SIZE in this case, and displays a warning if you attempt to use this older form of delete.

Using Dynamic Arrays

Strings are, of course, character arrays, and it should come as no surprise that new and delete also can be used to create and free dynamic arrays of any type. Listing 12.12, NEWARRAY.CPP, demonstrates.

Listing 12.12. NEWARRAY.CPP (Declares arrays with new).

```
 1:  #include <iostream.h>
 2:
 3:  #define COUNT 100  // Number of integers
 4:
 5:  main()
 6:  {
 7:    int *array;  // Array of integers
 8:    int i;       // Array index
 9:
10:    array = new int[COUNT];
11:
12:  // Fill array
13:    for (i = 0; i < COUNT; i++)
14:      array[i] = i;
15:
16:  // Display array contents
17:    for (i = 0; i < COUNT; i++) {
18:      cout.width(8);
19:      cout << array[i];
20:    }
21:    delete[] array;
22:    return 0;
23:  }
```

In this example, line 7 declares a pointer array to int. Line 10 uses new to allocate space for 100 int values. The array is then filled with values from 0 to 99, and displayed in eight-character columns by a for loop at lines 17–20. Line 21 deletes the array, using empty brackets in the expression delete[], as in the preceding listing, to tell the compiler that an array, and not just one int, is being deleted. Actually, Borland C++ permits line 21 to be written without the brackets as

```
delete array;  // ???, but okay in Borland C++
```

Multidimensional Dynamic Arrays

To declare a pointer to a two- or three-dimensional array (or one with more dimensions), specify the number of elements in the second and subsequent positions. For example, suppose you want to allocate space for a 10-by-20 array of double values. You begin by declaring

```
int (*matrix)[20];
```

which states that matrix is a pointer to an array of 20 integers. You must use parentheses around (*matrix) because the array brackets have higher precedence than the pointer symbol *. The integers don't exist just yet; all you've done is tell the compiler that matrix addresses an array of a certain size. To allocate memory for the 10-by-20 matrix, and assign the array's address to matrix, use the statement

```
matrix = new int[10][20];
```

Operator new allocates memory for the array. The resulting address is assigned to matrix. To create an 8-by-8-by-8 cube, use the statements

```
int (*matrix)[8][8];
matrix = new int[8][8][8];
```

This declaration of matrix specifies the second and third array dimensions, telling the compiler that matrix is to address an 8-by-8 array of integers. The new expression specifies all three dimensions, allocating space for a specific *number* of 8-by-8 arrays—in other words, a three-dimensional cube.

When allocating space for a multidimensional array, the first subscript may be a variable, but the second and subsequent subscripts must be constants. If an int v equals 40, for instance, these lines:

```
int (*matrix)[20];
matrix = new int[v][20];
```

allocate space for a two-dimensional, 40-by-20 array of int values addressed by matrix. Delete multidimensional arrays of any size as though they had only one dimension:

```
delete[] matrix;
```

Trapping Out-of-Memory Errors

If new cannot fulfill a request to allocate space for a dynamic variable, the operator returns null. Usually, you should test new's result by comparing it to the NULL macro like this:

```
int *p = new int[100];   // Allocate array of 100 integers
if (p == NULL)           // If allocation fails
  Error();               //  call error function.
```

For better control over out-of-memory errors, you can install a function that is called before new returns null. First, design the function, which requires no arguments and returns nothing. The function might simply display an error message and end:

```
void OutOfMemory(void)
{
  cerr << "\nMemory allocation request failed\n";
  exit(1);
}
```

Writing to the cerr output stream is equivalent to writing to the ANSI C stderr output file. Under normal conditions, the system's standard error output cannot be redirected, and writing to cerr helps ensure that error messages are displayed on-screen rather than sent to a file where they might be missed.

Next, preferably early in main(), call set_new_handler(), prototyped in new.h, and pass as an argument the error function name:

```
#include <new.h>
main()
{
  set_new_handler(OutOfMemory);
  ...
}
```

If new fails to allocate a requested object, the Borland C++ memory manager calls the new error function. If that function returns, the allocation request is repeated, possibly leading to another call to the error handler if that request again fails. A better error handler could attempt to delete some memory held in reserve, and permit new to retry its request.

> **NOTE:** Chapter 15, "Advanced Topics in C++," discusses another, and probably better, way to deal with out-of-memory errors. Using a technique called operator overloading, it's possible to provide custom programming for the new and delete operators, thus gaining control over how these operators allocate memory.

Function Overloading

Even if you are just getting started programming, you have probably faced the demanding job of thinking up new function names. Sure, you can invent any old name for a function—the compiler greets a function named f29q() with the same enthusiasm as it greets one named BattingAverage(). Humans, however, tend to comprehend the latter name.

In a large program, coming up with good function names is no joking matter. Consider a drawing program that has to draw umpteen shapes. Each drawing function needs a unique name, leading to programs strewn with functions such as DrawEllipse, DrawCircle, DrawSquare, DrawLine, and so on. The code probably also has numerous variables named ellipse, circle, square, and line, and the resulting code looks as though it has developed a bad stammer:

```
DrawEllipse(ellipse);
DrawCircle(circle);
DrawSquare(square);
DrawLine(line);
```

Wouldn't it be great if you could use the *same* function name—let's call it Draw()—to draw all shapes? Then, you could simply write

```
Draw(ellipse);
Draw(circle);
Draw(square);
Draw(line);
```

This is the kind of clarity that function overloading can bring to programs. In C++, multiple functions may have the same names as long as they differ in at least one parameter. The functions are "overloaded" because, though named the same, they perform multiple jobs. The many Draw() functions in our hypothetical graphics program are still separate and distinct, and are written just as other non-overloaded functions, but the C++ compiler recognizes them by *the way they are used,* not only by their names.

A simple example demonstrates how function overloading can help simplify a program's text. Listing 12.13, OVERLOAD.CPP, uses overloaded functions to display the square of three values, each of a different type.

Listing 12.13. OVERLOAD.CPP (Demonstrates function overloading).

```
 1:  #include <iostream.h>
 2:
 3:  int square(int a);
 4:  double square(double a);
 5:  long double square(long double a);
 6:
 7:  main()
 8:  {
 9:    int x = 10;
10:    double y = 20;
11:    long double z = 30;
12:
13:    cout << square(x) << '\n';
14:    cout << square(y) << '\n';
15:    cout << square(z) << '\n';
16:    return 0;
17:  }
18:
19:  int square(int a)
20:  {
21:    return a * a;
22:  }
23:
24:  double square(double a)
25:  {
26:    return a * a;
27:  }
28:
29:  long double square(long double a)
30:  {
31:    return a * a;
32:  }
```

Three overloaded square() functions are prototyped at lines 3–5. Each function has the identical name, but is considered distinct because each also differs in at least one parameter. Each is implemented at lines 19–32 as a separate function, just as each would be if their names were not the same.

Lines 13–15 illustrate how overloaded functions can clarify a program's meaning. Despite the different data types involved, it's obvious that each statement displays the square of an argument. This is much neater than having separate squareInt(), squareDouble(), and squareLongDouble() function names. Of course, it's up to you to overload functions that perform more or less the same jobs. If you name *every* function in your program the same (provided each one differs by at least one argument), your code might be as incomprehensible as a novel written using only one word.

Default Function Arguments

A relatively obscure, but important, C++ technique provides default argument values to function parameters. This can be useful when function calls typically need to supply only some, but not always all, arguments. Suppose you need a function that returns the sum of four int values, like this:

```
int sum(int a, int b, int c, int d)
{
  return a + b + c + d;
}
```

To call the function with only two argument values—let's call them v1 and v2—you need to supply zeros to the other two unused parameters:

```
cout << sum(v1, v2, 0, 0);
```

This is no great imposition, but it does require you to look up sum()'s documentation to determine what values to supply to unused parameters. Mistakenly passing −1 or another value to parameters c and d, which a careless programmer might do, causes the function to return the wrong sum.

Default function arguments are designed to guard against this condition by supplying values for unspecified arguments. To declare a default value, follow the parameter with an equal sign and a value in the function's prototype:

```
int sum(int a, int b, int c = 0, int d = 0);
```

Declared like this, sum() requires only two arguments, but can have up to four. The default values must come last in the function's parameter list, and must appear only in the function's prototype. If arguments are not specified for c and d, those parameters are given the default values listed in the prototype. These statements are now allowed:

```
cout << sum(1, 2);        // a == 1, b == 2, c == 0, d == 0
cout << sum(1, 2, 3);     // a == 1, b == 2, c == 3, d == 0
cout << sum(1, 2, 3, 4);  // a == 1, b == 2, c == 3, d == 4
```

Listing 12.14, CENTER.CPP, shows a more practical example of default function arguments. The program uses the CRT.C module from Chapter 11, "Input and Output." Copy CRT.C to your current working directory and rename the file CRT.CPP. (Installing the supplied disk stores a copy of crt.h and CRT.C, renamed CRT.CPP, in the same directory as CENTER.CPP). Compile with the DOS command **bcc -c crt**. You must recompile the module for use with C++ programs. The CRT module's *statements* are no different, but the compiled CRT.OBJ file must contain the correct information for linking to C++ programs. After compiling CRT, compile and link CENTER with the command **bcc center crt.obj**. Run the program, and enter a small string, which is centered on-screen in a variety of styles, selected by default function arguments.

Listing 12.14. CENTER.CPP (Uses default function arguments).

```
1:  #include <iostream.h>
2:  #include <stdio.h>
3:  #include <string.h>
4:  #include "crt.h"
5:
6:  void Center(int x, int y, char *s, int width = 0, int fill = '-');
7:
8:  main()
9:  {
10:    char s[128];   // String to center
11:    int length;    // Length of string
12:
13:    cout << "Enter a string: ";
14:    cin.getline(s, 128);
15:    length = strlen(s);
```

continues

Listing 12.14. continued

```
16:    clrscr();
17:    Center(40, 10, s);                    // All defaults
18:    Center(40, 12, s, length + 8);        // One default
19:    Center(40, 14, s, length + 16, '*');  // No defaults
20:    CrtGotoxy(0, 23);
21:    return 0;
22:  }
23:
24:  void Center(int x, int y, char *s, int width, int fill)
25:  {
26:    int wd2;     // Width divided by 2
27:    int c;       // for-loop control variable
28:
29:    if (width > 0) {
30:      wd2 = width / 2;
31:      for (c = x - wd2; c <= x + wd2; c++)
32:        CrtPokew(y, c, (CRT_NORMAL * 256) + fill);
33:    }
34:    CrtGotoxy(x - (strlen(s) / 2), y);
35:    cputs(s);
36:  }
```

Function Center() (see line 6) uses several parameters to center a string on-screen. The function's parameters are

int x, int y	Coordinate (x,y) around which the string is centered.
char *s	A pointer to a null-terminated string.
int width = 0	The horizontal width in which the string should be centered. If nonzero, this many characters centered at (x,y) are displayed using the character value indicated by parameter fill.
int fill = '-'	A character value displayed around the centered string.

Lines 17–19 demonstrate different ways to call Center(). Line 17 is the simplest case, using default values for width and fill, which have no effect on the output. Line 18 supplies a width value, causing the string to be centered with default dashes on either side. Line 19 supplies arguments to all parameters, overriding the defaults.

References

In Chapter 9, "Pointers," you learned how to create pointers as aliases that address other variables. These lines:

```
int i = 1234;
int *p = &i;
```

declare an `int` variable `i` initialized to 1234, and an `int` pointer `p`, initialized to the address of `i`. Given these declarations, these two statements:

```
cout << "i == " << i << '\n';
cout << "i == " << *p << '\n';
```

each display `i`'s value. The expression `*p` dereferences `p`, telling the compiler to use the value that `p` addresses.

Using pointers as aliases for other values poses the danger that, if a statement alters the address stored in the pointer, that pointer no longer refers to the same value. If such a change is unintentional, a serious bug might result. Also, to use a pointer's addressed value requires dereferencing the pointer, leading to confusing code studded with asterisks.

C++ offers a safer alternative to pointer aliases. By declaring a *reference* variable, you create an object that, like a pointer, refers to another value, but unlike a pointer, is permanently tied to its alter ego. A reference to a value *always* refers to that value.

There are three main uses for references: as variables, as function parameters, and as function results.

References as Variables

As a variable, a reference *refers* to another value. You probably won't use references this way in practice, but the technique demonstrates how references work. Compile and run Listing 12.15, REFVAR.CPP, which shows four ways to address and display an integer value.

Listing 12.15. REFVAR.CPP (Demonstrates reference variables).

```
 1:  #include <iostream.h>
 2:
 3:  main()
 4:  {
 5:    int ivar = 1234;    // Variable assigned value
 6:    int *iptr = &ivar;  // Pointer assigned ivar's address
 7:    int &iref = ivar;   // Reference associated with ivar
 8:    int *p = &iref;     // Pointer assigned iref's address
 9:
10:    cout << "ivar  == " << ivar << '\n';
11:    cout << "*iptr == " << *iptr << '\n';
12:    cout << "iref  == " << iref << '\n';
13:    cout << "*p    == " << *p << '\n';
14:    return 0;
15:  }
```

Lines 5–8 declare four variables. First is a simple `int`, `ivar`, initialized to 1234. Next is a pointer to `int`, named `iptr`, and assigned the address of `ivar`. The third declaration creates a reference. The line

```
int &iref = ivar;
```

declares `iref` as a reference to an `int`. To `iref`, the declaration assigns `ivar`—not `ivar`'s value, but its address in memory. Following the declaration, `iref` points to `ivar` much like a pointer. As line 12 shows, the statement

```
cout << "iref  == " << iref << '\n';
```

displays 1234, `ivar`'s value. It does so by using the reference `iref` to refer to `ivar`'s location in memory.

The fourth declaration at line 8 creates another pointer, `p`, assigned the address stored in `iref`. Lines 6 and 8 have identical results: Both lines create pointers that address `ivar`. As line 13 proves, dereferencing the pointer with the expression `*p` accesses `ivar`'s value. Figure 12.2 illustrates the relationships of the variables in Listing 12.15. As the illustration suggests, using `iref` is similar to using a dereferenced pointer such as `*p`. Both expressions access `ivar`'s value, 1234.

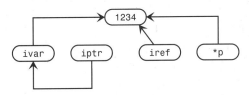

Figure 12.2. Relationships of variables in Listing 12.15, REFVAR.CPP.

Remember one rule when using references: *Once initialized, a reference may not be reassigned.* In REFVAR.CPP, you cannot declare a new integer variable and set `iref` to refer to it:

```
int anotherInt;
iref = anotherInt;   // ???
```

This does not cause `iref` to refer to `anotherInt`. It assigns `anotherInt`'s value to the object to which `iref` refers—in other words, to `ivar`. You may also assign new literal values to the object of a reference. For example, this statement:

```
iref = 4321;
```

changes `ivar`'s value to 4321. You might find these rules easier to memorize if you think of references as unchanging aliases, similar—but not identical—to pointer aliases.

As a related rule, references must be initialized in their declarations. Line 7, for example, cannot be written

```
int &iref;   // ???
```

Unlike a pointer, which can be declared in an uninitialized state, or set to null if the pointer does not address valid data, a reference must always refer to an object. There is no equivalent of a null pointer for a reference.

NOTE: References do not have to be preinitialized in four special cases: when declared `extern`, when used as function parameters, when used as function return types, or in class declarations. (See Chapter 13, "Programming with Classes.")

No operators apply directly to references. Operators apply only to referenced objects. If you add this statement to Listing 12.15, between lines 13 and 14:

```
iref++;
```

the compiler generates code to increment `ivar`, the variable to which `iref` refers. The statement does not affect `iref` directly in any way.

References may also refer to constants; however, you may not assign literal values directly to a reference. The declaration

```
int &iref = 1234;   // ???
```

does not compile because 1234 is not an object to which `iref` can refer. You may, however, declare a `const` reference to a legitimate object with programming such as

```
int x = 1234;          // Declare and initialize int object
const int &iref = x;   // Declare const reference iref for x
```

References as Function Parameters

Despite having intriguing properties, on their own, reference variables are rarely of much use. Rather than use a reference to refer to another variable, you may as well just use the variable itself.

As function parameters, however, references are far more versatile, and offer a handy alternative to pointer parameters. Listing 12.16, BOX.CPP, demonstrates how to use references this way, creating function parameters that refer to the actual arguments that statements pass to those parameters. The program is similar to BOX.C from Chapter 11, "Input and Output." Compare the two listings to see how BOX.CPP uses reference parameters where the original program used pointers.

NOTE: Listing 12.16 requires the CRT.OBJ module, compiled as explained earlier, for Listing 12.14, CENTER.CPP. Compile BOX.CPP with the command **bcc box crt.obj**.

Listing 12.16. BOX.CPP (Demonstrates reference function parameters).

```
 1:  #include <iostream.h>
 2:  #include "crt.h"
 3:
 4:  void GetCoords(int &toprow, int &topcol, int &botrow, int &botcol);
 5:  void DrawBox(int toprow, int topcol, int botrow, int botcol);
 6:
 7:  main()
 8:  {
 9:    int toprow, topcol, botrow, botcol;
10:
11:    GetCoords(toprow, topcol, botrow, botcol);
12:    CrtGotoxy(0, 0);
13:    CrtEeop();
14:    DrawBox(toprow, topcol, botrow, botcol);
15:    CrtGotoxy(0, 23);
16:    return 0;
17:  }
18:
19:  void GetCoords(int &toprow, int &topcol, int &botrow, int &botcol)
20:  {
21:    cout << "\nEnter top row and column (ex: 3 7): ";
22:    cin >> toprow >> topcol;
23:    cout << "Enter bottom row and column (ex: 20 64): ";
24:    cin >> botrow >> botcol;
25:  }
26:
27:  void DrawBox(int toprow, int topcol, int botrow, int botcol)
28:  {
29:    CrtBox(0, CRT_NORMAL, toprow, topcol, botrow, botcol);
30:  }
```

Function GetCoords() is prototyped at line 4. The function declares four int reference parameters, toprow, topcol, botrow, and botcol. Line 11 calls GetCoords(), passing as arguments the four int variables declared at line 9. Inside the function (see lines 19–25), two input stream statements read values directly into the arguments passed to GetCoords(). The reference parameters *refer* directly to those arguments.

Reference and pointer parameters are closely related. In fact, references can be implemented internally by a C++ compiler as pointers. To hammer home the idea, consider this small function:

```
void f(int *ip)
{
  *ip = 1234;
}
```

Inside the function, pointer ip addresses an argument passed to the function with a statement such as

```
f(&ivar);   // Pass ivar by address
```

In the function, the statement *ip = 1234; assigns 1234 to ivar, which is passed by address to f(). Now consider the same function using a reference parameter:

```
void f(int &ir)
{
  ir = 1234;
}
```

Pointer ip is replaced by a reference ir, to which the function assigns 1234. Assignments like this give values to the referenced object. The statement

```
f(ivar);  // Pass ivar by reference
```

passes ivar *by reference* to f(), causing ir to refer to ivar, thus setting ivar to 1234.

References as Function Results

Functions may return references to objects, provided those objects persist when the function is not active. (In other words, functions may not return references to local automatic variables.) A function declared as

```
double &ref(double d);
```

requires one double argument and returns a reference to a double object, presumably one that is declared elsewhere.

Listing 12.17, REFFUNC.CPP, demonstrates how to use reference functions to hide a data structure's internal representation. The technique is important in large projects, especially when data structures might change, possibly causing a conventional ANSI C program to require extensive modifications. C++ reference functions can reduce these kinds of maintenance chores by providing access to structures such as arrays without tying the code to the data's physical properties. Compile and run the program, and when prompted, enter an index value from 0 to 9, and then enter a floating-point value. The program inserts your entry into an array of double values. To end the program, press Enter at the prompt.

Listing 12.17. REFFUNC.CPP (Demonstrates reference functions).

```
 1:  #include <iostream.h>
 2:  #include <stdlib.h>
 3:  #include <string.h>
 4:
 5:  #define FALSE 0
 6:  #define TRUE 1
 7:  #define SIZE 10
 8:  #define BUFLEN 20
 9:
10:  double &ref(int index);
11:  void ShowArray(void);
12:
13:  double array[SIZE];
14:
15:  main()
16:  {
17:    int done = FALSE, index;
18:    char buffer[BUFLEN];
19:
20:    for (index = 0; index < SIZE; index++)
21:      ref(index) = index;  // Assign to reference function!
22:    while (!done) {
23:      ShowArray();
24:      cout << "\nEnter index from 0 to 9, Enter to quit: ";
25:      cin.getline(buffer, BUFLEN);
26:      done = (strlen(buffer) == 0);
27:      if (!done) {
28:        index = atoi(buffer);
29:        cout << "Enter floating point value: ";
30:        cin.getline(buffer, BUFLEN);
31:        ref(index) = atof(buffer);
32:      }
```

continues

Listing 12.17. continued

```
33:    }
34:    return 0;
35:  }
36:
37:  double &ref(int index)
38:  {
39:    if ((index < 0) || (index >= SIZE))
40:      index = 0;
41:    return array[index];  // Return reference to array element
42:  }
43:
44:  void ShowArray(void)
45:  {
46:    cout << "\nArray:\n";
47:    for (int i = 0; i < SIZE; i++)
48:      cout << "[" << i << "] == " << array[i] << '\n';
49:  }
```

A global array of double values is declared at line 13. In a larger program, this array might be stored in a separate module. Although the program displays and inserts values into this array, it does so without referring directly to the global data structure anywhere in function main(). Thanks to a reference function, it is possible to change the internal storage of the double values (perhaps using a linked list rather than an array), and the program still operates as before, without a single change to any of main()'s statements.

Line 10 declares a reference function named ref(). The function returns a reference to a double object identified by an int parameter index. Because the function returns a reference to a double object, the function name may appear on the left side of an assignment operator, as shown at line 21. This is probably the most common use for reference functions. The statement at line 21 assigns a value to the double object referred to by ref(index). Exactly how that object is stored is immaterial. The reference function hides the data's internal representation.

Line 31 shows another use of the reference function, assigning the double result from function atof() to ref(index). If ref were an array, this statement might be written as

```
ref[index] = atof(buffer);
```

A change to the data's storage mechanism, then, would require a corresponding change to the code, which in turn requires additional testing, debugging, and so on. Reference functions can help reduce such undesirable changes.

The reference function is implemented at lines 37–42. An `if` statement forces `index` into the proper range, after which the `return` statement at line 41 returns a reference to one of the `double` values in the global `array`. It's important to understand that line 41 does *not* return a `double` value. It returns a *reference* to a `double` object. If `ref()` returns a `double` value, then the function could not be used on the left side of an assignment operator, as it is in `main()`.

Summary

- C++ is more than just an object-oriented version of C. C++ has many features that improve and extend C. Most of what you have learned so far about ANSI C applies to C++, and most ANSI C programs are C++ compatible. C++'s more advanced features, however, are not found in ANSI C.

- Compiling a program file named with the extension .CPP indicates to Borland C++ that the file contains C++ programming. Header file extensions don't matter. Some C++ programmers name their header files with the extension .hpp. This book uses .h.

- C++ recognizes all ANSI C keywords, operators, and other language elements. C++ adds several new keywords and operators to ANSI C.

- Function prototypes are required in C++ programs. Before a statement may call a function, the compiler must have processed that function's prototype.

- Other new C++ features include stricter type checking, a reduced need for `typedef`, and the definition of a `char` as an 8-bit byte. In C++, literal characters such as `'X'` are type `char`. In ANSI C, literal characters are type `int`.

- Use the C++ comment symbol, `//`, to begin a comment that extends to the end of the current line. C++ and ANSI C comments (using brackets `/*` and `*/`) may be mixed in the same program. C++ comments may be nested inside ANSI C comments.

- I/O streams use the `<<` (put to) and `>>` (get from) operators to write and read data. The output stream `cout` is tied to the system's standard output. The input stream `cin` is tied to the standard input. Use output stream `cerr` to display error messages on the console.

- The safest way to read character strings into buffers is to call an input stream's get() member function. Use cin.get() or cin.getline() to read strings from the system's standard input. Member functions belong to a class—one of C++'s major contributions to programming (see Chapter 13, "Programming with Classes").

- Use member functions such as cout.width() to set the column width for a subsequent output stream statement. Use modifiers dec, hex, and oct to specify decimal, hexadecimal, and octal output formats. You can also call standard functions such as sprintf() to prepare strings for writing to output streams.

- Declarations may appear anywhere in any C++ statement block. You can, for example, declare a variable inside a for loop statement's braces. Such a variable's scope extends only to its declaring block. You must declare variables, however, before you can use them.

- When a local variable has the same name as a global variable, the local name hides the global name. Use the scope resolution operator :: to unhide a global variable. If a local variable is named count, the expression ::count refers to a global count.

- Some C++ authorities recommend using const rather than #define to declare symbolic constants. The compiler can check the data types of const objects in expressions. Also, Turbo Debugger recognizes const, but not #defined, names. Global const values, however, occupy space in the program's data segment and require time-wasting memory references to use. In practice, and despite published advice to the contrary, C++ programmers use #define just as successfully as C programmers do.

- An inline function's statements are injected directly into the compiled code in place of a function call. Use inline functions to avoid making function calls, which can waste time inside tight loops that must run as fast as possible. Be aware that the inline keyword, such as register, is only a suggestion to the compiler, not an ironclad command. An inline function may or may not be compiled inline. (Inline functions are never compiled inline when preparing code for debugging.)

- Use the operators new and delete to allocate and free heap memory for dynamic variables. In C++ programs, new and delete take the place of conventional memory-management functions such as malloc(), calloc(), free(), and others. You may still use these functions in C++ programs. Memory allocated by `new`, however, *must* be freed by `delete`. Memory allocated by `malloc()` must be freed by `free()`.

- Function names may be overloaded. That is, a program may have two or more functions of the same names as long as those functions differ in at least one parameter. Function overloading helps reduce the need to invent arbitrarily unique function names such as `DrawCircle` and `DrawEllipse`. It's your responsibility to use function overloading sensibly. It's probably never wise to name *all* functions the same!

- Default function arguments supply values for parameters. Declare default values after any other parameters listed in the function's prototype.

- A reference, declared with `&`, *refers* to another object. Unlike a pointer alias, which also can refer to an object, a reference must be initialized when declared (except in certain cases), and a reference may not be made to refer to a different object later on.

- References are typically used to declare function parameters that refer to the actual arguments passed to the function. In this way, references are similar to pointer parameters, but are easier to use. References are also sometimes returned as function results—a useful technique for hiding data storage details, thus allowing those details to be changed without requiring corresponding changes to the code.

Exercises

12.1 Using I/O streams, write a filter program that converts a text file to all uppercase.

12.2 Revise Listing 12.4, GETVAL.CPP, to repeat its prompt upon detecting an error on the input stream.

12.3 Design and test an inline function `min()`, which returns the lesser of two integer values.

12.4 Using the `min()` inline function from the preceding exercise, write a benchmark program that reports the amount of time saved compared to a normal function call.

12.5 Design a set of overloaded functions that return the absolute value of an `int`, a `long`, and a `double` value.

12.6 In Chapter 9, "Pointers," Listing 9.11, READSTR.C, includes a function that reads a string into a dynamic variable stored on the heap. Rewrite this program using C++'s new operator and I/O streams.

12.7 Modify Listing 12.17, REFFUNC.CPP, to store `double` values in a linked list rather than an array. The program should operate exactly as before, and thanks to the use of a reference function, statements in `main()` should not require any modifications.

13

Programming with Classes

You'd have to be living facedown in a moon crater not to have heard about object-oriented programming, or OOP as it is comically known. OOP is the programming paradigm of the 1990s, the model (some say) upon which all the world's software soon will be built. There are still a few doubters who resist the move to OOP, but the predictions of OOP's wide acceptance appear to be coming true, and those who ignore OOP risk missing the major contribution of C++ to programming—the class.

Simply stated, a class is an object-oriented tool for creating new data types. C++ has many built-in types such as int, double, and char. Classes give you the means to create new types that, due in part to OOP principles, behave in ways nearly identical to those that come with the language.

Why Use Object-Oriented Programming?

Many experts agree that OOP and C++ classes help reduce complexity, especially in large programs of about 10,000 or more lines. OOP also encourages programmers to reuse existing code rather than rewrite functions from scratch. It's common for conventional C programmers to rewrite the same code over and over because *it's too much trouble to reuse existing, tested modules.* C++ classes are easy to reuse and extend, and OOP code tends to evolve from existing modules the way trees grow by extending their branches. Rather than replant low-level code into every new program, with OOP you write programs that grow naturally from your current crop of tested modules.

If this is your initial exposure to OOP, don't be concerned if OOP's advantages elude you at first. C++ lets you learn OOP at your own speed. Unlike so-called "pure" OOP languages such as SmallTalk and Actor, C++ is a hybrid programming language that combines conventional and OOP methods. This means you can use what you already know about C++ while you learn OOP; you don't have to choke down all of OOP's details at once.

This chapter, as well as Chapter 14, "Inheritance and Polymorphism," and Chapter 15, "Advanced Topics in C++," present basic information about C++ classes and explain how classes mesh with OOP's three main benefits:

    Encapsulation
    Inheritance
    Polymorphism

Understanding the importance of encapsulation requires a brief trip back to conventional C programming. C++ classes and encapsulation can unclog one of conventional programming's most common and most constricting bottlenecks—a change to a fundamental data structure in a program nearing completion.

Trouble in Paradise

Conventional C programming techniques often make programmers work harder than necessary. For instance, consider how you might represent the date and time—a typical task that many, if not most, programs need to do. In ANSI C, you could declare a struct like this:

```
struct TTime {
  int year;
  int month;
  int day;
  int hour;
  int minute;
};
```

TTime's members store the component values of a single date and time. The extra T in TTime stands for *type*, a convention that helps distinguish data type names from others. Given this structure, you can declare a TTime variable such as

```
TTime appointment;
```

Notice that C++ does not require the struct keyword before TTime as in ANSI C. Given this declaration, you can assign values to appointment's members with statements such as

```
appointment.year = 1996;
appointment.month = 7;
appointment.day = 14;
appointment.hour = 8;
appointment.minute = 30;
```

A program that uses lots of TTime structures probably needs functions to display dates and times, to change structure members, to compare two dates, and so on. You could write a display function like this:

```
void Display(struct TTime *tp)
{
  char buffer[32];
  sprintf(buffer, "Date: %02d/%02d/%04d  Time: %02d:%02d\n",
    tp->month, tp->day, tp->year, tp->hour, tp->minute);
  cout << buffer;
}
```

To display a date and time, a statement can pass to Display() the address of a TTime structure such as appointment:

```
Display(&appointment);
```

So far, all is well in paradise. Consider, however, a typical problem that can cause carefully written conventional code to fall from grace. After designing a struct like

TTime and writing a zillion date and time functions, you discover a superior way to store the date and time that would greatly improve your program's runtime speed. For example, you might use a long integer that represents the number of seconds from a fixed date. This change also makes it possible to use date and time library functions that recognize the date and time stored in this way.

Too bad you didn't think of this great idea earlier! To change the program's representation at this late stage, you have to

- Modify the TTime structure, deleting the current members and adding a single new long integer member. (You might even decide not to use a structure after all.)

- Revise all functions such as Display() that declare TTime parameters or that return TTime structures, pointers, or references.

- Hunt for and modify statements that assign or use component values in TTime structures. These statements must be revised to use the new date and time format.

In a large program with thousands of lines, the prospect of tracking down every use of TTime is disheartening. The change to the data structure forces you to revise code that has already been tested, thus requiring new debugging sessions and wasting valuable development time. The old rule of thumb is *let the data structure the code.* In the real world, however, data specifications are likely to change during a program's development, making extra work for programmers.

With conventional programming, the data representations you choose early in a program's development limit your freedom to make changes later. With OOP, data may change with only limited effects on the code. C++ classes can restrict a program's access to internal data storage details, so changes to data representations do not necessarily affect every use of that information. Consider how you might store the date and time in a class and take advantage of these benefits.

Introducing the Class

A class is a kind of structure that encapsulates data and functions into a handy package. (See Figure 13.1.)

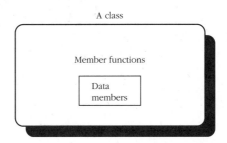

Figure 13.1. A class encapsulates data and functions.

Here's the previous TTime structure rewritten as a class and encapsulating data and functions:

```
class TTime {
public:                 // Access specifier
  int year;             // Data member
  int month;            //     "     "
  int day;              //     "     "
  int hour;             //     "     "
  int minute;           //     "     "
  void Display(void);   // Member function
};
```

The class looks very much like the TTime struct, except that it begins with the class keyword. Again, by convention, the extra *T* in the class name reminds you that TTime is a data type. Braces enclose the six members of the class, which are preceded by public, one of three access specifiers that limit the ways programs may use members of a class. Later, you'll examine two other access specifiers, private and protected. The public access specifier makes the members available to all users of the class.

Data members in a class are exactly like data members in a struct. Data members such as year, month, and day may be variables, pointers, references, arrays, structures, and so on. They may also be class objects. However, members may not use the storage class specifiers auto, extern, or register.

Class member functions such as Display() are declared as function prototypes. Presumably, member functions such as Display() in TTime perform some kind of operation on the class's data members. The actual function statements are provided at another place in the program.

Listing 13.1, CLASS1.CPP, uses the TTime class in a C++ program and demonstrates how to implement a member function. Compile the program and run it to display a sample date and time.

Listing 13.1. CLASS1.CPP (Demonstrates TTime class).

```
 1:  #include <iostream.h>
 2:  #include <stdio.h>
 3:
 4:  class TTime {
 5:  public:                  // Access specifier
 6:    int year;              // Data member
 7:    int month;             //    "    "
 8:    int day;               //    "    "
 9:    int hour;              //    "    "
10:    int minute;            //    "    "
11:    void Display(void);   // Member function
12:  };
13:
14:  main()
15:  {
16:    TTime appointment;   // Object of type TTime
17:
18:    appointment.month = 7;        // Initialize object data members
19:    appointment.day = 14;
20:    appointment.year = 1996;
21:    appointment.hour = 8;
22:    appointment.minute = 30;
23:    cout << "Appointment == ";
24:    appointment.Display();        // Call member function
25:    cout << '\n';
26:    return 0;
27:  }
28:
29:  void TTime::Display(void)
30:  {
31:    char s[32];
32:    sprintf(s, "Date: %02d/%02d/%04d  Time: %02d:%02d\n",
33:      month, day, year, hour, minute);
34:    cout << s;
35:  }
```

Lines 4–12 declare the TTime class. Typically, class declarations are written in header files, but you may also insert them directly into a program module as done here.

Skip to lines 29–35, where the Display() member function is implemented. There are two main differences between a member function's implementation and the implementation of a common function:

- The member function name is prefaced by the class name and a scope resolution operator. The function header void TTime::Display(void) tells the compiler that Display() is a member of the TTime class. Because the class name uniquely qualifies the member function's name, the program may have other functions and other class member functions named Display() without conflict.

- Inside the member function, statements have direct access to the class's members. For example, lines 32–33 refer directly to the month, day, year, hour, and minute data members of the TTime class.

The main program uses the TTime class much as it would any other data type. First, line 16 declares appointment as an object of type TTime. The declaration creates a class object, also called an *instance,* of the class type. The class TTime is a mere schematic that describes the format of the class members. You must create an object such as appointment of the class type in order to use the class.

Next, lines 18–22 assign values to appointment's data members, initializing a date and time. Line 24 then calls the Display() member function, which displays appointment's date and time. All these lines use dot notation to reference a member of the class object. Use dot notation to refer to a class object's public data members (those preceded by the public access specifier) just as you refer to the members of a struct object. When such a member is a function (see line 24), C++ calls the function, which typically performs some action upon the class object's data. Line 24, for example, calls the Display() function to display the value of the data members in appointment. A program might have other TTime class objects declared as

```
TTime today;
TTime tomorrow;
TTime yesterday;
```

These objects could be assigned values and then displayed with the statements

```
today.Display();        // Display value of today class object
tomorrow.Display();     // Display value of tomorrow class object
yesterday.Display();    // Display value of yesterday class object
```

> **NOTE:** C++ permits structures and unions as well as classes to have member functions. In fact, in CLASS1.CPP, if you change `class` to `struct` and remove the `public` access specifier, the program works as before. (Members of a `struct` or `union` are public by default.) In practice, however, member functions are rarely of much practical use in structures and unions, and are therefore more commonly declared in classes.

CLASS1.CPP does nothing to prevent the problem with changes to data representations mentioned earlier. All data members in the TTime class are public, and are therefore directly accessible by statements such as those at lines 18–22. A change to the class's data members would require reprogramming all such statements—the sort of extra work that can cause software release dates to slip.

Listing 13.2, CLASS2.CPP, declares a new and improved TTime class that uses member functions to access a class object's data members. The new class permits the data members to change more readily than before, helping to keep the project on course.

Listing 13.2. CLASS2.CPP (New and improved TTime class).

```
 1:  #include <iostream.h>
 2:  #include <stdio.h>
 3:
 4:  class TTime {
 5:  private:
 6:    int year;
 7:    int month;
 8:    int day;
 9:    int hour;
10:    int minute;
11:  public:
12:    void Display(void);
13:    void GetTime(int &m, int &d, int &y, int &hr, int &min);
14:    void SetTime(int m, int d, int y, int hr, int min);
15:  };
16:
```

```
17:   main()
18:   {
19:     TTime appointment;
20:     int month, day, year, hour, minute;
21:
22:     appointment.SetTime(7, 14, 1996, 8, 30);
23:     cout << "Appointment == ";
24:     appointment.Display();
25:     appointment.GetTime(month, day, year, hour, minute);
26:     appointment.SetTime(month, day, year, ++hour, minute);
27:     cout << "Next hour   == ";
28:     appointment.Display();
29:     return 0;
30:   }
31:
32:   void TTime::Display(void)
33:   {
34:     char s[32];
35:     sprintf(s, "Date: %02d/%02d/%04d  Time: %02d:%02d\n",
36:       month, day, year, hour, minute);
37:     cout << s;
38:   }
39:
40:   void TTime::GetTime(int &m, int &d, int &y, int &hr, int &min)
41:   {
42:     m = month;     // Return data members to caller
43:     d = day;
44:     y = year;
45:     hr = hour;
46:     min = minute;
47:   }
48:
49:   void TTime::SetTime(int m, int d, int y, int hr, int min)
50:   {
51:     month = m;     // Assign arguments to data members
52:     day = d;
53:     year = y;
54:     hour = hr;
55:     minute = min;
56:   }
```

The new TTime class has three additions. First, the private access specifier (line 5) makes the int data members (lines 6–10) private to the class. Because of this change, only class member functions may refer directly to these data members. Remember this rule: *A class's private members are available only to members of that class. Private members are invisible outside of the class.*

> **NOTE:** Members of a class are private by default, and technically speaking, line 5 in CLASS2.CPP is not required. For clarity, however, it's a good idea to mark private members with an explicit private access specifier.

A class may have multiple private and public sections, which may be in any order. You can repeat the private and public access specifiers (see lines 5 and 11) as many times as you want in a class declaration. Although not shown here, member functions may also be declared in a private section, but are more commonly public. You'll investigate a third access specifier, protected, in Chapter 14, "Inheritance and Polymorphism."

Two other additions to TTime are the GetTime() and SetTime() member functions (lines 13–14). Along with Display(), the three member functions limit access to the class's private parts. The only legitimate way to use TTime's private data members is to call one of the class's public member functions. As a direct result of encapsulating data and functions in a class, if the data representation changes, only the class's member functions need to be rewritten. Similarly, if a problem develops, debugging can begin with an examination of the class member functions because no other functions or statements in the program have direct access to TTime's private members. Figure 13.2 shows these concepts with arrows indicating access paths to a class's public and private members. Notice that functions in a class have access to one another—in other words, two class functions may call each other.

Lines 40–56 implement the two new member functions, GetTime() and SetTime(). As with Display(), the class name and scope resolution operator TTime:: preface the function names, informing the compiler that these functions belong to the class. The program could declare other GetTime() and SetTime() functions and member functions in other classes without conflicting with those that belong to TTime.

Inside the member function implementations, statements have direct access to the class's data members month, day, year, hour, and minute. (See Figure 13.2.) In GetTime(), for example, lines 42–46 pass the values of the class object's component members back to the caller's arguments by way of the five `int` reference parameters. In `SetTime()`, value parameters are assigned to the class object's data members.

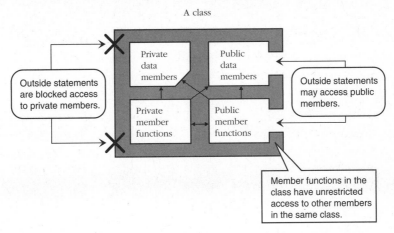

Figure 13.2. Classes restrict access to private members.

In the main program, because `TTime`'s data members are private to the class, it is no longer possible to assign values directly to a class object. For example, this statement from CLASS1.CPP:

```
appointment.month = 7;   // ???
```

does not compile in CLASS2.CPP because `month` is private to the `TTime` class and is therefore directly usable only by members of the same class. If you try to compile this statement, the compiler complains that "`TTime::month` is not accessible in function `main()`."

In the new program, to assign values to the `appointment` class object requires calling a member function. For example, line 22 executes the statement

```
appointment.SetTime(7, 14, 1996, 8, 30);
```

which sets `appointment`'s date and time to July 14, 1996, at 8:30. Similarly, line 25 calls `GetTime()` to copy `appointment`'s data member values to local variables declared at line 20. These values are then passed back to `SetTime()` with the `hour` incremented, thus upping the `appointment`'s hour. (Obviously, this is not the ideal way to change a date and time, but you'll take care of that problem later.)

Using Member Functions

Most classes are best declared in header files, which various modules can include to share the same classes. The next several listings expand the TTime class and illustrate a common way to declare and implement classes and programs in multiple modules.

Listing 13.3, time1.h, declares a new TTime class, similar to the one in CLASS2.CPP, but with a couple of additional member functions. As before, the new class has several private data members. Like most software projects under development, this program has a few inefficiencies. No matter—the problem of changing the class's data representation is easily dealt with, as you will soon see.

Listing 13.3. time1.h (Declares TTime class in a header file).

```
 1:  /* time1.h -- TTime class declaration */
 2:
 3:  #ifndef __TIME1_H
 4:  #define __TIME1_H  1  /* Prevent multiple #includes */
 5:
 6:  class TTime {
 7:  private:
 8:    int month;
 9:    int day;
10:    int year;
11:    int hour;
12:    int minute;
13:  public:
14:    void Display(void);
15:    void GetTime(int &m, int &d, int &y, int &hr, int &min);
16:    void SetTime(int m, int d, int y, int hr, int min);
17:    char *GetSTime(void);
18:    void ChangeTime(long nminutes);
19:  };
20:
21:  #endif  /* __TIME1_H */
```

Lines 3, 4, and 21 prevent the time1.h header file from being included more than once. (You saw this same trick in Chapter 11, "Input and Output," in Listing 11.2, crt.h.) Storing the TTime class declaration in a header file makes the class readily available to other modules.

A separate module, Listing 13.4, TIME1.CPP, implements the TTime class member functions. This organization of classes into headers and implementation files is typical. Declare one or more classes in a header file ending in .h, and implement the class member functions in a separate file ending in .CPP. To compile this module from DOS, enter **bcc -c time1**. To compile from an IDE, make TIME1.CPP's window current, and press Alt+F9.

Listing 13.4. TIME1.CPP (Implements the TTime class).

```
 1:  /* time1.cpp -- TTime class implementation */
 2:
 3:  #include <iostream.h>
 4:  #include <stdio.h>
 5:  #include <dos.h>
 6:  #include <string.h>
 7:  #include "time1.h"
 8:
 9:  // Display date and time
10:  void TTime::Display(void)
11:  {
12:    char s[30];
13:    sprintf(s, "Date: %02d/%02d/%04d  Time: %02d:%02d",
14:      month, day, year, hour, minute );
15:    cout << s << '\n';
16:  }
17:
18:  // Return current date and time data members
19:  void TTime::GetTime(int &m, int &d, int &y, int &hr, int &min)
20:  {
21:    m = month;     // Pass object's data members to caller
22:    d = day;
23:    y = year;
24:    hr = hour;
25:    min = minute;
26:  }
```

continues

Listing 13.4. continued

```
27:
28:   // Set date and time data members
29:   void TTime::SetTime(int m, int d, int y, int hr, int min)
30:   {
31:     month = m;      // Assign arguments to object's data members
32:     day = d;
33:     year = y;
34:     hour = hr;
35:     minute = min;
36:   }
37:
38:   // Return string representation of date and time
39:   char *TTime::GetSTime(void)
40:   {
41:     char buffer[40];  // Plenty of space
42:     char *cp;   // Pointer to function result
43:
44:     sprintf(buffer, "Date: %02d/%02d/%04d  Time: %02d:%02d\n",
45:       month, day, year, hour, minute );
46:     cp = strdup(buffer);  // Trim to smallest possible size
47:     return cp;
48:   }
49:
50:   // Add nminutes (which may be negative) to current time
51:   void TTime::ChangeTime(long nminutes)
52:   {
53:     struct date ds;
54:     struct time ts;
55:     long timeinsecs;
56:
57:     ds.da_year = year;
58:     ds.da_mon = month;
59:     ds.da_day = day;
60:     ts.ti_hour = hour;
61:     ts.ti_min = minute;
62:     ts.ti_sec = 0;
63:     ts.ti_hund = 0;
64:     timeinsecs = dostounix(&ds, &ts);
65:     timeinsecs += (nminutes * 60);
66:     unixtodos(timeinsecs, &ds, &ts);
```

```
67:    year = ds.da_year;
68:    month = ds.da_mon;
69:    day = ds.da_day;
70:    hour = ts.ti_hour;
71:    minute = ts.ti_min;
72:  }
```

Before examining how TIME1.CPP implements the TTime class, compile and run Listing 13.5, APPOINT1.CPP, a sample program that uses the class to display a page from a fictitious appointment calendar. (Lucky for you, your calendar shows no appointments—you have the entire day to yourself.) To compile the program from DOS, enter **bcc appoint1 time1**, or you can enter **bcc appoint1 time1.obj** if you have already compiled the TIME1 module.

NOTE: From an IDE, the easiest way to compile APPOINT1.CPP is to use Project|Open to create a new project named APPOINT1.PRJ. Use the Project|Add command to add APPOINT1.CPP and TIME1.CPP to the project. You can then press F9 to compile and link the program. You can also press Ctrl+F9 to compile and run the program. To compile other multifile programs in this chapter using an IDE, create a project and add the main program (the one containing function main()). Then add one or more .CPP modules used by the program. You don't have to add .h header files to projects.

Listing 13.5. APPOINT1.CPP (Displays a sample appointment calendar).

```
1:  #include <iostream.h>
2:  #include <stdio.h>
3:  #include "time1.h"
4:
5:  main()
6:  {
7:    TTime appointment;
8:
```

continues

Listing 13.5. continued

```
 9:    appointment.SetTime(7, 21, 1996, 8, 30);
10:    for (int slots = 1; slots <= 17; slots++) {
11:      appointment.Display();
12:      appointment.ChangeTime(30);
13:    }
14:    return 0;
15:  }
```

Line 3 includes time1.h, making the TTime class declaration available to the program. Line 7 declares an appointment class object of type TTime. Line 9 assigns to appointment date and time component values, after which a for loop displays a series of appointments, 30 minutes apart. Line 12 calls the ChangeTime() member function to add 30 minutes to the date and time in appointment. The program directly references no class data members. In all cases, the program calls member functions to perform actions on appointment.

Now that you've seen how to use the TTime class, skip back to TIME1.CPP (Listing 13.4), which implements the class member functions. Some of the programming is repeated from before. New member functions are GetSTime() (lines 39–48), which returns a string representation of a TTime object's date and time, and ChangeTime() (lines 51–72), which adds or subtracts a specified number of minutes from an object's date and time.

These two new member functions are prefaced with TTime:: to identify them to the compiler as members of the TTime class. Member function GetSTime() calls sprintf() (see line 44) to prepare a string with the private data members month, day, year, hour, and minute inserted with the appropriate punctuation. Line 46 then calls strdup() to copy this raw string to a new one on the heap. Line 47 returns a pointer to this string, which the program can delete by calling free().

Member function ChangeTime() calls two library functions, dostounix() and unixtodos(), to convert the class object's date and time to and from a long integer format. This makes it easy for line 65 to add or subtract the specified number of minutes passed to the member function as parameter nminutes. In the main program (Listing 13.5, line 12), the statement

```
appointment.ChangeTime(30);
```

calls the ChangeTime() member function for the appointment class object to advance the object's time by 30 minutes.

When a statement such as this calls a member function, C++ passes to the function the address of the object, in this case, the address of `appointment`. Inside the member function, the object's address is available through a special keyword named `this`. All member functions receive a `this` pointer, which addresses the class object for which the member function was called. In Listing 13.5, line 12 passes to member function `ChangeTime()` a `this` pointer that addresses `appointment`. Literally speaking, `this` is how member functions refer to the class objects for which they are called.

You may use `this` as a pointer to an object of the class type. For example, line 21 of Listing 13.4 in member function `GetTime()` could be written as

```
m = this->month;
```

Translated to plain English, this statement assigns to reference parameter `m` the value of the `month` data member in the class object addressed by `this`. In most cases, however, you do not need to use `this` explicitly. The statement

```
m = month;
```

refers by default to the `month` data member in the class object addressed by `this`.

Modifying Private Data Members

Better ways to represent data often become apparent midway in the mad dash to a software project's deadline. As suggested earlier, storing the date and time as the number of seconds from a fixed date (typically January 1, 1970 on DOS systems) is convenient and allows the use of other library functions that use this same date and time format.

Member function `ChangeTime()` in Listing 13.4 converts the date and time data members to a `long` integer (`timeinsecs`), thus wasting time and effort if this function is called frequently. Obviously, this function could be simplified if the date and time were already in `long` integer format.

Listings 13.6, time2.h, 13.7, TIME2.CPP, and 13.8, APPOINT2.CPP, make this change to `TTime`'s data representation. Compile the program as you did APPOINT1.CPP and TIME1.CPP, but use the filenames APPOINT2.CPP and TIME2.CPP.

Listing 13.6. time2.h (Modified TTime class).

```
 1:  /* time2.h -- TTime class declaration */
 2:
 3:  #ifndef __TIME2_H
 4:  #define __TIME2_H  1  /* Prevent multiple #includes */
 5:
 6:  class TTime {
 7:  private:
 8:    long dt;  // Date and time in seconds from January 1, 1970
 9:  public:
10:    void Display(void);
11:    void GetTime(int &m, int &d, int &y, int &hr, int &min);
12:    void SetTime(int m, int d, int y, int hr, int min);
13:    char *GetSTime(void);
14:    void ChangeTime(long nminutes);
15:  };
16:
17:  #endif  /* __TIME2_H */
```

Class TTime in time2.h is identical to TTime in time1.h, but declares only a single long private data member, dt. Gone are the individual month, day, year, hour, and minute component values. Despite this change, however, *the public member functions are the same,* and thus, statements that use the TTime class need no modifications.

The member functions themselves must be revised, but at least the revision work is limited to a set of easily identified functions. Listing 13.7, TIME2.CPP, carries out this task.

Listing 13.7. TIME2.CPP (Implements modified TTime class).

```
 1:  /* time2.cpp -- TTime class implementation */
 2:
 3:  #include <iostream.h>
 4:  #include <time.h>
 5:  #include <dos.h>
 6:  #include <string.h>
 7:  #include "time2.h"
 8:
```

```
 9:  // Display date and time
10:  void TTime::Display(void)
11:  {
12:    cout << ctime(&dt);
13:  }
14:
15:  // Return current date and time data members
16:  void TTime::GetTime(int &m, int &d, int &y, int &hr, int &min)
17:  {
18:    struct date ds;
19:    struct time ts;
20:
21:    unixtodos(dt, &ds, &ts);
22:    y = ds.da_year;
23:    m = ds.da_mon;
24:    d = ds.da_day;
25:    hr = ts.ti_hour;
26:    min = ts.ti_min;
27:  }
28:
29:  // Set dt data member
30:  void TTime::SetTime(int m, int d, int y, int hr, int min)
31:  {
32:    struct date ds;
33:    struct time ts;
34:
35:    ds.da_year = y;
36:    ds.da_mon = m;
37:    ds.da_day = d;
38:    ts.ti_hour = hr;
39:    ts.ti_min = min;
40:    ts.ti_sec = 0;
41:    ts.ti_hund = 0;
42:    dt = dostounix(&ds, &ts);
43:  }
44:
45:  // Return string representation of date and time
46:  char *TTime::GetSTime(void)
47:  {
48:    char *cp = strdup(ctime(&dt));
49:    return cp;
```

continues

Listing 13.7. continued

```
50:  }
51:
52:  // Add nminutes (which may be negative) to current time
53:  void TTime::ChangeTime(long nminutes)
54:  {
55:    dt += (nminutes * 60);
56:  }
```

The new module greatly improves the old, and has shrunk in size. Now that the date and time are stored as a long integer, line 12 simply calls the library function ctime() to convert the date and time to an ASCII string. Member functions GetTime() and PutTime() are somewhat more complex than before, because they now have to convert the date and time to and from individual parameters, using the unixtodos() and dostounix() library functions described earlier.

Member functions GetSTime() and ChangeTime() are vastly improved (see Lines 46–56). GetSTime() passes the result of ctime() directly to strdup() to return the date and time as a string. Best of all, ChangeTime() is now reduced to a single statement. Because the date and time are in the proper form, there's no need for all the conversion statements in the former version.

Changing data formats to simplify code is a time-honored programming optimization technique. With OOP and C++ classes, a change to a fundamental data structure does not necessarily require corresponding changes to statements that use that information. As demonstrated by Listing 13.8, APPOINT2.CPP, the main program in the sample project is oblivious to the major modifications made to the TTime class.

The new main program, APPOINT2.CPP, is identical to APPOINT1.CPP, except that line 3 includes header time2.h rather than time1.h. In this small example, the real benefits of OOP are practically nil. Even a 10,000-line program, however, with hundreds of TTime class objects would require no more effort to modify than this sample! Encapsulating data and functions in a class localizes changes to code by restricting access to data, thus minimizing the potential amount of revisions required later if the data representation changes.

Listing 13.8. APPOINT2.CPP (Displays sample appointment calendar).

```
 1:  #include <iostream.h>
 2:  #include <stdio.h>
 3:  #include "time2.h"
 4:
 5:  main()
 6:  {
 7:    TTime appointment;
 8:
 9:    appointment.SetTime(7, 21, 1996, 8, 30);
10:    for (int slots = 1; slots <= 17; slots++) {
11:      appointment.Display();
12:      appointment.ChangeTime(30);
13:    }
14:    return 0;
15:  }
```

Inline Member Functions

So far, you've seen relatively simple examples of class declarations. C++ offers many other goodies that you can use in classes. For example, using member functions to access class data members rightly brings up the concern of efficiency. Calling a member function like SetTime() to assign values to a class object's data members takes more time than simply assigning values directly to those members—if, that is, they were public.

Although that observation is true, remember that one of the major goals of using classes is to restrict access to data, and therefore promote easier maintenance in the future. How much are a few function calls worth to the stability of your program and the ease of making future modifications?

In most cases, calling member functions instead of accessing class data members directly has little significant impact on a program's performance. There are times, however, when utmost efficiency is required. For those times, C++ permits classes to declare inline member functions. Though inline member functions are used exactly as others, no function calls are made in the compiled code. Rather, an inline member function's statements *are inserted directly into the compiled program.* (See Figure 13.3.)

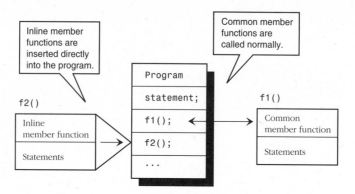

Figure 13.3. An inline member function's statements are inserted directly into the program.

Listing 13.9, time3.h, redeclares the TTime class using a few inline member functions (lines 14 and 17–22).

Listing 13.9. time3.h (Redeclares TTime class with inline member functions).

```
 1:  /* time3.h -- TTime class declaration */
 2:
 3:  #ifndef __TIME3_H
 4:  #define __TIME3_H  1  /* Prevent multiple #includes */
 5:
 6:  #include <iostream.h>
 7:  #include <time.h>
 8:  #include <string.h>
 9:
10:  class TTime {
11:  private:
12:    long dt;  // Date and time in seconds from January 1, 1970
13:  public:
14:    void Display(void) { cout << ctime(&dt); }
15:    void GetTime(int &m, int &d, int &y, int &hr, int &min);
16:    void SetTime(int m, int d, int y, int hr, int min);
17:    char *GetSTime(void)
18:    {
19:      char *cp = strdup(ctime(&dt));
```

```
20:     return cp;
21:   }
22:   void ChangeTime(long nminutes) { dt += (nminutes * 60); }
23: };
24:
25: #endif  /* __TIME3_H */
```

As a result of the inline member functions in time3.h, the class's implementation in Listing 13.10, TIME3.CPP, is much simpler than before.

Listing 13.10. TIME3.CPP (Implements TTime class's non-inline member functions).

```
1:  /* time3.cpp -- TTime class implementation */
2:
3:  #include <dos.h>
4:  #include "time3.h"
5:
6:  // Return current date and time data members
7:  void TTime::GetTime(int &m, int &d, int &y, int &hr, int &min)
8:  {
9:    struct date ds;
10:   struct time ts;
11:
12:   unixtodos(dt, &ds, &ts);
13:   y = ds.da_year;
14:   m = ds.da_mon;
15:   d = ds.da_day;
16:   hr = ts.ti_hour;
17:   min = ts.ti_min;
18: }
19:
20: // Set dt data member
21: void TTime::SetTime(int m, int d, int y, int hr, int min)
22: {
23:   struct date ds;
24:   struct time ts;
25:
26:   ds.da_year = y;
```

continues

Listing 13.10. continued

```
27:     ds.da_mon = m;
28:     ds.da_day = d;
29:     ts.ti_hour = hr;
30:     ts.ti_min = min;
31:     ts.ti_sec = 0;
32:     ts.ti_hund = 0;
33:     dt = dostounix(&ds, &ts);
34:   }
```

Because inline member functions are used no differently than normal member functions, the main program requires no modifications. Listing 13.11, APPOINT3.CPP, is identical to APPOINT2.CPP, but includes time3.h at line 3 rather than time2.h. Compile the entire program by entering the DOS command **bcc appoint3 time3**. In an IDE, you can create and compile a project of the files APPOINT3.CPP and TIME3.CPP.

Listing 13.11. APPOINT3.CPP (Displays sample appointment calendar).

```
 1:   #include <iostream.h>
 2:   #include <stdio.h>
 3:   #include "time3.h"
 4:
 5:   main()
 6:   {
 7:     TTime appointment;
 8:
 9:     appointment.SetTime(7, 21, 1996, 8, 30);
10:     for (int slots = 1; slots <= 17; slots++) {
11:       appointment.Display();
12:       appointment.ChangeTime(30);
13:     }
14:     return 0;
15:   }
```

Line 14 in time3.h (Listing 13.9) shows a typical inline member function declaration. For reference, here's a shortened version of the TTime class declaration:

```
class TTime {
private:
  long dt;
public:
  void Display(void) { cout << ctime(&dt); }
...
};
```

Member function `Display()`'s statements are written directly in braces after the member function header in the class declaration. Notice the placement of the semicolon, which comes after the `cout` output stream statement. This format is consistent with C++'s rules, which state that semicolons terminate declarations and statements. You might find this format easier to learn by writing the inline member function using an indented style:

```
class TTime {
private:
  long dt;
public:
  void Display(void)
  {
    cout << ctime(&dt);
  }
...
};
```

Either format works equally well, but to save space, most inline functions are written on one or two run-together lines, as shown earlier.

Statements that call the inline `Display()` member function do not generate a function call in the compiled code. For example, if you declare a class object and assign it a date and time:

```
TTime today;
today.SetTime(4, 19, 1998, 6, 0);
```

you can then call the `Display()` member function for the `today` class object:

```
today.Display();
```

Despite appearances, the program is compiled as though you had written

```
cout << ctime(&today.dt);
```

Of course, you can't actually write such a statement because `dt` is a private data member of `TTime`, and therefore cannot be accessed outside of the class.

> **NOTE:** As with common inline functions, C++ may or may not inject inline member functions directly into the compiled code. For example, if an inline member function is too complex, the compiler may choose to compile it as a normal member function. Keeping your inline member functions as short as possible is the best way to ensure that their statements are actually inserted inline.

Most inline member functions are declared directly in a class, as demonstrated in Listing 13.9 at line 14. You may also declare inline member functions by using the `inline` keyword in the module's implementation. For example, to convert `TTime`'s `GetTime()` to an inline member function, you can revise the function implementation in Listing 13.10 to

```
inline void TTime::GetTime(int &m, int &d, int &y, int &hr, int &min)
{
  ...
}
```

Simply tacking on `inline` to a member function, however, may not produce the expected results because *an inline member function's implementation must be seen by the compiler before that function is called.* In most cases, inline member functions are best encoded directly in class declarations.

Overloaded Member Functions

In Chapter 12, "Introducing C++," you learned how to overload functions by declaring multiple functions of the same names that differ in at least one parameter. You may use a similar technique to overload a class's member functions.

Overloaded member functions are particularly useful when some (but not all) of a member function's parameters are needed. For example, as currently designed, `TTime`'s `SetTime()` function requires five integer arguments. To set the date and time to January 15, 1997, at 11:45, you must write

```
TTime anyTime;
anyTime.SetTime(1, 15, 1997, 11, 45);
```

Suppose, however, you want to set only the date, letting the class default to the current time. Currently, there is no easy way to initialize `TTime` in this way.

Overloading SetTime() with differing numbers of parameters makes it possible for the program to pass zero or more arguments, as in the statement

```
anyTime.SetTime(1, 15, 1997);
```

Listing 13.12, time4.h, shows the new TTime class and several overloaded SetTime() member functions.

Listing 13.12. time4.h (Shows TTime class with overloaded member functions).

```
 1:  /* time4.h -- TTime class declaration */
 2:
 3:  #ifndef __TIME4_H
 4:  #define __TIME4_H  1  /* Prevent multiple #includes */
 5:
 6:  #include <iostream.h>
 7:  #include <time.h>
 8:  #include <string.h>
 9:
10:  class TTime {
11:  private:
12:    long dt;  // Date and time in seconds from January 1, 1970
13:  public:
14:    void Display(void) { cout << ctime(&dt); }
15:    void GetTime(int &m, int &d, int &y, int &hr, int &min);
16:    void SetTime(int m, int d, int y, int hr, int min);
17:    void SetTime(int m, int d, int y, int hr);
18:    void SetTime(int m, int d, int y);
19:    void SetTime(int m, int d);
20:    void SetTime(int m);
21:    void SetTime(void);
22:    char *GetSTime(void)
23:    {
24:      char *cp = strdup(ctime(&dt));
25:      return cp;
26:    }
27:    void ChangeTime(long nminutes) { dt += (nminutes * 60); }
28:  };
29:
30:  #endif  /* __TIME4_H */
```

Lines 16–21 declare six overloaded SetTime() member functions. Each member function has the same name and differs in at least one parameter—the minimum requirements for the compiler to distinguish among them. Even though each member function has the same name, however, each is distinct and must be implemented separately, as Listing 13.13, TIME4.CPP, shows.

Listing 13.13. TIME4.CPP (Implements overloaded member functions).

```
1:  /* time4.cpp -- TTime class implementation */
2:
3:  #include <dos.h>
4:  #include "time4.h"
5:
6:  // Return current date and time data members
7:  void TTime::GetTime(int &m, int &d, int &y, int &hr, int &min)
8:  {
9:    struct date ds;
10:   struct time ts;
11:
12:   unixtodos(dt, &ds, &ts);
13:   y = ds.da_year;
14:   m = ds.da_mon;
15:   d = ds.da_day;
16:   hr = ts.ti_hour;
17:   min = ts.ti_min;
18: }
19:
20: // Set dt data member
21: void TTime::SetTime(int m, int d, int y, int hr, int min)
22: {
23:   struct date ds;
24:   struct time ts;
25:
26:   getdate(&ds);  // Get current date and time
27:   gettime(&ts);
28:   if (y >= 0) ds.da_year = y;
29:   if (m >= 0) ds.da_mon = m;
30:   if (d >= 0) ds.da_day = d;
31:   if (hr >= 0) ts.ti_hour = hr;
32:   if (min >= 0) ts.ti_min = min;
```

```
33:     ts.ti_sec = 0;
34:     ts.ti_hund = 0;
35:     dt = dostounix(&ds, &ts);
36:  }
37:
38:  void TTime::SetTime(int m, int d, int y, int hr)
39:  {
40:     SetTime(m, d, y, hr, -1);
41:  }
42:
43:  void TTime::SetTime(int m, int d, int y)
44:  {
45:     SetTime(m, d, y, -1, -1);
46:  }
47:
48:  void TTime::SetTime(int m, int d)
49:  {
50:     SetTime(m, d, -1, -1, -1);
51:  }
52:
53:  void TTime::SetTime(int m)
54:  {
55:     SetTime(m, -1, -1, -1, -1);
56:  }
57:
58:  void TTime::SetTime(void)
59:  {
60:     SetTime(-1, -1, -1, -1, -1);
61:  }
```

The new, fully equipped SetTime() member function at lines 21–36 calls library functions getdate() and gettime() for the system's current date and time. This new version of SetTime() assigns to the class object's data members any parameter values that are greater than or equal to zero, thus leaving the current default values alone for any parameters that are less than zero. If today is a class object of type TTime, the statement

```
today.SetTime(1, 15, 1998, -1, -1);
```

sets today's date to January 15, 1998, but uses the current hour and minute because those two arguments are set to –1.

Because the function is overloaded, there's no need to enter the two negative argument placeholders. You can simply write

```
today.SetTime(1, 15, 1998);
```

In this case, the overloaded member function with three `int` parameters is called (see lines 43–46), which supplies the missing negative values. The compiler knows which of the overloaded `SetTime()` member functions to call based on the number and types of arguments used in the statement. The other overloaded member functions are similarly implemented in terms of the five-parameter, fully equipped `SetTime()`. For example, the statement

```
today.SetTime();
```

calls the no-parameter overloaded `SetTime()` member function at lines 58–61, which calls the five-parameter version to set `today` to the system's current date and time.

Listing 13.14, OVERMF.CPP, demonstrates how to use the overloaded `TTime` member functions. Compile this program with the DOS command **bcc overmf time4**, or in an IDE, create and compile a project with the files OVERMF.CPP and TIME4.CPP.

Listing 13.14. OVERMF.CPP (Demonstrates using overloaded member functions).

```
1:  #include <iostream.h>
2:  #include <stdio.h>
3:  #include "time4.h"
4:
5:  main()
6:  {
7:    TTime appointment;
8:
9:    appointment.SetTime();
10:   appointment.Display();
11:   appointment.SetTime(8);
12:   appointment.Display();
13:   appointment.SetTime(8, 1);
14:   appointment.Display();
15:   appointment.SetTime(8, 1, 1996);
16:   appointment.Display();
17:   appointment.SetTime(8, 1, 1996, 8);
```

```
18:     appointment.Display();
19:     appointment.SetTime(8, 1, 1996, 8, 30);
20:     appointment.Display();
21:     return 0;
22: }
```

Lines 9–20 call each of the overloaded SetTime() member functions, passing from zero to five arguments, and also call Display(). When you run the program, the interspersed calls to Display() show the results of each call to SetTime().

Default Member Function Parameters

Numerous overloaded member functions such as those at lines 16–21 in Listing 13.12 are useful, but they often lead to confusing code. In some cases, default member function parameters can reduce the number of member functions required while still permitting statements to specify a variable number of arguments.

Chapter 12, "Introducing C++," explained default parameters for common functions. Default member function parameters are exactly the same as those you learned about before, but they appear in a class declaration. Listing 13.15, time5.h, revises the TTime class's SetTime() member function to use default parameter values.

Listing 13.15. time5.h (Revises TTime to use default member function parameters).

```
1: /* time5.h -- TTime class declaration */
2:
3: #ifndef _ _TIME5_H
4: #define _ _TIME5_H  1  /* Prevent multiple #includes */
5:
6: #include <iostream.h>
7: #include <time.h>
8: #include <string.h>
9:
10: class TTime {
11: private:
12:     long dt;  // Date and time in seconds from January 1, 1970
```

continues

Listing 13.15. continued

```
13:   public:
14:     void Display(void) { cout << ctime(&dt); }
15:     void GetTime(int &m, int &d, int &y, int &hr, int &min);
16:     void SetTime(int m = -1, int d = -1, int y = -1,
17:       int hr = -1, int min = -1);
18:     char *GetSTime(void)
19:     {
20:       char *cp = strdup(ctime(&dt));
21:       return cp;
22:     }
23:     void ChangeTime(long nminutes) { dt += (nminutes * 60); }
24:   };
25:
26:   #endif   /* _ _TIME5_H */
```

Each of SetTime()'s parameters at lines 16–17 is assigned a default value of –1, which is used for any unspecified arguments in calls to this member function. Default parameter values must follow any other parameters in the member function's declaration. Given a TTime class object named today, the statement

```
today.SetTime(1, 15, 1998);
```

passes January 15, 1998, to SetTime()'s first three parameters. Because unspecified parameters assume the declared default values, the last two arguments are invisibly set to –1, and the preceding statement is compiled as though it had been written

```
today.SetTime(1, 15, 1998, -1, -1);
```

Implementing the new TTime class is now much simpler than with the overloaded SetTime() member functions. Listing 13.16, TIME5.CPP, shows the result.

The default member function parameter values are not listed in the function's header at line 21. Default values may appear only in the member function's declaration.

Listing 13.17, DEFAULT.CPP, uses the new TTime class, demonstrating that in this case, the default member function parameters allow a variable number of arguments to be passed to SetTime(). The end result is the same as the overloaded example presented earlier, but the class implementation is far simpler.

Listing 13.16. TIME5.CPP (Implements a simplified TTime class).

```
1:  /* time5.cpp -- TTime class implementation */
2:
3:  #include <dos.h>
4:  #include "time5.h"
5:
6:  // Return current date and time data members
7:  void TTime::GetTime(int &m, int &d, int &y, int &hr, int &min)
8:  {
9:    struct date ds;
10:   struct time ts;
11:
12:   unixtodos(dt, &ds, &ts);
13:   y = ds.da_year;
14:   m = ds.da_mon;
15:   d = ds.da_day;
16:   hr = ts.ti_hour;
17:   min = ts.ti_min;
18:  }
19:
20:  // Set dt data member
21:  void TTime::SetTime(int m, int d, int y, int hr, int min)
22:  {
23:    struct date ds;
24:    struct time ts;
25:
26:    getdate(&ds);   // Get current date and time
27:    gettime(&ts);
28:    if (y >= 0) ds.da_year = y;
29:    if (m >= 0) ds.da_mon = m;
30:    if (d >= 0) ds.da_day = d;
31:    if (hr >= 0) ts.ti_hour = hr;
32:    if (min >= 0) ts.ti_min = min;
33:    ts.ti_sec = 0;
34:    ts.ti_hund = 0;
35:    dt = dostounix(&ds, &ts);
36:  }
```

Listing 13.17. DEFAULT.CPP (Uses default member function parameters).

```
 1:  #include <iostream.h>
 2:  #include <stdio.h>
 3:  #include "time5.h"
 4:
 5:  main()
 6:  {
 7:    TTime appointment;
 8:
 9:    appointment.SetTime();
10:    appointment.Display();
11:    appointment.SetTime(8);
12:    appointment.Display();
13:    appointment.SetTime(8, 1);
14:    appointment.Display();
15:    appointment.SetTime(8, 1, 1996);
16:    appointment.Display();
17:    appointment.SetTime(8, 1, 1996, 8);
18:    appointment.Display();
19:    appointment.SetTime(8, 1, 1996, 8, 30);
20:    appointment.Display();
21:    return 0;
22:  }
```

Constructors and Destructors

Until now, class objects have been uninitialized at birth. Consider any one of the preceding TTime classes. The declaration

TTime anyTime;

creates a class object anyTime of type TTime, but does not initialize that object's data members. If you forget to initialize the class object, the statement

anyTime.Display();

is likely to output garbage, or at the very least, an incorrect date and time.

Classes may declare one or more constructors to initialize class objects automatically when the object is created, thus practically eliminating errors caused by using uninitialized data. Classes may also declare a destructor (but only one) that is called to perform clean-up duties when a class object goes out of scope. Constructors and destructors are similar to common member functions, but are rarely called directly by program statements. C++ calls constructors and destructors automatically to initialize and clean up class objects.

Listing 13.18, time6.h, declares yet one more version of the TTime class. The new class has two constructors to initialize newly created TTime class objects. It also has a destructor to clean up old TTime class objects that are scheduled to go out of scope.

Listing 13.18. time6.h (Declares TTime class with constructors and a destructor).

```
 1:  /* time6.h -- TTime class declaration */
 2:
 3:  #ifndef __TIME6_H
 4:  #define __TIME6_H  1  /* Prevent multiple #includes */
 5:
 6:  #include <iostream.h>
 7:  #include <time.h>
 8:  #include <string.h>
 9:
10:  class TTime {
11:  private:
12:    long dt;  // Date and time in seconds from January 1, 1970
13:    char *dts;  // Date and time as a string
14:    void DeleteDts(void);  // Delete dts pointer
15:  public:
16:    TTime();                                  // Constructor
17:    TTime(int m, int d = -1, int y = -1,      // Constructor
18:      int hr = -1, int min = -1);
19:    ~TTime();                                 // Destructor
20:    void Display(void) { cout << ctime(&dt); }
21:    void GetTime(int &m, int &d, int &y, int &hr, int &min);
22:    void SetTime(int m = -1, int d = -1, int y = -1,
23:      int hr = -1, int min = -1);
24:    const char *GetSTime(void);
25:    void ChangeTime(long nminutes)
```

continues

Listing 13.18. continued

```
26:     { dt += (nminutes * 60); DeleteDts(); }
27: };
28:
29: #endif  /* __TIME6_H */
```

Constructors are declared as member functions with no return value and zero or more parameters of any type (but not of the constructor's own class). Constructors are typically declared in a public section, but may be inserted anywhere in a class. Constructors always have the same name as the class in which they are declared. They may optionally be coded inline.

Line 16 declares TTime() as TTime's class constructor. Because the constructor declares no parameters, it is called the default constructor. Lines 17–18 declare a second overloaded constructor for TTime. This constructor is also named the same as the class, but this time it declares five int parameters, the last four of which are given default values of –1. TTime also declares a destructor at line 19, explained later.

> **NOTE:** The C++ compiler automatically and invisibly inserts a default constructor and a destructor into classes that have no constructors or destructors.

In addition to its constructors and destructor, the new TTime class has two other new features. A second private data member at line 13 adds a char pointer, dts, to the class. This pointer is intended to address a string representation of the date and time. As you'll see later, keeping the date and time in string form helps lighten the class's memory management duties, and may improve runtime performance. Line 14 adds a private member function, DeleteDts(), which deletes any memory addressed by the dts pointer. Member functions that are private may be called only by other member functions in the class, but like other private members, are not accessible on the outside. There is no way, then, for an errant program statement to call DeleteDtr() and delete the memory addressed by dts. Only members of the class are so privileged.

Before looking at an example of a constructor in use, examine TTime's implementation in Listing 13.19, TIME6.CPP.

Listing 13.19. TIME6.CPP (Implements TTime).

```
1:  /* time6.cpp -- TTime class implementation */
2:
3:  #include <dos.h>
4:  #include "time6.h"
5:
6:  // Default constructor
7:  TTime::TTime()
8:  {
        dts = NULL;   // No current string
                      1);
```

```
                                 int y, int hr, int min)
                       nt string
                       );


                                 string owned by object


                       id)
                     e string owned by object
                     ointer to null
32:
33:  // Return current date and time data members
34:  void TTime::GetTime(int &m, int &d, int &y, int &hr, int &min)
35:  {
36:    struct date ds;
37:    struct time ts;
38:
39:    unixtodos(dt, &ds, &ts);
```

continues

Listing 13.19. continued

```
40:    y = ds.da_year;
41:    m = ds.da_mon;
42:    d = ds.da_day;
43:    hr = ts.ti_hour;
44:    min = ts.ti_min;
45:  }
46:
47:  // Set dt data member
48:  void TTime::SetTime(int m, int d, int y, int hr, int min)
49:  {
50:    struct date ds;
51:    struct time ts;
52:
53:    getdate(&ds);   // Get current date and time
54:    gettime(&ts);
55:    if (y >= 0) ds.da_year = y;
56:    if (m >= 0) ds.da_mon = m;
57:    if (d >= 0) ds.da_day = d;
58:    if (hr >= 0) ts.ti_hour = hr;
59:    if (min >= 0) ts.ti_min = min;
60:    ts.ti_sec = 0;
61:    ts.ti_hund = 0;
62:    dt = dostounix(&ds, &ts);
63:    DeleteDts();   // Delete any current string
64:  }
65:
66:  const char *TTime::GetSTime(void)
67:  {
68:    if (dts)        // Return current string if there is one
69:      return dts;
70:    dts = strdup(ctime(&dt));
71:    return dts;
72:  }
```

Lines 7–11 implement TTime's default constructor, TTime(). As with all member functions, the implementation's header is prefaced with the class name and a scope resolution operator. Though the header TTime::TTime() appears to suffer from a bad case of mirror imaging, it properly identifies the TTime() constructor as belonging to the TTime class (see Figure 13.4).

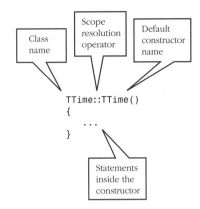

Figure 13.4. A default constructor's parts and pieces.

Statements in a constructor may use the same kinds of programming as found in other member and nonmember functions. Typically, however, a constructor limits its duties to assigning initial values to class data members, to allocating memory owned by class objects, and so on. In this case, line 16 sets char pointer dts to NULL, indicating that the pointer does not yet address a valid string. Because C++ calls the constructor automatically to initialize an object of the TTime class, *all such objects are guaranteed to have initialized dts pointers.* The constructor also calls the SetTime() member function with default arguments of –1 (see line 10), thus initializing the class object to the current date and time.

The second overloaded constructor is implemented at lines 14–18. Similar to the default constructor, but declaring date and time parameters, this constructor can be used to assign any initial values to a class object. Overloaded constructors are similar to overloaded member functions. In any class, you can declare as many constructors as needed, provided they differ from one another by at least one parameter. Constructors must have the same name as their declaring class, and are therefore overloaded by definition.

Using Constructors

Not all classes need constructors, but most classes have at least one. Other classes might have a dozen constructors or more. The purpose of a constructor is to provide clearly defined initializations for class objects. Listing 13.20, CONSTRUC.CPP, demonstrates how TTime's constructors initialize TTime objects.

Listing 13.20. CONSTRUC.CPP (Uses TTime's constructors).

```
 1:  #include <iostream.h>
 2:  #include <stdio.h>
 3:  #include "time6.h"
 4:
 5:  main()
 6:  {
 7:    TTime t1;
 8:    TTime t2(8);
 9:    TTime t3(8, 1);
10:    TTime t4(8, 1, 1996);
11:    TTime t5(8, 1, 1996, 8);
12:    TTime t6(8, 1, 1996, 8, 30);
13:
14:    t1.Display();
15:    t2.Display();
16:    t3.Display();
17:    t4.Display();
18:    t5.Display();
19:    t6.Display();
20:    return 0;
21:  }
```

Lines 7–12 declare six class objects of type TTime. C++ automatically calls a class's constructor when an object of the class is created. For example, when the program allocates storage for t1 as declared at line 7, the default constructor is called automatically to initialize the object.

> **HINT:** Compile and run CONSTRUC.CPP in Turbo Debugger. (Use the DOS commands **bcc -v construc time6** and **td construc.**) Press F7 repeatedly to single-step through the program's statements. For each of the six class objects declared at lines 7–12, C++ calls the appropriate constructor to initialize the object's data members.

Lines 8–12 declare and initialize class objects t2 through t6 using explicit arguments in parentheses. These declarations resemble earlier examples that declared

TTime class objects and then called member function SetTime() to assign values to the object's data members. By using a constructor, however, these jobs are automatically carried out at the time the objects are created. With constructors, class objects are guaranteed to be initialized, thus helping to prevent one of programming's most common mistakes—using uninitialized variables.

Using Destructors

Another sample program uses the TTime class from time6.h and TIME6.CPP (Listings 13.18 and 13.19), and shows how a destructor is used to clean up class objects that are scheduled to go out of scope. Compile Listing 13.21, DESTRUC.CPP, as you have others (use the DOS command **bcc destruc time6.obj**, or create an IDE project consisting of DESTRUC.CPP and TIME6.CPP).

Listing 13.21. DESTRUC.CPP (Uses TTime's destructor).

```
 1:  #include <iostream.h>
 2:  #include <stdio.h>
 3:  #include "time6.h"
 4:
 5:  void f(void);
 6:
 7:  main()
 8:  {
 9:    f();
10:    return 0;
11:  }
12:
13:  void f(void)
14:  {
15:    TTime today;
16:    const char *sp;
17:
18:    sp = today.GetSTime();
19:    cout << "First time: " << sp;
20:    sp = today.GetSTime();
21:    cout << "Second time: " << sp;
22:  }
```

DESTRUC's `main()` function calls another function `f()`, implemented at lines 13–22. Inside the function, line 15 declares an automatic `TTime` class object, `today`, local to the function's scope. Because local automatic objects are created when their declaring functions are called, C++ calls the `TTime()` default constructor for `today` as part of the function's startup duties. This action occurs *every time the function is called*. (You might want to verify this fact by running DESTRUC in Turbo Debugger.)

Lines 18–21 call the `GetSTime()` member function for the `today` class object. The member function's result is saved in a local `char` pointer `sp`. Look back to Listing 13.19, TIME6.CPP, where `GetSTime()` is implemented (lines 66–72). The member function first checks whether data member `dts` is null. If not, it returns `dts`; otherwise it calls `strdup()` and `ctime()` to convert the current date and time to a string, saving the string's address in `char` pointer `dts`, a private data member of the class. Subsequent calls to `GetSTime()` therefore use a previously allocated string. This reduces the number of times the same date and time string is allocated space on the heap, a refinement that should reduce heap fragmentation and help keep the code running quickly.

Because a `TTime` class object owns a `dts` pointer to a memory block allocated on the heap, the class must carefully manage this memory. Objects of type `TTime` must not be allowed to go out of scope without returning any owned memory to the heap, or that memory would be unrecoverable, possibly leading to an out-of-memory error. Also, if a `TTime` class object's date and time change—by calls to `ChangeTime()` and `SetTime()`, for example—a non-null `dts` pointer must be deleted and set to null, so it will be reallocated on the next call to `GetSTime()`.

Skip back to time6.h (Listing 13.18) and examine line 19, which declares a destructor for the `TTime` class. Destructors are usually declared in a class's public section, but don't have to be. A class may have only one destructor, which is named the same as its declaring class (as are any constructors), but is preceded by a tilde character (~), used in mathematics to represent *difference*. Destructors are the antithesis of constructors—what a constructor constructs, a destructor can destroy.

Implement a destructor as you do other class member functions. You may optionally code a destructor inline. TIME6.CPP (Listing 13.19) implements the `TTime` class destructor at lines 21–24, repeated here for reference:

```
TTime::~TTime()
{
  delete dts;  // Delete string owned by object
}
```

As with constructors and member functions, the destructor's name ~TTime() is prefaced by the class name and a scope resolution operator TTime::, identifying the destructor as a member of the TTime class. The single statement in TTime's destructor deletes dts. (It's not necessary to test whether dts is null; the delete operator ignores null pointer arguments.)

When an object of a class goes out of scope, C++ automatically calls that object's class destructor if it has one. This gives objects the opportunity to clean up after themselves—deleting any memory allocated by a constructor or member function, for instance.

> **HINT:** Remember—constructors build; destructors destroy. A class may have many constructors, and programs may therefore build objects in many different ways. However, a class may have only one destructor. If you need different ways to destroy objects, a destructor can call member functions, use a switch statement, or take other actions to change how the destructor operates based on various conditions.

The Life of an Object

Class objects can be global or local to a function. Like variables of common types, objects of a class type can also be addressed by pointers and referred to by references. Think of classes as new data types, and use them accordingly, just as you do variables of other types.

The nature of an object—that is, whether it's global, local, addressed by a pointer, and so on—affects when that object's class constructors and destructor are called. When an object is created, C++ automatically calls that object's default constructor, or it calls another constructor that you specify in the object's declaration. When an object goes out of scope, C++ calls that object's destructor. Figure 13.5 represents these actions in a time line, marking typical events in the life of an object.

The following notes help clarify exactly when constructors and destructors are called for class objects of various kinds.

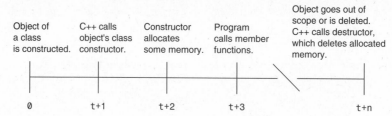

Figure 13.5. Events that occur during a typical object's lifetime.

Global Class Objects

A global class object's class constructor is called before function `main()` begins to run. This action ensures that all global class objects are initialized before the program formally starts. Using the `TTime` class (see Listings 13.18, time6.h, and 13.19, TIME6.CPP), the global declaration

```
TTime today;
```

creates a global object `today` of the class `TTime`. Before calling `main()`, C++ calls `TTime`'s default constructor for `today`, which assigns the current date and time to the object.

To initialize a global `TTime` class object for a specific date and time, declare the object like this:

```
TTime someTime(9, 4, 1953, 10, 45);
```

The presence of an initializer list in parentheses causes C++ to search `TTime` for a constructor that can accept the specified initializing arguments. In this case, C++ calls `TTime`'s overloaded constructor (see Listing 13.18, lines 17–18), which initializes `someTime` to September 4, 1953, at 10:45. Again, this action occurs before `main()` is called.

A global object's class destructor is normally called as part of the program's shutdown duties after any `atexit()` functions finish (see Chapter 22, "Functions and Examples"). Destructors are not called, however, if the program ends by calling `abort()`.

Local Class Objects

Automatic class objects declared locally to a function are created when the function is called and destroyed when the function ends. Like variables of common types, automatic class object data members are stored on the stack. In this function:

```
void anyFunction(void)
{
  TTime now;  // Initialized on each entry to function
  ...
}
```

the default TTime constructor is called to initialize the class object now to the current date and time each time the function is called.

When the function ends, C++ calls TTime's destructor for the now object, thus giving the object the chance to clean up after itself before it goes out of scope.

If you call exit() to end a program, global class object destructors are called normally, but destructors for any existing automatic variables local to a function (including those local to main()) are *not* called.

Pointers to Objects

A pointer may address a dynamic class object, which is typically allocated heap space by new. You can declare a pointer pToday to a class object of type TTime:

```
TTime *pToday;
```

This might be a global declaration or it might be local to a function. Like all pointers, pToday must be initialized before use, usually by using new:

```
pToday = new TTime;
```

In this statement, operator new allocates heap space for an object of type TTime. The address of that object's first byte is assigned to pToday. In addition, C++ calls the object's default constructor, which, in this example, initializes the object to the current date and time.

To use pointers to class objects, dereference them as you do pointers to objects of other types. For example, this statement displays the date and time for the TTime class object addressed by pToday:

```
pToday->Display();
```

Classes resemble structures, so when using pointers to class objects, you'll most often use the -> operator to refer to an addressed object's member. However, you can also use the * dereference operator with class object pointers. For example, this statement:

```
sp = (*pToday).GetSTime();
```

553

assigns to `sp` (declared as `const char *sp;`) the result of member function `GetSTime()` for the class object addressed by `pToday`. However, the following statement:

```
sp = pToday->GetSTime();
```

is easier to write, clearer to read, and performs the identical service.

C++ calls a dynamic class object's destructor when that object is deleted. The statement

```
delete pToday;
```

deletes the object addressed by `pToday`, returning that object's memory to the heap for other uses. Just before the object is destroyed, C++ calls the class destructor, which can take advantage of the opportunity to delete any memory that the object happens to own. In the case of the `TTime` class, for instance, the destructor can delete the memory addressed by pointer `dts`.

> **NOTE:** Do not confuse the life of a pointer with the life of an addressed object. A global pointer exists for the duration of the program, but it may address a multitude of class objects created by `new` and destroyed by `delete`. Similarly, an automatic pointer declared locally to a function is created when the function runs and destroyed when the function ends. However, *the objects addressed by pointers have global scope and must be deleted explicitly.* In a function `f()`, if you call `new` to create an object on the heap, that object remains in memory even after the function ends. You must explicitly delete any such object if you don't want it to remain in memory after the function returns.

Reference Objects

Class objects may be declared as references. Suppose you declare a global `TTime` class object as

```
TTime today;  // Global today object
```

Later in the program, you can declare a reference to `today` like this:

```
TTime &rToday = today;  // Reference to today
```

The reference rToday is an alias for today, and may be used in today's stead. For example, each of these two statements displays today's date and time:

```
rToday.Display();
today.Display();
```

Because references refer to an existing object, the class constructor is not called when the reference comes into scope, nor is the destructor called when the reference goes out of scope. These actions occur when the object itself is created and destroyed.

NOTE: References are more commonly declared as function parameters. In practice, they are rarely used as described in this section.

Parameter Objects

You may pass class objects, pointers to class objects, and class object references as arguments to functions. Classes are data types, and you can declare function parameters of them as you do other parameters. Here's a sample:

```
void anyFunction(TTime t)
{
  t.Display();
}
```

Function anyFunction() has a single parameter t of type TTime. The function calls t's Display() member function to display the parameter's date and time. A program can declare a class object of type TTime:

```
TTime today;
```

and then pass that object by value to anyFunction():

```
anyFunction(today);
```

Functions may also declare class pointer parameters. Passing large class objects by value to functions causes those objects to occupy an undesirable amount of stack space. In such cases, a pointer parameter is more efficient:

```
void anyFunction(TTime *tp)
{
  tp->Display();
}
```

To call this version of anyFunction(), a statement passes the address of a TTime class object rather than the object itself:

```
anyFunction(&today);
```

Probably, this is the most common method for passing objects to functions. However, function parameters may be declared as class object references. The results are similar to what you can achieve with pointer parameters, but inside the function, no pointer dereferences are required. Here's yet one more version of anyFunction(), this time using a reference parameter to an object of class TTime:

```
void anyFunction(TTime &tr)  // tr is a reference parameter
{
  tr.Display();  // Call Display for object that tr references
}
```

Elsewhere in the program, you can pass a TTime class object directly to anyFunction's reference parameter:

```
anyFunction(today);
```

One disadvantage of reference parameters is that statements such as this appear to pass argument today by value. The fact that a reference to today is passed to anyFunction() is not clear from the text.

Object Function Results

Functions may return a class object directly, as a pointer, or as a reference. Least common is a function that returns a TTime class object directly:

```
TTime newTime(void)
{
  TTime t;
  return t;
}
```

Local object t (initialized automatically by a constructor call when the function begins) is returned directly. A statement could call newTime() like this:

```
TTime anotherTime = newTime();
```

which copies newTime()'s function result to anotherTime. This technique offers few advantages, and it's just as easy to create a new TTime object without calling a function:

```
TTime anotherTime;  // Same as above
```

More commonly, functions return pointers and references to class objects. For instance, here's a function that allocates a new TTime class object on the heap and returns the object's address:

```
TTime *newTimeP(void)
{
  TTime *p = new TTime;  // Allocate and initialize object
  return p;  // Return address of object as function result
}
```

Inside the function, a TTime pointer p is assigned the address of a TTime class object allocated by new. The pointer exists only inside the function, but the object addressed by the pointer has global scope; therefore, the function may return its address. A statement can call newTime() to obtain a new object and assign the object's address to a TTime pointer such as tp:

```
TTime *tp = newTimeP();
```

Finally, functions may return references to class objects. You might use a reference function to refer to an existing object such as a global TTime today:

```
TTime &newTimeR(void)
{
  return today;
}
```

Elsewhere, you can declare a TTime reference and assign newTimeR()'s result to it:

```
TTime &tr = newTimeR();
```

Reference tr is now an alias for today, and can be used in a statement:

```
tr.Display();
```

The reference function also can be used directly in a statement. For example, the program can call newTimeR() to display today's date and time:

```
newTimeR().Display();
```

This technique is especially useful when a function such as newTimeR() performs a search operation, perhaps returning a reference to one of several TTime class objects based on some specified criteria.

Arrays of Class Objects

Just as you can declare arrays of common data types, you can declare arrays of class objects. For example, this declaration creates an array of ten TTime objects:

```
TTime tenTimes[10];
```

There's only one hard-and-fast rule to remember: *Class objects to be stored in arrays must have default constructors.* When an array of class objects such as tenTimes comes into being, C++ calls the class default constructor once for *each* object in the array. In the case of tenTimes, C++ calls TTime's default constructor ten times, thus initializing objects tenTimes[0] through tenTimes[9] to the current date and time.

A sample program, Listing 13.22, OBARRAY1.CPP, demonstrates how to use simple arrays of class objects. The program uses the TTime class defined earlier in time6.h. Compile the program from DOS with the command **bcc obarray1 time6**, or create and compile an IDE project consisting of the files OBARRAY1.CPP and TIME6.CPP.

Listing 13.22. OBARRAY1.CPP (Demonstrates arrays and the default constructor).

```
 1:  #include <iostream.h>
 2:  #include <stdio.h>
 3:  #include "time6.h"
 4:
 5:  main()
 6:  {
 7:    TTime tarray[6];
 8:
 9:    for (int i = 0; i < 6; i++)
10:      tarray[i].Display();
11:    return 0;
12:  }
```

Line 7 declares an array tarray of six TTime objects. When you run OBARRAY1, you see six equivalent dates and times, indicating that C++ called the class constructor to initialize each array element. (Run the program in Turbo Debugger—use the DOS commands **bcc -v obarray1 time6** and **td obarray1**—and press F7 repeatedly to trace the statements, verifying that TTime's constructor is called six times.)

If you want C++ to call a different constructor, you must explicitly initialize each array element. You can do this directly in the array's declaration as Listing 13.23, OBARRAY2.CPP, demonstrates. Compile the program as you did OBARRAY1.

Listing 13.23. OBARRAY2.CPP (Declares arrays and alternate constructors).

```
 1:  #include <iostream.h>
 2:  #include <stdio.h>
 3:  #include "time6.h"
 4:
 5:  main()
 6:  {
 7:    TTime tarray[6] = {
 8:      { TTime() },
 9:      { TTime(8) },
10:      { TTime(8, 1) },
11:      { TTime(8, 1, 1996) },
12:      { TTime(8, 1, 1996, 8) },
13:      { TTime(8, 1, 1996, 8, 30) }
14:    };
15:    for (int i = 0; i < 6; i++)
16:      tarray[i].Display();
17:    return 0;
18:  }
```

Lines 7–14 declare an array of six TTime objects, just as in OBARRAY1. In this case, however, the arrayed objects are initialized by specifying constructors inside braces, similar to the way you would initialize elements in an array of structs. Line 8 initializes the object at tarray[0] by calling TTime's default constructor. Lines 9–13 initialize the other arrayed objects by calling the overloaded constructor.

There's no easy way to initialize some arrayed class objects using the default constructor and some using an alternate constructor. If you need to do that, it's probably best to declare the array as in OBARRAY1, then reinitialize selected objects as needed. Except for small arrays, the technique illustrated in OBARRAY2 is too unwieldy to be of much practical use.

Arrays of class objects may also be stored on the heap and addressed with pointers. Some extra care is needed in this case to manage the array. Listing 13.24, OBARRAY3.CPP, demonstrates the idea. Compile it as you did OBARRAY1.

Listing 13.24. OBARRAY3.CPP (Manages dynamic arrays of class objects).

```
 1:  #include <iostream.h>
 2:  #include <stdio.h>
 3:  #include "time6.h"
 4:
 5:  main()
 6:  {
 7:    TTime *tarrayP;
 8:
 9:    tarrayP = new TTime[6];  // Allocate dynamic array
10:    for (int i = 0; i < 6; i++)
11:      tarrayP[i].Display();
12:    delete[] tarrayP;  // Note special form of delete[]
13:    return 0;
14:  }
```

Line 7 declares a TTime class object pointer tarrayP. To initialize the pointer, line 9 uses new, allocating an array of six TTime objects on the heap, assigning to tarrayP the address of the array's first object. In conjunction with the call to new, C++ automatically calls TTime's default constructor six times to initialize each of the arrayed objects.

As you should with other dynamic objects, you should delete dynamic class object arrays after you are done using them. However, deleting such arrays leads to a problem. Due to the C and C++ inability to distinguish between pointers and arrays, programs must use a special form of delete[] to ensure that, when deleting a dynamic array of class objects, any destructor for those objects is properly called. If line 12 in OBARRAY3 had been written

```
delete tarrayP;  // ???
```

the compiler does not know whether tarrayP addresses a single TTime class object or an array of them. To inform the compiler that tarrayP addresses an array, add empty brackets to delete:

```
delete[] tarrayP;  // Delete array of TTime class objects
```

This special command ensures that the class destructor is called for each object in the array.

> **NOTE:** Past versions of C++ required you to specify the number of arrayed class objects being deleted. In the past, you would use a statement such as `delete[6] tarrayP;` to delete an array of six `TTime` class objects addressed by `tarrayP`. This technique is no longer permitted, and Borland C++ ignores any value inside `delete[]`'s brackets. If you specify an array size in brackets, the compiler warns you that "Array size for 'delete' ignored in function x()."

Summary

- Object-oriented programming, or OOP, helps programmers to reduce complexity and to reuse existing code.

- In C++, the principles of OOP are embodied in the class, a tool for creating new data types that behave much as built-in types such as `int` and `double`. Use objects of a class as you do objects of other data types.

- Classes are similar to structures, but may have data and function members. Classes encapsulate data and functions, thus controlling access to a program's data.

- Use the `public` access specifier to make class members available to all users of a class. Use the `private` access specifier to make class members private. Only the class's own member functions may directly access private data members and call private member functions. Chapter 14, "Inheritance and Polymorphism," introduces a third access specifier, `protected`.

- Members of a class are private by default. However, for clarity, it's best to use the `private` access specifier to identify private members.

- Class member functions are implemented like normal functions, but their headers include the class name and a scope resolution operator. For a class `T`, a member function declared as `void f(void);` is implemented using the header `void T::f(void)`, identifying to the compiler that function `f()` is a member of class `T`.

- Every class member function receives a hidden parameter named `this`, which addresses the object for which the member function is called. For an object x of class T, in a member function `T::f()`, `this` addresses x. Usually, it's not necessary to use `this` in statements because member functions can directly access a class object's members.

- Class objects may be declared globally or locally to functions. Class objects may also be created by `new`, stored on the heap, and addressed by pointers. You may also declare references to class objects.

- Functions may declare class object parameters, which can be value parameters, pointers, or references. Functions may also return class objects, but they more commonly return pointers and references to class objects.

- Inline member functions inject their statements directly into the compiled code. The `inline` keyword, however, is merely a suggestion to the compiler, which may or may not take the hint to compile inline functions in line. Writing short inline functions is the best way to prevent the compiler from treating inline declarations as common member functions.

- Like common functions, member functions may be overloaded. A class may declare an unlimited number of functions that have the same name, provided each function differs in at least one parameter. Overloaded member functions help reduce the number of symbols programmers have to think up for similar operations. However, overloaded member functions are distinct from one another, and they must be implemented individually.

- Member functions may declare default parameter values for unspecified arguments.

- A class may declare one or more constructors to provide automatic initialization for class objects. A constructor is named the same as its class and has no return type. A class's default constructor has no parameters. Other constructors may declare one or more parameters, usually to provide initial values to class objects. Constructor parameters may be of any type, but not of the constructor's own class. C++ calls one of a class's constructors when an object of the class is created.

- A class may declare a destructor (but only one). A destructor typically deletes pointer variables addressed by class object data members, but it may perform other cleanup duties. C++ calls the class destructor when an object of the class goes out of scope or is deleted.

- Programs may create arrays of class objects. The class must have a default constructor, which C++ calls once for each object in the array. Arrays may also be declared and initialized with explicit calls to overloaded constructors.

- When arrays of class objects go out of scope, C++ automatically calls the class destructor for each arrayed object.

- Dynamic arrays of class objects may be created by new, stored on the heap, and addressed by pointers. However, because C and C++ do not distinguish between pointers and arrays, you must use delete[] (with empty brackets), not delete (without brackets), to delete dynamic class object arrays. This form of delete ensures that the class destructor is called for each arrayed object.

Exercises

> **NOTE:** For all exercises that refer to the TTime class, use the declaration in time6.h (Listing 13.18) and implementation in TIME6.CPP (Listing 13.19).

13.1 Invent a button class such as you might use in a simulation that requires on/off switches. Your class should have appropriate member functions to control button class objects.

13.2 Using the TTime class (see Listings 13.18 and 13.19), write a program DT.CPP that displays the current date and time.

13.3 Starting with your answer to Exercise 13.2, write a statement to change your object's date to tomorrow at the same time.

13.4 Using the TTime class, write a program named DAY.CPP that reports the day of the week for any date entered on the DOS command line. For example, the command **day jan 5 1997** should report the specified date's day of the week.

13.5 Add member functions to the TTime class to get and change the date and time using a long integer argument representing the number of seconds from January 1, 1970. Also add a constructor to initialize a TTime class object using a long integer seconds value. You may use inline member functions in your answer.

13.6 Create a class that can store a string on the heap. It should be possible to pass a string to an object of your class, and later, to retrieve a pointer to that same string. It should also be possible to modify a class object's string. Use constructors and a destructor to provide for any necessary automatic object initialization and deinitialization.

13.7 Write a program that uses your string object from Exercise 13.6 to read and display a text file.

Inheritance and Polymorphism

In the preceding chapter, you learned how classes encapsulate data and functions into one handy package. As you will discover in this chapter, classes can do much more. Using an OOP technique called inheritance, you can build new classes from existing ones just as a builder constructs a skyscraper out of brick, stone, and other relatively simple building materials. You'll also investigate polymorphism—a technique that uses inheritance along with another new C++ feature called a virtual member function.

Single Inheritance

Single inheritance describes the relationship between one class that is derived from another. (See Figure 14.1.) The class at the top of the hierarchy is the *base class*. The other class is the *derived class*.

Many classes might be derived from a single base class. Even so, as Figure 14.2 illustrates, such relationships are still of the single-inheritance variety because each new class derives from a single base. Later in this chapter, you'll investigate multiple inheritance, in which one class is derived from multiple base classes.

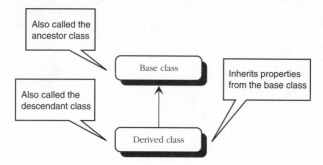

Figure 14.1. Single inheritance.

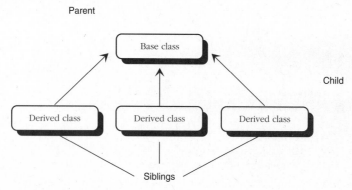

Figure 14.2. Multiple classes derived from a single base.

A variety of terms describe classes that are related through inheritance. A base class is often called an *ancestor*, and a derived class is often called a *descendant*. Grandparent, parent, and child also conveniently describe class relationships. In Figure 14.2, the derived classes are siblings because they share the same parent. Terms used less frequently include *subclass* (base) and *superclass* (derived), but these technical words are usually more confusing than helpful.

A derived class may itself be a base class from which additional classes are derived. Despite the apparent complexity of the class hierarchy in Figure 14.3, all the illustrated relationships use single inheritance because all derived classes possess only one parent each. There is no set limit on the number of classes that may be derived from one another. You can build derivations of classes upon classes until they reach the sky.

A derived class inherits data members and member functions—but not constructors or a destructor—from its base class. In Figure 14.3, for instance, derived class A inherits properties from the base class at the top of the heirarchy. Derived class B inherits those properties plus any new ones in class A. Derived class C inherits properties from the top base class and from derived classes A and B. Later, you'll encounter some refinements to this rule. In general, though, a derived class begins its existence with a copy of its base class's members, including any members inherited from more distantly related classes.

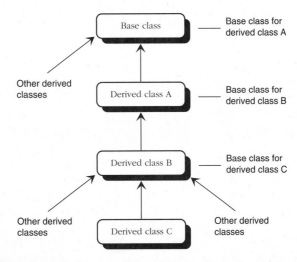

Figure 14.3. A derived class may be a base class for other derivations.

Declaring Derived Classes

A few examples demonstrate the mechanism of inheritance. Consider a base class, TBase, declared as

```
class TBase {
private:
  int count;  // Represents private class data
public:
  TBase() { count = 0; }
  void SetCount(int n) { count = n; }
  int GetCount(void) { return count; }
};
```

Though not of any practical use, TBase's members resemble those typically found in C++ classes from which new classes might be derived. Member count represents the class's private data. Only TBase member functions may refer directly to count. The default constructor, TBase(), initializes count to zero. Member function SetCount() assigns count a new value. Member function GetCount() returns count's present value. To keep the code simple, TBase's constructor and two member functions are written inline and require no separate implementations.

Suppose you need a new class that contains all of TBase's properties yet can increment and decrement a class object's value by a specified amount. You could rewrite the original class, but that might not be practical in a large project, especially when many programmers are involved. Such a change might not even be possible if TBase is part of a commercial class library to which the source code is unavailable. Rather than modify TBase, you can derive a new class from it and add the features you need:

```
class TDerived: public TBase {
public:
  TDerived(): TBase() { }
  void ChangeCount(int n) { SetCount(GetCount() + n); }
};
```

The derived class is named TDerived. Immediately following the derived class name are a colon and one of the keywords public, protected, or private. After those elements is the name of a base class (TBase) from which TDerived receives its inheritance. Figure 14.4 illustrates the parts and pieces of TDerived and its constructor.

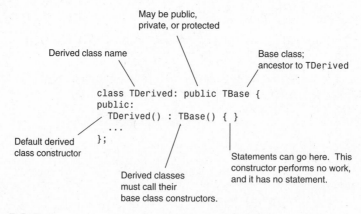

Figure 14.4. Some parts and pieces of a derived class.

A public base class's public members remain public in the derived class. In a derived class declaration that begins as

```
class TDerived: public TBase {
```

all of TBase's public members become public members in TDerived. Any private members in TBase remain private to their original declaring class, and TDerived may not access those members in TBase. You may also declare a base class to be private:

```
class TDerived: private TBase {
```

In this case, all public members in TBase become private members in TDerived. Subsequent derivations of TDerived may not access any members in TBase. Later, you'll look at a third type of base class specifier, protected.

Using Derived Class Constructors

Closely examine TDerived's constructor, TDerived(). A derived class typically provides a constructor if its base class has one. Also, a derived class constructor must call a base class constructor. (C++ can automatically insert default constructors, destructors, and calls to these members as needed for many classes.) In TDerived, the line

```
TDerived(): TBase() { }
```

declares the derived class's constructor TDerived() and calls the base class constructor using the special form :TBase(). You don't call base class constructors in statements; you call them by specifying their names following a derived class constructor declaration.

In this example, the new TDerived class constructor performs no new duties and accordingly is implemented as a null inline function with an empty pair of braces. A constructor may execute statements, however. In this case, TDerived's constructor might be declared inline as

```
TDerived(): TBase() { cout << "I am being initialized\n"; }
```

However, you do not have to implement derived constructors inline, and you could also declare TDerived() like this:

```
class TDerived: public TBase {
public:
  TDerived();  // Derived constructor
  void ChangeCount(int n) { SetCount(GetCount() + n); }
};
```

You must then implement the declared constructor, TDerived(), separately. If the new constructor has no new tasks to perform, you could write it like this:

```
TDerived::TDerived()   // Constructor header
  : TBase()            // Calls base class constructor
{
  // Derived constructor's statements go here
}
```

The first line of this constructor's implementation begins with the class name and a scope resolution operator (TDerived::), followed by the constructor's name (TDerived()). Because the TDerived class is derived from class TBase, the new constructor must call the base class constructor as shown. This call ensures that any data members inherited from the base class are properly initialized. In this case, the base class constructor sets the private count member to zero.

Using Derived Class Member Functions

The derived class inherits count from the base class. Because count is private to TBase, however, TDerived cannot directly access that member. Only members of the same class may access a class's private members. TDerived could, however, declare its own private members. For example, suppose the class is declared as

```
class TDerived: public TBase {
private:
  int secondCount;
public:
  TDerived();  // Derived constructor
  void ChangeCount(int n) { SetCount(GetCount() + n); }
};
```

TDerived inherits TBase's properties, including the base class's private count member. The new class adds a new private member secondCount. To initialize the new member, the constructor might now be implemented as

```
TDerived::TDerived()   // Constructor header
  : TBase()            // Initialize TBase data member(s)
{
  secondCount = 0;     // Initialize TDerived data member
}
```

The call to constructor TBase() initializes a TBase class object. The derived class constructor's assignment to secondCount initializes a TDerived object. The base class constructor must be called first, thus ensuring that any inherited members are initialized before any new members in the derived class. Figure 14.5 illustrates the relationship between TBase and TDerived.

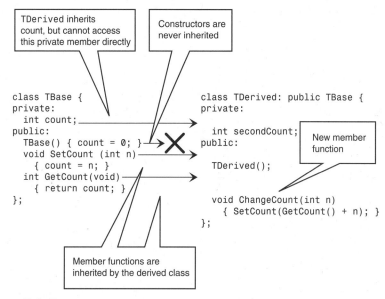

Figure 14.5. The relationship between TBase and TDerived.

The new TDerived class also declares a ChangeCount public member function for incrementing or decrementing the count value inherited from TBase. However, because count is private to TBase, ChangeCount() cannot access that member directly. You could *not* write ChangeCount() as

```
void ChangeCount(int n) { count += n; }  // ???
```

That statement won't compile because count is private to the base class, and only members of TBase can access count directly. To modify count, ChangeCount can call nonprivate inherited member functions such as SetCount() and GetCount():

```
void ChangeCount(int n) { SetCount(GetCount() + n); }
```

Introducing Protected Members

A *protected class member* is a cross between a private and a public member. Like private members, protected members are accessible only to other class member functions. Outside of the class, protected members are invisible. Like public members, protected members are inherited by derived classes and are accessible to member functions in the derived class. Figure 14.6 illustrates the relationship between derived and base classes and their private, protected, and public members.

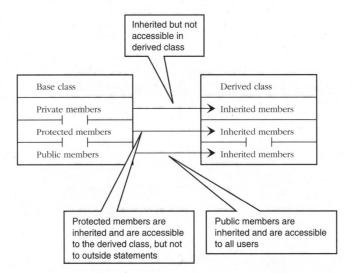

Figure 14.6. Private, protected, and public members in base and derived classes.

Keep the following rules in mind when deciding whether to make members private, protected, or public:

- A private member is accessible only to members of the class in which the private member is declared.

- A protected member is accessible to members of its own class and to any members in a derived class.

- A public member is accessible to the class's own members, to a derived class's members, and to all other users of the class.

> **NOTE:** Chapter 15, "Advanced Topics in C++," explains how *friends* of a class can alter these rules.

You may have as many private, protected, and public sections in a class as you need, and the sections may occur in any order. (However, if an inline member function refers to another member, that member must be declared before the inline member function is implemented.) Consider this class:

```
class TAnyClass {
private:
  int A;          // Accessible only to TAnyClass members
  void fa(void);  //      "          "        "        "
protected:
  int B;          // Accessible to TAnyClass and derived class members
  void fb(void);  //      "          "        "        "
public:
  int C;          // Accessible to all members and users
  void fc(void);  //      "          "        "        "
};
```

Data member A is private to TAnyClass and is accessible only to other members of the class—that is, member functions fa(), fb(), and fc() may access A directly. However, outside statements and even member functions in a derived class may never refer directly to A. In addition, member function fa() may be called only by other members of TAnyClass. No outside statement may call fa(), which is the exclusive and private property of TAnyClass.

Data member B and member function fb() are protected. These members are accessible to other members of TAnyClass and to any members in a derived class. However, outside the class, protected members have private status. No outside statements may access B or fb().

Data member C and member function fc() are public, and may be accessed directly by all TAnyClass members, by members in a derived class, and by statements outside the class. Public members are always accessible to all users of the class.

The private, protected, or public access specifiers may also preface a base class name in a derived class declaration. Using TAnyClass, a derived class can be declared as

```
class TDerived: public TAnyClass {
  // New data members, member functions, constructors, etc.
};
```

The `public` specifier may be replaced by `private` or `protected`. If none of these specifiers is used, members of the inherited class default to private status. The specifier affects the status of inherited members. In a derived class,

- A public base class's members retain their public, protected, and private access specifications.

- A protected base class's public members become protected members of the derived class. Protected and private members retain their original access specifications.

- A private base class's members all become private members in the derived class, regardless of those members' original access specifications.

The third case—a base class declared as private to a derived class—has the most profound effect on inherited members. In the following base class:

```
class TBase {
protected:
  int x;
public:
  int y;
  ...
};
```

if you derive a new class like this:

```
class TDerived: private TBase {  // Note "private" status
public:
  void f(void);
};
```

member function `f()` may access members x and y inherited from TBase. However, because TBase is declared as a private base class of TDerived, the status of members x and y change to private. In a subsequent derivation such as

```
class TDescendant: public TDerived {
public:
  void g(void);
};
```

member function g() may not access members x and y, despite these members' original protected and public status.

Qualifying Selected Members

A base class specifier potentially affects all inherited members. For instance, given this class A:

```
class A {
public:
  int x;
  A() { cout << "Inside A's constructor\n"; x = 0; }
  void Display(void) { cout << "x == " << x << '\n'; }
};
```

class B can inherit A as a private base class:

```
class B: private A {
public:
  B(): A() { cout << "Inside B's constructor\n"; }
};
```

Because A is declared private to B, all of A's formerly public members are now private members of B. This means that subsequent derived classes of B or any statements outside of B cannot call the Display() member function inherited from A. These lines compile and run correctly:

```
A objectA;
objectA.Display();  // Okay. Display() is public to A
```

But the following lines cause the compiler to complain that "'A::Display()' is not accessible..."

```
B objectB;
objectB.Display();  // ??? Display() is private to B
```

If you want to make only some inherited members private to a derived class, you can selectively qualify one or more members. Suppose you want class A's public int x member to become a private member of B, but you want A's public Display() member function to remain public in B so outside statements can call it. To do this, specify base class A as a private member of B as you did before, but in B's public section, qualify the inherited members you want to remain public:

```
class B: private A {
public:
  A::Display;  // Selectively qualify Display()
  B(): A() { cout << "Inside B's constructor\n"; }
};
```

The expression `A::Display;` in B's public section tells the compiler that this member, which was declared in A, should retain its public status. The inherited `int x` data member becomes a private member of B as it did before, but `Display()` remains public. The earlier attempt to call `Display()` for a B class object now compiles and works correctly:

```
B objectB;
objectB.Display();  // Display() is a public member of B
```

Using Constructors and Destructors

As mentioned earlier, a derived class typically provides a constructor if its base class has one, and a base class constructor must be called in order to initialize any data members in the base class.

Destructors, on the other hand, do not require such strict handling. A derived class needs to supply a destructor only if the derived class has any members that require deleting when an object of the derived class goes out of scope. Consider a base class declared as

```
class TBase {
private:
  char *basep;
public:
  TBase(const char *s) { basep = strdup(s); }
  ~TBase() { delete basep; }
  const char *GetStr(void) { return basep; }
};
```

This `TBase` class has one private data member, a pointer `basep` to a character string. The class constructor calls library function `strdup()` to copy a string argument to the heap, assigning the address of the allocated memory to `basep`. The destructor `~TBase()` deletes this memory block when an object of type `TBase` goes out of scope. Creating a class object like

```
TBase president("George Washington");
```

passes the string `"George Washington"` to the class constructor, which copies the string to the heap and assigns the string's address to president's `basep` data member. To display president's string, you could use the statement

```
cout << president.GetStr();
```

When president goes out of scope, the class destructor deletes the string that was copied onto the heap by the constructor. Figure 14.7 illustrates how president appears in memory.

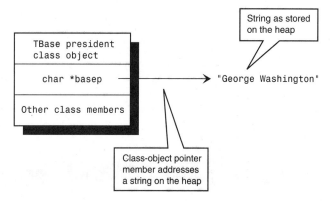

Figure 14.7. An object of type TBase in memory.

Consider what happens in a new class derived from TBase. The derived class might be declared as

```
class TDerived: public TBase {
private:
  char *uppercasep;
public:
  TDerived(const char *s);
  ~TDerived() { delete uppercasep; }
  const char *GetUStr(void) { return uppercasep; }
};
```

To its inheritance from TBase, TDerived adds a private char pointer data member named uppercasep to address an uppercase copy of the string stored by TBase. The derived class destructor deletes this new string. TDerived's constructor might be implemented as

```
TDerived::TDerived(const char *s)
  : TBase(s)  // Call base constructor
{
  uppercasep = strupr(strdup(s));  // Initialize TDerived data
}
```

The constructor calls TBase's constructor, which copies the string addressed by s to the heap and initializes the basep pointer to address the copied string. After completing this step, the derived class constructor makes another copy of the string, converts its characters to uppercase by calling strupr(), and assigns to uppercasep the address of the copied string.

If you now create an object of type TDerived, you create two copies of a string, one unchanged and one in uppercase. You might use a declaration such as

```
TDerived president("George Washington");
```

and then execute statements like these:

```
cout << "Original string: " << president.GetStr() << '\n';
cout << "Uppercase string: " << president.GetUStr() << '\n';
```

The first output statement displays the original unchanged copy of the string "George Washington". The second output statement displays the copy of that string in uppercase as initialized by the derived class constructor:

```
Original string: George Washington
Uppercase string: GEORGE WASHINGTON
```

Figure 14.8 illustrates how this new president class object is organized in memory.

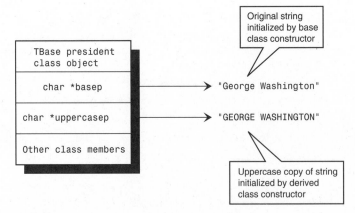

Figure 14.8. An object of type TDerived in memory.

A derived class object such as president must carefully delete any memory that it allocates. In Figure 14.8, president owns two memory blocks. When the object goes out of scope, its destructor deletes this memory and returns it to the heap for reuse.

The TBase class destructor deletes the memory addressed by data member basep. For simplicity, the destructor is coded inline:

```
~TBase() { delete basep; }
```

Similarly, the TDerived destructor deletes the memory addressed by data member uppercasep. Again, an inline declaration keeps the code simple:

```
~TDerived() { delete uppercasep; }
```

Unlike constructors, a destructor in a derived class does not explicitly call the base class destructor. (It is possible, however, for a program to call a destructor as a common member function. See Chapter 15, "Advanced Topics in C++.") C++ calls destructors automatically when objects of a class go out of scope. In Figure 14.8, for example, when president goes out of scope, C++ first calls the derived class destructor, which executes the statement

```
delete uppercasep;
```

Next, C++ calls the base class destructor, which executes the statement

```
delete basep;
```

As you can see, the two strings are deleted in the reverse order in which they were constructed. An easy way to remember the order that constructors and destructors are called is to think of a hierarchy of base and derived classes as floors in a building (see Figure 14.9). Base class constructors are called before derived class constructors, thus constructing derived objects from the ground up—similar to the way skyscrapers are built from the foundation to the clouds. When a derived class object goes out of scope, its destructors run in the reverse order, tearing an object apart by calling derived class destructors before destructors in base classes, much as a destruction crew demolishes a real building from the penthouse down.

Using Replacement Member Functions

As you've seen, a derived class typically provides new data and function members. But it may also replace member functions inherited from a base class. Suppose you declare class TBase like this:

```
class TBase {
private:
  char *sptr;
```

```
public:
  TBase(const char *s) { sptr = strdup(s); }
  ~TBase() { delete sptr; }
  void Display(void) { cout << sptr << '\n'; }
};
```

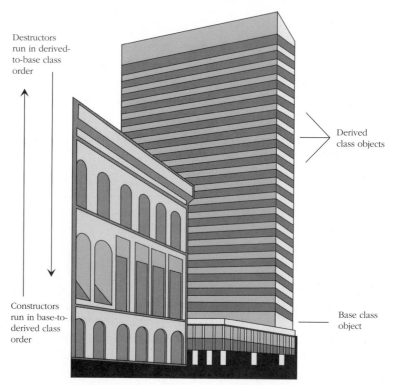

Destructors run in derived-to-base class order

Constructors run in base-to-derived class order

Derived class objects

Base class object

Figure 14.9. Like buildings, objects are constructed from the ground up and destroyed from the top down.

The class is similar to others you've seen in this chapter. The TBase() constructor calls strdup() to copy a string argument to the heap and addresses the allocated memory with private member sptr. The destructor ~TBase() deletes this addressed memory when a TBase object goes out of scope. Member function Display() displays the addressed string using an inline output stream statement. You could declare a TBase object as

```
TBase state("California");
```

and then display state's string with the statement

```
state.Display();
```

Later in this program's development, suppose you decide that all such strings should be labeled with the string "State:". You could accomplish that with the two statements

```
cout << "State: ";
state.Display();
```

but you would have to make similar modifications throughout the program. A better solution is to derive a new class from TBase and replace the inherted Display() member function with a modified version. You could write the derived class as

```
class TState: public TBase {
public:
  TState(const char *s): TBase(s) { }
  void Display(void);  // Replacement function
};
```

In addition to a constructor, the derived class declares a member function Display(). Because this member is identical to the base class Display(), the new member function replaces the inherited one. You might implement the replacement member function as

```
void TState::Display(void)
{
  cout << "State: ";  // New statement
  TBase::Display();    // Call replaced member function
}
```

The replacement Display() member function outputs the "State: " preface and calls the base class's Display() to finish the string. Prefacing Display() with TBase:: tells the compiler to call the member function in TBase.

Declaring and using a class object like this:

```
TState state("Ohio");
state.Display();
```

displays the string "State: Ohio"

A similar trick applies to constructors in derived classes. Suppose you need a few classes for various state names. You could design a class for each state, such as this one:

```
class TPennsylvania: public TState {
public:
  TPennsylvania(): TState("Pennsylvania") { }
};
```

The TPennsylvania class is derived from TState. The new constructor, which declares no parameters, passes the literal string "Pennsylvania" to the base class constructor. These lines:

```
TPennsylvania Pennsylvania;
Pennsylvania.Display();
```

create an object named Pennsylvania and display the state's name.

Constructors also might add additional parameters. Perhaps you need a class that, in addition to recording a state's name, also stores its population. You could derive the new class from TState:

```
class TPopulation: public TState {
private:
  long population;
public:
  TPopulation(long n, const char *name);
  void Display(void);
};
```

TPopulation's constructor specifies a long parameter for the state's population and a const char pointer for its name. You could write the constructor as

```
TPopulation::TPopulation(long n, const char *name)
  : TState(name)
{
  population = n;
}
```

The derived class calls the base class constructor, passing name to TState() to initialize the string portion of the derived class object. After that step, the constructor saves the long parameter n in the derived class's private population data member.

To display the state's name and its population, you could write the replacement Display() member function as

```
void TPopulation::Display(void)
{
```

```
    TState::Display();
    cout << "Population == " << population << '\n';
}
```

Elsewhere in the program, you could create and use a TPopulation class object to display a state's name and population:

```
TPopulation Nebraska(1570000, "Nebraska");
Nebraska.Display();
```

Using Inheritance

So far, this chapter has presented several academic facts about inheritance, derived classes, constructors, and destructors. A "real life" example illustrates how to put these concepts to work in real programs. With inheritance, you can derive a new class that augments the properties of an existing class. Rather than write code from scratch, with classes and inheritance you can sometimes build programs that take advantage of existing code more easily than with conventional function libraries.

Borland C++ contains an extensive class library. (See Chapter 17, "Borland's Class Library.") One class named Timer is tailor-made for timing events. In this section, you'll build a derived class that enhances Timer and creates a general-purpose benchmark class, which you might use to test algorithms, I/O throughput, or other speed-sensitive code.

Ignoring the class's private members—which a derived class can't use anyway—the Timer class is declared in file timer.h as

```
class Timer
{
public:
    Timer();        // Constructor
    void start();   // Start timing
    void stop();    // Stop timing
    void reset();   // Reset the timer
    int status();   // 0==not time; 1==timing in progress
    double time();  // Elapsed time in milliseconds
    static double resolution();  // See Chapter 15
private:
    ...
};
```

> **NOTE:** Static member functions are described in Chapter 15, "Advanced Topics in C++." For now, ignore the Timer class's static member function resolution().

Assuming that you installed Borland C++ using the default directory names, the complete declaration for the Timer class is located in C:\BORLANDC\ CLASSLIB\INCLUDE. The source code module TIMER.CPP is located in C:\BORLANDC\CLASSLIB\SOURCE. Examine these files to learn more about how Timer is programmed.

Interestingly, the Timer class module has a built-in test program that you can compile and run. To try this program from DOS, change to the directory containing TIMER.CPP. Then, enter the command **bcc -DTEST_TIMER -I..\include timer**. The -D option defines a symbol TEST_TIMER that engages the test program, which is normally not compiled. The -I command specifies the directory where timer.h is located. After compiling, run TIMER. The program displays a report of the timer's accuracy:

```
Resolution: 8.39e-07
   0 ms., actual time = 0.024674 seconds.
 100 ms., actual time = 0.127362 seconds.
 200 ms., actual time = 0.222327 seconds.
 300 ms., actual time = 0.314453 seconds.
 400 ms., actual time = 0.393548 seconds.
 500 ms., actual time = 0.465171 seconds.
 600 ms., actual time = 0.630901 seconds.
 700 ms., actual time = 0.738385 seconds.
 800 ms., actual time = 0.775155 seconds.
 900 ms., actual time = 0.836996 seconds.
```

These figures suggest that Timer isn't very accurate, but it's still useful for timing events to an accuracy of about one-tenth of a second.

Building a Class for all Benchmarks

Now that a base class has been located and tested, the next step is to derive a new class from Timer. The class needs a constructor along with member functions to call a test function and to report the elapsed time for a specified number of tests. Listing 14.1, bench.h, shows one way to design a class with these characteristics.

Listing 14.1. bench.h (TBench **class declaration**).

```
 1:  /* bench.h -- TBench class declaration */
 2:
 3:  #ifndef __BENCH_H
 4:  #define __BENCH_H  1   /* Prevent multiple #includes */
 5:
 6:  #include <timer.h>
 7:
 8:  typedef void (* testfn)(void);
 9:
10:  class TBench: public Timer {
11:  public:
12:    TBench(): Timer() { }
13:    void Benchmark(long numTests, testfn tf);
14:    void Report(void);
15:  };
16:
17:  #endif  /* __BENCH_H */
```

Class TBench is derived from Timer. The TBench() constructor (line 12) calls the base class Timer's constructor, but adds no new statements to construct TBench objects. Member function Benchmark() (line 13) lists two parameters: numTests, equal to the number of tests to perform, and tf, a pointer to the test function, which must return void and have no parameters (see typedef at line 8). A second member function, Report() at line 14, displays test results.

Listing 14.2, BENCH.CPP, implements the TBench derived class.

Listing 14.2. BENCH.CPP (TBench **class implementation**).

```
 1:  /* bench.cpp -- TBench class implementation */
 2:
 3:  #include <stdio.h>
 4:  #include "bench.h"
 5:
```

continues

Listing 14.2. continued

```
 6:   // Call testfunction tf a total of numTests times
 7:   void TBench::Benchmark(long numTests, testfn tf)
 8:   {
 9:     printf("Running %ld tests...", numTests);
10:     reset();      // Reset timer to zero
11:     start();      // Start timing
12:     while (--numTests >= 0)
13:       (* tf)();   // Call user test function
14:     stop();       // Stop timing
15:     puts("\nTests completed");
16:   }
17:
18:   // Display test results
19:   void TBench::Report(void)
20:   {
21:     double result = time();
22:     if (result < resolution())
23:       puts("Results too small for accuracy");
24:     printf("Elapsed time == %6f sec.\n", result);
25:   }
```

Lines 7–16 implement member function Benchmark(). After displaying the number of tests to perform, the function resets and starts the timer by calling inherited member functions reset() and start().

Lines 12–13 repeatedly call the test function addressed by pointer tf. After the final test is performed, line 14 calls another inherited member function, stop(), which halts the timer. Line 15 displays a brief message to let users know the tests are finished.

Lines 19–25 implement the other TBench member function, Report(). Line 21 assigns to result the value of inherited member function time(). Lines 22–23 display a message if the elapsed time is too small to be trustworthy. (If you see this message, try increasing the number of tests.) Line 24 displays the benchmark's results in seconds.

To use the TBench class, create an object and pass to Benchmark() the number of tests to perform and a test function's address. Next, call Report(). Listing 14.3, TBENCH.CPP, demonstrates these steps and serves as a shell for your own benchmarks. To compile TBENCH.CPP and the BENCH.CPP module requires linking to the library file TCLASDBS.LIB, which contains the Timer class's compiled code. If you are using the command-line compiler, enter the following two lines into a file TURBOC.CFG (or edit that file if it exists in your BORLANDC\BIN directory):

```
-Ic:\borlandc\classlib\include;c:\borlandc\include
-Lc:\borlandc\classlib\lib;c:\borlandc\lib
```

Next, from DOS, enter the command **bcc tbench bench tclasdbs.lib**, or make sure the above directories are listed in an IDE. Then create and compile a project consisting of the files TBENCH.CPP and BENCH.CPP.

NOTE: If you installed the supplied diskette, you can compile TBENCH using the MAKE file TBENCH.MAK (not listed here). Change to the directory that contains TBENCH.CPP and at a DOS prompt enter **make -ftbench.mak**. The Borland C++ MAKE.EXE utility must be in the current path, and you might have to edit the drive and directories in TBENCH.MAK. (See Chapter 20, "DOS Tools and Techniques," for more information about MAKE.EXE.)

Listing 14.3. TBENCH.CPP (Test the TBench class).

```
 1:  #include <iostream.h>
 2:  #include <stdio.h>
 3:  #include "bench.h"
 4:
 5:  #define NUMTESTS 20000
 6:
 7:  void Testfn(void);
 8:
 9:  main()
10:  {
11:    TBench test;
12:
13:    cout << "Testing sprintf() function\n";
14:    test.Benchmark(NUMTESTS, Testfn);
15:    test.Report();
16:    return 0;
17:  }
```

continues

Listing 14.3. continued

```
18:
19:  void Testfn(void)
20:  {
21:    char buffer[80];
22:    double d = 3.14159;
23:
24:    sprintf(buffer, "%lf", d);
25:  }
```

Line 11 declares a TBench object named test. Because C++ calls the object's constructor (which calls the base class Timer constructor), you can be certain that the test object is properly initialized and is therefore ready for use. After displaying a brief message, the program calls member function Benchmark() (line 14) and passes the number of tests to perform and the address of a test function. Line 15 calls test's Report() member function to display the test results. The test function (lines 19–25) calls sprintf() just for demonstration. For a different time trial, replace Testfn()'s contents with other statements. Running the program displays a report:

```
Testing sprintf() function
Running 20000 tests...
Tests completed
Elapsed time == 4.118690 sec.
```

> **HINT:** When beginning a new program, look for one or more classes with some of the capabilities you need. Use the existing classes as bases to derive new classes. To these new classes you can add constructors, destructors, data members, and member functions so the existing classes can do your bidding. This is not to suggest that OOP makes programming simple, but with OOP and C++ classes, at least you simplify the job of reusing existing code.

Polymorphism

Few subjects in OOP raise a beginning programmer's eyebrows higher than polymorphism—actually a simple concept with a fancy name. Borrowed from biology, the term *polymorphism* describes related organisms that can assume a variety of forms. In C++, polymorphic class objects addressed by pointers can appear to change form at runtime. By doing so, these objects alter the program's outcome.

C++ makes polymorphism possible with the application of a rule that you should memorize, stick on the refrigerator, tattoo on your arm, or simply never forget: *A base class pointer may address an object of that class or an object of any class derived from the base.* (See Figure 14.10.)

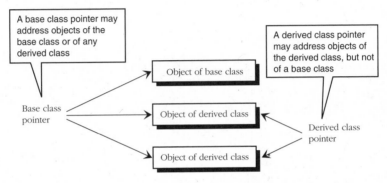

Figure 14.10. A base class pointer may address a derived class object.

This rule is a one-way street. In other words, a pointer to a derived class object may not address an object of a base class. A good way to keep this rule straight in your mind is to think of classes as building blocks stacked on top of one another. A base class typically declares various data members, which a derived class inherits. Given a pointer to a base class (the first block), the compiler expects to find those inherited members in an addressed object of the derived class type (a second block inserted under the first). (See Figure 14.11.)

Again using the analogy of two blocks—one block representing the base class and two blocks representing a derived class and its base—it would make no sense for a derived-class pointer to address a base class object. The derived-class pointer addresses a "two-block" object. It can't address the base class "single block" because the program might attempt to read or write data to the nonexistent "second block" found only in the derived class object.

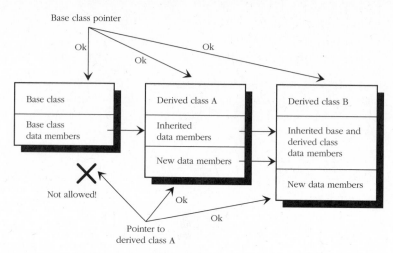

Figure 14.11. A base class pointer can address data members inherited by a derived class.

Introducing Virtual Member Functions

Polymorphism uses a new C++ feature that you haven't seen before, virtual functions. Keeping in mind the class pointer rules stated in the preceding section, consider a simple object, which declares a data member, a constructor, and a member function:

```
class TValue {
protected:
  int value;
public:
  TValue(int n) { value = n; }
  int GetValue(void) { return value; }
};
```

You can declare and use a TValue object, which stores and regurgitates an integer value on demand:

```
TValue x(10);                    // Initialize TValue object x
cout << x.GetValue() << '\n';    // Displays 10
```

Next, derive a new class from TValue. For demonstration purposes, the derived class multiplies the base class value by a specified amount. Let's call the class TMult:

```
class TMult: public TValue {
protected:
  int multiplier;
public:
  TMult(int n, int m): TValue(n) { multiplier = m; }
  int GetValue(void) { return value * multiplier; }
};
```

TMult replaces its inherited member function GetValue() with a new function that returns value * multiplier. If you declare an object of type TMult and call its GetValue() member function, the result—as you might expect—is the product of the two values used to initialize the object:

```
TMult y(10, 2);                   // Initialize TMult object y
cout << y.GetValue() << '\n';  // Displays 20
```

Consider what happens now if you address a TSingle or a TDouble object with a pointer. You can declare and initialize a TValue pointer tvp like this:

```
TValue *tvp = new TValue(10);
```

and call the GetValue() member function for the addressed object:

```
cout << tvp->GetValue() << '\n';  // Displays 10
```

Of course, you can also declare a pointer to the derived class TMult and call the replacement GetValue() member function:

```
TMult *tmp = new TMult(10, 2);
cout << tmp->GetValue() << '\n';  // Displays 20
```

Applying the C++ rule about pointers and derived classes, you also can declare a pointer to the base class:

```
TValue *basep;  // Pointer to a TValue object
```

and then assign the address of a derived object to that pointer:

```
basep = new TMult(10, 2);  // !!! Address a derived object
```

Pointer basep was declared to address an object of class TValue, but this statement creates a derived TMult object and assigns the object's address to basep. What do you suppose happens if you execute the following statement?

```
cout << basep->GetValue() << '\n';  // ??? Displays 10
```

This statement compiles, but it does not produce the expected result, 20. As far as C++ knows, pointer basep addresses a TValue object. Therefore, C++ calls the

GetValue() member function in the base class TValue. But we want C++ to call the GetValue() member function for the derived object that the pointer actually addresses.

The solution to this predicament is to declare GetValue() as a virtual member function. Calls to virtual member functions are linked at runtime (by a technique known as *late binding*). Calls to run-of-the-mill member functions are linked at compile time (*early binding*). Virtual member functions and late binding make it possible for objects to determine their own behavior at runtime—the chief characteristic of polymorphism.

> **NOTE:** Borland C++ statically links virtual member functions if it can safely do so without negatively affecting any uses of those functions. The compiler performs this optimization automatically.

Listing 14.4, POLY.CPP, declares the TValue and TMult classes as described earlier, but with one change. In the new classes, GetValue() is declared as a virtual member function.

Listing 14.4. POLY.CPP (Demonstrates polymorphism).

```
 1:  #include <iostream.h>
 2:
 3:  class TValue {
 4:  protected:
 5:    int value;
 6:  public:
 7:    TValue(int n) { value = n; }
 8:    virtual int GetValue(void) { return value; }
 9:  };
10:
11:  class TMult: public TValue {
12:  protected:
13:    int multiplier;
14:  public:
15:    TMult(int n, int m): TValue(n) { multiplier = m; }
16:    virtual int GetValue(void) { return value * multiplier; }
17:  };
18:
```

```
19:  main()
20:  {
21:    TValue *basep;
22:
23:    basep = new TValue(10);
24:    cout << basep->GetValue() << '\n';  // Displays 10
25:    delete basep;
26:
27:    basep = new TMult(10, 2);            // !!!
28:    cout << basep->GetValue() << '\n';  // !!! Displays 20
29:    delete basep;
30:
31:    return 0;
32:  }
```

Lines 8 and 16 preface GetValue()'s declaration with the keyword virtual. This informs the compiler that calls to GetValue() are to be linked at runtime. Technically, the addresses of the two GetValue() virtual member functions are stored in an internal table. When statements call virtual member functions, C++ looks up the correct function addresses from this table. If you think this lookup action takes time, you are correct. Using virtual member functions might reduce the program's performance, although in practice, serious slowdowns are rare.

Virtual member functions are inherited by derived classes, as are common member functions. However, once declared virtual, a member function's declaration may not change. In other words, to add new programming to GetValue(), derived class TMult (lines 11–17) must declare this member function exactly as TValue does (lines 3–9).

When you run POLY, you see two values, 10 and 20, on-screen—the results of calling the two GetValue() virtual member functions. Line 21 declares a pointer basep to class TValue. Line 23 calls new to create a TValue object, which is initialized to the value 10 (line 24).

After deleting this object (line 25), line 27 creates an object of the derived class TMult. Because of C++'s class-pointer rule, basep may address an object of this derived class, even though the pointer was declared to address a TValue object. Because basep addresses a TMult object, line 28 displays the value 20.

Carefully compare the output statements at lines 24 and 28. Ignoring the comments at the ends of the lines, you can see that the two statements are exactly identical. If the two statements are identical, however, how can they produce different output? Answer: The addressed objects determine for themselves which of the two virtual GetValue() member functions to call. Even more importantly, this decision is made by the program at runtime, not by the compiler or programmer.

> **NOTE:** You will encounter many more samples of polymorphism and virtual member functions in future examples. Don't be concerned, however, if you are struggling with the concept. Most programmers don't grasp the significance of virtual functions and polymorphism until they use these techniques for a period of time.

It may be helpful to think of polymorphism as a response to a message. For instance, in classical OOP terms, an expression such as

```
basep->GetValue();
```

sends a "message" named GetValue() to the object addressed by basep. Upon receiving this message, the object responds in some predetermined way. Most importantly, that same message could be sent to other objects that determine their own responses (or they might ignore the message). Regardless of the type of object that basep addresses, the object itself responds in its programmed fashion to the GetValue() message.

Using Pure Virtual Member Functions

A pure virtual member function is an unfinished placeholder that a derived class is expected to complete. Declare a pure virtual member function as you normally would, but follow its declaration in a class with = 0. For example, in this class

```
class AbstractClass {
public:
  virtual void f1(void);       // Normal virtual member function
  virtual void f2(void) = 0;   // Pure virtual member function
  ...
};
```

f2() is a pure virtual member function. The compiler does not require the implementation of f2() as it does of other member functions declared in a class.

When a class contains one or more pure virtual member functions, it is called an *abstract class*. Like an abstract idea, an abstract class describes an unrealized concept. An abstract class is a kind of schematic from which you are expected to build one or more derived classes. With C++, you cannot create objects of an abstract class type. For example, you could not declare an object of type `AbstractClass`. If you try to compile the line

```
AbstractClass myObject;   // ???
```

the compiler tells you that it "Cannot create an instance of class 'AbstractClass.'" However, other member functions in `AnyClass` may call a pure virtual member function. For instance, member function `f1()` could call `f2()`:

```
void AbstractClass::f1(void)
{
  f2();   // Call pure virtual member function
  ...     // Other statements in f1()
}
```

To use the abstract class, you must derive a new class from it:

```
class MyClass: public AbstractClass {
public:
  virtual void f2(void);   // Former pure virtual member function
  ...
};
```

The derived `MyClass` inherits the pure virtual member function, but declares it without `= 0`. (Including the suffix would cause `MyClass` to become an abstract class.) Elsewhere, you must implement member function `f2()`:

```
void MyClass::f2(void)
{
  ...   // Statements in member function
}
```

Calls to the original pure virtual member function—as made in this case by `AnyClass::f1()`, for example—are now redirected to `MyClass::f2()`. Simply by implementing a pure virtual member function in a derived class, you can plug in code that other members can call, without requiring those other members to be revised or even recompiled. Pure virtual member functions operate like hooks onto which you can attach your own code.

Now that all pure virtual member functions are accounted for, the compiler accepts objects of type `MyClass`:

```
MyClass myObject;
```

Executing the statement

```
myObject.f1();
```

calls the inherited f1(), which calls f2() in MyClass.

The next several listings show a practical example of a pure virtual member function and an abstract class. The class, TSet, can store simple sets of objects of an unspecified type. Listing 14.5, set.h, declares the class along with a few other items.

Listing 14.5. set.h (TSet class declaration).

```
 1:  // set.h -- TSet class declaration
 2:
 3:  #ifndef __SET_H
 4:  #define __SET_H  1    // Prevent multiple #includes
 5:
 6:  class TElem;
 7:  typedef TElem* PTElem;
 8:  typedef PTElem* PPTElem;
 9:
10:  class TSet;
11:  typedef TSet* PTSet;
12:
13:  class TSet {
14:  private:
15:    int max;       // Maximum number of elements
16:    int index;     // Set array index
17:    PPTElem set;   // Pointer to array of PTElem pointers
18:  protected:
19:    virtual int CompareElems(PTElem p1, PTElem p2) = 0;
20:  public:
21:    TSet(int n)
22:      { max = n; index = 0; set = new PTElem[n]; }
23:    virtual ~TSet()
24:      { delete[] set; }
25:    void AddElem(PTElem p);
26:    int HasElem(PTElem p);
27:  };
28:
29:  #endif   // __SET_H
```

To make `TSet` as versatile as possible, the class needs to store objects of an unspecified class. As line 6 shows, C++ permits incomplete class declarations that have no bodies:

```
class TElem;   // Incomplete class declaration
```

Given this declaration, `TElem` objects can be listed in function parameters, returned by functions, and so on. Later, of course, the program must specify a real class for `TElem`. However, the incomplete class declaration makes it possible to write the `TSet` class without knowing in advance what kind of class objects are to be stored in the set.

Lines 7–8 declare two optional symbols, which help keep program listings easy to read. `PTElem` is declared as an alias for `TElem*`. In other words, `PTElem` is a pointer to an object of type `TElem`. Similarly, `PPTElem` is declared as an alias for a `PTElem` pointer—that is, a pointer *to a pointer to* a `TElem` object. The `TSet` class uses `PPTElem` to create a dynamically sized array of `PTElem` pointers.

Lines 10–11 use similar declarations to specify an incomplete `TSet` class and an alias symbol `PTSet` as a pointer to a `TSet` object. The only reason for declaring `TSet` incompletely at line 10 is to permit the subsequent `typedef` declaration to compile.

The `TSet` class declaration comes next (lines 13–27). Three private data members hide the class's inner details. In this version of `TSet`, a set is stored as a dynamically sized array of `PTElem` pointers, using a `PPTElem` pointer to address the array. (Member `set` is literally a pointer to an array of pointers to `TElem` objects.) Members `max` and `index` are used to manage this array.

HINT: Because all `TSet`'s data members are private to the class, they could be changed at a later time without affecting outside code. When designing classes, it's often useful to choose a simple, if not ideally efficient, method for storing class data. As long as you make that data private to the class, you can always change it later without affecting any programming outside the class.

Line 19 declares a pure virtual member function, `CompareElems`, as a protected member of `TSet`. Pure virtual member functions also can be public, but are often protected because a derived class is expected to finish them. `CompareElems()` is supposed to return zero if two `TElem` objects addressed by pointers `p1` and `p2` are identical. Obviously, you can't complete `CompareElems()` yet because you don't know what a TElem class contains. However, by using pure virtual member functions, you can at least finish the generic programming needed by TSet.

That programming is declared and partially implemented at lines 22–26. The inline class constructor (lines 21–22) initializes the class's private data members and calls new to allocate an array of PTElem pointers. The class destructor (lines 23–24) deletes this memory, cleaning up any TSet objects before they go out of scope.

Member functions AddElem() and HasElem() (lines 25–26) are not appropriate for inline treatment. The class's implementation module (Listing 14.6, SET.CPP) completes these functions. (You can compile this much of the program, but to use the class, you must supply a host program. An example follows in the next section.)

Listing 14.6. SET.CPP (TSet class implementation).

```
 1:  // set.cpp -- TSet class implementation
 2:
 3:  #include <iostream.h>
 4:  #include <stdlib.h>
 5:  #include "set.h"
 6:
 7:  // Add element to set. (Aborts program on error!)
 8:  void TSet::AddElem(PTElem p)
 9:  {
10:    if (set == NULL) {
11:      cout << "\nERROR: Out of memory";
12:      exit(1);
13:    }
14:    if (index >= max) {
15:      cout << "\nERROR: Set limit exceeded";
16:      exit(1);
17:    }
18:    set[index] = p;
19:    ++index;
20:  }
21:
22:  // Returns true if element at p is in the set
23:  int TSet::HasElem(PTElem p)
24:  {
25:    if (set == NULL)
26:      return 0;  // No elements in a null set
27:    for (int i = 0; i < index; i++)
```

```
28:        if (CompareElems(p, set[i]) == 0)
29:          return 1;  // Element is in set
30:      return 0;  // Element is not in set
31:    }
```

SET.CPP implements TSet's two member functions, AddElem() and HasElem(). Interestingly, these functions are written before the design of the elements on which they operate. All that's known about the elements is that they are of an unspecified class named TElem.

Even so, AddElem() (lines 8–20) adds a TElem object addressed by parameter p to the set. Lines 10–17 check for error conditions and halt the program if insufficient memory is available or if the set is full. (A more sophisticated class would provide better error handling, but this minimal design will do for the example.) Lines 18–19 store the TElem object addressed by p in the set array.

Member function HasElem() (lines 23–31) returns *true* if the passed TElem object is currently in the set. HasElem() calls the class's pure virtual member function CompareElems() at line 28. Although this function does not yet exist, it's okay to call it! A derived class must eventually supply the real programming in order to compare two elements. Because of the virtual member functions and polymorphism, the statement at line 28 can call that as yet unsupplied code.

The next program, TSET.CPP (Listing 14.7), supplies the missing pieces in TSet and TElem to create a set of strings equal to the names of the months that have 30 days: April, June, November, and September. The program illustrates how virtual member functions and abstract classes can provide the basic designs of a program that will be completed later. Compile the program and the SET module with the DOS command **bcc tset set**. You also can create and compile an IDE project consisting of the files TSET.CPP and SET.CPP.

Listing 14.7. TSET.CPP (Test TSet **class).**

```
1:   #include <iostream.h>
2:   #include <string.h>
3:   #include "set.h"
4:
5:   class TElem {
6:   private:
```

continues

Listing 14.7. continued

```
 7:    char *sp;   // Pointer to element string
 8:  public:
 9:    TElem(const char *s) { sp = strdup(s); }
10:    virtual ~TElem() { delete sp; }
11:    virtual const char *GetString(void) { return sp; }
12:  };
13:
14:  class TMySet: public TSet {
15:  protected:
16:    virtual int CompareElems(PTElem p1, PTElem p2);
17:  public:
18:    TMySet(int n): TSet(n) { }
19:  };
20:
21:  void Test(const char *s, PTSet setp);
22:
23:  main()
24:  {
25:    TMySet thirties(12);  // A set of 12 TElem objects
26:
27:    thirties.AddElem(new TElem("Sep"));
28:    thirties.AddElem(new TElem("Apr"));
29:    thirties.AddElem(new TElem("Jun"));
30:    thirties.AddElem(new TElem("Nov"));
31:    Test("Jan", &thirties);
32:    Test("Feb", &thirties);
33:    Test("Mar", &thirties);
34:    Test("Apr", &thirties);
35:    Test("May", &thirties);
36:    Test("Jun", &thirties);
37:    Test("Jul", &thirties);
38:    Test("Aug", &thirties);
39:    Test("Sep", &thirties);
40:    Test("Oct", &thirties);
41:    Test("Nov", &thirties);
42:    Test("Dec", &thirties);
43:    return 0;
44:  }
45:
46:  // Report whether string s is in the set at setp
```

```
47:   void Test(const char *s, PTSet setp)
48:   {
49:     TElem testElem(s);
50:
51:     if (setp->HasElem(&testElem))
52:       cout << s << " is in the set\n";
53:     else
54:       cout << s << " is not in the set\n";
55:   }
56:
57:   // Return zero if two TElems are equal; nonzero if not
58:   int TMySet::CompareElems(PTElem p1, PTElem p2)
59:   {
60:     return (stricmp(p1->GetString(), p2->GetString()));
61:   }
```

The first step in using the TSet class is to write a TElem class. Objects of the TElem class are stored in the set. Lines 5–12 declare a sample TElem class that can store a string value. All of the class's member functions are written inline.

Lines 14–19 derive a new class, TMySet, from the abstract TSet. The new class constructor performs no new duties, so it simply calls the base class TSet() constructor. Most importantly, line 16 declares a virtual member function CompareElems(), which was declared as a pure virtual member function in TSet().

Skip to the end of the listing where CompareElems() is implemented. The completed function calls library function stricmp() to compare two strings. These strings are obtained by calling the TElem GetString() member function (also see line 11). When line 51 calls HasElems(), that member function calls the completed CompareElems() at lines 58–61. You might want to run the finished program in Turbo Debugger and trace this function call to observe how the program redirects it to CompareElems().

This example of virtual member functions and abstract classes leads to some interesting observations:

- The SET module can be compiled ahead of time and inserted into a class library. Users do not require the source code file SET.CPP of the TSet class. The host program needs only set.h.

- Another program can use the TSet class to store a set of different TElem class objects. You do not need to recompile SET.CPP for each new use of the class.

TSet provides some rudimentary set operations. It's up to a user of the class to fill in the details.

- On the downside, when designing abstract classes such as TSet, programmers usually add numerous virtual member functions in case they are needed. When designing abstract classes, try to provide only the minimum required members instead of attempting to cover every possible base. If your classes are too complex, other programmers (or even you at a later date) may be discouraged from deriving new classes from them.

Using Virtual Destructors

Member functions and destructors—but not constructors—may be virtual. A virtual destructor typically is used when one class needs to delete objects of a derived class that are addressed by pointers to a base class. For example, consider this class, which can store a string value:

```
class TBase {
private:
  char *sp1;
public:
  TBase(const char *s)
    { sp1 = strdup(s); }
  virtual ~TBase()
    { delete sp1; }
};
```

The TBase class constructor allocates space for a string by calling strdup() and stores the new string's address in sp1. The virtual destructor deletes this memory when an object of type TBase goes out of scope.

Next, derive a new class from TBase:

```
class TDerived: public TBase {
private:
  char *sp2;
public:
  TDerived(const char *s1, const char *s2): TBase(s1)
    { sp2 = strdup(s2); }
  virtual ~TDerived()
    { delete sp2; }
};
```

The new class stores a second string that sp2 addresses. The new constructor calls TBase(), passes one string to the base class, and allocates some additional memory for a second string, which is deleted by the class destructor.

When a TDerived object goes out of scope, it's important that both strings be deleted. Suppose you declare a pointer to TBase but assign it the address of a TDerived object—this is perfectly allowable because, as you've learned before, a base class pointer may address an object of that class or of any derived class. The program at this stage looks like this:

```
TBase *pbase;
pbase = new TDerived("String 1", "String 2");
```

Consider what happens later when the program deletes the object addressed by pbase:

```
delete pbase;  // !!!
```

The compiler was told that pbase addresses a TBase object, and the program normally would call TBase's destructor when the addressed object is deleted. However, pbase actually addresses a TDerived object, and that class's destructor must be called as well as the one in the base class.

Because the destructors are declared to be virtual, calls to them are linked at runtime, and the object itself determines which destructor should be called. If the destructors were not virtual, however, only the base class destructor would be called, leaving the second string on the heap and causing a serious bug.

Multiple Inheritance

So far in this chapter, derived and base classes have been related by single inheritance. Multiple inheritance describes a more complex relationship in which a single class inherits the data members and member functions from more than one base class. Figure 14.12 illustrates the concept of multiple inheritance.

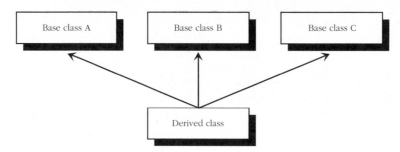

Figure 14.12. Multiple inheritance

Loading the Bases

To derive a new class from multiple base classes, list the base class names after the new one. If A, B, and C are classes, a new class D could inherit all of them like this:

```
class D: public A, public B, public C {
  ...
};
```

You can also declare multiple base classes as private or protected to a derived class. Or, you can use a mix of specifiers:

```
class D: protected A, public B, C {
  ...
};
```

Base class C defaults to private status, but for clarity, it's best to state explicitly a base class's private, protected, or public status. The same rules listed earlier for single inheritance apply to multiple inherited base classes.

The difference in multiple inheritance is that a derived class receives all of the inheritable properties from all of the listed base classes. In the event of a name conflict (two base classes declaring a member function of the same name, for example) use the scope resolution operator to specify which member you intend to use. For instance, suppose classes A and B each have a public Display() member function. In the derived class:

```
class D: public A, public B {
public:
  void f(void);
  ...
};
```

member function `f()` must specify which of the conflicting `Display()` functions to use. It does this by prefacing function calls with the appropriate class name and a scope resolution operator:

```
void D::f(void)
{
  Display();       // ??? Ambiguous; won't compile
  A::Display();    // Call A's member function
  B::Display();    // Call B's member function
}
```

Using Multiple Base Class Constructors

A class derived from multiple base classes might also need to call multiple base class constructors. If A, B, and C are classes with default constructors, a derived class D can call those constructors like this:

```
class D: public A, public B, public C {
public:
  D(): A(), B(), C() { }  // Inline constructor
  ...
};
```

Or, the constructor can be declared

```
class D: public A, public B, public C {
public:
  D();  // Externally implemented constructor
  ...
};
```

and implemented separately, typically in another file:

```
D::D()
  : A(), B(), C()
{
  ... // Statements in constructor D()
}
```

Of course, the constructors may have various parameters not shown here. The constructors are called in the order in which their base classes are declared. However, it's generally unwise to devise classes that depend on other class objects to be constructed in a particular order. As a rule, classes should operate as independently of each other as possible.

NOTE: Suppose a class depends on other class objects to be initialized in a certain order. Instead of having one class inherit other class properties, you might declare the dependent classes as data members of a new class. The new class could then control when and how the dependent members are initialized.

Using Virtual Base Classes

Derived classes and their bases form a class hierarchy that can grow tremendously complex even in relatively simple programs. A base class can be inherited by one or more other classes that in turn can become base classes for still more classes. All of these classes are consequently related by single or multiple inheritance as though they were biblical characters begatting one another until no one can tell who is related to whom.

It's easy to understand how conflicts arise in a complex class hierarchy, especially when multiple inheritance is involved. One of the most common conflicts occurs when a derived class inherits too many copies of a particular base—like lottery winners, for example, who suddenly acquire more "cousins" than they previously knew existed.

To demonstrate how derived classes can get into inheritance trouble, examine the classes from the following program in Listing 14.8, FRANCH.CPP. The program uses familiar relationships between fictitious companies and three fictitious franchisees: Bob, Ted, and Alice. The program may seem a bit silly, but borrowing familiar relationships from the real world helps to explain a typical and often exasperating problem with multiple inheritance.

Listing 14.8. FRANCH.CPP (Multiple inheritance and franchisees).

```
1:  /* franch.cpp */
2:
3:  #include <iostream.h>
4:  #include <string.h>
5:
6:  class Company {
7:  private:
8:    char *name;
9:  public:
10:   Company(const char *s) {
11:     name = strdup(s);
12:     cout << " In constructor for ";
13:     Display();
14:   }
15:   virtual ~Company() {
16:     cout << " In destructor for ";
17:     Display();
18:     delete name;
19:   }
20:   void Display(void) { cout << name << '\n'; }
21: };
22:
23: class Jennys: public Company {
24: public:
25:   Jennys(): Company("Jenny's") { }
26: };
27:
28: class McDougles: public Company {
29: public:
30:   McDougles(): Company("McDougles") { }
31: };
32:
33: class BurgerQueen: public Company {
34: public:
35:   BurgerQueen(): Company("BurgerQueen") { }
36: };
37:
```

continues

Listing 14.8. continued

```
38:  class Bob
39:    : public Jennys,
40:      public McDougles {
41:  };
42:
43:  class Ted
44:    : public McDougles,
45:      public BurgerQueen {
46:  };
47:
48:  class Alice
49:    : public Jennys,
50:      public McDougles,
51:      public BurgerQueen {
52:  };
53:
54:  main()
55:  {
56:    Bob *bobp;
57:    Ted *tedp;
58:    Alice *alicep;
59:
60:    cout << "\nInitializing Bob's restaurant\n";
61:    bobp = new Bob;
62:    cout << "Initializing Ted's restaurant\n";
63:    tedp = new Ted;
64:    cout << "Initializing Alice's restaurant\n";
65:    alicep = new Alice;
66:
67:    cout << "\nDeleting Bob's restaurant\n";
68:    delete bobp;
69:    cout << "Deleting Ted's restaurant\n";
70:    delete tedp;
71:    cout << "Deleting Alice's restaurant\n";
72:    delete alicep;
73:
74:    return 0;
75:  }
```

Figure 14.13 illustrates the relationships among the classes in FRANCH.CPP. At the root of the hierarchy is the Company class, which serves as a base class for three derived classes: Jennys, McDougles, and BurgerQueen. Each of these "company" classes is derived from Company, and each class therefore inherits a name data member (see line 8) and a Display() member function (line 20).

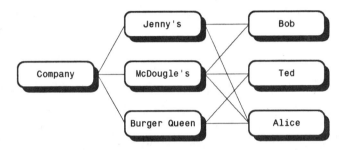

Figure 14.13. Class hierarchy in program FRANCH.CPP.

The three adventurous investors, Bob, Ted, and Alice, are declared as classes (lines 38–52). Class Bob derives his culinary empire from two Company classes, Jennys and McDougles. Class Ted derives his fortunes from McDougles and BurgerQueen. Alice, the most ambitious soul in the group, takes on the three Company classes: Jennys, McDougles, and BurgerQueen. When you run the program, you see a report that indicates which constructors and destructors run at what times as they initialize and destroy three class objects, one for each franchisee (lines 56–58).

> **HINT:** When debugging your own code, you might use output statements similar to those in FRANCH.CPP. Displaying a message in a constructor, destructor, or member function often provides useful feedback about a complex class hierarchy's organization.

The class hierarchy in FRANCH.CPP seems simple enough. But a subtle problem with the class relationships arises if another class is derived from the group of companies and investors. Suppose another corporation purchases some of the parent companies and selected franchisees. As in the real world of corporate finance, the complex relationships among companies and people can easily get out of hand.

Consider a `Corporation` class that attempts to inherit the `McDougles` company along with franchisees `Ted` and `Alice`:

```
class Corporation
  : public McDougles,  // ???
    public Ted,
    public Alice {
public:
  ...
};
```

Refer back to Figure 14.13 and you can see why this `Corporation` can never get off the ground. (The code does not even compile.) `Ted` and `Alice` already derive in part from `McDougles`. When `Corporation` attempts to do the same, it ends up with multiple `McDougles` base classes. At this point, the compiler warns you that "`McDougles` is inaccessible because [it is] also in `Ted`."

When you receive a similar warning for a complex set of related classes, try to identify those base classes which require only a single object. In the case of `Corporation`, it makes sense to have only one `McDougles` company. Even though `Ted` is derived from `McDougles`, it is the same `McDougles` from which `Corporation` is attempting to derive. In the process of acquiring `Ted`'s assets, the `Corporation` does not end up with two separate `McDougles` parent companies. There's only one such parent, which is related to `Corporation` directly and indirectly through `Ted`.

In similar (but less frivolous) situations, in which a multiply derived class requires only one copy of a multiply inherited base class, you can reduce those bases to one instance by declaring them all to be virtual base classes. In a class hierarchy, there is only one copy of a virtual base class object, even when that object's class is inherited more than once.

Listing 14.9, CONGLOM.CPP, demonstrates how to form a `Corporation` class that uses virtual base classes and solves the problem of a proliferation of `McDougles` base classes.

Listing 14.9. CONGLOM.CPP (Loading the bases).

```
1:  /* conglom.cpp */
2:
3:  #include <iostream.h>
4:  #include <string.h>
5:
```

```
 6:   class Company {
 7:   private:
 8:     char *name;
 9:   public:
10:     Company(const char *s) {
11:       name = strdup(s);
12:       cout << " In constructor for ";
13:       Display();
14:     }
15:     virtual ~Company() {
16:       cout << " In destructor for ";
17:       Display();
18:       delete name;
19:     }
20:     void Display(void) { cout << name << '\n'; }
21:   };
22:
23:   class Jennys: public Company {
24:   public:
25:     Jennys(): Company("Jenny's") { }
26:   };
27:
28:   class McDougles: public Company {
29:   public:
30:     McDougles(): Company("McDougles") { }
31:   };
32:
33:   class BurgerQueen: public Company {
34:   public:
35:     BurgerQueen(): Company("BurgerQueen") { }
36:   };
37:
38:   class Bob
39:     : virtual public Jennys,
40:       virtual public McDougles {
41:   };
42:
43:   class Ted
44:     : virtual public McDougles,
45:       virtual public BurgerQueen {
46:   };
```

continues

Listing 14.9. continued

```
47:
48:  class Alice
49:    : virtual public Jennys,
50:      virtual public McDougles,
51:      virtual public BurgerQueen {
52:  };
53:
54:  class Corporation
55:    : virtual public McDougles,
56:      public Ted,
57:      public Alice {
58:  private:
59:    char *name;
60:  public:
61:    Corporation(): McDougles(), Ted(), Alice()
62:      { name = "Conglomerate Industries"; }
63:    void Display(void) { cout << name << '\n'; }
64:  };
65:
66:  main()
67:  {
68:    cout << "\nForming a corporation\n";
69:    Corporation *cp;
70:    cp = new Corporation;
71:    cp->Display();
72:    delete cp;
73:    return 0;
74:  }
```

Class Company is unchanged, as are Jennys, McDougles, and BurgerQueen. Bob, Ted, and Alice, however, require modifications to prevent future derivations from ending up with too many copies of their parent base classes. For example, Bob is now declared as

```
class Bob
  : virtual public Jennys,
    virtual public McDougles {
};
```

Adding `virtual` to the listed base classes tells the compiler that, in a subsequent derivation which also inherits either `Jennys` or `McDougles`, there should be only one instance of those two base classes. Similarly, `Ted` and `Alice` (see lines 43–52) specify their base classes to be `virtual`.

You can now form class `Corporation` (lines 54–64). As before, the class inherits bases `McDougles`, `Ted`, and `Alice`. By specifying `McDougles` as a virtual base class, however, only one copy of that `Company` class exists in the final result, despite the fact that `Ted` and `Alice` are also derived from `McDougles`.

NOTE: `Ted` and `Alice` could also be declared as virtual base classes at lines 56–57. This is required only if a subsequent derivation of `Corporation` also inherits those classes.

Using Borland's ObjectBrowser

There's nothing like a few diagrams to help explain the relationships among a set of derived classes. If you have Microsoft Windows, you can use ObjectBrowser in Borland C++ for Windows 3.1 (or Turbo C++ for Windows 3.0) to display related classes and their members. Because BCW and TCW can compile and run most DOS programs in a graphics window, you can use the browser whether you are writing a Windows or a DOS application. (BCW and TCW cannot create DOS .EXE code files, however.)

To experiment with ObjectBrowser, start BCW and open CONGLOM.CPP (Listing 14.9). Select the Compiler command in the Options menu and choose Advanced code generation. Make sure you select **D**ebug info in .OBJs and **B**rowser info in .OBJs. Using Options|Linker|Settings, also select Include debug information.

You can now compile the program (press F9). After a successful compilation, use the **Browse** menu's **Classes** command for a graphics display of the program's class hierarchy (see Figure 14.14). As you can see, because the program includes iostream.h, the browser also shows the relationships among I/O stream classes.

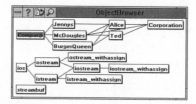

Figure 14.14. BCW's browser showing the classes from CONGLOM.CPP.

Summary

- Single inheritance describes the relationship between one class that is derived from another. Many classes may be derived from a single base class.

- Multiple inheritance describes the relationship of a class that is derived from more than one base class.

- Derived classes may serve as base classes for subsequent derivations. There is no set limit on the number of classes that may be derived from other classes.

- A protected class member is a cross between a private and a public member. Like a private member, a protected member is not accessible outside the class. Like a public member, a protected member is available to a derived class that inherits that member from a base class.

- A derived class inherits all present data members and member functions—but not constructors or destructors—from a base class.

- A derived class must call a base class constructor—if it has one—to initialize data members in the base class portion of a derived object.

- A base class's public and protected members are inherited and are accessible in a derived class. The private members of a base class remain private to the base class and are not accessible in the derived class.

- Derived classes may declare public, protected, or private base classes. These access specifiers can change the access status (public, protected, and private) of inherited members.

- You may selectively qualify inherited members. For example, if a derived class declares a private base class, all of the base class's members become private to the derived class. Selected inherited members, however, may be qualified to remain public.

- Destructors are normally provided in derived classes only if those classes declare data members that require deletion when an object of the derived class goes out of scope. However, destructors may perform other cleanup chores. C++ automatically calls class destructors (and constructors) as needed.

- Constructors in a base class are called before constructors in a class derived from that base. Destructors are called in the opposite order: a derived class destructor is called before a base class destructor. Objects of derived classes are constructed in base-to-derived class order and destroyed in derived-to-base class order.

- Derived classes may provide replacements for member functions inherited from a base class. These member functions have the same names as their inherited functions, but may possess the same or a different set of parameters.

- A pointer to a base class may address an object of that class or of any class derived from that base. Using such a pointer, a statement may call a virtual member function, which is linked at runtime to the actual object that the pointer addresses. The addressed object may therefore change form without requiring the pointer statement to be recompiled—an effect known as polymorphism.

- Destructors and member functions may be virtual, but constructors are not. C++ links virtual member functions and virtual destructors at runtime by consulting an internal address table.

- A pure virtual member function declaration ends with = 0. Any class that contains one or more pure virtual member functions is called an abstract class and cannot create objects. A derived class is expected to inherit an abstract class and provide programming for all pure virtual member functions.

- Multiple inheritance can lead to highly complex class hierarchies. One of the most common problems with multiple inheritance is a derived class that inherits too many copies of a distant base-class relative. To fix this problem, you may declare the base class as virtual, limiting to one the number of base class objects existing in the derived class object.

- You can use Borland's ObjectBrowser in Borland C++ for Windows 3.1 (or Turbo C++ for Windows 3.0) to inspect complex class hierarchies. Though ObjectBrowser requires Microsoft Windows, you can use it to browse classes in DOS and Windows applications.

Exercises

14.1 Write a series of related classes appropriate for a screen entry program such as a name-and-address database. Aim for generic classes that can prompt for and return values of a variety of data types at specified locations on-screen. (The purpose of this exercise is for you to think about class hierarchies. Your answer does not need to read and write information in disk files.)

14.2 Derive a new class from the TBench class (Listings 14.1 and 14.2) that performs a series of tests for a specified number of repetitions and reports the average elapsed time for all tests.

14.3 Design and test a class that can store a set of integer values from 0 to 15 using one bit per value. The class should have member functions to add, delete, extract, and display set values. Use virtual member functions, constructors, and destructors where appropriate. The class should display a binary value such as 0100100011001011, where 1 represents items in the set.

14.4 Design a class that can store a list of objects of an unspecified class type.

14.5 Using your answer from Exercise 14.4, write a program that can store and display a disk directory as a list of string objects.

14.6 Starting with the classes in the answer to Exercise 14.5, use multiple inheritance to derive a new class that displays a directory and can store a wildcard string. For example, initializing the new directory object with the string "*.CPP" should display all .CPP files in the current directory and should also store this wildcard string for future reference.

15

Advanced Topics in C++

Learning to program computers is like learning to walk. When you can stand without toppling over, the real work begins—figuring out how to get from point A to point B.

Now that you've learned most of what ANSI C and C++ have to offer, you might be wondering about your next destination. With the knowledge you have acquired so far, you should be able to design and complete a sizeable application. But don't end your studies just yet. In this chapter, you'll meet advanced C++ topics such as operator overloading, streamable classes, templates, and other techniques that may prove invaluable to your future programming treks.

Friends

One of OOP's main gifts is the encapsulation of data in classes. You've seen many examples of this *data-hiding* concept in previous listings, and you've considered its benefits of reduced maintenance chores and easier debugging.

Like many rules in life and programming, however, those of data hiding are made to be broken. In C++, you can break encapsulation's rules by using *friends,* although you do so at some risk to your program's welfare. Declaring a friend of a class is like giving a pal a copy of your house key. If you go away for the weekend, don't be surprised on your return to discover your buddy asleep on the couch and the refrigerator seriously depleted.

C++ classes can declare two kinds of friends. An entire class may be a friend of another class, or a single function may be declared as a friend. The following sections describe both of these friendly C++ techniques.

> **NOTE:** If friends have a counterpart in C++, it's the goto statement. Like goto, a friend enables you to break the rules intended to help you write reliable code. Don't interpret the following sections as an endorsement of friends. Top C++ programmers avoid using friends unless absolutely necessary.

Friend Classes

A class may declare another class as a friend. The first class (the one that declares the friend) gives another class (the friend) permission to access all private and protected members of the first class. Public members are always accessible, so you don't need to declare a class a friend to give it access to public members.

Typically, friend classes are used when two unrelated classes require access to the class's private or protected parts. Suppose you declare this class:

```
class AClass {
private:
  double value;  // Private data member
public:
  AClass() { value = 3.14159; }
};
```

Class AClass contains a single private member, value, of type double. To that member, the class constructor assigns the value 3.14159. Except for that action, the class provides no means to change or even to inspect a class object's value. The private data member is as safe from harm as a bear cub by its mother's side.

Next, suppose you declare another class that contains an object of AClass as a data member:

```
class BClass {
private:
  AClass anObject;  // AClass object data member
public:
  void ShowValue(void)
    { cout << anObject.value; }   // ???
};
```

Member anObject of type AClass is private to BClass. Member function ShowValue() attempts to display anObject's value. However, the declaration doesn't compile because value is private to AClass, and only member functions in AClass may access value.

Changing value's private access specifier to protected in AClass would not solve the problem. A protected member is available to its declaring class and to any derived class. Although BClass owns an object of type AClass, the two classes are unrelated, and BClass's members cannot access AClass's private and protected members. Of course, you could make value public in AClass, but that would also make value available to all statements.

A better solution is to make BClass a friend of AClass. Objects of BClass can access value and any other private and protected members, but statements outside the two classes are still prevented from entering AClass's restricted areas. To make this change, use the friend keyword inside the class to which the other class needs access. In this example, BClass must access the private value member inside AClass. So to give BClass permission to use that private data, AClass can declare BClass as a friend. Here's the new AClass declaration:

```
class AClass {
  friend class BClass;  // BClass is a friend of AClass
private:
  double value;  // Accessible by AClass and BClass members!
public:
  AClass() { value = 3.14159; }
};
```

The only difference from the previous declaration is the line friend class BClass. This tells the compiler to grant BClass access to AClass's private and protected members. Other statements in other classes and in the main program still can't use AClass's private and protected declarations. Only BClass has a backstage pass to

AClass's private rooms. In this manner, you may declare any number of classes as friends. The only restriction is that the friend keyword must appear inside a class declaration. A few other facts are worth remembering:

- A class must name all of its friends in advance.

- The class containing the private and protected data is the one that declares another class to be a friend, thus giving that friend special access to the normally hidden members of the declaring class. A class can never declare itself to be a friend of another class.

- The friend class may be declared before or after the class that declares the friend. The order of the declarations is unimportant, but the friend class is typically declared last so the friend's inline member functions can refer to the other class's private or protected parts.

- Derived classes of the friend do not inherit special access to the original class's private and protected members. Only the specifically named friend has that permission.

- A derived class may be a friend of its base class, although in such cases, using protected members in the base accomplishes the same goal of giving the friend access to restricted members in a base class.

Listing 15.1, FRIEND.CPP, demonstrates how a friend class can access another class's private and protected members.

Listing 15.1. FRIEND.CPP (Using a friend class).

```
 1:  #include <iostream.h>
 2:
 3:  class Pal {
 4:    friend class Buddy;  // Buddy is a friend of Pal
 5:  private:
 6:    int x;     // Accessible to Pal and Buddy members
 7:  protected:
 8:    void doublex(void) { x *= x; }  // Accessible to Pal and Buddy
 9:  public:
10:    Pal() { x = 100; }     // Accessible to all users
11:    Pal(int n) { x = n; }  //    "    "    "    "    "
12:  };
13:
14:  class Buddy {
```

```
15:  private:
16:    Pal palObject;  // Accessible only to Buddy's members
17:  public:
18:    void ShowValues(void);  // Accessible to all users
19:  };
20:
21:  main()
22:  {
23:    Buddy aBuddy;
24:
25:    aBuddy.ShowValues();
26:    return 0;
27:  }
28:
29:  void Buddy::ShowValues(void)
30:  {
31:    Pal aPal(1234);
32:
33:    cout << "\nBefore, palObject.x == " << palObject.x;
34:    palObject.doublex();
35:    cout << "\nAfter, palObject.x  == " << palObject.x;
36:    cout << "\naPal.x == " << aPal.x << '\n';
37:  }
```

FRIEND begins by declaring a class named Pal. Line 4 states that a second class Buddy is a friend of Pal. Because of this line, Buddy's member functions may access the private and protected members of Pal objects. However, Pal may not access any private or protected members in Buddy.

At line 16, the Buddy class declares an object of the Pal class. As you can see when you run the code, even though Buddy is unrelated to Pal, member function ShowValues() can directly access Pal's private member x and protected member function doublex (see lines 29–37).

Mutual Friend Classes

Two classes can declare each other as friends, giving each class access to the other's private and protected members. Of course, this also destroys the barriers that prohibit access to a class's restricted members. The frequent need for classes to befriend other classes signifies a poorly designed class hierarchy. Most classes are better off as strangers to one another.

For two classes to become mutual friends, each class must list the other as a friend, giving both classes access to each other's private and protected members. For `AClass` and `BClass` to be mutual friends, their declarations could be written as

```
class BClass;  // Optional incomplete class declaration

class AClass {
  friend class BClass;    // BClass may access all AClass members
  // ... other members
};

class BClass {
  friend class AClass;    // AClass may access all BClass members
  // ... other members;
};
```

Any member functions in either class may now access the private and protected members in an object of the other class. If the first class refers to the second class by name—in a member function parameter, for example—you may need to use an incomplete class declaration as done here for `BClass`. This allows `AClass` to declare `BClass` data members and member function parameters even though `BClass`'s complete declaration comes later.

Friend Functions

A friend function is similar to—but less onerous than—a friend class. Declaring a function as a friend of a class gives that function access to private and protected members in class objects. The friend function may be a common C++ function or a class member.

In a typical design, a friend function declares parameters of classes to which the function owes its friendship. Inside the friend function, statements can then access normally hidden members in class-object arguments that are passed to the function.

Listing 15.2, FRIENDFN.CPP, demonstrates how to declare and use a typical friend function for two classes.

FRIENDFN declares two classes, One and Two. An incomplete class declaration at line 3 allows One to refer to Two. Lines 6 and 14 declare a friend function named Show(). Because each class declares Show() as a friend, statements in Show() are granted access to the private and protected members in classes One and Two. (The classes listed here have no protected sections, but if they did, the friend declaration would allow access to those members.)

Listing 15.2. FRIENDFN.CPP (Using a friend function).

```
 1:  #include <iostream.h>
 2:
 3:  class Two;   // Incomplete class declaration
 4:
 5:  class One {
 6:    friend void Show(One &c1, Two &c2);
 7:  private:
 8:    char *s1;   // Accessible to One and Show()
 9:  public:
10:    One() { s1 = "Testing "; }
11:  };
12:
13:  class Two {
14:    friend void Show(One &c1, Two &c2);
15:  private:
16:    char *s2;   // Accessible to Two and Show()
17:  public:
18:    Two() { s2 = "one, two, three"; }
19:  };
20:
21:  main()
22:  {
23:    One c1;
24:    Two c2;
25:
26:    Show(c1, c2);
27:    return 0;
28:  }
29:
30:  void Show(One &c1, Two &c2)
31:  {
32:    cout << c1.s1 << c2.s2 << '\n';
33:  }
```

Function Show()'s declarations include reference parameters c1 and c2 of the two class types. Because Show() is a friend of those classes, statements inside Show() can access private and protected members in class-object arguments that are passed to Show().

For example, the implementation for Show() (lines 30–33) displays the values of the strings addressed by pointers s1 and s2. Because Show() is a friend of the two classes, it can refer directly to the s1 and s2 data members, which are private to their respective classes. Other "unfriendly" functions would not be allowed similar access to those hidden members.

Friend Member Functions

A friend function can also be a class member. In a typical case, a class declares a member function of another class as a friend. The friend member function can access the declaring class's private and protected members.

Listing 15.3, FRIENDMF.CPP (that's MF for member function), shows the basic strategy for using friend member functions.

Listing 15.3. FRIENDMF.CPP (Using a friend member function).

```
 1:  #include <iostream.h>
 2:
 3:  class One;  // Incomplete class declaration
 4:
 5:  class Two {
 6:  private:
 7:    char *s2;  // Accessible to Two's members
 8:  public:
 9:    Two() { s2 = "one, two, three"; }
10:    void Show(One &c1);
11:  };
12:
13:  class One {
14:    friend void Two::Show(One &c1);
15:  private:
16:    char *s1;  // Accessible to One and Two::Show
17:  public:
```

```
18:   One() { s1 = "Testing "; }
19:   };
20:
21:   main()
22:   {
23:     One c1;
24:     Two c2;
25:
26:     c2.Show(c1);
27:     return 0;
28:   }
29:
30:   void Two::Show(One &c1)
31:   {
32:     cout << c1.s1 << s2 << '\n';
33:   }
```

As in FRIENDFN (Listing 15.2), the new program FRIENDMF declares two classes One and Two. Line 10 declares Show() as a member function of class Two. Class One declares that same member function as a friend (line 14) using the class name and a scope resolution operator (Two::) to tell the compiler where it can find Show().

The order of the two classes is reversed from the earlier listing because the class that prototypes the member function must be declared before the class that specifies the member function as a friend. In order for One to declare Two::Show() as a friend of the class, Two's declaration must have been seen by the compiler.

Another difference is the way Show() refers to private data in the two classes (see lines 30–33). The member declares only one reference parameter, One &c1. Because Show() is a member of class Two, it can access all members of Two directly. The expression c1.s1 in the output stream statement at line 32 is allowed because Show() is a friend of class One, of which s1 is a private data member. Show() can refer to s2 directly because this member belongs to class Two, the same class that declares Show().

Because Show() is a member of Two, the member function now has a this pointer that addresses the class object for which the member function was called. Consequently, the program must define an object of class Two (line 24) and then call Show() for that object (line 26).

Operator Overloading

The topic of operator overloading has been smothered in a lot of unnecessary mumbo jumbo. Simply stated, operator overloading makes it possible to define actions for class objects in expressions that use common operators such as plus (+) and minus (–). With appropriately overloaded operators, you can declare a class such as TAnyClass, and define some objects of that class type:

```
TAnyClass c1, c2, c3;
```

You can use these objects in expressions such as

```
c3 = c1 + c2;
```

To understand operator overloading, it helps to review what you know about operators in general. The common plus sign operator (+), of course, sums two values. The minus sign (–) subtracts two values. These and other symbols are called *binary operators* because they require two arguments. Others such as the not operator (!), are *unary*—they require only one argument. Unary minus (–) is another example. The expression -count negates count's value.

Operator overloading makes it possible to add new data types to the built-in types that C++ operators are designed to handle. Overloaded operators are declared as common friend functions or as class member functions. The following sections explain how to write and use overloaded binary and unary operator member functions.

Overloading Operator Functions

A simple example illustrates operator overloading for a hypothetical class named ZZ:

```
class ZZ {
public:
  friend ZZ operator+(ZZ a, ZZ b);
  friend ZZ operator-(ZZ a, ZZ b);
  friend ZZ operator*(ZZ a, ZZ b);
  friend ZZ operator/(ZZ a, ZZ b);
  // ... other public, private, and protected members
};
```

ZZ declares four overloaded operator friend functions. (In practice, ZZ might declare other public, private, and protected members.) The function names are operator+(),

`operator-()`, `operator*()`, and `operator/()`. Normally, you can't use symbols like +, -, *, and / in identifiers, but for the purpose of overloading operators, in C++ a function name can consist of the word `operator` and one of the symbols in Table 15.1.

Table 15.1. Operators that may be overloaded.

*	/	+	–	%	^	&	¦
~	!	,	=	<	>	<=	>=
++	--	<<	>>	==	!=	&&	¦¦
*=	/=	%=	^=	&=	¦=	+=	-=
<<=	>>=	->	->*	[]	()	new	delete

Operators +, -, *, and & may be overloaded for binary and unary expressions. Operators ., .*, ::, ?:, and `sizeof` may not be overloaded. In addition, =, (), [], and -> must be implemented as nonstatic member functions. (We'll examine static member functions later in this chapter.)

The hypothetical class `ZZ` declares operator functions for the first four operators in the table. Each function has the general form

```
friend ZZ operator+(ZZ a, ZZ b);
```

The function is declared as a friend of the class, which gives `operator+()` access to the class's private and protected members. The function returns type `ZZ` (it could return another type) so that its result may be assigned to another `ZZ` object. (Assigning one object to another brings some tricky subjects into play; they are discussed later in this chapter.) Most importantly, the function's name `operator+()` identifies the function as the method by which expressions that use the plus operator can process objects of the class. Presumably, `operator+()` adds two objects in a way that is appropriate for the `ZZ` class.

NOTE: The compiler does not enforce mathematical concepts for overloaded operators. For clarity, you should define addition-like actions for overloaded plus operators, multiplication-like actions for overloaded times operators, and so on. If you sidestep tradition (defining a plus sign that multiplies rather than adds, for example), the results are likely to be confusing.

The operator+() function name bothers some people upon first encounter. Remember, operator+() is simply the function's name. If you named the function feeblewitz() rather than operator+(), you could write a statement such as

```
feeblewitz(a, b);
```

where a and b are objects of type ZZ. Replacing feeblewitz with operator+, you can call an overloaded operator function with the statement

```
operator+(a, b);   // Same as feeblewitz(a, b)
```

There is no difference between those two function calls—only the function names are different. However, as an overloaded operator, operator+() can also be called in an expression that uses a plus sign. For example, this statement is exactly equivalent to the preceding function call:

```
a + b;   // Same as operator+(a, b);!
```

The expressions a + b and operator+(a, b) perform exactly the same jobs, and they generate exactly the same code. The only reason for using one form over the other is clarity. Operator overloading adds nothing to C++ that you don't already know. It simply enables you to use objects in expressions rather than pass objects to functions.

A working example of a class that uses overloaded operators helps illustrate these concepts. Listing 15.4, STROPS.CPP, contains the beginnings of a class that can store integer values in string form. By using overloaded operators, the program can evaluate expressions that add and subtract strings as their equivalent numeric values.

Listing 15.4. STROPS.CPP (Overloaded operator functions).

```
 1:   #include <iostream.h>
 2:   #include <stdlib.h>
 3:   #include <string.h>
 4:
 5:   class TStrOp {
 6:   private:
 7:     char value[12];
 8:   public:
 9:     TStrOp() { value[0] = 0; }
10:     TStrOp(const char *s);
11:     long GetValue(void) { return atol(value); }
12:     friend long operator+(TStrOp a, TStrOp b);
```

```
13:     friend long operator-(TStrOp a, TStrOp b);
14:  };
15:
16:  main()
17:  {
18:    TStrOp a = "1234";
19:    TStrOp b = "4321";
20:
21:    cout << "\nValue of a == " << a.GetValue();
22:    cout << "\nValue of b == " << b.GetValue();
23:    cout << "\na + b +  6 == " << (a + b + 6);
24:    cout << "\na - b + 10 == " << (a - b + 10)
25:         << '\n';
26:    return 0;
27:  }
28:
29:  TStrOp::TStrOp(const char *s)
30:  {
31:    strncpy(value, s, 11);
32:    value[11] = 0;
33:  }
34:
35:  long operator+(TStrOp a, TStrOp b)
36:  {
37:    return (atol(a.value) + atol(b.value));
38:  }
39:
40:  long operator-(TStrOp a, TStrOp b)
41:  {
42:    return (atol(a.value) - atol(b.value));
43:  }
```

Running STROPS displays

```
Value of a == 1234
Value of b == 4321
a + b +  6 == 5561
a - b + 10 == -3077
```

Before examining the program's class and its overloaded operator functions, take a look at function main(). Lines 18–19 declare two objects, a and b, of type TStrOp. The objects are initialized with literal strings, and could have been written as

```
TStrOp a("1234");
TStrOp b("4321");
```

Though the objects obviously represent string values, the expressions at lines 23 and 24 add and subtract the objects directly:

```
(a + b + 6)
(a - b + 10)
```

You normally can't use strings or objects in such expressions; operator overloading expands C++'s knowledge of the kinds of data types it can add and subtract.

Two friend functions declared in lines 12–13 overload the plus and minus operators for pairs of TStrOp class objects. The declarations are similar to those in the hypothetical ZZ class explained earlier. However, in this case, the functions return type long. Typically, overloaded operator functions return the same type as their class (or a reference to a class object), but that's not a requirement. Overloaded operator functions, just like other functions, can return any data types.

Examine the overloaded operator implementations at lines 35–43. Because the functions were declared as friends and not as member functions, their implementations are identical to other common C++ functions. The only differences are the special function names operator+ and operator-, which permit the compiler to evaluate expressions that use plus and minus operators and TStrOp class objects.

Because the operator functions are friends, they can access the private and protected parts of TStrOp objects. This fact enables the functions to convert the value string member in the two parameters a and b to a long integer. Those conversions are handled by calling the standard atol (ASCII to long) function prototyped in stdlib.h. The functions simply return the addition or subtraction of the converted values.

Overloading Operator Member Functions

Overloaded functions can be members of a class, as demonstrated in Listing 15.5, STROPS2.CPP. This program is similar to STROPS (Listing 15.4), but illustrates how to overload operators as member functions.

Listing 15.5. STROPS2.CPP (Shows overloaded operator member functions).

```
 1:  #include <iostream.h>
 2:  #include <stdlib.h>
 3:  #include <string.h>
 4:
 5:  class TStrOp {
 6:  private:
 7:    char value[12];
 8:  public:
 9:    TStrOp() { value[0] = 0; }
10:    TStrOp(const char *s);
11:    long GetValue(void) { return atol(value); }
12:    long operator+(TStrOp b);
13:    long operator-(TStrOp b);
14:  };
15:
16:  main()
17:  {
18:    TStrOp a = "1234";
19:    TStrOp b = "4321";
20:
21:    cout << "\nValue of a == " << a.GetValue();
22:    cout << "\nValue of b == " << b.GetValue();
23:    cout << "\na + b +  6 == " << (a + b + 6);
24:    cout << "\na - b + 10 == " << (a - b + 10)
25:         << '\n';
26:    return 0;
27:  }
28:
29:  TStrOp::TStrOp(const char *s)
30:  {
31:    strncpy(value, s, 11);
32:    value[11] = 0;
33:  }
34:
35:  long TStrOp::operator+(TStrOp b)
36:  {
37:    return (atol(value) + atol(b.value));
38:  }
```

continues

Listing 15.5. continued.

```
39:
40:  long TStrOp::operator-(TStrOp b)
41:  {
42:    return (atol(value) - atol(b.value));
43:  }
```

Examine the overloaded operator member functions declared at lines 12–13 and implemented in lines 35–43. Because the functions are members of class TStrOp, they already have access to the class's private and protected members, so there's no need to specify them as friends of the class. In addition, the overloaded operator member functions receive a this pointer to the object for which the functions are called. The functions therefore need only single parameters, not two as before. To add two string values, operator+() sums the long equivalents of the expressions this->value and b.value.

Operator functions and member functions require the proper numbers of parameters. You cannot declare operator+() at line 12 like this:

```
long operator+(TStrOp a, TStrOp b);  // ???
```

This line does not compile because operator+() is a member of the TStrOp class, and as a member function it receives a this pointer to a class object. Including this, parameters a and b total three parameters, and an overloaded binary operator such as operator+() is permitted only two. To add two TStrObj objects, operator+() sums *this.value and b.value (see line 37). It doesn't need a third parameter. Member function operator-() also receives a this pointer, and therefore needs only one other parameter to overload the binary subtraction operator (lines 40–43).

Overloading Unary Operators

Unary operators such as unary plus and unary minus require only one argument. You can overload these and other unary operators with techniques similar to those illustrated in the preceding sections.

As with binary operators, you can declare an overloaded unary operator function as a friend or as a member of a class. An overloaded unary operator friend function declares only one parameter of the class type (it needs only one value on which to operate). For example, add this declaration to STROPS2.CPP (Listing 15.5) just above private: at line 6:

```
friend long operator-(TStrOp a);
```

Even though line 13 already overloads the minus operator, because the new declaration specifies only one parameter, there is no conflict. The member function at line 13 receives an invisible this parameter. The new nonmember function does not receive a this pointer. To implement the new unary minus nonmember function, add these lines after function main():

```
long operator-(TStrOp a)
{
  return -atol(a.value);
}
```

Because unary operator-() is a friend of the class, the return statement may directly access the private value member in the TStrOp parameter a. The function is now complete, and the compiler can evaluate unary minus expressions involving objects of the class type. For an example, add the following statement to main() (after line 20 is a good place):

```
cout << "\n-a    == " << -a;
```

Compile the modified program and run. As you can see, the expression -a is replaced by the long negation of a's string member. You have taught C++ how to negate a long value that's represented in string form!

As with overloaded binary operators, you can also declare overloaded unary operators as member functions. Start with a fresh copy of STROPS2.CPP and add the following declaration above line 14 (before TStrOp's closing brace):

```
long operator-(void);
```

This member function declaration is similar to the friend unary function you added a moment ago. Because all member functions receive a this pointer, the new operator-() member function declares no parameters and operates directly on the long equivalent of this->value. This is demonstrated in the function's implementation, which you can insert after main():

```
long TStrOp::operator-(void)
{
  return -atol(value);  // i.e. -atol(this->value)
}
```

The overloaded member function returns the long negation of value. Use it in expressions such as the following, which you can insert into main():

```
cout << "\n-a    == " << -a;
```

Type Conversions

You can supply your own type-conversion rules to convert objects automatically to other types. For example, suppose you declare and initialize an object of the TStrOp class from STROPS2 (Listing 15.5):

```
TStrOp myValue = "9876";
```

The TStrOp class stores a string that can be used as an equivalent long integer in addition and subtraction expressions. You might logically attempt to assign the myValue object to a long variable:

```
long x = myValue;  // ???
```

That doesn't compile, however, because TStrOp does not provide for converting a string to a long. A solution is to use an overloaded conversion operator to translate a TStrOp object to another data type.

Conversion operators take the form operator TYPE() where TYPE is the data type to which you want to convert objects of the class. For example, to provide a type conversion rule for translating TStrOp objects to long, insert this inline function inside the class's public section:

```
operator long() { return atol(value); }
```

This is a special use for the operator keyword that C++ provides specifically for creating new type-conversion rules. With the new rule in place, it's now possible to assign an object of type TStrOp to a long variable, pass a TStrOp object to a long function parameter, and so on.

Array Subscript Operator

You can overload the array subscript operator [] to provide array-like access to a class's data members, even though that data might be stored as individual members or on a list. A simple example, Listing 15.6, SSOP.CPP, demonstrates how to overload [] for a class that stores four integer values as separate data members.

Though simplistic, class PseudoArray contains all of the necessary pieces required to overload the array subscript operator. The class declares four private int members at lines 5–8. Line 13 declares a member function operator[] with one unsigned parameter. The parameter serves as the array index, and it can be any data type.

Listing 15.6. SSOP.CPP (Overloading the subscript operator).

```
 1:  #include <iostream.h>
 2:
 3:  class PseudoArray {
 4:  private:
 5:    int value0;
 6:    int value1;
 7:    int value2;
 8:    int value3;
 9:  public:
10:    PseudoArray(int v0, int v1, int v2, int v3)
11:      { value0 = v0; value1 = v1; value2 = v2; value3 = v3; }
12:    int GetInt(unsigned i);
13:    int operator[](unsigned i);
14:  };
15:
16:  main()
17:  {
18:    PseudoArray pa(10, 20, 30, 40);
19:
20:    for (int i = 0; i <= 3; i++)
21:      cout << "pa[" << i << "] == " << pa[i] << '\n';
22:    return 0;
23:  }
24:
25:  int PseudoArray::GetInt(unsigned i)
26:  {
27:    switch (i) {
28:      case 0: return value0;  // Note: break not needed
29:      case 1: return value1;  //   "    "    "    "    "
30:      case 2: return value2;  //   "    "    "    "    "
31:      case 3: return value3;  //   "    "    "    "    "
32:    default: return value0;
33:    }
34:  }
35:
36:  int PseudoArray::operator[](unsigned i)
37:  {
38:    return GetInt(i);
39:  }
```

Line 12 shows the usual method for accessing a class's private data through a member function, GetInt(), which returns one of the class's integer values. You can declare an object of the class and display the second value with the statements

```
PseudoArray pa(10, 20, 30, 40);
cout << "Value #2 == " << pa.GetInt(1);  // Call member function
```

That's the usual way to "get to" a class's private data. However, because the class overloads the subscript operator, you can also use the statement

```
cout << "Value #2 == " << pa[1];  // Use pa as an array!
```

Line 21 shows another example. The expressions pa[1] and pa[i] appear to access pa as an array, although pa is actually a class object. Overloading the subscript operator makes it possible to use array indexing (a handy and clear way to access multiple values) rather than call member functions for an object of a class.

Keep in mind that overloaded array indexes can be any data types. For example, you can replace line 13 with

```
int operator[](char c);
```

and then use character array indexes such as 'A' to 'D' to index the array, with 'A' being the initial index—an atypical construction in common C or C++ arrays, which usually require zero-based index values. In a sense, by overloading [] and using characters for indexes, you are establishing an association between a set of characters and a set of values, creating what's known as an *associative array.* You might implement the overloaded operator[] member function like this:

```
int PseudoArray::operator[](char c)
{
  return GetInt(c - 'A');
}
```

You can then use a char variable as an array index. For example, after making the preceding changes, replace lines 20–21 with

```
for (char c = 'A'; c <= 'D'; c++)
  cout << "pa[" << c << "] == " << pa[c] << '\n';
```

Function Call Operator

Overloading the function call operator () effectively makes a class object appear to be a callable function. The overloaded operator() may return a typed value or void, and it may optionally declare parameters. It must be a nonstatic class member. Here's a sample class with an overloaded function call operator that returns an `int` value:

```
class TAnyClass {
  int x;
public:
  int operator()(void);
  TAnyClass(int n) { x = n; }
};
```

`TAnyClass` overloads the function call operator with the declaration `int operator()(void);`. You could replace `void` with a parameter list. Implement the overloaded member function in the usual way:

```
int TAnyClass::operator()(void)
{
  return x;
}
```

In this example, `operator()` returns the `int x` data member of a `TAnyClass` object. A program might use the class like this:

```
main()
{
  TAnyClass object = 100;
  int q = object();  // Looks like a function call!
  cout << q;
  return 0;
}
```

The second statement appears to call a function named `object()`, but it actually executes the statement `object.operator()();`.

Class-Member-Access Operator

The unary class-member-access operator, `->`, is overloaded as `operator->()`. It must be a nonstatic class member function. Here's how you might overload `->` for `TAnyClass`:

```
class TAnyClass {
  int x, y;
public:
  TAnyClass(int xx, int yy) { x = xx; y = yy; }
```

```
  TAnyClass* operator->();
  int GetX(void) { return x; }
  int GetY(void) { return y; }
};
```

The `operator->()` member function must return an object, a reference, or a pointer to an object of the class type. In this case, it returns a `TAnyClass` pointer. The operator might be implemented as

```
TAnyClass* TAnyClass::operator->()
{
  cout << "\nAccessing member: ";
  return this;
}
```

This shows how to use an overloaded `->` operator as a debugging device. The overloaded operator displays a brief message before returning `this`, which addresses the object for which the member function is called. The main program can apply the overloaded operator to a `TAnyClass` object as shown here:

```
main()
{
  TAnyClass t(100, 200);
  cout << t->GetX() << '\n';
  cout << t->GetY() << '\n';
  return 0;
}
```

The two output stream statements use the overloaded `->` operator to access member functions `GetX()` and `GetY()` for a `TAnyClass` object `t`. These statements actually execute as though they had been written

```
cout << (t.operator->())->GetX() << '\n';
cout << (t.operator->())->GetY() << '\n';
```

Consequently, the program displays labels before the values returned by `GetX()` and `GetY()`:

```
Accessing member: 100
Accessing member: 200
```

Increment and Decrement Operators

In earlier versions of C++, it was impossible to define separate overloaded operations for postfix and prefix ++ and -- operators. The distinction is now possible, as TAnyClass shows:

```
class TAnyClass {
  int x;
public:
  TAnyClass(int xx) { x = xx; }
  int operator++() { return ++x; }      // Prefix ++object
  int operator++(int) { return x++; }   // Postfix object++
  int operator--() { return --x; }      // Prefix --object
  int operator--(int) { return x--; }   // Postfix object--
  int GetX(void) { return x; }
};
```

Member function operator++() defines a prefix increment operator for an object of type TAnyClass. This member function has no parameters. Member function operator++(int) defines a postfix increment operator for a TAnyClass object. C++ assigns zero to the single int parameter.

The demonstration functions are implemented inline, but they could be implemented separately. For an object v of type TAnyClass, the expression ++v calls the overloaded prefix ++ operator, in effect executing the statement x.operator++();. The expression v++ calls the overloaded postfix ++ operator, and executes as though written x.operator++(0);. The decrement operators work similarly.

To experiment with the above class, add it to a C++ program with the following main() function:

```
main()
{
  TAnyClass t(100);
  cout << "t == " << t.GetX() << "; ++t == " << ++t << '\n';
  cout << "t == " << t.GetX() << "; t++ == " << t++ << '\n';
  cout << "t == " << t.GetX() << "; --t == " << --t << '\n';
  cout << "t == " << t.GetX() << "; t-- == " << t-- << '\n';
  return 0;
}
```

Other Operator Overloading Concerns

As you learn more about operator overloading, keep the following facts in mind.

- C++ does not "understand" the meaning of an overloaded operator. It's your responsibility to provide meaningful overloaded operator functions.

- C++ is not able to derive complex operators from simple ones. In a class with overloaded operator functions `operator*()` and `operator=()`, C++ can't evaluate the expression a `*=` b unless you also overload `operator*=()`.

- Never change the syntax of an overloaded operator. Binary operators must remain binary. Unary operators must remain unary. It is not possible, for example, to create a unary division operator because no such built-in capability exists for division in C++.

- You can't invent new operators. You can overload only the operators listed in Table 15.1.

- You can't overload preprocessing symbols # and ##.

Overloading and Memory Management

ANSI C programs use `malloc()` and `free()` along with similar library functions to allocate and deallocate memory blocks on the heap. By contrast, C++ programs use the operators new and delete. Below the hatch, most C++ implementations define new and delete internally by calling `malloc()` and `free()`. Some C++ programmers therefore assume no significant differences exist between the ANSI C and C++ techniques.

That's a dangerous assumption, however, because new and delete are operators, not functions. As operators, new and delete may be overloaded to specify new memory management facilities for objects of a class. By overloading new and delete, you gain total control over how objects are allocated memory.

> **WARNING:** Never call `free()` to deallocate an object constructed by `new`, and never call `malloc()` to allocate memory that's later freed by `delete`. Mixing ANSI C and C++ memory management techniques may appear to work in some cases, but the program could fail if `new` and `delete` are overloaded for a class, or if Borland changes how these operators are implemented in a future compiler release.

Overloading *new*

You can overload `new` just as you can other operators such as + and =. Overloading `new` in a class declaration tells the compiler that from now on you will take care of memory allocation requests for objects of the class.

To overload `new`, insert a function prototype of the form `void * operator new(size_t size);`. Future uses of `new` to allocate space for class objects are directed to the overloaded function. The function should return the address of space allocated for the object. If no space is available, the function should return null (zero).

Listing 15.7, OVERNEW.CPP, is a simple but complete example that overloads `new` to allocate space for objects. Instead of storing the objects on the heap, the program stuffs them into a global buffer. You could use a similar technique to allocate space for objects stored in other locations—on disk, for example, or in custom memory hardware.

> **NOTE:** Line 6 in OVERNEW.CPP issues a `#pragma warn -aus` command. This instructs the compiler to turn off warnings for unused variables that are declared in the program for demonstration purposes only.

The overloaded `new` function declared at line 13 and implemented at lines 38–48 checks whether space is available in the global buffer. If not, the function returns 0, which causes `new` to return null. (The program doesn't check for this condition, but you should do that in a real setting, of course.) If space is available, the global `index` is incremented by the size of the memory request that is passed to the `new` function in the `size` parameter. The function then returns the address of the newly allocated space.

Listing 15.7. OVERNEW.CPP (Overloading new).

```cpp
 1:  #include <iostream.h>
 2:
 3:  // Following "pragma" turns off the compiler's warning about unused
 4:  // variables, which appear in the program for demonstration only
 5:
 6:  #pragma warn -aus
 7:
 8:  class BrandNew {
 9:  private:
10:    int x;
11:  public:
12:    BrandNew();
13:    void * operator new(size_t size);
14:  };
15:
16:  char buf[512];
17:  int index;
18:
19:  main()
20:  {
21:    cout << "\nCreating local instance";
22:    BrandNew b1;
23:
24:    cout << "\nAllocating space via new";
25:    BrandNew *b2 = new BrandNew;
26:    BrandNew *b3 = new BrandNew;
27:    BrandNew *b4 = new BrandNew;
28:    BrandNew *b5 = new BrandNew;
29:    return 0;
30:  }
31:
32:  BrandNew::BrandNew()
33:  {
34:    cout << "\nInside constructor";
35:    x = index;
36:  }
37:
38:  void *BrandNew::operator new(size_t size)
39:  {
40:    cout << "\nInside overloaded new. Size == " << size;
41:    if (index >= 512 - sizeof(BrandNew))
```

```
42:     return 0;
43:   else {
44:     int k = index;
45:     index += sizeof(BrandNew);
46:     return &buf[k];
47:   }
48: }
```

Overloading *delete*

The delete operator is the other side of the memory allocation coin. As with new, you can overload delete to trap deletions of objects addressed by pointers.

An overloaded delete operator function's prototype must be in the form

```
void operator delete(void *p);
```

where p is the address of the object being deleted. Alternatively, you may declare the function using the form

```
void operator delete(void *p, size_t size);
```

With this second form, C++ passes in size the number of bytes to dispose.

To add an overloaded delete function to the BrandNew class in OVERNEW (Listing 15.7), add this member function declaration to the class's public section:

```
void operator delete(void *p);
```

Next, append the function's implementation to the end of the listing:

```
void BrandNew::operator delete(void *p)
{
  cout << "\nDeleting object at " << p;
}
```

An output statement displays the address of each object being deleted. Because the program's objects are not stored on the heap, the overloaded delete operator doesn't actually delete any memory. You also need a few statements to delete some objects. Insert these lines into main() just above the return statement:

```
delete b2;
delete b3;
delete b4;
delete b5;
```

When you run the program, the message tells you exactly when the overloaded delete operator is called to action. This example is just for demonstration, and in a complete application, delete should dispose of deleted memory blocks for future uses of the overloaded new. (See also the section "Placing Objects at Specific Addresses" later in this chapter.)

> **NOTE:** To use the C++ memory manager to allocate heap space for objects that override new, preface the operator with a double colon. For example, the line BrandNew *x = ::new BrandNew bypasses the overloaded new operator for BrandNew objects. Similarly, ::delete calls the C++ default memory deallocator.

Setting the *new* Error Handler

Normally, if new can't fulfill a request for memory, the operator returns null. To change this default action, assign an error-function address to the C++ _new_handler pointer, defined as

```
typedef void (*vfp)(void);
vfp _new_handler;
```

Using a typedef is optional, but it improves the clarity of the declarations. The error function returns void and requires no arguments. Assign an error function by calling set_new_handler(), prototyped in new.h as

```
vfp set_new_handler(vfp);
```

Design your error handler as an ordinary C++ function. You might, for example, halt a program with an out-of-memory error message:

```
void memerr(void)
{
  fputs("\n\nOut of memory\n", stderr);
  exit(1);
}
```

To have new call memerr() for memory errors, pass the function's address to set_new_handler() like this:

```
set_new_handler(memerr);
```

> **NOTE:** See also `set_new_handler()` in Chapter 22, "Functions and Examples."

Copying Class Objects

When copying one class object to another object of a compatible type, the results can be unexpected, especially for classes that declare pointer data members. There are four trouble spots to consider:

- When one object is used to initialize a newly defined object of the same class.

- When an object is passed to a function's value parameter of the class type.

- When a function returns a class object (as opposed to an object reference or pointer).

- When a statement assigns one object to another.

The first three cases construct and initialize new copies of class objects from existing objects. The fourth case assigns an existing object to another previously defined object.

> **NOTE:** Keep in mind the distinction between copying an object and assigning one object to another. The first three situations listed above construct new objects by calling a class constructor. In the fourth case, assigning one object to another does not construct a new object, and therefore no constructor is called.

After copying an object, all may seem well, but troubles might arise if the class objects contain pointer data members. Copying such objects might cause duplicate pointers to address the same locations in memory. Deleting one of those pointers might cause others to address freed memory. Worse yet, deleting the same space more than once in a class destructor might corrupt the heap.

C++ provides two mechanisms for ensuring that classes with pointer members are copied and assigned safely: memberwise initialization and memberwise assignment.

Memberwise Initialization

When an object is used to initialize a new object of a class, C++ copies each data member from the existing object to the new one. For example, here's a simple class with no pointer members:

```
class TAnyClass {
private:
  int i;
  double r;
public:
  TAnyClass()
    { i = 0; r = 0; }
  TAnyClass(int ii, double rr)
    { i = ii; r = rr; }
};
```

In practice, TAnyClass needs other member functions to access its private data members i and r, but the example illustrates how object copying works. The class declares two inline constructors. The default constructor TAnyClass() initializes members i and r to zero. An alternate constructor initializes a class object with explicit values. You can declare TAnyClass objects v1 and v2:

```
TAnyClass v1;
TAnyClass v2(100, 3.14159);
```

You can also use an existing object such as v2 to initialize a new object v3:

```
TAnyClass v3 = v2;
```

This copies v2 to v3 by performing a memberwise initialization of v3's data members. In other words, v2's data members are copied one by one to v3's members as though you had written

```
TAnyClass v3;
v3.i = v2.i;    // For illustration only
v3.r = v2.r;    // "    "    "    "
```

NOTE: The second and third statements in the preceding example are for illustration only. Because the class data members are private, these statements do not compile.

Memberwise initialization of a new class object occurs also when you pass an object to a function's value parameter and when a function returns a class object. If any of these actions causes a pointer data member to be duplicated, a serious bug might arise. The next section explains how to stay out of duplicate-pointer trouble.

The Copy Constructor

You can provide a copy constructor for constructing objects that are copied from other objects. The constructor can perform whatever actions are needed to create a safe object copy—one that doesn't accidentally duplicate a pointer. (Borland C++ creates a copy constructor as needed for classes that don't explicitly declare one.)

Declare a copy constructor as CLASS(const CLASS&). Like all constructors, a copy constructor cannot be virtual and is not inherited by a derived class. Here's a new version of TAnyClass class with a pointer data member and a copy constructor:

```
#include <string.h>
class TAnyClass {
private:
  int i;      // Private data member
  double r;   // Private data member
  char *s;    // Private pointer member!
public:
  TAnyClass()
    { i = 0; r = 0; s = NULL; }
  TAnyClass(int ii, double rr, const char *ss)
    { i = ii; r = rr; s = strdup(ss); }
  ~TAnyClass() { delete s; }
  const char *GetStr(void) { return s; }
  TAnyClass(TAnyClass &copy);  // Copy constructor
};
```

The copy constructor TAnyClass(TAnyClass &copy) has the same name as its class (TAnyClass) and declares a reference &copy to a TAnyClass object, the one that's being copied to this one. Elsewhere in the program (or inline with the declaration), implement the copy constructor:

```
TAnyClass::TAnyClass(TAnyClass &copy)
{
  cout << "Inside TAnyClass's copy constructor\n";
  i = copy.i;
  r = copy.r;
  if (copy.s)
    s = strdup(copy.s);
  else
    s = NULL;
}
```

The output stream statement isn't necessary. It is useful, however, during debugging for showing exactly when the copy constructor runs. The next two statements copy members i and r from copy to the new object. To deal with a string addressed by pointer s, strdup() allocates fresh heap memory for a copy of the original string. Or, if copy's pointer is null, the new object's pointer is assigned NULL. For copied TAnyClass objects, there is no longer any danger that two or more s pointers might accidentally address the same memory. The program can now use statements such as

```
TAnyClass v1;
TAnyClass v2(1, 2, "A test string");
TAnyClass v3 = v2;  // Calls copy constructor
```

C++ calls the TAnyClass copy constructor automatically for the first three situations listed earlier: when an object is used to initialize a newly constructed TAnyClass object (illustrated by the third line above), when a statement passes an object to a function parameter, or when a function returns a class object.

Unfortunately, the class still is not completely safe. When a statement directly assigns one object to another, you must again consider what happens if those objects contain pointer members. The next section explains how to handle this problem.

> **NOTE:** C++ calls copy contructors also for class object arguments passed by value to functions, and for functions that return class objects.

Memberwise Assignment

Assigning a class object to another object might cause pointer data members to address the same locations in memory—a dangerous situation to avoid at all costs. Consider this program fragment, which uses TAnyClass from the preceding section:

```
TAnyClass v1;
TAnyClass v2(1, 2, "A test string");
v1 = v2;  // ???
```

After defining v1 with default values and defining v2 with explicit arguments, an assignment statement copies v2 to v1. But look out! The assignment does not call any class constructor for v1, not even the class's copy constructor. If the class declares or inherits any pointer data members, the copied pointers now address the same location in memory, almost certainly causing a major bug if that memory is deleted in a destructor.

A copy constructor can't solve this problem because the objects involved have already been constructed. C++ calls constructors to initialize new objects, not when assigning one object to another.

Fortunately, you can easily cure this problem by overloading the assignment operator, =. Use a declaration of the form void operator=(const CLASS&). For example, to add an overloaded assignment operator function to TAnyClass, modify the class from the preceding section as follows:

```
class TAnyClass {
private:
  int i;      // Private data member
  double r;   // Private data member
  char *s;    // Private pointer member!
public:
  ...         // See preceding TAnyClass declaration
  void operator=(const TAnyClass &copy);  // Assigment operator
};
```

The operator= declaration overloads the assignment operator, specifying a constant reference parameter copy of type TAnyClass. The parameter refers to the object being copied. In other words, if a and b are TAnyClass objects, in the assignment a = b, copy refers to b. Implement the overloaded assignment function like this:

```
void TAnyClass::operator=(const TAnyClass &copy)
{
  cout << "\nInside TAnyClass's operator= function";
  if (this == &copy)
    return;
  delete s;
  i = copy.i;
  r = copy.r;
  s = strdup(copy.s);
}
```

As before, the output statement is just for debugging. The first `if` statement compares the `this` pointer to the address of the `copy` reference parameter. This catches an accidental assignment of the same object to itself. If you attempt to execute

```
TAnyClass v1, v2;
v1 = v1;
```

the overloaded assignment operator simply ends without performing any actions.

The second `if` statement deletes the space (if any) currently allocated to pointer s. (It is not an error to delete a null pointer, so it is not necessary to check whether s is null before using `delete`.)

The other assignments in the overloaded function are identical to those in the copy constructor presented earlier. The next section explains how to avoid this kind of duplication by making a copy constructor and overloaded assignment operator cooperate.

Calling *operator=* from a Copy Constructor

You can easily avoid wasteful duplications in a copy constructor and overloaded assignment operator. Inside the copy constructor, simply call the overloaded `operator=` function by assigning the copied object to `*this`:

```
TAnyClass::TAnyClass(TAnyClass &copy)
{
  s = NULL;       // Initialize any pointers to null!
  *this = copy;   // Calls overloaded assignment operator
}
```

It's vital to initialize any members (usually pointers) that the overloaded assignment operator inspects. If s were not assigned NULL, for example, that pointer might have an unpredictable value, causing the overloaded assignment function to delete unallocated memory. Needless to say, that's likely to cause a few problems.

Advanced I/O Streams

By overloading the input and output stream operators >> and <<, you can add one or more classes to the kinds of data types that the compiler recognizes for I/O stream statements. The following sections explain how to create streamable classes and explain a few other I/O stream topics.

Formatting Output

iostream.h declares one input and three output stream objects as follows:

```
extern istream_withassign _Cdecl cin;    // Input stream object
extern ostream_withassign _Cdecl cout;   // Output stream object
extern ostream_withassign _Cdecl cerr;   // Error output stream object
extern ostream_withassign _Cdecl clog;   // Buffered error output object
```

The classes istream_withassign and ostream_withassign are ultimately derived from the granddaddy I/O stream class, ios. You don't need to study every detail about these classes to use them in programs, but if you are interested, Borland C++ includes the complete and extensive source code for I/O streams.

The stream classes perform formatted I/O with built-in error-handling. I/O streams support the fundamental data types char, short, int, long, char* (a null-terminated string, for example), float, double, long double, and void* (displayed as an address value).

Keep in mind that cin, cout, cerr, and clog are objects. Their respective classes define overloaded input and output stream operators, making I/O stream statements possible:

```
cin >> v;   // Read variable v from standard input
cout << v;  // Write v to the standard output
```

As you've seen in other examples, you can cascade multipart I/O stream statements using a statement such as

```
cout << "Balance == $" << balance << " (dollars)\n";
```

To format output, you can set one or more flags in an I/O stream object (see the declaration for class ios in iostream.h). Use the class flags(), setf(), and unsetf() member functions to manipulate these flags directly. For example, to output an unsigned value in hexadecimal, you can set cout's hex flag by calling the ios class member function setf():

```
unsigned v = 12345;
cout << "Before: " << v << '\n';   // Output in default (decimal)
cout.setf(cout.hex);               // Modify output stream
cout << "After:  " << v << '\n';   // Output in hexadecimal
```

Although this works, there are easier methods for formatting output streams, as demonstrated next.

Using Manipulators

Including the iomanip.h header file (which includes iostream.h if necessary) makes available several manipulators that are useful for constructing formatted output and reading formatted input. For example, you can use the hex manipulator to output a value in hexadecimal:

```
unsigned v = 12345;
cout << "In hexadecimal v == " << hex << v << '\n';
cout << "In decimal v == " << dec << v << '\n';
```

The last line uses the dec manipulator to return cout's output format to decimal. You can also manipulate input streams. These statements read a value in hex and display that same value in decimal:

```
cout << "Enter value in hex: ";
cin >> hex >> v;
cout << "Value in decimal == " << dec << v;
```

Table 15.2 lists the I/O manipulators defined in iomanip.h.

Some manipulators accept a parameter. For example, setbase(int n) formats a value using radix n. (If n is zero, output defaults to decimal and input defaults to ANSI C specifications for literal integers.)

An output-stream manipulator function returns type ostream&—in other words, a reference to an ostream object. You can write your own manipulators by including iostream.h and defining an ostream& function. Here's how you might define a bell manipulator for an output stream:

Table 15.2. Input and output stream manipulators.

Manipulator	Effect
dec	Decimal conversion
hex	Hexadecimal conversion
oct	Octal conversion
ws	Extract whitespace characters
endl	Inserts new line; flushes stream
ends	Inserts null-terminator in string
flush	Flushes output stream
setbase(int n)	Sets radix to n (0, 8, 10, or 16)
resetiosflags(long f)	Clears formatting bits specified by f
setiosflags(long f)	Sets formatting bits specified by f
setfill(int c)	Uses c for justification fill character
setprecision(int n)	Sets floating-point precision to n
setw(int n)	Sets field width to n

```
ostream& bell(ostream& os) {
  return os << "\a";  // '\a' is the bell escape code
}
```

The bell() function returns ostream& and declares an ostream& parameter, os. This design allows the function to be cascaded in a multipart output stream statement:

```
cout << bell << "Ding!";
```

You can also call a stream object's member functions to adjust formatting. For instance, to display an int variable v right-justified in an 8-character column, you can write

```
cout.width(8);
cout << v << '\n';  // Displays v in 8 columns
cout << v << '\n';  // Displays v using default justification
```

The width() modifier is short-lived, and affects only the next output statement. Other member functions include fill(char c) which sets justification filler to character c and precision(int n) which sets floating-point precision to n.

Overloading Output Streams

Normally, output streams can handle only simple data types—int, long, double, char *, and so on. By overloading the output stream operator <<, you can easily add your own classes to the data types that output stream statements are designed to use.

Listing 15.8, POINTOUT.CPP, creates a streamable class named TPoint with two int values, x and y, representing a coordinate, perhaps on a graphics display. The program overloads the output stream operator so it can write TPoint objects in output stream statements as shown at lines 20 and 23.

Listing 15.8. POINTOUT.CPP (Classes and output streams).

```
 1:  #include <iostream.h>
 2:
 3:  class TPoint {
 4:  private:
 5:    int x, y;
 6:  public:
 7:    TPoint() { x = y = 0; }
 8:    TPoint(int xx, int yy) { x = xx; y = yy; }
 9:    void PutX(int xx) { x = xx; }
10:    void PutY(int yy) { y = yy; }
11:    int GetX(void) { return x; }
12:    int GetY(void) { return y; }
13:    friend ostream& operator<<(ostream& os, TPoint &p);
14:  };
15:
16:  main()
17:  {
18:    TPoint p;
19:
20:    cout << p << '\n';
21:    p.PutX(100);
22:    p.PutY(200);
```

```
23:     cout << p << '\n';
24:     return 0;
25:  }
26:
27:  ostream& operator<<(ostream& os, TPoint &p)
28:  {
29:     os << "x == " << p.x << ", y == " << p.y;
30:     return os;
31:  }
```

Line 13 overloads the output stream operator by declaring a friend member function operator<<(). This friend member function returns ostream& and declares two parameters: os, of type ostream&, and p, a reference to a TPoint object.

Because operator<<() is a friend of TPoint, the statement at line 29 may directly access the x and y data members in the object addressed by reference p. Note that this line is itself an output stream statement, which writes the values of the two data members plus two literal strings to the ostream reference os. Finally, the function returns os. Running the program displays

```
x == 0, y == 0
x == 100, y == 200
```

Because operator<<() returns an ostream reference, it's possible to cascade multiple objects in a single output stream statement. For example, if p1, p2, and p3 are TPoint objects, you can display their values with

```
cout << p1 << "; " << p2 << "; " << p3;
```

Internally, such statements are executed by making multiple function calls to the overloaded output-stream operators. The preceding line is executed as though it were written

```
((((cout << p1) << "; ") << p2) << "; ") << p3;
```

Aren't you glad you don't have to type all those parentheses?

Overloading Input Streams

Overloading the input stream operator >> is also possible and effectively teaches C++ how to input objects of a class. Listing 15.9, POINTIN.CPP, adds input streamability to the POINTOUT.CPP sample program in the preceding section.

Listing 15.9. POINTIN.CPP (Classes and input streams).

```
 1:  #include <iostream.h>
 2:
 3:  class TPoint {
 4:  private:
 5:    int x, y;
 6:  public:
 7:    TPoint() { x = y = 0; }
 8:    TPoint(int xx, int yy) { x = xx; y = yy; }
 9:    void PutX(int xx) { x = xx; }
10:    void PutY(int yy) { y = yy; }
11:    int GetX(void) { return x; }
12:    int GetY(void) { return y; }
13:    friend ostream& operator<<(ostream& os, TPoint &p);
14:    friend istream& operator>>(istream& is, TPoint &p);
15:  };
16:
17:  main()
18:  {
19:    TPoint p;
20:
21:    cout << p << '\n';
22:    p.PutX(100);
23:    p.PutY(200);
24:    cout << p << '\n';
25:    cout << "\nEnter x and y values: ";
26:    cin >> p;
27:    cout << "\nYou entered: " << p;
28:    return 0;
29:  }
30:
31:  ostream& operator<<(ostream& os, TPoint &p)
32:  {
33:    os << "x == " << p.x << ", y == " << p.y;
34:    return os;
35:  }
36:
37:  istream& operator>>(istream& is, TPoint &p)
38:  {
39:    is >> p.x >> p.y;
40:    return is;
41:  }
```

Line 14 declares an input stream friend member function operator>>() for the TPoint class. The function is similar to the output stream operator declared above, but uses istream in place of ostream.

The function's implementation (see lines 37–41) reads values for x and y using the istream reference s. The function returns is so it can be cascaded in multipart input stream statements.

Running the program prompts for x and y values. Type two integers separated by a space. The input stream statement at line 26 stores both values you enter in the class object, which line 27 displays.

Templates

Just as a class is a schematic for building objects, a *template* is a schematic for building functions and classes. Templates are especially useful in class libraries that are shared among many programmers. Sometimes also called parameterized types, templates provide specifications for functions and classes, but not the actual implementation details.

> **NOTE:** Templates are experimental. AT&T has proposed them for a future C++ version 3.0 specification. Borland C++ 3.0 and 3.1 currently implement the most recent AT&T C++ version 2.1 specification, but include templates as a native feature. Be aware that template syntax may change in a future compiler release.

Template Functions

A function template describes the generic properties of a function—similar to a recipe for a cake. Typically declared in a header file, a template function has the general form

```
template<class T> void f(T param)
{
  // Function body
}
```

The function begins with `template<class T>`, which specifies to the compiler that T is a user-defined type. (You can change T to another name if you want.) At least one T parameter is needed to give the function some data on which to operate. You might also specify a pointer (`T *param`) or reference (`T &param`). The function can declare multiple parameters and return a value of type T:

```
template<class T> T f(int a, T b)
{
  // Function body
}
```

This version of template function `f()` returns type T and has two parameters, an `int` named a and an unspecified T object named b. The template's user supplies the actual data type for T. For example, a program might specify the prototype:

```
double f(int a, double b);
```

If this were a common function, you would have to supply an implementation for the function. Because `f()` is a template function, however, the compiler implements the function's code—in this case replacing the placeholder T with `double`.

An example clarifies how templates can reduce the size and complexity of programs by providing generic functions that are implemented by the compiler. Listing 15.10, minmax.h, declares two useful function templates, `min()` and `max()`.

Listing 15.10. minmax.h (Function templates `min` and `max`).

```
 1:  // minmax.h -- Function templates for min and max
 2:
 3:  #ifndef __MINMAX_H
 4:  #define __MINMAX_H  1  /* Prevent multiple #includes */
 5:
 6:  template<class T> T max(T a, T b)
 7:  {
 8:    if (a > b)
 9:      return a;
10:    else
11:      return b;
12:  }
13:
14:  template<class T> T min(T a, T b)
15:  {
16:    if (a < b)
17:      return a;
```

```
18:    else
19:      return b;
20:  }
21:
22:  #endif   /* __MINMAX_H */
```

Study line 6 closely. It states that T is an unspecified type, which a template function max() returns. In addition, max() requires two T arguments. The function's statements at lines 8–11 are schematics for the real statements that are generated later when T's actual type is specified. Function template min() is declared similarly.

You can use more than one placeholder. To declare max() with two different possible types, you could write

```
template<class T1, class T2> T1 max(T1 a, T2 b)
```

This version of max() returns a value of type T1 and requires two arguments, one of type T1 and one of type T2.

A program uses template functions simply by issuing prototypes, which the compiler uses to write the actual function bodies. Listing 15.11, FTEMPLAT.CPP, illustrates how this works.

Listing 15.11. FTEMPLAT.CPP (Using function templates).

```
1:   #include <iostream.h>
2:   #include "minmax.h"
3:
4:   int max(int a, int b);
5:   double max(double a, double b);
6:   char max(char a, char b);
7:
8:   main()
9:   {
10:    int i1 = 100, i2 = 200;
11:    double d1 = 3.14159, d2 = 9.87654;
12:    char c1 = 'A', c2 = 'z';
13:
14:    cout << "max(i1, i2) == " << max(i1, i2) << '\n';
15:    cout << "max(d1, d2) == " << max(d1, d2) << '\n';
16:    cout << "max(c1, c2) == " << max(c1, c2) << '\n';
17:    return 0;
18:  }
```

Lines 4–6 declare three prototypes for template function max(). These lines provide the compiler with the information it needs to implement three overloaded max() functions. Each max() function returns a different data type and requires pairs of arguments of that same type. The main program calls the max() functions at lines 14–16. You use template functions as you do common functions.

Template Classes

Template classes are even more powerful than template functions. A class template provides the skeleton for a generic class to be implemented later. As with template functions, template classes are typically declared in a header file. Listing 15.12, db.h, demonstrates how to write a template class—in this case, one that can store a small database of records.

Listing 15.12. db.h (Class template TDatabase).

```
 1:  // db.h — TDatabase template class declaration
 2:
 3:  #ifndef __DB_H
 4:  #define __DB_H  1  /* Prevent multiple #includes */
 5:
 6:  template<class T>
 7:  class TDatabase {
 8:  private:
 9:    T *rp;       // Records pointer
10:    int num;     // Number of records
11:  public:
12:    TDatabase(int n)
13:      { rp = new T[num = n]; }
14:    ~TDatabase()
15:      { delete[] rp; }
16:    void DoNothing(void);
17:    T &GetRecord(int recnum);
18:  };
19:
20:  template<class T>
21:  void TDatabase<T>::DoNothing(void)
22:  {
23:  }
24:
```

```
25:   template<class T>
26:   T &TDatabase<T>::GetRecord(int recnum)
27:   {
28:     T *crp = rp;  // Current record ptr = records pointer
29:     if (0 <= recnum && recnum < num)
30:       while (recnum-- > 0)
31:         crp++;
32:     return *crp;
33:   }
34:
35:   #endif  /* __DB_H */
```

A template class is declared using the general form

```
template<class T> class TDatabase {
  // private, protected, and public members
}
```

T refers to an unspecified type that is supplied by the template's user. (You can change T to another identifier if you want.) T is a placeholder that might later be replaced by a built-in type, another class, a pointer type, and so on. TDatabase is the name of the template class. For clarity, declare the template's header on separate lines:

```
template<class T>
class TAnyClass {
  ...
}
```

You can also specify more than one placeholder:

```
template<class T1, class T2, class T3>
class TAnotherClass {
  ...
}
```

The template class can use T to declare data members, member function return values, parameters, and other items of an unspecified type. For example, in TDatabase, line 9 declares a pointer named rp of type T:

```
T *rp;
```

At this stage, T's real nature is unknown, and the program can use T only in completely generic ways. Nevertheless, TDatabase's constructor at lines 12–13 allocates an array of T objects, assigning the address of the array to rp and also setting a data member num equal to the number of requested records. (For simplicity, the class ignores any memory-allocation errors that might occur.) Line 15 deletes this array, using the special form delete[] to ensure that a destructor is called in case the array holds class objects.

Line 17 declares a member function GetRecord(), which returns a reference to an object of type T that is identified by record number recnum. This is another totally generic operation and does not require any knowledge of T's eventual type.

Template class member functions can be implemented inline as demonstrated by TDatabase's constructor and destructor. Or, they can be implemented separately. Because these template class member functions are still only declarations, however, they normally go in a header file, not in a separate module. DoNothing()—which, as its name implies, doesn't do much—shows the form that implements a template class member function:

```
template<class T>
void TDatabase<T>::DoNothing(void)
{
}
```

The member function's header is prefaced with template<class T>. Next comes the function return type (void), the class name (TDatabase<T>), and a scope resolution operator (::). Last are the function declaration (DoNothing(void)) and body (empty in this case). Use this sample as a guide to writing your own template class member functions.

Lines 25–33 show a more sophisticated template class member function, along with statements that perform the function's activities. GetRecord() returns a reference to an object of type T. Inside the function, a T pointer crp is assigned rp. In other words, crp addresses the first record stored in the TDatabase object. Line 29 checks whether recnum is in the proper range. If so, a while loop at lines 30–31 decrements recnum to zero and advances crp to each record in the database.

Examine line 31 carefully. Incrementing a typed pointer p with the expression p++ advances the pointer by the number of bytes of the object that p addresses. In TDatabase, even though the type of object addressed by crp is unknown, the expression crp++ is perfectly acceptable. Later, when an actual type is supplied for the template class, the compiler can generate the proper instructions to increment crp by sizeof(T). In the absence of template classes, similar generic statements are difficult to write.

Line 32 returns the dereferenced value of crp—in other words, a reference to whatever object crp addresses. This completes the template class, which makes no assumptions about the type of data it contains.

The next step is to use the template to create a database class object that can store some records. Listing 15.13, CTEMPLAT.CPP, puts the TDatabase template class to work.

Listing 15.13. CTEMPLAT.CPP (Using class templates).

```
 1:   #include <iostream.h>
 2:   #include <string.h>
 3:   #include "db.h"
 4:
 5:   class TRecord {
 6:   private:
 7:     char name[41];
 8:   public:
 9:     TRecord()
10:       { name[0] = 0; }
11:     TRecord(const char *s)
12:       { Assign(s); }
13:     void Assign(const char *s)
14:       { strncpy(name, s, 40); }
15:     char *GetName(void)
16:       { return name; }
17:   };
18:
19:   main()
20:   {
21:     int rn;                     // Record number index
22:     TDatabase<TRecord> db(3);    // Database of 3 TRecords
23:     TDatabase<TRecord*> dbp(3);  // Database of 3 TRecord pointers
24:     TDatabase<TRecord> *pdb;     // Pointer to db of TRecords
25:     TDatabase<TRecord*> *ppdb;   // Pointer to db of TRecord ptrs
26:
27:     cout << "\n\nDatabase of 3 TRecords\n";
28:     db.GetRecord(0).Assign("George Washington");
29:     db.GetRecord(1).Assign("John Adams");
30:     db.GetRecord(2).Assign("Thomas Jefferson");
```

continues

Listing 15.13. continued.

```
31:    for (rn = 0; rn <= 2; rn++)
32:      cout << db.GetRecord(rn).GetName() << '\n';
33:
34:    cout << "\n\nDatabase of 3 TRecord pointers\n";
35:    dbp.GetRecord(0) = new TRecord("George Bush");
36:    dbp.GetRecord(1) = new TRecord("Ronald Reagan");
37:    dbp.GetRecord(2) = new TRecord("Jimmy Carter");
38:    for (rn = 0; rn <= 2; rn++)
39:      cout << dbp.GetRecord(rn)->GetName() << '\n';
40:
41:    cout << "\n\nPointer to database of 3 TRecords\n";
42:    pdb = new TDatabase<TRecord>(3);
43:    pdb->GetRecord(0).Assign("John Adams");
44:    pdb->GetRecord(1).Assign("Thomas Jefferson");
45:    pdb->GetRecord(2).Assign("Aaron Burr");
46:    for (rn = 0; rn <= 2; rn++)
47:      cout << pdb->GetRecord(rn).GetName() << '\n';
48:
49:    cout << "\n\nPointer to database of 3 TRecord pointers\n";
50:    ppdb = new TDatabase<TRecord *>(3);
51:    ppdb->GetRecord(0) = new TRecord("Dan Quayle");
52:    ppdb->GetRecord(1) = new TRecord("George Bush");
53:    ppdb->GetRecord(2) = new TRecord("Walter Mondale");
54:    for (rn = 0; rn <= 2; rn++)
55:      cout << ppdb->GetRecord(rn)->GetName() << '\n';
56:
57:    return 0;
58:  }
```

After including the TDatabase template class header file db.h (line 3), the program declares a class TRecord—the one to be stored as objects in a TDatabase instance. The TRecord class is simplistic and declares only a single name character array as a data member. But TRecord could be any class, as TDatabase makes no assumptions about the kinds of objects it can store.

Lines 22–25 show four ways to create class objects from a class template. The line

```
TDatabase<TRecord> db(3);
```

defines an object named db of the template class type TDatabase and specifies TRecord as the class that is to replace T throughout the template. The parenthetical (3) is db's initializer, passed to the TDatabase constructor.

You can also define a database of other values—you don't have to use class types. For example, the following defines a database of 100 double values:

```
TDatabase<double> dbd(100);
```

Because it is designed to store objects of any type, TDatabase is called a *container class*. Usually, the best template container classes are fully generic, although that ideal is often difficult to achieve.

Lines 23–25 show how to create some other kinds of template class instances. Line 23 declares a TDatabase object dbp of three TRecord pointers. Line 24 declares pdb as a pointer to a TDatabase object of an unspecified number of TRecord objects. Line 25 declares a similar pointer to a database of TRecord pointers to TRecord objects. These examples should cover most kinds of objects you might want to create for other class templates.

The program uses the TDatabase object as it would any nontemplate. For example, line 28:

```
db.GetRecord(0).Assign("George Washington");
```

calls GetRecord(0) to obtain a reference to record number zero. The line then calls that object's Assign() member function to give it a string value.

Lines 34–55 show how to use the other TDatabase objects. Line 35 is particularly interesting:

```
dbp.GetRecord(0) = new TRecord("George Bush");
```

Because GetRecord() returns a reference to an object, it can be used on the left side of an assignment statement. In this case, a new TRecord object is constructed and its address is assigned to database record number zero as referred to by GetRecord().

Note that in all of these examples, you do not need typecasts to inform the compiler about the data types used by TDatabase. Despite the template's generic nature, it is possible to avoid using typecasts yet still create classes that can handle a variety of data types.

> **HINT:** It's probably best not to construct template classes from scratch. Instead, you might design TDatabase to use specific TRecord objects. Then, after debugging TDatabase, you can convert it to a general-purpose template. Converting regular classes to templates in this manner helps to identify a class's true generic capabilities—a challenge that is often the most difficult aspect of creating useful templates.

Odds and Ends

All computer languages have valuable features that are rarely used. You probably won't employ the following techniques often, but then again, you might find one or more of these C++ odds and ends just what you need.

Pointers to Member Functions

You can address class member functions with pointers, but not in the same way you address common functions (see Chapter 9, "Pointers"). Member functions are called in reference to objects of a class, and they receive a hidden this pointer. For these reasons, addressing member functions with pointers requires new techniques.

A member function pointer is bound to its class name. For example, for a class TFirstClass, you might declare a pointer to a member function like this:

```
double (TFirstClass::*myfnptr)(void);
```

This states that myfnptr addresses a TFirstClass member function that requires no input and returns double. To declare myfnptr as a pointer to a member function that returns void and has two int parameters, you can write

```
void (TFirstClass::*myfnptr)(int, int);
```

These declarations do not specify which member function myfnptr addresses, only the form of the function that may be assigned to the pointer variable. It's still necessary to create an object of the class and to assign the address of a class member of the appropriate form to the pointer.

Listing 15.14, MFNPTR.CPP, shows the basic steps required to define and use pointers to member functions.

Listing 15.14. MFNPTR.CPP (Pointers to member functions).

```
 1:  #include <iostream.h>
 2:  #include <iomanip.h>
 3:
 4:  class TFirstClass {
 5:  private:
 6:    int count;
 7:  public:
 8:    TFirstClass() { count = 0; }
 9:    int Access(void);
10:  };
11:
12:  int (TFirstClass::*myfnptr)(void);
13:
14:  main()
15:  {
16:    int i;
17:    TFirstClass fc;
18:
19:    cout << "\nCall Access the normal way:\n";
20:    for (i = 0; i < 9; i++)
21:      cout << setw(8) << dec << fc.Access();
22:    cout << "\n\nCall Access via the member function pointer\n";
23:    myfnptr = &TFirstClass::Access;
24:    for (i = 0; i < 9; i++)
25:      cout << setw(8) << dec << (fc.*myfnptr)();
26:    cout << "\n\nMember function pointer and a dynamic instance\n";
27:    TFirstClass *fp = new TFirstClass;
28:    for (i = 0; i < 9; i++)
29:      cout << setw(8) << dec << (fp->*myfnptr)();
30:    return 0;
31:  }
32:
33:  int TFirstClass::Access(void)
34:  {
35:    return count++;
36:  }
```

Line 12 declares `myfnptr` as a pointer to a TFirstClass member function that requires no arguments and returns an `int` value. The pointer may address any TFirstClass member function of that design.

In function `main()`, line 17 declares a TFirstClass object `fc`. Line 21 calls the TFirstClass `Access()` member function for object `fc` in the usual way. (`Access()` merely increments and returns a private data member, just to give the program something to do.)

Line 25 shows how to call `Access()` by addressing the member function with pointer `myfnptr`. To initialize the pointer, line 23 assigns to `myfnptr` the address of the `Access()` member function in TFirstClass. You could also replace the pointer declaration (line 12) and the assignment (line 23) with a single statement, either globally or in `main()`:

```
int (TFirstClass::*myfnptr)(void) = &TFirstClass::Access;
```

When calling an addressed member function, you must follow two rules:

1. Refer to an object of the class.

2. Surround the function call with parentheses.

For example, if `n` is an `int` variable and `fc` is a TFirstClass object, the following line copies to `n` the result returned by `Access()`:

```
n = (fc.*myfnptr)();
```

The double character symbol `.*` is called the *pointer-to-member* operator and is used to dereference a member function pointer for a class object. The parentheses around `(fc.*myfnptr)` are required because the function-call operator `()` has higher precedence than `.*`. The statement listed above is exactly equivalent to the more common statement

```
n = fc.Access();
```

You can also call member functions via pointers when objects are addressed by other pointer variables. For example, refer back to lines 27–29 in MFNPTR (Listing 15.14). First, pointer `fp` is assigned the address of a new TFirstClass object. Then, the expression

```
(fp->*myfnptr)();
```

in the output stream statement at line 29 calls the `Access()` member function for the object addressed by `fp`. The triple character symbol `->*` is a second kind of pointer-to-member operator. Again, the extra parentheses are needed because `()` has higher precedence than `->*`. The preceding statement is exactly equivalent to

```
fp->Access();
```

In addition to addressing member functions with pointers, it's also possible to address other public data members. For example, if `TFirstClass` had a public `double` member named `balance`, you could define a pointer to that member as

```
double TFirstClass::*dataPtr;
```

Pointer `dataPtr` is declared to address any public `double` data member in class `TFirstClass`. To initialize the pointer, use a statement such as

```
dataPtr = &TFirstClass::balance;
```

Or you could define the pointer and assign the address of the `balance` member in one easy motion:

```
double TFirstClass::*dataPtr = &TFirstClass::balance;
```

Either way, `dataPtr` now addresses the `balance` member in `TFirstClass`. Actually, `dataPtr` does not hold the address of a memory location; instead, it holds the offset where the `balance` member is stored in a `TFirstClass` object. It is still necessary to refer to the addressed data member through a class object. These statements, for instance, initialize and display `balance`'s value:

```
fc.balance = 1234.56;
cout << "\nBalance=" << fc.*dataPtr;
```

The notation `fc.*dataPtr` is similar to the notation used to call a member function, and it uses the pointer-to-member operator `.*`. The expression does not require extra parentheses, however, because it contains no conflicting operators.

Static Members

A static member function typically performs a global action or initializes global data for all objects of a class. To declare a static member function, precede a normal class member function declaration with the keyword `static`.

```
class TAnyClass {
public:
  static void GlobalInit(void);
  ...
};
```

Static member functions may not be virtual. Implement the static member function as you do others, prefacing the function name with the class name and a scope resolution operator:

```
void TAnyClass::GlobalInit(void)
{
  // Statements to perform
}
```

The static member function may perform any statements, however it does not receive a this pointer, and it cannot access any normal data or function members in the class. A program calls a static member function by referring, not to an object, but to the class name:

```
TAnyClass::GlobalInit();  // Call GlobalInit() static function
```

Presumably, a static member function like GlobalInit() performs actions that affect all objects of type TAnyClass.

Classes can also declare static data members. For example, in this class:

```
class TAnyClass {
private:
  static char c;  // Static data member
public:
  char GetC(void) { return c; }
};
```

member c is declared as a private static char variable. (Static data members can also be protected or public.) Only one copy of TAnyClass::c exists regardless of how many TAnyClass objects the program defines. The program must define and initialize the static member, usually with a global definition such as

```
char TAnyClass::c = 'q';
```

In effect, c is a global variable that is accessible only to TAnyClass member functions. You can next define a TAnyClass object that uses c. These statements, for example, define an object x and call the class GetC() member function, which displays the character 'q':

```
TAnyClass x;
cout << x.GetC();  // Displays static c data member
```

Placing Objects at Specific Addresses

You might occasionally need to store an object at a specific location, perhaps in a global buffer in a data segment. Such objects persist beyond the scope of their declarations and are sometimes called "persistent objects."

Listing 15.15, PERSIST.CPP, demonstrates how to store an object at a specific address. The program also shows how to call a destructor directly—an uncommon technique that may be necessary to delete objects that are created by an overloaded new operator that bypasses the default memory allocator.

Listing 15.15. PERSIST.CPP (Stores persistent object in a buffer).

```
 1:  #include <iostream.h>
 2:
 3:  class TPersist {
 4:  private:
 5:    int x, y;
 6:  public:
 7:    TPersist(int a, int b) { x = a; y = b; } // Constructor
 8:    ~TPersist() { x = 0; y = 0; }  // Destructor
 9:    void *operator new(size_t, void *p) { return p; }
10:    friend ostream& operator<< (ostream &os, TPersist &p);
11:  };
12:
13:  char object[sizeof(TPersist)];
14:
15:  main()
16:  {
17:    TPersist *p = new(object) TPersist(10, 20);
18:    cout << *p;
19:    p->TPersist::~TPersist();  // Explicit call to destructor
20:    return 0;
21:  }
22:
23:  ostream& operator<< (ostream& os, TPersist &p)
24:  {
25:    os << "x == " << p.x << ", y == " << p.y;
26:    return os;
27:  }
```

Class TPersist (lines 3–11) overloads new in an unusual way. Rather than allocate memory to a pointer, the overloaded operator function simply returns its void pointer parameter p. The program uses new at line 17 to store a TPersist object in the global buffer defined at line 13. The expression new(object) calls the overloaded new member function, passing the char buffer object's address as an argument. Because the overloaded new operator simply returns p, this strange-looking statement in effect assigns object's address to p and also calls the TPersist constructor to initialize the newly allocated object in the buffer.

A good exercise is to run PERSIST in Turbo Debugger. Inspect the object buffer and single step the code by pressing F8. When the statement at line 17 executes, you'll see the values 10 and 20 stored in the global buffer—proving that the overloaded new bypasses the heap memory allocator.

Line 19 calls the class destructor for the object addressed by p. Because the object is stored in a global variable, it may be necessary to call the destructor this way in order to perform any cleanup duties. For nonvirtual destructors, use the statement form shown in the listing:

```
p->TPersist::~TPersist();  // Explicit call to destructor
```

C++ doesn't recognize the scope of the object stored in the buffer, and it can't call the object's class destructor automatically. Again, executing this statement in Turbo Debugger is instructive. When you do that, you see the destructor's inline statements set the object's data members to zero (see lines 8 and 19).

For virtual destructors—even those in objects of a derived class—you should be able to use the form

```
p->~TPersist();  // Explicit call to destructor
```

Unfortunately, however, this is currently not possible in Borland C++. (Calling destructors explicitly is not a highly regarded technique, so this deficiency is practically meaningless.)

Initializing Class Object Members

A constructor typically initializes data members for an object of a class. For example, TAnyClass declares two int data members x and y, and initializes those members with assignment statements in an inline constructor:

```
class TAnyClass {
private:
  int x, y;
public:
  TAnyClass() { x = 0; y = 0; }
  ...
};
```

Alternatively, you can initialize members as though they had constructors, writing

```
class TAnyClass {
private:
  int x, y;
public:
  TAnyClass(): x(0), y(0) { }
  ...
};
```

This form of the TAnyClass constructor assigns zero to x and y just as the assignments did in the previous example. The compiled code is the same for both forms, but the second form specifies initializers for data members before the body of the constructor is executed. (In this example, the constructor's body is empty.)

The technique is essential to initialize object members of another class. For example, suppose TAnyClass owns a data member object of class TNewClass, and that TNewClass's constructor requires an integer parameter:

```
class TNewClass {
  int x;
public:
  TNewClass(int n) { x = n; }
  ...
};
```

If TAnyClass declares a data member of type TNewClass, TAnyClass's constructor must initialize that object. Because constructors can't be called directly, the object must be initialized using the alternate form introduced earlier:

```
class TAnyClass {
private:
  int x;
  TNewClass z;  // Object data member
public:
```

```
TAnyClass(int n): z(n)   // Initialize z
  { x = n; }             // Initialize x
  ...
};
```

Member x is type int as before. Member z is an object of class TNewClass. TAnyClass's constructor declares an int parameter n, which is used to initialize z before the constructor's body runs. Inside the constructor, an assignment stores the value of n in x. In a class with multiple object data members, you can initialize them in a list separated with commas:

```
class TAnyClass {
private:
  int x;
  TNewClass a, b, z;  // Three object data members
public:
  TAnyClass(int n): a(n), b(n), z(n)  // Initialize a, b, and z
    { x = n; }                        // Initialize x
  ...
};
```

Nested Class Declarations

Items other than data and function members can nest inside class declarations. A class can declare a typedef symbol, a struct, or even another class. These *nested class declarations* are sometimes useful for providing declarations closely related to a specific class. Nested class declarations also permit two or more classes to declare identically named items that are distinguished by their respective class names.

Use a nested typedef to export a data type from inside a class. The following TAnyClass, for example, uses typedef to declare CLASS_COUNTER as an alias for int:

```
class TAnyClass {
public:
  typedef int CLASS_COUNTER;  // Nested typedef declaration
  static CLASS_COUNTER ClassCount;  // Static variable
public:
  TAnyClass() { ClassCount++; }
  ~TAnyClass() { ClassCount--; }
};
```

The class also declares a static CLASS_COUNTER variable named ClassCount. To define memory for this variable, the program needs a global declaration such as

```
TAnyClass::CLASS_COUNTER TAnyClass::ClassCount;
```

The class name prefaces the data type and variable name. Because TAnyClass provides the typedef CLASS_COUNTER, the program can define the variable ClassCount without any direct knowledge of the variable's underlying data type. With no extra help from the program, the class itself counts the number of its own constructed objects:

```
TAnyClass *cp1, *cp2, *cp3;  // Declare class-object pointers
cp1 = new TAnyClass;         // Construct class objects
cp2 = new TAnyClass;         //    "         "        "
cp3 = new TAnyClass;         //    "         "        "
cout << "There are " << TAnyClass::ClassCount << " objects\n";
```

The final statement displays 3. Here again, the class name prefaces the reference to ClassCount.

Complex nested declarations are also possible. A class can declare an inner struct:

```
class TAnyClass {
public:
  struct ClassStruct {
    int x;
    int y;
  };
};
```

The program can then define an object of type TAnyClass::ClassStruct:

```
TAnyClass::ClassStruct k;
```

Use k as you would a non-nested struct:

```
k.x = 1;
k.y = 2;
```

Extending these concepts further leads to a nested class declaration—one class declared inside another:

```
class TAnyClass {
public:
  class ClassClass {
    int x;
```

```
    int y;
  public:
    ClassClass() { x = 1; y = 2; }
    int GetX(void) { return x; }
    int GetY(void) { return y; }
  };
};
```

In this example, TAnyClass declares an inner class named ClassClass. A program might use the nested class like this:

```
TAnyClass::ClassClass k;
cout << "k.x == " << k.GetX() << '\n';
cout << "k.y == " << k.GetY() << '\n';
```

Other kinds of nested class declarations such as enumerated constants are also possible. The key to using nested class declarations is to remember always to preface references to nested items with the class name and a scope resolution operator. Other than this rule, you can use most nested class declarations as you do unnested ones.

The Object-Data Calling Convention

Borland C++ 3.1 includes an important new optimization that can greatly increase performance of object-oriented programs. As you have learned, class member functions receive a hidden this pointer, which addresses the object for which the member function is called. Defining a variable of a class named TAnyClass:

```
TAnyClass anyvar;
```

and calling a TAnyClass member function:

```
anyVar.AnyFunction();
```

passes to AnyFunction a this pointer that addresses anyvar. Literally speaking, "this" is how member functions address data members in class objects.

To avoid wasting time and memory by passing this on the stack, Borland C++ 3.1 can instead pass this in a register, thus saving the time it takes to push this onto the stack and, inside member functions, to refer to the stacked this pointer. Known as the *object-data calling convention,* this simple yet effective code optimization can make a world of difference in performance, especially in programs that can call many small member functions—a typical case for most object-oriented applications.

Near this pointers are passed in register si. Far this pointers are passed in ds:si, and the compiler automatically saves and restores ds as needed. To engage object-data calling, compile the program from a DOS prompt with option -po. You might, for instance, use the command

```
bcc -po myprog
```

You can also select object-data calling by using the IDE's Options| Compiler|Optimizations command, and selecting Object data calling.

Inside a program's text, to enable the convention, use this #pragma command:

```
#pragma option -po
```

Class declarations following that line use the object-data calling convention. To return to the previous setting for the -po option, use the command

```
#pragma option -po.
```

> **HINT:** Like other optimizations, the object-data calling convention doesn't guarantee positive results. One obvious negative effect is the elimination of si as a register variable. In some cases, you might discover that object-data calling worsens performance. For best results, test the effects on your code with and without object-data calling.

Summary

- Friends of a class are granted access to that class's private and protected members. Public members are always accessible; any friends may access them as well.

- Two classes may declare each other as friends. These mutual friends have full access to one another's private and protected members.

- A friend function is granted access to a class's private and protected members. Friend functions may be garden variety functions or members of a class.

- Overloading operators extends the kinds of built-in data types that C++ operators recognize. You can overload binary operators such as divide (/) and times (*), and you can overload unary operators such as minus (–) and not (~). With few exceptions, most C++ operators can be overloaded to permit objects of a class to be used in expressions involving those operators.

- Because new and delete are operators, they too can be overloaded to provide custom memory management facilities for class objects.

- Normally, new returns null if the operator can't satisfy a memory allocation request. You can modify this action by calling set_new_handler().

- Classes can declare a copy constructor, which C++ calls when an object initializes another object of the same class, when an object is passed to a function's value parameter and when a function returns a class object.

- Classes can overload the assignment operator, which C++ calls when an object of a class is assigned to another already constructed object of that same class.

- I/O streams are provided as classes derived from ios and declared in iostream.h. Four I/O stream objects are provided: cin, cout, cerr, and clog. The ios class and derivatives define input (>>) and output (<<) stream operators for all built-in C++ data types.

- I/O stream manipulators, declared in iomanip.h, make it possible to format input and output in I/O stream statements. You can also write your own manipulators.

- Classes can overload I/O stream operators to provide input and output capabilities for class objects. Programs can use objects of these classes in I/O stream statements.

- Templates are experimental, but they are implemented in Borland C++. Templates are useful for creating general-purpose functions and classes for which actual implementation details are supplied by the templates' users.

- Other C++ features covered in this chapter include pointers to member functions, static member functions, placing objects at specific addresses, calling destructors directly, initializing class object members, nesting class declarations, and engaging the object-data calling convention (introduced in Borland C++ 3.1).

Exercises

15.1 You are writing a simulation of an internal combustion engine. Devise two classes, one named TEngine, and one named TFuel with a private double data member level, which measures how much "fuel" is stored in a class object's tank. Using friends, declare your TFuel and TEngine classes so that TEngine can refer directly to Fuel's private level.

15.2 Add times (*) and divide (/) overloaded operator functions to the TStrOp class in STROPS.CPP, Listing 15.4.

15.3 Add ++ and -- overloaded operators to the TStrOp class in STROPS2.CPP, Listing 15.5. Implement prefix and postfix forms of these operators.

15.4 Declare and implement a double type-conversion operator for class TStrOp in STROPS2.CPP, Listing 15.5.

15.5 Given a class named TFruit and an object orange of type TFruit, use orange to initialize a new object named grapefruit.

15.6 Write the prototype for a copy constructor in the hypothetical TFruit class from Exercise 15.5.

15.7 Write an overloaded assignment operator for the TFruit class from Exercise 15.5.

15.8 Write a program that uses the min() template function from Listing 15.10.

15.9 Create a database of 100 random integers using the TDatabase template class from Listing 15.12. Use a for loop and output stream statement to display the object's values in 8-character columns.

Part 4

DOS and Windows Development Tools

PART 4

16

The Borland Graphics Interface

There are few areas in computer programming more satisfying than graphics. Programmers who spend their time designing graphics software live in a heaven of colors, shapes, animations, and three-dimensional objects, limited only by their imaginations and their computer's video displays.

With the Borland Graphics Interface (BGI), anyone can become a computer graphics artist, whether you write business software, games, simulations, or just like to have fun. Even simple programs can produce remarkable patterns, giving your programs an extra touch that text-only software can never match.

Introducing the Borland Graphics Interface

All PCs can display characters with fixed bit patterns stored in ROM or, sometimes, in RAM. Although a PC's extended ASCII characters have fixed-line and angle segments giving a limited ability to construct lines and boxes on text displays, the real excitement in computer graphics comes from the ability to control each display dot, called a picture element, or pixel.

Typical PC graphics displays offer resolutions from 320 x 200 pixels to 1024 x 768 pixels in as few as two to as many as 256 colors. That's anywhere from 64,000 to 786,432 pixels at your control. Also called an All Points Addressable (APA) display, a PC graphics screen is the Etch-A-Sketch of many a programmer's dreams.

Perhaps the most difficult aspect of PC graphics is writing programs to choose among the number of possible display formats, some of which do not exist on certain computer models. Borland C++ simplifies the process by automatically detecting and initializing the best graphics mode available. By following a few simple rules, you can write graphics software that runs correctly on all the graphics modes listed in Table 16.1.

Table 16.1. BGI graphics modes.

Mode	Description	Driver file
CGA	Color Graphics Adapter	CGA.BGI
MCGA	Multicolor Graphics Array	CGA.BGI
EGA	Enhanced Graphics Adapter	EGAVGA.BGI
VGA	Video Graphics Array	EGAVGA.BGI
Hercules	Hercules Monochrome Graphics	HERC.BGI
AT&T	AT&T 400-Line Graphics	ATT.BGI
PC3270	IBM PC 3270 Graphics	PC3270.BGI
IBM8514	IBM PC 8514 Graphics	IBM8514.BGI

Most of the programs in this chapter work best with an EGA or VGA color graphics adapter and an RGB (Red, Green, Blue) monitor. You can use CGA graphics or a less expensive color monitor, but the results may not be as colorful or as clear. On Hercules and similar monochrome graphics systems, you see only shades of green or amber instead of different hues. Standard IBM monochrome adapters cannot display graphics.

The right column in Table 16.1 lists the BGI disk files containing the object-code drivers for the graphics modes on the left. To run graphics programs, you need at least one BGI driver file. Compiling programs requires the graphics.h header file (usually stored in C:\BORLANDC\INCLUDE). To link BGI programs requires the GRAPHICS.LIB file (usually stored in C:\BORLANDC\LIB), which contains device-independent code for all BGI functions. When compiling programs from the command line, you must tell the linker to read GRAPHICS.LIB. For example, to compile a BGI program named GRAPH.CPP, enter the command

```
bcc graph graphics.lib
```

Text-mode IDE users should select Options|Linker, choose Libraries, and enable Graphics library. To debug BGI programs with Turbo Debugger, compile with the -v option and run the debugger with options -vg (full graphics save) and, if necessary, -vp (color palette save).

Another important disk file type ends in .CHR and contains information for drawing text characters on graphics displays. A .CHR file is also called (somewhat incorrectly) a font file. In typesetting, a font is one type size and style. In Borland C++ graphics, a font is a text style, which you can scale up or down to many different sizes. The word *font*, in this chapter, describes a text style in *all* possible sizes.

NOTE: You can't use Borland C++ for Windows to create BGI programs, but you can run compiled BGI programs in a DOS prompt window under Microsoft Windows 3.0 or 3.1. Depending on your system—if you are running Windows 3.1 in 386-Enhanced-Mode, for example—you might be able to display BGI graphics inside a graphical DOS prompt window. For best results, however, configure the DOS prompt for text-mode output. Microsoft Windows has its own set of graphics commands and techniques, introduced in Chapter 21, "Windows Tools and Techniques."

Initializing BGI Drivers

Listing 16.1, ITROUND.CPP (in-the-round), shows the correct way to initialize a graphics mode and draw a circle in the center of the screen.

> **NOTE:** Most programs in this chapter call getch() from conio.h to pause for you to press a key. Press Enter or another key to end a graphics example and return to the DOS prompt.

Listing 16.1. ITROUND.CPP (Demonstrates in-the-round BGI graphics).

```
 1:  #include <graphics.h>
 2:  #include <stdio.h>
 3:  #include <stdlib.h>
 4:  #include <conio.h>
 5:  main()
 6:  {
 7:    int gdriver = DETECT, gmode, gerr;
 8:    int xcenter, ycenter;
 9:    unsigned radius;
10:
11:    initgraph(&gdriver, &gmode, "c:\\borlandc\\bgi");
12:    gerr = graphresult();
13:    if (gerr != grOk) {
14:      printf("BGI error: %s\n", grapherrormsg(gerr));
15:      exit(gerr);
16:    }
17:    xcenter = getmaxx() / 2;
18:    ycenter = getmaxy() / 2;
19:    radius = getmaxy() / 4;
20:    setcolor(GREEN);
21:    circle(xcenter, ycenter, radius);
22:    getch();        // Wait for keypress before ending
23:    closegraph();   // Shut down BGI graphics
24:    return 0;
25:  }
```

If your system has EGA or VGA graphics, ITROUND should display a green circle in the center of the display. If you have a different graphics system and your circle is not green, don't worry—you'll learn about colors and how to change them later. If you don't see a circle, or if you receive an error message, check your installation options.

You must have the proper .BGI, .CHR, graphics.h, and GRAPHICS.LIB files available when using the compiler and when running a compiled BGI program.

> **NOTE:** If you can compile and run ITROUND, but don't see a circle and you're sure your system supports graphics, try changing setcolor()'s argument from GREEN to WHITE, or remove line 20.

ITROUND contains elements used in all BGI programs. Lines 7–16 automatically detect and initialize a graphics display mode, and report any errors. The first step is to set an integer variable gdriver to DETECT, a symbolic constant declared in graphics.h. Passing the initialized gdriver by address to initgraph() (line 11) automatically detects an ideal graphics mode. Function initgraph() stores the selected driver's number in gdriver and mode in gmode. (Later, you'll look more closely at these values and discover how to defeat automatic graphics-mode selection.) The simplest BGI initialization sequence is

```
int gdriver = DETECT, gmode;
initgraph(&gdriver, &gmode, "c:\\borlandc\\bgi");  // Note double '\\'!
```

Change the string argument to the path where you store .BGI driver and .CHR font files. If you don't store these files in C:\BORLANDC\BGI, you must make this change to every program in this chapter. Notice the double backslashes used in the pathname string, needed because \\ represents a *single* backslash character. Function initgraph() looks in the specified path first, then if the needed files aren't found, in the current directory. A null string instructs initgraph() to look only in the current drive and directory:

```
int gdriver = DETECT, gmode;
initgraph(&gdriver, &gmode, "");  // Look for BGI files in current dir
```

Function initgraph() loads the proper graphics BGI driver file from disk, initializes various internal variables, engages a video-display mode, and erases the screen.

Table 16.2 lists all BGI driver and mode constants. Most BGI drivers can handle several different modes with various resolutions and memory buffers (pages). A single page equals the amount of memory needed to hold all the pixels from one display. Multipage modes let you draw offscreen while viewing graphics on other screens—an especially useful technique for animation and slide-show programs.

Table 16.2. Graphics modes, resolutions, and pages.

Driver	Mode	Resolution	Pages
CGA	CGAC0	320 × 200, palette 0	1
	CGAC1	320 × 200, palette 1	1
	CGAC2	320 × 200, palette 2	1
	CGAC3	320 × 200, palette 3	1
	CGAHI	640 × 200	1
MCGA	MCGAC0	320 × 200, palette 0	1
	MCGAC1	320 × 200, palette 1	1
	MCGAC2	320 × 200, palette 2	1
	MCGAC3	320 × 200, palette 3	1
	MCGAMED	640 × 200	1
	MCGAHI	640 × 480	1
EGA	EGALO	640 × 200, 16 colors	4
	EGAHI	640 × 350, 16 colors	2
EGA64	EGA64LO	640 × 200, 16 colors	1
	EGA64HI	640 × 350, 4 colors	1
EGAMONO	EGAMONOHI	640 × 350	1–4*
VGA	VGALO	640 × 200, 16 colors	4
	VGAMED	640 × 350, 16 colors	2
	VGAHI	640 × 480, 16 colors	1
HECMONO	HERCMONOHI	720 × 348, monochrome	2
ATT400	ATT400C0	320 × 200, palette 0	1
	ATT400C1	320 × 200, palette 1	1
	ATT400C2	320 × 200, palette 2	1
	ATT400C3	320 × 200, palette 3	1

Driver	Mode	Resolution	Pages
	ATT400MED	640×200	1
	ATT400HI	640×400	1
PC3270	PC3270HI	720×350	1
IBM8514	IBM8514LO	640×480, 256 colors	n/a
	IBM8514HI	1024×768, 256 colors	n/a

64K on card = 1 page; 256K = 4 pages.

Initializing Graphics the Hard Way

If you don't care to have a graphics mode selected automatically, you can choose a different mode by assigning a driver from Table 16.2 to gdriver and a mode to gmode before calling initgraph(). For example, the following code initializes EGA low-resolution, 640 x 200, 16-color graphics:

```
int gdriver = EGA, gmode = EGALO;
initgraph(&gdriver, &gmode, "c:\\borlandc\\bgi");
```

When manually selecting graphics modes this way, it's up to you to determine what graphics hardware the computer has. Usually, it's best to let Borland C++ automatically select a graphics mode for you, but you might want to include an option in your programs to let people select specific modes. Be careful with this technique. Initializing unavailable display modes can hang the computer, forcing you to reboot or, in some cases, to shut off power.

One way to avoid such problems is to call detectgraph() rather than pass the default DETECT constant to initgraph(). Function detectgraph() checks the hardware and sets integer variables gdriver and gmode to suggested values. Unlike initgraph(), however, detectgraph() does not initialize the display. The initialization sequence now becomes

```
detectgraph(&gdriver, &gmode);    // Find "ideal" driver and mode
initgraph(&gdriver, &gmode, "");  // Initialize graphics
```

This is identical to passing DETECT to initgraph(), but because most graphics drivers support more than one configuration, detectgraph() gives you the chance to initialize the display for a different mode. You might use this idea, for instance, to detect CGA graphics but initialize the display to 640 x 200 resolution rather than the default 320 x 200:

```
detectgraph(&gdriver, &gmode);      // Find "ideal" driver and mode
if (gdriver == CGA) {               // If driver is CGA...
  gmode = CGAHI;                    //   select high resolution mode
  initgraph(&gdriver, &gmode, "");  // Initialize graphics
  // Graphics statements
}
```

Another possibility is to call function getmaxmode() after initgraph() to find the range of modes supported by an automatically selected driver. To select another display mode, you can then pass a value in the range zero to getmaxmode() to setgraphmode(), which clears the display and selects a specified graphics mode. For example, this initializes graphics for the highest possible mode number:

```
detectgraph(&gdriver, &gmode);      // Find "ideal" driver and mode
initgraph(&gdriver, &gmode, "");    // Initialize graphics
if (graphresult == grOk) {          // If no errors are detected
  setgraphmode(getmaxmode());       //   select highest possible mode
  // Graphics statements
};
```

Another way to detect a driver's maximum mode number is to call getmoderange(), which returns two int values representing the low and high modes for a graphics driver. Unlike getmaxmode(), getmoderange() may be called before initgraph() as in this fragment, which selects the lowest possible mode number for the default graphics driver:

```
int gdriver, gmode, lomode, himode;
detectgraph(&gdriver, &gmode);              // Find "ideal" driver and mode
getmoderange(gdriver, &lomode, &himode);    // Get range of modes
initgraph(&gdriver, &lomode, "");           // Initialize to lowest mode
```

Be aware that getmoderange() works with only standard-issue drivers. Function getmaxmode(), however, returns the maximum mode number for BGI *and* custom drivers supplied by third-party vendors.

You can also pass –1 to getmoderange() after calling initgraph() to obtain all possible mode ranges for a selected driver. You might use this technique to switch to a different mode from an automatically selected one:

```
int gdriver = DETECT, gmode, lomode, himode;
initgraph(&gdriver, &gmode, "");        // Initialize default graphics
if (graphresult() == grOk) {            // If no errors are detected
  getmoderange(-1, &lomode, &himode);   // Get ranges for current driver
  setgraphmode(himode);                 // Change to highest mode
  // Graphics statements
};
```

Detecting Graphics Errors

The final step in preparing a graphics mode is to check whether initgraph() detected any errors. This and other BGI functions save an internal error code that describes an operation's success or failure. Function graphresult() returns this error code and resets the internal value to zero. Calling graphresult() twice or more in succession returns a valid error code only the first time around.

Lines 12–16 in ITROUND show the correct way to check graphresult(). First, assign the function result to an int variable such as gerr. All graphics errors are either zero or negative. If gerr is not equal to the enumerated constant grOk, line 14 displays an appropriate error message returned by grapherrormsg(). Table 16.3 lists graphics error values and messages. You could decode these values and display your own messages, but it's easier to call grapherrormsg() and use the default strings. The function also fills empty parentheses with filenames (see error values –3 and –8, for example).

Table 16.3. Graphics error numbers and messages.

Constant	Value	Error string
grOk	0	No error
grNoInitGraph	−1	(BGI) graphics not installed
grNotDetected	−2	Graphics hardware not detected
grFileNotFound	−3	Device driver file not found ()
grInvalidDriver	−4	Invalid device driver file ()
grNoLoadMem	−5	Not enough memory to load driver
grNoScanMem	−6	Out of memory in scan fill

continues

Table 16.3. continued

Constant	Value	Error string
grNoFloodMem	−7	Out of memory In flood fill
grFontNotFound	−8	Font file not found ()
grNoFontMem	−9	Not enough memory to load font
grInvalidMode	−10	Invalid graphics mode for selected driver
grError	−11	Graphics error
grIOerror	−12	Graphics I/O error
grInvalidFont	−13	Invalid font file ()
grInvalidFontNum	−14	Invalid font number
grInvalidVersion	−18	Invalid version

Displaying Driver and Mode Names

After initializing graphics with initgraph(), you can call getdrivername() for the name of the selected driver and getmodename(gmode) for the name of mode gmode.

To see how these functions work, replace lines 17–21 of ITROUND with the following:

```
outtextxy(0, 0, getdrivername());
outtextxy(0, 20, getmodename(gmode));
```

The outtextxy() function displays a text string at a specified location. You'll see this function again later.

Detecting Screen Resolution

After successfully initializing a BGI program, the screen is clear and ready for drawing. A few statements, repeated here from ITROUND (lines 17–19), detect the display's maximum resolution and prepare three useful values:

692

```
xcenter = getmaxx() / 2;
ycenter = getmaxy() / 2;
radius = getmaxy() / 4;
```

Functions getmaxx() and getmaxy() return the display's maximum horizontal (X) and vertical (Y) coordinate values. By designing your programs around these values, you write graphics code that works correctly in different resolutions. Here, int variables xcenter and ycenter are set to the midpoint of the display's X and Y axes, and the unsigned radius is set to one-quarter the height.

Lines 20 and 21 in ITROUND draw the circle, calling setcolor() to choose a drawing color and circle() to draw the figure in that color. The three arguments passed to circle() specify the circle's X and Y center coordinate and radius.

Switching Between Text and Graphics

To return to the display mode in effect before calling initgraph(), end your BGI programs by calling closegraph(). If you don't do this, you may leave the video interface stuck in a graphics mode, requiring users to reboot or to use the DOS MODE command to return to a text display.

Function closegraph() also removes from memory the BGI driver previously loaded by initgraph(). To return to graphics after calling closegraph() requires repeating all the BGI initialization steps. To switch back and forth between text and graphics modes more easily, use the method demonstrated in Listing 16.2, MIXEDMOD.CPP.

Listing 16.2. MIXEDMOD.CPP (Switches between graphics and text modes).

```
1:  #include <graphics.h>
2:  #include <stdio.h>
3:  #include <stdlib.h>
4:  #include <conio.h>
5:  main()
6:  {
7:    int gdriver = DETECT, gmode, gerr;
8:    int xcenter, ycenter;
```

continues

Listing 16.2. continued

```
 9:
10:    initgraph(&gdriver, &gmode, "c:\\borlandc\\bgi");
11:    gerr = graphresult();
12:    if (gerr != grOk) {
13:      printf("BGI error: %s\n", grapherrormsg(gerr));
14:      exit(gerr);
15:    }
16:    xcenter = getmaxx() / 2;
17:    ycenter = getmaxy() / 2;
18:    setcolor(CYAN);
19:    rectangle(xcenter - 50, ycenter - 50, xcenter + 50, ycenter + 50);
20:    outtext("This is the graphics page. Press Enter...");
21:    getch();
22:    restorecrtmode();
23:    printf("This is the text page. Press Enter...");
24:    getch();
25:    setgraphmode(gmode);
26:    circle(xcenter, ycenter, ycenter / 2);
27:    outtext("Back on the graphics page. Press Enter...");
28:    getch();
29:    closegraph();
30:    return 0;
31:  }
```

Lines 18–19 change the drawing color to cyan (blue-green) and display a box by calling rectangle(), declared in graphics.h as

```
void far rectangle(int left, int top, int right, int bottom);
```

Coordinate (left,top) specifies the upper-left corner and (right,bottom) the lower-right corner of a rectangle drawn in the current color. Line 20 displays a line of text. Function outtext() is roughly equivalent to cputs() or puts(), but does not recognize escape codes such as '\n' or '\t'.

After you press Enter or another key, line 22 calls restorecrtmode() to return temporarily to the text display. After you press Enter once more, line 25 calls setgraphmode(), passing as an argument the same gmode value originally returned by initgraph(). This restores the display to graphics for the circle() command at line 26.

Unless you are using a monochrome or CGA graphics mode, notice that the cyan color selected in line 18 changes (probably to white) when switching back to graphics in line 25. Also, the rectangle is gone. As these observations indicate, function setgraphmode() erases the display and resets all graphics parameters to their default settings.

Graphics Defaults

After changing colors and selecting other graphics features, to restore default conditions, call graphdefaults(), which does not erase the display. If you need to detect the current graphics mode, call getgraphmode(). Rather than keep a global gmode variable as in MIXEDMOD, you could write

```
int tempgmode = getgraphmode();
restorecrtmode();
// Text display commands
setgraphmode(tempgmode);
```

This fragment saves the current graphics mode in tempgmode, and then restores text mode with restorecrtmode(). Passing tempgmode to setgraphmode() returns to graphics, erases the display, and resets BGI defaults, after which tempgmode is no longer needed.

Viewports and Coordinates

Every graphics display pixel has a unique x and y location, or coordinate. The x-axis is horizontal; y is vertical. The pixel in the upper-left corner of the display is identified by the coordinate (0,0). Positive x coordinates move to the right. Positive y coordinates move down. In the vertical direction, this is the reverse of common mathematics notation where positive values move up along the y-axis.

All coordinate values in Borland C++ graphics are signed integers. As the inner rectangle in Figure 16.1 shows, the visible portion of the graphics display is merely a restricted view of the entire *logical* surface, or plane, on which programs can draw. This restricted area is called a *viewport*. Graphics are normally clipped to remain inside the current viewport; graphics outside are invisible.

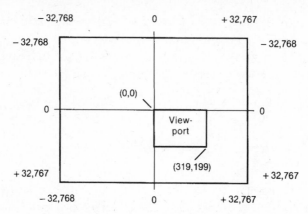

Figure 16.1. A viewport defines the visible area of the logical coordinate surface, or plane.

An internal coordinate, called the *current point* (CP), represents the location where many graphics operations begin. The CP might be at the beginning of a line, or it might be the position where text appears. CP is initialized to (0,0). To find CP, call getx() and gety().

The total number of horizontal coordinate values equals getmaxx() + 1. The total number of vertical coordinate values equals getmaxy() + 1. By using these functions rather than fixed limits, you can write programs that work correctly in any resolution.

Clearing the Viewport

To clear the viewport to the current background color, call clearviewport(). To clear the viewport and reset CP to (0,0), call cleardevice(). To clear the viewport, reset CP, and restore default BGI settings, call clearviewport() followed by graphdefaults(). Calling cleardevice() in this case is redundant.

Changing the Viewport

There are two main reasons to change the viewport as illustrated in Figure 16.1. You can restrict drawing to a portion of the display, protecting graphics in other locations. You can shift the *origin*—the viewport's top-left corner—making some kinds of graphics operations easier to write.

Listing 16.3, RESTRICT.CPP, calls `setviewport()` to restrict drawing to a small rectangle in the upper-left corner at coordinates (0,0) to (100,75). Lines drawn inside this rectangle are visible; lines drawn outside have their wings clipped.

Listing 16.3. RESTRICT.CPP (Restricts viewport to upper-left corner).

```
 1:  #include <graphics.h>
 2:  #include <stdio.h>
 3:  #include <stdlib.h>
 4:  #include <conio.h>
 5:  #define CLIPOFF 0
 6:  #define CLIPON 1    // Could be any nonzero value
 7:  main()
 8:  {
 9:    int gdriver = DETECT, gmode, gerr;
10:    initgraph(&gdriver, &gmode, "c:\\borlandc\\bgi");
11:    gerr = graphresult();
12:    if (gerr != grOk) {
13:      printf("BGI error: %s\n", grapherrormsg(gerr));
14:      exit(gerr);
15:    }
16:    setviewport(0, 0, 100, 75, CLIPON);
17:    while (!kbhit()) {
18:      setcolor(1 + random(getmaxcolor()));
19:      line(random(getmaxx()), random(getmaxy()),
20:           random(getmaxx()), random(getmaxy()));
21:    }
22:    getch();
23:    closegraph();
24:    return 0;
25:  }
```

Function `setviewport()` requires five `int` arguments. The first four arguments define the new viewport's rectangle. The fifth argument can be any nonzero value to clip graphics to the new viewport, or zero not to clip drawing. (See lines 5–6 and 16.)

Experiment with different coordinate values in line 16 and change `CLIPON` to `CLIPOFF` so you can see the difference clipping makes.

A new viewport's upper-left corner is located at the relative coordinate (0,0). These statements:

```
setviewport(100, 50, 200, 150, CLIPON);
putpixel(0, 0, WHITE);
```

plot a point at the *relative* viewport location (0,0), which appears at the *absolute* screen coordinate (100,50).

To reset the viewport to full screen and erase the display, call `graphdefaults()` followed by `clearviewport()`. You can also call `setviewport()` like this:

```
setviewport(0, 0, getmaxx(), getmaxy(), CLIPON);
```

To determine the current viewport's dimensions, call `getviewsettings()` passing the address of a `viewporttype` structure, declared in graphics.h as

```
struct viewporttype {
  int left, top, right, bottom;
  int clip;
};
```

Pass to `getviewsettings()` a pointer to a `viewporttype` structure:

```
viewporttype v;
getviewsettings(&v);
```

Another useful viewport setting is the *aspect ratio*, equal to a single pixel's width divided by its height. BGI functions take the display's aspect ratio into account when drawing circles and arcs. If the BGI didn't compensate for the display's aspect ratio, a round circle would look oval.

NTSC (National Television Standard Code) standard aspect ratio is 4:3, suggesting an ideal display with a multiple of four pixels wide by a multiple of three pixels tall, a ratio of 1.333. In some VGA modes, the aspect ratio is very nearly 1.000—pixels are just about square. In 640 x 350 EGA mode, the aspect ratio is 0.7750—nowhere near the ideal.

Notice that the aspect ratio is *not* equal to the horizontal divided by the vertical *resolutions*. A display's resolution is unrelated to its aspect ratio. To find the current aspect ratio, call `getaspectratio()` and pass the addresses of two `int` variables:

```
int xaspect, yaspect;
getaspectratio(&xaspect, &yaspect);
```

The function assigns the current aspect ratio values to the two integer variables, xaspect and yaspect. Listing 16.4, ASPECT.CPP, displays the aspect ratio for the current graphics mode.

Listing 16.4. ASPECT.CPP (Displays current aspect ratio).

```
 1:  #include <graphics.h>
 2:  #include <stdio.h>
 3:  #include <iostream.h>
 4:  #include <stdlib.h>
 5:  #include <conio.h>
 6:  #include <iomanip.h>
 7:  main()
 8:  {
 9:    int gdriver = DETECT, gmode, gerr;
10:    int xaspect, yaspect;
11:    initgraph(&gdriver, &gmode, "c:\\borlandc\\bgi");
12:    gerr = graphresult();
13:    if (gerr != grOk) {
14:      printf("BGI error: %s\n", grapherrormsg(gerr));
15:      exit(gerr);
16:    }
17:    restorecrtmode();
18:    getaspectratio(&xaspect, &yaspect);
19:    cout << "graph driver = " << gdriver << '\n';
20:    cout << "graph mode   = " << gmode << '\n';
21:    cout << "xaspect      = " << xaspect << '\n';
22:    cout << "yaspect      = " << yaspect << '\n';
23:    cout << "aspect ratio = " << setprecision(3) <<
24:      (double)xaspect / (double)yaspect << '\n';
25:    return 0;
26:  }
```

In EGA 640 x 350 mode, ASPECT displays the following information:

```
Graph driver  = 3
Graph mode    = 1
Xaspect       = 7750
Yaspect       = 10000
Aspect ratio  = 0.775
```

These values indicate that, for graphics driver 3 in mode 1, a one-unit-tall pixel is 0.775 of a unit wide. Assuming the aspect ratio is less than zero, multiplying the height of a line by the display's aspect ratio compensates for the disparity, making it possible to draw equal-length vertical and horizontal lines even though they require different numbers of pixels. Listing 16.5, EQUALS.CPP, demonstrates this technique.

Listing 16.5. EQUALS.CPP (Compensates for a display's aspect ratio).

```
 1:  #include <graphics.h>
 2:  #include <stdio.h>
 3:  #include <stdlib.h>
 4:  #include <conio.h>
 5:  #include <math.h>
 6:
 7:  void DrawLines(int x, int y, int len, double ratio);
 8:
 9:  main()
10:  {
11:    int gdriver = DETECT, gmode, gerr;
12:    int xaspect, yaspect;
13:    double ratio = 1.0;  // No adjustment
14:
15:    initgraph(&gdriver, &gmode, "c:\\borlandc\\bgi");
16:    gerr = graphresult();
17:    if (gerr != grOk) {
18:      printf("BGI error: %s\n", grapherrormsg(gerr));
19:      exit(gerr);
20:    }
21:    DrawLines(25, 25, 75, ratio);
22:    getaspectratio(&xaspect, &yaspect);
23:    ratio = (double)xaspect / (double)yaspect;
24:    DrawLines(110, 110, 75, ratio);
25:    getch();
26:    closegraph();
27:    return 0;
28:  }
29:
```

```
30:  void DrawLines(int x, int y, int len, double ratio)
31:  {
32:    line(x, y, x + len, y);  // Horizontal line
33:    line(x, y, x, y + ceil(len * ratio));  // Vertical line
34:  }
```

EQUALS draws two right angles. The first in the upper-left corner is not adjusted for the display's aspect ratio. Unless your display's pixels are perfectly square, the vertical line is probably longer than the horizontal because pixels in most display modes are taller than they are wide.

For the second right angle at lower-right, the program adjusts the vertical line length by the aspect ratio, calculated at line 23. This adjustment draws equal-length horizontal and vertical lines. If you measure these lines, however, don't be too surprised if the results are imperfect. Differences in display monitors can also affect the apparent aspect ratio.

If the default aspect ratio is not correct—in other words, if circles aren't perfectly round—call setaspectratio() with two parameters representing the X and Y axes. The actual values aren't too important. It's the *ratio* of X to Y that matters. For instance, to change the display ratio to the NTSC standard 4:3, a ratio of 1.333, you can use the statement

```
setaspectratio(4, 3);
```

Shifting the Origin

By turning off clipping and moving the viewport so that (0,0) is at dead center, you can write graphics that use both negative and positive coordinate values. In effect, you divide the viewport into quadrants. Figure 16.2 shows the relationship of this new viewport to the entire coordinate plane.

Shifting the origin requires a small trick: Turn off clipping and set the viewport so that the absolute center of the screen becomes the new (0,0) coordinate:

```
#define CLIPOFF 0
#define CLIPON 1
int xcenter = getmaxx() / 2;
int ycenter = getmaxy() / 2;
setviewport(xcenter, ycenter, getmaxx(), getmaxy(), CLIPOFF);
```

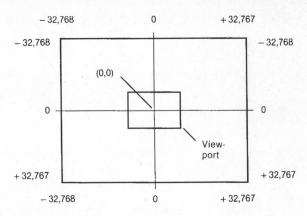

Figure 16.2. Changing the viewport and placing (0,0) at center divides the display into quadrants.

Passing CLIPON to setviewport() would restrict drawing to the lower-right quadrant. With clipping off, the other three quadrants are usable. Figure 16.3 shows an exploded view of the center portion of Figure 16.2. As illustrated, four combinations of coordinate values locate points in each quadrant:

- (–X, –Y) Upper-left quadrant.

- (–X, +Y) Lower-left quadrant.

- (+X, –Y) Upper-right quadrant.

- (+X, +Y) Lower-right quadrant.

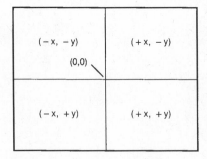

Figure 16.3. With (0,0) at the center, positive and negative coordinates specify points in four quadrants.

Plotting Points

Two fundamental routines display and read individual pixels:

```
void far putpixel(int x, int y, int color);
unsigned far getpixel(int x, int y);
```

Function putpixel() displays one dot at location (x,y) in the specified color number. Function getpixel() returns a pixel's current color. A color value represents the pixel's logical color, and is not necessarily equal to the pixel's actual storage value in memory or its visible hue.

Listing 16.6, TWINKLER.CPP, demonstrates how to use putpixel() and getpixel().

Listing 16.6. TWINKLER.CPP (Demonstrates putpixel() and getpixel()).

```
 1:  #include <graphics.h>
 2:  #include <stdio.h>
 3:  #include <stdlib.h>
 4:  #include <time.h>
 5:  #include <conio.h>
 6:  main()
 7:  {
 8:    int gdriver = DETECT, gmode, gerr;
 9:    int x, y, xmax, ymax;
10:    unsigned color;
11:
12:    initgraph(&gdriver, &gmode, "c:\\borlandc\\bgi");
13:    gerr = graphresult();
14:    if (gerr != grOk) {
15:      printf("BGI error: %s\n", grapherrormsg(gerr));
16:      exit(gerr);
17:    }
18:    xmax = getmaxx();
19:    ymax = getmaxy();
20:    randomize();
21:    while (!kbhit()) {
22:      x = random(xmax);
23:      y = random(ymax);
```

continues

Listing 16.6. continued

```
24:        color = random(getmaxcolor());
25:        if (getpixel(x, y) != BLACK)
26:          putpixel(x, y, BLACK);
27:        else
28:          putpixel(x, y, color);
29:      }
30:    getch();          // Read pending keypress
31:    closegraph();
32:    return 0;
33:  }
```

The program displays dots at random locations unless getpixel() discovers a dot already there. Line 24 calls getmaxcolor() to determine the maximum available color number. Line 26 turns a pixel off by painting it black. The effect is to create a display full of pixels, evenly distributed like sand on the beach. Let the program run for several minutes. This makes a good test of the random number generator as well as checking your monitor's ability to resolve individual pixels.

Drawing Lines

You could draw lines by plotting individual pixels along a path between two coordinates. It's easier—and much faster—to call one of the BGI's three line generators: line(), lineto(), and linerel().

Function line() connects two points, (x1,y1) and (x2,y2), and is declared in graphics.h as

```
void far line(int x1, int y1, int x2, int y2);
```

The two points can be anywhere, even off screen, although you see lines only in the visible portion of the current viewport. Listing 16.7, GRBORDER.CPP, uses line() to draw a border around the graphics display.

Rather than specify both line end points, as GRBORDER does at lines 18–21, you can call lineto() to draw a line from CP to any other location:

```
lineto(x, y);  // Draw line from CP to (x,y)
```

Listing 16.7. GRBORDER.CPP (Draws a border around a graphics display).

```
 1:  #include <graphics.h>
 2:  #include <stdio.h>
 3:  #include <stdlib.h>
 4:  #include <conio.h>
 5:  main()
 6:  {
 7:    int gdriver = DETECT, gmode, gerr;
 8:    int xmax, ymax;
 9:
10:    initgraph(&gdriver, &gmode, "c:\\borlandc\\bgi");
11:    gerr = graphresult();
12:    if (gerr != grOk) {
13:      printf("BGI error: %s\n", grapherrormsg(gerr));
14:      exit(gerr);
15:    }
16:    xmax = getmaxx();
17:    ymax = getmaxy();
18:    line(0, 0, xmax, 0);
19:    line(xmax, 0, xmax, ymax);
20:    line(xmax, ymax, 0, ymax);
21:    line(0, ymax, 0, 0);
22:    getch();
23:    closegraph();
24:    return 0;
25:  }
```

You can also use `linerel()` to draw lines a relative distance from CP—useful for drawing shapes at a variety of locations. For example, this draws a 50-unit horizontal line starting at CP:

```
linerel(50, 0);
```

Drawing lines with `lineto()` or `linerel()` moves CP to the line's new end point. Drawing with `line()` does *not* update CP. Because `lineto()` has fewer parameters than `line()`, it runs a tiny bit faster—enough to make a noticeable difference in speed when you have many lines to draw.

Another way to change CP before drawing lines is to call `moveto()`. The statements

```
moveto(x1, y1);
lineto(x2, y2);
```

have the identical effect as

```
line(x1, y1, x2, y2);
```

Relative Lines

Two functions move CP to a new coordinate relative to the present CP. Function `moverel()` moves CP invisibly; `linerel()` moves CP and draws a line. With these functions, it's easy to design figures that display correctly at any position. The functions are declared in graphics.h as

```
void far moverel(int dx, int dy);
void far linerel(int dx, int dy);
```

Parameters `dx` (delta X) and `dy` (delta Y) represent the requested change in X and Y. Positive values move down and to the right; negative values move up and to the left.

Listing 16.8, RELATIVE.CPP, uses these functions to draw a design centered relatively to any point (X,Y). Because of the `moverel()` and `linerel()` statements, the same figure (see function `DrawFigure()` at lines 33–44) is easily drawn at any screen location.

Listing 16.8. RELATIVE.CPP (Draws shape using relative line commands).

```
 1:  #include <graphics.h>
 2:  #include <stdio.h>
 3:  #include <stdlib.h>
 4:  #include <time.h>
 5:  #include <conio.h>
 6:  #include <dos.h>
 7:
 8:  void DrawFigure(int x, int y, int size);
 9:
10:  main()
11:  {
```

```
12:     int gdriver = DETECT, gmode, gerr;
13:     int xmax, ymax;
14:
15:     initgraph(&gdriver, &gmode, "c:\\borlandc\\bgi");
16:     gerr = graphresult();
17:     if (gerr != grOk) {
18:       printf("BGI error: %s\n", grapherrormsg(gerr));
19:       exit(gerr);
20:     }
21:     xmax = getmaxx();
22:     ymax = getmaxy();
23:     randomize();
24:     while (!kbhit()) {
25:       delay(100);
26:       DrawFigure(random(xmax), random(ymax), 10 + random(40));
27:     }
28:     getch();
29:     closegraph();
30:     return 0;
31:   }
32:
33:   void DrawFigure(int x, int y, int size)
34:   {
35:     moveto(x, y);
36:     moverel(x - size, y - size);
37:     linerel(size, 0);
38:     linerel(0, size);
39:     linerel(-size, 0);
40:     linerel(0, -size);
41:     linerel(size, size);
42:     moverel(0, -size);
43:     linerel(-size, size);
44:   }
```

Stylish Lines

Two functions, getlinesettings() and setlinestyle(), examine and change three line characteristics: style, pattern, and thickness. The line style can be one of the following enumerated constants as declared in graphics.h:

```
enum line_styles {
   SOLID_LINE   = 0,   // Solid lines
   DOTTED_LINE  = 1,   // Dotted lines
   CENTER_LINE  = 2,   // Dashed and dotted lines
   DASHED_LINE  = 3,   // Dashed lines
   USERBIT_LINE = 4,   // User-defined line bit pattern
};
```

The first four constants specify solid, dotted, alternating dash-dot, and dashed lines. The fifth constant makes it possible to specify some other bit pattern. Other enumerated constants represent normal or thick line widths:

```
enum line_widths {
  NORM_WIDTH  = 1,   // One pixel-wide lines
  THICK_WIDTH = 3,   // Three-pixel-wide lines
};
```

These are the only automatic thicknesses available. To draw two-pixel-wide lines, you have to draw two lines of normal width.

Call `setlinestyle()` to change line styles and thickness. For example, these statements draw a fat dash-dot center line, dividing the top and bottom of the display:

```
setlinestyle(CENTER_LINE, 0, THICK_WIDTH);
line(0, getmaxy() / 2, getmaxx(), getmaxy() / 2);
```

The second `setlinestyle()` parameter (0 in the example) is significant only when the first parameter equals USERBIT_LINE. In this case, the second parameter is the word bit pattern you want the line generator to use. For example, here's how you might display a faint line of sparse dots in the center of the screen:

```
unsigned pattern = 0x1010;
setlinestyle(USERBIT_LINE, pattern, NORM_WIDTH);
line(0, getmaxy() / 2, getmaxx(), getmaxy() / 2);
```

The pattern value equals 0x1010, or in binary, 0001 0000 0001 0000. Each 1 in pattern becomes a dot on-screen; each 0 an invisible point that is not plotted.

To read the current line style settings, call `getlinesettings()` with the address of a `linesettingstype` structure declared in graphics.h as

```
struct linesettingstype {
  int linestyle;
  unsigned upattern;
  int thickness;
};
```

The three members equal the three arguments most recently passed to setlinestyle(). Call getlinesettings() to preserve the current line style:

```
linesettingstype style;    // Define style structure
getlinesettings(&style);   // Preserve current settings
// Set new line styles and draw lines
// Next, restore saved settings
setlinestyle(style.linestyle, style.upattern, style.thickness);
```

Selecting Colors

Different graphics modes can display different numbers of colors. CGA modes can show up to four colors. EGA and VGA modes can display up to 16 colors. Other BGI drivers (look for them on CompuServe, electronic bulletin boards, and other online services) can display 256 colors on some VGA and SVGA (super VGA) hardware. IBM 8514 adapters can also display 256 colors.

In all these displays, a *palette* controls which actual colors (or shades of gray on monochrome systems) you see on-screen. Changing palettes instantly changes the colors of points already visible. You can't draw a few shapes in one set of colors and then change palettes to get more colors. Changing palettes merely instructs the video hardware to use certain colors.

A BGI palette is an array of color values. The indexes to each arrayed value represent *color numbers*—the values programs use to specify line, point, and fill colors. BGI defines color constants in the COLORS enumeration:

```
enum COLORS {
  BLACK, BLUE, GREEN, CYAN, RED, MAGENTA,
  BROWN, LIGHTGRAY, DARKGRAY, LIGHTBLUE,
  LIGHTGREEN, LIGHTCYAN, LIGHTRED, LIGHTMAGENTA,
  YELLOW, WHITE
};
```

When you draw in a certain color, such as red, the actual color you see depends on the color value of palette[RED]. If you change that color value to blue, all red points currently on display—as well as those drawn later—are colored blue. graphics.h declares a palette as a palettetype structure:

```
#define MAXCOLORS 15
struct palettetype {
  unsigned char size;
  signed char colors[MAXCOLORS + 1];
};
```

709

A palettetype structure starts with an unsigned char member size, which indicates how many bytes follow. In other words, the actual size of the colors array varies for different modes but is never greater than MAXCOLORS + 1. To determine the number of available colors, call getmaxcolor(). To load a palettetype structure with the contents of an in-memory palette, call getpalette():

```
palettetype pt;     // Palette structure
getpalette(&pt);    // Pass address of pt to getpalette()
```

> **NOTE:** Function getpalette() does not work with the IBM-8514 BGI driver.

Function getpalette() initializes the size member in pt and inserts color values into the colors array. You can pass a modified palette to setallpalette():

```
pt.colors[1] = BROWN;
setallpalette(&pt);
```

A value of −1 in the colors array causes no change to a color. Because of this, you can change some colors while leaving others alone, as in this sample:

```
palettetype pt;
pt.size = getmaxcolor() + 1;
for (int i = 0; i <= pt.size; i++)
  pt.colors[i] = -1;
pt.colors[1] = BROWN;
setallpalette(&pt);
```

An easier way to change a single color entry is to call setpalette(). This also changes the second color to brown:

```
setpalette(1, BROWN);
```

The first parameter (1) is an index to the color palette array. Index 0 refers to the background color. The second parameter is the color value, an int ranging from −128 to +127. After this statement, passing 1 to setcolor() draws in brown, or in whatever actual color or gray shade this value produces in one or another graphics mode.

In many programs, palettetype structures are useful for preparing several different palettes and switching among them quickly by calling setallpalette(). To change individual palette entries, call the simpler setpalette().

The Default Palette

The BGI package maintains a copy of the original palette initialized by `initgraph()`. To read this palette, call `getdefaultpalette()`, which returns a pointer to a `palettetype` structure. Call the function like this:

```
palettetype far *ppt;
ppt = getdefaultpalette();  // Assign default palette address to ppt
```

Changing Display Colors

It's wise to call `getmaxcolor()` early in your program. The function returns the maximum color number (palette index) that you can pass to `setcolor()`.

Color number 0 is the background color. Values from 1 to `getmaxcolor()` equal the full range of color numbers you can use. Listing 16.9, RANDLINE.CPP, demonstrates `getmaxcolor()` and also calls `getmaxx()` and `getmaxy()` to fill the screen with randomly positioned lines in randomly selected colors for any display mode.

Listing 16.9. RANDLINE.CPP (Draws colored lines at random).

```
 1:  #include <graphics.h>
 2:  #include <stdio.h>
 3:  #include <stdlib.h>
 4:  #include <conio.h>
 5:  #include <dos.h>
 6:  main()
 7:  {
 8:    int gdriver = DETECT, gmode, gerr;
 9:    int cmax, xmax, ymax;
10:
11:    initgraph(&gdriver, &gmode, "c:\\borlandc\\bgi");
12:    gerr = graphresult();
13:    if (gerr != grOk) {
14:      printf("BGI error: %s\n", grapherrormsg(gerr));
15:      exit(gerr);
16:    }
17:    cmax = getmaxcolor();
18:    xmax = getmaxx() + 1;
19:    ymax = getmaxy() + 1;
20:    randomize();
```

continues

Listing 16.9. continued

```
21:    while (!kbhit()) {
22:      delay(100);
23:      setcolor(1 + random(cmax));   // 1 .. getmaxcolor()
24:      lineto(random(xmax),          // 0 .. getmaxx()
25:             random(ymax));         // 0 .. getmaxy()
26:    }
27:    getch();
28:    closegraph();
29:    return 0;
30:  }
```

Remove line 22 to increase the speed of this example, slowed for effect. Line 23 calls setcolor() to select a color at random with an index value of one to getmaxcolor(). Because zero represents the background color, this scheme prevents drawing invisible lines.

If you need to determine the current drawing color, call getcolor() and assign the function's result to an int variable:

```
int thecolor;
thecolor = getcolor();
```

In the Background

Two other color functions examine and change the background color, which always has the color palette number 0 no matter what actual color you see. This statement changes the background to cyan:

```
setbkcolor(CYAN);  // Change background color
```

Calling setbkcolor() is equivalent to changing the palette entry for color number 0:

```
setpalette(0, CYAN);  // Change background color
```

These functions have an immediate visual effect. You don't have to clear the screen or perform any other steps to see the new background color. Lines and other shapes are preserved and appear on top of the new background—as long as they aren't the same color as the background, of course. To determine the current background color, call `getbkcolor()`:

```
int backgroundcolor;
backgroundcolor = getbkcolor();
```

Setting the Write Mode

Changing the write mode affects the method used to poke pixels into the display. Normally, functions such as `drawpoly()`, `line()`, `linerec()`, `lineto()`, and `rectangle()`—some of which you haven't yet seen—simply turn on the appropriate pixels to draw lines and other shapes. To set the write mode to XOR (exclusive OR), call `setwritemode()` with the predefined constant `XOR_PUT`:

```
setwritemode(XOR_PUT);
```

To change the write mode back to normal, pass `COPY_PUT` to `setwritemode()`:

```
setwritemode(COPY_PUT);
```

After setting the write mode to `XOR_PUT`, redrawing a line in the same color erases the line. This is useful in graphics programs that display shapes on top of other shapes. With `XOR_PUT`, you can draw and erase a shape simply by drawing it twice.

Drawing Shapes

The BGI package offers three basic shapes, all composed of lines: rectangles, bars, and polygons. You can also fill a shape's insides with various patterns and colors. In the case of bars, you can display a pseudo-three-dimensional box, popular for business graphs.

Rectangles

Rectangles are the easiest shapes to draw. Pass the coordinates of the upper-left and lower-right corners of the area to enclose. Then call `rectangle()`, declared as

```
void far rectangle(int x1, int y1, int x2, int y2);
```

A few simple statements use `rectangle()` to outline the display for any graphics mode:

```
int xmax = getmaxx();
int ymax = getmaxy();
rectangle(0, 0, xmax, ymax);  // Outline screen
```

Bars

A simple bar, typically used for drawing bar graphs, is just a rectangle painted with a color and a bit pattern. When drawing these and other filled shapes, it's helpful to think of the color as the *paint* and the bit pattern as the *brush*. The statement

```
bar(x1, y1, x2, y2);
```

has the same effect as calling `rectangle()` with these coordinates and then filling the box with the current paint (white, unless you change it) and brush pattern (normally solid).

Function `setcolor()` does not affect a filled shape's paint color. To select a bar's fill color, call `setfillstyle()` like this:

```
setfillstyle(SOLID_FILL, BLUE);
```

This function requires two arguments. The first is a pattern selector, which can be one of the enumerated constants listed in the leftmost column in Table 16.4 and declared in enum `fill_patterns` in graphics.h. The second argument is the paint color to use for filling shapes.

If the standard brush patterns don't suit your tastes, you can create your own with `setfillpattern()`. Pass to this function the address of an 8-byte array, which you might define as

```
char pattern[8];  // Custom fill pattern
```

A custom fill pattern is an 8 x 8 block, with each bit corresponding to one pixel. Initialize a `pattern` array with bit values:

```
pattern[0] = 0x00;  // 00000000
pattern[1] = 0x3c;  // 00111100
pattern[2] = 0x24;  // 00100100
pattern[3] = 0x24;  // 00100100
pattern[4] = 0x24;  // 00100100
pattern[5] = 0x24;  // 00100100
```

```
pattern[6] = 0x3c;  // 00111100
pattern[7] = 0x00;  // 00000000
```

Enable the custom bit pattern by calling `setfillpattern()`:

```
setfillpattern(pattern, BLUE);
```

To preserve the current fill pattern, call `getfillpattern()`, passing the address of an 8-byte array. You can then restore a modified pattern with `setfillpattern()`:

```
char pattern[8];
int color = BLUE;
getfillpattern(pattern);  // Save current fill pattern
// Change fill pattern and draw shapes
setfillpattern(pattern, color);  // Restore pattern and select a color
```

Table 16.4. Pattern constants for `setfillstyle()`.

Constant	Value	Fill effect
EMPTY_FILL	0	Background color
SOLID_FILL	1	Solid color
LINE_FILL	2	Lines (———)
LTSLASH_FILL	3	Thin slashes (///)
SLASH_FILL	4	Thick slashes (///)
BKSLASH_FILL	5	Thick backslashes (\\\)
LTBKSLASH_FILL	6	Thin backslashes (\\\)
HATCH_FILL	7	Light hatch marks
XHATCH_FILL	8	Heavy hatch marks
INTERLEAVE_FILL	9	Interleaved lines
WIDE_DOT_FILL	10	Sparse dots
CLOSE_DOT_FILL	11	Dense dots
USER_FILL	12	Previous SetFillPattern

To preserve the current fill pattern *and* color, call `getfillsettings()`. This function requires the address of a `fillsettingstype` structure declared in graphics.h as

```
struct fillsettingstype {
  int pattern;
  int color;
};
```

After calling `getfillsettings()`, you can restore both the original pattern and color by passing the members of this structure to `setfillstyle()`:

```
fillsettingstype settings;
getfillsettings(&settings);
// Select patterns and colors, and draw filled shapes
setfillstyle(settings.pattern, settings.color);
```

Three-Dimensional Bars

Similar to `bar`, function `bar3d()` draws a pseudo-three-dimensional box with three visible sides. The box has no depth and is technically called an *orthographic projection*. Even so, this object is useful for breathing some realism into an otherwise boring two-dimensional bar chart. Listing 16.10, FANCYBAR.CPP, uses `bar3d()` to display a series of three-dimensional bars.

Listing 16.10. FANCYBAR.CPP (Demonstrates `bar3d()` function).

```
 1:  #include <graphics.h>
 2:  #include <stdio.h>
 3:  #include <stdlib.h>
 4:  #include <conio.h>
 5:
 6:  #define TOPOFF 0    // No top on bars
 7:  #define TOPON 1     // Put a lid on (any nonzero value is okay)
 8:  #define DEPTH 14    // Adjust to affect pseudo depth
 9:  #define NUMBARS 9   // Adjust to affect number of bars
10:
11:  main()
12:  {
13:    int gdriver = DETECT, gmode, gerr;
14:    int width, height;
15:    int i, x1, y1, x2, y2, xmax, ymax;
16:
17:    initgraph(&gdriver, &gmode, "c:\\borlandc\\bgi");
```

```
18:    gerr = graphresult();
19:    if (gerr != grOk) {
20:      printf("BGI error: %s\n", grapherrormsg(gerr));
21:      exit(gerr);
22:    }
23:    xmax = getmaxx();
24:    ymax = getmaxy();
25:    randomize();
26:    width = xmax / NUMBARS;
27:    height = ymax - (ymax / 4);
28:    for (i = 1; i <= NUMBARS; i++) {
29:      x1 = width * (i - 1);
30:      y1 = DEPTH + random(height);
31:      x2 = x1 + (width / 2);
32:      y2 = ymax - (ymax / 6);
33:      bar3d(x1, y1, x2, y2, DEPTH, TOPON);
34:    }
35:    getch();
36:    closegraph();
37:    return 0;
38:  }
```

The face of each bar is filled with a solid color (probably white). The top and right sides are outlined. To change the number of bars, adjust NUMBARS. To change the depth of the pseudo-three-dimensional effect, change DEPTH.

You can change bar patterns the same way you changed the brushes and paint colors in earlier examples. Use either setfillstyle() or setfillpattern(). For example, to fill the bars with red slashes, insert this statement between lines 27 and 28:

```
setfillstyle(SLASH_FILL, RED);
```

When you run this modified program, bars are filled with red slashes instead of solid white—a definite improvement. Notice that the bar outlines remain white, unaffected by setfillstyle(). To change outline colors, call setcolor(). Add this statement after setfillstyle():

```
setcolor(YELLOW);
```

You now should see red-faced, slash-filled bars, outlined in yellow. On older CGA graphics systems, you might see the reverse—yellow faces outlined in red. This just goes to show that you can't trust the names of color constants to hold true for all graphics modes!

Polygons

A polygon is any enclosed shape with sides of straight lines. Triangles and boxes are polygons. Because there are easy ways to draw such simple shapes, however, a polygon is usually a more complex multisided object.

In memory, a polygon is an array of (x,y) coordinates—two integers per point. The array can be any size within practical limits; the more points you have, the longer it takes to draw the figure. Unlike some other graphics types, there is no predefined polygon structure. Probably, it's best to use an array of `pointtype` structures:

```
pointtype polygon[10];  // Array of 10 pointtype structures
```

Each `pointtype` structure has two int members, x and y. To fix the starting point of the polygon to (0,0), you could write

```
polygon[0].x = 0;
polygon[0].y = 0;
```

Listing 16.11, STARSTRU.CPP, calls BGI's `drawpoly()` function to display a five-point star, stored in a global array of `pointtype` structures.

Listing 16.11. STARSTRU.CPP (Draws a star with `drawpoly()`).

```
 1:  #include <graphics.h>
 2:  #include <stdio.h>
 3:  #include <stdlib.h>
 4:  #include <conio.h>
 5:
 6:  pointtype polygon[6] = {
 7:    { 50,  0},
 8:    { 90, 75},
 9:    {  0, 25},
10:    {100, 25},
11:    { 10, 75},
12:    { 50,  0}
13:  };
14:
15:  main()
16:  {
17:    int gdriver = DETECT, gmode, gerr;
18:    initgraph(&gdriver, &gmode, "c:\\borlandc\\bgi");
19:    gerr = graphresult();
```

```
20:    if (gerr != grOk) {
21:      printf("BGI error: %s\n", graphErrormsg(gerr));
22:      exit(gerr);
23:    }
24:    setcolor(CYAN);
25:    drawpoly(6, (const int *)polygon);
26:    getch();
27:    closegraph();
28:    return 0;
29:  }
```

The first argument passed to drawpoly() (see line 25) tells how many coordinates follow—in this case, six. The second argument is the address of the pointtype array. Unfortunately, drawpoly()'s second parameter is declared as const int far* (far pointer to a constant int), and a typecast is needed, as shown at line 25, to pass an array of pointtype structures to the function. Notice that this five-point object (see lines 6–13) requires *six* entries to close the shape. Replace line 25 with the following to see what happens if you forget this important rule:

```
drawpoly(5, (const int *)polygon);   // ???
```

Filled Polygons

You can fill polygons with patterns and colors the same way you fill two- and three-dimensional bars. Use setfillstyle() and setfillpattern() to select a brush and paint, but call fillpoly() rather than drawpoly(). For a test, replace line 25 in STARSTRU with these statements:

```
setfillstyle(INTERLEAVE_FILL, LIGHTBLUE);
fillpoly(5, (const int *)polygon);
```

The 5 is not a mistake. Function fillpoly() operates differently than drawpoly(). Painting a polygon with an unconnected side would leak paint all over the screen, so fillpoly() automatically closes polygons for you.

Flood Filling

So far, you've learned how to draw and fill regular shapes such as boxes, bars, and polygons connected with straight sides. To fill other shapes, use floodfill(), declared:

```
void far floodfill(int x, int y, int border);
```

Coordinate (x,y) specifies a *seed*, which can be anywhere inside a closed shape. Parameter `border` is the color of the lines that outline the shape, which must be completely enclosed. If the shape has gaps in its border, the paint leaks into the surrounding areas, possibly filling the screen and ruining your drawing. Change the paint color and brush with `setfillstyle()` and `setfillpattern()` as you did in previous examples.

Circular Shapes

Three useful functions round out the BGI set of basic graphics commands: `arc()`, `circle()`, and `ellipse()`. A variant of these routines, `pieslice()`, makes it easy to draw pie-chart graphics or pie-slice wedges for other purposes.

Arcs and Circles

To draw an arc, specify a starting (X,Y) coordinate, equal to the center of the circle containing the arc. Also specify the starting and ending angles of imaginary spokes that radiate from the arc's center to its two ends. Finally, specify a radius, the length of a spoke. The complete definition for function `arc()` is

```
void far arc(int x, int y, int stangle, int endangle, int radius);
```

Figure 16.4 shows how `arc()`'s parameters define an arc. On-screen, only the heavy line is visible. The center point is at (X,Y). The starting angle (`stangle`) is labeled A. The ending angle (`endangle`) is at B. The `radius` is the dotted line *r*. Angles and the radius must be positive integers or zero. An angle of zero is at 3 o'clock, with greater angles rotating counterclockwise.

Listing 16.12, RAINBOW.CPP, draws a rainbow (not true to nature's colors, however) by cycling through all available colors and calling `arc()`.

Listing 16.12. RAINBOW.CPP (Draws a rainbow-like shape with `arc()`).

```
1:  #include <graphics.h>
2:  #include <stdio.h>
3:  #include <stdlib.h>
```

```
 4:   #include <conio.h>
 5:
 6:   main()
 7:   {
 8:     int gdriver = DETECT, gmode, gerr;
 9:     int cmax, color, x, y, radius;
10:
11:     initgraph(&gdriver, &gmode, "c:\\borlandc\\bgi");
12:     gerr = graphresult();
13:     if (gerr != grOk) {
14:       printf("BGI error: %s\n", grapherrormsg(gerr));
15:       exit(gerr);
16:     }
17:     x = getmaxx() / 2;
18:     y = getmaxy() / 2;
19:     cmax = getmaxcolor();
20:     radius = y;
21:     for (color = 1; color <= cmax; color++) {
22:       setcolor(color);
23:       arc(x, y, 0, 180, radius);
24:       y += 10;
25:     }
26:     getch();
27:     closegraph();
28:     return 0;
29:   }
```

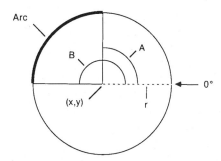

Figure 16.4. Of the many parameters that specify arcs, only the arc itself (the heavy line here) is visible.

As Figure 16.4 shows, arcs have three important coordinates: the center point, the starting point of the first pixel in the arc, and the ending point of the last pixel. Call getarccoords() after drawing an arc to get these points. Listing 16.13, GETARC.CPP, demonstrates how to do this with a program that draws a figure similar to the illustration in Figure 16.4.

Listing 16.13. GETARC.CPP (Gets arc coordinates).

```
 1:  #include <graphics.h>
 2:  #include <stdio.h>
 3:  #include <stdlib.h>
 4:  #include <conio.h>
 5:
 6:  main()
 7:  {
 8:    int gdriver = DETECT, gmode, gerr;
 9:    int xcenter, ycenter, stangle, endangle, radius;
10:    struct arccoordstype ac;
11:
12:    initgraph(&gdriver, &gmode, "c:\\borlandc\\bgi");
13:    gerr = graphresult();
14:    if (gerr != grOk) {
15:      printf("BGI error: %s\n", grapherrormsg(gerr));
16:      exit(gerr);
17:    }
18:    xcenter = getmaxx() / 2;
19:    ycenter = getmaxy() / 2;
20:    radius = getmaxy() / 3;
21:    stangle = 0;
22:    endangle = 59;
23:    setcolor(BROWN);
24:    circle(xcenter, ycenter, radius);
25:    setcolor(WHITE);
26:    arc(xcenter, ycenter, stangle, endangle, radius);
27:    getarccoords(&ac);
28:    setcolor(BLUE);
29:    line(ac.x, ac.y, ac.xstart, ac.ystart);
30:    line(ac.x, ac.y, ac.xend, ac.yend);
```

```
31:    getch();
32:    closegraph();
33:    return 0;
34:  }
```

Structure arccoordstype (used in GETARC at line 10) is declared in graphics.h as

```
struct arccoordstype {
  int x, y;
  int xstart, ystart, xend, yend;
};
```

Six integer members locate the center, starting, and ending points associated with the arc most recently drawn. GETARC uses this information to draw a blue wedge inside a brown circle with a white arc. (Depending on your display type, of course, you might see different colors.)

The program also demonstrates the BGI circle() function, which has three parameters:

```
void far circle(int x, int y, int radius);
```

Function circle() draws a circle (what else?) centered at (x,y) with the specified radius.

Ellipses

An ellipse in BGI terms is any oval shape, including perfectly round circles. You can also draw a portion of an oval, similar to arc()'s output, but with finer control over the results. One function, ellipse(), draws all these shapes, and is declared as

```
void far ellipse(int x, int y, int stangle, int endangle,
  int xradius, int yradius);
```

The (x,y) coordinate is at the center of the ellipse (or ellipse-like arc). Angles stangle and endangle correspond to A and B in Figure 16.4, and have the same purpose as arc()'s similar angle parameters. The last two parameters control the ellipse's width (xradius) and height (yradius).

Unlike circle(), ellipse() does not compensate for the display's aspect ratio. Depending on the display mode, even if xradius equals yradius, the ellipse might not be circular. To draw a circle with ellipse(), you must adjust the shape's radii to be proportional to the display's aspect ratio.

Listing 16.14, OVALTINE.CPP, demonstrates `ellipse()` while drawing an interesting pseudo-three-dimensional shape. A `while` loop (lines 24–29) varies the ellipse's horizontal and vertical radii to draw successive ovals from fat to skinny and short to tall.

Listing 16.14. OVALTINE.CPP (Demonstrates `ellipse()` function).

```
 1:  #include <graphics.h>
 2:  #include <stdio.h>
 3:  #include <stdlib.h>
 4:  #include <conio.h>
 5:
 6:  main()
 7:  {
 8:    int gdriver = DETECT, gmode, gerr;
 9:    int xmax, ymax, xradius, yradius;
10:    int xcenter, ycenter;
11:
12:    initgraph(&gdriver, &gmode, "c:\\borlandc\\bgi");
13:    gerr = graphresult();
14:    if (gerr != grOk) {
15:      printf("BGI error: %s\n", grapherrormsg(gerr));
16:      exit(gerr);
17:    }
18:    xmax = getmaxx();
19:    ymax = getmaxy();
20:    xcenter = xmax / 2;
21:    ycenter = ymax / 2;
22:    yradius = ycenter / 4;
23:    xradius = xcenter / 2;
24:    while (xradius > 40) {
25:      setcolor(1 + (xradius % (getmaxcolor() + 1)));
26:      ellipse(xcenter, ycenter, 0, 360, xradius, yradius);
27:      xradius--;
28:      yradius++;
29:    }
30:    getch();
31:    closegraph();
32:    return 0;
33:  }
```

Filled Ellipses

Function `fillellipse()` operates much like other filled-shape functions such as `fillpoly()` or the general-purpose `floodfill()`. Function `fillellipse()` has four parameters:

```
void far fillellipse(int x, int y, int xradius, int yradius);
```

The parameters are similar to those in `ellipse()`. Function `fillellipse()` can't fill partial ellipses, however, so it doesn't need `ellipse()`'s angle values, which are used to draw partial arcs. Use `setfillstyle()` to modify an ellipse's fill pattern and color.

To see how `fillellipse()` works, replace lines 22–29 in OVALTINE with the following statements, which draw a tennis racket (or maybe it's a fly swatter).

```
yradius = ycenter / 2;
xradius = xcenter / 4;
setcolor(WHITE);
setfillstyle(HATCH_FILL, LIGHTRED);
fillellipse(xcenter, yradius, xradius, yradius);
setfillstyle(SOLID_FILL, WHITE);
bar(xcenter - 8, yradius * 2, xcenter + 8, ymax);
```

Filled Partial Ellipses

Another function, with the somewhat unusual name `sector()`, has the identical parameters as `ellipse()`:

```
void far sector(int x, int y, int stangle, int endangle,
  int xradius, int yradius );
```

Function `sector()` draws a full or partial ellipse filled with the current pattern and color initialized by `setfillstyle()`. Except for filling what it draws, `sector()` is the same as `ellipse()`. Adjust the two angle parameters, `stangle` and `endangle` to draw filled partial ellipses.

To see how `sector()` differs from `fillellipse()`, make a fresh copy of OVALTINE and replace lines 22–29 with the following statements, which draw an umbrella (or maybe it's a mushroom).

```
yradius = ycenter / 2;
xradius = xcenter / 3;
setcolor(WHITE);
```

```
setfillstyle(HATCH_FILL, LIGHTGREEN);
sector(xcenter, yradius * 2, 0, 180, xradius, yradius);
setfillstyle(SOLID_FILL, WHITE);
bar(xcenter - 8, yradius * 2, xcenter + 8, ymax);
```

A Slice of Pie

A highly specialized function, `pieslice()`, makes it easy to draw pie charts—one of the more common shapes needed in business graphics programming. Function `pieslice()` is declared as

```
void far pieslice(int x, int y, int stangle, int endangle,
  int radius);
```

Except for its name, `pieslice()` is identical to `arc()`. In fact, that's what a pie slice is—a filled arc, or wedge, with its end points joined at the center (see Figure 16.4).

Each slice of pie has an outline color, selected by `setcolor()`, and a fill pattern and interior color, set by `setfillstyle()` or `setfillpattern()` as for other filled shapes. If you don't want outlined pie wedges, use the same colors for the interior and outline. Listing 16.15, SWEETYPI.CPP, draws a pie chart from a set of data points.

Listing 16.15. SWEETYPI.CPP (Draws a pie chart from a data set).

```
1:  #include <graphics.h>
2:  #include <stdio.h>
3:  #include <stdlib.h>
4:  #include <conio.h>
5:  #include <math.h>
6:
7:  #define ENTRIES 8    // Number of wedges
8:
9:  struct Wedge {
10:    int stAngle;      // A wedge's starting angle
11:    int endAngle;     // A wedge's ending angle
12:  };
13:  typedef struct Wedge *WedgePtr;
14:
15:  // Global variables
```

```
16:   double pieData[ENTRIES] =
17:     { 12.0, 5.0, 7.0, 29.0, 13.0, 22.0, 8.0, 4.0 };
18:   Wedge wedgeData[ENTRIES];
19:   double percentage[ENTRIES];
20:
21:   // Function prototypes
22:   void Calculate(void);
23:   void DisplayChart(int cmax, int xcenter, int ycenter, int radius);
24:
25:   main()
26:   {
27:     int gdriver = DETECT, gmode, gerr;
28:     int xcenter, ycenter, radius;
29:
30:     initgraph(&gdriver, &gmode, "c:\\borlandc\\bgi");
31:     gerr = graphresult();
32:     if (gerr != grOk) {
33:       printf("BGI error: %s\n", grapherrormsg(gerr));
34:       exit(gerr);
35:     }
36:     xcenter = getmaxx() / 2;
37:     ycenter = getmaxy() / 2;
38:     radius = getmaxy() / 3;
39:     Calculate();
40:     DisplayChart(getmaxcolor(), xcenter, ycenter, radius);
41:     getch();
42:     closegraph();
43:     return 0;
44:   }
45:
46:   // Calculate wedge parameters
47:   void Calculate(void)
48:   {
49:     int i, arcAngle;
50:     WedgePtr wp;
51:     int startAngle = 0;
52:     double total = 0;
53:
54:     for (i = 0; i < ENTRIES; i++)
55:       total += pieData[i];
```

continues

Listing 16.15. continued

```
56:    for (i = 0; i < ENTRIES; i++) {
57:      percentage[i] = pieData[i] / total;
58:      if (i == ENTRIES - 1)
59:        arcAngle = 360;
60:      else
61:        arcAngle = startAngle + ceil(percentage[i] * 360.0);
62:      wp = &wedgeData[i];
63:      wp->stAngle = startAngle;
64:      wp->endAngle = arcAngle;
65:      startAngle = wp->endAngle;
66:    }
67:  }
68:
69:  // Display the pie chart
70:  void DisplayChart(int cmax, int xcenter, int ycenter, int radius)
71:  {
72:    int i;
73:    WedgePtr wp;
74:
75:    for (i = 0; i < ENTRIES; i++) {
76:      setfillstyle(SOLID_FILL, (i % cmax + 1));
77:      wp = &wedgeData[i];
78:      pieslice(xcenter, ycenter,
79:        wp->stAngle, wp->endAngle, radius);
80:    }
81:  }
```

The program's data is stored in a global double array (lines 16–17), but could just as well be loaded from a disk file. SWEETYPI displays a pie chart by calculating the percentage of 360° for each data value (lines 56–66) along with the pie-slice angles, stored in an array of Wedge structures (lines 9–13 and 18). After calculating percentages and angles, function DisplayChart() (lines 70–81) calls setfillstyle() and pieslice() to display each wedge.

On monochrome monitors, the wedge divisions might be difficult to see. To fix this problem, use different fill patterns. You might change line 76 to

```
setfillstyle(1 + (i % 11), i % cmax + 1);
```

With this change, each wedge is filled with a different color *and* pattern, making the pie chart visible on most types of graphics displays.

Bitmaps

Three functions—imagesize(), getimage(), and putimage()—copy and display bitmaps (arrays of pixels) anywhere on-screen. The functions are declared in graphics.h as

```
unsigned far imagesize(int left, int top, int right, int bottom);
void far getimage(int left, int top, int right, int bottom,
  void far *bitmap);
void far putimage(int left, int top, const void far *bitmap, int op);
```

Function imagesize() calculates the number of bytes required to store a bitmap with its upper-left corner at (left,top) and its lower-right corner at (right,bottom). Function getimage() copies a bitmap plus its width and height from the display to a buffer addressed by pointer bitmap. It is your responsibility to ensure this buffer is large enough to store the image—usually by calling imagesize(). Function putimage() copies a bitmap from memory to the display. The op parameter is one of the following enumerated values:

```
enum putimage_ops {
  COPY_PUT,              // Direct copy
  XOR_PUT,               // image XOR screen
  OR_PUT,                // image OR screen
  AND_PUT,               // image AND screen
  NOT_PUT                // NOT image
};
```

Listing 16.16, DEVELOP.CPP, demonstrates these functions, drawing a small green house with drawpoly(), then copying that image over and over to create a rapidly expanding development of little green houses.

Listing 16.16. DEVELOP.CPP (Demonstrates bitmaps).

```
1:  #include <graphics.h>
2:  #include <stdio.h>
3:  #include <stdlib.h>
4:  #include <conio.h>
```

continues

Listing 16.16. continued

```
 5:   #include <alloc.h>
 6:
 7:   pointtype house[9] = {
 8:     { 0, 50}, { 0, 25}, {25,  0}, {50, 25}, { 1, 25},
 9:     {50, 50}, {50, 26}, { 1, 50}, {50, 50}
10:   };
11:
12:   main()
13:   {
14:     int gdriver = DETECT, gmode, gerr;
15:     int xmax, ymax;
16:     void *image;
17:
18:     initgraph(&gdriver, &gmode, "c:\\borlandc\\bgi");
19:     gerr = graphresult();
20:     if (gerr != grOk) {
21:       printf("BGI error: %s\n", grapherrormsg(gerr));
22:       exit(gerr);
23:     }
24:     xmax = getmaxx();
25:     ymax = getmaxy();
26:     setcolor(GREEN);
27:     drawpoly(9, (const int *)house);
28:     image = malloc(imagesize(0, 0, 50, 50));  // Reserve memory
29:     if (image) {
30:       getimage(0, 0, 50, 50, image);  // Copy image from screen
31:       while (!kbhit())
32:         putimage(random(xmax), random(ymax), image, COPY_PUT);
33:     }
34:     getch();
35:     closegraph();
36:     return 0;
37:   }
```

After drawing the house to be replicated (line 27), the program calls malloc() and imagesize() to reserve space for a buffer to hold the image as a bitmap (line 28). Function getimage() copies the house to the buffer. Lines 31–32 copy that same image to random locations until you press a key to end the program.

BGI Text Fonts

There are two kinds of graphics fonts: bitmapped and vectored, or *stroked*. The default font is bitmapped—its character shapes are stored as fixed bit patterns. All other fonts are stroked, formed out of individual line segments. Table 16.5 lists BGI's fonts.

Table 16.5. BGI text fonts.

Constant	Value	Type	Disk file
BOLD_FONT	10	Stroked	BOLD.CHR
COMPLEX_FONT	8	Stroked	LCOM.CHR
DEFAULT_FONT	0	Bitmap	none
EUROPEAN_FONT	9	Stroked	EURO.CHR
GOTHIC_FONT	4	Stroked	GOTH.CHR
SANS_SERIF_FONT	3	Stroked	SANS.CHR
SCRIPT_FONT	5	Stroked	SCRI.CHR
SIMPLEX_FONT	6	Stroked	SIMP.CHR
SMALL_FONT	2	Stroked	LITT.CHR
TRIPLEX_FONT	1	Stroked	TRIP.CHR
TRIPLEX_SCR_FONT	7	Stroked	TSCR.CHR

The advantage of using a stroked font becomes obvious when you enlarge characters. Because their patterns are formed of line segments, stroked characters retain their relative shapes as they grow larger. The humps of a B stay round no matter how large they become. Also, the lines in a character have the same thicknesses in all font sizes. The vertical lines in an uppercase I, for example, may grow taller but they won't get fatter.

Bitmapped fonts are different. As a bitmapped character grows, jagged edges along diagonals become more pronounced. Each bit—normally a single pixel in the font's default size—grows in all directions, making lines grow fatter as well as taller. You probably have seen this effect on paper banners created by dot matrix printers. The larger the character, the blockier it looks.

Bitmapped fonts have one important advantage over stroked fonts—they are faster to display. Because a stroked character is composed of individually drawn lines, it takes longer to display than a bitmapped image.

An example shows how to load and use character fonts. Listing 16.17, GRAPHTEX.CPP, displays BGI font names in those fonts.

Listing 16.17. GRAPHTEX.CPP (Demonstrates BGI fonts).

```
 1:  #include <graphics.h>
 2:  #include <stdio.h>
 3:  #include <stdlib.h>
 4:  #include <conio.h>
 5:
 6:  void DisplayText(int *y, int font, const char *name);
 7:
 8:  main()
 9:  {
10:    int gdriver = DETECT, gmode, gerr;
11:    int y = 0;
12:
13:    initgraph(&gdriver, &gmode, "c:\\borlandc\\bgi");
14:    gerr = graphresult();
15:    if (gerr != grOk) {
16:      printf("BGI error: %s\n", grapherrormsg(gerr));
17:      exit(gerr);
18:    }
19:    DisplayText(&y, DEFAULT_FONT, "Default");
20:    DisplayText(&y, TRIPLEX_FONT, "Triplex");
21:    DisplayText(&y, SMALL_FONT, "Small");
22:    DisplayText(&y, SANS_SERIF_FONT, "Sans serif");
23:    DisplayText(&y, GOTHIC_FONT, "Gothic");
24:    DisplayText(&y, SCRIPT_FONT, "Script");
25:    DisplayText(&y, SIMPLEX_FONT, "Simplex");
26:    DisplayText(&y, TRIPLEX_SCR_FONT, "Triplex SCR");
27:    DisplayText(&y, COMPLEX_FONT, "Complex");
28:    DisplayText(&y, EUROPEAN_FONT, "European");
29:    DisplayText(&y, BOLD_FONT, "Bold");
30:    getch();
31:    closegraph();
32:    return 0;
```

```
33:  }
34:
35:  void DisplayText(int *y, int font, const char *name)
36:  {
37:    char buffer[80];
38:    int size;
39:
40:    if (font == SMALL_FONT)
41:      size = 4;
42:    else
43:      size = 2;
44:    settextstyle(font, HORIZ_DIR, size);
45:    sprintf(buffer, "%s font", name);
46:    outtextxy(0, *y, buffer);
47:    *y += textheight("M") + 4;
48:  }
```

Lines 19–29 call `DisplayText` to change fonts and display a small string. Line 44 calls `settextstyle()` to select a font using one of the constants from Table 16.5. The second `settextstyle()` argument specifies the font's direction, either `HORIZ_DIR` for horizontal text or `VERT_DIR` for vertical (rotated) text. The third parameter specifies the font's relative size.

After preparing a string to display (line 45), `outtextxy()` displays that string at a specified coordinate. You can also call `outtext()` to display a string at the current position (CP). For horizontal text, function `outtext()` advances the horizontal (X) component of the CP to the end of the displayed string. Function `outtextxy()` does not change CP.

Text Justification

Use `settextjustify()` to change where `outtext()` displays text in relation to CP, or to the coordinate passed to `outtextxy()`. The function is declared as

```
void far settextjustify(int horiz, int vert);
```

The `horiz` parameter determines whether text starts at CP and moves right, starts at the center, or starts at the right and moves left. The `vert` parameter determines whether text is above, below, or centered at CP. For `horiz`, use one of the first three text_just enumerated constants; for vert, use one of the last three (CENTER_TEXT is listed twice, but defined once):

```
enum text_just {
  LEFT_TEXT   = 0,  // Horizontal (horiz) parameter
  CENTER_TEXT = 1,  //     "     "     "    "    "
  RIGHT_TEXT  = 2,  //     "     "     "    "    "
  BOTTOM_TEXT = 0,  // Vertical (vert) parameter
/*CENTER_TEXT = 1,  //     "     "     "    "    "   */
  TOP_TEXT    = 2   //     "     "     "    "    "
};
```

Nine combinations of these values change where text displays in relation to CP. Listing 16.18, JUSTIFY.CPP, demonstrates all nine selections. Run the program and press Enter to display a line of text at different locations relative to CP, which is represented as a small cross.

Listing 16.18. JUSTIFY.CPP (Demonstrates BGI text justification).

```
 1:  #include <graphics.h>
 2:  #include <stdio.h>
 3:  #include <stdlib.h>
 4:  #include <conio.h>
 5:
 6:  #define ESC 27  // ASCII Esc character
 7:  #define TEST_STRING "Justification test. Press a key."
 8:
 9:  main()
10:  {
11:    int gdriver = DETECT, gmode, gerr;
12:    int xcenter, ycenter, horiz, vert;
13:    char c, s[11];
14:
15:    initgraph(&gdriver, &gmode, "c:\\borlandc\\bgi");
16:    gerr = graphresult();
17:    if (gerr != grOk) {
18:      printf("BGI error: %s\n", grapherrormsg(gerr));
19:      exit(gerr);
20:    }
21:    xcenter = getmaxx() / 2;
22:    ycenter = getmaxy() / 2;
```

```
23:     for (vert = 0; vert <= 2; vert++) {
24:       for (horiz = 0; horiz <= 2; horiz++) {
25:         clearviewport();
26:         settextjustify(LEFT_TEXT, TOP_TEXT);
27:         setcolor(WHITE);
28:         sprintf(s, "horiz == %d", horiz);
29:         outtextxy(0,  0, s);
30:         sprintf(s, "vert  == %d", vert);
31:         outtextxy(0, 25, s);
32:         settextjustify(horiz, vert);
33:         setcolor(RED);
34:         outtextxy(xcenter, ycenter, TEST_STRING);
35:         setcolor(WHITE);
36:         line(xcenter, ycenter - 2, xcenter, ycenter + 2);
37:         line(xcenter - 2, ycenter, xcenter + 2, ycenter);
38:         if ((c = getch()) == ESC)
39:           break;
40:       }
41:       if (c == ESC)
42:         break;
43:     }
44:     closegraph();
45:     return 0;
46:   }
```

Lines 26–31 display the current horiz and vert justification values. Line 32 calls settextjustify() to change the justification setting for the subsequent outtextxy() statement in line 34. Lines 36–37 draw the small reference cross.

Text Width and Height

To determine how many pixels a character occupies on-screen in the current font and size, call functions textheight() and textwidth(). For example, to set an integer n to the height of a capital M in the current font, use the statement

```
int n = textheight("M");
```

To set n to the width of a string, write

```
int n = textwidth("How wide is this string?");
```

Function `textheight()` makes it possible to display multiple lines of text in different fonts and sizes, separated by an equal amount of space. For example, this fragment displays two strings separated vertically by exactly four pixels:

```
int y = 0;
outtextxy(0, y, "String number one");
y += textheight("M") + 4;
outtextxy(0, y, "String number two");
```

A capital M is usually the largest character in a font, so an M character is typically used to calculate relative text heights and sizes. See also GRAPHTEX (Listing 16.17) for an example of how to space lines of multifont text.

Controlling Font Size

For finer control over character width and height, call `setusercharsize()`, declared as

```
void far setusercharsize(int multx, int divx,
  int multy, int divy);
```

The four parameters specify two ratios, which specify text width and height in the current style and size set by `settextstyle()`. The horizontal ratio equals `multx` / `divx`. The vertical ratio equals `multy` / `divy`. A ratio of 1.0 causes no change. A ratio less than 1.0 reduces the horizontal or vertical size. A ratio greater than 1.0 increases the size. For example, this fragment displays text in normal and half-wide sizes:

```
setusercharsize(1, 1, 1, 1);
settextstyle(TRIPLEX_FONT, HORIZ_DIR, USER_CHAR_SIZE);
outtextxy(0, 0, "Normal width");
setusercharsize(1, 2, 1, 1);
settextstyle(TRIPLEX_FONT, HORIZ_DIR, USER_CHAR_SIZE);
outtextxy(0, 40, "Half width");
```

The first call to `setusercharsize()` configures text output to its default size. After calling `setusercharsize()`, you must call `settextstyle()` to choose a font and direction. Rather than the usual size parameter, specify `USER_CHAR_SIZE`, a symbolic constant equal to zero.

The second call to `setusercharsize()` in this example configures text output to half normal width. In this case, `multx` equals one and `divx` equals two, a ratio of 1:2 or 0.5. Notice that you must again call `settextstyle()` after changing ratios. To display text twice as wide, use the statement

```
setusercharsize(2, 1, 1, 1);
```

That specifies a ratio of 2:1 or 2.0—twice as wide as 1:1. Here's another example:

```
setusercharsize(2, 1, 4, 1);
```

Subsequent text output is now twice as wide (2:1) and four times as tall (4:1) as normal.

Reading Text Parameters

To determine current text settings, pass the address of a textsettingstype structure to gettextsettings(). The structure is declared as

```
struct textsettingstype {
  int font;
  int direction;
  int charsize;
  int horiz;
  int vert;
};
```

Function gettextsettings() fills a textsettingstype structure with the current text parameters. You might use the function to save the current settings, change to a new font and size, display some text, and then restore the original settings:

```
textsettingstype ts;
gettextsettings(&ts);
// change settings and display text
settextstyle(ts.font, ts.direction, ts.charsize);
settextjustify(ts.horiz, ts.vert);
```

Creating Stand-Alone Graphics Applications

Unless you write code for programmers, most of your program's customers won't have Borland's BGI driver and CHR font files. You can distribute those files with your finished application, or you can create a stand-alone .EXE code file that combines drivers, fonts, code, and data into one .EXE code file.

Creating a complete BGI .EXE file takes extra time, and is best done as a final step in building a finished application. First, use the BGIOBJ.EXE utility to translate selected .CHR font and .BGI driver files into linkable .OBJ code files. The BGIOBJ utility is stored in your BORLANDC\BGI directory (not BORLANDC\BIN). Its syntax is

```
BGIOBJ [/F] <source> <destination[.OBJ]> <public name>
  <segment-name>  <segment-class>
```

Except for unusual circumstances, you can use default font and driver names. For example, to create SANS.OBJ from the font file SANS.CHR, enter the command

```
bgiobj sans
```

Don't specify a filename extension. BGIOBJ knows the names of BGI font and driver files. The program reports the number of converted bytes, filenames, and a public symbol:

```
13596 bytes from 'SANS.CHR' converted into 'SANS.OBJ',
public name = '_sansserif_font'.
```

To create a linkable .OBJ file for the EGAVGA.BGI driver, enter the command

```
bgiobj egavga
```

Again, no filename extension is needed. BGIOBJ reports

```
5554 bytes from 'EGAVGA.BGI' converted into 'EGAVGA.OBJ',
public name = '_EGAVGA_driver'.
```

You now have two new files, SANS.OBJ and EGAVGA.OBJ. Perform these steps for every font and driver that you need. Next, link the resulting .OBJ files into your program. There are two ways to accomplish this step. You can make C:\BORLANDC\LIB the current directory, then add the .OBJ files to a copy of GRAPHICS.LIB with a command such as

```
tlib graphics +..\bgi\sans +..\bgi\egavga
```

This assumes your .OBJ files are stored in C:\BORLANDC\BGI. Alternatively, you can manually link the .OBJ files to your compiled code file:

```
bcc myprog graphics.lib sans.obj egavga.obj
```

Either way, the font and driver .OBJ file bytes are linked to your program's finished .EXE code file. Unlike common .OBJ files, however, converted fonts and drivers do *not* contain callable functions. Linking them as .OBJ files merely combines them with the finished executable code. So that BGI functions can find the linked fonts and drivers, the program has to register them. That's "register" as in "registering to vote." To register a driver, call `registerbgidriver()`. To register a font, call `registerbgifont()`. Perform these steps *before* calling `initgraph()`. For example, your program could execute the statements

```
if (registerbgidriver(EGAVGA_driver) < 0) error();
if (registerbgifont(sansserif_font) < 0) error();
```

The functions return a negative error code if not successful. Arguments passed to the functions are the public symbols reported by BGIOBJ, minus the leading underscore. These symbols are declared as pseudo function names near the end of graphics.h like this:

```
void EGAVGA_driver(void);
void sansserif_font(void);
```

Never call these functions! They are prototyped *only* to give BGI functions the locations of the linked-in font and driver .OBJ files. Because the files are linked to the finished .EXE code file, the corresponding .CHR and .BGI files are no longer needed, and do not have to be distributed separately with your application.

After registering fonts and drivers, call `initgraph()` as usual, but with one difference. You no longer have to specify a pathname. You might also perform your own mode detection, or select a specific mode and driver:

```
int gdriver = VGA, gmode = VGAHI;
initgraph(&gdriver, &gmode, "");
```

When linking multiple fonts and drivers, it's possible to exceed the 64K limit imposed on a code segment. If this happens, use BGIOBJ's /F option to create far-code segments:

```
bgiobj /F sans
bgiobj /F egavga
```

Combine the resulting .OBJ files into GRAPHICS.LIB, or specify the filenames to the command-line BCC compiler as explained earlier. Because the .OBJ files now reside in separate code segments, you must call `registerfarbgidriver()` and `registerfarbgifont()` to register them:

```
if (registerfarbgidriver(EGAVGA_driver_far) < 0) error();
if (registerfarbgifont(sansserif_font_far) < 0) error();
```

Pass as arguments the `far` forms of the pseudo function names as shown here.

> **NOTE:** See file UTIL.DOC in your BORLANDC\DOC directory for more information about using BGIOBJ.EXE and linking fonts and drivers into .EXE code files.

Summary

- The Borland Graphics Interface (BGI) provides graphics functions for all popular (and some not-so-popular) all-points-addressable PC graphics displays.

- Files ending in .BGI contain BGI drivers for specific video hardware. For example, file EGAVGA.BGI stores the driver code for EGA and VGA displays.

- Files ending in .CHR contain BGI fonts, which are scalable to any size.

- Function `initgraph()` can automatically detect and initialize an ideal graphics mode. Or, you can initialize specific modes to select among a variety of resolutions, colors, and pages for multipage modes.

- Pixel coordinates have unique (X,Y) locations. X coordinate values are sequenced positively from left to right. Y coordinate values are sequenced positively from top to bottom. Coordinate (0,0) locates the pixel at the top-left corner of the display.

- Absolute coordinates are at fixed locations. Logical coordinates are relative to the current viewport, and may be positive or negative.

- Viewports may be clipped to prevent drawing outside of their borders. You can also shift a viewport's origin and turn off clipping to divide a display into quadrants with coordinate (0,0) at center.

- BGI graphics functions can plot points and draw lines, rectangles, circles, ellipses, and arcs. You can also draw filled boxes, pie slices, and polygons. Scan this chapter for examples of most such functions, and also see Chapter 22, "Functions and Examples," for more information about specific BGI routines.

- Colors are represented as indexes into a palette, which controls the actual colors displayed. Visible colors depend upon color palette entries and the video mode.

- Bitmaps are copies of pixels as stored in memory. BGI functions are provided to copy portions of a graphics display to memory and to transfer in-memory bitmaps to the screen.

- There are two kinds of BGI fonts: bitmapped and vectored, or stroked. Bitmapped fonts display quickly, but look blocky in large sizes. Stroked fonts display more slowly, but retain their good looks when resized.

- Use the BGIOBJ.EXE utility to convert .CHR font and .BGI driver files to linkable .OBJ code files. With this technique, you can build fonts and drivers directly into a finished application's .EXE code file.

Borland's Class Library

Borland's class library provides ready-made *container* classes that you can plug into programs for managing all sorts of data collections. Like conventional arrays and lists, container classes are general-purpose vessels for storing data. Container classes are object-oriented, however, and can be extended through inheritance and polymorphism to accommodate many different types of objects and tasks.

This chapter introduces Borland's class library, which supplies you with several varieties of containers and related classes. Two versions of the class library are provided: Object-based and template-based. The template-based library is more versatile, but the Object-based classes are easier to use, so I'll begin there.

Object-Based Classes

Figure 17.1 illustrates the relationships among the classes in the Object-based class library. Most classes are derived from the Object class. Iterator classes are derived from ContainerIterator and are used to perform repetitive tasks for a container's contents. MemBlocks and MemStack stand alone. Bold monospace names are called *instance classes* and may be used directly to construct objects. Names in regular monospace are *abstract classes,* which contain one or more pure virtual member functions. An abstract class must be inherited by a derived class before it can be used to construct objects.

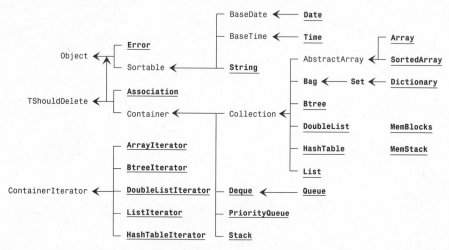

Figure 17.1. Borland's class library.

There's an Object-based container class that can handle almost any data storage task. Table 17.1 lists the instance classes from Figure 17.1 and gives a brief description of what each class can do.

Table 17.1. Instance classes in Borland's class library.

Class name	Description
Array	Unsorted random-access collections that resemble conventional arrays.
Association	Associates a value and a key object. Typically stored in a Dictionary object and used in key searches.
Bag	Like an Array, stores an unsorted collection, but may have more than one copy of the same object.
Btree	B-tree key retrieval class, often used in database programs to provide fast key searches.

Class name	Description
Date	General-purpose date class, useful for storing and outputting formatted dates.
Deque	A "double-ended queue," a classic data structure that functions as a restricted linear list where data enters and leaves only at the list ends.
Dictionary	Used to store Association objects, forming a database of values identified by unique lookup keys.
DoubleList	A classic doubly-linked list.
Error	Failed attempts to construct Object-based objects using new return a pointer to a static Error instance called theErrorObject. The NOOBJECT macro is defined as *(Object::ZERO) where Object::ZERO is a pointer to the global Error instance. NOOBJECT serves the same purpose as a null pointer and is used to occupy invalid or unused container class slots.
HashTable	An unsorted collection of objects stored and retrieved using hash values returned by the container class member function HashValue().
List	A classic singly-linked list.
MemBlocks	Fixed-block memory allocation class used for managing container class memory. Normally not used directly in applications.
MemStack	Provides "mark-and-release" heap memory management for containers. Using this technique, heap memory operates in a stack-like manner rather than in its typical linked-list fashion. The result is faster heap memory operations with the potential loss of the standard memory manager's general versatility.
PriorityQueue	A sequenced container of sortable objects. Typically used to implement scheduling algorithms using GIFO (greatest in, first out) or SIFO (smallest in, first out) data structures.

continues

Table 17.1. continued

Class name	Description
Queue	A container of objects forming a FIFO (first in, first out) data structure. New objects enter a queue from one end and exit from the other.
Set	A collection of unique objects. Only one instance of any particular object can be a member of a set.
SortedArray	Identical to an Array, but automatically maintains objects in sorted order. Objects stored in a SortedArray container must be derived from Sortable.
Stack	A container of objects forming a LIFO (last in, first out) data structure. New objects enter and leave a stack from only one end.
String	Dynamic string. String objects are sortable and can be stored in alphabetic order in SortedArray containers.
Time	General-purpose time class, useful for storing and outputting formatted times.

In addition to the instance classes in Table 17.1, the Object-based library provides five iterator classes, one for each main container class: ArrayIterator, BtreeIterator, DoubleListIterator, HashTableIterator, and ListIterator. Iterator classes are used internally by the container class member functions forEach(), firstThat(), and lastThat() to perform actions on the objects in a container. You also can use iterator classes to create your own external iterator objects for looping through a container's contents.

Table 17.2 lists the Object-based library's abstract classes. You can't construct objects of these classes. Instead, you must derive new classes using at least one of these classes as a base. All the instance classes in Table 17.1 (and iterator classes) are derived from one or more of the abstract classes listed in Table 17.2.

Table 17.2. Abstract classes in Borland's class library.

Class name	Description
AbstractArray	Provides array-like services, including an overloaded subscript operator for accessing array objects using integer indexes.
BaseDate	Derived from Sortable to provide basic date capabilities for the Date class.
BaseTime	Derived from Sortable to provide basic time capabilities for the Time class.
Collection	A specialized abstract derivative of the Container class. Collections differ from Containers primarily in their capability to search for objects based on their values and to provide the basis for random-access data structures. For example, the Array class is derived in part from Collection, but the Stack class, which provides nonrandom access to stored objects, is derived from Container.
Container	The base class for all container classes, including specialized Collections. Container is derived directly from Object.
ContainerIterator	A friend of Container, and therefore capable of accessing all Container class members. Provides iterators for performing operations on one or more of a container's objects.
Object	The ancestor of all major class library classes. Objects to be stored in containers must be of classes derived from Object (but see the section "Template-Based Classes" later in this chapter).

continues

Table 17.2. continued

Class name	Description
Sortable	Base class for all objects to be stored in a sorted container such as SortedArray. Note that Sortable is not a container and does not store other objects. A Sortable object can be compared with other objects of the same kind. For example, a String object is derived from Sortable and therefore can be compared with other String objects, stored in SortedArray containers, and so on.
TShouldDelete	Specifies object ownership rules to containers that are scheduled to be destroyed. Also controls the automatic deletion of objects removed from containers. Tells container classes whether to delete owned objects automatically when the containers go out of scope.

Compiling Class Library Applications

When compiling programs that use Object-based classes, include the necessary header files and link them to an appropriate library. You can specify library files in an IDE project or you can type their names for the command-line compiler (or include the names in a MAKE or batch file). For example, a program that uses the Array class includes the array.h header:

```
#include <iostream.h>
#include <array.h>
main()
{
  ...
}
```

Be sure to add C:\BORLANDC\CLASSLIB\INCLUDE (or the equivalent directory where you store class library header files) to the IDE's directory settings. For the command line compiler, edit or prepare a TURBOC.CFG text file containing commands such as

```
-Ic:\borlandc\classlib\include;c:\borlandc\include
-Lc:\borlandc\classlib\lib;c:\borlandc\lib
```

In the IDE, specify an appropriate class library filename in the program's project, or use the Options|Linker|Libraries command to select the Static "Container Class Library" checkbox. Each of the three supplied .LIB files contains a different version of the compiled classes. The three files are

- TCLASDBS.LIB—Use this to debug and to trace member function calls. Specify TCLASDBS.LIB in an IDE project or a DOS command such as **bcc -v myprog tclasdbs.lib**.

- TCLASDLL.LIB—Use this only with Microsoft Windows for a shareable Dynamic Link Library (DLL) form of compiled class member functions. Must be used with any ObjectWindows-based program that also uses OWL.DLL (see Chapter 21, "Windows Tools and Techniques").

- TCLASSS.LIB—Use this for normal linking of small memory model applications. Specify TCLASSS.LIB in an IDE project or compile your program with a DOS command such as **bcc myprog tclasss.lib**. The third S in TCLASSS.LIB stands for "small-memory model."

> **NOTE:** Library files are supplied for small memory model programs. For other memory models, recompile the library according to instructions in MAKEFILE, usually found in C:\BORLANDC\CLASSLIB. For example, enter the command **make -DMDL=1** to build the large-memory-model class library. If you receive errors from the linker about missing files, use the **-DINCLUDE=** and **-DLIB=** options to specify include and library directories. If you still receive errors, check whether you have defined an INCLUDE environment variable. If so, either delete the variable or make sure that INCLUDE specifies the directories C:\BORLANDC\CLASSLIB\INCLUDE; C:\BORLANDC\INCLUDE.

Using the Class Library

A short example demonstrates how to use Borland's class library. Listing 17.1, SORTTEXT.CPP, reads and sorts a text file using classes SortedArray and String to perform most of the work. To compile the listing, follow the instructions in the preceding section. (Configure the IDE's directories and linker options and create a project with SORTTEXT.CPP and TCLASSS.LIB. Or, from a DOS prompt, enter **bcc sorttext tclasss.lib**.) Run the program and supply the name of a text file to sort. For example, enter **sorttext sorttext.cpp >temp.txt** to sort SORTTEXT.CPP and store the results in TEMP.TXT. *Warning: The output file TEMP.TXT is overwritten without notice.*

Listing 17.1. SORTTEXT.CPP (Demonstrates **Object-based** classes).

```
 1:  // Common includes
 2:  #include <iostream.h>
 3:  #include <stdio.h>
 4:  #include <stdlib.h>
 5:
 6:  // Class library includes
 7:  #include <strng.h>
 8:  #include <sortarry.h>
 9:
10:  #define BUFSIZE 128
11:
12:  main(int argc, char *argv[])
13:  {
14:    FILE *f;                 // Input file
15:    char buffer[BUFSIZE];    // Buffer for reading text lines
16:    char *cp;                // Misc pointer for buffer fixup
17:    SortedArray array(500);  // Array of 500 Objects
18:    String *sp;              // Pointer to a String object
19:
20:    if (argc <= 1) {
21:      puts("No file name specified");
22:      exit(1);
23:    }
24:
25:  // Open file
26:    f = fopen(argv[1], "r");
27:    if (!f) {
28:      printf("Error opening %s\n", argv[1]);
29:      exit(2);
30:    }
```

```
31:
32:  // Read file into String array
33:    while (fgets(buffer, BUFSIZE, f)) {
34:      cp = strchr(buffer, '\n');
35:      if (cp)
36:        *cp = NULL;              // Replace newline with null
37:      sp = new String(buffer);   // Construct String object
38:      array.add(*sp);            // Add object to array
39:    }
40:
41:  // Output array contents
42:    for (sizeType i = 0; i < array.getItemsInContainer(); i++)
43:      cout << array[i] << endl;
44:    fclose(f);
45:    return 0;
46:  }
```

Lines 7 and 8 include the class library header files strng.h and sortarry.h. The program uses conventional techniques to open a text file specified on the command line (lines 25–30). If no errors are detected, lines 33–39 execute a while loop that reads each line of text into a char buffer. Lines 34–36 replace a possible newline character with NULL.

Line 37 uses buffer to create a String class library object addressed by pointer sp, which line 38 adds to array, an object of type SortedArray (see line 17). These two lines demonstrate the class library's utility. Only two statements are needed to construct a sortable string in memory, to add the string to an array, and to maintain the array's contents in alphabetical order.

Lines 42–46 display the array's contents. A for loop cycles index i from zero to one less than the value returned by member function getItemsInContainer(). Call this same member function to determine the number of objects in any Container-based class.

Line 43 is the most interesting one in the program, though at first glance the statement may seem common. The statement uses subscripting in the expression array[i] to access one String object. (The endl symbol is a synonym for the explicit newline character '\n'.) The AbstractArray class from which SortedArray is derived overloads the subscript operator so that objects can be accessed using familiar array-like expressions. Polymorphism is also at work here, giving output stream statements the capability to recognize String objects, all without requiring you to specify what kind of data array contains. Therefore, you could change the type of data stored in array without having to modify expressions such as this one—a bonus you'll appreciate in large programs when data specifications change.

Class Library Study Tips

At first, just grasping the scope and purpose of the class library's umpteen classes and jillion member functions may seem as impossible as holding onto a greased pig in a mud puddle. The following are a few suggestions that will help keep things from slipping out of hand:

- Read the class header files, typically stored in C:\BORLANDC\CLASSLIB \INCLUDE. You might want to print a reference copy of all .h files in this directory. Become generally familiar with class and member function names and try to identify common and similarly named members in various classes.

- Study public and protected class members. Ignore any private declarations. For example, in file abstarry.h, the header file for class AbstractArray, there's no need to ponder the class's private declarations because these items are not accessible outside the class.

- Focus on the obvious. Most member function names use descriptive mnemonics. For example, Array::addAt() adds a new object at a specified position. A good way to learn how class members work is to make logical assumptions based on member function names and then write a short sample program to test your assumptions.

- Many classes are derived from others, and studying just one class is often not enough to learn its capabilities. For example, Array inherits an objectAt() member function from AbstractArray—a fact you would miss if you examined only Array's declaration.

- Run test programs compiled with the -v option for Turbo Debugger. Use the debugger's View|Hierarchy command to investigate class relationships. Tracing member function calls through a tangled web of derived classes often reveals much about how the classes work.

- Microsoft Windows users can use **B**rowse menu commands in Borland C++ for Windows to explore the class hierarchy and examine data members and member functions. Compile programs using the -v option to enable browsing.

- To solve puzzles and riddles (such as "When does member function X call function Y?" and "Should a member function call an inherited base class function?"), read the class source code in C:\BORLANDC\CLASSLIB \SOURCE. Reading the class library's source code is also a great way to pick up tips and techniques you can use for writing your own classes.

Developing Class Consciousness

After you become generally familiar with the classes in the class library, you'll discover that all classes naturally divide into three main categories: noncontainer classes, container classes, and helper classes.

Not every class in the Object-based library is a container. Noncontainer classes include Object, String, Date, Time, Error, Sortable, and Association, none of which is designed to store instances of other objects. The abstract Object and Sortable classes are used to derive other classes for constructing objects to store in containers.

Container classes include Array, Bag, Btree, Deque, Dictionary, DoubleList, HashTable, List, PriorityQueue, Queue, Set, SortedArray, and Stack, which can store objects of any class descended from Object. (Later in this chapter, you'll see how template class containers can store objects of any data type.)

Helper classes include TShouldDelete, ListIterator (and other iterator classes derived from ContainerIterator), MemBlocks, and MemStack. These classes are used internally by other classes or in conjunction with one or more container class objects. You'll rarely use helper classes directly.

The special noncontainer class, Error, is provided for the sole purpose of constructing a global object named theErrorObject. The symbolic constant NOOBJECT is defined as a pointer to theErrorObject. NOOBJECT serves the same purpose as a null pointer—that is, providing a unique value that stands for "nothing is stored here." Empty Array slots, for example, are filled with NOOBJECT pointers.

The Ancestor of All Classes: *Object*

To store your own data in containers, start by deriving a new class from Object, the ancestor of all classes in the class library. Your new class must provide certain member functions such as isA(), which identifies the class numerically, and nameOf(), which gives the class a string name. Object classes also must provide a hash value, although this can be zero if you don't plan on storing class instances in a HashTable container.

Listing 17.2, gobs.h (graphics objects), shows the correct way to derive a new class from Object.

Listing 17.2. gobs.h (Graphics objects).

```
 1:  // gobs.h -- Header file for gobs.cpp (graphics objects)
 2:
 3:  #ifndef __GOBS_H
 4:  #define __GOBS_H  1   // Prevent multiple #includes
 5:
 6:  #include <clstypes.h>
 7:  #include <object.h>
 8:
 9:  const GObjectClass = __firstUserClass + 1;
10:
11:  class GObject: public Object {
12:  public:
13:  // Constructor
14:    GObject(int xx1, int yy1, int xx2, int yy2, int ccolor)
15:      : x1(xx1), y1(yy1), x2(xx2), y2(yy2), color(ccolor) { }
16:  // Required pure virtual member function replacements
17:    virtual classType isA() const { return GObjectClass; }
18:    virtual char *nameOf() const { return "GObject"; }
19:    virtual hashValueType hashValue() const { return 0; }
20:    virtual int isEqual(const Object&) const { return 0; }
21:    virtual void printOn(ostream&) const { return; }
22:  // New pure virtual member function
23:    virtual void Display(void) = 0;
24:  protected:
25:    int x1, y1, x2, y2;
26:    int color;
27:  };
28:
29:  class GLine: public GObject {
30:  public:
31:    GLine(int xx1, int yy1, int xx2, int yy2, int ccolor)
32:      : GObject(xx1, yy1, xx2, yy2, ccolor) { }
```

```
33:    virtual void Display(void);
34:  };
35:
36:  class GRectangle: public GObject {
37:  public:
38:    GRectangle(int xx1, int yy1, int xx2, int yy2, int ccolor)
39:      : GObject(xx1, yy1, xx2, yy2, ccolor) { }
40:    virtual void Display(void);
41:  };
42:
43:  class GCircle: public GObject {
44:  public:
45:    GCircle(int xx1, int yy1, int rradius, int ccolor)
46:      : GObject(xx1, yy1, 0, 0, ccolor), radius(rradius) { }
47:    virtual void Display(void);
48:  protected:
49:    int radius;
50:  };
51:
52:  #endif  // __GOBS_H
```

NOTE: To keep these examples simple, a few required elements have been omitted. In a complete application, each class derived from Object might have to provide isA(), nameOf(), hashValue(), and other member functions, depending on how those classes are to be used.

Line 9 defines constant GObjectClass equal to __firstUserClass + 1. Give all your Object-derived classes similar unique identifying values, starting with __firstUserClass, an enumerated symbol in clstypes.h.

The header file then declares GObject as a class derived from Object. The new class is abstract and can be used to declare additional classes for drawing graphics shapes as introduced in Chapter 16, "The Borland Graphics Interface." A constructor (lines 14–15) initializes GObject instances with properties common to many graphics objects.

Lines 17–21 implement pure virtual member functions inherited from Object. (The functions are written inline to save space, but because they are virtual, they are compiled to common non-inline functions.) Member function isA() returns the class numeric identifier, GObjectClass; nameOf() returns the class name as a string; and hashValueType(), isEqual(), and printOn() return dummy values (or they return without performing any action) because these functions aren't needed. All pure virtual member functions must be implemented, however, so that objects of classes derived from GObject can be constructed.

To its inheritance, the new class declares a pure virtual member function, Display() (line 23), and a few protected data members (lines 25–26). Derived classes such as GLine, GRectangle, and GCircle (lines 29–50) build on GObject and use these new members as shown in the class implementation, Listing 17.3, GOBS.CPP.

Listing 17.3. GOBS.CPP (Graphics object class implementations).

```
 1:  // gobs.cpp -- graphics object implementations
 2:
 3:  #include <graphics.h>
 4:  #include "gobs.h"
 5:
 6:  void GLine::Display(void)
 7:  {
 8:    setcolor(color);
 9:    line(x1, y1, x2, y2);
10:  }
11:
12:  void GRectangle::Display(void)
13:  {
14:    setcolor(color);
15:    rectangle(x1, y1, x2, y2);
16:  }
17:
18:  void GCircle::Display(void)
19:  {
20:    setcolor(color);
21:    circle(x1, y1, radius);
22:  }
```

Each of the classes derived from GObject defines a Display() member function, calling appropriate BGI functions to draw a line, a rectangle, and a circle. This completes the graphics objects. Next, you need an appropriate container for storing a series of graphics shapes—in other words, a picture. Listing 17.4, GBAG.CPP, shows one way to proceed. Compile the program from a DOS prompt with the command **bcc gbag gobs graphics.lib tclasss.lib**, or specify files GBAG.CPP, GOBS.CPP, GRAPHICS.LIB, and TCLASSS.LIB in an IDE project. You might also have to tell the compiler where to locate the files GRAPHICS.LIB and TCLASSS.LIB.

NOTE: GBAG.CPP requires a graphics display. The program does not work on standard monochrome display adapters.

Listing 17.4. GBAG.CPP (Graphics object container demonstration).

```
1:  #include <graphics.h>
2:  #include <stdio.h>
3:  #include <stdlib.h>
4:  #include <conio.h>
5:  #include <bag.h>
6:  #include "gobs.h"
7:
8:  class GBag: public Bag {
9:  public:
10: // Constructor
11:    GBag(int anUpper): Bag(anUpper) { }
12: // New member functions
13:    void AddGObject(GObject *gp);
14:    void DisplayAll(void);
15: };
16:
17: void DisplayGObject(Object &g, void *);
18:
19: main()
20: {
21:   int gdriver = DETECT, gmode, gerr;
```

continues

Listing 17.4. continued

```
22:    int xmax, ymax;
23:    GBag ga(4);  // Bag of four GObjects
24:
25:    initgraph(&gdriver, &gmode, "c:\\borlandc\\bgi");
26:    gerr = graphresult();
27:    if (gerr != grOk) {
28:      printf("BGI error: %s\n", grapherrormsg(gerr));
29:      exit(gerr);
30:    }
31:    xmax = getmaxx();
32:    ymax = getmaxy();
33:    ga.AddGObject(new GRectangle(0, 0, xmax, ymax, WHITE));
34:    ga.AddGObject(new GLine(0, 0, xmax, ymax, RED));
35:    ga.AddGObject(new GLine(xmax, 0, 0, ymax, RED));
36:    ga.AddGObject(new GCircle(xmax / 2, ymax / 2, xmax / 3, BLUE));
37:    ga.DisplayAll();
38:    getch();
39:    closegraph();
40:    return 0;
41: }
42:
43: void GBag::AddGObject(GObject *gp)
44: {
45:    add(*gp);
46: }
47:
48: void DisplayGObject(Object &g, void *)
49: {
50:    ((GObject &)g).Display();
51: }
52:
53: void GBag::DisplayAll(void)
54: {
55:    forEach(DisplayGObject, NULL);
56: }
```

You might use any of the class library's container classes to store a series of graphics shapes. This program uses a Bag, an unordered collection container that can store more than one copy of the same object. (`Bag` is the base class for `Set`, which restricts owned objects to unique values.)

Rather than use `Bag` directly—as SORTTEXT (Listing 17.1) used `Array`—the program derives a new class, `GBag`, from the `Bag` class (lines 8–15). The new class adds two member functions: `AddGObject`, which inserts a graphics object addressed by pointer `gp`, and `DisplayAll()`, which calls the `Display()` member function for each of the bagged graphics objects.

In the main program, line 23 defines a `GBag` object named `ga`, which is capable of storing four `GObject` class instances. Those instances (one rectangle, two lines, and a circle) are created at lines 33–36 by the new operator and passed to `ga`'s `AddGObject()` member function. Line 37 calls the bag's `DisplayAll()` member function to display the picture.

Performing these actions requires only a few simple statements. Line 45 inserts a new graphics object by calling `add()`, a member function inherited from the `Bag` class. Function `add()` requires a reference to an object, provided by dereferencing pointer `gp` in `AddGObject()`. (I wrote the example this way to demonstrate how to add pointer-addressed objects to containers.)

`DisplayGObject()` (lines 48–51) is not a class member. This conventional function, prototyped at line 17, calls a `GObject`'s `Display()` member function. Because `Display()` is virtual, the object itself determines which `Display()` is actually called—a good example of polymorphism.

Member function `DisplayAll()` (lines 53–56) demonstrates how to call an iteration function—in this case, `forEach()`—inherited from `Bag`. The program passes to `forEach()` the address of a function declared as shown by `DisplayGObject`. This function is called once for every bagged graphics object. A second pointer argument can be used to address other data (or a class object) and is passed to the called function. In this case, no other data is needed, and line 55 sets the second argument to `NULL`.

You can write similar programs in many different ways, of course, but using container classes offers several benefits. Member functions are short and easy to read. The program is devoid of complex nested loops and `if` statements—common breeding grounds for bugs. You can easily change `Bag` to `Array` at line 8 to store graphics objects in an array-like collection. No other changes to existing code are required. The program also makes good use of polymorphism, calling a virtual member function such as `Display()` without having to decode the actual object data types. The identical code draws rectangles, circles, and lines, and it also can draw future graphics shapes derived from `GObject`.

Object Ownership

When one object owns another—whether addressed by a pointer, declared as a data member, or owned by any other means—it's vital to plan what happens when the owned object or its owner goes out of scope. It wouldn't be beneficial to have a container destroy an object that was still in use. Such an act would be similar to switching off the ignition while driving down the freeway during rush hour. The likely collisions are not pleasant to imagine.

There are four main cases to consider, which are illustrated in Figure 17.2. A container and its objects can have global scope, local scope (that is, defined as automatic variables in a function), or a mixture of scopes. Objects might also be stored dynamically in heap memory and addressed by pointers. A container might even own a mix of objects, each with a potentially different scope.

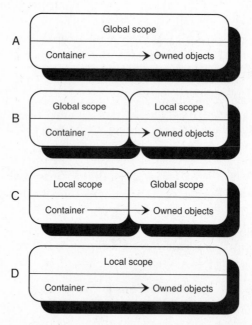

Figure 17.2. Containers and owned objects can have global or local scope, or a potentially confusing mix.

By default, when a container is destroyed, any objects owned by the container are destroyed automatically. This plan works great when the container and its objects share the same scope (cases A and D in Figure 17.2). When the container and its objects are in different scopes, however, the rules become more complex. In the figure's case B, any owned objects must be deleted from the global container before those objects can safely go out of scope—when their defining function ends, for example. In case C, it might be necessary to prevent the local container from destroying the global objects it owns—assuming that those objects are to remain active after the container's defining function returns.

Refer back to Figure 17.1 to see how the class library provides for these situations. `Association` and `Container` are derived from `Object` and `TShouldDelete`, an example of multiple inheritance. Class `TShouldDelete` gives containers a clean way to specify whether they should automatically delete owned objects or let the program handle that chore.

Suppose you declare an `Array` object. To tell that object not to delete its collected objects, use programming such as

```
#include <array.h>         // Include Array class declaration
Array myArray(10);         // Array of 10 objects
myArray.ownsElements(0);   // Objects are not to be destroyed
```

Passing 0 to `ownsElements()`, a member function inherited by all containers via `TShouldDelete`, tells the container that it should not assume ownership of its stored objects. When the container goes out of scope, it does not delete those objects (because it doesn't own them). To reset a container to its default condition that automatically deletes owned objects, pass 1 to `ownsElements()`:

```
myArray.ownsElements(1);   // Delete owned objects automatically
```

To determine a container's current object-ownership status, call `ownsElements()` as an `int` function. The function returns 1 if it owns its objects and therefore deletes them automatically. It returns 0 if it does not assume ownership of its objects:

```
if (myArray.ownsElements() == 0)
  // myArray does not automatically delete its objects
```

Ownership also comes into play at other times. `Container` classes, for instance, provide a member function, `flush()`, that removes all objects from a container. Pass to `flush()` one of three enumerated constants declared publicly by `TShouldDelete` as

```
enum DeleteType {NoDelete, DefDelete, Delete};
```

Because `DeleteType` is declared inside the `TShouldDelete` class, outside of a derived class, you must specify the class name to reference the enumerated constants:

```
#include <shddel.h>
myArray.flush(TShouldDelete::NoDelete);
myArray.flush(TShouldDelete::DefDelete);
myArray.flush(TShouldDelete::Delete);
```

Each of these statements removes myArray's objects. Specify NoDelete to remove, but not destroy, the objects. Pass DefDelete to remove objects but destroy them only if the container owns the objects. Pass Delete to flush() to remove and destroy a container's objects.

Use similar programming when you call a Collection class's detach() member function. If myObject is an instance of any Object-derived class, you can add it to myArray and then detach the object by writing

```
myArray.add(myObject);
...
myArray.detach(myObject);
```

Function detach() searches for myObject and detaches it if it is found. (If the object is not found, it's not in the collection anyway, so any search error is safely ignored.) To detach and delete the object, specify Delete as the second argument:

```
myArray.detach(myObject, TShouldDelete::Delete);
```

The default action detaches but does not delete the object (the opposite of how flush() works). To specify the default condition explicitly, you can write

```
myArray.detach(myObject, TShouldDelete::NoDelete);  // Default
```

Sequence Containers

A sequence container provides order-dependent storage for objects. The Stack, Deque, Queue, and PriorityQueue classes are sequences because they insert objects in specified orders. Sequences also cannot search for objects. Instead, they provide restricted access to objects via member functions.

The most common example of a sequence container is a Stack. You need to include a few header files:

```
#include <iostream.h>
#include <strng.h>
#include <stack.h>
```

Then declare a stack object:

```
Stack myStack;
```

Next, create a few objects to store in myStack. For simplicity, use a few String pointers:

```
String *s1 = new String("One");
String *s2 = new String("Two");
String *s3 = new String("Three");
```

The String class is derived from Object, so objects of type String can be stored in a Stack sequence container. To store objects in myStack, call the push() member function and pass the dereferenced pointers as arguments:

```
myStack.push(*s1);
myStack.push(*s2);
myStack.push(*s3);
```

To remove data from myStack, call pop() until the stack becomes empty:

```
while (!myStack.isEmpty())
  cout << myStack.pop() << endl;
```

Popping objects from a stack does not automatically delete those objects. If the stacked objects are addressed by pointers, to pop and delete them, write the loop as

```
while (!myStack.isEmpty()) {
  Object &r = myStack.pop();  // Pop object from stack
  cout << r << endl;  // Or other action on r
  delete &r;  // Delete popped object
}
```

Local reference r is assigned to each object popped as a reference from myStack. After using r (here its value is passed to the output stream object cout), delete destroys the removed object.

Collection Containers

Collections are higher-order containers. Derived from the Container class, Collection classes are either unordered or ordered. Unordered collections include Bag, HashTable, List, DoubleList, and AbstractArray (the base class for Array). Ordered collections include Btree and SortedArray. Also, Set and Dictionary are derived from Bag.

Unsorted collection classes can store any `Object`-derived objects. Sorted collections can store only objects of classes derived from `Sortable`—the `String` class, for example.

Use `hasMember()` and `findMember()` member functions to locate objects in collections. For example, you can construct a `SortedArray`:

```
SortedArray myArray(100);
```

and then, after adding some objects to `myArray` (see SORTTEXT.CPP, Listing 17.1), you can determine whether a given object is present:

```
String testString("My dog has fleas");
if (myArray.hasMember(testString))
  cout << "Better take your dog to the Vet\n";
```

Likewise, to locate a specific object, call `findMember()`, which returns `NOOBJECT` if the target object is not in the collection:

```
Object &r = myArray.findMember(testString);
if (r != NOOBJECT)
  cout << r << endl;
```

Iterations

There are two ways to use iterator classes such as `ListIterator` and `ArrayIterator`. You can call a container's iteration member functions `firstThat()`, `lastThat()`, and `forEach()`, or you can construct an iterator object to provide your own iterations for the objects stored in a container.

Iteration member functions—the easier of the two techniques—create their own internal iterator objects, which require no actions on your part. As demonstrated earlier in GBAG.CPP (Listing 17.4, line 55), the iteration member function `forEach()` calls a function for every object owned by a container. To `forEach()`, pass the address of an `iterFuncType` function, defined in clstypes.h as

```
typedef void (*iterFuncType)(class Object &, void *);
```

The function receives a reference to every object in the container along with a `void *` pointer, which can address data of your choosing. For example, to call an `iterFuncType` function `myFunc` and pass the address of a global variable `myGlobalData` for a container `myContainer`, you could call `forEach()` like this:

```
myContainer.forEach(myFunc, &myGlobalData);
```

To `firstThat()` and `lastThat()`, pass the address of the slightly different `condFuncType` function, defined as

```
typedef int (*condFuncType)(const class Object &, void *);
```

This function should return true (nonzero) if the referenced object satisfies a condition. As before, the `void *` pointer parameter can address data of your choice. You might design a `condFuncType` function like this:

```
int myCondFunc(const class Object &r, void *p)
{
  if (((myClass &)r).AnyFunction() == *(myDataType *)p)
    return 1;
  else
    return 0;
}
```

In this hypothetical example, `myCondFunc()` returns true if the object's `AnyFunction()` returns a value equal to whatever is addressed by p.

The container's `findFirst()` member function calls the target function until it returns true, or until the container runs out of objects. You might call `findFirst()` like this:

```
SortedArray myContainer(10);
int myGlobalData = 123;
...
Object &r = myContainer.firstThat(myCondFunc, &myGlobalData);
```

The final statement assigns to r a reference to the first object in `myContainer` that satisfies the condition programmed into `myCondFunc`. The `findLast()` iteration function works similarly but locates the last object of a collection that satisfies a programmed condition.

The second and more difficult way to perform an iterated operation for a container's objects is to create an external iterator object. Iterator classes such as `ContainerIterator` overload the `++` operator, which you can use to access a container's objects sequentially without concern for how those objects are stored in memory. To demonstrate external iterators, replace member function `DisplayAll()` in GBAG.CPP (Listing 17.4) with

```
void GBag::DisplayAll(void)
{
  ContainerIterator &ci = initIterator();
  while (ci != 0)
```

```
    ((GObject &)ci++).Display();
  delete &ci;
}
```

The first statement in `DisplayAll()` defines a reference `ci` of the class `ContainerIterator` and assigns to `ci` the result of `initIterator()`, a member function that all container classes provide. This step prepares the iterator object (`ci`) to sequentially access the container's owned objects.

A `while` loop inspects `ci`'s integer value, an action made possible by `ContainerIterator`'s overloading of type `int`. If `ci` is nonzero, it refers to an object in the container for which the `Display()` member function is called. Operator `++` increments `ci` to access the next contained object. Finally, `delete` destroys the iterator object referenced by `ci`.

Template-Based Classes

Borland's template-based class library provides the same container classes and member functions as the `Object`-based library, but it offers additional benefits. For one, template-based containers can store any kind of data, not only objects of classes derived from `Object`. For another, you can select a container's internal storage methods. For example, you might construct a set as a vector (an array of juxtaposed values), or you could implement a set as a linked list. Being able to choose how a container stores data makes it possible to select the best storage method for your application.

On the down side, templates take longer to compile than the equivalent `Object`-based classes. For shorter compile times, it's a good idea to develop your applications using the `Object`-based library and then, after you squash the bugs in your code, convert your containers to the more versatile templates. With templates it's possible to clone the entire `Object`-based library, so you relinquish no capabilities when switching between the two techniques.

> **NOTE:** See Chapter 15, "Advanced Topics in C++," for general information about writing and using C++ templates.

Template class library files are named beginning with BIDS (for "Borland International Data Structure") and usually are stored in C:\BORLANDC\ CLASSLIB\LIB. When linking template-based code, specify these .LIB files:

- BIDSDBS.LIB: Use this for debugging with Turbo Debugger, similar to the `Object`-based TCLASDBS.LIB.

- BIDSDLL.LIB: Use this only with Microsoft Windows for a shareable Dynamic Link Library (DLL) form of the template class library. Equivalent to TCLASDLL.LIB.

- BIDSS.LIB: Use this for normal linking of small memory model applications. Follow the instructions in C:\BORLAND\CLASSLIB\MAKEFILE to build library files for other memory models. Equivalent to TCLASSS.LIB.

ADTs and FDSs

A container class is known as an *abstract data type* (ADT). The `Stack` class is an ADT because it provides functions such as `push()` and `pop()` that do not depend on the stack's implementation details. A stack might be constructed as a linked list, or it could be designed as a vector. A stack's internal implementation has nothing to do with the stack's "stackness."

Lists and vectors, however, are inseparable from their internal storage methods and are referred to as *fundamental data structures* (FDS). Loosely defined, an FDS is any structure that can be used to implement an ADT. For example, a `Stack` class (the ADT) might be implemented using a linked list (the FDS). Together, the combination of an ADT and an FDS provide a complete container class template.

All ADT template containers (`Stack`, `Queue`, `Deque`, `Bag`, `Set`, `Array`, and `SortedArray`) are implemented as `Vectors` (an FDS). The `Stack` class is implemented as a `Vector` or a `List`. `Queues` and `Deques` are implemented as `Vectors` or `DoubleLists`. There are also sorted and counted FDSs that can be used to implement ADTs in direct (object storing) and indirect (pointer storing) versions.

Using Template Classes

Template classes look complex at first glance, but they are not difficult to use. Best of all, template containers can store almost anything. Listing 17.5, INTSET.CPP, demonstrates how to use a template class to construct a set of integer values.

Listing 17.5. INTSET.CPP (A template-based set of integers).

```
1:  #include <iostream.h>
2:  #include <iomanip.h>
3:  #include <sets.h>
4:
5:  main()
6:  {
7:    BI_SetAsVector<int> intset;
8:
9:    intset.add(2);
10:   intset.add(7);
11:   intset.add(12);
12:   for (int i = 1; i <= 14; i++) {
13:     cout << setw(2) << i << ": is ";
14:     if (!intset.hasMember(i))
15:       cout << "not ";
16:     cout << "in the set\n";
17:   }
18:   return 0;
19: }
```

Line 7 declares intset as a set of int values, stored as a vector. To store a different kind of value in a set, just change the data type in angle brackets. Here's how you might store a set of double values:

BI_SetAsVector<double> doubleset;

You also can specify a class as the container's data type. Suppose you have a class named myClass. You can store a set of myClass objects (perhaps derived from String) like this:

BI_SetAsVector<myClass> myClassSet;

Use templates the way you use Object-based classes. For instance, to add elements to intset (lines 9–11), call the Set class's add() member function. Line 14 calls hasMember() to determine whether a given value is stored in intset.

Template-Naming Conventions

ADT and FDS template classes use a sophisticated naming convention composed of various symbols. Table 17.3 lists the terms used in template class names.

Table 17.3. Template class-name symbols.

Term	Description
BI_	Borland International
I	Indirect (no I == direct)
C	Counted
S	Sorted
O	Object-based nonpolymorphic
TC	Object-based polymorphic
ADT	Stack ¦ Queue ¦ Deque ¦ Bag ¦ Set ¦ Array ¦ SArray
FDS	Vector ¦ List ¦ DoubleList
Imp	Implementation
<T>	User-specified object type

FDSs are defined in header files vectimp.h, listimp.h, and dlistimp.h. FDS template names use the form:

```
BI_[I][C¦S][FDS[Iterator]]Imp<T>
```

Square-bracketed items are optional. A vertical bar (¦) means "or." Italics indicate an item that is to be replaced by one of several symbols. For example, *FDS* could be replaced with Vector, List, or DoubleList. From this layout, you can construct a variety of FDS template names. For example, BI_IVectorImp<T> specifies an indirect vector implementation for objects of the user-defined type T. Not all symbol combinations are possible. Table 17.4 lists the complete set of FDS class template names.

FDS templates come in two flavors: direct and indirect. Direct-storage templates store objects directly. Indirect-storage templates store pointers to objects. The two types of containers are used similarly, although you must be careful to feed them the correct items (either objects or pointers).

Table 17.4. Fundamental data structure (FDS) template class names.

FDS template class	Description
BI_VectorImp<T>	Vector
BI_CVectorImp<T>	Counted vector
BI_SVectorImp<T>	Sorted vector
BI_IVectorImp<T>	Indirect vector
BI_ICVectorImp<T>	Indirect counted vector
BI_ISVectorImp<T>	Indirect sorted vector
BI_ListImp<T>	Singly-linked list
BI_IListImp<T>	Indirect singly-linked list
BI_SListImp<T>	Sorted singly-linked list
BI_ISListImp<T>	Indirect sorted singly-linked list
BI_DoubleListImp<T>	Doubly-linked list
BI_IDoubleListImp<T>	Indirect doubly-linked list
BI_SDoubleListImp<T>	Sorted doubly-linked list
BI_ISDoubleListImp<T>	Indirect sorted doubly-linked list

Direct-storage container classes require objects that can be copied and that have default constructors. Common types such as int and double are compatible with these requirements because, conceptually, an int has a default constructor even though the int data type is not implemented as a C++ class. Of course, C++ knows how to copy int values.

Indirect-storage container classes store pointers to objects, and because C++ already knows how to copy pointers, the addressed objects do not require copy constructors. Indirect-storage container classes can store pointers to any kind of object.

Associated with the FDS template classes are several iterator classes, listed in Table 17.5.

Table 17.5. Template iterator classes.

Iterator class name	Description
BI_VectorIteratorImp<T>	Direct Vector iterator
BI_IVectorIteratorImp<T>	Indirect Vector iterator
BI_ListIteratorImp<T>	Direct List iterator
BI_IListIteratorImp<T>	Indirect List iterator
BI_DoubleListIteratorImp<T>	Direct DoubleList iterator
BI_IDoubleListIteratorImp<T>	Indirect DoubleList iterator

Now for the ADT templates—the abstract data types implemented in terms of specific FDSs. The template library's ADTs are defined in header files stacks.h, queues.h, deques.h, bags.h, sets.h, and arrays.h. Note the trailing *s* in these file names. stacks.h (plural) defines stack template classes; stack.h (singular) defines the Object-based Stack class.

ADT template names follow this format (see Table 17.3):

BI_[I]*ADTAsFDS*<T>

The syntax is a kind of menu from which you can order a smorgasbord of ADTs implemented with specific FDSs. For instance, BI_QueueAsDoubleList calls for the "Borland International Queue ADT class implemented as a DoubleList FDS." The trailing <T> represents a user-specified type T, which can be any data type or class. BI_SetAsVector stores a set of objects directly as a vector. BI_ISetAsVector stores a set of indirect pointers as a vector, and so on.

In addition to these templates, which enable you to supply a data type for <T>, two more template variations mirror the capabilities of the Object-based class library. Using the symbols from Table 17.3, these additional template names have the general form:

BI_[O¦TC]*ADTAsFDS*

An O or a TC preface is required in these names. The Object-based nonpolymorphic templates (O preface) use no virtual member functions; thus, they give programs a potential performance boost but lose polymorphic behavior. The Object-based polymorphic templates (TC preface) exactly duplicate the Object-based library, including virtual member functions.

Note that these two kinds of templates do not end with <T>, and therefore do not give you the opportunity to specify the type of objects to be stored in a container. These templates are intended to mirror the Object-based classes in all ways, and thus stored objects must be of classes derived from Object. The template class BI_OBagAsVector, for example, combines a Bag ADT implemented as a Vector FDS in a nonpolymorphic fashion (no virtual member functions). The template class BI_TCBagAsVector is also a Bag container, but it is implemented polymorphically as a Vector and is exactly equivalent to the Object-based Bag class. Objects stored in these containers must be derived from the Object class.

In other words, these two declarations are functionally equivalent:

```
Bag oldBag;              // An Object-based Bag container
BI_TCBagAsVector newBag; // Same ol' bag as a brand new template
```

Math Classes

Classes make it possible to add new data types to the C++ language. Two math classes, complex and bcd, demonstrate the power of this capability by providing two numeric data types for constructing complex and binary-coded decimal numbers. The two classes implement a wide range of overloaded operators and mathematical functions such as +, *, sin(), sqrt(), and others. Technically, complex and bcd are not part of the container class library, but it's convenient to discuss them here. Only C++ programs, but not ANSI C programs, can use the complex and bcd classes.

To use the complex class, include header complex.h. You can then define variables of type complex, just as you define variables of built-in types such as int and double. Listing 17.6, COMPLEX.CPP, demonstrates how to use the complex class.

Listing 17.6. COMPLEX.CPP (Demonstrates the complex class).

```
1:  #include <iostream.h>
2:  #include <complex.h>
3:
4:  main()
5:  {
6:    complex number = -2;
7:    complex result = sqrt(number);
```

```
 8:    cout << "complex sqrt(-2) == " << result;
 9:    return 0;
10: }
```

Line 6 defines a `complex` variable named `number`, initialized to –2. Line 7 defines a second `complex` variable, `result`, initialized to the square root of `number`. Function `sqrt()` is defined as a friend of the `complex` class, and when passed a `complex` value, the `sqrt()` function returns a `complex` result. Line 8 displays the program's result in an output stream statement. Such statements are possible because the `complex` class overloads the input and output stream operators.

A similar class, `bcd`, adds binary-coded decimals to C++. A binary-coded decimal value stores floating-point numbers as individual decimal digits. This format eliminates round-off errors in decimal floating-point values. Of course, a repeating-decimal value such as 123.33333... might still be rounded when stored in `bcd` format, but round-off *errors* associated with binary floating-point data types such as `real` and `double` are effectively eliminated by the `bcd` class.

One problem with binary-coded decimals concerns speed. Typically, expressions with floating-point values evaluate faster than similar expressions with binary-coded decimals. The `bcd` class also limits precision to 17 decimal digits, equivalent to the approximate range of 1e+125 to 1e–125.

Despite these disadvantages, binary-coded decimal numbers are typically used in accounting programs, where just one missing penny might cause managers and treasurers to consider changing their vocations. Listing 17.7, BCD.CPP, shows how to use the `bcd` class.

Listing 17.7. BCD.CPP (Demonstrates the `bcd` class).

```
1:  #include <iostream.h>
2:  #include <iomanip.h>
3:  #include <bcd.h>
4:  #include <math.h>
5:
6:  #define MAX 10
7:
8:  main()
9:  {
```

continues

Listing 17.7. continued

```
10:    bcd array[MAX], sum = 0, avg;
11:    int i;
12:
13:    for (i = 0; i < MAX; i++)
14:      array[i] = (i + 1) * M_PI;
15:    for (i = 0; i < MAX; i++) {
16:      sum += array[i];
17:      cout << "bcd array[" << i << "] == " << array[i] << endl;
18:    }
19:    avg = sum / MAX;
20:    cout << "For " << MAX << " bcd numbers:" << endl;
21:    cout << "bcd sum == " << sum << endl;
22:    cout << "average == " << avg << endl;
23:    bcd rounded = bcd(real(avg), 2);
24:    cout << "average rounded to 2 places == " << rounded << endl;
25:    return 0;
26:  }
```

Line 10 defines an array of 10 bcd numbers, a sum (initialized to 0), and avg. As this line shows, you use bcd numbers as you use other data types in C++. You can assign values to bcd variables (line 14, for instance, assigns the result of an expression to array[i]). You can add, subtract, multiply, and divide bcd values (see lines 16 and 19 for a couple of samples), and you can display bcd values in output stream statements (lines 20–22 and 24).

NOTE: For more information about the complex and bcd classes, examine their declarations in header files complex.h and bcd.h. These files are typically stored in the C:\BORLANDC\INCLUDE directory.

Summary

- Container classes are general-purpose vessels for storing data collections. Unlike conventional arrays and lists, container class arrays, lists, bags, and other structures are object-oriented and can be extended through inheritance and polymorphism.

- Borland's container class library comes in two forms: Object-based and template-based. Object-based classes are easier to use and compile quickly, but they offer less versatility and (possibly) reduced performance. Template-based classes require more effort to use and more time to compile, but they are more versatile and give potentially better performance.

- Data objects stored in Object-based containers must be of a class derived from Object. Template-based containers can store objects of any class or even values of built-in types such as int and double.

- Not all classes are containers. The class library naturally comprises three categories: noncontainer classes, container classes, and helper classes. Only container classes such as Array, Bag, Deque, and others can store object collections. Noncontainers such as Object and String are not capable of owning objects. Helper classes such as TShouldDelete, ListIterator, and MemStack provide internal services to various class member functions and are rarely used directly.

- It's important to consider the consequences of object ownership. Normally, when a container object is destroyed, it automatically destroys the objects it contains. Call the TShouldDelete class's ownsElements() member function (inherited by all container classes) to specify whether a container should destroy its owned objects automatically.

- Sequence containers provide order-dependent storage for objects. The Stack, Deque, Queue, and PriorityQueue classes are examples of sequence containers. These containers cannot search for objects, nor can they provide random access to objects.

- Collections are higher-level containers. Unordered collection classes include Array, Bag, HashTable, List, and DoubleList. Ordered collections include Btree and SortedArray. Collection classes provide hasMember() and findMember() search functions.

- Iteration member functions forEach(), findFirst(), and findNext() perform actions for a container's objects. You also can create your own external iterator class objects to access a container's contents.

- Template classes provide the same container classes and member functions as in the Object-based library. Template containers, however, can store any kind of data, not only objects of classes derived from Object.

- A container class template is known as an abstract data type, or ADT. An ADT is any structure that is independent of its storage mechanism. For example, a stack is an ADT because a stack can be implemented in a variety of ways.

- A storage mechanism class template is known as a fundamental data structure, or FDS. An FDS is defined by its physical characteristics and can be used to implement an ADT. Lists, doubly-linked lists, and vectors are FDSs.

- The template class library makes it possible to select an ADT implemented with a particular FDS. Not all combinations of ADTs and FDSs are provided.

- Direct and indirect (pointer) versions of template container classes are available. Direct-storage templates require objects to have default constructors and to have the capability of being copied. Indirect-storage templates store pointers to objects and do not carry these same restrictions.

- Additional templates mirror the Object-based class library, offering the option of nonpolymorphic containers (no virtual member functions) or exact replicas of the Object-based classes, including virtual member functions.

- Use the complex class to construct complex numbers. Use the bcd class to store decimal floating-point values as binary-coded decimals, eliminating round-off errors typically associated with floating-point binary data types such as real and double.

Turbo Vision

What is Turbo Vision and do you need it? Answering the first question is easy: Turbo Vision is a class library for constructing complex software interfaces with pull-down menus, overlapping windows, dialog boxes, and similar features that are standard equipment for modern commercial DOS software.

Answering the second question—do you need Turbo Vision—is more difficult. Some programmers find Turbo Vision to be the ideal application environment, or *framework*. Others discover that Turbo Vision leads to a dead end—it's definitely not for everyone. If you are writing graphics software, for example, you can probably skip this chapter. Turbo Vision is designed to work best in text mode, and its primary purpose is to provide text-based user interfaces powered by *event-driven technology*— a term you'll explore later in more detail.

> **NOTE:** If you are not familiar with C++ classes, you should read chapters 12–15 before continuing. Programming with Turbo Vision requires a thorough understanding of C++ classes and object-oriented programming.

While digging into this chapter, keep in mind that Turbo Vision is a highly sophisticated class library. A single chapter cannot possibly cover all that Turbo Vision has to offer! The goal of this chapter is not to replace Borland's 534-page reference, but to present a fast-paced introduction to Turbo Vision programming techniques. After reading the chapter, you can decide whether you should spend more time studying the official documentation, references, and examples.

Introducing Turbo Vision

Before learning to use Turbo Vision, you need to tighten a few nuts and bolts to prepare the IDE and command-line compilers for Turbo Vision programming.

Parts and Pieces

If you installed Borland C++ in the default directories, Turbo Vision's files are stored in subdirectories nested in C:\BORLANDC\TVISION. Table 18.1 lists each directory and describes its files.

Table 18.1. Turbo Vision directories.

Directory	Description of files
DEMOS	Demonstration programs.
DOCDEMOS	Listings from Borland's *Turbo Vision User's Guide.*
HELP	Help compiler for preparing your own online help windows in Turbo Vision applications.
INCLUDE	Header files for Turbo Vision classes.
LIB	TV.LIB object-code library file, which must be linked to all Turbo Vision programs.
OBJECT	This directory is used only for rebuilding Turbo Vision object-code (.OBJ) files; otherwise the directory has no files and is normally empty.
SOURCE	Source code .CPP, .ASM, and related files. Use MAKEFILE to rebuild the library.

Figure 18.1 illustrates the relationships between significant Turbo Vision classes, minus a few relatively minor classes that aren't typically used directly in applications. Derived classes are to the right of their bases. Thus `TMenuBar` is derived from `TMenuView`, which is derived from `TView`, `TObject`, and `TStreamable`. Several miscellaneous classes are listed at upper-right column of figure 18.1.

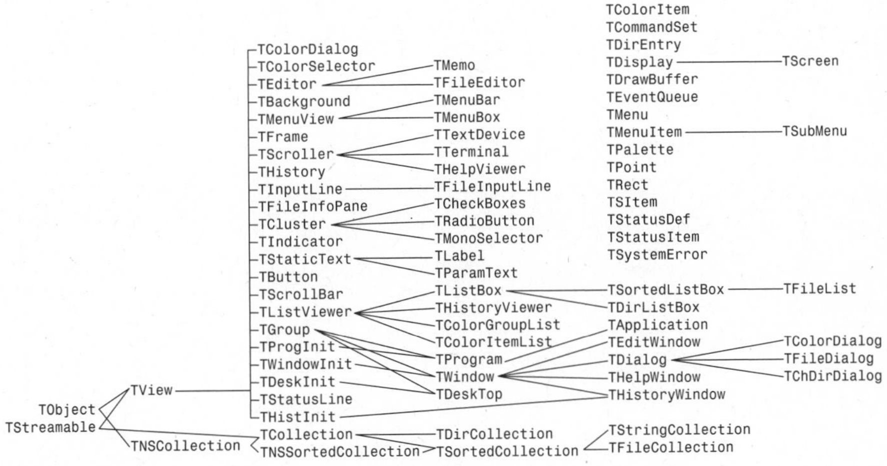

Figure 18.1. Turbo Vision class hierarchy.

Table 18.2 lists Turbo Vision's header files and documents the classes that each file declares. Programs don't usually need to include these headers directly. Instead, they include tv.h and use #define statements to import the necessary classes.

Table 18.2. Turbo Vision header files and classes.

Header file	Purpose	Classes declared
app.h	Application wrappers	TApplication, TBackground,TDeskInit, TDeskTop, TProgInit, TProgram
buffers.h	Video memory buffers	TBufListEntry, TVMemMgr
colorsel.h	Color and palette selection	TColorDialog, TColorDisplay, TColorGroup, TColorGroupList, TColorItem, TColorItemList, TColorSelector, TMonoSelector

continues

Table 18.2. continued

Header file	Purpose	Classes declared
config.h	Miscellaneous parameters	none
dialogs.h	Dialogs and controls	TButton, TCheckBoxes, TCluster, TDialog, THistInit, THistory, THistoryViewer, THistoryWindow, TInputLine, TLabel, TListBox, TParamText, TRadioButtons, TSItem, TStaticText
drawbuf.h	Screen manager interface	TDrawBuffer
editors.h	Text editors	TEditor, TEditWindow, TFileEditor, TIndicator, TMemo
help.h	Online help	TCrossRef, THelpFile, THelpIndex, THelpTopic, THelpViewer, THelpWindow, TParagraph
menus.h	Pull-down menus	TMenuItem, TSubMenu, TMenu, TMenuView, TMenuBar, TMenuBox, TStatusItem, TStatusDef, TStatusLine
msgbox.h	Messages and input dialog functions	MsgBoxText
objects.h	Miscellaneous classes	TCollection, TPoint, TRect, TSortedCollection
resource.h	String collections and resources	TResourceCollection, TResourceFile, TStrIndexRec, TStringCollection, TStringList, TStrListMaker
stddlg.h	Standard file dialogs	TChDirDialog, TDirCollection, TDirEntry, TDirListBox, TFileCollection, TFileDialog, TFileInfoPane, TFileInputLine, TFileList, TSortedListBox
system.h	Low-level mouse and event classes	TDisplay, TEventQueue, THWMouse, TMouse, TScreen, TSystemError

Header file	Purpose	Classes declared
textview.h	Scrollable text-based views	`otstream`, `TTerminal`, `TTextDevice`
tkeys.h	Keyboard constants	none
tobjstrm.h	Streamable base classes	`fpbase`, `fpstream`, `ifpstream`, `iopstream`, `ipstream`, `ofpstream`, `opstream`, `pstream`, `TPReadObjects`, `TPWObj`, `TPWrittenObjects`, `TStreamable`, `TStreamableClass`, `TStreamableTypes`
ttypes.h	Miscellaneous `typedef` and `class` declarations	none
tv.h	Main Turbo Vision header	none (includes other headers as needed)
tvobjs.h	Low-level and internal nonstreamable classes	`TNSCollection`, `TNSSortedCollection`, `TObject`
util.h	Miscellaneous function prototypes	none
views.h	Window and view (that is, output) classes	`TCommandSet`, `TFrame`, `TGroup`, `TListViewer`, `TPalette`, `TScrollBar`, `TScroller`, `TView`, `TWindow`, `TWindowInit`

Configuring the IDE

To compile Turbo Vision programs, you can use the text-based IDE but not Borland C++ for Windows. Three main IDE settings are required:

- Select the large memory model by using the **O**ptions menu and Compiler|Code-generation commands.

- Link to TV.LIB by using the **O**ptions menu and Linker|Libraries commands and selecting Turbo-Vision.

- Designate the proper directories by using the **Options** menu and **Directories** command. The include and library directories respectively should be

```
c:\borlandc\tvision\include;c:\borlandc\include
c:\borlandc\tvision\lib;c:\borlandc\lib
```

In addition, Turbo Vision programs that also use Borland's class library must specify C:\BORLANDC\CLASSLIB directories. In that case, the two directories should be as follows (type the first and second lines all on one line):

```
c:\borlandc\tvision\include;c:\borlandc\classlib\include;
  c:\borlandc\include
c:\borlandc\tvision\lib;c:\borlandc\classlib\lib;c:\borlandc\lib
```

Configuring the Command-Line Compiler

To use the command-line compiler for Turbo Vision programming, create or edit a TURBOC.CFG text file, and store it in the current directory. At a minimum, the file should specify the large memory model and appropriate include and library directories. Separate multiple directory names with semicolons as in the preceding section, or for better clarity, type them on separate lines. Here's the bare minimum TURBOC.CFG file you need to compile the programs in this chapter:

```
-ml
-Ic:\borlandc\tvision\include
-Ic:\borlandc\classlib\include      (optional)
-Ic:\borlandc\include
-Lc:\borlandc\tvision\lib
-Lc:\borlandc\classlib\lib          (optional)
-Lc:\borlandc\lib
```

The two references to CLASSLIB directories are needed only for the WINDMENU.CPP example. Turbo Vision programs do not require linking to Borland's class library.

After preparing a TURBOC.CFG file, compile and link Turbo Vision listings as you do others, but specify the library file TV.LIB. For example, to compile and link a program named TVAPP.CPP, enter the command **bcc tvapp tv.lib**. If TVAPP.CPP uses other modules, include their names like this: **bcc tvapp module1 module2 tv.lib**. Or, if the modules are already compiled, use a command such as **bcc tvapp module1.obj module2.obj tv.lib**.

Event-Driven Programming

Conventional programs typically spend time waiting for events to happen. The standard library's getchar() function, for example, does not return until a character is available from stdin (usually after a key is struck). When a statement calls getchar(), all other activities are put on hold until the expected event arrives.

Event-driven programs turn the tables on conventional user-interface techniques. Rather than pause for expected events, an event-driven program responds to any and all events as they occur. Figure 18.2 compares conventional and event-driven user-interface concepts.

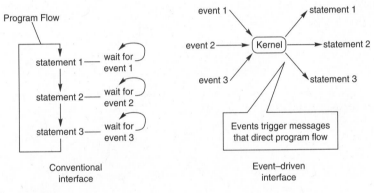

Figure 18.2. Conventional versus event-driven interfaces.

In a typical event-driven program, a core subroutine (or a collection of routines often called a kernel) intercepts various events such as mouse-button clicks, keypresses, and other external happenings. In response to these events, the kernel generates one or more messages, which are passed to modules for processing. In Turbo Vision, these conceptual event-driven modules are constructed as class objects. Member functions in object classes respond to event messages passed as arguments.

The Turbo Vision Desktop

Listing 18.1, DESK.CPP, is a bare-bones Turbo Vision application with a pull-down menu at the top, a status line at the bottom, and a blank desktop where other items can appear. Figure 18.3 shows DESK with its pull-down menu open to reveal a single command. Compile the listing from DOS with the command **bcc desk tv.lib**. Like all Turbo Vision programs, DESK recognizes a mouse and works with nearly any make and model of color or monochrome displays. If you don't have a mouse (or if you hate meeses to pieces), select menu commands by pressing Alt and a highlighted letter, or press F10 and use cursor keys to move the menu's highlight bar. Press Enter to execute a highlighted command. To quit the program, use the File menu's Exit command, click the mouse pointer on the Alt-X label in the status line, or press **Alt-X**.

Figure 18.3. DESK.CPP's display.

There are several main parts to DESK.CPP. Study the listing closely—most Turbo Vision programs have similar parts. Lines 1–11 include header files that declare various classes and other items. Rather than include headers directly, however, Turbo Vision programs define symbolic constants such as Uses_TApplication and Uses_TStatusLine. TApplication and TStatusLine are class names. Defining Uses_... symbols for every Turbo Vision class used in a program (plus Uses_TKeys and Uses_TDeskTop in most cases), and including tv.h (see line 11), automatically loads the necessary header files.

Listing 18.1. DESK.CPP (Creates a bare-bones Turbo Vision application).

```
 1:  #define Uses_TApplication
 2:  #define Uses_TStatusLine
 3:  #define Uses_TStatusDef
 4:  #define Uses_TStatusItem
 5:  #define Uses_TMenuBar
 6:  #define Uses_TSubMenu
 7:  #define Uses_TMenuItem
 8:  #define Uses_TKeys
 9:  #define Uses_TRect
10:  #define Uses_TDeskTop
11:  #include <tv.h>
12:
13:  class TAnyApp: public TApplication
14:  {
15:  public:
16:    TAnyApp(): TProgInit(
17:      TAnyApp::initStatusLine,
18:      TAnyApp::initMenuBar,
19:      TAnyApp::initDeskTop) { }
20:    static TStatusLine *initStatusLine(TRect r);
21:    static TMenuBar *initMenuBar(TRect r);
22:  };
23:
24:  // Initialize application's status line
25:  TStatusLine *TAnyApp::initStatusLine(TRect r)
26:  {
27:    r.a.y = r.b.y - 1;
28:    return new TStatusLine(r,
29:      *new TStatusDef(0, 0xFFFF)+
30:      *new TStatusItem("", kbF10, cmMenu)+
31:      *new TStatusItem("~Alt-X~ Exit", kbAltX, cmQuit)
32:    );
33:  }
34:
35:  // Initialize application's pull-down menus
36:  TMenuBar *TAnyApp::initMenuBar(TRect r)
37:  {
38:    r.b.y = r.a.y + 1;
```

continues

Listing 18.1. continued

```
39:    return new TMenuBar(r,
40:      *new TSubMenu("~F~ile", kbAltF)+
41:      *new TMenuItem("E~x~it", cmQuit, kbAltX, hcNoContext, "Alt-X")
42:    );
43:  }
44:
45:  main()
46:  {
47:    TAnyApp app;
48:    app.run();
49:    return 0;
50:  }
```

> **NOTE:** Don't worry about accidentally loading the same headers more than once. The tv.h and other header files are designed to ignore unnecessary Uses_TClass symbols.

Skip down to the end of DESK's listing, where you'll find a short main() function. All Turbo Vision programs have similar main bodies, looking much like DESK's:

```
main()
{
  TAnyApp app;
  app.run();
  return 0;
}
```

The first line declares app as an object of type TAnyApp, a class derived from TApplication. This class is often called "the TApplication class," and it serves as a wrapper that envelopes a Turbo Vision application. Defining a TApplication object is all that's required to initialize a Turbo Vision program.

The second line calls the run() member function for your program's TApplication class object, in this example, app. Calling run() executes a Turbo Vision program.

The third line returns zero, but it could return an error code if necessary.

> **HINT:** If you discover a need to insert more than these three statements into main(), you are probably missing the point of Turbo Vision. *No* main() function needs to have any additional code, regardless of how complex the program.

The program's TApplication class TAnyApp is derived at lines 13–22. The constructor at lines 16–19 may seem unusual until you investigate TApplication's base class, TProgram, which is multiply derived from TGroup and TProgInit. All of these classes except TProgInit have default constructors, so only TProgInit()'s constructor is called explicitly.

To this constructor are passed the addresses of three member functions, initStatusLine(), initMenuBar(), and initDeskTop(), which initialize the program's status line, menu bar, and blank desktop. You may provide replacement member functions for these initializers, but you'll normally supply only initStatusLine() and initMenuBar(). Each function receives a TRect object that indicates the display size.

TRect is another Turbo Vision class with two data members, a and b, both of type TPoint, which declares two int members x and y. TPoint describes a single display coordinate; TRect uses two TPoint objects to describe a rectangle's upper-left and lower-right corners. The classes don't display anything; they merely represent screen locations, with coordinate (0,0) at the extreme upper left. Figure 18.4 illustrates how these classes represent points and rectangles.

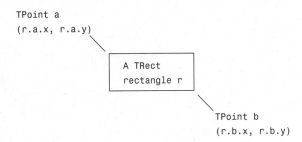

Figure 18.4. TRect and TPoint classes describe a rectangle.

File objects.h declares the TRect and TPoint classes, and it might be helpful for you to examine their declarations now. You'll see many examples of TRect and TPoint class objects in Turbo Vision programs.

In DESK, member function `initStatusLine()` sets `r.a.y` (the `TPoint` object a's y member) to `r.b.y` minus one (see line 27). After this step, `r` describes a thin rectangle at the display's bottom—the typical location for a status line. The expression `r.b.y - r.a.y` equals the height of the rectangle in characters—one character tall in this case. (If `r.a.y` equaled `r.b.y`, the rectangle would have zero height, and the status line would not appear!) Member function `initStatusLine()` returns the address of a `TStatusLine` object, constructed at lines 28–32 using `r` as the line's size and location.

These statements may seem odd, but they are simply Turbo Vision's way of creating a linked list, in this case, a list of items to appear on the status line. Three expressions use the `new` operator to construct objects of classes `TStatusDef` and `TStatusItem`. The objects are "added" together by plus signs (+), which are overloaded to allow creating linked lists using addition.

An object of class `TStatusDef` heads the status line list. In this example, arguments `0` and `0xFFFF` represent the range of help-context values for which other status items are displayed.

Lines 30–31 construct objects of class `TStatusItem`. The class constructor requires at least three items: a string for a status line label, a hot key symbol such as `kbF10`, and a command constant such as `cmMenu`, which associates a label with a command. Use tilde characters in the label to specify highlighted text.

Line 30 adds an invisible status label, keyed to function key F10 and associated with the command `cmMenu`. Pressing F10, then, opens the program's menu. Line 31 specifies the label Alt-X Exit, using tilde characters (~) to highlight Alt-X. Constant kbAltX designates a hot key, which is associated with cmQuit. See file tkeys.h for a complete list of key constants. If you do not want to associate a hot key with a menu command or status line entry, use the symbol kbNoKey.

Similar programming appears at lines 36–43, which implement TAnyApp's initMenuBar member function. Line 38 adjusts TRect to place the menu bar at the display's top. Lines 39–42 create a linked list of TSubMenu (menu bar label) and TMenuItem (command name) class objects.

The TSubMenu class constructor requires at least two items: a string (with optional highlighting tildes), and a key constant such as kbAltF. The TMenuItem constructor requires a string, a command value (cmQuit), a key constant (kbAltX), a help context (hcNoContext if the program has no online help), and a string to be displayed next to the command as a reminder of its associated hot key, "Alt-X" here (see Figure 18.3).

After you feel comfortable with DESK's parts and pieces, consider how the program works. There aren't any loops or explicit function calls—except, that is, for main()'s app.run() statement at line 48. This is an event-driven program, remember. When you select a command, that event triggers a message, which is passed to another TApplication member function named handleEvent(). The next section shows how to use handleEvent() to respond to commands selected from a pull-down menu. At the same time, we'll investigate another key Turbo Vision subject—how to open a window.

Menus, Commands, and Windows

Without a doubt, windowed interfaces have won the battle to define a standard software display. That's not *Microsoft Windows,* but windows in general. Turbo Vision creates text-based windows, illustrated in Figure 18.5, which is a snapshot of the next program, ONEWIND.

Turbo Vision windows have titles, close buttons in the upper left border, zoom buttons at upper right, and a size bar at lower right, which you can click and drag with a mouse pointer. An active window's borders are double-lined; inactive windows have single-line borders. You can drag windows to new locations, resize them, and so on. These and other operations are probably "old hat" to most PC users.

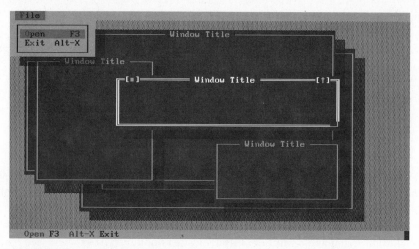

Figure 18.5. ONEWIND's display, showing several windows open on Turbo Vision's desktop.

Opening Windows

Listing 18.2, ONEWIND.CPP, illustrated in Figure 18.5, opens one or more windows on Turbo Vision's desktop. Compile ONEWIND from DOS with the command **bcc onewind tv.lib**. The program requires a mouse. If you don't have one, you can still run the program, open windows, and exit. You must use a mouse, however, to move, resize, zoom, and close windows. (Later, you'll add full keyboard capabilities to a similar but expanded program.)

Listing 18.2. ONEWIND.CPP (Constructs Turbo Vision windows).

```
 1:   #define Uses_TApplication
 2:   #define Uses_TStatusLine
 3:   #define Uses_TStatusDef
 4:   #define Uses_TStatusItem
 5:   #define Uses_TMenuBar
 6:   #define Uses_TSubMenu
 7:   #define Uses_TMenuItem
 8:   #define Uses_TKeys
 9:   #define Uses_TRect
10:   #define Uses_TDeskTop
11:   #define Uses_TWindow
```

```
12:   #include <tv.h>
13:   #include <stdlib.h>
14:
15:   #define cmOpen 100
16:
17:   int Rnd(int low, int high);
18:   void RandomRect(TRect &r);
19:
20:   class TAnyApp: public TApplication
21:   {
22:   public:
23:     TAnyApp(): TProgInit(
24:       TAnyApp::initStatusLine,
25:       TAnyApp::initMenuBar,
26:       TAnyApp::initDeskTop) { }
27:     static TStatusLine *initStatusLine(TRect r);
28:     static TMenuBar *initMenuBar(TRect r);
29:     virtual void handleEvent(TEvent& event);
30:     void OpenWindow(void);
31:   };
32:
33:   // Return random int between low and high
34:   int Rnd(int low, int high)
35:   {
36:     return (low + random(high - low + 1));
37:   }
38:
39:   // Randomize coordinates in r. Assumes r.a.x = r.a.y = 0
40:   void RandomRect(TRect &r)
41:   {
42:     int x, y, xd2, yd2;
43:
44:     x = r.b.x;
45:     y = r.b.y;
46:     xd2 = (x / 2) - 8;
47:     yd2 = (y / 2) - 6;
48:     r.a.x = Rnd(0, xd2);
49:     r.a.y = Rnd(0, yd2);
50:     r.b.x = Rnd(xd2 + 16, x);
51:     r.b.y = Rnd(yd2 + 12, y);
52:   }
```

continues

Listing 18.2. continued

```
53:
54:   // Initialize application's status line
55:   TStatusLine *TAnyApp::initStatusLine(TRect r)
56:   {
57:     r.a.y = r.b.y - 1;
58:     return new TStatusLine(r,
59:       *new TStatusDef(0, 0xFFFF)+
60:       *new TStatusItem("", kbF10, cmMenu)+
61:       *new TStatusItem("~Open~ F3", kbF3, cmOpen)+
62:       *new TStatusItem("~Alt-X~ Exit", kbAltX, cmQuit)
63:     );
64:   }
65:
66:   // Initialize application's pull-down menus
67:   TMenuBar *TAnyApp::initMenuBar(TRect r)
68:   {
69:     r.b.y = r.a.y + 1;
70:     return new TMenuBar(r,
71:       *new TSubMenu("~F~ile", kbAltF)+
72:       *new TMenuItem("~O~pen", cmOpen, kbF3, hcNoContext, "F3")+
73:       *new TMenuItem("E~x~it", cmQuit, kbAltX, hcNoContext, "Alt-X")
74:     );
75:   }
76:
77:   // Respond to event messages
78:   void TAnyApp::handleEvent(TEvent& event)
79:   {
80:     TApplication::handleEvent(event);
81:     if (event.what == evCommand) {
82:       switch (event.message.command) {
83:         case cmOpen:
84:           OpenWindow();
85:           break;
86:         default:
87:           return;
88:       }
89:       clearEvent(event);
90:     }
91:   }
92:
93:   // Open a window of random size and location
```

```
 94:   void TAnyApp::OpenWindow()
 95:   {
 96:     TRect r;        // Rectangle for specifying window size
 97:     TWindow *w;     // Pointer to TWindow object
 98:
 99:     r = deskTop->getExtent();              // Get desktop size
100:     RandomRect(r);                         // Create random TRect
101:     w = new TWindow(r, "Window Title", 0); // Construct window
102:     deskTop->insert(w);                    // Insert into desktop
103:   }
104:
105:   main()
106:   {
107:     TAnyApp app;
108:     app.run();
109:     return 0;
110:   }
```

Compare ONEWIND's listing with DESK's and you'll find many similarities. Lines 1–13 define Uses_... symbols for the classes used in the program, and include the tv.h and stdlib.h header files.

Lines 17–18 prototype two functions that initialize a TRect object using random coordinate values. Purely to keep things interesting, ONEWIND calls these functions to open windows at random locations and sizes. See also lines 33–52.

TAnyApp, derived from TApplication, is nearly the same as in the previous listing, but adds two member functions: handleEvent() and OpenWindow(). The first is inherited; the second is new. (Following this book's convention, where possible, new functions are capitalized so you can tell them apart from most built-in library functions and inherited members.)

Member function initStatusLine() (lines 55–64) should also be familiar. Only line 61 is new. It adds the label Open, which you can select by pressing F3 or by clicking the mouse pointer. Similarly, initMenuBar() prepares the program's menu, and it too has only one new line (72). Most Turbo Vision programs have similar initStatusLine() and initMenuBar() member functions.

The program's two newcomers, handleEvent() (lines 78–91) and OpenWindow() (lines 94–103), demonstrate how Turbo Vision programs respond to event messages and how they can throw open a window. Function handleEvent() receives a single argument, a reference named event to a TEvent structure, declared in system.h as

```
struct TEvent
{
  ushort what;                // Describes event's nature (e.g. evCommand)
  union
  {
    MouseEventType mouse;  // Information about mouse events
    KeyDownEvent keyDown;  // Information about keyboard events
    MessageEvent message;  // Information about other message events
  };
  void getMouseEvent();    // Called by TProgram::getEvent()
  void getKeyEvent();      //      "     "    "     "     "     "
};
```

TEvent's what data member describes the kind of event that handleEvent() receives. This member equals a command constant such as evCommand, which indicates the event is a menu command. Other ev... constants such as evMouseDown and evKeyDown describe other event types.

Depending on what's value, the subsequent union contains one of three possible other structures: mouse, keyDown, or message. (You can find these struct declarations in system.h.)

Finally in TEvent, there are two member functions. Though unusual, structs can have member functions just like classes. Unlike classes, however, structs cannot use inheritance or polymorphism.

Getting back to ONEWIND, handleEvent()'s first job is to pass its TEvent parameter to TApplication::handleEvent() (see line 80), thus giving the ancestor class object the opportunity to handle its own events. After this step, the program inspects event.what. If this member equals evCommand, then event's message member (third in TEvent's union) holds the command value. Based on the command's value, a switch statement at lines 82–88 calls another function, which can be a member of TAnyApp or a plain function.

Lines 83–85, for instance, call the OpenWindow() member function for a command equal to cmOpen. Because this is not a standard command, as is cmQuit, the program defines at line 15 cmOpen as a unique value. Turbo Vision reserves command values ranges of 0–99 and 256–999. You may use any other values for your own command constants.

When handling event messages, you must observe two precautions. First, handleEvent() should simply return for any messages that it does not explicitly handle. Line 87, for example, returns for any command values that are not recognized. Second, call clearEvent as at line 89 for any event messages that you do handle. This TView member function sets event.what to evNothing, thus cancelling the event and preventing it from causing any subsequent actions.

> **NOTE:** The TCommandSet class accepts command values in the range of 0–255. This class is useful for specifying sets of commands, and for that reason, it's best to use 100 through 255 for your program's command constants.

That covers in general how Turbo Vision programs receive and respond to command events. ONEWIND's other new member function, OpenWindow() (lines 94–103), creates and displays a text-based window on the desktop. The member function declares two local variables, TRect r for sizing windows, and a pointer w for addressing a TWindow class object.

The first step in creating that object is to define its size and position. Line 99 begins the process by initializing r to the display's size. All TApplication derivatives inherit a deskTop pointer to a TDeskTop object. Calling that object's getExtent() member function (inherited from TView) as demonstrated here initializes r to the display's size. Line 100 calls RandomRect() to adjust r to a random size and location within these boundaries.

Armed with the adjusted TRect object, it's now possible to create a window. Line 101 does that by constructing a TWindow class object, passing to TWindow's constructor the initialized r, a title string, and a window number (zero for none). This step creates the window object, but it doesn't display the window or make it active. To do that, the window is inserted into the desktop by the statement

```
deskTop->insert(w);
```

Inserting objects into other objects is a common Turbo Vision technique. Member function insert() receives a pointer argument such as the TWindow pointer w, and adds the addressed object to its list of various other owned objects. Once an object is inserted into the desktop, the program can forget about it. The desktop takes care of manipulating the window and deleting the class object at the appropriate time.

Resist the urge to keep track of your own TWindow objects. Instead, insert them into the desktop and move on to other parts of your program. Event-driven programs don't require you to keep track of windows, *which operate independently in response to events as they occur.*

ONEWIND graphically demonstrates this concept. You can open one, two, a dozen, even hundreds of windows, shuffle them around (if you have a mouse), and perform other actions. These events are handled inside Turbo Vision, but of course, you can deal with some of these events yourself. The next program shows how.

Writing a Window Menu

Like real desks, a Turbo Vision desktop is easily buried under an avalanche of windows, documents, and other items. Multiwindow programs need a Window menu with commands that can tile, cascade, and perform other window-organization tasks.

Listing 18.3, WINDMENU.CPP, implements a complete Window menu (see Figure 18.6) with appropriate hot keys. If you use the Borland C++ text-based IDE, most of these commands and keys should be familiar. Keyboard lovers can press Ctrl+F5 and then use cursor keys with and without pressing a Shift key to move and size windows. Press F5 to zoom windows to full screen and back, F6 to select the next window (in creation order), and Alt+F3 to close the active window. You can also select windows by pressing Alt and the window's number. WINDMENU limits you to opening 12 windows, for no other reason than to show how that's done. You can open any number of windows within reasonable limits, but the Alt key can select only windows numbered 1 through 9. Also try the program's tile and cascade commands, which redisplay windows in neat sections or fanned out like a deck of cards.

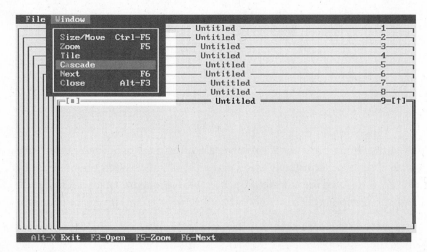

Figure 18.6. A Window menu manages WINDMENU's multiple windows.

Listing 18.3. WINDMENU.CPP (Implements a Window menu).

> **NOTE:** Change the drive letter and path in line 1 to refer to the Borland
> C++ class library resource.h header as installed on your system.

```
 1:  #include <C:\borlandc\classlib\include\resource.h>
 2:  #include <sets.h>              // Class library header
 3:
 4:  #define Uses_TApplication
 5:  #define Uses_TStatusLine
 6:  #define Uses_TStatusDef
 7:  #define Uses_TStatusItem
 8:  #define Uses_TMenuBar
 9:  #define Uses_TSubMenu
10:  #define Uses_TMenuItem
11:  #define Uses_TKeys
12:  #define Uses_TRect
13:  #define Uses_TDeskTop
14:  #define Uses_TWindow
15:  #define Uses_TCommandSet
16:  #include <tv.h>                // Turbo Vision header
17:
18:  #define cmOpen 100             // File:Open command id
19:  #define NOTITLE "Untitled"     // Untitled window title
20:  #define MAXWINDOWS 12          // Maximum number of windows
21:
22:  // Global variables
23:
24:  int numWindows;               // Number of windows now open
25:  BI_SetAsVector<short> windowNums(MAXWINDOWS); // Set of window #s
26:  TCommandSet tileCmdSet, openCmdSet;  // Various command-id sets
27:
28:  // The application class
29:  class TAnyApp: public TApplication
30:  {
31:  public:
32:    TAnyApp(int argc, char *argv[]);
```

continues

Listing 18.3. continued

```
33:    static TStatusLine *initStatusLine(TRect r);
34:    static TMenuBar *initMenuBar(TRect r);
35:    virtual void idle();
36:    void TileWindows(void);
37:    void CascadeWindows(void);
38:    virtual void handleEvent(TEvent& event);
39:    void OpenWindow(const char *wtitle);
40:    int GetWindowNumber(void);
41: };
42:
43: // The application window class
44: class TAnyWindow: public TWindow
45: {
46: public:
47:    TAnyWindow(const TRect &r, const char *wtitle, short wNum);
48:    virtual void close();
49:    void PutWindowNumber(void);
50: };
51:
52: // TAnyApp member functions
53:
54: // Construct TAnyApp object and initialize global variables
55: TAnyApp::TAnyApp(int argc, char *argv[])
56:    : TProgInit(
57:      TAnyApp::initStatusLine,
58:      TAnyApp::initMenuBar,
59:      TAnyApp::initDeskTop)
60: {
61:    tileCmdSet += cmTile;      // Init command-id sets for
62:    tileCmdSet += cmCascade;   //   enabling and disabling menu
63:    openCmdSet += cmOpen;      //   commands.
64:    if (argc > 1)
65:      OpenWindow(argv[1]);     // Open window from DOS prompt
66: }
67:
68: // Initialize application's status line
69: TStatusLine *TAnyApp::initStatusLine(TRect r)
70: {
71:    r.a.y = r.b.y - 1;
72:    return new TStatusLine(r,
```

```
73:       *new TStatusDef(0, 0xFFFF)+
74:       *new TStatusItem("", kbF10, cmMenu)+
75:       *new TStatusItem("~Alt-X~ Exit", kbAltX, cmQuit)+
76:       *new TStatusItem("~F3~-Open", kbF3, cmOpen)+
77:       *new TStatusItem("~F5~-Zoom", kbF5, cmZoom)+
78:       *new TStatusItem("~F6~-Next", kbF6, cmNext)
79:     );
80:   }
81:
82:   // Initialize application's pull-down menus
83:   TMenuBar *TAnyApp::initMenuBar(TRect r)
84:   {
85:     r.b.y = r.a.y + 1;
86:     return new TMenuBar(r,
87:       *new TSubMenu("~F~ile", kbAltF)+
88:       *new TMenuItem("~O~pen", cmOpen, kbF3, hcNoContext, "F3")+
89:           newLine()+
90:       *new TMenuItem("E~x~it", cmQuit, kbAltX, hcNoContext,
91:                     "Alt-X")+
92:       *new TSubMenu("~W~indow", kbAltW)+
93:       *new TMenuItem("~S~ize/Move", cmResize, kbCtrlF5,
94:           hcNoContext, "Ctrl-F5")+
95:       *new TMenuItem("~Z~oom", cmZoom, kbF5, hcNoContext, "F5")+
96:       *new TMenuItem("~T~ile", cmTile, kbNoKey)+
97:       *new TMenuItem("C~a~scade", cmCascade, kbNoKey)+
98:       *new TMenuItem("~N~ext", cmNext, kbF6, hcNoContext, "F6")+
99:       *new TMenuItem("~C~lose", cmClose, kbAltF3, hcNoContext,
100:                    "Alt-F3")
101:     );
102:   }
103:
104:  // Return true if view addressed by P is tileable
105:  Boolean IsTileable(TView *p, void *)
106:  {
107:    if ((p->options & ofTileable) == ofTileable)
108:      return True;
109:    else
110:      return False;
111:  }
112:
113:  // Perform various commands when event queue is empty
```

continues

Listing 18.3. continued

```
114:   void TAnyApp::idle()
115:   {
116:     TApplication::idle();
117:     if (deskTop->firstThat(IsTileable, NULL))
118:       enableCommands(tileCmdSet);
119:     else
120:       disableCommands(tileCmdSet);
121:   }
122:
123:   // Tile all open windows on desktop
124:   void TAnyApp::TileWindows(void)
125:   {
126:     TRect r = getExtent();
127:     r.grow(0, -1);
128:     r.move(0, -1);
129:     deskTop->tile(r);
130:   }
131:
132:   // Cascade all open windows on desktop
133:   void TAnyApp::CascadeWindows(void)
134:   {
135:     TRect r = getExtent();
136:     r.grow(0, -1);
137:     r.move(0, -1);
138:     deskTop->cascade(r);
139:   }
140:
141:   // Respond to event messages
142:   void TAnyApp::handleEvent(TEvent& event)
143:   {
144:     TApplication::handleEvent(event);
145:     if (event.what == evCommand) {
146:       switch (event.message.command) {
147:         case cmOpen:
148:           OpenWindow(NOTITLE);
149:           break;
150:         case cmTile:
151:           TileWindows();
152:           break;
153:         case cmCascade:
```

```
154:         CascadeWindows();
155:         break;
156:      default:
157:         return;
158:      }
159:    clearEvent(event);
160:   }
161: }
162:
163: // Open a new numbered window on the desktop
164: void TAnyApp::OpenWindow(const char *wtitle)
165: {
166:   TRect r = deskTop->getExtent();
167:   r.a.x = r.a.y = numWindows++;
168:   TAnyWindow *w = new TAnyWindow(r, wtitle, GetWindowNumber());
169:   deskTop->insert(w);
170:   if (numWindows >= MAXWINDOWS)
171:     disableCommands(openCmdSet);
172: }
173:
174: // Get next window number for a new window to use
175: int TAnyApp::GetWindowNumber(void)
176: {
177:   for (short i = 1; i <= MAXWINDOWS; i++)
178:     if (!windowNums.hasMember(i)) {
179:       windowNums.add(i);
180:       return i;
181:     }
182:   return wnNoNumber;
183: }
184:
185: // TAnyWindow member functions
186:
187: // Construct TAnyWindow objects
188: TAnyWindow::TAnyWindow(const TRect &r, const char *wtitle,
189:   short wNum):
190:   TWindow(r, wtitle, wNum),
191:   TWindowInit(TAnyWindow::initFrame)
192: {
193:   options |= ofTileable;
194: }
```

continues

Listing 18.3. continued

```
195:
196:    // Close window and return its number to global set
197:    void TAnyWindow::close()
198:    {
199:      TWindow::close();    // Call ancestor function to close
200:      PutWindowNumber();   // Return window's number to global set
201:      numWindows--;        // Reduce number of windows
202:      enableCommands(openCmdSet);  // Enable File:Open command
203:    }
204:
205:    // Make window's number available for future windows
206:    void TAnyWindow::PutWindowNumber(void)
207:    {
208:      if (1 <= number && number <= MAXWINDOWS)
209:        windowNums.detach(number);
210:    }
211:
212:    main(int argc, char *argv[])
213:    {
214:      TAnyApp app(argc, argv);
215:      app.run();
216:      return 0;
217:    }
```

WINDMENU uses the BI_SetAsVector<> template class from Borland's class library, requiring lines 1–2 to include file resource.h and sets.h. Unfortunately, Turbo Vision also has a resource.h file, and therefore, line 1 uses an explicit directory to load the proper file. Using Turbo Vision and the class library together is not officially supported by Borland, but seems to work. Still, beware of other possible conflicts.

At the end of the listing is a slightly modified main() function, which defines argc and argv parameters for importing command-line arguments. These are passed to TAnyApp's constructor.

Four global variables keep track of window numbers and various command sets. Variable numWindows (line 24) counts the number of open windows. Line 25 declares a set windowNums of short integer values, using the BI_SetAsVector<> class template. The set holds used window numbers so that new windows can be assigned unused values. Line 26 declares two more sets of the Turbo Vision class TCommandSet. Sets tileCmdSet and openCmdSet hold menu command values so these commands can be enabled (displayed normally) and disabled (displayed in grayed text) to indicate whether they are active.

When the program constructs its TApplication object, TAnyApp's constructor (lines 55–66) initializes the global TCommandSets (lines 61–63). The += operator is overloaded to insert command constant values into sets. The set titleCmdSet, for instance, is given a set of two commands: cmTile and cmCascade. The set openCmdSet has only one command value, cmOpen.

If a command-line argument is entered, the TAnyApp constructor calls OpenWindow() (line 65). This demonstrates how a program can optionally open a named file on startup. (Try running the program with a command such as **windmenu test.txt**. The file does not have to exist and is not actually opened.)

Class TAnyApp (lines 29–41) declares a constructor (line 32) and a few new members: idle(), TileWindows(), CascadeWindows(), and GetWindowNumber(). A second class, TAnyWindow (lines 44–50) is derived from TWindow. Create your own windows in a similar fashion. TAnyWindow inherits close() to perform additional work when windows are closed—in this example, deleting their numbers from the global windowNums set. To perform that action, the class also declares a new member function PutWindowNumber().

The program's status line (lines 69–80) and menu bar (lines 83–102) functions are similar to those you've seen before, but initMenuBar() is more complex. In the function, TSubMenu class objects (see lines 87 and 92) insert multiple menu names into the menu bar. Commands in those menus follow as TMenuItem objects. Line 89 demonstrates how to add a cosmetic separator line between commands (see Figure 18.7).

Any program has moments where there's not much to do. When no events are pending, Turbo Vision calls TApplication::idle(). Extend this function as at lines 114–121 to perform actions during your program's "quiet time." In this case, WINDMENU uses idle() to enable and disable various menu commands. Line 118 calls enableCommands, passing a TCommandSet variable to display those commands normally and allow them to be selected. Line 120 calls disableCommands, passing a similar variable to display commands in grayed text and prevent their selection. Line 117 determines whether any windows can be tiled, in which case the tileCmdSet commands are enabled. The desktop's firstThat() member function calls a nonmember function IsTileable (lines 105–111), which examines a window's options data member, returning True if a flag named ofTileable is set.

Figure 18.7. WINDMENU's File menu with a separator line dividing two commands.

To respond to menu command events, the program's handleEvent() member function (lines 142–161) operates as you've seen in other examples, but recognizes more commands. No matter how many menu commands there are in your program, you program them as shown here. In response to the Window menu's Tile command, handleEvent() calls TileWindows() (lines 124–130). For the Cascade command, the function calls CascadeWindows() (lines 133–139).

These two member functions are similar. Each begins by initializing a TRect object to the extent of the desktop, then calling the object's grow() and move() members to adjust that rectangle to outline the space between the menu bar and status line, keeping windows within these lines. Line 129 then calls the desktop's tile() member function to display windows in kitchen-floor-tile fashion. Line 138 calls cascade() to display windows cascaded on top of one another.

To make windows tileable, TAnyWindow's constructor (lines 188–194) sets bit ofTileable in the TWindow object's options data field. (This is the same flag checked by function IsTileable().)

When opening new windows, TAnyApp's OpenWindow() member function (lines 164–172) initializes a TRect object r, increments numWindows, and uses new to construct a TAnyWindow object. Function GetWindowNumber() returns a window number not in the global windowNums set (see lines 168 and 175–183). After inserting the new window into the desktop (line 169), the program calls disableCommands() for the openCmdSet (which contains only cmOpen) to disable the File|Open command. When the maximum number of windows is open, the command is disabled, preventing any more windows from being opened.

When a window is closed, Turbo Vision calls the window object's `close()` virtual member function. `TAnyWindow()` enhances the stock function by first calling the ancestor's `close()` (line 199). It then detaches the window's number from the global set (lines 200 and 206–210), decrements `numWindows`, and enables the File|Open command. (It doesn't matter if the command is already enabled.)

You should now have a clearer picture of how to write a Turbo Vision application with menus, commands, and multiple overlapping pop-up windows. So far, however, our windows have been as empty as a politician's promises. To display text in a window, Turbo Vision programs use another object called a view.

Window Views

A view is an object of class `TView`, and is typically inserted into a `TWindow` object to provide a window's visible content. Despite their obvious differences, windows and views are related through inheritance. The `Window` class derives in part from `TGroup`, which is itself derived from `TView`. In other words, not only can a window *own* a view, a window *is* a view, typically inserted into the desktop for display.

Figure 18.8 illustrates these concepts, showing that the desktop can own a window, which can own a view. At first, this layering of windows and views may seem overly complex, but it provides a sensible way for Turbo Vision programs to separate window-frame actions from the operations involving a window's contents.

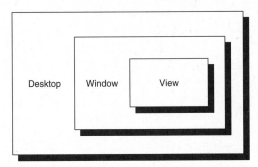

Figure 18.8. The desktop typically owns a window, which might own a view.

Listing 18.4, DISPLAY.CPP, demonstrates how to insert a view into a window. The program displays a few lines of text that you might recognize (see Figure 18.9). The program also demonstrates how to create a single, fixed window—an atypical technique that's especially useful in reducing a Turbo Vision program's complexity when you don't need multiple overlapping windows.

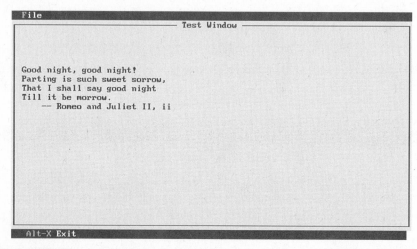

Figure 18.9. DISPLAY.CPP uses a view to display text in a window.

Listing 18.4. DISPLAY.CPP (Displays text in a window view).

```
 1:  #define Uses_TApplication
 2:  #define Uses_TStatusLine
 3:  #define Uses_TStatusDef
 4:  #define Uses_TStatusItem
 5:  #define Uses_TMenuBar
 6:  #define Uses_TSubMenu
 7:  #define Uses_TMenuItem
 8:  #define Uses_TKeys
 9:  #define Uses_TRect
10:  #define Uses_TDeskTop
11:  #define Uses_TWindow
12:  #include <tv.h>
13:
14:  class TAnyApp: public TApplication
```

```
15:   {
16:   public:
17:     TAnyApp();
18:     static TStatusLine *initStatusLine(TRect r);
19:     static TMenuBar *initMenuBar(TRect r);
20:   };
21:
22:   class TAnyWindow: public TWindow
23:   {
24:   public:
25:     TAnyWindow(const TRect &r, const char *wtitle, short wNum);
26:   };
27:
28:   class TAnyView: public TView
29:   {
30:   public:
31:     TAnyView(const TRect &r);
32:     virtual void draw();
33:   protected:
34:     char *textArray[5];
35:   };
36:
37:   // Construct TAnyApp object
38:   TAnyApp::TAnyApp(): TProgInit(
39:     TAnyApp::initStatusLine,
40:     TAnyApp::initMenuBar,
41:     TAnyApp::initDeskTop)
42:   {
43:     TRect r = getExtent();
44:     r.grow(0, -1);
45:     insert(new TAnyWindow(r, "Test Window", wnNoNumber));
46:   }
47:
48:   // Initialize application's status line
49:   TStatusLine *TAnyApp::initStatusLine(TRect r)
50:   {
51:     r.a.y = r.b.y - 1;
52:     return new TStatusLine(r,
53:       *new TStatusDef(0, 0xFFFF)+
54:       *new TStatusItem("", kbF10, cmMenu)+
55:       *new TStatusItem("~Alt-X~ Exit", kbAltX, cmQuit)
```

continues

Listing 18.4. continued

```
56:     );
57:   }
58:
59:   // Initialize application's pull-down menus
60:   TMenuBar *TAnyApp::initMenuBar(TRect r)
61:   {
62:     r.b.y = r.a.y + 1;
63:     return new TMenuBar(r,
64:       *new TSubMenu("~F~ile", kbAltF)+
65:       *new TMenuItem("E~x~it", cmQuit, kbAltX, hcNoContext, "Alt-X")
66:     );
67:   }
68:
69:   // Construct TAnyWindow objects
70:   TAnyWindow::TAnyWindow(const TRect &r, const char *wtitle,
71:     short wNum):
72:     TWindow(r, wtitle, wNum),
73:     TWindowInit(TAnyWindow::initFrame)
74:   {
75:     TRect cr = getClipRect();
76:     setState(sfShadow, False);
77:     cr.grow(-1, -1);
78:     TView *vp = new TAnyView(cr);
79:     insert(vp);
80:   }
81:
82:   // Construct window's view
83:   TAnyView::TAnyView(const TRect &r):
84:     TView(r)
85:   {
86:     growMode = gfGrowHiX + gfGrowHiY;
87:     textArray[0] = "Good night, good night!";
88:     textArray[1] = "Parting is such sweet sorrow,";
89:     textArray[2] = "That I shall say good night";
90:     textArray[3] = "Till it be morrow.";
91:     textArray[4] = "    -- Romeo and Juliet II, ii";
92:   }
93:
94:   // Display window-view's contents
95:   void TAnyView::draw()
```

```
96:   {
97:     TView::draw();
98:     for (int y = 0; y <= 4; y++)
99:       writeStr(1, y + 4, textArray[y], 1);
100:  }
101:
102:  main()
103:  {
104:    TAnyApp app;
105:    app.run();
106:    return 0;
107:  }
```

Most of DISPLAY is similar to other programs in this chapter. A major new addition is the TAnyView class (lines 28–35), derived from TView. Turbo Vision programs derive classes from TView in order to provide objects for window contents. The class declares a constructor (line 31) and it inherits and extends a virtual draw() member function (line 32), which Turbo Vision calls whenever the view needs to be updated. Line 34 stores a few char pointers to give the view something to display.

The concept of updating windows on demand in a draw() member function is vital. Event-driven programs must be able to re-create their displays at the drop of a hat. There's just no telling when another window might come along, obscure a view, and then move aside, requiring the formerly covered window to be redisplayed. In Turbo Vision, you don't display items in windows. You provide views that can draw themselves whenever necessary.

TAnyApp's constructor shows how to insert a single fixed-size window into an application. Lines 43–44 prepare a TRect object for the window's size and location. Line 45 then inserts a TAnyWindow object created by new. The TAnyWindow constructor (lines 70–80) calls getClipRect() inherited from TView to initialize r. The clipping rectangle represents a view's minimum space that needs drawing—at this stage, the entire window surface.

Line 76 calls setState to alter the window's state flag, which you should not access directly. Various sf... constants refer to bits in this flag. The statement here turns off the window's shadow, which provides a pseudo-three-dimensional effect for multiple overlapping windows, but looks odd for a fixed-size single window. (Remove the line, recompile, and run the program to see the problem, which might not be apparent on all types of video hardware.)

Line 78 constructs the window's view object, passing TRect cr to TAnyView's constructor. The resulting pointer is then inserted into the TAnyWindow object (line 79). This is all that's required to construct and attach a view to a window. The view wakes up as needed when an event requires the window to be updated. Also, because the window owns the view, it deletes the TView object when it's no longer needed, just as the desktop deletes its owned windows automatically.

The TAnyView class needs a minimum of two items. A constructor (lines 83–92) prepares the view's growMode flag, assigning gfGrowHiX + gfGrowHiY bits to enable the view to grow and shrink with its parent window. (The window in this example can't be resized, but you'll normally want views to change size along with their parent windows this way.) The TAnyView constructor also initializes the view's text pointers. In your own views, you can store whatever data you need to display. There aren't any fixed rules about what kind of data a view object can contain.

The second requirement for all TView objects is to provide a draw() member function (lines 95–100). First, call the ancestor's draw() (line 97), which erases the view by overwriting it with blank characters. After that step, a for loop calls writeStr() to display TAnyView's strings. You can't use printf() and similar output statements to display text in Turbo Vision windows. You must instead use one of several TView member functions, all of which begin with write.

For example, call writeChar() to display a single character, writeLine() to write one or more lines, or writeStr() to write a single string. You can find these functions documented in the Turbo Vision User's Guide, in Borland's online help, and in the views.h header file. Function writeStr() is declared as

```
void writeStr(short x, short y, const char *str, uchar color);
```

Set x and y to the window-relative coordinate where the first character of the string addressed by str should appear. Set color to a color palette number, which is not a color attribute, but an index that represents a relative color number. Set color to 1 as at line 99 to display text in its normal foreground color for this view. Zero represents the view's background color.

For most Turbo Vision applications, specifying colors is a simple matter of using an appropriate color index in a writeStr() or similar statement. Sophisticated applications can do more, however, as demonstrated next.

Color Palettes

A color value in Turbo Vision is merely an index into a table called a palette that determines actual visible colors. In Turbo Vision, you don't specify colors directly. You specify palette indexes to make one item's color the same as another item's color. The colors you see depend on your monitor type, video mode, and color scheme, selected automatically when a Turbo Vision program starts.

Color Mapping

A few modifications to DISPLAY.CPP (Listing 18.4) demonstrate how to use Turbo Vision color palettes. Copy DISPLAY.CPP to a new file named CDISPLAY.CPP. (The copied and edited CDISPLAY.CPP file is supplied on the book's accompanying diskette. If you have the disk, copy DISPLAY.CPP to a different filename such as XDISPLAY.CPP so you can make the changes as suggested in this section. Then replace CDISPLAY with XDISPLAY in the following instructions.) Load the copied file into your editor.

> **NOTE:** The following sections assume that you have a color monitor. On monochrome displays, you won't see all the effects mentioned here.

Change line 99 in the original listing to

```
writeStr(1, y + 4, textArray[y], y + 1);
```

Using `y + 1` rather than a literal color value selects color indexes 1 through 5 for each displayed string. Compile and run the modified program. (From DOS, enter **bcc cdisplay tv.lib.**) The text lines are now painted in different colors, except for the last two lines which are the same color for reasons that will become clear later.

To select an actual color, Turbo Vision maps palette index values, starting with the palette in the current view, and reaching back to the palettes in the view's owners. At the end of this chain is a grandaddy palette that contains the actual display attributes. (You can find these palettes in app.h by searching for the symbols `cpColor`, `cpBlackWhite`, and `cpMonochrome`.) Eventually, this mapping strategy translates palette indexes into actual color attributes. For convenience, palettes are defined as character strings like this:

```
#define myColors "\x3\x8\x9"
```

Another modification to CDISPLAY.CPP shows how to use a similar palette string to customize a view's colors. First, add this virtual member function declaration to class TAnyView, just after `virtual void draw();`:

```
virtual TPalette& getPalette() const;
```

Member function `getPalette()` is inherited from TView. The ancestor function simply returns null, indicating that no palette mapping is in effect for this view (thus the view uses the default color scheme). Implement a replacement `getPalette()` function like this:

```
#define cpAnyView "\x1\x2\x3\x4\x5"
TPalette& TAnyView::getPalette() const
{
  static TPalette palette(cpAnyView, sizeof(cpAnyView) - 1);
  return palette;
}
```

First, #define a palette mapping string such as cpAnyView. Pass this string and its size, minus one, to a TPalette constructor, and return the resulting static object. When Turbo Vision needs a color, it calls `getPalette()` and uses the returned TPalette object to map palette index entries. In this example, the colors are unchanged from before because the string "\x1\x2\x3\x4\x5" simply maps index 1 to 1, 2 to 2, 3 to 3, 4 to 4, and 5 to 5. (The first index digit in a palette is 1, not 0.)

To customize a view's colors, modify cpAnyView's mapping. For example, you could reverse the indexes, changing the string to

```
#define cpAnyView "\x5\x4\x3\x2\x1"
```

As you might expect, reversing the palette mappings reverses the colors of the text lines in the window. As you can see when you run the modified program, the view's background color is also affected. The background color uses the first palette index (1), which is now mapped to the owner's fifth palette entry. To keep the background the same, but change other text colors, map 1 to 1 like this:

```
#define cpAnyView "\x1\x3\x2\x1\x2"
```

Now the background returns to its default setting (Blue on color monitors) because the palette maps 1 to 1 (the first entry in the string). The other index mappings provide different colors for the view's strings.

When customizing colors, you must provide one value for each possible index that might be used. (Borland's Turbo Vision User's Guide lists the required number of palette entries and their uses for all views, windows, and so on.) Try this faulty string to see what happens if you don't provide enough entries in a palette:

```
#define cpAnyView "\x4"  // ???
```

The background of the window's view now changes to cyan because the first (and only) color palette index maps the background (always 1) to 4. Worse, all text except for the first line is now bright red. In text modes, the foreground might also be flashing. This effect indicates a palette mapping error caused by an output routine (writeStr() in this case) using an unmapped palette index.

Understanding Color Palettes

Keep in mind that all color palette translations occur at runtime and depend on a view's owners, not on class inheritance, a common misconception. Typically, a window owns a view, and the view's colors are therefore mapped to the window's. Those color indexes are in turn mapped to the window's owner, and so on, eventually reaching the program's TApplication object, where palette indexes are ultimately translated to actual color attributes. The application's desktop object, of type TDeskTop, defines a null palette, which Turbo Vision recognizes as the end of the line when mapping palette indexes.

Figure 18.10 shows how color mapping works in Turbo Vision. At the bottom of the figure is the palette returned by TAnyView's getPalette() member function. (If you are following along, change cpAnyView's string to "\x1\x3\x5\x6\x7" to make CDISPLAY.CPP match the figure.)

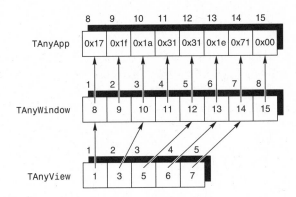

Figure 18.10. Color mapping in Turbo Vision.

The index values 1, 2, 3, 4, and 5 shown above the bottom row of boxes in Figure 18.10 are the palette indexes used in writeStr() and similar output member functions. The values inside the boxes are the palette string values to which the indexes are translated. To map an index to a visible color, Turbo Vision begins with the current view, in this case, TAnyView. Suppose, for example, a writeStr() statement specifies color index 3. That value is mapped to 5, the third entry in TAnyView's palette.

Because TAnyView is owned by a TAnyWindow object, the mapping continues. Turbo Vision takes the 5 it just obtained from TAnyView's palette and uses that value as an index into the owner's palette, in this case an object of type TAnyWindow. Finding a decimal 12 at the fifth entry in this palette, Turbo Vision performs another mapping, extracting the twelfth entry in the palette of the TAnyWindow object's owner, TAnyApp. Here the mapping stops, resulting in an actual attribute value of 0x31. (The top of the figure shows only a portion of the full attribute palette.) This attribute value is poked directly into the text screen's video display memory.

It should now be clear why, when you first modified the original DISPLAY.CPP, the last two lines of text came out in the same color. Those two lines were colored using TAnyWindow's index values 4 and 5, which map to 11 and 12 (see middle of Figure 18.10). The two indexes ultimately map to the same attribute, 0x31, in TAnyApp's palette.

Selecting Default Colors

The preceding sections assume you have a color display, and even though color monitors are becoming increasingly popular, not all CRTs are color. Commercial programs must provide the means to configure their displays for black and white (also called gray scale) and monochrome output.

In most cases, Turbo Vision detects the display hardware and initializes the screen accordingly. You should still give users the option to select an alternate configuration in case autodetection fails on an unusual display, or to allow people to configure a laptop's gray-scale monitor, or just to satisfy a whim. (Maybe somebody with a color display would *rather* see black and white text. Who knows?)

To change display modes, make sure system.h is included by adding this definition at the top of the program:

```
#define Uses_TScreen
```

Next, call TProgram's setScreenMode() member function (inherited by TApplication). To throw the display into black and white, for example, use the statement

```
setScreenMode(TDisplay::smBW80);
```

Constant smBW80 is one of several defined in the TDisplay class as a member of the enumeration videoModes:

```
class TDisplay
{
public:
...
  enum videoModes {
    smBW80    = 0x0002,
    smCO80    = 0x0003,
    smMono    = 0x0007,
    smFont8x8 = 0x0100
  };
...
};
```

Because videoModes is defined in TDisplay, you must specify the class name to access the values: smBW80 for black and white displays (useful for LCD screens), smCO80 for color displays, or smMono for monochrome display adapters. To the first two of these constants, add smFont8x8 to select 43- or 50-line modes on EGA and VGA displays. For example, for most VGA adapters, this selects 50-line color output:

```
setScreenMode(TDisplay::smCO80 + TDisplay::smFont8x8);
```

Dialogs and Controls

You are probably familiar with dialog boxes. They are special-purpose windows that programs can use to communicate with users. A typical dialog box contains controls—objects such as buttons, scroll bars, check boxes, and input areas—that are useful for selecting options, entering filenames, and other tasks. Dialogs are like bulletin boards where programs can post information and get input.

Standard Dialogs

Turbo Vision provides several ready-to-use dialogs. These standard dialogs include a message box, file selection dialogs, and a directory changer. Figure 18.11 shows Turbo Vision's file dialog, typically displayed by selecting a program's File|Open command.

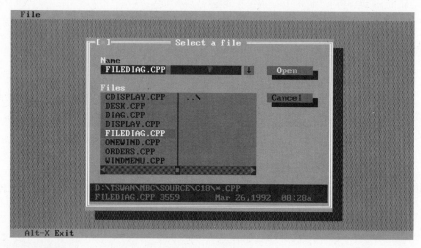

Figure 18.11. Turbo Vision's standard file dialog.

Listing 18.5, FILEDIAG.CPP, demonstrates how to add a file dialog to programs. It also uses two other related dialogs: one for naming new files to be saved to disk, and another to change directories.

Listing 18.5. FILEDIAG.CPP (Demonstrates standard file menu dialogs).

```
 1:  #define Uses_TApplication
 2:  #define Uses_TStatusLine
 3:  #define Uses_TStatusDef
 4:  #define Uses_TStatusItem
 5:  #define Uses_TMenuBar
 6:  #define Uses_TSubMenu
 7:  #define Uses_TMenuItem
 8:  #define Uses_TKeys
 9:  #define Uses_TRect
10:  #define Uses_TDeskTop
11:  #define Uses_TFileDialog
```

```
12:   #define Uses_TChDirDialog
13:   #define Uses_MsgBox
14:   #include <tv.h>
15:
16:   #define cmOpen 100
17:   #define cmSave 101
18:   #define cmSaveAs 102
19:   #define cmChangeDir 103
20:
21:   class TFileApp: public TApplication
22:   {
23:   public:
24:     TFileApp(): TProgInit(
25:       TFileApp::initStatusLine,
26:       TFileApp::initMenuBar,
27:       TFileApp::initDeskTop) { }
28:     static TStatusLine *initStatusLine(TRect r);
29:     static TMenuBar *initMenuBar(TRect r);
30:     void ChangeDir(void);
31:     void OpenFile(void);
32:     void SaveFile(void);
33:     void SaveFileAs(void);
34:     virtual void handleEvent(TEvent& event);
35:   };
36:
37:   // Initialize application's status line
38:   TStatusLine *TFileApp::initStatusLine(TRect r)
39:   {
40:     r.a.y = r.b.y - 1;
41:     return new TStatusLine(r,
42:       *new TStatusDef(0, 0xFFFF)+
43:       *new TStatusItem("", kbF10, cmMenu)+
44:       *new TStatusItem("~Alt-X~ Exit", kbAltX, cmQuit)
45:     );
46:   }
47:
48:   // Initialize application's pull-down menus
49:   TMenuBar *TFileApp::initMenuBar(TRect r)
50:   {
51:     r.b.y = r.a.y + 1;
52:     return new TMenuBar(r,
```

continues

817

Listing 18.5. continued

```
53:         *new TSubMenu("~F~ile", kbAltF)+
54:         *new TMenuItem("~O~pen...", cmOpen, kbNoKey)+
55:         *new TMenuItem("~C~lose", cmClose, kbNoKey)+
56:         *new TMenuItem("~S~ave", cmSave, kbNoKey)+
57:         *new TMenuItem("Save ~a~s...", cmSaveAs, kbNoKey)+
58:         *new TMenuItem("Change ~d~ir...", cmChangeDir, kbNoKey)+
59:         newLine()+
60:         *new TMenuItem("E~x~it", cmQuit, kbAltX, hcNoContext, "Alt-X")
61:     );
62: }
63:
64: // Execute change-directory dialog
65: void TFileApp::ChangeDir(void)
66: {
67:   TChDirDialog *cdp;
68:
69:   cdp = new TChDirDialog(cdNormal, 100);
70:   if (validView(cdp)) {
71:     deskTop->execView(cdp);
72:     delete cdp;
73:   }
74: }
75:
76: // Select existing filename using file dialog
77: void TFileApp::OpenFile(void)
78: {
79:   TFileDialog *fdp;
80:   char buffer[128];
81:
82:   fdp = new TFileDialog("*.*", "Select a file", "~N~ame",
83:       fdOpenButton, 101);
84:   if (validView(fdp)) {
85:     if (deskTop->execView(fdp) != cmCancel) {
86:       fdp->getFileName(buffer);
87:       messageBox(buffer, mfInformation + mfOKButton);
88:     }
89:     delete fdp;
90:   }
91: }
92:
```

```
 92:
 93:  // Save named file or reroute to SaveFileAs()
 94:  void TFileApp::SaveFile(void)
 95:  {
 96:  /*
 97:    if (fileIsNamed)        // If file was named previously
 98:      WriteFileToDisk();    // then write it to disk
 99:    else
100:  */
101:      SaveFileAs();         // Else default to SaveFileAs()
102:  }
103:
104:  // Save file under a new or selected name
105:  void TFileApp::SaveFileAs(void)
106:  {
107:    TFileDialog *fdp;
108:    char buffer[128];
109:
110:    fdp = new TFileDialog("*.*", "Save file as", "~N~ame",
111:                          fdOKButton, 102);
112:    if (validView(fdp)) {
113:      if (deskTop->execView(fdp) != cmCancel) {
114:        fdp->getFileName(buffer);
115:        messageBox(buffer, mfInformation + mfOKButton);
116:        // Check here if overwriting existing file
117:      }
118:      delete fdp;
119:    }
120:  }
121:
122:  // Respond to event messages
123:  void TFileApp::handleEvent(TEvent& event)
124:  {
125:    TApplication::handleEvent(event);
126:    if (event.what == evCommand) {
127:      switch (event.message.command) {
128:        case cmOpen:
129:          OpenFile();
130:          break;
131:        case cmSave:
132:          SaveFile();
```

continues

Listing 18.5. continued

```
133:            break;
134:          case cmSaveAs:
135:            SaveFileAs();
136:            break;
137:          case cmChangeDir:
138:            ChangeDir();
139:            break;
140:          default:
141:            return;
142:        }
143:        clearEvent(event);
144:     }
145:  }
146:
147:  main()
148:  {
149:     TFileApp app;
150:     app.run();
151:     return 0;
152:  }
```

The change directory dialog is simple to use, as member function ChangeDir() demonstrates (lines 65–74). Pointer cdp addresses a TChDirDialog object, constructed by new at line 69. The first argument selects dialog options, cdNormal for immediate use, cdNoLoadDir not to load the current directory (assuming you'll do so by other means), or cdHelpButton to display an additional Help button in the dialog if you have provided online help.

An if statement calls validView() to test whether the dialog is usable. (You can call validView(), a member of TProgram, to test any just created view. It returns true if the view is valid and ready for use.)

Line 71 shows how to execute a modal dialog—one that demands attention and must be closed before other program activities may continue. Calling the desktop's execView() member function executes the dialog, displaying it, handling all keyboard and mouse activity, closing the dialog window, and so on. This particular dialog also lets users change the current drive and directory.

After execView() returns, line 72 deletes the TChDirDialog object. The dialog was not inserted into a view; therefore, it must be deleted explicitly.

Displaying a standard file dialog is not much more difficult, but there's one additional step: extracting a filename selected in the dialog's Name input area (see Figure 18.11). The dialog is created and executed (lines 82–85), but this time execView()'s result is inspected. If the function returns cmCancel, the dialog's Cancel button was selected; otherwise, the dialog object holds a selected filename, obtained by calling its getFileName() member (line 86).

Global function messageBox(), declared in msgbox.h, displays the selected filename as confirmation. (A complete program would open the file and construct a window to display its contents.) To messageBox(), pass a string and one or more mf... constants, selecting various options. Line 87 specifies an information message box with an Ok button. An error message dialog might use the options mfError + mfCancelButton.

Member function SaveFileAs() displays one other standard dialog, typically used to select new filenames. The program's SaveFile() member function (lines 94–102) shows one way to default to this dialog if an unnamed file is saved. (The program simulates file I/O and doesn't actually open any files or write any data to disk. The commented-out statements at lines 96–100 suggest how you might save a real file in a complete application.)

Constructing Your Own Dialogs

Standard dialogs only go so far. Eventually, you'll want to create your own dialog boxes. The next several listings show how, implementing a fictitious pizza parlor order-entry application. Figure 18.12 shows the program's order dialog in action.

Before running the complete program, you need to enter and compile a support module with three dialog functions that you might find useful in your own code. Listing 18.6, diag.h, lists the function prototypes.

Listing 18.6. diag.h (Creates a header for DIAG.CPP).

```
1:  // diag.h -- Header file for dialog functions in diag.cpp
2:
3:  void AboutProgram(TDeskTop *deskTop, const char *programTitle);
4:  int Yes(TDeskTop *deskTop, const char *prompt);
5:  void ErrorMessage(TDeskTop *deskTop, int errNumber,
6:    const char *errMessage);
```

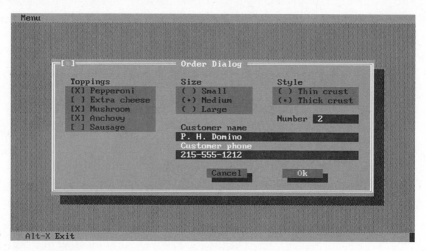

Figure 18.12. Order-entry dialog from the ORDERS program.

Listing 18.7, DIAG.CPP, implements the three functions: AboutProgram(), Yes(), and ErrorMessage(). The first of these displays an about-box dialog, typically used to show a program's copyright notice and author. The Yes() function prompts users for yes or no responses. ErrorMessage() displays (you guessed it) error messages. Figure 18.13 shows a sample about-box dialog, taken from the ORDERS demonstration.

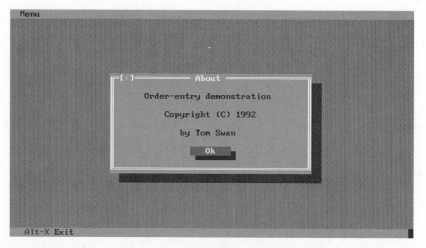

Figure 18.13. Sample about-box dialog from the ORDERS program.

Listing 18.7. DIAG.CPP (Implements auxiliary Turbo Vision dialog functions).

```
1:  // diag.cpp -- Dialog support functions
2:
3:  #define Uses_TDeskTop
4:  #define Uses_TDialog
5:  #define Uses_TStaticText
6:  #define Uses_TButton
7:  #include <tv.h>
8:  #include <stdio.h>
9:  #include <string.h>
10: #include <dos.h>
11: #include "diag.h"
12:
13: // Display "About Program" dialog box
14: void AboutProgram(TDeskTop *deskTop, const char *programTitle)
15: {
16:    TDialog *dp;  // Pointer to about-box dialog object
17:    TRect r(0, 0, 40, 11);  // Initial uncentered dialog size
18:    char buffer[128];
19:
20:    dp = new TDialog(r, "About");
21:    if (!dp)
22:      return;
23:    dp->options |= ofCentered;
24:    strcpy(buffer, "\n\003");
25:    strcat(buffer, programTitle);
26:    strcat(buffer, "\n \n");
27:    strcat(buffer, "\003Copyright (C) 1992\n \n");
28:    strcat(buffer, "\003by Tom Swan");
29:    r.grow(-1, -1);  // Shrink rectangle
30:    dp->insert(new TStaticText(r, buffer));
31:    dp->insert(new TButton(TRect(15, 8, 25, 10 ), "O~k~",
32:      cmOK, bfDefault));
33:    deskTop->execView(dp);
34:    delete dp;
35: }
36:
37: // Prompt user for Yes or No answer. Returns true for Yes
38: int Yes(TDeskTop *deskTop, const char *prompt)
```

continues

Listing 18.7. continued

```
39:    {
40:      TDialog *dp;
41:      TRect r(0, 0, 60, 7);
42:      char buffer[128];
43:      int result;
44:
45:      dp = new TDialog(r, "Please answer Yes or No");
46:      if (!dp)
47:        return 0;
48:      dp->options |= ofCentered;
49:      r.grow(-1, -2);
50:      strcpy(buffer, "\003");
51:      strcat(buffer, prompt);
52:      dp->insert(new TStaticText(r, buffer));
53:      dp->insert(new TButton(TRect(35, 4, 43, 6),
54:        "~N~o", cmNo, bfNormal));
55:      dp->insert(new TButton(TRect(17, 4, 26, 6),
56:        "~Y~es", cmYes, bfDefault));
57:      result = (deskTop->execView(dp) == cmYes);
58:      delete dp;
59:      return result;
60:    }
61:
62:    // Display error message
63:    void ErrorMessage(TDeskTop *deskTop, int errNumber,
64:      const char *errMessage)
65:    {
66:      TDialog *dp;
67:      TRect r(0, 0, 60, 7);
68:      char buffer[128];
69:
70:      sprintf(buffer, "Error %d", errNumber);
71:      dp = new TDialog(r, buffer);
72:      if (!dp)
73:        return;
74:      dp->options |= ofCentered;
75:      r.grow(-1, -2);
76:      strcpy(buffer, "\003");
77:      strcat(buffer, errMessage);
78:      dp->insert(new TStaticText(r, buffer));
```

```
79:    dp->insert(new TButton(TRect(20, 4, 40, 6),
80:      "O~k~", cmOK, bfNormal));
81:    sound(440);
82:    delay(200);
83:    nosound();
84:    deskTop->execView(dp);
85:    delete dp;
86: }
```

Each dialog in DIAG is constructed as an object of class TDialog (see lines 20, 45, and 71). Lines 31–32, 52–56, and 74–80 demonstrate how to insert control objects into dialog boxes. For example, the statement

```
dp->insert(new TStaticText(r, buffer));
```

inserts a TStaticText object into the dialog addressed by dp at the location specified by TRect object r, using the string buffer. This control simply displays a static string inside a dialog box. Other controls require different arguments, but are inserted similarly. This line:

```
dp->insert(new TButton(TRect(15, 8, 25, 10 ), "O~k~",
  cmOK, bfDefault));
```

inserts a TButton object, and shows a different way to pass a TRect object to a control's constructor.

After inserting various control objects into a dialog box, call the desktop's execView() member function to execute it. The function's return value equals the command identifier of the button used to close the dialog. (See lines 33, 57, and 84.) It's up to you whether to act on this value or ignore it.

A Sample Turbo Vision Application

The following program, Listing 18.8, ORDERS.CPP, isn't 100% complete (that would take too much space), but it should give you a running start toward finishing your own Turbo Vision applications. Before compiling this program, enter or locate on disk diag.h and DIAG.CPP from the preceding section. Then, enter or locate on disk ORDERS.CPP and compile with the DOS command **bcc orders diag tv.lib**. Or, list ORDERS.CPP and DIAG.CPP in an IDE project.

Listing 18.8. ORDERS.CPP (Demonstrates dialog boxes).

```
 1:  #define Uses_TApplication
 2:  #define Uses_TStatusLine
 3:  #define Uses_TStatusDef
 4:  #define Uses_TStatusItem
 5:  #define Uses_TMenuBar
 6:  #define Uses_TSubMenu
 7:  #define Uses_TMenuItem
 8:  #define Uses_TKeys
 9:  #define Uses_TRect
10:  #define Uses_TDeskTop
11:  #define Uses_TWindow
12:  #define Uses_TDialog
13:  #define Uses_TCheckBoxes
14:  #define Uses_TSItem
15:  #define Uses_TLabel
16:  #define Uses_TRadioButtons
17:  #define Uses_TInputLine
18:  #define Uses_TButton
19:  #include <tv.h>           // Turbo Vision header
20:  #include "diag.h"         // Various dialog functions
21:
22:  #define cmAbout 100       // Menu command ids
23:  #define cmSave  101
24:  #define cmOrder 102
25:
26:  #define ONUMBER_LEN 4     // Input string lengths
27:  #define ONAME_LEN 64
28:  #define OPHONE_LEN 64
29:
30:  // Order record to match order-entry dialog box
31:
32:  struct OrderInfo {
33:    ushort oToppings;              // Toppings check boxes
34:    ushort oSize;                  // Size radio buttons
35:    ushort oStyle;                 // Style radio buttons
36:    char oNumber[ONUMBER_LEN];     // Number input box
37:    char oName[ONAME_LEN];         // Customer name input box
38:    char oPhone[OPHONE_LEN];       // Customer phone input box
39:  };
40:
41:  OrderInfo order;          // Global order structure
```

```
42:    void NewOrder(void);      // Function to initialize order
43:
44:    // The application class
45:    class TOrderApp: public TApplication
46:    {
47:    public:
48:      TOrderApp();
49:      static TStatusLine *initStatusLine(TRect r);
50:      static TMenuBar *initMenuBar(TRect r);
51:      void SaveOrder(void);
52:      ushort OrderDialog(void);
53:      virtual void handleEvent(TEvent& event);
54:    };
55:
56:    // Initialize global order structure
57:    void NewOrder()
58:    {
59:      order.oToppings = 0;
60:      order.oSize = 0;
61:      order.oStyle = 0;
62:      order.oNumber[0] = 0;
63:      order.oName[0] = 0;
64:      order.oPhone[0] = 0;
65:    }
66:
67:    // Construct TOrderApp object and initialize global variables
68:    TOrderApp::TOrderApp()
69:      : TProgInit(
70:        TOrderApp::initStatusLine,
71:        TOrderApp::initMenuBar,
72:        TOrderApp::initDeskTop)
73:    {
74:    }
75:
76:    // Initialize application's status line
77:    TStatusLine *TOrderApp::initStatusLine(TRect r)
78:    {
79:      r.a.y = r.b.y - 1;
80:      return new TStatusLine(r,
81:        *new TStatusDef(0, 0xFFFF)+
82:        *new TStatusItem("", kbF10, cmMenu)+
```

continues

827

Listing 18.8. continued

```
83:        *new TStatusItem("~Alt-X~ Exit", kbAltX, cmQuit)
84:      );
85:  }
86:
87:  // Initialize application's pull-down menus
88:  TMenuBar *TOrderApp::initMenuBar(TRect r)
89:  {
90:    r.b.y = r.a.y + 1;
91:    return new TMenuBar(r,
92:     *new TSubMenu("~M~enu", kbAltM)+
93:      *new TMenuItem("~A~bout", cmAbout, kbNoKey)+
94:      *new TMenuItem("~S~ave", cmSave, kbNoKey)+
95:      *new TMenuItem("~O~rder", cmOrder, kbNoKey)+
96:        newLine()+
97:      *new TMenuItem("E~x~it", cmQuit, kbAltX, hcNoContext,"Alt-X")
98:      );
99:  }
100:
101:  // Dummy "save order" function
102:  void TOrderApp::SaveOrder(void)
103:  {
104:    if (Yes(deskTop, "Save this order?"))
105:      NewOrder();  // Clear dialog if Yes button selected
106:  }
107:
108:  // Create and execute order-entry dialog
109:  ushort TOrderApp::OrderDialog(void)
110:  {
111:    TDialog *dp;    // Pointer to dialog object
112:    TView *vp;      // Pointer to view object for creating controls
113:    TRect r;        // Miscellaneous rectangle for sizing
114:    ushort result;  // Value of button used to close dialog
115:
116:    // Create dialog object
117:    dp = new TDialog(TRect(0, 0, 64, 15), "Order Dialog");
118:    if (!dp)
119:      return cmCancel;
120:    dp->options |= ofCentered;  // Center dialog window
121:
122:    // Create toppings check boxes
```

```
123:    vp = new TCheckBoxes(TRect(3, 3, 21, 8),
124:      new TSItem("Pepperoni",
125:      new TSItem("Extra cheese",
126:      new TSItem("Mushroom",
127:      new TSItem("Anchovy",
128:      new TSItem("Sausage",NULL) )))));
129:    dp->insert(vp);
130:    dp->insert(new TLabel(TRect(3, 2, 21, 3), "Toppings", vp));
131:
132:    // Create Size radio buttons
133:    vp = new TRadioButtons(TRect(25, 3, 40, 6),
134:      new TSItem("Small",
135:      new TSItem("Medium",
136:      new TSItem("Large", NULL) )));
137:    dp->insert(vp);
138:    dp->insert(new TLabel(TRect(25, 2, 40, 3), "Size", vp));
139:
140:    // Create Style radio buttons
141:    vp = new TRadioButtons(TRect(44, 3, 61, 5),
142:      new TSItem("Thin crust",
143:      new TSItem("Thick crust", NULL) ));
144:    dp->insert(vp);
145:    dp->insert(new TLabel(TRect(44, 2, 61, 3), "Style", vp));
146:
147:    // Create Number, Name, and Phone input boxes
148:    vp = new TInputLine(TRect(52, 6, 61, 7), ONUMBER_LEN);
149:    dp->insert(vp);
150:    dp->insert(new TLabel(TRect(44, 6, 51, 7), "Number", vp));
151:
152:    vp = new TInputLine(TRect(25, 8, 61, 9), ONAME_LEN);
153:    dp->insert(vp);
154:    dp->insert(new TLabel(TRect(25, 7, 61, 8),
155:      "Customer name", vp));
156:
157:    vp = new TInputLine(TRect(25, 10, 61, 11), OPHONE_LEN);
158:    dp->insert(vp);
159:    dp->insert(new TLabel(TRect(25, 9, 61, 10),
160:      "Customer phone", vp));
161:
162:    // Create Cancel and Ok buttons
163:    vp = new TButton(TRect(30, 12, 40, 14),
```

continues

Listing 18.8. continued

```
164:        "Cancel", cmCancel, bfNormal);
165:    dp->insert(vp);
166:    vp = new TButton(TRect(45, 12, 55, 14),
167:        "O~k~", cmOK, bfDefault);
168:    dp->insert(vp);
169:
170:    // Execute dialog
171:    dp->setData(&order);
172:    result = deskTop->execView(dp);
173:    if (result != cmCancel)
174:      dp->getData(&order);
175:    delete dp;
176:    return result;
177: }
178:
179: // Respond to event messages
180: void TOrderApp::handleEvent(TEvent& event)
181: {
182:    TApplication::handleEvent(event);
183:    if (event.what == evCommand) {
184:      switch (event.message.command) {
185:        case cmAbout:
186:          AboutProgram(deskTop, "Order-entry demonstration");
187:          break;
188:        case cmSave:
189:          ErrorMessage(deskTop, 999, "Feature not implemented");
190:          break;
191:        case cmOrder:
192:          if (OrderDialog() == cmCancel)
193:            NewOrder();     // Clear dialog if cancelled
194:          else
195:            SaveOrder();    // Else call dummy save function
196:          break;
197:        default:
198:          return;
199:      }
200:      clearEvent(event);
201:    }
202: }
203:
```

```
204:  main()
205:  {
206:    TOrderApp app;
207:    app.run();
208:    return 0;
209:  }
```

Most Turbo Vision techniques used in ORDERS have been covered elsewhere in this chapter. New sections show how to use the dialog-box functions in module DIAG (Listings 18.6 and 18.7), and how to send information to and from dialog controls.

Line 104 demonstrates DIAG's Yes() function, which displays a message and returns true if the dialog box's Yes button is selected. To see a sample of this dialog box, use the program's Menu|Order command and press Enter. Select either the Yes or No button to close the resulting dialog.

See line 186 for an example of DIAG's AboutProgram() function, which displays the information-only dialog shown in Figure 18.13. Line 189 calls DIAG's ErrorMessage() dialog to display an error message, in this case informing users that the program's Menu|Save command isn't yet implemented. (Try using that command to see and hear a sample error message.)

The program's main feature is its order-entry dialog, illustrated in Figure 18.12. Though more complex, the dialog uses the identical techniques you've seen before, but with one major difference. A struct named OrderInfo stores values represented by the dialog's controls (see lines 32–39).

Function NewOrder() (lines 57–65) zeros a global order structure of type OrderInfo (line 41). The order and types of members in the OrderInfo structure match the order and types of controls in the program's dialog. This fact is vital. A dialog's associated data structure *must* match the dialog's controls exactly, or data might be copied to unprotected memory locations. (If Turbo Vision has an Achilles heel, this is it. Any errors in a dialog's structure are likely to cause major bugs.)

Table 18.3 lists Turbo Vision's control class types and their associated data types. Use these types to declare members of a dialog's data structure for holding control values.

Table 18.3. Control class data structure member types.

Class	Associated data type
TButton	none
TCheckBoxes	ushort
TInputLine	char string[n]
TLabel	none
TRadioButtons	ushort
TStaticText	none

Member function OrderDialog() (lines 109–177) constructs the order-entry dialog using the techniques you examined earlier in the DIAG module. After inserting various controls, the program calls the dialog's setData() member function (line 171), passing the address of the order structure. Turbo Vision copies the members of this structure to the dialog's controls in the order in which those controls were inserted into the dialog box. The controls, then, first appear with the values stored in order.

After calling execView() to execute the dialog (line 172), if that function did not return cmCancel (indicating that the user selected the Cancel button), member function getData() is called to copy the control values back to order. After this step, any information entered into dialog controls is now stored in order, which the program could print, save to a disk file, or use in any other way.

Summary

- Turbo Vision is a class library for constructing complex software interfaces with pull-down menus, overlapping windows, dialog boxes, and other modern conveniences.

- Turbo Vision is designed to work best in text mode, and to mirror the capabilities of graphical user interfaces such as Microsoft Windows.

- Under the hood, a Turbo Vision program is event driven—that is, driven by messages sent in response to events such as mouse clicks and keyboard keystokes.

- The Turbo Vision desktop typically consists of three main players: a menu bar at the top, a status line at the bottom, and a blank desktop surface in the middle where other items appear.

- To create a window, in which you might display information, derive a class from TWindow. In response to a menu command (or some other event), create an object of your TWindow derived class and insert it into the desktop. You don't have to keep track of window objects. The desktop does that for you.

- Define a handleEvent() member function to intercept messages relating to events.

- Multiwindow programs need a **W**indow menu to help users organize a potentially messy desktop. Turbo Vision provides window cascading and tiling features that put any number of windows back into formation. (See Listing 18.3.)

- A TView object is used to provide TWindow objects text or other data to display. To create a view, derive a class from TView, construct an object of your derived class, and insert it into a TWindow object (which is typically inserted into the desktop).

- Colors in Turbo Vision applications are represented by index numbers. Palettes of indexed color values are mapped to a view's owners' palettes, eventually translating relative indexes into actual display attributes. Colors in Turbo Vision are not hues; they are relative values that you can use to paint one display item using the same color scheme as another item.

- Normally, Turbo Vision programs automatically select an appropriate display type and color scheme. You can modify these startup parameters, however, and you can select black-and-white displays, 43- and 50-line modes, and so forth.

- Dialogs are like bulletin boards. They give programs a handy place to communicate with users. Turbo Vision dialogs are represented by TDialog class objects. Ready-to-use dialogs are provided to select filenames, change directories, and display messages.

- You can construct your own dialogs and insert into them a variety of control objects such as buttons, labels, check boxes, and so forth. Each of these controls has an associated Turbo Vision class.

Assembly Language Optimizations

Despite advances in high-level languages such as C and C++, assembly language continues to play an important role in computer programming. Only with assembly language can a programmer communicate with a computer on its own level—through the language of the processor, often called *machine language*.

Most compiled Borland C++ programs run well enough straight from the compiler; they don't need any help from assembly language. There are times, however, when a sprinkling of low-level code can improve a high-level C++ application. Assembly language can help you

- Optimize selected critical statements, those on which a program depends most heavily.

- Access hardware at the bit level.

- Implement interrupt service routines (ISRs).

These suggestions are not the exclusive domain of assembly language but are areas where a little assembly language often comes in handy. Borland C++ offers you three ways to use assembly language with C++ programs:

- You can compile a program to an assembly language file.

- You can insert inline asm statements into a program's text.

- You can write external modules assembled by Turbo Assembler (TASM).

This chapter examines these choices and shows examples of each.

C Function Anatomies

When using assembly language, you take over the compiler's usual task of translating C and C++ statements into machine code. By assuming the role of compiler, you can gain a great deal of control over the final results, but you must accept a tremendous responsibility. Writing assembly language programs is like cooking with atoms and molecules rather than eggs and flour. An assembly language programmer is a kind of software chemist. You can mix processor instructions in whatever way you wish, but it's up to you to ensure a palatable outcome.

> **NOTE:** This chapter assumes you are familiar with 80x86 assembly language mnemonics, general purpose registers, segment registers, the stack pointer, bits, bytes, and other low-level concerns. If you are lost already, you might need to study an assembly language tutorial and come back to this chapter another time. (See Bibliography.)

Compiling to Assembly Language

Before jumping into your own assembly language functions, it's helpful to look at the code Borland C++ generates. You can also use this method to examine the compiler's output, whether for curiosity's sake or to investigate wayward statements on their most fundamental levels.

Normally, the compiler converts C and C++ statements directly into processor instructions. Using option -B with the command-line compiler translates a program into an assembly language text file. For a program named MYPROG.CPP, the command **bcc -B myprog** creates MYPROG.ASM with the compiled output in assembly language form. After compiling, BCC runs TASM to assemble MYPROG.ASM into object code, after which it deletes MYPROG.ASM. You can also insert the line

```
#pragma inline
```

in a program module to achieve the same result. (The #pragma directive gives a private command such as inline to the compiler.)

In the past, the only reason to use the -B option was to assemble inline assembly language statements inserted directly into a C or C++ program. Today, the compiler has its own built-in assembler, obsoleting -B except for compiling older programs. You can also use -B with -Ename, where name identifies an alternate assembler such as the Microsoft Macro Assembler (MASM).

A related and potentially more valuable option, -S, also generates assembly language output, but does not run TASM and does not delete the created .ASM file. Examining the instructions in this file is a great way to learn how the compiler converts high-level statements to low-level processor code. You can also modify the assembly language text before assembling, perhaps to experiment with a low-level optimization. For a program file MYPROG.CPP, type **bcc -S myprog** to create MYPROG.ASM. Edit or examine this file, then with TASM.EXE in the current path (it's usually stored in C:\BORLANDC\BIN), finish compiling with the command **bcc myprog.asm**.

Functions that Return *void*

Use the -S option to compile a program with a simple C function that returns void. Enter Listing 19.1, VOIDF.CPP, and at a DOS prompt type **bcc -S voidf**. Load the resulting VOIDF.ASM file into your editor.

Ignoring several miscellaneous lines at the beginning of the generated assembly language file (lines which declare macros, arrange the program's segments, and include debugging information), Listing 19.2, VOIDF.ASM, shows the resulting VOIDF.ASM file's assembly language commands.

Listing 19.1. VOIDF.CPP (Compile this program using the -s option).

```
 1:  #include <stdio.h>
 2:
 3:  void f(void);
 4:
 5:  main()
 6:  {
 7:    f();
 8:    return 0;
 9:  }
10:
11:  void f(void)
12:  {
13:    int x = 123;
14:    printf("x == %d\n", x);
15:  }
```

> **NOTE:** Don't bother entering or assembling VOIDF.ASM. You can more easily create your own unmodified copy by compiling Listing 19.1 with the -s option. On disk, VOIDFM.ASM (M for modified) contains Listing 19.2. I added the explanatory comments to the right of most lines.

Listing 19.2. VOIDF.ASM (Contains commented assembly language for VOIDF.CPP).

```
 1:  _TEXT   segment byte public 'CODE'     ; Beginning of code segment
 2:      ;
 3:      ;   main()
 4:      ;
 5:          assume  cs:_TEXT               ; Assembler directive
 6:  _main   proc    near                   ; Start of main() function
 7:          push    bp                     ; Save base pointer register
 8:          mov     bp,sp                  ; Set bp equal to sp
 9:      ;
10:      ;   {
```

```
11:      ;        f();
12:      ;
13:          call    near ptr @f$qv        ; Call function f()
14:      ;
15:      ;     return 0;
16:      ;
17:          xor     ax,ax                 ; Set return value ax to 0
18:          jmp     short @1@58           ; A useless instruction!
19: @1@58:
20:      ;
21:      ;     }
22:      ;
23:          pop     bp                    ; Restore base pointer
24:          ret                           ; Return to caller
25: _main   endp                          ; End of main() function
26:      ;
27:      ;     void f(void)
28:      ;
29:          assume  cs:_TEXT              ; Assembler directive
30: @f$qv   proc    near                  ; Start of function f()
31:          push    bp                    ; Save base pointer register
32:          mov     bp,sp                 ; Set bp equal to sp
33:          sub     sp,2                  ; Reserve stack space for x
34:      ;
35:      ;     {
36:      ;       int x = 123;
37:      ;
38:          mov     word ptr [bp-2],123   ; Assign 123 to int x
39:      ;
40:      ;       printf("x == %d\n", x);
41:      ;
42:          push    word ptr [bp-2]       ; Push value of x
43:          mov     ax,offset DGROUP:s@   ; Push address of string
44:          push    ax                    ;   s stored in data seg
45:          call    near ptr _printf      ; Call printf() function
46:          pop     cx                    ; Remove item from stack
47:          pop     cx                    ; Remove item from stack
48:      ;
49:      ;     }
50:      ;
51:          mov     sp,bp                 ; Reset stack pointer
```

continues

Listing 19.2. continued

```
52:              pop      bp                       ; Restore bp register
53:              ret                               ; Return to caller
54: @f$qv        endp
55:              ?debug   C E9                     ; Debugging information
56:              ?debug   C FA00000000             ;  for Turbo Debugger
57: _TEXT        ends
58: _DATA        segment word public 'DATA'        ; Global data segment
59: s@           label    byte                     ; Label for printf() string
60:              db       'x == %d'                ; The printf() string
61:              db       10                       ; A newline character
62:              db       0                        ; String null terminator
63: _DATA        ends                              ; End of global data seg
64: _TEXT        segment byte public 'CODE'        ; Keeps segments in order,
65: _TEXT        ends                              ;  or possibly extraneous
66:              public   _main                    ; Export _main symbol
67:              public   @f$qv                    ; Export function f()
68:              extrn    _printf:near             ; Import printf() function
69: _s@          equ      s@                       ; Not used in this code
70:              end                               ; End of listing
```

The generated text shows key instructions that you must provide when writing your own assembly language functions. The main() function begins at line 6 with a proc directive, which assigns label _main to this location, a near address. (In other memory models, a function's address might be far.) In assembly language, public symbols such as main have a leading underscore (_main). Line 7 saves the value of register bp on the stack and then sets bp equal to sp, the stack pointer. Register bp addresses items stored on the stack and is typically assigned the stack pointer on entry to a function.

Line 13 calls the program's f() function, specifying a near address at label @f$qv. The compiler invents such labels as needed. Notice that the original C++ text appears as comments at lines 9–12. These comments appear above the related assembly language.

Lines 17–19 implement main()'s return statement. Exclusive ORing (xor) register ax with itself sets that register to zero, the value to be returned (see line 15). The jmp instruction at line 18 is obviously useless—it merely jumps to the immediately following address. As this demonstrates, nonsense instructions sometimes creep into the compiler's output. In critical cases, you can optimize these statements by rewriting them in assembly language (as you'll see later in this chapter).

Finally, main() ends at lines 23–24, restoring the originally saved value of bp (undoing the effect of line 7) and returning to main()'s caller—that is, the startup code that's linked to this compiled module to create the finished .EXE code file.

That brings you to function f() (lines 30–54). Because other functions might use register bp, the first duty is to save this register by pushing it onto the stack (line 31). After that, to address this function's local variables and any parameters (this example has none), the program assigns stack pointer sp to bp (line 32). These are the identical steps taken at the start of main(). Most functions begin similarly.

Line 33 lowers the stack pointer by two, reserving that many bytes on the stack for the function's int x local variable (line 36). A mov instruction at line 38 deposits the literal value 123 into this space. Notice how the statement uses bp to address the local variable.

The function's printf() statement comes next at lines 42–47. The code pushes x onto the stack along with the address of string s, stored in the program's data segment. This string is the literal one that appears in VOIDF.CPP (line 14 in Listing 19.1, line 40 in Listing 19.2). The compiler collects all such strings and stores them in the program's data segment. It also invents labels such as s to address unnamed objects.

With the proper arguments on the stack, the assembled function next calls printf() at line 45. By convention, the library function's name in assembly language is _printf. Upon returning from printf(), the two pop instructions at lines 46–47 remove the arguments pushed onto the stack before the call, a design known as the *C calling convention*.

NOTE: In the C calling convention, compiled programs push arguments onto the stack before calling a function, after which the caller removes the arguments to prevent the stack from overflowing. In the alternate Pascal calling convention (used, for example, by Microsoft Windows programs), the called function removes arguments from the stack. The C calling convention permits passing a variable number of arguments to a function, but bloats the object code with stack adjustment instructions. The Pascal calling convention reduces code file size, but permits passing only fixed numbers of arguments to functions.

Function f() ends at lines 51–53 by first setting the stack pointer equal to bp, which undoes the reservation of stack space back at line 33. At this point, int x ceases to exist. Line 52 restores the saved bp register, after which a ret instruction returns to f()'s caller.

Among other duties, the remaining lines specify debugging information (lines 55–56), store the printf()'s literal string in the program's data segment (lines 59–62), export public symbols (lines 66–67), and import the external library printf() function (line 68).

Even in this simple example, there's a lot going on below the surface! You should be getting the idea that digging into compiled output is painstaking work. Be sure the results are worth the effort before embarking on similar journeys into your program's lower levels.

Functions that Return Values

When a function returns a value, it does so internally in one of several ways, passing word values in ax, byte values in al. Functions pass far pointers in registers dx:ax with dx holding the segment and ax holding the offset address components. Floating-point values are passed on the 80x87 math coprocessor stack. Structures are passed directly on the stack. Arrays are passed by address.

Many variations of return-value schemes exist. To determine exactly how to handle a specific return type, compile a short example using the -S option and examine the resulting assembly language. It's pointless to memorize a lot of return-value rules, which might change in future compiler releases. Always examine the actual output of a sample function before making any assumptions about how low-level compiled code works.

Class Member Functions

Class objects and their class member functions complicate the assembly language story. Take a look at a sample program with a simple class, Listing 19.3, CLASSF.CPP. Compile with the command **bcc -S classf** and examine the resulting assembly language statements in CLASSF.ASM.

Listing 19.3. CLASSF.CPP (Compile with the -s option).

```
 1:  #include <stdio.h>
 2:
 3:  class TClass {
 4:  public:
 5:    int x;
 6:    void SetX(int n);
 7:    int GetX(void);
 8:  };
 9:
10:  main()
11:  {
12:    TClass q;
13:
14:    q.SetX(123);
15:    printf("q.GetX() == %d\n", q.GetX());
16:    return 0;
17:  }
18:
19:  void TClass::SetX(int n)
20:  {
21:    x = n;
22:  }
23:
24:  int TClass::GetX(void)
25:  {
26:    return x;
27:  }
```

Sample class TClass at lines 3–8 declares one public data member (int x) and two member functions to set and get the data member's value. In assembly language, member function SetX() looks like this:

```
push    bp                      ; Save bp
mov     bp,sp                   ; Address stack with bp
push    si                      ; Save si, used next
mov     si,word ptr [bp+4]      ; Address object via 'this' with si
mov     ax,word ptr [bp+6]      ; Assign function parameter to ax
mov     word ptr [si],ax        ; Assign ax to object's x member
pop     si                      ; Restore si
pop     bp                      ; Restore bp
ret                             ; Return to caller
```

As usual, instructions save bp and set the register equal to the stack pointer sp for addressing values on the stack, in this case, parameter int n (line 19 in Listing 19.3). After saving si, the program uses bp to set si to the this pointer, passed to all nonstatic class member functions. The this pointer addresses the object for which a statement called a nonstatic member function—in this case, the object q declared back at line 12 in main(). After preparing si to this's value, the program assigns to ax the value at [bp+6], which addresses parameter n. The program then assigns this value to word ptr [si], an address reference to the first word of object q (addressed by si). Finally, the program restores registers si and bp before the function returns.

The important lesson to remember is that nonstatic class member functions receive a this pointer to the object for which a statement called those functions. In assembly language, it's up to you to use this to locate objects in memory.

Writing Inline BASM code

Now that you've investigated a few sample programs in assembly language, you can begin to think about writing your own. You can proceed in two ways. The first is to use the built-in assembler (BASM) to insert inline assembly language statements in your program's text. The second is to write external modules for assembling separately with TASM into object-code files you can link with your compiled program. This section explains BASM's ins and outs. It's by far the easiest way to add assembly language to C and C++ programs.

Despite its attractive ease of use, however, BASM lacks some of TASM's advanced capabilities:

- BASM does not have macros.

- BASM cannot assemble 80386- or 80486-specific instructions.

- BASM does not recognize ideal mode, TASM's enhanced assembly language syntax.

- BASM has only a limited set of assembler directives for reserving memory.

If you need these features, you must use the stand-alone TASM assembler. Keep in mind, however, that you can use the C and C++ compilers to deal with many situations that require advanced TASM commands in a stand-alone assembly language program. It's probably best, for example, to reserve space for variables using C and C++ declarations, to which you can refer by name in assembly language statements. If you need to assemble 80386 or 80486 instructions, however, or if you prefer to use ideal mode, you must use TASM.

NOTE: If your assembly language statements use any 80186 or 80286 instructions, use the -1 option when compiling with BCC. If your statements use any protected mode 80286 instructions, use the -2 option.

Writing *asm* Statements

An inline asm statement injects one or more processor instruction bytes directly into a program's compiled output. Use asm statements to insert snippets of assembly language, perhaps to optimize a key statement or to access hardware registers. An asm statement has the general form

```
asm mnemonic [operands] [;]
```

The asm keyword comes first, followed by an assembly language mnemonic such as mov or shl. Any required operands come next—one or more register names, for example, or an address reference. An optional semicolon ends the statement, which may also end with a new line. Unlike stand-alone assembly language, semicolons do not begin comments. In TASM modules, for instance, this statement ends with a comment:

```
mov  ax, cx   ; Set ax equal to cx
```

The equivalent BASM statement is a little different:

```
asm  mov  ax, cx;  /* Set ax equal to cx */
```

You must use C or C++ comments to document asm statements. A semicolon terminates the statement, but is optional. You could write

```
asm  mov  ax, cx   /* Set ax equal to cx */
```

You can also use C++ comments:

```
asm  mov  ax, cx   // Set ax equal to cx
```

Surround multiple asm statements with braces. Each asm statement is a C statement, and the rules for forming compound statements apply to asm as they do for if, while, and other constructions:

```
asm {
  push bp        // Save bp on stack
  mov  bp,sp     // Set bp equal to sp
  ...            // Insert other asm statements here
  pop bp         // Restore bp
}
```

You can use semicolons to separate multiple asm statements on one line and save a little space in your program's text. Use this popular trick to push and pop selected registers:

```
asm {
  push ax; push bx; push cx; push dx
  ...  // Insert other statements here
  pop dx; pop cx; pop bx; pop ax
}
```

Global asm statements—those appearing outside of any function—assemble to the program's data segment. There's not much call for the technique, but if you want to inject some code into a data segment, you can do so. Just write your asm statements outside of any function implementations.

Local asm statements—those appearing inside a function implementation—are assembled by BASM into the code stream at that position. The compiler prevents most conflicts between BASM's output and nearby C++ statements, but it's wise to examine the before and after compiled output using the -S option to ensure success.

Optimizing Functions

The primary reason for adding assembly language to C++ programs is to improve performance. First, using your own tests—or even better, profiling a program with Turbo Profiler—identify those functions in your program that share a proportionally large amount of the total operating time. Optimizing these critical functions in assembly language might significantly boost your program's performance.

> **NOTE:** Frederick P. Brooks in "The Mythical Man-Month" speculates all speed problems can be solved by translating one to five percent of a program into optimized assembly language. Optimizing the rest of the program is likely to produce negligible results.

Consider a simple example, a function MySquare() that returns the square of an int value:

```
int MySquare(int n)
{
  return n * n;
}
```

Use the -S option to compile a program with this function. The results in assembly language (with explanatory comments added) are

```
        push    bp                      ; Save base pointer register
        mov     bp,sp                   ; Address stack with bp
        mov     bx,word ptr [bp+4]      ; Move int n into bx
        mov     ax,bx                   ; Transfer bx to ax
        imul    bx                      ; Multiply ax * bx
        jmp     short @2@58             ; Jump to next location
@2@58:
        pop     bp                      ; Restore base pointer register
        ret                             ; Return to caller
```

There are two obvious inefficiencies in this code. First, int n (located at offset bp+4 on the stack) is moved into register bx and then immediately transferred into ax. Why not move int n directly into ax? Second, a jmp instruction uselessly jumps to the very next address, most likely skipping code that in other circumstances would appear at this location.

Compiled code is filled with similar inefficiencies, which at first glance appear to be gross errors that a competent assembly language programmer would never make. Keep in mind, however, that unless function MySquare() enjoys critical status, these wasteful instructions probably have no perceptible effect on the program's performance.

On the other hand, if MySquare() occupies a large proportion of the program's total operating time, optimizing the function for peak performance should produce a respectable payoff. Using the compiler-generated assembly language as a guide, you can rewrite the function with an asm statement as Listing 19.4, INLINEFN.CPP, demonstrates.

Listing 19.4. INLINEFN.CPP (Optimizes MySquare() with an asm statement).

```
1:  #include <stdio.h>
2:
3:  int MySquare(int n);
4:
5:  main()
6:  {
7:    int i;
8:    int array[10];
9:
10:   for (i = 0; i < 10; i++)
11:     array[i] = MySquare(i);
12:   for (i = 0; i < 10; i++)
13:     printf("array[%d] == %d\n", i, array[i]);
14:   return 0;
15: }
16:
17: // Prevent "Function should return value" warning
18: #pragma warn -rvl
19:
20: int MySquare(int n)
21: {
22: /*
23:   return n * n;
24: */
25:   asm {
26:     mov ax, word ptr n
27:     imul bx
28:   }
29: }
30:
31: // Restore prevented warning to previous state
32: #pragma warn .rvl
```

Lines 22–24 convert function MySquare's original multiplication statement into a comment. When optimizing your own functions, *never delete the original code.*

Someday in the future, you might need to port the program to another computer system, perhaps one that does not have an 80x86 processor. Simply remove the comment brackets and delete any asm statements to convert them back to C or C++.

Lines 25–28 show MySquare()'s optimized assembly language. The first statement moves parameter n into ax. You don't have to calculate n's offset address (that is, using an address expression such as [bp+4]). You can reference any parameter or variable name and let BASM insert an appropriate address reference.

Line 27 multiplies ax by bx, leaving the result in registers dx (high-order value) and ax (low-order value) as the function's result. Evidently, because the modified function does not execute an explicit return, the superfluous jmp instruction is also eliminated.

Unfortunately, the compiler now warns you MySquare() is missing a return statement. Though harmless, the warning is annoying and you might want to defeat it by using a #pragma warn directive as demonstrated at line 18. The directive

```
#pragma warn -rvl
```

turns off the warning. The directive

```
#pragma warn +rvl
```

turns it on. After either such command, you can write

```
#pragma warn .rvl
```

to restore a warning to its previous status. You can issue this same warning on the command line using an option such as -wrvl. Other warning combinations (there are dozens) are documented in Borland's reference manuals.

After optimizing a function such as MySquare(), it's wise to examine the final results. To verify the compiler's output, again compile the code using the -S option and scan the assembly language. Here's the new MySquare():

```
push  bp
mov   bp,sp
mov   ax, word ptr [bp+4]
imul  bx
pop   bp
ret
```

Compare this code with the previous example prior to optimization. The integer parameter is moved directly into ax and the superfluous jmp instruction is gone. The compiler saves, initializes, and restores bp. It also supplies a ret instruction.

As you can also see from this small example, optimizing a function takes much time and care. Don't waste *your* critical time optimizing code that already works as fast as necessary.

Executing Jumps

An assembly language jump instruction such as jmp or jnl continues a program at a specified address. In stand-alone TASM programs, labels identify jump-target locations. In BASM, asm jump instructions can transfer control only to C or C++ labels such as targeted by gotos. In fact, an asm jump instruction *is* a goto statement.

Because target labels are written in C or C++, they must appear outside of asm statements. Suppose, for example, you want to insert a copyright notice into the code stream rather than in a data segment where such notice is more likely to be found and modified by a software pirate. You can encode a jmp instruction around the text like this:

```
asm {
  jmp L1
  db 13,10,'(C) 1992 by Tom Swan',0
}
L1:
asm {
  // ... Additional instructions
}
```

The jmp L1 instruction skips the db (define bytes) directive, which inserts a carriage return (13), line feed (10), and copyright string into the code (note the single quotes and explicit NULL termination byte 0 at the end of the string). The target label L1 appears after the initial asm statement, which might be followed by C and C++ statements or another asm statement as shown here.

You can also use relative jump instructions such as jnz, jl, and others. If any targets are unreachable by these "near" jump instructions, they abort the program abnormally. For example, if you write

```
asm jne TARGET
```

BASM assembles that instruction (jump if not equal) unchanged only if the distance from this location to TARGET is within −128 and +127 bytes backward or forward. If the target label is located farther away, BASM inserts a jump to the program's abnormal-termination entry point. You can fix the problem by converting the conditional jump to the equivalent code:

```
asm je TEMP
asm jmp TARGET
TEMP:
```

The effect is to skip the unconditional jmp instruction if the opposite condition holds. Together, the je and jmp instructions perform the identical job as the original jne jump, but can "hit" targets farther away.

BASM automatically optimizes unconditional jmp instructions. If you write

```
asm jmp LABEL
```

and if LABEL refers to an address within −128 and +127 bytes, BASM uses the most efficient 2-byte jmp instruction possible. If the target label is farther away, however, BASM uses a less efficient 3-byte jmp.

You can override these optimizations by prefacing labels with NEAR PTR and FAR PTR. For example, to force a FAR jump to a nearby label, you can write

```
asm jmp FAR PTR LABEL
```

Accessing Variables

In asm statements, you may reference local, global, and register variables by name. You may also refer directly to function parameters. It may be necessary, however, to use WORD PTR and BYTE PTR overrides for loading 16- and 8-bit values into registers. For an int variable or parameter count, the instruction

```
asm mov ax, count
```

is equivalent to

```
asm mov ax, WORD PTR count
```

To move count's first byte into a byte-sized register, you must supply the override:

```
asm mov al, BYTE PTR count
```

Use the similar override DWORD PTR with LES instructions and with indirect far calls to load 32-bit pointers—that is, "double word" values.

You may use registers si and di in asm statements without conflicting with register variables. If an asm statement uses si or di, the compiler does not assign register variables to those registers.

Accessing Structure Members

Inline asm statements may refer to structure members by name. You must be careful, however, to consider whether an instruction needs a value (a memory reference) or an address (the member's relative offset).

Suppose you declare a structure TPoint with two int members x and y. Using a typedef (not required in C++, but useful in ANSI C code), you design the struct like this:

```
typedef struct point {
  int x;
  int y;
} TPoint;
```

You next declare a global or local variable cursor of type TPoint:

```
TPoint cursor;
```

In C and C++ statements, the expressions cursor.x and cursor.y refer to cursor's members. In asm statements, you can use similar expressions. This loads into register ax the value of cursor's y member:

```
asm mov ax, WORD PTR cursor.y  // Load y's value into ax
```

To refer to y's offset address relative to the structure's first byte, use the OFFSET keyword:

```
asm mov bx, OFFSET cursor.y  // Load y's offset into bx
```

You can also address structures with registers. Here's how to prepare registers ds:di to address cursor and load member y's value into ax:

```
asm {
  mov di, OFFSET cursor    // Move cursor's location into di
  mov ax, [di].y           // Move member y's value into ax
}
```

Register ds already addresses the program's global data segment. Only di needs initializing. The compiler assumes y is a member of the TPoint structure cursor. A conflict might arise, however, if another structure declares a y member. You can resolve the problem by preceding the member with the struct's name in parentheses:

```
asm {
  mov di, OFFSET cursor    // Move cursor's location into di
  mov ax, [di].(TPoint)y   // Tell assembler which struct to use
}
```

Writing External Turbo Assembler Modules

Inline BASM statements are especially appropriate for small optimizations—a few instructions here and there, or a lone function that needs a performance boost. More sophisticated assembly language work requires the additional capabilities of the stand-alone Turbo Assembler.

TASM is a remarkable product. It can assemble complete applications written entirely in assembly language. It also boasts a variety of options and directives that range from simple memory reservation instructions to sophisticated macro facilities. TASM even has a kind of class structure, which you can use to write object-oriented assembly language modules.

TASM's main value for C and C++ programmers, however, is in creating .OBJ (object code) modules for linking to compiled programs. You can prototype a C or C++ function, write statements to call that function, and then implement the function completely in assembly language.

As with inline BASM code, external assembly language modules require much care and effort to construct. Be sure the results are worth the trouble; don't convert all or most of your code to assembly language in hopes of better performance. Identify the critical code and concentrate on making that code run as fast as possible.

Using the H2ASH Utility

One of the most difficult jobs in writing external assembly language modules is developing an interface to a program's data structures. Assembly language isn't designed to accommodate C structures, arrays, strings, and C++ classes, so you may have to use a few tricks for accessing objects of these and other types from assembly language statements.

853

The utility H2ASH.EXE can help reduce the amount of time you spend answering the question, "How do I access my program's data using assembly language directives and instructions?" H2ASH converts a C or C++ header file's declarations into an equivalent .ASH (assembly language header) file containing equivalent TASM declarations and equates. You can use these declarations to access your program's data or as guides to writing your own directives.

H2ASH supports most C constructs and C++ classes. It expands `#include` files and can take advantage of ideal mode—TASM's improved MASM-like syntax. Unfortunately, H2ASH does not recognize multiple inheritance, virtual base classes, or templates. It also issues warnings for items such as macros that don't translate easily to TASM directives. Consider H2ASH as a guide to, but not the last word on, translating C and C++ declarations to assembly language.

> **NOTE:** For more information about the H2ASH utility, read the text file H2ASH.TSM typically located in the C:\BORLANDC\DOC directory.

To learn how to use H2ASH, process a few sample header files. For example, locate the db.h header (Listing 11.15) from Chapter 11, "Input and Output." With that file in the current directory, enter **h2ash db.h** to create a new file DB.ASH with equivalent TASM directives. Because db.h includes stdio.h, H2ASH converts symbols in that header file as well as those in db.h. (As H2ASH runs, it may warn you from time to time about macros or other items that can't be converted.)

Though the results are imperfect, H2ASH skillfully translates most items. For instance, db.h defines these symbolic constants:

```
#define FALSE 0
#define TRUE 1
#define NAMELEN 30
#define ADDRLEN 30
#define CSZLEN 30
#define PHONELEN 13
```

H2ASH translates these symbols to the equivalent TASM directives:

```
FALSE     EQU   0
TRUE      EQU   1
```

```
NAMELEN    EQU   30
ADDRLEN    EQU   30
CSZLEN     EQU   30
PHONELEN   EQU   13
```

H2ASH also digests more complex declarations. Consider db.h's original struct, which declares members for a sample database record:

```
typedef struct record {
   union {
      long numrecs;
      long custnum;
   } info;
   char name[NAMELEN];
   char addr[ADDRLEN];
   char csz[CSZLEN];
   char phone[PHONELEN];
   double balance;
} Record;
```

Converting this structure to equivalent TASM directives is easy with H2ASH, which outputs the following equivalent TASM directives:

```
tag$1     UNION
numrecs   DD      ?
custnum   DD      ?
tag$1     ENDS


record    STRUC
info      tag$1   <>
name      DB      30 DUP ( ? )
addr      DB      30 DUP ( ? )
csz       DB      30 DUP ( ? )
phone     DB      13 DUP ( ? )
balance   DQ      ?
record    ENDS
```

In addition to translating existing names such as numrecs and phone, H2ASH creates any needed symbols such as tag$1. It also creates declarations for calling a C or C++ program's prototyped functions:

```
GLOBAL C CreateDB     :NEAR
GLOBAL C OpenDB       :NEAR
GLOBAL C ReadRecord   :NEAR
GLOBAL C WriteRecord  :NEAR
```

Writing External TASM Modules

The following programs demonstrate how to write an external assembly language module. Listing 19.5, TESTTIME.CPP, calls a function Timer() to access the computer's timer count, stored in low memory at address 0000:046C and updated regularly by a BIOS subroutine. Don't compile the program yet. You'll do that later after constructing the external Timer() module.

Listing 19.5. TESTTIME.CPP (Tests Timer() function).

```
 1:  #include <conio.h>
 2:  #include "timer.h"
 3:
 4:  main()
 5:  {
 6:    while (!kbhit()) {
 7:      gotoxy(1, wherey());
 8:      cprintf("%ld   ", Timer());
 9:    }
10:    getch();   // Throw away keypress
11:    return 0;
12:  }
```

The program doesn't do much—it just provides a vehicle for testing the Timer() function to be written in assembly language. Line 2 includes the function's header, Listing 19.6, timer.h.

Listing 19.6. timer.h (Creates Timer() function header).

```
1:  // timer.h -- Header file for timer.cpp
2:
3:  extern "C" {
4:
5:    long Timer(void);
6:
7:  }
```

External function prototypes in C++ programs are usually declared inside an `extern "C" { }` directive. This disables a process called *name mangling* by which C++ transforms function names into unique strings that permit linkers to verify the types of arguments passed to functions. The function name `Timer()`, for instance, is mangled to `@Timer$qv`. Such names are difficult to read, and it's probably best to use unmangled external function names in assembly language modules. (The ANSI-C compiler does not mangle function names, so this advice applies only to C++ programs.)

> **HINT:** If you must use mangled symbols (perhaps you need to maintain and use a function in C++ and assembly-language forms), write a dummy function that has no instructions and compile with option -S to produce an assembly language file complete with mangled symbols. Use this file as a shell, which you can fill with your function's instructions.

Next comes the assembly language module, which provides the executable instructions for the external `Timer()` function. Listing 19.7, TIMER.ASM, implements `Timer()` using TASM's ideal-mode syntax.

Listing 19.7. TIMER.ASM (Implements `Timer()` assembly language module).

```
 1:               IDEAL
 2:               MODEL small
 3:
 4:               CODESEG
 5:               PUBLIC _Timer
 6:
 7:  PROC    _Timer
 8:               xor     ax, ax                  ; Set ax to 0000
 9:               mov     es, ax                  ; Set es to 0000
10:               mov     di, 0046cH              ; Set di to 046C
11:               mov     ax, [WORD PTR es:di]    ; Get low-order timer
12:               mov     dx, [WORD PTR es:di+2]  ; Get high-order timer
13:               ret                             ; Return to caller
14:  ENDP
15:
16:  END
```

Line 2 shows an important consideration: selecting a memory model. You must use the same memory model for external modules and their host programs (see Chapter 20, "DOS Tools and Techniques"). Inside the code segment (begun with the CODESEG keyword at line 4), declare the external function name in a PUBLIC directive. Preface the public name with an underscore—C's standard convention for public symbols.

Write the function as you would a stand-alone assembly language subroutine, usually inside PROC and ENDP directives (lines 7–14). It's your responsibility to return any needed values in the appropriate registers, preserve the stack, save and restore registers bp and ds, and take care of other low-level jobs. In this case, the function returns a long int value in the register pair ax:dx (lines 11–12). There's no reason to save and restore bp and the stack pointer sp because the function uses no stack-based parameters or variables.

You now possess the necessary components to assemble and compile the example. With TASM.EXE and the BCC.EXE command-line compiler in the current path, and with the files TESTTIME.CPP, timer.h, and TIMER.ASM in the current directory, type **bcc testtime timer.asm** from a DOS prompt. The C++ compiler first compiles TESTTIME.CPP to TESTTIME.OBJ, then TASM assembles TIMER.ASM to TIMER.OBJ. Finally, the linker joins the object-code files to create TESTTIME.EXE. Run the program and press any key to stop the repeating timer.

To assemble modules separately, use TASM's /ml option to generate case-sensitive public symbols. For example, enter **tasm /ml timer** to assemble TIMER.ASM to TIMER.OBJ, compile TESTTIME.CPP with **bcc -c testtime** and link the modules with **bcc testtime.obj timer.obj**.

Though not shown in these samples, assembly language modules often need to export data as well as code. Use a DATASEG directive to begin a data segment and specify a public symbol for a global variable:

```
        IDEAL
        MODEL small
        DATASEG                 ; Start data segment
        PUBLIC _MyVar
_MyVar  DW      0               ; A word-size variable
        CODESEG
; Insert module's functions here
END
```

In the C++ host, declare MyVar (minus the underscore) in an extern directive:

```
extern int MyVar;
```

858

You can then use MyVar as though it had been defined in a C++ module. You don't have to use the "C" option in the extern directive as you do with functions because C++ doesn't mangle variable names.

To access C++ variables from inside an external assembly language module, use a similar EXTRN directive. For example, given the global variable

```
int Global;
```

an assembly language module can refer to Global as an external WORD _Global like this:

```
        IDEAL
        MODEL small
        DATASEG
        EXTRN _Global:WORD  ; External word-size variable
; Insert other data directives here
        CODESEG
; Insert module's functions here
END
```

Listing 19.8, TIMER.MSM, shows an alternate MASM-style Timer() function. Assemble this module with the command **tasm /ml timer.msm**, and then compile and link as before with the command **bcc testtime timer.obj**.

Listing 19.8. TIMER.MSM (Demonstrates Timer() function in MASM syntax).

```
 1:         .MODEL small
 2:
 3:         .CODE
 4:         PUBLIC _Timer
 5:
 6: _Timer  PROC
 7:         xor     ax, ax
 8:         mov     es, ax
 9:         mov     di, 0046cH
10:         mov     ax, WORD PTR [es:di]
11:         mov     dx, WORD PTR [es:di+2]
12:         ret
13: _Timer  ENDP
14:
15: END
```

Using Interrupts

Interrupts tell a program to stop what it's doing, do something else for a while, then pick up where it left off. A hardware device might generate an interrupt signal to notify the computer of external events such as a keypress or a mouse click. An Interrupt Service Routine (ISR) responds to the interrupt signal and returns to the interrupted program by executing an `iret` (interrupt return) instruction. You can write ISRs in C and C++, but most programmers use assembly language to ensure top speed.

You can also call ISRs with assembly language `int` instructions. For example, to use a DOS function, programs call the DOS dispatcher using an instruction such as

```
asm int 0x21   // Call DOS function dispatcher
```

Down in a PC's lower reaches is a table of 32-bit address values called *vectors*. Executing a software interrupt instruction causes the 80x86 processor to push registers and flags onto the stack and transfer control to the address stored in the table at the interrupt number's location. The program vectors to the ISR subroutine like a car careening around a hidden curve.

Calling DOS Functions

Using the built-in BASM assembler, asm statements can easily call DOS functions. Use the technique illustrated by Listing 19.9, BASMWELC.CPP, which displays the string "Welcome to BASM!$" in two ways: by calling a C function and by calling the DOS print-string subroutine.

Listing 19.9. BASMWELC.CPP (Calls DOS to output a string).

```
 1:  #include <stdio.h>
 2:
 3:  // Dollar-sign (ASCII$) and null-terminated (ASCIIZ) string
 4:  char message[] = "Welcome to BASM!$";
 5:
 6:  main()
 7:  {
 8:    puts(message);  // Display ASCIZ string
 9:    asm {
10:      mov ah, 9              // Select DOS function number 9
```

```
11:        mov dx, OFFSET message   // Address ASCII$ string
12:        int 0x21                 // Call DOS via 0x21 interrupt
13:    }
14:    return 0;
15: }
```

All DOS functions have identifying numbers such as 9, the DOS print-string function. In this program's asm statement, line 10 loads the DOS function number into register ah, assigns to dx the offset address of the string's first character, and calls the DOS function dispatcher with the instruction int 0x21 at line 12.

> **NOTE:** Consult a DOS programming reference for other DOS function numbers and their requirements (see Bibliography).

Due to DOS function 9's unusual requirements, the string must be terminated with a dollar sign character ($), a leftover from DOS's ancestor CP/M operating system. When you run the program, you see line 8 display the entire string including its dollar sign terminator. You also see the asm statement display the string, but without the trailing dollar sign.

Calling BIOS Functions

Another set of routines provides I/O services for a PC's hardware components. A collection of ISRs and other subroutines are stored in ROM and are known as the basic input-output system, or BIOS. For the most part, you call these routines using software interrupt instructions.

> **WARNING:** BIOS routines perform critical hardware operations, including low-level floppy and hard disk drive services. Be extremely careful when calling these routines. The smallest error in calling a BIOS routine can erase an entire disk full of information. Never call BIOS routines without first backing up all important data.

Listing 19.10, BIGC.CPP, demonstrates how to call a BIOS interrupt—in this case, one that changes the shape of the cursor. Compile and run the program to alter your cursor from its usual skinny appearance to a large size model that's easier to see on a crowded screen. (Reboot to restore the original cursor shape.)

Listing 19.10. BIGC.CPP (Changes to a large-model cursor).

```
 1:  main()
 2:  {
 3:    asm {
 4:      mov ch, 0      // Set cursor top row
 5:      mov cl, 7      // Set cursor bottom row
 6:      mov ah, 1      // Select video BIOS routine #1
 7:      int 0x10       // Call BIOS to change cursor shape
 8:    }
 9:    return 0;
10:  }
```

A single asm statement at lines 3–8 performs this program's main duty: calling the BIOS video routine to alter the text display's cursor shape. First, lines 4–5 load registers ch and cl with scan-line values, representing the number and position of the horizontal CRT lines that comprise the visible cursor. (If you look closely at the text cursor, you might see these lines on some types of displays.) Experiment with these two values to construct a variety of cursor shapes.

Line 6 loads into register ah the identifying number for the BIOS video ISR's cursor-shape routine. After these preparatory steps, line 7 calls the BIOS ISR by executing int 0x10, similar to the way the preceding program called the DOS function dispatcher. A large cursor should appear as soon as you run the program. Unfortunately, the cursor may revert back to its former shape due to other programs changing but not restoring the cursor size.

Writing Interrupt Service Routines

In addition to calling DOS and BIOS functions, you can write your own ISRs. To simplify the process, Borland C++ provides an interrupt keyword that converts a void function into an ISR. In C and C++ programs, write an interrupt function like this:

```
void interrupt AnyName(unsigned bp, unsigned di, unsigned si,
                       unsigned ds, unsigned es, unsigned dx,
                       unsigned cx, unsigned bx, unsigned ax,
                       unsigned ip, unsigned cs, unsigned flags)
{
  // ... C or C++ statements
}
```

The unsigned parameters provide access to register values stored on the stack. In the case of a hardware interrupt, these values should not be disturbed as they represent the interrupted program's state. In fact, for most hardware ISRs, you probably do not need to declare any parameters. Software interrupts, however, typically pass information in registers, accessible in interrupt functions through the listed parameters. You may include only the parameters you need, but you must include them in the order shown. Thus, if your program needs register ax, it still must include parameters bp through ax.

The compiler adds some of its own code to interrupt functions. In compiled form, interrupt functions begin with the preamble

```
push  ax          ; Save registers
push  bx
push  cx
push  dx
push  es
push  ds
push  si
push  di
push  bp
mov   bp,DGROUP   ; Set bp to data segment address
mov   ds,bp       ; Initialize DS to program's data segment
mov   bp,sp       ; Address local data via bp
```

In addition to saving registers and preparing bp for addressing local variables and parameters, the compiler copies the program's data segment address into ds. This vital step ensures that interrupt functions can locate their program's global data. Remember, a hardware interrupt might be called at any moment, at which time ds might address some other program's data.

The statements in the function come next, followed by cleanup instructions before the ISR ends:

```
pop    bp          ; Restore saved registers
pop    di
pop    si
pop    ds
pop    es
pop    dx
pop    cx
pop    bx
pop    ax
iret               ; Return to interrupted program
```

After restoring register values pushed earlier onto the stack, the function executes `iret`, which transfers control back to the interrupted program, or in the case of a software interrupt, to the location following an `int` instruction. Registers and flags saved on the stack by the interrupt signal or instruction are also restored at this time.

Listing 19.11, MULTIP.CPP, demonstrates how to write and install an interrupt function written with inline asm instructions. The program taps into the PC's interrupt 0x1c vector, which normally does nothing but is called on a regular basis by the BIOS function awakened by the system's internal clock. Cycling at approximately 18.2 times per second, interrupt 0x1c gives you a handy hook on which to hang actions to be executed regularly while the rest of the program continues unaware of any interruptions. In MULTIP, the interrupt is programmed to display the time at the upper-right corner of the text display while you enter test strings. Press Enter to end the program and remove the ISR from memory.

NOTE: If you have a monochrome display adapter, change `0xb800` at line 5 to `0xb000`.

Listing 19.11. MULTIP.CPP (Demonstrates an interrupt service routine).

```
1:  #include <stdio.h>
2:  #include <dos.h>
3:  #include <string.h>
4:
5:  #define DISPSEG 0xb800   // Use 0xb000 for monochrome display
6:
```

```
 7:  // Global variable for saving original 0x1c interrupt vector
 8:  void interrupt (far *oldVector)(...);
 9:
10:  // Function prototypes
11:  void InitInterrupt(void);
12:  void DoWhateverYouWant(void);
13:  void DeinitInterrupt(void);
14:  void interrupt ShowTime(...);
15:
16:  main()
17:  {
18:    setcbrk(0);   // Prevent ending program by pressing Ctrl+C
19:    InitInterrupt();
20:    DoWhateverYouWant();
21:    DeinitInterrupt();
22:    return 0;
23:  }
24:
25:  // Redirect interrupt vector to our own service routine
26:  void InitInterrupt(void)
27:  {
28:    oldVector = getvect(0x1c);  // Save current vector
29:    setvect(0x1c, ShowTime);     // Set vector to ShowTime()
30:  }
31:
32:  // ShowTime() runs concurrently with this sample function
33:  void DoWhateverYouWant(void)
34:  {
35:    int i, done = 0;
36:    char s[128];
37:
38:    while (!done) {
39:      puts("\n\nEnter a string (Enter to quit):");
40:      gets(s);
41:      done = (strlen(s) == 0);
42:      if (!done) {
43:        for (i = 0; i < 40; i++)
44:          puts(s);
45:      }
46:    }
47:  }
```

continues

Listing 19.11. continued

```
48:
49:    // Restore original interrupt vector before program ends
50:    void DeinitInterrupt(void)
51:    {
52:      setvect(0x1c, oldVector);
53:    }
54:
55:    // Interrupt 0x1c service routine. Poke time into display.
56:    void interrupt ShowTime(...)
57:    {
58:      asm {
59:        xor ax, ax                        // ax <- 0000
60:        mov ds, ax                        // ds <- 0000
61:        mov ax, [0x046d]                  // get timer div 256
62:        mov bx, DISPSEG                   // bx = display addr
63:        mov ds, bx                        // ds = display addr
64:        mov word ptr [0x009a], 0x0f07c    // display '¦'
65:        mov bh, 0x70                      // attribute = reversed
66:        push ax                           // save timer value
67:        xchg ah, al                       // ah = timer hi mod 256
68:        aam                               // make unpacked bcd
69:        or ax, 0x3030                     // convert to ascii
70:        mov bl, ah                        // move digit to bl
71:        mov [0x0096], bx                  // display 1st hr digit
72:        mov bl, al                        // move digit to bl
73:        mov [0x0098], bx                  // display 2nd hr digit
74:        pop ax                            // restore timer value
75:        mov cx, 0x0f06                    // calc ax / 4.26
76:        mul ch                            //   ax <- ax * 15
77:        shr ax, cl                        //   ax <- ax / 64
78:        aam                               // make unpacked bcd
79:        or ax, 0x3030                     // convert to ascii
80:        mov bl, ah                        // move digit to bl
81:        mov [0x009C], bx                  // display 1st min digit
82:        mov bl, al                        // move digit to bl
83:        mov [0x009e], bx                  // display 2nd min digit
84:      }
85:    }
```

When poking the address of a custom ISR into the PC's interrupt vector table, you should almost always preserve the original vector for restoring later. To save the old vector, declare a variable like this:

```
void interrupt (far *oldVector)(...);
```

In English, this line declares oldVector as a far pointer to a void interrupt function that receives a variable number of arguments—represented in C++ as a three-dot ellipsis in parentheses; in ANSI C, as an empty pair of parentheses. To preserve an interrupt vector, assign to oldVector the value returned from getvect() as line 28 demonstrates. Call setvect() (line 29), then, to redirect interrupts to your custom routine. Another call to setvect() (line 52) restores the saved interrupt vector before the program ends.

Lines 33–47 prompt you to enter a string, displayed several times in a for loop. This code gives the program something to do while the ISR executes in the background—a simple but effective form of multiprocessing using a timer interrupt. Run the program and spend a few minutes typing strings. Despite the fact that function DoWhateverYouWant() has control, the program's ISR automatically updates the displayed time.

The ShowTime() ISR (lines 56–85) uses a single inline asm statement to decode the current time, translate the binary coded decimal (BCD) result to ASCII, and poke the digits directly into the display's video buffer. Comments in the listing explain the purpose of each instruction.

It's difficult to imagine a function that is more system-dependent than ShowTime(), which is unlikely to run correctly on any computer other than a true-blue, 100-percent compatible IBM PC with a common monochrome or graphics display. The function would certainly fail on nonstandard hardware.

Such is the nature of assembly language. Programs written in assembly language are intimately tied to their host machine. Despite this restriction, however, when used skillfully, a little assembly language can go a long way towards optimizing your programs to run as fast as possible in the smallest amount of space.

Summary

- With assembly language you can optimize critical statements to run as fast as possible, you can access hardware at the bit level, and you can code interrupt service routines (ISRs) for top speed.

- Use the -S option to compile a program to an assembly language text file. Examine the file to learn how the compiler translates high-level statements to machine language.

- The primary reason for adding assembly language to programs is to improve the performance of critical code—typically a small percentage of a program's total instructions. Identify your program's critical code (perhaps by using Turbo Profiler), and optimize those instructions with assembly language. Optimizing a program's noncritical code typically gives little or no performance benefits.

- Borland's built-in assembler (BASM) assembles inline asm statements in C and C++ programs. Terminate an inline statement with a semicolon or a new line. Enclose multiple inline statements in braces.

- BASM lacks sophisticated TASM features such as macros, 80386 and 80486 instructions, ideal mode, and advanced directives. Nevertheless, BASM is more than adequate for most assembly language tasks.

- Inline BASM statements recognize C and C++ comments. Unlike stand-alone assembly language programs, BASM comments do not begin with semicolons.

- For more sophisticated assembly language work, write external modules that you assemble with TASM and link to compiled C and C++ programs. With this method, you can take advantage of TASM's advanced features such as ideal mode and macros. You also gain complete control over the low-level instructions in assembled functions.

- Use the H2ASH utility to simplify translating high-level items, #defines, structures, and such to equivalent assembly language declarations. The utility is a useful, though imperfect, tool.

- Interrupts temporarily halt a program to perform another task. Every interrupt has an identifying number that serves as an index into a table of ISR vectors (addresses) in low memory.

- Hardware devices such as keyboards and a mouse generate interrupt signals, causing the processor to pass control to the associated ISR vector. A hardware interrupt can occur at any time.

- Software ISRs operate like subroutines. Programs call a software ISR with an assembly language `int` instruction. Call the DOS function dispatcher, for example, with the instruction `int 0x21`. You can also call BIOS routines using software interrupts, but use extreme caution; the BIOS contains many low-level subroutines that, if misused, can cause the permanent loss of data.

- You can code your own interrupt service routines in C or C++, but most programmers use assembly language for the best possible performance.

DOS Tools and Techniques

Borland C++ supplies a variety of DOS development tools that can help you become a better programmer. This chapter covers some of the more useful tools and describes how to use three advanced programming techniques: optimizations, memory models, and overlays.

DOS Tools

Professional programmers use utility programs such as MAKE, PRJ2MAK, TLIB, Turbo Debugger, Turbo Profiler, and others like GREP and TOUCH to make the most of their development systems and to save time. Of all the many utilities that come with Borland C++, these rank highest with the pros.

Using MAKE

Complex programs with dozens of modules are difficult to compile and link by hand. To automate compilation, you can build an IDE project (see Chapter 2, "The

Integrated Environment" and Chapter 4, "Borland C++ for Windows"), you can write a batch file of the necessary commands, or you can use a more sophisticated tool called MAKE.

Batch files are useful for compiling small programs with a few modules, but for larger programs, MAKE saves you time and aggravation by issuing only the minimum number of commands that keep an entire project up to date. Suppose you modify four files in a 16-module program. MAKE examines the dates and times of your program's source and object-code files and automatically recompiles only the four modified files plus any other files that depend on the modified files.

The Borland C++ MAKE utility reads a text file (called the MAKE file) that contains compiler and linker commands. Actually, MAKE can issue any DOS command and it can run most programs and utilities. Typical MAKE files have three kinds of commands: macros, dependency rules, and DOS command lines:

- *Macros* are optional but save typing and can increase a MAKE file's clarity. MAKE-file macros are similar to #defined symbols in a C or C++ program.

- *Dependency rules* state which files depend on others. In Chapter 14, "Inheritance and Polymorphism," for example, the BENCH.EXE file *depends on* BENCH.OBJ—if you change BENCH.CPP (see Listing 14.2), you must recreate BENCH.EXE in order to keep the object code file up to date with its source.

- MAKE issues *DOS commands* when it detects a dependent file that is out of date relative to other files on which the file depends. Typically, MAKE issues command-line compiler and linker commands, but it can give any valid DOS command.

Listing 20.1, TBENCH.MAK, is a simple MAKE file that uses these three concepts to compile and link Chapter 14's BENCH.CPP and TBENCH.CPP programs (Listings 14.2 and 14.3).

Listing 20.1. TBENCH.MAK (MAKE file for Chapter 14's TBENCH and BENCH).

```
1:  # TBENCH.MAK -- Make file for TBench program and class
2:
3:  library=c:\borlandc\classlib\lib;c:\borlandc\lib
4:  include=c:\borlandc\classlib\include;c:\borlandc\include
5:
```

```
 6:  tbench.exe: tbench.obj bench.obj
 7:    bcc -L$(library) tbench.obj bench.obj tclasdbs.lib
 8:  tbench.obj: tbench.cpp
 9:    bcc -c -I$(include) tbench
10:  bench.obj: bench.cpp bench.h
11:    bcc -c -I$(include) bench
```

From DOS, change to Chapter 14's directory where you store the files bench.h, BENCH.CPP, TBENCH.CPP, and TBENCH.MAK. Type **make -ftbench.mak** to run MAKE and have it process the commands in TBENCH.MAK. If nothing seems to happen, delete the .OBJ and .EXE files in the directory and try again. The program might already be up-to-date, in which case MAKE correctly performs no actions.

> **NOTE:** If you don't specify a filename with the -f option, MAKE attempts to read a file named MAKEFILE in the current directory.

Line 1 in TBENCH.MAK is a comment, which begins with #. MAKE ignores comment lines. Lines 3 – 4 declare two macros, library and include. Modify the listed pathnames to match your installation. MAKE replaces the expressions $(library) and $(include) with the associated text. You don't have to use macros in MAKE files, but they can save a lot of typing.

Lines 6, 8, and 10 state three dependency rules. This line:

```
tbench.exe: tbench.obj bench.obj
```

states that TBENCH.EXE depends on TBENCH.OBJ and BENCH.OBJ. If TBENCH.EXE's file date and time are earlier than either of the two listed .OBJ files or if TBENCH.EXE does not exist, MAKE issues the command on the subsequent line, which must begin with one or more blanks:

```
  bcc -L$(library) tbench.obj bench.obj tclasdbs.lib
```

The expression -L$(library) expands to -LC:\BORLANDC\... using the value associated with the library macro. The -L option gives the linker the location of any required .LIB and .OBJ files. The sample specifies TCLASDBS.LIB, which contains the code for the Timer class. The command links the specified .OBJ and .LIB files to create or recreate TBENCH.EXE.

Similar commands in TBENCH.MAK keep the program's other files up-to-date. In general, every file on which another depends requires a dependency rule and a DOS command to create that file. These lines:

```
tbench.obj: tbench.cpp
  bcc -c -I$(include) tbench
bench.obj: bench.cpp bench.h
  bcc -c -I$(include) bench
```

keep TBENCH.OBJ and BENCH.OBJ up to date. The first line states that TBENCH.OBJ depends on TBENCH.CPP. If TBENCH.OBJ's date and time are earlier than TBENCH.CPP or if TBENCH.OBJ does not exist, MAKE issues the command on the subsequent line, which compiles TBENCH.C to create TBENCH.OBJ using the -c (compile only) option.

The third line in the previous code states that BENCH.OBJ depends on BENCH.CPP and bench.h. If either of those two file's dates and times are more recent than BENCH.OBJ, a change must have been made to one of the text files, and MAKE issues the command on the next line to compile or recompile the BENCH module.

MAKE sorts out all such dependencies and issues the minimum number of commands in the correct sequence to compile and link an entire project. Try this experiment. After running MAKE as suggested earlier, load bench.h into your editor and enter an inconsequential change. Save the file to disk. (You can also type **touch bench.h** to update the file's date and time using the TOUCH.EXE utility.) From DOS, enter **make -ftbench.mak**. MAKE issues commands to compile BENCH.CPP and then gives another command to link the resulting object-code files to create TBENCH.EXE. Next, try a similar experiment, but this time modify or **touch tbench.cpp**. MAKE determines that BENCH.OBJ is current, so this time it compiles only TBENCH.CPP before linking.

NOTE: Another useful command is **make -n -ftbench.mak**. The -n option tells MAKE to display but not issue commands. Use this option to inspect the commands that MAKE will give without actually executing those commands. (This is especially useful when debugging a recalcitrant MAKE file.) You might also rename TBENCH.MAK to MAKEFILE, with no extension. You then can just type **make** to run MAKE.

Using PRJ2MAK

IDE project files are easy to use, but they don't provide the detailed documentation that many software companies require their programmers to keep. If you are an IDE fan, use the PRJ2MAK utility to convert .PRJ project files to equivalent .MAK files that you can process with MAKE. You can also print the resulting .MAK files for documenting file dependencies.

Try using PRJ2MAK on one of the project files from Chapter 13, "Programming with Classes." To convert APPOINT1.PRJ to a MAKE file, for example, change to that chapter's directory and enter `prj2mak appoint1`. PRJ2MAK reads APPOINT1.PRJ and creates a new file APPOINT1.MAK, which you can use with the command `make -fappoint1.mak`.

Compiling programs with a MAKE file generated by PRJ2MAK creates one or more temporary files in the current directory and also creates a configuration file with options and directory information. The preceding command, for example, creates APPOINT1.CFG. You can delete or edit this file as you wish.

Using TLIB

Library files are convenient for storing multiple .OBJ object-code files, perhaps from a library of common modules. As an added benefit, the linker can extract multiple files from libraries much more quickly than it can read the individual .OBJ files from disk. Use the TLIB utility to insert and extract .OBJ files in .LIB libraries.

Given the files A.OBJ, B.OBJ, and C.OBJ, combine them into a library named MYLIB.LIB with this command, entered at a DOS prompt:

```
tlib mylib.lib +a.obj +b.obj +c.obj
```

If MYLIB.LIB doesn't exist, TLIB creates it. To replace existing modules in a library, use -+ as in

```
tlib mylib.lib -+b.obj
```

A MAKE file might include such a command (preceded by at least one blank) to update a library upon recompiling B.OBJ's source module.

To extract a library file to a new .OBJ file, use the * command

```
tlib mylib.lib *b.obj
```

To remove a module, use -. To extract and remove a module from a library file, use -*. Use these commands with extreme caution. Keep backup copies of library files from which you remove modules.

Use TLIB's /E option to create an extended dictionary, which helps the TLINK linker load modules quickly. Use the /C option to add mixed case symbols to libraries (two modules, for example, that have symbols such as FALSE, false, and False that differ only in case). Don't use /C or /E for libraries that will be used with other linkers. Use them only for TLINK.

For a list of a library's contents and public symbols, enter a command such as **tlib mylib.lib,con** or **tlib mylib.lib,temp.txt**. To print a report, enter **tlib mylib.lib,prn**. You must follow the library name with a comma and output filename for this option to work.

Other Useful Tools

Chapter 3, "The Command-Line Environment," and Chapter 4, "Borland C++ for Windows," introduce Turbo Debugger and Turbo Profiler. It's truly amazing how many programmers never use these important development tools. Don't neglect these valuable programs!

Spend time now learning how to use the debugger and profiler. Instead of hunting for bugs in your source code, use Turbo Debugger to isolate problems and identify their causes. Instead of optimizing functions at random in hopes of improving performance, use Turbo Profiler to identify critical code and rewrite those sections in assembly language. If you follow these two suggestions, you'll save many hours of frustration.

Another useful tool is GREP, which searches for strings in text files at blazing speed. Use GREP to identify files that contain variables, functions, and other symbols. For example, to locate library header files with the word false, change to C:\BORLANDC\INCLUDE and enter **grep -li false *.h**. The -li command means "list filenames and ignore case."

Use the TOUCH utility to update file dates and times. The command **touch *.*** provides the current date and time for every file in the current directory. Software companies typically use TOUCH to update files before producing a master diskette. The resulting directory looks clean, and any out-of-date files stick out like neon signs.

Finally, if there's a kitchen sink among Borland C++ utilities, TDUMP is a virtual bathtub. Undoubtedly the result of torturous object-file investigations conducted by Borland programmers, TDUMP rivals the *New York Times* in voluminous output. Enter `tdump file` for a listing of a file's contents, probably in hexadecimal, or enter `tdump tdump.exe` for the lowdown on TDUMP.EXE's executable code layouts. Use TDUMP's –v (verbose) option if you really like to read long reports. Type `tdump` alone for a list of the program's many options. You're on your own with this mostly undocumented tool, but do try it. You might find it useful for uncovering a file's hidden secrets.

Optimizations

Borland C++ is an optimizing compiler. Version 3.0's command line and text IDE compilers offer a full range of optimizations. Version 3.1 adds those same optimizations to Borland C++ for Windows. Turbo C++ for Windows 3.0 lacks the sophisticated optimizations of the command-line and IDE compilers.

As you probably realize, nobody has yet written the perfect compiler. Perhaps no one ever will. Computers are smart, but humans are smarter, and only human programmers are capable of finding the best software solutions to problems.

Although far from perfect, modern compilers do a better job than ever before of generating efficient code. Simply stated, to optimize code, the compiler first translates one or more high level statements and then examines the generated instructions one byte at a time. In this process, certain patterns emerge. The compiler might discover an assignment of a memory value to a register that's copied back to that same location in the very next instruction. Obviously, the compiler can delete these and other wasteful instructions.

If you were writing your own compiler, you'd want to know why such inefficiencies occur in compiled code. As a programmer, you are mostly interested in having the compiler remove wasteful instructions so that you don't have to rewrite the statements in assembly language. This section describes some of the optimizations you can order Borland C++ to make to your compiled programs and points out some of the pitfalls.

When and If to Optimize

Some programmers optimize their programs just before shipping a product. Others optimize at every step along the development path. Which is the right approach for you? In addition to answering that question, you need to choose whether to optimize modules for speed or for size. Small programs tend to run more slowly than large ones, typically because loops (which reduce program size) add significant overhead to a program's total operating time. Small, fast programs are desirable, but in terms of optimization techniques, *small* and *fast* are often incompatible words.

When choosing optimizations, keep the following suggestions in mind:

- Optimizing takes time: In Borland C++, it takes as much as 50 percent longer to compile the same program with speed optimizations than it does without them. It takes about 20 percent longer when optimizing for size. For faster compilation times, turn off all optimizations.

- Optimizations might cause bugs to appear or in some cases might even lead to new bugs. Many programmers continually optimize their code in order to test programs in their final distributed forms. If you wait until the last moment to optimize, the theory goes, a bug might skip your attention. On the other hand, during early prototyping, saving time is more important than fixing bugs, and you can probably turn off optimizations until sometime later during the program's development.

- Try multiple optimization techniques. You might discover that different modules benefit from different optimizations. You might, for instance, optimize some modules for size and others for speed. Be selective and use Turbo Profiler to prove the wisdom of your decisions.

- Turbo Debugger recognizes optimized code, but be aware that conflicts can arise among statements with bugs, the debugger, and optimized instructions. If a bug won't hold still, try debugging with and without optimizations. Differences in the compiled code might provide useful clues.

- Above all else, use good programming techniques. Don't rely on optimizations to do your job! Your skills as a programmer are the best optimizing tools you have. Use register variables wisely, employ inline functions and inline class member functions, have sound reasons for declaring member functions virtual, and test different algorithms for solving specific problems. The QuickSort algorithm, for example, is not always faster than other sorting methods.

Optimizing for Speed or Size

In the IDE, choose Options|Compiler|Optimizations and select one of the two buttons Fastest Code or Smallest Code. Clicking either button selects a combination of options in the large panel at left (Figure 20.1) and the smaller panels at right. Toggle individual options on and off to fine-tune results.

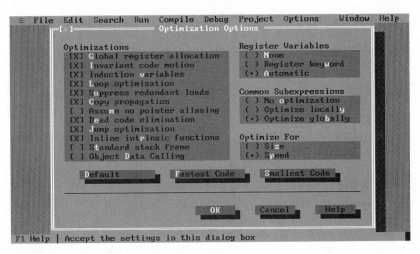

Figure 20.1. The IDE's optimizations panel.

Borland C++ for Windows 3.1 has similar optimization panels; Turbo C++ for Windows 3.0 offers far fewer choices. You can also select these same options with the command line compiler (see Appendix C). Use -02 to optimize for speed; -01 for size. (Those are capital Os, not zeros.) To disable all optimizations, use -0d. You can specify multiple options separately or string them together. The option -0abc is the same as the three options -0a -0b -0c. Rather than enter these and other options manually, it's probably best to insert them in a TURBOC.CFG configuration file.

Register Optimizations

You can select from three register optimizations (Figure 20.1). In the Register Variables panel, select None for no register variables (or use the -r- command-line option), Register keyword (-rd) for using register variables only where specified in the source, or Automatic (-r, the default) to recognize the register keyword and to have the compiler choose other register variables for you.

To select candidate variables to store in registers, the compiler examines one expression or statement block at a time and attempts to determine the "live range" of all variables within the block's scope. For example, in these hypothetical statements:

```
void f(void)
{
  int y;
  for (int i = 0; i < 10; i++)
    y += SomeFunction(i);
  int x = SomeOtherFunction(y);
  printf("x == %d\n", x);
}
```

the compiler could store x and i in the same register because these values are not alive concurrently—that is, they are not in use at the same times. Variables y and i would require separate registers because they live in the same statement blocks.

In addition to determining live ranges for variables, the compiler keeps track of any temporary registers that it requires for various instructions. It then performs a *global register optimization* to determine if any free registers remain for storing variables. Registers ax, bc, cx, dx, si, di, and es are available for this purpose (only si and di are preserved across function calls). Select global register optimization from the optimization panel (Figure 20.1) or use the -0e command-line option. (Option -02 includes -0e.)

Another useful register optimization switch is -z (Suppress redundant loads in the IDE). With this option, if the compiler detects that a register already has a certain value, it suppresses instructions that would store that same value in that register.

Dead Code

Use -0b (Dead code elimination in the IDE) to delete assignments to unused variables. This optimization also eliminates variables assigned values that are never used.

> **NOTE:** Complex macro expansions and conditional compilation instructions might cause dead code to creep into your programs, so it's wise to test the before- and aftereffects of this optimization even if you regularly delete dead-code statements, as careful programmers should do.

A similar optimization moves invariant statements outside of loops. If you do something silly like this:

```
for (int i = 0; i < 100; i++) {
  count = 100;    // invariant statement
  AnyFunction(i);
}
```

the compiler moves the invariant assignment to count outside of the loop.

Eliminating Common Subexpressions

A common subexpression typically occurs when you reference the same structure member more than once. Suppose you have a structure with substructure member v that has an int count member. Given a pointer p that addresses the outer structure, you write an if statement to test whether count's value is in the range 0 to 9:

```
if ((p->v.count >= 0) && (p->v.count < 10 ))
  // ... do something
```

In order to address count, the compiler generates code to calculate the structure's address, the offset to member v, and the offset to count. The two common subexpressions, p->v.count, cause the program to repeat this calculation twice to evaluate the expression—a gross waste of time. Experienced programmers eliminate such waste by using a temporary variable:

```
int t = p->v.count;
if ((t >= 0) && (t < 10))
  // ... do something
```

The compiler's common subexpression eliminator performs this kind of optimization for you. You have three choices (see Figure 20.1): No optimization, Optimize locally (-0c), or Optimize globally (-0g). Local suppression works only within compound statement blocks. Global suppression attempts to optimize entire functions.

Generally, you should use global suppression for the best speed. This choice, however, can swell code-file size if the compiler creates numerous temporary variables to hold subexpression values. In that case, try switching to local subexpression elimination, which should reduce code-file size but might cause a loss of performance.

Optimizations and Pointer Aliasing

Never mention pointer aliasing to a compiler author unless you are prepared to spend the rest of the evening discussing code generation anomalies. Pointers give programmers plenty of trouble; they give optimizing-compiler authors nightmares and hangovers.

When a pointer addresses a variable in memory, if the compiler stores that variable in a register, an assignment via the pointer throws the register and associated memory location out of synch. Recognizing this fact, the compiler normally does not perform subexpression elimination across statements that involve potentially dangerous pointer expressions. It avoids the same traps when performing copy propogation—an optimization technique that "remembers" values assigned to expressions and uses those values instead of repeating the same expressions later.

You can tell the compiler not to take precautions for pointer aliasing by enabling the IDE's Assume no pointer aliasing option (see Figure 20.1) or by using the -Oa command-line switch. This tack might put some wind into your code's sails, but it could also sink the ship. Of all the available optimization techniques, assuming there are no aliased pointers is one of the ways most likely to produce hard-to-find bugs. Use this option with care.

Fast Function Calls

This optimization can give some kinds of programs a tremendous performance boost by passing to functions some argument values in registers instead of pushing those values onto the stack. To have the compiler perform fast function calls whenever possible, use the IDE's Options|Compiler|Entry/Exit Code command and select the Register Calling Convention. Use the -pr option with the command-line compiler.

You can also force specific functions to accept register arguments. Preface the function's name with the _fastcall modifier:

```
int _fastcall square(int n);
```

Use the same modifier in the function prototype and its implementation:

```
int _fastcall square(int n)
{
  return n * n;
}
```

Calls to square() pass n in a register such as ax instead of pushing the argument value onto the stack. Instead of addressing the parameter on the stack, which takes extra time, the function's compiled code simply uses the register value.

Inline String Functions

In theory, Chapter 19's advice about optimizing a program's critical code sounds clean and simple. In practice, you might discover your program's critical code is buried deep inside a precompiled library function. Optimizing library functions in assembly language is an unappealing task, but fortunately, there's an alternative—at least for the string and memory functions in Table 20.1. Using a special option, you can have the compiler insert inline code for these functions.

Table 20.1. Potential inline string and memory functions.

alloca	memcpy	stpcpy	strcpy	strncpy
fabs	memset	strcat	strlen	strnset
memchr	rotl	strchr	strncat	strrchr
memcmp	rotr	strcmp	strncmp	

To inline memory and string functions, use the -Oi command-line compiler option, or select Inline intrinsic functions in the IDE's optimization panel (Figure 20.1). Your program's code files may balloon in size, but they might also run faster if many statements call these common library routines.

Choosing a Memory Model

The great myth about memory models is that, by selecting a larger model, you give your programs extra RAM. Nonsense. Under DOS, all memory is available to all programs in all memory models. A memory model simply changes the methods that the compiler uses (and that also you can use) to address data and to store and call functions. A memory model is an addressing scheme, not a memory supplier.

> **NOTE:** Memory models also affect the methods by which Microsoft Windows programs address data and code (see Chapter 21, "Windows Tools and Techniques"). Here again, memory models do not affect the quantity of available memory.

The following sections describe each of Borland C++'s six memory models: tiny, small, medium, compact, large, and huge. Each section illustrates a memory model using a horizontal diagram with lower addresses to the left and higher addresses to the right. These illustrations differ from the standard vertical drawings that ambiguously place addresses at the top or bottom and lead to confusion about whether segments grow up or down. (In some of these illustrations, stacks "grow down" and "shrink up," a confusing mixture of terms.) In this chapter's memory model diagrams, arrows indicate the direction in which segments expand—left toward lower addresses, right toward higher ones. Shaded areas indicate free memory.

The following notes explain more about the parts and labels in memory model diagrams.

- The phrase _TEXT segment 'CODE' refers to the symbol and name assigned to a compiled segment, using standard linker terminology. A program's "text" is its code.

- The phrase _DATA segment 'DATA' refers to initialized global data where the program stores global variables. The huge model names data segments 'FAR_DATA'.

- The phrase _BSS segment 'BSS' refers to uninitialized global data.

- The number 64K means "up to 64K." Memory segments may be as small as 16 bytes or as large as 64K (exactly 65,536 bytes). Regardless of memory model, code and data segments can never be larger than 64K each.

- Segment registers cs, ds, and ss point to the base locations of the program's code, data, and stack segments. In some models, multiple segment registers address the same location. In others, segments are distinct. The stack pointer sp indicates the top of the stack, which moves in the arrow's direction as statements push new data onto the stack and in the opposite direction as statements pop data from the stack. Programs begin with the stack pointer initialized at the highest possible offset address within the stack segment.

- DGROUP is an assembly language term that groups multiple segments into a single segment up to 64K. Some memory models combine the stack, heap, and data segments in DGROUP, thus limiting those segments to a combined total maximum of 64K bytes.

- Access heap memory through malloc() and new. To access far heap memory, use far memory allocation functions such as farmalloc(). To access the far heap with new, you can overload the operator to call farmalloc(), but it may be just as well to select a model with no far heap, in which case all unused memory is available through malloc() and new.

- In models that support multiple data or code segments (or both), the word sfile_... indicates the segment's unique name, created from the module's filename. An ellipsis in these models (medium, large, and huge) indicates that multiple segments of the type at left may appear at this location.

- Near pointers are 16-bit offsets from a segment base. Far pointers are full 32-bit pointers and include segment and offset words. Near functions use similar 16-bit call and ret instructions. Far functions use 32-bit calls and retf (far return) instructions. In general, near pointers and functions are faster than far equivalents.

- Select a memory model using the IDE's Options|Compiler|Code generation command, or use the command-line compiler's -mx option, where x is one of the letters t (tiny), s (small), m (medium), c (compact), l (large), or h (huge). For example, the command **bcc -ml myprog** compiles MYPROG.CPP using the large memory model. All modules, including any library routines, must use the same memory model. In some cases, this means you might have to rebuild a library before you can link your program. Also, some libraries require you to use a specific memory model.

The Tiny Model

The tiny memory model (see Figure 20.2) creates a .COM-style program, a relic from MS-DOS's early days originally intended to provide an upgrade path for CP/M applications. (MS-DOS was originally modeled after Digital Research's now obsolete CP/M operating system for 8088-based computers.)

In the tiny model, every scrap of the program's data, code, stack space, and heap occupy a single memory segment up to 64K bytes long. All pointers and function addresses are near.

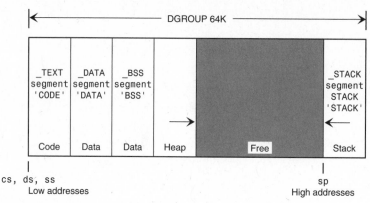

Figure 20.2. The tiny memory model.

Microsoft discourages programmers from creating .COM code files, although this model has proven useful for utilities that need to load quickly and conserve disk space. On the other hand, despite their apparently small file sizes, tiny memory model programs always occupy a full 64K segment, if available, even when less memory would do the job. Small memory model programs might therefore occupy less RAM than the equivalent tiny model programs.

> **NOTE:** When compiling with BCC.EXE, use the two options -mt and -lt. The first selects the tiny memory model; the second passes option /t to the linker. If you do not use -lt with BCC (or /t with TLINK), the linker displays "Warning: No stack." To complete the compilation, use the DOS EXE2BIN utility—for example, type **exe2bin myprog.exe myprog.com**. It's probably best, however, to have TLINK create .COM files directly.

The Small Model

The small memory model (see Figure 20.3) stores code in a separate segment up to 64K bytes long. Global data, the stack, and the heap occupy one additional segment. Remaining memory is available through far-heap allocation functions.

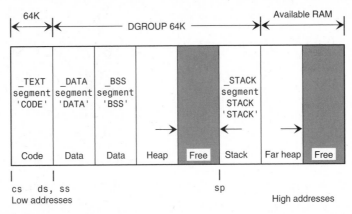

Figure 20.3. The small memory model.

Small model programs are appropriate for short tests, examples (such as many of the listings in this book), and utility programs. All pointers and functions are near, giving this model the best possible speed advantages. The compiler uses the small memory model by default.

This model limits programs to one 64K segment of code, but more importantly, provides only up to 64K for all global data, the heap, and the stack. To gain more memory requires using nonstandard far-heap allocation functions, making this model unattractive for writing portable applications that have large data requirements.

The Medium Model

The medium memory model (see Figure 20.4) improves on the small model by permitting multiple code segments, each of which can occupy up to 64K bytes. As with small model programs, global data, the heap, and the stack must fit in one 64K segment, making this model inappropriate for data-intensive programs.

Pointers are near in the medium model, but function addresses are far. Generally, the medium model is best for programs with many functions but only minimum amounts of data. Medium model code segments can be overlays.

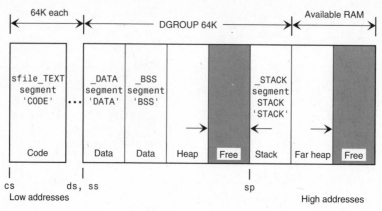

Figure 20.4. The medium memory model.

The Compact Model

The compact memory model (see Figure 20.5) might be the all-around best choice for small- to medium-size programs, especially when performance is important. Code and global data have separate segments, each up to 64K bytes long. The stack also has its own segment, and the heap occupies whatever memory remains.

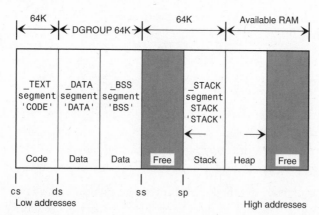

Figure 20.5. The compact memory model.

Functions are near in this model, but pointers are far in order to access the potentially large amount of memory on the heap. If your program has a moderate amount of code but needs to work with large amounts of data, the compact model might be the ideal choice.

The Large Model

The large memory model (see Figure 20.6) is the same as the compact model but permits multiple code segments. Because of this, large model programs use far functions and far pointers by default.

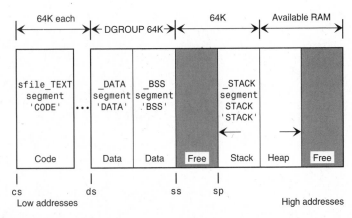

Figure 20.6. The large memory model.

The large model is similar to the model that Turbo Pascal programs use. In programs with large amounts of data and many functions, the large model might be the best choice. Of all models, this one tends to take the best advantage of 80x86 segmented memory (in real mode, that is). Code segments can be overlays.

The Huge Model

The huge memory model (see Figure 20.7) extends the large memory model by permitting multiple code and data segments. Programs with massive global data needs and many functions can use this model. Pointers and functions are far by default.

The huge model is useful for programs with many large static arrays or other structures. Even so, individual data segments can be no larger than 64K. Code segments can be overlays.

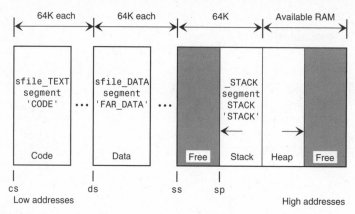

Figure 20.7. The huge memory model.

Near and Far Pointers

Memory models affect the default near and far sizes of pointers and function addresses. Table 20.2 lists the default pointer, function address, and this pointer sizes for Borland C++'s six memory models. Near pointers are relative to the segment base register ds; near function addresses are relative to the code segment register cs. Near pointers can address code and data within 64K of their segment base. Far pointers include segment and offset values and can directly address any location in a PC's first megabyte of RAM.

Table 20.2. Pointer, function, and this-pointer sizes.

Memory Model	Pointer size	Functions	this pointer
Tiny	near	near	near
Small	near	near	near
Medium	near	far	near
Compact	far	near	far
Large	far	far	far
Huge	far	far	far

In any memory model, you can selectively override near and far default sizes to address data and code in whatever way you wish. You can, for example, declare a far pointer in a small memory model program, which uses near pointers by default. You can also declare functions to be near in a large memory model program, thus improving performance by calling functions with relatively fast `call` instructions that use 16-bit offset addresses. One exception: you can't override the `this` pointer's default near or far status.

> **NOTE:** Be careful when overriding the near and far default sizes of function addresses and pointers. Calls to near functions are possible only from within the same code segment, and near pointers might require you to initialize a segment register. The compiler generates correct code only for default pointer and function address sizes. The results of any overrides are your responsibility.

To override a pointer's default size, declare it with a near or far keyword. Here are a few samples:

```
double far *dfp;    // Far pointer to a double value
int near *inp;      // Near pointer to an integer
char *c;            // Default size pointer to a char or string
```

In the absence of near or far, the compiler uses the default size for the current memory model. Pointer c might be near or far depending on the memory model, but dfp is always far; inp is always near.

You can also declare huge pointers, which are normalized far pointers with unique segment and offset values. Normalized pointers have offset values in the range of 0 to 15. Declare huge pointers with the huge modifier:

```
double huge *p1;    // Huge pointer to a double value
double huge *p2;    // Second huge pointer to a double value
```

Because the compiler normalizes huge pointers, it's safe to compare them in relational expressions. The statement

```
if (p1 < p2)
  DoSomething();
```

executes DoSomething() if the address value of p1 is less than the address value of p2. You can similarly compare near pointers.

You cannot safely compare far pointers, however, because two unnormalized far pointers can differ in value but address the same location! In hexadecimal, the address values 0000:0010 and 0001:0000 point to the same byte in memory. It's senseless to compare these unnormalized far pointers.

Segment Pointers

An obscure type of pointer, called a segment pointer, is a kind of near-and-far hybrid. Declare a segment pointer with the _seg modifier:

```
double _seg *sp;     // Segment pointer to a double value
```

Segment pointers have an assumed offset of 0000, and thus occupy only 16 bits but can address all of a PC's first megabyte of RAM (in 16-byte minimum-size chunks).

Don't confuse segment pointers with pointers declared using one of the segment overrides: _cs, _ds, and _es. Use these overrides to create near pointers as offsets from a nonstandard segment register. For example, to create a pointer dp into the stack, you can declare it as

```
double _ss *dp;     // Pointer to double stored on the stack
```

This pointer's assumed segment register is ss rather than the usual ds. Replace _ss with _cs to address code-segment data, or use _es to create pointers that address data stored relative to es, which you would have to initialize somehow. Beware of these refinements—they are tricky to use correctly. Poking around in the system stack is like traversing a mine field on a pogo stick. You might be better advised to take a safer course (in other words, using standard pointer techniques).

Near and Far Functions

Pointers are not the only kinds of address modifications you can make. You can also declare functions to be near or far independently of a memory model. For a function prototyped as

```
void AnyFunction(void);
```

the compiler inserts a near ret or a far retf instruction at the function's exit point depending on the current model's default treatment for function addresses. It also uses near or far addresses in calls to the function. To force the compiler to use far addressing, add the far keyword before the function name:

```
void far AnyFunction(void);
```

You can also force functions to be near:

```
void near AnyFunction(void);
```

Near functions might be useful in the medium, large, and huge memory models, which use far function calls and returns by default. Compiled calls to near functions require only 16-bit addresses and are somewhat faster than far functions. This is especially true for recursive functions, which perform better and use less stack space when declared to be near.

> **NOTE:** Don't make trouble for yourself by forcing all intersegment function calls to be near. Profile your code to ensure that any modifications to a function's near or far status are truly worth the effort.

Programs that use the huge memory model give functions the additional task of locating the module's data segment. Each segment in a huge model program has its own private data segment, and thus every function must initialize register ds to address that module's global data. In addition to the usual startup code that prefaces compiled functions, the compiler adds the instructions

```
push ds          ; Save current data segment
mov  ax,X_DATA   ; Assign ax the module's data segment address
mov  ds,ax       ; Move ax into segment register ds
```

The function also executes pop ds before returning to its caller. Functions might suffer a drop in performance from this additional overhead, which you can eliminate by using the large memory model and storing your data on the heap.

Sometimes, functions in other memory models need to initialize ds to locate the program's data. In such cases, use the _loadds modifier in the function's header:

```
void _loadds AnyFunction(void);
```

The compiler treats this function as it does in huge memory model programs, adding instructions to the function's compiled code to save and initialize ds.

Overlays and VROOMM

VROOMM is the sound that the price of Borland's stock usually makes on Wall Street. It's also Borland's "Virtual Runtime Object-Oriented Memory Manager," otherwise known as the overlay loader. Use VROOMM to load one or more code segments as needed into memory, leaving other code segments on disk. Assuming that not all code segments need to be in memory at once, overlays make it possible to run programs that have more code than available RAM.

VROOMM includes features for storing code overlays in expanded and extended memory. Executable code, however, always runs in a PC's lower 640K of memory. VROOMM is not a DOS extender. It's an overlay manager that you can use to run massive programs in relatively small spaces.

Here are some key observations to keep in mind when using overlays:

- The smallest possible overlay is one code segment. This does not mean, however, that overlays are each 64K bytes long. Overlay segments can occupy anywhere from 16 to 64K, although most fall somewhere in between. Generally, small overlays perform better than large ones. Ideally, all of a program's overlay segments are similar in size.

- You can overlay only code segments. You cannot overlay data or stack segments or any part of the heap.

- Overlay programs must use the medium, large, or huge memory models. In other words, VROOMM works only with memory models that support multiple code segments (which makes perfect sense because the smallest overlay is a segment). You cannot overlay tiny, small, or compact programs.

- VROOMM maintains a memory buffer in which code overlays reside on their way in and out of RAM. In the default arrangement, the overlay buffer exists between the stack and far heap in medium model programs (see Figure 20.4) and between the stack and heap in large and huge programs (see Figures 20.6 and 20.7). The default buffer size is about twice as large as the largest overlay segment.

- You can optionally swap overlay segments to expanded or extended RAM. VROOMM makes the process nearly automatic (more on this later). Using these options permits programs to take advantage of extra RAM on modern

PCs but still run on RAM-starved PCs of old (last month's models, for example).

- The overlay manager installs its own control code in private segments. The space that these segments take should pay you back many times in space saved by using overlays. So for all practical purposes, you can ignore VROOMM's overhead.

- VROOMM uses interrupt vector 0x3f for its dynamic segment loader. Don't touch this interrupt!

- You don't need to take any special actions to call functions in overlay segments. You write your programs the same with or without overlays. VROOMM makes overlay management transparent to programmers—almost transparent, that is. When calling a function in an overlay module, all currently active functions must be far. If function A calls function B which calls function C in an overlay segment, A and B must be far or the program will crash. VROOMM walks the stack looking for function return addresses, and it expects those addresses to be far. Using the near function modifier in overlay programs, even in nonoverlay segments, is extremely hazardous.

- External assembly language functions that are included in overlay object-code modules must be far.

- VROOMM permits multiple overlay segments to occupy memory concurrently. A function in overlay A can call another function in overlay B, which might call yet another function in overlay C. Some other overlay managers permit only one overlay module in memory at a time, thus preventing overlay functions from calling one another. VROOMM does not impose any similar restrictions.

- Never overlay interrupt service routines, critical functions that are called repeatedly, or similar code that must be in RAM at all times or that programs call frequently. Overlaying every one of a program's code segments is usually unwise.

- The stand-alone and IDE Turbo Debuggers support overlays. You debug overlaid programs no differently from others. Use the stand-alone debugger's View|Module command to select among a program's multiple code segments.

- Microsoft Windows overlays code segments as needed, and in enhanced mode on computers with 80386 or better processors, Windows can even virtualize data by swapping memory segments to and from disk. VROOMM isn't needed, therefore, and doesn't work for Windows programs. (DOS programs running in a Windows DOS-prompt window, however, can use overlays the same as they can under plain DOS.)

Writing Overlay Modules

A few simple listings demonstrate how to construct overlay segments and programs. First, Listings 20.2, root.h, and 20.3, ROOT.CPP, present a main program that calls three functions, OvlA(), OvlB(), and OvlC(). Each function, to be presented later, exists in a separate overlay code segment.

Listing 20.2. root.h.

```
1:  #include <iostream.h>
2:  #include <conio.h>
3:
4:  void OvlA(void);
5:  void OvlB(void);
6:  void OvlC(void);
```

Listing 20.3. ROOT.CPP.

```
1:  #include "root.h"
2:
3:  main()
4:  {
5:    cout << "Enter root program\n";
6:    cout << "Press Enter to call overlay A...";
7:    getch();
8:    OvlA();
9:    cout << "Press Enter to call overlay B...";
10:   getch();
11:   OvlB();
12:   cout << "Press Enter to call overlay C...";
13:   getch();
14:   OvlC();
15:   return 0;
16: }
```

Next come the three overlay modules in Listings 20.4, OVLA.CPP, 20.5, OVLB.CPP, and 20.6, OVLC.CPP. Nothing in the modules themselves indicates their status as overlays.

Listing 20.4. OVLA.CPP.

```
1:  #include "root.h"
2:
3:  void OvlA(void)
4:  {
5:    cout << "\nWelcome to Overlay A!\n";
6:    cout << "Press any key to exit Overlay A...";
7:    getch();
8:    cout << '\n';
9:  }
```

Listing 20.5. OVLB.CPP.

```
1:  #include "root.h"
2:
3:  void OvlB(void)
4:  {
5:    cout << "\nWelcome to Overlay B!\n";
6:    cout << "Press any key to exit Overlay B...";
7:    getch();
8:    cout << '\n';
9:  }
```

Listing 20.6. OVLC.CPP.

```
1:  #include "root.h"
2:
3:  void OvlC(void)
4:  {
5:    cout << "\nWelcome to Overlay C!\n";
6:    cout << "Press any key to exit Overlay C...";
7:    getch();
8:    cout << '\n';
9:  }
```

You could compile these modules into a single nonoverlaid program. To do that, enter the command

```
bcc -ml root ovla ovlb ovlc
```

To compile the modules as overlays, use the -Y and -Yo (a lowercase letter o, not a zero) like this:

```
bcc -ml -Y root -Yo ovla ovlb ovlc
```

You must use the -Y option to compile overlaid modules, and you must select an appropriate memory model, -ml, here. In addition, use the -Yo option to compile selected modules as separate overlay code segments. In this command, OVLA, OVLB, and OVLC are compiled and linked as three separate code segment overlays. ROOT is not an overlay segment. Turn off overlay code generation with -Yo-. Suppose for example that only OVLA and OVLB, but not OVLC, are to be overlays. In this case use the command

```
bcc -ml -Y root -Yo ovla ovlb -Yo- ovlc
```

Normally, options immediately follow **bcc**. Option -Yo- may appear between filenames on the command line. These options pass to the linker the /o option, which tells TLINK to link in the VROOMM overlay manager from file OVERLAY.LIB (usually stored in C:\BORLANDC\LIB). If you run TLINK separately, specify /o to link overlaid programs.

To build overlaid applications in the text-based IDE, follow these steps:

1. Create a project for your application. Using the listings in this section, you might create a project named ROOT.PRJ and add to it the files ROOT.CPP, OVLA.CPP, OVLB.CPP, and OVLC.CPP.

2. Use the Options|Application command and select the DOS Overlay button.

3. Select an overlay module in the Project window, choose the Project|Local options command, and enable "Overlay this module" near the bottom of the window. Repeat this step for each project module to be treated as a separate code overlay segment.

This should be all you need to do to create most overlaid programs. You might also want to use the Options|Compiler|Code generation command to select the Medium, Large, or Huge memory model. Selecting the Options|Application button in step 2 changes the memory model to medium and sets other individual options. Don't repeat step 2 after changing to a new memory model or selecting other options.

> **NOTE:** You can't build overlaid applications using Borland C++ for Windows 3.1 (or Turbo C++ for Windows 3.0) because Windows code segments are overlaid automatically. You never need to use VROOMM in Windows programs. The preceding instructions apply only to the text-based IDE.

Managing Overlay Memory

Programs with many small overlay segments might benefit from a larger overlay buffer. To increase the buffer's size, assign a value equal to the buffer size in 16-byte paragraphs to _ovrbuffer in your program's main() function. For example, to reserve a 4096-byte buffer for ROOT.CPP (Listing 20.3), add this statement between lines 4 and 5:

```
unsigned _ovrbuffer = 256;   // 256 * 16 == 4096 bytes
```

Ignore the warning that "'_ovrbuffer' is assigned a value that is never used...." Use #pragma warn -aus or the IDE's Options|Compiler|Messages command to turn off this warning.

Overlays in Expanded and Extended Memory

Look up functions _OvrInitEms() and _OvrInitExt() in Chapter 22, "Functions and Examples." Use these functions in overlaid programs to enable swapping of code segments to expanded and extended RAM.

All PCs, XTs, and ATs can use expanded, or "page-frame" memory. In this memory system, additional RAM is made available as pages that appear in a "window," a reserved location somewhere in the upper reaches of memory. Commands sent to the memory hardware bring various pages of memory into this window. Call _OvrInitEms() to automatically detect and use expanded memory for overlays.

Systems with 80286, 80386, or 80486 processors can use extended memory, which resides at addresses above the first megabyte of RAM available on all PCs. Extended memory is available only by using the processor's protected mode. Call _OvrInitExt() to automatically detect and use extended memory for overlays.

Summary

- Use the MAKE utility to automate compilation of multimodule projects. MAKE reads a "MAKE file" (which you can name MAKEFILE) typically containing three types of items: macros, dependency rules, and DOS commands. With a properly constructed MAKE file, after modifying selected files in a program, a single DOS command such as `make -fmyfile.mak` issues the minimum number of commands required to bring the program's .EXE code file up to date.

- Use PRJ2MAK to convert IDE project files to equivalent MAKE files, which you can use with MAKE or print for documenting your program's file dependencies.

- Use the TLIB utility to create and manage library .LIB files, containing one or more .OBJ object-code files. The linker can load libraries more quickly than individual .OBJ files.

- Borland C++ has many other useful tools including Turbo Debugger and Turbo Profiler (see Chapters 3 and 4), GREP (useful for searching text files), TOUCH (for updating file dates and times), and the wordy, but intriguing, do-it-all, know-it-all utility, TDUMP.

- Optimizing compilers revise their generated code in order to remove wasteful instructions. Optimizing takes time, and some programmers postpone optimizing code until just before finishing a program. Other programmers optimize at every stage, on the grounds that the code you distribute tomorrow is the code you should test today.

- You can optimize for speed or size, but not both. Generally, reducing code file size means giving up performance. Extra performance typically causes code file sizes to grow.

- A memory model is an addressing scheme, not a memory supplier. Choosing a larger memory model does not make more memory available to programs; it changes the organization of code and data in memory and selects default methods by which statements access data and call functions.

- Borland C++'s six memory models are tiny, small, medium, compact, large, and huge.

- In any memory model, you can force pointers and functions to be near or far, and you can use other modifiers to create segment pointers and to load the ds register in functions. The responsibility for mixing near and far addressing techniques is yours.

- VROOMM is Borland's Virtual Runtime Object-Oriented Memory Manager, otherwise known as the overlay loader. Use VROOMM to build overlaid programs that have more code than could possibly fit into RAM at one time.

- The smallest VROOMM overlay module is a single code segment. VROOMM supports only the medium, large, and huge memory models as these are the only models that permit multiple code segments.

- VROOMM maintains an overlay buffer for keeping overlaid segments on their way in and out of RAM. You can also swap overlay segments to expanded and extended memory.

21

Windows Tools and Techniques

Microsoft Windows 3.0 and 3.1 offer programmers an exciting new market for their programs. Software users have for years demanded better memory management, graphical user interfaces (GUIs), multitasking, and virtual memory. Windows has these features and more, and with Version 3.1's improved speed and stability, there's every reason to believe that Windows' popularity will continue to grow.

With Borland C++ you can write complete Windows applications with all the usual elements—pull-down menus, dialog boxes, graphics, controls, and so on. This chapter gives you a flying start to developing your own Windows programs.

Borland C++ 3.1 fully supports all new Windows 3.1 features, including the STRICT option (for better compile-time type checking), TrueType fonts, common dialogs, and object linking and embedding (OLE). You can use Borland C++ 3.0 to compile and run this chapter's listings, but you must have Borland C++ 3.1 to call Windows 3.1 functions.

Most programs in this chapter use ObjectWindows, Borland's Windows class library nicknamed OWL. You can write conventional nonobject-oriented Windows programs with Borland C++, but due to Windows' event-driven nature, OWL's classes and Windows fit together naturally. OWL programs tend to be shorter, easier to understand, and, most important, easier to maintain than Windows programs written conventionally in C.

> **NOTE:** You can use Borland C++ 3.0 or 3.1's text-based IDE or the command-line compiler to create Windows applications. Most Windows programmers, however, also are Windows *users,* and this chapter assumes that you are using Turbo C++ for Windows 3.0 or Borland C++ for Windows 3.1. See Chapter 4, "Borland C++ for Windows," for more information about using these integrated development environments (IDEs). Any references in this chapter to BCW 3.1 also apply to TCW 3.0 unless otherwise noted.

OWL's Class Hierarchy

Figure 21.1 diagrams OWL's class hierarchy. All OWL classes derive from class Object defined in Borland's class library (see Chapter 17, "Borland's Class Library"). Except for TModule, from which the application wrapper class TApplication derives, all other OWL classes are derived, using multiple inheritance, from TStreamable and Object. The TStreamable class provides I/O-stream capabilities, and because most OWL classes inherit TStreamable, you can read and write most OWL objects in stream statements using the << and >> operators.

On the second tier from the left in Figure 21.1 are TModule, TWindowsObject, and TScroller. Use TScroller to scroll a window's contents up, down, left, and right using standard scroll bar controls. TModule provides application services; all OWL programs rely on a single instance of the TApplication class, which is derived from TModule.

In the middle of the second tier is TWindowsObject, probably OWL's all-around most important class. You never use TWindowsObject directly. Instead, you create objects of derived classes such as TDialog to create dialog boxes and TWindow to create overlapping windows. Other classes that derive from these two provide standard dialogs, multiple document interfaces (MDI), and controls.

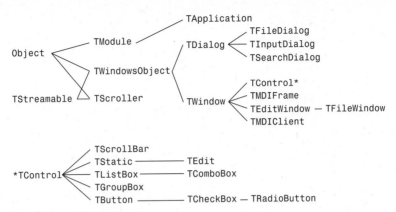

Figure 21.1. The ObjectWindows class hierarchy.

TControl extends the class hierarchy with a set of specialized classes that interface with common Windows control elements such as scroll bars, static text items, editable text, list and combo boxes, group boxes, buttons, check boxes, and radio buttons.

While learning about OWL, keep its main goal in mind: to provide a framework for building programs, not to plaster new code over every inch of the Windows API. There are, for example, no TBitmap or TLine classes. To display bitmaps, lines, and other graphics shapes, you call Windows API functions just as you do in nonOWL programs. OWL doesn't write your code for you. It provides an object-oriented base, or framework, on which to build programs. OWL is like a prefabricated building's frame. The big pieces come ready-made, but it's still your job to install the wiring, lay the carpet, and paint the walls.

Developing Windows Applications

You can use the small, medium, or large memory models to develop Windows applications. You can't use the tiny or huge models. Borland C++ 3.0 can compile Windows applications that use the compact memory model. Borland C++ 3.1 can no longer use the compact model for OWL programs.

Windows programs require a definition file, usually named the same as the program's main module but ending in .DEF. If you don't supply a definition file, BCW uses OWL.DEF in C:\BORLANDC\OWL\LIB by default, but it also warns you about this condition to guard against accidentally compiling with the default settings. Supply an explicit .DEF file to turn off this warning. You can use Listing 21.1, OWLWELC.DEF, with all of this chapter's listings, except where noted.

Listing 21.1. OWLWELC.DEF (Definition file for this chapter's programs).

```
1:  EXETYPE WINDOWS
2:  CODE PRELOAD MOVEABLE DISCARDABLE
3:  DATA PRELOAD MOVEABLE MULTIPLE
4:  HEAPSIZE 4096
5:  STACKSIZE 5120
```

Listing 21.2, OWLWELC.CPP, shows an OWL program's bare-minimum layout. Compilation instructions follow the listing.

Listing 21.2. OWLWELC.CPP (Bare-minimum OWL application).

```
1:  #include <owl.h>
2:
3:  // The TApplication class
4:  class TWelcomeApp: public TApplication
5:  {
6:  public:
7:    TWelcomeApp(LPSTR aName, HANDLE hInstance, HANDLE hPrevInstance,
8:      LPSTR lpCmdLine, int nCmdShow) : TApplication(aName, hInstance,
9:      hPrevInstance, lpCmdLine, nCmdShow) {};
10:   virtual void InitMainWindow();
11: };
12:
13: // Initialize the application's main window
14: void TWelcomeApp::InitMainWindow()
15: {
16:   MainWindow = new TWindow(NULL, "Welcome to ObjectWindows");
17: }
18:
19: // Equivalent to a DOS program's main() function
20: int PASCAL WinMain(HANDLE hInstance, HANDLE hPrevInstance,
```

```
21:    LPSTR lpCmdLine, int nCmdShow)
22:  {
23:    TWelcomeApp WelcomeApp("OWLWelcome", hInstance, hPrevInstance,
24:      lpCmdLine, nCmdShow);
25:    WelcomeApp.Run();
26:    return WelcomeApp.Status;
27:  }
```

To compile and run OWLWELC, use Project|Open to load OWLWELC.PRJ from disk and press Crtl+F9. You also can compile (F9) and then use the Windows File Manager to run the resulting OWLWELC.EXE file. If you don't have the diskette that came with this book, type in the listing or change to its directory and, using BCW, open a new project named OWLWELC.PRJ. To the project, add OWLWELC.DEF and OWLWELC.CPP. Use Options|Application to select Windows App, and then use Options|Linker|Libraries to select Static for Container, ObjectWindows, and Standard class libraries. (You also may use the dynamic link library, or DLL, versions of these libraries, but in that case, you must select all three DLLs, not just one or two.) Also use Options|Directories to set Include Directories to

```
C:\BORLANDC\OWL\INCLUDE;C:\BORLANDC\CLASSLIB\INCLUDE;C:\BORLANDC\INCLUDE
```

and Library Directories to

```
C:\BORLANDC\OWL\LIB;C:\BORLANDC\CLASSLIB\LIB;C:\BORLANDC\LIB
```

You then should be able to compile and run the example. If you receive errors and are using BCW and Windows 3.1, use Options|Compiler|Code generation and enter **WIN30** into the Defines input box. This symbol enables BCW to compile OWL programs written for Windows 3.0. Specify WIN31 to compile OWL programs for Windows 3.1 *or* 3.0. Define only one symbol, never both. TCW does not recognize either symbol, but defining them for TCW does no harm.

NOTE: Project files can be exchanged between the text-based and Windows IDEs. Command-line compiler users might want to use the BCW IDE at first and then process .PRJ files with PRJ2MAK (see Chapter 20, "DOS Tools and Techniques") to create equivalent MAKE files. Be sure to close the project in the IDE first. Using PRJ2MAK on a few sample applications is the easiest way to learn the correct command-line options to use for compiling and linking OWL applications.

After compiling and running OWLWELC, you should see the window in Figure 21.2. You can move and resize the window, zoom it to full screen or shrink it to an icon, and open its system menu. To close the window, and thus end the OWLWELC program, select that menu's Close command or press Alt+F4.

Figure 21.2. OWLWELC's bare-minimum window.

Let's see exactly how the listing displays its main window—the essential ingredient in all Windows programs. In the listing, class TWelcomeApp derives from TApplication. All OWL programs have a similar TApplication class. The class constructor passes several parameters to the ancestor constructor, but it performs no new duties and therefore is most easily defined inline (lines 7–9). The TWelcomeApp class provides a replacement for the inherited member function InitMainWindow(). All OWL TApplication classes must do the same.

InitMainWindow()'s job is to create a TWindow (or a derivative) class object to serve as the program's main window. This class object interfaces with the *Windows* window element, which OWL registers and creates by calling Windows API functions. Line 16 shows a typical way to create a program's main window, assigning the address of a TWindow object to member MainWindow in the program's TApplication object. The NULL argument tells TWindow that this object has no owner—a fact that is true of all main windows. The string serves as the window's title.

Finally, in OWLWELC is the program's main body, function WinMain() at lines 20–27. WinMain() is a Windows program's equivalent of a DOS program's main() function. All Windows programs begin at the first statement in WinMain(). In a conventional Windows program, WinMain() is typically long and complex, and you must explicitly register a window class to initialize the program and start its ball rolling. OWL takes care of these steps for you, requiring you to perform only three actions. No matter how complex, an OWL application's WinMain() function

- Constructs an object of the program's TApplication class derivative, TWelcomeApp, here.

- Calls the TApplication class Run() member function to initialize the program's main window and engage its message loop, which dispatches Windows messages.

- Returns the TApplication Status member (or another int value) indicating success (zero) or failure (nonzero) to the task that started the program.

Using Message-Response Functions

Windows is an event-driven environment. Deep inside, Windows intercepts events such as mouse clicks and key presses, for which it sends descriptive messages to windows. Messages are commands that tell programs to perform certain actions, such as drawing graphics or responding to menu selections. Instead of concerning yourself about *when* you should perform your program's tasks, in Windows' event-driven climate you simply decide what to do upon receiving a message.

Classes go hand in hand with the concept of event-driven programming. You build classes that operate independently of other classes, responding to messages in no particular order. To relate class objects to Windows messages, Borland C++ provides message-response member functions (also known as *response functions*). The compiler stores a table of addresses to a class's response functions, indexed by values related to Windows messages.

> **NOTE:** Borland C++'s message response mechanism extends class syntax in a nonstandard way, although Borland has stated its intention to propose response functions to the ANSI committee charged with preparing an official C++ specification. The message-response mechanism, technically known as *dynamically dispatchable virtual tables* (DDVT), is available to all applications, not only to Windows or OWL programs. DDVTs might be useful in other event-driven environments, for example.

A message response function looks like a pure virtual member function declaration, which ends with = 0;. For example, to use the class

```
class AbstractClass {
public:
  virtual void f1(void);
  virtual void f2(void) = 0;  // Pure virtual member function
  ...
};
```

you must derive a new class from AbstractClass and provide a fully implemented f2()
member function. A message response function ends with a similar nonzero value in
brackets:

```
class ResponseClass {
public:
  virtual void f3() = [123];  // Response function
  ...
};
```

For this class, the compiler creates a DDVT table entry keyed to the ID value
123. In the case of an OWL program, a response function receives a reference
parameter of type RTMessage (a typedef symbol that stands for TMessage &). In OWL,
you program response functions like this:

```
class OWLClass {
public:
  virtual void WMLButtonDown(RTMessage msg)
    = [WM_FIRST + WM_LBUTTONDOWN];
  ...
};
```

WM_FIRST is one of several constants that define a range of ID values associated
with various Windows messages such as WM_LBUTTONDOWN, which Windows issues upon
sensing a left-mouse-button-click event. The value in brackets relates the function,
WMLButtonDown(), to the message. Simply stated, when you click the mouse, OWL calls
the function. With response functions, event handling is as simple as that. The
function's msg parameter contains information about specific messages. For mouse
clicks, msg provides the mouse cursor's coordinates. For keypress events, msg contains
an ASCII character, and so on. For some messages, you simply ignore msg, although
you still must declare its RTMessage type as the function's parameter.

Device-Independent Graphics

Listing 21.3, SKETCH.CPP, demonstrates how to use message response functions and also shows how OWL programs can draw graphics in windows. Load SKETCH.PRJ from disk into BCW, or build a new project as you did for OWLWELC, copying OWLWELC.DEF to SKETCH.DEF and setting options as explained earlier.

Listing 21.3. SKETCH.CPP (Sketch with the mouse using response functions).

```
 1:  #include <owl.h>
 2:
 3:  class TSketchApp: public TApplication
 4:  {
 5:  public:
 6:    TSketchApp(LPSTR aName, HANDLE hInstance, HANDLE hPrevInstance,
 7:      LPSTR lpCmd, int nCmdShow) : TApplication(aName, hInstance,
 8:      hPrevInstance, lpCmd, nCmdShow) {};
 9:    virtual void InitMainWindow();
10:  };
11:
12:  _CLASSDEF(TSketchWin)
13:  class TSketchWin: public TWindow
14:  {
15:  public:
16:    HDC dc;                    // Handle to display context
17:    BOOL dragging;             // True if clicking and dragging mouse
18:    TSketchWin(PTWindowsObject aParent, LPSTR aTitle);
19:    virtual LPSTR GetClassName()
20:      { return "TSketchWin"; }
21:    virtual void GetWindowClass(WNDCLASS &aWndClass);
22:    virtual void WMLButtonDown(RTMessage msg)
23:      = [WM_FIRST + WM_LBUTTONDOWN];
24:    virtual void WMMouseMove(RTMessage msg)
25:      = [WM_FIRST + WM_MOUSEMOVE];
26:    virtual void WMLButtonUp(RTMessage)
27:      = [WM_FIRST + WM_LBUTTONUP];
28:    virtual void WMLButtonDblClk(RTMessage)
29:      = [WM_FIRST + WM_LBUTTONDBLCLK];
30:  };
```

continues

Listing 21.3. continued

```
31:
32:   // Initialize TSketchApp's main window
33:   void TSketchApp::InitMainWindow()
34:   {
35:     MainWindow = new TSketchWin(NULL, "Sketch - Double click to clear");
36:   }
37:
38:   // Construct the application's main window
39:   TSketchWin::TSketchWin(PTWindowsObject aParent, LPSTR aTitle)
40:     : TWindow(aParent, aTitle)
41:   {
42:     dragging = FALSE;
43:   }
44:
45:   // Modify Windows class for this object's window element
46:   void TSketchWin::GetWindowClass(WNDCLASS &aWndClass)
47:   {
48:     TWindow::GetWindowClass(aWndClass); // Let ancestor initialize AWndClass
49:     aWndClass.style |= CS_DBLCLKS;      // Enable double-click mouse messages
50:   }
51:
52:   // Respond to left-mouse-button click
53:   void TSketchWin::WMLButtonDown(RTMessage msg)
54:   {
55:     if (!dragging) {
56:       dragging = TRUE;
57:       SetCapture(HWindow);
58:       dc = GetDC(HWindow);
59:       MoveTo(dc, msg.LP.Lo, msg.LP.Hi);
60:     }
61:   }
62:
63:   // Respond to mouse movement
64:   void TSketchWin::WMMouseMove(RTMessage msg)
65:   {
```

```
66:    if (dragging)
67:       LineTo(dc, msg.LP.Lo, msg.LP.Hi);
68:  }
69:
70:  // Respond to release of left mouse button
71:  void TSketchWin::WMLButtonUp(RTMessage)
72:  {
73:    if (dragging) {
74:       ReleaseCapture();
75:       ReleaseDC(HWindow, dc);
76:       dragging = FALSE;
77:    }
78:  }
79:
80:  // Respond to mouse double-click messages
81:  void TSketchWin::WMLButtonDblClk(RTMessage)
82:  {
83:    InvalidateRect(HWindow, NULL, TRUE);
84:  }
85:
86:  int PASCAL WinMain(HANDLE hInstance, HANDLE hPrevInstance,
87:    LPSTR lpCmd, int nCmdShow)
88:  {
89:    TSketchApp SketchApp("Sketch", hInstance, hPrevInstance,
90:      lpCmd, nCmdShow);
91:    SketchApp.Run();
92:    return SketchApp.Status;
93:  }
```

SKETCH's TApplication class, TSketchApp (lines 3–10), is similar to OWLWELC's similar class. This time, however, the program also provides a TWindow class derivative, TSketchWin, at lines 12–30. Most OWL programs declare a similar TWindow-based class to customize the program's main window. In this case, OWLWELC adds data members to keep track of the mouse button's status (BOOL dragging) and to provide a display context (dc) for directing graphics functions to draw in this program's window.

> **NOTE:** The _CLASSDEF() macro at line 12 creates several typedef aliases for TSketchWin pointers and references such as PTSketchWin (equivalent to TSketchWin *), RTSketchWin (equivalent to TSketchWin &), and others. The macro saves you the trouble of entering typedef declarations to create these symbols, and it also lends clarity and consistency to the program's source text. See the end of file _defs.h in C:\BORLANDC\INCLUDE for a list of the typedef symbols that _CLASSDEF() creates.

Several response functions at lines 22–29 intercept selected mouse messages. OWL calls function WMMouseMove() when you move the mouse. It calls WMLButtonDblClk() when you double-click the left mouse button. Declaring response functions as shown here links a TWindow class object to specific Windows messages.

The program initializes its main window as in OWLWELC (see lines 33–36), but this time it constructs an object of the derived TSketchWin class rather than TWindow. The TSketchWin constructor (lines 18 and 39–43) calls the ancestor constructor to initialize the window object and sets dragging to FALSE. When the program begins, it therefore assumes that the user is not dragging the mouse.

To enable double-clicking, member function GetWindowClass (see lines 21 and 46–50) initializes a Windows WNDCLASS structure with OWL's default window attributes, then sets bit CS_DBLCLKS in the window's class style (line 49). Don't confuse a Windows window class with a C++ class—they have little in common. A window class is a structure that programs register with Windows in order to create visible windows (and controls, dialogs, and so on) on-screen. A C++ class is a program element that in OWL programs often is associated with a *Windows* window element. To register a new window class with Windows, provide a GetWindowClass() member function along with a unique name returned by GetClassName(). If you don't provide GetClassName(), OWL will not call GetWindowClass().

The three response functions at lines 53–78 respond to left-mouse-button-down messages, left-mouse-button-up messages, and mouse movements to draw lines in the window as you click and drag the mouse. (Consult a Windows API reference for details about Windows functions such as SetCapture() and ReleaseCapture(). See bibliography.) As another example, response function WMLButtonDblClk() at lines 81–84 calls the Windows API function InvalidateRect() to erase the window's contents by declaring it to be invalid—that is, in need of updating.

Using Turbo Debugger for Windows

A good way to learn more about how SKETCH and other OWL programs work is to run them under control of Turbo Debugger for Windows (TDW). You can start TDW from the Windows Program Manager, but you can run it more easily from BCW by using the Run|Debugger command. TDW is a Windows program, but it uses the computer's text display to show source code, variables, expressions, and other details. The debugger closely resembles Turbo Debugger for DOS, but it includes Windows-related commands and features.

NOTE: Perhaps someday we will be fortunate enough to have a GUI debugger that will show programs and debugging information together on the same display. Unfortunately, that day hasn't yet arrived, although you might be able to attach a second monochrome monitor to your computer to display TDW's output. Be aware, however, that taking this action might force a 16-bit video adapter to run in the monochrome card's 8-bit mode, seriously curtailing display performance.

If you have two PCs connected by an RS232 null-modem serial cable, you can also debug programs remotely. In Windows, run WRSETUP.EXE to configure the remote system, then start WREMOTE.EXE on that same system. On the other computer, after compiling your program with debugging information saved to the resulting .EXE code file, enter a command such as `td -r myapp` from a DOS prompt. You can also run TDINST.EXE to configure TD for remote debugging, in which case you do not need to type -r. If all goes as planned, the program MYAPP.EXE is copied from the development computer to the remote Windows system. That system runs the program while you view the debugger's screen on your other computer. Notice that, when debugging in remote mode, you run the DOS debugger, TD, from a DOS prompt (or a DOS-prompt window). The Windows debugger, TDW, does not have a remote debugging option.

After successfully compiling and trying SKETCH, run the debugger and try a few experiments. These tips will help guide you through your own future debugging sessions:

- Set a breakpoint (F2) on the statement in `WMLButtonDblClk()`, and press F9 to run the program. Draw a sample sketch and double-click the left mouse button. The debugger returns when OWL calls the function in response to the mouse event.

- When the debugger returns, use the View|Windows Messages command and enter `HWindow` (simply typing opens the necessary input dialog). Select the Handle option and close the dialog(s). Continue running by pressing F9, then double-click to activate the breakpoint. Again use View|Window Messages to inspect the recorded messages.

- You can set similar breakpoints in other response functions (or whatever functions you need to inspect). Try setting a breakpoint on function `WMLButtonDown()`. Run the program and click the mouse pointer in the window. When the debugger returns, inspect the `msg` parameter—it contains the location of the mouse pointer.

- Before debugging, save any open documents in *all* running programs. A debugging session is a trip into the unknown. Take as many steps as you can to protect your development system from harm. (Setting up for remote debugging offers the highest level of protection, because the code being debugged runs on the remote computer, not on your valuable development system.)

- Try always to run Windows programs to completion when operating the debugger. If you must abort a program prematurely, reboot as soon as possible. Halting programs in midstream can leave DOS or Windows or both in unstable states. This fact is especially true of Windows 3.0 running with versions of DOS earlier than 5.0.

Using WinSight

Another useful debugging tool is the WinSight utility, which displays messages for any or all running applications. Figure 21.3 shows WinSight's window behind the SKETCH program's.

Tracing a program's message flow is a great way to learn how Windows works, and it also can provide clues for hunting bugs. To use WinSight, after compiling and running this chapter's SKETCH program, run WinSight from the Program Manager and follow these suggestions:

- Select the Spy|Find Window command and slowly move the mouse pointer to SKETCH's window. As you move the mouse from window to window, WinSight shows each window's handle and other information. Use Spy|Open Detail to see more facts about selected windows.

- After selecting SKETCH's window, use the Messages|Options command to limit tracing to Mouse messages. You can trace all messages, but doing so produces reams of data and can slow system performance to a crawl. In most cases, limit tracing to a small number of message types.

- Select the Start! command to begin tracing messages for the selected window. Move the mouse back to SKETCH's window and click to bring the window forward. (For best results, adjust the SKETCH and WinSight windows so that you can see both on-screen.) Click and drag the mouse inside SKETCH to draw a shape. As you do, WinSight shows you the messages that Windows generates for mouse-click and mouse-move events.

- To stop tracing, select the Stop! command, which replaces Start! while tracing.

Figure 21.3. WinSight inspecting SKETCH's message flow.

NOTE: WinSight traces messages received via the Windows functions, `GetMessage()` and `SendMessage()`. The utility can't trace messages, such as `WM_INITDIALOG`, passed directly to the program's functions.

WinSpector

Borland C++ 3.1 comes with another debugging utility, WinSpector (see Figure 21.4). Use WinSpector to inspect conditions that exist after a program halts with a general protection (GP) fault. These errors are also called UAEs, or Unrecovereable Application Errors. They are typically caused by a program that attempts to read or write memory beyond the application's defined boundaries, or that executes an illegal instruction code. When Windows receives a UAE, it displays a system error message and halts the offending program.

Figure 21.4. The WinSpector utility.

To install WinSpector, run it from the Program Manager; or, in Windows 3.1, drag the utility's icon to the StartUp window. (In Windows 3.0, to run WinSpector automatically, add WINSPCTR.EXE to the WIN.INI file's load command.) When developing Windows programs, it's probably best to start WinSpector and leave it running in the background for the entire session.

When a system-level error occurs, WinSpector awakens. While the trail of the GP fault is still warm, the program quickly takes a snapshot of various conditions, register values, and other system-level elements, all of which might help you to determine where your code went awry. Double-click on WinSpector's icon to display a report on recent errors.

Use the Set **P**refs button to select WinSpector's options. You can write information about trapped conditions to a log file, append new information to old logs (probably the best choice to keep a history list of goings on), and set other options to dump stack frame information, add your own comments, and so on.

Deciphering the contents of a WinSpector snapshot requires a great deal of knowledge about Windows, DOS, and PC internals. If you don't comprehend a

WinSpector log file, you probably aren't ready to use the information anyway. In fact, if you are just getting started with Windows programming, WinSpector's reports might be more confusing than helpful. Even for advanced programmers, a WinSpector snapshot (called a *core dump* in programming's ancient days) still provides only vague clues about a bug. The reports don't tell you what statements in your code committed a crime. They just show you what the victim looks like after the deed has been done.

> **NOTE:** At one point, WinSpector was called Dr. Frank, and its icon resembled Dr. Frankenstein's infamous monster. For a short time, a version of Dr. Frank was publicly available on CompuServe, but the program was deleted when Borland decided to include WinSpector with the 3.1 compiler. Personally, I liked the name Dr. Frank better—after all, debugging Windows code can provide you with more chills than a horror film. At Borland, less ghoulish heads prevailed, however, and Dr. Frank became WinSpector. (Officially, that's "spector" as in "inspector," but the true story behind the program's new name is that "WinSpector" is phonetically, if not literally, the specter of its former monstrous self).

Menus, Icons, and Other Resources

Resources are structures that describe the attributes of various on-screen elements. Resources include menu commands, dialog boxes, buttons, check boxes, icons, and keyboard "hot key" accelerators. You design all of these and other resources separately, then combine them with your compiled program.

There are many ways to accomplish that same end. In the early days of Windows programming, developers created resources with text-file script commands. A resource compiler such as Microsoft's RC.EXE translated these .RC script files into .RES binary resource files, then bound the result into the compiled program's .EXE image.

NOTE: Borland C++ 3.1 now includes Borland's own resource compiler, BRC.EXE. Use the program as you do RC.EXE—that is, enter a command such as **brc myfile.rc** to compile a resource script. Enter **brc** alone for a list of options. BRC calls two other code files, BRCC.EXE and RLINK.EXE, which together are functionally equivalent to Microsoft's RC.EXE utility. Unlike RC, however, BRC can bind multiple resource (.RES) files into an executable code file, and the Borland program also does a better job of detecting resource ID conflicts. (See file MANUAL.RW in your Borland C++ DOC subdirectory for more information about using BRC.EXE.)

You can still write resource scripts in these old-fashioned ways, but it's much easier to use a tool such as Borland's Resource Workshop (RW), supplied with Borland C++ 3.1 and Application Frameworks (see Figure 21.5). With RW, you construct your resources on-screen as you want them to appear. You then can create an .RC script file or a compiled .RES binary file, ready for attaching to your code.

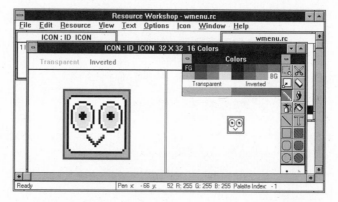

Figure 21.5. Design resources directly with Resource Workshop.

That step requires some forethought. The simplest course is to create .RES files directly (use RW's File|Preferences command and select the Multi-save .RES check box). Add the .RES file to your program's project to have the compiler bind the resources directly into the linked .EXE code file.

It's also possible to add .RC script text files to a project, in which case TCW 3.0 calls RC.EXE to compile the resource commands into a binary .RES file. The new BCW 3.1 can compile .RC script files directly; it doesn't require RC.EXE to be online. If you compile with the command-line compiler, you must run RC.EXE to bind a resource file to your compiled code. In fact, you must run RC.EXE on your program's .EXE code file *even if your program does not use any resources.*

NOTE: This chapter does not list .RC script files for sample listings. The files are included on disk, however, along with binary .RES files ready for binding. Icon files (.ICO) also are provided on disk. Use RW to open the .RC script files to examine sample resources.

The next program uses resources to construct a pull-down menu and an About-Box dialog—a common place to insert a copyright notice or other miscellaneous information about the program (see Figure 21.6). Several files make up the demonstration, including Listing 21.4, wmenu.h (the program's header file), and Listing 21.5, WMENU.CPP (the program's source text). In addition to these two files, on disk you'll find WMENU.DEF (linker definition file), WMENU.ICO (About-Box and desktop icon image), WMENU.PRJ (IDE project file), WMENU.RC (resources in script form for loading into RW), and WMENU.RES (resources in binary form). As you can see, there are many component files in a Windows program!

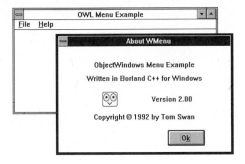

Figure 21.6. wmenu's main window and About-Box dialog.

Listing 21.4. wmenu.h (WMENU's header file).

```
 1:  // Resource ID values
 2:
 3:  #define ID_MENU 100
 4:  #define ID_ABOUT 100
 5:  #define ID_ACC 100
 6:  #define ID_ICON 100
 7:
 8:  // Menu-command ID values
 9:
10:  #define CM_FILEEXIT 102
11:  #define CM_HELPABOUT 201
```

Listing 21.5. WMENU.CPP (An OWL program with menu and dialog resources).

```
 1:  #include <owl.h>
 2:  #include "wmenu.h"
 3:
 4:  class TWMenuApp: public TApplication
 5:  {
 6:  public:
 7:    TWMenuApp(LPSTR aName, HANDLE hInstance, HANDLE hPrevInstance,
 8:      LPSTR lpCmd, int nCmdShow) : TApplication(aName, hInstance,
 9:      hPrevInstance, lpCmd, nCmdShow) {};
10:    virtual void InitInstance();
11:    virtual void InitMainWindow();
12:  };
13:
14:  class TWMenuWin: public TWindow
15:  {
16:  public:
17:    TWMenuWin(PTWindowsObject aParent, LPSTR aTitle);
18:    virtual void GetWindowClass(WNDCLASS& aWndClass);
19:    virtual LPSTR GetClassName()
20:      { return "TWMenuWin"; }
21:    virtual void CMFileNew(RTMessage)
22:      = [CM_FIRST + CM_FILENEW];
23:    virtual void CMFileExit(RTMessage)
```

```
24:       = [CM_FIRST + CM_FILEEXIT];
25:    virtual void CMHelpAbout(RTMessage)
26:       = [CM_FIRST + CM_HELPABOUT];
27: };
28:
29:
30: // Initialize this program instance
31: void TWMenuApp::InitInstance()
32: {
33:    TApplication::InitInstance();
34:    HAccTable = LoadAccelerators(hInstance, MAKEINTRESOURCE(ID_ACC));
35: }
36:
37: // Initialize TWMenuApp's main window
38: void TWMenuApp::InitMainWindow()
39: {
40:    MainWindow = new TWMenuWin(NULL, "OWL Menu Example");
41: }
42:
43: // Construct a TWMenuWin object
44: TWMenuWin::TWMenuWin(PTWindowsObject aParent, LPSTR aTitle)
45:    : TWindow(aParent, aTitle)
46: {
47:    AssignMenu(ID_MENU);
48:    Attr.X = GetSystemMetrics(SM_CXSCREEN) / 8;
49:    Attr.Y = GetSystemMetrics(SM_CYSCREEN) / 8;
50:    Attr.H = Attr.Y * 6;
51:    Attr.W = Attr.X * 6;
52: }
53:
54: // Return window "class" information
55: void TWMenuWin::GetWindowClass(WNDCLASS& aWndClass)
56: {
57:    TWindow::GetWindowClass(aWndClass);
58:    aWndClass.hIcon = LoadIcon(GetApplication()->hInstance,
59:       MAKEINTRESOURCE(ID_ICON));
60: }
61:
62: // Respond to the File menu's New command
63: void TWMenuWin::CMFileNew(RTMessage)
64: {
```

continues

Listing 21.5. continued

```
65:    MessageBeep(0);   // Not implemented!
66:  }
67:
68:  // Respond to the File menu's Exit command
69:  void TWMenuWin::CMFileExit(RTMessage)
70:  {
71:    CloseWindow();   // Proper way to close an OWL window
72:  }
73:
74:  // Respond to the Help menu's About OWLWMenu command
75:  void TWMenuWin::CMHelpAbout(RTMessage)
76:  {
77:    GetApplication()->ExecDialog(new TDialog(this, ID_ABOUT));
78:  }
79:
80:  int PASCAL WinMain(HANDLE hInstance, HANDLE hPrevInstance,
81:    LPSTR lpCmd, int nCmdShow)
82:  {
83:    TWMenuApp WMenuApp("WMenu", hInstance, hPrevInstance,
84:      lpCmd, nCmdShow);
85:    WMenuApp.Run();
86:    return WMenuApp.Status;
87:  }
```

There's a new member function, InitInstance(), in WMENU's TApplication class, TWMenuApp (lines 4–12). InitInstance() is appropriate for program-instance-related tasks, in this case, to load a keyboard accelerator table of menu key definitions such as F3 and Alt+X (see lines 31–35). OWL calls InitInstance() for each program instance—that is, for each new copy of a program. You can run one, two, or several copies of WMENU, for example, and in each case, OWL calls the application's InitInstance() member function. Only one copy of the program's code ever exists in RAM, but each copy receives its own data segment, so you probably don't need to take special precautions to guard against global-data conflicts. Not shown is a similar function, which you can declare in your TApplication derived class as

```
virtual void InitApplication();
```

Implement this member function for tasks to perform *only the first time an application runs.* By using InitApplication() and InitInstance(), you can write programs that users can run many times for working on separate documents while sharing the same code in memory, thus conserving RAM.

WMENU's TWMenuWin constructor (lines 44–52) loads the program's menu by passing its resource identifier ID_MENU to AssignMenu. You usually store constants like ID_MENU in a header file such as wmenu.h, which RW can create and maintain automatically. It's possible to name resources using strings, but symbolic constants take less memory.

In addition to loading the program's menu, the constructor assigns position, width, and height values to members of structure Attr (see lines 48–51). The window isn't yet visible at this stage in the program, so these changes take effect later.

As in SKETCH, GetWindowClass modifies one of the window class's default values, in this case loading the program's icon resource and attaching it to the window class's hIcon member (lines 58–59). hIcon is a *handle*—an integer value that Windows uses to identify various items stored internally. Visible windows have handles, too, named HWindow in OWL programs.

Skip down briefly to WMENU's WinMain() function (lines 80–87). Look familiar? Except for the class and object names, this is the identical main program in SKETCH and OWLWELC. No matter how complex the application, you construct a WinMain() function in this same way.

That leaves the program's response functions, declared at lines 21–26. Take a close look at the first such function, CMFileNew(), repeated here for reference:

```
virtual void CMFileNew(RTMessage)
  = [CM_FIRST + CM_FILENEW];
```

CMFileNew() uses the same design as the response functions in SKETCH. This time, however, the ID value in brackets equals the command-message base constant CM_FIRST plus the command's ID value assigned in the resource, CM_FILENEW. When you select WMENU's File|New command, Windows generates a WM_COMMAND message that includes CM_FILENEW's integer value. Normally you create your own menu-command identifiers (see wmenu.h, Listing 21.4). In this case, however, OWL provides CM_FILENEW along with a few other menu commands available to programs that include owl.h. Use the same identifiers in RW by adding or including the owlrc.h header in the resource script project.

> **NOTE:** If you have trouble adding headers to RW resource projects, set an INCLUDE environment variable to *base*\OWL\INCLUDE;*base*\INCLUDE where *base* usually is C:\BORLANDC. You might also include *base*\CLASSLIB\INCLUDE. Be careful not to introduce a conflict between RW and MAKE, which also recognizes an INCLUDE variable. (If you receive errors while rebuilding Borland C++ standard and class library sources, an INCLUDE variable setting might be the culprit.)

After declaring response functions for various Windows messages and, in this case, for WMENU's commands, implement each command to perform whatever actions you want. For instance, CMFileNew()'s implementation at lines 63–66 responds to the File|New command. WMENU's menu is just for show, so this function merely calls MessageBeep(0) to sound a brief alarm. (The zero is required for reasons known only to Microsoft's programmers.) MessageBeep() is handy for inserting audible debugging clues in programs. If you aren't sure whether a function runs, add a MessageBeep() statement at a strategic spot.

Lines 69–72 similarly implement the CMFileExit() response function. Selecting WMENU's File|Exit command runs this function, which calls member function CloseWindow(). Always call CloseWindow() to close a TWindow class object. Don't call PostQuitMessage(0), as you might do in a conventional Windows program. Calling CloseWindow() gives OWL the opportunity to perform cleanup chores before ending the application.

Finally in WMENU, function CMHelpAbout() responds to the Help|About command. This function displays the program's About-Box dialog—an example of a *modal dialog box*. Modal dialogs are essential to Windows programming. Let's take a closer look at them.

Modal Dialogs

A modal dialog is so named because it throws the program into a *mode* that disables subactivities until you close the dialog window. Modal dialogs are like young children. They demand all of a program's attention, and you must respond to them before you can use other program commands and features.

Modal dialogs do not, however, prevent you from switching to another application. The modal or modeless state of a dialog applies only to the host application, not to other independently running programs. (More on this later.)

To activate a modal dialog, use a command such as

```
GetApplication()->ExecDialog(new TDialog(this, ID_ABOUT));
```

The statement calls GetApplication(), a member function inherited from TWindowsObject, the ancestor to TWindow and thus ancestor to every window, control, and dialog object in an OWL program. GetApplication() returns a pointer to the program's TApplication class object, for which you can call another function, ExecDialog(), to display modal dialog boxes. To ExecDialog() pass the address of a TDialog class object (or of a derived class) constructed with two arguments: this representing the address of the parent object (in this case the address of the TWMenuWin object for this program's main window) and a resource identifier (either a numeric constant such as ID_ABOUT or a string, depending on how you named the dialog resource in RW).

That single (if somewhat involved) statement is all you need in order to activate any modal dialog. OWL and Windows take care of the rest, displaying the dialog, handling keyboard and mouse events, clicking buttons, toggling check boxes, and so on.

When you close the dialog, because you passed this to the TDialog constructor (see line 77 in WMENU.CPP), the owning object deletes the TDialog object from memory. Generally, when a class constructor declares a parent window pointer parameter (see TDialog's constructor in your *ObjectWindows for C++ User's Guide* or in BCW's online help), the parent deletes the object automatically.

Modeless Dialogs

Modeless dialogs look like the modal variety, but they behave as child windows—those that belong to another parent window. Modeless dialogs are like older children. They operate independently of their parents and do not prevent you from using the program's menus and other features.

Designing modeless dialogs is no different from designing modal ones. In fact, any modal dialog can become a modeless one without any changes to its resource. Using modeless dialogs, however, is trickier. As an example, compile and run WMENU.CPP (Listing 21.5) so you know that the program works. Then, delete or change to a comment line 77 in CMHelpAbout(), which calls ExecDialog().

Next, add the following declaration to function CMHelpAbout():

```
PTDialog D;   // Pointer to modeless dialog instance
```

Pointer D, of type PTDialog (an alias for TDialog *), will address an object of type TDialog. Use this object to create, initialize, and display the program's About-Box dialog. Add these lines also to CMHelpAbout():

```
D = new TDialog(this, ID_ABOUT);
D->EnableAutoCreate();
GetApplication()->MakeWindow(D);
D->Show(SW_SHOW);
```

After making these changes, compile and run the program. Now you can open a gaggle of About-Box dialogs, and you can use the program's menus even when the dialogs are active.

The first statement uses operator new to construct a TDialog object. Instead of passing that object's address to ExecDialog() as before, however, the function calls its EnableAutoCreate() member function, inherited from TWindowsObject. This step prepares the TDialog object to create the *Windows* window element that corresponds to the class object. To create that element, the program next calls the application's MakeWindow() member function, passing it the address of the modeless TDialog object.

At this point, there are two elements in memory: the TDialog class object and a Windows window element associated with that object. To make the window visible, the final statement calls the TDialog class's Show() member function, inherited from TWindowsObject. To Show() you can pass various constants (SW_SHOW here). (Look up these constants in BCW's online help.)

NOTE: If you haven't yet taken advantage of the extensive online help provided with BCW, you're missing one of the great sources of information on OWL programming. The online help text documents every member in every OWL class.

Windows and Graphics

In addition to providing a graphical user interface, Windows gives programmers a rich library of device-independent graphics functions. Collectively known as the Graphics

Device Interface (GDI), these functions work independently of any specific output device. This means you can use the same `Rectangle()` function to draw rectangles in windows and also print rectangles on paper, or perhaps draw them on a plotter.

Key to Windows GDI graphics is the concept of a display context, represented by a handle of type `HDC`. A display context joins a device (such as the display) using a device driver (software provided by Windows or by a hardware manufacturer) to an internal structure represented by the `HDC` handle. To draw on a device, you initialize or otherwise obtain a handle to a display context and pass that handle to a GDI function such as `Rectangle()`. If all goes as planned, a glorious rectangle appears soon thereafter.

Listing 21.6, GRDEMO.CPP, demonstrates how to add a `Paint()` member function to a `TWindow` derived class for drawing shapes in windows. The program also illustrates an important GDI concept—that all Windows programs must be able to re-create their window contents on demand.

Listing 21.6. GRDEMO.CPP (OWL graphics demonstration).

```
 1:  #include <owl.h>
 2:  #include <string.h>
 3:
 4:  class TGrDemoApp: public TApplication
 5:  {
 6:  public:
 7:    TGrDemoApp(LPSTR aName, HANDLE hInstance, HANDLE hPrevInstance,
 8:      LPSTR lpCmd, int nCmdShow) : TApplication(aName, hInstance,
 9:      hPrevInstance, lpCmd, nCmdShow) {};
10:    virtual void InitMainWindow();
11:  };
12:
13:  _CLASSDEF(TGrDemoWin)
14:  class TGrDemoWin: public TWindow
15:  {
16:  public:
17:    TGrDemoWin(PTWindowsObject aParent, LPSTR aTitle)
18:      : TWindow(aParent, aTitle) { }
19:    virtual void Paint(HDC PaintDC, PAINTSTRUCT &);
20:  };
21:
```

continues

Listing 21.6. continued

```
22:  // Initialize TGrDemoApp's main window
23:  void TGrDemoApp::InitMainWindow()
24:  {
25:    MainWindow = new TGrDemoWin(NULL, "Graphics Demonstration");
26:  }
27:
28:  // Paint or repaint window's contents on demand
29:  void TGrDemoWin::Paint(HDC PaintDC, PAINTSTRUCT &)
30:  {
31:    HBRUSH newbrush, oldbrush;
32:    char msg[] = " This rectangle MIGHT be orange!";
33:
34:    newbrush = CreateSolidBrush(RGB(255, 127, 0));
35:    oldbrush = SelectObject(PaintDC, newbrush);
36:    Rectangle(PaintDC, 25, 25, 250, 175);
37:    SelectObject(PaintDC, oldbrush);
38:    TextOut(PaintDC, 25, 200, msg, strlen(msg));
39:    DeleteObject(newbrush);
40:  }
41:
42:  int PASCAL WinMain(HANDLE hInstance, HANDLE hPrevInstance,
43:    LPSTR lpCmd, int nCmdShow)
44:  {
45:    TGrDemoApp GrDemoApp("GrDemo", hInstance, hPrevInstance,
46:      lpCmd, nCmdShow);
47:    GrDemoApp.Run();
48:    return GrDemoApp.Status;
49:  }
```

Compile and run GRDEMO (using the supplied GRDEMO.PRJ project on disk). The program displays a rectangle and a string. On color displays, the rectangle should be orange. These shapes appear in the window courtesy of TGrDemoWin's Paint() member function declared at line 19.

OWL calls Paint() in response to a WM_PAINT message from Windows, which indicates that a window requires updating. To Paint() OWL passes two arguments: an initialized display context, PaintDC, and a reference to a PAINTSTRUCT structure containing information about the update region. Windows normally clips drawing to the window's boundaries, so in Paint(), you can simply draw your entire window's contents. You don't have to calculate which parts of a window require updating.

Sophisticated applications, however, might need to use the supplied information to restrict drawing to on-screen elements in order to improve display speeds.

The ancestor `TWindow::Paint()` is just a place holder, so there's no need to call it. To color the rectangle, lines 34–35 obtain a solid brush from Windows, assigning the brush object's handle to `newbrush`. Calling `SelectObject()` inserts the new brush into the display context, and returns the current brush handle restored in a similar statement at line 37. Object's like brushes and pens (used to color lines) take memory. Always delete them by calling `DeleteObject()` as shown at line 39.

To display the rectangle, `Paint()` calls `Rectangle()` at line 36, passing the display context `PaintDC` and the shape's coordinates. Line 38 draws a line of text by calling the Windows `TextOut()` function.

Because Windows might call on your window to update its contents at any time, you cannot draw in windows and expect those shapes to remain on display for any length of time. In Windows graphics, you must keep track of *every* displayed object, perhaps by storing their coordinates in an array or inserting shape objects into a list. In a `TWindow` class derivative, declare a `Paint()` member function that draws your window's shapes. Follow this concept religiously to keep your windows in shape.

DLLs and Custom Controls

A Dynamic Link Library, or DLL, is a kind of runtime programming library—a module of functions that multiple programs can share. Only one copy of a DLL ever exists in RAM, no matter how many programs use it. You might also use DLLs for multilanguage programming. As soon as they are compiled, DLLs are available to all Windows programs—provided, that is, that the DLL conforms to expected data formats such as floating-point representations. In fact, Windows itself is largely composed of several DLLs.

One intriguing use for DLLs is in custom controls. You can design a control, compile it to a DLL, and then plug the control into a dialog box just as you can buttons, check boxes, scroll bars, and other built-in controls. In the next few listings, you'll implement a sample DLL with a pie-shaped control, useful in a status dialog that you might include in an installation utility or in any program that performs lengthy activities. Figure 21.7 shows a sample dialog with the custom pie-shaped control indicating the elapsed time of a dummy test operation.

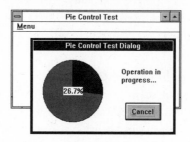

Figure 21.7. A custom control DLL in service.

The first of several related listings is Listing 21.7, piectrl.h, the DLL's header file. Several #define statements define constants as WM_USER plus values from zero to three. These are called *user-defined messages*—those that programs use to communicate with the DLL's control window. Two other constants, PIE_BACKCOLOR and PIE_FORECOLOR, serve as selectors for the WM_CTLCOLOR message, which the control sends to host programs to request color values. In that way, each program that uses the DLL can color the custom control differently.

Listing 21.7. piectrl.h.

```
1:  // Resource ID values
2:
3:  #define PIE_SETLIMIT (WM_USER + 0)
4:  #define PIE_GETLIMIT (WM_USER + 1)
5:  #define PIE_SETINDEX (WM_USER + 2)
6:  #define PIE_GETINDEX (WM_USER + 3)
7:  #define PIE_BACKCOLOR 100
8:  #define PIE_FORECOLOR 101
```

Like executable Windows programs, a DLL requires a definition .DEF file. As Listing 21.8, PIECTRL.DEF, shows, the first line, LIBRARY PIECTRL, tells the linker to create a .DLL rather than an .EXE code file.

Listing 21.8. PIECTRL.DEF.

```
1:  LIBRARY PIECTRL
2:  EXETYPE WINDOWS
3:  CODE PRELOAD MOVEABLE DISCARDABLE
4:  DATA PRELOAD MOVEABLE SINGLE
5:  HEAPSIZE 1024
```

The DLL's source module is shown in Listing 21.9, PIECTRL.CPP. To compile the DLL, load its project file into BCW (PIECTRL.PRJ is supplied on this book's accompanying disk) and press F9. You can't run a DLL. You have to write another program to load and use the library.

> **NOTE:** PIECTRL.CPP uses the stricter definitions in windows.h, as supplied by Borland C++ 3.1 to support Windows 3.1. If you are using Turbo C++ for Windows 3.0, enable lines 18–19 (remove the leading // comment indicators), delete lines 22–23 (or convert them to comments), enable lines 100–101, and delete or comment-out lines 105–106. These changes are necessary because, where WORD parameters were permitted under Version 3.0 (of Windows and Borland C++), new UINT (unsigned integer) parameters are now required.

Listing 21.9. PIECTRL.CPP.

```
 1:  #include <windows.h>
 2:  #include <stdio.h>
 3:  #include <string.h>
 4:  #include <math.h>
 5:  #include "piectrl.h"
 6:
 7:  #define CLASS_NAME "PieCtrl"    // Custom control class name
 8:  #define EXTRA_BYTES 4           // Extra bytes in window instance
 9:  #define PIE_LIMIT 0             // Offset to instance Limit value
10:  #define PIE_INDEX 2             // Offset to instance Index value
11:
12:  // Function prototypes
13:  double Radians(double w);
14:  BOOL RegisterPieCtrl(HANDLE hInstance);
15:  void Paint(HDC DC, HWND hWindow);
16:
17:  // Turbo C++ for Windows 3.0
18:  // LONG FAR PASCAL PieWndFn(HWND hWindow, WORD wMsg, WORD wParam,
19:  //   LONG lParam);
20:
```

continues

Listing 21.9. continued

```
21:   // Borland C++ for Windows 3.1
22:   LONG FAR PASCAL PieWndFn(HWND hWindow, UINT wMsg, UINT wParam,
23:     LONG lParam);
24:
25:   // Global variable
26:   HANDLE hModuleInstance = NULL;
27:
28:   // Return radians in angle w
29:   double Radians(double w)
30:   {
31:     int iw = floor(w);
32:     return (abs(iw % 360) * M_PI / 180.0);
33:   }
34:
35:   // Register the custom control window with Windows
36:   BOOL RegisterPieCtrl(HANDLE hInstance)
37:   {
38:     WNDCLASS w;   // Windows "window class" structure
39:
40:     w.cbClsExtra = 0;
41:     w.cbWndExtra = EXTRA_BYTES;
42:     w.hbrBackground = 0;
43:     w.hIcon = 0;
44:     w.hInstance = hInstance;
45:     w.hCursor = LoadCursor(0, IDC_ARROW);
46:     w.lpfnWndProc = PieWndFn;
47:     w.lpszClassName = CLASS_NAME;
48:     w.lpszMenuName = 0;
49:     w.style = CS_HREDRAW ¦ CS_VREDRAW ¦ CS_GLOBALCLASS;
50:     return RegisterClass(&w);
51:   }
52:
53:   // Paint pie control
54:   void Paint(HDC DC, HWND hWindow)
55:   {
56:     RECT r;
57:     HBRUSH brush;
58:     WORD tHeight, center;
59:     double dLimit, dIndex;
60:     int xEnd, yEnd, xStart, yStart;
```

```
61:    double percent, dRadius, endAngle, startAngle = 270.0;
62:    char s[20];
63:
64:    SaveDC(DC);
65:    GetClientRect(hWindow, &r);
66:    if (r.right > r.bottom)
67:      r.right = r.bottom;
68:    else if (r.bottom > r.right)
69:      r.bottom = r.right;
70:    dRadius = r.right;
71:    center = r.right / 2;
72:    dLimit = SendMessage(hWindow, PIE_GETLIMIT, 0, 0);
73:    dIndex = SendMessage(hWindow, PIE_GETINDEX, 0, 0);
74:    percent = dIndex / dLimit;
75:    sprintf(s, "%0.1f%%", (percent * 100.0));
76:    endAngle = startAngle + (percent * 360.0);
77:    xEnd = center + floor(dRadius * cos(Radians(endAngle)));
78:    yEnd = center + floor(dRadius * sin(Radians(endAngle)));
79:    xStart = center + floor(dRadius * cos(Radians(startAngle)));
80:    yStart = center + floor(dRadius * sin(Radians(startAngle)));
81:    brush = (HBRUSH) SendMessage(GetParent(hWindow),
82:      WM_CTLCOLOR, DC, MAKELONG(hWindow, PIE_BACKCOLOR));
83:    SelectObject(DC, brush);
84:    Pie(DC, r.left, r.top, r.right, r.bottom,
85:      xEnd, yEnd, xStart, yStart);
86:    if (dLimit != dIndex) {
87:      brush = (HBRUSH) SendMessage(GetParent(hWindow),
88:        WM_CTLCOLOR, DC, MAKELONG(hWindow, PIE_FORECOLOR));
89:      SelectObject(DC, brush);
90:      Pie(DC, r.left, r.top, r.right, r.bottom,
91:        xStart, yStart, xEnd, yEnd);
92:    }
93:    tHeight = HIWORD(GetTextExtent(DC, s, 1));
94:    SetTextAlign(DC, TA_CENTER);
95:    TextOut(DC, center, center - tHeight / 2, s, strlen(s));
96:    RestoreDC(DC, -1);
97:  }
98:
99:  // Turbo C++ for Windows 3.0
100: // LONG FAR PASCAL PieWndFn(HWND hWindow, WORD wMsg, WORD wParam,
101: //   LONG lParam)
```

continues

Listing 21.9. continued

```
102:
103:   // Pie control "window function" i.e. message dispatcher
104:   // Borland C++ for Windows 3.1
105:   LONG FAR PASCAL PieWndFn(HWND hWindow, UINT wMsg, UINT wParam,
106:     LONG lParam)
107:   {
108:     long result = 0L;
109:     PAINTSTRUCT ps;
110:
111:     switch (wMsg) {
112:       case WM_CREATE:
113:         SendMessage(hWindow, PIE_SETLIMIT, 100, 0);
114:         SendMessage(hWindow, PIE_SETINDEX, 0, 0);
115:         break;
116:       case WM_GETDLGCODE:
117:         result = DLGC_STATIC;
118:         break;
119:       case WM_PAINT:
120:         BeginPaint(hWindow, &ps);
121:         Paint(ps.hdc, hWindow);
122:         EndPaint(hWindow, &ps);
123:         break;
124:       case PIE_SETLIMIT:
125:         if (GetWindowWord(hWindow, PIE_LIMIT) != wParam) {
126:           SetWindowWord(hWindow, PIE_LIMIT, wParam);
127:           InvalidateRect(hWindow, NULL, FALSE);
128:           UpdateWindow(hWindow);
129:         }
130:         break;
131:       case PIE_GETLIMIT:
132:         result = GetWindowWord(hWindow, PIE_LIMIT);
133:         break;
134:       case PIE_SETINDEX:
135:         if (GetWindowWord(hWindow, PIE_INDEX) != wParam) {
136:           SetWindowWord(hWindow, PIE_INDEX, wParam);
137:           InvalidateRect(hWindow, NULL, FALSE);
138:           UpdateWindow(hWindow);
139:         }
140:         break;
141:       case PIE_GETINDEX:
142:         result = GetWindowWord(hWindow, PIE_INDEX);
```

```
143:        break;
144:      default:
145:        result = DefWindowProc(hWindow, wMsg, wParam, lParam);
146:        break;
147:    }
148:    return result;
149:  }
150:
151:  // Windows Exit Procedure (WEP) for DLLs
152:  int FAR PASCAL WEP(int nSystemExit)
153:  {
154:    switch (nSystemExit) {
155:      case WEP_SYSTEM_EXIT:
156:        break;                    // System shut down
157:      case WEP_FREE_DLL:
158:        break;                    // DLL released
159:    }
160:    UnregisterClass(CLASS_NAME, hModuleInstance);
161:    return 1;
162:  }
163:
164:  // DLL rough equivalent to a DOS program's main() function
165:  int FAR PASCAL LibMain(HANDLE hModule, WORD /*wDataSeg*/,
166:    WORD /*wHeapSize*/, LPSTR /*lpszCmdLine*/)
167:  {
168:    hModuleInstance = hModule;
169:    return RegisterPieCtrl(hModule);
170:  }
```

Lines 165–170 at the end of the listing reveal a key difference between DLLs and executable Windows programs. In place of the usual WinMain(), a DLL has a LibMain() function. When Windows first loads a DLL, it calls this function to initialize the library. Typically, as done here, LibMain() saves the DLL's instance handle in a global variable and registers the DLL's window—in this case, the custom pie-control window.

Registration takes place at lines 36–51. Several statements assign values to a WNDCLASS structure, passed by address to the Windows RegisterClass() function. Line 47 specifies the class name, which a dialog box or other window can use to reference the custom control. Registering the window makes its design parameters available to any and all programs.

The only remaining job is to respond to messages passed to the control's window function—that is, the function charged with receiving the control window's messages and taking appropriate actions. Function PieWndFn() (lines 105–149) handles all messages sent to a custom pie control window. In listing order, the control's messages and line numbers are:

- WM_CREATE (112) is called during the control window's initialization. Sends two user-defined messages to itself, setting the control's maximum range to 100 and the current index to zero. The "limit" might represent a total time estimate, the number of files to be copied, or some other number of operations to be performed. The "index" is the amount of time or other unit from zero to "limit" that has passed.

- WM_GETDLGCODE (116) returns DLGC_STATIC, telling Windows not to send any keyboard messages to this window.

- WM_PAINT (119) draws the control's shape on demand, calling BeginPaint() to initialize a PAINTSTRUCT structure (see line 109) and provides a display context (member hdc in the structure). To avoid cluttering the program with drawing commands, line 121 calls a local function, Paint(), to draw the control (see lines 54–97). Finally, line 122 calls EndPaint(), releasing the display context and countering the earlier BeginPaint() statement. (OWL takes similar steps in calling a TWindow class Paint() member function in response to a WM_PAINT message.)

- PIE_SETLIMIT (124) implements one of the control's user-defined messages, in this case setting the maximum limit for the control.

- PIE_GETLIMIT (131) is another user-defined message that returns the current control limit value.

- PIE_SETINDEX (134) sets the control's index, which can range from zero to the current limit.

- PIE_GETINDEX (141) returns the control's current index value.

Finally in PIECTRL, function WEP() (Windows Exit Procedure) shuts down the DLL. Windows calls WEP() when the last exiting program to use the DLL frees it from memory, and also as part of Windows' shutdown sequence. As shown at lines 152–162, you can inspect parameter nSystemExit to take different actions for each of these conditions. In this case, the DLL requires no special actions, and you can remove these lines. Line 160 calls `UnregisterClass()` to delete the class name from Windows before the DLL disappears from RAM.

That finishes the custom control DLL. Now you need a program to use it. Before writing the code, you need to design a dialog box to hold the custom control. (The accompanying disk includes the complete resource in file PIETEST.RES.) To create your own dialogs, follow these steps:

1. Start RW's dialog editor, either by creating a new dialog resource or by selecting an existing one from the current project.

2. Select RW's static-text control. RW doesn't recognize your custom pie control, so you'll insert a static-text item into the dialog, then bind it to the custom control window's class.

3. Size and position the static-text item. The custom pie control uses the smaller resource dimension to calculate its diameter, so the end result is always circular, even if the static-text item isn't perfectly square.

4. Press and hold the Ctrl key while you double-click the mouse pointer inside the static-text item. This obscure RW command opens the control's Generic Control Style dialog box.

5. In that dialog, set Class to `"PieCtrl"`. You must type the surrounding double quotes. Close the dialog and save the project.

You have just told RW to associate the dummy static-text control with a window registered under the name "PieCtrl." You won't see the actual control in RW. At runtime, in the course of creating the program's dialog, Windows searches for a window class to match each of the dialog's controls, including the custom pie-shaped control. So that Windows finds the custom control's class name (`"PieCtrl"`), the host program loads PIECTRL.DLL, which, as mentioned before, initializes and registers the custom control window class. If the DLL is already in memory, Windows ignores any command to load another copy. Thus, only one copy of the same DLL ever exists in RAM.

Listing 21.10, pietest.h (resource ID header file), and Listing 21.11, PIETEST.CPP (host program), carry out these final steps in the process of using a custom control. The program displays the dialog box in Figure 21.7.

Listing 21.10. pietest.h.

```
1:  // Resource ID values
2:
3:  #define ID_MENU 100
4:  #define ID_DIALOG 100
5:  #define ID_PIECTRL 1
6:
7:  // Menu-command ID values
8:
9:  #define CM_TEST 101
```

Listing 21.11. PIETEST.CPP.

```
1:  #include <owl.h>
2:  #include "piectrl.h"
3:  #include "pietest.h"
4:
5:  #define PIE_CTRL_DLL "PIECTRL.DLL"   // Name of custom control DLL
6:  #define EM_DLLNOTFOUND 1             // DLL not found error code
7:  #define END_TIME 15                  // Max time for test dialog
8:
9:  // Function prototype
10: void Delay(long mSecs);
11:
12: class TPieApp: public TApplication
13: {
14: private:
15:   HANDLE libHandle;
16: public:
17:   TPieApp(LPSTR aName, HANDLE hInstance, HANDLE hPrevInstance,
18:     LPSTR lpCmd, int nCmdShow);
19:   ~TPieApp();
20:   virtual void Error(int errorCode);
21:   virtual void InitMainWindow();
22: };
23:
24: _CLASSDEF(TPieWin)
25: class TPieWin: public TWindow
26: {
```

```
27:  private:
28:    BOOL testing;
29:  public:
30:    TPieWin(PTWindowsObject AParent, LPSTR ATitle);
31:    virtual BOOL CanClose();
32:    virtual void CMTest(RTMessage)
33:      = [CM_FIRST + CM_TEST];
34:  };
35:
36:  _CLASSDEF(TPieDlg)
37:  class TPieDlg: public TDialog
38:  {
39:  private:
40:    HBRUSH backBrush, foreBrush;
41:  public:
42:    BOOL continueFlag;
43:    TPieDlg(PTWindowsObject aParent, int resourceID);
44:    ~TPieDlg();
45:    void Start(WORD endTime);
46:    void Update(WORD time);
47:    virtual void Cancel(RTMessage)
48:      = [ID_FIRST + IDCANCEL];
49:    virtual void WMCtlColor(RTMessage msg)
50:      = [WM_FIRST + WM_CTLCOLOR];
51:  };
52:
53:  void Delay(long mSecs)
54:  {
55:    long mark = GetTickCount() + mSecs;
56:    while (GetTickCount() <= mark) ;
57:  }
58:
59:  // Construct TPieApp application object
60:  TPieApp::TPieApp(LPSTR aName, HANDLE hInstance, HANDLE hPrevInstance,
61:    LPSTR lpCmd, int nCmdShow) : TApplication(aName, hInstance,
62:    hPrevInstance, lpCmd, nCmdShow)
63:  {
64:    libHandle = LoadLibrary(PIE_CTRL_DLL);
65:    if (libHandle < 32)
66:      Status = EM_DLLNOTFOUND;
```

continues

Listing 21.11. continued

```
 67:   }
 68:
 69:   // Destroy TPieApp application object
 70:   TPieApp::~TPieApp()
 71:   {
 72:     if (libHandle >= 32)
 73:       FreeLibrary(libHandle);
 74:   }
 75:
 76:   // Handle startup errors
 77:   void TPieApp::Error(int errorCode)
 78:   {
 79:     if (errorCode == EM_DLLNOTFOUND) {
 80:       MessageBox(NULL, "Can't find PIECTRL.DLL", "Application Error",
 81:         MB_APPLMODAL | MB_ICONSTOP | MB_OK);
 82:       exit(errorCode);
 83:     } else
 84:       TApplication::Error(errorCode);
 85:   }
 86:
 87:   // Initialize TPieApp's main window
 88:   void TPieApp::InitMainWindow()
 89:   {
 90:     MainWindow = new TPieWin(NULL, "Pie Control Test");
 91:   }
 92:
 93:   // Construct TPieWin objects
 94:   TPieWin::TPieWin(PTWindowsObject AParent, LPSTR ATitle)
 95:     : TWindow(AParent, ATitle)
 96:   {
 97:     AssignMenu(ID_MENU);
 98:     testing = FALSE;
 99:   }
100:
101:   // Return true if okay to close window
102:   BOOL TPieWin::CanClose()
103:   {
104:     return ~testing;
105:   }
106:
```

```
107:   // Respond to menu's test command
108:   void TPieWin::CMTest(RTMessage)
109:   {
110:     PTPieDlg d;       // Pointer to modeless dialog
111:     unsigned time;    // Local time unit counter
112:     BOOL finished;    // Operation completed flag
113:
114:     if (testing)      // Prevent recursion
115:       return;
116:     testing = TRUE;                        // Prevent app from ending
117:     d = (PTPieDlg)GetApplication()->MakeWindow(new TPieDlg(this, ID_DIALOG));
118:     if (d == NULL)                         // Exit if above failed
119:       return;
120:     d->Show(SW_NORMAL);
121:     d->Start(END_TIME);                    // Initialize custom control
122:     time = 0;                              // Initialize local time
123:     finished = FALSE;                      // Initialize done flag
124:     while ((finished == FALSE) && (d->continueFlag)) {
125:       d->Update(time);                     // Update custom control position
126:       Delay(500);          // *** Insert your operation or fn call here
127:   //    MessageBeep(0);                    // Optional audible feedback
128:       if (++time > END_TIME)               // Count time passed and set flag
129:         finished = TRUE;
130:     }
131:     if (IsWindow(d->HWindow))              // Close dialog if necessary
132:       d->CloseWindow();
133:     testing = FALSE;                       // Permit application to end
134:   }
135:
136:   // Construct TPieDlg objects and initialize custom control colors
137:   TPieDlg::TPieDlg(PTWindowsObject aParent, int resourceID)
138:     : TDialog(aParent, resourceID)
139:   {
140:     EnableKBHandler();
141:     continueFlag = TRUE;
142:     backBrush = CreateSolidBrush(RGB(16, 0, 16));
143:     foreBrush = CreateSolidBrush(RGB(255, 0, 0));
144:   }
```

continues

Listing 21.11. continued

```
145:
146:   // Destroy TPieDlg objects and delete color brushes
147:   TPieDlg::~TPieDlg()
148:   {
149:     DeleteObject(backBrush);
150:     DeleteObject(foreBrush);
151:   }
152:
153:   // Initialize dialog's pie control values
154:   void TPieDlg::Start(WORD endTime)
155:   {
156:     SendDlgItemMessage(HWindow, ID_PIECTRL, PIE_SETLIMIT, endTime, 0);
157:     SendDlgItemMessage(HWindow, ID_PIECTRL, PIE_SETINDEX, 0, 0);
158:     continueFlag = TRUE;
159:   }
160:
161:   // Update pie control and execute background tasks
162:   void TPieDlg::Update(WORD time)
163:   {
164:     MSG msg;
165:
166:     SendDlgItemMessage(HWindow, ID_PIECTRL, PIE_SETINDEX, time, 0);
167:     while (PeekMessage(&msg, 0, 0, 0, PM_REMOVE)) {
168:       if (~IsDialogMessage(HWindow, &msg)) {
169:         TranslateMessage(&msg);
170:         DispatchMessage(&msg);
171:       }
172:     }
173:   }
174:
175:   // Prepare to shut down dialog prematurely
176:   void TPieDlg::Cancel(RTMessage)
177:   {
178:     continueFlag = FALSE;
179:   }
180:
181:   // Respond to control's request for color information
182:   void TPieDlg::WMCtlColor(RTMessage msg)
183:   {
```

```
184:    switch (msg.LP.Hi) {
185:      case PIE_BACKCOLOR:
186:        msg.Result = backBrush;
187:        break;
188:      case PIE_FORECOLOR:
189:        msg.Result = foreBrush;
190:        break;
191:      default:
192:        DefWndProc(msg);
193:        break;
194:    }
195:  }
196:
197:  int PASCAL WinMain(HANDLE hInstance, HANDLE hPrevInstance,
198:    LPSTR lpCmd, int nCmdShow)
199:  {
200:    TPieApp PieApp("PieTest", hInstance, hPrevInstance,
201:      lpCmd, nCmdShow);
202:    PieApp.Run();
203:    return PieApp.Status;
204:  }
```

The TPieApp class constructor (lines 60–67) calls LoadLibrary() to load
PIECTRL.DLL. If that succeeds, the DLL's custom "PieCtrl" window class is
initialized and registered with Windows.

Function CMTest() (lines 108–134) displays the program's modeless dialog box
and calls various member functions for the dialog's class, TPieDlg, declared at lines 37–
51. This class, derived from TDialog, communicates with the custom pie control by
sending it messages. Meanwhile, as the dummy operation delay at line 126 shows, you
can call a function or perform any other action while the custom pie control slices itself
down to nothing.

Any program that loads a DLL should free that library before ending. TPieApp's
destructor at lines 70–74 demonstrates one way to accomplish this step. Freeing the
DLL in the application's destructor ensures that this task is completed no matter how
the program ends.

New Features in Windows 3.1.

Released early in 1992, Windows 3.1 makes many improvements and enhancements to Version 3.0. Some of the most important new features include

- *Better performance.* Windows 3.1 runs faster and displays text and graphics more quickly.

- *Improved reliability.* Errors that lead to an Unrecoverable Application Error (UAE) are less likely to hang the system or require rebooting.

- *Object-linking and embedding (OLE).* Programs can share information with this communications protocol, by which users can create documents using editors in multiple OLE-aware applications.

- *Common dialog boxes.* You can use built-in color, font, file, printer, and other dialogs, so you don't have to reinvent the same old "dialog wheels" in every new program.

- *TrueType fonts.* Use these scalable fonts for better looking displays, and to improve text display speed. Because TrueType fonts are scalable, they look similar at different resolutions, providing "what you see is what you get," or WYSIWYG, output.

There are other new features and improvements in Windows 3.1, but these are at the top of the heap. The next sections explain how to compile Windows 3.1 code, and list sample programs that demonstrate two popular Windows 3.1 newcomers—common dialog boxes and TrueType fonts.

Compiling OWL Programs

OWL is compatible with Windows 3.0 and 3.1. To compile Windows 3.0 programs (which run also under Windows 3.1), define the symbol WIN30 using Options|Compiler|Code generation. To compile Windows 3.1 programs, define WIN31. You must define WIN31 to use Windows 3.1 functions.

If you are using Windows 3.1, you can also define the STRICT symbol before including owl.h or windows.h. Defining STRICT helps the compiler do a better job of checking function argument types. Because Windows uses unsigned integers for many different purposes, it's easy to pass functions the wrong type of data—a window handle, for instance, instead of a display context. Without STRICT, the program compiles with no warning of impending disaster. With STRICT, the compiler catches many data-type mismatch errors.

To engage STRICT type checking, select the Options|Compiler|Code generation command and enter **STRICT;WIN31** into the Defines input box. If you receive compiler errors for code that previously compiled, you can usually repair the problem by following these suggestions:

- Use HINSTANCE rather than the generic HANDLE data type in your TApplication class constructor for the hInstance and hPrevInstance parameters.

- Use HINSTANCE rather than HANDLE also for the two instance parameters in function WinMain().

- Double check function parameter and return types. Code that previously compiled might cause an error unless function types are declared exactly as required. Use BCW's online help to verify function declarations.

- Use an explicit typecast for assigning the results of functions such as SelectObject(), which can return several different types of handles. For example, if oldBrush and newBrush are type HBRUSH, use the following statement:

```
oldBrush = (HBRUSH)SelectObject(DC, newBrush);
```

NOTE: The sample Windows 3.1 programs in this chapter have associated .PRJ project files on disk that define the STRICT and WIN31 symbols. The sample Windows 3.0 programs listed previously in this chapter do not use STRICT.

Accessing Common Dialogs

Listing 21.12, COMMON.CPP, demonstrates how to use each of the nine common dialogs in Windows 3.1. Load the COMMON.PRJ project file into BCW and press Ctrl+F9 to compile and run the demo. Select a dialog from the program's Dialogs menu, which has seven commands, one for each dialog. There are only seven commands because the Print command displays a basic printer dialog, from which you can select two additional printer setup dialogs.

One of the niftiest common dialogs presents a color palette for selecting and customizing colors. Figure 21.8. shows the common color dialog, which looks a lot more exciting on a color display than it does in black and white here.

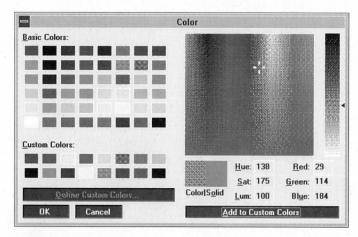

Figure 21.8. Common color dialog.

Listing 21.12. COMMON.CPP (Displays nine common dialogs).

```
 1:  #include <commdlg.h>
 2:  #include <owl.h>
 3:  #include <string.h>
 4:  #include "common.h"
 5:
 6:  #define EM_BADVERSION -100
 7:
 8:  class TCommApp: public TApplication
 9:  {
10:  public:
```

```
11:    TCommApp(LPSTR aName, HINSTANCE hInstance, HINSTANCE hPrevInstance,
12:      LPSTR lpCmd, int nCmdShow) : TApplication(aName, hInstance,
13:      hPrevInstance, lpCmd, nCmdShow) {};
14:    virtual void Error(int ErrorCode);
15:    virtual void InitInstance();
16:    virtual void InitMainWindow();
17:  };
18:
19:  class TCommWin: public TWindow
20:  {
21:  protected:
22:    // Color dialog members
23:    COLORREF color;         // Selected color
24:    COLORREF aColors[16];   // Custom color array
25:    // Font dialog member
26:    LOGFONT font;           // Logical font
27:    // File dialog members
28:    char fileName[256];     // Current filename
29:    char filterStr[81];     // File filter list
30:    int filterIndex;        // Number of filter for dlg list box
31:    // Find and replace dialog data members
32:    HWND hFindDlg;          // Find-and-replace dialog handle
33:    char findStr[41];       // Current find string (find and replace dlg)
34:    char replaceStr[41];    // Current replace string (replace dlg only)
35:    FINDREPLACE fr;         // Find-and-replace dialog structure
36:  public:
37:    TCommWin(PTWindowsObject AParent, LPSTR ATitle);
38:    virtual void GetWindowClass(WNDCLASS& AWndClass);
39:    virtual LPSTR GetClassName()
40:      { return "TCommWin"; }
41:    virtual void CMFileExit(RTMessage)
42:      = [CM_FIRST + CM_FILEEXIT];
43:    virtual void CMDialogsColor(RTMessage)
44:      = [CM_FIRST + CM_DIALOGSCOLOR];
45:    virtual void CMDialogsFont(RTMessage)
46:      = [CM_FIRST + CM_DIALOGSFONT];
47:    virtual void CMDialogsOpen(RTMessage)
48:      = [CM_FIRST + CM_DIALOGSOPEN];
```

continues

949

Listing 21.12. continued

```
49:    virtual void CMDialogsSaveAs(RTMessage)
50:      = [CM_FIRST + CM_DIALOGSSAVEAS];
51:    virtual void CMDialogsPrint(RTMessage)
52:      = [CM_FIRST + CM_DIALOGSPRINT];
53:    virtual void CMDialogsFind(RTMessage)
54:      = [CM_FIRST + CM_DIALOGSFIND];
55:    virtual void CMDialogsReplace(RTMessage)
56:      = [CM_FIRST + CM_DIALOGSREPLACE];
57:    virtual void CMHelpAbout(RTMessage)
58:      = [CM_FIRST + CM_HELPABOUT];
59:  };
60:
61:  // Respond to startup errors
62:  void TCommApp::Error(int ErrorCode)
63:  {
64:    if (ErrorCode == EM_BADVERSION)
65:      MessageBox(0, "Requires Windows 3.1 or later",
66:        "Version Error", MB_APPLMODAL ¦ MB_ICONSTOP ¦ MB_OK);
67:    else
68:      TApplication::Error(ErrorCode);
69:  }
70:
71:  // Detect Windows version number. Halt if < 3.1.
72:  void TCommApp::InitInstance()
73:  {
74:    DWORD version;
75:    char majorRev, minorRev;
76:    BOOL okay;
77:
78:    version = GetVersion();
79:    majorRev = LOBYTE(LOWORD(version));
80:    minorRev = HIBYTE(LOWORD(version));
81:    if (majorRev  < 3) okay = FALSE; else
82:    if (majorRev == 3) okay = (minorRev >= 1); else
83:    if (majorRev  > 3) okay = TRUE;  // I hope!
84:    if (okay)
85:      TApplication::InitInstance();
86:    else
```

```
 87:        Status = EM_BADVERSION;
 88:  }
 89:
 90:  // Initialize the application's window
 91:  void TCommApp::InitMainWindow()
 92:  {
 93:    MainWindow = new TCommWin(NULL, "Common Dialogs");
 94:  }
 95:
 96:  // Construct the application's window object
 97:  TCommWin::TCommWin(PTWindowsObject AParent, LPSTR ATitle)
 98:    : TWindow(AParent, ATitle)
 99:  {
100:    int i;
101:
102:    AssignMenu(ID_MENU);
103:    Attr.X = GetSystemMetrics(SM_CXSCREEN) / 8;
104:    Attr.Y = GetSystemMetrics(SM_CYSCREEN) / 8;
105:    Attr.H = Attr.Y * 6;
106:    Attr.W = Attr.X * 6;
107:  // Initialize color dialog data members
108:    color = RGB(0, 0, 0);  // Initial color
109:    for (i = 0; i <= 15; i++)  // Set custom colors to white
110:      aColors[i] = RGB(255, 255, 255);
111:  // Initialize logical font data members
112:    memset(&font, 0, sizeof(font));
113:  // Initialize filename and list-box filters (wild cards)
114:    fileName[0] = 0;
115:    if (LoadString(GetApplication()->hInstance, STR_FILEFILTERS,
116:        filterStr, sizeof(filterStr)) == 0)
117:      filterStr[0] = 0;
118:    else {
119:      // Must set a variable to the initial length of filterStr
120:      // because the for loop changes the string's apparent length
121:      int fslen = strlen(filterStr);
122:      for (i = 0; i < fslen; i++)
123:        if (filterStr[i] == '|')
124:          filterStr[i] = 0;
125:    }
```

continues

Listing 21.12. continued

```
126:    filterIndex = 1;
127: // Initialize find and replace data members
128:    hFindDlg = 0;
129:    findStr[0] = 0;
130:    replaceStr[0] = 0;
131: }
132:
133: // Modify window class to use custom icon
134: void TCommWin::GetWindowClass(WNDCLASS& AWndClass)
135: {
136:    TWindow::GetWindowClass(AWndClass);
137:    AWndClass.hIcon = LoadIcon(GetApplication()->hInstance,
138:      MAKEINTRESOURCE(ID_ICON));
139: }
140:
141: // Exit program by closing the main window
142: void TCommWin::CMFileExit(RTMessage)
143: {
144:    CloseWindow();
145: }
146:
147: // DIALOG #1: Common color dialog
148: void TCommWin::CMDialogsColor(RTMessage)
149: {
150:    CHOOSECOLOR cc;
151:    COLORREF tempColors[16];
152:    int i;
153:
154:    memset(&cc, 0, sizeof(cc));
155:    for (i = 0; i <= 15; i++)
156:      tempColors[i] = aColors[i];
157:    cc.lStructSize = sizeof(CHOOSECOLOR);
158:    cc.hwndOwner = HWindow;
159:    cc.Flags = CC_RGBINIT ¦ CC_FULLOPEN;
160:    cc.rgbResult = color;
161:    cc.lpCustColors = tempColors;
162:    if (ChooseColor(&cc)) {
163:      color = cc.rgbResult;
164:      for (i = 0; i <= 15; i++)
165:        aColors[i] = tempColors[i];
```

```
166:     }
167:   }
168:
169:   // DIALOG #2: Common font-selection dialog
170:   void TCommWin::CMDialogsFont(RTMessage)
171:   {
172:     CHOOSEFONT cf;
173:     LOGFONT tempFont;
174:
175:     memset(&cf, 0, sizeof(cf));
176:     tempFont = font;  // Copy current font
177:     cf.lStructSize = sizeof(CHOOSEFONT);
178:     cf.hwndOwner = HWindow;
179:     cf.Flags = CF_INITTOLOGFONTSTRUCT ¦ CF_BOTH ¦ CF_EFFECTS;
180:     cf.lpLogFont = &tempFont;
181:     cf.rgbColors = color;  // Selected by Color dialog
182:     if (ChooseFont(&cf)) {
183:       font = *cf.lpLogFont;
184:     }
185:   }
186:
187:   // DIALOG #3: Common file-open dialog
188:   void TCommWin::CMDialogsOpen(RTMessage)
189:   {
190:     OPENFILENAME fn;
191:     char tempName[256];
192:
193:     memset(&fn, 0, sizeof(fn));
194:     strcpy(tempName, fileName);  // Copy current filename
195:     fn.lStructSize = sizeof(OPENFILENAME);
196:     fn.hwndOwner = HWindow;
197:     fn.Flags = OFN_PATHMUSTEXIST ¦ OFN_FILEMUSTEXIST;
198:     fn.lpstrFile = tempName;  // Address current filename
199:     fn.nMaxFile = sizeof(fileName);
200:     fn.lpstrFilter = filterStr;  // Address file filters
201:     fn.nFilterIndex = filterIndex;  // Filter for list box
202:     if (GetOpenFileName(&fn)) {
203:       strcpy(fileName, (const char *)fn.lpstrFile); // Save selected filename
204:       filterIndex = fn.nFilterIndex;  // Save selected filter #
205:     }
```

continues

Listing 21.12. continued

```
206:  }
207:
208:  // DIALOG #4: Common file-save-as dialog
209:  void TCommWin::CMDialogsSaveAs(RTMessage)
210:  {
211:    OPENFILENAME fn;
212:    char tempName[256];
213:
214:    memset(&fn, 0, sizeof(fn));
215:    strcpy(tempName, fileName);  // Copy current filename
216:    fn.lStructSize = sizeof(OPENFILENAME);
217:    fn.hwndOwner = HWindow;
218:    fn.Flags = OFN_OVERWRITEPROMPT;
219:    fn.lpstrFile = tempName;  // Address current filename
220:    fn.nMaxFile = sizeof(fileName);
221:    fn.lpstrFilter = filterStr;  // Address file filters
222:    fn.nFilterIndex = filterIndex;  // Filter for list box
223:    if (GetSaveFileName(&fn)) {
224:      strcpy(fileName, (const char *)fn.lpstrFile);  // Save selected filename
225:      filterIndex = fn.nFilterIndex;  // Save selected filter #
226:    }
227:  }
228:
229:  // DIALOGS #5-7: Common printer, setup, and options dialogs
230:  void TCommWin::CMDialogsPrint(RTMessage)
231:  {
232:    PRINTDLG pd;
233:
234:    memset(&pd, 0, sizeof(pd));
235:    pd.lStructSize = sizeof(PRINTDLG);
236:    pd.hwndOwner = HWindow;
237:    pd.Flags = PD_RETURNDC;  // PD_PRINTSETUP for setup dialog
238:    if (PrintDlg(&pd)) {
239:      // ... Print using pd.hDC device context
240:      DeleteDC(pd.hDC);
241:      if (pd.hDevMode != 0)
242:        GlobalFree(pd.hDevMode);
243:      if (pd.hDevNames != 0)
244:        GlobalFree(pd.hDevNames);
245:    }
```

```
246:   }
247:
248:   // DIALOG #8: Common find-text dialog
249:   void TCommWin::CMDialogsFind(RTMessage)
250:   {
251:     if (hFindDlg) {
252:       SendMessage(hFindDlg, WM_CLOSE, 0, 0);   // Close dialog if open
253:       hFindDlg = 0;
254:     }
255:     memset(&fr, 0, sizeof(fr));
256:     fr.lStructSize = sizeof(FINDREPLACE);
257:     fr.hwndOwner = HWindow;
258:     fr.lpstrFindWhat = findStr;
259:     fr.wFindWhatLen = sizeof(findStr);
260:     hFindDlg = FindText(&fr);
261:   }
262:
263:   // DIALOG #9: Common replace-text dialog
264:   void TCommWin::CMDialogsReplace(RTMessage)
265:   {
266:     if (hFindDlg) {
267:       SendMessage(hFindDlg, WM_CLOSE, 0, 0);   // Close dialog if open
268:       hFindDlg = 0;
269:     }
270:     memset(&fr, 0, sizeof(fr));
271:     fr.lStructSize = sizeof(FINDREPLACE);
272:     fr.hwndOwner = HWindow;
273:     fr.lpstrFindWhat = findStr;
274:     fr.wFindWhatLen = sizeof(findStr);
275:     fr.lpstrReplaceWith = replaceStr;
276:     fr.wReplaceWithLen = sizeof(replaceStr);
277:     hFindDlg = ReplaceText(&fr);
278:   }
279:
280:   // Display this program's about-box dialog
281:   void TCommWin::CMHelpAbout(RTMessage)
282:   {
283:     GetApplication()->ExecDialog(new TDialog(this, ID_ABOUT));
284:   }
285:
```

continues

Listing 21.12. continued

```
286:  int PASCAL WinMain(HINSTANCE hInstance, HINSTANCE hPrevInstance,
287:    LPSTR lpCmd, int nCmdShow)
288:  {
289:    TCommApp CommApp("CommApp", hInstance, hPrevInstance,
290:      lpCmd, nCmdShow);
291:    CommApp.Run();
292:    return CommApp.Status;
293:  }
```

Line 1 includes the commdlg.h header. This file declares symbols, structures, functions, and other odds and ends related to common dialogs.

Before activating the dialogs, the program determines the Windows version number. Member function InitInstance() in class TCommApp (lines 72–88) calls GetVersion() and sets two char variables to the major and minor Windows revision numbers. If Windows 3.0 or earlier is detected, line 87 sets Status to EM_BADVERSION, causing OWL to abort the program's startup phase and call Error() at lines 62–69.

HINT: You can use the resource compiler utility RC.EXE with option -31 to mark a Windows code file for use only with Windows 3.1. I prefer to perform version checks in the program, however, which give my programs better control over their use with future Windows versions.

The COMMON.CPP listing has many short functions (lines 148–278), one for each common dialog. (Function CMDialogsPrint displays three printer setup dialogs.) The functions are similar, and after studying one of them, CMDialogsColor (lines 148–167), you should be able to figure out how the others operate.

The first step in using a common dialog is to prepare a supplied structure containing members that specify options and parameters. The color selection dialog, for instance, uses a CHOOSECOLOR structure, defined in the sample program as cc at line 150. Fill this structure with zero bytes as done here at line 154, setting all members to default values. You can then assign values to selected structure members and ignore other members you don't need.

Lines 157–161, for example, assign new values to members of the cc CHOOSECOLOR structure. Generally, the first three members shown here are required:

- 1StructSize Assign to this member the size in bytes of the dialog's structure (CHOOSECOLOR in this case).

- hwndOwner Assign to this member the handle of the window that owns the dialog as a child window. In an OWL program, use a TWindow object's HWindow member.

- Flags Assign to this member one or more option flags using a logical-OR expression. Line 159 selects option CC_RGBINIT and CC_FULLOPEN. These options instruct the dialog to use the current color assigned to member rgbResult, and to display the full color-selection dialog rather than an abbreviated version without a 256-color palette.

Try modifying line 159 to assign only CC_RGBINIT to cc.Flags. The resulting color dialog lacks the 256-color palette, but displays more quickly. Windows provides dozens of similar options that alter the style, fields, and other features of common dialogs. These options are covered in the Windows 3.1 API documentation and in BCW's online help.

After initializing a common dialog structure's members, call the appropriate function such as ChooseColor (see line 162) to display the dialog box. Pass the address of an initialized dialog structure, &cc in the sample listing. Extract values from structure members if the function returns true—indicating that the user accepted the dialog's settings (typically by clicking the OK button or pressing Enter). If the dialog function returns false, the user has cancelled the dialog and you should ignore any modified structure member values.

Line 163 extracts a selected color from member cc.rgbResult, assigning this value to a class member color declared at line 23. Examine the other dialog members declared below this line. Comments in the listing explain the purpose of each member. Lines 164–165 extract an array of color values, storing these in aColors, another class member. As these statements demonstrate, retrieving common dialog selections requires only a few simple assignments.

Table 21.1. lists common dialog functions, purpose, type (modal or modeless), and associated structure for each of the nine common dialogs. As mentioned before, the printer setup dialog has three parts, so there are only seven entries in the table. For additional details on these functions and structures, consult BCW's online help and search for the function names.

Table 21.1. Common dialog functions and structures.

Function	Purpose	Type	Structure
ChooseColor()	Select one or more colors	Modal	CHOOSECOLOR
ChooseFont()	Select fonts and styles	Modal	CHOOSEFONT
FindText()	Find text in a document	Modeless	FINDREPLACE
GetOpenFileName()	Select an existing filename	Modal	OPENFILENAME
GetSaveFileName()	Select a new filename	Modal	OPENFILENAME
PrintDlg()	Choose printer options (three-part dialog)	Modal	PRINTDLG
ReplaceText()	Find and replace text in a document	Modeless	FINDREPLACE

TrueType Fonts

TrueType fonts repair one of the most glaring deficiencies of earlier Windows versions—displaying fonts in the same relative sizes on different display and printer resolutions. TrueType fonts are scalable fonts—they are composed of points and "hints" that explain to an output device how to outline and fill in character patterns. TrueType characters are independent of output resolution. The same TrueType symbols on a low-quality 640 x 480 display should appear in the same relative sizes (more or less) on a fancy 1024 x 768 monitor.

Another advantage of TrueType fonts is increased display speed. The first time Windows displays a TrueType font character, it draws the character's pattern and creates a temporary bitmapped version of that pattern in memory. The next time the same character is needed, Windows uses the in-memory bitmap, vastly improving display speed. (It takes far less time to move pixels en masse onto the screen than it does to draw the equivalent lines and filled shapes.) You may have noticed TrueType's two-speed gearshift when using a word processor. Displaying a paragraph the first time takes a few seconds. Displaying that same paragraph again takes only a fraction of the original time because Windows uses the in-memory character bitmaps on the second and subsequent go-arounds.

Figure 21.9. shows a sample display of the next program, Listing 21.13, TTFONT.CPP. The program demonstrates how to select and use TrueType fonts to display text in a window. Load the program's TTFONT.PRJ project file into BCW and press Ctrl+F9 to compile and run. Use the program's Font menu to open a common font dialog (see Figure 21.10.) and select a new font and style.

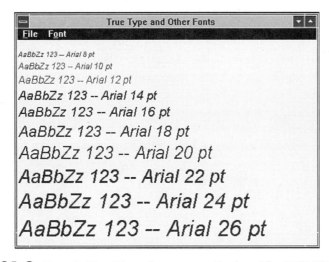

Figure 21.9. Sample TrueType-font text as displayed by TTFONT.CPP.

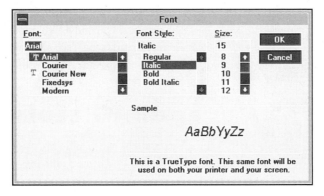

Figure 21.10. Common font dialog.

Listing 21.13. TTFONT.CPP (Displays TrueType fonts).

```
 1:  #include <commdlg.h>
 2:  #include <owl.h>
 3:  #include <stdio.h>
 4:  #include <string.h>
 5:  #include "ttfont.h"
 6:
 7:  #define EM_BADVERSION -100
 8:
 9:  class TFontApp: public TApplication
10:  {
11:  public:
12:    TFontApp(LPSTR aName, HINSTANCE hInstance, HINSTANCE hPrevInstance,
13:      LPSTR lpCmd, int nCmdShow) : TApplication(aName, hInstance,
14:      hPrevInstance, lpCmd, nCmdShow) {};
15:    virtual void Error(int ErrorCode);
16:    virtual void InitInstance();
17:    virtual void InitMainWindow();
18:  };
19:
20:  class TFontWin: public TWindow
21:  {
22:  private:
23:    LOGFONT font;          // Logical font
24:    COLORREF fontColor;  // Font foreground color
25:  public:
26:    TFontWin(PTWindowsObject AParent, LPSTR ATitle);
27:    virtual void CMFileExit(RTMessage)
28:      = [CM_FIRST + CM_FILEEXIT];
29:    virtual void CMFontChoose(RTMessage)
30:      = [CM_FIRST + CM_FONTCHOOSE];
31:    virtual void Paint(HDC PaintDC, PAINTSTRUCT &);
32:  };
33:
34:  // Respond to startup errors
35:  void TFontApp::Error(int ErrorCode)
36:  {
37:    if (ErrorCode == EM_BADVERSION)
38:      MessageBox(0, "Requires Windows 3.1 or later",
39:        "Version Error", MB_APPLMODAL | MB_ICONSTOP | MB_OK);
40:    else
```

```
41:       TApplication::Error(ErrorCode);
42:  }
43:
44:  // Detect Windows version number. Halt if < 3.1.
45:  void TFontApp::InitInstance()
46:  {
47:    DWORD version;
48:    char majorRev, minorRev;
49:    BOOL okay;
50:
51:    version = GetVersion();
52:    majorRev = LOBYTE(LOWORD(version));
53:    minorRev = HIBYTE(LOWORD(version));
54:    if (majorRev  < 3) okay = FALSE; else
55:    if (majorRev == 3) okay = (minorRev >= 1); else
56:    if (majorRev  > 3) okay = TRUE;  // I hope!
57:    if (okay)
58:      TApplication::InitInstance();
59:    else
60:      Status = EM_BADVERSION;
61:  }
62:
63:  // Initialize the application's window
64:  void TFontApp::InitMainWindow()
65:  {
66:    MainWindow = new TFontWin(NULL, "True Type and Other Fonts");
67:  }
68:
69:  // Construct the application's window object
70:  TFontWin::TFontWin(PTWindowsObject AParent, LPSTR ATitle)
71:    : TWindow(AParent, ATitle)
72:  {
73:    AssignMenu(ID_MENU);
74:    Attr.X = GetSystemMetrics(SM_CXSCREEN) / 8;
75:    Attr.Y = GetSystemMetrics(SM_CYSCREEN) / 8;
76:    Attr.H = Attr.Y * 6;
77:    Attr.W = Attr.X * 6;
78:    memset(&font, 0, sizeof(font));
79:    font.lfHeight = 20;  // Required!
80:    font.lfWeight = FW_NORMAL;
81:    font.lfCharSet = ANSI_CHARSET;
```

continues

Listing 21.13. continued

```
82:    font.lfOutPrecision = OUT_DEFAULT_PRECIS;
83:    font.lfClipPrecision = CLIP_DEFAULT_PRECIS;
84:    font.lfQuality = PROOF_QUALITY;
85:    font.lfPitchAndFamily = VARIABLE_PITCH;
86:    strcpy(font.lfFaceName, "Arial");  // Required!
87:    fontColor = GetSysColor(COLOR_WINDOWTEXT);
88:  }
89:
90:  // Exit program by closing the main window
91:  void TFontWin::CMFileExit(RTMessage)
92:  {
93:    CloseWindow();
94:  }
95:
96:  // Choose new font
97:  void TFontWin::CMFontChoose(RTMessage)
98:  {
99:    CHOOSEFONT cf;      // Choose-font dialog structure
100:   LOGFONT tempFont;   // Temporary copy of TFontWin's logical font struct
101:
102:   memset(&cf, 0, sizeof(cf));          // Fill struct with 0s
103:   tempFont = font;                     // Copy TFontWin's logical font
104:   cf.lStructSize = sizeof(CHOOSEFONT); // Assign structure size
105:   cf.hwndOwner = HWindow;              // Assign parent window handle
106:   cf.Flags = CF_INITTOLOGFONTSTRUCT | CF_BOTH;  // Select dialog options
107:   cf.lpLogFont = &tempFont;            // Assign address of tempFont
108:   cf.rgbColors = fontColor;            // Assign foreground color
109:   if (ChooseFont(&cf)) {               // Activate common font dialog
110:     font = *cf.lpLogFont;             // Use this font for text
111:     fontColor = cf.rgbColors;         // Use selected foreground color
112:     InvalidateRect(HWindow, NULL, TRUE);  // Redisplay window contents
113:   }
114: }
115:
116: // Paint the window's contents
117: void TFontWin::Paint(HDC PaintDC, PAINTSTRUCT &)
118: {
119:   int len, x, y, points;
```

```
120:    char testString[256];
121:    char pointsStr[4];
122:    int endOfTestString;
123:    long textExtent;
124:    int mapModeOldH;
125:    HFONT fontH, fontOldH;
126:    LOGFONT tempFont;
127:
128:    x = 10;
129:    y = 0;
130:    strcpy(testString, "AaBbZz 123 -- ");
131:    endOfTestString = strlen(testString);
132:    tempFont = font;  // Copy selected logical font
133:    SetTextColor(PaintDC, fontColor);
134:    SetBkColor(PaintDC, GetSysColor(COLOR_WINDOW));
135:    // Set graphics mapping to 1 unit = 1/1440 inch,
136:    // or 1/20 of a typesetting point, equal to 1/72 inch.
137:    mapModeOldH = SetMapMode(PaintDC, MM_TWIPS);
138:    points = 8;
139:    while (points <= 32) {
140:      tempFont.lfHeight = -points * 20;  // At 20 twips per point
141:      fontH = CreateFontIndirect(&tempFont);
142:      fontOldH = (HFONT)SelectObject(PaintDC, fontH);
143:      testString[endOfTestString] = 0;   // Delete old font name
144:      sprintf(&testString[endOfTestString],
145:        "%s %d pt", font.lfFaceName, points);
146:      len = strlen(testString);
147:      textExtent = GetTextExtent(PaintDC, testString, len);
148:      y = y + HIWORD(textExtent) + 5;    // Adjust Y using char height
149:      TextOut(PaintDC, x, -y, testString, len);
150:      SelectObject(PaintDC, fontOldH);   // Restore saved font handle
151:      DeleteObject(fontH);               // Delete new font handle
152:      points += 2;
153:    }
154:    SetMapMode(PaintDC, mapModeOldH);     // Restore saved mapping mode
155:  }
156:
157:  int PASCAL WinMain(HINSTANCE hInstance, HINSTANCE hPrevInstance,
158:    LPSTR lpCmd, int nCmdShow)
159:  {
```

continues

Listing 21.13. continued

```
160:    TFontApp FontApp("TTFontApp", hInstance, hPrevInstance,
161:        lpCmd, nCmdShow);
162:    FontApp.Run();
163:    return FontApp.Status;
164: }
```

To store the current font and color, the program's TWindow class derivative, TFontWin (lines 20–32) includes two data members, font of type LOGFONT and fontColor of type COLORREF.

The first of these two types is called a *logical font structure*. It contains various members that describe a font's characteristics. Before using the font to display text, request a handle to a font that most closely resembles the parameters in the logical font structure. If possible, Windows satisfies the requested parameters with an exact match. If the requested font doesn't exist, however, Windows selects another font that, with luck, closely resembles your choice. Although this font-matching scheme seems reasonable, the results are often disappointing. For best results, you should use logical fonts that exactly match those available.

One way to satisfy this goal is to provide users with a font selection dialog. The sample program's CMFontChoose() member function (lines 97–114) provides this service with a common font-selection dialog. The function resembles the one you examined in the preceding section for selecting colors. After initializing a CHOOSEFONT structure (see lines 99, 102, and 104–108), function ChooseFont() (line 109) displays the font selection dialog illustrated in Figure 21.10. If the function returns true, lines 110–112 save the selected logical font and color, then invalidate the window, causing it to be redrawn by member function Paint() (lines 117–155).

Examine Paint() closely. It contains sample statements that show how to display text using TrueType fonts. Select appropriate background and foreground colors (lines 133–134) and then call SetMapMode() to change pixel mapping to MM_TWIPS as demonstrated at line 137.

This special mode maps a graphics display unit to 1/1440 of an inch, equal to 1/20 of a typesetting point, which is about 1/72 of an inch. (The word TWIP is a loose acronym for "twentieth of a point.") With MM_TWIPS mapping in effect, you can select font heights using points rather than a fixed number of pixels, causing text to be displayed in about the same relative size regardless of output resolution.

Line 140 shows how to select a font's point size, commonly expressed as a negative value. Set the logical font to 20 times the desired point size (because there are 20 points in a TWIP). Pass the address of the logical font structure to `CreateFontIndirect()` and assign the resulting handle to an `HFONT` variable. Pass this variable and the display context to `SelectObject()`, selecting the font for subsequent text output functions such as `TextOut()` (see line 149). When you are done using a font, reselect the previously selected font by again calling `SelectObject()` and then delete the unneeded font handle (lines 150–151). You should also restore the display context's mapping mode (line 154).

The remaining statements in the sample program's `Paint()` member function calculate the coordinates where lines of text appear in the window. To calculate text coordinates, call `GetTextExtent()` with a display context, string, and string length as demonstrated at line 147. The function returns a `long` value. For the selected font and string, the high word of this `long` value equals the maximum character height. The low word equals the string's length. Using these values (extracted with the help of the `HIWORD` and `LOWORD` macros) you can calculate (x,y) coordinates to pass to `TextOut()`. For better control over text location, you might also have to call the Windows functions `SetTextAlign()` and `SetTextJustification()` (not shown in the sample listing—look these up in BCW's online help).

Summary

- The Windows graphical user interface, or GUI, features multitasking capabilities and device-independent graphics. Windows provides a rapidly expanding market for software developers.

- Borland C++ fully supports Windows 3.0 and 3.1 programming. To write Windows applications, you can use the command-line compiler, the text IDE, or Borland C++ for Windows. For most Windows applications, BCW is the best choice.

- ObjectWindows, or OWL, is Borland's class library for Windows software development. With OWL, you program Windows using an object-oriented framework that interfaces with common elements such as graphical windows and dialogs.

- All OWL programs are based on a class derived from TApplication. Windows are derived from TWindow. Use message-response functions in TWindow objects to respond to messages generated by Windows.

- Turbo Debugger for Windows (TDW) resembles the DOS Turbo Debugger (TD). TDW is a Windows application that runs your code, displays variables, sets breakpoints, and performs other tasks that can help you find the causes of bugs. TDW runs in text mode, not in a graphical window.

- WinSight is another useful debugging tool. Use WinSight to investigate message flow from Windows to and from your program.

- Faulty program statements might cause Windows to halt a program with a system error. Install WinSpector to trap these errors and display detailed information that might help locate the cause of problems. WinSpector creates a text-file log that you can examine for a detailed error report.

- Most Windows programs have resources such as pull-down menus and dialog boxes. Design these and other resources with Resource Workshop. You can also write resource script files and compile them with the RC.EXE utility.

- Modal dialogs capture the program's attention. You must close a modal dialog before you can use other program features.

- Modeless dialogs resemble the modal kind, but do not prohibit using other program commands while the modeless dialog is on display.

- A display context associates graphics output with a device such as a graphical window on a display monitor, a printer, or a plotter. Pass a display context to Graphics Device Interface (GDI) functions to draw lines, shapes, text, and other graphical output.

- A Dynamic Link Library is a collection of functions that many programs can share. Only one copy of a DLL ever exists in memory regardless of how many programs use the library.

- The newly released Windows 3.1 runs fast and is more reliable than Version 3.0. New features include object-linking and embedding (OLE), common dialog boxes, and TrueType fonts.

Part 5

Function
Encyclopedia

22

Functions and Examples

In this chapter is a complete alphabetic reference to the Borland C++ standard function library. Most sections have these six parts:

1. *Syntax.* The function's prototype as declared in a library header file such as stdio.h. For simplicity, system macros such as _Cdecl and _FARFUNC from header file prototypes are not included. (These and similar macros, if non-null, affect the compiled code but have no bearing on a function's use.)

2. *Include.* One or more header files such as stdio.h that declare the function's prototype, related symbolic constants, structures, and so on. To use a function in your programs, insert a directive such as

```
#include <stdio.h>
```

3. *Description.* An explanation of the function's purpose, use, return value, and possible errors.

4. *Parameters.* If the function declares parameters, each is listed here in declaration order. Consult this section for information about the types of arguments you need to pass to a function. Functions with no parameters do not have a Parameters section.

5. *See also.* One or more cross references to other related functions.

6. *Example.* A complete example of the function in a C or C++ program, or a reference to another example that uses this function along with one or more others.

The following notes explain a few conventions used throughout the reference. In addition, they suggest how to compile BGI graphics examples.

- The reference includes corrections and omissions to Borland's official documentation. The purpose of the reference is not to replace Borland's manuals, however, but to provide a fast-access portable guide to the standard library. For complete information, consult this chapter *and* Borland's manuals.

- Examples begin with a comment that gives the associated filename. Functions with short names have similar file entries—the example for atof(), for instance, is stored in file ATOF.CPP. A few long function identifiers have abbreviated filenames.

- To keep examples short, symbolic constants define argument values, which in practice would be entered by users or read from data files. The purpose of the examples is to show functions in use, not to serve as samples of award-winning programming technique. Noncritical error conditions are therefore sometimes ignored, statements are repeated rather than inserted into separate functions, and other shortcuts are taken.

- Also to save space, examples do not have blank lines between declarations, function prototypes, and other elements—as do most of the book's numbered listings.

- For read-only files, many examples use their own filenames (see access(), for example). Run these examples with their text files in the current directory.

- A few examples are not given for extremely sensitive functions such as those that could wipe out your hard drive if you mistype an argument value. Nevertheless, you should exercise caution when running any examples that read from or write to disk. *Always keep backup copies of your important files.*

- Some functions that are identical in purpose (and can be implemented as macros) are listed but are not described. For example, the description for _dos_allocmem() tells you to "See allocmem" because these two functions have identical results.

- Many math functions have `double`, `long double`, and `complex` versions. Because these functions have similar uses, most examples demonstrate only the `double` models.

- Some functions have near and far versions. In most cases, and for the best compatibility with other C and C++ compilers, use the near versions and select an appropriate memory model (see Chapter 20, "DOS Tools and Techniques").

- Unless otherwise stated, strings are expected to contain ASCII characters and end with a null terminating byte.

- To compile BGI graphics examples for functions such as `bar()`, you might have to modify the `initgraph()` statement's pathname (`"c:\\borlandc\\bgi"` by default). Set the path to the location of the compiler's .BGI and .CHR files, and enter double backslashes to separate directories in literal pathname strings. Compile graphics examples from DOS with the command **bcc filename graphics.lib**. Of course, all graphics examples require a graphics display—they do not work on monochrome monitors. For best results, most examples require an EGA- or VGA-compatible adapter. See Chapter 16, "The Borland Graphics Interface," for more information about BGI graphics.

abort   Terminate program

Syntax   `void abort(void);`

Include   stdlib.h

Description   Writes "Abnormal program termination" to `stderr` and ends program via `_exit(3)`.

See also   `atexit, _c_exit, _cexit, exit, _exit, raise, signal, spawn...`

Example
```
/* abort.cpp */
#include <stdio.h>
#include <stdlib.h>
main()
{
  int errorCode;
  printf("Enter error code or 0: ");
  scanf("%d", &errorCode);
  if (errorCode != 0)
    abort();
  else
```

```
      puts("No error detected");
    return 0;
  }
```

abs   Absolute value

Syntax   `int abs(int x);`
         `double abs (complex x);`

Include   math.h, complex.h

Description   Returns the absolute (nonnegative) value of x. Complex version is prototyped in complex.h.

Parameters   **int x** Any integer from –32767 to +32767. The argument –32768 is returned as –32768.

complex x An instance of the complex class.

See also   cabs, ceil, ceill, complex, fabs, floor, floorl, labs

Example
```
/* abs.cpp */
include <stdio.h>
#include <math.h>
main()
{
  int x = -123;
  printf("%d\n", x);
  printf("%d\n", abs(x));
  return 0;
}
```

absread   Read sector absolute

Syntax   `int absread(int drive, int nsects, long lsect, void *buffer);`

Include   dos.h

Description   Reads raw disk sector data (up to 64K in number) at absolute positions, whether the sectors belong to a file, a directory, or are unused. Calls DOS interrupt 0x25. Returns 0 for success, –1 for error and sets global errno to register AX from DOS.

Parameters   **int drive** Drive number (0==A:, 1==B:, ...).

int nsects Number of sectors to read.

long lsect First sector number.

void *buffer Buffer to hold sector data.

See also   abswrite, biosdisk, _dos_read, read

Example

```
/* absread.cpp */
#include <stdio.h>
#include <dos.h>
#define SIZE 512    // Bytes per sector
#define NUMSECT 4   // Number sectors to read
#define DRIVE 2     // 0==A:, 1==B:, 2==C:, etc.
#define SECTOR 100  // Starting logical sector
main()
{
  unsigned char buffer[SIZE * NUMSECT];
  int err;
  err = absread(DRIVE, NUMSECT, SECTOR, &buffer);
  if (err == 0)
    puts("Read successful");
  else
    puts("Error detected");
  return err;
}
```

abswrite   Write sector absolute

Syntax   `int abswrite(int drive, int nsects, long lsect, void *buffer);`

Include   dos.h

Description   Writes raw data to sectors (up to 64K in number) at absolute positions with no regard to files or directories that might be stored there. *Use with extreme caution.* Parameters are identical to absread's, except that data travels from the buffer to disk. Calls DOS interrupt 0x26. Returns 0 for success, −1 for error and sets global errno to register AX from DOS. No example is shown due to this function's dangerous nature.

See also   absread, biosdisk, _dos_write, write

access   Determine file access

Syntax   `int access(const char *filename,int amode);`

Include   io.h

Description   Determines access mode for a file or directory. Returns 0 if requested access is allowed, –1 for error and sets global `errno` to `ENOENT` if the file doesn't exist, or `EACCES` if access is denied. Typically used to detect whether a file or directory exists.

Parameters   `const char *filename` File or path to test.

                  `int amode` Mode: 0–exits, 1–executable (ignored), 2–writeable, 4–readable, 6–readable and writeable.

See also   chmod, fopen, fstat, stat

Example

```
/* access.cpp */
#include <stdio.h>
#include <io.h>
#define FILENAME "access.cpp"
main()
{
  int result;
  result = access(FILENAME, 0);
  if (result == 0)
    puts(FILENAME" exists");
  else
    puts(FILENAME" does not exist");
  return 0;
}
```

acos, acosl   Arc cosine

Syntax

```
double acos(double x);
long double acosl(long double x);
complex acos(complex x);
```

Include   math.h, complex.h

Description   Calculates arc cosine of x.

See also   asin, atan, atan2, complex, cos, matherr, sin, tan

Example

```
/* acos.cpp */
#include <stdio.h>
#include <math.h>
#define V 0.25
```

```
main()
{
  printf("Arc cosine of %lf == %lf\n", V, acos(V));
  return 0;
}
```

alloca   Allocate stack space

Syntax   `void *alloca(size_t size);`

Include   malloc.h

Description Allocates temporary stack space, which might be used for any purpose and is similar to space allotted to a local variable. Returns a pointer to the reserved space, or null if `size` bytes are not available. Allocated space is deleted automatically when the function ends. Do not call `alloca()` in an expression passed as an argument to another function, because this is likely to corrupt the stack.

Parameters `size_t size` The number of bytes to allocate.

See also   `malloc`

Example
```
/* alloca.cpp */
#include <stdio.h>
#include <malloc.h>
#include <string.h>
#define SIZE 128
void f(void);
main()
{
  printf("SP before calling f() == %#x\n", _SP);
  f();
  printf("SP after calling f() == %#x\n", _SP);
  return 0;
}

void f(void)
{
  char *p;
  char dummy[1];
  dummy[0] = 0;   // Ensure proper stack frame
  puts(" Enter function f()");
```

```
    printf(" SP before alloca() == %#x\n", _SP);
    p = (char *)alloca(SIZE);
    if (p) {
      printf(" SP after alloca() == %#x\n", _SP);
      strcpy(p, " A string on the stack");
      puts(p);
    }
}
```

allocmem   Allocate DOS memory

Syntax   `int allocmem(unsigned size, unsigned *segp);`

Include   dos.h

Description   Allocates memory by calling DOS function 0x48. Reserved space is paragraph aligned. Do not use this function in conjunction with `malloc()`. If successful, `allocmem()` returns −1. Any other value indicates failure, and represents the number of paragraphs that can be allocated on a subsequent attempt.

Parameters   **unsigned size** Requested block size in paragraphs.

unsigned *segp Pointer to a 2-byte word. If the function is successful, this word is set to the segment address of the reserved memory.

See also   `calloc, coreleft, _dos_allocmem, freemem, malloc, setblock`

Example
```
/* allocmem.cpp */
#include <stdio.h>
#include <dos.h>
#define NPARAGRAPHS 32  // Number of paragraphs
main()
{
  int result;    // Function result
  unsigned seg;  // Passed by address to allocmem()
  printf("Allocating %d paragraphs\n", NPARAGRAPHS);
  result = allocmem(NPARAGRAPHS, &seg);
  if (result == -1) {
    puts("Allocation successful");
    freemem(seg);  // Free allocated paragraphs
  } else
    puts("Allocation failed");
  return 0;
}
```

arc   Draw arc

Syntax   `void far arc(int x, int y, int stangle, int endangle, int radius);`

Include   graphics.h

Description   Draws a circular arc in the current drawing color on a graphics display.

Parameters   `int x`, `int y` Center coordinate.

`int stangle` Starting angle in degrees.

`int endangle` Ending angle in degrees.

`int radius` Radius from center in pixels.

See also   `circle, ellipse, fillellipse, getarccoords, getaspectratio, pieslice, sector`

Example
```cpp
/* arc.cpp */
#include <graphics.h>
#include <stdio.h>
#include <stdlib.h>
#include <conio.h>
main()
{
  int gdriver = DETECT, gmode, gerr;
  int maxX, x, y;
  initgraph(&gdriver, &gmode, "c:\\borlandc\\bgi");
  gerr = graphresult();
  if (gerr != grOk) {
    printf("BGI error: %s\n", grapherrormsg(gerr));
    exit(gerr);
  }
  maxX = getmaxx();
  y = 10;
  for (x = 25; x < maxX - 75; x++) {
    setcolor(x % 16);
    arc(x, y, y % 360, x % 360, x / 10);
    y += x % 2;
  }
  getch();
  closegraph();
  return 0;
}
```

arg   Angle of number in complex plane

Syntax   `double arg(complex x);`

Include   complex.h

Description   Returns angle in radians of number in the complex plane.

See also   `complex, norm, polar`

Example
```
/* arg.cpp */
#include <stdio.h>
#include <complex.h>
main()
{
  double y = 4.2;
  double x = 3.1;
  complex z = complex(x,y);
  printf("Angle in radians == %f\n", arg(z));
  return 0;
}
```

asctime   ASCII date and time

Syntax   `char *asctime(const struct tm *tblock);`

Include   time.h

Description   Converts to a 26-character string the date and time in a structure addressed by `tblock`. Returns the address of the string, a static variable. Multiple calls to `asctime()` overwrite this variable, and you should copy the converted string for safekeeping.

Parameters   **const struct tm *tblock** See time.h for the structure's members. Store date and time information in tm, and pass to the function to convert to a string.

See also   `ctime, difftime, ftime, gmtime, localtime, mktime, strftime, stime, time, tzset`

Example
```
/* asctime.cpp */
#include <stdio.h>
#include <time.h>
#include <dos.h>
#include <string.h>
main()
```

```
{
    struct tm t;           // time.h date and time structure
    struct time dt;        // dos.h time structure
    struct dosdate_t dd;   // dos.h date structure
    char ts[26];           // holds result
    gettime(&dt);          // read the current time
    _dos_getdate(&dd);     // read the current date
    t.tm_sec   = dt.ti_sec;      // Seconds
    t.tm_min   = dt.ti_min;      // Minutes
    t.tm_hour  = dt.ti_hour;     // Hour
    t.tm_mday  = dd.day;         // Day
    t.tm_mon   = dd.month - 1;   // Month
    t.tm_year  = dd.year - 1900; // Year
    t.tm_wday  = dd.dayofweek;   // Day of week
    t.tm_yday  = 0;   // Unused day of year
    t.tm_isdst = 0;   // Unused "is daylight savings time"
    strcpy(ts, asctime(&t));
    puts(ts);
    return 0;
}
```

asin, asinl   Arc sine

Syntax   double asin(double x);
long double asinl(long double x);
complex asin(complex x);

Include   math.h, complex.h

Description   Returns arc sine of x.

See also   acos, atan, atan2, complex, cos, matherr, matherr, sin, tan

Example
```
/* asin.cpp */
#include <stdio.h>
#include <math.h>
#define V 0.25
main()
{
    printf("Arc sine of %lf == %lf\n", V, asin(V));
    return 0;
}
```

assert   Abort if assertion fails

Syntax   `void assert(int test);`

Include   assert.h

Description   A macro used for debugging. Tests a condition and aborts program if that condition fails.

Parameters   **int test** True or false expression. If expression is false (zero), function halts program. If expression is true (nonzero), program continues normally.

See also   `abort, exit`

Example
```
/* assert.cpp */
#include <stdio.h>
#include <assert.h>
#include <stdlib.h>
main()
{
  char buffer[128];
  int testValue;
  printf("Enter test value 0 or 1: ");
  gets(buffer);
  testValue = atoi(buffer);
  assert((testValue == 0) || (testValue == 1));
  puts("Program ending normally");
  return 0;
}
```

atan, atanl   Arc tangent

Syntax
```
double atan(double x);
long double atanl(long double x);
complex atan(complex x);
```

Include   math.h, complex.h

Description   Returns arc tangent of x.

See also   `acos, asin, atan2, complex, cos, sin, tan`

Example
```
/* atan.cpp */
#include <stdio.h>
#include <math.h>
```

```
#define V 0.25
main()
{
  printf("Arc tangent of %lf == %lf\n", V, atan(V));
  return 0;
}
```

atan2, atan2l   Arc tangent of y/x

Syntax
```
double atan2(double y, double x);
long double atan2l(long double y, long double x);
```

Include   math.h

Description   Returns arc tangent of y/x.

See also   acos, asin, atan, cos, sin, tan

Example
```
/* atan2.cpp */
#include <stdio.h>
#include <math.h>
#define X 80.0
#define Y 45.0
main()
{
  double at2 = atan2(Y, X);
  printf("Arc tangent of %lf/%lf == %lf\n", Y, X, at2);
  return 0;
}
```

atexit   Register exit function

Syntax   `int atexit(void(* func)(void));`

Include   stdlib.h

Description   Registers an exit function, which runs when the program ends, but before DOS regains control. Programs might call atexit() multiple times to register up to 32 exit functions. Returns zero if successful; nonzero if function cannot be registered.

Parameters   **void(* func)(void)** Pointer to exit function that has no parameters.

See also   abort, exit, spawn...

Example
```
/* atexit.cpp */
#include <stdio.h>
#include <stdlib.h>
void f1(void);
void f2(void);
main()
{
  atexit(f1);   // Register exit function f1()
  atexit(f2);   // Register exit function f2()
  return 0;
}

void f1(void)
{
  puts("Exit function #1");
}

void f2(void)
{
  puts("Exit function #2");
}
```

atof   ASCII to floating-point

Syntax   `double atof(const char *s);`

Include   math.h

Description   Converts a string to a `double` floating-point value. Returns value or +/-HUGE_VAL for errors, setting errno to ERANGE.

Parameters   **const char *s** Pointer to string to convert.

See also   atoi, atol, _atold, cgets, gets, strtod

Example
```
/* atof.cpp */
#include <stdio.h>
#include <math.h>
main()
{
  char buffer[128];
  double result;
  printf("Enter double value to convert: ");
  gets(buffer);
```

```
    result = atof(buffer);
    printf("Result == %f\n", result);
    return 0;
}
```

atoi   ASCII to integer

Syntax   `int atoi(const char *s);`

Include   stdlib.h

Description   Converts string to an int value. Returns value or zero if string cannot be converted.

Parameters   **const char *s** Pointer to string to convert.

See also   atof, atol, cgets, gets, strtod

Example
```
/* atoi.cpp */
#include <stdio.h>
#include <stdlib.h>
main()
{
  char buffer[128];
  int result;
  printf("Enter integer value to convert: ");
  gets(buffer);
  result = atoi(buffer);
  printf("Result == %d\n", result);
  return 0;
}
```

atol   ASCII to long

Syntax   `long atol(const char *s);`

Include   stdlib.h

Description   Converts string to long value. Returns value or zero if string cannot be converted.

Parameters   **const char *s** Pointer to string to convert.

See also   atof, atoi, cgets, gets, strtod, strtol, strtoul

Example
```
/* atol.cpp */
#include <stdio.h>
#include <stdlib.h>
main()
{
  char buffer[128];
  long result;
  printf("Enter long value to convert: ");
  gets(buffer);
  result = atol(buffer);
  printf("Result == %ld\n", result);
  return 0;
}
```

_atold   ASCII to long double

Syntax   `long double _atold(const char *s);`

Include   stdlib.h

Description   Converts string to a `long double` value. Returns value or zero if string cannot be converted.

Parameters   **const char *s** Pointer to string to convert.

See also   atof, atoi, atol, cgets, gets, strtod

Example
```
/* _atold.cpp */
#include <stdio.h>
#include <math.h>
main()
{
  char buffer[128];
  long double result;
  printf("Enter long double value to convert: ");
  gets(buffer);
  result = _atold(buffer);
  printf("Result == %Lf\n", result);
  return 0;
}
```

bar   Draw bar

Syntax   `void far bar(int left, int top, int right, int bottom);`

Include   graphics.h

Description   Draws filled rectangular bar on graphics display. Bar is filled with current fill pattern and color.

Parameters   `int left, int top` Top-left coordinate of bar.

             `int right, int bottom` Bottom-right coordinate of bar.

See also   `bar3d, rectangle, setcolor, setfillstyle`

Example
```cpp
/* bar.cpp */
#include <graphics.h>
#include <stdio.h>
#include <stdlib.h>
#include <conio.h>
main()
{
  int gdriver = DETECT, gmode, gerr;
  int x1, y1, x2, y2;
  initgraph(&gdriver, &gmode, "c:\\borlandc\\bgi");
  gerr = graphresult();
  if (gerr != grOk) {
    printf("BGI error: %s\n", grapherrormsg(gerr));
    exit(gerr);
  }
  x1 = getmaxx() / 2;   // Center screen
  y1 = getmaxy() / 4;   // Lower mid screen
  x2 = x1 + 25;         // Width of bar
  y2 = y1 * 2;          // Height of bar
  setfillstyle(1, 3);   // Pattern, Color
  bar(x1, y1, x2, y2);  // Draw filled bar
  getch();
  closegraph();
  return 0;
}
```

bar3d   Draw 3D bar

Syntax   `void far bar3d(int left, int top, int right, int bottom,`
                 `int depth, int topflag);`

Include   graphics.h

985

Description   Draws three-dimensional bar, similar to bar(), but having simulated depth as well as width and height.

Parameters   **int left, int top** Top-left coordinate of bar.

int right, int bottom Bottom-right coordinate of bar.

int depth Controls depth of simulated 3-D effect.

int topflag Set to zero for a topless bar, or to nonzero to put a lid on the graphic.

See also   bar, rectangle, setcolor, setfillstyle, setlinestyle

Example
```cpp
/* bar3d.cpp */
#include <graphics.h>
#include <stdio.h>
#include <stdlib.h>
#include <conio.h>
#define FALSE 0
#define TRUE 1
main()
{
  int gdriver = DETECT, gmode, gerr;
  int x1, y1, x2, y2, depth, top;
  initgraph(&gdriver, &gmode, "c:\\borlandc\\bgi");
  gerr = graphresult();
  if (gerr != grOk) {
    printf("BGI error: %s\n", grapherrormsg(gerr));
    exit(gerr);
  }
  x1 = getmaxx() / 2;    // Center screen
  y1 = getmaxy() / 4;    // Lower mid screen
  x2 = x1 + 25;          // Width of bar
  y2 = y1 * 2;           // Height of bar
  depth = 10;            // Depth of illusion
  top = TRUE;            // NOT a topless bar!
  setfillstyle(1, 3);    // Pattern, Color
  bar3d(x1, y1, x2, y2, depth, top);  // Draw filled 3D bar
  getch();
  closegraph();
  return 0;
}
```

bcd   Binary coded decimal

Syntax
```
bcd bcd(int x);
bcd bcd(double x);
bcd bcd(double x, int decimals);
```

Include   bcd.h

Description   Converts x to an instance of the binary coded decimal (bcd) class. Arithmetic operators are overloaded to allow common expressions involving bcd numbers.

See also   `real, complex, imag`

Example
```
/* bcd.cpp */
#include <stdio.h>
#include <bcd.h>
#define ACCOUNT 857.56
#define PAYMENT 54.25
main()
{
  bcd balance = bcd(ACCOUNT - PAYMENT);
  cout << "Balance == " << balance << '\n';
  return 0;
}
```

bdos   DOS system call

Syntax   `int bdos(int dosfun, unsigned dosdx, unsigned dosal);`

Include   dos.h

Description   Calls low-level DOS function. Returns value of register AX following call to DOS. Use for DOS functions that require integer arguments in register DX.

Parameters   **int dosfun** DOS function number.

unsigned dosdx Value for DX word register.

unsigned dosal Value for AL byte register.

See also   `bdosptr, geninterrupt, int86, int86x, intdos, intdosx`

Example
```
/* bdos.cpp */
#include <stdio.h>
```

```
#include <dos.h>
main()
{
  int verify = getverify() ^ 1;
  puts("Toggle disk-write verification");
  puts("Enter VERIFY before & after to test");
  bdos(0x2e, 0, verify);
  return 0;
}
```

bdosptr   DOS system call

Syntax   `int bdosptr(int dosfun, void *argument, unsigned dosal);`

Include   dos.h

Description Calls low-level DOS function. Returns value of register AX following call to DOS. Use for DOS functions that require pointer arguments in register DX or DS:DX. Returns −1 on error and sets `errno` and `_doserrno`.

Parameters **int dosfun** DOS function number.

              void *argument Address required by DOS function.

              unsigned dosal Value for AL byte register.

See also   bdos, geninterrupt, int86, int86x, intdos, intdosx

Example
```
/* bdosptr.cpp */
#include <stdio.h>
#include <dos.h>
#define BUFLEN 40
main()
{
  int len;
  char buffer[BUFLEN];
  buffer[0] = BUFLEN - 2;
  buffer[1] = 0;
  printf("Enter a string: ");
  bdosptr(0x0a, buffer, 0);
  len = buffer[1];
  buffer[len + 2] = 0;
  printf("\nbuffer == %s", &buffer[2]);
  printf("\nlen    == %d\n", buffer[1]);
```

```
      return 0;
    }
```

bioscom   Perform serial I/O

Syntax   `int bioscom(int cmd, char abyte, int port);`

Include   bios.h

Description   Executes serial, RS-232, communications commands. To use this function, consult a DOS reference for details of interrupt function 0x14. A similar function, `_bios_serialcom()`, is also prototyped in bios.h.

Parameters   `int cmd` 0–set port parameters to `abyte`; 1–send char in `abyte`; 2–receive char; 3–return port status.

`char abyte` Baud rate, parity, and other flags.

`int port` I/O port number 0–COM1, 1–COM2, and so forth.

Example
```
/* bioscom.cpp */
#include <stdio.h>
#include <stdlib.h>
#include <bios.h>
#define COM1 0
#define STATUS 3
main()
{
  int status = bioscom(STATUS, 0, COM1);
  printf("Status of COM1 == %#x\n", status);
  return 0;
}
```

biosdisk   BIOS disk drive services

Syntax   `int biosdisk(int cmd, int drive, int head, int track,`
            `int sector, int nsects, void *buffer);`

Include   bios.h

Description   Calls interrupt 0x13 to perform direct disk operations. Caution: This low-level function is for advanced work only, not for normal file handling. Consult a DOS or PC reference for the use of this interrupt and its parameters. A similar function, _bios_disk() (not shown) uses a diskinto_t structure, defined in bios.h, to specify arguments to the function.

Parameters **int cmd** One of several commands, for example, 2 to read disk sectors, 5 to format a disk track.

int drive Drive number.

int head Drive's head number.

int track Drive's track number.

int sector Drive's sector number.

int nsects Number of sectors.

void *buffer Address of a destination buffer.

See also absread, abswrite

Example
```cpp
/* biosdisk.cpp */
/* --------------------------------------- */
/* WARNING: Enter this program carefully!!! */
/* biosdisk() can DESTROY disk drive data!!! */
/* --------------------------------------- */
#include <stdio.h>
#include <bios.h>
#include <conio.h>
#define DRIVE 0  // 0==A:, 1==B:, 2==C:, etc.
#define HEAD 0
#define TRACK 1
#define SECTOR 1
#define SECTORSIZE 512
#define NUMSECTORS 4
#define SIZE (SECTORSIZE * NUMSECTORS)
#define DISKREAD 2
main()
{
  char buffer[SIZE];
  int result;
  puts("Insert scratch floppy in drive A:");
  puts("Press Enter to read from disk");
  getch();
  result = biosdisk(DISKREAD, DRIVE, HEAD, TRACK,
    SECTOR, NUMSECTORS, buffer);
```

```
        if (result == 0)
          puts("Disk read successful");
        else
          puts("Error detected");
        return 0;
    }
```

biosequip   Check equipment

Syntax   `int biosequip(void);`

Include   bios.h

Description   Returns integer via BIOS interrupt 0x11, which describes various facts about the computer. A similar function, `_bios_equiplist()`, is also declared in bios.h. The value returned by `biosequip()` corresponds to the following bit-field structure:

```
struct equipment {
  unsigned hasdiskette : 1;
  unsigned hascoprocessor: 1;
  unsigned planar : 2;
  unsigned videomode : 2;
  unsigned numfloppy : 2;
  unsigned hasdma: 1;
  unsigned numserial : 3;
  unsigned gameadaptor : 1;
  unsigned serialprinter: 1;
  unsigned numprinters : 2;
};
```

Example
```
/* biosequi.cpp */
#include <stdio.h>
#include <bios.h>
struct equipment {
  unsigned hasdiskette : 1;
  unsigned hascoprocessor: 1;
  unsigned planar : 2;
  unsigned videomode : 2;
  unsigned numfloppy : 2;
  unsigned hasdma: 1;
  unsigned numserial : 3;
  unsigned gameadaptor : 1;
```

```
    unsigned serialprinter: 1;
    unsigned numprinters : 2;
};
union twotypes {
  struct equipment eq;   /* The bit field structure */
  int k;                 /* Same bytes as an integer */
};
main()
{
  union twotypes t;
  t.k = biosequip();   /* Get list as integer */
  printf("\nNumber of printers           %d", t.eq.numprinters);
  printf("\nGame adaptor installed (1)  %d", t.eq.gameadaptor);
  printf("\nNumber of serial ports       %d", t.eq.numserial);
  printf("\nNumber of diskette drives    ");
  if (t.eq.hasdiskette)
    printf("%d", t.eq.numfloppy + 1);
  else
    printf("0");
  printf("\nInitial video mode (2)      %d", t.eq.videomode);
  printf("\nPlanar RAM size (3)         %d", t.eq.planar);
  printf("\n\n(1): 0=FALSE, 1=TRUE");
  printf("\n(2): 1=40x25 color, 2=80x25 color, 3=monochrome");
  printf("\n(3): 3=64K on XTs\n");
  return 0;
}
```

bioskey   Direct keyboard interface

Syntax   `int bioskey(int cmd);`

Include   bios.h

Description   Calls BIOS interrupt 0x16 to provide direct keyboard services. Consult a DOS or PC reference for information on this interrupt and its arguments. Another function prototyped in bios.h, `_bios_keybrd()`, also provides low-level keyboard services.

Parameters   **int cmd** 0–return ASCII character; 1–test for keystroke; 2–request shift key status.

Example   `/* bioskey.cpp */`

```
#include <stdio.h>
#include <bios.h>
main()
{
  printf("Press any key to continue...");
  while (bioskey(1) == 0) ;  // Wait for keypress
  printf("\nbioskey(0) == %#x\n", bioskey(0));
  return 0;
}
```

biosmemory   Return memory size

Syntax   `int biosmemory(void);`

Include   bios.h

Description   Calls BIOS interrupt 0x12 and returns size of memory, not including the video display buffer, or any expanded or extended memory on AT or higher-class computers. Return value is in 1024-byte blocks. A similar bios.h function, _bios_memsize, is also prototyped in bios.h.

Example
```
/* biosmemo.cpp */
#include <stdio.h>
#include <bios.h>
main()
{
  int mem = biosmemory();
  printf("Main memory == %dK bytes\n", mem);
  return 0;
}
```

biosprint   Print using BIOS

Syntax   `int biosprint(int cmd, int abyte, int port);`

Include   bios.h

Description   Calls BIOS interrupt 0x17 to access the printer by communicating directly with the specified port. Consult a DOS or PC reference for more information about this interrupt and its parameters. A similar function, _bios_printer, is also prototyped in bios.h.

Parameters **int cmd** 0–print character int abyte; 1–initialize port; 2–read port or printer status.

int abyte Must be in range 0 to 255.

int port 0–LPT1:, 1–LPT2:, etc.

Example
```
/* biosprin.cpp */
#include <stdio.h>
#include <bios.h>
#define LPT1 0  // LPT2 == 1
#define CMD 2   // Read status
main()
{
  int status = biosprint(CMD, 0, LPT1);
  printf("Printer status == %#x\n", status);
  return 0;
}
```

biostime   Read or set BIOS timer

Syntax `long biostime(int cmd, long newtime);`

Include bios.h

Description Reads or changes the BIOS timer, which cycles at the approximate rate of 18.2 ticks per second, beginning with zero at midnight. The timer is used for informal tasks such as shutting off diskette motors after a certain number of seconds (more or less), but is not accurate enough for time-critical operations. A similar function, _bios_timeofday(), is also prototyped in bios.h.

Parameters **int cmd** 0–return time; 1–set time to newtime.

long newtime Used only if cmd equals 1.

Example
```
/* biostime.cpp */
/* ----------------------------------- */
/* NOTE: Compile with bcc -O- biostime */
/* to disable optimizations.           */
/* ----------------------------------- */
#include <stdio.h>
#include <bios.h>
#define CMD 0  // Read timer
main()
```

```
{
  long t1, t2;
  int i, j;
  printf("Executing 500000 for loops...");
  t1 = biostime(CMD, 0);
  for (i = 0; i < 25000; i++)
    for (j = 0; j < 20; j++) ;
  t2 = biostime(CMD, 0);
  printf("\nTimer ticks == %d\n", t2 - t1);
  return 0;
}
```

brk   Change data-segment allocation

Syntax   `int brk(void *addr);`

Include   alloc.h

Description   Increases a program's heap space by moving the end of the current data segment (called the break value). After calling `brk()` successfully, `coreleft()` returns a larger value than before. Returns zero for success and −1 for error, setting `errno` to ENOMEM (error—not enough memory).

Parameters   **void *addr** New break-value address, usually obtained by calling `malloc()` before allocating any variables on the heap.

See also   coreleft, sbrk

Example
```
/* brk.cpp */
#include <stdio.h>
#include <alloc.h>
#define SIZE 1024
main()
{
  char *p = (char *)malloc(1);
  printf("coreleft() before brk() == %u bytes\n", coreleft());
  if (brk(p + SIZE) == 0)
    printf("coreleft() after brk()  == %u bytes\n", coreleft());
  else
    puts("Error detected");
  return 0;
}
```

bsearch   Binary search

Syntax   `void *bsearch(const void *key, const void *base, size_t nelem, size_t width, int (*fcmp)(const void *, const void *));`

Include   stdlib.h

Description   Searches a sorted array using the binary-search algorithm to minimize the number of comparisons required to find a match. Returns zero if search argument is not found; otherwise, returns the matching item's address. When searching an array of duplicate items, a matching item is not necessarily the first in the array. As demonstrated in the example, `bsearch()` requires you to supply a comparison function, similar to that used by `qsort()`. Your function is passed two pointers, A and B, to elements in the array to be searched, and must return −1 if A < B, zero if A == B, or +1 if A > B.

Parameters   **const void *key** Pointer to search key, of the same data type (usually) as the items stored in the array.

const void *base Pointer to array containing items sorted in low-to-high order.

size_t nelem The number of elements in the array.

size_t width The size in bytes of each element in the array.

int (*fcmp)(const void *, const void*) Comparison function. See example.

See also   lfind, lsearch, qsort

Example
```cpp
/* bsearch.cpp */
#include <stdio.h>
#include <stdlib.h>
#include <string.h>
char *array[] = {
  "Boston",
  "Chicago",
  "Cincinnati",
  "Los Angeles",
  "Miami",
  "New York",
  "Philadelphia"
};
```

```
#define WIDTH (sizeof(array[0]))
#define NELEM (sizeof(array) / sizeof(array[0]))
int Compare(const void *a, const void *b);
main()
{
  char buffer[128];   // Input string buffer
  char **p;           // Result of bsearch()
  char *key;          // Search key pointer
  key = buffer;
  printf("Enter search string: ");
  gets(buffer);
  p = (char **)bsearch(&key, array, NELEM, WIDTH, Compare);
  if (p)
    printf("Found %s\n", *p);
  else
    printf("%s not found\n", buffer);
  return 0;
}

int Compare(const void *a, const void *b)
{
  return stricmp(*(char **)a, *(char **)b);
}
```

cabs, cabsl Absolute value of complex number

Syntax ```
double cabs(struct complex z);
long double cabsl(struct _complexl z);
```

*Include*  math.h

*Description*  Calculates absolute value of a complex number. Function cabs() returns type double. Function cabsl() returns long double. The first example below shows how to use cabs() in C programs; the second shows how to achieve similar results in C++ programs without using cabs().

*See also*  abs, complex, fabs, labs, matherr

*Examples*  ```
/* cabs.c */
#include <stdio.h>
#include <math.h>
```

```
main()
{
  struct complex z = {2.0, 1.0};
  double result;
  result = cabs(z);
  printf("cabs(%.2lf:%.2lf) == %.2lf", z.x, z.y, result);
  return 0;
}

/* cabs.cpp */
#include <stdio.h>
#include <math.h>
#include <complex.h>
main()
{
  complex z(1.0, 2.0);
  double result;
  result = abs(z);  // NOT cabs() for C++!
  printf("cabs(%.2lf:%.2lf) == %.2lf", real(z), imag(z), result);
  return 0;
}
```

calloc Allocate and clear memory

Syntax   `void *calloc(size_t nitems, size_t size);`

Include stdlib.h

Description Allocates a block of memory up to 64K long on the heap and sets every byte in the block to zero. Returns null if not successful; otherwise, returns the address of the first allocated byte.

Parameters **size_t nitems** Number of items to allocate.

size_t size Size in bytes of one item.

See also `farcalloc, free, malloc, realloc`

Example
```
/* calloc.cpp */
#include <stdio.h>
#include <stdlib.h>
#define SIZE 128
main()
```

```
{
  char *s = (char *)calloc(1, SIZE);
  if (s == NULL)
    puts("Error in calloc()");
  else {
    printf("Enter a string: ");
    gets(s);
    printf("Your string is: %s\n", s);
    free(s);
  }
  return 0;
}
```

ceil, ceill   Round up

Syntax
```
double ceil(double x);
long double ceill(long double x);
```

Include   math.h

Description   Returns smallest integer not less than x. In other words, rounds x up to next highest value. Two versions are provided: Use ceil() to round double values and ceill() to round long double values.

See also   floor, floorl, fmod, modf

Example
```
/* ceil.cpp */
#include <stdio.h>
#include <math.h>
main()
{
  char buffer[128];
  double d;
  printf("Enter a floating-point value: ");
  gets(buffer);
  d = atof(buffer);
  printf("Original value: %f\n", d);
  printf("ceil(value)   : %f\n", ceil(d));
  return 0;
}
```

_c_exit   Cleanup without exit

Syntax   `void _c_exit(void);`

Include   process.h

Description   Performs same cleanup services as _exit(), but does not end the program. The function performs only one job: It restores interrupt vectors saved by the program's startup code.

See also   abort, _cexit, exit, _exit

Example
```
/* _c_exit.cpp */
#include <stdio.h>
#include <process.h>
#include <dos.h>
void DispPointer(const char *message, void far *p);
main()
{
  void far *p;
  p = (void far *)_dos_getvect(0);
  DispPointer("Before _c_exit() vector 0 == ", p);
  _c_exit();
  p = (void far *)_dos_getvect(0);
  DispPointer("After _c_exit() vector 0  == ", p);
  return 0;
}

void DispPointer(const char *message, void far *p)
{
  printf("%s%04x:%04x\n", message, FP_SEG(p), FP_OFF(p));
}
```

_cexit   Cleanup without exit

Syntax   `void _cexit(void);`

Include   process.h

Description   Similar to _c_exit(), _cexit() performs the same cleanup services as exit(), but does not end the program. It does not close any open files, but writes any buffered data to disk, calls any exit functions (see atexit()), and restores saved interrupt vectors.

See also   abort, atexit, _c_exit, exit

Example
```
/* _cexit.cpp */
#include <stdio.h>
#include <process.h>
#include <dos.h>
void DispPointer(const char *message, void far *p);
main()
{
  void far *p;
  p = (void far *)_dos_getvect(0);
  DispPointer("Before _cexit() vector 0 == ", p);
  _cexit();
  p = (void far *)_dos_getvect(0);
  DispPointer("After _cexit() vector 0  == ", p);
  return 0;
}

void DispPointer(const char *message, void far *p)
{
  printf("%s%04x:%04x\n", message, FP_SEG(p), FP_OFF(p));
}
```

cgets **Read string from console**

Syntax `char *cgets(char *str);`

Include conio.h

Description Reads a character string into a specially prepared `char` array, addressed by `str`. Call `textbackground()` and `textcolor()` to set text colors for `cgets()` to use. The function returns a pointer to the entered string, located at `str[2]`. The maximum number of characters entered is limited to the stated maximum. Users must press Enter to end input. A newline character is not stored in the string. The function uses direct-video I/O and its output is not redirectable.

Parameters **char *str** Points to specially prepared `char` buffer. Set `str[0]` to the maximum number of characters to read including a terminating null. The function stores the actual number of characters entered (not including the terminating null) into `str[1]`. The first character of the entered string (which can be a null string) begins at `str[2]`.

See also cputs, getch, getche, gets, textbackground, textcolor

Example

```
/* cgets.cpp */
#include <stdio.h>
#include <conio.h>
#define SIZE 23   // Room for 20 characters
main()
{
  char buffer[SIZE];
  char *result;
  buffer[0] = SIZE - 2;  // Including null terminator
  printf("Enter up to 20 characters: ");
  result = cgets(buffer);
  printf("\nResult = %s", result);
  return 0;
}
```

_chain_intr   Chain to interrupt

Syntax   void _chain_intr(void(interrupt far *newhandler)());

Include   dos.h

Description   Callable only by C interrupt functions, _chain_intr() passes control from one interrupt service routine (ISR) to another. The target ISR receives register values that were passed to the first ISR (the one that calls the function). The target ISR may return directly from the interrupt—it does not have to return control to the calling ISR. Typically used by TSRs to hook new code into an exiting interrupt vector, such as the PC's keyboard ISR.

Parameters   **interrupt far *newhandler** Address of target ISR.

See also   _dos_getvect, _dos_setvect, _dos_keep, enable, geninterrupt, getvect, setvect

Example

```
/* _chain_i.cpp */
#include <dos.h>
#include <stdio.h>
#define INTNO 0xff  // Any unused interrupt vector
typedef void interrupt (*isrfp)(...);

void interrupt isr2()
{
  _enable();  // Enable interrupts
  puts("Inside function isr2()");
```

```
}

void interrupt isr1()
{
  _enable();  // Enable interrupts
  puts("Inside function isr1()");
  _chain_intr((isrfp)isr2);  // Chain to isr2()
}

main()
{
  isrfp oldvect = _dos_getvect(INTNO);
  _dos_setvect(INTNO, (isrfp)isr1);
  geninterrupt(INTNO);  // Call isr1() via interrupt
  _dos_setvect(INTNO, oldvect);
  return 0;
}
```

chdir Change directory

Syntax   `int chdir(const char *path);`

Include   dir.h

Description Change current DOS directory to the path string addressed by parameter path. Returns zero for success and –1 for error, setting errno to ENOENT (path or filename not found).

Parameters **const char *path** Pointer to the path string that may contain drive and directory names. Use double backslashes to separate drive and subdirectory names. Examples of acceptable path strings include: `"c:\\"`, `"a:\\backup"`, `"c:\\borlandc\\include"`.

See also _chdrive, getcurdir, getcwd, getdisk, mkdir, rmdir, setdisk

Example
```
/* chdirx.cpp */
/* --------------------------------- */
/* NOTE: Program name changed to avoid */
/* conflict with DOS CHDIR command.    */
/* --------------------------------- */
#include <stdio.h>
#include <dir.h>
main()
{
```

```
char path[128];
printf("Enter new path: ");
gets(path);
if (chdir(path))  // i.e. if not successful
  perror(path);   // print system error
return 0;
}
```

_chdrive   Change drive

Syntax   `int _chdrive(int drive);`

Include   direct.h

Description   Change current disk drive. Does not alter current path on the new or former drive.

Parameters   **int drive** Set to 1 for drive A:, 2 for B:, 3 for C:, and so forth.

See also   `chdir, _dos_getdrive, _dos_setdrive, getdisk, getdrive, setdisk`

Example
```
/* _chdrive.cpp */
#include <stdio.h>
#include <direct.h>
#include <conio.h>
#define DRIVEA 1
main()
{
  printf("Insert diskette in A: and press Enter...");
  getch();
  _chdrive(DRIVEA);
  return 0;
}
```

_chmod   Change file attributes

Syntax   `int _chmod(const char *path, int func [, int attrib]);`

Include   dos.h, io.h

Description   Reads or writes DOS file attributes (often called file-access modes). Returns file attribute if successful; otherwise, returns −1 and sets errno to ENOENT (file not found) or EACCES (access denied, for example, write-protected).

Parameters   `const char *path` Pointer to filename string that might contain drive and path information.

`int func` 0–return file's current attribute; 1–change file's attribute to attrib.

`int attrib` New attribute if func == 1, else not specified. Set attrib to any logical-ORed combination of the constants FA_RDONLY, FA_HIDDEN, FA_SYSTEM, FA_LABEL, FA_DIREC, or FA_ARCH.

See also   `chmod, creat, findfirst, findnext`

Example
```cpp
/* _chmod.cpp */
#include <stdio.h>
#include <dos.h>
#include <io.h>
void pattrib(int hasattrib, int c);
main()
{
  char path[128];
  int attributes;
  printf("Enter filename: ");
  gets(path);
  attributes = _chmod(path, 0);  // Third param not needed
  if (attributes == -1)
    perror(path);
  else {
    printf("%s attributes: ", path);
    pattrib(attributes & FA_RDONLY, 'r');
    pattrib(attributes & FA_HIDDEN, 'h');
    pattrib(attributes & FA_SYSTEM, 's');
    pattrib(attributes & FA_LABEL, 'l');
    pattrib(attributes & FA_DIREC, 'd');
    pattrib(attributes & FA_ARCH, 'a');
  }
  return 0;
}

void pattrib(int hasattrib, int c)
{
  if (hasattrib)
    putchar(c);
  else
    putchar('-');
}
```

chmod   Change file access mode

Syntax   `int chmod(const char *path, int amode);`

Include   sys\stat.h

Description Changes a file's access mode by altering its directory attributes. Returns 0 for success and –1 for error (see _chmod for `errno` error codes).

Parameters **const char *path** Pointer to filename string that might contain drive and path information.

int amode One of the three expressions S_IWRITE (write permission), S_IREAD (read-only permission), or S_IREAD|S_WRITE (read or write permission).

See also   `access, _chmod, fstat, open, sopen, stat`

Example
```
/* chmod.cpp */
#include <stdio.h>
#include <io.h>
#include <sys\stat.h>
#define FILENAME "CHMOD.CPP"
main()
{
  int result;
  printf("Setting %s mode to read and write\n", FILENAME);
  result = chmod(FILENAME, S_IREAD | S_IWRITE);
  if (result)  // i.e. if not successful
    perror(FILENAME);
  return 0;
}
```

chsize   Change file size

Syntax   `int chsize(int handle, long size);`

Include   io.h

Description Changes an open file's size. Increasing a file's size with `chsize()` is faster than writing dummy blocks after the end of an existing file—a common trick employed by database systems to reserve disk space for data. Decreasing a file's size with `chsize()` truncates the file, throwing away any information currently stored beyond the file's new end. The file must be opened with write-permission enabled. Extended portions of files are filled with null bytes. Returns zero for success; −1 for error, setting errno to EACCESS (access denied) or EBADF (bad file number).

Parameters   `int handle` Handle to file, opened with write-permission enabled.

       `long size` New size in bytes.

See also   close, _creat, creat, open

Example

```
/* chsize.cpp */
#include <stdio.h>
#include <io.h>
#include <sys\stat.h>
#define FILENAME "test.dat"
main()
{
  int handle, result;
  handle = creat(FILENAME, S_IREAD ¦ S_IWRITE);
  if (handle == -1)
    perror(FILENAME);
  else {
    result = chsize(handle, 1024);
    if (result)
      perror("chsize()");
    close(handle);
  }
  return 0;
}
```

circle   Draw circle

Syntax   `void far circle(int x, int y, int radius);`

Include   graphics.h

Description   Draw a circle on graphics display. Use `setaspectratio` if circle does not appear round.

Parameters   `int x` Circle's center X coordinate.

       `int y` Circle's center Y coordinate.

int radius Circle's radius (distance in pixels from center to circumference).

See also   arc, ellipse, sector, setaspectratio

Example

```
/* circle.cpp */
#include <graphics.h>
#include <stdio.h>
#include <stdlib.h>
#include <conio.h>
main()
{
  int gdriver = DETECT, gmode, gerr;
  int xmax, ymax, radius, color;
  initgraph(&gdriver, &gmode, "c:\\borlandc\\bgi");
  gerr = graphresult();
  if (gerr != grOk) {
    printf("BGI error: %s\n", grapherrormsg(gerr));
    exit(gerr);
  }
  xmax = getmaxx();
  ymax = getmaxy();
  radius = 10;
  color = 0;
  while (radius < (xmax / 4)) {
    setcolor(color % 16);
    circle(xmax / 2, ymax / 2, radius);
    radius += 5;
    color++;
  }
  getch();
  closegraph();
  return 0;
}
```

_clear87   Clear floating-point status word

Syntax   unsigned int _clear87 (void);

Include   float.h

Description Clears current status of 80x87 floating-point exception handler. Returns current status before clearing.

See also `_control87`, `_fpreset`, `_status87`

Example
```cpp
/* _clear87.cpp */
#include <stdio.h>
#include <float.h>
main()
{
  double d = DBL_MIN;  // Smallest double
  float f;             // Uninitialized float
  printf("1. 80x87 status == %#x\n", _status87());
  f = d;       // Force loss of precision
  printf("2. 80x87 status == %#x\n", _status87());
  _clear87();  // Reset internal error status
  printf("3. 80x87 status == %#x\n", _status87());
  d = f;       // Eliminate "f not used" warning
  return 0;
}
```

cleardevice Clear graphics screen

Syntax `void far cleardevice(void);`

Include graphics.h

Description Clears graphics display to current background color and moves current position to (0,0).

See also `clearviewport`, `setbkcolor`

Example
```cpp
/* cleardev.cpp */
#include <graphics.h>
#include <stdio.h>
#include <stdlib.h>
#include <conio.h>
#define FALSE 0
main()
{
  int gdriver = DETECT, gmode, gerr;
  int c, xmax, ymax, cmax, done = FALSE;
  puts("Press Esc to halt; Enter to clear device");
  puts("Press Enter now to begin...");
```

```
      getch();
      initgraph(&gdriver, &gmode, "c:\\borlandc\\bgi");
      gerr = graphresult();
      if (gerr != grOk) {
        printf("BGI error: %s\n", grapherrormsg(gerr));
        exit(gerr);
      }
      xmax = getmaxx();
      ymax = getmaxy();
      cmax = getmaxcolor();
      randomize();
      while (!done) {
        setcolor(random(cmax));
        lineto(random(xmax), random(ymax));
        if (kbhit()) {
          c = getch();
          if (c == 13)
            cleardevice();
          else
            done = (c == 27);
        }
      }
      closegraph();
      return 0;
    }
```

clearerr   Reset error indication

Syntax   void clearerr(FILE *stream);

Include   stdio.h

Description   Resets to zero the specified stream's error and end-of-file values. Following a file error, call clearerr() to permit further I/O on the stream.

Parameters   **FILE *stream** Pointer to file stream such as returned by fopen().

See also   eof, feof, ferror, perror, rewind

Example   /* clearerr.cpp */
#include <stdio.h>
main()
{

```
char c;
fread(&c, 1, 1, stdprn);
printf("Before, ferror() == %d\n", ferror(stdprn));
clearerr(stdprn);
printf("After, errno == %d\n", ferror(stdprn));
return 0;
}
```

clearviewport   Clear current viewport

Syntax   void far clearviewport(void);

Include   graphics.h

Description Erase current viewport to the background color and position the current
              pointer (CP) to relative coordinate (0,0).

See also   cleardevice, getviewsettings, setviewport

Example
```
/* clearvie.cpp */
#include <graphics.h>
#include <stdio.h>
#include <stdlib.h>
#include <conio.h>
#define MESSAGE "Press Enter to clear viewport..."
main()
{
  int gdriver = DETECT, gmode, gerr;
  int xmax, ymax;
  initgraph(&gdriver, &gmode, "c:\\borlandc\\bgi");
  gerr = graphresult();
  if (gerr != grOk) {
    printf("BGI error: %s\n", grapherrormsg(gerr));
    exit(gerr);
  }
  xmax = getmaxx();
  ymax = getmaxy();
  setcolor(YELLOW);
  line(0, 0, xmax / 2, ymax / 2);
  outtextxy(0, ymax - textheight(MESSAGE), MESSAGE);
  while (getch() != 13) ;  // Wait for Enter key
  clearviewport();
  outtext("<-- cp is here");
  outtextxy(0, ymax - textheight("m"), "Press Enter to quit");
```

```
    while (getch() != 13) ;  // Wait for Enter key
    closegraph();
    return 0;
}
```

clock   Determine processor time

Syntax   `clock_t clock(void);`

Include   time.h

Description   Returns a value that represents the amount of time that has passed since a program began running. Returns −1 for systems that lack an internal timer. In Borland C++, but not necessarily on other ANSI C installations, type `clock_t` is a `typedef` alias for a `long int`.

See also   gettime, time

Example
```
/* clock.cpp */
#include <stdio.h>
#include <time.h>
#include <dos.h>
main()
{
  clock_t t1, t2, t3;
  t1 = clock();
  delay(500);
  t2 = clock();
  t3 = t2 - t1;
  printf("Clock ticks for 500ms delay == %lu\n", t3);
  printf("500 mx delay in seconds == %f\n", t3 / CLK_TCK);
  return 0;
}
```

_close, close   Close file

Syntax   `int _close(int handle);`
           `int close(int handle);`

Include   io.h

Description   Closes an open file identified by `handle`. Returns 0 for success and −1 for error.

Parameters   **int handle** File handle such as returned by open().

See also   creat, creatnew, dup, fclose, open, sopen

Example
```cpp
/* close.cpp */
#include <stdio.h>
#include <string.h>
#include <io.h>
#include <fcntl.h>
#include <sys\stat.h>
main()
{
  int handle;
  char *fname = strdup(tmpnam(NULL));
  char buffer[128];
  memset(buffer, 0xff, sizeof(buffer));
  handle = open(fname, O_CREAT, S_IREAD | S_IWRITE);
  if (handle) {
    printf("Writing to file %s\n", fname);
    write(handle, buffer, sizeof(buffer));
    close(handle);
  }
  return 0;
}
```

closedir   Close directory stream

Syntax   void closedir(DIR *dirp);

Include   dirent.h

Description   Closes a directory stream opened previously by opendir.

Parameters   **DIR *dirp** Pointer to directory stream, such as returned by opendir.

See also   findfirst, findnext, opendir, readdir, rewinddir

Example
```cpp
/* closedir.cpp */
#include <stdio.h>
#include <dirent.h>
main()
{
  DIR *d = opendir(".");
  struct dirent *dp;
  while ((dp = readdir(d)) != NULL)
```

```
    puts(dp->d_name);
  closedir(d);
  return 0;
}
```

closegraph   Shut down graphics system

Syntax   `void far closegraph(void);`

Include   graphics.h

Description   Closes BGI graphics. Frees all internal memory structures, fonts, graphics drivers, flood-fill buffer (created by `setgraphbufsize()`), and so forth. Also restores display mode that was in effect prior to calling `initgraph()`.

See also   `initgraph, setgraphbufsize`

Example
```
/* closegra.cpp */
#include <graphics.h>
#include <stdio.h>
#include <stdlib.h>
#include <conio.h>
main()
{
  int gdriver = DETECT, gmode, gerr;
  initgraph(&gdriver, &gmode, "c:\\borlandc\\bgi");
  gerr = graphresult();
  if (gerr != grOk) {
    printf("BGI error: %s\n", grapherrormsg(gerr));
    exit(gerr);
  }
  setcolor(4);              // Set drawing color
  circle(175, 85, 50);     // x, y, radius
  getch();                 // Pause
  closegraph();            // End graphics display
  puts("End of program");
  return 0;
}
```

clreol Clear to end of line

Syntax   `void clreol(void);`

Include   conio.h

Description   Clears text display from cursor position to end of the line (that is, to the right edge of the current text window).

See also   `clrscr, delline, gotoxy, window`

Example
```
/* clreol.cpp */
#include <stdio.h>
#include <conio.h>
main()
{
  int i, j;
  char s[128];
  for (i = 1; i <= 24; i++)
    for (j = 1; j <= 80; j++)
      putch('x');  // Fill screen
  gotoxy(10, 10);
  printf("Enter your name: ");
  clreol();          // Make space for gets()
  gets(s);
  gotoxy(1, 25);
  return 0;
}
```

clrscr Clear screen

Syntax   `void clrscr(void);`

Include   conio.h

Description   Erases the current text window. Positions cursor at its home position, at coordinate (1,1) in the upper-left corner of the text window.

See also   `clreol, delline, gotoxy, window`

Example
```
/* clrscr.cpp */
#include <stdio.h>
#include <conio.h>
main()
{
  int i, j;
```

```
    clrscr();  // Erase display and "home" the cursor
    for (i = 1; i <= 24; i++)
      for (j = 1; j <= 80; j++)
        putch('x');  // Fill screen with x characters
    puts("\nPress Enter to end program");
    while (getch() != 13) ;
    clrscr();          // Clear screen again
    gotoxy(1, 25);     // Put cursor on bottom line
    return 0;
}
```

complex   Create complex number

Syntax   `complex complex(double real, double imag);`

Include   complex.h

Description   The `complex` class constructor creates a complex number with real and imaginary parts. The class provides overloaded mathematics operators such as +, -, *, and /, which you can use in expressions involving `complex` class instances. In order to use the `complex` class, however, your program must be written using C++. Plain ANSI C programs may use `struct complex` and function `cabs()` (absolute value of a complex number), but all other operations must be written from scratch.

Parameters   **double real** Real part of complex number to be created.

double imag Imaginary part of complex number to be created. Defaults to zero if not specified.

See also   abs, acos, arg, asin, atan, atan2, cabs, conj, cos, cosh, imag, log, log10, norm, polar, pow, real, sin, sinh, sqrt, tan, tanh

Example   See cabs.

conj   Return complex conjugate of complex number

Syntax   `complex conj(complex x);`

Include   complex.h

Description   Returns a `complex` class instance equal to an instance constructed as `complex(real(x), -imag(x))`.

| Parameters | **complex x** Instance of class `complex` for which the complex conjugate is desired. |

| See also | cabs, complex, imag, real |

Example
```
/* conj.cpp */
#include <stdio.h>
#include <complex.h>
main()
{
  complex x(1.0, 2.0);
  cout << "x == " << x << "\n";
  cout << "conj(x) == " << conj(x) << "\n";
  cout << "complex(real(x), -imag(x)) == ";
  cout << complex(real(x), -imag(x)) << "\n";
  return 0;
}
```

_control87   Floating-point control word

| Syntax | unsigned int _control87(unsigned int newcw, unsigned int mask); |

| Include | float.h |

Description
Returns or modifies the floating-point control word, a bitwise value of various flags and settings relating to the 80x87 math coprocessor or emulator. The function returns the current control word value (if `mask` is zero), or the new control word value if changed (`mask` is nonzero).

Parameters
unsigned int newcw New control word bits. To change a bit in the internal control word, the bit must have a corresponding 1 bit in the `mask`.

unsigned int mask Logical mask. For every bit equal to 1, `_control87` sets the internal control word bit to the corresponding bit in `newcw`. No changes to the internal control word are made for `mask` bits equal to zero. Set `mask` to zero to read the current control word (returned as the function result) without making any changes.

| See also | _clear87, _fpreset, _status87 |

Example   `/* _control.cpp */`

```
#include <stdio.h>
#include <float.h>
main()
{
  double d1 = 1, d2 = 0;
  _control87(MCW_EM, MCW_EM);  // Mask divide-by-zero errs
  d1 /= d2;  // Despite divide by zero, program continues
  printf("_status87() == %lu\n", _status87());
  _clear87();
  return 0;
}
```

coreleft   Return unused RAM memory

Syntax   `unsigned coreleft(void);`
            `unsigned long coreleft(void);`

Include   alloc.h

Description   Returns amount of heap space never before used. This value represents
            a true picture of available memory only if no objects have been allocated
            and freed. An accurate tally of available RAM requires walking the
            heap (see `heapwalk()`). In small memory models, `coreleft` returns an
            unsigned value. In large memory models, `coreleft` returns an unsigned
            `long` value.

See also `allocmem, brk, farcoreleft, heapwalk, malloc`

Example   ```
/* coreleft.cpp */
#include <stdio.h>
#include <alloc.h>
main()
{
  printf("coreleft() == %lu", coreleft());
  return 0;
}
```

## cos, cosl   Calculate cosine

*Syntax*    `double cos(double x);`
            `long double cosl(long double x);`
            `complex cos(complex x);`
```

Include	math.h, complex.h
Description	Calculates cosine of x.
See also	acos, asin, atan, atan2, complex, matherr, sin, tan
Example	

```
/* cos.cpp */
#include <stdio.h>
#include <math.h>
#define V 0.25
main()
{
  printf("Cosine of %lf == %lf\n", V, cos(V));
  return 0;
}
```

cosh, coshl   Calculate hyperbolic cosine

Syntax
```
double cosh(double x);
long double coshl(long double x);
complex cosh(complex x);
```

Include   math.h, complex.h

Description   Calculates hyperbolic cosine of x, equal to (ex + e-x)/2. The complex version returns a complex class instance constructed as (exp(x) + exp(-x))/2.

See also   acos, asin, atan, atan2, complex, cos, sin, sinh, tan, tanh

Example
```
/* cosh.cpp */
#include <stdio.h>
#include <math.h>
#define V 0.25
main()
{
  printf("Hyperbolic cosine of %lf == %lf\n", V, cosh(V));
  return 0;
}
```

country   Return country-dependent information

Syntax   struct COUNTRY *country(int xcode, struct country *cp);

Include   dos.h

Description   DOS stores a variety of internal facts that programs can use to alter the way data is formatted according to regional demands. For example, in Europe, dates are typically formatted as day/month/year; in the United States, dates are written month/day/year. Use country() to interrogate DOS for its country-dependent information. This function returns a COUNTRY structure declared as:

```
struct COUNTRY {
    int   co_date;        // Date format
    char  co_curr[5];     // Currency symbol
    char  co_thsep[2];    // Thousands separator
    char  co_desep[2];    // Decimal point
    char  co_dtsep[2];    // Date value separator
    char  co_tmsep[2];    // Time value separator
    char  co_currstyle;   // Currency style
    char  co_digits;      // Currency significant digits
    char  co_time;        // Time format
    long  co_case;        // Upper- and lowercase map
    char  co_dasep[2];    // General purpose data separator
    char  co_fill[10];    // Unused
};
```

Most COUNTRY members have obvious meanings. Member co_date is 0 for USA month/day/year dates, 1 for European day/month/year dates, or 2 for Japanese year/month/day format. Member co_curstyle is 0 if the currency symbol (co_curr[5]) should precede values with no intervening space, 1 if the symbol should follow a value with no intervening space, 2 if the symbol and one space should precede values, or 3 if a space and symbol should follow values. Member co_case addresses a function that performs lowercase to uppercase mapping for characters with ASCII values from 0x80 to 0xff.

Parameters   **int xcode** Country code or zero. USA–0, Europe–1, Japan–2.

struct country *cp Set to (struct COUNTRY *)–1 to change the current country to the nonzero value of xcode. Any other nonzero cp value should address a COUNTRY structure. If xcode is zero, country() fills with current country-dependent information returned by DOS function 0x38. If xcode is nonzero, *cp is filled with the specified country's information.

See also   intdos

Example
```
/* country.cpp */
#include <stdio.h>
#include <dos.h>
main()
{
  struct COUNTRY info;
  double balance = 123.45;
  country(0, &info);
  printf("Balance = %s%.2f\n", info.co_curr, balance);
  return 0;
}
```

cprintf   Write formatted output to screen

Syntax   `int cprintf(const char *format[, argument, ...]);`

Include   conio.h

Description   Display formatted output via direct-video routines. See `printf()` for more information. Function `cprintf()` does not recognize the newline escape code `"\n"`, or the carriage-return and line-feed code `"\r\n"`. Use `gotoxy()` to position the cursor before and after calling `cprintf()`.

Parameters   **const char *format** Format string containing text to display along with escape codes in the form `%d`, `%8.2f`, and so on. Use the escape code `"\n\r"` to begin a new line.

argument, ... A comma-separated list of argument values of appropriate data types. One value for each escape code in the preceding format string *must* be specified.

See also   clreol, clrscr, cputs, gotoxy, fprintf, printf, sprintf, vprintf

Example
```
/* cprintf.cpp */
#include <stdio.h>
#include <conio.h>
#include <limits.h>
main()
{
  char *s = "Maximum integer ==";
  int v = INT_MAX;
  clrscr();
  cputs("Testing cprintf()");
```

```
    gotoxy(1, 10);
    cprintf("%s%8d", s, v);
    gotoxy(1, 12);
    cprintf("Minimum integer ==%8d", INT_MIN);
    gotoxy(1, 24);
    return 0;
}
```

cputs   Write string to screen

Syntax   `int cputs(const char *str);`

Include   conio.h

Description Writes a string directly to the video display buffer, or lacking memory-mapped video, by calling BIOS routines. Does not start a new display line. Returns last character displayed.

Parameters **const char *str** Pointer to null-terminated character string to be displayed.

See also   cgets, cprintf, fputs, gotoxy, puts

Example
```
/* cputs.cpp */
#include <stdio.h>
#include <conio.h>
#include <string.h>
#define MESSAGE "Journey to the Center of the Screen"
void Center(int y, const char *s);
main()
{
  clrscr();
  Center(10, MESSAGE);
  gotoxy(1, 24);
  return 0;
}

void Center(int y, const char *s)
{
  gotoxy(40 - strlen(s) / 2, y);
  cputs(s);
}
```

_creat   Create file

Syntax   `int _creat(const char *path, int attrib);`

Include   io.h, dos.h

Description   Creates a new file with a specified attribute. See the similar `_dos_creat()` function for more information.

Parameters   **const char *path** Pointer to new filename string.

   int attrib Attribute (see `_dos_creat()`).

See also   `_chmod, chsize, _close, close, creat, creatnew, creattemp, _dos_creat`

Example
```cpp
/* _creat.cpp */
#include <stdio.h>
#include <io.h>
#include <dos.h>
#include <string.h>
main()
{
  int handle;
  char *fname = strdup(tmpnam(NULL));
  char buffer[128];
  memset(buffer, 0xff, sizeof(buffer));
  handle = _creat(fname, FA_NORMAL);
  if (handle) {
    printf("Writing to file %s\n", fname);
    write(handle, buffer, sizeof(buffer));
    close(handle);
  }
  return 0;
}
```

creat   Create file

Syntax   `int creat(const char *path, int amode);`

Include   sys\stat.h, io.h

Description   Creates new file. If successful, returns nonnegative integer handle for use with other functions—`read()` and `write()`, for example. Returns −1 if an error is detected. Before calling `creat()`, set global `_fmode` variable to `O_TEXT` if creating a text file, or to `O_BINARY` if creating a binary file.

Parameters   **const char *path** Pointer to null-terminated filename string, which may contain a drive and directory paths.

int amode Set to S_IWRITE to open file for writing, S_IREAD to open for reading only, or (S_IREAD | S_IWRITE) to open for reading and writing.

See also   close, _creat, creatnew, creattemp, dup, fopen, open, read, write

Example

```
/* creat.cpp */
#include <stdio.h>
#include <io.h>
#include <sys\stat.h>
#include <string.h>
main()
{
  int handle;
  char *fname = strdup(tmpnam(NULL));
  char buffer[128];
  memset(buffer, 0xff, sizeof(buffer));
  handle = creat(fname, S_IREAD | S_IWRITE);
  if (handle) {
    printf("Writing to file %s\n", fname);
    write(handle, buffer, sizeof(buffer));
    close(handle);
  }
  return 0;
}
```

creatnew Create new file

Syntax   int creatnew(const char *path, int attrib);

Include   io.h, sys\stat.h

Description   Same as _creat() and _dos_creat(), but if the file specified by path already exists, the file is not overwritten and creatnew() returns –1. Returns nonnegative file handle if successful and –1 if not. Requires DOS 3.0 or a later version.

Parameters   **const char *path** Pointer to null-terminated filename string, which may contain a drive and directory paths.

int attrib Specifies the new file's directory attributes using a logical-OR combination of any of the FA_xxxx constants declared in dos.h (see also Chapter 11, "Input and Output," Table 11.4).

See also   close, _creat, creat, creattemp, _dos_creat, dup, open

Example
```cpp
/* creatnew.cpp */
#include <stdio.h>
#include <io.h>
#include <sys\stat.h>
main()
{
  int handle;
  char *fname = "CREATNEW.CPP";
  handle = creatnew(fname, S_IREAD | S_IWRITE);
  if (handle < 0)
    printf("%s already exists\n", fname);
  else
    printf("%s created\n", fname);
  return 0;
}
```

creattemp   Create temporary file

Syntax   `int creattemp(char *path, int attrib);`

Include   io.h, dos.h

Description   Creates a temporary file with a unique name in the directory specified by path. The file is opened for reading and writing in binary mode. Returns nonnegative file handle if successful and −1 if not. Requires DOS 3.0 or a later version.

Parameters   **const char *path** Pointer to null-terminated filename string, which may contain a drive and directory path information.

int attrib Specifies the new file's directory attributes using any of the FA_xxxx constants declared in dos.h (see also Chapter 11, "Input and Output," Table 11.4).

See also   close, _creat, creat, creatnew, dup, open

Example
```cpp
/* creattem.cpp */
#include <stdio.h>
#include <io.h>
#include <dos.h>
#include <conio.h>
main()
```

```
    {
      int handle;
      puts("Insert scratch diskette in A:.");
      printf("Press Enter to create temporary file...");
      while (getch() != 13) ;
      handle = creattemp("A:\\", FA_NORMAL);
      if (handle < 0)
        puts("\nError creating temporary file");
      else
        puts("\nTemporary file created in A:\\");
      return 0;
    }
```

cscanf Scan and format input from console

Syntax   `int cscanf(char *format[, address, ...]);`

Include   conio.h

Description   Direct-video version of `scanf()` that can be used to input text information and convert it to binary forms. Returns number of input fields read. See `scanf()` for more information.

Parameters   **char *format** Pointer to formatting string, containing specifiers in the form "%s", "%f", and so on.

address, ... The address of a variable of a suitable type for holding information converted from text to binary form. Variables *must* be passed by address. It is a grievous error not to supply the correct number of variables in the expected types. Beware!

See also   cgets, fscanf, scanf, sscanf

Example
```
/* cscanf.cpp */
#include <stdio.h>
#include <conio.h>
main()
{
  int a, b, c;
  clrscr();
  gotoxy(1, 10);
  cputs("Enter three integers (ex. 44 12 83): ");
  cscanf("%d%d%d", &a, &b, &c);
```

```
      gotoxy(1, 12);
      cprintf("Your values are %d %d %d\n", a, b, c);
      return 0;
}
```

ctime   Convert date and time to string

Syntax   `char *ctime(const time_t *time);`

Include   time.h

Description   Returns a character string representation of the date and time information addressed by pointer `time`. Use function `tzset()` (time-zone set) to modify `daylight` and `timezone` global variables, which affect `ctime()`'s result. The function returns a pointer to a static `char` buffer. Subsequent calls to `ctime()` use the same buffer, which should be copied using `strdup()` or a similar string function for safekeeping.

Parameters   **const time_t *time** Pointer to a `time_t` value, such as returned by the `time()` function.

See also   `asctime, ftime, getdate, gettime, gmtime, localtime, time, tzset`

Example
```
/* ctime.cpp */
#include <stdio.h>
#include <time.h>
main()
{
  time_t theTime;
  time(&theTime);
  printf("The time is %s\n", ctime(&theTime));
  return 0;
}
```

ctrlbrk   Set control-break

Syntax   `void ctrlbrk(int (*handler)(void));`

Include   dos.h

Description   Install a Ctrl+Break interrupt handler. The handler is free to execute a `longjump()` to anywhere in the program.

Parameters   **int (*handler)(void)** Pointer to interrupt function, which can return zero to end the program immediately.

See also   getcbrk, signal

Example
```
/* ctrlbrk.cpp */
#include <stdio.h>
#include <stdlib.h>
#include <dos.h>
int CtrlBreakHandler(void);
main()
{
  char buffer[128];

  ctrlbrk(CtrlBreakHandler);
  printf("Enter string or press Ctrl+Break: ");
  gets(buffer);
  puts("Ending program normally");
  return 0;
}

int CtrlBreakHandler(void)
{
  puts("!!! Ctrl+Break hander entered !!!");
  exit(1);    // Abort program
  return 0;   // Never executed. Avoids warning
}
```

delay Pause

Syntax   `void delay(unsigned milliseconds);`

Include   dos.h

Description   Suspends normal program operation for the specified number of milliseconds. Reasonably accurate, but might be affected by other system activity. For example, under Windows, the actual amount of the delay could depend on system-level multitasking settings. The function is typically used in between calls to sound() and nosound() in order to sound a tone for a specific length of time.

Parameters   **unsigned milliseconds** The amount of delay in milliseconds. A value of 1000 delays the program for about one second.

See also   nosound, sleep, sound

Example
```
/* delay.cpp */
#include <stdio.h>
#include <dos.h>
#include <string.h>
main()
{
  char *s = "Slow down and smell the flowers.";
  for (int i = 0; i < strlen(s); i++) {
    delay(250);
    putchar(s[i]);
  }
  return 0;
}
```

delline   Delete line

Syntax   `void delline(void);`

Include   conio.h

Description   Delete line at cursor. Moves other lines that follow the deleted line (if there are any) up and displays a blank line at bottom of screen or current window.

See also   `clreol, clrscr, gotoxy, insline, window`

Example
```
/* delline.cpp */
#include <stdio.h>
#include <conio.h>
main()
{
  clrscr();
  for (int i = 1; i <= 24; i++)
    printf("This is line #%d.\n", i);
  puts("\nPress any key 10 times.");
  gotoxy(1, 10);
  for (i = 1; i <= 10; i++) {
    getch();    // Wait for keypress
    delline();  // Delete line at cursor
  }
  gotoxy(1, 24);
  return 0;
}
```

detectgraph   Detect graphics modes

Syntax   `void far detectgraph(int far *graphdriver, int far *graphmode);`

Include   graphics.h

Description   Determines a system's graphics capability. Always use this function prior to initializing BGI graphics. Given a choice of graphics modes, the function selects the highest possible standard resolution that can give the best results.

Parameters   **int far *graphdriver** A pointer to an integer. Set to zero to request autodetection. Set to a nonzero value to select an ideal or specific graphics mode. See Chapter 17, "Borland's Class Library," for more information.

int far *graphmode A pointer to an integer. If graphdriver equals zero, graphmode is set to the highest possible resolution for the system's graphics display. If graphdriver is not zero, graphmode specifies a specific mode for a multimode display adapter. See graphics_modes in graphics.h and also Chapter 17 for more information.

See also   `graphresult, initgraph`

Example

```
/* detectgr.cpp */
#include <graphics.h>
#include <stdio.h>
#include <stdlib.h>
#include <conio.h>
main()
{
  int gdriver, gmode, gerr;
  int xmax, ymax;
  detectgraph(&gdriver, &gmode);
  initgraph(&gdriver, &gmode, "c:\\borlandc\\bgi");
  gerr = graphresult();
  if (gerr != grOk) {
    printf("BGI error: %s\n", grapherrormsg(gerr));
    exit(gerr);
  }
  xmax = getmaxx();
  ymax = getmaxy();
  setcolor(3);
  circle(xmax / 2, ymax / 2, xmax / 4);
```

```
    getch();
    closegraph();
    return 0;
}
```

difftime   Difference between two times

Syntax   `double difftime(time_t time2, time_t time1);`

Include   time.h

Description   Returns the difference between `time1` and `time2`. The time interval is system-dependent.

Parameters   **time_t time2** A `long` value such as returned by the `time()` function that is greater than or equal to `time1`.

time_t time1 A `long` value such as returned by `time()` that is less than or equal to `time2`.

See also   `asctime, ctime, gmtime, localtime, time, timezone, tzset`

Example
```
/* difftime.cpp */
#include <stdio.h>
#include <time.h>
#include <conio.h>
#include <string.h>
main()
{
  char *s = "How much wood could a woodchuck "
    "chuck if a woodchuck could chuck wood?";
  char buffer[128];
  time_t t1, t2;
  clrscr();
  puts("Type the following sentence.");
  puts("pressing Enter ONLY at the end.");
  gotoxy(1, 10);
  cputs(s);
  gotoxy(1, 15);
  cputs("Enter sentence now:");
  gotoxy(1, 17);
  t1 = time(NULL);
  gets(buffer);
  t2 = time(NULL);
```

```
        gotoxy(1, 24);
        if (strcmp(buffer, s) != 0)
          puts("ERROR: Mistakes in typing detected.");
        printf("Typing time == %.1f seconds.\n", difftime(t2, t1));
        return 0;
      }
```

disable, _disable   Disable interrupts

Syntax   `void disable(void);`
            `void _disable(void);`

Include   dos.h

Description   Disable interrupts, except for nonmaskable interrupts (NMI).

See also   `enable, getvect, setvect`

Example
```
/* disable.cpp */
#include <stdio.h>
#include <dos.h>
main()
{
  puts("Interrupts enabled.");
  disable();
  puts("Interrupts disabled.");
  enable();
  puts("Interrupt reenabled.");
  return 0;
}
```

div   Divide two integers

Syntax   `div_t div(int numer, int denom);`

Include   stdlib.h

Description   Divides integer number by denom. Returns quotient and remainder in a div_t structure declared as:

```
typedef struct {
  int quot;        /* Quotient */
  int rem;         /* Remainder */
} div_t;
```

Parameters   **int numer** Numerator.

         int demom Denominator.

See also   ldiv

Example

```
/* div.cpp */
#include <stdio.h>
#include <stdlib.h>
main()
{
  int v1 = 100, v2 = 17;
  div_t result;
  result = div(v1, v2);
  printf("%d / %d == %d\n", v1, v2, result.quot);
  printf("Remainder == %d\n", result.rem);
  return 0;
}
```

_dos_allocmem   Allocate DOS memory

Syntax   unsigned _dos_allocmem(unsigned size, unsigned *segp);

Include   dos.h

Description   See allocmem.

_dos_close   Close DOS file

Syntax   unsigned _dos_close(int handle);

Include   dos.h

Description   Close file associated with handle such as returned by _dos_open(). Returns zero for success and a DOS error code for failure.

Parameters   **int handle** Handle of open file.

See also   _dos_creat, _dos_open, _dos_read, _dos_write

Example

```
/* _dos_clo.cpp */
#include <stdio.h>
#include <stdlib.h>
#include <dos.h>
#include <string.h>
main()
{
```

```
  int handle;    // File handle
  unsigned num;  // Number of bytes written
  char *fname = strdup(tmpnam(NULL));
  char buf[] = "Write me to disk, please!";
  if (_dos_creat(fname, _A_NORMAL, &handle) != 0) {
    perror(fname);
    exit(1);
  }
  printf("Writing to file %s\n", fname);
  if (_dos_write(handle, buf, strlen(buf), &num) != 0) {
    perror(fname);
    exit(2);
  }
  _dos_close(handle);
  printf("%d bytes written to %s\n", num, fname);
  return 0;
}
```

_dos_creat   Create DOS file

Syntax unsigned _dos_creat(const char *path, unsigned attr,
   int *handlep);

Include dos.h

Description Create a new DOS file, overwriting any existing file of the same name. Returns zero for success and a DOS error code for failure.

Parameters **const char *path** Pointer to pathname string, which may contain drive and directory information.

unsigned attr Logical-OR of _A_NORMAL (plain file), _A_RDONLY (read only), _A_HIDDEN (hidden), or _A_SYSTEM (system), or other _A_xxxx constants declared in dos.h. (Note: You can use FA_xxxx and _A_xxxx constants interchangeably. The _A_xxxx constants are provided for compatibility with Microsoft C. The FA_xxxx constants are unique to Borland C++.)

int *handlep Address of int variable. If function is successful, it stores the new open file's handle at this location.

See also creat, fopen, _dos_close, _dos_creatnew

Example See _dos_close.

_dos_creatnew   Create DOS file

Syntax   unsigned _dos_creatnew(const char *path, int attrib,
            int *handlep);

Include   dos.h

Description   Same as _dos_creat() but does not overwrite an existing file.

See also   _dos_close, _dos_creat, _dos_getfileattr, _dos_setfileattr

Example
```cpp
/* _dos_cre.cpp */
#include <stdio.h>
#include <stdlib.h>
#include <dos.h>
#include <string.h>
main()
{
  int handle;     // File handle
  char fname[128];
  puts("Create new filename");
  printf("Enter filename: ");
  gets(fname);
  if (strlen(fname) == 0)
    return 0;
  if (_dos_creatnew(fname, _A_NORMAL, &handle) != 0) {
    printf("%s already exists.\n", fname);
    exit(1);
  }
  _dos_close(handle);
  printf("Blank file %s created.\n", fname);
  return 0;
}
```

dosexterr   Get extended DOS error information

Syntax   int dosexterr(struct DOSERROR *eblkp);

Include   dos.h

Description   Call after any DOS function reports an error. Returns de_exterror. Inserts extended DOS error information into a DOSERROR structure declared as:

```
struct DOSERROR {
  int   de_exterror;
  char  de_class;
  char  de_action;
  char  de_locus;
};
```

Parameters   **struct DOSERROR *eblkp** Pointer to extended DOSERROR structure. Consult a DOS reference for function 0x59 for more information about this structure's members.

See also   clearerr, perror, strerror

Example
```
/* dosexter.cpp */
#include <stdio.h>
#include <stdlib.h>
#include <dos.h>
main()
{
  int handle;
  struct DOSERROR eblk;
  char *fname = "DOSEXTER.CPP";  // Program's own file
  if (_dos_creatnew(fname, _A_NORMAL, &handle) != 0) {
    printf("%s already exists.\n", fname);
    dosexterr(&eblk);
    puts("Extended error information");
    puts(--------------------------");
    printf("de_exterror == %d\n", eblk.de_exterror);
    printf("de_class    == %d\n", eblk.de_class);
    printf("de_action   == %d\n", eblk.de_action);
    printf("de_locus    == %d\n", eblk.de_locus);
    exit(1);
  }
  _dos_close(handle);
  printf("Blank file %s created.\n", fname);
  return 0;
}
```

_dos_findfirst   Search DOS directory

Syntax   unsigned _dos_findfirst(const char *path, int attrib, struct find_t *ffblk);

Include   dos.h

Description   Begin directory search. Calls DOS function 0x4e. Returns zero if successful or nonzero if an error is detected or if no files are found.

Parameters   **const char *path** Pointer to path string, which may contain wildcard characters '*' and '?'.

int attrib Logical-OR combination of any of the _A_xxxx constants declared in dos.h.

struct find_t *ffblk Pointer to find_t structure, which may be passed to _dos_findnext() to continue searching for additional matching files.

See also   chdir, _dos_findnext, findfirst, findnext, getcwd

Example
```
/* _dos_fin.cpp */
#include <stdio.h>
#include <string.h>
#include <dos.h>
main(int argc, char *argv[])
{
  struct find_t fb;
  char *path = "*.*";
  int done;
  if (argc > 1)
    path = strdup(argv[1]);
  done = _dos_findfirst(path, _A_NORMAL, &fb);
  while (!done) {
    puts(fb.name);
    done = _dos_findnext(&fb);
  }
  return 0;
}
```

_dos_findnext   Continue DOS directory search

Syntax   unsigned _dos_findnext(struct find_t *ffblk);

Include   dos.h

Description   After successfully calling _dos_findfirst(), you may call _dos_findnext() to continue searching for additional files. Returns 0 if successful, or nonzero if an error is detected or if there are no more matching files.

Parameters **struct find_t *ffblk** Pointer to find_t structure as filled in by preceding call to _dos_findfirst().

See also chdir, _dos_findfirst, findfirst, findnext, getcwd

Example See _dos_findfirst.

_dos_freemem Free DOS memory

Syntax unsigned _dos_freemem(unsigned segx);

Include dos.h

Description Frees memory allocated by _dos_allocmem().

Parameters **unsigned segx** Segment address as returned by _dos_allocmem() or _dos_setblock().

See also _dos_allocmem, _dos_setblock

Example
```cpp
/* _dos_fre.cpp */
#include <stdio.h>
#include <dos.h>
#define NPARAGRAPHS 32   // Number of paragraphs
main()
{
  int result;    // Function result
  unsigned seg;  // Passed by address to allocmem()
 printf("Allocating %d paragraphs\n", NPARAGRAPHS);
  result = _dos_allocmem(NPARAGRAPHS, &seg);
  if (result == 0) {
    puts("Allocation successful. Freeing memory.");
    _dos_freemem(seg);   // Free allocated paragraphs
  } else {
    puts("Allocation failed");
    printf("%u paragraphs could be allocated.\n", seg);
  }
  return 0;
}
```

_dos_getdate Get DOS system date

Syntax void _dos_getdate(struct dosdate_t *datep);

Include dos.h

Description   Fills in a dosdate_t structure with the current system date declared in dos.h as:

```
struct dosdate_t {
    unsigned char day;          /* 1-31 */
    unsigned char month;        /* 1-12 */
    unsigned int  year;         /* 1980 - 2099 */
    unsigned char dayofweek;    /* 0 - 6 (0=Sunday) */
};
```

Parameters   **struct dosdate_t *datep** Pointer to dosdate_t structure. After calling _dos_getdate(), this structure's members equal the current system date, provided the system has a clock or the user has set the date properly.

See also   _dos_setdate, getdate, setdate

Example
```
/* _dos_gda.cpp */
#include <stdio.h>
#include <dos.h>
const char *dow[7] = {
    "Sun", "Mon", "Tue", "Wed", "Thu", "Fri", "Sat"
};
const char *months[12] = {
    "Jan", "Feb", "Mar", "Apr", "May", "Jun",
    "Jul", "Aug", "Sep", "Oct", "Nov", "Dec"
};
main()
{
    struct dosdate_t dt;
    _dos_getdate(&dt);
    printf("%s %d-%s-%d\n",
        dow[dt.dayofweek], dt.day, months[dt.month], dt.year);
    return 0;
}
```

_dos_getdiskfree   Get DOS disk free space

Syntax   unsigned _dos_getdiskfree(unsigned char drive,
            struct diskfree_t *dtable);

Include   dos.h

Description Determines amount of free space available on a disk drive. Fills in structure `diskfree_t` declared in dos.h as

```
struct diskfree_t {
  unsigned total_clusters;
  unsigned avail_clusters;
  unsigned sectors_per_cluster;
  unsigned bytes_per_sector;
};
```

Parameters **unsigned char drive** 0–current drive, 1–A:, 2–B:, 3–C:, and so on.

struct diskfree_t *dtable Pointer to `diskfree_t` structure, filled in by function. Total bytes free equals `(long)avail_clusters * (long)sectors_per_cluster * (long)bytes_per_sector`.

See also _dos_getdrive, getdfree, getdisk, _getdrive

Example
```
/* _dos_gdi.cpp */
#include <stdio.h>
#include <stdlib.h>
#include <dos.h>
main()
{
  unsigned long freeSpace;
  struct diskfree_t free;
  if (_dos_getdiskfree(0, &free) != 0) {
    puts("Error checking disk free space");
    exit(1);
  }
  freeSpace = (long)free.avail_clusters *
      (long)free.bytes_per_sector
      * (long)free.sectors_per_cluster;
  printf("Free space on drive = %lu bytes", freeSpace);
  return 0;
}
```

_dos_getdrive Get current DOS drive

Syntax void _dos_getdrive(unsigned *drivep);

Include dos.h

Description Get current drive number.

Parameters   **unsigned *drivep** Pointer to unsigned integer set to 1 for drive A:, 2 for B:, 3 for C:, and so on.

See also   _dos_setdrive, getcwd

Example

```
/* _dos_gdr.cpp */
#include <stdio.h>
#include <dos.h>
main()
{
  unsigned drive;
  _dos_getdrive(&drive);
  printf("Drive number == %d\n", drive);
  printf("Drive letter == %c:\n", ('A' - 1) + drive);
  return 0;
}
```

_dos_getfileattr   Get DOS file attributes

Syntax   int _dos_getfileattr(const char *path, unsigned *attribp);

Include   dos.h

Description   Retrieves attributes for specified file. Returns zero for success and a DOS error code for failure.

Parameters   **const char *path** Pointer to null-terminated path string, which may contain drive and directory information, but no wildcards.

   unsigned *attribp Pointer to an unsigned variable to hold the file's attribute bits identified by the _A_xxxx constants declared in dos.h.

See also   chmod, _dos_setfileattr, stat

Example

```
/* _dos_gfi.cpp */
#include <stdio.h>
#include <dos.h>
main()
{
  unsigned attrib;
  char fname[128];
  printf("Enter filename: ");
  gets(fname);
  if (_dos_getfileattr(fname, &attrib) != 0)
    printf("%s not found.\n", fname);
```

```
    else {
      printf("%s's archive bit == ", fname);
      if ((attrib & _A_ARCH) == _A_ARCH)
        puts("ON");
      else
        puts("OFF");
    }
    return 0;
}
```

_dos_getftime   Get DOS file date and time

Syntax   `unsigned _dos_getftime(int handle, unsigned *datep,`
        `unsigned *timep);`

Include   dos.h

Description   Retrieves specified file's date and time at the moment of its most recent update. Returns zero for success and a DOS error code for failure.

Parameters   **int handle** An open file handle such as returned by _dos_open().

        unsigned *datep Pointer to unsigned variable to hold the date. Bits 0–4 hold the day; 5–8 the month, and 9–15 the number of years since 1980 (14 is 1994, for example).

        unsigned *timep Pointer to unsigned variable to hold the time. Bits 0–4 hold the number of seconds divided by 2, 5–10 the minutes, and 11–15 the hour.

See also   _dos_gettime, _dos_setftime, _dos_settime, fstat, stat

Example
```
/* _dos_gft.cpp */
#include <stdio.h>
#include <stdlib.h>
#include <dos.h>
#include <fcntl.h>

typedef struct dosfdate {
  unsigned day:5;
  unsigned month:4;
  unsigned year:7;
} Dosdate;
```

```
typedef struct dosftime {
  unsigned seconds:5;
  unsigned minutes:6;
  unsigned hours:5;
} Dostime;

main()
{
  Dosdate date;
  Dostime time;
  int handle;
  char fname[128];
  printf("Enter filename: ");
  gets(fname);
  if (_dos_open(fname, O_RDONLY, &handle) != 0) {
    perror(fname);
    exit(1);
  }
  if (_dos_getftime(handle,
    (unsigned *)&date, (unsigned *)&time) != 0)
    puts("Error reading date and time");
  else {
    printf("FILE=%s DATE=%d/%d/%d TIME=%d:%02d\n",
      fname, date.month, date.day, date.year + 1980,
      time.hours, time.minutes);
  }
  _dos_close(handle);
  return 0;
}
```

_dos_gettime   Get DOS system time

Syntax   `void _dos_gettime(struct dostime_t *timep);`

Include   dos.h

Description   Read current system time into a dostime_t structure declared as

```
struct dostime_t {
  unsigned char hour;      /* Hours */
  unsigned char minute;    /* Minutes */
  unsigned char second;    /* Seconds */
  unsigned char hsecond;   /* Hundredths of seconds */
};
```

Parameters   **struct dostime_t *timep** Pointer to dostime_t structure to hold the current time.

See also   _dos_getftime, _dos_settime

Example
```
/* _dos_gti.cpp */
#include <stdio.h>
#include <dos.h>
main()
{
  int hour;
  struct dostime_t theTime;
  char *ampm = "pm";
  _dos_gettime(&theTime);
  hour = theTime.hour;
  if (hour < 12)
    ampm = "am";
  else
    if (hour > 12)
      hour -= 12;
  printf("The hour is %d %s\n", hour, ampm);
  return 0;
}
```

_dos_getvect   Get DOS interrupt vector

Syntax   `void interrupt(far *_dos_getvect(unsigned interruptno))();`

Include   dos.h

Description   Get four-byte vector for the specified interrupt number. An interrupt vector is a pointer that is stored in low memory and is used to address various system interrupt handlers in DOS and in the ROM BIOS.

Parameters   **unsigned interruptno** Interrupt number. See a DOS or PC reference for more information.

See also   _c_exit, _dos_setvect, getvect, setvect

Example
```
/* _dos_gve.cpp */
#include <stdio.h>
#include <dos.h>
main()
{
  void far *v;
```

```
    v = (void far *)_dos_getvect(9);
    printf("Vector 9 == %04x:%04x\n", FP_SEG(v), FP_OFF(v));
    return 0;
}
```

_dos_keep   Terminate and stay resident

Syntax   `void _dos_keep(unsigned char status, unsigned size);`

Include   dos.h

Description   See `keep`.

_dos_open   Open DOS file

Syntax   `unsigned _dos_open(const char *path, unsigned oflags,`
`    int *handlep);`

Include   dos.h

Description   Open specified file for reading and writing. Returns zero for success and a DOS error code for failure.

Parameters   **const char *path** Pointer to null-terminated filename string, which may contain drive and path information, but no wildcards.

unsigned oflags Open-mode constants (see fcntl.h) plus file-sharing constants (see share.h).

int *handlep Pointer to int variable in which _dos_open() stores the open file's handle.

See also   _dos_close, _dos_creat, _dos_read, _dos_write

Example   See _dos_getftime.

_dos_read   Read from DOS file

Syntax   `unsigned _dos_read(int handle, void far *buffer, unsigned len,`
`    unsigned *nreadp);`

Include   dos.h

Description   Read data from open file. Returns zero for success and a DOS error code for failure.

Parameters   **int handle** Handle to open file such as returned by _dos_open().

void far *buffer Pointer to variable at least len bytes long. If the function is successful, it stores file data into this buffer. Must be a far pointer.

unsigned len Number of bytes to read from disk.

unsigned *nreadp If function is successful, the number of bytes actually read (which may differ from the number requested) is stored into the unsigned variable addressed by this pointer.

See also   _dos_open, _dos_write, read, write

Example
```
/* _dos_rea.cpp */
#include <stdio.h>
#include <stdlib.h>
#include <dos.h>
#include <fcntl.h>
#include <alloc.h>
#include <io.h>
#include <limits.h>
#define fname "_DOS_REA.CPP"  // Reads own file
main()
{
  int handle;            // File handle
  char *p;               // Data pointer
  unsigned nread;        // Number of bytes actually read
  long len;              // Number of bytes requested
  unsigned ulen;         // Same as len as unsigned int
  unsigned readresult;   // Function result
  if (_dos_open(fname, O_RDONLY, &handle) != 0) {
    perror(fname);
    exit(1);
  }
  len = filelength(handle);
  if (len > UINT_MAX) {
    puts("File too long for program");
    exit(2);
  }
  ulen = (unsigned)len;
  p = (char far *)malloc(ulen);  // Allocate data buffer
  if (!p) {
    puts("File too large for available memory");
```

```
          exit(2);
      }
      // Read entire file into buffer
      readresult = _dos_read(handle, p, ulen, &nread);
      if ((readresult != 0) || (nread != ulen)) {
        puts("Error reading file");
        exit(3);
      }
      puts(p);  // Displays entire file!
      _dos_close(handle);
      return 0;
  }
```

_dos_setblock   Modify allocated block

Syntax unsigned _dos_setblock(unsigned newsize, unsigned segx, unsigned *maxp);

Include dos.h

Description Modifies size of memory segment allocated by _dos_allocmem(). Returns 0 for success and a DOS error code for failure.

Parameters **unsigned newsize** New requested segment size.

unsigned segx Segment address as returned by _dos_allocmem().

unsigned *maxp Pointer to unsigned variable. In the event of a failure to reallocate memory in the requested size, _dos_setblock() stores at this location the maximum possible block-reallocation size.

See also _dos_allocmem, _dos_freemem

Example
```
/* _dos_sbl.cpp */
#include <stdio.h>
#include <dos.h>
#define NPARAGRAPHS 32  // Number of paragraphs
#define NEWSIZE 64      // Requested paragraphs
main()
{
  int result;    // Function result
  unsigned seg;  // Passed by address to allocmem()
  unsigned max;  // Maximum possible size
  printf("Allocating %d paragraphs\n", NPARAGRAPHS);
  result = _dos_allocmem(NPARAGRAPHS, &seg);
```

```
      if (result == 0) {
        puts("Allocation successful. Reallocating.");
        if (_dos_setblock(NEWSIZE, seg, &max) != 0) {
          puts("Reallocation failed");
          printf("Maximum paragraphs = %lu\n", max);
        } else
          puts("Reallocation successful");
        _dos_freemem(seg);   // Free allocated paragraphs
      } else {
        puts("Allocation failed");
        printf("%u paragraphs could be allocated.\n", seg);
      }
      return 0;
    }
```

_dos_setdate   Set DOS system date

Syntax unsigned _dos_setdate(struct dosdate_t *datep);

Include dos.h

Description Change system date according to member values in the specified dosdate_t structure (see _dos_getdate() for format). Returns zero for success and nonzero for failure.

Parameters **struct dosdate_t *datep** Pointer to dosdate_t structure containing the new system date.

See also _dos_getdate, _dos_getfdate, _dos_setfdate

Example
```
/* _dos_sda.cpp */
#include <stdio.h>
#include <dos.h>
main()
{
  struct dosdate_t dt;
// Don't run program unless you want to change
// your computer's system date!
  return 0;  // Remove to change date.
  dt.day   = 1;
  dt.month = 1;
  dt.year  = 2000;
  if (_dos_setdate(&dt) != 0)
    puts("Error setting date");
```

```
      else
      puts("Date set to 1/1/2000");
      return 0;
}
```

_dos_setdrive Set current DOS drive

Syntax   void _dos_setdrive(unsigned drive, unsigned *ndrivesp);

Include   dos.h

Description Change current drive.

Parameters **unsigned drive** Number of desired drive: 1=A:, 2=B:, 3=C:, and so on.

unsigned *ndrivesp Total number of available drives is stored at the unsigned variable addressed by this pointer.

See also   _dos_getdrive

Example
```
/* _dos_sdr.cpp */
#include <stdio.h>
#include <dos.h>
#include <conio.h>
main()
{
  unsigned ndrives;
  _dos_setdrive(0, &ndrives);
  printf("System has %u disk drives.\n", ndrives);
  puts("\nInsert scratch disk in A:");
  printf("Press Enter to change to A:");
  getch();
  _dos_setdrive(1, &ndrives);
  return 0;
}
```

_dos_setfileattr Set DOS file attributes

Syntax   unsigned _dos_setfileattr(const char *path, unsigned attr);

Include   dos.h

Description Sets specified file attributes to value of attr's low byte. Returns zero for success and a DOS error code for failure.

Parameters   **const char *path** Pointer to null-terminated filename string, which may contain drive and directory information, but no wildcards.

unsigned attr New attribute value in low byte.

See also   _dos_getfileattr

Example

```
/* _dos_sfi.cpp */
#include <stdio.h>
#include <dos.h>
#define FNAME "_DOS_SFI.CPP"  // Program's own name
main()
{
  unsigned attrib;
  if (_dos_getfileattr(FNAME, &attrib) != 0)
    printf("%s not found", FNAME);
  else {
    attrib |= FA_ARCH;  // Set attribute bit
    if (_dos_setfileattr(FNAME, attrib) != 0)
      printf("Can't set %s's archive bit\n", FNAME);
    else
      printf("%s's archive bit set\n", FNAME);
  }
  return 0;
}
```

_dos_setftime Set DOS file date and time

Syntax   `unsigned _dos_setftime(int handle, unsigned date, unsigned time);`

Include   dos.h

Description   Change an open file's date and time. Returns zero for success and a DOS error code for failure.

Parameters   **int handle** Handle to open file such as returned by _dos_open().

unsigned date New date value. Bits 0–4 hold the day; 5–8 the month, and 9–15 the number of years since 1980 (for example, 14 is 1994).

unsigned time New time value. Bits 0–4 hold the number of seconds divided by 2, 5–10 the minutes, and 11–15 the hour.

See also   _dos_getftime, _dos_gettime, _dos_settime

Example
```
/* _dos_sft.cpp */
#include <stdio.h>
#include <stdlib.h>
#include <dos.h>
#include <fcntl.h>
#define FNAME "_DOS_SFT.CPP"
main()
{
  unsigned date = 0, time = 0;
  int handle;
  if (_dos_open(FNAME, O_RDONLY, &handle) != 0) {
    perror(FNAME);
    exit(1);
  }
  if (_dos_setftime(handle, date, time) != 0) {
    perror(FNAME);
    exit(2);
  }
  _dos_close(handle);
  printf("%s's date and time have been zeroed\n", FNAME);
  return 0;
}
```

_dos_settime   Set DOS system time

Syntax   unsigned _dos_settime(struct dostime_t *timep);

Include   dos.h

Description   Change system time to values specified by members of a dostime_t structure (see _dos_gettime() for declaration).

Parameters   **struct dostime_t *timep** Pointer to dostime_t structure containing new time information.

See also   _dos_getftime, _dos_gettime, _dos_setftime

Example
```
/* _dos_sti.cpp */
#include <stdio.h>
#include <dos.h>
main()
{
  struct dostime_t ti;
```

```
// Don't run program unless you want to change
// your computer's system time!
  return 0;  // Remove to change time.

  ti.hour = 0;
  ti.minute = 0;
  ti.second = 0;
  ti.hsecond = 0;
  if (_dos_settime(&ti) != 0)
    puts("Error setting time");
  else
    puts("Time zeroed");
  return 0;
}
```

_dos_setvect   Set DOS interrupt vector

Syntax   void _dos_setvect(unsigned interruptno, void interrupt(*isr)());

Include   dos.h

Description   Change interrupt vector. Typically used to hook new code onto existing BIOS and DOS interrupt service routines.

Parameters   **unsigned interruptno** Interrupt number.

void interrupt(*isr)() Far pointer to new interrupt service routine.

See also   _dos_getvect

Example
```
/* _dos_sve.cpp */
#include <stdio.h>
#include <dos.h>
#include <conio.h>
#define INTR 0x1c
#define FALSE 0
void interrupt (*oldhandler)(...);
void interrupt newhandler(...);
int count;
main()
{
  int done = FALSE;
  clrscr();
  cputs("Press Esc to quit");
```

```
   gotoxy(1, 8);
  cputs("Timer interrupt in effect");
   oldhandler = _dos_getvect(INTR);
   _dos_setvect(INTR, newhandler);
   while (!done) {
     gotoxy(10, 10);
     cprintf("%d", count);
     clreol();
     if (kbhit())
       done = (getch() == 27);
   }
   _dos_setvect(INTR, oldhandler);
   gotoxy(1, 25);
   return 0;
}

void interrupt newhandler(...)
{
  count++;
  oldhandler();
}
```

_dos_write   Write to DOS file

Syntax unsigned _dos_write(int handle, void far *buffer, unsigned len,
          unsigned *nwritten);

Include dos.h

Description Write date to open file. Returns zero for success and a DOS error code for failure.

Parameters **int handle** Handle to open file such as returned by _dos_open().

void far *buffer Pointer to buffer containing at least len bytes to be written to the file.

unsigned len Number of bytes to write starting with byte addressed by buffer.

unsigned *nwritten If function is successful, it stores in the variable addressed by this pointer the number of bytes actually written. The number of bytes actually written may be fewer than the number requested if, for example, an error occurs while writing.

See also   _dos_creat, _dos_open, _dos_read

Example   See _dos_close.

dostounix   Convert date and time to UNIX format

Syntax   `long dostounix(struct date *d, struct dostime *t);`

Include   dos.h

Description   UNIX stores dates and times in a `long` integer equal to the number of seconds GMT (Greenwich Mean Time) since the witching hour (00:00:00, otherwise known as midnight) on January 1, 1970. Because DOS is incapable of using dates and times prior to January 1, 1980, 00:00:00, you may not pass dates earlier than that to `dostounix`.

Parameters   **struct date *d** Pointer to a `date` structure containing the date to convert to unix format. See `getdate()` and dos.h for declaration.

struct dostime *t Pointer to a `time` structure containing the time to convert to unix format. See `gettime()` and dos.h for declaration.

See also   getdate, gettime, unixtodos

Example
```
/* dostouni.cpp */
#include <stdio.h>
#include <dos.h>
#include <time.h>
main()
{
  time_t utime;
  struct time t;
  struct date d;
  struct tm *gmtp, *loctp;
  gettime(&t);
  getdate(&d);
  utime = dostounix(&d, &t);
  gmtp = gmtime(&utime);
  loctp = localtime(&utime);
  printf("\nGMT time == %s\n", asctime(gmtp));
  printf("Local time == %s\n", asctime(loctp));
  return 0;
}
```

drawpoly   Draw outline of polygon

Syntax `void far drawpoly(int numpoints, int far *polypoints);`

Include graphics.h

Description Draws polygon of a specified number of points on graphics display in current line style, color, and mode. Does not close polygon automatically. For a closed shape, the last point must be the same as the first.

Parameters `int numpoints` Number of (x,y) coordinate pairs in the array addressed by `polypoints`.

`int far *polypoints` Pointer to an array of (x,y) coordinate pairs. Each value in the array is an `int`. The entire array should be at least `numpoints` `* 2 * sizeof(int)` bytes long.

See also `fillpoly, floodfill, setcolor, setlinestyle, setwritemode`

Example
```
/* drawpoly.cpp */
#include <graphics.h>
#include <stdio.h>
#include <stdlib.h>
#include <conio.h>
main()
{
  int gdriver = DETECT, gmode, gerr;
  int xmax, ymax, xmaxd4, ymaxd4;
  pointtype polypoints[3];
  initgraph(&gdriver, &gmode, "c:\\borlandc\\bgi");
  gerr = graphresult();
  if (gerr != grOk) {
    printf("BGI error: %s\n", grapherrormsg(gerr));
    exit(gerr);
  }
  xmax = getmaxx();
  ymax = getmaxy();
  xmaxd4 = xmax / 4;
  ymaxd4 = ymax / 4;
  polypoints[0].x = xmaxd4;
  polypoints[0].y = ymaxd4;
  polypoints[1].x = xmax - xmaxd4;
  polypoints[1].y = ymaxd4;
  polypoints[2].x = xmax / 2;
  polypoints[2].y = ymax - ymaxd4;
```

```
    polypoints[3] = polypoints[0];
    setcolor(12);
    drawpoly(4, (int far *)polypoints);    // connect coordinates
    getch();
    closegraph();
    return 0;
}
```

dup   Duplicate file handle

Syntax   `int dup(int handle);`

Include   io.h

Description   Returns a new file handle based on `handle`. Typically used to flush an open file without having to close the file. To use `dup()` this way, first duplicate the file's handle, then close the duplicate, leaving the original handle open. If successful, function returns new file handle and if not successful, it returns −1.

Parameters   **int handle** Handle to open file such as returned by `open()`.

See also   close, creat, creatnew, _dos_close, _dos_open, dup2, fflush, flushall, fopen, open

Example
```
/* dup.cpp */
#include <stdio.h>
#include <stdlib.h>
#include <dos.h>
#include <io.h>
#include <string.h>
main()
{
  int handle;      // Original file handle
  int duphandle;   // Duplicate handle
  unsigned num;    // Number of bytes written to disk
  char *fname = strdup(tmpnam(NULL));
  char buf[] = "Write me to disk, please!";
  if (_dos_creat(fname, _A_NORMAL, &handle) != 0) {
    perror(fname);
    exit(1);
  }
  printf("Writing to file %s\n", fname);
```

```
if (_dos_write(handle, buf, strlen(buf), &num) != 0) {
  perror(fname);
  exit(2);
}
duphandle = dup(handle);  // Duplicate handle
if (duphandle != -1)
  _dos_close(duphandle);   // Flush file to disk
_dos_close(handle);        // File is still open
return 0;
}
```

dup2   Duplicate handle to handle

Syntax   int dup2(int oldhandle, int newhandle);

Include   io.h

Description   Similar to a DOS standard file redirection command, dup2() duplicates an existing file handle (oldhandle) so that a new handle (newhandle) takes on the old file's characteristics. Use dup() to duplicate an existing new handle for safekeeping. Returns zero for success and −1 for failure.

Parameters   **int oldhandle** Handle to file such as returned by open(). This handle is the one that you want to duplicate. In other words, oldhandle is the file to which you want to redirect another file handle.

int newhandle Handle to file such as returned by open(). Or, this handle may also be a standard file handle such as stdout (newhandle == 1). This is the handle that you want to have take on the characteristics of oldhandle—in other words, newhandle is the file to be redirected to another file handle. If file associated with newhandle is open, the file is closed before being redirected.

See also   close, creat, creatnew, _dos_close, _dos_open, dup, fopen, open

Example
```
/* dup2.cpp */
#include <stdio.h>
#include <stdlib.h>
#include <io.h>
#include <string.h>
#include <dos.h>
#define STDOUT_H 1  // stdout handle number
```

```
main()
{
  int handle, savehandle;
  char *fname = strdup(tmpnam(NULL));
  if (_dos_creat(fname, _A_NORMAL, &handle) != 0) {
    perror(fname);
    exit(1);
  }
  savehandle = dup(STDOUT_H);
  dup2(handle, STDOUT_H);
  puts("Redirected to the temporary file!");
  dup2(savehandle, STDOUT_H);
  printf("Type %s to see redirected text\n", fname);
  return 0;
}
```

ecvt Convert floating-point number to string

Syntax   `char *ecvt(double value, int ndig, int *dec, int *sign);`

Include   stdlib.h

Description Converts specified `double value` to a null-terminated string. Returns address of static buffer, which is overwritten on subsequent function calls. To preserve the returned string, use `strcpy()` or another string function to copy the characters to another location. The same static string buffer is also used (and overwritten) by `fcvt()`.

Parameters **double value** Floating-point value to convert.

int ndig Number of digit characters desired in the result.

int *dec Pointer to integer, in which `ecvt()` stores the relative position of the decimal point. (The resulting string does *not* contain a decimal-point character.) A negative value indicates a decimal point to the left of the string's first digit.

int *sign Function sets this integer to zero if `value` is positive or zero. Sets `*sign` to nonzero if `value` is negative.

See also   atof, fcvt, gcvt, sprintf

Example   /* ecvt.cpp */
           #include <stdio.h>

```
#include <stdlib.h>
#include <math.h>
#include <string.h>
main()
{
  double value = M_PI;
  char *result;
  int decimal, sign;
  result = strdup(ecvt(value, 10, &decimal, &sign));
  printf("Orignal value == %f\n", value);
  printf("Result string == %s\n", result);
  printf(" decimal       == %d\n", decimal);
  printf(" sign          == %d\n", sign);
  return 0;
}
```

ellipse   Draw an ellipse or arc

Syntax   `void far ellipse(int x, int y, int stangle, int endangle,`
          `int xradius, int yradius);`

Include   graphics.h

Description   Draws an elliptical arc on the graphics display. Outline of arc is in the current line thickness and color. The current line style except for its thickness is ignored (that is, the arc's outline is always solid).

Parameters   `int x, int y` The (x,y) coordinate of the arc's center.

`int stangle` Starting angle in degrees from 0 to 360. Set stangle to 0 and endangle to 360 to draw a complete ellipse. Angles run counter-clockwise; zero degrees is at 3 o'clock.

`int endangle` Ending angle of the arc.

`int xradius` Horizontal distance from center to arc in pixels.

`int yradius` Vertical distance from center to arc in pixels.

See also   `arc, circle, fillellipse, sector, setcolor, setlinestyle`

Example
```
/* ellipse.cpp */
#include <graphics.h>
#include <stdio.h>
#include <stdlib.h>
#include <time.h>
```

1059

```
#include <conio.h>
#include <math.h>
main()
{
  int gdriver = DETECT, gmode, gerr;
  int xmax, ymax, radius;
  randomize();
  initgraph(&gdriver, &gmode, "c:\\borlandc\\bgi");
  gerr = graphresult();
  if (gerr != grOk) {
    printf("BGI error: %s\n", grapherrormsg(gerr));
    exit(gerr);
  }
  xmax = getmaxx();
  ymax = getmaxy();
  radius = 10;
  while (radius < ymax / 2) {
    setcolor(1 + abs(random(getmaxcolor())));
    ellipse(xmax / 2, ymax / 2, 0, 360, radius, 50);
    ellipse(xmax / 2, ymax / 2, 0, 360, 50, radius);
    radius += 10;
  }
  getch();
  closegraph();
  return 0;
}
```

_ _emit_ _   Insert literal code

Syntax   void _ _emit_ _(argument, ...);

Include   dos.h

Description   Inserts one or more bytes directly into the compiler's object-code output. In effect, _ _emit_ _() gives you the opportunity to "play compiler." The bytes you insert are added to the program's compiled code with no regard whatsoever of their correctness or suitability. Screw up just one byte, and your program will crash—it's as simple as that. (Inline assembly language is *much* safer than this relatively poor method for injecting machine code instructions into the compiler's output. See Chapter 19, "Assembly Language Optimizations.")

Parameters   **argument** A byte in the range of 0x0 to 0xff, or a word value in the range of 0x0 to 0xffff. To output a 16-bit word in the range 0x0 to 0xff, use an unsigned typecast. For example, `__emit__(0x2);` inserts a *byte* equal to 2 into the code stream; `__emit__((unsigned)0x2);` injects a *word* equal to 2. You may also specify the address of a variable. If the variable is local to a function, or if it is a function parameter, one byte is injected if the value's address offset is from −128 to 128 bytes from the location specified by register BP; otherwise, two bytes are written. You must specify at least one argument to `__emit__()`, but you may specify several arguments separated with commas.

See also `disable, enable, int86, int86x, intdos, intdosx, intr`

Example
```
/* __emit__.cpp */
#include <stdio.h>
main()
{
  __emit__(0xFA);  // CLI (clear interrupts)
  __emit__(0xFB);  // STI (set interrupts)
  return 0;
}
```

enable   Enable interrupts

Syntax `void enable(void);`

Include dos.h

Description Enables hardware interrupts. Typically used only after using `disable()` to turn off interrupts, except for nonmaskable interrupts (NMI), which cannot be disabled.

See also `disable, getvect, setvect, _dos_getvect, _dos_setvect`

Example See `disable`.

eof   End of file

Syntax `int eof(int handle);`

Include io.h

Description Returns true (1) if the file identified by `handle` is positioned at the file's end. Returns false (0) if the file is not at its end. Returns −1 if an error occurs, and sets errno to EBADF (bad file number).

Parameters `int handle` Open file handle, such as returned by `open()`.

See also   clearerr, close, feof, ferror, open, perror, read, write

Example

```
/* eof.cpp */
#include <stdio.h>
#include <stdlib.h>
#include <io.h>
main(int argc, char *argv[])
{
  FILE *fp;     // File stream
  int handle;   // Handle to same file
  char c;       // For reading file content
  if (argc <= 1) {
    puts("No file specified");
    exit(1);
  }
  fp = fopen(argv[1], "r");
  if (!fp)
    perror(argv[1]);
  else {
    handle = fileno(fp);
    do {
      read(handle, &c, 1);  // Read a character
      putchar(c);                // Write to stdout
    } while (!eof(handle));
    fclose(fp);
  }
  return 0;
}
```

exec...   Execute task

Syntax

```
int execl(char *path, char *arg0, *arg1, ..., *argn, NULL);
int execle(char *path, char *arg0, *arg1, ..., *argn, NULL,
   char **env);
int execlp(char *path, char *arg0, *arg1, ..., *argn, NULL);
int execlpe(char *path, char *arg0, *arg1, ..., *argn, NULL,
   char **env);
int execv(char *path, char *argv[]);
int execve(char *path, char *argv[], char **env);
int execvp(char *path, char *argv[]);
int execvpe(char *path, char *argv[], char **env);
```

Include   process.h

Description   Executes tasks, otherwise known as child processes. Use one of these functions to run another program, or run COMMAND.COM to issue a DOS command from within a program. The function names are mnemonic. Functions named with "e" accept a pointer to a new environment; other functions inherit the parent process's environment. Functions named with "l" pass their arguments as separate char * strings. Functions named with "p" search for the target program file in the system PATH directories. Functions named with "v" pass arguments as a variable-length array of char *. Except for these differences, the functions essentially perform the same job.

Parameters   **char *path** Pointer to null-terminated string equal to the name of the program to execute. Include .EXE or .COM filename extension. May also include drive and directory information.

char *arg0, ... *argn Argument strings to be passed individually to the executed child task. The first argument should be the program's name, and is usually the same as path.

NULL Marks the end of the preceding argument list.

char **env Pointer to environment string pointers.

char *argv[] Pointer to variable-length array of argument string pointers.

See also   searchpath, spawn..., system

Example
```
/* exec.cpp */
#include <stdio.h>
#include <stdlib.h>
#include <conio.h>
#include <process.h>
main()
{
  char *cmd;  // Pointer to command.com
  printf("Press Enter for directory...");
  getch();
  cmd = getenv("COMSPEC");
  execl(cmd, cmd, "/c dir *.*", NULL);
  perror("exec():");  // Executes only if execl() fails
  return 0;
}
```

_exit Exit program unconditionally

Syntax `void _exit(int status);`

Include stdlib.h

Description Terminates program immediately. Does not close any open files, does not flush any modified output buffers to disk, and does not execute any exit functions installed by `atexit()`. Use this low-level terminator only in extreme situations. Normally, to end programs immediately, call `exit()` (no leading underscore).

Parameters **int status** Value to pass back to DOS COMMAND.COM (or to another parent process). Available via DOS `errorlevel` variable.

See also `abort, atexit, exit, keep`

Example
```
/* _exit.cpp */
#include <stdio.h>
#include <stdlib.h>
main(int argc)
{
  if (argc <= 1) {
    puts("Ending via _exit(1)");
    fcloseall();  // Close any open files
    _exit(1);     // Exit without closing files
  }
  return 0;  // Executed if argument specified
}
```

exit Exit program

Syntax `void exit(int status);`

Include stdlib.h

Description Terminates program immediately. Closes any open files, flushes any modified output buffers to disk, and executes any exit functions installed by `atexit()`.

Parameters **int status** Value to pass back to DOS COMMAND.COM (or to another parent process). Available via DOS `errorlevel` variable. Note: The example's filename is EXITX.CPP, which avoids a conflict with the DOS EXIT command.

See also   abort, atexit, _exit, keep

Example
```cpp
/* exitx.cpp */
#include <stdio.h>
#include <stdlib.h>
main(int argc, char *argv[])
{
  int i;
  if (argc <= 1) {
    puts("No arguments entered");
    exit(1);
  }
  for (i = 0; i < argc; i++)
    puts(argv[i]);
  return 0;
}
```

exp, expl   Exponential

Syntax
```cpp
double exp(double x);
long double expl(long double x);
complex exp(complex x);
```

Include   math.h, complex.h

Description   Exponential of *ex*. Macro M_E declared in math.h gives the value of *e* as 2.71828182845904523536. Errors from exp() return HUGE_VAL. Errors from expl() return LHUGE_VAL. Underflow errors return 0.0.

See also   complex, frexp, ldexp, log, log10, matherr, pow, pow10, sqrt

Example
```cpp
/* exp.cpp */
#include <stdio.h>
#include <math.h>
main()
{
  double x;
  char buffer[128];
  printf("Enter exponent: ");
  gets(buffer);
  x = atof(buffer);
  printf("e ^ %.3lf == %lf\n", x, exp(x));
  return 0;
}
```

fabs, fabsl   Floating-point absolute value

Syntax
```
double fabs(double x);
long double fabsl(long double x);
```

Include   math.h

Description   Returns absolute (unsigned) equivalent of a floating-point value x.

Parameters   **double x** Any double value.

long double x Any long double value.

See also   abs, cabs, labs

Example
```
/* fabs.cpp */

#include <stdio.h>
#include <math.h>
main()
{
  double x = -123.321;
  printf("%lf\n", x);
  printf("%lf\n", fabs(x));
  return 0;
}
```

farcalloc   Allocate far heap memory

Syntax   `void far *farcalloc(unsigned long nunits, unsigned long unitsz);`

Include   alloc.h

Description   Allocates and clears memory on the far heap. In large memory models—compact, large, and huge—farcalloc() operates similarly to calloc(), but requires unsigned long arguments. Cannot be used in tiny model programs (which do not have a far heap). Returns pointer to allocated memory, or null if memory request cannot be fulfilled.

Parameters   **unsigned long nunits** Number of elements, each unitsz bytes long, to allocate.

unsigned long unitsz Size of one element in bytes.

See also   calloc, farcoreleft, farfree, farmalloc, malloc

Example
```
/* farcallo.cpp */
#include <stdio.h>
#include <alloc.h>
main()
{
  char far *p;    // Pointer to far-heap buffer
  p = (char far *)farcalloc(1024, 1);  // Allocate buffer
  if (p) {
    p[0] = 'A';  //  Assign "ABC" to buffer, which is
    p[1] = 'B';  //    null terminated because farcalloc()
    p[2] = 'C';  //    fills allocated memory with zeros.
    printf("Far string == %Fs\n", p);
    farfree(p);
  }
  return 0;
}
```

farcoreleft   Unused far heap memory

Syntax   `unsigned long farcoreleft(void);`

Include   alloc.h

Description   Returns number of bytes never used on the far heap. After allocating and freeing any far-heap memory, `farcoreleft()` does not give an accurate account of available memory.

See also   `coreleft, farheapcheckfree, farmalloc, farheapwalk`

Example
```
/* farcorel.cpp */
#include <stdio.h>
#include <alloc.h>
void Report(const char *message);
main()
{
  void far *p;
  Report("at start");
  p = farmalloc(1024 * sizeof(int));  // Space for 1024 ints
  Report("after farmalloc()");
  farfree(p);
  Report("after farfree()");
  return 0;
}
```

```
void Report(const char *message)
{
  printf("farcoreleft() %s == %lu\n", message,
farcoreleft());
}
```

farfree   Free far heap memory

Syntax `void farfree(void far *block);`

Include alloc.h

Description Frees block of memory allocated by `farmalloc()` or `farcalloc()`.

Parameters **void far *block** Far pointer to memory to be freed.

See also `farcalloc, farmalloc`

Example See `farcoreleft`.

farheapcheck   Check far heap

Syntax `int farheapcheck(void);`

Include alloc.h

Description Performs diagnostic on far heap's allocated and freed memory blocks. Walks the far heap, and checks every block for errors. Returns zero or positive value for success and a negative value for failure. Return value may be one of the constants _HEAPEMPTY (if no used or freed blocks exist on the far heap), _HEAPOK (if the heap checks out), or _HEAPCORRUPT (if an error is detected).

See also heapcheck

Example
```
/* farheapc.cpp */
#include <stdio.h>
#include <alloc.h>
#define MSIZE 1024
long FarHeapSize(void);
main()
{
  long result;
  void far *p1 = farmalloc(MSIZE);  // Allocate 3 buffers
  void far *p2 = farmalloc(MSIZE);
```

```
        void far *p3 = farmalloc(MSIZE);
        farfree(p2);   // Dispose of middle buffer
        result = FarHeapSize();
        if (result == -1)
          puts("Error in far heap");
        else
          printf("Far heap size == %ld bytes", result);
        farfree(p1);
        farfree(p3);
        return 0;
      }

      long FarHeapSize(void)
      {
        unsigned long count;
        struct farheapinfo info;
        info.ptr = NULL;
        if (farheapcheck() != _HEAPOK)
          return -1L;
        count = farcoreleft();
        while (farheapwalk(&info) == _HEAPOK)
          if (info.in_use == 0)
            count += info.size;
        return count;
      }
```

farheapcheckfree   Check far heap free blocks

Syntax   `int farheapcheckfree(unsigned int fillvalue);`

Include   alloc.h

Description   Similar to `farheapcheck()`, but examines only freed blocks for errors. Returns same constants as `farheapcheck()` plus `_BADVALUE` if any value not equal to `fillvalue` is found in a freed block. Typically used after calling `farheapfillfree()`.

Parameters   **unsigned int fillvalue** Value to compare with freed blocks, usually assigned test values by `farheapfillfree()`.

See also   `farheapcheck`, `farheapfillfree`, `farheapwalk`

Example
```
/* farheapf.cpp */
#include <stdio.h>
#include <alloc.h>
#define SIZE 10  // Number of buffers to allocate
#define BUFSIZE 64  // Size of buffers in bytes
main()
{
  char far *pa[SIZE];
  int test;
  for (int i = 0; i < SIZE; i++)
    pa[i] = (char far *)farmalloc(BUFSIZE);  // Allocate bufs
  for (i = 0; i < SIZE; i += 2)
    farfree(pa[i]);  // Free every other buffer
  test = farheapfillfree(1);   // Fill free bufs with test
value
  if (test < 0)
    puts("Error filling free blocks");
  test = farheapcheckfree(1);  // Compare buffers
  if (test > 0)
    puts("Far free blocks pass inspection");
  else
    puts("Error detected in far heap free blocks");
  return 0;
}
```

farheapchecknode   Check far heap node

Syntax `int farheapchecknode(void *node);`

Include alloc.h

Description Checks validity of a memory block, which can be active or freed. If the memory block is freed, however, the function may report error _BADNODE if the memory manager has combined the freed block with an adjacent available space. Returns negative value for success and a positive value for failure.

Parameters **void *node** Pointer to memory block to be tested.

See also farheapcheck, farheapwalk, heapchecknode

Example
```
/* farheapn.cpp */
#include <stdio.h>
#include <alloc.h>
```

```
#define MSIZE 1024
void Report(int result, const char *message);
main()
{
  long result;
  void far *p1 = farmalloc(MSIZE);   // Allocate 3 buffers
  void far *p2 = farmalloc(MSIZE);
  void far *p3 = farmalloc(MSIZE);
  farfree(p2);  // Dispose of middle buffer
  result = farheapchecknode(p1);   // Test allocated block
  Report(result, "Allocated block: ");
  result = farheapchecknode(p2);   // Test freed block
  Report(result, "Freed block: ");
  farfree(p1);
  farfree(p3);
  return 0;
}

void Report(int result, const char *message)
{
  printf(message);
  switch (result) {
    case _HEAPEMPTY:
      puts("No far heap"); break;
    case _HEAPCORRUPT:
      puts("Far heap is corrupted"); break;
    case _BADNODE:
      puts("Bad or freed far heap block"); break;
    case _FREEENTRY:
      puts("Free far heap block"); break;
    case _USEDENTRY:
      puts("Used far heap block"); break;
  }
}
```

farheapfillfree   Fill far heap free blocks

Syntax   `int farheapfillfree(unsigned int fillvalue);`

Include   alloc.h

Description   Fills freed far heap blocks with specified value. Typically used before calling `farheapcheckfree()` to perform a heap diagnostic.

Parameters **unsigned int fillvalue** Value to assign to freed heap blocks.

See also farheapcheckfree, farheapwalk, heapfillfree

Example See farheapcheckfree.

farheapwalk   Walk far heap blocks

Syntax int farheapwalk(struct farheapinfo *hi);

Include alloc.h

Description Walks the heap's allocated and freed memory blocks. Always call farheapcheck() to check the heap before calling farheapwalk(), which operates correctly only if the heap is not corrupted. Fills a farheapinfo structure with information about examined blocks. The structure is declared in alloc.h as

```
struct farheapinfo {
  void huge *ptr;        // Pointer to block
  unsigned long size;    // Size of block in bytes
  int in_use;            // True if used; false if freed
};
```

Returns _HEAPEMPTY (if there are no far heap blocks to walk), _HEAPOK (if the heap status is valid), or _HEAPEND (after reaching the last block). Function is typically used to determine total amount of far heap space available.

Parameters **struct farheapinfo *hi** Pass by address to function. Set member ptr to null for the first call, then pass the returned structure in subsequent calls to walk additional heap blocks.

See also farheapcheck, heapwalk

Example See farheapcheck.

farmalloc   Allocate far heap memory

Syntax void far *farmalloc(unsigned long nbytes);

Include alloc.h

Description Allocates one or more bytes of far heap space, up to all available memory. Returns a far pointer to allocated block, or null if the memory request cannot be fulfilled. Does not work in the tiny memory model (which has no far heap).

Parameters   `unsigned long nbytes` Number of bytes to allocate.

See also   `farcalloc, farcoreleft, farfree, farrealloc, malloc`

Example   See `farcoreleft`.

farrealloc   Reallocate far heap block

Syntax   `void far *farrealloc(void far *oldblock, unsigned long nbytes);`

Include   alloc.h

Description   Modifies size of a block allocated on the far heap by `farmalloc()` or `farcalloc()`. Returns address of modified block, which might not be at the same location as the original. If the reallocation request fails (probably because enough memory is not available), the function returns null.

Parameters   `void far *oldblock` Pointer to memory block to be reallocated.

`unsigned long nbytes` New requested block size, which may be less or greater than the current block's size.

See also   `farcalloc, farmalloc, realloc`

Example
```
/* farreall.cpp */
#include <stdio.h>
#include <alloc.h>
void Report(const char *message);
main()
{
  void far *p;
  Report("Before first allocation");
  p = farmalloc(1024);  // Allocate 1024-byte buffer
  Report("After first allocation");
  p = farrealloc(p, 2048); // Increase block size
  Report("After first reallocation");
  p = farrealloc(p, 512);  // Decrease block size
  Report("After second reallocation");
  return 0;
}
```

```
void Report(const char *message)
{
  puts(message);
  printf(" far core left == %lu\n", farcoreleft());
}
```

fclose   Close stream

Syntax   `int fclose(FILE *stream);`

Include   stdio.h

Description   Closes an open file stream, such as returned by `fopen()`. If the stream was opened for writing, any modified data held in memory is flushed to disk before closing the file. After closing a file, its `FILE *` value is no longer valid, and must not be used. Returns zero for success; `EOF` for failure.

Parameters   **FILE *stream** File stream previously opened by `fopen()` or a similar function.

See also   close, fcloseall, fdopen, fflush, flushall, fopen, freopen

Example
```
/* fclose.cpp */
#include <stdio.h>
#include <stdlib.h>
main(int argc, char *argv[])
{
  FILE *fp;
  char buffer[256];
  if (argc <= 1) {
    puts("No file specified");
    exit(1);
  }
  fp = fopen(argv[1], "r");
  if (!fp)
    puts("Error opening file");
  else {
    while (fgets(buffer, 255, fp) != NULL)
      fputs(buffer, stdout);
    fclose(fp);
  }
  return 0;
}
```

fcloseall   Close open streams

Syntax   `int fcloseall(void);`

Include   stdio.h

Description   Closes all open FILE * streams, but not standard I/O files stdin, stdout, stdprn, stderr, or stdaux. Returns number of streams closed, or EOF if an error was detected.

See also   `fclose, flushall, fopen, freopen`

Example   See _exit.

fcvt   Convert floating point to string

Syntax   `char *fcvt(double value, int ndig, int *dec, int *sign);`

Include   stdlib.h

Description   Identical to ecvt() except that rounding conforms to FORTRAN–F specifications.

Parameters   See ecvt.

See also   `atof, _atold, ecvt, gcvt, sprintf`

Example   See ecvt.

fdopen   Associate stream with handle

Syntax   `FILE *fdopen(int handle, char *type);`

Include   stdio.h

Description   Returns a FILE * stream for an open file handle such as returned by creat(), dup(), dup2(), or open(). Returns null if the file cannot be opened as a stream.

Parameters   **int handle** An open file handle.

   char *type File mode string, identical to fopen() mode strings. The specified mode must match the file identified by handle. For example, the string "w" opens the file for writing. Add "t" to a mode string ("wt" for instance) to specify text mode; add "b" as in "wb" for binary mode. In the absence of "t" or "b", the file mode is governed by global variable _fmode. See fopen() for specific string.

See also   _dos_open, fclose, fopen, freopen, open

Example
```cpp
/* fdopen.cpp */
#include <stdio.h>
#include <stdlib.h>
#include <io.h>
#include <sys\stat.h>
#include <fcntl.h>
main(int argc, char *argv[])
{
  int handle;  // File handle
  FILE *fp;     // Same file as a stream
  char buffer[256];
  if (argc <= 1) {
    puts("No file specified");
    exit(1);
  }
  handle = open(argv[1], O_RDONLY | O_TEXT, S_IREAD);
  if (handle == NULL)
    puts("Error opening file");
  else {
    fp = fdopen(handle, "rt");  // handle to stream
    while (fgets(buffer, 255, fp) != NULL)
      fputs(buffer, stdout);
  }
  close(handle);
  return 0;
}
```

feof   End of file stream

Syntax   int feof(FILE *stream);

Include   stdio.h

Description   Returns true (nonzero) if the specified file stream's internal pointer is positioned beyond the file's last byte, usually due to a preceding I/O operation on the stream. Returns false if the file's internal pointer is not at the end of the file. Implemented as a macro.

Parameters   **FILE *stream** Any open file stream, such as returned by fopen().

See also   clearerr, eof, ferror, fopen, rewind

Example
```
/* feof.cpp */
#include <stdio.h>
#include <stdlib.h>
main(int argc, char *argv[])
{
  FILE *fp;            // File stream
  char buffer[128];  // For reading text lines
  if (argc <= 1) {
    puts("No file specified");
    exit(1);
  }
  fp = fopen(argv[1], "r");
  if (!fp)
    perror(argv[1]);
  else {
    while (!feof(fp))
      if (fgets(buffer, 255, fp) != NULL)
        fputs(buffer, stdout);
    fclose(fp);
  }
  return 0;
}
```

ferror   Stream error

Syntax   `int ferror(FILE *stream);`

Include   stdio.h

Description   Returns true (nonzero) if any errors have occurred for the specified stream. Returns false (zero) if no errors have been detected.

Parameters   **FILE *stream** Any open file stream, such as returned by fopen().

See also   clearerr, eof, feof, fopen, perror, rewind

Example
```
/* ferror.cpp */
#include <stdio.h>
#include <stdlib.h>
#define FNAME "FERROR.CPP"
main()
{
  FILE *fp;
  puts("Opening FERROR.CPP for reading");
```

```
  fp = fopen(FNAME, "r");
  if (!fp) {
    puts("Can't open "FNAME);
    exit(1);
  }
  puts("Attempting to write to file");
  fputs("Force file error", fp);
  if (ferror(fp))
    puts("File stream error detected!");
  fclose(fp);
  return 0;
}
```

fflush   Flush stream

Syntax   `int fflush(FILE *stream);`

Include   stdio.h

Description   Writes any modified file buffers to disk for the specified stream. Does not close the file. Call this function periodically in any program that keeps output files open for long periods of time. After calling `fflush()`, the file and any in-memory buffers are "in synch."

Parameters   **FILE *stream** Any open file stream, such as returned by `fopen()`.

See also   `fclose, flushall, fwrite, setbuf, setvbuf`

Example
```
/* fflush.cpp */
#include <stdio.h>
#include <stdlib.h>
#include <string.h>
#include <conio.h>
main()
{
  FILE *inpf, *outf;
 char buffer[255];
  char *fname = strdup(tmpnam(NULL));
  outf = fopen(fname, "w");  // Create temporary file
  inpf = fopen("FFLUSH.CPP", "r");  // Open this file
  if (!(inpf ¦¦ outf)) {
    puts("Error opening files");
    exit(1);
  }
```

```
    printf("Writing to %s", fname);
    while (fgets(buffer, 255, inpf) != NULL)
      fputs(buffer, outf);
    printf("\nPress Enter to flush output file");
    getch();
    fflush(outf);
    printf("\nFile is flushed. Closing file.");
    fclose(outf);
    fclose(inpf);
    printf("\nList file %s then delete.", fname);
    return 0;
  }
```

fgetc   Get character

Syntax   `int fgetc(FILE *stream);`

Include   stdio.h

Description   Reads one character from specified stream. Returns character value if successful. Returns EOF if the file's internal pointer is positioned beyond the end of the file. Also returns EOF if any errors are detected.

Parameters   **FILE *stream** Any open file stream, such as returned by fopen(), opened for reading in a text mode.

See also   fgetchar, fputc, fputs, fread, fwrite, perror

Example
```
/* fgetc.cpp */
#include <stdio.h>
#include <stdlib.h>
main(int argc, char *argv[])
{
  FILE *fp;  // File stream
  int c;     // Holds each char from file
  if (argc <= 1) {
    puts("No file specified");
  exit(1);
  }
  fp = fopen(argv[1], "r");
  if (!fp)
    puts("Error opening file");
  else {
    while ((c = fgetc(fp)) != EOF)
```

```
        fputc(c, stdout);
      fclose(fp);
    }
    return 0;
  }
```

fgetchar   Get character

Syntax   `int fgetchar(void);`

Include   stdio.h

Description   Reads one character from the standard input file `stdin`. Equivalent to `fgetc(stdin)`. Returns character or `EOF` if the file pointer is positioned beyond its end, or if an error occurs.

See also   `fgetc, fputchar, getchar`

Example
```
/* fgetchar.cpp */
#include <stdio.h>
#include <stdlib.h>
#include <string.h>
main()
{
  FILE *fp;  // File stream
  char *fname = strdup(tmpnam(NULL));
  int c;     // Holds characters written to disk
  fp = fopen(fname, "w");  // Create new file
  if (!fp)
    puts("Error writing to file");
  else {
    printf("%s created. Enter text to store in\n", fname);
    printf("file. Press Ctrl+Z and Enter to end.\n");
    while ((c = fgetchar()) != EOF)
      fputc(c, fp);
    fclose(fp);
    printf("\nList %s to see results.\n", fname);
    puts("You may delete this file.");
  }
  return 0;
}
```

fgetpos   Get file pointer

Syntax   `int fgetpos(FILE *stream, fpos_t *pos);`

Include   stdio.h

Description   Copies the specified file's data pointer to the `fpos_t` variable addressed by pos. This value represents the offset in bytes from the beginning of the file to the location where the next I/O operation would take place. Identifier `fpos_t` is defined in Borland C++ as a `typedef` alias for `long`. The function returns zero for success, −1 for failure, and sets errno to EBADF (bad file number). Borland C++'s Library Reference specifies error EINVAL (invalid argument), but this error code is rarely seen.

Parameters   **FILE *stream** Any open file stream, such as returned by `fopen()`.

fpos_t *pos Pointer to a `fpos_t` variable to hold the file's internal pointer.

See also   `fseek, fsetpos, ftell, lseek, tell`

Example
```
/* fgetpos.cpp */
#include <stdio.h>
#include <stdlib.h>
#define FNAME "FGETPOS.CPP"
void Report(FILE *f, const char *message);
main()
{
  FILE *fp = fopen(FNAME, "r");
  char buffer[256];
  if (!fp) {
    puts("Error opening "FNAME);
    exit(1);
  }
  Report(fp, "Before reading file");
  fgets(buffer, 255, fp);
  Report(fp, "After reading file");
  fclose(fp);
  return 0;
}

void Report(FILE *f, const char *message)
{
  fpos_t pos;
```

```
    puts(message);
    if (fgetpos(f, &pos) != 0) {
      puts("Error accessing file");
      fclose(f);
      exit(1);
    }
    printf(" File position == %ld\n", pos);
}
```

fgets   Get string

Syntax   `char *fgets(char *s, int n, FILE *stream);`

Include   stdio.h

Description   Reads characters up to and including the next newline character or at most n – 1. Other characters form a file stream to the location addressed by `char *s`. Appends a newline character if read plus a null character to the end of the string. Returns `char *s` for success and null for failure.

Parameters   `char *s` Pointer to `char` buffer at least n bytes long.

   `int n` Maximum number of characters including a terminating null to read into the location addressed by s.

   `FILE *stream` Any open file stream, such as returned by `fopen()`, opened for reading in a text mode.

See also   cgets, fputs, gets

Example   See fclose.

filelength   Get file size

Syntax   `long filelength(int handle);`

Include   io.h

Description   Returns the size of a file in bytes, or –1 if there is an error.

Parameters   `int handle` File handle such as returned by `open()`.

See also   fopen, lseek, open

Example   `/* fileleng.cpp */`
   `#include <stdio.h>`

```
#include <stdlib.h>
#include <io.h>
#include <fcntl.h>
main(int argc, char *argv[])
{
  int handle;
  long flen;
  if (argc <= 1) {
    puts("Enter file name to find length\n");
    exit(1);
  }
  handle = open(argv[1], O_RDONLY | O_BINARY);
  if (handle < 0) {
    perror(argv[1]);
    exit(1);
  }
  flen = filelength(handle);
  printf("%s is %ld bytes long.\n", argv[1], flen);
  close(handle);
  return 0;
}
```

fileno   Convert file stream to handle

Syntax   int fileno(FILE *stream);

Include   stdio.h

Description   Returns a handle for a file stream. Use this function to convert a stream for functions that require a handle.

Parameters   **FILE *stream** Pointer to open file stream.

See also   fdopen, fopen, freopen, open

Example
```
/* fileno.cpp */
#include <stdio.h>
#include <io.h>
char buffer[] = "Write me to stderr using a handle\n";
main()
{
  int handle = fileno(stderr);
  write(handle, &buffer, sizeof(buffer));
  return 0;
}
```

fillellipse Draw filled ellipse

Syntax `void far fillellipse(int x, int y, int xradius, int yradius);`

Include graphics.h

Description Draws a filled ellipse on the graphics display using the current filling color and pattern.

Parameters `int x`, `int y` Center (x,y) coordinate.

  `int xradius` Horizontal radius.

  `int yradius` Vertical radius.

See also `arc, circle, ellipse, pieslice, setaspectratio, setfillstyle`

Example
```
/* fillelli.cpp */
#include <graphics.h>
#include <stdio.h>
#include <stdlib.h>
#include <time.h>
#include <conio.h>
main()
{
  int gdriver = DETECT, gmode, gerr;
  int x, direction, count, xmax, ymax;
  initgraph(&gdriver, &gmode, "c:\\borlandc\\bgi");
  gerr = graphresult();
  if (gerr != grOk) {
    printf("BGI error: %s\n", grapherrormsg(gerr));
    exit(gerr);
  }
  xmax = getmaxx();
  ymax = getmaxy();
  x = 20;
  direction = 1;
  count = 5;
  randomize();
  setcolor(WHITE);
  while (!kbhit()) {
    if ((x > xmax - 50) || (x <= 0)) {
      direction *= -1;
      count += 5;
    }
```

```
      setfillstyle(random(12), 1 + abs(random(getmaxcolor())));
      fillellipse(x, ymax / 2,
        count + random(xmax / 6),
        count + random(ymax / 4));
      x += (50 * direction);
    }
    getch();
    closegraph();
    return 0;
  }
```

fillpoly   Draw filled polygon

Syntax   void far fillpoly(int numpoints, int far *polypoints);

Include   graphics.h

Description   Draws a filled polygon on the graphics display using the current filling color and pattern. The polygon's outline uses the current line color and style.

Parameters   **int numpoints** Number of nodes in the polygon.

int far *polypoints Pointer to an array of 16-bit integers, each pair representing an (x,y) coordinate. There must be at least numpoints integer pairs in the array.

See also   drawpoly, floodfill, setcolor, setfillstyle, setlinestyle

Example
```
/* fillpoly.cpp */
#include <graphics.h>
#include <stdio.h>
#include <stdlib.h>
#include <time.h>
#include <dos.h>
#include <conio.h>
#define NUMPOINTS 13
main()
{
  int gdriver = DETECT, gmode, gerr;
  char pat[8] = {0x11, 0x22, 0x44, 0x88, 0x11, 0x22, 0x44, 0x88};
  int xmax, ymax, i;
  pointtype polypoints[NUMPOINTS];
```

```
  initgraph(&gdriver, &gmode, "c:\\borlandc\\bgi");
  gerr = graphresult();
  if (gerr != grOk) {
    printf("BGI error: %s\n", grapherrormsg(gerr));
    exit(gerr);
  }
  xmax = getmaxx();
  ymax = getmaxy();
  randomize();
  while (!kbhit()) {
    clearviewport();
    for (i = 0; i < NUMPOINTS; i++) { // Create random polygon
      polypoints[i].x = abs(random(xmax));
      polypoints[i].y = abs(random(ymax));
    }
    polypoints[NUMPOINTS - 1] = polypoints[0];  // Complete shape
    setcolor(1 + random(getmaxcolor()));
    drawpoly(NUMPOINTS, (int *)&polypoints);  // Connect the dots
    setfillpattern(pat, 1 + random(getmaxcolor()));
    fillpoly(NUMPOINTS, (int *)&polypoints);  // Fill polygon
    delay(3000);  // Pause between screens
  }
  getch();
  closegraph();
  return 0;
}
```

findfirst   Search directory

Syntax   `int findfirst(const char *pathname, struct ffblk *ffblk,`
`int attrib);`

Include   dir.h, dos.h

Description   Begins the directory search. Calls DOS function 0x4e. Returns zero if successful, or −1 if an error is detected or if no files are found.

Parameters   **const char *pathname** Pointer to a path string, which may contain wild card characters '*' and '?'.

struct ffblk *ffblk Pointer to ffblk structure, which may be passed to findnext() to continue searching for additional matching files.

int attrib Logical-OR combination of any of the FA_xxxx constants declared in dos.h.

See also   _dos_findfirst, findnext

Example
```
/* findfirs.cpp */
#include <stdio.h>
#include <string.h>
#include <dir.h>
#include <dos.h>
main(int argc, char *argv[])
{
  struct ffblk fb;
  char *path = "*.*";
  int done;
  if (argc > 1)
    path = strdup(argv[1]);
  done = findfirst(path, &fb, FA_NORMAL);
  while (done == 0) {
    puts(fb.ff_name);
    done = findnext(&fb);
  }
  return 0;
}
```

findnext   Continue directory search

Syntax   int findnext(struct ffblk *ffblk);

Include   dir.h

Description   After successfully calling findfirst(), you may call findnext() to continue searching for additional files. Returns 0 if successful, or −1 if an error is detected or if there are no more matching files.

Parameters   **struct ffblk *ffblk** Pointer to ffblk structure filled in by preceding call to findfirst().

See also   _dos_findnext, findfirst

Example   See findfirst.

floodfill   Fill graphics area

Syntax   `void far floodfill(int x, int y, int border);`

Include   graphics.h

Description   Fills an area of any shape on the graphics screen with the current filling color and pattern. The function works with all graphics drivers except IBM-8514.

Parameters   **int x**, **int y** Coordinate of the seed. Used as the starting place for filling.

int border Color of the border surrounding the area to be filled. The seed (x,y) coordinate must be inside this area. Any breaks in the border cause the "paint" to leak, possibly flooding the screen.

See also   `drawpoly, fillellipse, fillpoly, pieslice, setfillstyle`

Example
```
/* floodfil.cpp */
#include <graphics.h>
#include <stdio.h>
#include <stdlib.h>
#include <conio.h>
#define OUTLINECOLOR YELLOW
void Box(int x1, int y1, int x2, int y2);
main()
{
  int gdriver = DETECT, gmode, gerr;
  char pat[8] = {0x11, 0x22, 0x44, 0x88, 0x88, 0x44, 0x22, 0x11};
  int cx, cy, xmaxd4, ymaxd4, xmax, ymax;
  initgraph(&gdriver, &gmode, "c:\\borlandc\\bgi");
  gerr = graphresult();
  if (gerr != grOk) {
    printf("BGI error: %s\n", grapherrormsg(gerr));
    exit(gerr);
  }
  xmax = getmaxx();
  ymax = getmaxy();
  xmaxd4 = xmax / 4;
  ymaxd4 = ymax / 4;
  cx = xmax / 2;
  cy = ymax / 2;
  setcolor(OUTLINECOLOR);
  Box(xmaxd4, ymaxd4, xmax - xmaxd4, ymax - ymaxd4);
```

```
      ellipse(cx, cy, 0, 360, xmaxd4 / 2, ymaxd4 / 2);
// Fill space around the ellipse
    getch();  // Press any key to continue
    setfillpattern(pat, LIGHTCYAN);
    floodfill(xmaxd4 + 1, ymaxd4 + 1, OUTLINECOLOR);
// Fill space inside the ellipse
    getch();  // Press any key to continue
    setfillpattern(pat, RED);
    floodfill(cx, cy, OUTLINECOLOR);
    getch();
    closegraph();
    return 0;
}

void Box(int x1, int y1, int x2, int y2)
{
    moveto(x1, y1);
    lineto(x2, y1);
    lineto(x2, y2);
    lineto(x1, y2);
    lineto(x1, y1);
}
```

floor, floorl   Round down

Syntax
```
double floor(double x);
long double floorl(long double x);
```

Include   math.h

Description   Returns largest integer not greater than x. In other words, rounds x down to next lowest value. Two versions are provided: Use `floor()` to round `double` values and `floorl()` to round `long double` values.

See also   ceil, fmod, modf

Example
```
/* floor.cpp */
#include <stdio.h>
#include <math.h>
main()
{
    char buffer[128];
    double d;
    printf("Enter a floating point value: ");
```

```
        gets(buffer);
        d = atof(buffer);
        printf("Original value: %f\n", d);
        printf("floor(value)  : %f\n", floor(d));
        return 0;
      }
```

flushall   Flush all streams

Syntax   `int flushall(void);`

Include   stdio.h

Description   Flushes all open file streams, writing to disk any modified data held in memory buffers. Database applications can call `flushall()` periodically in the program's main menu loop to ensure that all file data is written to disk. Leaves file streams open. Returns the current number of active I/O file streams.

See also   fclose, fcloseall, fflush, fopen, fwrite

Example
```
/* flushall.cpp */
#include <stdio.h>
#include <stdlib.h>
#include <string.h>
#include <conio.h>
main()
{
  FILE *inpf, *outf;
  char buffer[255];
 char *fname = strdup(tmpnam(NULL));
 outf = fopen(fname, "w"); // Create temporary file
  inpf = fopen("FLUSHALL.CPP", "r");  // Open this file
  if (!(inpf || outf)) {
    puts("Error opening files");
    exit(1);
  }
  printf("Writing to %s", fname);
  while (fgets(buffer, 255, inpf) != NULL)
    fputs(buffer, outf);
  printf("\nPress Enter to flush all files");
  getch();
  flushall();
```

```
      printf("\nAll files are flushed.");
      fclose(outf);
      fclose(inpf);
      printf("\nList file %s then delete.", fname);
      return 0;
    }
```

_fmem...   Far memory functions

Syntax
```
void far *far _fmemccpy(void far *dest, const void far *src,
    int c, size_t n);
void far *far _fmemchr(const void far *s, int c, size_t n);
int far _fmemcmp(const void far *s1, const void far *s2,
    size_t n);
void far *far_fmemcpy(void far *dest, const void far *src,
    size_t n);
int far _fmemicmp(const void far *s1, const void far *s2,
    size_t n);
void far *far _fmemset(void far *s, int c, size_t n);
```

Include mem.h

Description Far versions of various memory functions that operate similarly to their near-pointer counterparts, but use and return far pointers. Refer to individual functions in the *See also* list for more information and examples.

See also memccpy, memchr, memcmp, memcpy, memicmp, memset

fmod, fmodl   Floating point modulus

Syntax
```
double fmod(double x, double y);
long double fmodl(long double x, long double y);
```

Include math.h

Description Returns x modulo y, equal to the remainder after dividing y into x. Use fmod() for double values and fmodl() for long doubles.

See also ceil, div, floor, fmod, modf

Example
```
/* fmod.cpp */
#include <stdio.h>
#include <math.h>
```

```
main()
{
  double v1 = 100, v2 = 17.5;
  double result;
  result = fmod(v1, v2);
  printf("fmod(%lf, %lf) == %lf\n", v1, v2, result);
  return 0;
}
```

fnmerge   Build pathname

Syntax   `void fnmerge(char *path, const char *drive, const char *dir,`
            `const char *name, const char *ext);`

Include   dir.h

Description   Concatenates the strings addressed by drive, dir, name, and ext char
            pointers, storing the completed pathname at the location addressed by
            path. Except for path, the component char pointers may be null or they
            may address null strings, in which case that component is skipped. Adds
            a colon to the drive letter unless it is already followed by a colon.
            Appends a backslash to any directory name and prefaces an extension
            with a period if necessary. The maximum length of the resulting string,
            including a null terminator, is defined by the constant MAXPATH declared
            in dir.h. (Currently, MAXPATH equals 80.)

Parameters   **char *path** Pointer to a buffer at least MAXPATH bytes long. The resulting
            path string is stored at this location.

            const char *drive Pointer to a drive letter, which may optionally end
            with a colon.

            const char *dir Pointer to one or more directory names, separated by
            single backslashes, and optionally beginning or ending with a backslash.

            const char *name Pointer to a filename of no more than eight charac-
            ters.

            const char *ext Pointer to a file extension of no more than three
            characters plus an optional preceding period.

See also   fnsplit, _fullpath, _makepath

Example   /* fnmerge.cpp */
            #include <stdio.h>

```
#include <dir.h>
main()
{
  char *drive = "C:";
  char *dir = "\\BORLANDC\\INCLUDE";
  char *name = "DOS";
  char *ext = "H";
  char path[MAXPATH];
  fnmerge(path, drive, dir, name, ext);
  printf("Merged path = %s", path);
  return 0;
}
```

fnsplit   Parse pathname

Syntax   int fnsplit(const char *path, char *drive, char *dir, char *name, char *ext);

Include   dir.h

Description   Separates the components of a pathname string into drive, directory, filename, and file extension. Use constants MAXDRIVE, MAXDIR, MAXPATH, MAXFILE, and MAXEXT, defined in dir.h, to define char buffers of the correct sizes to hold the function's results. Returns coded int value, with bits corresponding to the constants WILDCARDS, EXTENSION, FILENAME, DIRECTORY, and DRIVE. Function results containing one or more of these bits set to one indicate the presence of that component in the original string.

Parameters   **const char *path** Pointer to the pathname to be separated. Any missing components (for example, a missing drive letter) are ignored.

char *drive Pointer to string buffer at least MAXDRIVE bytes long. A drive letter and colon are stored at this location.

char *dir Pointer to string buffer at least MAXDIR bytes long. One or more directory names, separated by single backslashes, and beginning and ending with backslashes, are stored at this location.

char *name Pointer to a string buffer at least MAXFILE bytes long. A filename is stored at this location.

char *ext Pointer to a string buffer at least MAXEXT bytes long. A file extension preceded by a period is stored at this location.

See also   fnmerge, _fullpath, _splitpath

Example
```
/* fnsplit.cpp */
#include <stdio.h>
#include <dir.h>
main()
{
  char *path = "C:\\BORLANDC\\INCLUDE\\*.H";
  char drive[MAXDRIVE];
  char dir[MAXDIR];
  char name[MAXFILE];
  char ext[MAXEXT];
  int result;
  result = fnsplit(path, drive, dir, name, ext);
  puts("The original path is:");
  printf(" path  : %s\n", path);
  puts("The path's components are:");
  printf(" drive : %s\n", drive);
  printf(" dir   : %s\n", dir);
  printf(" name  : %s\n", name);
  printf(" ext   : %s\n", ext);
  if ((result && WILDCARDS) == WILDCARDS)
    puts("Wild cards detected in path");
  return 0;
}
```

fopen   Open file stream

Syntax   FILE *fopen(const char *filename, const char *mode);

Include   stdio.h

Description   Opens an existing file or creates a new one. If it is successful, fopen()
returns a FILE stream pointer that should be saved in a variable for use
with other file functions. Any errors return null.

Parameters   **const char *filename** Pointer to a filename string that may contain
drive and directory information, but may not contain any wild cards.

const char *mode A pointer to a string equal to one of the modes listed
in the following table. Add t to any of these modes to access a text file.
Add b for binary files. For example, the mode string "rb" opens a file for

reading in binary mode. The mode string `"a+t"` opens a text file ready for appending new information to the end of the file. The mode string `"a+t"` is equivalent to `"at+"`.

`fopen()` **mode strings**

Mode	Binary	Text	Use
`"r"`	`"rb"`	`"rt"`	Opens an existing file for reading.
`"w"`	`"wb"`	`"wt"`	Creates a new file for writing. Overwrites any existing file of the specified name.
`"a"`	`"ab"`	`"at"`	Opens a file for appending new information to the end of the file.
`"r+"`	`"r+b"`	`"r+t"`	Opens an existing file for reading and writing.
`"w+"`	`"w+b"`	`"w+t"`	Creates a new file for reading and writing. Overwrites any existing file of the specified name.
`"a+"`	`"a+b"`	`"a+t"`	Opens a file for appending new information to the end of the file. If the file does not exist, a new file is created of the specified name.

See also   `creat`, `fclose`, `ferror`, `fread`, `fseek`, `fwrite`, `open`, `perror`, `rewind`, `setbuf`, `setmode`, `strerror`

Example   See `fclose`.

FP_OFF   Get far address offset

Syntax   `unsigned FP_OFF(void far *p);`

Include   dos.h

Description   Provided as a macro, `FP_OFF()` returns the offset portion of a far address.

Parameters   `void far *p` Any far pointer.

See also   FP_SEG, MK_FP

Example

```
/* FP_OFF.cpp */
#include <stdio.h>
#include <dos.h>
void DispPointer(void far *p);
main()
{
  char far *p;
  p = new char[128];
  printf("After allocating memory, p == ");
  DispPointer(p);
  delete p;
  p = NULL;
  printf("After setting p to NULL, p == ");
  DispPointer(p);
  return 0;
}
void DispPointer(void far *p)
{
  printf("%04x:%04x\n", FP_SEG(p), FP_OFF(p));
}
```

_fpreset   Reinitialize floating–point math

Syntax   void _fpreset(void);

Include   float.h

Description   Resets the floating–point math package or an 80x87 math coprocessor. Typically used in conjunction with system, exec..., and spawn... functions, which execute child processes that might affect the math package's status. Calling _fpreset() after executing a child process returns the math package or coprocessor to a stable state.

See also   _clear87, _control87, exec..., spawn..., _status87, system

Example

```
/* _fpreset.cpp */
#include <stdio.h>
#include <float.h>
main()
{
```

```
double d = DBL_MIN;   // Smallest double
float f;              // Uninitialized float
printf("1. 80x87 status == %#x\n", _status87());
f = d;        // Force loss of precision
printf("2. 80x87 status == %#x\n", _status87());
_fpreset();   // Reset floating-point package
printf("3. 80x87 status == %#x\n", _status87());
d = f;        // Eliminate "f not used" warning
return 0;
}
```

fprintf   Write formatted output

Syntax `int fprintf(FILE *stream, const char *format[, argument, ...]);`

Include stdio.h

Description Writes formatted text output to a file stream opened for writing or appending in text mode. Returns the number of bytes written to the stream. Returns EOF if any errors are detected. The format string and arguments are identical in format to those used by printf().

Parameters **FILE *stream** Pointer to a file stream such as that returned by fopen(). The function's output is written to this stream.

const char *format Pointer to a format string that may include literal text along with format specifiers prefaced with %, such as %d or &f. See printf() for more information on the many possible formats available.

argument, ... One argument for each format specifier in the format string. The argument's value is converted to text according to the format specifier and inserted into the output text.

See also cprintf, fscanf, fputc, fputs, printf, sprintf

Example
```
/* fprintf.cpp */
#include <stdio.h>
#include <dos.h>
main()
{
  double d = 3.14159;
  char *s = "A string";
```

```
long v = 1234567;
fprintf(stdout, "Double value == %lf\n", d);
fprintf(stdout, "String value == %s\n", s);
fprintf(stdout, "Long value == %ld\n", v);
fprintf(stdout, "Address of v == %#04x:%#04x\n",
  FP_SEG(&v), FP_OFF(&v));
return 0;
}
```

FP_SEG   Get far address segment

Syntax   `unsigned FP_SEG(void far *p);`

Include   dos.h

Description Provided as a macro, `FP_SEG()` returns the segment portion of a far address.

Parameters **void far *p** Any far pointer.

See also   `FP_OFF`, `MK_FP`

Example   See `FP_OFF`.

fputc   Write character to a stream

Syntax   `int fputc(int c, FILE *stream);`

Include   stdio.h

Description Writes a single character to the specified stream. Returns the value of c for success and EOF for failure.

Parameters **int c** The character value to write.

FILE *stream A stream pointer such as that returned by `fopen()`. The character is written to this stream.

See also   `fgetc`, `fputchar`, `fputs`, `putc`

Example   See `fgetc`.

fputchar Put character on stdout

Syntax   `int fputchar(int c);`

Include stdio.h

Description Writes a single character to stdout. Returns the value of c for success and EOF for failure. Defined as `fputc(c, stdout)`.

Parameters **int c** The character value to write.

See also fgetchar, fputc, fputs, putchar

Example
```
/* fputchar.cpp */
#include <stdio.h>
main()
{
  int c;
  puts("Display the alphabet");
  for (c = 'A'; c <= 'Z'; c++)
    fputchar(c);
  return 0;
}
```

fputs Put string on stream

Syntax   `int fputs(const char *s, FILE *stream);`

Include stdio.h

Description Writes a null-terminated string of characters to the specified stream. Returns nonnegative value for success and EOF for failure.

Parameters **const char *s** Pointer to a null-terminated string to write to the output stream.

FILE *stream Pointer to a file stream such as that returned by fopen().

See also fgets, fprintf, fputc, gets, puts

Example See fclose.

fread   Read data from stream

Syntax   `size_t fread(void *ptr, size_t size, size_t n, FILE *stream);`

Include   stdio.h

Description   Reads data from a file stream starting at the current file pointer. After reading data, `fread()` leaves the file pointer positioned after the last byte read. You may call `fseek()` to position the file pointer before reading. `fread()` returns the number of items read. The number of bytes read equals the function result times the number of bytes per item. Returns zero if unsuccessful or if the file pointer is at the end of the file.

Parameters   **void *ptr** Pointer to a destination buffer. Function transfers bytes from the file stream to this location, which must be large enough to hold the requested data.

size_t size The size in bytes of one item to be read from the file stream.

size_t n The number of items to read.

FILE *stream A pointer to an open file stream such as that returned by `fopen()`.

See also   fopen, fwrite, fprintf, fseek

Example
```
/* fread.cpp */
#include <stdio.h>
#include <stdlib.h>
int array[100];  // Array of 100 ints equal to zero
main()
{
// Create temporary file in "w+b" mode
  FILE *tempf = tmpfile();
  if (!tempf) {
    perror("Can't open temporary file");
    exit(1);
  }
// Write 100 integers to file
  for (int index = 0; index < 100; index++)
    fwrite(&index, sizeof(int), 1, tempf);
// Read integers into array
  rewind(tempf);
  fread(&array, sizeof(int), 100, tempf);
  puts("Array after reading from disk");
```

```
      for (index = 0; index < 100; index++)
        printf("%8d", array[index]);
      rmtmp();  // Close and erase temporary file
      return 0;
    }
```

free   Free allocated block

Syntax   `void free(void *block);`

Include   alloc.h

Description   Frees a block of memory previously allocated by `malloc()`, `calloc()`, or a similar memory allocator. The memory is returned to the heap for use by subsequent memory requests. After freeing a block, a program must not use that memory.

Parameters   **void *block** Pointer to memory block to be freed. After being passed to `free()`, the pointer must not be used except to hold the address of freshly allocated memory.

See also   `calloc, freemem, malloc, realloc, strdup`

Example
```
/* free.cpp */
#include <stdio.h>
#include <stdlib.h>
#include <string.h>
main()
{
  char *original = "An original string";
  char *copy;  // Pointer to copy of original string
// Allocate memory to hold copy of original string
  copy = (char *)malloc(strlen(original) + 1);
  if (copy == NULL) {
    puts("Error allocating memory");
    exit(1);
  }
  strcpy(copy, original);  // Transfer original to copy
  strupr(copy);  // Convert copy to uppercase
  printf("Original == %s\n", original);
  printf("Copy     == %s\n", copy);
  free(copy);  // Free memory occupied by copy of string
  return 0;
}
```

freemem   Free DOS memory block

Syntax   `int freemem(unsigned segx);`

Include   dos.h

Description   Frees memory allocated by `allocmem()`. Returns zero for success and −1 for failure.

Parameters   **unsigned segx** Segment address such as that returned by `allocmem()` or `setblock()`.

See also   `allocmem, _dos_allocmem, _dos_freemem, free, setblock`

Example   See `allocmem`.

freopen   Associate new file with stream

Syntax   `FILE *freopen(const char *filename, const char *mode,`
           `FILE *stream);`

Include   stdio.h

Description   Closes a currently open file stream and associates that stream with a new named file. Typically used to redirect `stdin`, `stdout`, and `stderr` streams.

Parameters   **const char *filename** Pointer to the new filename string to be associated with the file stream.

   const char *mode Pointer to one of the mode strings listed in the *Description* of `fopen()`. This is the mode to be used for the newly opened file.

   FILE *stream The open file stream to be associated with a new named file.

See also   `fclose, fopen`

Example
```
/* freopen.cpp */
#include <stdio.h>
#include <stdlib.h>
#include <string.h>
main()
{
```

```
      FILE *outf;
      char *fname = strdup(tmpnam(NULL));
   // Redirect stderr to temporary output file
      outf = freopen(fname, "w", stderr);
      if (outf == NULL) {
        puts("Error opening temporary file");
        exit(1);
      }
      fputs("Simulated error message\n", stderr);
      fputs("written to file via stderr.\n", stderr);
      fclose(outf);
      printf("\nList file %s then delete.\n", fname);
      return 0;
   }
```

frexp, frexpl   Split mantissa and exponent

Syntax   ```
double frexp(double x, int *exponent);
long double frexpl(long double x, int *exponent);
```

*Include*    math.h

*Description*  Returns the mantissa $m$ of a floating point value such that $0.5 <= m < 1.0$. Stores int exponent $n$ at the location addressed by pointer exponent. The original value equals m * 2n. Use frexp() for double arguments and frexpl() for long doubles.

*Parameters*  **double x**, **long double x** Floating point value to be split into a mantissa and exponent.

**int *exponent** Function stores the exponent into the int value addressed by this pointer. The function returns the value's mantissa directly.

*See also*    exp, ldexp, pow, matherr

*Example*    ```
/* frexp.cpp */
#include <stdio.h>
#include <math.h>
main()
{
  double pi = M_PI;
  double mantissa;
```

```
    int exponent;
    mantissa = frexp(pi, &exponent);
    printf("Original value  == %lf\n", pi);
    printf("Mantissa        == %lf\n", mantissa);
    printf("Exponent        == %d\n", exponent);
    printf("%lf * 2^^%d == %lf\n", mantissa, exponent,
      (mantissa * pow(2, exponent)));
    return 0;
}
```

fscanf   Scan and format stream input

Syntax `int fscanf(FILE *stream, const char *format[,address, ...]);`

Include stdio.h

Description Reads text from a stream, converting data to binary according to format specifiers embedded in the `format` string. Values are transferred to the locations specified by the address arguments.

Parameters **FILE *stream** Pointer to open a file stream such as that returned by `fopen()`. Characters are read from this stream.

const char *format Pointer to a format string that should include one or more format specifiers preceded by %. See `scanf()` for more information about the allowable specifiers.

address, ... One address pointer for each format specifier. Data is converted from text to binary, and stored in these locations, which must be large enough to hold the expected values.

See also atof, fprintf, scanf, sscanf, vfscanf, vscanf, vsscanf

Example
```
/* fscanf.cpp */
#include <stdio.h>
main()
{
  double v;
  puts("Enter a floating point value");
  fscanf(stdin, "%lf", &v);  // Note address-of operator!
  printf("Value == %lf\n", v);
  return 0;
}
```

fseek Reposition file pointer

Syntax   `int fseek(FILE *stream, long offset, int whence);`

Include   stdio.h

Description   Moves a file stream's internal pointer, thus affecting the location of a subsequent read or write operation on the file. Returns zero for success and nonzero for failure.

Parameters   **FILE *stream** Pointer to an open file stream such as that returned by `fopen()`.

long offset For binary files, this is the number of bytes to move the file pointer in the direction indicated by whence. For text files, this value must be zero or a value returned by `ftell()`. Set offset to a negative value to move the file pointer backwards (toward the beginning of the file).

int whence Set to SEEK_SET to move the file pointer offset bytes from the beginning of the file. Set to SEEK_CUR to move the file pointer relative to its current position. Set to SEEK_END to move the file pointer a specified number of bytes from the end of the file.

See also   fgetpos, fopen, fsetpos, ftell, lseek, rewind, tell

Example
```cpp
/* fseek.cpp ( <- 'p' is 12th character ) */
#include <stdio.h>
#include <stdlib.h>
main()
{
  FILE *inf;
  char c;
// Open text file in binary mode
  inf = fopen("FSEEK.CPP", "rb");
  if (inf == NULL) {
    perror("Unable to open FSEEK.CPP");
    exit(1);
  }
// Seek to 12th byte from file beginning
  if (fseek(inf, 11, SEEK_SET) != 0)
    perror("Error during file seek");
```

```
        else {
          fread(&c, 1, 1, inf);
          printf("12th character == %c", c);
        }
        fclose(inf);
        return 0;
      }
```

fsetpos   Position file pointer

Syntax   `int fsetpos(FILE *stream, const fpos_t *pos);`

Include   stdio.h

Description   Restores a file stream's internal pointer to the position returned by a preceding call to `fgetpos()`. Returns zero for success and nonzero for failure.

Parameters   **FILE *stream** Pointer to a file stream such as that returned by `fopen()`.

const fpos_t *pos Pointer to an `fpos_t` structure prepared by a preceding call to `fgetpos()`.

See also   fgetpos, fseek, ftell, ungetc

Example
```
/* fsetpos.cpp */
#include <stdio.h>
main()
{
  FILE *inf;   // Input file stream
  fpos_t pos;  // File position
  char buffer[128];
  inf = fopen("FSETPOS.CPP", "rb");
  fgets(buffer, 128, inf);
  printf("First string == %s\n", buffer);
  fgetpos(inf, &pos);  // Save current position
  fgets(buffer, 128, inf);
  printf("Second string == %s\n", buffer);
  fsetpos(inf, &pos);  // Restore saved position
  fgets(buffer, 128, inf);
  printf("String after fsetpos == %s\n", buffer);
  fclose(inf);
  return 0;
}
```

_fsopen   Open shared file

Syntax   FILE *_fsopen(const char *filename, const char *mode, int shflg);

Include   stdio.h, share.h

Description   Similar to fopen(), but uses the DOS SHARE program to enable multi-user file sharing. SHARE must be installed for _fsopen() to take advantage of file sharing. Returns a pointer to a file stream if successful and null for failure.

Parameters   **const char *filename** Pointer to a filename string, which may contain drive and directory information, but may not contain any wild cards.

const char *mode Pointer to one of the mode strings listed in the description of fopen(). This is the mode to be used for the newly opened file.

int shflg Share flag composed of one of the constants listed in the following table and declared in share.h.

_fsopen() **share flags**

Constant	Value	Effect on other users
SH_COMPAT	0X0000	Set compatibility mode
SH_DENYRW	0X0010	Deny reading and writing
SH_DENYWR	0X0020	Deny writing
SH_DENYRD	0X0030	Deny reading
SH_DENYNONE	0X0040	Deny nothing
SH_DENYNO	SH_DENYNONE	Same as SH_DENYNONE

See also   close, creat, open, fclose, fopen, fread, fwrite, read, write

Example
```
/* _fsopen.cpp */
#include <stdio.h>
#include <stdlib.h>
#include <share.h>
main(int argc, char *argv[])
{
  FILE *fp;
```

```
      char buffer[256];
      if (argc <= 1) {
        puts("No file specified");
        exit(1);
      }
  // Open shared file; deny write access
      fp = _fsopen(argv[1], "r", SH_DENYWR);
      if (!fp)
        puts("Error opening file");
      else {
        while (fgets(buffer, 255, fp) != NULL)
          fputs(buffer, stdout);
        fclose(fp);
      }
      return 0;
  }
```

fstat   File status

Syntax   int fstat(int handle, struct stat *statbuf);

Include   sys\stat.h

Description   Use this function to find out information about a file identified by a handle. Returns 0 for success and −1 for failure. Facts about the file are stored in a stat structure, declared in sys\stat.h as

```
struct stat
{
  short st_dev;      // Drive number or handle for device (for
                     // example, PRN)
  short st_ino;      // Unused
  short st_mode;     // Mode bit mask using S_xxxx constants
  short st_nlink;    // Always equal to 1
  int   st_uid;      // Unused
  int   st_gid;      // Unused
  short st_rdev;     // Identical to st_dev
  long  st_size;     // Size of file in bytes (0 for devices)
  long  st_atime;    // Time of most recent file change in
                     // seconds from 1970
  long  st_mtime;    // Identical to st_atime
  long  st_ctime;    // Identical to st_atime
};
```

Parameters **int handle** Handle of an open file such as that returned by open().

struct stat *statbuf Pointer to stat structure as listed in *Description*.

See also access, chmod, stat

Example

```
/* fstat.cpp */
#include <stdio.h>
#include <stdlib.h>
#include <sys\stat.h>
#include <io.h>
#include <fcntl.h>
#include <time.h>
main(int argc, char *argv[])
{
  char *fname;
  struct stat statbuf;
  int handle, result;
  if (argc <= 1) {
    puts("No file specified");
    exit(1);
  }
  fname = argv[1];
  handle = open(fname, O_RDONLY | O_TEXT);
  if (handle == NULL) {
    perror(fname);
    exit(1);
  }
// Get info about open file associated with handle
  result = fstat(handle, &statbuf);
  if (result != 0) {
    printf("Error getting stats for %s\n", fname);
    exit(1);
  }
  printf("Information about %s\n", fname);
  printf("Drive number  : %d\n", statbuf.st_dev);
  printf("Size in bytes : %ld\n", statbuf.st_size);
  printf("Was updated   : %s\n", ctime(&statbuf.st_atime));
  close(handle);
  return 0;
}
```

_fstr... Far string functions

Syntax
```
char far *far _fstrcat(char far *dest, const char far *src);
char far *far _fstrchr(const char far *s, int c);
int far _fstrcmp(const char far *s1, const char far *s2);
char far *far _fstrcpy(const char far *dest,
  const char far *src);
size_t far _fstrcspn(const char far *s1, const char far *s2);
char far *far _fstrdup(const char far *s);
int far _fstricmp(const char far *s1, const char far *s2);
size_t far _fstrlen(const char far *s);
char far *far _fstrlwr(char far *s);
char far *far _fstrncat(char far *dest, const char far *src,
  size_t maxlen);
int far _fstrncmp(const char far *s1, const char far *s2,
  size_t maxlen);
char far *far _fstrncpy(char far *dest, const char far *src,
  size_t maxlen);
int far _fstrnicmp(const char far *s1, const char far *s2,
  size_t maxlen);
char far *far _fstrnset(char far *s, int c, size_t n);
char far *far _fstrpbrk(const char far *s1,
  const char far *s2);
char far *far _fstrrchr(const char far *s, int c);
char far *far _fstrrev(char far *s);
char far *far _fstrset(char far *s, int c);
size_t far _fstrspn(const char far *s1, const char far *s2);
char far *far _fstrstr(const char far *s1,
  const char far *s2);
char far *far _fstrtok(char far *s1, const char far *s2);
char far *far _fstrupr(char far *s);
```

Include   string.h

Description   Far versions of various string functions, which operate similarly to their near counterparts but use and return far char pointers. The functions are also declared far. Refer to individual functions in the *See also* list for more information and examples.

See also   strcat, strchr, strcmp, strcpy, strcspn, strdup, stricmp, strlen, strlwr, strncat, strncmp, strncpy, strnicmp, strnset, strpbrk, strrchr, strrev, strset, strspn, strstr, strtok, strupr

ftell   Get file pointer

Syntax   long int ftell(FILE *stream);

Include   stdio.h

Description   Returns a file stream's internal pointer, equal to the offset in bytes from the beginning of a binary file to the byte affected by the next I/O operation. This value can be passed to fseek(), for example, to position the file pointer a certain number of bytes ahead or back. You may also use ftell() on text files, but the value returned does not necessarily represent a byte offset into the file.

Parameters   **FILE *stream** Pointer to an open file stream such as that returned by fopen().

See also   fgetpos, fopen, fseek, fsetpos, lseek, rewind, tell

Example
```
/* ftell.cpp */
#include <stdio.h>
main()
{
  FILE *inf;  // Input file stream
  long pos;   // File position
  char buffer[128];
  inf = fopen("FTELL.CPP", "rb");
  fgets(buffer, 128, inf);  // Read first line of file
  printf("First string  == %s\n", buffer);
  pos = ftell(inf);
  printf("File position == %ld\n", pos);
  rewind(inf);
  pos = ftell(inf);
  printf("Position after rewind == %ld\n", pos);
  fclose(inf);
  return 0;
}
```

ftime   Get current time

Syntax   `void ftime(struct timeb *buf);`

Include   sys\timeb.h

Description   Stores current date and time in a `timeb` structure declared in sys\timeb.h as

```
struct timeb {
  long  time;     // Number of seconds from GMT January 1, 1970
  short millitm;  // Milliseconds equal to time.ti_hund * 10
  short timezone; // Difference in minutes between GMT and
                  //   local time
  short dstflag;  // 1--daylight savings in effect; 0--
                  //   standard time
};
```

Parameters   **struct timeb *buf** Pointer to a `timeb` structure as listed in the description.

See also   `asctime`, `ctime`, `_dos_gettime`, `_dos_settime`, `gmtime`, `localtime`, `stime`, `time`, `tzset`

Example
```
/* ftime.cpp */
#include <stdio.h>
#include <time.h>
#include <sys\timeb.h>
main()
{
  timeb thetime;
  ftime(&thetime);
  printf("The date and time are: %s", ctime(&thetime.time));
  printf("Timezone == %d\n", thetime.timezone);
  printf("Daylight saving flag == %d\n", thetime.dstflag);
  return 0;
}
```

_fullpath   Complete relative pathname

Syntax   `char * _fullpath(char *buffer, const char *path, int buflen);`

Include   stdlib.h

Description Expands a partial path into a fully qualified pathname that includes drive and directory information. Returns pointer to resulting `char` buffer for success and null for failure.

Parameters **char *buffer** Pointer to a character buffer. If null, a buffer of no greater than _MAX_PATH bytes is allocated by calling malloc(). Constant _MAX_PATH is declared in stdlib.h. You may free this buffer by calling free().

const char *path Pointer to the original partial pathname. May contain directory pseudonyms ".\" and "..".

int buflen Maximum number of characters to be stored in buffer. Ignored if buffer is null.

See also fnmerge, fnsplit, _makepath, _splitpath

Example
```
/* _fullpat.cpp */
#include <stdio.h>
#include <stdlib.h>
main(int argc, char *argv[])
{
  char *path;
  if (argc <= 1) {
    puts("Error: no file name specified");
    exit(1);
  }
  printf("File name as entered: %s\n", argv[1]);
  path = _fullpath(NULL, argv[1], 0);
  if (path == NULL)
    puts("Error expanding path name");
  else
    printf("Full path name: %s\n", path);
  return 0;
}
```

fwrite   Write data to stream

Syntax size_t fwrite(const void *ptr, size_t size, size_t n,FILE *stream);

Include stdio.h

Description Writes one or more bytes to a file stream opened in binary mode. For writing to text files, use fprintf(), fputc(), fputs(), or a similar function. Returns the number of items written. The number of bytes written equals the function result times `size`.

Parameters `const void *ptr` Pointer to source data to be written to the file.

`size_t size` The size in bytes of one data item.

`size_t n` The number of data items, each having `size` bytes, to be written to the file.

`FILE *stream` Pointer to a file stream opened in binary mode.

See also `fopen, fprintf, fputc, fputs, fread`

Example See `fread`.

gcvt   Convert floating point to string

Syntax `char *gcvt(double value, int ndec, char *buf);`

Include stdlib.h

Description Using the same internal programming as `printf()` and similar functions that can output `double` floating-point values in ASCII, `gcvt()` converts a `double` value to a null-terminated ASCII string and returns `buf`. The result, stored at the location addressed by `buf`, has `ndec` decimal places in FORTRAN F format:

`[+/-] [zeros] [digit...] ['.'] [digit...]`

or if that format cannot accurately represent `value`, the result is in `printf()` E style (that is, scientific notation):

`[+/-] digit ['.'] [digit...] 'E' sign [digit...]`

Parameters `double value` Floating-point value to convert to ASCII.

`int ndec` Number of requested decimal places. The result is not guaranteed to have this many digits after the decimal point. A maximum of 18 digits may be requested.

`char *buf` Pointer to character buffer to hold the result. Allow plenty of space and, after calling `gcvt()`, use `strdup()` or a similar string function to trim the result.

See also `ecvt, fcvt, printf, sprintf`

Example
```
/* gcvt.cpp */
#include <stdio.h>
#include <stdlib.h>
#include <math.h>
#include <string.h>
#define NDEC 6   // Number of decimal places
main()
{
  double value = M_PI;
  char buffer[128];   // Temporary buffer
  char *copy;   // Pointer to result
  gcvt(value, NDEC, buffer);
// Copy raw string in buffer to heap
  copy = strdup(buffer);
  if (copy == NULL) {
    puts("Error copying string");
    exit(1);
  }
  printf("Original value == %lf\n", value);
  printf("String == %s\n", copy);
  printf("Length == %d chars\n", strlen(copy));
  free(copy);
  return 0;
}
```

geninterrupt Generate software interrupt

Syntax   void geninterrupt(int intr_num);

Include   dos.h

Description   Inserts a software interrupt instruction into the compiled code. Use with extreme caution.

Parameters   **int intr_num** Interrupt number.

See also   bdos, bdosptr, disable, enable, getvect, int86, intdos, intr

Example
```
/* geninter.cpp */
#include <stdio.h>
#include <dos.h>
main()
{
```

```
    puts("Output character via DOS function 2");
    printf("The character is: ");
    _AH = 2;    // DOS function: output char
    _DL = '@';  // Char value
    geninterrupt(0x21);  // Call DOS interrupt 0x21
    return 0;
}
```

getarccoords   Get arc coordinates

Syntax void far getarccoords(struct arccoordstype far *arccoords);

Include graphics.h

Description After calling arc(), you can call getarccoords() to retrieve information about the displayed arc. The example displays an arc, then calls getarccoords() to locate the arc's center, starting, and ending coordinates, which are marked onscreen with small Xs. graphics.h declares arccoordstype as

```
struct arccoordstype {
  int x, y;
  int xstart, ystart, xend, yend;
};
```

Parameters **struct arccoordstype far *arccoords** Pointer to an arccoordstype structure, filled in by the function. Members x and y locate the arc's center; xstart and ystart represent the starting coordinate of the arc's one end; xend and yend represent the ending coordinate of the arc's other end.

See also arc, ellipse, fillellipse, pieslice, sector

Example
```
/* getarcco.cpp */
#include <graphics.h>
#include <stdio .h>
#include <stdlib.h>
#include <conio.h>
void drawx(int x, int y);
main()
{
  int gdriver = DETECT, gmode, gerr;
  int xmax, ymax;
  struct arccoordstype arccoords;
```

```
initgraph(&gdriver, &gmode, "c:\\borlandc\\bgi");
gerr = graphresult();
if (gerr != grOk) {
  printf("BGI error: %s\n", grapherrormsg(gerr));
  exit(gerr);
}
xmax = getmaxx();
ymax = getmaxy();
setcolor(YELLOW);
arc(xmax / 2, ymax / 2, 45, 135, ymax / 4);
getarccoords(&arccoords);
setcolor(RED);
drawx(arccoords.x, arccoords.y);
setcolor(BLUE);
drawx(arccoords.xstart, arccoords.ystart);
setcolor(GREEN);
drawx(arccoords.xend, arccoords.yend);
getch();
closegraph();
return 0;
}

void drawx(int x, int y)
{
  line(x - 5, y, x + 5, y);
  line(x, y - 5, x, y + 5);
}
```

getaspectratio   Graphics aspect ratio

Syntax   `void far getaspectratio(int far *xasp, int far *yasp);`

Include   graphics.h

Description   Graphics shapes must be adjusted to compensate for display pixels that are not perfectly square for all display modes and monitors. If this were not done, circles would not be round, and squares would be rectangular. The function assigns values to two `int` parameters that represent the current graphics driver's aspect ratio. The example displays a square box adjusted for the display's aspect ratio. The result may still not be square, however, depending on the settings of the monitor's horizontal or vertical sizes.

Parameters   **int far *xasp** Pointer to an int. The function assigns the X (numerator) component of the current aspect ratio to this value.

int far *yasp Pointer to an int. The function assigns the Y (denominator) component of the current aspect ratio to this value.

See also   arc, circle, ellipse, getmaxx, getmaxy, setaspectratio

Example
```
/* getaspec.cpp */
#include <graphics.h>
#include <stdio.h>
#include <stdlib.h>
#include <conio.h>
main()
{
  int gdriver = DETECT, gmode, gerr;
  int xlen, ylen, xasp, yasp;
  double ratio;
  initgraph(&gdriver, &gmode, "c:\\borlandc\\bgi");
  gerr = graphresult();
  if (gerr != grOk) {
    printf("BGI error: %s\n", grapherrormsg(gerr));
    exit(gerr);
  }
  getaspectratio(&xasp, &yasp);
  ratio = (double)xasp / (double)yasp;
  setcolor(YELLOW);
  xlen = 100.0 / ratio;      // Adjust xlen }
  ylen = 100;
  line(0, 0, xlen, 0);       // Draw box }
  line(xlen, 0, xlen, ylen);
  line(xlen, ylen, 0, ylen);
  line(0, ylen, 0, 0);
  getch();
  closegraph();
  return 0;
}
```

getbkcolor   Graphics background color

Syntax   int far getbkcolor(void);

Include   graphics.h

Description   Returns the color value of the graphics background. Use setbkcolor() to modify this color (usually black when a graphics program begins). The example changes background colors about once a second until you press a key to end the demonstration.

See also   getcolor, getmaxcolor, getpalette, setallpalette, setbkcolor

Example
```cpp
/* getbkcol.cpp */
#include <graphics.h>
#include <stdio.h>
#include <stdlib.h>
#include <conio.h>
#include <dos.h>
main()
{
  int gdriver = DETECT, gmode, gerr;
  int xmax, ymax, xmaxd4, ymaxd4;
  initgraph(&gdriver, &gmode, "c:\\borlandc\\bgi");
  gerr = graphresult();
  if (gerr != grOk) {
    printf("BGI error: %s\n", grapherrormsg(gerr));
    exit(gerr);
  }
  xmax = getmaxx();
  ymax = getmaxy();
  xmaxd4 = xmax / 4;
  ymaxd4 = ymax / 4;
  while (!kbhit()) {
    setbkcolor(random(getmaxcolor()));
    setfillstyle(HATCH_FILL, getbkcolor() + 1);
    bar(xmaxd4, ymaxd4, xmax - xmaxd4, ymax - ymaxd4);
    delay(1000);
  }
  getch();
  closegraph();
  return 0;
}
```

getc Get character from stream

Syntax   int getc(FILE *stream);

Include   stdio.h

Description   Returns next character (if any) from the specified input stream. When reading from stdin, users must press Enter after typing a character. Returns EOF for an end-of-file error.

Parameters   **FILE *stream** Any file stream opened in text mode for reading.

See also   fgetc, getch, getchar, getche, gets, putc, putchar, puts, ungetc

Example
```
/* getc.cpp */
#include <stdio.h>
main()
{
  char c;
  printf("Input a character: ");
  c = getc(stdin);
  printf("\nCharacter == %c", c);
  printf("\nASCII hex == %#x", c);
  printf("\nASCII dec == %d\n", c);
  return 0;
}
```

getcbrk   Get control break setting

Syntax   int getcbrk(void);

Include   dos.h

Description   Returns DOS's Ctrl+Break setting: 0 if off and 1 if on. Executes DOS function 0x33.

See also   ctrlbrk, setcbrk

Example
```
/* getcbrk.cpp */

#include <stdio.h>
#include <dos.h>
main()
{
  int result;
  result = getcbrk();
  printf("Crtl+Break switch is ");
  if (result == 0)
    puts("OFF");
  else
    puts("ON");
```

```
        return 0;
    }
```

getch   Get character without echo

Syntax   `int getch(void);`

Include   conio.h

Description   Returns the next character entered at the keyboard, or the next character waiting in the system's typeahead buffer. Does not display the character.

See also   cgets, cscanf, getc, getchar, getche, kbhit

Example
```
/* getch.cpp */
#include <stdio.h>
#include <conio.h>
#define ASCII_ESC 27  // Esc key in ASCII
void ascii(char c);
main()
{
  int done = 0;
  char c;
  puts("Key test. Press Esc to quit.");
  while (!done) {
    c = getch();
    ascii(c);
    if (!c)
      ascii(getch());
    done = (c == ASCII_ESC);
    puts("");  // Start new display line
  }
  return 0;
}

void ascii(char c)
{
  printf("%c (%#x)", c, c);
}
```

getchar   Get character from stdin

Syntax   `int getchar(void);`

Include   stdio.h

Description   Returns a character value (if any) from stdin, or EOF for an end-of-file error. Users must press Enter after typing a character. Implemented as a macro.

See also   fgetc, fgetchar, getc, getch, getche, gets, ungetc

Example
```
/* getchar.cpp */
#include <stdio.h>
main()
{
  char c;
  printf("Input a character: ");
  c = getchar();
  printf("\nCharacter == %c", c);
  printf("\nASCII hex == %#x", c);
  printf("\nASCII dec == %d\n", c);
  return 0;
}
```

getche   Get character and echo

Syntax   int getche(void);

Include   conio.h

Description   Same as getch(), but displays the returned character at the current cursor position.

See also   cgets, cscanf, getc, getch, getchar, kbhit

Example
```
/* getche.cpp */
#include <stdio.h>
#include <conio.h>
#define ASCII_ESC 27   // Esc key in ASCII
main()
{
  char c = 0;
  puts("Press keys or Esc to quit");
  while (c != ASCII_ESC) {
    puts("");
    c = getche();
    if (!c) {
```

```
      c = getche();
      printf(" (function key)");
    }
  }
  return 0;
}
```

getcolor   Get drawing color

Syntax   `int far getcolor(void);`

Include   graphics.h

Description   Returns current graphics drawing color.

See also   getbkcolor, getmaxcolor, getpalette, setcolor, setpalette

Example
```cpp
/* getcolor.cpp */
#include <graphics.h>
#include <stdio.h>
#include <stdlib.h>
#include <conio.h>
#include <dos.h>
main()
{
  int gdriver = DETECT, gmode, gerr;
  int xmax, ymax, xmaxd4, ymaxd4;
  initgraph(&gdriver, &gmode, "c:\\borlandc\\bgi");
  gerr = graphresult();
  if (gerr != grOk) {
    printf("BGI error: %s\n", grapherrormsg(gerr));
    exit(gerr);
  }
  xmax = getmaxx();
  ymax = getmaxy();
  xmaxd4 = xmax / 4;
  ymaxd4 = ymax / 4;
  while (!kbhit()) {
    setlinestyle(SOLID_LINE, SOLID_FILL, THICK_WIDTH);
    setcolor(1 + random(getmaxcolor()));
    rectangle(xmaxd4, ymaxd4, xmax - xmaxd4, ymax - ymaxd4);
    setbkcolor(getcolor() + 1);
    delay(1000);
  }
```

```
      getch();
      closegraph();
      return 0;
    }
```

getcurdir   Get current directory for drive

Syntax   `int getcurdir(int drive, char *directory);`

Include   dir.h

Description Stores the current directory pathname for any drive at the location addressed by `directory`. Returns 0 for success and –1 for failure.

Parameters **int drive** Drive number. 0–current, 1–A:, 2–B:, and so on.

char *directory Pointer to `char` buffer at least `MAXDIR` bytes long. Function stores current directory pathname at this location.

See also   `chdir, findfirst, findnext, _getdcwd, getcwd, getdisk, mkdir, rmdir`

Example
```
/* getcurdi.cpp */
#include <stdio.h>
#include <dir.h>
main()
{
  char dir[MAXDIR];
  int cd = getcurdir(0, dir);
  if (cd == 0)
    printf("Current dir == %s\n", dir);
  else
    puts("Error reading current directory");
  return 0;
}
```

getcwd   Get current working directory

Syntax   `char *getcwd(char *buf, int buflen);`

Include   dir.h

Description Stores the current directory pathname for the current drive at the location addressed by `buf`. Returns `buf` or null for an error.

Parameters **char *buf** Pointer to char buffer at least buflen bytes long, including room for the string's null terminator. May be set to null, in which case getcwd() allocates and fills a buffer of buflen bytes. Call free() to delete this buffer.

int buflen Size of the destination buffer in bytes.

See also chdir, findfirst, findnext, getcurdir, getdisk, mkdir, rmdir

Example
```
/* getcwd.cpp */
#include <stdio.h>
#include <dir.h>
#include <alloc.h>
main()
{
  char *dp;
  dp = getcwd(NULL, MAXPATH);
  if (dp == NULL)
    puts("Error reading directory");
  else {
    printf("Current dir == %s", dp);
    free(dp);
  }
  return 0;
}
```

getdate   Get system date

Syntax void getdate(struct date *datep);

Include dos.h

Description Get current date. Fills a date structure declared in dos.h as

```
struct date {
  int da_year;  // Year--1980
  char da_day;  // Day of the month
  char da_mon;  // Month (1--Jan, 2--Feb, ..., 12--Dec)
};
```

Parameters **struct date *datep** A pointer to a date structure as listed in the description.

See also ctime, _dos_getdate, _dos_setdate, gettime, setdate, settime

Example

```
/* getdate.cpp */
#include <stdio.h>
#include <dos.h>
main()
{
  date today;
  getdate(&today);
  printf("Today is %d/%d/%d\n",
    today.da_mon, today.da_day, today.da_year);
  return 0;
}
```

_getdcwd   Get current directory for drive

Syntax   `char *_getdcwd(int drive, char *buffer, int buflen);`

Include   direct.h

Description   Stores the current directory pathname for any drive. Returns `buffer` address for success and null for failure.

Parameters   **int drive** Drive number. 0–current, 1–A:, 2–B:, and so on.

char *buffer Pointer to `char` array at least `buflen` bytes long. Set `buffer` to null to have _getdcwd call `malloc()` to allocate a buffer of `buflen` bytes and store the pathname there. Call `free()` to delete this allocated memory.

int buflen Size in bytes of `char` array addressed by `buffer`, or the size of the desired buffer if `buffer` is null.

See also   chdir, getcwd, _getdrive

Example

```
/* _getdcwd.cpp */
#include <stdio.h>
#include <conio.h>
#include <direct.h>
#include <ctype.h>
main()
{
  int drive;
  char *cp;
  printf("Enter drive letter (A, B, C, etc.): ");
```

```
    drive = 1 + (toupper(getche()) - 'A');
    cp = _getdcwd(drive, NULL, MAXPATH);
    if (cp)
      printf("\n\n%s\n", cp);
    else
      puts("\n\nError reading drive");
    return 0;
  }
```

getdefaultpalette   Get graphics palette

Syntax   `struct palettetype *far getdefaultpalette(void);`

Include   graphics.h

Description   Returns a pointer to the graphics palette originally initialized by a graphics driver.

See also   `getpalette, getpalettesize, initgraph, setallpalette, setpalette`

Example
```
/* getdefau.cpp */
#include <graphics.h>
#include <stdio.h>
#include <stdlib.h>
#include <conio.h>
#include <dos.h>
main()
{
  int gdriver = DETECT, gmode, gerr;
  int i, j, xmax, ymax;
  palettetype far *newpalette, far *savedpalette;
  initgraph(&gdriver, &gmode, "c:\\borlandc\\bgi");
  gerr = graphresult();
  if (gerr != grOk) {
    printf("BGI error: %s\n", grapherrormsg(gerr));
    exit(gerr);
  }
  xmax = getmaxx();
  ymax = getmaxy();
  i = 1;
  j = 1;
  savedpalette = getdefaultpalette();
  newpalette = savedpalette;
```

```
while (i < ymax / 2) {
  delay(100);
  setcolor(1 + (j % (newpalette->size - 1)));
  ellipse(xmax / 2, ymax / 2, 0, 360, i, ymax / 3);
  i = i + 4;
  j++;
}
while (!kbhit()) {
  delay(100);
  j = newpalette->colors[newpalette->size - 1];
  for (i = newpalette->size - 1; i >= 1; i--)
    newpalette->colors[i] = newpalette->colors[i - 1];
  newpalette->colors[1] = j;
  setallpalette(newpalette);
}
setallpalette(savedpalette);
getch();
closegraph();
return 0;
}
```

getdfree   Get free disk space

Syntax   `void getdfree(unsigned char drive, struct dfree *dtable);`

Include   dos.h

Description   Stores a disk's size and other information in a `dfree` structure declared in dos.h as

```
struct dfree {
  unsigned df_avail;   // Number of clusters available
  unsigned df_total;   // Total number of clusters on drive
  unsigned df_bsec;    // Number of bytes per sector
  unsigned df_sclus;   // Number of sectors per cluster
};
```

Parameters   **unsigned char drive** Drive number. 0–current drive, 1–A:, 2–B:, and so on.

struct dfree *dtable Pointer to `dfree` structure as listed in the description. The function sets `df_sclus` to 0xFFFF if it can't access the specified drive.

See also   fstat, getfat, getfatd, stat

Example

```
/* getdfree.cpp */
#include <stdio.h>
#include <stdlib.h>
#include <dos.h>
main()
{
  dfree freeinfo;
  long free;
  getdfree(0, &freeinfo);
  if (freeinfo.df_sclus == 0xFFFF) {
    puts("Error getting drive information");
    exit(1);
  }
  puts("Free space on current drive:");
  printf(" Available clusters == %u\n", freeinfo.df_avail);
  printf(" Total clusters ... == %u\n", freeinfo.df_total);
  printf(" Bytes per sector   == %u\n", freeinfo.df_bsec);
  printf(" Sectors per cluster == %u\n", freeinfo.df_sclus);
  free = (long)freeinfo.df_avail *
    (long)freeinfo.df_bsec * (long)freeinfo.df_sclus;
  printf("Total free space = %lu bytes\n", free);
  return 0;
}
```

getdisk   Get current drive

Syntax   `int getdisk(void);`

Include   dir.h

Description   Returns current disk drive number: 0 for drive A:, 1 for B:, 2 for C:, and so on. Functions getdisk() and _getdrive() both call _dos_getdrive().

See also   _dos_getdrive, getcurdir, getcwd, setdisk

Example

```
/* getdisk.cpp */
#include <stdio.h>
#include <dir.h>
main()
{
  int drive = getdisk();
  printf("Current drive == %c:\n", 'A' + drive);
  return 0;
}
```

_getdrive   Get drive number

Syntax	`int _getdrive(void);`
Include	direct.h or dos.h
Description	Similar to `getdisk`, but returns the current drive as 1 for A:, 2 for B:, 3 for C:, and so on.
See also	`getdisk`
Example	

```
/* _getdriv.cpp */

#include <stdio.h>
#include <direct.h>
main()
{
  int drive = _getdrive();
  printf("Current drive == %c:\n", 'A' + drive - 1);
  return 0;
}
```

getdrivername   Get graphics driver name

Syntax	`char *far getdrivername(void);`
Include	graphics.h
Description	Returns a pointer to the name of the current graphics driver as an ASCII string.
See also	`grapherrormsg`, `graphresult`, `initgraph`
Example	

```
/* getdrive.cpp */
#include <graphics.h>
#include <stdio.h>
#include <stdlib.h>
main()
{
  int gdriver = DETECT, gmode, gerr;
  initgraph(&gdriver, &gmode, "c:\\borlandc\\bgi");
  gerr = graphresult();
  if (gerr != grOk) {
    printf("BGI error: %s\n", grapherrormsg(gerr));
    exit(gerr);
```

```
    }
    char *name = getdrivername();
    closegraph();
    printf("Graphics driver is: %s\n", name);
    return 0;
}
```

getdta   Get disk transfer address

Syntax   `char far *getdta(void);`

Include   dos.h

Description   Returns a far pointer to the DOS disk transfer address (DTA). For small- and medium-model programs, `getdta`'s result assumes that the DTA is in the program's data segment. No such assumption is made for other memory models.

See also   `setdta`

Example
```
/* getdta.cpp */
#include <stdio.h>
#include <dos.h>
main()
{
    char far *cp;
    cp = getdta();
    printf("Disk transfer address (DTA) == %Fp\n", cp);
    return 0;
}
```

getenv   Get environment string

Syntax   `char *getenv(const char *name);`

Include   stdlib.h

Description   Returns a pointer to a specified environment variable, or null if the variable can't be found.

Parameters   **const char *name** Pointer to environment variable string—COMSPEC, for example. Function returns this variable's setting if found in the environment.

See also   `exec, getpsp, putenv`

Example   See exec.

getfat Get file allocation table

Syntax   `void getfat(unsigned char drive, struct fatinfo *dtable);`

Include   dos.h

Description   Fills a `fatinfo` structure with information about a specified drive's file allocation table (FAT). The `fatinfo` structure is declared in dos.h as

```
struct fatinfo {
  char     fi_sclus;   // Number of sectors per cluster
  char     fi_fatid;   // FAT ID value
  unsigned fi_nclus;   // Total number of clusters
  int      fi_bysec;   // Number of bytes per cluster
};
```

Member `fi_fatid` is set to 0xF8 if the drive is fixed. Other values indicate a removable disk. See a DOS reference to function 0x1C for more information.

Parameters   **unsigned char drive** Drive number. 0–current drive, 1–A:, 2–B:, and so on.

struct fatinfo *dtable Pointer to `fatinfo` structure, filled in by `getfat()`.

See also   `getdfree, getfatd`

Example
```
/* getfat.cpp */
#include <stdio.h>
#include <conio.h>
#include <dos.h>
void report(int drive);
main()
{
  puts("Insert diskettes into all floppy drives");
  printf("and press any key for FAT info");
  getch();
  report(1);  // A:
  report(2);  // B:
  report(3);  // C:
  return 0;
}
```

```
void report(int drive)
{
  fatinfo fat;
  getfat(drive, &fat);
  printf("\nDrive %c", 'A' + drive - 1);
  if (fat.fi_sclus < 0)
    puts(" is unreadable or unformatted");
  else {
    if (fat.fi_fatid & 0x80) {
      puts("'s characteristics:");
      switch ((unsigned char)fat.fi_fatid) {
        case 0xfd: puts("360K"); break;
        case 0xf9: puts("1.2M"); break;
        case 0xf0: puts("1.44M"); break;
        default: puts("Hard drive or other");
      }
    }
  }
}
```

getfatd   Get default file allocation table

Syntax   void getfatd(struct fatinfo *dtable);

Include   dos.h

Description   Identical to getfat() for the current drive.

Example
```
/* getfatd.cpp */
#include <stdio.h>
#include <dos.h>
main()
{
  fatinfo fat;
  getfatd(&fat);
  if (fat.fi_sclus < 0)
    puts("Error reading current drive");
  else
    printf("Sectors per cluster == %u\n", fat.fi_sclus);
  return 0;
}
```

getfillpattern   Get user fill pattern

Syntax   `void far getfillpattern(char far *pattern);`

Include   graphics.h

Description   Transfers the current graphics fill pattern to the location addressed by pattern.

Parameters   **char far *pattern** Pointer to an 8-byte array.

See also   `getfillsettings, setfillpattern`

Example
```
/* getfillp.cpp */
#include <graphics.h>
#include <stdio.h>
#include <stdlib.h>
#include <conio.h>
main()
{
  int gdriver = DETECT, gmode, gerr;
  char pattern[8];  // Fill pattern is an 8-byte array
  initgraph(&gdriver, &gmode, "c:\\borlandc\\bgi");
  gerr = graphresult();
  if (gerr != grOk) {
    printf("BGI error: %s\n", grapherrormsg(gerr));
    exit(gerr);
  }
  getfillpattern(pattern);
  closegraph();
  puts("Fill pattern:");
  for (int i = 0; i < 8; i++)
    printf("pattern[%d] == %#x\n", i, pattern[i]);
  return 0;
}
```

getfillsettings   Get fill pattern and color

Syntax   `void far getfillsettings(struct fillsettingstype far *fillinfo);`

Include   graphics.h

Description   Fills in a `fillsettingstype` structure with the current graphics fill pattern ID number and fill color. The structure is declared in graphics.h as

```
struct fillsettingstype {
  int pattern;  // Fill pattern ID number
  int color;    // Fill color
};
```

Fill pattern IDs are enumerated symbols of type enum fill_patterns declared in graphics.h. In alphabetic order, these symbols and their associated values are the following:

Enumerated symbol	Value	Fill pattern
BKSLASH_FILL	5	\\\ fill (thick lines)
CLOSE_DOT_FILL	11	Closely spaced dot fill
EMPTY_FILL	0	Fill with background color
HATCH_FILL	7	Light hatch fill
INTERLEAVE_FILL	9	Interleaving line fill
LINE_FILL	2	-- fill
LTBKSLASH_FILL	6	\\\ fill
LTSLASH_FILL	3	/// fill
SLASH_FILL	4	/// fill (thick lines)
SOLID_FILL	1	Fills with solid fill color
USER_FILL	12	User-defined fill
WIDE_DOT_FILL	10	Widely spaced dot fill
XHATCH_FILL	8	Heavy crosshatch fill

Parameters **struct fillsettingstype far *fillinfo** Pointer to a fillsettingstype structure as listed in *Description*.

See also getfillpattern, setfillpattern, setfillstyle

Example
```
/* getfills.cpp */
#include <graphics.h>
#include <stdio.h>
#include <stdlib.h>
#include <conio.h>
main()
```

```
   {
     int gdriver = DETECT, gmode, gerr;
     fillsettingstype fst;
     initgraph(&gdriver, &gmode, "c:\\borlandc\\bgi");
     gerr = graphresult();
     if (gerr != grOk) {
       printf("BGI error: %s\n", grapherrormsg(gerr));
       exit(gerr);
     }
     getfillsettings(&fst);
     closegraph();
     printf("Pattern == %#x\n", fst.pattern);
     printf("Color   == %#x\n", fst.color);
     return 0;
   }
```

getftime   Get file date and time

Syntax   `int getftime(int handle, struct ftime *ftimep);`

Include   io.h

Description   Gets a file's date and time as listed in the directory. Returns zero for success and −1 for failure. Fills an `ftime` bit-field structure declared in io.h as

```
struct ftime {
  unsigned ft_tsec  : 5;   // Seconds in two-second intervals
  unsigned ft_min   : 6;   // Minute
  unsigned ft_hour  : 5;   // Hour
  unsigned ft_day   : 5;   // Day
  unsigned ft_month : 4;   // Month
  unsigned ft_year  : 7;   // Year
};
```

Parameters   **int handle** Opens a file handle such as that returned by open().

struct ftime *ftimep Pointer to an `ftime` structure as listed in *Description*.

See also   open, setftime

Example
```
/* getftime.cpp */
#include <stdio.h>
#include <stdlib.h>
```

```
#include <io.h>
main(int argc, char *argv[])
{
  FILE *f;
  ftime ft;
  if (argc <= 1) {
    puts("No filename specified");
    exit(1);
  }
  f = fopen(argv[1], "rb");
  if (!f) {
    printf("Can't open file %s\n", argv[1]);
    exit(2);
  }
  getftime(fileno(f), &ft);
  printf("%s %02d/%02d/%d %02d:%02d\n",
    argv[1], ft.ft_month, ft.ft_day, ft.ft_year,
    ft.ft_hour, ft.ft_min);
  fclose(f);
  return 0;
}
```

getgraphmode   Current graphics mode

Syntax   `int far getgraphmode(void);`

Include   graphics.h

Description   Returns the current graphics mode as set by `initgraph()`. See Chapter 17, "Borland's Class Library," for a list of graphics modes, declared as type `enum graphics_modes` in graphics.h.

See also   `detectgraph, initgraph, getmoderange, restorecrtmode, setgraphmode`

Example
```
/* getgraph.cpp */
#include <graphics.h>
#include <stdio.h>
#include <stdlib.h>
#include <conio.h>
main()
{
  int gdriver = DETECT, gmode, gerr;
  int oldmode;
  initgraph(&gdriver, &gmode, "c:\\borlandc\\bgi");
```

```
    gerr = graphresult();
    if (gerr != grOk) {
      printf("BGI error: %s\n", grapherrormsg(gerr));
      exit(gerr);
    }
    setcolor(LIGHTMAGENTA);
    rectangle(100, 100, 150, 150);
    outtextxy(0, 0, "This is the graphics page");
    outtextxy(0, 20, "Press any key to continue...");
    getch();
    oldmode = getgraphmode();
    restorecrtmode();
    puts("This is on the text page");
    printf("Press any key to continue...");
    getch();
    setgraphmode(oldmode);
    rectangle(100, 100, 150, 150);
    outtextxy(0, 40, "Back on the graphics page");
    outtextxy(0, 60, "Press any key to continue...");
    getch();
    closegraph();
    return 0;
  }
```

getimage   Copy bit image to memory

Syntax   `void far getimage(int left, int top, int right, int bottom,`
           `void far *bitmap);`

Include graphics.h

Description Copies a portion of the graphics screen into a buffer addressed by
bitmap. The captured image rectangle is defined by the four int
parameters. Pixels from the graphics display memory are copied to
memory along with width and height information.

The format of the transferred information depends on the current
graphics mode. For best results, call imagesize() to allocate a buffer of
an appropriate size, which you can pass to getimage(). To restore a
saved image, call putimage().

Parameters **int left, int top** The image's upper-left (X,Y) coordinate.

int right, int bottom The image's lower-right (X,Y) coordinate.

void far *bitmap Pointer to a buffer large enough to hold the requested bitmap image.

See also   getpixel, imagesize, putimage, putpixel

Example
```
/* getimage.cpp */
#include <graphics.h>
#include <stdio.h>
#include <stdlib.h>
#include <time.h>
#include <conio.h>
#define X1 100
#define Y1 100
#define X2 227
#define Y2 163
main()
{
  int gdriver = DETECT, gmode, gerr;
  int xmax, ymax;
  int x, y, xsize, ysize, i;
  void far *image;
  initgraph(&gdriver, &gmode, "c:\\borlandc\\bgi");
  gerr = graphresult();
  if (gerr != grOk) {
    printf("BGI error: %s\n", grapherrormsg(gerr));
    exit(gerr);
  }

  xmax = getmaxx();
  ymax = getmaxy();
  randomize();
  for (i = 1; i <= 100; i++) {
  // Draw a few lines at random }
    setcolor(1 + random(getmaxcolor()));
    lineto(random(xmax), random(ymax));
  }
  image = new char[imagesize(X1, Y1, X2, Y2)];
  if (image) {
    getimage(X1, Y1, X2, Y2, image);  // Copy display image
    clearviewport();
    xsize = 1 + (X2 - X1);
    ysize = 1 + (Y2 - Y1);
    x = 0;
```

```
    while (x < xmax) {
      y = 0;
      while (y < ymax) {
        putimage(x, y, image, COPY_PUT);  // Replicate image
        y = y + ysize;
      }
      x = x + xsize;
    }
  }
  getch();
  closegraph();
  return 0;
}
```

getlinesettings Get current line settings

Syntax void far getlinesettings(struct linesettingstype far *lineinfo);

Include graphics.h

Description Fills in a linesettingstype structure with the current graphics line style, pattern, and thickness. The structure is declared in graphics.h as

```
struct linesettingstype {
  int linestyle;       // An enum line_styles value
  unsigned upattern;   // Line pattern if linestyle == USERBIT_LINE
  int thickness;       // 1-NORM_WIDTH, 3-THICK_WIDTH (3 pixels wide)
};
```

Member linestyle is one of the following enum line_styles symbols, declared in graphics.h:

Enumerated symbol	Value	Line style
CENTER_LINE	2	Alternating small and large dashes
DASHED_LINE	3	Dashed lines
DOTTED_LINE	1	Dotted lines
SOLID_LINE	0	Solid lines
USERBIT_LINE	4	User dot/dash pattern

Parameters   **struct linesettingstype far *lineinfo** Pointer to a linesettingstype structure as listed in *Description*.

See also   setlinestyle

Example
```
/* getlines.cpp */
#include <graphics.h>
#include <stdio.h>
#include <stdlib.h>
#include <conio.h>
main()
{
  int gdriver = DETECT, gmode, gerr;
  linesettingstype lineinfo;
  int height;
  char s[128];
  initgraph(&gdriver, &gmode, "c:\\borlandc\\bgi");
  gerr = graphresult();
  if (gerr != grOk) {
    printf("BGI error: %s\n", grapherrormsg(gerr));
    exit(gerr);
  }
  height = textheight("M");
  getlinesettings(&lineinfo);
  outtextxy(0, 0, "Default line settings:");
  sprintf(s, "Line style == %d", lineinfo.linestyle);
  outtextxy(0, height * 2, s);
  sprintf(s, "Pattern .. == %u", lineinfo.upattern);
  outtextxy(0, height * 4, s);
  sprintf(s, "Thickness  == %d", lineinfo.thickness);
  outtextxy(0, height * 6, s);
  outtextxy(0, height * 8, "Press any key...");
  getch();
  closegraph();
  return 0;
}
```

getmaxcolor   Return maximum color value

Syntax   int far getmaxcolor(void);

Include   graphics.h

Description   Returns maximum graphics color value.

See also   getbkcolor, getcolor, getpalette, setcolor

Example
```
/* getmaxco.cpp */
#include <graphics.h>
#include <stdio.h>
#include <stdlib.h>
#include <conio.h>
main()
{
  int gdriver = DETECT, gmode, gerr;
  int x, y, xmax, ymax, color;
  initgraph(&gdriver, &gmode, "c:\\borlandc\\bgi");
  gerr = graphresult();
  if (gerr != grOk) {
    printf("BGI error: %s\n", grapherrormsg(gerr));
    exit(gerr);
  }
  xmax = getmaxx();
  ymax = getmaxy();
  x = 0;
  y = 0;
  rectangle(0, 0, xmax, ymax);
  for (color = 1; color <= getmaxcolor(); color++) {
    setcolor(color);
    line(x, 0, x, ymax);
    line(0, y, xmax, y);
    x += (xmax / getmaxcolor());
    y += (ymax / getmaxcolor());
  }
  getch();
  closegraph();
  return 0;
}
```

getmaxmode   Maximum graphics mode

Syntax   int far getmaxmode(void);

Include   graphics.h

Description Similar to getmoderange(), getmaxmode(). Returns the maximum value you can pass to setgraphmode(), typically to select different display adapter options. Unlike getmoderange(), which works only for BGI graphics drivers, getmaxmode() works for all drivers, even those from other vendors.

See also getmodename, getmoderange, setgraphmode

Example

```
/* getmaxmo.cpp */
#include <graphics.h>
#include <stdio.h>
#include <stdlib.h>
#include <conio.h>
main()
{
  int gdriver = DETECT, gmode, gerr;
  int xmax, ymax, maxmode;
  char far *driver;
  initgraph(&gdriver, &gmode, "c:\\borlandc\\bgi");
  gerr = graphresult();
  if (gerr != grOk) {
    printf("BGI error: %s\n", grapherrormsg(gerr));
    exit(gerr);
  }
  xmax = getmaxx();
  ymax = getmaxy();
  maxmode = getmaxmode();
  driver = getdrivername();
  closegraph();
  printf("Default driver is %s\n", driver);
  printf("X max = %d\n", xmax);
  printf("Y max = %d\n", ymax);
  printf("Maximum mode = %d\n", maxmode);
  return 0;
}
```

getmaxx, getmaxy Maximum graphics coordinates

Syntax
```
int far getmaxx(void);
int far getmaxy(void);
```

Include graphics.h

Description Return maximum X (getmaxx()) and Y (getmaxy()) graphics coordinate values. Values are zero-based, so if getmaxx() returns 639, there are 640 pixels available horizontally.

See also getx, gety, moveto

Example
```
/* getmaxxy.cpp */
#include <graphics.h>
#include <stdio.h>
#include <stdlib.h>
#include <conio.h>
main()
{
  int gdriver = DETECT, gmode, gerr;
  int xmax, ymax, xmin, ymin;
  initgraph(&gdriver, &gmode, "c:\\borlandc\\bgi");
  gerr = graphresult();
  if (gerr != grOk) {
    printf("BGI error: %s\n", grapherrormsg(gerr));
    exit(gerr);
  }
  xmax = getmaxx();
  ymax = getmaxy();
  xmin = 0;
  ymin = 0;
  while ((xmax > 0) && (ymax > 0)) {
    setcolor(1 + random(getmaxcolor()));
    line(xmin, ymin, xmax, ymin);
    line(xmax, ymin, xmax, ymax);
    line(xmax, ymax, xmin, ymax);
    line(xmin, ymax, xmin, ymin);
    xmax--;
    ymax--;
    xmin++;
    ymin++;
  }
  getch();
  closegraph();
  return 0;
}
```

getmodename   Get graphics mode name

Syntax `char *far getmodename(int mode_number);`

Include graphics.h

Description Returns pointer to the specified graphics mode name as an ASCII string.

Parameters **int mode_number** Any value from 0 to the value returned by getmaxmode().

See also `getdrivername, getmaxmode, getmoderange`

Example
```cpp
/* getmoden.cpp */
#include <graphics.h>
#include <stdio.h>
#include <stdlib.h>
#include <conio.h>
main()
{
  int gdriver = DETECT, gmode, gerr;
  initgraph(&gdriver, &gmode, "c:\\borlandc\\bgi");
  int i, y, height;
  char s[128];
  gerr = graphresult();
  if (gerr != grOk) {
    printf("BGI error: %s\n", grapherrormsg(gerr));
    exit(gerr);
  }
  height = textheight("M") + 8;
  sprintf(s, "Graphics driver is: %s", getdrivername());
  outtextxy(0, 0, s);
  y = height;
  for (i = 0; i <= getmaxmode(); i++) {
    sprintf(s, "mode %d : %s", i, getmodename(i));
    outtextxy(0, y, s);
    y += height;
  }
  outtextxy(0, y, "Press any key to end...");
  getch();
  closegraph();
  return 0;
}
```

getmoderange Get graphics mode range

Syntax   `void far getmoderange(int graphdriver, int far *lomode,`
        `int far *himode);`

Include   graphics.h

Description   Returns a range of possible mode values for a specified graphics driver, corresponding to a symbol in enum `graphics_drivers` (see initgraph). Works only for BGI graphics drivers. See getmaxmode() for a similar function that can handle all graphics drivers, even those from other vendors. An out-of-range `graphdriver` value sets `lomode` and `himode` to −1.

Parameters   `int graphdriver` Graphics driver value, −1 for current graphics driver.

    `int far *lomode` Pointer to an int, which the function sets to the lowest possible mode value that can be passed to setgraphmode().

    `int far *himode` Pointer to an int, which the function sets to the highest possible mode value that can be passed to setgraphmode().

See also   getgraphmode, getmaxmode, getmodename, initgraph, setgraphmode

Example
```
/* getmoder.cpp */
#include <graphics.h>
#include <stdio.h>
char *modenames[10] = {
  "CGA      ", "MCGA     ", "EGA      ", "EGA64    ",
  "EGAMono  ", "Reserved ", "HercMono ", "Att400   ",
  "VGA      ", "PC3270   "
};
main()
{
  int graphdriver, lomode, himode;
  puts("Graphics Driver Mode Ranges\n");
  for (graphdriver = 0; graphdriver < 10; graphdriver++) {
    getmoderange(graphdriver + 1, &lomode, &himode);
    printf("%s == %2d ... %2d\n",
      modenames[graphdriver], lomode, himode);
  }
  return 0;
}
```

getpalette   Get current palette

Syntax   `void far getpalette(struct palettetype far *palette);`

Include   graphics.h

Description   Fills in a `palettetype` structure with the current graphics palette. The structure is declared in graphics.h as

```
#define MAXCOLORS 15
struct palettetype {
  unsigned char size;
  signed char colors[MAXCOLORS + 1];
};
```

Sets member `size` to the number of palette colors. Sets `colors` to the palette color values. For example, after the program calls `getpalette()`, `colors[CYAN]` is the actual color value used for the `CYAN` color. Does not work with the IBM-8514 graphics driver.

Parameters   **`struct palettetype far *palette`** Pointer to a `palettetype` structure as listed in *Description*.

See also   `getbkcolor, getcolor, getdefaultpalette, getmaxcolor, getpalettesize, setallpalette, setpalette, setrgbpalette`

Example   `/* getpalet.cpp */`

```
#include <graphics.h>
#include <stdio.h>
#include <stdlib.h>
#include <conio.h>
main()
{
  int gdriver = DETECT, gmode, gerr;
  int h, i, xmax;
  palettetype palette;
  char s[128];
  initgraph(&gdriver, &gmode, "c:\\borlandc\\bgi");
  gerr = graphresult();
  if (gerr != grOk) {
    printf("BGI error: %s\n", grapherrormsg(gerr));
    exit(gerr);
  }
  xmax = getmaxx();
  getpalette(&palette);
```

```
    h = textheight("M") + 8;
    outtextxy(0, 0, "   Index  Palette.colors[i]  Sample");
    for (i = 0; i <= palette.size - 1; i++) {
      moveto(0, (i + 1) * h);
      sprintf(s, "Color #%2d == ", i);
      outtext(s);
      sprintf(s, "%3d : ", palette.colors[i]);
      outtext(s);
      setfillstyle(SOLID_FILL, i);
      bar(getx(), gety(), xmax, gety() + 4);
    }
    getch();
    closegraph();
    return 0;
}
```

getpalettesize   Get current palette size

Syntax `int far getpalettesize(void);`

Include graphics.h

Description Returns the size of the current graphics color palette in bytes. Equivalent to the maximum number of available colors.

See also setpalette, setallpalette

Example `/* getpales.cpp */`

```
#include <graphics.h>
#include <stdio.h>
#include <stdlib.h>
#include <conio.h>
#include <dos.h>
main()
{
  int gdriver = DETECT, gmode, gerr;
  int i, xmax, ymax;
  initgraph(&gdriver, &gmode, "c:\\borlandc\\bgi");
  gerr = graphresult();
  if (gerr != grOk) {
    printf("BGI error: %s\n", grapherrormsg(gerr));
    exit(gerr);
  }
```

```
    xmax = getmaxx();
    ymax = getmaxy();
    for (i = 1; i <= 100; i++) {
      setcolor(1 + random(getmaxcolor() - 1));
      line(abs(random(xmax)),
           abs(random(ymax)),
           abs(random(xmax)),
           abs(random(ymax)));
    }
    while (!kbhit()) {
      if (i >= getpalettesize())
        i = 1;
      else
        i++;
      delay(10);
      setpalette(i, 1 + random(getmaxcolor() - 1));
    }
    getch();
    closegraph();
    return 0;
}
```

getpass   Read password

Syntax   `char *getpass(const char *prompt);`

Include   conio.h

Description Displays a string addressed by `prompt` and returns a password string
              entered by the user. Typing is not echoed to the display.

Parameters **const char *prompt** Pointer to a prompt string, displayed at the current
              cursor location.

See also   `cgets, getch`

Example   `/* getpass.cpp */`

```
#include <stdio.h>
#include <conio.h>
#include <string.h>
main()
{
  char *password;
```

```
  int done = 0;
  while (!done) {
    password = getpass("What is the password? ");
    done = !stricmp(password, "password");
    if (!done)
      puts("Incorrect! (Hint: try PASSWORD)");
  }
  puts("Correct!");
  return 0;
}
```

getpid   Get process ID

Syntax   `unsigned getpid(void);`

Include   process.h

Description   In a multitasking operating system such as UNIX, `getpid()` might return a task's unique process ID number. In MS-DOS, the function returns the segment address of a program's PSP (program segment prefix).

See also   `exec...`, `getpsp`

Example   `/* getpid.cpp */`

```
#include <stdio.h>
#include <process.h>
main()
{
  unsigned pid = getpid();
  printf("Process ID == %#X\n", pid);
  return 0;
}
```

getpixel   Get pixel color

Syntax   `unsigned far getpixel(int x, int y);`

Include   graphics.h

Description   Returns a value that represents a pixel's color at the specified coordinate.

Parameters   `int x, int y` Coordinate of the target pixel.

See also   getimage, putimage, putpixel

Example   /* getpixel.cpp */

```cpp
#include <graphics.h>
#include <stdio.h>
#include <stdlib.h>
#include <time.h>
#include <conio.h>
#define FALSE 0
#define BORDER_COLOR RED
void box(int x1, int y1, int x2, int y2);
main()
{
  int gdriver = DETECT, gmode, gerr;
  int i, xmax, ymax, x, y, pendown;
  initgraph(&gdriver, &gmode, "c:\\borlandc\\bgi");
  gerr = graphresult();
  if (gerr != grOk) {
    printf("BGI error: %s\n", grapherrormsg(gerr));
    exit(gerr);
  }
  xmax = getmaxx();
  ymax = getmaxy();
  randomize();
  for (i = 1; i <= 15; i++)
    box(random(xmax), random(ymax),
        random(xmax), random(ymax));
  for (x = 0; x <= xmax; x++) {
    pendown = FALSE;
    for (y = 0; y <= ymax; y++)
      if ((getpixel(x, y)     == BORDER_COLOR) &&
          (getpixel(x + 1, y) == BORDER_COLOR))
        pendown = !pendown;
      else if (pendown)
        putpixel(x, y, random(getmaxcolor()));
  }
  getch();
  closegraph();
  return 0;
}
```

```
void box(int x1, int y1, int x2, int y2)
{
  setcolor(BORDER_COLOR);
  line(x1, y1, x2, y1);
  line(x2, y1, x2, y2);
  line(x2, y2, x1, y2);
  line(x1, y2, x1, y1);
}
```

getpsp   Get program segment prefix

Syntax   `unsigned getpsp(void);`

Include   dos.h

Description   Returns the segment address value of the program's PSP (program segment prefix). Calls DOS function 0x62.

See also   `getenv, getpid`

Example
```
/* getpsp.cpp */
#include <stdio.h>
#include <dos.h>
main()
{
  unsigned psp = getpsp();
  printf("Program segment prefix (PSP) == %#X\n", psp);
  return 0;
}
```

gets   Get string from stdin

Syntax   `char *gets(char *s);`

Include   stdio.h

Description   Reads characters including whitespace from the standard input until receiving a newline character, which is replaced by null. Successive characters are stored at the location addressed by s. Returns s or null on end of file or any errors. There is no way to specify to gets() the maximum number of characters to read.

Parameters   **char *s** Addresses a buffer large enough to hold expected input. The resulting string is null-terminated.

See also   cgets, ferror, fgets, fopen, fputs, fread, getc, puts, scanf

Example

```
/* gets.cpp */
#include <stdio.h>
main()
{
  char buffer[128];
  printf("Enter a string: ");
  gets(buffer);
  printf("\nYour string is: %s\n", buffer);
  return 0;
}
```

gettext   Copy text to memory

Syntax

```
int gettext(int left, int top, int right, int bottom,
    void *destin);
```

Include   conio.h

Description   Copies one or more characters and attributes from a text-mode display to a buffer. Typically used to save a portion of a display for restoring later by calling puttext().

Parameters   **int left, int top** Absolute screen coordinates of the upper-left corner location of the display rectangle to be copied. Coordinate (1,1) represents the display's extreme upper-left corner.

int right, int bottom The bottom-right corner location of the display rectangle to be copied.

void *destin The address of a buffer large enough to hold the copied text and attributes. Each character requires two bytes of storage. The minimum required buffer size equals (H * W * 2) bytes where *H* is the height and *W* is the width in characters of the display rectangle to be copied.

See also   getpixel, movetext, putpixel, puttext

Example

```
/* gettext.cpp */
#include <stdio.h>
#include <conio.h>
#define ROWS 25  // Number of display rows
#define COLS 80  // Number of display columns
```

```
#define BUFSIZE (ROWS * COLS * 2)
main()
{
  int i;
  void *save;
  clrscr();
  for (i = 0; i < 20; i++)
    printf("This is test string number %d\n", i);
  save = new char[BUFSIZE];
  if (save) {
    gettext(1, 1, COLS, ROWS, save);
    printf("\nPress any key to erase screen");
    getch();
    clrscr();
    printf("\nPress any key to restore screen");
    getch();
    clrscr();
    puttext(1, 1, COLS, ROWS, save);
    gotoxy(1, ROWS - 1);
  }
  return 0;
}
```

gettextinfo   Get text mode information

Syntax   void gettextinfo(struct text_info *r);

Include   conio.h

Description   Fills in a text_info structure with information about the current text-mode display. The structure is declared in conio.h as

```
struct text_info {
  unsigned char winleft;        // Window's left border
  unsigned char wintop;         // Window's top border
  unsigned char winright;       // Window's right border
  unsigned char winbottom;      // Window's bottom border
  unsigned char attribute;      // Current text attribute
  unsigned char normattr;       // Default normal attribute
  unsigned char currmode;       // Current display mode
  unsigned char screenheight;   // Display height in characters
  unsigned char screenwidth;    // Display width in characters
```

```
                unsigned char curx;              // Cursor X coordinate after gotoxy()
                unsigned char cury;              // Cursor Y coordinate after gotoxy()
            };
```

Parameters   **struct text_info *r** Pointer to a text_info structure, which the
function fills with information about the current display mode. The
win... members specify the current window size and location (see
function window()). The currmode member can be one of the constants
BW40, BW80, C40, C80, or C4350 where *BW* stands for black-and-
white (monochrome) and *C* stands for color. Comments in *Description*
explain the other members.

See also   gotoxy, textattr, textbackground, textcolor, textmode, wherex,
wherey, window

Example
```
/* gettexti.cpp */
#include <stdio.h>
#include <conio.h>
main()
{
  text_info ti;
  char *s;
  gettextinfo(&ti);
  switch (ti.currmode) {
    case BW40:  s = "BW40"; break;
    case BW80:  s = "BW80"; break;
    case C40:   s = "C40"; break;
    case C80:   s = "C80"; break;
    case C4350: s = "C4350"; break;
    default: s = "Unknown";
  }
  printf("Current text mode is %s\n", s);
  return 0;
}
```

gettextsettings   Get graphics font

Syntax   void far gettextsettings(struct textsettingstype far
*texttypeinfo);

Include   graphics.h

Description Fills a `textsettingstype` structure with miscellaneous information about a graphics display's text settings. The structure is declared in graphics.h as

```
struct textsettingstype {
  int font;                 // BGI font ID
  int direction;            // Text display orientation
  int charsize;             // Size as passed to settextstyle()
  int horiz;                // Horizontal justification
  int vert;                 // Vertical justification
};
```

Parameters **struct textsettingstype far *texttypeinfo** Pointer to a textsettingstype structure for holding the function's result.

See also outtext, outtextxy, registerbgifont, settextjustify, settextstyle, setusercharsize, textheight, textwidth

Example
```
/* gettexts.cpp */
#include <graphics.h>
#include <stdio.h>
#include <stdlib.h>
#include <conio.h>
void outint(int *y, int h, char *s, int v);
main()
{
  int gdriver = DETECT, gmode, gerr, h, y;
  textsettingstype ts;
  initgraph(&gdriver, &gmode, "c:\\borlandc\\bgi");
  gerr = graphresult();
  if (gerr != grOk) {
    printf("BGI error: %s\n", grapherrormsg(gerr));
    exit(gerr);
  }
  gettextsettings(&ts);
  h = textheight("M") + 4;
  y = 0;
  outint(&y, h, "font .........", ts.font);
  outint(&y, h, "direction ....", ts.direction);
  outint(&y, h, "charsize .....", ts.charsize);
  outint(&y, h, "horiz ........", ts.horiz);
  outint(&y, h, "vert .........", ts.vert);
  getch();
```

```
  closegraph();
  return 0;
}

void outint(int *y, int h, char *s, int v)
{
  char buffer[40];
  sprintf(buffer, "%s %d", s, v);
  outtextxy(0, *y, buffer);
  *y += h;
}
```

gettime   Get system time

Syntax void gettime(struct time *timep);

Include dos.h

Description Fills in a time structure with the current system time. The structure is declared in dos.h as

```
struct time {
  unsigned char ti_min;    // Minutes
  unsigned char ti_hour;   // Hours
  unsigned char ti_hund;   // Hundredths of seconds
  unsigned char ti_sec;    // Seconds
};
```

Parameters **struct time *timep** Pointer to a time structure for holding the function's result.

See also asctime, _dos_gettime, getdate, setdate, settime, stime, time

Example See asctime.

getvect   Get interrupt vector

Syntax void interrupt(*getvect(int interruptno))();

Include dos.h

Description Returns an interrupt vector as a far pointer to an interrupt function. Typically used with interrupt as defined in dos.h to call an interrupt service routine. Interrupt vectors are stored as pointers to interrupt service routines, which are called when an interrupt signal is received or when a software interrupt instruction is executed. An interrupt's number is an index to an array of such pointers stored in low memory.

Parameters   **int interruptno** Interrupt number, from 0 to 255, used as an index to the array of far pointers, or vectors, stored in low memory.

See also   disable, enable, geninterrupt, setvect

Example
```
/* getvect.cpp */
#include <stdio.h>
#include <dos.h>
main()
{
  void far *p = getvect(0);
  printf("Divide by zero ISR address == %Fp\n", p);
  return 0;
}
```

getverify   DOS verify flag

Syntax   int getverify(void);

Include   dos.h

Description   Returns the state of the DOS read/write verify flag. If true (nonzero), verification is on. If false (zero), verification is off. When on, following a disk write, DOS rereads the disk to check for a possible bad-sector error. When off, DOS does not follow disk writes with reads. Verification checks only that the disk is readable. Information written to disk is not compared with the information's source.

See also   getcbrk, setcbrk, setverify

Example
```
/* getverif.cpp */
#include <stdio.h>
#include <dos.h>
main()
{
  int verify = getverify();
  printf("Verify toggle is ");
  if (verify)
    puts("ON");
  else
```

```
    puts("OFF");
  return 0;
}
```

getviewsettings   Get current viewport

Syntax `void far getviewsettings(struct viewporttype far *viewport);`

Include graphics.h

Description Fills a `viewporttype` structure with information about the current graphics display viewport. The structure is declared in graphics.h as

```
struct viewporttype {
  int left, top, right, bottom;   // Viewport rectangle
  int clip;                       // True if clipping in effect
};
```

Parameters **struct viewporttype far *viewport** Pointer to a `viewporttype` structure filled in by the function.

See also `clearviewport, getx, gety, graphdefaults, setviewport`

Example
```
/* getviews.cpp */
#include <graphics.h>
#include <stdio.h>
#include <stdlib.h>
#include <conio.h>
main()
{
  int gdriver = DETECT, gmode, gerr;
  viewporttype vp;
  initgraph(&gdriver, &gmode, "c:\\borlandc\\bgi");
  gerr = graphresult();
  if (gerr != grOk) {
    printf("BGI error: %s\n", grapherrormsg(gerr));
    exit(gerr);
  }
  getviewsettings(&vp);
  rectangle(vp.left, vp.top, vp.right, vp.bottom);
  moveto(10, vp.bottom / 2);
  outtext("Clipping = ");
```

1159

```
        if (vp.clip)
          outtext("TRUE");
        else
          outtext("FALSE");
        getch();
        closegraph();
        return 0;
      }
```

getw   Get integer from stream

Syntax   `int getw(FILE *stream);`

Include   stdio.h

Description   Gets the next binary integer word value from the specified stream. The file should be opened for reading in binary, not text, mode. Returns EOF on errors or end of file. However, because EOF's value is an integer, you must call `feof()` to detect an end-of-file condition, and `ferror()` to detect errors.

Parameters   **FILE *stream** Pointer to a file stream opened for reading in binary mode.

See also   fopen, fread, putw

Example
```
/* getw.cpp */
#include <stdio.h>
#include <stdlib.h>
main()
{
  FILE *f;
  int w;
  f = tmpfile();
  if (!f) {
    puts("Error opening temporary file");
    exit(1);
  }
  puts("Creating temporary file of 100 integers");
  for (w = 0; w < 100; w++)
    putw(w, f);
  rewind(f);
  puts("Reading temporary file");
  w = getw(f);
  while (!feof(f)) {
```

```
      printf("%8d", w);
      w = getw(f);
    }
    return 0;
  }
```

getx, gety   Return graphics coordinate

Syntax   `int far getx(void);`
`int far gety(void);`

Include   graphics.h

Description   Together, the two functions return the graphics display's current position (CP), the (X,Y) location where a shape will appear for most drawing and text graphics output functions.

See also   getmaxx, getmaxy, getviewsettings, lineto, moveto, outtext

Example
```
/* getxy.cpp */
#include <graphics.h>
#include <stdio.h>
#include <stdlib.h>
#include <conio.h>
main()
{
  int gdriver = DETECT, gmode, gerr;
  char s[80];
  initgraph(&gdriver, &gmode, "c:\\borlandc\\bgi");
  gerr = graphresult();
  if (gerr != grOk) {
    printf("BGI error: %s\n", grapherrormsg(gerr));
    exit(gerr);
  }
  putpixel(getmaxx() / 2, getmaxy() / 2, BLUE);
  sprintf(s, "getx()==%d gety()==%d", getx(), gety());
  outtext(s);
  moveto(getmaxx() / 2, getmaxy() / 2);
  outtext("->");
  sprintf(s, "getx()==%d gety()==%d", getx(), gety());
  outtext(s);
  getch();
  closegraph();
  return 0;
}
```

gmtime Greenwich mean time

Syntax `struct tm *gmtime(const time_t *timer);`

Include time.h

Description Returns a pointer to a static tm structure with a specified local time in seconds from January 1, 1970 converted to Greenwich mean time (GMT). The tm structure, which is overwritten by each call to gmtime(), is declared in time.h.

Parameters **const time_t *timer** A pointer to a time_t value, such as that returned by the time function. Borland C++ defines time_t as equivalent to long.

See also asctime, ctime, ftime, localtime, stime, time, tzset

Example See dostounix.

gotoxy Position cursor

Syntax `void gotoxy(int x, int y);`

Include conio.h

Description Moves the text display cursor to a specified coordinate relative to the current window. Ignores invalid arguments.

Parameters **int x**, **int y** Window coordinate. The window's upper-left corner is identified by the coordinate (1,1).

See also wherex, wherey, window

Example
```
/* gotoxy.cpp */
#include <stdio.h>
#include <conio.h>
#include <dos.h>
#include <string.h>
#define NOWAIT 0   // No pause
#define WAIT 3000  // 3-second pause
void Center(int wait, int *y, const char *s);
main()
{
  int y = 8;
  clrscr();
  Center(WAIT, &y, "You can drive");
  Center(WAIT, &y, "a mile a minute");
```

```
    Center(WAIT, &y, "but there's no");
    Center(WAIT, &y, "future in it.");
    Center(NOWAIT, &y, "(From a sign on the PA turnpike)");
    gotoxy(1, 24);
    return 0;
}

void Center(int wait, int *y, const char *s)
{
    gotoxy(1, *y);
    clreol();
    gotoxy(40 - (strlen(s) / 2), *y);
    cprintf(s);
    *y += 2;
    delay(wait);
}
```

graphdefaults   Reset graphics

Syntax   `void far graphdefaults(void);`

Include   graphics.h

Description   After changing various graphics settings, call `graphdefaults()` to reset the graphics display to its startup state as initialized by `initgraph`. Restores the viewport to full screen and sets the current position to (0,0). Restores startup colors, drawing styles and patterns, and text font and directory. The example displays circles at random clipped to a small square space at the display's upper-left corner. Press the Spacebar to call `graphdefaults()` and reset the viewport to fullscreen.

See also   initgraph, setgraphmode

Example
```
/* graphdef.cpp */
#include <graphics.h>
#include <stdio.h>
#include <stdlib.h>
#include <conio.h>
#define FALSE 0
#define TRUE 1
#define BLANK ' '
#define ESC 27
```

```
main()
{
  int gdriver = DETECT, gmode, gerr;
  int done;
  char ch;
  initgraph(&gdriver, &gmode, "c:\\borlandc\\bgi");
  gerr = graphresult();
  if (gerr != grOk) {
    printf("BGI error: %s\n", grapherrormsg(gerr));
    exit(gerr);
  }
  setviewport(10, 10, 110, 110, TRUE);
  done = FALSE;
  while (!done) {
    setcolor(1 + random(getmaxcolor()));
    circle(random(getmaxx()), random(getmaxy()), random(25));
    if (kbhit()) {
      if ((ch = getch()) == BLANK)
        graphdefaults();
      else
        done = (ch == ESC);
    }
  }
  closegraph();
  return 0;
}
```

grapherrormsg   Graphics error message

Syntax
: `char *far grapherrormsg(int errorcode);`

Include
: graphics.h

Description
: Returns a pointer to a string description of the specified error code.

Parameters
: **int errocode** An error code such as that returned by `graphresult()`.

See also
: `initgraph`, `graphresult`

Example
:
```
/* grapherr.cpp */
#include <graphics.h>
#include <stdio.h>
#include <stdlib.h>
#include <conio.h>
```

```
void outstr(int *y, int h, const char *s);
main()
{
  int gdriver = DETECT, gmode, gerr;
  int h, e, y;
  char s[80];
  initgraph(&gdriver, &gmode, "c:\\borlandc\\bgi");
  gerr = graphresult();
  if (gerr != grOk) {
    printf("BGI error: %s\n", grapherrormsg(gerr));
    exit(gerr);
  }
  h = textheight("M") + 2;
  y = 0;
  outstr(&y, h, "Graphics error messages");
  y += h;
  for (e = 0; e >= -18; e--) {
    sprintf(s, "%03d : %s", e, grapherrormsg(e));
    outstr(&y, h, s);
  }
  getch();
  closegraph();
  return 0;
}

void outstr(int *y, int h, const char *s)
{
  outtextxy(1, *y, s);
  *y += h;
}
```

_graphfreemem   Free graphics memory

Syntax   `void far _graphfreemem(void far *ptr, unsigned size);`

Include   graphics.h

Description   Deletes memory allocated by _graphgetmem(). The default function calls free(). Override this default by defining your own function as listed in *Syntax*. The example installs _graphfreemem() and _graphgetmem() functions to show the startup and shutdown memory-management tasks executed by the graphics system.

1165

Parameters   **void far *ptr** Pointer to the memory block to be freed.

unsigned size Size of the member block in bytes.

See also   _graphgetmem, setgraphbufsize

Example
```
/* _graphfr.cpp */
#include <graphics.h>
#include <stdio.h>
#include <stdlib.h>
#include <conio.h>
#include <alloc.h>
int grflag;   // True after graphics initialized
main()
{
  int gdriver = DETECT, gmode, gerr;
  int h, y;
  initgraph(&gdriver, &gmode, "c:\\borlandc\\bgi");
  gerr = graphresult();
  if (gerr != grOk) {
    printf("BGI error: %s\n", grapherrormsg(gerr));
    exit(gerr);
  }
  grflag = 1;
  h = textheight("M") + 2;
  y = getmaxy() / 2;
  outtextxy(10, y, "In graphics mode");
  outtextxy(10, y + h, "Press any key to end...");
  getch();
  grflag = 0;
  closegraph();
  return 0;
}

void far * far _graphgetmem(unsigned size)
{
  char buffer[40];
  sprintf(buffer, "_graphgetmem() size==%u", size);
  if (grflag)
    outtextxy(0, 0, buffer);
  else
    puts(buffer);
  getch();
```

```
   return farmalloc(size);
}

void far _graphfreemem(void far *ptr, unsigned size)
{
  char buffer[40];
  sprintf(buffer, "_graphfreemem() size==%u", size);
  if (grflag)
    outtextxy(0, textheight("M") + 2, buffer);
  else
    puts(buffer);
  getch();
  farfree(ptr);
}
```

_graphgetmem   Allocate graphics memory

Syntax `void far *far _graphgetmem(unsigned size);`

Include graphics.h

Description Some graphics functions—`floodfill()`, for instance—call
`_graphgetmem()` to allocate temporary memory buffers. The default
function calls `malloc()` to obtain this memory from the heap. To
override the default allocator, implement your own `_graphgetmem()`
function as prototyped in *Syntax*. Graphics functions then call your
function when they need some memory. The function returns a
pointer to the allocated memory or null if the requested number of
bytes is not available. When redefining this function, you also should
provide a custom `_graphfreemem()` function to delete allocated
memory.

Parameters **unsigned size** Number of bytes requested.

See also `_graphfreemem`, `initgraph`, `setgraphbufsize`

Example See `_graphfreemem`.

graphresult   Graphics error code

Syntax `int far graphresult(void);`

Include graphics.h

Description   Call this function to check for errors after using one of the graphics functions listed under *See also.* Save `graphresult()`'s returned value in an int variable, because calling the function resets the graphics system's internal error code to grOK (that is, no error). The function result can be passed to `grapherrormsg()` to obtain a text description of an error condition.

See also   detectgraph, drawpoly, fillpoly, floodfill, grapherrormsg, initgraph, pieslice, registerbgidriver, registerbgifont, setallpalette, setcolor, setfillstyle, setgraphmode, setlinestyle, setpalette, settextjustify, settextstyle, setusercharsize, setviewport, setvisualpage

Example
```cpp
/* graphres.cpp */
#include <graphics.h>
#include <stdio.h>
#include <stdlib.h>
#include <conio.h>
main()
{
  int gdriver = DETECT, gmode, gerr;
  int fn;
  printf("Font number? ");
  scanf("%d", &fn);
  initgraph(&gdriver, &gmode, "c:\\borlandc\\bgi");
  gerr = graphresult();
  if (gerr != grOk) {
    printf("BGI error: %s\n", grapherrormsg(gerr));
    exit(gerr);
  }
  setcolor(LIGHTBLUE);
  settextstyle(fn, 0, 4);
  if (graphresult() == grOk)
    outtext("Font selected");
  else
    outtext("Error in settextstyle()");
  getch();
  closegraph();
  return 0;
}
```

harderr, _harderr   Hardware error handler

Syntax   ```
void harderr(int (*handler)());
void _harderr(int (far *handler)());
```

*Include*   dos.h

*Description*   Use one of these functions to attach a hardware error routine to a program. The error routine is called indirectly in response to DOS interrupt 0x24. The two functions have similar purposes but different forms. The hardware error function for harderr() is prototyped as

```
int handler(int errval, int ax, int bp, int si);
```

Parameter errval is the DOS error code (passed in register DI for interrupt 0x24). Parameters ax, bp, and si are copies of the AX, BP, and SI register values assigned by DOS. Parameter ax is negative for general device errors and nonnegative for disk errors, in which case (ax & 0x00ff) equals the offending drive number (0–A:, 1–B:, 2–C:, and so on). Parameters bp (segment) and si (offset) address the header of the software device driver for the device that reported the error to DOS. The handler function may elect to return 0 to ignore the error condition, 1 to have DOS retry the operation that caused the error, or 2 to have DOS abort the faulty operation. Or, the function may call hardresume() or hardretn() to exit. (See the descriptions for these two functions in this chapter.)

The error function for _harderr() is prototyped as

```
void far handler(unsigned deverr, unsigned errval,
  unsigned far *devhdr);
```

Parameter deverr equals the device error code passed by DOS in register AX for interrupt 0x24. If bit 15 of deverr equals 1, a general device error was reported; if bit 15 equals 0, a disk error has occurred and (deverr & 0x00ff) equals the offending drive number (0–A:, 1–B:, 2–C:, and so on). Parameter errval equals the DOS error code passed in register DI. Pointer parameter devhdr addresses the header of the software device driver for the device that reported the error condition to DOS. Unlike harderr(), _harderr() does not return a value and must instead exit by calling _hardretn or _hardresume.
```

Either handler may call DOS functions 0x01 through 0x0C (or any C or C++ functions that call *only* these DOS routines). Calls to any other DOS functions corrupt DOS and cause serious problems. Calling standard I/O or UNIX-equivalent I/O functions is never allowed in a hardware error handler.

The two examples attempt to open a file on drive A:. HARDERR.CPP demonstrates how to use harderr() and associated functions. _HARDERR.CPP demonstrates how to use the similar _harderr() and its kin. Run either example, remove any diskette from A:, and press a key to begin the test. To retry the file-open operation, answer *yes* to the prompt. Answer *no* to end the demonstration.

Parameters   **int (*handler)()** Pointer to a hardware error function as prototyped in *Description*. Calling harderr() sets up internal code that calls this function upon detecting a DOS interrupt 0x24.

int (far *handler)() Explicit far pointer to a hardware error function as prototyped in *Description*.

See also   getvect, hardresume, _hardresume, hardretn, _hardretn, setvect

Example (harderr)
```
/* harderr.cpp */
#include <stdio.h>
#include <dos.h>
#include <conio.h>
#define IGNORE 0
#define RETRY 1
#define ABORT 2
int errfn(int errval, int ax, int bp, int si);
main()
{
  FILE *f;
  harderr(errfn);
  puts("Remove any diskette from drive A:");
  printf("and press any key to continue...");
  getch();
  puts("\nOpening a file on drive A:");
  f = fopen("A:TEMP.$$$", "r");
  printf("\nfopen() return value == %p\n", f);
  return 0;
}
```

```
int errfn(int errval, int ax, int bp, int si)
{
  int drive;
  char ch;
  char s[80];
  if (ax < 0) {
    cputs("Device error");
    hardretn(ABORT);
  }
  drive = ax & 0x0ff;
  sprintf(s,
    "Error #%d on %c: (ax==%#x bp==%#x si==%#x). Try again?",
    errval, 'A' + drive, ax, bp, si);
  gotoxy(1, wherey());
  clreol();
  cputs(s);
  ch = getch();
  if (ch == 'y' || ch == 'Y')
    hardresume(RETRY);
  else
    hardresume(ABORT);
  return ABORT;
}
```

Example (_harderr)
```
/* _harderr.cpp */
#include <stdio.h>
#include <dos.h>
#include <conio.h>
void far errfn(unsigned deverr, unsigned errval,
  unsigned far *devhdr);
main()
{
  FILE *f;
  _harderr(errfn);
  puts("Remove any diskette from drive A:");
  printf("and press any key to continue...");
  getch();
  puts("\nOpening a file on drive A:");
  f = fopen("A:TEMP.$$$", "r");
  printf("\nfopen() return value == %p\n", f);
  return 0;
}
```

```
void far errfn(unsigned deverr, unsigned errval,
  unsigned far *devhdr)
{
  int drive;
  char ch;
  char s[80];
  if (deverr & 0x8000) {
    cputs("Device error");
    _hardretn(_HARDERR_ABORT);
  }
  drive = deverr & 0x0ff;
  sprintf(s,
    "Error #%d on %c: (deverr==%d header==%Fp). Try again?",
    errval, 'A' + drive, deverr, devhdr);
  gotoxy(1, wherey());
  clreol();
  cputs(s);
  ch = getch();
  if (ch == 'y' || ch == 'Y')
    _hardresume(_HARDERR_RETRY);
  else
    _hardresume(_HARDERR_ABORT);
}
```

hardresume, _hardresume Return to DOS

Syntax   `void hardresume(int axret);`
`void _hardresume(int rescode);`

Include   dos.h

Description   Function `hardresume()` may be called by a hardware error handler prepared by `harderr()`. Calling `hardresume()` exits the error handler and passes axret to DOS. The error handler may also elect to return a value, as described in the notes to function `harderr()`.

Function `_hardresume()` may be called by a hardware error handler prepared by `_hardresume()`. Calling `_hardresume()` exits the error handler and passes rescode to DOS. This type of error handler must exit by calling either `_hardresume()` or `_hardretn()` (also described in this chapter).

Parameters   **int axret** Set to 0 to have DOS ignore the condition that caused the error handler to be called. Set to 1 to have DOS retry the faulty operation. Set to 2 to have DOS abort the operation.

int rescode Set to _HARDERR_ABORT to abort the program by calling DOS's Ctrl+Break interrupt routine 0x23. Set to _HARDERR_IGNORE to have DOS ignore the error condition, to _HARDERR_RETRY to have DOS retry the operation, or to _HARDERR_FAIL to have DOS abort (fail) the operation but not the program.

See also   harderr, _harderr, hardretn, _hardretn

Example   See harderr and _harderr.

hardretn, _hardretn Return to application

Syntax   void hardretn(int retn);
             void _hardretn(int retn);

Include   dos.h

Description   Function hardretn() may be called by a hardware error handler prepared by harderr(). Calling hardretn() returns directly to the application I/O statement that caused the error to occur.

Function _hardretn() may be called by a hardware error handler prepared by _harderr(). Calling _hardretn() returns directly to the application I/O statement that caused the error to occur.

Parameters   **int retn** Specify the value to be returned by the I/O function that caused the hardware error handler to be called. For DOS functions less than 0x38, the retn value is returned in register AL to I/O functions that return a Boolean success-or-fail result. For DOS functions greater than or equal to 0x38, the retn value represents a DOS error code and is returned along with the carry flag set to indicate that an error has occurred.

See also   harderr, _harderr, hardresume, _hardresume

Example   See harderr and _harderr.

heapcheck   Check and verify heap

Syntax   `int heapcheck(void);`

Include   alloc.h

Description   Call `heapcheck()` to test the validity of allocated and freed memory blocks on the heap. Equivalent to `farheapcheck()` in large memory model programs. Returns _HEAPEMPTY (1) if there is no heap or _HEAPOK (2) if there is a heap and its memory blocks are verified to be error-free. Returns _HEAPCORRUPT (–1) if any errors are detected.

See also   `farheapcheck, heapcheckfree, heapchecknode, heapfillfree, heapwalk`

Example   See `heapwalk`.

heapcheckfree   Check heap free blocks

Syntax   `int heapcheckfree(unsigned int fillvalue);`

Include   alloc.h

Description   After calling `heapfillfree()` to fill all freed heap memory blocks to a specified value, call `heapcheckfree()` to verify the heap's stability. If `heapcheckfree()` returns _HEAPEMPTY (1), there is no heap. If the function returns _HEAPOK (2), then all freed blocks are verified. A return value of _HEAPCORRUPT (–1) indicates a serious error with the heap's structure. A value of _BADVALUE (–3) indicates that another value other than the specified fill value was found in a freed memory block.

Parameters   **unsigned int fillvalue** Value to be compared to values in freed memory blocks. Specify the same value as that passed to `heapfillfree()`.

See also   `farheapcheckfree, heapfillfree, heapwalk`

Example
```
/* heapchec.cpp */
#include <stdio.h>
#include <alloc.h>
void Report(const char *s, int result);
main()
{
  int result;
  void *p1 = malloc(1024);
  void *p2 = malloc(1024);
  void *p3 = malloc(1024);
```

```
                void *p4 = malloc(1024);
                void *p5 = malloc(1024);
                free(p2);
                free(p4);
                result = heapfillfree(0xffff);
                Report("After filling free blocks with 0xffff", result);
                result = heapcheckfree(0xffff);
                Report("After checking free blocks with 0xffff", result);
                result = heapcheckfree(0);
                Report("After checking free blocks with 0", result);
                free(p1);
                free(p3);
                free(p5);
                return 0;
            }

            void Report(const char *s, int result)
            {
              printf("%s: ", s);
              switch (result) {
                case _HEAPEMPTY:
                  puts("Heap empty");
                  break;
                case _HEAPOK:
                  puts("Heap is OK");
                  break;
                case _HEAPCORRUPT:
                  puts("Heap is corrupted");
                  break;
                case _BADVALUE:
                  puts("Bad value in heap");
                  break;
              }
            }
```

heapchecknode Check and verify heap node

Syntax   `int heapchecknode(void *node);`

Include   alloc.h

Description   Checks the validity of an allocated or freed memory block on the heap. Returns _HEAPEMPTY (1) if there is no heap, _HEAPCORRUPT (−1) if the heap is corrupted, _BADNODE (−2) if an error is detected in the target node or if that node has been deleted and combined with another deleted block, _FREEENTRY (3) if the block has been freed and no errors are detected, or _USEDENTRY (4) if the block is in use and no errors are detected. Note that in the case of a deleted node, a return value of _BADNODE does not necessarily indicate a corrupted heap, but rather that the memory manager has combined the deleted block with another adjacent block.

Parameters   **void *node** Pointer to the memory block to be tested.

See also   farheapchecknode

Example
```cpp
/* heapnode.cpp */
#include <stdio.h>
#include <alloc.h>
void Report(const char *s, int result);
main()
{
  int result;
  void *p1 = malloc(1024);
  void *p2 = malloc(1024);
  void *p3 = malloc(1024);
  result = heapchecknode(p2);
  Report("After malloc()", result);
  free(p2);
  result = heapchecknode(p2);
  Report("After free()", result);
  free(p1);
  free(p3);
  result = heapchecknode(p2);
  Report("After freeing all nodes", result);
  return 0;
}

void Report(const char *s, int result)
{
  printf("%s: ", s);
  switch (result) {
    case _HEAPEMPTY:
      puts("Heap empty");
```

```
          break;
        case _HEAPCORRUPT:
          puts("Heap is corrupted");
          break;
        case _BADNODE:
          puts("Can't find node");
          break;
        case _FREEENTRY:
          puts("Free node");
          break;
        case _USEDENTRY:
          puts("Used node");
          break;
      }
    }
```

heapfillfree   Fill free heap blocks

Syntax   `int heapfillfree(unsigned int fillvalue);`

Include   alloc.h

Description   Fills freed memory blocks (if there are any) with a specified word value. Usually followed by a call to `heapcheckfree()` to verify values stored in freed memory blocks. Also can be used during debugging to make freed blocks easy to find by searching for byte values in memory. Returns `_HEAPEMPTY` (1) if there is no heap, `_HEAPOK` (2) if no errors are detected, or `_HEAPCORRUPT` (−1) if the heap is corrupted.

Parameters   **unsigned int fillvalue** Value to be stored in all freed memory blocks.

See also   `farheapfillfree, heapcheckfree`

Example   See `heapcheckfree`.

heapwalk   Access heap nodes

Syntax   `int heapwalk(struct heapinfo *hi);`

Include   alloc.h

Description   Typically used in a loop to walk the heap by stepping through allocated and freed memory blocks in their linked-list order. Before calling `heapwalk()` for the first time, always call `heapcheck()` to verify that the heap is not corrupted. If heapcheck() does not return _HEAPOK, do *not* call heapwalk(). Returns _HEAPEMPTY (1) if there is no heap, _HEAPOK (2) if no errors are detected so far, or _HEAPEND (5) upon reaching the end of the heap. Fills in members of a heapinfo structure declared in alloc.h as

```
struct heapinfo
{
  void _FAR *ptr;        // Pointer to node or null
  unsigned int size;     // Size of node in bytes
  int in_use;            // True if allocated; false if freed
};
```

Parameters **struct heapinfo *hi** Pointer to a heapinfo structure as listed in *Description*. Set hi.ptr to 0 (null) before the initial call to heapwalk(); thereafter, pass the same unmodified structure to heapwalk() until all blocks are located.

See also farheapwalk, heapcheck

Example
```
/* heapwalk.cpp */
#include <stdio.h>
#include <alloc.h>
void Report(char *s);
long NearHeapSize(void);
main()
{
  void *p1;
  void *p2;
  Report("Before calling malloc()");
  p1 = malloc(1024);
  Report("After allocating 1024 bytes");
  p2 = malloc(1024);
  Report("After allocating another 1024 bytes");
  free(p1);
  Report("After freeing 1024 bytes");
  free(p2);
  Report("After freeing another 1024 bytes");
  return 0;
}

void Report(char *s)
{
```

```
      long result;
      puts(s);
      result = NearHeapSize();
      if (result < 0)
        puts("- No near heap or error!");
      else
        printf("- Near heap size = %lu\n", result);
    }

    // Walk heap and return free space available
    long NearHeapSize(void)
    {
      unsigned long count;
      struct heapinfo info;

      info.ptr = NULL;
      if (heapcheck() != _HEAPOK)
        return -1L;
      count = coreleft();
      while (heapwalk(&info) == _HEAPOK)
        if (info.in_use == 0)
          count += info.size;
      return count;
    }
```

highvideo Select high-intensity characters

Syntax void highvideo(void);

Include conio.h

Description Sets the current attribute's high-intensity bit to display text in bright, or high-intensity, mode. Affects only direct-video output routines prototyped in conio.h.

See also cprintf, cputs, gettextinfo, lowvideo, normvideo, textattr, textcolor

Example
```
/* highvide.cpp */
#include <stdio.h>
#include <conio.h>
main()
{
```

```
  clrscr();
  puts("Demonstrate highvideo() and lowvideo()");
  puts("-------------------------------------");
  for (int color = 0; color <= 15; color++) {
    highvideo();
    cprintf("Color==%2d", color);
    textcolor(color);
    cputs("  High video  ");
    lowvideo();
    cputs("Low video");
    gotoxy(1, wherey() + 1);  // Pseudo new line
  }
  return 0;
}
```

hypot, hypotl   Hypotenuse of right triangle

Syntax   `double hypot(double x, double y);`
           `long double hypotl(long double x, long double y);`

Include   math.h

Description   Calculates length z of the hypotenuse of a right triangle with sides of lengths x and y according to the formula $z^2 = x^2 + y^2$ for $z \geq 0$.

Parameters   **double x, double y** Lengths of two sides forming a right angle.

long double x, long double y Same as the preceding but for use with the `long double` function hypotl().

See also   cos, sin, tan

Example
```
/* hypot.cpp */
#include <stdio.h>
#include <stdlib.h>
#include <math.h>
main(int argc, char *argv[])
{
  if (argc <= 2) {
    puts("Enter HYPOT X Y. (ex. HYPOT 30 40)");
    exit(1);
  }
```

```
    double x = atol(argv[1]);
    double y = atol(argv[2]);
    double z = hypot(x, y);
    printf("Length of hypotenuse == %lf\n", z);
    return 0;
}
```

imag   Imaginary of complex number

Syntax   `double imag(complex x);`

Include   complex.h

Description Returns an imaginary part of a complex number composed of real and imaginary components. The `complex` class is declared in complex.h.

Parameters **complex x** An instance of the `complex` class.

See also   `cabs, complex, conj, real`

Example
```
/* imag.cpp */
#include <iostream.h>
#include <complex.h>
main()
{
  complex q(4.5, 5.2);
  cout << "complex q == " << q << '\n';
  cout << "real(q)   == " << real(q) << '\n';
  cout << "imag(q)   == " << imag(q) << '\n';
  return 0;
}
```

imagesize   Bitmap size

Syntax   `unsigned far imagesize(int left, int top, int right, int bottom);`

Include   graphics.h

Description Returns the number of bytes required to save a copy of the graphics display outlined by the specified arguments. Images that require more than one 64K segment of storage cause `imagesize()` to return –1. The example uses `imagesize()` along with `getimage()` and `putimage()` to take a block of randomly displayed pixels on a "roller coaster" ride.

Parameters **int left**, **int top** Coordinate of the image's upper-left corner.

int right, **int bottom** Coordinate of the image's lower-right corner.

See also getimage, putimage

Example
```cpp
/* imagesiz.cpp */
#include <graphics.h>
#include <stdio.h>
#include <stdlib.h>
#include <time.h>
#include <conio.h>
#include <math.h>
#include <alloc.h>
#define X1 100
#define Y1 100
#define X2 227
#define Y2 163
double radians(unsigned angle);
main()
{
  int gdriver = DETECT, gmode, gerr;
  int xmax, ymax, cmax, x, y, i;
  void *image;
  initgraph(&gdriver, &gmode, "c:\\borlandc\\bgi");
  gerr = graphresult();
  if (gerr != grOk) {
    printf("BGI error: %s\n", grapherrormsg(gerr));
    exit(gerr);
  }
  xmax = getmaxx();
  ymax = getmaxy();
  cmax = getmaxcolor();
  randomize();
  for (i = 1; i <= 30000; i++)
    putpixel(random(xmax), random(ymax), random(cmax));
  image = malloc(imagesize(X1, Y1, X2, Y2));  // Reserve memory
  if (image) {
    getimage(X1, Y1, X2, Y2, image);  // Copy display image
    clearviewport();
    y = 0;
    for (x = 0; x <= xmax - (X2 - X1); x++, y++)
```

```
        putimage(x, 100 + floor(sin(radians(y)) * 50.0),
            image, COPY_PUT);
    }
    getch();
    closegraph();
    return 0;
}

double radians(unsigned angle)
{
    return abs(angle % 360) * M_PI / 180.0;
}
```

initgraph   Initialize graphics

Syntax   `void far initgraph(int far *graphdriver,`
        `int far *graphmode, char far *pathtodriver);`

Include   graphics.h

Description   Initializes the Borland Graphics Interface (BGI) software and prepares the video interface for displaying graphics. Loads a BGI graphics driver into memory according to one of the following constants:

Graphics driver constants for the `initgraph()` function.

Constant	Value
DETECT	0 (Request automatic graphics detection)
CGA	1
MCGA	2
EGA	3
EGA64	4
EGAMONO	5
IBM8514	6
HERCMONO	7

continues

Constant	Value
ATT400	8
VGA	9
PC3270	10

After calling initgraph(), use graphresult() to determine whether graphics have been properly initialized. See Chapter 16, "The Borland Graphics Interface," for more information on using initgraph() and BGI graphics.

Parameters   **int far *graphdriver** Pointer to an int variable, normally initialized to DETECT prior to calling initgraph() in order to select the best possible graphics mode for the system. The function assigns one of the driver constants from the table in *Description* to this variable. You also can request an explicit graphics mode by initializing graphdriver to a driver constant, but then you are responsible for ensuring that the system is capable of supporting the requested display mode.

int far *graphmode Pointer to an int variable, normally filled in by initgraph() to the highest-quality resolution supported by the automatically selected or explicitly specified driver. Can also be set to an explicit driver mode constant.

char far *pathtodriver Pointer to the directory path where BGI drivers are stored. Drivers might also be in the current directory, in which case pathtodriver should be set to null.

See also   closegraph, detectgraph, getdrivername, getgraphmode, getmoderange, graphdefaults, graphresult, installuserdriver, registerbgidriver, registerbgifont, setgraphmode

Example   See arc, imagesize, and other BGI graphics examples.

inp   Input byte from hardware port

Syntax   int inp(unsigned portid);

Include   conio.h

Description   Reads and returns a byte value from the specified hardware port. If conio.h is included, inp() is defined as a macro unless the symbol inp is undefined with #undef, in which case inp() is encoded as a function.

Parameters   **unsigned portid** Hardware port number.

See also   inport, inportb, inpw, outp, outport, outportb, outpw

Example
```
/* inp.cpp */
#include <stdio.h>
#include <conio.h>
main()
{
  int printstatus;
  unsigned port = 0x03bd;
  printstatus = inp(port);
  cprintf("Printer status = %d", printstatus);
  return 0;
}
```

inport   Input word from hardware port

Syntax   unsigned inport(unsigned portid);

Include   dos.h

Description   Reads and returns a word value from the specified hardware port.

Parameters   **unsigned portid** Hardware port number.

See also   inp, inportb, inpw, outp, outport, outportb, outpw

Example
```
/* inport.cpp */
#include <stdio.h>
#include <dos.h>
main()
{
  unsigned portzero;
  unsigned port = 0;
  portzero = inport(port);
  printf("Port zero = %u", portzero);
  return 0;
}
```

inportb   Input byte from hardware port

Syntax   `unsigned char inportb(unsigned portid);`

Include   dos.h

Description   Similar to `inp()` but prototyped in the dos.h header. Reads and returns a byte value from the specified hardware port. If dos.h is included, `inportb()` is defined as a macro unless the symbol `inportb` is undefined with `#undef`, in which case `inportb()` is encoded as a function.

Parameters   **unsigned portid** Hardware port number.

See also   inp, inport, inpw, outp, outport, outportb, outpw

Example
```
/* inportb.cpp */
#include <stdio.h>
#include <dos.h>
main()
{
  unsigned char printstatus;
  unsigned port = 0x03bd;
  printstatus = inportb(port);
  printf("Printer status = %u", printstatus);
  return 0;
}
```

inpw   Input word from hardware port

Syntax   `unsigned inpw(unsigned portid);`

Include   conio.h

Description   Reads and returns a word value from the specified hardware port. If conio.h is included, `inpw()` is defined as a macro unless the symbol `inpw` is undefined with `#undef`, in which case `inpw()` is encoded as a function.

Parameters   **unsigned portid** Hardware port number.

See also   inp, inport, inportb, outp, outport, outportb, outpw

Example
```
/* inpw.cpp */
#include <stdio.h>
#include <conio.h>
main()
{
```

```
    unsigned portzero;
    unsigned port = 0;
    portzero = inpw(port);
    cprintf("Port zero = %d", portzero);
    return 0;
}
```

insline   Insert blank line

Syntax   `void insline(void);`

Include   conio.h

Description   Inserts a blank line in the text display window at the current cursor row. The blank line's attribute is displayed in the current background color. Shifts any lines below down one row.

See also   `clreol, delline, gotoxy, window`

Example
```
/* insline.cpp */
#include <stdio.h>
#include <conio.h>
#include <dos.h>
main()
{
  int y;
  clrscr();
  for (y = 1; y <= 25; y++) {
    gotoxy(1, y);
    cputs("Row row row your boat, gently down the stream");
  }
  gotoxy(1, 8);
  highvideo();
  cputs("Inserting blank lines");
  clreol();
  delay(1000);
  for (y = 8; y <= 18; y++) {
    gotoxy(1, y);
    delay(500);
    insline();
  }
  gotoxy(1, 25);
  return 0;
}
```

installuserdriver   Install graphics driver

Syntax   int far installuserdriver(char far *name,
            int huge (*detect)(void));

Include   graphics.h

Description   Installs a third-party BGI-compatible graphics driver for use by initgraph and other BGI graphics functions. Returns a value that can be passed to initgraph()'s graphdriver parameter.

Parameters   **char far *name** Pointer to the driver's filename.

int huge (*detect)(void) Pointer to an optional automatic mode detection function or null if no such function exists. If non-null, this pointer must address an int function with no parameters. The function should return grError (−11) to report any errors or a positive graphics mode number for success, in which case initgraph attempts to initialize the specified hardware display mode.

See also   initgraph, graphresult, registerbgidriver, registerbgifont

Example
```
/* insuserd.cpp */
#include <graphics.h>
#include <stdio.h>
#include <stdlib.h>
#include <conio.h>
int huge detect3DG(void);
main()
{
  int udriver, gdriver, gmode, gerr;
  udriver = installuserdriver("3DG.BGI", detect3DG);
  if (udriver != grOk) {
    puts("Unable to install 3DG.BGI driver");
    exit(1);
  }
/* -- Method #1 (pass udriver to initgraph()): */
/* gdriver = udriver; */
/* --z Method #2 (let initgraph() auto-detect driver): */
  gdriver = DETECT;
// Next statement calls detect3DG!
  initgraph(&gdriver, &gmode, "c:\\borlandc\\bgi");
  gerr = graphresult();
  if (gerr != grOk) {
```

```
        printf("BGI error: %s\n", grapherrormsg(gerr));
    exit(gerr);
    }
// Insert graphics code here
    closegraph();
    return 0;
}

#define DRIVERFOUND 0  // Always false for demo only
#define DEFAULTMODE 3  // Default display mode

// The following is for demonstration purposes only. In a real
// setting, the function would attempt to detect a video
// hardware mode and return a mode value or grError. In this
// demonstration, the function always returns an error, and
// the compiler generates warnings about "unreachable" code
// because the if statement is always false.

int huge detect3DG(void)
{
    if (DRIVERFOUND)        // Ignore compiler warning: demo only
        return DEFAULTMODE; // Tell initgraph() mode to use
    else
        return grError;     // Signal error to initgraph()
}
```

installuserfont   Install graphics font

Syntax   int far installuserfont(char far *name);

Include   graphics.h

Description Installs a user-supplied font file ending in .CHR. If successful, the
              function returns a value that can be passed to settextstyle() to select
              the font. If not successful, the function returns grError.

Parameters **char far *name** Pointer to the BGI font's filename.

See also   installuserdriver, settextstyle

Example   /* insuserf.cpp */
              #include <graphics.h>

```
#include <stdio.h>
#include <stdlib.h>
#include <conio.h>
main()
{
  int ufont, gdriver = DETECT, gmode, gerr;
  int x, y, size;
  char s[40];
  initgraph(&gdriver, &gmode, "c:\\borlandc\\bgi");
  gerr = graphresult();
  if (gerr != grOk) {
    printf("BGI error: %s\n", grapherrormsg(gerr));
    exit(gerr);
  }
  ufont = installuserfont("SIMP.CHR");
  if (ufont <= 0)
    ufont = SANS_SERIF_FONT;
  x = 0;
  y = 0;
  for (size = 1; size <= 7; size++) {
    settextstyle(ufont, HORIZ_DIR, size);
    y = 4 + y + textheight("M");
    sprintf(s, "Testing font size %d", size);
    outtextxy(x, y, s);
  }
  getch();
  closegraph();
  return 0;
}
```

int86   Software interrupt

Syntax   `int int86(int intno, union REGS *inregs, union REGS *outregs);`

Include   dos.h

Description Executes a software interrupt. Returns the value of the AX register after the interrupt returns. If the processor's carry flag is set, int86 assigns an error code to the global _doserrno variable.

Parameters **int intno** Software interrupt number.

union REGS *inregs Pointer to REGS structure. Assign values to this structure's members, which int86() copies to the real processor registers before executing the software interrupt.

union REGS *outregs After the interrupt returns, int86() copies the real processor registers into the REGS structure addressed by outregs. For many software interrupts, a nonzero cflag member in outregs indicates an error. The inregs and outregs pointers can address the same REGS structure.

See also bdos, bdosptr, geninterrupt, getvect, int86x, intdos, intdosx, intr, setvect

Example
```
/* int86.cpp */
#include <dos.h>
char dosstring[] = "A dollar-sign terminated string$";
main()
{
  union REGS registers;
  registers.h.ah = 9;
  registers.x.dx = FP_OFF(dosstring);
  int86(0x21, &registers, &registers);
  return 0;
}
```

int86x   Extended software interrupt

Syntax `int int86x(int intno, union REGS *inregs, union REGS *outregs, struct SREGS *segregs);`

Include dos.h

Description Similar to int86(), but includes a third parameter, segregs, which addresses a structure that specifies segment register values to be copied to the DS and ES registers before executing the software interrupt. See int86() for descriptions of the first three parameters. Returns AX.

Parameters **struct SREGS *segregs** Pointer to SREGS structure with members ds and es set to segment values to be copied into the real processor registers DS and ES before the software interrupt is executed. After the software interrupt returns, int86x() sets the segregs members ds and es to the DS and ES register values, and restores the original DS register value. It does not restore ES.

See also   bdos, bdosptr, geninterrupt, getvect, intdos, intdosx, int86, intr, segread, setvect

Example
```cpp
/* int86x.cpp */
#include <dos.h>
char dosstring[] = "A dollar-sign terminated string$";
main()
{
  union REGS registers;
  struct SREGS segments;
  registers.h.ah = 9;
  registers.x.dx = FP_OFF(dosstring);
  segments.ds = FP_SEG(dosstring);
  int86x(0x21, &registers, &registers, &segments);
  return 0;
}
```

intdos   DOS interrupt

Syntax   `int intdos(union REGS *inregs, union REGS *outregs);`

Include   dos.h

Description   Calls a DOS function by executing software interrupt 0x21. Returns the value of the processor's AX register after the DOS function returns.

Parameters   **union REGS *inregs** Pointer to REGS structure. Assign the DOS function number to inregs->h.ah plus any other required register values to this structure's members, which intdos() copies to the real processor registers before calling DOS.

union REGS *outregs After the DOS function returns, intdos() copies the real processor registers into the REGS structure addressed by outregs. For many functions, a nonzero cflag member in outregs indicates an error. The inregs and outregs pointers can address the same REGS structure.

See also   bdos, bdosptr, geninterrupt, int86, int86x, intdosx, intr

Example
```cpp
/* intdos.cpp */
#include <dos.h>
char dosstring[] = "A dollar-sign terminated string$";
main()
```

```
{
  union REGS registers;
  registers.h.ah = 9;
  registers.x.dx = FP_OFF(dosstring);
  intdos(&registers, &registers);
  return 0;
}
```

intdosx   Extended DOS interrupt

Syntax   `int intdosx(union REGS *inregs, union REGS *outregs,`
            `    struct SREGS *segregs);`

Include   dos.h

Description   Similar to intdos(), but includes a third parameter, segregs, which
addresses a structure that specifies segment register values to be copied
to the DS and ES registers before calling DOS. See intdos() for
descriptions of the first two parameters. Returns AX.

Parameters   **struct SREGS *segregs** Pointer to SREGS structure with members ds and
es set to segment values to be copied into the real processor registers DS
and ES before the DOS function is called. After DOS returns, intdosx()
sets the segregs members ds and es to the DS and ES register values and
restores the original DS register value. It does not restore ES.

See also   bdos, bdosptr, geninterrupt, int86, int86x, intdos, intr, segread

Example
```
/* intdosx.cpp */
#include <dos.h>
char dosstring[] = "A dollar-sign terminated string$";
main()
{
  union REGS registers;
  struct SREGS segments;
  registers.h.ah = 9;
  registers.x.dx = FP_OFF(dosstring);
  segments.ds = FP_SEG(dosstring);
  intdosx(&registers, &registers, &segments);
  return 0;
}
```

intr   Software interrupt

Syntax   `void intr(int intno, struct REGPACK *preg);`

Include   dos.h

Description   Similar to `int86()` and `int86x()`. Executes a software interrupt.

Parameters   **int intno** Software interrupt number.

struct REGPACK *preg Pointer to a `REGPACK` structure containing pseudo register values to be copied to the real processor registers before the software interrupt is executed. After the interrupt returns, `intr()` copies the real processor registers back to this structure, which you can examine for any values returned by the interrupt service routine.

See also   geninterrupt, getvect, int86, int86x, intdos, intdosx, setvect

Example
```cpp
/* intr.cpp */
#include <dos.h>
char dosstring[] = "A dollar-sign terminated string$";
main()
{
  struct REGPACK registers;
  registers.r_ax = 9 << 8;   // Shift 9 into pseudo AH register
  registers.r_dx = FP_OFF(dosstring);
  registers.r_ds = FP_SEG(dosstring);
  intr(0x21, &registers);
  return 0;
}
```

ioctl   I/O control

Syntax   `int ioctl(int handle, int func [, void *argdx, int argcx]);`

Include   io.h

Description   Executes DOS function 0x44 to communicate directly with a device driver. Results vary on different systems, and the DOS function differs significantly from the UNIX `ioctl()` function. The function's return value depends on the driver function. A return value of −1 indicates an error and sets the global `errno` variable to `EINVAL` (invalid argument), `EBADF` (bad file number), or `EINVDAT` (invalid data).

Parameters   **int handle** Handle to a file such as that returned by open(). Can be used only with func parameter values 0, 6, and 7.

int func Device driver function selector. 0–get info, 1–set info, 2–read bytes, 3–write bytes, 4–read bytes with handle equal to drive (0–default, 1–A:, 2–B:, and so on), 5–write bytes with handle equal to drive as for function 4, 6–get input status, 7–get output status, 8–test for removable media (DOS 3.0), 11–set sharing conflict retry count (DOS 3.0). See a DOS reference for more information about DOS function 0x44 and specific function values.

void *argdx Pointer to an optional argument to be addressed by registers DS:DX before calling DOS.

int argcx Optional value to be copied to register CX before calling DOS.

See also   intdos, intdosx, open

Example
```cpp
/* ioctl.cpp */
#include <stdio.h>
#include <stdlib.h>
#include <io.h>
#include <ctype.h>
main(int argc, char *argv[])
{
  if (argc <= 1) {
    puts("Enter IOCTL x: to test whether");
    puts("drive x: is removable.");
    exit(1);
  }
  char driveletter = toupper(argv[1][0]);
  int drive = 1 + (driveletter - 'A');
  int isfixed = ioctl(drive, 8, 0, 0);
  printf("Drive %c: is ", driveletter);
  if (isfixed)
    puts("fixed");
  else
    puts("removable");
  return 0;
}
```

is... Character classification macros

Syntax
```
int isalnum(int c);
int isalpha(int c);
int isascii(int c);
int iscntrl(int c);
int isdigit(int c);
int isgraph(int c);
int islower(int c);
int isprint(int c);
int ispunct(int c);
int isspace(int c);
int isupper(int c);
int isxdigit(int c);
```

Include ctype.h

Description These macros return nonzero (true) if character c is a member of a specified set of characters. The macros return zero (false) if the character is not a member of the specified set. The macros are table-driven and very fast. You can undefine one or more function names using #undef to encode them as nonmacro functions. The following table explains the purpose of each macro.

Character classification macros.

Function	Character c is...
isalnum	Alphanumeric (a digit or an uppercase or lowercase letter)
isalpha	Alphabetic (an uppercase or lowercase letter)
isascii	ASCII ($0 \leq c \leq 0x7e$)
iscntrl	ASCII control code (0x7f or 0x00 to 0x1f)
isdigit	A digit from '0' to '9'
isgraph	Printable but nonspace ($0x21 \leq c \leq 0x7e$)
islower	A lowercase letter from 'a' to 'z'
isprint	Printable or space ($0x20 \leq c \leq 0x7e$)
ispunct	A punctuation symbol

Function	Character c is...
isspace	A "whitespace" character: space, tab, carriage return, new line, vertical tab, or form feed
isupper	An uppercase letter from 'A' to 'Z'
isxdigit	A hexadecimal digit '0' to '9', 'A' to 'F', or 'a' to 'f'

Parameters   **int c** The test character.

See also   toascii, tolower, toupper

Example

```cpp
/* is.cpp */
#include <stdio.h>
#include <stdlib.h>
#include <ctype.h>
main(int argc, char *argv[])
{
  if (argc <= 1) {
    puts("Enter IS x to determine the");
    puts("nature of character x.");
    exit(1);
  }
  char c = argv[1][0];
  printf("Character %c is:\n", c);
  if (isalpha(c) ) puts("alphabetical");
  if (isascii(c) ) puts("ASCII");
  if (iscntrl(c) ) puts("a control");
  if (isdigit(c) ) puts("a digit");
  if (isgraph(c) ) puts("printable nonspace");
  if (islower(c) ) puts("lowercase");
  if (isprint(c) ) puts("printable including space");
  if (ispunct(c) ) puts("a punctuation mark");
  if (isspace(c) ) puts("a space");
  if (isupper(c) ) puts("uppercase");
  if (isxdigit(c)) puts("a hex digit");
  return 0;
}
```

isatty   Check for device type

Syntax   `int isatty(int handle);`

Include   io.h

Description   Returns nonzero if the hardware device associated with a file handle is a terminal, a console, a printer, or a serial port. Returns zero if the device is none of these types.

Parameters   `int handle` File handle such as that returned by `open()`, or a standard file handle such as `stdout`.

See also   `fileno, open`

Example
```
/* isatty.cpp */
#include <stdio.h>
#include <io.h>
main()
{
  int handle = fileno(stdout);
  printf("Standard output (stdout) is ");
  if (!isatty(handle))
    puts("not");
  puts("\na terminal, console, printer, or serial device");
  return 0;
}
```

itoa   Convert integer to string

Syntax   `char *itoa(int value, char *string, int radix);`

Include   stdlib.h

Description   Converts an `int` value to a null-terminated string. Returns a pointer to the resulting string.

Parameters   `int value` The value to be converted. If `value` is negative, a minus sign precedes the result only if `radix` equals 10.

`char *string` A pointer to a `char` buffer large enough to hold the result. Depending on the `radix` value, `itoa()` can return up to 17 bytes.

`int radix` The number base to use for the conversion, from 2 to 36.

See also   `atoi, atol, ltoa, ultoa`

Example
```
/* itoa.cpp */
#include <stdio.h>
#include <stdlib.h>
main()
{
  char result[17];
  int value = 23677;
  itoa(value, result, 10);
  printf("value in decimal == %s\n", result);
  itoa(value, result, 16);
  printf("value in hex     == %s\n", result);
  itoa(value, result, 2);
  printf("value in binary  == %s\n", result);
  return 0;
}
```

kbhit Check for keystroke

Syntax `int kbhit(void);`

Include conio.h

Description Returns true (nonzero) if a character is waiting in the system's keyboard type-ahead buffer. Typically followed by a call to getch() or getche() to read the waiting character. Returns false (zero) if no character is waiting to be read.

See also `getch, getche`

Example
```
/* kbhit.cpp */
#include <stdio.h>
#include <conio.h>
#include <ctype.h>
main()
{
  printf("Press a key to continue...");
  while (!kbhit()) /* wait */ ;
  char c = getch();
  puts("");
  if (isprint(c))
    printf("You entered character %c\n", c);
  else
```

```
        puts("You entered a nonprintable character");
      return 0;
    }
```

keep Terminate and stay resident

Syntax `void keep(unsigned char status, unsigned size);`

Include dos.h

Description Terminates the current program and tells DOS to make that program resident. The TSR (terminate and stay resident) program runs in the background, usually by trapping keyboard or other interrupts, and performs actions that modify the computer's operation while DOS and other programs run. Because DOS is a single-tasking operating system, however, a TSR is not an independent task but rather an extension of DOS, and great care is needed to avoid conflicts between the TSR, DOS, and other programs.

The function calls DOS function 0x31, as does the similar function `_dos_keep()`. Functions `keep` and `_dos_keep()` restore modified interrupt vectors before calling DOS function 0x31. Function `_dos_keep()` also executes any registered exit functions and flushes open file buffers. Function `keep()` does not perform these additional tasks.

Parameters **unsigned char status** Exit code passed to DOS in register AL.

unsigned size Program size in 16-byte paragraphs passed to DOS in register DX.

See also `abort, atexit, exit, flushall`

labs Long absolute value

Syntax `long int labs(long int x);`

Include math.h

Description Returns the absolute (nonnegative) value of a long integer.

Parameters **long int x** The candidate value. If x is negative, `labs()` returns x's positive equivalent. If x is positive, `labs()` returns x unchanged.

See also `abs, cabs, fabs`

Example
```
/* labs.cpp */
#include <stdio.h>
#include <math.h>
main()
{
  long value = -4321;
  printf("Original long value == %ld\n", value);
  value = labs(value);
  printf("Absolute value      == %ld\n", value);
  return 0;
}
```

ldexp   Long double exponent

Syntax
```
double ldexp(double x, int exp);
long double ldexpl(long double x, int exp);
```

Include   math.h

Description   Returns x * 2exp.

Parameters   **double x, long double x** The double (ldexp()) or long double (ldexpl) value to multiply by a power of 2.

int exp The power by which to raise 2 before multiplying by x.

See also   exp, frexp, modf, pow, pow10

Example
```
/* ldexp.cpp */
#include <stdio.h>
#include <stdlib.h>
#include <math.h>
main(int argc, char *argv[])
{
  double v, result;
  int exp;
  if (argc <= 2) {
    puts("Enter LDEXP x exp to compute x * 2^^exp");
    exit(1);
  }
  v = atof(argv[1]);
  exp = atoi(argv[2]);
  result = ldexp(v, exp);
```

```
    printf("%lf * 2^^%d == %lf\n", v, exp, result);
    return 0;
}
```

ldiv   Divide two longs

Syntax   `ldiv_t ldiv(long int numer, long int denom);`

Include   stdlib.h

Description Divides two `long` values and returns the result as a structure declared in
              stdlib.h as

```
typedef struct {
   long quot;        // Quotient
   long rem;         // Remainder
} ldiv_t;
```

Parameters **long int numer** Numerator (value to be divided by denom)

              long int denom Denominator (value by which numer is divided)

See also   div

Example
```
/* ldiv.cpp */
#include <stdio.h>
#include <stdlib.h>
main()
{
  long l1 = 4321;
  long l2 = 1234;
  ldiv_t result;
  result = ldiv(l1, l2);
  printf("%ld / %ld == %ld and a remainder of %ld\n",
    l1, l2, result.quot, result.rem);
  return 0;
}
```

lfind   Linear search

Syntax   `void *lfind(const void *key, const void *base, size_t *num,`
              `size_t width, int (*fcmp)(const void *, const void *));`

Include   stdlib.h

Description   Searches a table of records using a comparison routine that you must supply. The table does not have to be sorted. Returns the address of the first matching record or null if the search key isn't found.

Parameters   `const void *key` Pointer to the search key.

`const void *base` Pointer to the beginning of the table or another location where the search is to begin.

`size_t *num` Pointer to a value of type `size_t` equal to the number of records in the table to be searched.

`size_t width` The size in bytes of one record in the table. All records in the table must be of the same size.

`int (*fcmp)(const void *, const void *)` Pointer to a comparison function, which should return zero if the elements addressed by the two void pointer parameters are equal, or nonzero if the two elements are unequal. The comparison function needs to examine records only for equality.

See also   bsearch, lsearch, qsort

Example
```
/* lfind.cpp */
#include <stdio.h>
#include <stdlib.h>
#include <string.h>
#define NUMELEMS 4
typedef char *Pchar;
typedef char **PPchar;
char *cp[NUMELEMS] = {
   "California",
   "Pennsylvania",
   "Arizona",
   "Florida"
};
int compare(Pchar a, PPchar b);
main()
{
   size_t numelems = NUMELEMS;
   Pchar searchkey = "Arizona";
   PPchar result;
   result = (PPchar)lfind(searchkey, cp, &numelems,
      sizeof(void *), (int(*)(const void*, const void*))compare);
```

```
  if (result)
    printf("Result == %s\n", *result);
  else
    printf("%s not found\n", searchkey);
  return 0;
}

int compare(Pchar key, PPchar b)
{
  return stricmp(key, *b);
}
```

line   Draw line

Syntax   `void far line(int x1, int y1, int x2, int y2);`

Include   graphics.h

Description   Draws a line with end points at (x1, y1) and (x2, y2) in the current drawing color, style, and thickness. Does not update the current position.

Parameters   **int x1, y1** Starting coordinate.

int x2, y2 Ending coordinate.

See also   getlinesettings, linerel, lineto, setcolor, setlinestyle, setwritemode

Example
```
/* line.cpp */
#include <graphics.h>
#include <stdio.h>
#include <stdlib.h>
#include <conio.h>
#include <dos.h>
main()
{
  int gdriver = DETECT, gmode, gerr;
  int cmax, xmin, ymin, xmax, ymax;
  initgraph(&gdriver, &gmode, "c:\\borlandc\\bgi");
  gerr = graphresult();
  if (gerr != grOk) {
    printf("BGI error: %s\n", grapherrormsg(gerr));
    exit(gerr);
  }
```

```
      cmax = getmaxcolor();
      xmax = getmaxx();
      ymax = getmaxy();
      xmin = 0;
      ymin = 0;
      while ((xmin < xmax) ¦¦ (ymin < ymax)) {
        delay(25);
        setcolor(random(cmax));
        line(xmin, ymin, xmax, ymin);
        line(xmin, ymax, xmax, ymax);
        xmin++;
        ymin++;
        xmax--;
        ymax--;
      }
      getch();
      closegraph();
      return 0;
    }
```

linerel   Draw relative line

Syntax   `void far linerel(int dx, int dy);`

Include   graphics.h

Description   Draws a line to a location relatively distant from the current position `(x, y)` in the current color, style, and thickness. One end point of the resulting line is at `(x, y)`; the other end point is at `(x + dx, y + dy)`.

Parameters   `int dx` Relative horizontal distance from current position.

`int dy` Relative vertical distance from current position.

See also   `line, lineto, setcolor, setlinestyle, setwritemode`

Example
```
/* linerel.cpp */
#include <graphics.h>
#include <stdio.h>
#include <stdlib.h>
#include <time.h>
#include <conio.h>
main()
```

```
{
  int gdriver = DETECT, gmode, gerr;
  int cmax, xmax, ymax, color;
  initgraph(&gdriver, &gmode, "c:\\borlandc\\bgi");
  gerr = graphresult();
  if (gerr != grOk) {
    printf("BGI error: %s\n", grapherrormsg(gerr));
    exit(gerr);
  }
  cmax = getmaxcolor();
  xmax = getmaxx();
  ymax = getmaxy();
  randomize();
  while (!kbhit()) {
    moveto(0, 0);
    color = 1 + random(cmax);
    while (xmax > 1) {
      setcolor(random(color));
      linerel(xmax, 0);
      linerel(0, ymax);
      linerel(-xmax, 0);
      linerel(0, -ymax);
      xmax -= 2;
      ymax -= 2;
      moveto(getx() + 1, gety() + 1);
    }
  }
  getch();
  closegraph();
  return 0;
}
```

lineto Draw connected line

Syntax `void far lineto(int x, int y);`

Include graphics.h

Description Draws a line from the current position to a new location at (x, y) in the current color, style, and thickness. Sets the current position to (x, y).

Parameters `int x, int y` Line end coordinate.

See also `line, linerel, moveto, setcolor, setlinestyle, setwritemode`

Example
```
/* lineto.cpp */
#include <graphics.h>
#include <stdio.h>
#include <stdlib.h>
#include <conio.h>
#include <dos.h>
#define MAXLINES 125
#define TIMEDELAY 50
void lines(int n);
int cmax, xmax, ymax;
main()
{
  int gdriver = DETECT, gmode, gerr;
  initgraph(&gdriver, &gmode, "c:\\borlandc\\bgi");
  gerr = graphresult();
  if (gerr != grOk) {
    printf("BGI error: %s\n", grapherrormsg(gerr));
    exit(gerr);
  }
  cmax = getmaxcolor();
  xmax = getmaxx();
  ymax = getmaxy();
  while (!kbhit())
    lines(1);
  getch();
  closegraph();
  return 0;
}

void lines(int n)
{
  int x1, y1, x2, y2;

  if (kbhit())
    return;
  delay(TIMEDELAY);
  if (n < MAXLINES) {
    x1 = getx();
    y1 = gety();
    setcolor(1 + random(cmax));
    x2 = random(xmax);
    y2 = random(ymax);
```

```
      lineto(x2, y2);
      lines(n + 1);    // Call self recursively
   }
   delay(TIMEDELAY);
   setcolor(BLACK);
   line(x1, y1, x2, y2);
}
```

localeconv   Current locale

Syntax   `struct lconv *localeconv(void);`

Include   locale.h

Description   Returns a pointer to a locale structure of type `lconv` as declared in locale.h. Members of this structure describe "country-specific" information such as the decimal point character to use in floating-point numbers, the currency symbol, and other regional facts.

See also   `setlocale`

Example
```
/* localeco.cpp */
#include <stdio.h>
#include <locale.h>
main()
{
   lconv *lp;
   double balance = 4567.98;
   setlocale(LC_ALL, "C");
   lp = localeconv();
   printf("Balance == %s%lf\n", lp->int_curr_symbol, balance);
   return 0;
}
```

localtime   Convert date and time to structure

Syntax   `struct tm *localtime(const time_t *timer);`

Include   time.h

Description   Converts a time value to a static structure of type `tm` declared in time.h as

```
struct tm
{
  int tm_sec;     // Seconds
  int tm_min;     // Minutes
  int tm_hour;    // Hour
  int tm_mday;    // Day of month
  int tm_mon;     // Month (1==January)
  int tm_year;    // Year
  int tm_wday;    // Day of week (0==Sunday)
  int tm_yday;    // Day of year (0==January 1)
  int tm_isdst;   // True if daylight savings in effect
};
```

Parameters   `const time_t *timer` Pointer to `time_t` value such as that returned by the `time()` function.

See also   `asctime, ctime, ftime, gmtime, stime, time, tzset`

Example
```
/* localtim.cpp */
#include <stdio.h>
#include <time.h>
main()
{
  time_t thetime;
  tm *timep;
  time(&thetime);
  timep = localtime(&thetime);
  printf("The time is %02d:%02d\n",
    timep->tm_hour, timep->tm_min);
  return 0;
}
```

lock   Set file-sharing locks

Syntax   `int lock(int handle, long offset, long length);`

Include   io.h

Description   Locks file regions using functions in DOS 3.0 and higher. Requires DOS's SHARE.EXE code to be loaded. Returns zero for success and −1 for failure, and sets `errno` to `EACCES`.

Parameters   `int handle` Handle to a file such as that returned by `open()`.

long offset Offset from the beginning of the file, specifying the beginning of the location to lock.

long length Number of bytes to lock starting from offset.

See also   fileno, open, sopen, unlock

Example
```
/* lock.cpp */
#include <stdio.h>
#include <stdlib.h>
#include <conio.h>
#include <io.h>
#include <fcntl.h>
#define FILENAME "LOCK.CPP"
void pause(const char *msg);
main()
{
  int handle, lockstatus;
  puts("Opening file");
  handle = open(FILENAME, O_RDONLY | O_BINARY);
  if (handle < 0) {
    printf("Error opening %s\n", FILENAME);
    exit(1);
  }
  pause("lock first byte of file");
  lockstatus = lock(handle, 0, 1);   // Lock first byte of file
  if (lockstatus < 0)
    puts("Error detected. SHARE installed?");
  else {
    puts("First byte of file locked");
    pause("unlock file");
    lockstatus = unlock(handle, 0, 1);   // Unlock first byte
    if (lockstatus < 0)
      puts("Error unlocking file!");
    else
      puts("File unlocked");
  }
  puts("Closing file");
  close(handle);
  return 0;
}
```

```
void pause(const char *msg)
{
  printf("Press any key to %s...", msg);
  getch();
  puts("");
}
```

locking   File-sharing locks

Syntax   `int locking(int handle, int cmd, long length);`

Include   io.h

Description   Locks or unlocks file regions using functions in DOS 3.0 or later versions. Requires SHARE.EXE to be loaded. Returns zero for success and –1 for failure and sets errno to `EBADF` (bad file number), `EACCES` (region already locked/unlocked), `EDEADLOCK` (failure after ten locking attempts), or `EINVAL` (bad cmd value or SHARE.EXE not loaded).

Parameters   `int handle` Handle to a file such as that returned by open().

`int cmd` One of the following constants: `LK_LOCK` or `LK_RLCK` (attempt to lock region ten times per second before reporting failure), `LK_NBLCK` or `LK_NBRLCK` (attempt to lock region and report failure immediately), or `LK_UNLCK` (unlock region).

`long length` Number of bytes to lock starting from offset.

See also   fileno, _fsopen, open, sopen

Example
```
/* locking.cpp */
#include <stdio.h>
#include <stdlib.h>
#include <conio.h>
#include <io.h>
#include <fcntl.h>
#include <sys\locking.h>
#define FILENAME "LOCKING.CPP"
main()
{
  int handle, lockstatus;
  long flen;
  printf("Opening %s\n", FILENAME);
  handle = open(FILENAME, O_RDONLY | O_BINARY);
```

```
          if (handle < 0) {
            printf("Error opening %s\n", FILENAME);
            exit(1);
          }
          flen = filelength(handle);
          lockstatus = locking(handle, LK_LOCK, flen);   // Lock whole file
          if (lockstatus < 0)
            puts("Error detected. SHARE installed?");
          else {
            puts("Entire file is locked");
            printf("Press any key to unlock and quit...");
            getch();
            puts("");
            lockstatus = locking(handle, LK_UNLCK, flen);   // Unlock file
            if (lockstatus < 0)
              puts("Error unlocking file!");
            else
              puts("File unlocked");
          }
          puts("Closing file");
          close(handle);
          return 0;
        }
```

log   Natural logarithm

Syntax   double log(double x);
           complex log(complex x);
           long double logl(long double x);

Include   math.h, complex.h

Description   Returns natural logarithm of x.

Parameters   **double x** Candidate value of type double (log).

complex x Candidate instance of class complex (complex log).

long double x Candidate value of type long double (logl).

See also   complex, exp, ldexp, log10, pow, pow10, sqrt

Example
```
/* log.cpp */
#include <stdio.h>
#include <stdlib.h>
#include <math.h>
main(int argc, char *argv[])
{
  double x;
  if (argc <= 1) {
    puts("Enter LOG x to calculate natural logarithm of x");
    exit(1);
  }
  x = atof(argv[1]);
  printf("Natural logarithm of %lf == %lf\n", x, log(x));
  return 0;
}
```

log10 Base-10 logarithm

Syntax
```
double log10(double x);
complex log10(complex x);
long double log10l(long double x);
```

Include math.h, complex.h

Description Returns base ten logarithm of x.

Parameters **double x** Candidate value of type double (log10).

complex x Candidate instance of class complex (complex log10).

long double x Candidate value of type long double (log10l).

See also complex, exp, ldexp, log, pow, pow10, sqrt

Example
```
/* log10.cpp */
#include <stdio.h>
#include <stdlib.h>
#include <math.h>
main(int argc, char *argv[])
{
  double x;
  if (argc <= 1) {
    puts("Enter LOG10 x to calculate base-10 logarithm of x");
```

```
      exit(1);
    }
    x = atof(argv[1]);
    printf("Base-10 logarithm of %lf == %lf\n", x, log10(x));
    return 0;
}
```

longjmp   Nonlocal goto

Syntax   `void longjmp(jmp_buf jmpb, int retval);`

Include   setjmp.h

Description   Restores the program state as captured by a preceding call to `setjmp()`.
The function that called `setjmp()` must be active or `longjmp()`'s result
is undefined. Overlaid programs cannot use `longjmp()`. Typically used
to implement coroutines or error-handlers.

Parameters   **jmp_buf jmpb** A structure of type `jmp_buf` as declared in setjmp.h.

int retval Value to pass back as `setjmp()`'s return value.

See also   ctrlbrk, setjmp, signal

Example
```
/* longjmp.cpp */
#include <stdio.h>
#include <stdlib.h>
#include <setjmp.h>
#define MAXLOOPS 10
void coroutine1(void);
void coroutine2(void);
long iteration;
jmp_buf jumpinfo;
main()
{
  int value = setjmp(jumpinfo);
  if (value != 0)
    coroutine1();
  coroutine2();    // A "no-loop" loop
  return 0;
}

void coroutine1(void)
{
```

```
      puts("In coroutine #1");
      if (++iteration == MAXLOOPS)
        exit(0);  // Optional; prevents runaway program
    }

    void coroutine2(void)
    {
      puts("In coroutine #2");
      longjmp(jumpinfo, 1);
    }
```

lowvideo   Select low-intensity characters

Syntax   `void lowvideo(void);`

Include   conio.h

Description   Resets the current attribute's high-intensity bit to display text in dim, or low-intensity, mode. Affects only direct-video output routines prototyped in conio.h. Does not affect any characters currently onscreen.

See also   `cprintf`, `cputs`, `gettextinfo`, `highvideo`, `normvideo`, `textattr`, `textcolor`

Example   See `highvideo`.

_lrotl, _lrotr   Rotate left, rotate right

Syntax   `unsigned long _lrotl(unsigned long val, int count);`
`unsigned long _lrotr(unsigned long val, int count);`

Include   stdlib.h

Description   Function `_lrotl` returns `val` rotated left by count bits. Function `_lrotr` returns `val` rotated right by count bits.

Parameters   **unsigned long val** Value to be rotated.

       int count Number of bits by which to rotate `val`.

See also   `_rotl`, `_rotr`

Example
```
/* _lrotlr.cpp */
#include <stdio.h>
#include <stdlib.h>
```

```
main()
{
  unsigned long v = 123, n;
  printf("Original value == %lu\n", v);
  n = _lrotl(v, 3);
  printf("Value rotated left by 3 == %lu\n", n);
  n = _lrotr(v, 2);
  printf("Value rotated right by 2 == %lu\n", n);
  return 0;
}
```

lsearch   Linear search

Syntax   void *lsearch(const void *key, void *base, size_t *num,
             size_t width, int (*fcmp)(const void *, const void*));

Include   stdlib.h

Description   Like lfind(), lsearch() searches a table for a matching record, but if
the target key is not located, lsearch() appends to the end of the table
the record addressed by key.

Parameters   See lfind.

See also   bsearch, lfind, qsort

Example
```
/* lsearch.cpp */
#include <stdio.h>
#include <stdlib.h>
#define NUMELEMS 10  // Leave room for additions
double array[NUMELEMS] = { 1.1, 2.2, 3.3, 4.4 };
size_t numelems = 4;
int compare(double *key, double *arg);
void lookup(double key);
void display(const char *msg);
main()
{
  lookup(2.2);  // Look up value in array
  lookup(9.9);  // Look up value not in array
  return 0;
}

int compare(double *key, double *arg)
{
```

```
    if (*key == *arg)
      return 0;
    else
      return -1;
}


void lookup(double key)
{
  double *result;
  printf("\nSearching for %.1lf\n", key);
  display("before");
  result = (double *)lsearch(&key, array, &numelems,
    sizeof(double), (int(*)(const void*, const void*))compare);
  if (result)
    printf("Result == %.1lf\n", *result);
  display("after");
}


void display(const char *msg)
{
  printf("Array %s. Number elements == %d\n", msg, numelems);
  for (int i = 0; i < numelems; i++)
    printf(" [%.1lf]", array[i]);
  puts("");
}
```

lseek   Move file pointer

Syntax `long lseek(int handle, long offset, int fromwhere);`

Include io.h or stdio.h

Description Changes the current file position. Returns the new position as an offset in bytes from the file's beginning, or −1 if any errors are detected, and sets errno to `EBADF` (bad file handle) or `EINVAL` (invalid argument).

Parameters **int handle** File handle such as that returned by open().

long offset Offset in bytes by which to change the current file position. The effect depends on the value of fromwhere. If fromwhere equals `SEEK_CUR`, offset can be positive to move the current position forward, or negative to move backward.

int fromwhere One of the three constants declared in io.h and stdio.h: SEEK_SET (set new position to file beginning plus offset bytes), SEEK_CUR (set new position to current position plus offset bytes), or SEEK_END (set new position to end of file minus offset bytes).

See also   filelength, fileno, fseek, ftell, open

Example
```cpp
/* lseek.cpp ( <- 'p' is 12th character ) */
#include <stdio.h>
#include <stdlib.h>
#include <io.h>
#include <fcntl.h>
#define SEEKERR -1L
main()
{
  int handle;
  char c;
// Open text file in binary mode
  handle = open("LSEEK.CPP",O_BINARY | O_RDONLY);
  if (handle == NULL) {
    puts("Unable to open FSEEK.CPP");
    exit(1);
  }
// Seek to 12th byte from file beginning
  if (lseek(handle, 11, SEEK_SET) == SEEKERR)
    puts("Error during file seek");
  else {
    read(handle, &c, 1);
    printf("12th character == %c", c);
  }
  close(handle);
  return 0;
}
```

ltoa   Convert long to string

Syntax   char *ltoa(long value, char *string, int radix);

Include   stdlib.h

Description   Converts a long value to a null-terminated string. Returns a pointer to the resulting string.

Parameters   **long value** The value to be converted. If value is negative, a minus sign precedes the result only if radix equals 10.

char *string A pointer to a char buffer large enough to hold the result. Depending on the radix value, itoa() can return up to 33 bytes.

int radix The number base to use for the conversion, from 2 to 36.

See also   atoi, atol, itoa, ultoa

Example
```
/* ltoa.cpp */
#include <stdio.h>
#include <stdlib.h>
main()
{
  char buffer[33];
  long v = 0xFACEL;
  printf("Original value in hex == %#lx\n", v);
  ltoa(v, buffer, 2);  // Convert v to binary string
  printf("Value in binary == %s\n", buffer);
  return 0;
}
```

_makepath   Make DOS pathname

Syntax
```
void _makepath(char *path, const char *drive, const char *dir,
    const char *name, const char *ext);
```

Include   stdlib.h

Description   Creates a DOS pathname from various component arguments. Ignores null arguments.

Parameters   **char *path** Pointer to a string buffer at least _MAX_PATH bytes long. The function stores its result in this location as a null-terminated string in the form "D:\DIR\SUBDIR\NAME.EXT".

const char *drive Pointer to a null-terminated string containing a drive letter such as 'C' or a drive letter and colon such as 'D:'.

const char *dir Pointer to a null-terminated string containing one or more directory names separated by backslashes. The function appends a backslash to the end of this string if necessary.

const char *name Pointer to a null-terminated string specifying a filename without an extension.

const char *ext Pointer to a null-terminated string specifying a filename extension. The function inserts a period before this string if necessary.

See also   _fullpath, getcwd, _splitpath

Example

```
/* _makepat.cpp */
#include <stdio.h>
#include <stdlib.h>
main()
{
  char *drive = "C:";
  char *dir   = "\\BORLANDC\\INCLUDE";
  char *name  = "STDLIB";
  char *ext   = ".H";
  char path[_MAX_PATH];
  _makepath(path, drive, dir, name, ext);
  printf("Path == %s\n", path);
  return 0;
}
```

malloc   Allocate memory

Syntax   void *malloc(size_t size);

Include   stdlib.h or alloc.h

Description   Allocates a block of memory from the heap. When you are finished using the allocated memory, pass its pointer to free() in order to return that memory to the heap for use by subsequent calls to malloc(). The function returns a pointer to the allocated memory, or it returns null if the requested number of bytes is not available.

In small memory models, the heap consists of addresses from the end of the global data segment to the beginning of the area reserved for the stack. In large memory models, the heap consists of all conventional (not extended or expanded) memory not used by the program's data, code, and stack.

Parameters   size_t size Number of bytes to allocate. If size equals zero, malloc() returns null.

See also   `allocmem, calloc, coreleft, far..., free, heapwalk, realloc`

Example   See free.

matherr   Math error handler

Syntax   `int matherr(struct exception *e);`
           `int _matherrl(struct _exceptionl *e);`

Include   math.h

Description   Called by the math library in response to math errors. To trap these calls, simply define a `matherr()` or a `_matherrl()` function as prototyped here. Function `matherr()` is called for floating-point errors; function `_matherrl()` is called for `long double` floating-point errors. The functions are passed `exception` or `_exceptionl` structures that describe the nature of the math error. These structures are declared in math.h as

```
struct exception
{
  int type;
  char _FAR *name;
  double arg1, arg2, retval;
};

struct _exceptionl
{
  int type;
  char _FAR *name;
  long double arg1, arg2, retval;
};
```

In these structures, the `type` member indicates the kind of error: `DOMAIN` (domain or range error), `SING` (singularity), `OVERFLOW` (function result too large), `UNDERFLOW` (function result too small), or `TLOSS` (loss of significant digits). The `name` pointer addresses a string set to the name of the math function in which the error occurred. The `arg1` and `arg2` members are the original arguments passed to that function. For single-argument functions, `arg1` is the argument and `arg2` is undefined. The `retval` member is the default value to be returned by the error function. Your function should return this value, which equals one for `UNDERFLOW` and `TLOSS` error codes. Alternatively, return zero if an error cannot be resolved, or nonzero if the error is handled successfully.

Parameters   **struct exception *e** Pointer to a structure that describes the error (matherr).

struct _exception1 *e Pointer to a structure that describes the error (_matherr1).

See also   longjmp, setjmp

Example
```
/* matherr.cpp */
#include <stdio.h>
#include <math.h>
int matherr(struct exception *info);
main()
{
  double z = log(-1);  // ???
  printf("z == %lf\n", z);
  return 0;
}

int matherr(struct exception *info)
{
  if (info->type == DOMAIN) {
    puts("Math DOMAIN error detected");
    return 1;  // error handled here
  } else
    return 0;  // error not handled here
}
```

max   Return larger of two values

Syntax   (type) max(a, b);

Include   stdlib.h

Description   Implemented as a macro, max() returns the larger of the two values a or b. The type of the function is the same as the type of its arguments. The arguments and return value must be the same type. For C programs only. (Chapter 15, "Advanced Topics in C++," explains how to define a max() template for C++ programs.)

Parameters   **a**, **b** Argument values of any numeric type (int, long, double, and so on).

See also   min

Example
```c
/* max.c -- Note: MUST be a C, not a C++, program! */
#include <stdio.h>
#include <stdlib.h>
main()
{
  int a = 9, b = 45;
  int c = max(a, b);
  printf("max(%d, %d) == %d\n", a, b, c);
  return 0;
}
```

mblen   Multibyte character length

Syntax   int mblen(const char *s, size_t n);

Include   stdlib.h

Description   Returns one of three values: zero if s is null or if s addresses a null character (that is, a zero-length string), −1 if n bytes starting at s do not form a valid multibyte character depending on the current locale, or a positive nonzero value equal to the number of bytes that form a valid multibyte character.

Parameters   **const char *s** Pointer to a multibyte character.

size_t n Maximum number of bytes to examine starting at a location addressed by s.

See also   mbstowcs, mbtowc, setlocale

Example
```cpp
/* mblen.cpp */
#include <stdio.h>
#include <stdlib.h>
main()
{
  if (mblen(NULL, 0))
    puts("Multibyte chars are state dependent");
  else
    puts("Multibyte chars are not state dependent");
  return 0;
}
```

mbstowcs Multibyte string to array

Syntax `size_t mbstowcs(wchar_t *pwcs, const char *s, size_t n);`

Include stdlib.h

Description Processes up to n entries of a multibyte character string addressed by s and stores the converted characters in an array of wchar_t elements at the location addressed by pwcs. In Borland C++, wchar_t is the same as char. Returns the number of processed elements or −1 if any errors are detected.

Parameters **wchar_t *pwcs** Pointer to a destination array, filled with a maximum of n elements of type wchar_t.

const char *s Pointer to a source string containing multibyte characters.

size_t n Maximum number of elements to examine in the source.

See also mblen, mbtowc, setlocale

Example
```
/* mbstowcs.cpp */
#include <stdio.h>
#include <stdlib.h>
main()
{
  wchar_t target[80];
  char *source = "A string";
  int result = mbstowcs(target, source, 80);
  printf("result == %d\n", result);
  printf("target == %s\n", target);
  return 0;
}
```

mbtowc Multibyte string to code

Syntax `int mbtowc(wchar_t *pwc, const char *s, size_t n);`

Include stdlib.h

Description Examines up to n elements of a multibyte character addressed by s. If that character is valid, the function converts it to an equivalent wchar_t value, which is stored at the location addressed by pwc. Returns zero if s is null or addresses a null character, −1 if any errors are detected, or a positive nonzero value equal to the number of bytes in the converted multibyte character.

Parameters   **wchar_t *pwc** Pointer to the destination for holding the function result.

const char *s Pointer to the source string containing a multibyte character.

size_t n Maximum number of elements to examine in the source.

See also   mblen, mbstowcs, setlocale

Example
```c
/* mbtowc.cpp */
#include <stdio.h>
#include <stdlib.h>
main()
{
  wchar_t target[80];
  char *source = "A string";
  int result = mbtowc(target, source, 80);
  printf("result == %d\n", result);
  printf("target == %s\n", target);
  return 0;
}
```

memccpy, _fmemccpy   Copy characters

Syntax
```c
void *memccpy(void *dest, const void *src, int c, size_t n);
void far * far _fmemccpy(void far *dest, const void far *src,
    int c, size_t n);
```

Include   mem.h

Description   Copies memory from a source location to a destination until character c is copied, or until n bytes have been copied. Returns the address following c in the destination, or if c was not copied, returns null. Function _fmemccpy() is the far-pointer version.

Parameters   **void *dest** Pointer to the destination.

const void *src Pointer to the source.

int c Character that when transferred should end copying.

size_t n Maximum number of bytes to copy.

See also   memchr, memcmp, memcpy, memicmp, memmove, memset

Example
```cpp
/* memccpy.cpp */
#include <stdio.h>
#include <mem.h>
#include <string.h>
main()
{
  char *source = "Original string";
  char dest[80];
  char *p;
  p = (char *)memccpy(dest, source, 'l', strlen(source));
  *p = NULL;
  printf("Original string == %s\n", source);
  printf("Copy of string  == %s\n", dest);
  return 0;
}
```

memchr, _fmemchr   Search memory for character

Syntax
```cpp
void *memchr(const void *s, int c, size_t n);
void far * far _fmemchr(const void far *s, int c, size_t n);
```

Include   mem.h

Description   Searches for a character c in a block of memory. If the character is found, memchr() returns its address. If the character is not found, the function returns null. Function _fmemchr() is the far-pointer version.

Parameters   **const void *s** Pointer to memory in which to search for a character.

int c The character to find.

size_t n Maximum number of bytes to search, starting at a location addressed by s.

See also   memccpy, memcmp, memcpy, memicmp, memmove, memset

Example
```cpp
/* memchr.cpp */
#include <stdio.h>
#include <mem.h>
#include <string.h>
main()
```

```
{
  char *path = "C:\\BORLANDC\\BIN";
  char *dir;
  printf("Original string == %s\n", path);
  dir = (char *)memchr(path, '\\', strlen(path));
  if (dir)
    printf("Directory == %s\n", dir);
  return 0;
}
```

memcmp, _fmemcmp   Compare memory

Syntax
```
int memcmp(const void *s1, const void *s2, size_t n);
int far _fmemcmp(const void far *s1, const void far *s2,
  size_t n);
```

Include   mem.h

Description   Compares memory bytes as unsigned char strings, which do not have to be null-terminated. Returns a negative result if the string at s1 is alphabetically less than the string at s2. Returns zero if the two strings are equal. Returns a positive value if the string at s1 is alphabetically greater than the string at s2. Function _fmemcmp() is the far-pointer version.

Parameters   **const void *s1** Pointer to the first string of character bytes.

const void *s2 Pointer to the second string of character bytes.

size_t n Maximum number of bytes to compare.

See also   memccpy, memchr, memcpy, memicmp, memmove, memset

Example
```
/* memcmp.cpp */
#include <stdio.h>
#include <mem.h>
main()
{
  char b1[] = "String #1";
  char b2[] = "String #2";
  int result = memcmp(b1, b2, 6);
  if (result == 0)
```

```
        printf("First 6 chars of %s and %s are equal\n", b1, b2);
      return 0;
    }
```

memcpy, _fmemcpy   Copy nonoverlapping memory

Syntax   `void *memcpy(void *dest, const void *src, size_t n);`
`void far *far _fmemcpy(void far *dest, const void far *src,`
`   size_t n);`

Include   mem.h

Description   Copies an array of bytes from a source to a destination. If any bytes in these two locations overlap, the results are not defined (see `memmove()`). Function `_fmemcpy()` is the far-pointer version.

Parameters   **void *dest** Pointer to the destination.

const void *src Pointer to the source.

size_t n Number of bytes to copy from the source location to the destination.

See also   memccpy, memchr, memcmp, memicmp, memmove, memset, movedata, movemem

Example
```
/* memcpy.cpp */
#include <stdio.h>
#include <mem.h>
#include <string.h>
main()
{
  char *source = "Original string";
  char dest[80];
  memcpy(dest, source, strlen(source) + 1);
  printf("Original string == %s\n", source);
  printf("Copy of string  == %s\n", dest);
  return 0;
}
```

memicmp, _fmemicmp   Compare memory ignoring case

Syntax
```
int memicmp(const void *s1, const void *s2, size_t n);
int far _fmemicmp(const void far *s1, const void far *s2,
  size_t n);
```

Include   mem.h

Description   Same as memcmp() and _fmemcmp(), but ignores case when comparing two strings that do not have to be null-terminated. Function _fmemicmp() is the far-pointer version.

Parameters   See memcmp.

See also   memccpy, memchr, memcmp, memcpy, memmove, memset

Example
```
/* memicmp.cpp */
#include <stdio.h>
#include <mem.h>
#include <string.h>
main()
{
  char b1[] = "CASELESS COMPARE";
  char b2[] = "caseless compare and extras";
  int result = memicmp(b1, b2, strlen(b1));
  printf("string 1 == %s\n", b1);
  printf("string 2 == %s\n", b2);
  if (result == 0)
    puts("strings begin the same");
  else
    puts("strings differ");
  return 0;
}
```

memmove, _fmemmove   Copy memory

Syntax
```
void *memmove(void *dest, const void *src, size_t n);
void far * far _fmemmove(void far *dest, const void far *src,
  size_t n);
```

Include   mem.h

Description Copies an array of bytes from a source to a destination. Unlike `memcpy()`, `memmove()` correctly copies any overlapping bytes in these two locations. Function `_fmemmove()` is the far-pointer version.

Parameters **`void *dest`** Pointer to the destination.

`const void *src` Pointer to the source.

`size_t n` Number of bytes to copy from the source to the destination.

See also `memccpy, memchr, memcmp, memcpy, memicmp, memset, movedata, movemem`

Example
```cpp
/* memmove.cpp */
#include <stdio.h>
#include <mem.h>
#include <string.h>
main()
{
  char s[] = "     Leading spaces";
  char *p;
  printf("Original string == %s\n", s);
  p = s;
  while (*p == ' ')
    p++;
  if (*p)
    memmove(s, p, strlen(p) + 1);
  else
    s[0] = NULL;
  printf("New string == %s\n", s);
  return 0;
}
```

memset, _fmemset Set memory

Syntax `void *memset(void *s, int c, size_t n);`
`void far * far _fmemset(void far *s, int c, size_t n);`

Include mem.h

Description Fills memory with a byte value. Function `_fmemset()` is the far-pointer version.

Parameters **`void *s`** Pointer to the first byte to be filled.

`int c` Character to store in memory.

size_t **n** Number of bytes to set to character c, starting with the byte at the location addressed by s.

See also   memccpy, memchr, memcmp, memcpy, memicmp, memmove

Example
```
/* memset.cpp */
#include <stdio.h>
#include <mem.h>
main()
{
  char buffer[80];
  buffer[79] = NULL;
  memset(buffer, '@', 79);
  puts(buffer);
  return 0;
}
```

min   Return smaller of two values

Syntax   (type) min(a, b);

Include   stdlib.h

Description   Implemented as a macro, min() returns the smaller of the two values a or b. The type of the function is the same as the type of its arguments. The arguments and return value must be the same type. For C programs only. (Chapter 15, "Advanced Topics in C++," explains how to define a min() template for C++ programs.)

Parameters   **a, b** Argument values of any numeric type (int, long, double, and so on).

See also   max

Example
```
/* min.c -- Note: MUST be a C, not a C++, program! */
#include <stdio.h>
#include <stdlib.h>
main()
{
  int a = 9, b = 45;
  int c = min(a, b);
  printf("min(%d, %d) == %d\n", a, b, c);
  return 0;
}
```

mkdir   Make directory

Syntax   `int mkdir(const char *path);`

Include   dir.h

Description   Creates a new disk directory. Returns zero for success and –1 for failure and sets `errno` to `EACCES` (access denied) or `ENOENT` (no such directory). The `EACCES` error indicates that the directory already exists. The `ENOENT` error typically means that a higher-level subdirectory in the path does *not* exist. If path addresses the string `"C:\D1\D2\D3"`, `mkdir()` can create a directory, D3, in the path C:\D1\D2 only if those nested directories already exist. (Note: To avoid a conflict with the DOS `MKDIR` command, the example is named MKDIRX.CPP.)

Parameters   `const char *path` Pointer to a null-terminated string specifying the directory name. The string can contain drive and subdirectory information, but only the final directory name in a nested path is created.

See also   chdir, getcurdir, getcwd, rmdir

Example
```
/* mkdirx.cpp */
#include <stdio.h>
#include <stdlib.h>
#include <dir.h>
main(int argc, char *argv[])
{
  if (argc <= 1) {
    puts("Enter MKDIRX DIR to create new directory");
    exit(1);
  }
  if (mkdir(argv[1]) == 0)
    printf("%s created", argv[1]);
  else
    printf("%s not created", argv[1]);
  return 0;
}
```

MK_FP   Make far pointer

Syntax   `void far *MK_FP(unsigned seg, unsigned ofs);`

Include   dos.h

Description Use this macro to create and return a far, 32-bit pointer with segment and offset words. In a C program, the macro's result can be assigned to any far pointer variable. In a C++ program, assigning the function to a typed pointer requires using a typecast expression.

Parameters **unsigned seg** Segment address value.

unsigned ofs Offset address value.

See also FP_OFF, FP_SEG, movedata, segread

Example
```
/* mk_fp.cpp */
#include <stdio.h>
#include <dos.h>
main()
{
  void far *p;
  p = MK_FP(0xB000, 0x0100);
  printf("Pointer value == %#06x:%#06x\n",
    FP_SEG(p), FP_OFF(p));
  return 0;
}
```

mktemp Make unique filename

Syntax char *mktemp(char *template);

Include dir.h

Description Returns a pointer to a filename guaranteed to be unique in the current directory. Any errors return null.

Parameters **char *template** Pointer to a null-terminated string that must end with six 'X' characters. The function replaces these characters in the original string with the string "AA.AAA" and then checks the directory for a file of that name. If the string is a unique filename, the function returns template. For example, if the original string is "QXXXXXX", mktemp() modifies this string to "QAA.AAA" and searches for that filename. If the file exists, mktemp() modifies the string to "QAA.AAB" and tries again.

See also tempnam, tmpfile, tmpnam

Example
```
/* mktemp.cpp */
#include <stdio.h>
#include <dir.h>
```

```
main()
{
  char *tempname = "QQXXXXXX";
  if (mktemp(tempname) == NULL)
    puts("Error creating temporary filename");
  else
    printf("Temporary filename == %s\n", tempname);
  return 0;
}
```

mktime   Convert time to calendar format

Syntax   `time_t mktime(struct tm *t);`

Include   time.h

Description   Converts members of a tm date-and-time structure to a `time_t` value, the same type returned by the `time()` function. Returns a `time_t` value, which in Borland C++ is equivalent to a long integer equal to the number of seconds from January 1, 1970 to the specified date and time. Allowable dates and times range from January 1, 1970 at 00:00:00 (that is, at midnight) to January 19, 2038 at 03:14:07. See `localtime()` or time.h for the `struct tm` declaration.

Parameters   **`struct tm *t`** Pointer to a tm structure containing members such as tm_year and tm_hour set to the desired date and time. Out-of-range values are automatically adjusted before converting.

See also   localtime, strftime, time

Example
```
/* mktime.cpp */
#include <stdio.h>
#include <stdlib.h>
#include <mem.h>
#include <time.h>
char *dayofweek[7] = {
  "Sun", "Mon", "Tue", "Wed", "Thu", "Fri", "Sat" };
main()
{
  struct tm ts;
  memset(&ts, 0, sizeof(struct tm));
  ts.tm_mday = 31;
  ts.tm_mon = 11;
```

```
   ts.tm_year = 99;
   ts.tm_isdst = -1;
   if (mktime(&ts) == -1) {
     puts("Error converting time");
     exit(1);
   }
   printf("Date == %d/%d/%d\n",
     ts.tm_mon + 1, ts.tm_mday, ts.tm_year + 1900);
   printf("Day of week == %s\n",
     dayofweek[ts.tm_wday]);
   return 0;
}
```

modf, modfl   Split floating point

Syntax
```
double modf(double x, double *ipart);
long double modfl(long double x, long double *ipart);
```

Include   math.h

Description   Separates a double (modf()) or long double (modfl()) value into its integer and fractional parts. The functions store the integer value at the location addressed by ipart, and they return the fractional portion of the original value.

Parameters   **[long] double x** Original double or long double value to separate.

[long] double *ipart Pointer to a double or a long double variable in which the function deposits the original value's integer part.

See also   fmod, ldexp

Example
```
/* modf.cpp */
#include <stdio.h>
#include <math.h>
main()
{
  double v = 3.14159;
  double ipart;
  double fpart = modf(v, &ipart);
  printf("Original double value    == %.5lf\n", v);
  printf("Value's integer part     == %.0lf\n", ipart);
  printf("Value's fractional part == %.5lf\n", fpart);
  return 0;
}
```

1235

movedata   Copy bytes

Syntax   `void movedata(unsigned srcseg, unsigned srcoff, unsigned dstseg, unsigned dstoff, size_t n);`

Include   mem.h

Description   Copies bytes from a source location to a destination. Works correctly for all memory models. The source and destination addresses must not overlap.

Parameters   `unsigned srcseg` Source segment address.

`unsigned srcoff` Source offset address.

`unsigned dstseg` Destination segment address.

`unsigned dstoff` Destination offset address.

`size_t n` Number of bytes to move from the source to the destination.

See also   `FP_OFF, memcpy, memmove, MK_FP, movmem, segread`

Example
```
/* movedata.cpp */
#include <stdio.h>
#include <mem.h>
#include <dos.h>
#include <string.h>
main()
{
  char b1[80] = "String to be moved";
  char b2[80];
  movedata(FP_SEG(&b1), FP_OFF(&b1),
    FP_SEG(&b2), FP_OFF(&b2), strlen(b1) + 1);
  printf("Original string == %s\n", b1);
  printf("Copy of string  == %s\n", b2);
  return 0;
}
```

movmem   Move memory

Syntax   `void movmem(void *src, void *dest, unsigned length);`

Include   mem.h

Description Copies bytes from a source location to a destination. The source and destination addresses can overlap. (Note: Compare the example with `memmove()`'s similar program.)

Parameters **`void *src`** Pointer to the source from which bytes are copied.

`void *dest` Pointer to the destination to which bytes are copied.

`unsigned length` Number of bytes to copy from the source to the destination.

See also `memcpy, memmove, movedata`

Example
```
/* movmem.cpp */
#include <stdio.h>
#include <mem.h>
#include <string.h>
main()
{
  char s[] = "     Leading spaces";
  char *p;
  printf("Original string == %s\n", s);
  p = s;
  while (*p == ' ')
    p++;
  if (*p)
    movmem(p, s, strlen(p) + 1);
  else
    s[0] = NULL;
  printf("New string == %s\n", s);
  return 0;
}
```

moverel   Move relative

Syntax `void far moverel(int dx, int dy);`

Include graphics.h

Description Moves the current position (x, y) to (x + dx, y + dy).

Parameters **`int dx`** Relative horizontal distance from the current position.

`int dy` Relative vertical distance from the current position.

See also `linerel, moveto`

Example
```
/* moverel.cpp */
#include <graphics.h>
#include <stdio.h>
#include <stdlib.h>
#include <conio.h>
main()
{
  int gdriver = DETECT, gmode, gerr;
  initgraph(&gdriver, &gmode, "c:\\borlandc\\bgi");
  gerr = graphresult();
  if (gerr != grOk) {
    printf("BGI error: %s\n", grapherrormsg(gerr));
    exit(gerr);
  }
  moveto(10, getmaxy() / 2);
  for (int i = 1; i <= 36; i++) {
    setcolor(1 + random(getmaxcolor()));
    circle(getx(), gety(), getx());
    moverel(i, 0);
  }
  getch();
  closegraph();
  return 0;
}
```

movetext   Move text rectangle

Syntax
```
int movetext(int left, int top, int right, int bottom,
    int destleft, int desttop);
```

Include conio.h

Description Moves characters within a defined rectangle to a new location on the text display. The source and destination rectangles might overlap. Typically used to make a pseudo "window" appear to move from one location to another. Coordinate arguments are absolute, and are not relative to any defined window (see window() function).

Parameters **int left, int top** The top-left coordinate of the source rectangle.

int right, int bottom The bottom-right coordinate of the source rectangle.

int destleft, **int desttop** The top-left coordinate of the destination rectangle to which the source rectangle is moved.

See also gettext, puttext, window

Example
```
/* movetext.cpp */
#include <stdio.h>
#include <stdlib.h>
#include <conio.h>
main()
{
  clrscr();
  while (!kbhit()) {
    gotoxy(1, 1);
    textcolor(random(16));
    cputs("Borland C++");
    movetext(1, 1, 11, 2, 1 + random(80), 1 + random(25));
  }
  getch();
  gotoxy(1, 25);
  return 0;
}
```

moveto   Move graphics CP

Syntax void far moveto(int x, int y);

Include graphics.h

Description Moves the internal current position (CP) to the viewport coordinate (x,y), affecting the origin of graphics functions such as lineto().

Parameters **int x**, **int y** Desired CP coordinate.

See also lineto, moverel, outtext

Example
```
/* moveto.cpp */
#include <graphics.h>
#include <stdio.h>
#include <stdlib.h>
#include <conio.h>
#include <dos.h>
void Outline(int xmax, int ymax);
main()
```

```
{
  int gdriver = DETECT, gmode, gerr;
  int y, xmax, ymax, cmax;
  initgraph(&gdriver, &gmode, "c:\\borlandc\\bgi");
  gerr = graphresult();
  if (gerr != grOk) {
    printf("BGI error: %s\n", grapherrormsg(gerr));
    exit(gerr);
  }
  xmax = getmaxx();
  ymax = getmaxy();
  cmax = getmaxcolor();
  moveto(xmax / 2, ymax / 2);
  y = ymax / 2;
  Outline(xmax, ymax);
  while (!kbhit()) {
    delay(50);
    setcolor(1 + random(cmax));
    lineto(1 + random(xmax - 2), 1 + random(ymax - 2));
    y += random(15);
    if (y >= ymax) {
      y = 1;
      moveto(getx(), y);
    }
  }
  getch();
  closegraph();
  return 0;
}

void Outline(int xmax, int ymax)
{
  int oldx, oldy;
  oldx = getx();
  oldy = gety();
  moveto(0, 0);
  lineto(xmax, 0);
  lineto(xmax, ymax);
  lineto(0, ymax);
  lineto(0, 0);
  moveto(oldx, oldy);
}
```

norm   Square of absolute value

Syntax   `double norm(complex x);`

Include   complex.h

Description Returns `real(x) * real(x) + imag(x) * imag(x)`.

Parameters `complex x` A complex number with real and imaginary parts.

See also   `abs`, `arg`, `complex`, `polar`

Example
```cpp
/* norm.cpp */
#include <iostream.h>
#include <complex.h>
main()
{
  complex x(1.2, 2.1);
  cout << "complex x == " << x << '\n';
  cout << "norm(x) == " << norm(x) << '\n';
  return 0;
}
```

normvideo   Select normal intensity characters

Syntax   `void normvideo(void);`

Include   conio.h

Description Resets text display background and foreground colors to their startup values. Affects only text output functions prototyped in conio.h.

See also   `highvideo`, `lowvideo`, `textattr`, `textbackground`, `textcolor`

Example
```cpp
/* normvide.cpp */
#include <stdio.h>
#include <conio.h>
main()
{
  clrscr();
  puts("Text attributes  Columns=textcolor, Rows=textbackground");
  puts("First character=lowvideo, Second character=highvideo");
  puts("----------------------------------------------------");
```

```
    printf("\n\n ");
    for (int i = 0; i <= 15; i++)
      printf("%4d", i);
    for (int bcolor = 0; bcolor <= 15; bcolor++) {
      puts("");
      printf("%2d", bcolor);
      for (int fcolor = 0; fcolor <= 15; fcolor++) {
        normvideo();
        cprintf(" ");
        textcolor(fcolor);
        textbackground(bcolor);
        lowvideo();
        cputs(" a");
        highvideo();
        cputs("a");
      }
    }
    normvideo();
    return 0;
  }
```

nosound   Turn off sound

Syntax   `void nosound(void);`

Include   dos.h

Description   Call `nosound()` to stop a tone begun by function `sound()`.

See also   `delay, sound`

Example
```
/* nosound.cpp */
#include <conio.h>
#include <dos.h>
main()
{
  clrscr();
  for (int i = 1; i <= 10; i++) {
    delay(150);
    cprintf("%4c", 14);
    sound(2000);
    delay(150);
```

```
    nosound();
  }
  return 0;
}
```

_open   Open a file

Syntax   `int _open(const char *filename, int oflags);`

Include   fcntl.h, io.h

Description   Opens a specified file in binary mode for reading and writing. Returns a positive file handle if successful and −1 if an error occurs.

Parameters   `const char *filename` Pointer to a null-terminated filename string, which may contain drive and path information, but no wild cards.

`unsigned oflags` Open-mode constants (see fcntl.h) plus file-sharing constants (see share.h).

See also   `_dos_open`, `open`, `_read`, `sopen`, `write`

Example
```cpp
/* _open.cpp */
#include <stdio.h>
#include <stdlib.h>
#include <fcntl.h>
#include <io.h>
main(int argc, char *argv[])
{
  int handle;  // File handle
  char c;      // Holds bytes from file
  if (argc <= 1) {
    puts("Filename required");
    exit(1);
  }
  handle = _open(argv[1], O_RDONLY);
  if (handle == -1) {
    perror(argv[1]);
    exit(2);
  }
  printf("\nReading bytes from %s\n\n", argv[1]);
  while (!eof(handle))
    if (_read(handle, &c, 1) == 1)
      printf(" %#04x ", c);
```

```
  _close(handle);
  return 0;
}
```

open   Open a file

Syntax   `int open(const char *path, int access [, unsigned mode]);`

Include   fcntl.h, sys\stat.h, io.h

Description Opens a file in a specified mode. The opened file can be read from or written to, depending on the access used.

Parameters **const char *path** Pointer to a null-terminated filename string.

int access One of the fcntl.h constants O_RDONLY (read only), O_WRONLY (write only), or O_RDWR (read and write) logically ORed with an appropriate combination of the constants O_APPEND (add data to end of file), O_CREAT (create new file), O_TRUNC (rewrite an existing file), O_EXCL (with O_CREAT prevents recreating an existing file), O_BINARY (open in binary mode), or O_TEXT (open as text).

unsigned mode Required only if access includes O_CREAT. Set to one of the expressions S_IWRITE (statements may write to file), S_IREAD (statements may read from file), or S_IWRITE | S_IREAD (statements may read and write file data).

See also   close, creat, creatnew, creattemp, dup, dup2, fopen, lseek, lock, _open, read, sopen, write

Example
```cpp
/* open.cpp */
#include <stdio.h>
#include <stdlib.h>
#include <fcntl.h>
#include <sys\stat.h>
#include <io.h>
main(int argc, char *argv[])
{
  int handle;  // File handle
  char c;      // Holds bytes from file
  if (argc <= 1) {
    puts("Filename required");
    exit(1);
```

```
    }
    handle = open(argv[1], O_RDONLY | O_BINARY);
    if (handle == -1) {
      perror(argv[1]);
      exit(2);
    }
    printf("\nReading bytes from %s\n\n", argv[1]);
    while (!eof(handle))
      if (read(handle, &c, 1) == 1)
        printf("  %#04x  ", c);
    close(handle);
    return 0;
}
```

opendir Open directory stream

Syntax `DIR *opendir(char *dirname);`

Include dirent.h

Description Opens a directory stream for reading filename entries with `readdir()`.

Parameters **char *dirname** Pointer to null-terminated directory name string.

See also `closedir, readdir, rewinddir`

Example See `closedir`.

outp Output byte to hardware port

Syntax `int outp(unsigned portid, int value);`

Include conio.h

Description Sends a byte to a hardware output port. Returns `value`.

Parameters **unsigned portid** Output port ID.

int value Byte value to send to port.

See also `inp, inpw, outport`

Example
```
/* outp.cpp */
#include <stdio.h>
#include <conio.h>
#define SETNMI 0x80
#define CLRNMI 0x00
```

```
main()
{
  unsigned portid = 0xa0;   // NMI (nonmaskable interrupt)
  puts("Setting NMI");
  outp(portid, SETNMI);     // Set NMI
  puts("Clearing NMI");
  outp(portid, CLRNMI);     // Clear NMI
  return 0;
}
```

outport   Output word to hardware port

Syntax   `void outport(unsigned portid, unsigned value);`

Include   dos.h

Description Sends a word to a hardware output port. See `outportb` for a similar
              example.

Parameters **unsigned portid** Output port ID.

              unsigned value Value to send to the port.

See also   `inport, inportb, outportb`

outportb   Output byte to hardware port

Syntax   `void outportb(unsigned portid, unsigned char value);`

Include   dos.h

Description Sends a byte to a hardware output port.

Parameters **unsigned portid** Output port ID.

              unsigned char value Value to send to port.

See also   `inport, inportb, outport`

Example
```
/* outportb.cpp */
#include <stdio.h>
#include <dos.h>
#define SETNMI 0x80
#define CLRNMI 0x00
main()
{
```

```
        unsigned portid = 0xa0;   // NMI (nonmaskable interrupt)
        puts("Setting NMI");
        outportb(portid, SETNMI);     // Set NMI
        puts("Clearning NMI");
        outportb(portid, CLRNMI);     // Clear NMI
        return 0;
    }
```

outpw   Output word to hardware port

Syntax   `unsigned outpw(unsigned portid, unsigned value);`

Include   conio.h

Description   Sends a word to a hardware output port. See outp for a similar example.

Parameters   **unsigned portid** Output port ID.

unsigned value Value to send to the port.

See also   `inp, inpw, outp`

outtext   Display string

Syntax   `void far outtext(char far *textstring);`

Include   graphics.h

Description   Displays a text string in graphics at the current position (CP), using the current font, direction, size, justification, and color. Updates CP to the end of the displayed string if horizontal justification equals LEFT_TEXT and if output direction is set to HORIZ_DIR.

Parameters   **char far *textstring** Far pointer to a null-terminated string.

See also   `gettextsettings, outtextxy, setbkcolor, setcolor, settextjustify, textheight, textwidth`

Example
```
/* outtext.cpp */
#include <graphics.h>
#include <stdio.h>
#include <stdlib.h>
#include <time.h>
#include <conio.h>
main()
{
```

1247

```
int gdriver = DETECT, gmode, gerr;
int charsize, y, cmax;
initgraph(&gdriver, &gmode, "c:\\borlandc\\bgi");
gerr = graphresult();
if (gerr != grOk) {
  printf("BGI error: %s\n", grapherrormsg(gerr));
  exit(gerr);
}
y = 0;
cmax = getmaxcolor();
randomize();
for (charsize = 1; charsize <= 8; charsize++) {
  setcolor(1 + random(cmax));
  moveto(0, y);
  settextstyle(1, 0, charsize);
  outtext("This is a test. abcdefg 1234567890");
  y += textheight("M") + 1;
}
getch();
closegraph();
return 0;
}
```

outtextxy   Display string at (x,y)

Syntax `void far outtextxy(int x, int y, char far *textstring);`

Include graphics.h

Description Same as `outtext()` but positions output at the specified (x,y) coordinate.

Parameters `int x`, `int y` Starting coordinate.

`char far *textstring` Far pointer to a null-terminated string.

See also outtext

Example `/* outtxtxy.cpp */`
`#include <graphics.h>`

```
#include <stdio.h>
#include <stdlib.h>
#include <time.h>
#include <conio.h>
main()
{
  int gdriver = DETECT, gmode, gerr;
  int charsize, y, cmax;
  initgraph(&gdriver, &gmode, "c:\\borlandc\\bgi");
  gerr = graphresult();
  if (gerr != grOk) {
    printf("BGI error: %s\n", grapherrormsg(gerr));
    exit(gerr);
  }
  y = 0;
  cmax = getmaxcolor();
  randomize();
  for (charsize = 3; charsize <= 9; charsize++) {
    setcolor(1 + random(cmax));
    settextstyle(2, 0, charsize);
    outtextxy(0, y, "This is a test. abcdefg 1234567890");
    y += textheight("M") + 1;
  }
  getch();
  closegraph();
  return 0;
}
```

_OvrInitEms   Initialize EMS overlays

Syntax   `int far _OvrInitEms(unsigned emsHandle, unsigned firstPage,`
`unsigned pages);`

Include   dos.h

Description   Detects the presence of EMS (Expanded Memory System) RAM and, if found, uses that memory for storing a program's overlays. Returns zero if successful. Requires medium, large, or huge memory model, and the -Y and -Yo options. To compile an example from DOS, for example, enter **bcc -ml -Y main -Yo ovla ovlb ovlc, ... ovln**.

Parameters   **unsigned emsHandle** Zero for automatic EMS detection, or nonzero to specify an EMS handle obtained by other means.

unsigned firstPage Zero if emsHandle is zero; otherwise an optional first page number.

unsigned pages If nonzero, specifies the maximum number of EMS pages to use for overlay swapping.

See also   _OvrInitExt

Example
```
/* _ovrems.cpp */
#include <stdio.h>
#include <dos.h>
#define PAGES 16
main()
{
#ifndef __MEDIUM__
  #ifndef __LARGE__
    #ifndef __HUGE__
       #error Medium, large, or huge model only
    #endif
  #endif
#endif
  printf("Allocating %dK bytes EMS RAM\n", PAGES * 16);
  if (_OvrInitEms(0, 0, PAGES) == 0)
    puts("EMS available for overlays");
  else
    puts("EMS not used for overlays");
  return 0;
}
```

_OvrInitExt   Initialize overlay extended memory

Syntax   int far _OvrInitExt(unsigned long startAddress,
       unsigned long length);

Include   dos.h

Description   Detects presence of extended RAM and, if found, uses that memory for storing a program's overlays. Returns zero if successful. Requires medium, large, or huge memory model, and the -Y and -Yo options. To compile an example from DOS, for example, enter **bcc -ml -Y main -Yo ovla ovlb ovlc, ... ovln.**

Parameters **unsigned long startAddress** Zero for automatic address selection. If nonzero, specifies starting address for extended memory.

unsigned long length Zero to allocate enough extended memory for all overlays. Nonzero to limit extended memory use to a specified amount.

See also _OvrInitEms

Example
```
/* _ovrext.cpp */
#include <stdio.h>
#include <dos.h>
main()
{
#ifndef __MEDIUM__
  #ifndef __LARGE__
    #ifndef __HUGE__
      #error Medium, large, or huge model only
    #endif
  #endif
#endif
  puts("Allocating extended RAM");
  if (_OvrInitExt(0, 0) == 0)
    puts("Extended RAM available for overlays");
  else
    puts("Extended RAM not used for overlays");
  return 0;
}
```

parsfnm   Parse filename

Syntax `char *parsfnm(const char *cmdline, struct fcb *fcb, int opt);`

Include dos.h

Description Old-style method for parsing a filename (usually extracted from the DOS command line) into a file control block (FCB). Early versions of DOS used FCBs for all file I/O, but the function is not recommended for new programs. Returns zero for failure; otherwise, it returns a nonzero pointer to the byte past the parsed filename string.

Parameters **const char *cmdline** Pointer to the command line to be parsed as a filename into an FCB.

struct fcb *fcb Pointer to the `fcb` structure to hold results and to be used in subsequent I/O.

int opt Register AL option for DOS function 0x29.

See also   _fullpath, _makepath

Example
```
/* parsfnm.cpp */
#include <stdio.h>
#include <stdlib.h>
#include <dos.h>
main(int argc, char *argv[])
{
  struct fcb fb;
  if (argc <= 1) {
    puts("Filename required");
    exit(1);
  }
  if (parsfnm(argv[1], &fb, 1))
    printf("File %s on drive %d\n", fb.fcb_name, fb.fcb_drive);
  else
    puts("Error parsing filename");
  return 0;
}
```

peek   Get word from memory

Syntax   `int peek(unsigned segment, unsigned offset);`

Include   dos.h

Description   Returns a word value from memory at the specified location.

(**Note:** When implemented as a macro, the `peek()` function in Borland C++ 3.0 does not work correctly. Do not use this function with Borland C++ 3.0.)

Parameters   **unsigned segment** Segment portion of target address.

unsigned offset Offset portion of target address.

See also   peekb, poke

Example
```
/* peek.cpp */
#include <stdio.h>
```

```
#include <dos.h>
#include <conio.h>
#define TIMER_OFS 0x046c
main()
{
  unsigned tick;
  puts("Reading system timer tick low word");
  puts("Press any key to quit");
  while (!kbhit()) {
    gotoxy(1, wherey());
    tick = peek(0, TIMER_OFS);
    cprintf("Timer == %05u", tick);
  }
  getch();  // Throw away keypress
  return 0;
}
```

peekb   Get byte from memory

Syntax   `char peekb(unsigned segment, unsigned offset);`

Include   dos.h

Description Returns a byte value from memory at the specified location.

(**Note:** When implemented as a macro, the `peekb()` function in Borland C++ 3.0 does not work correctly. Do not use this function with Borland C++ 3.0.)

Parameters **unsigned segment** Segment portion of target address.

unsigned offset Offset portion of target address.

See also   peek, pokeb

Example
```
/* peekb.cpp */
#include <stdio.h>
#include <dos.h>
#include <conio.h>
#define TIMER_OFS 0x046c
main()
{
  unsigned char tick;
  puts("Reading system timer tick low byte");
  puts("Press any key to quit");
```

```
while (!kbhit()) {
  gotoxy(1, wherey());
  tick = peekb(0, TIMER_OFS);
  cprintf("Timer == %03u", tick);
}
getch();  // Throw away keypress
return 0;
}
```

perror Print system error message

Syntax   void perror(const char *s);

Include   stdio.h

Description   Following an error by most library functions, call perror() to send to stderr a description of the error.

Parameters   **const char *s** Optional string to add to error message. Typically set to the program's filename.

See also   clearerr, _strerror, strerror

Example   See chdir, _open, open

pieslice Draw pie-slice wedge

Syntax   void far pieslice(int x, int y, int stangle, int endangle, int radius);

Include   graphics.h

Description   Draws a filled wedge with the sharp point at coordinate (x,y). Use setcolor() to color the wedge outline. Use setfillstyle() to select the wedge fill color and pattern. The example uses pieslice() to display a chart of the 16 colors available in EGA and VGA displays.

Parameters   **int x**, **int y** Center of the wedge (at its sharp point).

int stangle, **int endangle** Angles from the center that define wedge width. Greater angles run counterclockwise.

int radius Length of the wedge from the center.

See also   arc, circle, ellipse, getarccoords, sector, setcolor, setfillstyle, setfillpattern

Example
```
/* pieslice.cpp */
#include <graphics.h>
#include <stdio.h>
#include <stdlib.h>
#include <conio.h>
main()
{
  int gdriver = DETECT, gmode, gerr;
  int color, stangle, radius, xcenter, ycenter;
  initgraph(&gdriver, &gmode, "c:\\borlandc\\bgi");
  gerr = graphresult();
  if (gerr != grOk) {
    printf("BGI error: %s\n", grapherrormsg(gerr));
    exit(gerr);
  }
  xcenter = getmaxx() / 2;
  ycenter = getmaxy() / 2;
  radius = getmaxx() / 4;
  stangle = 0;
  for (color = 0; color <= 14; color++) {
    stangle += 24;
    setfillstyle(SOLID_FILL, color);
    pieslice(xcenter, ycenter, stangle, stangle + 24, radius);
  }
  getch();
  closegraph();
  return 0;
}
```

poke Put word into memory

Syntax `void poke(unsigned segment, unsigned offset, int value);`

Include dos.h

Description Insert integer into memory at a specified address.

(**Note:** When implemented as a macro, the poke() function in Borland C++ 3.0 or 3.1 does not work correctly. Do not use this function with Borland C++ 3.0 or 3.1.)

Parameters **unsigned segment** Segment portion of target address.

unsigned `offset` Offset portion of target address.

int `value` Integer value to poke into memory.

See also peek, pokeb

Example
```cpp
/* poke.cpp */
#include <stdio.h>
#include <dos.h>
int value;
void far *p = &value;
main()
{
  // A VERY roundabout way to assign 123 to value!
  poke(FP_SEG(p), FP_OFF(p), 123);
  printf("value == %d\n", value);
  return 0;
}
```

pokeb   Put byte into memory

Syntax   `void pokeb(unsigned segment, unsigned offset, char value);`

Include   dos.h

Description Insert byte into memory at a specified address.

(**Note:** When implemented as a macro, the `pokeb()` function in Borland C++ 3.0 or 3.1 does not work correctly. Do not use this function with Borland C++ 3.0 or 3.1.)

Parameters *unsigned* `segment` Segment portion of target address.

unsigned `offset` Offset portion of target address.

char `value` Byte value to poke into memory.

See also   peekb, poke

Example
```cpp
/* pokeb.cpp */
#include <stdio.h>
#include <dos.h>
char c;
void far *p = &c;
main()
{
```

```
    // A VERY roundabout way to assign 'X' to c!
    pokeb(FP_SEG(p), FP_OFF(p), 'X');
    printf("c == %c\n", c);
    return 0;
}
```

polar   Magnitude and angle to complex

Syntax   `complex polar(double mag, double angle);`

Include   complex.h

Description   Construct a complex object from a magnitude and an angle. Equivalent to a complex object constructed as `complex(mag * cos(angle), mag * sin(angle))`.

Parameters   **double mag** Magnitude, or absolute value.

   double angle The argument.

See also   `abs, arg, complex, norm`

Example
```
/* polar.cpp */
#include <iostream.h>
#include <complex.h>
#include <math.h>
main()
{
  double mag = 2.2;
  double angle = 45;
  complex x = polar(mag, angle);
  cout << "mag == " << mag << ", angle == " << angle << '\n';
  cout << "polar(mag, angle) == " << x << '\n';
  complex y = complex(mag * cos(angle), mag * sin(angle));
  cout << "equivalent expression == " << y << '\n';
  return 0;
}
```

poly   Polynomial

Syntax   `double poly(double x, int degree, double coeffs[]);`
`long double polyl(long double x, int degree,`
   `long double coeff[]);`

Include	math.h

Description Calculates a polynomial. Function `poly()` operates on and returns type `double`; `polyl()` is a `long double` version.

Parameters `double x` Argument value.

`int degree` Extent of coefficients.

`double coeff[]` Coefficients as an array of `double` or `long double` values from `coeff[0]` to `coeff[degree]`. Array values are stored in reverse compared to their use in the polynomial. Thus, in the Example, the coefficients for polynomial x^^3 + 3x^^2 + 4x + 6 (using ^^ to indicate superscripting) are stored as `coeff[0]==6.0`, `coeff[1]==4.0`, `coeff[2]==3.0`, and `coeff[3]==1.0`.

Example
```
/* poly.cpp */
#include <stdio.h>
#include <math.h>
#define DEGREE 3
#define X 3.5
main()
{
  double coeff[DEGREE + 1] = { 6.0, 4.0, 3.0, 1.0 };
  double q = poly(X, DEGREE, coeff);
  printf("x^^3 + 3x^^2 + 4x + 6 == %lf\n", q);
  printf("for x == %lf\n", X);
  return 0;
}
```

pow Calculate x to power of y

Syntax
```
double pow(double x, double y);
long double powl(long double x, long double y);
complex pow(complex x, complex y);
complex pow(complex x, double y);
complex pow(double x, complex y);
```

Include math.h, complex.h

Description Returns xy. Function `pow()` returns type `double`; function `powl()` is the `long double` version. The overloaded `complex pow()` functions accept any combination of `complex` and `double` arguments and return the equivalent of the expression

```
exp(y * log(x))
```

Parameters   **double x**, **double y** Argument values as `double` or `long double` floating-point values.

complex x, **complex y** Argument values as `complex` objects.

See also   complex, exp, log, pow10, sqrt

Example
```cpp
/* pow.cpp */
#include <stdio.h>
#include <stdlib.h>
#include <math.h>
main(int argc, char *argv[])
{
  if (argc <= 2) {
    puts("Enter POW X Y to calculate X^^Y");
    exit(1);
  }
  long double x = _atold(argv[1]);
  long double y = _atold(argv[2]);
  printf("%.3Lf^^%.3Lf == %Lg\n", x, y, powl(x, y));
  return 0;
}
```

pow10   Raise 10 to a power

Syntax
```cpp
double pow10(int p);
long double pow10l(int p);
```

Include   math.h

Description   Returns 10 raised to the power of p. Function `pow10()` returns a double value; function `pow10l()` returns `long double`.

Parameters   **int p** Power by which to raise 10.

See also   exp, log, pow

Example
```cpp
/* pow10.cpp */
#include <stdio.h>
#include <stdlib.h>
#include <math.h>
main(int argc, char *argv[])
{
```

```
  if (argc <= 1) {
    puts("Enter POW10 P to calculate 10^^P");
    exit(1);
  }
  int p = atoi(argv[1]);
  printf("10^^%d == %Lg\n", p, pow10l(p));
  return 0;
}
```

printf   Write formatted output

Syntax   `int printf(const char *format[, argument,...]);`

Include   stdio.h

Description   Boasting more options than a Mercedes, `printf()` is one of the most capable, if one of the more confusing, functions in the standard library. The `printf()` function's initial argument is a formatting string which usually contains text interspersed with conversion commands that are replaced with values formatted according to various and complex formulas. Zero or more arguments follow the formatting string, one argument per conversion command. The compiler does not verify the number of arguments or their data types. In other words, all formatting errors (many of which most C and C++ programmers make eventually) are your responsibility to prevent. The function returns the number of characters written to stdout, although this value usually is ignored.

A `printf()` statement might be as simple as

`printf("Display this string\n");`

but in this case, it's probably best to call `puts()` instead. A more typical `printf()` statement has at least two parameters—a formatting string and the name of a program variable:

`printf("Your balance is $%8.2f\n", balance);`

The statement displays the value of a double variable, balance, formatted in eight columns with two decimal places. The embedded conversion command `%8.2f` tells `printf()` to send to the standard output balance's formatted value. The \n escape code begins a new line. The other characters in the string are sent literally to stdout. If balance equals 159.72, the statement displays

`Your balance is $  159.72`

All formatting conversion commands begin with a percent sign (%) followed by various digits and symbols selected from a smorgasbord of options. Arguments are applied to conversion commands one by one, in left-to-right order. The formatting string conforms to this syntax:

```
% [flags] [width] [.precision] [F|N|h|1|L] conversion
```

A required percent sign begins a conversion command. Bracketed items are optional. The flags specify justification rules, plus and minus signs, decimal points, trailing zeros, and prefixes in octal or hexadecimal. The width specifies column size, padded with blanks or 0 digit characters. The precision, which must begin with a period, denotes numeric precision for floating-point values or the minimum number of digits for integers. One of several modifiers selects among size-related characteristics: F (far pointer), N (near pointer), h (short int), l (long), or L (long double). The required conversion character selects a data type.

The following sections describe each part of a printf() formatting string. When constructing formatting strings, to avoid confusion, select from one set of options at a time, using the preceding syntax as a guide to the order in which the following notes apply.

'%'   Embedded conversion commands must begin with a percent sign. To insert a percent-sign character into the output, type the symbol twice: %%.

[flags]   Flags are optional. If specified, flags can consist of one or more of the following characters:

Flags for the printf() function.

Flag	Description
–	Left-justifies output. Fills any remaining space to the right with blanks. Default output is right-justified.
+	Prefaces numeric values with a plus or minus sign. Usually, only negative values are prefaced with minus signs.
' '	Displays a blank in front of positive numeric values and a minus sign in front of negative ones. This is the default action, so don't combine a blank flag with +. Do not type the single quotes, only a single blank space.

continues

Flag	Description
#	If conversion is x or X, prefaces nonzero arguments with 0x or 0X, respectively. If conversion is o, prefaces result with 0. If conversion is e, E, or f, forces a decimal point to appear in the output (normally one prefaces only nonzero fractions). If conversion is g or G, a decimal point is forced into the output and trailing zeros are *not* truncated as they normally are.
[**width**]	Specifies a minimum column width. Normally, any extra space is filled with blanks. If the width value begins with the digit 0, however, any extra space is filled with 0 characters. The field width also can be the asterisk character, *, which causes the *next* int argument value to be used as the column width—a rare case in which a conversion command requires two arguments. With this command, you specify two values: an integer that represents the minimum width to use, and the value to be formatted within that column width. The width integer comes *before* the value being formatted. Specifying a 0 width pads output with leading 0s within a variable column width. There is never any danger of specifying fewer columns than are needed to display a value. Columns are enlarged as necessary to ensure that no values are truncated.
['.'**precision**]	If a period appears at this location in a formatting string, the next value represents the precision to use for the formatted result. The exact meaning of the precision depends on the type of item being formatted. An integer value follows the period. The default value is 0—that is, .0 is the same as specifying no precision. Default precisions are 1 for conversion characters d, i, o, u, x, and X; 6 for e, E, and f; a variable number of significant digits for g and G; and all characters for conversions s and c—that is, strings and characters.

If the conversion character is g or G, the precision represents the maximum number of significant digits in the formatted result. If conversion is e, E, or f, the precision equals the number of decimal places to use, and the final digit is rounded. If conversion is s, the precision stands for the maximum number of characters to use from the string. Precision has no effect on conversion character c (single characters are always displayed). If the conversion character is d, i, o, u, x, or X, at least the number of digits specified by the precision are output, padded at left as necessary with 0 digit characters.

Conversion The required conversion character tells printf() the type of an argument. It is up to you to supply an argument of the expected type. If you use a conversion character g, for example, then the argument must be a floating-point value. Probably the most common cause of problems with printf() statements is the application of the wrong type of argument for a specified conversion character.

The following table lists all possible conversion characters, of which only one can be used per command. Case is significant—a lowercase g is not the same as an uppercase G.

Conversion characters for the printf() function.

Conversion Character	Description
%	Outputs a percent symbol.
c	A character.
d	A signed decimal.
e	A double value to be formatted using scientific notation (for example, 1.0765e+10).
E	Same as e, but inserts an uppercase E into the result.
f	A double value to be formatted in decimal format, such as 123.45.

continues

1263

Conversion Character	Description
g	A double value to be formatted in either scientific or decimal notation. Automatically selects option f or e as needed to give the most accurate results in a reasonably small amount of space.
G	Same as g, but if scientific notation is used, the uppercase letter E appears in the result rather than a lowercase e.
i	Same as d—a signed decimal.
n	Treats the argument value as a pointer to an int variable in which printf() stores the number of characters written to stdout so far. The n conversion does not add any characters to the output.
o	An unsigned octal.
p	A pointer. In tiny, small, and medium memory models, pointers are formatted as offset hexadecimal values. In compact, large, and huge memory models, pointers are formatted as segment and offset hexadecimal values separated by a colon.
s	A null-terminated string. Specify a precision value to restrict output to a maximum number of characters.
u	An unsigned decimal.
x	An unsigned hexadecimal using the digits 0, 1, 2, 3, 4, 5, 6, 7, 8, and 9, and the lower-case letters a, b, c, d, e, and f.
X	Same as x, an unsigned hexadecimal, but using uppercase letters A, B, C, D, E, and F.

Parameters   `const char *format` Pointer to a null-terminated string (usually typed as a literal string directly in the `printf()` statement). The string's characters are passed unchanged to the standard output. Embedded conversion commands in the string (see preceding descriptions) are replaced with values formatted according to the rules for those commands and the argument data types.

               `argument, ...` One or more argument variables, literal values, constants, expressions, pointers, dereferenced pointers, function calls, and so on. At least one argument must be supplied for each conversion command in the preceding format string. Arguments are not checked for number or type, and they are evaluated in left-to-right order.

See also   `cprintf`, `ecvt`, `fprintf`, `fread`, `fscanf`, `putc`, `puts`, `putw`, `scanf`, `sprintf`, `vprintf`, `vsprintf`

Example
```cpp
/* printf.cpp */
#include <stdio.h>
main()
{
  int xint = 123;
  long xlong = 12345678L;
  char xchar = '@';
  char *xstring = "My dog has knees";
  double xdouble = 3.14159;
  long double xlongdouble = xdouble * xdouble;
  puts( "Sample printf() statements");
  puts( "VARIABLE          RESULT");
  printf("xint (decimal) == %d\n", xint);
  printf("xint (hex)     == %#x\n", xint);
  printf("xint (octal)   == %#o\n", xint);
  printf("xlong          == %ld\n", xlong);
  printf("xchar          == %c\n", xchar);
  printf("xstring        == %s\n", xstring);
  printf("xdouble        == %lf\n", xdouble);
  printf("xlongdouble(1) == %Le\n", xlongdouble);
  printf("xlongdouble(2) == %Lf\n", xlongdouble);
  return 0;
}
```

putc   Output character to stream

Syntax   `int putc(int c, FILE *stream);`

Include   stdio.h

Description   Sends a character to a file stream, such as stdout or a file opened by function fopen(). If successful, putc() returns c; otherwise, it returns EOF. The function is written as a macro.

Parameters   **int c** Character to write to the specified stream.

FILE *stream Any file stream opened for output.

See also   feof, fopen, fputc, fputch, fputchar, fputs, fwrite, getc, getchar, printf, putch, putchar, putw, vprintf

Example
```
/* putc.cpp */
#include <stdio.h>
main()
{
  for (int c = 32; c < 127; c++)
    putc(c, stdout);
  return 0;
}
```

putch   Display character

Syntax   `int putch(int c);`

Include   conio.h

Description   Pokes character c directly into the video buffer at the current cursor position. If successful, putch() returns c; otherwise, it returns EOF.

Parameters   **int c** Character to display.

See also   cprintf, cputs, getch, getche, gotoxy, putc, textbackground, textcolor

Example
```
/* putch.cpp */
#include <conio.h>
main()
{
  for (int c = 32; c <= 255 ; c++)
    putch(c);
  return 0;
}
```

putchar   Output character to stdout

Syntax   `int putchar(int c);`

Include   stdio.h

Description   Same as `putc()` but outputs c to stdout. Encoded as a macro that executes `putc(c, stdout)`. If successful, `putchar()` returns c; otherwise, it returns EOF.

Parameters   **int c** Character to write to stdout.

See also   putc

Example
```
/* putchar.cpp */
#include <stdio.h>
main()
{
  for (int c = 32; c < 127; c++)
    putchar(c);
  return 0;
}
```

putenv   Add string to environment

Syntax   `int putenv(const char *envvar);`

Include   stdlib.h

Description   Given an envvar string in the form `"name=value"`, `putenv()` searches for an environment variable name, and if it finds one, it inserts in the environment a pointer to the new string. Case is significant; thus, to `putenv()`, path and PATH are different names. Replaced environment strings are not overwritten or deleted. The function returns zero for success and −1 for failure.

If name is not found, the envvar pointer is appended to the environment. The startup code reserves space for as many as four such attachments. Additional variables cause `putenv()` to expand the environment, in which case the original env pointer passed as the third argument to `main()` becomes invalid.

Parameters   **const char *envvar** Pointer to a null-terminated string in the form `"name=value"`. For best results, pass only global or literal strings to envvar. Automatic string variables or dynamic strings allocated by malloc() or similar heap allocators must not be deleted or permitted to go out of scope after being passed to putenv().

See also   exec..., getenv

Example
```
/* putenv.cpp */
#include <stdio.h>
#include <stdlib.h>
void Display(const char *s);
main()
{
  puts("Before calling putenv()");
  Display("PUTENV");
  putenv("PUTENV=A test string");
  puts("After calling putenv()");
  Display("PUTENV");
  return 0;
}

void Display(const char *s)
{
  char *result = getenv(s);
  if (result)
    printf("%s == %s\n", s, result);
  else
    printf("%s not found in environment\n", s);
}
```

putimage   Display bitmap

Syntax   void far putimage(int left, int top, void far *bitmap, int op);

Include   graphics.h

Description   Copies a saved graphics bitmap image to the display. Normally, you save images with getimage() and then redisplay them with putimage(), perhaps at a different location. The Example shows how to use this technique to bounce a red rubber ball around onscreen.

Parameters   **int left**, **int top** Coordinate of the image rectangle's upper-left pixel.

void far *bitmap Pointer to the image data as saved by getimage().

int op One of the enumerated putimage_ops symbols COPY_PUT, XOR_PUT, OR_PUT, AND_PUT, or NOT_PUT, which select the logical operation that `putimage()` uses to combine image bits with graphics already on display.

See also   getimage, imagesize

Example
```cpp
/* putimage.cpp */
#include <graphics.h>
#include <stdio.h>
#include <stdlib.h>
#include <conio.h>
#define RADIUS 10
main()
{
  int gdriver = DETECT, gmode, gerr;
  int xc, yc, x1, y1, x2, y2, xmax, ymax;
  int diameter, dx, dy, x, y;
  void far *image;
  initgraph(&gdriver, &gmode, "c:\\borlandc\\bgi");
  gerr = graphresult();
  if (gerr != grOk) {
    printf("BGI error: %s\n", grapherrormsg(gerr));
    exit(gerr);
  }
  xmax = getmaxx();
  ymax = getmaxy();
  xc = xmax / 2;
  yc = ymax / 2;
  x1 = (xc - RADIUS) - 1;
  y1 = (yc - RADIUS) - 4;
  x2 = (xc + RADIUS) + 1;
  y2 = (yc + RADIUS) + 4;
  diameter = RADIUS + RADIUS;
  setcolor(WHITE);
  circle(xc, yc, RADIUS);              // Draw ball's outline
  setfillstyle(SOLID_FILL, RED);
  floodfill(xc, yc, WHITE);        // Color ball red
  image = new char[imagesize(x1, y1, x2, y2)];
  if (image) {
    getimage(x1, y1, x2, y2, image);  // Copy display image
    clearviewport();
    dx = 1;
    dy = 1;
    y = yc;
    x = xc;
```

```
      while (!kbhit()) {
        putimage(x, y, image, COPY_PUT);   // Display ball
        x += dx;
        y += dy;
        if ((y >= ymax - diameter) || (y <= 0))
          dy = -dy;
        if ((x >= xmax - diameter) || (x <= 0))
          dx = -dx;
      }
    }
    getch();
    closegraph();
    return 0;
  }
```

putpixel   Plot pixel

Syntax   `void far putpixel(int x, int y, int color);`

Include   graphics.h

Description Displays a single graphics pixel at a specified coordinate. The resulting color depends on the video mode.

Parameters **int x**, **int y** Coordinate at which to display the pixel.

              int color Pixel's suggested color.

See also   getpixel, putimage

Example
```
/* putpixel.cpp */
#include <graphics.h>
#include <stdio.h>
#include <stdlib.h>
#include <conio.h>
main()
{
  int gdriver = DETECT, gmode, gerr;
  int xmax, ymax, cmax, color;
  initgraph(&gdriver, &gmode, "c:\\borlandc\\bgi");
  gerr = graphresult();
  if (gerr != grOk) {
    printf("BGI error: %s\n", grapherrormsg(gerr));
    exit(gerr);
```

```
    }
    xmax = getmaxx();
    ymax = getmaxy();
    cmax = getmaxcolor();
    while (!kbhit()) {
      if (random(400) > 2)
        color = 0;
      else
        color = 1 + random(cmax);
      putpixel(random(xmax), random(ymax), color);
    }
    getch();
    closegraph();
    return 0;
}
```

puts   Output string to stdout

Syntax   `int puts(const char *s);`

Include   stdio.h

Description   Writes to the standard output the specified string plus a newline character.

Parameters   **const char *s** Pointer to a null-terminated string.

See also   cputs, fputs, gets, printf

Example
```
/* puts.cpp */
#include <stdio.h>
main()
{
  puts("Welcome to a program, the primary job");
  puts("of which is to bid you welcome!");
  return 0;
}.
```

puttext   Copy text to screen

Syntax   `int puttext(int left, int top, int right, int bottom,`
           `    void *source);`

Include   conio.h

Description   Copies to the display a text buffer saved by `gettext()`.

Parameters   `int left`, `int top` The upper-left corner of the display rectangle.

`int right`, `int bottom` The bottom-right corner of the display rectangle.

`void *destin` The address of a buffer initialized by `gettext()`.

See also   `gettext`, `movetext`, `window`

Example   See `gettext`.

putw   Output integer to stream

Syntax   `int putw(int w, FILE *stream);`

Include   stdio.h

Description   Writes an integer to a file stream. Returns `w` for success and `EOF` for failure. Because `EOF` might equal `w` (both are integer values), call `ferror()` to confirm a suspected `putw()` error.

Parameters   `int w` Integer to write to a file stream.

`FILE *stream` A file stream such as that opened by `fopen()`.

See also   `fwrite`, `getw`, `printf`

Example   See `getw`.

qsort   Quicksort

Syntax   `void qsort(void *base, size_t nelem, size_t width,`
`    int (*fcmp)(const void *, const void *));`

Include   stdlib.h

Description   Sorts a table of data elements using the Quicksort algorithm and a user-supplied comparison function.

Parameters   `void *base` Pointer to the base of the data element array.

`size_t nelem` Number of elements in the table.

`size_t width` Size in bytes of a single element.

`int (*fcmp)(const void *, const void *)` Pointer to a comparison function, to which `qsort()` passes two pointers that address elements in the table being sorted. The function should return −1 if the first parameter is less than the second, zero if the two parameters are equal, or +1 if the first parameter is greater than the second.

See also   bsearch, lfind, lsearch

Example
```cpp
/* qsort.cpp */
#include <stdio.h>
#include <stdlib.h>
#include <time.h>
#define SIZE 100
int compare(const void *a, const void *b);
void DisplayArray(void);
int array[SIZE];   // Array of integers
main()
{
  for (int i = 0; i < SIZE; i++)
    array[i] = rand();
  DisplayArray();
  qsort((void *)array, SIZE, sizeof(array[0]), compare);
  DisplayArray();
  return 0;
}

int compare(const void *a, const void *b)
{
  int aint = *(int *)a;
  int bint = *(int *)b;
  if (aint < bint)
    return -1;
  else if (aint > bint)
    return +1;
  else
    return 0;
}

void DisplayArray(void)
{
  puts("");
  for (int i = 0; i < SIZE; i++)
    printf("%8d", array[i]);
}
```

raise Send signal

Syntax `int raise(int sig);`

Include signal.h

Description Sends a signal, executing a signal handler to run if one has been installed by a preceding call to the `signal()` function. Typically used to implement error functions.

Parameters **int sig** Signal to be sent. One of the constants defined in signal.h: SIGABRT (force abnormal termination), SIGFPE (floating-point error), SIGILL (illegal operation), SIGINT (control-break interrupt), SIGSEGV (bounds violation), or SIGTERM (terminate program).

See also abort, signal

Example
```
/* raise.cpp */
#include <stdio.h>
#include <signal.h>
main(int argc, char *argv[])
{
  if (argc <= 1) {
    puts("Enter at least one argument");
    puts("e.g RAISE XYZ");
    raise(SIGTERM);  // Terminate program
  }
  printf("Argument == %s\n", argv[1]);
  return 0;
}
```

rand Random number

Syntax `int rand(void);`

Include stdlib.h

Description Returns an integer selected at random from the range zero to RAND_MAX.

See also random, randomize, srand

Example
```
/* rand.cpp */
#include <stdio.h>
#include <conio.h>
#include <stdlib.h>
```

```
#include <time.h>
main()
{
  puts("Press any key to stop");
  puts("random number generation...");
  randomize();  // Seed generator
  while (!kbhit()) {
    gotoxy(1, wherey());
    printf("%8d", rand());
  }
  getch();  // Throw away keypress
  return 0;
}
```

randbrd   Read random block

Syntax   `int randbrd(struct fcb *fcb, int rcnt);`

Include   dos.h

Description   Reads disk records from the file identified by a file control block (FCB), storing those records at the current disk transfer address (DTA). Calls DOS function 0x27. Requires the file control block's `fcb_recsize` and `fcb_random` members to be initialized as the Example demonstrates. Returns 0 (success), 1 (end of file), 2 (partial records read due to impending wrap-around of buffer address), 3 (partial record read at end of file). Consult a DOS reference for more information about function 0x27.

Parameters   `struct fcb *fcb` Pointer to a file control block, identifying an open file from which to read records.

`int rcnt` Number of records to read.

See also   fread, getdta, parsfnm, randbwr, read, setdta

Example
```
/* randbrd.cpp */
#include <stdio.h>
#include <stdlib.h>
#include <string.h>
#include <dos.h>
struct fcb fb;  // File control block
main()
{
  int result;
```

```c
  char far *olddta;
  char outbuf[256] = "Borland C++ and Application Frameworks";
  char inbuf[256];          // Uninitialized buffer
  fb.fcb_drive = 0;         // Default drive
  strcpy(fb.fcb_name, "TEMP    ");  // Filename
  strcpy(fb.fcb_ext, "$$$");    // Extension
  if ((bdosptr(0x16, &fb, 0) & 0x00ff) != 0) {    // Create file
    puts("Error creating file");
    exit(1);
  }
  fb.fcb_recsize = 128;  // Bytes per record
  setdta(outbuf);
  if (randbwr(&fb, 2) != 0) {         // Write to file
    puts("Error writing to file");
    exit(2);
  }
  if ((bdosptr(0x10, &fb, 0) & 0xff) != 0) {   // Close file
    puts("Error closing file");
    exit(3);
  }
  if ((bdosptr(0x0f, &fb, 0) & 0xff) != 0) {   // Reopen file
    puts("Error opening file");
    exit(4);
  }
  fb.fcb_random = 0L;   // Reset random record number
  setdta(inbuf);        // Address input buffer
  if (randbrd(&fb, 2) != 0) {        // Read file
    puts("Error reading from file");
    exit(5);
  }
  if ((bdosptr(0x10, &fb, 0) &0xff) != 0) {   // Close file
    puts("Error closing file");
    exit(3);
  }
  printf("Input buffer after reading:\n");
  puts(inbuf);
  return 0;
}
```

randbwr   Write random block

Syntax   `int randbrw(struct fcb *fcb, int rcnt);`

Include   dos.h

Description   Writes disk records to the file identified by a file control block (FCB) from the current disk transfer address (DTA). Calls DOS function 0x28. Returns 0 (success), 1 (disk full), or 2 (partial records written due to impending address wrap-around). Consult a DOS reference for more information.

Parameters   **struct fcb *fcb** Pointer to a file control block, identifying an open file to which to write records.

   int rcnt Number of records to write.

See also   `fwrite, getdta, parsfnm, randbrd, setdta, write`

Example   See randbrd.

random   Random number in range

Syntax   `int random(int num);`

Include   stdlib.h

Description   Returns an integer selected at random from the range `0 ... num - 1`. Encoded as a macro in stdlib.h.

Parameters   **int num** Upper limit plus one.

See also   `rand, randomize, srand`

Example
```
/* random.cpp */
#include <stdio.h>
#include <conio.h>
#include <stdlib.h>
#include <time.h>
unsigned long counts[4];
main()
{
  int n;
  double percent;
  unsigned long loops = 0;
  randomize();  // See random number generator
```

```
    puts("\nCount frequency of random numbers from 0 to 99.");
    puts("Press any key to stop counting...");
    while (!kbhit()) {
      n = random(100);
      gotoxy(1, wherey());
      cprintf("Random number==%5d  Loops==%lu", n, ++loops);
      if (n < 25) counts[0]++;
      if (n < 50) counts[1]++;
      if (n < 75) counts[2]++;
      counts[3]++;
    }
    getch();  // Throw away keypress
    puts("\n\n Range  :   Count Percentage");
    puts(    "---------------------------");
    for (n = 0; n < 4; n++) {
      percent = 100.0 * ((double)counts[n] / loops);
      printf("0 - %d :%8lu == %7.3lf%%\n",
        ((n + 1) * 25) - 1, counts[n], percent);
    }
    return 0;
}
```

randomize   Seed random numbers

Syntax   `void randomize(void);`

Include   stdlib.h, time.h

Description   Randomly seeds the random number generator, causing it to begin a new random sequence. Calls function `time()`—the reason for including time.h.

See also   rand, random, srand

Example   See rand, random.

_read   Read from file

Syntax   `int _read(int handle, void *buf, unsigned len);`

Include   io.h

Description   Reads bytes from a file. Calls DOS function 0x3f. Returns zero for success and a DOS error code for failure.

Parameters   `int handle` Handle to an open file.

`void *buf` Pointer to a buffer into which file data is copied.

`unsigned len` Maximum number of bytes to read.

See also   _dos_open, _dos_read, fread, fopen, _open, read, _write

Example   See _open.

read   Read from file

Syntax   `int read(int handle, void *buf, unsigned len);`

Include   io.h

Description   Reads bytes from a file. Returns the number of bytes read—zero if attempting to read past the end of the file or –1 for failure.

Parameters   `int handle` Handle to the open file.

`void *buf` Pointer to the buffer into which file data is copied.

`unsigned len` Maximum number of bytes to read.

See also   _dos_open, _dos_read, fread, fopen, _open, _read, _write

Example   See open.

real   Complex or BCD to real

Syntax   `double real(complex x);`
`double real(bcd x);`

Include   complex.h, bcd.h

Description   Returns the `double` real value of a `complex` class object, or the equivalent `double` value of a binary-coded decimal `bcd` class object.

Parameters   `complex x` An object of the `complex` class.

`bcd x` An object of the `bcd` class.

See also   abs, bcd, complex, imag

Example
```
/* real.cpp */
#include <stdio.h>
#include <complex.h>
```

```
#include <bcd.h>
main()
{
  bcd b(123456);
  complex c(1.2, 3.4);
  cout << "bcd b     == " << b << '\n';
  cout << "real(b)   == " << real(b) << '\n';
  cout << "complex c == " << c << '\n';
  cout << "real(c)   == " << real(c) << '\n';
  return 0;
}
```

realloc   Reallocate memory

Syntax `void *realloc(void *block, size_t size);`

Include stdlib.h

Description Expands or shrinks an existing memory block to a new size, or creates a new block. Copies existing block to a new location if necessary. Returns the address of the modified block and returns null for errors.

Parameters **void *block** Pointer to block to be resized, such as returned by a preceding call to malloc(). You may set block to null, in which case realloc() attempts to allocate a new block of the specified size.

size_t size The requested size in bytes for the reallocated memory block.

See also calloc, farcalloc, farmalloc, farrealloc, free, malloc

Example
```
/* realloc.cpp */
#include <stdio.h>
#include <stdlib.h>
main()
{
  void *p1;
  void *p2;
  puts("Allocating 128 bytes");
  p1 = malloc(128);         // Allocate 128 bytes
  if (p1) {
    puts("Resizing block to 256 bytes");
    p2 = realloc(p1, 256);  // Resize to 256 bytes
  }
```

```
  if (p2)
    delete p2;    // Delete resized block
  else
    delete p1;    // Or delete original if resizing failed
  return 0;
}
```

rectangle   Draw rectangle

Syntax   void far rectangle(int left, int top, int right, int bottom);

Include   graphics.h

Description   Draws a rectangle on the graphics display using the current line style, thickness, and color.

Parameters   **int left, int top** Coordinate of the rectangle's upper-left corner.

int right, int bottom Coordinate of the rectangle's lower-right corner.

See also   circle, bar, bar3d, setcolor, setlinestyle

Example
```
/* rectangl.cpp */
#include <graphics.h>
#include <stdio.h>
#include <stdlib.h>
#include <conio.h>
#include <dos.h>
main()
{
  int gdriver = DETECT, gmode, gerr;
  int xmax, ymax, cmax;
  initgraph(&gdriver, &gmode, "c:\\borlandc\\bgi");
  gerr = graphresult();
  if (gerr != grOk) {
    printf("BGI error: %s\n", grapherrormsg(gerr));
    exit(gerr);
  }
  xmax = getmaxx();
  ymax = getmaxy();
  cmax = getmaxcolor();
  while (!kbhit()) {
    delay(50);
    setcolor(1 + random(cmax));
```

```
        rectangle(random(xmax), random(ymax),
          random(xmax), random(ymax));
      }
      getch();
      closegraph();
      return 0;
    }
```

registerbgidriver Register custom BGI driver

Syntax   `int registerbgidriver(void (*driver)(void));`

Include   graphics.h

Description   Registers a custom BGI graphics driver, as might be supplied by a graphics display interface manufacturer and loaded into memory or installed in GRAPHICS.LIB. Not required for supplied drivers. Returns a handle to the driver or a negative error code. To use a registered driver, pass its handle to `initgraph()`.

(**Note:** The Example is for demonstration purposes only. Before the program will run, it requires modification and a custom graphics driver.)

Parameters   **void (*driver)(void)** Pointer to a void function requiring no parameters—i.e. the address of driver image in memory.

See also   initgraph, installuserdriver, installuserfont, registerbgifont

Example
```
/* rbgidriv.cpp */
#include <graphics.h>
#include <stdio.h>
#include <stdlib.h>
#include <conio.h>
// Following is for demonstration purposes only.
// Replace driver name with custom 3rd-party
// driver name as installed in GRAPHICS.LIB.
#define DRIVER EGAVGA_driver
main()
{
  int gdriver = DETECT, gmode, gerr;
  gerr = registerbgidriver(DRIVER);
```

```
    if (gerr < 0) {
      puts("Unable to register graphics driver");
      puts(grapherrormsg(gerr));
      exit(1);
    }
    initgraph(&gdriver, &gmode, "c:\\borlandc\\bgi");
    gerr = graphresult();
    if (gerr != grOk) {
      printf("BGI error: %s\n", grapherrormsg(gerr));
      exit(gerr);
    }
    while (!kbhit()) {
      setcolor(1 + random(getmaxcolor()));
      lineto(random(getmaxx()), random(getmaxy()));
    }
    getch();
    closegraph();
    return 0;
}
```

registerbgifont   Register custom BGI font

Syntax   `int registerbgifont(void (*font)(void));`

Include   graphics.h

Description   Registers a custom graphics font in memory. Not required for supplied fonts. Returns font handle or negative error code. To use a registered font, pass its handle to `settextstyle()`. To compile the example, change to C:\BORLANDC\BGI or the equivalent directory and enter `bgiobj goth` to convert GOTH.CHR to GOTH.OBJ. Change back to the example directory and enter **bcc rbgifont graphics.lib c:\borlandc\bgi\goth.obj**.

Parameters   **void (*font)(void)** Pointer to a `void` function requiring no parameters—that is the address of the font image in memory.

See also   initgraph, installuserdriver, installuserfont, registerbgidriver, settextstyle

Example
```
/* rbgifont.cpp */
#include <graphics.h>
#include <stdio.h>
```

```
#include <stdlib.h>
#include <conio.h>
#include <dos.h>
#define FONT gothic_font
char s[1];
main()
{
  int gdriver = DETECT, gmode, gerr;
  gerr = registerbgifont(FONT);
  if (gerr < 0) {
    puts("Unable to register font");
    puts(grapherrormsg(gerr));
    exit(1);
  }
  initgraph(&gdriver, &gmode, "c:\\borlandc\\bgi");
  gerr = graphresult();
  if (gerr != grOk) {
    printf("BGI error: %s\n", grapherrormsg(gerr));
    exit(gerr);
  }
  while (!kbhit()) {
    setcolor(1 + random(getmaxcolor()));
    s[0] = 33 + random(222);  // ASCII 33 ... 254
    s[1] = 0;
    delay(250);
    settextstyle(GOTHIC_FONT, HORIZ_DIR, 2 + random(14));
    outtextxy(random(getmaxx()), random(getmaxy()), s);
  }
  getch();
  closegraph();
  return 0;
}
```

remove   Remove file

Syntax   `int remove(const char *filename);`

Include   stdio.h

Description   Deletes a named file (if it exists). Returns zero for success and −1 for failure and sets errno to ENOENT (file not found) or EACCES (access denied). Encoded as a macro that calls `unlink()`.

Parameters   `const char *filename` Pointer to null-terminated string that represents the name of the file to be deleted.

See also   chmod, chsize, rename, unlink

Example
```
/* remove.cpp */
#include <stdio.h>
#include <io.h>
#include <sys\stat.h>
main()
{
  char tfname[L_tmpnam];
  tmpnam(tfname);
  printf("Creating temporary file %s\n", tfname);
  int handle = creat(tfname, S_IWRITE);
  if (handle) {
    puts("Closing temporary file");
    close(handle);
  }
  printf("Removing %s\n", tfname);
  remove(tfname);
  return 0;
}
```

rename   Rename file

Syntax   `int rename(const char *oldname, const char *newname);`

Include   stdio.h

Description   Changes a filename. Can also move a file from one directory to another (on the same drive only), without causing the file's contents to be copied. Returns zero for success and –1 for failure and sets errno to ENOENT (file not found), EACCES (access denied), or ENOTSAM (not same drive). The example is named RENAMER.CPP to avoid a conflict with the DOS RENAME command.

Parameters   `const char *oldname` Pointer to existing filename string. Can contain drive and directory path information but no wild cards.

`const char *newname` Pointer to new filename string. Can contain drive and directory path information but no wild cards. Any drive letter must be the same as used for oldname. If a different directory is given, the file is moved to that directory (if it exists) without causing the file's contents to be copied.

See also   `creat, chmod, chsize, remove`

Example

```
/* renamer.cpp */
#include <stdio.h>
#include <stdlib.h>
main(int argc, char *argv[])
{
  if (argc < 3) {
    puts("Use like DOS RENAME command.");
    puts("ex. RENAME MYFILE.TXT MYFILE.BAK");
    puts("Or, enter a directory to move files.");
    puts("ex. RENAME MYFILE.TXT C:\NEWDIR\MYFILE.TXT");
    exit(1);
  }
  if (rename(argv[1], argv[2]) == -1)
    printf("Error renaming %s to %s\n", argv[1], argv[2]);
  else
    printf("%s renamed to %s\n", argv[1], argv[2]);
  return 0;
}
```

restorecrtmode   Restore pre-graphics mode

Syntax   `void far restorecrtmode(void);`

Include   graphics.h

Description   Restores display mode in effect prior to calling `initgraph()` to initialize graphics. After calling `restorecrtmode()`, call `setgraphmode()` to return to graphics. Call `closegraph()`, *not* `restorecrtmode()`, to end graphics permanently.

See also   `closegraph, getgraphmode, initgraph, setgraphmode`

Example

```
/* restorec.cpp */
#include <graphics.h>
#include <stdio.h>
#include <stdlib.h>
#include <conio.h>
#define ASCII_ESC 27
```

```
main()
{
  int gdriver = DETECT, gmode, gerr;
  int xmax, ymax, cmaxp1;
  char c = 0;
  initgraph(&gdriver, &gmode, "c:\\borlandc\\bgi");
  gerr = graphresult();
  if (gerr != grOk) {
    printf("BGI error: %s\n", grapherrormsg(gerr));
    exit(gerr);
  }
  xmax = getmaxx();
  ymax = getmaxy();
  cmaxp1 = getmaxcolor() + 1;
  while (c != ASCII_ESC) {
    setgraphmode(gmode);
    while (!kbhit()) {
      setcolor(random(cmaxp1));
      circle(random(xmax), random(ymax), random(75));
    }
    c = getch();  // Throw away keypress
    restorecrtmode();
    clrscr();
    puts("Press Enter for graphics; Esc to quit...");
    c = getch();
  }
  closegraph();
  return 0;
}
```

rewind   Reset file pointer

Syntax   void rewind(FILE *stream);

Include   stdio.h

Description Resets a file stream's internal position to the beginning of the file. Typically used to reread a file from its first byte, or to prepare for writing new data over the beginning of an existing file. Also clears the file's end-of-file and error flags.

Parameters **FILE *stream** Pointer to open file stream such as returned by fopen().

1287

See also   fopen, fseek, fsetpos, ftell

Example   See fread.

rewinddir   Reset directory stream

Syntax   void rewinddir(DIR *dirp);

Include   dirent.h

Description   Resets open directory stream so that the next operation begins again with the first directory entry. The example uses rewinddir() to display the same directory twice.

Parameters   **DIR *dirp** Pointer to DIR structure as defined in dirent.h.

See also   closedir, findfirst, findnext, opendir, readdir

Example
```
/* rewinddi.cpp */
#include <stdio.h>
#include <dirent.h>
#include <dos.h>
main()
{
  DIR *d = opendir(".");
  struct dirent *dp;
  while ((dp = readdir(d)) != NULL)
    printf("%14s  ", dp->d_name);
  puts("\n\nPlay it again, Sam...\n");
  delay(2000);
  rewinddir(d);
  while ((dp = readdir(d)) != NULL)
    printf("%14s  ", dp->d_name);
  closedir(d);
  return 0;
}
```

rmdir   Remove directory

Syntax   int rmdir(const char *path);

Include   dir.h

Description   Deletes named directory, which must have no files and cannot be the current directory or a disk's root directory. Returns zero for success and

−1 for failure and sets errno to ENOENT (directory not found) or EACCES (access denied). The example is named RMDIRS.CPP to avoid a conflict with the DOS RMDIR command.

Parameters   `const char *path` Pointer to null-terminated string naming the directory to be removed.

See also   _chmod, chdir, getcurdir, getcwd, mkdir

Example
```
/* rmdirs.cpp */
#include <stdio.h>
#include <stdlib.h>
#include <dir.h>
main(int argc, char *argv[])
{
  if (argc <= 1 ) {
    puts("Enter directory name to remove");
    exit(1);
  }
  if (rmdir(argv[1]) == -1)
    printf("Unable to remove %s\n", argv[1]);
  else
    printf("%s removed\n", argv[1]);
  return 0;
}
```

rmtmp   Remove temporary files

Syntax   `int rmtmp(void);`

Include   stdio.h

Description   Closes and removes all temporary files previously created by one or more calls to tmpfile(). The current directory must be the same as when the temporary files were created. Temporary files in other directories are not removed. Returns the total number of temporary files closed and removed.

See also   remove, tmpfile, tmpnam

Example   See fread.

_rotl, _rotr   Rotate left, rotate right

Syntax
```
unsigned _rotl(unsigned value, int count);
unsigned _rotr(unsigned value, int count);
```

Include stdlib.h

Description Rotates bits in unsigned values left (_rotl()) or right (_rotr()). Returns rotated value.

Parameters **unsigned value** Value to be rotated left or right. Original variable is not modified.

int count Number of rotations.

See also _lrotl, _lrotr

Example
```
/* _rotlr.cpp */
#include <stdio.h>
#include <stdlib.h>
main(int argc, char *argv[])
{
  unsigned result;
  if (argc < 3) {
    puts("Enter value and rotation count");
    puts("ex. _ROTL 123 4");
    exit(1);
  }
  unsigned value = atoi(argv[1]);
  int count = atoi(argv[2]);
  result = _rotl(value, count);
  printf("%u rotated LEFT  %d times == %u\n",
    value, count, result);
  result = _rotr(value, count);
  printf("%u rotated RIGHT %d times == %u\n",
    value, count, result);
  return 0;
}
```

sbrk   Change data segment size

Syntax `void *sbrk(int incr);`

Include alloc.h

Description   Expands or shrinks the size of a program's data segment. Returns pointer to the former break value (the address following the end of the data segment). If sbrk() fails, it returns −1 and sets errno to ENOMEM (not enough memory).

Parameters   **int incr** If incr is positive, sbrk() attempts to expand the data segment by the specified number of bytes. If incr is negative, sbrk() attempts to shrink the data segment by the absolute value of the specified number of bytes.

See also   brk, coreleft

Example
```
/* sbrk.cpp */
#include <stdio.h>
#include <alloc.h>
void Report(const char *msg);
main()
{
  Report("\nBefore expanding data segment to 4K");
  sbrk(4000);
  Report("\nAfter expanding data segment to 4K");
  return 0;
}

void Report(const char *msg)
{
  puts(msg);
  printf("coreleft() == %ul\n", (unsigned long)coreleft());
}
```

scanf   Get formatted input from stdin

Syntax   int scanf(const char *format[, address, ...]);

Include   stdio.h

Description   Reads text input from stdin, translating input fields to binary according to conversion rules supplied by a format string. Stores the translated values at supplied addresses, usually referring to program variables. Returns the number of input fields successfully scanned, or returns EOF if attempting to read past the input's end of file.

The scanf() function is unforgiving of errors, the most common of which is neglecting to pass the *address* of an argument that follows the `format` string. Except for arrays (especially `char` arrays), always apply the `&` address of operator to arguments passed to `scanf()`. Between calls to `scanf()`, it might be necessary to call `fflush(stdin)` to reset the standard input file after any input errors.

The function's `format` string conforms to the following rules, expressed in Backus-Naur syntax. The symbol `::=` gives a name at left to a set of rules at right. Bracketed items are optional. A vertical bar means "or." The word *blank* stands for a blank character, *literal* for a nonblank character, and *number* for an integer value (in text form).

```
format string ::= [blank] [literal] [conversion rule]
conversion rule ::= % [*] [width] [h | l | L] [N | F] [type]
width ::= number;
type ::= % | c | d | D | e | E | f | F | g | G |
         i | I | n | o | O | p | s | u | U | x | X | [
```

These rules tell you that format strings can have whitespace characters (blanks), literal text, and conversion rules. Whitespace characters (blanks, tabs, and newline characters) cause `scanf()` to read and ignore those characters from the input. Non-whitespace characters cause the function to read and ignore matching non-whitespace characters from the input.

A conversion rule begins with a percent sign (`%`) and is followed by one or more other optional items in the order shown. Each conversion item is further described in the following sections.

[*]   An asterisk suppresses assigning a value to the input field argument.

[width]   Maximum number of characters to apply from the input during the translation of the current input field argument. Fewer but no more than this many characters are used in translating the field.

[h | l | L]   Force argument data type to be `short int` (`h`), `long int` (`l` for all integer arguments), `double` (`l` for all floating point arguments), or `long double` (`L` for all floating point arguments).

[N | F]   Force argument address to be near (`N`) or far (`F`).

Type   The following table lists conversion type characters, of which one must be supplied for every conversion rule. Case is significant (`D` and `d`, for example, specify different conversions).

Conversion characters for `scanf()` function.

Conversion Character	Description of argument field **v**
%	No conversion. Read and store a percent character.
c	`char *v` or `char v[n]` for a width n.
d	`int *v` in decimal.
D	`long *v` in decimal.
e	`float *v`.
E	`float *v`.
f	`float *v`.
g	`float *v`.
G	`float *v`.
i	`int *v` in decimal, octal, or hexadecimal.
I	`long *v` in decimal, octal, or hexadecimal.
n	`int *v` set to number of characters so far read from input.
o	`int *v` in octal.
O	`long *v` in octal.
p	`near *v` for tiny, small, and medium memory models in OFFSET format; `far *v` for compact, large, and huge models in SEGMENT:OFFSET format.
s	`char *v` to an array of `char`.
u	`unsigned int *v` in decimal.
U	`unsigned long *v` in decimal.
x	`int *v` in hexadecimal.
X	`int *v` in hexadecimal.

continues

Conversion Character	Description of argument field v
[	Begin regular expression, a set of characters in square brackets. The conversion rule %[xyz] scans for the characters x, y, and z. A preceding caret (^) means "not." Thus %[^xyz] scans for all characters not equal to x, y, or z. Define character ranges with a hyphen. The rule %[A-Z] scans for upper-case alphabetic characters from A to Z inclusively. You can also string multiple ranges together. The rule %[0-9A-Fa-f] scans for hexadecimal digits 0 through 9, A through F, and a through f. Character ranges must be ordered in ASCII from low to high. The rule %[0-9] specifies the digits 0 through 9; the rule %[9-0] specifies the digits 9 and 0 and a hyphen character (-).

> **NOTE:** Conversion characters e, E, f, g, and G are equivalent for all forms of floating point values.

Parameters   **const char *format** Pointer to null-terminated string containing one or more conversion rules and other characters as explained in the preceding description. Typically entered as a literal string directly in a scanf() statement.

address, ... Argument addresses, one per conversion rule in the preceding format string. Be sure to supply the *address* of arguments. Pass the int variable x, for example, as &x.

See also   atof, atoi, atol, cscanf, fscanf, getc, gets, printf, sscanf, vfscanf, vscanf, vsscanf

Example
```
/* scanf.cpp */
#include <stdio.h>
```

```
main()
{
  int i;
  puts("Enter an integer value in hex");
  scanf("%i", &i);
  printf("In decimal, you entered %d\n", i);
  return 0;
}
```

_searchenv   Search named path for file

Syntax   void _searchenv(const char *file, const char *varname,
           char *buf);

Include   stdlib.h

Description   Searches the current directory for the specified filename. If the file is not found, continues searching in each of the directories listed and separated by semicolons in an environment variable such as PATH or INCLUDE. If the file is found in any of these locations, _searchenv() stores the file's complete pathname at the location addressed by buf. If the file is not found, buf is set to a null string.

Parameters   **const char *file** Pointer to filename string.

const char *varname Pointer to environment variable name (PATH, LIB, INCLUDE, or similar) listing one or more directories that might contain the given file.

char *buf Pointer to an array of char large enough to hold any possible path specification, e.g. a string of MAX_PATH (80) characters.

See also   findfirst, findnext, getenv, putenv, searchpath

Example
```
/* _searche.cpp */
#include <stdio.h>
#include <stdlib.h>
#include <string.h>
main()
{
  char pathname[_MAX_PATH];
  puts("Searching for BCC.EXE along PATH");
  _searchenv("BCC.EXE", "PATH", pathname);
  if (strlen(pathname) == 0)
```

```
      puts("BCC.EXE not found");
    else
      puts(pathname);
    return 0;
  }
```

searchpath   Search system path for file

Syntax   `char *searchpath(const char *file);`

Include   dir.h

Description   Similar to _searchenv(), but searches for a filename in the current directory, and failing to find the file there, in each directory specified by the PATH environment variable. Returns a pointer to the file's complete pathname, or returns null if the file is not found. The returned string is stored in a static buffer that is reused by each call to searchpath().

Parameters   **const char *file** Pointer to filename string.

See also   _searchenv

Example
```
/* searchpa.cpp */
#include <stdio.h>
#include <dir.h>
main()
{
  char *pathname;
  puts("Searching for BCC.EXE along PATH");
  pathname = searchpath("BCC.EXE");
  if (pathname == NULL)
    puts("BCC.EXE not found");
  else
    puts(pathname);
  return 0;
}
```

sector   Draw elliptical wedge

Syntax   `void far sector(int x, int y, int stangle, int endangle,`
            `int xradius, int yradius);`

Include   graphics.h

Description   This strangely named sector() function operates like ellipse(), but fills an elliptical arc and wedge with the current fill pattern and color (see setfillstyle() and setfillpattern()). Use setcolor() to change the wedge's outline color. The parameters are identical to and have the same effects as the parameters for ellipse().

Parameters   See **ellipse**.

See also   arc, circle, ellipse, fillellipse, getarccoords, getaspectratio, pieslice, setfillpattern, setfillstyle

Example
```cpp
/* sector.cpp */
#include <graphics.h>
#include <stdio.h>
#include <stdlib.h>
#include <time.h>
#include <conio.h>
main()
{
  int gdriver = DETECT, gmode, gerr;
  int x, y, xmax, ymax, cmax, xsize, ysize;
  int xsized2, ysized2;
  randomize();
  initgraph(&gdriver, &gmode, "c:\\borlandc\\bgi");
  gerr = graphresult();
  if (gerr != grOk) {
    printf("BGI error: %s\n", grapherrormsg(gerr));
    exit(gerr);
  }
  xmax = getmaxx();
  ymax = getmaxy();
  cmax = getmaxcolor();
  xsize = xmax / 8;
  ysize = ymax / 4;
  xsized2 = xsize / 2;
  ysized2 = ysize / 2;
  y = ysized2;
  while (y < (ymax - ysized2)) {
    x = xsized2;
    while (x < (xmax - xsized2)) {
      setcolor(1 + random(cmax));
      setfillstyle(1 + random(11), 1 + random(cmax));
      sector(x, y, random(360), random(45),
```

```
            xsized2 - 6, ysized2 - 6);
        x += xsize;
      }
      y += ysize;
    }
    getch();
    closegraph();
    return 0;
}
```

segread   Read segment registers

Syntax   `void segread(struct SREGS *segp);`

Include   dos.h

Description Copies current segment register values (CS, DS, ES, and SS) to a structure defined in dos.h as

```
struct SREGS {
  unsigned int es;
  unsigned int cs;
  unsigned int ss;
  unsigned int ds;
};
```

Parameters **struct SREGS *segp** Pointer to SREGS structure.

See also   FP_OFF, FP_SEG, MK_FP

Example
```
/* segread.cpp */
#include <stdio.h>
#include <dos.h>
main()
{
  struct SREGS sr;
  segread(&sr);
  printf("CS == %#04x\n", sr.cs);
  printf("DS == %#04x\n", sr.ds);
  printf("ES == %#04x\n", sr.es);
  printf("SS == %#04x\n", sr.ss);
  return 0;
}
```

setactivepage   Set active graphics page

Syntax   `void far setactivepage(int page);`

Include   graphics.h

Description   Determines the memory page on which to draw graphics. Works only for graphics modes and hardware that support multiple graphics pages, such as EGA, VGA, and Hercules. Together, `setactivepage()` and `setvisualpage()` make it possible to design smooth animation sequences with a technique known as page swapping or ping ponging. The idea is to draw new graphics on an invisible page while viewing the most recent frame. Then, switch frames bringing the new graphics into view and preparing to draw on the other page.

The example draws a series of expanding circles, with each new set of circles forming a frame in the animation. To see the difference page swapping makes, set `visual` to 0, drawing and displaying on the same graphics page. Without page swapping, you can see each circle being formed. With page swapping, drawing occurs backstage—you see only the results.

Parameters   **int page** Page number to make visible.

See also   setvisualpage

Example
```
/* setactiv.cpp */
/* Note: Requires multipage EGA or VGA display */
#include <graphics.h>
#include <stdio.h>
#include <stdlib.h>
#include <conio.h>
main()
{
  int gdriver = VGA, gmode = VGAMED, gerr;  // VGA
/* int gdriver = EGA, gmode = EGAHI, gerr; */   // EGA
  int cmax, radius, xc, yc;
  int active, visual, temp;
  initgraph(&gdriver, &gmode, "c:\\borlandc\\bgi");
  gerr = graphresult();
  if (gerr != grOk) {
    printf("BGI error: %s\n", grapherrormsg(gerr));
    exit(gerr);
  }
```

```
      cmax = getmaxcolor();
      xc = getmaxx() / 2;
      yc = getmaxy() / 2;
      radius = 10;
      active = 0;
      visual = 1;
      setactivepage(active);
      while (!kbhit()) {
        if (radius == 10) {        // i.e. once per cycle
          setvisualpage(visual);
          setactivepage(active);
        }
        setcolor(1 + random(cmax));
        circle(xc, yc, radius);
        temp = active;
        active = visual;
        visual = temp;
        radius += 10;
        if (radius > yc)
          radius = 10;
      }
      getch();
      closegraph();
      return 0;
    }
```

setallpalette   Change palette colors

Syntax   `void far setallpalette(struct palettetype far *palette);`

Include   graphics.h

Description   Changes the current graphics palette to use the values in the addressed palettetype structure, defined in graphics.h as

```
#define MAXCOLORS 15
struct palettetype {
  unsigned char size;
  signed char colors[MAXCOLORS+1];
};
```

Calling `setallpalette()` immediately affects displayed colors. Set any palette entry to −1 to make no change to that entry. The Example shows how to use the function to achieve an animation effect simply by scrambling palette colors until you press a key to stop the program.

Parameters **struct palettetype far *palette** Pointer to palettetype structure containing new palette colors.

See also getpalette, getpalettesize, setpalette, setrgbpalette

Example
```cpp
/* setallpa.cpp */
#include <graphics.h>
#include <stdio.h>
#include <stdlib.h>
#include <conio.h>
#include <dos.h>
#include <time.h>
main()
{
  int gdriver = DETECT, gmode, gerr;
  int i, cmax, xmax, ymax;
  palettetype palette;
  initgraph(&gdriver, &gmode, "c:\\borlandc\\bgi");
  gerr = graphresult();
  if (gerr != grOk) {
    printf("BGI error: %s\n", grapherrormsg(gerr));
    exit(gerr);
  }
  xmax = getmaxx();
  ymax = getmaxy();
  cmax = getmaxcolor();
  randomize();
  for (i = 1; i <= 75; i++) {
    setcolor(1 + random(cmax));
    circle(random(xmax), random(ymax), random(100));
  }
  palette.size = cmax + 1;   // Number of colors in palette
  palette.colors[0] = -1;    // No change to background color
  while (!kbhit()) {
    delay(150);
    for (i = 1; i <= cmax; i++)
      palette.colors[i] = random(cmax + 1);
    setallpalette(&palette);
  }
  getch();
```

```
    closegraph();
    return 0;
}
```

setaspectratio Change graphics aspect ratio

Syntax `void far setaspectratio(int xasp, int yasp);`

Include graphics.h

Description Changes graphical aspect ratio—the relationship of a single pixel's width divided by its height. Affects the relative width and height of shapes such as circles and rectangles.

Parameters **int xasp** The horizontal width in unspecified units. The exact value is meaningless—it's the ratio of a pixel's width to its height that affects graphical output.

int yasp The vertical height in unspecified units.

See also getaspectratio

Example
```
/* setaspec.cpp */
#include <graphics.h>
#include <stdio.h>
#include <stdlib.h>
#include <conio.h>
void RoundAbout(int &y, int ch);
main()
{
  int gdriver = DETECT, gmode, gerr;
  int ch, y;
  initgraph(&gdriver, &gmode, "c:\\borlandc\\bgi");
  gerr = graphresult();
  if (gerr != grOk) {
    printf("BGI error: %s\n", grapherrormsg(gerr));
    exit(gerr);
  }
  ch = textheight("M");
  outtextxy(1, getmaxy() - ch - ch, "Press Enter to advance");
  y = 1;
```

```
    RoundAbout(y, ch);
    setaspectratio(1, 1);
    RoundAbout(y, ch);
    setaspectratio(1, 2);
    RoundAbout(y, ch);
    setaspectratio(2, 1);
    RoundAbout(y, ch);
    setaspectratio(3, 2);
    RoundAbout(y, ch);
    closegraph();
    return 0;
}

void RoundAbout(int &y, int ch)
{
    char c;
    char s[80];
    int xasp, yasp;
    getaspectratio(&xasp, &yasp);
    sprintf(s, "x==%d  y==%d  ratio==%lf", xasp, yasp,
      double(xasp) / double(yasp));
    outtextxy(1, y, s);
    circle(getmaxx() - (getmaxx() / 3),
      getmaxy() / 2, getmaxy() / 4);
    getch();
    y += ch + 5;
}
```

setbkcolor   Change graphics background color

Syntax   void far setbkcolor(int color);

Include   graphics.h

Description Change the graphics display's background color.

Parameters   **int color** Color value, used as an index into the current palette. At most times, setting color to zero changes the background to black, the default.

See also   getbkcolor, getcolor, setallpalette, setcolor, setpalette

Example
```
/* setbkcol.cpp */
#include <graphics.h>
#include <stdio.h>
#include <stdlib.h>
#include <conio.h>
#include <dos.h>
main()
{
  int gdriver = DETECT, gmode, gerr;
  int color;
  initgraph(&gdriver, &gmode, "c:\\borlandc\\bgi");
  gerr = graphresult();
  if (gerr != grOk) {
    printf("BGI error: %s\n", grapherrormsg(gerr));
    exit(gerr);
  }
  while (!kbhit()) {
    color = 0;
    while (color <= getmaxcolor()) {
      setbkcolor(color);
      delay(500);
      if (kbhit())
        color = getmaxcolor();
      color++;
    }
  }
  getch();
  closegraph();
  return 0;
}
```

setblock Modify memory block size

Syntax   `int setblock(unsigned segx, unsigned newsize);`

Include   dos.h

Description   Attempts to shrink or expand a DOS memory block (i.e. a segment) such as allocated by `allocmem()`. Returns −1 for success, or if the resizing request cannot be satisfied, returns the maximum number of 16-byte paragraphs available.

Parameters   **unsigned segx** Memory segment address as assigned by `allocmem()`.

        unsigned newsize Requested new size in 16-byte paragraphs for the memory block.

See also   allocmem, coreleft, _dos_allocmem, freemem, realloc

Example
```cpp
/* setblock.cpp */
#include <stdio.h>
#include <dos.h>
#define NPARAGRAPHS 32   // Number of paragraphs
main()
{
  int result;     // Function result
  unsigned seg;   // Passed by address to allocmem()
  printf("Allocating %d paragraphs\n", NPARAGRAPHS);
  result = allocmem(NPARAGRAPHS, &seg);
  if (result == -1) {
    puts("Allocation successful");
  } else {
    puts("Allocation failed");
    return 1;
  }
  puts("Attempting to double block size");
  result = setblock(seg, NPARAGRAPHS + NPARAGRAPHS);
  if (result == -1)
    puts("Block resizing successful");
  freemem(seg);  // Free allocated paragraphs
  return 0;
}
```

setbuf   Enable stream buffer

Syntax   void setbuf(FILE *stream, char *buf);

Include   stdio.h

Description   After opening a file stream (by calling `fopen()` usually), call `setbuf()` to attach an I/O buffer to the file. Files are normally buffered (except for nonredirected standard files `stdin` and `stdout`). Use this function to cancel buffering, to buffer an unbuffered file, or to use a program variable as a buffer for debugging.

Never call setbuf() after reading or writing to a file, or you risk losing data temporarily stored in an existing buffer. Always call setbuf() immediately after opening a file or after calling fseek(). An unbuffered file, however, can be buffered at any time. Also take care that the specified buffer remains valid during the time the file is open.

Parameters   **FILE *stream** An open file such as returned by fopen().

char *buf Pointer to new buffer to be used for I/O. The buffer must have BUFSIZ (512) bytes. Set buf to null to cancel buffering for the file.

See also   fopen, fseek, setvbuf

Example
```
/* setbuf.cpp */
#include <stdio.h>
char buffer[BUFSIZ];
main()
{
  setbuf(stdout, buffer);  // Use our buffer
  puts("Some text for our buffer");
  puts(buffer);  // Displays same string as above
  return 0;
}
```

setcbrk   Change control-break setting

Syntax   int setcbrk(int cbrkvalue);

Include   dos.h

Description   Turn Ctrl+Break checking on and off.

Parameters   **int cbrkvalue** 0–turn off Ctrl+Break checking. 1–turn on Ctrl+Break checking.

See also   getcbrk

Example
```
/* setcbrk.cpp */
#include <stdio.h>
#include <dos.h>
main()
{
  puts("Forcing Ctrl+Break checking ON");
  setcbrk(1);
  return 0;
}
```

setcolor   Change drawing color

Syntax   void far setcolor(int color);

Include   graphics.h

Description Change graphics drawing color. The Example displays a series of bars in all possible colors for the current graphics mode. The first bar is the same as the background and is, therefore, invisible.

Parameters **int color** Color number, used as an index into the current palette to determine the actual color.

See also   getbkcolor, getcolor, getmaxcolor, setallpalette, setbkcolor, setpalette

Example
```cpp
/* setcolor.cpp */
#include <graphics.h>
#include <stdio.h>
#include <stdlib.h>
#include <conio.h>
main()
{
  int gdriver = DETECT, gmode, gerr;
  int x, xmax, ymax, cmax, color, width, height;
  initgraph(&gdriver, &gmode, "c:\\borlandc\\bgi");
  gerr = graphresult();
  if (gerr != grOk) {
    printf("BGI error: %s\n", grapherrormsg(gerr));
    exit(gerr);
  }
  xmax = getmaxx();
  ymax = getmaxy();
  cmax = getmaxcolor();
  width = ((xmax + 1) / (cmax + 1)) / 2;
  height = ((ymax + 1) / 4);
  x = 0;
  for (color = 0; color <= cmax; color++) {
    setcolor(color);
    rectangle(x, ymax, x + width, height);
    setfillstyle(LTSLASH_FILL, color);
    floodfill(x + 1, ymax - 1, color);
    x += (width + width);
  }
```

```
    getch();
    closegraph();
    return 0;
}
```

_setcursortype   Change cursor style

Syntax   void _setcursortype(int cur_t);

Include   conio.h

Description Change cursor style or turn it off.

Parameters **int cur_t** One of the constants _NOCURSOR (turn off cursor), _SOLIDCURSOR (change cursor to block), _NORMALCURSOR (change cursor to normal underline).

See also   gotoxy, wherex, wherey

Example
```
/* _setcurs.cpp */
#include <stdio.h>
#include <conio.h>
main()
{
  char s[128];
  puts("Enter a string using a block cursor");
  _setcursortype(_SOLIDCURSOR);
  gets(s);
  _setcursortype(_NORMALCURSOR);
  puts("\nYour string is:");
  puts(s);
  return 0;
}
```

setdate   Change current date

Syntax   void setdate(struct date *datep);

Include   dos.h

Description Change system date.

Parameters **struct date *datep** Pointer to date structure containing the new date.

See also   getdate, gettime, settime

Example
```
/* setdate.cpp */
/* Finds day of week for this day next year */
/* Does not account for leap years */
#include <stdio.h>
#include <dos.h>
char *days[7] =
  {"Sun","Mon","Tues","Wednes","Thurs","Fri","Satur"};
main()
{
  struct date d;
  struct dosdate_t dd;
  getdate(&d);          // Get current date
  d.da_year++;          // Advance year
  setdate(&d);          // Set new date
  _dos_getdate(&dd);    // Get date and day of week
  printf("This day next year is on %sday\n",
    days[dd.dayofweek]);
  d.da_year--;          // Reset year
  setdate(&d);          // Restore date
  return 0;
}
```

setdisk   Change current disk drive

Syntax   int setdisk(int drive);

Include   dir.h

Description   Change current disk drive.

Parameters   **int drive** Drive number (0=A:, 1=B:, 2=C:, etc.)

See also   getdisk

Example
```
/* setdisk.cpp */
#include <stdio.h>
#include <dir.h>
main()
{
  setdisk(0);  // Change to A:
  return 0;
}
```

setdta   Set disk transfer address

Syntax   `void setdta(char far *dta);`

Include   dos.h

Description   Change the DOS disk transfer address (DTA).

Parameters   **char far *dta** New DTA.

See also   `getdta`

Example
```
/* setdta.cpp */
#include <stdio.h>
#include <dos.h>
main()
{
  char buffer[1024];   // I/O buffer
  char far *olddta;    // For saving current dta
  olddta = getdta();   // Get current dta
  setdta(buffer);      // Change dta to our buffer
  // ...                // I/O operations using dta
  setdta(olddta);      // Restore original dta
  return 0;
}
```

setfillpattern   Select custom fill pattern

Syntax   `void far setfillpattern(char far *upattern, int color);`

Include   graphics.h

Description   Changes the bit pattern and color used by various filled shape functions such as `bar()`, `fillellipse()`, `pieslice()`, and others.

Parameters   **char far *upattern** Eight-byte array of bits to use as the new fill pattern.

int color Color for filling shapes.

See also   `getfillpattern, getfillsettings, setfillstyle`

Example
```
/* setfillp.cpp */
#include <graphics.h>
#include <stdio.h>
#include <stdlib.h>
#include <conio.h>
```

```
#include <dos.h>
main()
{
  int gdriver = DETECT, gmode, gerr;
  int i, xc, yc, x1, y1, x2, y2;
  char pattern[8];
  initgraph(&gdriver, &gmode, "c:\\borlandc\\bgi");
  gerr = graphresult();
  if (gerr != grOk) {
    printf("BGI error: %s\n", grapherrormsg(gerr));
    exit(gerr);
  }
  xc = getmaxx() / 2;
  yc = getmaxy() / 2;
  x1 = xc - 50;
  y1 = yc - 50;
  x2 = xc + 50;
  y2 = yc + 50;
  while (!kbhit()) {
    setfillpattern(pattern, RED);
    bar(x1, y1, x2, y2);
    for (i = 0; i < 8; i++)
      pattern[i] = 1 + random(255);   // 1 .. 255
    delay(250);
  }
  getch();
  closegraph();
  return 0;
}
```

setfillstyle   Select fill pattern and color

Syntax   void far setfillstyle(int pattern, int color);

Include   graphics.h

Description   Same as setfillpattern(), but selects from a predetermined set of
possible fill patterns such as SLASH_FILL, XHATCH_FILL, and others (see
getfillsettings() for a complete list).

Parameters   **int pattern** Pattern constant.

int color Color for filling shapes.

See also   getfillpattern, getfillsettings, setfillpattern

Example

```
/* setfills.cpp */
#include <graphics.h>
#include <stdio.h>
#include <stdlib.h>
#include <conio.h>
main()
{
  int gdriver = DETECT, gmode, gerr;
  int xmax, ymax, cmax;
  initgraph(&gdriver, &gmode, "c:\\borlandc\\bgi");
  gerr = graphresult();
  if (gerr != grOk) {
    printf("BGI error: %s\n", grapherrormsg(gerr));
    exit(gerr);
  }
  xmax = getmaxx();
  ymax = getmaxy();
  cmax = getmaxcolor();
  while (!kbhit()) {
    setfillstyle(1 + random(11), 1 + random(cmax));
    bar(random(xmax), random(ymax),
      random(xmax), random(ymax));
  }
  getch();
  closegraph();
  return 0;
}
```

setftime   Set file date and time

Syntax   int setftime(int handle, struct ftime *ftimep);

Include   io.h

Description   Change open file's date and time as stored in the directory. Note that, if data is written to a file, closing that file also updates its date and time.

Parameters   **int handle** An open file's handle, such as returned by open().

struct ftime *ftimep Pointer to ftime structure, defined in io.h.

See also   getftime

Example

```cpp
/* setftime.cpp */
/* Change *.BAK file dates and times to 0-00-80 00:00a */
#include <stdio.h>
#include <dir.h>
#include <dos.h>
#include <io.h>
#include <fcntl.h>
#include <stdlib.h>
struct ftime zerodt;  // Zero date and time
main()
{
// *** To enable, remove lines starting here ********************
  puts("This program resets to 0-00-80 00:00a the dates");
  puts("and times of all *.BAK files in the current directory.");
  puts("Don't run this program unless you are sure you want");
  puts("to reset backup file dates and times!!!");
  exit(1);
// *** End removing lines here *********************************
  struct ffblk fb;
  char *path = "*.BAK";
  int done, handle;
  done = findfirst(path, &fb, FA_NORMAL);
  while (!done) {
    if ((fb.ff_attrib & FA_DIREC) == 0) {
      if ( (handle = open(fb.ff_name, O_RDONLY)) >= 0 ) {
        setftime(handle, &zerodt);
        printf("%s date/time zeroed\n", fb.ff_name);
        close(handle);
      }
    }
    done = findnext(&fb);
  }
  return 0;
}
```

setgraphbufsize Change graphics buffer size

Syntax `unsigned far setgraphbufsize(unsigned bufsize);`

Include graphics.h

Description Sets the size of an internal buffer used for graphics routines such as `floodfill()` and `fillpoly()`. You must call `setgraphbufsize()` before calling `initgraph()` or after calling `closegraph()`. Returns size of default buffer (normally 4096 bytes).

(**Warning:** Selecting a buffer that is too small can hang your computer, potentially causing a loss of information. Setting NEWSIZE to 800 in the Example, for instance, causes a system crash, and can also cause Microsoft Windows to halt. *Do not select a small buffer size with* `setgraphbufsize()` *unless you are prepared to reboot your computer!*)

Parameters **unsigned bufsize** Newly requested buffer size.

See also closegraph, fillpoly, floodfill, _graphfreemem, _graphgetmem, initgraph

Example
```cpp
/* setgbufs.cpp */
#include <graphics.h>
#include <stdio.h>
#include <stdlib.h>
#include <conio.h>
// WARNING: Setting the following to too small a value
// can cause serious bugs, including a violation
// of "system integrity" in Microsoft Windows!!!!
#define NEWSIZE 8192U  // New graphics buffer size
main()
{
  int gdriver = DETECT, gmode, gerr;
  int xmax, ymax, xmaxd2, ymaxd2;
  unsigned fnresult = setgraphbufsize(NEWSIZE);
  printf("Old buffer size == %u bytes. New size == %u bytes.\n",
    fnresult, NEWSIZE);
  puts("Press any key for graphics...");
  getch();
  initgraph(&gdriver, &gmode, "c:\\borlandc\\bgi");
  gerr = graphresult();
```

```
if (gerr != grOk) {
  printf("BGI error: %s\n", grapherrormsg(gerr));
  exit(gerr);
}
xmax = getmaxx();
ymax = getmaxy();
xmaxd2 = xmax / 2;
ymaxd2 = ymax / 2;
setcolor(WHITE);
circle(xmaxd2, ymaxd2, ymaxd2);
setfillstyle(CLOSE_DOT_FILL, BLUE);
floodfill(0, 0, WHITE);
floodfill(xmax, ymax, WHITE);
setfillstyle(XHATCH_FILL, GREEN);
floodfill(xmaxd2, ymaxd2, WHITE);
gerr = graphresult();
getch();
closegraph();
if (gerr != grOk)
  printf("BGI error: %s\n", grapherrormsg(gerr));
return 0;
}
```

setgraphmode   Switch to graphics mode

Syntax   void far setgraphmode(int mode);

Include   graphics.h

Description   Return to graphics mode after calling restorecrtmode().

Parameters   **int mode** Graphics mode such as returned by getgraphmode() or initialized by initgraph().

See also   getgraphmode, getmoderange, initgraph, restorecrtmode

Example
```
/* setgraph.cpp */
#include <graphics.h>
#include <stdio.h>
#include <stdlib.h>
#include <conio.h>
main()
```

```
{
    int gdriver = DETECT, gmode, gerr;
    int i, oldmode, xmax, ymax, cmax;
    initgraph(&gdriver, &gmode, "c:\\borlandc\\bgi");
    gerr = graphresult();
    if (gerr != grOk) {
        printf("BGI error: %s\n", grapherrormsg(gerr));
        exit(gerr);
    }
    xmax = getmaxx();
    ymax = getmaxy();
    cmax = getmaxcolor();
    oldmode = getgraphmode();
    restorecrtmode();
    puts("Ready for graphics!");
    printf("Press any key to continue...");
    getch();
    setgraphmode(oldmode);
    while (!kbhit()) {
        setcolor(random(1 + cmax));
        rectangle(random(xmax), random(ymax),
            random(xmax), random(ymax));
    }
    getch();
    closegraph();
    return 0;
}
```

setjmp   Enable nonlocal goto

Syntax   `int setjmp(jmp_buf jmpb);`

Include   setjmp.h

Description   Saves program state for a subsequent call to longjmp(). The state of a program consists of all segment register values, registers si and di, the stack and base pointer registers sp and bp, and the processor flags.

Parameters   **jmp_buf jmpb** The jump buffer of type jmp_buf, as defined in setjmp.h.

See also   longjmp, raise, signal

Example   See longjmp.

setlinestyle   Set line width and style

Syntax   void far setlinestyle(int linestyle, unsigned upattern,
　　int thickness);

Include   graphics.h

Description   Changes the thickness and bit pattern used by lineto(), linerel(),
line(), rectangle(), and other graphics functions that draw straight
lines. Does not affect outlines of circles and ellipses.

Parameters   **int linestyle** Set to SOLID_LINE, DOTTED_LINE, CENTER_LINE,
DASHED_LINE, or USERBIT_LINE.

unsigned upattern If linestyle equals USERBIT_LINE, a 16-bit value
with 1 bits where visible dots should appear and 0 bits where the
background should show through.

int thickness Set to NORM_WIDTH or THICK_WIDTH.

See also   getlinesettings, line, linerel, lineto, setwritemode

Example
```
/* setlines.cpp */
#include <graphics.h>
#include <stdio.h>
#include <stdlib.h>
#include <conio.h>
main()
{
  int gdriver = DETECT, gmode, gerr;
  int y, xmax;
  int linestyle, thickness;
  unsigned pattern;
  char s[80];
  initgraph(&gdriver, &gmode, "c:\\borlandc\\bgi");
  gerr = graphresult();
  if (gerr != grOk) {
    printf("BGI error: %s\n", grapherrormsg(gerr));
    exit(gerr);
  }
  xmax = getmaxx();
  y = 4;
  pattern = 0;   // Ignored unless linestyle == USERBIT_LINE
  for (thickness = 1; thickness <= 3; thickness++) {
    for (linestyle = 0; linestyle <= 3; linestyle++) {
```

```
            setcolor(RED);
            setlinestyle(linestyle, pattern, thickness);
            line(0, y, xmax, y);
            sprintf(s, "Style==%d  Pattern==%u  Thickness==%d",
              linestyle, pattern, thickness);
            setcolor(WHITE);
            outtextxy(0, y + 8, s);
            y += 28;
          }
          y += 14;
        }
        getch();
        closegraph();
        return 0;
      }
```

setlocale   Select a locale

Syntax `char *setlocale(int category, char *locale);`

Include locale.h

Description Officially supported, but has no practical effect. Returns previous "locale" string. Intended for use with functions such as `strcoll()`, which compares strings using a collating sequence for the current locale.

Parameters `int category` An `LC_...` constant representing a "locale." `LC_CTYPE` is the only supported option.

`char *locale` Pointer to a string or null.

See also `localeconv, mblen, mbtowc, mbstowcs, wcstombs, wctomb`

Example See `localeconv`.

setmem   Fill memory

Syntax `void setmem(void *dest, unsigned length, char value);`

Include mem.h

Description Fills memory with a value.

Parameters `void *dest` Pointer to memory block to be filled.

`unsigned length` Size of the memory block in bytes.

char **value** Value to store in memory.

See also   calloc, memset, strset

Example
```c
/* setmem.cpp */
#include <stdio.h>
#include <mem.h>
#define LEN 64
void Report(unsigned char *p, unsigned len, const char *s);
main()
{
  unsigned char *p = new char[LEN];
  Report(p, LEN, "Before filling");
  setmem(p, LEN, 0xff);
  Report(p, LEN, "After filling");
  delete p;
  return 0;
}

void Report(unsigned char *p, unsigned len, const char *s)
{
  unsigned int c;
  printf("\n\n%s\n", s);
  for (int i = 0; i < len; i++) {
    c = *p++;
    if (c == 0)
      printf("0x00     ");
    else
      printf("%#04x     ", c);
  }
}
```

setmode   Set file mode

Syntax   int setmode(int handle, int amode);

Include   io.h, fcntl.h

Description   Changes an open file's mode to binary or text. Returns previous mode for success and –1 for failure.

Parameters   **int** **handle** Open file's handle such as returned by open().

int **amode** File mode: O_BINARY or O_TEXT.

See also   creat, _dos_open, open

Example
```
/* setmode.cpp */
#include <stdio.h>
#include <io.h>
#include <fcntl.h>
#define FNAME "setmode.cpp"
main()
{
  int handle, c;
  handle = open(FNAME, O_BINARY);
  if (handle)
    if (setmode(handle, O_TEXT) != -1)
      while (!eof(handle))
        if (read(handle, &c, 1))
          putchar(c);
  return 0;
}
```

set_new_handler   Operator new error handler

Syntax   void (* set_new_handler(void (* my_handler)()))();

Include   new.h

Description   Assigns the address of a user function to be called if new fails to allocate a requested amount of memory. The user function can abort the program, or it can delete some memory (possibly reserved earlier as a safety pool) and return. If the memory request again fails, the handler is again called until the handler ends the program or frees additional memory. The statement set_new_handler(0) causes new to return null for memory allocation failures (the default action). Returns the address (null by default) of the previously assigned handler.

Parameters   **void (* my_handler)()** Pointer to a void function requiring no parameters—the function to be called by new. Set to null to reset new to its default action of returning null for memory allocation failures.

See also   malloc, free

Example
```
/* set_new_.cpp */
#include <stdio.h>
```

```
#include <stdlib.h>
#include <new.h>
void memerr(void);
main()
{
  set_new_handler(memerr);
  for (;;) {
    printf("Allocating 1024 bytes");
    void far *p = new[1024];
    printf(" at %p\n", p);
  }
}

void memerr(void)
{
  fputs("\n\nOut of memory\n", stderr);
  exit(1);
}
```

setpalette   Change palette color

Syntax   `void far setpalette(int colornum, int color);`

Include   graphics.h

Description   Changes one entry of the current color palette.

Parameters   **int colornum** Color palette index. 0 represents the first entry in the palette, 1 is the second, 2 is the third, and so on.

int color New color value to use for the palette entry specified by colornum. Actual color depends on video mode and hardware.

See also   getpalette, setallpalette, setbkcolor, setcolor, setrgbpalette

Example
```
/* setpalet.cpp */
#include <graphics.h>
#include <stdio.h>
#include <stdlib.h>
#include <conio.h>
#include <dos.h>
main()
{
```

```
int gdriver = DETECT, gmode, gerr;
int cmax, temp, c, y, xmax;
int colors[16];
initgraph(&gdriver, &gmode, "c:\\borlandc\\bgi");
gerr = graphresult();
if (gerr != grOk) {
  printf("BGI error: %s\n", grapherrormsg(gerr));
  exit(gerr);
}
xmax = getmaxx();
cmax = getmaxcolor();
y = 0;
setlinestyle(SOLID_LINE, 0, THICK_WIDTH);
for (c = 0; c <= cmax; c++) {
  colors[c] = c;                // Save colors in array
  setcolor(c);
  y += 20;
  line(0, y, xmax, y);          // Fill screen with lines
}
while (!kbhit()) {              // "Rotate" colors
  delay(150);                   // Adjust to change speed
  temp = colors[1];
  for (c = 1; c <= cmax; c++) {
    if (c == cmax)
      colors[c] = temp;
    else
      colors[c] = colors[c + 1];
    setpalette(c, colors[c]);
  }
}
getch();
closegraph();
return 0;
}
```

setrgbpalette   Define IBM-8514 colors

Syntax   void far setrgbpalette(int colornum, int red, int green, int blue);

Include   graphics.h

Description   Sets the red, green, and blue (RGB) color values for IBM-8514 and VGA 256-color displays. Also affects 16-color EGA and VGA modes. Uses only the least-significant 6 bits of the low bytes in each of the three int parameters. Because palette entries control the colors of pixels already on display, the function has an immediate visual effect.

Parameters   `int colornum` Color index from 0 to 255 (256-color modes) or 0 to 15 (other EGA and VGA modes).

`int red` New red component from 0 to 63.

`int green` New green component from 0 to 63.

`int blue` New blue component from 0 to 63.

See also   getpalette, setallpalette, setpalette

Example
```cpp
/* setrgbpa.cpp */
#include <graphics.h>
#include <stdio.h>
#include <stdlib.h>
#include <conio.h>
main()
{
  int gdriver = DETECT, gmode, gerr;
  int x, xmax, ymax, cmax, color, width, height;
  initgraph(&gdriver, &gmode, "c:\\borlandc\\bgi");
  gerr = graphresult();
  if (gerr != grOk) {
    printf("BGI error: %s\n", grapherrormsg(gerr));
    exit(gerr);
  }
  xmax = getmaxx();
  ymax = getmaxy();
  cmax = getmaxcolor();
  width = ((xmax + 1) / (cmax + 1)) / 2;
  height = ((ymax + 1) / 4);
  x = 0;
  for (color = 0; color <= cmax; color++) {
    setcolor(color);
    line(x, ymax, x, height);
    line(x + 1, ymax, x + 1, height);
    x += (width + width);
  }
```

```
while (!kbhit())
  for (color = 1; color <= cmax; color++)
    if (gdriver == IBM8514)
      setrgbpalette(color, random(65), random(65), random(65));
    else
      setpalette(color, random(cmax + 1));
getch();
closegraph();
return 0;
}
```

settextjustify   Graphics text justification

Syntax   `void far settextjustify(int horiz, int vert);`

Include   graphics.h

Description   Specifies location of graphics text output relative to the current position (CP). Advances CP beyond the displayed string's last pixel if `horiz` equals `LEFT_TEXT` and the current direction equals `HORIZ_DIR` (see `settextstyle()`). Affects justification of text displayed by `outtextxy()` or `outtext()` preceded by `moveto()`.

Parameters   **int horiz** One of the constants `LEFT_TEXT`, `CENTER_TEXT`, or `RIGHT_TEXT`. Specifies horizontal position of string relative to CP.

int vert One of the constants `BOTTOM_TEXT`, `CENTER_TEXT`, or `TOP_TEXT`.

See also   gettextsettings, outtext, settextstyle, textheight, textwidth

Example
```
/* settextj.cpp */
#include <graphics.h>
#include <stdio.h>
#include <stdlib.h>
#include <conio.h>
#define ASCII_ESC 27
main()
{
  int gdriver = DETECT, gmode, gerr;
  int xcenter, ycenter, horiz, vert;
  initgraph(&gdriver, &gmode, "c:\\borlandc\\bgi");
  gerr = graphresult();
  if (gerr != grOk) {
```

```
      printf("BGI error: %s\n", grapherrormsg(gerr));
      exit(gerr);
    }
    xcenter = getmaxx() / 2;
    ycenter = getmaxy() / 2;
    for (vert = 0; vert <= 2; vert++)
      for (horiz = 0; horiz <= 2; horiz++) {
        settextjustify(horiz, vert);
        clearviewport();
        setcolor(MAGENTA);
        outtextxy(xcenter, ycenter,
          "Happy new year! Press a key.");
        setcolor(WHITE);
        rectangle(xcenter, ycenter, xcenter + 1, ycenter + 1);
        if (getch() == ASCII_ESC) {
          closegraph();
          exit(0);
        }
      }
    getch();
    closegraph();
    return 0;
}
```

settextstyle   Graphics text style

Syntax   `void far settextstyle(int font, int direction, int charsize);`

Include   graphics.h

Description   Selects text characteristics for subsequent `outtext()` and `outtextxy()` statements.

Parameters   `int font` One of the built-in font names `BOLD_FONT`, `COMPLEX_FONT`, `DEFAULT_FONT`, `EUROPEAN_FONT`, `GOTHIC_FONT`, `SANS_SERIF_FONT`, `SCRIPT_FONT`, `SIMPLEX_FONT`, `SMALL_FONT`, `TRIPLEX_FONT`, `TRIPLEX_SCR_FONT`, or the name of a third-party font.

`int direction` Either `HORIZ_DIR` to display text horizontally or `VERT_DIR` to display text vertically.

`int charsize` Relative character size. Zero to select stroked (vectored) font default size or the size specified in a preceding `setusercharsize()` statement.

See also   gettextsettings, installuserfont, outtext, outtextxy, registerbgifont, settextjustify, setusercharsize, textheight, textwidth

Example

```
/* settexts.cpp */
#include <graphics.h>
#include <stdio.h>
#include <stdlib.h>
#include <conio.h>
#define SIZE 4
main()
{
  int gdriver = DETECT, gmode, gerr;
  int x, y;
  initgraph(&gdriver, &gmode, "c:\\borlandc\\bgi");
  gerr = graphresult();
  if (gerr != grOk) {
    printf("BGI error: %s\n", grapherrormsg(gerr));
    exit(gerr);
  }
  x = textwidth("M") * 4;
  y = textheight("M") * 2;
  settextstyle(SANS_SERIF_FONT, VERT_DIR, SIZE);
  outtextxy(x, y, "Going up");
  settextstyle(SANS_SERIF_FONT, HORIZ_DIR, SIZE);
  outtextxy(x, y, "    Stepping out");
  getch();
  closegraph();
  return 0;
}
```

settime   Set system time

Syntax   void settime(struct time *timep);

Include   dos.h

Description   Changes system time.

Parameters   **struct time *timep** Pointer to time structure containing the new time.

See also   ctime, _dos_settime, getdate, gettime, setdate, time

Example
```
/* settime.cpp */
#include <stdio.h>
#include <stdlib.h>
#include <dos.h>
struct time t;
main(int argc, char *argv[])
{
  if (argc <= 2) {
    puts("Enter hh mm to set the time");
    puts("ex. SETTIME 08 10");
    exit(1);
  }
  t.ti_hour = atoi(argv[1]);
  t.ti_min = atoi(argv[2]);
  settime(&t);
  gettime(&t);
  printf("The time is %02d:%02d:%02d",
    t.ti_hour, t.ti_min, t.ti_sec);
  return 0;
}
```

setusercharsize   Graphics text size

Syntax   `void far setusercharsize(int multx, int divx, int multy,`
           `int divy);`

Include   graphics.h

Description   Adjusts graphics text horizontal and vertical sizes. Uses a ratio less than
one to shrink characters smaller than normal. For example, if `multx/divx` equals 0.25, characters display one-fourth their normal width. If
`multy/divy` equals 3.5, characters display about 3.5 times their normal
height. After calling `setusercharsize()`, pass zero to `settextstyle()`'s
`charsize` parameter to use the new ratio.

Parameters   `int multx`, `int divx` Horizontal size ratio equal to `multx/divx`

`int multy`, `int divy` Vertical size ratio equal to `multy/divy`.

See also   `gettextsettings, outtext, outtextxy, settextjustify, settextstyle,`
`textheight, textwidth`

Example   `/* setuserc.cpp */`
`#include <graphics.h>`

```
#include <stdio.h>
#include <stdlib.h>
#include <conio.h>
main()
{
  int gdriver = DETECT, gmode, gerr;
  int hgt;
  initgraph(&gdriver, &gmode, "c:\\borlandc\\bgi");
  gerr = graphresult();
  if (gerr != grOk) {
    printf("BGI error: %s\n", grapherrormsg(gerr));
    exit(gerr);
  }
  setusercharsize(1, 1, 7, 2);
  settextstyle(SANS_SERIF_FONT, HORIZ_DIR, 0);
  outtextxy(0, 50, "Tall in the saddle");
  hgt = textheight("M");
  if (gdriver == CGA)
    setusercharsize(4, 3, 1, 1);
  else
    setusercharsize(8, 3, 1, 1);
  settextstyle(SANS_SERIF_FONT, HORIZ_DIR, 0);
  outtextxy(0, 60 + hgt, "Wide in the ride");
  getch();
  closegraph();
  return 0;
}
```

setvbuf   Assign buffering to stream

Syntax   int setvbuf(FILE *stream, char *buf, int type, size_t size);

Include   stdio.h

Description   Modifies I/O buffering. Buffered I/O stores data in temporary buffers, speeding throughput. Unbuffered I/O (character devices only) reads and writes data one character at a time, which typically gives poor performance but saves memory.

Except for redirected stdin and stdout files, file I/O is normally buffered. Call setvbuf() to attach or to automatically allocate a new program buffer to a file stream. The function returns zero for success and nonzero for failure.

Parameters **FILE *stream** Open file stream such as returned by fopen(). Or a predefined stream such as stdin or stdout.

char *buf Pointer to buffer, usually a char array. If null, setvbuf() allocates a buffer by calling malloc(). Automatically allocated buffers are freed upon closing the file.

int type One of the constants _IOFBF (full buffering—input reads full buffer; output writes entire buffer when full), _IOLBF (line buffering—same as full buffering but text output writes entire buffer upon receiving a newline character), or _IONBF (disable buffering).

size_t size Size of the new buffer in bytes up to 32767.

See also fflush, fclose, fopen, fread, fwrite, setbuf

Example
```
/* setvbuf.cpp */
#include <stdio.h>
#include <stdlib.h>
#define FNAME "setvbuf.cpp"
#define SIZE 2048
main()
{
  FILE *f = fopen(FNAME, "rt");
  char buffer[SIZE];
  if (!f) {
    perror(FNAME);
    exit(1);
  }
  if (setvbuf(f, buffer, _IOFBF, SIZE) != 0)
    puts("Unable to attach file buffer");
  else {
    puts("Reading file via buffered I/O...");
    while (!feof(f))
      putchar(getc(f));
  }
  return 0;
}
```

setvect Set interrupt vector

Syntax void setvect(int interruptno, void interrupt (*isr)());

Include dos.h

Description   Sets an interrupt vector to address an interrupt service routine (ISR).

Parameters   `int interruptno` Interrupt number.

`void interrupt (*isr)()` Pointer to ISR interrupt function.

See also   getvect

Example
```
/* setvect.cpp */
#include <stdio.h>
#include <dos.h>
#include <conio.h>
#define INTR 0x1c
#define FALSE 0
void interrupt (*oldhandler)(...);
void interrupt newhandler(...);
int count;
main()
{
  int done = FALSE;
  clrscr();
  cputs("Press Esc to quit");
  gotoxy(1, 8);
  cputs("Timer interrupt in effect");
  oldhandler = getvect(INTR);
  setvect(INTR, newhandler);
  while (!done) {
    gotoxy(10, 10);
    cprintf("%d", count);
    clreol();
    if (kbhit())
      done = (getch() == 27);
  }
  setvect(INTR, oldhandler);
  gotoxy(1, 25);
  return 0;
}

void interrupt newhandler(...)
{
  count++;
  oldhandler();
}
```

setverify   Set DOS verify flag

Syntax   `void setverify(int value);`

Include   dos.h

Description   Sets DOS verify flag on or off. With verification on, DOS rereads all data written to disk (but does not compare that data with the original information). With verification off, DOS does not reread disk writes.

Parameters   `int value` 0–turn off verification. 1–turn on verification.

See also   `getcbrk, getverify, setcbrk`

Example
```
/* setverif.cpp */
#include <stdio.h>
#include <dos.h>
main()
{
  puts("Forcing Verify flag ON");
  setverify(1);
  return 0;
}
```

setviewport   Change graphics viewport

Syntax   `void far setviewport(int left, int top, int right, int bottom, int clip);`

Include   graphics.h

Description   Defines graphics viewport and determines whether to clip output to that viewport's boundaries.

Parameters   `int left`, `int top` Absolute coordinate of the top-left viewport rectangle.

`int right`, `int bottom` Absolute coordinate of the bottom-right viewport rectangle.

`int clip` 0–do not clip output; nonzero–clip output.

See also   `cleardevice, clearviewport, getviewsettings, moveto`

Example
```
/* setviewp.cpp */
#include <graphics.h>
#include <stdio.h>
#include <stdlib.h>
```

```
#include <time.h>
#include <conio.h>
#define CLIP_ON 1
main()
{
  int gdriver = DETECT, gmode, gerr;
  int xmax, ymax, cmax, xcenter, ycenter, xcd2, ycd2;
  initgraph(&gdriver, &gmode, "c:\\borlandc\\bgi");
  gerr = graphresult();
  if (gerr != grOk) {
    printf("BGI error: %s\n", grapherrormsg(gerr));
    exit(gerr);
  }
  xmax = getmaxx();
  ymax = getmaxy();
  cmax = getmaxcolor();
  xcenter = xmax / 2;
  ycenter = ymax / 2;
  xcd2 = xcenter / 2;
  ycd2 = ycenter / 2;
  randomize();
  setviewport(xcenter - xcd2, ycenter - ycd2,
    xcenter + xcd2, ycenter + ycd2, CLIP_ON);
  while (!kbhit()) {
    setcolor(1 + random(cmax));
    lineto(random(xmax) - xcd2, random(ymax) - ycd2);
  }
  getch();
  closegraph();
  return 0;
}
```

setvisualpage   Set graphics visual page

Syntax   `void far setvisualpage(int page);`

Include   graphics.h

Description Determines the visible graphics page on multipage displays.

Parameters   **int page** Page number. Range depends on hardware capabilities and
current graphics mode.

See also   setactivepage

Example   See setactivepage.

setwritemode   Set graphics line-write mode

Syntax   void far setwritemode(int mode);

Include   graphics.h

Description   Selects logic by which new pixels are combined with pixels already on display. Affects output of drawpoly(), line(), linerel(), lineto(), and rectangle().

Parameters   **int mode** Either COPY_PUT (new pixels overwrite existing pixels) or XOR_PUT (new pixels are combined with existing pixels via the exclusive OR operator).

See also   drawpoly, line, linerel, lineto, rectangle, putimage

Example
```
/* setwrite.cpp */
#include <graphics.h>
#include <stdio.h>
#include <stdlib.h>
#include <time.h>
#include <conio.h>
struct Rec {
  int color;
  int x1, y1, x2, y2;
};
void SetValues(Rec *p, int c, int x, int y, int xx, int yy);
main()
{
  int gdriver = DETECT, gmode, gerr;
  int i, xmax, ymax, cmax;
  Rec v[10];
  initgraph(&gdriver, &gmode, "c:\\borlandc\\bgi");
  gerr = graphresult();
  if (gerr != grOk) {
    printf("BGI error: %s\n", grapherrormsg(gerr));
    exit(gerr);
  }
  randomize();
```

```
xmax = getmaxx();
ymax = getmaxy();
cmax = getmaxcolor();
setfillstyle(XHATCH_FILL, RED);
bar(0, 0, xmax, ymax);
for (i = 0; i < 10; i++)
  SetValues(&v[i], 1 + random(cmax),
    random(xmax), random(ymax),
    random(xmax), random(ymax));
setwritemode(XOR_PUT);
setlinestyle(SOLID_LINE, 0, THICK_WIDTH);
for (i = 0; i < 10; i++) {
  setcolor(v[i].color);
  line(v[i].x1, v[i].y1, v[i].x2, v[i].y2);
}
for (i = 9; i >= 0; i--) {
  getch();
  setcolor(v[i].color);
  line(v[i].x1, v[i].y1, v[i].x2, v[i].y2);
}
getch();
closegraph();
return 0;
}

void SetValues(Rec *p, int c, int x, int y, int xx, int yy)
{
  p->color = c;
  p->x1 = x;
  p->y1 = y;
  p->x2 = xx;
  p->y2 = yy;
}
```

signal Configure signal

Syntax   void (*signal(int sig, void (*func)(int sig[, int subcode])))(int);

Include   signal.h

Description   Installs user function to respond to raised signals, usually as part of a program's error handling. Returns address of replaced signal function.

Parameters **int sig** A constant such as SIGABRT (abort program abnormally), SIGFPE (floating-point error), SIGILL (illegal operation), SIGINT (Ctrl+Break interrupt), SIGSEGV (illegal memory segment access), or SIGTERM (terminate program).

void (*func)() Pointer to user function.

See also abort, _control87, ctrlbrk, exit, longjmp, raise, setjmp

Example
```c
/* signal.cpp */
#include <stdio.h>
#include <stdlib.h>
#include <signal.h>
void MyCtrlBreak(int);
main()
{
  char s[128];
  signal(SIGINT, MyCtrlBreak);
  while (0 == 0) {
    puts("Enter a string or press Ctrl+Break to quit");
    gets(s);
    printf("You entered: %s\n\n", s);
  }
}

void MyCtrlBreak(int)
{
  puts("\n\nCtrl+Break detected!");
  puts("Ending program via exit(1)");
  exit(1);
}
```

sin, sinl   Sine

Syntax
```c
double sin(double x);
complex sin(complex x);
long double sinl(long double x);
```

Include math.h, complex.h

Description Sine of x.

Parameters **double x** Argument value.

See also   acos, asin, atan, atan2, complex, cos, tan

Example
```
/* sin.cpp */
#include <stdio.h>
#include <math.h>
#define V 25.8
main()
{
  printf("Sine of %lf == %lf\n", V, sin(V));
  return 0;
}
```

sinh, sinhl   Hyperbolic sine

Syntax
```
double sinh(double x);
complex sinh(complex x);
long double sinhl(long double x);
```

Include   math.h, complex.h

Description   Hyperbolic sine of x.

Parameters   **double x** Argument value.

See also   acos, asin, atan, atan2, complex, cos, cosh, sin, tan, tanh

Example
```
/* sinh.cpp */
#include <stdio.h>
#include <math.h>
#define V 25.8
main()
{
  printf("Hyperbolic sine of %lf == %lf\n", V, sinh(V));
  return 0;
}
```

sleep   Suspend program

Syntax   void sleep(unsigned seconds);

Include   dos.h

Description   Pauses for one or more seconds.

Parameters **unsigned seconds** Number of seconds to pause. Accuracy limited to system clock "granularity"—about plus or minus one hundredth of a second.

See also delay

Example
```
/* sleep.cpp */
#include <stdio.h>
#include <dos.h>
char *sv[3] = { "Slow down", "You move", "Too fast" };
main()
{
  for (int i = 0; i < 3; i++) {
    sleep(1);
    puts(sv[i]);
  }
  return 0;
}
```

sopen   Open shared file

Syntax `int sopen(char *path, int access, int shflag[, int mode]);`

Include fcntl.h, sys\stat.h, share.h, io.h

Description Similar to open(), but opens a file to be shared by another process. Returns positive file handle for success and −1 for failure and sets errno to ENOENT (no such file or directory), EMFILE (too many files open), EACCES (access denied), EINVACC (invalid access code).

Parameters **char *path** Pointer to filename string, which may contain drive and path information.

int access One of the three constants O_RDONLY (read only), O_WRONLY (write only), O_RDWR (read and write) logically ORed with any one or more of the six constants O_APPEND (append to end of file), O_BINARY (open in binary mode), O_CREAT (create new file if it does not exist), O_EXCL (combine with O_CREAT to force error for existing file), O_TEXT (open in text mode), O_TRUNC (truncate file).

int shflag One of the constants SH_COMPAT (compatibility mode—in other words, no flags), SH_DENYNO (permit full read and write access), SH_DENYNONE (same as SH_DENYNO), SH_DENYRD (deny reading), SH_DENYRW (deny reading and writing), SH_DENYWR (deny writing).

int mode Specified only when access includes the O_CREAT option. Either of the two constants S_IWRITE (permit writing) or S_IREAD (permit reading), or the expression S_IREAD ¦ S_IWRITE (permit reading and writing).

See also access, chmod, close, creat, fstat, lock, lseek, open, stat, unlock, unmask

Example
```
/* sopen.cpp */
#include <stdio.h>
#include <stdlib.h>
#include <fcntl.h>
#include <sys\stat.h>
#include <share.h>
#include <io.h>
main(int argc, char *argv[])
{
  int handle;
  char c;
  if (argc <= 1) {
    puts("Enter name of text file to read.");
    puts("ex. SOPEN sopen.cpp");
    exit(1);
  }
  handle = sopen(argv[1], O_RDONLY ¦ O_TEXT, SH_DENYWR);
  if (handle == 0)
    perror(argv[1]);
  else {
    while (read(handle, &c, 1) > 0)
      putchar(c);
    close(handle);
  }
  return 0;
}
```

sound   Turn on tone

Syntax void sound(unsigned frequency);

Include dos.h

Description Begins sounding a tone at approximately the given frequency. Call nosound() to stop tone.

Parameters **unsigned frequency** Approximate frequency in hertz.

See also delay, nosound

Example
```
/* sound.cpp */
#include <stdio.h>
#include <conio.h>
#include <dos.h>
main()
{
  int freq;
  while (!kbhit()) {
    printf("Whoop... ");
    for (freq = 500; freq <= 900; freq++) {
      delay(1);
      sound(freq);
    }
    nosound();
    delay(75);
  }
  return 0;
}
```

spawnl, ...spawnvpe Create and run child processes

Syntax
```
int spawnl(int mode, char *path, char *arg0, arg1, ..., argn,
  NULL);
int spawnle(int mode, char *path, char *arg0, arg1, ...,
  argn, NULL, char *envp[]);
int spawnlp(int mode, char *path, char *arg0, arg1, ...,
  argn, NULL);
int spawnlpe(int mode, char *path, char *arg0, arg1, ...,
  argn, NULL, char *envp[]);
int spawnv(int mode, char *path, char *argv[]);
int spawnve(int mode, char *path, char *argv[],
  char *envp[]);
int spawnvp(int mode, char *path, char *argv[]);
int spawnvpe(int mode, char *path, char *argv[],
  char *envp[]);
```

Include   process.h, stdio.h

Description   These functions all perform a similar job—loading and running another program—in other words, "spawning" a child process. Each function requires a mode argument that specifies the relationship of the parent process to its child. Each function also requires a pointer path to the child's filename string.

The functions differ in their remaining parameters. Function spawnl() accepts a variable number of pointers to argument strings to be passed to the child process (as though those arguments were typed on the DOS command line). End the list with NULL. Function spawnlpe() adds to this list a pointer to a set of environment strings to be passed to the child.

The two functions spawnlp() and spawnlpe() are identical to spawnl() and spawnle() respectively. However, the p in the function names tells you that, in addition to searching for the child's file in the current directory, if the file is not found, all directories on the current PATH are also searched. Functions without p in their names search for child process files only in the current directory.

The two functions spawnv() and spawnve() accept a pointer to an array of char pointers to be passed as arguments to the child. These functions are handy for passing the arguments given to the parent on the DOS command line to the child arguments. Again, the two alternate functions spawnvp() and spawnvpe() are identical to spawnv() and spawnve() respectively, but search for the child's file in the current directory and if necessary all directories on the system PATH.

If successful, the spawn...() functions return the child process's exit status—in other words, the value passed by the child to exit() or returned by the child's main() return statement. If not successful, the functions return –1 and set errno to E2BIG (too many arguments), EINVAL (invalid argument), ENOENT (no such file or directory), ENOEXEC (error executing child process), or ENOMEM (not enough memory).

Parameters   **int mode** Required by all functions. Either of the constants P_WAIT (keep parent in memory until child finishes, then resume parent's execution), or P_OVERLAY (replace parent completely with child process, which ends by returning to the grandparent process, usually DOS). The constant P_NOWAIT (run child and parent concurrently) is defined but does not work for DOS programs.

char *path Required by all functions. Pointer to the child's filename string. May contain drive and directory information, but should normally specify only the filename (e.g. MYCHILD.EXE) to take advantage of the functions' file searching capabilities.

char *arg0, **arg1**, **...**, **argn** Required only by spawnl(), spawnle(), spawnlp(), and spawnlpe().

char *envp[] Required only by spawnle(), spawnlpe(), spawnve(), and spawnvpe().

char *argv[] Required only by spawnv(), spawnve(), spawnvp(), and spawnvpe().

See also   abort, atexit, chdir, _chdrive, getcurdir, getcwd, getenv, exit, exec..., putenv, _searchenv, searchpath, system

Example
```cpp
/* spawn.cpp */
#include <process.h>
#include <stdio.h>
#include <stdlib.h>
#include <conio.h>
main(int argc, char *argv[])
{
  int result;
  if (argc <= 1) {
    puts("Enter name of program to run");
    puts("ex. SPAWN SOUND.EXE");
    exit(1);
  }
  printf("Press any key to run child process...");
  getch();
  puts("");
  result = spawnl(P_WAIT, argv[1], NULL);
  if (result == -1)
    printf("Error running %s\n", argv[1]);
  else
    printf("\nReturned from child. Result == %d", result);
  return 0;
}
```

_splitpath Parse pathname

Syntax `void _splitpath(const char *path, char *drive, char *dir,`
`char *name, char *ext);`

Include stdlib.h

Description Separates a DOS pathname string into its components—in other words, drive letter, directory, filename, and extension.

Parameters **const char *path** Full or partial pathname string such as `"C:\\ANYDIR\\ANYFILE.EXT"` or `"\\...\\SUBDIR\\ANYFILE.EXT"`.

char *drive Pointer to char array _MAX_DRIVE bytes long, or null to skip storing any drive letter and colon.

char *dir Pointer to char array _MAX_DIR bytes long, or null to skip storing any directory information. Result includes leading and trailing backslashes.

char *name Pointer to char array _MAX_FNAME bytes long, or null to skip storing any filename information.

char *ext Pointer to char array _MAX_EXT bytes long, or null to skip storing any file extension information. Result includes preceding period.

See also _fullpath, _makepath, parsfnm

Example
```
/* _splitpa.cpp */
#include <stdio.h>
#include <stdlib.h>
main(int argc, char *argv[])
{
  char drive[_MAX_DRIVE];
  char dir[_MAX_DIR];
  char fname[_MAX_FNAME];
  char ext[_MAX_EXT];
  if (argc <= 1) {
    puts("Enter pathname to parse");
    puts("ex. _SPLITPA c:\\borlandc\\bin\\bcc.exe");
    exit(1);
  }
  _splitpath(argv[1], drive, dir, fname, ext);
  printf("Drive ........ %s\n", drive);
```

```
  printf("Directory .... %s\n", dir);
  printf("Filename .... %s\n", fname);
  printf("Extension .... %s\n", ext);
  return 0;
}
```

sprintf   Format values to string

Syntax   `int sprintf(char *buffer, const char *format[, argument, ...]);`

Include   stdio.h

Description   Same as `printf()`, but stores formatted arguments in a user-supplied string buffer. Returns number of bytes inserted into `buffer`, not including a terminating null.

Parameters   **char *buffer** Pointer to buffer for storing function's result. The buffer *must* be large enough to hold any possible expansion of the supplied arguments plus a null terminating byte.

const char *format Pointer to a formatting string containing whitespace, literal text, and conversion rules (see `printf()`).

argument, ... One or more argument values, with at least one argument per conversion rule in the `format` string.

See also   cprintf, fprintf, printf, scanf, vfprintf, vprintf, vsprintf

Example
```
/* sprintf.cpp */
#include <stdio.h>
main()
{
  char buffer[128];
  int i = 123;
  double d = 3.14159;
  char *s = "A string";
  sprintf(buffer, "i==%d  d==%lf  s==%s\n", i, d, s);
  puts(buffer);
  return 0;
}
```

sqrt, sqrtl   Square root

Syntax
```
double sqrt(double x);
complex sqrt(complex x);
long double sqrtl(long double x);
```

Include   math.h, complex.h

Description   Returns square root of an argument.

Parameters   **double x** Argument value.

See also   complex, exp, log, pow

Example
```
/* sqrt.cpp */
#include <stdio.h>
#include <stdlib.h>
#include <math.h>
main(int argc, char *argv[])
{
  if (argc <= 1) {
    puts("Enter value for square root");
    puts("ex. SQRT 64");
    exit(1);
  }
  double v = atof(argv[1]);
  printf("sqrt(%.2lf) == %.2lf\n", v, sqrt(v));
  return 0;
}
```

srand   Seed random number generator

Syntax   void srand(unsigned seed);

Include   stdlib.h

Description   The statement srand(n) seeds the random number generator to produce a random sequence n.

Parameters   **unsigned seed** Value to seed random number generator, producing a predictable random sequence (useful for debugging programs that use random numbers). To produce an unpredictable random sequence, set seed to a rapidly changing value such as the time of day.

See also   rand, random, randomize

Example
```
/* srand.cpp */
#include <stdio.h>
#include <stdlib.h>
void Display(const char *msg);
main()
{
  srand(9);
  Display("Random numbers for seed == 9");
  srand(9);
  Display("After reseeding with seed == 9");
  srand(2);
  Display("Random numbers for seed == 2");
  return 0;
}

void Display(const char *msg)
{
  puts("");
  puts(msg);
  for (int i = 0; i < 8; i++)
    printf("%8d", rand());
  puts("");
}
```

sscanf   Scan and format string input

Syntax
```
int sscanf(const char *buffer, const char *format[,
  address, ...]);
```

Include   stdio.h

Description   Same as scanf(), but takes input from a user-supplied string. Returns number of input fields scanned and converted.

Parameters   **const char *buffer** Pointer to string containing input to be scanned.

const char *format Pointer to format string with conversion rules that tell the function how to convert input fields (see scanf()).

address, ... One or more arguments passed by address. The function stores converted fields at these addresses, one per conversion rule in the format string.

See also   fscanf, printf, scanf, vfscanf, vscanf, vsscanf

Example
```
/* sscanf.cpp */
#include <stdio.h>
main()
{
  char *s;
  double d;
  printf("Enter floating point number: ");
  gets(s);
  sscanf(s, "%lf", &d);
  printf("Input as a string == %s\n", s);
  printf("Input as a double == %lf\n", d);
  printf("Input in scientific notation == %le\n", d);
  return 0;
}
```

stackavail   Available stack space

Syntax `size_t stackavail(void);`

Include malloc.h

Description Returns number of bytes available on the stack, equal to the amount of memory available to `alloca()`.

See also alloca, allocmem, coreleft, _dos_allocmem, farcoreleft, heapwalk, segread

Example
```
/* stackava.cpp */
#include <stdio.h>
#include <malloc.h>
void f(void);
void Report(const char *msg);
main()
{
  Report("Outside of function");
  f();
  return 0;
}

void f(void)
{
  char buffer[2048];   // Use some stack space
  buffer[0] = 0;       // Prevent compiler warning
```

```
    Report("Inside of function");
}

void Report(const char *msg)
{
  puts(msg);
  printf("Stack space == %u bytes\n", stackavail());
}
```

stat   Get file information

Syntax   `int stat(char *path, struct stat *statbuf);`

Include   sys\stat.h

Description Similar to `fstat()`, but uses a filename string rather than an open file's handle to obtain information about a file's status. Returns zero for success and −1 if the specified file is not found.

Parameters **char *path** Pointer to filename string, which may contain drive and directory information.

struct stat *statbuf Pointer to a stat structure for storing the function's result.

See also   access, chmod, fstat

Example   `/* stat.cpp */`

```
#include <stdio.h>
#include <stdlib.h>
#include <sys\stat.h>
#include <time.h>
main(int argc, char *argv[])
{
  char *fname;
  struct stat statbuf;
  if (argc <= 1) {
    puts("Enter filename");
    puts("ex. STAT stat.cpp");
    exit(1);
  }
  fname = argv[1];
  if (stat(fname, &statbuf) != 0) {
```

```
        printf("Error getting stats for %s\n", fname);
        exit(1);
    }
    printf("Information about %s\n", fname);
    printf("Drive number  : %d\n", statbuf.st_dev);
    printf("Size in bytes : %ld\n", statbuf.st_size);
    printf("Was updated   : %s\n", ctime(&statbuf.st_atime));
    return 0;
}
```

_status87   Floating-point status

Syntax   `unsigned int _status87(void);`

Include   float.h

Description Returns the floating-point status word for an 80x87 math coprocessor
              or emulator.

See also   `_clear87, _control87, _fpreset, raise, signal`

Example
```
/* _status8.cpp */
#include <stdio.h>
#include <float.h>
main()
{
  int result;
  double d = 3.14159;
  d *= d;   // Any floating point operation
  result = _status87();
  printf("80x87 status == %d\n", result);
  return 0;
}
```

stime   Set system date and time

Syntax   `int stime(time_t *p);`

Include   time.h

Description Change system date and time.

Parameters **time_t *p** Pointer to `time_t` value, equal to the number of elapsed
              seconds since GMT 00:00:00 on January 1, 1970.

See also   asctime, _dos_setftime, _dos_settime, ftime, gettime, gmtime, localtime, settime, time, tzset

Example

```
/* stime.cpp */
#include <stdio.h>
#include <stdlib.h>
#include <time.h>
#define SECS_PER_HOUR (60 * 60)
main(int argc, char *argv[])
{
  char c;
  time_t thetime;
  puts("Daylight savings adjustment\n");
  if (argc <= 1) {
    puts("Enter + to advance hour; - to retard");
    puts("ex. STIME + or STIME -");
    exit(1);
  }
  c = argv[1][0];   // i.e. first char of first arg
  time(&thetime);
  if (c == '+')
    thetime += SECS_PER_HOUR;
  else if (c == '-')
    thetime -= SECS_PER_HOUR;
  stime(&thetime);
  time(&thetime);
  printf("The time is %s\n", ctime(&thetime));
  return 0;
}
```

stpcpy   Copy string to string

Syntax   char *stpcpy(char *dest, const char *src);

Include   string.h

Description   Copies source string src and its null terminator to a destination string dest. Returns dest + strlen(src).

Parameters   **char *dest** Pointer to destination string large enough to hold the result.

            const char *src Pointer to null-terminated source string.

See also   strcpy, strncpy

Example
```
/* stpcpy.cpp */
#include <stdio.h>
#include <string.h>
main()
{
  char src[80] = "abcdefghij";
  char dst[80] = "1234567890";
  printf("Before: src==%s  dst==%s\n", src, dst);
  puts("Calling stpcpy(dst, src)");
  stpcpy(dst, src);
  printf("After : src==%s  dst==%s\n", src, dst);
  return 0;
}
```

strcat, _fstrcat   Concatenate strings

Syntax
```
char *strcat(char *dest, const char *src);
char far * far _fstrcat(char far *dest, const char far *src);
```

Include   string.h

Description   Concatenates (joins) a source string src to the end of an initialized destination string dest. Returns dest.

Parameters   **char *dest** Pointer to initialized destination string.

const char *src Pointer to source string to be copied to the end of the destination string.

See also   stpcpy, strcpy, strncat

Example
```
/* strcat.cpp */
#include <stdio.h>
#include <string.h>
main()
{
  char src[80] = "abcdefghij";
  char dst[80] = "1234567890";
  printf("Before: src==%s  dst==%s\n", src, dst);
  puts("Calling strcat(dst, src)");
  strcat(dst, src);
  printf("After : src==%s  dst==%s\n", src, dst);
  return 0;
}
```

strchr, _fstrchr   Scan string for character

Syntax
```
char *strchr(const char *s, int c);
char far * far _fstrchr(const char far *s, int c);
```

Include   string.h

Description   Searches a string s from front to back for the first occurrence of a character c. Returns a pointer to the character if found and null if not found.

Parameters   **const char *s** Pointer to target string.

int c Character for which to search. Set to null (ASCII 0) to have strchr() search for a string's null terminator.

See also   strcspn, strrchr, strspn, strstr

Example
```
/* strchr.cpp */
#include <stdio.h>
#include <string.h>
main()
{
  char src[80] = "abcdefghij";
  printf("String at src == %s\n", src);
  puts("Calling char *p = strchr(src, 'd')");
  char *p = strchr(src, 'd');
  printf("String at p   == %s\n", p);
  return 0;
}
```

strcmp   Compare strings

Syntax
```
int strcmp(const char *s1, const char *s2);
int far _fstrcmp(const char far *s1, const char far *s2);
```

Include   string.h

Description   Compares two strings. Returns a negative value if s1 < s2, zero if s1 == s2, or a positive value if s1 > s2.

Parameters   **const char *s1** Pointer to first string to be compared.

const char *s2 Pointer to second string to be compared.

See also   strchr, strcmpi, strcoll, stricmp, strncmp, strnicmp

Example
```
/* strcmp.cpp */
#include <stdio.h>
#include <stdlib.h>
#include <string.h>
main(int argc, char *argv[])
{
  char *p;
  if (argc <= 2) {
    puts("Enter two strings to compare");
    puts("ex. STRCMP stringa stringb");
    exit(1);
  }
  int result = strcmp(argv[1], argv[2]);
  if (result < 0)
    p = "is less than";
  else if (result > 0)
    p = "is greater than";
  else
    p = "equals";
  printf("%s %s %s", argv[1], p, argv[2]);
  return 0;
}
```

strcmpi   Compare strings ignoring case

Syntax   `int strcmpi(const char *s1, const char *s2);`

Include   string.h

Description   Same as strcmp() but ignores differences in upper- and lowercase. For compatibility with other C compilers, strcmpi() is implemented as a macro that translates directly to stricmp().

Parameters   See strcmp.

See also   strchr, strcmp, strcoll, stricmp, strncmp, strnicmp

Example
```
/* strcmpi.cpp */
#include <stdio.h>
#include <stdlib.h>
#include <string.h>
main(int argc, char *argv[])
{
```

```
  char *p;
  if (argc <= 2) {
    puts("Enter two strings to compare ignoring case");
    puts("ex. STRCMPI stringa stringb");
    exit(1);
  }
  int result = strcmpi(argv[1], argv[2]);
  if (result < 0)
    p = "is less than";
  else if (result > 0)
    p = "is greater than";
  else
    p = "equals";
  printf("%s %s %s", argv[1], p, argv[2]);
  return 0;
}
```

strcoll   Collate strings

Syntax   `int strcoll(char *s1, char *s2);`

Include   string.h

Description   Same as strcmp() but compares two strings using a collating sequence dictated by the current locale. (Borland C++ marginally supports the concept of a locale, and, therefore, this function is provided only for compatibility with other ANSI C compilers.)

Parameters   See strcmp.

See also   localeconv, setlocale, strcmp, stricmp, strncmp, strnicmp, strxfrm

Example
```
/* strcoll.cpp */
#include <stdio.h>
#include <stdlib.h>
#include <string.h>
main(int argc, char *argv[])
{
  char *p;
  if (argc <= 2) {
    puts("Enter two strings to collate");
    puts("ex. STRCOLL stringa stringb");
    exit(1);
  }
```

```
    int result = strcoll(argv[1], argv[2]);
    if (result < 0)
      p = "is less than";
    else if (result > 0)
      p = "is greater than";
    else
      p = "equals";
    printf("%s %s %s", argv[1], p, argv[2]);
    return 0;
}
```

strcpy   Copy string to string

Syntax   `char *strcpy(char *dest, const char *src);`
`char far * _fstrcpy(char far *dest, const char far *src);`

Include   string.h

Description   Copies a source string src and its null terminator to a destination string dest, overwriting any string in the destination. Returns dest.

Parameters   **char *dest** Pointer to destination, overwritten with a copy of the source string. The destination string does not have to be initialized.

const char *src Pointer to source string to be copied to the destination.

See also   stpcpy, strncpy

Example
```
/* strcpy.cpp */
#include <stdio.h>
#include <string.h>
main()
{
  char src[80] = "abcdefghij";
  char dst[80] = "1234567890";
  printf("Before: src==%s  dst==%s\n", src, dst);
  puts("Calling strcpy(dst, src)");
  strcpy(dst, src);
  printf("After : src==%s  dst==%s\n", src, dst);
  return 0;
}
```

strcspn, _fstrcspn   Subset string search

Syntax   `size_t strcspn(const char *s1, const char *s2);`
           `size_t far _fstrcspn(const char far *s1, const char far *s2);`

Include   string.h

Description   Returns the number of characters from a string s1 that are not also in a second string s2. Can be used in parsing data entry—counting a string's initial characters that do not contain a certain punctuation character, for example, or a file extension.

Parameters   **const char s1** String in which to search for characters that are not in string s2.

const char s2 String containing characters that stop the incremental search of string s1.

See also   strchr, strcspn, strrchr, strspn, strstr

Example
```
/* strcspn.cpp */
#include <stdio.h>
#include <string.h>
main()
{
  char *s = "filename.cpp";
  char *ext = ".cpp";
  printf("Original string s == %s\n", s);
  int result = strcspn(s, ext);
  s += result;
  printf("After calling strcspn s == %s\n", s);
  return 0;
}
```

_strdate   Convert date to string

Syntax   `char *_strdate(char *datestr);`

Include   time.h

Description   Stores the current date as a string in mm/dd/yy format. Returns datestr.

Parameters   **char *datestr** Pointer to destination at least nine bytes long to hold the function result.

See also   asctime, ctime, _strtime, time

Example

```
/* _strdate.cpp */
#include <stdio.h>
#include <time.h>
main()
{
  char sdate[9];
  _strdate(sdate);
  printf("The date is %s\n", sdate);
  return 0;
}
```

strdup, _fstrdup   Duplicate string

Syntax   char *strdup(const char *s);
               char far * far _fstrdup(const char far *s);

Include   string.h

Description Copies a string to a newly allocated memory block strlen(s) + 1 bytes
               long. Returns a pointer to the duplicated string. You can delete this
               string by passing the pointer to free(). Returns null if not enough
               memory is available for storing the duplicate string.

Parameters   **const char *s** Pointer to null-terminated string to be duplicated.

See also   malloc, free, strcpy

Example

```
/* strdup.cpp */
#include <stdio.h>
#include <string.h>
#include <alloc.h>
main()
{
  char *s = "abcdefghij";
  char *duplicate;
  printf("Original string == %s\n", s);
  duplicate = strdup(s);
  printf("Duplicate string == %s\n", duplicate);
  free(duplicate);  // Delete duplicated string
  return 0;
}
```

_strerror Create error string

Syntax `char * _strerror(const char *s);`

Include string.h or stdio.h

Description Creates an error message string from s, adding a colon, a blank, and a description of any current system error.

Parameters **const char *s** Your error message of no more than 94 characters to add to the system error message. If null, _strerror() returns a pointer to the most recent error code string.

See also perror, strerror

Example
```
/* _strerro.cpp */
#include <stdio.h>
#include <string.h>
main()
{
  char *p = _strerror("Test error message");
  printf("Error message == %s\n", p);
  p = _strerror(NULL);
  printf("Most recent error = %s\n", p);
  return 0;
}
```

strerror Create error string

Syntax `char *strerror(int errnum);`

Include stdio.h or string.h

Description Returns a pointer to an error message string identified by errnum. Adds a newline character to the end of the string.

Parameters **int errnum** Error number.

See also perror, _strerror

Example
```
/* strerror.cpp */
#include <stdio.h>
#include <string.h>
main()
{
  for (int e = 0; e < 21; e++)
```

```
        printf("Error #%02d: %s", e, strerror(e));
      return 0;
   }
```

strftime Store date and time in string

Syntax `size_t strftime(char *s, size_t maxsize, const char *fmt, const struct tm *t);`

Include time.h

Description Formats the date and time as a string using a conversion rule system similar to `printf()`'s. A format string (`fmt`) contains one or more rules that are replaced by date and time components. The format string can contain other nonrule characters as well. Returns number of characters inserted into the destination string.

Conversion rules consist of a percent sign (%) and a character from the following table.

Conversion rules for `strftime()`.

Conversion rules	Date and time components
%	Insert percent sign (%)
a	Day of week (abbreviated Sun, Mon, etc.)
A	Day of week unabbreviated
b	Month (abbreviated Jan, Feb, etc.)
B	Month unabbreviated
c	Date and time in `asctime()` format
d	Day of month (01 to 31)
H	Hour in 24-hour format (00 to 23)
I	Hour in 12-hour format (00 to 12)
j	Day of year (001 to 366)
m	Month number (1 to 12)
M	Minute (00 to 59)

Conversion rules	Date and time components
p	AM or PM
S	Second (00 to 59)
U	Week number (00 to 53) (Sunday starts week)
w	Day of week (0 to 6) (Sunday == 0)
W	Week number (00 to 53) (Monday starts week)
x	Date
X	Time
y	Year minus century (e.g. 68 for 1968)
Y	Full year (e.g. 1968)
Z	Time zone name (EST or EDT)

Parameters **char *s** Pointer to destination string for storing function result.

size_t maxsize Maximum number of characters to insert into destination string. Usually set to the size minus one of string s.

const char *fmt Pointer to format string containing literal text and conversion rules as explained in the description.

const struct tm *t Pointer to a tm structure containing the date and time to be formatted into a string.

See also asctime, ctime, localtime, mktime, time

Example
```
/* strftime.cpp */
#include <stdio.h>
#include <time.h>
#define SIZE 80
main()
{
  time_t t;
  struct tm *tp;
  char s[SIZE];
```

```
    time(&t);
    tp = localtime(&t);
    puts("");
    strftime(s, SIZE, "The date is %x\n", tp);
    puts(s);
    strftime(s, SIZE, "The time is %X\n", tp);
    puts(s);
    strftime(s, SIZE, "Today is %A\n", tp);
    puts(s);
    return 0;
}
```

stricmp, _fstricmp   Compare strings ignoring case

Syntax   `int stricmp(const char *s1, const char *s2);`
            `int far _fstricmp(const char far *s1, const char far *s2);`

Include   string.h

Description   Same as strcmp() but ignores case when comparing two strings.

Parameters   See strcmp().

See also   strcmp, strcmpi, strcoll, strncmp, strnicmp

Example
```
/* stricmp.cpp */
#include <stdio.h>
#include <stdlib.h>
#include <string.h>
main(int argc, char *argv[])
{
  char *p;
  if (argc <= 2) {
    puts("Enter two strings to compare ignoring case");
    puts("ex. STRICMP stringa stringb");
    exit(1);
  }
  int result = stricmp(argv[1], argv[2]);
  if (result < 0)
    p = "is less than";
  else if (result > 0)
    p = "is greater than";
```

```
      else
        p = "equals";
      printf("%s %s %s", argv[1], p, argv[2]);
      return 0;
    }
```

strlen, _fstrlen   String length

Syntax   `size_t strlen(const char *s);`
`size_t far _fstrlen(const char far *s);`

Include   string.h

Description Returns length of a string—in other words, the number of characters
preceding the string's null terminator.

Parameters **const char *s** Pointer to a null-terminated string.

See also strchr

Example
```
/* strlen.cpp */
#include <stdio.h>
#include <stdlib.h>
#include <string.h>
main(int argc, char *argv[])
{
  if (argc <= 1) {
    puts("Enter string");
    puts("ex. STRLEN myString");
    exit(1);
  }
  int len = strlen(argv[1]);
  printf("String == %s\n", argv[1]);
  printf("Length == %d character(s)\n", len);
  return 0;
}
```

strlwr, _fstrlwr   Convert string to lowercase

Syntax   `char *strlwr(char *s);`
`char far * far _fstrlwr(char far *s);`

Include   string.h

Description   Changes uppercase letters in a string to lowercase.

Parameters   **char *s** Pointer to null-terminated string.

See also   strupr, tolower, toupper

Example

```
/* strlwr.cpp */
#include <stdio.h>
#include <string.h>
main()
{
  char s[] = "ABCDEFGHIJKLMNOPQRSTUVWXYZ";
  printf("Before conversion s == %s\n", s);
  strlwr(s);
  printf("After conversion s  == %s\n", s);
  return 0;
}
```

strncat, _fstrncat   Concatenate strings

Syntax

```
char *strncat(char *dest, const char *src, size_t maxlen);
char far * far _fstrncat(char far *dest, const char far *src,
  size_t maxlen);
```

Include   string.h

Description   Concatenates (joins) up to maxlen characters from a source string src to the end of an initialized destination string dest.

Parameters   **char *dest** Pointer to initialized destination string.

                const char *src Pointer to source string.

                size_t maxlen Maximum number of characters to be copied from the source string to the end of the destination string.

See also   strcat, strcpy

Example

```
/* strncat.cpp */
#include <stdio.h>
#include <string.h>
main()
{
  char src[80] = "abcdefghij";
```

```
    char dst[80] = "1234567890";
    printf("Before: src==%s  dst==%s\n", src, dst);
    puts("Calling strncat(dst, src, 5)");
    strncat(dst, src, 5);
    printf("After : src==%s  dst==%s\n", src, dst);
    return 0;
}
```

strncmp, _fstrncmp   Compare partial strings

Syntax
```
int strncmp(const char *s1, const char *s2, size_t maxlen);
int far _fstrncmp(const char far *s1, const char far *s2,
    size_t maxlen);
```

Include   string.h

Description   Same as strcmp(), but compares only up to maxlen characters in the two strings.

Parameters   **const char *s1** Pointer to first string.

const char *s2 Pointer to second string.

size_t maxlen Maximum number of characters to compare.

See also   strcmp, strcoll, stricmp, strnicmp

Example
```
/* strncmp.cpp */
#include <stdio.h>
#include <stdlib.h>
#include <string.h>
main(int argc, char *argv[])
{
  char *p;
  if (argc <= 3) {
    puts("Enter two strings and a number to compare n chars");
    puts("ex. STRNCMP stringa stringb 4");
    exit(1);
  }
  int n = atoi(argv[3]);
  int result = strncmp(argv[1], argv[2], n);
```

```
  if (result < 0)
    p = "is/are less than";
  else if (result > 0)
    p = "is/are greater than";
  else
    p = "equal(s)";
  printf("%d chars of %s %s %s", n, argv[1], p, argv[2]);
  return 0;
}
```

strncmpi Compare partial strings ignoring case

Syntax `int strncmpi(const char *s1, const char *s2, size_t maxlen);`

Include string.h

Description Same as strncmp(), but ignores the difference between upper- and lowercase letters. Implemented for compatibility with other C compilers as a macro that translates to strnicmp().

Parameters See strnicmp.

See also strncmp, strnicmp

Example
```
/* strncmpi.cpp */
#include <stdio.h>
#include <stdlib.h>
#include <string.h>
main(int argc, char *argv[])
{
  char *p;
  if (argc <= 3) {
    puts("Enter two strings and a number to compare n chars");
    puts("ignoring case.");
    puts("ex. STRNCMPI stringa stringb 4");
    exit(1);
  }
  int n = atoi(argv[3]);
  int result = strncmpi(argv[1], argv[2], n);
  if (result < 0)
    p = "is/are less than";
```

```
      else if (result > 0)
        p = "is/are greater than";
      else
        p = "equal(s)";
      printf("%d chars of %s %s %s", n, argv[1], p, argv[2]);
      return 0;
    }
```

strncpy, _fstrncpy Copy partial strings

Syntax `char *strncpy(char *dest, const char *src, size_t maxlen);`
`char far * far _fstrncpy(char far *dest, const char far *src,`
`   size_t maxlen);`

Include string.h

Description Copies up to `maxlen` characters from a source string `src` to a destination string `dst`, overwriting any characters in the destination. If `maxlen` equals the size in bytes of the destination string (and the source string is at least that long), the destination string is not null terminated. If `maxlen` and the length of the source string exceed the size of the destination string, the end of the destination is overwritten, possibly destroying other data or code in memory. To avoid trouble, never set `maxlen` greater than the maximum number of characters that the destination can safely hold.

Parameters `char *dest` Pointer to destination of at least `maxlen` bytes.

`cont char *src` Pointer to source string to be copied to the destination.

`size_t maxlen` Maximum number of characters to copy from the source to the destination.

See also strcat, strcpy

Example
```
/* strncpy.cpp */
#include <stdio.h>
#include <string.h>
main()
{
  char src[80] = "abcdefghij";
  char dst[80] = "1234567890";
  printf("Before: src==%s  dst==%s\n", src, dst);
  puts("Calling strncpy(dst, src, 5)");
```

1365

```
    strncpy(dst, src, 5);
    printf("After : src==%s  dst==%s\n", src, dst);
    return 0;
}
```

strnicmp, _fstrnicmp   Partial caseless compare

Syntax   `int strnicmp(const char *s1, const char *s2, size_t maxlen);`
`int far _fstrnicmp(const char far *s1, const char far *s2,`
`  size_t maxlen);`

Include   string.h

Description Compares up to maxlen characters of two strings. Ignores differences between upper- and lowercase letters.

Parameters **const char *s1** Pointer to first string to be compared.

const char *s2 Pointer to second string to be compared.

size_t maxlen Maximum number of characters from both strings to be compared.

See also stricmp, strncmp, strncmpi

Example
```
/* strnicmp.cpp */
#include <stdio.h>
#include <stdlib.h>
#include <string.h>
main(int argc, char *argv[])
{
  char *p;
  if (argc <= 3) {
    puts("Enter two strings and a number to compare n chars");
    puts("ignoring case.");
    puts("ex. STRNICMP stringa stringb 4");
    exit(1);
  }
  int n = atoi(argv[3]);
  int result = strnicmp(argv[1], argv[2], n);
  if (result < 0)
    p = "is/are less than";
```

```
  else if (result > 0)
    p = "is/are greater than";
  else
    p = "equal(s)";
  printf("%d chars of %s %s %s", n, argv[1], p, argv[2]);
  return 0;
}
```

strnset, _fstrnset   Set characters in string

Syntax
```
char *strnset(char *s, int c, size_t n);
char far * far _fstrnset(char far *s, int c, size_t n);
```

Include   string.h

Description   Fills a string with one or more characters, stopping upon reaching a null byte in the string.

Parameters   **char *s** Pointer to string to be filled.

int c Character to store in string.

size_t n Maximum number of characters to be filled.

See also   memset, setmem, strset

Example
```
/* strnset.cpp */
#include <stdio.h>
#include <string.h>
main()
{
  char s[] = "1234567890";
  printf("Before filling s == %s\n", s);
  puts("Calling strnset(s, '@', 4)");
  strnset(s, '@', 4);
  printf("After filling  s == %s\n", s);
  return 0;
}
```

strpbrk, _fstrpbrk   Scan string for characters

Syntax
```
char *strpbrk(const char *s1, const char *s2);
char far * far _fstrpbrk(const char far *s1,
  const char far *s2);
```

Include   string.h

Description   Scans a string for a character from a set of one or more characters. Returns a pointer to the first matching character found, or null if no characters match.

Parameters   **const char *s1** Pointer to a string to be scanned.

                const char *s2 Pointer to a string containing a set of characters.

See also   strchr, strcmp

Example
```
/* strpbrk.cpp */
#include <stdio.h>
#include <string.h>
main()
{
  char *s1 = "Balance = $341.59";
  char *s2 = "$";
  printf("s1 == %s\n", s1);
  printf("s2 == %s\n", s2);
  puts("Calling char *s3 = strpbrk(s1, s2)");
  char *s3 = strpbrk(s1, s2);
  printf("s3 == %s\n", s3);
  return 0;
}
```

strrchr, _fstrrchr   Scan string reverse

Syntax
```
char *strrchr(const char *s, int c);
char far * far _fstrrchr(const char far *s, int c);
```

Include   string.h

Description   Same as strrchr(), but searches for the last instance of a given character c in a string s. Returns a pointer to the character if found, or null if not.

Parameters **const char *s** Pointer to string to be searched.

int c Character to look for in string.

See also strcspn, strchr, strpbrk

Example
```
/* strrchr.cpp */
#include <stdio.h>
#include <string.h>
main()
{
  char *s = "FILENAME.CPP";
  printf("s == %s\n", s);
  puts("Calling char *p = strrchr(s, '.')");
  char *p = strrchr(s, '.');
  printf("p == %s\n", p);
  return 0;
}
```

strrev, _fstrrev   Reverse string

Syntax
```
char *strrev(char *s);
char far * far _fstrrev(char far *s);
```

Include string.h

Description Reverses order of characters in string (except for its null terminator). Possibly useful for searching the ends of long strings for patterns. Reversing two strings, for example, and passing them to strstr() determines whether one string ends with another. Returns s.

Quote multiword strings passed to the example—type the command **strrev "a multiword string"**.

Parameters **char *s** Pointer to string to be reversed.

See also strstr

Example
```
/* strrev.cpp */
#include <stdio.h>
#include <stdlib.h>
#include <string.h>
main(int argc, char *argv[])
{
   if (argc <= 1) {
```

```
        puts("Enter string to reverse");
        puts("ex. STRREV your name");
        exit(1);
    }
    printf("Original string == %s\n", argv[1]);
    strrev(argv[1]);
    printf("Reversed string == %s\n", argv[1]);
    return 0;
}
```

strset, _fstrset   Set characters in string

Syntax   `char *strset(char *s, int c);`
`char far * far _fstrset(char far *s, int c);`

Include   string.h

Description   Assigns character c to all characters in string s, up to but not including the string's null terminator byte.

Parameters   **char *s** Pointer to string to be filled.

int c Character to store in string.

See also   `memset, setmem, strnset`

Example
```
/* strset.cpp */
#include <stdio.h>
#include <string.h>
main()
{
    char s[] = "1234567890";
    printf("Before filling s == %s\n", s);
    puts("Calling strset(s, '@')");
    strset(s, '@');
    printf("After filling  s == %s\n", s);
    return 0;
}
```

strspn, _fstrspn   Scan string subset

Syntax   `size_t strspn(const char *s1, const char *s2);`
`size_t far _fstrspn(const char far *s1, const char far *s2);`

Include	string.h
Description	Returns the number of characters from a string s1 that are also in a second string s2. Can be used in verifying data entry—counting a string's initial characters that are digits, for example.
Parameters	**const char *s1** Pointer to string to be scanned.
	const char *s2 Pointer to string containing characters to scan for in string s1.
See also	strcmp, strcspn

Example
```
/* strspn.cpp */
#include <stdio.h>
#include <string.h>
main()
{
  char *s = "filename.cpp";
  char *test = "abcdefghijklmnopqrstuvwxyz";
  printf("Original string s == %s\n", s);
  int result = strspn(s, test);
  s += result;
  printf("After calling strspn s == %s\n", s);
  return 0;
}
```

strstr, _fstrstr   Scan string for substring

Syntax
```
char *strstr(const char *s1, const char *s2);
char far * far _fstrstr(const char far *s1,
  const char far *s2);
```

Include	string.h
Description	Hunts for a string (s2) in another string (s1). Returns address of matching string's first character or null if the substring s2 is not found in s1.
Parameters	**const char *s1** Pointer to string in which to search for the substring addressed by s2.
	const char *s2 Pointer to substring to search for in the string addressed by s1.

See also   strchr, strcmp, strcspn, strspn

Example
```
/* strstr.cpp */
#include <stdio.h>
#include <string.h>
main()
{
  char *s1 = "filename.cpp";
  char *s2 = ".cpp";
  printf("s1 == %s\n", s1);
  printf("s2 == %s\n", s2);
  puts("Calling char *s3 = strstr(s1, s2)");
  char *s3 = strstr(s1, s2);
  printf("s3 == %s\n", s3);
  return 0;
}
```

_strtime   Convert time to string

Syntax   char *_strtime(char *timestr);

Include   time.h

Description   Stores the current time as a string in hh/mm/ss format. Returns timestr.

Parameters   **char *timestr** Pointer to destination at least nine bytes long to hold the function result.

See also   asctime, ctime, _strdate, time

Example
```
/* _strtime.cpp */
#include <stdio.h>
#include <time.h>
main()
{
  char stime[9];
  _strtime(stime);
  printf("The time is %s\n", stime);
  return 0;
}
```

strtod   String to double

Syntax   `double strtod(const char *s, char **endptr);`
             `long double _strtold(const char *s, char **endptr);`

Include   stdlib.h

Description Converts a floating point value in string form to a `double` or a `long double` binary value. Returns converted result for success and ±`HUGE_VAL` (`strtod()`) or ± `LHUGE_VAL` (`strtold()`) for errors.

Parameters **`const char *s`** Pointer to string containing a floating point value in text, either in decimal (such as `"123.45"`) or in scientific notation (such as `"4.5e-3"`).

`char **endptr` If non-null, `endptr` is set to the address of the character *after* the last character in s that participated in the conversion. Use this optional pointer to parse strings for multiple floating point values, perhaps separated by white space, commas, etc.

See also   atof, printf, sprintf, strtol

Example
```
/* strtod.cpp */
#include <stdio.h>
#include <stdlib.h>
#include <string.h>
main(int argc, char *argv[])
{
  if (argc <= 1) {
    puts("Enter double value");
    puts("ex. STRTOD 3.14159");
    exit(1);
  }
  char *endptr;
  double d = strtod(argv[1], &endptr);
  printf("Value in binary == %lf\n", d);
  if (strlen(endptr) > 0)
    printf("Scan stopped at: %s\n", endptr);
  return 0;
}
```

strtok, _fstrtok   Scan string for tokens

Syntax   `char *strtok(char *s1, const char *s2);`
`char far * far _fstrtok(char far *s1, const char far *s2);`

Include   string.h

Description   Divides a source string s1 into tokens (substrings), separated by one or more characters in a second string s2. Typically used to parse parameter lists of tokens separated by commas or other symbols. Returns address of token, or null if no match is found. Call repeatedly, passing the address of a source string s1 on the first call, then setting s1 to null on subsequent calls in order to continue parsing until the function returns null.

Parameters   `char *s1` Pointer to string to be tokenized. *Warning: This function directly modifies the source string by replacing separator characters with nulls.* Set to null to continue parsing the same string.

`const char *s2` Pointer to string containing one or more characters used as token separators in string s1.

See also   strcspn, strspn

Example
```
/* strtok.cpp */
#include <stdio.h>
#include <string.h>
main()
{
  char s[] = "filename,100,1/1/90";
  char *delimit = ",/";
  printf("Original string == %s\n", s);
  puts("As parsed into tokens:");
  char *p = strtok(s, delimit);
  while (p) {
    puts(p);
    p = strtok(NULL, delimit);
  }
  return 0;
}
```

strtol   Convert string to long

Syntax   `long strtol(const char *s, char **endptr, int radix);`

Include   stdlib.h

Description   Converts a `long` value in string form to a `long` binary value. The value in the string can be in decimal, octal, or hexadecimal, using standard C formatting (such as recognized by `printf()`, `scanf()`, and other similar functions.) Other radixes from 2 to 36 are also recognized. Returns converted result for success and sets a non-null `endptr` to the address following the last participating character; returns zero for errors and sets a non-null `endptr` equal to `s`.

Parameters   **const char *s** Pointer to a string containing a `long` integer value in text form. Can also contain other characters.

char **endptr If non-null, `endptr` is set to the address of the character *after* the last character in s that participated in the conversion. Use this optional pointer to parse strings for multiple `long` values, perhaps separated by white space, commas, etc.

int radix Set to a number from 2 to 36 to select a specific radix (number base) for the conversion—for example, use 2 for binary values, 10 for decimals, 16 for hexadecimals, etc. Letters from A to Z are recognized as numeric symbols for number bases exceeding 10. (Base 16 uses 0 to 9 and A to F, base 17 uses 0 to 9 and A to G, and so on.) Set `radix` to zero to have the function automatically detect and convert numbers using standard C formatting rules—in other words, decimals begin with a digit, octals begin with the letter o, and hexadecimals begin with `0x` or `0X`.

See also   atoi, atof, atol, printf, sprintf, strtoul

Example
```
/* strtol.cpp */
#include <stdio.h>
#include <stdlib.h>
#include <string.h>
#define RADIX 0   // Automatic radix detection
main(int argc, char *argv[])
{
  if (argc <= 1) {
    puts("Enter long value");
    puts("ex. STRTOD 0xF96C");
    exit(1);
  }
  char *endptr;
```

```
long l = strtol(argv[1], &endptr, RADIX);
printf("Value in binary == %ld\n", l);
if (strlen(endptr) > 0)
  printf("Scan stopped at: %s\n", endptr);
return 0;
}
```

strtoul   String to unsigned long

Syntax   unsigned long strtoul(const char *s, char **endptr, int radix);

Include   stdlib.h

Description   Same as strtol(), but converts unsigned long values from text to binary.

Parameters   See strtol.

See also   atoi, atof, atol, printf, sprintf, strtol

Example
```
/* strtoul.cpp */
#include <stdio.h>
#include <stdlib.h>
#include <string.h>
#define RADIX 0   // Automatic radix detection
main(int argc, char *argv[])
{
  if (argc <= 1) {
    puts("Enter unsigned long value");
    puts("ex. STRTOUL 98765");
    exit(1);
  }
  char *endptr;
  long l = strtoul(argv[1], &endptr, RADIX);
  printf("Value in binary == %lu\n", l);
  if (strlen(endptr) > 0)
    printf("Scan stopped at: %s\n", endptr);
  return 0;
}
```

strupr, _fstrupr   Convert string to uppercase

Syntax
```
char *strupr(char *s);
char far * far _fstrupr(char far *s);
```

Include   string.h

Description   Changes lowercase letters in a string to uppercase.

Parameters   **char *s** Pointer to null-terminated string.

See also   strlwr, tolower, toupper

Example
```
/* strupr.cpp */
#include <stdio.h>
#include <string.h>
main()
{
  char s[] = "abcdefghijklmnopqrstuvwxyz";
  printf("Before conversion s == %s\n", s);
  strupr(s);
  printf("After conversion s  == %s\n", s);
  return 0;
}
```

strxfrm   Transform string to string

Syntax   size_t strxfrm(char *s1, char *s2, size_t n);

Include   string.h

Description   Similar to strncpy(), but is said to "transform" up to n characters of one string s1 into another string s2. However, in effect, up to n characters (including a null terminating byte) from the second string s2 are simply copied to s1. Returns number of transformed (copied) characters.

Parameters   **char *s1** Pointer to destination string to be transformed.

     char *s2 Pointer to source string copied to destination.

     size_t n Maximum number of characters to transform.

See also   strcoll, strcpy, strncpy

Example
```
/* strxfrm.cpp */
#include <stdio.h>
#include <string.h>
main()
{
  char src[80] = "abcdefghij";
  char dst[80] = "1234567890";
  printf("Before: src==%s  dst==%s\n", src, dst);
  puts("Calling strxfrm(dst, src, 4)");
  strxfrm(dst, src, 4);
  printf("After : src==%s  dst==%s\n", src, dst);
  return 0;
}
```

swab   Swap bytes

Syntax `void swab(char *src, char *dest, int n);`

Include stdlib.h

Description Copies up to n characters, which must be an even number, from a source string `src` to a destination string `dest`, and swaps byte pairs while copying. Typically used to convert data between computers that store multibyte values in different orders—when transferring files to 80x86-based PCs that store values of lesser significance at lower addresses, for example, from other systems such as 68000-based Macintoshes that store values of greater significance at lower addresses.

Parameters **char *src** Pointer to source data containing an even number of bytes. Though typed as a char *, src can address data of any type. It doesn't have to address a null-terminated string.

char *dest Pointer to destination at least as large as the source data.

int n Maximum number of bytes to copy. Must be an even number.

See also strcpy

Example
```
/* swab.cpp */
#include <stdio.h>
#include <stdlib.h>
#include <string.h>
main()
{
```

```
char src[] = "Orignal data";
char dst[80];
int len = strlen(src);
if ((len & 1) == 1) {
  puts("Error: Source data length must be even");
  exit(1);
}
printf("Original data  == %s\n", src);
puts("Calling swab(src, dst, len)");
swab(src, dst, len);
printf("Converted data == %s\n", dst);
return 0;
}
```

system   System command

Syntax   int system(const char *command);

Include   stdlib.h

Description   Gives a system command as though typed at a DOS prompt. Loads and runs COMMAND.COM as a child process using the COMSPEC environment variable to locate COMMAND.COM's directory. The function can be used to run another program, in which case the program's executable code file must be in the current directory or in any directory listed on the system PATH. Returns zero for success and –1 for errors and sets errno to E2BIG (command string too large or contains too many arguments), ENOENT (file or directory not found), ENOEXEC (error executing child process), or ENOMEM (not enough memory for operation).

Parameters   **const char *command** Pointer to command string. If command is null, system() returns zero if the environment variable COMSPEC exists; otherwise, it returns 1. This special case does *not* detect the actual presence of the COMMAND.COM processor.

See also   exec..., getenv, putenv, _searchenv, searchpath, spawn...

Example
```
/* system.cpp */
#include <stdio.h>
#include <stdlib.h>
#include <conio.h>
main()
{
```

```
    puts("Press any key to execute tree command");
    getch();
    system("tree \\");  // Command == tree \
    puts("\nBack from system() tree command");
    return 0;
}
```

tan, tanl   Tangent

Syntax
```
double tan(double x);
complex tan(complex x);
long double tanl(long double x);
```

Include   math.h, complex.h

Description   Returns tangent of an argument value.

Parameters   **double x**, **long double x** Argument value.

complex x Instance of the complex class.

See also   acos, asin, atan, atan2, complex, cos, sin

Example
```
/* tan.cpp */
#include <stdio.h>
#include <math.h>
#define V 25.8
main()
{
  printf("Tangent of %lf == %lf\n", V, tan(V));
  return 0;
}
```

tanh, tanhl   Hyperbolic tangent

Syntax
```
double tanh(double x);
complex tanh(complex x);
long double tanhl(long double x);
```

Include   math.h, complex.h

Description   Returns hyperbolic tangent of an argument value.

Parameters **double x**, **long double x** Argument value.

complex x Instance of the complex class.

See also complex, cos, cosh, sin, sinh, tan

Example
```
/* tanh.cpp */
#include <stdio.h>
#include <math.h>
#define V 25.8
main()
{
  printf("Hyperbolic tangent of %lf == %lf\n", V, tanh(V));
  return 0;
}
```

tell   Get file position

Syntax long tell(int handle);

Include io.h

Description Returns an open file's current position, equal to the offset in bytes from the beginning of a file where the next I/O operation on that file will occur. Returns –1 for errors.

Parameters **int handle** Handle to open file such as returned by open().

See also fgetpos, ftell, lseek, open

Example
```
/* tell.cpp */
#include <stdio.h>
#include <stdlib.h>
#include <fcntl.h>
#include <io.h>
main()
{
  int handle; // Input file handle
  long pos;    // File position
  char buffer[128];
  handle = open("TELL.CPP", O_RDONLY | O_BINARY);
  if (handle == -1) {
    puts("Error opening file");
    exit(1);
  }
```

```
pos = tell(handle);
printf("At start of file, tell() == %ld\n", pos);
read(handle, buffer, 10);
pos = tell(handle);
printf("After reading 10 bytes tell() == %ld\n", pos);
close(handle);
return 0;
}
```

tempnam   Temporary filename

Syntax   char *tempnam(char *dir, char *prefix);

Include   stdio.h

Description   Returns the name of a new file guaranteed not to exist in one of several possible directories. The returned name contains complete drive and directory information. Use this name to create a temporary file, which is your responsibility to delete. The temporary filename string is allocated memory by malloc(). Call free() to delete this memory when you are done using the filename string.

In the course of creating a temporary filename, the function searches up to four directories in this order: a directory assigned to the TMP environment variable, the dir argument passed to tempnam(), the directory string defined by constant P_tmpdir in STDIO.H, or the current directory.

NOTE: P_tmpdir is defined as a null string in Borland C++, thus defaulting to the current directory. In effect, therefore, tempnam() actually searches only three, not four, directories.

Parameters   **char *dir** Pointer to directory string. This directory is searched only if the TMP environment variable is not set, if it refers to a nonexistent directory, or if an error occurs while attempting to create a temporary filename for the TMP directory. Set dir to null to skip searching an explicit directory.

`char *prefix` A pointer to a string containing up to five characters which may *not* include a period. The temporary filename begins with this text, to which the function adds additional characters to ensure the filename's uniqueness.

See also   free, getenv, mktemp, putenv, tmpfile, tmpnam

Example

```
/* tempnam.cpp */
#include <stdio.h>
#include <alloc.h>
main()
{
  char *fname = tempnam(NULL, "temp");
  printf("Temporary filename == %s\n", fname);
  free(fname);  // Delete temporary name from heap
  return 0;
}
```

textattr   Set text attributes

Syntax   void textattr(int newattr);

Include   conio.h

Description   Sets the text attribute word for output functions prototyped in conio.h. Equivalent to calling `textbackground()` and `textcolor()`.

Parameters   `int newattr` Attribute word to use for subsequent conio.h text output statements.

See also   cprintf, cputs, gettextinfo, highvideo, lowvideo, normvideo, putch, textbackground, textcolor

Example

```
/* textattr.cpp */
#include <conio.h>
#define ATTR ((RED << 4) | WHITE)
main()
{
  textattr(ATTR);
  cprintf("Attribute value == %#x\r\n", ATTR);
  normvideo();
  cputs("After resetting normal video attributes");
  clreol();
  return 0;
}
```

textbackground   Select text background color

Syntax   `void textbackground(int bkcolor);`

Include   conio.h

Description   Set background color or monochrome text attribute for text output functions prototyped in conio.h.

Parameters   **int bkcolor** Background color in range 0 to 7, or for clarity, one of the constants BLACK, BLUE, GREEN, CYAN, RED, MAGENTA, BROWN, or LIGHTGRAY.

See also   cprintf, cputs, gettextinfo, putch, textattr, textcolor

Example

```
/* textback.cpp */
#include <conio.h>
main()
{
  int c, color;
  clrscr();
  for (color = 0; color <= 15; color++) {
    textbackground(color);
    cprintf("\r\n");
    if (color < 8)
      lowvideo();
    else
      highvideo();
    for (c = 'A'; c <= 'Z'; c++)
      cprintf(" %c", c);
  }
  return 0;
}
```

textcolor   Select text foreground color

Syntax   `void textcolor(int fgcolor);`

Include   conio.h

Description   Set foreground color or monochrome text attribute for text output functions prototyped in conio.h.

Parameters   **int fgcolor** Foreground color in range 0 to 15, or for clarity, one of the constants BLACK, BLUE, GREEN, CYAN, RED, MAGENTA, BROWN, LIGHTGRAY,

DARKGRAY, LIGHTBLUE, LIGHTGREEN, LIGHTCYAN, LIGHTRED, LIGHTMAGENTA, YELLOW, or WHITE. Logically OR a color value with constant BLINK to enable flashing characters for some text modes.

See also cprintf, cputs, gettextinfo, highvideo, lowvideo, normvideo, putch, textattr, textbackground

Example
```
/* textcolo.cpp */
#include <conio.h>
main()
{
  int c, color;
  for (color = 0; color <= 15; color++) {
    textbackground(color);
    cprintf("\r\n");
    for (c = 'A'; c <= 'Z'; c++) {
      textcolor(c % 16);
      cprintf(" %c", c);
    }
  }
  normvideo();
  cprintf("\r\n");
  clreol();
  return 0;
}
```

textheight   String height in pixels

Syntax int far textheight(char far *textstring);

Include graphics.h

Description Returns height in pixels of a string to be displayed in graphics using the current font as selected by settextstyle().

Parameters **char far *textstring** Pointer to string to be displayed. Use "M" for general purpose height settings for a selected font.

See also gettextsettings, outtext, outtextxy, settextstyle, textwidth

Example
```
/* textheig.cpp */
#include <graphics.h>
#include <stdio.h>
#include <stdlib.h>
```

```
#include <conio.h>
#define MESSAGE "Happy Holidays"
main()
{
  int gdriver = DETECT, gmode, gerr;
  int xcenter, ycenter, x1, x2, y1, y2, h, w;
  initgraph(&gdriver, &gmode, "c:\\borlandc\\bgi");
  gerr = graphresult();
  if (gerr != grOk) {
    printf("BGI error: %s\n", grapherrormsg(gerr));
    exit(gerr);
  }
  xcenter = getmaxx() / 2;
  ycenter = getmaxy() / 2;
  settextjustify(CENTER_TEXT, CENTER_TEXT);
  settextstyle(TRIPLEX_FONT, HORIZ_DIR, 4);
  h = textheight(MESSAGE) + 4;
  w = textwidth(MESSAGE) + 4;
  x1 = xcenter - (w / 2);
  x2 = xcenter + (w / 2);
  y1 = ycenter - (h / 2);
  y2 = ycenter + (h / 2);
  setcolor(RED);
  rectangle(x1, y1, x2, y2);
  setcolor(GREEN);
  outtextxy(xcenter, ycenter, MESSAGE);
  getch();
  closegraph();
  return 0;
}
```

textmode   Engage text mode

Syntax   void textmode(int mode);

Include   conio.h

Description   Select a text display mode. Not for use with graphics (see instead restorecrtmode() and setgraphmode()). All modes are not available on all monitor types or video hardware.

Parameters   **int mode** Mode number. One of the constants BW40 (40-col black and white), C40 (40-col color), BW80 (80-col black and white), C80 (80-col color), MONO (monochrome), or C4350 (43- or 50-line EGA or VGA). Or, set to LASTMODE to return to a previously selected text mode.

See also   gettextinfo, restorecrtmode, setgraphmode, window

Example
```
/* textmode.cpp */
/* Note: Requires EGA or VGA video card */
#include <conio.h>
main()
{
  int color;
  struct text_info ti;
  gettextinfo(&ti);
  textmode(C4350);   // EGA==43 lines, VGA==50 lines
  clrscr();
  cputs("    Tiny text color demonstration\r\n");
  cputs("-------------------------------\r\n");
  for (color = 0; color <= 15; color++) {
    normvideo();
    cprintf("color=%2d", color);
    textcolor(color);
    cprintf("   Normal video    ");
    highvideo();
    cprintf("High video\r\n");
  }
  getch();   // Pause for keypress
  textmode(ti.currmode);
  return 0;
}
```

textwidth   String width in pixels

Syntax   `int far textwidth(char far *textstring);`

Include   graphics.h

Description   Returns width in pixels of a string to be displayed in graphics using the current font as selected by settextstyle().

Parameters   **char far *textstring** Pointer to string to be displayed. Use "M" for general-purpose width settings for a selected font.

See also   gettextsettings, outtext, outtextxy, settextstyle, textheight

Example

```
/* textwidt.cpp */
#include <graphics.h>
#include <stdio.h>
#include <stdlib.h>
#include <conio.h>
#define ASCII_RET 13
#define ASCII_ESC 27
main()
{
  int gdriver = DETECT, gmode, gerr;
  int xmax, ymax, c;
  char s[2] = " ";
  initgraph(&gdriver, &gmode, "c:\\borlandc\\bgi");
  gerr = graphresult();
  if (gerr != grOk) {
    printf("BGI error: %s\n", grapherrormsg(gerr));
    exit(gerr);
  }
  xmax = getmaxx();
  ymax = getmaxy();
  settextstyle(SANS_SERIF_FONT, HORIZ_DIR, 4);
  outtextxy(0, 0, "Type text; Esc to quit...");
  moveto(0, textheight("M") + 6);
  while ((c = getch()) != ASCII_ESC) {
    s[0] = c;
    outtext(s);
    if ((c == ASCII_RET) || (getx() + textwidth("M") > xmax)) {
      moveto(0, gety() + textheight("M") + 6);
      if (gety() + textheight("M") >= ymax)
        clearviewport(); // New page
    }
  }
  closegraph();
  return 0;
}
```

time   Get system time

Syntax   `time_t time(time_t *thetime);`

Include   time.h

Description   Returns current date and time expressed as the number of seconds elapsed since GMT 00:00:00 on January 1, 1970. The example is named TIMER.CPP to avoid conflicting with the DOS TIME command.

Parameters   `time_t *thetime` Optional pointer to a `time_t` variable, in which the current date and time are stored (the same value as returned by the function). Ignored if null.

See also   `asctime, ctime, difftime, ftime, gettime, gmtime, localtime, settime, stime, _strdate, strftime, _strtime, tzset`

Example
```
/* timer.cpp */
#include <stdio.h>
#include <time.h>
main()
{
  time_t thetime = time(NULL);
  printf("%s\n", ctime(&thetime));
  return 0;
}
```

tmpfile   Open temporary file

Syntax   `FILE *tmpfile(void);`

Include   stdio.h

Description   Names and creates a temporary file, opened for writing in binary mode. Creates file in the current directory, or if defined, in the directory specified by a TMP or TEMP environment variable. Never overwrites an existing file. The temporary file is automatically deleted when closed or when the program ends. Returns pointer to file stream for success and null for errors.

See also   `fopen, tmpnam`

Example   See `fread`.

tmpnam   Temporary filename

Syntax   `char *tmpnam(char *s);`

Include   stdio.h

Description   Returns pointer to a temporary filename, guaranteed to be unique in the current directory, or if defined, in a directory specified by the TMP or TEMP environment variables.

Parameters   **char *s** Optional pointer to string buffer at least L_tmpnam bytes long in which to store the function result. If s is non-null, tmpnam() returns s. If s is null, tmpnam() returns the address of static memory that is reused on subsequent calls to tmpnam().

See also   getenv, mktemp, putenv, tempnam, tmpfile

Example   See fflush.

toascii   Convert int to ASCII

Syntax   `int toascii(int c);`

Include   ctype.h

Description   Returns "pure" seven-bit ASCII value by forcing int c to the range 0 to 127.

Parameters   **int c** Character to be translated to pure ASCII.

See also   is..., tolower, toupper

Example
```
/* toascii.cpp */
#include <conio.h>
#include <ctype.h>
main()
{
  int c;
  cprintf("ASCII character values 159 to 255:\r\n");
  for (c = 159; c <= 255; c++)
    putch(c);
  cprintf("\r\n\r\n");
  cprintf("Same values filtered by toascii()\r\n");
  for (c = 159; c <= 255; c++)
    putch(toascii(c));
  return 0;
}
```

_tolower   Convert character to lowercase

Syntax   `int _tolower(int c);`

Include   ctype.h

Description Translates an ASCII letter character c to lowercase.

Parameters **int c** Character value A to Z to be translated to a to z respectively. Other characters give undefined results.

See also   `strlwr, strupr, tolower, _toupper, toupper`

Example
```
/* _tolower.cpp */
#include <stdio.h>
#include <ctype.h>
main()
{
  char *s = "ABCDEFGHIJKLMNOPQRSTUVWXYZ";
  printf("s == %s\n", s);
  puts("After _tolower()");
  for (int i = 0; s[i]; i++)
    s[i] = _tolower(s[i]);
  printf("s == %s\n", s);
  return 0;
}
```

tolower   Convert character to lowercase

Syntax   `int tolower(int c);`

Include   ctype.h

Description Returns lowercase equivalent of an ASCII character value c. Affects only alphabetic characters A to Z. Returns other characters unchanged.

Parameters **int c** ASCII character to be translated. All characters are allowed.

See also   `strlwr, strupr, _tolower, _toupper, toupper`

Example
```
/* tolower.cpp */
#include <stdio.h>
#include <ctype.h>
main()
```

```
{
  char *s = "ABCDEFGHIJKLMNOPQRSTUVWXYZ0123456789";
  printf("s == %s\n", s);
  puts("After tolower()");
  for (int i = 0; s[i]; i++)
    s[i] = tolower(s[i]);
  printf("s == %s\n", s);
  return 0;
}
```

_toupper Convert character to uppercase

Syntax   `int _toupper(int c);`

Include   ctype.h

Description   Translates an ASCII letter character c to uppercase.

Parameters   **int c** Character value a to z to be translated to A to Z respectively. Other characters give undefined results.

See also   `strlwr, strupr, _tolower, tolower, toupper`

Example
```
/* _toupper.cpp */
#include <stdio.h>
#include <ctype.h>
main()
{
  char *s = "abcdefghijklmnopqrstuvwxyz";
  printf("s == %s\n", s);
  puts("After _toupper()");
  for (int i = 0; s[i]; i++)
    s[i] = _toupper(s[i]);
  printf("s == %s\n", s);
  return 0;
}
```

toupper Convert character to uppercase

Syntax   `int toupper(int c);`

Include   ctype.h

Description Returns uppercase equivalent of an ASCII character value c. Affects only alphabetic characters a to z. Returns other characters unchanged.

Parameters **int c** ASCII character to be translated. All characters are allowed.

See also strlwr, strupr, _tolower, tolower, _toupper

Example
```
/* toupper.cpp */
#include <stdio.h>
#include <ctype.h>
main()
{
  char *s = "abcdefghijklmnopqrstuvwxyz0123456789";
  printf("s == %s\n", s);
  puts("After toupper()");
  for (int i = 0; s[i]; i++)
    s[i] = toupper(s[i]);
  printf("s == %s\n", s);
  return 0;
}
```

tzset   Set time zone

Syntax void tzset(void);

Include time.h

Description Sets the current time zone using the value of an optional environment variable TZ. From DOS, or in a batch file, you can set TZ to a string with a command such as

```
set TZ=EST5EDT
```

The TZ string, of which the default value is shown here, contains three items: a three-letter abbreviation for the time zone (EST=Eastern Standard Time, PST=Pacific Standard Time, and so on), the number of hours that this time zone differs plus or minus from GMT (Greenwich Mean Time) (EST=5, CST=6, MST=7, PST=8, continental Europe=–1, and so on), and an optional three-letter abbreviation representing the daylight saving time zone (EDT=Eastern daylight saving time, and so on).

Calling tzset() reads the TZ environment variable and sets the values of three global variables accordingly: daylight (true if daylight saving is in effect—that is, if the TZ variable ends with a three-letter suffix such as EDT), timezone (the difference in seconds between local time and GMT), and tzname (an array of pointers to timezone strings—tzname[0] addresses the TZ variable's preface string, such as "EST"; tzname[1] addresses the TZ variable's suffix string, such as "EDT").

See also asctime, ctime, ftime, gmtime, localtime, stime, _strdate, strftime, _strtime, time

Example
```
/* template.cpp */
#include <stdio.h>
#include <stdlib.h>
#include <time.h>
main()
{
  if (getenv("TZ") == NULL)
    putenv("TZ=EST5EDT");
  tzset();
  time_t t = time(NULL);
  printf("Date and time: %s", asctime(localtime(&t)));
  return 0;
}
```

ultoa   Convert unsigned long to string

Syntax char *ultoa(unsigned long value, char *string, int radix);

Include stdlib.h

Description Converts an unsigned long value to a string.

Parameters **unsigned long value** Value to be converted to a string.

char *string Pointer to char array at least 33 bytes long.

int radix A value from 2 to 36 to use for the converted value's number base.

See also itoa, ltoa

Example
```
/* ultoa.cpp */
#include <stdio.h>
#include <stdlib.h>
main()
{
```

```
unsigned long ul = 987654321L;
char result[33];
ultoa(ul, result, 10);
printf("Value in decimal == %s\n", result);
ultoa(ul, result, 16);
printf("Value in hexadecimal == %s\n", result);
return 0;
}
```

umask Set file permissions mask

Syntax   `unsigned umask(unsigned mode);`

Include io.h, sys\stat.h

Description Sets default file-access permissions for `creat()` and `open()`. Returns replaced mode value.

Parameters **unsigned mode** Either of the constants S_IREAD (permission to read) or S_IWRITE (permission to write), or the expression (S_READ ¦ S_IWRITE) (permission to read and write).

See also creat, open, sopen

Example
```
/* umask.cpp */
#include <stdio.h>
#include <fcntl.h>
#include <sys\stat.h>
#include <io.h>
#define FNAME "umask.cpp"   // Our own file
main()
{
  unsigned savedmask = umask(S_IREAD ¦ S_IWRITE);
  int handle = open(FNAME, O_TEXT);
  if (handle) {
    printf("%s opened\n", FNAME);
    close(handle);
  } else
    perror(FNAME);
  umask(savedmask);
  // ... Other I/O operations
  return 0;
}
```

ungetc   Return character to input stream

Syntax   `int ungetc(int c, FILE *stream);`

Include   stdio.h

Description   Pushes one character back to an input file stream. The next input operation on that same stream—getc() or fgetc(), for example— returns the pushed-back character. Only one such character can be pushed onto a file stream at a time. Functions fflush(), fseek(), fsetpos(), and rewind() delete any pushed-back character. Returns c for success and EOF for errors.

Parameters   **int c** Character to push back to a file stream.

     FILE *stream Pointer to an open file stream such as that returned by fopen().

See also   fgetc, fread, getc, getchar

Example
```
/* ungetc.cpp */
#include <stdio.h>
#include <string.h>
main()
{
  char s[128];
  puts("Enter a string");
  gets(s);
  if (strlen(s) > 0) {
    printf("Original string == %s\n", s);
    int c = s[strlen(s) - 1];
    printf("Pushing last character %c back to input\n", c);
    ungetc(c, stdin);
    printf("Result from getc() == %c\n", getc(stdin));
  }
  return 0;
}
```

ungetch   Return character to keyboard buffer

Syntax   `int ungetch(int c);`

Include   conio.h

Description   Similar to ungetc(), but pushes a character back to the keyboard buffer for reading with a conio.h input function such as getch(). Returns c for success and EOF for errors.

Parameters   **int c** Character to push back to the keyboard buffer.

See also   getch, getche

Example
```
/* ungetch.cpp */
#include <stdio.h>
#include <conio.h>
#include <string.h>
main()
{
  char s[128];
  puts("Enter a string");
  gets(s);
  if (strlen(s) > 0) {
    printf("Original string == %s\n", s);
    int c = s[strlen(s) - 1];
    printf("Pushing last character %c back to keyboard\n", c);
    ungetch(c);
    printf("Result from getch() == %c\n", getch());
  }
  return 0;
}
```

unixtodos   Convert UNIX date and time to DOS

Syntax   void unixtodos(long time, struct date *d, struct time *t);

Include   dos.h

Description   Translates a UNIX date and time long value to equivalent DOS date and time structures. The earliest supported time is 00:00:00 on January 1, 1980.

Parameters   **long time** Time and date in seconds from 00:00:00 on January 1, 1980.

             struct date *d Pointer to the date structure for holding the date portion of the function result.

struct time *t Pointer to the `time` structure for holding the time portion of the function result.

See also   `dostounix, time`

Example
```
/* unixtodo.cpp */
#include <stdio.h>
#include <dos.h>
#include <time.h>
main()
{
  time_t utime;
  struct time t;
  struct date d;
  time(&utime);
  unixtodos(utime, &d, &t);
  printf("The date is: %d/%d/%d\n",
    d.da_mon, d.da_day, d.da_year);
  printf("The time is: %02d:%02d:%02d\n",
    t.ti_hour, t.ti_min, t.ti_sec);
  return 0;
}
```

unlink   Delete file

Syntax   `int unlink(const char *filename);`

Include   dos.h or io.h or stdio.h

Description   Same as `remove()`. Deletes the named file. (*Unlink* is the UNIX term for *delete file*.) Returns zero for success and –1 for errors; sets `errno` to `EACCES` (access denied) or `ENOENT` (no such file or directory).

Parameters   **const char *filename** Pointer to the string representing the name of the file to delete. May contain drive and path information but no wildcards.

See also   `chmod, remove`

Example
```
/* unlink.cpp */

#include <stdio.h>
#include <io.h>
#include <sys\stat.h>
main()
{
```

```
char tfname[L_tmpnam];
tmpnam(tfname);
printf("Creating temporary file %s\n", tfname);
int handle = creat(tfname, S_IWRITE);
if (handle) {
  puts("Closing temporary file");
  close(handle);
}
printf("Unlinking (removing) %s\n", tfname);
unlink(tfname);
return 0;
}
```

unlock   **Release file-sharing locks**

Syntax   `int unlock(int handle, long offset, long length);`

Include   io.h

Description   Unlocks a lock placed earlier by `lock()`. Requires DOS 3.x and SHARE.EXE installed. Returns zero for success and –1 for errors.

Parameters   **int handle** File handle such as that returned by `open()`.

     long offset Offset in bytes from the start of the file to the beginning of the locked region.

     long length Length of the locked region in bytes.

See also   `lock, sopen`

Example   See `lock`.

utime   **Update file date and time**

Syntax   `int utime(char *path, struct utimbuf *times);`

Include   utime.h

Description   Changes a named file's date and time using a `utimbuf` structure declared in utime.h as

```
struct utimbuf
{
  time_t actime;   // Most recent access date and time
  time_t modtime;  // Most recent modification date and time
};
```

1399

Returns zero for success and –1 for errors; sets errno to EACCES (access denied), EMFILE (too many files open), or ENOENT (no such file or directory).

Parameters **char *path** Pointer to the string representing the name of the file to update. May include drive and path information but no wild cards.

struct utimbuf *times Pointer to the utimbuf structure, as explained in *Description*. DOS files do not support an access time; therefore, utime() uses only the structure's modtime member. It ignores member actime.

See also localtime, setftime, stat, time, tzset

Example
```
/* utime.cpp */
#include <stdio.h>
#include <stdlib.h>
#include <utime.h>
main(int argc, char *argv[])
{
  struct utimbuf utb;
  if (argc <= 1) {
    puts("Enter name of file to update");
    puts("to current date and time.");
    exit(1);
  }
  utb.actime = time(&utb.modtime);
  if (utime(argv[1], &utb) == 0)
    printf("%s updated", argv[1]);
  else
    printf("Error: %s not updated\n", argv[1]);
  return 0;
}
```

va_arg, va_end, va_start   Variable arguments

Syntax
```
type va_arg(va_list ap, type);
void va_end(va_list ap);
void va_start(va_list ap, lastfix);
```

Include   stdarg.h or varargs.h

Description   Use these "variable argument" macros to construct functions that accept a variable number of arguments, declared with the three-period ellipsis (...). For example, you might declare a function like this:

```
void AnyFunction(int FixedParam, ...);
```

Function `AnyFunction()` returns `void` and requires at least one `int` argument. The ellipsis indicates that, in addition to `FixedParam`, statements can pass one or more additional argument values of any type (except for values of type `char`, `unsigned char`, and `float`, which are promoted to other types and therefore are not allowed in variable argument lists).

Inside the function, special programming is needed to access these extra parameters. First, declare a variable of type `va_list` (a pointer to the parameter list), and initialize it with `va_start()`:

```
va_list vap;
va_start(vap, FixedParam);
```

Next, use `va_arg()` to extract one or more parameters of any type (except the excluded types mentioned earlier). Suppose, for example, that a statement passes two extra `int` values to the function. You can load these values into local variables like this:

```
int v1 = va_arg(vap, int);
int v2 = va_arg(vap, int);
```

Macro `va_arg()` requires two arguments: a `va_list` pointer (`vap`) and the type of argument to retrieve. If the number of arguments isn't known, use a sentinel to mark the end of the list. You might, for instance, pass a unique value such as −1 to multiparameter functions to end a list of preceding values. You could call the function like this:

```
AnyFunction(10, 9, 8, 7, 6, 5, 4, 3, 2, 1, 0, -1);
```

Assuming by prearrangement that −1 is the end-of-list sentinel, in `AnyFunction` use a loop to access the parameters:

```
void AnyFunction(int FixedParam, ...)
{
  va_list vap;  // Pointer to variable-argument list
  int v;        // Holds value of each argument
  printf("%d\n", FixedParam);  // Display fixed parameter
  va_start(vap, FixedParam);   // Begin accessing var-arg list
```

```
    while ((v = va_arg(vap, int)) != -1)  // Get one argument
      printf("%d\n", arg);  // Display argument value
    va_end(vap);  // Signal end of list
  }
```

The final step in the process passes the initialized vap pointer to va_end() to counter the preceding call to va_start().

Parameters **va_list ap** Pointer to the variable-argument list. Pass to va_start() to initialize, to va_arg() to retrieve the next parameter value, and to va_end() to signal the end of the parameter-retrieval process.

lastfix The address of the last (that is, the rightmost) typed parameter in the argument list. Pass to va_start() only.

type The data type to be returned by va_arg(). Can be different types on successive uses of va_arg(). Cannot be char, unsigned char, or float.

See also exec..., spawn..., v...printf, v...scanf

Example

```
/* va_arg.cpp */
#include <stdio.h>
#include <stdarg.h>
double Average(unsigned num, ...);
main()
{
  double result;
  result = Average(4, 75.5, 89.0, 62.5, 98.0);
  printf("Result = %lf\n", result);
  result = Average(3, 77.7, 88.8, 99.9);
  printf("Result = %lf\n", result);
  return 0;
}

// Return average of a set of double values
// Set num to the number of values that follow
double Average(unsigned num, ...)
{
  va_list vap;
  va_start(vap, num);
  double sum = 0.0;
  for (int i = 0; i < num; i++)
    sum += va_arg(vap, double);
```

```
      va_end(vap);
      return sum / num;
    }
```

vfprintf   Format output to stream

Syntax   `int vfprintf(FILE *stream, const char *format, va_list arglist);`

Include   stdio.h

Description   Same as `fprintf()`, but accepts a `va_list` pointer in place of the usual explicit argument values to be formatted to a file stream. Typically used in a function that declares a variable number of parameters (see `va_...()` macros).

Parameters   **`FILE *stream`** Pointer to a file stream such as that returned by `fopen()`.

    `const char *format` Pointer to a format string containing conversion rules and other text, as explained for function `printf()`.

    `va_list  arglist` A variable-argument list pointer initialized by `va_start()`.

See also   cprintf, fprintf, printf, scanf, sscanf, va_arg, va_end, va_start, vfscanf, vprintf, vscanf, vsprintf, vsscanf

Example
```
/* vfprintf.cpp */
#include <stdio.h>
#include <stdarg.h>
int MyPrintf(const char *format, ...);
main()
{
  int i = 123;
  double d = 3.14159;
  MyPrintf("int==%d  double=%lf\n", i, d);
  return 0;
}

int MyPrintf(const char *format, ...)
{
  va_list vap;
  va_start(vap, format);
  puts("Inside our own printf()-style function");
  int n = vfprintf(stdout, format, vap);
```

```
    va_end(vap);
    return n;
}
```

vfscanf   Scan and format input from stream

Syntax   `int vfscan(FILE *stream, const char *format, va_list arglist);`

Include   stdio.h

Description   Same as `fscanf()` but accepts a `va_list` pointer in place of the usual address arguments to which values are translated from a file stream. Typically used in a function that declares a variable number of parameters (see `va_...()` macros).

Parameters   **FILE *stream** Pointer to a file stream such as that returned by `fopen()`.

const char *format Pointer to a format string containing conversion rules and other text, as explained for function `scanf()`.

va_list arglist A variable-argument list pointer initialized by `va_start()`.

See also   cprintf, fprintf, printf, scanf, sscanf, va_arg, va_end, va_start, vfprintf, vprintf, vscanf, vsprintf, vsscanf

Example
```
/* vfscanf.cpp */
#include <stdio.h>
#include <stdarg.h>
int MyScanf(const char *prompt, const char *format, ...);
main()
{
  int i;
  double d;
  MyScanf("Enter integer and double values: ", "%d %lf", &i, &d);
  printf("i==%d  d==%lf\n", i, d);
  return 0;
}

int MyScanf(const char *prompt, const char *format, ...)
{
```

```
    va_list vap;
    va_start(vap, format);
    printf(prompt);
    int n = vfscanf(stdin, format, vap);
    va_end(vap);
    return n;
}
```

vprintf   Format output to stdout

Syntax   `int vprintf(const char *format, va_list arglist);`

Include   stdarg.h, stdio.h

Description   Same as `printf()`, but accepts a `va_list` pointer in place of the usual explicit argument values to be formatted to the standard output. Typically used in a function that declares a variable number of parameters (see `va_...()` macros).

Parameters   `const char *format` Pointer to a format string containing conversion rules and other text, as explained for function `printf()`.

`va_list  arglist` A variable-argument list pointer initialized by `va_start()`.

See also   cprintf, fprintf, printf, scanf, sscanf, va_arg, va_end, va_start, vfprintf, vfscanf, vscanf, vsprintf, vsscanf

Example
```
/* vprintf.cpp */
#include <stdio.h>
#include <stdarg.h>
int MyPrintf(const char *format, ...);
main()
{
  int i = 123;
  double d = 3.14159;
  MyPrintf("int==%d  double=%lf\n", i, d);
  return 0;
}

int MyPrintf(const char *format, ...)
{
  va_list vap;
  va_start(vap, format);
```

```
    puts("Inside our own printf()-style function");
    int n = vprintf(format, vap);
    va_end(vap);
    return n;
}
```

vscanf   Scan and format input from stdin

Syntax   `int vscanf(const char *format, va_list arglist);`

Include   stdarg.h, stdio.h

Description   Same as `scanf()` but accepts a `va_list` pointer in place of the usual address arguments to which values are translated from the standard input. Typically used in a function that declares a variable number of parameters (see `va_...()` macros).

Parameters   **const char *format** Pointer to a format string containing conversion rules and other text, as explained for function `scanf()`.

va_list arglist A variable-argument list pointer initialized by `va_start()`.

See also   cprintf, fprintf, printf, scanf, sscanf, va_arg, va_end, va_start, vfprintf, vfscanf, vprintf, vsprintf, vsscanf

Example
```
/* vscanf.cpp */
#include <stdio.h>
#include <stdarg.h>
int MyScanf(const char *prompt, const char *format, ...);
main()
{
  int i;
  double d;
  MyScanf("Enter integer and double values: ", "%d %lf", &i, &d);
  printf("i==%d  d==%lf\n", i, d);
  return 0;
}

int MyScanf(const char *prompt, const char *format, ...)
{
```

```
    va_list vap;
    va_start(vap, format);
    printf(prompt);
    int n = vscanf(format, vap);
    va_end(vap);
    return n;
}
```

vsprintf   Format output to string

Syntax   `int vsprintf(char *buffer, const char *format, va_list arglist);`

Include   stdarg.h, stdio.h

Description   Same as `sprintf()`, but accepts a `va_list` pointer in place of the usual explicit argument values to be formatted to a string buffer. Typically used in a function that declares a variable number of parameters (see `va_...()` macros).

Parameters   `char *buffer` Pointer to a char array large enough to hold the formatted result.

`const char *format` Pointer to a format string containing conversion rules and other text, as explained for the function `printf()`.

`va_list  arglist` A variable-argument list pointer initialized by `va_start()`.

See also   cprintf, fprintf, printf, scanf, sscanf, va_arg, va_end, va_start, vfprintf, vfscanf, vprintf, vscanf, vsscanf

Example
```
/* vsprintf.cpp */
#include <stdio.h>
#include <stdarg.h>
int MyPrintf(char *buf, const char *format, ...);
main()
{
  int i = 123;
  double d = 3.14159;
  char buf[80];
  MyPrintf(buf, "int==%d  double=%lf\n", i, d);
  printf("buf contents: %s\n", buf);
  return 0;
}
```

```
int MyPrintf(char *buf, const char *format, ...)
{
  va_list vap;
  va_start(vap, format);
  puts("Inside our own printf()-style function");
  int n = vsprintf(buf, format, vap);
  va_end(vap);
  return n;
}
```

vsscanf   Scan and format input from stream

Syntax   `int vsscanf(const char *buffer, const char *format,`
              `va_list arglist);`

Include   stdarg.h, stdio.h

Description Same as sscanf() but accepts a va_list pointer in place of the usual
              address arguments to which values are translated from a char buffer.
              Typically used in a function that declares a variable number of param-
              eters (see va_...() macros).

Parameters **const char *buffer** Pointer to a char array to be used as the source text.

              const char *format Pointer to a format string containing conversion
              rules and other text, as explained for function scanf().

              va_list arglist A variable-argument list pointer initialized by
              va_start().

See also   cprintf, fprintf, printf, scanf, sscanf, va_arg, va_end, va_start,
              vfprintf, vfscanf, vprintf, vscanf, vsprintf

Example
```
/* vsscanf.cpp */
#include <stdio.h>
#include <stdarg.h>
int MyScanf(char *buf, const char *format, ...);
main()
{
  int i;
  double d;
  char buf[128];
  printf("Enter integer and double values: ");
```

```
  gets(buf);
  MyScanf(buf, "%d %lf", &i, &d);
  printf("i==%d  d==%lf\n", i, d);
  return 0;
}

int MyScanf(char *buf, const char *format, ...)
{
  va_list vap;
  va_start(vap, format);
  int n = vsscanf(buf, format, vap);
  va_end(vap);
  return n;
}
```

wcstombs   Wide array to multibyte string

Syntax   `size_t wcstombs(char *s, const wchar_t *pwcs, size_t n);`

Include   stdlib.h

Description Translates up to n multibyte characters in a `wchar_t` (wide-character type) array to a `char` string. Intended for use with `setlocale()`, but as currently implemented, simply copies the characters at `pwcs` to a buffer at `s`, adding a null-terminating byte if necessary, and has little practical use. Returns the number of characters translated.

Parameters **char *s** Destination string pointer.

const wchar_t *pwcs Pointer to source data, a multibyte character array.

size_t n Maximum number of characters to translate.

See also   mblen, mbstowcs, mbtowc, setlocale, wctomb

Example
```
/* wcstombs.cpp */
#include <stdio.h>
#include <stdlib.h>
main()
{
  char s[80];
  wchar_t *pwcs = "Test string";
  wcstombs(s, pwcs, 80);
```

```
  printf("s == %s\n", s);
  return 0;
}
```

wctomb   Wide to multibyte character

Syntax   `int wctomb(char *s, wchar_t wc);`

Include   stdlib.h

Description Supposedly translates a wide character wc to a char pointer destination, returning the number of bytes required to represent the multibyte character in the current locale. As presently implemented, however, simply copies wc to the location addressed by s, and has little practical use. Returns zero if s is null. Returns 1 if s is non-null.

Parameters **char *s** Destination pointer or null.

wchar_t wc Character to be translated.

See also mblen, mbstowcs, mbtowc, setlocale, wcstombs

Example
```
/* wctomb.cpp */
#include <stdio.h>
#include <stdlib.h>
main()
{
  char s[80];
  wchar_t wc = '@';
  int result = wctomb(s, wc);
  printf("result == %d\n", result);
  printf("s[0] == %c\n", s[0]);
  return 0;
}
```

wherex, wherey   Cursor position

Syntax   `int wherex(void);`
`int wherey(void);`

Include   conio.h

Description Returns the horizontal (wherex()) and vertical (wherey()) cursor positions for text display modes only.

See also   gettextinfo, gotoxy

Example

```cpp
/* wherexy.cpp */
#include <conio.h>
void GoUp(void);
void GoLeft(void);
main()
{
  int x, i;
  clrscr();
  gotoxy(40, 12);
  cputs(" <-- Center of screen");
  gotoxy(40, 12);
  for (i = 1; i <= 4; i++)
    GoUp();
  for (i = 1; i <= 15; i++)
    GoLeft();
  x = wherex();
  cputs(" <-- up 4, left 15");
  gotoxy(x, wherey());
  getch();
  gotoxy(1, 24);
  return 0;
}

void GoUp(void)
{
  gotoxy(wherex(), wherey() - 1);
}

void GoLeft(void)
{
  gotoxy(wherex() - 1, wherey());
}
```

window   Text window

Syntax   void window(int left, int top, int right, int bottom);

Include   conio.h

Description Limits conio.h text-output functions to a portion of a text-mode display. Not for use with graphics modes. Has no visual effect (that is, does *not* display a window border).

Parameters `int left`, `int top` Top-left coordinate of the new restricted output rectangle. Subsequent calls to gotoxy() are relative to this coordinate.

`int right`, `int bottom` Bottom-right coordinate of the new restricted output rectangle.

See also clreol, clrscr, delline, gettextinfo, gotoxy, insline, movetext, puttext, textmode

Example
```
/* window.cpp */
#include <stdlib.h>
#include <conio.h>
#include <dos.h>
void RandText(void);
main()
{
  int y1 = 11, y2 = 11, y3 = 13;
  clrscr();
  while (!kbhit()) {
    window(1, 1, 26, 11);
    gotoxy(1, y1);
    RandText();
    y1 = wherey();
    window(20, 13, 45, 23);
    gotoxy(1, y2);
    RandText();
    y2 = wherey();
    window(50, 5, 75, 17);
    gotoxy(1, y3);
    RandText();
    y3 = wherey();
  }
  getch();                   // Throw away keypress
  textmode(LASTMODE);        // Reset to full screen
  gotoxy(1, 24);             // Position cursor at bottom
  return 0;
}
```

```
void RandText(void)
{
  int i;
  delay(75);
  for (i = 1; i <= 25; i++) {
    textcolor(1 + random(15));
    putch(32 + random(144));
  }
  cprintf("\r\n");
}
```

_write   Write to file

Syntax   `int _write(int handle, void *buf, unsigned len);`

Include   io.h

Description   Same as write(), except for these three differences: writes only to binary files, does not convert line feed control codes to carriage return and line feed pairs, and does not position the internal file pointer to the end of the file for files opened using option O_APPEND.

Parameters   See write.

See also   `creat, lseek, open, _read, write`

Example   See write.

write   Write to file

Syntax   `int write(int handle, void *buf, unsigned len);`

Include   io.h

Description   General-purpose output function for files identified by an integer handle. Can write text and binary data up to 65,534 bytes at a time. Writes data to the current file position, as set, for example, by lseek(). For files opened using the O_APPEND option, write() sets the internal file pointer to the end of the file prior to each write operation.

Using the function with binary files writes unmodified data. With text files, the function translates line feed control codes to carriage return and line feed pairs—DOS's dual-character end-of-line markers.

Returns the number of bytes successfully written, or −1 for errors and sets errno to EACCES (access denied) or EBADF (bad file handle). For text files, the number of returned bytes counts carriage return and line feed pairs as *one* byte, not two.

Parameters   **int handle** File handle such as that returned by open().

void *buf Pointer to a buffer or other variable containing data to write to the file.

unsigned len Number of bytes to write, starting with the byte addressed by buf.

See also   creat, dup, lseek, open, read, _write

Example
```cpp
/* write.cpp */
#include <stdio.h>
#include <io.h>
#include <mem.h>
#include <sys\stat.h>
#include <fcntl.h>
char buf[80] = "Introducing\nThe Write Stuff\nby Tom Swan\n";
main()
{
  char fname[L_tmpnam];
  int wresult;
  tmpnam(fname);
  printf("Creating temporary file %s\n", fname);
  int handle = creat(fname, S_IREAD ¦ S_IWRITE);
  if (handle) {
    setmode(handle, O_BINARY);
    puts("Writing data to file");
    wresult = write(handle, buf, sizeof(buf));
    printf("Function wrote %d bytes to file\n", wresult);
    close(handle);
    setmem(buf, sizeof(buf), 0);  // Erase data buffer
    puts("Reopening file");
    handle = open(fname, O_BINARY, S_IREAD);
    read(handle, buf, sizeof(buf));
    close(handle);
    puts("\nBuffer contents...\n");
    puts(buf);
    remove(fname);
  }
  return 0;
}
```

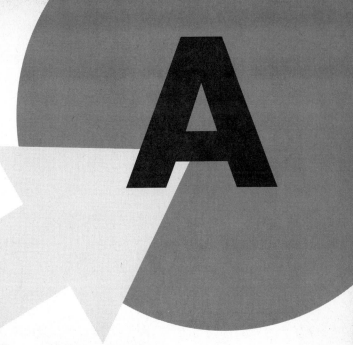

Extended ASCII Characters

Dec	Hex	OEM (DOS)	ANSI (Windows)	Dec	Hex	OEM (DOS)	ANSI (Windows)
000	00			010	0A	◙	□
001	01	☺	□	011	0B	♂	□
002	02	☻	□	012	0C	♀	□
003	03	♥	□	013	0D	♪	□
004	04	◆	□	014	0E	♫	□
005	05	♣	□	015	0F	¤	□
006	06	♠	□	016	10	▶	□
007	07	•	□	017	11	◀	□
008	08	◘	□	018	12	↕	□
009	09	○	□	019	13	‼	□

Dec	Hex	OEM (DOS)	ANSI (Windows)	Dec	Hex	OEM (DOS)	ANSI (Windows)
020	14	¶	□	044	2C	,	,
021	15	§	□	045	2D	–	–
022	16	▬	□	046	2E	.	.
023	17	↕	□	047	2F	/	/
024	18	↑	□	048	30	0	0
025	19	↓	□	049	31	1	1
026	1A	→	□	050	32	2	2
027	1B	←	□	051	33	3	3
028	1C	∟	□	052	34	4	4
029	1D	↔	□	053	35	5	5
030	1E	▲	□	054	36	6	6
031	1F	▼	□	055	37	7	7
032	20			056	38	8	8
033	21	!	!	057	39	9	9
034	22	"	"	058	3A	:	:
035	23	#	#	059	3B	;	;
036	24	$	$	060	3C	<	<
037	25	%	%	061	3D	=	=
038	26	&	&	062	3E	>	>
039	27	'	'	063	3F	?	?
040	28	(	(	064	40	@	@
041	29	)	)	065	41	A	A
042	2A	*	*	066	42	B	B
043	2B	+	+	067	43	C	C

Dec	Hex	OEM (DOS)	ANSI (Windows)	Dec	Hex	OEM (DOS)	ANSI (Windows)
068	44	D	D	092	5C	\	\
069	45	E	E	093	5D	]	]
070	46	F	F	094	5E	^	^
071	47	G	G	095	5F	_	_
072	48	H	H	096	60	`	`
073	49	I	I	097	61	a	a
074	4A	J	J	098	62	b	b
075	4B	K	K	099	63	c	c
076	4C	L	L	100	64	d	d
077	4D	M	M	101	65	e	e
078	4E	N	N	102	66	f	f
079	4F	O	O	103	67	g	g
080	50	P	P	104	68	h	h
081	51	Q	Q	105	69	i	i
082	52	R	R	106	6A	j	j
083	53	S	S	107	6B	k	k
084	54	T	T	108	6C	l	l
085	55	U	U	109	6D	m	m
086	56	V	V	110	6E	n	n
087	57	W	W	111	6F	o	o
088	58	X	X	112	70	p	p
089	59	Y	Y	113	71	q	q
090	5A	Z	Z	114	72	r	r
091	5B	[	[	115	73	s	s

Dec	Hex	OEM (DOS)	ANSI (Windows)	Dec	Hex	OEM (DOS)	ANSI (Windows)
116	74	t	t	140	8C	î	Œ
117	75	u	u	141	8D	ì	□
118	76	v	v	142	8E	Ä	□
119	77	w	w	143	8F	Å	□
120	78	x	x	144	90	É	□
121	79	y	y	145	91	æ	'
122	7A	z	z	146	92	Æ	'
123	7B	{	{	147	93	ô	"
124	7C	¦			148	94	ö	"
125	7D	}	}	149	95	ò	•
126	7E	˜	˜	150	96	û	–
127	7F	⌂	□	151	97	ù	—
128	80	Ç	□	152	98	ÿ	˜
129	81	ü	□	153	99	Ö	™
130	82	é	,	154	9A	Ü	š
131	83	â	ƒ	155	9B	¢	›
132	84	ä	"	156	9C	£	œ
133	85	à	…	157	9D	¥	□
134	86	å	†	158	9E	P$_t$	□
135	87	ç	‡	159	9F	ƒ	Ÿ
136	88	ê	ˆ	160	A0	á	
137	89	ë	‰	161	A1	í	¡
138	8A	è	Š	162	A2	ó	¢
139	8B	ï	‹	163	A3	ú	£

Dec	Hex	OEM (DOS)	ANSI (Windows)	Dec	Hex	OEM (DOS)	ANSI (Windows)
164	A4	ñ	¤	188	BC	⌡	$\frac{1}{4}$
165	A5	Ñ	¥	189	BD	⨆	$\frac{1}{2}$
166	A6	ª	¦	190	BE	⌐	$\frac{3}{4}$
167	A7	º	§	191	BF	┐	¿
168	A8	¿	¨	192	C0	└	À
169	A9	⌐	©	193	C1	⊥	Á
170	AA	¬	ª	194	C2	┬	Â
171	AB	$\frac{1}{2}$	«	195	C3	├	Ã
172	AC	$\frac{1}{4}$	¬	196	C4	—	Ä
173	AD	¡	—	197	C5	┼	Å
174	AE	«	®	198	C6	╞	Æ
175	AF	»	¯	199	C7	╟	Ç
176	B0	▨	°	200	C8	╚	È
177	B1	▤	±	201	C9	╔	É
178	B2	▉	²	202	CA	╩	Ê
179	B3	│	³	203	CB	╦	Ë
180	B4	┤	´	204	CC	╠	Ì
181	B5	╡	µ	205	CD	═	Í
182	B6	╢	¶	206	CE	╬	Î
183	B7	╖	•	207	CF	╧	Ï
184	B8	╕	,	208	D0	╨	Ð
185	B9	╣	¹	209	D1	╤	Ñ
186	BA	║	º	210	D2	╥	Ò
187	BB	╗	»	211	D3	╙	Ó

Dec	Hex	OEM (DOS)	ANSI (Windows)	Dec	Hex	OEM (DOS)	ANSI (Windows)
212	D4	╘	Ô	234	EA	Ω	ê
213	D5	╒	Õ	235	EB	δ	ë
214	D6	╓	Ö	236	EC	∞	ì
215	D7	╟	×	237	ED	ø	í
216	D8	╪	ø	238	EE	ε	î
217	D9	┘	Ù	239	EF	η	ï
218	DA	┌	Ú	240	F0	≡	δ
219	DB	█	Û	241	F1	±	ñ
220	DC	▄	Ü	242	F2	≥	ò
221	DD	▌	Ý	243	F3	≤	ó
222	DE	▐	Þ	244	F4	⌠	ô
223	DF	▀	ß	245	F5	⌡	õ
224	E0	α	à	246	F6	÷	ö
225	E1	β	á	247	F7	≈	÷
226	E2	Γ	â	248	F8	°	ø
227	E3	π	ã	249	F9	█	ù
228	E4	Σ	ä	250	FA	▪	ú
229	E5	σ	å	251	FB	√	û
230	E6	μ	æ	252	FC	ⁿ	ü
231	E7	γ	ç	253	FD	²	ý
232	E8	Φ	è	254	FE	▪	þ
233	E9	ø	é	255	FF	a	ÿ

Compiler (BCC) Options

Option	Default	3.0	3.1	Description
+*fname*		•	•	Use *fname* instead of TURBOC.CFG
@*fname*		•	•	Read options from file *fname*
-1-	•	•	•	Enable 8088/8086 instructions
-1		•	•	Enable 80186 instructions
-2		•	•	Enable 80286 instructions
-3			•	Enable 80386 instructions
-a-	•	•	•	Byte alignment
-a		•	•	Word alignment
-A		•	•	Limit to ANSI keywords
-A-	•	•	•	Enable Borland C++ keywords

continues

Option	Default	3.0	3.1	Description
-AK		•	•	Limit to standard K&R C keywords
-AT		•	•	Same as -A-
-AU		•	•	Limit to UNIX C keywords
-b-		•	•	Byte-size enumerated constants
-b	•	•	•	Word-size enumerated constants
-B		•	•	Compile to .ASM file and assemble
-c		•	•	Compile to .OBJ file; do not link
-C-	•	•	•	Disable nested comments
-C		•	•	Enable nested comments
-d-	•	•	•	Do not merge duplicate strings
-d		•	•	Merge duplicate strings
-D*name*		•	•	Define *name* as null string
-D*name=str*		•	•	Define *name* as string *str*
-e*fname*		•	•	Create linked *fname*.EXE code file
-E*fname*		•	•	Call assembler *fname* (default=TASM)
-f-		•	•	Disable floating point emulation
-f	•	•	•	Enable floating point emulation
-f287		•	•	Enable 80287 coprocessor instructions
-f87		•	•	Enable 8087 coprocessor instructions
-ff-		•	•	Disable fast floating point
-ff	•	•	•	Enable fast floating point
-Fc		•	•	Generate COMDEFs (ANSI C only. Not permitted for C++)
-Ff		•	•	Automatically create far variables

Option	Default	3.0	3.1	Description
–Ff=*size*		•	•	Same as –Ff and set threshold=*size*
–Fm		•	•	Same as –Fc –Ff –Fs
–Fs		•	•	Assume ds equals ss
–g*num*		•	•	Stop after *num* warnings
–G–	•	•	•	Optimize for size
–G		•	•	Optimize for speed
–h		•	•	Enable fast huge-pointer arithmetic
–H–	•	•	•	Disable precompiled headers
–H		•	•	Enable precompiled headers
–H=*fname*		•	•	Enable precompiled header file *fname*
–Hu		•	•	Use, don't create, precompiled headers
–i*num*		•	•	Set maximum identifier length to *num*
–I*path*		•	•	Set include-file directories to *path*
–j*num*		•	•	Stop after *num* errors
–Jg	•	•	•	Template publics; merge duplicates
–Jgd		•	•	Template publics; duplicates = error
–Jgx		•	•	Template external references
–k	•	•	•	Create standard stack frames
–K–	•	•	•	Default char is signed
–K		•	•	Default char is unsigned
–l-*opt*		•	•	Suppress linker option *opt*

continues

Option	Default	3.0	3.1	Description
-lopt		•	•	Pass option(s) opt to linker
-Lpath		•	•	Set library-file directories to path
-mc		•	•	Select compact memory model
-mh		•	•	Select huge memory model
-ml		•	•	Select large memory model
-mm		•	•	Select medium memory model
-mm!		•	•	Same as -mm and assume ds != ss
-ms	•	•	•	Select small memory model
-ms!		•	•	Same as -ms and assume ds != ss
-mt		•	•	Select tiny memory model
-mt!		•	•	Same as -mt and assume ds != ss
-M		•	•	Tell linker to create map file
-npath		•	•	Set output directory to path
-N		•	•	Enable stack-overflow checking
-ofname		•	•	Compile to fname.OBJ
-O		•	•	Optimize unnecessary jumps
-O1		•	•	Optimize for smallest size
-O2		•	•	Optimize for fastest speed
-Oa		•	•	Assume no pointer aliasing
-Ob		•	•	Optimize dead code
-Oc		•	•	Optimize local common subexpressions
-Od		•	•	Disable all optimizations
-Oe		•	•	Optimize global register allocation

Option	Default	3.0	3.1	Description
-Og		•	•	Optimize global common subexpressions
-Oi		•	•	Inline intrinsic functions
-Ol		•	•	Optimize loops to REP/STOS...
-Om		•	•	Optimize invariant code from loops
-Op		•	•	Optimize copy propagation
-Os		•	•	Optimize for smaller instructions
-Ot		•	•	Optimize for faster instructions
-Ov		•	•	Optimize loop induction variables
-Ox		•	•	Optimize for speed (for Microsoft C/C++ compatibility)
-p-	•	•	•	Enable C calling convention
-p		•	•	Enable Pascal calling convention
-po	•		•	Enable object-data calling convention
-pr		•	•	Enable _fastcall calling convention. Requires main() to be declared as int cdecl main(). In Windows, requires -WE option.
-P-ext		•	•	C & C++ compile; default extension ext
-Pext		•	•	C++ compile; default extension ext
-P-	•	•	•	Automatic C (.C) or C++ (.CPP) compile
-P		•	•	Force C++ compile
-Qe	•	•	•	Use all available expanded (EMS) RAM

continues

Option	Default	3.0	3.1	Description
-Qe-		•	•	Do not use expanded (EMS) RAM
-Qx		•	•	Use extended RAM
-r-		•	•	Disable register variables
-r	•	•	•	Enable register variables
-rd		•	•	Enable declared register variables only
-R		•	•	Create ObjectBrowser symbols
-S		•	•	Compile to .ASM file
-T-		•	•	Disable preceding assembler options
-Tstr		•	•	Pass str option to TASM
-tDc		•	•	Compile and link to .COM file
-tDe	•	•	•	Compile and link to .EXE file
-tW		•	•	Compile for Windows (see -W)
-u-		•	•	Disable identifier underscores
-u	•	•	•	Enable identifier underscores
-Uname		•	•	Undefine name
-v		•	•	Create Turbo Debugger symbols
-V		•	•	Enable smart C++ virtual tables
-V0		•	•	External C++ virtual tables
-V1		•	•	Public C++ virtual tables
-Va		•	•	Pass class args as temp references
-Vb		•	•	Virt base class ptr size = this size
-Vc		•	•	No hidden member functions (BC 2.0)
-Vf		•	•	Enable far C++ virtual tables
-vi	•	•	•	Expand inline functions
-Vmd		•	•	Smallest size member pointers

Option	Default	3.0	3.1	Description
–Vmm		•	•	Multiple inheritance mem ptrs okay
–Vmp		•	•	Use declared member pointer precision
–Vms		•	•	Single inheritance mem ptrs okay
–Vmv		•	•	No member pointer restrictions
–Vo		•	•	Same as –Va –Vb –Vc –Vp –Vt –Vv
–Vp		•	•	Pascal member functions get this first
–Vs		•	•	Local C++ virtual tables
–Vt		•	•	BC++ 2.0 virtual table pointers
–Vv		•	•	Disable class layout changes
–w–*msg*		•	•	Disable warning *msg*
–w*msg*		•	•	Enable warning *msg*
–w		•	•	Disable warnings
–W		•	•	Windows .OBJ; all functions exportable
–WD		•	•	Windows DLL .OBJ; all functions exportable
–WDE		•	•	Windows DLL .OBJ; declared functions exportable
–WE		•	•	Windows .OBJ; explicit functions exportable
–WS		•	•	Windows .OBJ; enable smart callbacks
–X		•	•	Disable IDE auto-make information
–y		•	•	Add line numbers to symbol table
–Y		•	•	Enable code overlays

continues

Option	Default	3.0	3.1	Description
-Yo		•	•	Overlay the following module(s)
-zA*name*		•	•	Set code class to *name*
-zB*name*		•	•	Set BSS class to *name*
-zC*name*		•	•	Code segment *name*
-zD*name*		•	•	BSS segment *name*
-zE*name*		•	•	Far segment *name*
-zF*name*		•	•	Far class *name*
-zG*name*		•	•	BSS group *name*
-zH*name*		•	•	Far group *name*
-zP*name*		•	•	Code group *name*
-zR*name*		•	•	Data segment *name*
-zS*name*		•	•	Data group *name*
-zT*name*		•	•	Data class *name*
-z*name**	•	•	•	Use default name for segment *name*
-Z		•	•	Optimize redundant register loads

Linker (TLINK) Options

Option	Default	5.0	5.1	Description
/3		•	•	Enable linking to 32-bit modules
/A=num	512	•	•	Set segment alignment to num bytes
/C		•	•	Case sensitive EXPORTS and INPORTS
/c		•	•	Case significant public, extern symbols
/d		•	•	Warn about duplicate library symbols
/e		•	•	Ignore library extended dictionary
/i		•	•	Include uninitialized data segments
/Lpath		•	•	Search path for library files
/l		•	•	Add line numbers to map file

continues

Option	Default	5.0	5.1	Description
/m		•	•	Create map file with public symbols
/n		•	•	Disable use of default libraries
/o		•	•	Overlay next modules or libraries
/o–	•	•	•	Stop linking overlay segments
/oovy		•	•	Link code segments of class *ovy*
/o#hex	3f	•	•	Change overlay interrupt to *hex*
/P		•	•	Pack code segments
/P=num	8192	•	•	Pack code segments up to *num* bytes
/s		•	•	Add segment information to map file
/t		•	•	Link to .COM file (tiny memory model)
/Td	•	•	•	Link to DOS .EXE code file
/Tdc		•	•	Link to DOS .COM file
/Tde		•	•	Link to DOS .EXE code file
/Tw		•	•	Link to Windows .EXE or .DLL file
/Twd		•	•	Link to Windows .DLL file
/Twe		•	•	Link to Windows .EXE file
/v		•	•	Add Turbo Debugger symbols to output
/x	•	•	•	Do not create map file
/ye	•	•	•	Swap to expanded (EMS) RAM
/ye–		•	•	Do not swap to expanded (EMS) RAM
/yx		•	•	Swap to 8MB maximum of extended RAM
/yx+		•	•	Swap to all available extended RAM
/yxnum		•	•	Swap to *num* K of extended RAM

Operator Precedence and Associativity

Level	Operators	Evaluation Order
1.(high)	() . [] -> ::	left-to-right
2.	* & ! ~ ++ -- + - sizeof new delete	right-to-left
3.	.* ->*	left-to-right
4.	* / %	left-to-right
5.	+ -	left-to-right
6.	<< >>	left-to-right
7.	< <= > >=	left-to-right
8.	== !=	left-to-right

continues

Level	Operators	Evaluation Order
9.	&	left-to-right
10.	^	left-to-right
11.	¦	left-to-right
12.	&&	left-to-right
13.	¦¦	left-to-right
14.	?:	right-to-left
15.	= *= /= += -= %= <<= >>= &= ^= ¦=	right-to-left
16.(low)	,	left-to-right

Operators at the top of the table have higher precedence than operators below. In expressions, beginning with arguments in the innermost set of parentheses (if any), programs evaluate operators of higher precedence before evaluating operators of lower precedence.

Unary plus (+) and unary minus (−) are at level 2, and have precedence over arithmetic plus and minus at level 5. The & symbol at level 2 is the address-of operator; the & symbol at level 9 is the bitwise AND operator. The * symbol at level 2 is the pointer-dereference operator; the * symbol at level 4 is the multiplication operator. In the absence of clarifying parentheses, operators on the same level are evaluated according to their left-to-right or right-to-left evaluation order.

C and C++
Keywords

Keyword	ANSI C	ANSI C++	Borland C++	Keyword	ANSI C	ANSI C++	Borland C++
_AH			•	_CL			•
_AL			•	_CS			•
_asm			•	_cs			•
_AX			•	_CX			•
_BH			•	_DH			•
_BL			•	_DI			•
_BP			•	_DL			•
_BX			•	_DS			•
_cdecl			•	_ds			•
_CH			•	_DX			•

continues

Keyword	ANSI C	ANSI C++	Borland C++	Keyword	ANSI C	ANSI C++	Borland C++
_ES			•	const	•	•	•
_es			•	continue	•	•	•
_export			•	default	•	•	•
_far			•	delete		•	•
_fastcall			•	do	•	•	•
_FLAGS			•	double	•	•	•
_huge			•	else	•	•	•
_interrupt			•	enum	•	•	•
_loadds			•	extern	•	•	•
_near			•	far			•
_pascal			•	float	•	•	•
_saveregs			•	for	•	•	•
_seg			•	friend		•	•
_SI			•	goto	•	•	•
_SP			•	huge			•
_SS			•	if	•	•	•
_ss			•	inline		•	•
asm	•	•	•	int	•	•	•
auto	•	•	•	interrupt			•
break	•	•	•	long	•	•	•
case	•	•	•	near			•
cdecl			•	new		•	•
char	•	•	•	operator		•	•
class		•	•	pascal			•

Keyword	ANSI C	ANSI C++	Borland C++	Keyword	ANSI C	ANSI C++	Borland C++
private		•	•	switch	•	•	•
protected		•	•	template		•	•
public		•	•	this		•	•
register	•	•	•	typedef	•	•	•
return	•	•	•	union	•	•	•
short	•	•	•	unsigned	•	•	•
signed	•	•	•	virtual		•	•
sizeof	•	•	•	void	•	•	•
static	•	•	•	volatile	•	•	•
struct	•	•	•	while	•	•	•

Bibliography

Borland International, Inc. *Open Architechture Handbook.* Borland, 1991.

Brooks, Frederick P., Jr. *The Mythical Man-Month.* Addison-Wesley Publishing Company, 1982.

Duncan, Ray. *Advanced MS-DOS.* Microsoft Press, 1986.

Ellis, Margaret A., and Bjarne Stroustroup. *The Annotated C++ Reference Manual.* Addison-Wesley Publishing Company, 1990.

Intel Corporation. *iAPX 86/88, 186/188 User's Manual.* Box 58130, Santa Clara, CA 95052-8130, (800) 548-4725.

Kernighan, Brian W., and Dennis M. Ritchie. *The C Programming Language, 2nd Ed.* Prentice Hall, 1988.

Knuth, Donald E., *The Art of Computer Programming. Vol. 1, Fundamental Algorithms; Vol. 2, Seminumerical Algorithms; Vol. 3, Sorting and Searching.* Addison-Wesley Publishing Company, 1973.

Norton, Peter, and Paul Yao. *Windows 3.0 Power Programming Techniques.* Bantam Computer Books, 1990.

Petzold, Charles. *Programming Windows.* Microsoft Press, 1990.

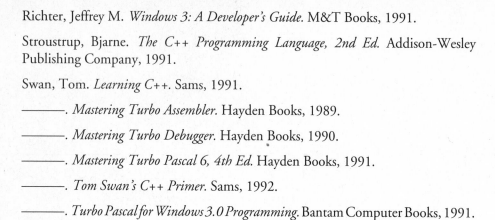
Richter, Jeffrey M. *Windows 3: A Developer's Guide.* M&T Books, 1991.

Stroustrup, Bjarne. *The C++ Programming Language, 2nd Ed.* Addison-Wesley Publishing Company, 1991.

Swan, Tom. *Learning C++.* Sams, 1991.

————. *Mastering Turbo Assembler.* Hayden Books, 1989.

————. *Mastering Turbo Debugger.* Hayden Books, 1990.

————. *Mastering Turbo Pascal 6, 4th Ed.* Hayden Books, 1991.

————. *Tom Swan's C++ Primer.* Sams, 1992.

————. *Turbo Pascal for Windows 3.0 Programming.* Bantam Computer Books, 1991.

Answers to Part 2 Exercises

Chapter 5, "Data: What a Program Knows"

5.1 With no headers or a return value—just an empty `main()` function—the absolutely smallest possible C program is

```
main(){}
```

If you purchased the disk, you can find this program in TEENSY.C. Compiling the program produces the warning "Function should return a value in function main." This warning is caused by the lack of a `return` statement in `main()`. To eliminate the warning, you can declare `main()` as returning `void`. For example, instead of the preceding example, you can write TEENSY.C as

```
void main(){}
```

5.2 Delete line 7 and change line 5 to

```
int value = 1234;
```

5.3 In both cases, k equals –31616. In the first case, 2,000,000 (1000 * 2000) is truncated to fit into int k. In the second case, however, even though 2,000,000 is well within the range of a long type, the compiler multiplies the two literal int constants to produce an int result, which is also truncated before being assigned to long k. To force a long result, and a correct answer, you must specify at least one of the constants to be long, as demonstrated by the following program:

```
/* klong.c */

#include <stdio.h>

main()
{
  long k;

  k = 1000 * 2000;
  printf("k = %ld\n", k);   /* -31616 */
  k = 1000L * 2000;
  printf("k = %ld\n", k);   /* 2000000 */
  k = 1000 * 2000L;
  printf("k = %ld\n", k);   /* 2000000 */
  k = 1000L * 2000L;
  printf("k = %ld\n", k);   /* 2000000 */
  return 0;
}
```

5.4 In DIVERR.C, value is declared as a global variable, and is therefore initialized to 0 at the start of the program. Division by 0 is not allowed, and the expression 100 / value halts the program with an error.

5.5
```
/* hiname.c */

#include <stdio.h>

main()
{
  char name[128];
```

```
      printf("What is your name? ");
      gets(name);
      printf("Hello %s\n", name);
      return 0;
    }
```

5.6   `/* goodcode.c */`

```
    #include "stdio.h"

    main()
    {
      int ivalue;
      double fvalue;

      ivalue = 32767;
      fvalue = 3.14159;
      printf("ivalue = %d\n", ivalue);
      printf("fvalue = %f\n", fvalue);
      return 0;
    }
```

5.7   `/* mile.c */`

```
    #include <stdio.h>
    #include <stdlib.h>

    main()
    {
      double kilometers;
      char string[128];

      printf("Convert kilometers to miles\n");
      printf("How many kilometers? ");
      gets(string);
      kilometers = atof(string);
      printf("Miles = %f\n", kilometers * (1 / 1.609344));
      return 0;
    }
```

5.8

```
/* unsigned.c */

#include <stdio.h>
#include <stdlib.h>

main()
{
  int value;
  char string[128];

  printf("Enter a value: ");
  gets(string);
  value = atoi(string);
  printf("Original value = %d\n", value);
  printf("Unsigned equivalent = %u\n", value);
  printf("Hexadecimal equivalent = %#x\n", value);
  return 0;
}
```

5.9 Two possible answers are:

```
enum {SUN, MON, TUE, WED, THU, FRI, SAT};
typedef enum {SUN, MON, TUE, WED, THU, FRI, SAT} DaysOfWeek;
```

5.10

```
/* circum.c */

#include <stdio.h>
#include <stdlib.h>
#include <math.h>

main()
{
  char response[128];

  printf("Calculate circumference of a circle.");
  printf("\nDiameter? ");
  gets(response);
  printf("Circumference = %f\n", M_PI * atof(response));
  return 0;
}
```

Chapter 6, "Action: What a Program Does"

6.1 In the answer, the expression (`value % 2`) equals the remainder of the integer division `value / 2`, and is zero only if `value` is evenly divisible by 2. Because zero represents false, the `if` statement selects the first following `printf()` statement if (`value % 2`) evaluates to a nonzero value. There are other correct answers. For example, the expression (`value & 1`) is true (nonzero) if `value` is odd because ANDing `value` with 1 isolates the binary value's least significant bit, which is 0 if the value is even, or 1 if not.

```
/* oddeven.c */

#include <stdio.h>

main()
{
  int value;

  printf("Enter value: ");
  scanf("%d", &value);
  if (value % 2)
    printf("Value is odd\n");
  else
    printf("Value is even\n");
  return 0;
}
```

6.2 Exclusive ORing 88 with –1 (0xffff hexadecimal) gives the same answer as the complement of 88. This is true because exclusive ORing any value with 0xffff toggles all 0 bits in that value to 1 and all 1 bits to 0. To prove these results, run TXOR.C (Listing 6.6) and enter 88 –1 (two separate values separated by one blank). Then run TCOMP.C (Listing 6.9) and enter 88. Compare the reported hexadecimal and binary values.

6.3
```
/* ascii2.c */

#include <stdio.h>

main()
```

```
{
  unsigned char c;

  c = 32;
  while (c < 128) {
    if ((c % 32) == 0) printf("\n");
    printf("%c", c);
    c++;
  }
  printf("\n");
  return 0;
}
```

6.4 There are many correct answers. One uses a do-while statement to call getchar() repeatedly until the response is correct. To test YESNO2.C, change TESTYN.BAT's yesno command to yesno2.

```
/* yesno2.c */

#include <stdio.h>
#include <stdlib.h>
#include <ctype.h>

main()
{
  char answer;

  printf("\nType Y for yes, N for no: ");
  do {
    answer = toupper(getchar());
  } while ((answer != 'Y') && (answer != 'N'));
  if (answer == 'Y')
    exit(1);
  else if (answer == 'N')
    exit(0);
  printf("This statement never executes!\n");
  return 99;  /* This statement doesn't execute either! */
}
```

6.5 The answer PRMPT.C uses a *flag* to control a `while` loop. A flag is a true-false value such as `goodResponse`, initialized to 0 (false). After prompting for input, the program sets `goodResponse` to the result of a logical expression that determines whether `response` is within the range of 1 to 100.

```c
/* prmpt.c */

#include <stdio.h>
#include <stdlib.h>

main()
{
  int goodResponse = 0;
  int response;
  char answer[128];

  while (!goodResponse) {
    printf("Enter value from 1 to 100: ");
    gets(answer);
    response = atoi(answer);
    goodResponse = ((1 <= response) && (response <= 100));
    if (!goodResponse)
      printf("ERROR: Try again!\n");
  }
  printf("Final value == %d\n", response);
  return 0;
}
```

6.6 The statement `value &= 0x001f` is equivalent to `value = value & 0x001f`. Applying the bitwise AND operator `&` to `value` using a mask of 0x001f strips `value`'s upper 8 bits, forcing those bits to 0, and therefore limiting the result to 8 significant bits, which can represent the range 0 to 31 in decimal.

```c
/* limit.c */

#include <stdio.h>
#include <stdlib.h>

main()
{
  unsigned value;
  char answer[128];
```

```
    printf("Enter value: ");
    gets(answer);
    value = atoi(answer);
    value &= 0x001f;   // value = value & 0x001f
    printf("Limited value == %d\n", value);
    return 0;
}
```

6.7 The answer uses C's modulus operator % to determine whether the remainder of an integer division is 0.

```
/* evendiv.c */

#include <stdio.h>
#include <stdlib.h>

main()
{
  int a, b, c, d;
  char answer[128];

  printf("Enter integer A: ");
  gets(answer);
  a = atoi(answer);
  printf("Enter integer B: ");
  gets(answer);
  b = atoi(answer);
  c = a / b;  /* c equals a divided by b */
  d = a % b;  /* d equals a modulo b (i.e. the remainder) */
  printf("%d / %d == %d\n", a, b, c);
  printf("%d %% %d == %d\n", a, b, d);
  if (d)
    printf("%d does not divide evenly into %d\n", b, a);
  else
    printf("%d divides evenly into %d\n", b, a);
  return 0;
}
```

6.8
```
/* wcountdn.c */

#include <stdio.h>

main()
```

```
{
  int counter;

  printf("while count\n");
  counter = 10;
  while (counter >= 1) {
    printf("%d\n", counter);
    counter--;
  }
  return 0;
}
```

6.9 There are many correct solutions. The one shown here in CELSIUS2.C uses a technique to be introduced in Chapter 7, "Functions: Divide and Conquer." After including header file conio.h (Borland C++'s direct-video console library), the program uses the expression c = getche() to get and echo a character from the keyboard, and assign that character to c. When c equals N for "No, don't continue," the program ends.

```
/* celsius2.c */

#include <stdio.h>
#include <math.h>
#include <conio.h>
#include <ctype.h>

main()
{
  double fdegrees, cdegrees;
  char answer[128];
  int done = 0;
  int c;

  printf("Fahrenheit to Celsius conversion");
  while (!done) {
    printf("\n\nDegrees Fahrenheit? ");
    gets(answer);
    fdegrees = atof(answer);
    cdegrees = ((fdegrees - 32.0) * 5.0) / 9.0;
    printf("Degrees Celsius = %.3f\n", cdegrees);
    printf("\n\nDo you want to enter another temperature? ");
    c = getche();
```

```
      done = (toupper(c) == 'N');  /* done is true if c equals 'N' */
    }
    return 0;
  }
```

6.10

```c
/* fact.c */

#include <stdio.h>
#include <stdlib.h>

main()
{
  int value = 0;
  double result;
  char answer[128];

  printf("Factorial demonstration\n");
  while (value >= 0) {
    printf("Value? (-1 to quit) ");
    gets(answer);
    value = atoi(answer);
    if (value >= 0) {
      result = 1;
      while (value > 0) {
        result *= value;
        value--;
      }
      printf("Factorial = %f\n", result);
    }
  }
  return 0;
}
```

Chapter 7, "Functions: Divide and Conquer"

7.1 Declare int value parameters for each function, and pass arguments such as 20 and 10. Inside the functions, use the parameter values as for loop limits.

```
/* fncount2.c */

#include <stdio.h>

void CountUp(int value);
void CountDown(int value);

main()
{
  CountUp(20);
  CountDown(10);
  return 0;
}

void CountUp(int value)
{
  int i;

  printf("\n\nCounting up to %d\n", value);
  for (i = 1; i <= value; i++)
    printf("%8d", i);
}

void CountDown(int value)
{
  int i;

  printf("\n\nCounting down from %d\n", value);
  for (i = value; i >= 1; i--)
    printf("%8d", i);
}
```

7.2 Include the math.h header to make M_PI available. Then implement the formula for a sphere's volume as shown here in function VolOfSphere(). Study how the function calls another function, Cube(), for the cube of an argument value.

```
/* sphere.c */

#include <stdio.h>
#include <math.h>
```

```
double Cube(double n);
double VolOfSphere(double r);
int FindVolume(void);

main()
{
  int done = 0;

  puts("Volume of a sphere");
  while (!done)
    done = !FindVolume();
  return 0;
}

double Cube(double n)
{
  return n * n * n;
}

double VolOfSphere(double r)
{
  return (4.0 * M_PI * Cube(r)) / 3.0;
}

int FindVolume(void)
{
  char answer[128];
  double radius;

  printf("\nRadius? (0 to quit) ");
  gets(answer);
  radius = atof(answer);
  if (radius != 0.0)
    printf("Volume == %1.3f\n", VolOfSphere(radius));
  return radius;   /* i.e. TRUE if radius != 0.0 */
}
```

7.3 The program limits input to values 14 or less. With larger values, the program takes a long time to finish or may hang.

```
/* harmony.c */

#include <stdio.h>
```

```
#include <stdlib.h>

double harmonics(double limit);

main()
{
  double limit, terms;
  char answer[128];

  printf("Harmonic series terms\n");
  printf("Enter limit (1...14) ");
  gets(answer);
  limit = atof(answer);
  if (limit > 14.0) {
    printf("Too large\n");
    exit(1);
  }
  terms = harmonics(limit);
  printf("Terms == %f\n", terms);
  return 0;
}

double harmonics(double limit)
{
  double sum, count;

  sum = count = 0.0;
  while (sum <= limit) {
    count++;
    sum += 1.0 / count;
  }
  return count;
}
```

7.4 There are many correct solutions. The one shown here prevents function GetValue() from returning unless a correct response is given.

```
/* range.c */

#include <stdio.h>
#include <stdlib.h>
```

```
#define FALSE 0
#define TRUE 1

int GetValue(int min, int max);

main()
{
  int n;

  n = GetValue(10, 100);
  printf("You entered %d\n", n);
  return 0;
}

int GetValue(int min, int max)
{
  int done = FALSE;
  int result;
  char answer[128];

  while (!done) {
    printf("Enter value from %d to %d: ", min, max);
    gets(answer);
    result = atoi(answer);
    done = ((min <= result) && (result <= max));
  }
  return result;
}
```

7.5 The function Amps() duplicates the formula for amperes given a voltage and resistance, passed as arguments to the function's parameters.

```
/* current.c */

#include <stdio.h>
#include <stdlib.h>

double Amps(double voltage, double resistance);

main()
{
  double voltage, resistance;
```

```
    printf("Calculate current in Amperes\n");
    printf("Voltage? ");
    scanf("%lf", &voltage);
    printf("Resistance in ohms? ");
    scanf("%lf", &resistance);
    printf("Current == %f amperes\n", Amps(voltage, resistance));
    return 0;
}

double Amps(double voltage, double resistance)
{
    return voltage / resistance;
}
```

7.6 The header file metrics.h defines the conversion factors as constants. File METRICS.C completes the program, adding one function per command.

```
/* metrics.h */

#include <conio.h>

#define FALSE 0
#define TRUE 1
#define CENT_PER_INCH 2.54
#define INCHES_PER_CENT 0.3937
#define FEET_PER_METER 3.28084
#define METERS_PER_FOOT 0.3048
#define MILES_PER_KILOMETER 0.621
#define KILOMETERS_PER_MILE 1.609

/* Function prototypes */

void DisplayMenu(void);
int MenuSelection(void);
double GetValue(void);
void InchesToCentimeters(void);
void CentimetersToInches(void);
void FeetToMeters(void);
void MetersToFeet(void);
void MilesToKilometers(void);
void KilometersToMiles(void);
```

```c
/* metrics.c */

#include <stdio.h>
#include <stdlib.h>
#include "metrics.h"

main()
{
  int quitting = FALSE;

  printf("Welcome to Metrics\n");
  while (!quitting) {
    DisplayMenu();
    switch(MenuSelection()) {
      case 1:
        InchesToCentimeters();
        break;
      case 2:
        CentimetersToInches();
        break;
      case 3:
        FeetToMeters();
        break;
      case 4:
        MetersToFeet();
        break;
      case 5:
        MilesToKilometers();
        break;
      case 6:
        KilometersToMiles();
        break;
      case 9:
        quitting = TRUE;
        break;
      default:
        printf("\nSelection error!\a\n");
    }
  }
  return 0;
}
```

```
/* Function implementations */

void DisplayMenu(void)
{
  printf("\nMenu\n");
  printf("----\n");
  printf("1 -- Inches to centimeters\n");
  printf("2 -- Centimeters to inches\n");
  printf("3 -- Feet to meters\n");
  printf("4 -- Meters to feet\n");
  printf("5 -- Miles to kilometers\n");
  printf("6 -- Kilometers to miles\n");
  printf("9 -- Quit\n");
}

int MenuSelection(void)
{
  printf("\nSelection? (Don't press ENTER!): ");
  return (getche() - '0');
}

double GetValue(void)
{
  double value;   /* Temporary place to store value */

  printf("\nValue to convert? ");
  scanf("%lf", &value);
  return value;
}

void InchesToCentimeters(void)
{
  double value;   /* Holds value passed back from GetValue */
  double result;  /* Holds computed result */

  printf("\nInches to Centimeters\n");
  value = GetValue();
  result = value * CENT_PER_INCH;
  printf("%.3f inches == %.3f centimeters\n", value, result);
}

void CentimetersToInches(void)
```

```
{
  double value;
  double result;

  printf("\nCentimeters to Inches\n");
  value = GetValue();
  result = value * INCHES_PER_CENT;
  printf("%.3f centimeters == %.3f inches\n", value, result);
}

void FeetToMeters(void)
{
  double value;
  double result;

  printf("\nFeet to Meters\n");
  value = GetValue();
  result = value * METERS_PER_FOOT;
  printf("%.3f feet == %.3f meters\n", value, result);
}

void MetersToFeet(void)
{
  double value;
  double result;

  printf("\nMeters to Feet\n");
  value = GetValue();
  result = value * FEET_PER_METER;
  printf("%.3f meters == %.3f feet\n", value, result);
}

void MilesToKilometers(void)
{
  double value;
  double result;

  printf("\nMiles to Kilometers\n");
  value = GetValue();
  result = value * MILES_PER_KILOMETER;
  printf("%.3f miles == %.3f kilometers\n", value, result);
}
```

```
void KilometersToMiles(void)
{
  double value;
  double result;

  printf("\nKilometers to Miles\n");
  value = GetValue();
  result = value * KILOMETERS_PER_MILE;
  printf("%.3f kilometers == %.3f miles\n", value, result);
}
```

7.7 A function such as InRange comes in handy when you need to test for the condition min <= n <= max. The function returns true (nonzero) if *n* ranges between two values, represented in the solution by constants MIN and MAX. If InRange returns false (zero), then *n* is outside of that range.

```
/* inrange.c */

#include <stdio.h>

#define MIN 10
#define MAX 100

int InRange(int min, int max, int n);

main()
{
  int number;

  printf("Enter an integer value: ");
  scanf("%d", &number);
  printf("Number is ");
  if (!InRange(MIN, MAX, number))
    printf("not ");
  printf("in range %d to %d\n", MIN, MAX);
  return 0;
}

int InRange(int min, int max, int n)
{
  return ((min <= n) && (n <= max));
}
```

7.8 An error function is something practically all programs need. The one shown here is adequate, though frivolous, for most error-message displays. A for loop in the main program displays all of the currently listed error messages, plus one, showing how the function handles unknown error codes.

```c
/* error.c */

#include <stdio.h>

#define MAXERR 5

void DisplayError(int errCode);

main()
{
  int errCode;

  for (errCode = 0; errCode <= MAXERR + 1; errCode++)
    DisplayError(errCode);
  return 0;
}

void DisplayError(int errCode)
{
  printf("Error #%d: ", errCode);
  switch (errCode) {
    case 0:
      puts("No error.");
      break;
    case 1:
      puts("Saved too late! Changes are gone.");
      break;
    case 2:
      puts("You must be joking.");
      break;
    case 3:
      puts("Sorry. I can't do that, Dave.");
      break;
    case 4:
      puts("Look at the mess you've made now!");
      break;
```

```
      case 5:
        puts("Tsk tsk <sigh>.");
        break;
      default:
        puts("Unknown, but it doesn't look good.");
  }
}
```

7.9 The answer uses a `static` local variable, `errCount`, declared inside `DisplayError` and initialized to 0. A new `printf()` statement in that function displays and increments `errCount` each time the function is called. Because `static` variables retain their values between function calls, `errCount` keeps track of how many times the function was called. Just for demonstration purposes, the main program's `for` loop counts down from `MAXERR + 1` to 0. The `switch` statement's cases are the same as in Exercise 7.8, and are not repeated here.

```
/* errcount.c */

#include <stdio.h>

#define MAXERR 5

void DisplayError(int errCode);

main()
{
  int errCode;

  for (errCode = MAXERR + 1; errCode >= 0; errCode--)
    DisplayError(errCode);
  return 0;
}

void DisplayError(int errCode)
{
  static unsigned errCount = 0;

  printf("Error #%d code %d: ", errCount++, errCode);
  switch (errCode) {
    ...  /* See previous exercise */
  }
}
```

7.10 The solution uses code similar to Exercise 6.10, but implements the factorial formula as a double function. You might want to copy the function and its prototype to another file for use in any program that needs to compute factorials.

```
/* factfn.c */

#include <stdio.h>
#include <stdlib.h>

double factorial(int number);

main()
{
  int value = 0;
  char answer[128];

  printf("Factorial function demonstration\n");
  while (value >= 0) {
    printf("Value? (-1 to quit) ");
    gets(answer);
    value = atoi(answer);
    if (value >= 0)
      printf("Factorial = %f\n", factorial(value));
  }
  return 0;
}

double factorial(int number)
{
  double value = 1;

  while (number > 1)
    value *= number--;
  return value;
}
```

Chapter 8, "Data Structures"

8.1

```c
/* strlen.c */

#include <stdio.h>

int StringLen(char s[]);

main()
{
  char s[] = "The string's length is: ";

  printf("%s%d\n", s, StringLen(s));
  return 0;
}

int StringLen(char s[])
{
  int len = 0;
  while (s[len] != 0)
    len++;
  return len;
}
```

8.2

```c
/* rotate.c */

#include <stdio.h>

#define SIZE 5

void Rotate(int data[], int numEntries);
void Display(int data[], int numEntries);

main()
{
  int i, data[SIZE];

  for (i = 0; i < SIZE; i++)
```

```
        data[i] = i + 1;
    Display(data, SIZE);
    Rotate(data, SIZE);
    Display(data, SIZE);
    Rotate(data, SIZE);
    Display(data, SIZE);
    return 0;
}

void Rotate(int data[], int numEntries)
{
    int i, temp;

    temp = data[numEntries - 1];
    for (i = numEntries - 1; i > 0; i--)
        data[i] = data[i - 1];
    data[0] = temp;
}

void Display(int data[], int numEntries)
{
    int i;

    for (i= 0; i < numEntries; i++)
        printf("%4d", data[i]);
    puts("");
}
```

8.3
```
/* average.c */

#include <stdio.h>
#include <stdlib.h>
#include <time.h>

#define SIZE 14

long data[SIZE];

void DisplayValues(long data[], int numEntries);
long Average(long data[], int numEntries);
```

```
main()
{
  int i;

  randomize();
  for (i = 0; i < SIZE; i++)
    data[i] = rand();
  DisplayValues(data, SIZE);
  printf("Average value: %ld\n", Average(data, SIZE));
  return 0;
}

void DisplayValues(long data[], int numEntries)
{
  int i;

  for (i = 0; i < numEntries; i++)
    printf("%2d: %ld\n", i, data[i]);
}

long Average(long data[], int numEntries)
{
  long result;
  int i;

  result = 0;
  for (i = 0; i < numEntries; i++)
    result += data[i];
  return (result / numEntries);
}
```

8.4 CARDS.C fills an array, deck, of Card structures, then calls a function, Shuffle(), to mix up the deck. The function uses a simple but effective algorithm that can scramble any array of items: A for loop makes one pass through the array and swaps every element with another selected at random. This method is fast and is just as effective as fan-shuffling a real deck of cards by hand.

```
/* cards.c */

#include <stdio.h>
#include <stdlib.h>
```

```c
#include <conio.h>
#include <time.h>

#define NCARDS 52
#define JACK 11
#define QUEEN 12
#define KING 13
#define ACE 14

typedef enum suit {SPADE, HEART, CLUB, DIAMOND} Suit;

typedef struct card {
  Suit cd_suit;   /* Card suit */
  int cd_value;   /* 2...ACE */
} Card;

void ShowDeck(void);
void Shuffle(void);
void SwapCard(int c1, int c2);

Card deck[NCARDS];

main()
{
  Suit st;
  int v;
  int c = 0;

  randomize();
  for (st = SPADE; st <= DIAMOND; st++)
    for (v = 2; v <= ACE; v++) {
      deck[c].cd_suit = st;
      deck[c].cd_value = v;
      c++;
    }
  puts("Before shuffling");
  ShowDeck();
  Shuffle();
  puts("\nPress a key...");
  getch();  /* Wait for keypress */
  puts("\nAfter shuffling");
  ShowDeck();
```

```
    return 0;
}

void ShowDeck(void)
{
  int c, v;

  for (c = 0; c < NCARDS; c++) {
    v = deck[c].cd_value;
    if (v < JACK)
      printf("%12d-", deck[c].cd_value);
    else
      switch (v) {
        case JACK:  printf("%12s-", " Jack"); break;
        case QUEEN: printf("%12s-", "Queen"); break;
        case KING:  printf("%12s-", " King"); break;
        case ACE:   printf("%12s-", " Ace"); break;
      }
    switch (deck[c].cd_suit) {
      case SPADE:   printf("Spade  "); break;
      case HEART:   printf("Heart  "); break;
      case CLUB:    printf("Club   "); break;
      case DIAMOND: printf("Diamond"); break;
    }
  }
}

void Shuffle(void)
{
  int c;

  for (c = 0; c < NCARDS; c++)
    SwapCard(c, random(NCARDS));
}

void SwapCard(int c1, int c2)
{
  Card t;

  t = deck[c1];
  deck[c1] = deck[c2];
  deck[c2] = t;
}
```

8.5

```c
/* spos.c */

#include <stdio.h>

int spos(char s[], char c);

main()
{
  int result;

  result = spos("abcd", 'c');
  printf("Result = %d\n", result);
  return 0;
}

/* Return pos of c in s; -1 if c not found */
int spos(char s[], char c)
{
  int i = 0;

  while (s[i] != NULL) {
    if (s[i] == c)
      return i;
    i++;
  }
  return -1;
}
```

8.6

```c
/* phone.c */

#include <stdio.h>

typedef struct telnum {
  unsigned areaCode;
  unsigned exchange;
  unsigned number;
} Telnum;

typedef struct twonums {
  Telnum voice;
  Telnum fax;
```

```
} Twonums;

void ShowNum(Telnum t);

main()
{
  Telnum myPhone;
  Twonums twoPhones;

  myPhone.areaCode = 900;
  myPhone.exchange = 555;
  myPhone.number = 1212;
  printf("myPhone == ");
  ShowNum(myPhone);
  twoPhones.voice.areaCode = 717;
  twoPhones.voice.exchange = 627;
  twoPhones.voice.number = 1911;
  twoPhones.fax.areaCode = 717;
  twoPhones.fax.exchange = 627;
  twoPhones.fax.number = 4715;
  printf("Business voice == ");
  ShowNum(twoPhones.voice);
  printf("Business fax == ");
  ShowNum(twoPhones.fax);
  return 0;
}

void ShowNum(Telnum t)
{
  printf("%d/%d-%d\n", t.areaCode, t.exchange, t.number);
}
```

8.7

```
/* cphone.c */

#include <stdio.h>

typedef struct telnum {
  unsigned areaCode;
  unsigned exchange;
  unsigned number;
} Telnum;
```

```
int TelnumsEqual(Telnum t1, Telnum t2);

main()
{
  Telnum myPhone, yourPhone;

  myPhone.areaCode = 900;
  myPhone.exchange = 555;
  myPhone.number = 1212;
  yourPhone = myPhone;
  if (TelnumsEqual(myPhone, yourPhone))
    puts("Numbers are equal");
  else
    puts("Numbers are not equal");
  puts("Modifying myPhone");
  myPhone.number = 1234;
  if (TelnumsEqual(myPhone, yourPhone))
    puts("Numbers are equal");
  else
    puts("Numbers are not equal");
  return 0;
}

int TelnumsEqual(Telnum t1, Telnum t2)
{
  return ((t1.areaCode == t2.areaCode) &&
    (t1.exchange == t2.exchange) &&
    (t1.number == t2.number));
}
```

8.8

```
/* aphone.c */

#include <stdio.h>
#include <stdlib.h>
#include <time.h>

typedef struct telnum {
  unsigned areaCode;
  unsigned exchange;
  unsigned number;
```

```
} Telnum;

void ShowNum(Telnum t);

main()
{
  Telnum phoneArray[100];
  int i;

  /* Initialize phoneArray values here */

  for (i = 0; i < 100; i++)
    ShowNum(phoneArray[i]);

  return 0;
}

void ShowNum(Telnum t)
{
  printf("%d/%d-%d\n", t.areaCode, t.exchange, t.number);
}
```

8.9 The solution in BITS.C is somewhat unorthodox, and it is highly system-dependent. Nevertheless, it demonstrates an extreme use for bit-field structures. Wordbits is a struct with 16 single-bit members, each corresponding to a bit in a 16-bit word. To make this structure easier to use, a union AWord is also declared. The main program shows how to set and display word and bit values in these structures.

```
/* bits.c */

#include <stdio.h>

typedef struct wordbits {
  unsigned b0:1;
  unsigned b1:1;
  unsigned b2:1;
  unsigned b3:1;
  unsigned b4:1;
  unsigned b5:1;
  unsigned b6:1;
  unsigned b7:1;
```

```
        unsigned b8:1;
        unsigned b9:1;
        unsigned b10:1;
        unsigned b11:1;
        unsigned b12:1;
        unsigned b13:1;
        unsigned b14:1;
        unsigned b15:1;
      } Wordbits;

      typedef union aword {
        unsigned w_value;
        Wordbits w_bits;
      } Aword;

      main()
      {
        Aword aw;

        aw.w_value = 0;
        aw.w_bits.b1 = 1;
        printf("Word value = %d\n", aw.w_value);
        aw.w_bits.b15 = 1;
        printf("Word value = %d\n", aw.w_value);
        printf("Bit #15 = %d\n", aw.w_bits.b15);
        printf("Bit #4 = %d\n", aw.w_bits.b4);
        return 0;
      }
```

8.10

```
      /* matrix.c */

      #include <stdio.h>

      #define SIZE 10

      void ShowMatrix(void);

      int matrix[SIZE][SIZE];

      main()
      {
```

```
   int n, m;

   for (n = 0; n < SIZE; n++)
     for (m = 0; m < SIZE; m++)
       if (n == m)
         matrix[n][m] = 1;
       else
         matrix[n][m] = 0;
   ShowMatrix();
   return 0;
}

void ShowMatrix(void)
{
   int n, m;

   for (n = 0; n < SIZE; n++) {
     puts("");
     for (m = 0; m < SIZE; m++)
       printf("%d  ", matrix[n][m]);
   }
}
```

Chapter 9, "Pointers"

9.1 This problem is similar to Exercise 8.1, but uses pointers in the solution
SLEN.C. Function slen() employs a well-known pointer trick for examining
characters in a string. The expression (*s++) dereferences pointer s to a single
character, which becomes the value of the expression (ending the while loop—
in this case on reaching the string's terminating null). The expression also
increments the pointer, causing it to address the next character in the string.
Keeping count of the number of loops executed computes the string's length.

```
/* slen.c */

#include <stdio.h>

unsigned slen(const char *s);

main()
```

```
{
  char *s = "Mastering Borland C++";

  printf("Length of string == %u", slen(s));
  return 0;
}

unsigned slen(const char *s)
{
  unsigned len = 0;

  while (*s++)
    len++;
  return len;
}
```

9.2 In MAKENULL.C, the statement *str = NULL; is exactly equivalent to str[0] = NULL;.

```
/* makenull.c */

#include <stdio.h>

main()
{
  char str[10] = "ABCDEFGHIJ";

  printf("Before, str == %s\n", str);
  *str = NULL;
  printf("After, str == %s\n", str);
  return 0;
}
```

9.3 MEMCHECK.C is one of many possible solutions. The program allocates a maximum size block of memory and fills it with test values. It then rereads each byte, checking for the expected values. There is no need to free the allocated memory, because the program ends immediately after the test is finished.

```
/* memcheck.c */

#include <stdio.h>
#include <alloc.h>
#include <stdlib.h>
```

```
main()
{
  unsigned long len, i;
  unsigned char far *p;
  unsigned char far *q;

  len = farcoreleft();
  printf("Memory checker\n");
  printf("Allocating %lu bytes\n", len);
  p = (unsigned char far *)farmalloc(len);
  if (p == NULL) {
    printf("Error allocating memory\n");
    exit(1);
  }
  printf("Filling memory...");
  q = p;
  for (i = 0; i < len; i++, q++)
    *q = i % 256;
  printf("\nChecking memory...");
  q = p;
  for (i = 0; i < len; i++, q++)
    if (*q != i % 256) {
      printf("\nError at byte %lu\n", i);
      exit(2);
    }
  printf("\nNo errors detected\n");
  return 0;
}
```

9.4 For safety, in DELARRAY.C, after deleting each array pointer, function `DeleteArray()` sets the pointers to null. This action makes it possible to determine whether the pointers address allocated memory and prevent the use of a freed pointer.

```
/* delarray.c */

#include <stdio.h>
#include <alloc.h>

void DeleteArray(void *array[], unsigned num);
```

```
main()
{
  char *buffers[4];

  printf("Start. Coreleft == %lu\n", coreleft());
  buffers[0] = malloc(128);
  buffers[1] = malloc(1024);
  buffers[2] = malloc(64);
  buffers[3] = malloc(512);
  printf("After malloc(). Coreleft == %lu\n", coreleft());
  DeleteArray((void *)buffers, 4);
  printf("After DeleteArray(). Coreleft == %lu\n", coreleft());
  return 0;
}

void DeleteArray(void *array[], unsigned num)
{
  unsigned i;

  for (i = 0; i < num; i++)
    if (array[i]) {
      free(array[i]);
      array[i] = NULL;
    }
}
```

9.5 It's always a good idea to test whether `malloc()` or a similar function returns null, indicating an out-of-memory error or a damaged heap. The modified READSTR.C is much safer than the listing in the chapter (see comments `/* !!! */`).

```
/* readstr.c */

#include <stdio.h>
#include <stdlib.h>
#include <string.h>

#define MAX 3     /* Maximum number of strings */

char *ReadString(void);
```

```
main()
{
  int i;              /* Array index */
  char *array[MAX]; /* Array of MAX char pointers */

  printf("Enter %d strings:\n", MAX);
  for (i = 0; i < MAX; i++) {
    array[i] = ReadString();
    if (array[i] == NULL) {                    /* !!! */
      puts("Error allocating string");
      exit(1);
    }
  }
  puts("\n\nYour strings are:\n");
  for (i = 0; i < MAX; i++)
    puts(array[i]);
  return 0;
}


char *ReadString(void)
{
  char *p;            /* p is a pointer to a char array */
  char buffer[128]; /* buffer for reading each string */

  gets(buffer);
  p = (char *)malloc(1 + strlen(buffer));
  if (p)                                        /* !!! */
    strcpy(p, buffer);
  return p;
}
```

9.6 The answer in INCP.C uses the expression (*p)++ to increment the value addressed by p. The expression *p++ is *not* correct, as this would increment the pointer, not the addressed value.

```
/* incp.c */

#include <stdio.h>

main()
{
  int i = 123;
  int *p = &i;
```

```
        printf("Before, i == %d\n", i);
        (*p)++;
        printf("After, i == %d\n", i);
        return 0;
    }
```

9.7 Examine function swapbytes() in SWAP.C. The function declares two void * pointers and a size integer. Using a temporary variable, swapbytes() exchanges the addressed bytes while advancing the pointers until size is decremented to zero.

```c
/* swap.c */

#include <stdio.h>
#include <stdlib.h>
#include <string.h>

typedef struct rec {
  char *title;
  char *author;
  int pages;
} Rec;

void swapbytes(void *p1, void *p2, unsigned size);
void showrecs(char *s);

Rec r1, r2;              /* Two Rec global variables */

main()
{
  r1.title  = "The C++ Programming Language";
  r1.author = "Bjarne Stroustrup";
  r1.pages  = 669;
  r2.title  = "Mastering Turbo Pascal 6.0";
  r2.author = "Tom Swan";
  r2.pages  = 1084;
  showrecs("Before");
  swapbytes(&r1, &r2, sizeof(r1));
  showrecs("After");
  return 0;
}
```

```
void swapbytes(void *p1, void *p2, unsigned size)
{
  unsigned char t;     /* Temporary place to hold each byte */

  while (size-- > 0) {
    t = *(char *)p1;
    *((char *)p1)++ = *(char *)p2;
    *((char *)p2)++ = t;
  }
}

void showrecs(char *s)
{
  printf("\n\n%s\n============", s);
  printf("\nr1.title  = %s", r1.title);
  printf("\nr1.author = %s", r1.author);
  printf("\nr1.pages  = %d", r1.pages);
  printf("\n\nr2.title  = %s", r2.title);
  printf("\nr2.author = %s", r2.author);
  printf("\nr2.pages  = %d\n", r2.pages);
}
```

9.8 Similar to HEAPNEAR.C, the solution HEAPMAX.C walks the heap in function HeapMax() to find the largest free space. The function returns that value or the result of coreleft(), whichever is larger.

```
/* heapmax.c */

#include <stdio.h>
#include <alloc.h>

void Report(char *s);
long HeapMax(void);

main()
{
  void *p1;
  void *p2 = NULL;

  Report("Before calling malloc()");
  while ((p1 = malloc(1024)) != NULL)
```

```
    p2 = p1;
  Report("After allocating memory");
  if (p2) free(p2);
  Report("After calling free()");
  return 0;
}

void Report(char *s)
{
  long result;

  puts(s);
  result = HeapMax();
  if (result < 0)
    puts("- No near heap or error!");
  else
    printf("- Maximum free space = %lu\n", result);
}

/* Return maximum free space or -1 for error */
long HeapMax(void)
{
  unsigned long count;
  struct heapinfo info;

  info.ptr = NULL;
  if (heapcheck() != _HEAPOK)
    return -1L;
  count = coreleft();
  while (heapwalk(&info) == _HEAPOK)
    if ((info.in_use == 0) && (info.size > count))
      count = info.size;
  return count;
}
```

9.9 QSUD.C demonstrates another way to use command-line arguments. Parameter argv is a pointer to an array of pointers to command-line argument
strings. The expression argv[1] addresses the second arrayed pointer. The
expression argv[1][0] addresses the first character addressed by the second
arrayed pointer. Because of the relationship between pointers and arrays, you
may use array subscripts with pointers when convenient, as it is here.

```
/* qsud.c */

#include <stdio.h>
#include <stdlib.h>
#include <time.h>

#define ARRAYSIZE 100

int compare(const void *a, const void *b);
void FillArray(void);
void DisplayArray(void);
void SortArray(int n);
void Instruct(void);

int array[ARRAYSIZE];   /* Array of integers */
int lessThan;           /* -1 to sort up; +1 to sort down */

main(int argc, char *argv[])
{
  if (argc <= 1)
    Instruct();
  if (argv[1][0] == '-') {
    if (argv[1][1] == 'd')
      lessThan = +1;
    else if (argv[1][1] == 'u')
      lessThan = -1;
    else
      Instruct();
  } else
    Instruct();
  FillArray();
  DisplayArray();
  SortArray(ARRAYSIZE);
  DisplayArray();
  return 0;
}

void Instruct(void)
{
  puts("QSorter Up and Down (qsud)");
  puts("Enter qsud -u to sort up.");
  puts("Enter qsud -d to sort down.");
  exit(0);
```

```
      }

      int compare(const void *a, const void *b)
      {
        int aint = *(int *)a;
        int bint = *(int *)b;
        if (aint < bint)
          return lessThan;
        else if (aint > bint)
          return ~lessThan;
        else
          return 0;
      }

      /* Fill global array with values taken at random */
      void FillArray(void)
      {
        int i;

        srand((unsigned)time(NULL));         /* Randomize */
        for (i = 0; i < ARRAYSIZE; i++)      /* Fill array */
          array[i] = rand();
      }

      void DisplayArray(void)
      {
        int i;

        puts("");  /* Start new display line */
        for (i = 0; i < ARRAYSIZE; i++)
          printf("%8d", array[i]);
      }

      void SortArray(int n)
      {
        if (n > 1)
          qsort((void *)array, n, sizeof(array[0]), compare);
      }
```

9.10 The system-dependent solution RESETCNS.C operates only on IBM PCs and 100-percent compatibles. It uses a pointer, kp, to the keyboard flags information stored at hexadecimal 0x0040:0x0017. Combined with the Keyboard bit-field structure, resetting the Caps Lock, Num Lock, and Scroll Lock keys is a simple matter of reading the existing flags, setting the three appropriate fields to zero, and copying the result back to memory.

```
/* resetcns.c */

#include <stdio.h>
#include <dos.h>

typedef struct keyboard {
  unsigned shiftRight : 1;      /* Keyboard flags */
  unsigned shiftLeft  : 1;
  unsigned ctrl       : 1;
  unsigned alt        : 1;
  unsigned scrollLock : 1;
  unsigned numLock    : 1;
  unsigned capsLock   : 1;
  unsigned insert     : 1;
  unsigned            : 8;      /* Not used */
} Keyboard;

main()
{
  Keyboard far *kp;  /* Pointer to keyboard struct */
  Keyboard keys;     /* Copy of key values */

  kp = (Keyboard far *)MK_FP(0x0040, 0x0017);
  keys = *kp;
  keys.capsLock = 0;
  keys.numLock = 0;
  keys.scrollLock = 0;
  *kp = keys;
  return 0;
}
```

Chapter 10, "Strings"

10.1 The answer, function strudup() in STRUDUP.C, uses two string functions: strdup() to create a duplicate copy of the string passed as an argument to the function; and strupr() to convert the copy to uppercase. A pointer to the copied string is returned as the function's result.

```
/* strudup.c */

#include <stdio.h>
#include <alloc.h>
#include <string.h>

char *strudup(const char *s);

main()
{
  char *s = "String with Upper- and Lowercase letters.";
  char *p;  /* Pointer to result from strudup() */

  p = strudup(s);
  if (p) {
    printf("Original string: %s\n", s);
    printf("Copy of string : %s\n", p);
    free(p);  /* Free duplicate string addressed by p */
  }
  return 0;
}

char *strudup(const char *s)
{
  char *p = strdup(s);   /* Make duplicate of string s */
  if (p)                 /* If duplication succeeds, */
    strupr(p);           /*  convert it to uppercase. */
  return (p);            /* Return NULL or ptr to duplicate. */
}
```

10.2 The solution (see function stracmp() in SARRAYS.C) compares two string arrays by calling strcmp() for each arrayed string. Notice how the initial array is declared as a global, preinitialized array of char * pointers to a series of literal strings—a useful device for storing short, fixed string lists in programs.

```
/* sarrays.c */

#include <stdio.h>
#include <string.h>
#include <mem.h>

char *a1[] = {     /* Array of char pointers */
```

```
    "Philadelphia",
    "Los Angeles",
    "New York",
    "Cincinnati",
    "Miami",
    "Boston",
    "Chicago"
};

#define MAX (sizeof(a1) / sizeof(a1[0]))

char *a2[MAX];      /* Two uninitialized arrays */
char *a3[MAX];

int stracmp(char *a[], char *b[], int max);

main()
{
  memcpy(a2, a1, sizeof(a2));  /* Copy pointers in a1 to a2 */
  memcpy(a3, a1, sizeof(a3));  /* Copy pointers in a1 to a3 */
  a3[2] = "Phoenix";           /* Change one pointer in a3 */
  if (stracmp(a1, a2, MAX))
    puts("a1 != a2");
  else
    puts("a1 == a2");
  if (stracmp(a1, a3, MAX))
    puts("a1 != a3");
  else
    puts("a1 == a3");
  return 0;
}

/* Return 0 if string arrays are equal; -1 if not */
int stracmp(char *a[], char *b[], int max)
{
  int i;

  for (i = 0; i < max; i++)
    if (strcmp(a[i], b[i]))
      return -1;
  return 0;
}
```

10.3 STRSORT.C uses the same preinitialized string array from the answer to Exercise 10.2. The array is sorted—not by moving the strings themselves, but by moving the char * pointers that address the strings. Because pointers tend to take less room than strings (and also because all the char * pointers are the same size), sorting the pointers is much faster than sorting the addressed characters directly.

```c
/* strsort.c */

#include <stdio.h>
#include <stdlib.h>
#include <string.h>

char *array[] = {     /* Array of char pointers */
  "Philadelphia",
  "Los Angeles",
  "New York",
  "Cincinnati",
  "Miami",
  "Boston",
  "Chicago"
};

#define MAX (sizeof(array) / sizeof(array[0]))

void Display(const char *message);
int Compare(const void *a, const void *b);
void SortArray(int n);

main()
{
  Display("Before sorting:");
  SortArray(MAX);
  Display("After sorting:");
  return 0;
}

void Display(const char *message)
{
  int i;

  puts("");
```

```
    puts(message);
    puts("----------------");
    for (i = 0; i < MAX; i++)
      puts(array[i]);
}

int Compare(const void *a, const void *b)
{
  return strcmp(*(char **)a, *(char **)b);
}

void SortArray(int n)
{
  if (n > 1)
    qsort((void *)array, n, sizeof(array[0]), Compare);
}
```

10.4 The simplest solution is to delete `static` from line 7 of Listing 10.4, GETS.C. Declaring the buffer as a local variable places it onto the stack. Any recursive calls to `GetStringAt()` now receive their own buffer. The disadvantage of this method is that many large buffers can quickly deplete the program's limited stack space. Another possible solution, therefore, is to store the buffer on the heap (be sure to free the buffer before the function ends). However, this too can fail if the heap is full or damaged. Only a static buffer is guaranteed to exist at runtime.

10.5 The search for .TXT isn't needed, although in many cases programs do need to search for specific filename extensions as demonstrated in EXT2.C. The solution is shown here in EXT3.C.

```
/* ext3.c */

#include <stdio.h>
#include <string.h>

main()
{
  char fileName[128];
  char *p;

  printf("Enter filename: ");
  gets(fileName);
  printf("As entered: %s\n", fileName);
```

```
    strupr(fileName);
    p = strchr(fileName, '.');
    if (p)
      *p = NULL;   /* Delete any other extension */
    strcat(fileName, ".TXT");
    printf("Final filename: %s\n", fileName);
    return 0;
  }
```

10.6 There are many correct solutions to this problem, which demonstrates several important string-function skills. The answer shown here in WORDSORT.C (see function SortWords()) prepares an input string for sorting with the library qsort() function. SortWords() begins by duplicating the original string. String function strtok() then tokenizes the copy into multiple substrings. Each token's address is stored in a local array of char * pointers, which is then sorted using techniques similar to those in Exercise 10.3's answer. However, to ignore case, WORDSORT's Compare() function calls stricmp() rather than strcmp(). After tokenizing the input string, its individual words are concatenated in reverse order into a new buffer, allocated on the heap by malloc(). The address of this buffer is returned as the function result after freeing the temporary copy of the original string.

```
/* wordsort.c */

#include <stdio.h>
#include <stdlib.h>
#include <string.h>

int Compare(const void *a, const void *b);
char *SortWords(const char *s);

main()
{
  char buffer[128];  /* Input string buffer */
  char *result;      /* Pointer to sorted copy of original */

  printf("Enter string: ");
  gets(buffer);
  printf("Original string: %s\n", buffer);
  result = SortWords(buffer);
  if (result)
    printf("After sorting  : %s\n", result);
```

```
    return 0;
}

int Compare(const void *a, const void *b)
{
  return stricmp(*(char **)a, *(char **)b);
}

/* Return copy of string s with up to 50 words sorted
   into reverse alphabetic order */
char *SortWords(const char *s)
{
  int numWords = 0;
  char *result = NULL;
  char *array[50];
  char *copy;

/* Make duplicate copy of string */
  copy = strdup(s);
  if (!copy)
    return NULL;

/* Tokenize the duplicate */
  array[0] = strtok(copy, " ");
  while (array[numWords])
    array[++numWords] = strtok(NULL, " ");

/* Sort string if it contains at least two words */
  if (numWords > 1) {
    qsort((void *)array, numWords, sizeof(array[0]), Compare);
    result = (char *)malloc(strlen(s) + 1);
    *result = NULL;
    while (numWords--) {
      strcat(result, array[numWords]);
      if (numWords)
        strcat(result, " ");
    }
  }
  free(copy);
  return result;
}
```

10.7 Function `strdel()` in STRDEL.C shows one possible solution. After checking that the original string and substring parameters are not null strings (in which case there is nothing for the function to do), `strstr()` finds the position of the substring in the main string. If the substring is found, `memmove()` moves the characters beyond the substring (including the string's terminating null) upward, thus deleting the substring's characters.

(**Note:** Pointer p addresses the substring located by `strstr()`. The expression `strlen(p)` equals the number of characters starting from the substring to the end of the original string.)

```c
/* strdel.c */

#include <stdio.h>
#include <string.h>
#include <mem.h>

char *strdel(char *string, const char *substring);

main()
{
  char string[128];
  char substring[128];

  printf("Enter string: ");
  gets(string);
  printf("Enter substring to delete: ");
  gets(substring);
  strdel(string, substring);
  printf("Result is   : %s\n", string);
  return 0;
}

char *strdel(char *string, const char *substring)
{
  char *p;
  int len;

  if (strlen(string) && strlen(substring)) {
    p = strstr(string, substring);
    if (p) {
      len = strlen(substring);
```

```
      memmove(p, p + len, 1 + strlen(p) - len);
    }
  }
  return string;
}
```

Chapter 11, "Input and Output"

11.1 After compiling SKIP.C, run it with a command such as skip <file.txt >prn, which redirects FILE.TXT to the printer. You can also use SKIP.C to add form feed control codes to files. To do that, enter a command such as skip <oldfile.txt >newfile.txt.

```
/* skip.c */

#include <stdio.h>

#define ASCIIFF 12    /* ASCII form feed control code */
#define LPP 55        /* Maximum lines per page */
#define MAXC 256      /* Maximum chars per line */

int GetLine(char *line);
void NewPage(int *lnp);

main()
{
  char line[MAXC];    /* Line of text */
  int ln = 0;         /* Line number */

  while (GetLine(line) != EOF) {
    if (++ln >= LPP)
      NewPage(&ln);   /* Start new page if necessary */
    puts(line);       /* Output one line */
  }
  if (ln != 0)
    NewPage(&ln);     /* Finish partial page */
  return 0;
}
```

```
int GetLine(char *line)
{
  int i = 0, c;

  c = getchar();
  while ((c != '\n') && (c != EOF)) {
    if (i < MAXC - 1)
      line[i++] = c;
    c = getchar();
  }
  line[i] = NULL;
  return c;
}

void NewPage(int *lnp)
{
  putchar(ASCIIFF);   /* Issue form feed */
  putchar('\n');      /* Issue carriage return */
  *lnp = 0;           /* Reset line number */
}
```

11.2 FSORT.C reads a file twice: first to calculate the number of lines and to
allocate enough memory for the file's contents and an array of char * pointers;
and the second time to load the file's text into memory. Sorting is a simple
matter of calling qsort() and writing the results back to disk. After compiling
the program, enter a command such as fsort file.txt to sort FILE.TXT and
preserve a copy of the original as FILE.BAK.

```
/* fsort.c */

#include <stdio.h>
#include <stdlib.h>
#include <string.h>

#define ASCIICR 13   /* ASCII carriage return */

void Error(const char *message);
int Compare(const void *a, const void *b);
char *NewExt(const char *fname, const char *ext);

main(int argc, char *argv[])
{
```

```
      char *inpfname, *bakfname, *outfname;
      FILE *inpf, *outf;
      char buffer[256];
      unsigned i, lines, size;
      char *p;        /* Miscellaneous char * pointer */
      char *datap;    /* Addresses file data in memory */
      char *datapc;   /* Copy of datap */
      char **array;   /* Array of line char * addresses */

      if (argc <= 1) {
        puts("Must enter text filename");
        exit(1);
      }

  /* Make filenames and open files */
      inpfname = strdup(argv[1]);
      bakfname = NewExt(inpfname, ".BAK");
      if (!bakfname)
        Error("Memory allocation failed");
      outfname = tempnam(".", "~");
      remove(bakfname);
      outf = fopen(outfname, "w+");
      if (!outf)
        Error(outfname);
      inpf = fopen(inpfname, "r+");
      if (!inpf)
        Error(inpfname);

  /* Count lines and get file size */

      lines = 0;
      size = 0;
      while (fgets(buffer, 255, inpf) != NULL) {
        lines++;                       /* Count lines */
        p = strchr(buffer, ASCIICR);  /* Search for cr */
        if (p)                         /* If found, */
          *p = NULL;                   /*  replace with NULL */
        size += strlen(buffer) + 1;   /* Compute size */
      }
      if (lines <= 1)
        Error("File must have at least two lines");
```

```
    /* Allocate room for file and a char * array */

      datap = (char *)malloc(size);
      array = (char **)malloc(lines);
      if ((datap == NULL) || (array == NULL))
        puts("Not enough memory available");

    /* Read file, assign string addresses to array, and sort */

      lines = 0;
      rewind(inpf);    /* Reset file to beginning */
      datapc = datap;  /* Use copy of data pointer */
      while (fgets(buffer, 255, inpf) != NULL) {
        p = strchr(buffer, ASCIICR);   /* Search for cr */
        if (p)                         /* If cr found, */
          *p = NULL;                   /*  replace with NULL */
        strcpy(datapc, buffer);        /* Copy string to buffer */
        array[lines] = datapc;         /* Save string address */
        datapc += strlen(buffer) + 1;  /* Advance data pointer */
        lines++;                       /* Advance array index */
      }
      qsort((void *)array, lines, sizeof(array[0]), Compare);

    /* Write output to new file */

      for (i = 0; i < lines; i++)
        fputs(array[i], outf);

    /* Close files and back up original */

      fclose(inpf);
      fclose(outf);
      rename(inpfname, bakfname);
      rename(outfname, inpfname);
      printf("%s sorted\n", inpfname);
      printf("Backup copy saved as %s\n", bakfname);
      return 0;
    }

    void Error(const char *message)
    {
      if (errno == 0)
```

```
      printf("Internal error: %s", message);
    else
      perror(message);   /* Print system error */
    exit(1);
  }

  int Compare(const void *a, const void *b)
  {
    return strcmp(*(char **)a, *(char **)b);
  }

  /* Return copy of filename with new extension */
  char *NewExt(const char *fname, const char *ext)
  {
    char *p;      /* Pointer to string result */
    int fnlen;  /* Filename length minus any extension */

    if (fname == NULL)
      return NULL;
    fnlen = strcspn(fname, ".");   /* Where is "."? */
    if (fnlen == 0)
      fnlen = strlen(fname);
    p = (char *)calloc(1, fnlen + strlen(ext) + 1);
    if (p) {
      strncpy(p, fname, fnlen);   /* Copy fname minus extension */
      strcat(p, ext);             /* Concatenate new extension */
    }
    return p;   /* Return pointer to new filename (or NULL) */
  }
```

11.3 JOIN.C opens two files for reading, and creates a third file for writing. It reads file number one, writes its lines to file number three, then repeats that process for the second file. The original files are undisturbed. Compile the program, then run it with a command such as `join f1.txt f2.txt f3.txt` to create a new file F3.TXT from F2.TXT and F1.TXT.

```
  /* join.c */

  #include <stdio.h>
  #include <stdlib.h>

  void Error(const char *message);
```

```c
main(int argc, char *argv[])
{
  FILE *f1, *f2, *f3;
  char buffer[256];

  if (argc < 4) {
    puts("Enter join FILE1 FILE2 FILE3 to create");
    puts("a new FILE3 from text in FILE1 + FILE2.");
    puts("WARNING: FILE3 is overwritten without notice!");
    exit(1);
  }
  f1 = fopen(argv[1], "r");    /* Open file #1 for reading */
  if (!f1)
    Error(argv[1]);
  f2 = fopen(argv[2], "r");    /* Open file #2 for reading */
  if (!f2)
    Error(argv[2]);
  f3 = fopen(argv[3], "w");    /* Create file #3 for writing */
  if (!f3)
    Error(argv[3]);
  while (fgets(buffer, 255, f1) != NULL)  /* Read file #1 */
    fputs(buffer, f3);                    /* Write to file #3 */
  while (fgets(buffer, 255, f2) != NULL)  /* Read file #2 */
    fputs(buffer, f3);                    /* Write to file #3 */
  fclose(f1);  /* Close files */
  fclose(f2);
  fclose(f3);
  printf("%s + %s -> %s", argv[1], argv[2], argv[3]);
  return 0;
}

void Error(const char *message)
{
  if (errno == 0)
    printf("Internal error: %s", message);
  else
    perror(message);  /* Print system error */
  exit(1);
}
```

11.4 SPLIT.C reads an input file, then creates successive files ending with the extension .nnn where *nnn* is a number from 000 to 999. Each file has 150 or fewer lines (adjustable by modifying constant MAXLINES). Be careful with this program: It creates lots of files and does not warn about erasing existing files of the same names. To test the program, create a temporary subdirectory, and copy to the directory a large file such as Borland C++'s README file. Then enter a command such as split readme to divide the original text into a series of smaller files.

```c
/* split.c */

#include <stdio.h>
#include <stdlib.h>
#include <string.h>

#define MAXLINES 150    /* Maximum lines per output file */

void Error(const char *message);
FILE *OpenNewFile(const char *fname, int fnum);

main(int argc, char *argv[])
{
  FILE *inpf, *outf;
  char buffer[256];
  int fileNumber = 1;
  int lines = 0;

  if (argc < 2) {
    puts("Enter split FILE to create multiple");
    puts("smaller files FILE.001, FILE.002, etc.");
    puts("WARNING: Output files are overwritten without notice!");
    exit(1);
  }
  inpf = fopen(argv[1], "r");  /* Open file for reading */
  if (!inpf)
    Error(argv[1]);
  printf("Splitting %s\n", argv[1]);
  outf = OpenNewFile(argv[1], fileNumber);
  while (fgets(buffer, 255, inpf) != NULL) {
    lines++;
```

```
      if (lines >= MAXLINES) {
        printf(" %d line(s)\n", lines);
        fclose(outf);
        outf = OpenNewFile(argv[1], ++fileNumber);
        lines = 1;
      }
      fputs(buffer, outf);
    }
    printf(" %d line(s)\n", lines);
    fclose(inpf);
    fclose(outf);
    return 0;
}

void Error(const char *message)
{
  if (errno == 0)
    printf("Internal error: %s", message);
  else
    perror(message);   /* Print system error */
  exit(1);
}

FILE *OpenNewFile(const char *fname, int fnum)
{
  int fnlen;      /* Filename length minus any extension */
  char *p;        /* New filename pointer */
  char ext[5];    /* New extension */
  FILE *f;        /* Temporary output file pointer */

  sprintf(ext, ".%03d", fnum);   /* Create ext 001, 002, ... */
  fnlen = strcspn(fname, ".");   /* Where is "."? */
  if (fnlen == 0)
    fnlen = strlen(fname);
  p = (char *)calloc(1, fnlen + 5);  /* fname + ".nnn" */
  if (!p)
    Error("Memory allocation failed");
  strncpy(p, fname, fnlen);        /* Copy fname to *p */
  strcat(p, ext);                  /* Attach new extension */
  f = fopen(p, "w");               /* Create output file */
  if (!f)
    Error(p);
```

```
      printf(" -> %s", p);          /* Display filenames */
      free(p);                      /* Free filename memory */
      return f;                     /* Return open file pointer */
   }
```

11.5 Compile and run LC.C as you do other filters. For example, to convert a file MYFILE.TXT to lowercase and store the result in NEWFILE.TXT, enter the command lc <myfile.txt >newfile.txt.

```
/* lc.c */

#include <stdio.h>
#include <ctype.h>

main()
{
   int c;

   while ((c = getchar()) != EOF)
      putchar(tolower(c));
   return 0;
}
```

11.6 The answer, CUSTBAL.C, requires module DB.OBJ to compile. Make sure db.h and DB.C are in the current directory (a copy of these files is in the ANSWER subdirectory if you purchased the diskette—if not, use MAKEDB and ADDREC to create your own sample file). Compile the program with the DOS command bcc custbal.c db.c, or if you already compiled DB.OBJ, enter bcc custbal.c db.obj. Run the program and enter DB.DAT or another database filename for a sum of the account balances.

```
/* custbal.c */

#include <stdlib.h>
#include "db.h"

main()
{
   char path[128];
   FILE *dbf;
   Record rec;
   long numrecs, recnum;
   double sum = 0.0;
```

```
      printf("Database filename? ");
      gets(path);
      dbf = OpenDB(path, &rec);
      if (!dbf) {
        printf("Can't open %s\n", path);
        exit(1);
      }
      numrecs = rec.info.numrecs;
      printf("\nNumber of records == %lu\n\n", numrecs);
      for (recnum = 1; recnum <= numrecs; recnum++)
        if (ReadRecord(dbf, recnum, &rec))
          sum += rec.balance;
      printf("Total balances = $%8.2f\n", sum);
      fclose(dbf);
      return 0;
    }
```

11.7 Compile and run DTREE.C from the directory where you want to begin a subdirectory tree listing. If there are no subdirectories in the current one, DTREE simply ends without displaying any text. The program uses a recursive function, ShowPaths(), to scan all directories starting at the current level and proceeding to all nested subdirectories. To perform this apparent feat of skill (which is just a simple trick), ShowPaths() detects a directory name by examining a file's attribute. If bit FA_DIREC is set in the attribute, and if the filename is not "." or "..", then this is a subdirectory. The function calls chdir() to change to that directory, and then calls itself recursively to continue scanning on this new level. When done with all filenames on a level, the function ends, unwinding the recursion. To keep DOS straight at this stage, the function calls chdir(".."), which steps back one level higher.

(**Note:** This method works *only* if no changes are made to any directories during the scan. In programs that must scan multiple nested directory paths while writing files and directories, the entire directory should be loaded into RAM before any such changes are made.)

```c
/* dtree.c */

#include <stdio.h>
#include <dir.h>
#include <dos.h>


void ShowPaths(int level);
```

```
main()
{
  ShowPaths(0);   /* Start ball rolling */
  return 0;
}

void ShowPaths(int level)
{
  int i, done;
  struct ffblk fb;

  done = findfirst("*.*", &fb, FA_DIREC);
  while (!done) {
    if (((fb.ff_attrib & FA_DIREC) == FA_DIREC) &&
         (fb.ff_name[0] != '.')) {
      for (i = 0; i < level * 2; i++)
        putchar(' ');           /* Write leading blanks */
      puts(fb.ff_name);         /* Write dir name */
      chdir(fb.ff_name);        /* Change to next dir */
      ShowPaths(level + 1);     /* Call self recursively */
      chdir("..");              /* Return to previous level */
    }
    done = findnext(&fb);       /* Do next filename */
  }
}
```

11.8 NARCH.C uses the same recursive directory scanning technique demonstrated in the answer to Exercise 11.7. While scanning, function ScanPath() keeps track of file sizes and other information for all files that have their archive bit set. The program also calls getdfree() to determine the number of bytes per cluster, using this information to calculate the total disk space occupied by all files. This is necessary because files are stored in whole clusters only—simply adding the file sizes does not give an accurate answer because most files have some wasted space at the end of their final cluster.

```
/* narch.c (sizes of files not archived) */

#include <stdio.h>
#include <stdlib.h>
#include <dir.h>
#include <dos.h>
```

```
void ScanPath(void);

unsigned long sum;      /* Sum of file sizes */
unsigned long nclust;   /* Sum of file clusters */
long bpc;               /* Bytes per cluster */
unsigned fcount;        /* File count */
unsigned ndirs = 1;     /* Directory count */

main()
{
  struct dfree free;

  getdfree(0, &free);
  if (free.df_sclus == 0xFFFF) {
    puts("Disk read error");
    exit(1);
  }
  bpc = (long)free.df_bsec * (long)free.df_sclus;
  printf("Scanning for unarchived files");
  ScanPath();
  printf("\n%u directories scanned\n", ndirs);
  printf("%u files are not backed up\n", fcount);
  printf("Bytes per cluster == %lu\n", bpc);
  printf("Total file sizes == %lu bytes\n", sum);
  printf("Total file clusters == %lu\n", nclust);
  printf("Total disk space occupied == %lu bytes\n",
    nclust * bpc);
  return 0;
}

void ScanPath(void)
{
  int done;
  struct ffblk fb;
  ldiv_t d;   /* Holds ldiv() result */

  done = findfirst("*.*", &fb, FA_DIREC);
  while (!done) {
    if ((fb.ff_attrib & FA_ARCH) == FA_ARCH) {
      fcount++;                        /* Count files */
      sum += fb.ff_fsize;              /* Add file sizes */
      d = ldiv(fb.ff_fsize, bpc);      /* Calculate clusters */
```

```
      nclust += d.quot;              /* Add to cluster sum */
      if (d.rem != 0)                /* Files are stored in */
        nclust++;                    /*  whole clusters only */
    }
    if (((fb.ff_attrib & FA_DIREC) == FA_DIREC) &&
        (fb.ff_name[0] != '.')) {
      putchar('.');         /* Display feedback */
      ndirs++;              /* Count number of directories */
      chdir(fb.ff_name);    /* Change to next directory */
      ScanPath();           /* Call self recursively */
      chdir("..");          /* Return to previous directory */
    }
    done = findnext(&fb);
  }
}
```

Answers to Part 3 Exercises

Chapter 12, "Introducing C++"

12.1 The solution is nearly identical to program FILTER.CPP (Listing 12.3), but it calls function toupper() to convert characters to uppercase before writing them to the standard output with cout.put(). Function toupper() is prototyped in ctype.h. Compile TOUPPER, and then from DOS, run the program with a command such as **toupper <toupper.cpp**.

```
/* toupper.cpp */

#include <iostream.h>
#include <ctype.h>

main()
{
```

```
      char c;

      while (cin.get(c))
        cout.put(toupper(c));
      return 0;
    }
```

12.2 GETVAL2.CPP uses a modified `test()` function, which returns TRUE if no errors have been detected. If `cin.good()` is FALSE, something is wrong with the input stream. In that event, after displaying an error message, `test()` clears the stream's state by calling `cin.clear()`. It also reads the pending newline character into a local `char` variable c.

```
/* getval2.cpp */

#define FALSE 0
#define TRUE 1

#include <iostream.h>
#include <stdlib.h>
#include <ctype.h>

int test(void);

main()
{
  double fp;  // A floating point value
  long k;     // A long int value

  do {
    cout << "Enter a floating point value: ";
    cin >> fp;
  } while (!test());
  cout << "Value entered is: " << fp << '\n';
  do {
    cout << "Enter an integer value: ";
    cin >> k;
  } while (!test());
  cout << "Value entered is: " << k << '\n';
  return 0;
}
```

```
int test(void)
{
  char c;

  if (!cin.good()) {
    cout << "Error detected" << '\n';
    cin.clear();   // Clear error flags
    cin >> c;      // Eat newline character
    return FALSE;
  }
  return TRUE;
}
```

12.3 Inline functions are typically stored in header files, as demonstrated by min.h here. Enter that file separately. Enter, save, and compile MIN.CPP, which demonstrates how to use min().

```
/* min.h -- Header file for min.cpp */

inline int min(int a, int b)
{
  if (a <= b)
    return a;
  else
    return b;
}



/* min.cpp */

#include <iostream.h>
#include "min.h"

main()
{
  int x, y;

  cout << "X? ";
  cin >> x;
```

```
    cout << "Y? ";
    cin >> y;
    cout << "min(a, b) == " << min(x, y) << '\n';
    return 0;
}
```

12.4 The solution, MINBENCH.CPP, calls function `clock()`, prototyped in time.h. (For a complete description of `clock()`, see Chapter 22, "Functions and Examples.") Before compiling MINBENCH, you might need to adjust `const ITERATIONS`, set to 500,000 loops. This value produces reasonable results for a 16Mhz 80386SX-based system, but can be set lower to reduce the program's running time for a slower system, or set higher for a faster processor. The program includes min.h from Exercise 12.3, and calls `inline min()` 500,000 times. For comparison, another loop calls a similar non-inline function `fmin()`.

(**Note:** If you run this program under Turbo Debugger, the reported times for the inline and non-inline functions are the same, proving that the compiler converts inline functions to normal ones for debugging.)

```
/* minbench.cpp */

#include <iostream.h>
#include <time.h>
#include "min.h"

int fmin(int a, int b);
void mark(clock_t &start);
void report(clock_t start, const char *message);

const long ITERATIONS = 500000;  // Adjust as necessary

main()
{
  int z;          // Throw-away integer
  long i;         // For-loop control variable
  clock_t start;  // Starting time for benchmark

  cout << "Testing...";
  mark(start);
```

```
    for (i = 0; i < ITERATIONS; i++)
      z = fmin(1, 2);
    report(start, "Normal function calls");

    cout << "Testing...";
    mark(start);
    for (i = 0; i < ITERATIONS; i++)
      z = min(1, 2);
    report(start, "Inline function calls");
    i = z;  // So compiler doesn't complain that z is not used
    return 0;
  }

  int fmin(int a, int b)
  {
    if (a <= b)
      return a;
    else
      return b;
  }

  void mark(clock_t &start)
  {
    start = clock();  // Mark starting time
  }

  void report(clock_t start, const char *message)
  {
    clock_t stop = clock();  // Mark ending time
    cout << '\n' << message << '\n';
    cout << " elapsed time == " <<
      (stop - start) / CLK_TCK << " seconds\n";
  }
```

12.5 Compile the solution, ABS.CPP, with the DOS command **bcc -v abs**, then load the code into Turbo Debugger with the command **td abs**. Set breakpoints at the beginning of each overloaded `absolute()` function, and press F9 to run. As you respond to the program's prompts, the debugger halts the code in each of the overloaded functions. Although the three `absolute()` functions have the same name, the compiler distinguishes among them by their different parameters.

```cpp
/* abs.cpp */

#include <iostream.h>

int absolute(int x);
long absolute(long x);
double absolute(double x);

main()
{
  int ivalue;
  long lvalue;
  double fvalue;

  cout << "Enter integer: ";
  cin >> ivalue;
  cout << " absolute() == " << absolute(ivalue) << '\n';
  cout << "Enter long integer: ";
  cin >> lvalue;
  cout << " absolute() == " << absolute(lvalue) << '\n';
  cout << "Enter floating point value: ";
  cin >> fvalue;
  cout << " absolute() == " << absolute(fvalue) << '\n';
  return 0;
}

int absolute(int x)
{
  if (x < 0)
    return -x;
  else
    return x;
```

```
}

long absolute(long x)
{
  if (x < 0)
    return -x;
  else
    return x;
}

double absolute(double x)
{
  if (x < 0)
    return -x;
  else
    return x;
}
```

12.6 The modified READSTR.CPP uses C++ comments in place of the ANSI C comments from the original listing. The new program also uses I/O stream statements instead of calling STDIO functions.

(**Note:** C++ purists would also recommend changing #define MAX 3 to a true constant declared as const int MAX = 3;. However, the benefits gained from such a change are debatable.)

```
/* readstr.cpp */

#include <iostream.h>
#include <string.h>

#define MAX 3        // Maximum number of strings

char *ReadString(void);

main()
{
  int i;                   // Array index
  char *array[MAX];  // Array of MAX char pointers
```

```
    cout << "Enter " << MAX << " strings:\n";
    for (i = 0; i < MAX; i++)
      array[i] = ReadString();
    cout << "\n\nYour strings are:\n";
    for (i = 0; i < MAX; i++)
      cout << array[i];
    return 0;
  }

char *ReadString(void)
{
  char *p;          // p is a pointer to a char array
  char buffer[128]; // buffer for reading each string

  cin.getline(buffer, sizeof(buffer));
  p = new char[1 + strlen(buffer)];
  strcpy(p, buffer);
  return p;
}
```

12.7 The new program, REFFUNC2.CPP, has four main changes: struct
customer has a new customer * pointer field named next, database is a
pointer to a list rather than an array, function FillDataBase() creates a linked-
list of customer structures, and reference function BalanceOf() searches the
list. Functions main() and Currency() are unchanged, and the program
operates no differently than before despite the major change to the techniques
used to store information.

```
/* reffunc2.cpp */

#include <iostream.h>
#include <stdio.h>
#include <stdlib.h>
#include <string.h>

#define FALSE 0
#define TRUE 1
#define SIZE 10   // Number of records in database
#define SLEN 40   // String length
```

```
struct customer {
  char name[SLEN];
  double balance;
  customer *next;   // Pointer to next customer
};

void FillDatabase(void);
const double &BalanceOf(const char *name);
const char *Currency(double d);

customer *database;   // Array is now a list pointer

main()
{
  char custname[SLEN];
  int done = FALSE;

  FillDatabase();
  cout << "Enter `Customer-X' where X = A, B, C, etc." << '\n';
  cout << "Or, press Enter to end program." << '\n';
  while (!done) {
    cin.getline(custname, SLEN);
    done = (strlen(custname) == 0);
    if (!done)
      cout << Currency(BalanceOf(custname)) << '\n';
  }
  return 0;
}

/* Fill database with sample values and display */
void FillDatabase(void)
{
  customer *cp;   // Pointer to new customer struct

  randomize();
  for (int i = 0; i < SIZE; i++) {
    cp = new customer;   // Allocate memory for new customer
    if (!cp) {
```

```
            cerr << "\nOut of memory\n";
            exit(1);
        }
        strcpy(cp->name, "Customer-X");
        cp->name[9] = 'A' + i;   // "A, B, ..., Z"
        cp->balance = rand() * 0.01;
        cout << cp->name
            << Currency(cp->balance) << '\n';
        if (database == NULL) {
            database = cp;          // Create new list
            cp->next = NULL;        // There is no "next" struct
        } else {
            cp->next = database;    // Insert customer into list
            database = cp;          // Change list head to new insert
        }
    }
}


/* Return reference to customer balance */
const double &BalanceOf(const char *name)
{
    static const double errval = -1;
    customer *cp;

    cp = database;
    while (cp != NULL) {
        if (stricmp(cp->name, name) == 0)
            return cp->balance;
        cp = cp->next;
    }
    return errval;
}

const char *Currency(double d)
{
    static char buffer[40] = "";
    sprintf(buffer, " $%8.2f", d);
    return buffer;
}
```

Chapter 13, "Programming with Classes"

13.1 Listing BUTTON.CPP shows only one of many possible solutions.

```cpp
/* button.cpp */

#include <iostream.h>

#define OFF 0
#define ON 1

class TButton {
private:
  int state;                   // Data member
public:
  TButton();                   // Constructor
  TButton(int initialState);   // Overloaded constructor
  int GetState(void);          // Member function
  void SetState(int newState); //    "       "
  void Toggle(void);           //    "    '  "
  void Display(void);          //    "       "
};

void Show3Buttons(TButton &b1, TButton &b2, TButton &b3);

main()
{
  TButton b1;  // Initialized via default constructor
  TButton b2(ON);  // Initialize b2 to ON state
  TButton b3(OFF);  // Initialize b3 to OFF state

  cout << "After initializing three TButton objects\n";
  Show3Buttons(b1, b2, b3);
  b1.SetState(ON);
```

```
        cout << "After setting b1's state to ON\n";
        Show3Buttons(b1, b2, b3);
        b1.Toggle();
        b2.Toggle();
        b3.Toggle();
        cout << "After toggling b1, b2, and b3\n";
        Show3Buttons(b1, b2, b3);
        return 0;
}

// Common function to display 3 button references
void Show3Buttons(TButton &b1, TButton &b2, TButton &b3)
{
    cout << " Button b1: ";
    b1.Display();  // Call button's member function
    cout << " Button b2: ";
    b2.Display();
    cout << " Button b3: ";
    b3.Display();
}

// Default constructor
TButton::TButton()
{
    state = OFF;  // Initialize button to OFF state
}

// Alternate constructor
TButton::TButton(int initialState)
{
    state = initialState;  // Initialize button to specified state
}

// Return current button state
int TButton::GetState(void)
{
    return state;
}
```

```
void TButton::SetState(int newState)
{
  state = newState;
}

void TButton::Toggle(void)
{
  if (state == OFF)
    state = ON;
  else
    state = OFF;
}

void TButton::Display(void)
{
  cout << "state == ";
  if (state == OFF)
    cout << "OFF\n";
  else
    cout << "ON\n";
}
```

13.2 The TTime class constructor automatically initializes a class object to the current date and time. The solution is simple: just declare a TTime object (today in DT.CPP) and call the object's Display() member function.

```
/* dt.cpp */

#include <iostream.h>
#include "time6.h"

main()
{
  TTime today;
  today.Display();
  return 0;
}
```

13.3 Add the following line to DT.CPP after declaring the TTime object today:

```
today.ChangeTime(24 * 60);  // i.e. 24 hours later
```

13.4 The TTime class can already display the day of the week (see DT.CPP in Exercise 13.2, for example). DAY.CPP converts command-line arguments into numeric form, checks for input errors, and assigns a date to a TTime class object. Calling that object's Display() member function displays the day of the week for that date. As a bonus, DAY.CPP lists a handy function, GetMonth(), that converts a month name such as JAN or APR to an integer value, with January equal to 1, February 2, and so on.

```cpp
/* day.cpp */

#include <iostream.h>
#include <stdlib.h>
#include <string.h>
#include "time6.h"

const char months[] = "decnovoctsepaugjuljunmayaprmarfebjan";

void CheckDate(int month, int day, int year);
int GetMonth(const char *amonth);
void Error(const char *s);

main(int argc, char *argv[])
{
  int month, day, year;

  if (argc <= 3)
    Error("Enter a date such as jan 5 1997");
  strlwr(argv[1]);  // Convert month name to lowercase
  month = GetMonth(argv[1]);
  day = atoi(argv[2]);
  year = atoi(argv[3]);
  CheckDate(month, day, year);
  TTime theDate(month, day, year);
  theDate.Display();
  return 0;
}

// Halt with error if any params are bad
void CheckDate(int month, int day, int year)
```

```
{
  if ((month < 1) || (month > 12))
    Error("Bad month value");
  if ((day < 1) || (day > 31))
    Error("Bad day value");
  if (year < 1970)
    Error("Bad year value");
}

// Convert monthname string to integer
int GetMonth(const char *amonth)
{
  char *s = strstr(months, amonth);
  if (s == NULL)
    Error("Bad month name");
  return (strlen(s) / 3);
}

// Display error message and exit program
void Error(const char *s)
{
  cout << "\nError: " << s << '\n';
  exit(1);
}
```

13.5 The new TTime constructor and member functions GetSeconds() and PutSeconds() are written inline, although these could be written normally. New lines are marked with the comment // NEW at the end. Use TIME6.CPP to compile the new TTime class declaration.

```
/* time7.h -- TTime class declaration */

#ifndef __TIME7_H
#define __TIME7_H  1  /* Prevent multiple #includes */

#include <iostream.h>
#include <time.h>
#include <string.h>
```

```
class TTime {
private:
  long dt;  // Date and time in seconds from January 1, 1970
  char *dts;  // Date and time as a string
  void DeleteDts(void);  // Delete dts pointer
public:
  TTime();                                    // Constructor
  TTime(int m, int d = -1, int y = -1,        // Constructor
    int hr = -1, int min = -1);
  TTime(long seconds) { dt = seconds; }  // NEW
  ~TTime();                                   // Destructor
  void Display(void) { cout << ctime(&dt); }
  long GetSeconds(void) { return dt; }  // NEW
  void SetSeconds(long newSeconds) { dt = newSeconds; }  //NEW
  void GetTime(int &m, int &d, int &y, int &hr, int &min);
  void SetTime(int m = -1, int d = -1, int y = -1,
    int hr = -1, int min = -1);
  const char *GetSTime(void);
  void ChangeTime(long nminutes)
    { dt += (nminutes * 60); DeleteDts(); }
};


#endif  /* __TIME7_H */
```

13.6 Most of the TStr (Type String) class member functions are simple one-statement models, and are therefore declared inline. The class is implemented here in separate modules. File tstr.h declares the class. TSTR.CPP implements the destructor and a member function. TESTSTR.CPP is a test program that uses the class. Compile the program and module with the DOS command **bcc teststr tstr**, or create and compile an IDE project consisting of the files TESTSTR.CPP and TSTR.CPP.

Class TStr stores a single private data member, s, as a pointer to char. The default constructor TStr() sets s to NULL, thus ensuring that s is initialized to a known value for all TStr class objects. An alternate constructor TStr(char *ss); provides a method to initialize a TStr class object to a specific string (see TESTSTR.CPP, which immediately follows tstr.h, for an example).

Member function GetStr() returns the value of data member s. Member function PutStr() (see TSTR.CPP) deletes any current string addressed by s and creates a new one by calling the string library function strdup().

The TStr class destructor deletes any addressed string to clean up a TStr class object before it goes out of scope. The destructor is implemented in module TSTR.CPP, but it could also be written inline. A useful experiment is to run TESTTSTR.CPP in Turbo Debugger (use commands **bcc -v testtstr tstr** and **td testtstr**). Set a breakpoint on the destructor in module TSTR.CPP and run the program to detect when C++ calls the TStr destructor to delete addressed strings.

```
/* tstr.h -- TStr class declaration */

#ifndef __TSTR_H
#define __TSTR_H  1  /* Prevent multiple #includes */

#include <string.h>

class TStr {
private:
  char *s;   // Pointer to class object's string
public:
  TStr() { s = NULL; }
  TStr(char *ss) { s = strdup(ss); }
  ~TStr();
  const char *GetStr(void) { return s; }
  void PutStr(const char *ss);
};

#endif  /* __TSTR_H */



/* tstr.cpp -- Implementation of TStr class */

#include "tstr.h"

// Destructor
TStr::~TStr()
{
  delete s;
}
```

```
// Change string to ss
void TStr::PutStr(const char *ss)
{
  delete s;
  s = strdup(ss);
}



/* testtstr.cpp */

#include <iostream.h>
#include "tstr.h"

main()
{
  TStr nullString;
  TStr myName("Tom Swan");
  TStr anyString;

  anyString.PutStr("Any 'ol string");
  cout << "The three strings are:\n";
  cout << " nullString == " << nullString.GetStr() << '\n';
  cout << " myName == " << myName.GetStr() << '\n';
  cout << " anyString == " << anyString.GetStr() << '\n';
  anyString.PutStr(myName.GetStr());
  cout << "After copying myName to anyString\n";
  cout << " myName == " << myName.GetStr() << '\n';
  cout << " anyString == " << anyString.GetStr() << '\n';
  return 0;
}
```

13.7 For simplicity, RTEXT.CPP reads a text file of up to 200 lines into an array of TStr class objects. The purpose of this exercise is not to provide a sophisticated file reader, but to have you think about the methods for creating multiple class objects in a program. One way to improve the code would be to design a new class object that can store a list or array of strings as a data member. That way, the data representation could change without affecting most of the programming.

```
/* rtext.cpp */
#include <iostream.h>
#include <stdio.h>
#include <stdlib.h>
#include "tstr.h"

void Error(const char *s);

#define MAXSTRINGS 200
TStr sarray[MAXSTRINGS];

main(int argc, char *argv[])
{
  FILE *inf;
  char buffer[256];
  int index = 0;
  if (argc <= 1)
    Error("Specify text filename to read");
// Open file
  inf = fopen(argv[1], "r");
  if (inf == NULL)
    Error("Can't open file");
// Read file into array of TStr objects
  while (fgets(buffer, 255, inf) != NULL) {
    sarray[index].PutStr(buffer);
    if (++index >= MAXSTRINGS)
      Error("File too large");
  }
  fclose(inf);
// Display strings in array
  for (int i = 0; i < index; i++)
    cout << sarray[i].GetStr();
  return 0;
}

void Error(const char *s)
{
  puts(s);
  exit(1);
}
```

Chapter 14, "Inheritance and Polymorphism"

14.1 The following program is by no means a complete screen designer but could serve as a starting place for a more sophisticated utility. Class TText can store and display a string at a specified x,y coordinate, using any foreground or background color as declared in conio.h. Class TData derives from TText but adds the capability of prompting for new strings. A third class TScEntry owns two data member pointers. One pointer addresses an object of type TText and is used to display a label such as Name or Address. A second pointer addresses an object of type TData—the input field where users can enter data associated with this label.

```cpp
/* screen.cpp */

#include <iostream.h>
#include <stdlib.h>
#include <string.h>
#include <conio.h>

#define BLANK ' '          // Blank ASCII character
#define MAXLEN 64          // All time input maximum length
#define FLABEL YELLOW      // Foreground label color
#define BLABEL CYAN        // Background label color
#define FDATA WHITE        // Foreground data color
#define BDATA BLACK        // Background data color

void Error(const char *s);

// Display text with attributes on screen
class TText {
protected:
  int x, y;                // Coordinate
  int fcolor, bcolor;      // Fore and background colors
  char *string;            // Pointer to text string
```

```
public:
  TText(int xc, int yc, int fore, int back, const char *s);
  virtual ~TText() { delete string; }
  void PutString(const char *s);
  void Erase(void);
  void Display(void);
};

// Derive a data-entry object from TText
class TData: public TText {
public:
  TData(int xc, int yc, int fore, int back, const char *s)
    : TText(xc, yc, fore, back, s) { }
  const char *GetText(int maxlen);
};

// One screen entry with label and data entry objects
class TScEntry {
protected:
  TText *labelp;  // Pointer to a TText object
  TData *datap;   // Pointer to a TData object
public:
  TScEntry(int xc, int yc,
    const char *labelStr, const char *dataStr);
  ~TScEntry() { delete labelp; delete datap; }
  void Display(void);
  void Edit(void);
};

main()
{
  TScEntry *screen[3];  // Array of TScEntry objects
  int i;  // screen array index

  clrscr();
  screen[0] = new TScEntry(4, 4, "Name: ", "Tom Swan");
  screen[1] = new TScEntry(4, 6, "Company: ", "Swan Software");
  screen[2] = new TScEntry(4, 8, "Address: ", "Lititz, PA");
  for (i = 0; i < 3; i++)  // Display screen
    screen[i]->Display();
```

```
    for (i = 0; i < 3; i++)   // Edit entries
      screen[i]->Edit();
    for (i = 0; i < 3; i++)   // Delete objects
      delete screen[i];
    gotoxy(1, 24);
    return 0;
  }


  // Halt program after displaying error message
  void Error(const char *s)
  {
    gotoxy(1, 24);
    cout << '\n' << s << '\n';
    exit(1);
  }


  // Construct a TText object
  TText::TText(int xc, int yc, int fore, int back, const char *s)
  {
    if (s == NULL)
      Error("Null string pointer passed to TText constructor");
    x = xc;
    y = yc;
    fcolor = fore;
    bcolor = back;
    string = strdup(s);
  }


  // Change a TText object's string
  void TText::PutString(const char *s)
  {
    if (s == NULL)
      Error("Null string pointer passed to PutString");
    Erase();
    delete string;        // Delete current string
    string = strdup(s);   // Copy new string to heap
  }


  // Erase current string display
  void TText::Erase()
```

```
{
  int len = strlen(string);
  gotoxy(x, y);
  for (int i = 0; i < len; i++)
    putch(BLANK);
}

// Display TText object
void TText::Display()
{
  Erase();                     // Clear area on-screen
  gotoxy(x, y);                // Position cursor
  textcolor(fcolor);           // Set foreground color
  textbackground(bcolor);      // Set background color
  cputs(string);               // Display the string
}

// Return new data entry
const char *TData::GetText(int maxlen)
{
  char buffer[MAXLEN + 3];   // Raw input buffer

  if ((maxlen > MAXLEN) || (maxlen <= 0))
    maxlen = MAXLEN;           // Adjust maxlen if necessary
  Erase();                     // Clear entry area
  gotoxy(x, y);                // Position cursor
  buffer[0] = maxlen;          // Set length for cgets()
  cgets(buffer);               // Get string
  if (buffer[1] > 0)           // If length of input > 0
    PutString(&buffer[2]);     //   insert new string into object
  Display();                   // Make sure display is "right"
  return string;               // Return new or old string
}

// Construct a TScEntry object
TScEntry::TScEntry(int xc, int yc,
  const char *labelStr, const char *dataStr)
{
  int len = strlen(labelStr) + 1;  // Data entry position
  labelp = new TText(xc, yc, FLABEL, BLABEL, labelStr);
```

```
    datap = new TData(xc + len, yc, FDATA, BDATA, dataStr);
    if ((labelp == NULL) || (datap == NULL))
      Error("Out of memory in TScEntry constructor");
  }


// Display TScEntry's label and data
void TScEntry::Display(void)
{
  labelp->Display();   // Display entry label
  datap->Display();    // Display current data
}


// Edit TScEntry's data (not saved)
void TScEntry::Edit(void)
{
  datap->GetText(30);   // 30 == maximum input length
}
```

14.2 To compile AVERAGE.CPP, follow the instructions in the chapter for
TBENCH.CPP (see Listing 14.3), but replace TBENCH with AVERAGE.
The new program derives a class TAverage from TBench. The TAverage constructor specifies the number of repeated tests to perform (numSets). During
each test, the program displays the elapsed time, saved in a private data
member, result. TAverage's Display() member function displays the average
elapsed time by dividing result by sets.

```
/* average.cpp -- Average test results */

#include <iostream.h>
#include <stdio.h>
#include "bench.h"

#define NUMTESTS 20000
#define NUMSETS 3

class TAverage: public TBench {
private:
  long sets;
  double result;
```

```
public:
  TAverage(long numSets): TBench()
    { sets = numSets; result = 0; }
  void Benchmark(long numTests, testfn tf);
  void Report(void);
};

void Testfn(void);

main()
{
  TAverage test(NUMSETS);

  cout << "Testing sprintf() function\n";
  test.Benchmark(NUMTESTS, Testfn);
  test.Report();
  return 0;
}

void Testfn(void)
{
  char buffer[80];
  double d = 3.14159;

  sprintf(buffer, "%lf", d);
}

void TAverage::Benchmark(long numTests, testfn tf)
{
  long numSets = sets;

  while (numSets--) {
    TBench::Benchmark(numTests, tf);
    TBench::Report();
    result += time();
  }
}

void TAverage::Report(void)
{
  printf("Total elapsed time == %6f sec\n", result);
```

```
        printf("Average for %ld sets == %6f sec\n", sets, result / sets);
    }
```

14.3 Compile the following three files with the DOS command **bcc tbitset bitset**, or create and compile an IDE project consisting of the files BITSET.CPP and TBITSET.CPP (which are listed after bitset.h). Class TBitSet (declared in bitset.h) stores an unsigned 16-bit value and has various member functions that can set, reset, and extract bits in this value. See comments in the listings for more information about how the class operates.

```
/* bitset.h -- TBitSet class declaration */

#ifndef __BITSET_H
#define __BITSET_H  1  /* Prevent multiple #includes */

typedef unsigned int WORD;  // Assumes 16-bit integers

#define TRUE 1
#define FALSE 0

class TBitSet {
private:
  WORD bitset;
protected:
  int IndexOkay(char n)
    { if (n <= 15) return TRUE; return FALSE; }
public:
  TBitSet() { bitset = 0; }
  void Add(char n);
  void Delete(char n);
  int HasBit(char n);
  char Extract(char n);
  void Display(void);
};

#endif  /* __BITSET_H */


/* bitset.cpp -- TBitSet class implementation */
```

```
#include <iostream.h>
#include "bitset.h"

// Set nth bit in bitset to 1
void TBitSet::Add(char n)
{
  if (IndexOkay(n))
    bitset |= 1 << n;   // i.e. OR 1 shifted left n times
}

// Set nth bit in bitset to 0
void TBitSet::Delete(char n)
{
  if (IndexOkay(n))
    bitset &= ~(1 << n);  // i.e. AND NOT 1 shifted left n times
}

// Return TRUE if nth bit in bitset == 1
int TBitSet::HasBit(char n)
{
  if (!IndexOkay(n))
    return FALSE;
  if ((bitset & 1 << n) != 0)
    return TRUE;
  return FALSE;
}

// Return nth bit in bitset (1 or 0; 9==error)
char TBitSet::Extract(char n)
{
  if (!IndexOkay(n))
    return 9;  // Indexing error
  if (HasBit(n))
    return 1;
  return 0;
}
```

```
// Display bitset as a binary value
void TBitSet::Display(void)
{
  for (int i = 15; i >= 0; i--) {
    if (((i + 1) % 4) == 0)
      cout << ' ';
    cout << (int)Extract(i);
  }
}


/* tbitset.cpp -- Test TBitSet class */

#include <iostream.h>
#include "bitset.h"

main()
{
  TBitSet bits;

  bits.Add(0);       // Set bits 0, 2, 4, and 15
  bits.Add(2);
  bits.Add(4);
  bits.Add(15);
  bits.Display();    // Display set as a binary value
  bits.Delete(2);    // Reset bit 2
  cout << '\n';
  bits.Display();
  return 0;
}
```

14.4 There are four files in the solution listed here. File item.h declares an Item
class, which has a private data member that can address an object of this same
class. Item's member functions are declared inline. File list.h (listed immediately following item.h) declares class TList, which derives from Item. (This
allows TList class objects to be linked to other TList class objects, although
this feature isn't demonstrated here.) LIST.CPP (listed immediately following
list.h) implements the TList class. Finally, TLIST.CPP (listed immediately
following LIST.CPP) demonstrates how to use TList. Compile the test
program and its modules with the DOS command **bcc tlist list**.

```
/* item.h -- Item class declaration */

#ifndef __ITEM_H
#define __ITEM_H  1    // Prevent multiple #includes

class Item;
typedef Item* PItem;

class Item {
private:
  PItem next;           // Addresses next item
public:
  Item() { next = NULL; }
  virtual ~Item() { }
  PItem GetNext(void) { return next; }
  void PutNext(PItem p) { next = p; }
};

#endif    // __ITEM_H


/* list.h -- TList class declaration */

#ifndef __LIST_H
#define __LIST_H  1    // Prevent multiple #includes

#include <stdlib.h>
#include "item.h"

class TList;
typedef TList* PTList;

class TList: public Item {
private:
  PItem anchor;          // Anchors list head
  PItem cip;             // Current item pointer
public:
// Constructor and destructor
  TList(): Item() { anchor = cip = NULL; }
  virtual ~TList();
// Inline member functions
  int ListEmpty(void)
```

```
     { return (anchor == NULL); }
   PItem CurrentItem(void)
     { return cip; }
   void ResetList(void)
     { cip = anchor; }
// Other member functions
   void InsertItem(PItem ip);
   PItem NextItem(void);
};

#endif    // __LIST_H


/* list.cpp -- TList class implementation */

#include <stddef.h>
#include "list.h"

// Destructor. Delete any listed Item objects
TList::~TList()
{
  PItem p;  // Pointer to Item object

  while(anchor) {
    p = anchor;             // Address item at anchor
    anchor = p->GetNext();  // Move anchor to next item
    delete p;               // Delete item at p
  }
}

// Insert into list a new Item object addressed by ip
void TList::InsertItem(PItem ip)
{
  if (ip == NULL)       // Ignore request to insert
    return;             //   a NULL item.
  ip->PutNext(anchor);  // Item addresses former anchor
  anchor = cip = ip;    // Anchor and cip address new item
}
```

```
// Move current Item pointer to next object
PItem TList::NextItem(void)
{
  if (cip != NULL)          // If list is not empty
    cip = cip->GetNext();   //  set cip to item at right.
  return cip;               // Return current item pointer.
}


/* tlist.cpp -- Test TList class */

#include <iostream.h>
#include "list.h"

class TMyItem : public Item {
private:
  int value;
public:
  TMyItem(int n) { value = n; }
  void PutValue(int n) { value = n; }
  int GetValue(void) { return value; }
};

void ShowList(void);

PTList lp = new TList;

main()
{
  int i;

  cout << "\nAfter allocating new list";
  ShowList();
  cout << "\n\nInsert 10 items into the list";
  for (i = 1; i <= 10; i++)
```

```
      lp->InsertItem(new TMyItem(i));
    ShowList();
    return 0;
  }

  void ShowList(void)
  {
    cout << "\nITEMS IN LIST: ";
    if (lp->ListEmpty()) {
      cout << "List is empty";
      return;
    }
    lp->ResetList();
    PItem ip = lp->CurrentItem();
    while (ip) {
      cout << ((TMyItem *)ip)->GetValue() << " ";
      ip = lp->NextItem();
    }
    cout << '\n';
  }
```

14.5 The solution uses the Item and TList classes from Exercise 14.4. File direct.h declares two classes. TStrItem can store a string (used later to hold filenames). TDirectory derives from TList. Notice how simple this class is. All the list mechanisms are in TList. TDirectory's only job is to read the disk directory and insert filenames in the the list of TStrItem objects. Compile test program TDIRECT.CPP with the DOS command **bcc tdirect direct list**. Run the program with a command such as **tdirect *.cpp** to display all .CPP files in the current directory.

```
  /* direct.h -- TDirectory class declaration */

  #ifndef __DIRECT_H
  #define __DIRECT_H 1    // Prevent multiple #includes

  #include <string.h>
  #include "item.h"
  #include "list.h"
```

```
class TStrItem;
typedef TStrItem* PTStrItem;

class TStrItem: public Item {
private:
  char *sp;  // String pointer
public:
  TStrItem(const char *s) { sp = strdup(s); }
  virtual ~TStrItem() { delete sp; }
  virtual const char *GetString(void) { return sp; }
};

class TDirectory: TList {
public:
  TDirectory(const char *wildcard);
  void Display(void);
};

#endif   // __DIRECT_H


/* direct.cpp -- TDirectory class implementation */

#include <iostream.h>
#include <dir.h>
#include <dos.h>
#include <string.h>
#include "item.h"
#include "list.h"
#include "direct.h"

TDirectory::TDirectory(const char *wildcard)
{
  struct ffblk fb;  // File entry structure
  int done;         // True when done reading entries

  done = findfirst(wildcard, &fb, FA_NORMAL | FA_DIREC);
```

```
    while (!done) {
      strlwr(fb.ff_name);       // Convert name to lowercase
      InsertItem(new TStrItem(fb.ff_name));  // Insert into list
      done = findnext(&fb);     // Do next entry
    }
}

void TDirectory::Display(void)
{
  PItem p;

  ResetList();
  p = CurrentItem();
  while (p) {
    cout << ((PTStrItem)p)->GetString() << '\n';
    p = NextItem();
  }
}



/* tdirect.cpp -- Display disk directory */

#include <iostream.h>
#include "direct.h"

main(int argc, char *argv[])
{
  char *wildcard;

  if (argc <= 1)
    wildcard = "*.*";
  else
    wildcard = argv[1];
  TDirectory *dp = new TDirectory(wildcard);
  dp->Display();
  delete dp;
  return 0;
}
```

14.6 Class TNamedDirectory inherits two base classes, TStrItem and TDirectory. The new class's constructor passes a string argument to the constructors for each of the base classes. Member function Display() in TNamedDirectory calls TDirectory's Display() member function to display the directory entries, and then calls GetString() from TStrItem to display the original wildcard string used to initialize the object. Compile this program with the command **bcc nameddir direct list**, then run TNAMEDDIR for a list of all .CPP files in the current directory.

```cpp
/* nameddir.cpp */

#include <iostream.h>
#include "direct.h"

class TNamedDirectory: public TStrItem, public TDirectory {
public:
  TNamedDirectory(const char *s)
    : TStrItem(s), TDirectory(s) { }
  void Display(void);
};

main()
{
  TNamedDirectory dir("*.cpp");
  dir.Display();
  return 0;
}

void TNamedDirectory::Display(void)
{
  TDirectory::Display();
  cout << '\n' << "Above directory of "
       << GetString() << '\n';
}
```

Chapter 15, "Advanced Topics in C++"

15.1 The solution is to make TEngine a friend class of TFuel. That way, TEngine may access TFuel's private level data member.

```cpp
/* fuel.cpp */

#include <iostream.h>

class TFuel {
  friend class TEngine;   // "TEngine may access
private:                  //    TFuel's restricted parts"
  double level;
public:
  TFuel(double n) { level = n; }
};

class TEngine {
private:
  TFuel myFuel;
public:
  TEngine(double n): myFuel(n) { }
  double GetFuelLevel(void)
    { return myFuel.level; }  // Access private data!
};

main()
{
  TEngine engine(1024);
  cout << "Fuel == " << engine.GetFuelLevel() << " units";
  return 0;
}
```

15.2 Make the following modifications to the program.

```
class TStrOp {
  // ... Other declarations
  friend long operator*(TStrOp a, TStrOp b);
  friend long operator/(TStrOp a, TStrOp b);
};

long operator*(TStrOp a, TStrOp b)
{
  return (atol(a.value) * atol(b.value));
}

long operator/(TStrOp a, TStrOp b)
{
  return (atol(a.value) / atol(b.value));
}
```

15.3 Make the following modifications to the program. Notice how `sprintf()` is called to reconvert incremented and decremented values back into strings. (The following lines are extracted from file STROPS3.CPP on the accompanying diskette.)

```
#include <stdio.h>

class TStrOp {
  // ... Other declarations
  long operator++();      // Prefix ++x
  long operator++(int);   // Postfix x++
  long operator--();      // Prefix --x
  long operator--(int);   // Postfix x--
};

long TStrOp::operator++()  // Prefix
{
  long t = atol(value);
  sprintf(value, "%ld", ++t);
  return t;
}
```

```
long TStrOp::operator++(int)   // Postfix
{
  long t = atol(value);
  sprintf(value, "%ld", (t + 1));
  return t;
}

long TStrOp::operator--()   // Prefix
{
  long t = atol(value);
  sprintf(value, "%ld", --t);
  return t;
}

long TStrOp::operator--(int)   // Postfix
{
  long t = atol(value);
  sprintf(value, "%ld", (t - 1));
  return t;
}
```

15.4
```
operator double() { return atof(value); }
```

15.5
```
TFruit orange;
TFruit grapefruit = orange;
```

15.6
```
TFruit(TFruit &copy);
```

15.7
```
void operator=(const TFruit &copy);
```

15.8 To use a template function, all you need to do is declare one or more suitable prototypes, as done here for three min() functions.

```
/* usemin.cpp */

#include <iostream.h>
#include "minmax.h"

int min(int a, int b);
double min(double a, double b);
char min(char a, char b);
```

```
main()
{
  int i1 = 100, i2 = 200;
  double d1 = 3.14159, d2 = 9.87654;
  char c1 = 'A', c2 = 'z';

  cout << "min(i1, i2) == " << min(i1, i2) << '\n';
  cout << "min(d1, d2) == " << min(d1, d2) << '\n';
  cout << "min(c1, c2) == " << min(c1, c2) << '\n';
  return 0;
}
```

15.9 The TDatabase template class is capable of storing any type of data, including class objects (such as TRecord in the chapter), but also simpler int or double values. The solution defines dbd as a database of 100 integers. A cout.width(8); statement sets output width to eight columns.

```
/* intdb.cpp */

#include <iostream.h>
#include <stdlib.h>
#include "db.h"

main()
{
  int rn;  // Record number index

  TDatabase<int> dbd(100);
  cout << "\n\nDatabase of ints\n";
  for (rn = 0; rn <= 99; rn++)
    dbd.GetRecord(rn) = rand();
  for (rn = 0; rn <= 99; rn++) {
    cout.width(8);
    cout << dbd.GetRecord(rn);
  }
  return 0;
}
```

Index

E

Programming Tools

EMS provides the world's largest and best collection of PD/Shareware for PC pros, extensively indexed and ZIPed for best value. Save time and money, learn techniques, and stop reinventing! Thirty-day guarantee.

Many of the programming tools found on the accompanying disk also can be found on the C++ Utility Directory from EMS Professional Shareware Libraries. The C++ Utility Directory is a comprehensive directory of available C++ compiler utilities for serious users and developers. This directory is the result of hundreds of hours of data collection, checking, and preparation.

The current C++ Utility Directory library contains 670 public domain and Shareware utility programs for PC programmers compressed with PKZIP to fit onto a single CD-ROM, 104 360K diskettes, or 26 1.44M diskettes. Updated quarterly, the library includes a database directory of all the PD/Shareware C++ utilities in the library as well as all known commercial C++ utility products.

For more information regarding the EMS Professional Shareware Libraries for 1-2-3, AutoCAD, ASM, BASIC, C, C++, dBASE (dBASE and Compilers), xBASE source code applications, DOS Utilities, DTP/Ventura, Child and Adult Education, Games, Hardware Demo, Home PC Applications, Novell Netware, OS/2, Turbo Pascal, Paradox, PCX Clipart, Sound Effects, Visual Basic, UNIX, Windows 3.X, WordPerfect, and our database of 31,091 PC products and the 12,476 companies that make them, contact

EMS Professional Shareware Libraries
4505 Buckhurst Court
Olney, MD 20832

Voice: (301) 924-3594
Fax: (301) 963-2708

International customers may contact France (16)1-34194308; Germany 0611/846225; United Kingdom (0763) 244114; Austria/Eastern Europe 43-1-5874600-0; Singapore 65-7777911; Bahrain/Arabic (973)244544.

Installing the Diskette

The diskette bound into the back cover contains all of the book's listings. Also included are several programs that are not in the book.

> **NOTE:** The files on the diskette are compressed. Before you can use the files, you must decompress them by using the supplied utility, LHARC.EXE.

Follow these steps to decompress and install the book's listings and other files onto your hard drive:

1. Create a directory on your hard drive to hold the decompressed files. (I call my directory MBC for Mastering Borland C++.) For example, enter the commands

    ```
    c:
    md \mbc
    ```

2. Copy all files from the diskette to your newly created directory. For example, with the diskette in drive A:, enter the command

    ```
    copy a:\*.* c:\mbc
    ```

3. Remove the diskette from A:. Change to the newly created directory on your hard drive, and run the supplied UNPACK.BAT program to complete the installation. For example, enter the commands

    ```
    c:
    cd \mbc
    unpack
    ```

4. After you see the message "Done," you can delete the .LZH compressed files and the UNPACK.BAT batch file. Enter the commands

    ```
    del *.lzh
    del unpack.bat
    ```

5. For instructions about compiling the programs, see the README file (load it into Borland C++ or another text editor). All programs are supplied in text form as printed in this book—you must compile the programs before you can run them.